MEMOIRS

°° OF °°

EASTERN ARKANSAS

COMPRISING

A Condensed History of the State, a Number of Biographies of Distinguished Citizens of the same, a Brief Descriptive History of each of the Counties named herein, and numerous Biographical Sketches of the Prominent Citizens of such Counties.

ILLUSTRATED.

CHICAGO, NASHVILLE AND ST. LOUIS:
THE GOODSPEED PUBLISHING CO.
1890.

NEW MATERIAL COPYRIGHT 1978
The Rev.Silas Emmett Lucas,Jr.

SOUTHERN HISTORICAL PRESS
%The Rev.S.Emmett Lucas,Jr.
Post Office Box 738
Easley, South Carolina 29640

ISBN 0-89308-080-2

PREFACE.

THIS beautiful volume has been prepared in response to the popular demand for the preservation of local history and biography. The method of preparation followed is the most successful and the most satisfactory yet devised —the most successful in the enormous number of volumes circulated, and the most satisfactory in the general preservation of personal biography and family record, conjointly with local history. The number of volumes now being distributed seems fabulous. Careful estimates place the number circulated in Ohio at 50,000 volumes; Pennsylvania, 60,000; New York, 75,000; Indiana, 40,000; Illinois, 40,000; Iowa, 30,000; Missouri, 25,000; Kansas, 20,000; Tennessee, 20,000; Kentucky, 25,000; Georgia, 20,000; Alabama, 20,000, and all the other States at the same proportionate rate. The entire State of Arkansas, which until recently had scarcely been touched by the historian, is now being rapidly written.

The design of the present extensive biographical and historical research is to gather and preserve in attractive form, while fresh with the evidence of truth, the enormous fund of perishing occurrence. In gathering the matter for the historical sketches of the counties, it was thought wisest, owing to the limited space, to collate and condense only the most valuable items, by reason of which such sketches are a credit to the book, and of permanent worth.

In the preparation of this volume the Publishers have met with nothing but courtesy and assistance from the public. Nothing promised is omitted, and much not promised is given. About fifty pages of State history were guaranteed; over twice that number are given. Special care was employed and great expense incurred to render the volume accurate. In all cases the personal sketches were submitted by mail, and in most instances were corrected and returned by the subjects themselves. Coming as they do from the most illustrious families of the State —all worthy citizens from the upper, middle and lower classes—they form in themselves the most complete account of the Eastern Counties ever written, and their great value to future generations will be warmly acknowledged by all thoughtful people. With many thanks to their friends for the success of such a difficult enterprise, the Publishers respectfully tender this fine volume to their patrons.

THE PUBLISHERS.

January, 1890.

CONTENTS.

CONTENTS.

CHAPTER XV.

White County—Location and Description—Boundary Lines—Topography and Geology—Water Supply—Drainage—Streams—Timber—Soil—Resources—Lumber Interests—Census Enumeration—Taxable Property—Live Stock Industry—Real and Personal Property —Railroad Facilities—Population—Era of Settlement—County Organization—Seat of Justice and Public Buildings—County Officers—Politics—Court Affairs—Roll of Attorneys—Civil War History— Towns and Villages—Schools—Churches—Biographical.

O the pleasant days of old, which so often people praise!
True, they wanted all the luxuries that grace our modern days;
Bare floors were strewed with rushes, the walls let in the cold;
O how they must have shivered in those pleasant days of old.—*Brown.*

WHITE COUNTY is located in the northeast part of Central Arkansas, and is bounded north by Cleburne, Independence and Jackson Counties, east by Woodruff, south by Prairie and Lonoke, and west by Faulkner.

Its boundary lines are as follows: Beginning in Range 3 west, at the point where White River crosses the line dividing Townships 9 and 10 north; thence west on the township line to the line dividing Ranges 5 and 6 west; thence north on the range line to the line dividing Townships 10 and 11 north; thence west on the township line to the line dividing Ranges 7 and 8 west; thence south on the range line to Little Red River; thence up said river, in a westerly direction, following its meanders, to the middle of Range 8 west; thence south on section lines to the line dividing Townships 8 and 9 north; thence west on the township line to the line dividing Ranges 10 and 11 west; thence south on the range line to Cypress Creek in Township 5 north; thence down Cypress Creek following its meanders to the line dividing Ranges 5 and 6 west; thence north on the range line to the line dividing Townships 5 and 6 north; thence east on the township line to White River; thence up White River following its meanders to the last crossing of the line dividing Townships 7 and 8 north; thence west on the township line to the southwest corner of Section 35, Township 8 north, Range 4 west; thence north on section lines until White River is again intersected; thence up the river following its meanders to the place of beginning; containing an area of 1,015 square miles, or 650,000 acres. Of this about 12,000 acres belong to the United States, 27,000 to the State, 81,000 to the St. Louis, Iron Mountain & Southern Railway Company, and the balance to individuals. Only about 10 per cent of the land is improved. Prices range from $5 to $25 per acre for improved, and from $1 to $10 for unimproved property.

The face of the county is somewhat rolling,

8

with three-fifths hilly and two-fifths level. The course of the streams show that the general trend is toward the southeast; White River, forming the eastern boundary line, is navigable for large vessels to points above. All the other streams of the county empty into this river. Little Red River enters from the northwest, and flows in an easterly and southeasterly direction through these limits and empties into White River near the line dividing Townships 6 and 7 north. It so divides the county as to leave about one-third of its area to the northeast and two-thirds to the southwest. Glaize Creek makes its appearance from the north, in Range 5 west, and flows thence in a direction east of south, emptying into White River a short distance above the mouth of Red River. Bayou Des Arc rises in the county's western part and, flowing southeasterly, finds an outlet in Cypress Creek at the southern boundary near the line between Ranges 6 and 7 west. Cypress Creek, which forms most of the southern boundary, runs in a general eastern direction and empties into White River at a point southeast of the county. These, the principal streams in this territory, together with their several tributaries, supply the entire drainage of the immediate region. Little Red River is navigable at all seasons of the year as far as West Point, and in high water it has been ascended to a point opposite Searcy. The United States has recently completed a dredge and two other boats at Judsonia, making necessary preparations to dredge and enlarge the river that it may be navigable at all seasons up to Judsonia.

There are numerous springs throughout the county, from which flows the purest of water. The most noted possessing mineral properties are the White Sulphur, Chalybeate and Alum Springs, at Searcy; the Armstrong Spring, nine miles west, and Griffin's Spring, four miles south. Well water of the best quality can be obtained at nearly all points at a moderate depth. The supply of water for family use is had from wells, springs and cisterns. Of timber, many varieties are common here, such as white, black, red, post, Spanish and overcup oak, black walnut, hickory, ash, cedar, pine, pecan, cypress and sweet and black gum.

Valuable white oak grows abundantly in nearly all parts of the county.

The most conspicuous geological feature of the county is the escarpment of sandstone along the bluffs of Little Red River, known as the "Bee Rock." The sandstone forming the cliffs in the foreground of this landscape is part of the conglomerate and millstone grit formation that intervenes between the overlying coal measures proper, and the underlying subcarboniferous limestone. The pebbly sandstones and millstone grit, which occur along the escarpments of Little Red River, attaining a thickness of from 150 to 200 feet, impart wild and romantic scenery for many miles along the banks of the stream. The dip of these sandstones at the old Patterson Mill is one and one-half to two degrees to the south, or a little west of south. In digging wells in the vicinity of Searcy, a blackish gray, indurated, argillo-siliceous shale is encountered, containing small scales of disseminated mica. This material is brittle and crumbles, by exposure, to a clay. Similar shales are struck, usually ten feet below the surface, under the red land situated west of Searcy. The first ten feet passed through, generally consists of soil, subsoil and gravel overlaying the shales. The red soil of these level farming lands is quite productive, yielding good crops of cotton, corn, wheat and the finest oats in ordinary seasons: 800 to 1,500 pounds of cotton in the seed to the acre, 20 to 25 bushels of wheat, and 40 to 60 bushels of oats, when there are seasonable rains.* This description of land covers a large proportion of the area of the county. The bottom lands along the streams are largely alluvial and exceedingly productive. The soil of that portion not previously mentioned, is composed of vegetable mold, sand and clay, and with proper cultivation all the lands of the county, excepting some thin soil on the ridges, yield abundantly.

There are some mineral deposits, such as iron, manganese, lead and coal here, but they have not yet been developed in paying quantities. It is thought, however, that a few of these ores may be found to exist to that extent which will warrant their mining.

---

* Quotations from State Geological Report.

Among the resources of the county, lumbering constitutes a considerable industry, there being many saw and shingle mills throughout its territory. Manufacturing has also been commenced; there is a wagon factory at Searcy, and a fruit-canning factory, and a factory for the manufacture of fruit boxes and crates at Judsonia.

Agriculture is here, as elsewhere, the leading occupation, but both horticulture and the raising of live stock are beginning to receive attention. The agricultural products are cotton, corn, wheat, oats, rye, peas, grass, potatoes, turnips, sorghum, etc. "Cotton is King," and is raised largely to the exclusion of other crops. Farming might, perhaps, be carried on more scientifically, as the lands have been cropped from year to year, some of them for half a century, without a proper rotation, with but very little fertilizing matter being returned to the soil. Clover and the tame grasses succeed well, and are most profitable for refertilizing the lands.

In 1880 there were 2,319 farms in White County, 83,679 acres of improved lands, and the value of all farm products for the year 1879 amounted to $925,392. The cereal and vegetable productions were as follows: Indian corn, 444,893 bushels; oats, 95,359 bushels; rye, 399 bushels; wheat, 17,-220 bushels; hay, 295 tons; cotton, 11,821 bales; Irish potatoes, 14,876 bushels; sweet potatoes, 23,098 bushels; tobacco, 28,184 pounds. These actual statistics taken from the reports of the United States census show conclusively what the soil is best adapted for.

In the cultivation of sweet potatoes and tobacco the county then ranked as third in the State, in Irish potatoes fifth, and in cotton fourteenth. The number of head of live stock, as given by the same census report, was: Horses 3,048; mules and asses 1,860; neat cattle 15,944; sheep 5,388; hogs 29,936. The abstract for taxable property for 1888 shows the following: Horses 4,157; mules and asses 2,052; neat cattle 19,839; sheep 3,678; hogs 23,330. Of the first four grades of animals there was a large increase from 1880 to 1888, a probable decrease being noticed in the other two. Perhaps the decrease in sheep is real, while that in hogs is only apparent, for the reason that the abstract of taxable property shows the number on hand when the property was assessed and does not include those slaughtered and sold during the year, as is the case with the census report.

Live stock is receiving considerable attention of late, and the county is well adapted to its growth. Improved breeds are being introduced to a great extent. Horses, mules, cattle and hogs succeed best, and sheep do tolerably well. The stock business is steadily increasing and will be one of the most profitable industries of this locality in the near future.

The county's horticultural resources (especially the raising of small fruits) are being developed to a considerable extent along the line of the St. Louis, Iron Mountain & Southern Railway. Peaches, plums, strawberries, raspberries and blackberries are already quite extensively raised and shipped from Bradford, Russell, Judsonia and Beebe. These fruits are all grown to perfection; apples and pears, however, do not succeed as well. Grapes are also grown and used to some extent in the manufacture of domestic wine. The increasing demand for fruits will make this variety a leading industry here.

It is very evident that owing to natural resources, mildness of climate, the trifling cost of fuel, and the small amount of feed and care required to winter live stock, a farmer can live much cheaper and with greater pecuniary profit hereabouts, than in the cold settlements of the north and northwest. The industrious poor man desiring to emigrate to a new country, where may be had a home of his own, will do well to investigate the many advantages offered by this and contiguous portions of Arkansas, before venturing with his all into cold and forbidding regions of less favored localities. Let a farmer practice the same economy and industry here that usually prevail in Indiana, Illinois and other Northern States and he will find it comparatively easy to gain a competency within a few years.

In 1880, the real estate of White County was assessed for taxation at $1,850,394 and the personal property at $744,821, making a total of

$2,595,215, on which the total amount of taxes charged for all purposes was $32,633. In taxable wealth it then ranked as fourth in the State. In 1888, the real-estate assessment was $2,440,883, and personal property $1,252,715, aggregating $3,693,598. The total amount of taxes charged thereon for all purposes was $56,407.88. These figures bear evidence that from 1880 to 1888 the taxable wealth of the county increased a little over 42 per cent—a most encouraging showing.

The St. Louis, Iron Mountain & Southern Railroad enters White County about five miles west of its northeast corner, and runs thence through the limits in a southwesterly direction, its length here being about thirty-nine miles. It was completed in 1872. Soon after the Searcy & West Point Railroad was constructed, running from West Point to Searcy, and crossing the St. Louis, Iron Mountain & Southern at Kensett. The cars on this road are drawn between Searcy and Kensett by an engine, and between Kensett and West Point by horses. Its length is ten and a half miles. The Memphis branch of the St. Louis, Iron Mountain & Southern Railroad connects Memphis with the main line at Bald Knob in the county's northeast part, its length being about ten miles, thus making the combined length of railroads within the county sixty-one miles or more. These roads, together with White River as a navigable outlet, afford excellent transportation facilities.

The population of White County, according to the United States census reports, has been as follows at the various decades mentioned: 1840, 920; 1850, 2,619; 1860, 8,316; 1870, 10,347; 1880, 17,794. Immigration to the county since 1880 has been so large that at the present its population must considerably exceed 20,000. The colored population was, in 1860, 1,435; in 1870, 1,200; in 1880, 2,032, at about which figure it still remains.

The Royal Colony, consisting of several families from Tennessee, was founded by James Walker and Martin Jones at the head of Bull Creek, in the northwest part of what is now White County. Lower down on Bull Creek were the settlements of Fielding and Frederick Price. Lewis Vongrolman founded a German settlement on Big Creek and Little Red River with John Magness, Philip Hilger, James King, the Wishes, Yinglings and others. Philip Hilger established and kept the "Hilger's Ferry" across Little Red River, on the old military road leading from Cape Girardeau to Little Rock. Farther north, near the Independence County line, was the Pate Settlement, founded by Lovic Pate. Alfred Arnold, John Akin and John Wright founded the settlement on Little Red River below where West Point is situated. Near the present town of Judsonia was a settlement founded by William Cook and Henry R. Vanmeter. Reuben Stephens settled in the Pate Settlement on the creek that now bears his name. Samuel Guthrie and John Dunaway also settled in that neighborhood.

The list just given includes the names of some of the most prominent pioneer settlers, all of whom according to the best information now obtainable, located in their respective places during the decade of the 20's. Others soon followed, and by the date of the organization of the county, 1836, all parts of the territory composing it were more or less sparsely settled. By reference to the population previously stated it will be seen that the settlement, until since the close of the Civil War, continued slow and gradual. Since 1880 there has been a large influx from the northern and eastern States. Most of the early settlers came from Tennessee and other southern States. The early county officers and all mentioned elsewhere in connection with the organization of the county were, of course, pioneer settlers. The names of those likewise prominent in county affairs will be found in subsequent pages of this volume.

White County was organized in accordance with the provisions of an act of the legislature of Arkansas Territory, approved October 23, 1835. The first sessions of court were held at the house of David Crise, on the place now known as the McCreary farm, three and a half miles east of Searcy. The organization of the county was completed early in 1836.

The place where the courts were first held, and the site of Searcy became competing points for the location of the permanent seat of justice. The commissioners who located the seat of justice were John Arnold, Jesse Terry, Byram Stacy, David Crise and Reuben Stephens. A majority of them were in favor of locating it at Searcy, where it has ever since remained. Soon after the site was selected, a log-cabin court house was erected at a point about 100 yards southwest of the present court house, and the first term of the circuit court was held therein in November, 1838. The next court house was a two-story frame, erected on the site of the present one. A short time before the Civil War this was moved away preparatory to erecting a new one. It now stands two blocks south of the public square and is known as the Chambliss House. The war coming on, the proceedings for the erection of the new court house were stopped, and until the present one was erected, the courts were held in the Masonic Hall at the southeast corner of the public square. In 1868 the county court appropriated $25,000 for the erection of a new court house, and for that amount the contract was let to Wyatt Sanford of Searcy, who erected the present court house in 1869-70. It is a large and substantial two-story building, the first story containing cross halls, a large fire-proof vault and county offices, being constructed of stone, and the second, containing the court room, of brick. Above the center of the building is a handsome tower containing a "town clock."

The first county jail was made of hewed logs, ten inches square, and was two stories high. The first story or "dungeon" was entered by means of a trap door from above. It stood on the same lot on which the present jail stands. The second jail, built on the same lot, was a one-story brick building containing four iron cells and cost $1,800. Becoming unsafe it was removed. The present jail and jailer's residence, standing about 100 yards northwest of the court house, was erected in 1882-83 by James E. Winsett at a cost of about $3,800. It is a two-story brick building containing three iron cells, a dungeon, and jailer's residence. The county owns a "poor farm" on which the paupers are supported. It consists of 120 acres, with ample buildings, and is located one and a half miles east of Searcy.

The following official directory contains names of the county's public servants with date of term of service annexed from date of organization to the present:

Judges: Samuel Guthrie, 1836–42; William Cook, 1842–44; Samuel Guthrie, 1844–46; M. Sanders, 1846–50; P. H. McDaniel, 1850–52; J. F. Batts, 1852–54; John Hutches, 1854–56; L. S. Poe, 1856–58; William Hicks, 1858–60; R. M. Exum, 1860–61; John Hutches, 1861–62; M. Sanders, 1862–64; John Hutches, 1864–66; M. Sanders, 1866–72; A. M. Foster, 1874–78; L. M. Jones, 1878–82; F. P. Laws, 1882–84; R. H. Goad, 1884–88; N. H. West, present incumbent, elected in 1888.

Clerks: P. W. Roberts, 1836–38; J. W. Bond, 1838–44; E. Guthrie, 1844–46; J. W. Bond, 1846–48; Samuel Morgan, 1848–52; R. S. Bell, 1852–56; Dandridge McRae, 1856–62; J. W. Bradley, 1862–68; J. A. Cole, 1868–72; A. P. Sanders, 1872–80; J. J. Bell, 1880–84; L. C. Canfield, 1884–88; C. S. George, present incumbent, elected in 1888. From 1872 to 1874, Allen Mitchel was circuit clerk, and from 1880 to 1882, T. C. Jones was county clerk, and from 1882 to 1884, J. R. Jobe was county clerk, and from 1884 to 1886, R. H. McCullough was circuit clerk. J. J. Bell is the present circuit clerk.

Sheriffs: P. Crease, 1836–38; William Cook, 1838–40; Milton Sanders, 1840–44; T. J. Lindsey, 1844–46; J. G. Robbins, 1846–50; J. M. Bowden, 1850–52; J. G. Robbins, 1852–54; R. M. Exum, 1854–60; J. W. Bradley, 1860–62; B. B. Bradley, 1862–64; W. C. Petty, 1864–66; J. G. Robbins, 1866–67; W. C. Petty, 1867–72; N. B. Petty, 1872–78; B. C. Black, 1878–84; J. H. Ford, 1884–88; R. W. Carnes, present incumbent, elected in 1888.

Treasurers: Michael Owens, 1836–38; John Arnold, 1838–42; James Bird, 1842–44; T. R. Vanmeter, 1844–46; J. Belew, 1846–48; J. M. Johnson, 1848–50; E. Neaville, 1850–52; W. T. Gilliam, 1852–54; W. B. Isbell, 1854–56; John Critz, 1856–60; S. B. Barnett, 1860–68; R. J.

Rogers, 1868–72; W. A. B. Jones, 1872–74; M. B. Pearson, 1874–80; D. L. Fulbright, 1880–84; J. M. Smith, 1884–88; J. G. Walker, present incumbent, elected in 1888.

Coroners: M. H. Blue, 1836–40; Hiram O'Neale, 1840–42; Samuel Beeler, 1842–44; D. Dobbins, 1844–46; E. K. Milligan, 1850–52; G. W. Davis, 1852–56; Alex Cullum, 1856–58; T. T. Britt, 1858–60; W. G. Sanders, 1860–72; T. L. Miller, 1872–74; Z. T. Haley, 1874–82; J. P. Baldock, 1882–84; J. H. Claiborne, 1884–86; J. M. Carter, 1886–88; Frank Blevins, present incumbent, elected in 1888.

Surveyors: S. Arnold, 1836–52; I. M. Moore, 1852–54; Thomas Moss, 1854–56; W. B. Holland, 1856–60; Thomas Moss, 1860–64; W. B. Holland, 1864–66; Thomas Moss, 1866–68; J. O. Hurt, 1868–72; Pres. Steele, 1872–74; J. P. Steele, 1874–76; Thomas Moss, 1876–80; B. S. Wise, present incumbent, elected in 1880, and served continuously since.

Assessors:* T. W. Leggett, 1868–70; I. S. Chrisman, 1870–72; J. H. Black, 1872–74; D. L. Fulbright, 1874–76; B. B. Bradley, 1876–84; J. J. Deener, 1884–88; G. W. Dobbins, present incumbent, elected in 1888.

Delegates in Constitutional Conventions: 1836, W. Cummins, A. Fowler and J. McLean, for Pulaski, White and Saline Counties; 1861, held March 4 to 21, and May 6 to June 3, J. N. Cypert; 1864, held January 4 to 23, not represented; 1868, J. N. Cypert and Thomas Owen; 1874, J. N. Cypert and J. W. House.

The first State senator for White County was R. C. Byrd, and the first representative in the house was Martin Jones.

The number of votes cast at the late elections for several candidates, as stated below, will show the political aspect of the county. At the September election 1888, for Governor, James P. Eagle, Democrat, 1,608; C. N. Norwood, combined opposition, 1,949. November election in 1888, for president, Cleveland, Democrat, 1,948; Harrison, Republican, 550; Streeter, Union Labor, 249; Fiske, Prohibition, 45.

* This office was not established until 1868.

The various courts held in the county are county, probate, circuit and chancery. The regular sessions of these bodies are held as follows: County court, commencing on the first Monday of January, April, July and October; probate, on the second Monday of the same months; circuit, on the third Monday of January and July; chancery, on the second Monday of June and December. The chancery court was made a separate court by an act of the General Assembly approved March 15, 1887, and was attached to the First chancery district, composed of Lonoke, Pulaski, Faulkner and White Counties. Prior to that time the circuit court had jurisdiction of all chancery business.

The legal bar (local) of White County is composed of the following-named attorneys: W. R. Coody, J. N. Cypert, D. McRae, B. Isbell, John B. Holland, S. Brundidge, Jr., J. F. Rives, Sr., J. F. Rives, Jr., E. Cypert, John M. Battle, John T. Hicks, J. D. DeBois, C. D. James and J. E. Russ.

Upon the approach of the Civil War a strong Union sentiment prevailed in White County, and when the Hon. J. N. Cypert was elected representative in the State convention held in March, 1861, he was instructed to, and did, vote against the secession of the State from the Federal Union. Afterward, when the "dogs of war" were let loose, and President Lincoln called upon the State for its quota of the first 75,000 troops for the Union army, the sentiment materially changed, and the people concluded to cast their lot in general with the Southern project of establishing a separate Confederacy. To this end companies of soldiers began to be organized, and in 1861, five companies first commanded, respectively, by Capts. F. M. Chrisman, John C. McCauley, Henry Blakemore, J. N. Cypert and J. A. Pemberton, and in 1862 three companies first commanded, respectively, by James McCauley, B. C. Black and Boothe Jones, were enlisted and organized within the county for the Confederate army. All were infantry companies except that of Capt. Chrisman, which was cavalry. Capt. James McCauley's company was mounted infantry. Some individuals joined commands outside of the county. No troops were organized within this territory for the Federal army, but a very few persons who refused to yield their Union sentiments left the county and enlisted as their principles dictated.

In 1862, when a division of the Federal army was moving from Batesville to Helena, an escort of its forage train, numbering about 500 men, was suddenly attacked at Whitney's Lane, five miles east of Searcy, by about 150 Confederates under Capt. Johnson. The latter made a bold and sudden attack and then retired, losing only about five men, while the Federals lost from fifty to 100. This was the only fight worthy of mention within the county. The county was overrun by scouting and foraging parties of both armies, and much provision was thus taken from the citizens. Three or four men were killed in the county during the war by scouts.

White County contains within its territory a number of towns of prominent local importance, besides those whose size has given them substantial reputation in the outside world. Of these Beebe is a flourishing place situated on the St. Louis, Iron Mountain & Southern Railroad, about sixteen miles southwest of Searcy. It began to build in the spring of 1872 (upon the completion of the railroad), but did not improve much until 1880, when it had reached a population of 428, and since then it has more than doubled in population. It has ten general, four grocery, three drug, two hardware, one furniture, two millinery and one notion store; also the White County Bank, two hotels, several boarding houses, two meat markets, two blacksmith and wagon shops, one saw and grist mill combined, two cotton-gins, two livery stables, railroad depot, postoffice, one photograph gallery, a fruit evaporator, five church edifices for the white and two for the colored people, a public school-house, five physicians, a dentist, two weekly newspapers, etc., etc. The Beebe Argus, published by W. B. Barnum, is an eight-column folio, Democratic in politics, and has for its motto: "A school-house on every hilltop and not a saloon in the valley." The Arkansas Hub is a seven-column folio, published by Sam J. Crabtree, and is independent in politics. Both of these

papers are ably edited and are well sustained, proving important factors in the influence of the community. Beebe is the center of one of the best fruit growing regions on the line of the St. Louis, Iron Mountain & Southern Railway, and ships a vast amount of fruit, especially small fruits, berries, tomatoes and the like, to the city markets. It is incorporated and has a full line of corporate officers. It also has lodges of the Masonic and Odd Fellow fraternities. It is thirty-three miles from Little Rock.

Bradford is a shipping station on the St. Louis, Iron Mountain & Southern Railroad, near the northern boundary of the county. It contains four general, one drug and one millinery store, one grist and one saw mill, a public school-house, two blacksmith shops, two physicians and a lodge each of Masons, Knights of Honor and Triple Alliance. The school-house is used for religious meetings. The population is about 100.

Bald Knob is situated in the northeastern part of White County, on the St. Louis, Iron Mountain & Southern Railroad at the junction of the Memphis branch. It contains three general, one hardware and grocery, one grocery, one drug and grocery and a millinery store, a grist-mill and a saw-mill, school-house, etc., etc.

Garner and Higginson are shipping stations on the St. Louis, Iron Mountain & Southern Railroad, the former about ten miles south of Searcy, and the latter five miles southeast.

Judsonia, formerly Prospect Bluff, is located on the west side of the St. Louis, Iron Mountain & Southern Railroad, and on the north bank of Little Red River. It is a comparatively old town. About the year 1870 a colony from the East settled there, and secured the change of the name of the town from Prospect Bluff to that of Judsonia. The place now contains four general, one dry goods, three grocery, one hardware, one hardware and furniture, one harness, one millinery and two drug stores; also a music store, meat market, two blacksmith shops, a wagon shop, a fruit and vegetable canning factory, fruit-box factory, two sawmills, a grist-mill and cotton-gin, a grist-mill and wool-carding mill, a tanyard, two hotels, a restaurant, a bakery, two livery stables, two church edifices for the white and two for the colored people; also a public school-house for the white and another for the colored people, three physicians, a lodge each of several secret and benevolent societies, a newspaper, the Judsonia Weekly Advance, etc., etc. The Advance is a six-column folio published by Berton W. Briggs, and has for its motto, "Overcome prejudice. Let free thought and free speech be encouraged." The Judsonia University is also located at this place. [See Schools.]

The White County Agricultural and Industrial Fair Association was organized at Judsonia in 1883, and grounds fitted up where exhibitions are held in the fall of the year.

The first fair was held in October, 1883. That of the past fall was a successful one. The present officers are Capt. D. L. McLeod, president; James L. Moore, vice-president; Charles D. James, secretary, and J. S. Kelley, treasurer. Messrs. D. L. McLeod, J. D. DeBois, J. S. Eastland, S. N. Ladd, Willis Meadows, James L. Moore, E. C. Kinney and J. S. Kelley are directors.

Judsonia's location in the midst of a wonderful fruit-growing community gives it prominent intercourse with the outside world. In 1889 immense shipments of fruit were made from this point, and in 1888 some 96,000 packages found their way to different sections. This will be the head of navigation on Little Red River when the Government shall have finished its work of improvement, for which appropriation was made.

Judsonia, like Beebe, is located in the center of a great fruit-growing region, is surrounded with many small fruit farms, and ships immense quantities of fruits, berries, tomatoes, etc., to the city markets. The town is incorporated and has a mayor and other corporate officers. It had a population of 267 in 1880, and now boasts of about 600, besides a dense population on the small fruit farms adjoining and surrounding it.

Kensett is situated on the St. Louis, Iron Mountain & Southern Railroad, at the crossing of the Searcy & West Point Railroad, four and a half miles east of Searcy. It contains the railroad depot, a general store, postoffice, hotel, a grocery,

blacksmith shop, a church edifice and a few dwelling houses.

Russell is a station on the St. Louis, Iron Mountain & Southern Railroad, between Bradford and Bald Knob. It contains two general stores, a drug and a millinery store, a saw-mill, grist-mill, cotton-gin, railroad depot, postoffice, etc.

There are some other small villages in the county containing a postoffice, general store, etc.

Searcy, the county seat, is situated in the geographical center of the county, at the western terminus of the Searcy & West Point Railroad. Its origin has been given in connection with the organization of the county. It was established in 1836, and a Mr. Howerton opened the first hotel in a double log-house south of what is now Spring Park. Moses Blew opened the first store, and was soon joined in the mercantile business by John W. Bond. At the beginning of the Civil War the place contained about six business places facing the public square. Its business was almost wholly destroyed during the war period, but revived soon thereafter. It now contains thirteen general, four grocery, three drug, two hardware, one furniture, one undertaking, one harness and saddle, two millinery stores, two meat markets, two restaurants, a bakery, two hotels and several boarding-houses, two grist and planing mills and cotton-gins combined, a wagon factory, two livery stables, six church edifices—three for the white and three for the colored people—a lodge each of Masons, Odd Fellows and Knights and Ladies of Honor, a Woman's Christian Temperance Union, Woman's Aid and Woman's Missionary Society, seven physicians, a dentist, three tailors, jewelers, etc. In addition to the interests mentioned, there are the Searcy Male and Female College, the Galloway Female College and three public schools—two for white and one for the colored people. One of the public school-houses, used by the former, was built for a male and the other for a female academy. Two weekly newspapers are also published here, the Arkansas Beacon and the White County Wheel. The former is a five-column quarto, published by Holland & Jobe. It is now in its eleventh volume, and is Democratic in politics. The

Strother E. Dent

WOODRUFF COUNTY, ARKANSAS.

latter is also a five-column quarto, published by R. A. Dowdy. It is in its second volume, and is published in the interest of the labor movement. These journals faithfully represent the interests of this section.

Spring Park, at Searcy, inclosing several acres, is located near the center of the city. It contains three never-failing mineral springs—White Sulphur, Chalybeate and Alum. The former of these have the most health-giving qualities, aiding digestion and curing constipation. This park contains bath-houses, is shaded by natural forest trees and is a very pleasant retreat for all persons. The town of Searcy is laid out "square with the world," its streets running east and west and north and south. It is beautifully located and is substantially built up, both in its churches, colleges, residences and business houses—the latter being mostly of brick. The healthfulness of location of the place is all that could be desired. The city is an educational center, and, especially a summer health resort, as many health and pleasure-seekers spend their summer months here. Its population is estimated at from 1,500 to 2,000. The residences are generally owned by the occupants, and there are very few renters, probably less than in any town of its size in the State. The town is incorporated and has a full complement of corporate officers.

West Point is situated on an eminence on the south side of Little Red River, at the eastern terminus of the Searcy & West Point Railroad. It was laid out in 1850 by J. M. West, hence its name, West Point, it being the point to which the river was navigable at all seasons of the year. At the beginning of the Civil War it had attained a population of 350 and did an immense amount of business, being the distributing point for a large scope of country to the westward. During the war period it lost nearly all its business, but afterward revived and flourished until the Iron Mountain Railroad was completed through the county. Then it again lost its prosperity, and in 1880 its population had run down to 123. Its population is now about 150. It contains three general stores, a drug store, a grist-mill and cotton-gin, a black-smith and wood shop, a church edifice, a public school-house and the railroad depot. It is supplied with a daily mail.

The advancement made in the cause of education in White County, under the free school system, is best shown by the following statistics as given in the report of the State superintendent of public instruction for the year ending June 30, 1888:

Scholastic population: White, males 3,384, females 3,173, total 6,557; colored, males 410, females 404, total 814. Number of pupils taught in the public schools: White, males 2,159, females 1,971, total 4,150; colored, males 295, females 283, total 578. Number of school districts, 101; districts reporting enrollment, 76; number of districts voting tax, 44. Number of teachers employed: Males 86, females 41, total 127. Average monthly salaries paid teachers: First grade, males $50, females $40; second grade, males $45, females $35; third grade, males $30, females $27.50. Amount expended for the support of the public schools: For teachers' salaries, $20,500.79; for building and repairing, $3,275; for treasurers' commissions, $565.60; total $24,341.39.

Assuming these statistics to be correct, only 63 per cent of the white and 71 per cent of the colored scholastic population were taught in the public schools. It must be noticed, however, that out of the 101 school districts, twenty-five failed to report the enrollment in the schools, which if ascertained and added to those that made reports, would largely increase the per cent of scholastic population attending. The fact that the school law does not compel full statistical reports to be made, is a strong argument in favor of its revision. Education for the masses is growing in popularity.

On July 23, 1888, a normal institute was opened at Searcy by Prof. T. S. Cox, conductor. This institute was in all respects a grand success. Its beginning noted the presence of thirty-four teachers, though seventy-one were in attendance at the close. A strong effort had been put forth by the county examiner, Mr. B. P. Baker, to secure a large attendance, and his energies in the work was the cause of bringing out nearly all the progressive teachers of the county, and many others friendly to education. Great interest was manifested, and much good work accomplished.

The Searcy Male and Female College is a chartered institution for the higher education of young men and women. The building is located within a campus of five acres, on a beautiful site in Searcy, convenient to the public square, and yet sufficiently removed to avoid the noise and bustle of business. It was organized in 1883, by Prof. W. H. Tharp (who conceived the idea of starting a reputable educational institution), and it at once become recognized as a school of a high order. Gen. D. McRae is president and Col. V. H. Henderson is secretary and treasurer of the board of trustees, and W. H. Tharp is president of the faculty. The members of the faculty are selected from colleges and universities of national reputation and most of them have supplemented their college or university course by thorough normal training, and hence in their teaching are prepared to use the most approved methods. Following the Preparatory Department is the Collegiate Department, divided into these Schools: Ancient Languages, Modern Languages, History, Natural Sciences, Mathematics, Philosophy and Belles-Lettres, Engineering, Elocution, Biblical History, Pianoforte, Vocal Culture, Harmony, Theory and Art.

A Normal Class is also taught, and the college cadets are organized into a company under the immediate supervision of the instructor in military tactics, Lieut. Albert J. Dabney (U. S. Naval Academy) commanding company.

The buildings consist of college hall, president's office and mathematics, a two-story boarding hall, music and art department, primary department, president's residence and cooking department, all separate, the dining-hall being under college hall. The history of the founding of this institution is most interesting. Prof. Tharp was aided in his work of starting the school by Prof. Conger of Ouachita College, Arkadelphia, the latter serving eighteen months as one of the principals. Subsequently Prof. Tharp was left in entire charge. Upon starting thirty-seven pupils were enrolled. A noticeable growth attended the worthy efforts of the founder and last year 204 pupils were in attendance. The capacity of the college has been doubled and still more room is needed. Its graduates have included persons of ability and influence, who have attained to prominence in their varied walks. The collegiate course is being strengthened and improved yearly, and every effort is being made to make this the leading educational institution of the State.

Galloway Female College was organized in the spring of 1888, under supervision of the several Conferences of the Methodist Episcopal Church, South, in the State of Arkansas. The citizens of Searcy secured its location by subscribing $25,000 toward its erection. The college building stands between a half and three-fourths of a mile southeast of the court house, on an eminence in a beautiful native forest, consisting of eighteen acres. It was erected in 1888–89, and consists of the main building and an east, west and north wing, with the kitchen department on the east side of the north wing, and its entire length from east to west is about 200 feet. Above the southern or front entrance is a tower eighty feet high. The building, the walls of which are constructed of brick on a rock foundation, has four stories above the basement, and contains a chapel 48x60 feet in size and twenty feet in height, five recitation rooms, a dining-room forty-eight feet square and twelve feet high, two double parlors, four reception halls, sixty-four bed-rooms, three bath-rooms, eleven halls and a kitchen with four rooms, storeroom and pantry. In the basement is the furnace room with two engines. The building in general is heated with steam, the rooms are all supplied with fire-places, and it is lighted with gas. The corner, or memorial stone, sets in the south wall, east of the main entrance, and has on its face the following inscription:

Galloway Female College.
C. B. Galloway, Bishop.

Building Committee.
P. A. Robertson,   G. B. Greer,
B. P. Baker,   A. W. Yarnell,
J. E. Skillern.

Elliott & Elliott,   A. B. Melton,
Builders,   Architect.

Near the building is a superior bored well, ninety-three feet deep, with sixty feet of water in it. The grounds cost $2,000, and the building about $32,000. The building is well supplied with piazzas, and is exceedingly well ventilated. R. W. Erwin is president of the college. The first session opened in September, 1889. Too much can not be said in favor of the location of this college, on account of the healthfulness of Searcy, the morality of its people, and many other advantages.

Judsonia University is a Baptist school located at Judsonia. It was founded by the colony that came from the East and located about the year 1870. The school-house is a large frame structure. The faculty is composed of five teachers. It is a good school and has the advantages of being in a quiet, moral town, removed from the vices and temptations of large cities.

The several religious denominations of White County are the Methodist Episcopal, Methodist Episcopal, South, Baptist, Presbyterian, Cumberland Presbyterian and Christian.

Of the Methodist Episcopal Church, South, there are the following: Searcy Station, Rev. J. M. Talkington, pastor, with a membership of 210; Searcy Circuit, consisting of six appointments, Rev. E. M. Baker, pastor, membership 386; El Paso Circuit, consisting of four appointments, Rev. H. F. Harvey, pastor, membership about 250; Lebanon Circuit, consisting of seven appointments, Rev. W. A. Pendergrass, pastor, membership 356; Bradford Circuit, consisting of seven appointments, Rev. C. H. Cary, pastor, membership 164; Beebe and West Point, C. H. Gregory, pastor, membership 225; Red River Circuit, only three appointments in this county, Rev. James A. Brown, pastor, membership about 150; and Kentucky Valley Circuit, with six appointments, Rev. M. B. Corrigan, pastor, membership 359; thus making an aggregate of 2,100 members. The Sunday-schools of this denomination have also a large membership. These organizations all belong to Searcy District of the White River Conference, of which Rev. George M. Hill is the presiding elder.

Of the Methodist Episcopal Church there is Beebe Station, Rev. R. R. Fletcher, pastor, membership 44; Judsonia Station, Rev. George H. Feese, pastor, membership 118; and Bald Knob Circuit, consisting of four appointments in White County and one in Jackson, Rev. F. M. Hughes, pastor. These comprise all the organizations of this denomination within White County, and all belong to the Little Rock District of the Arkansas Conference.

The Baptist Church organizations, pastors and memberships within the county, are as follows: Beebe, Isom P. Langley, 134; Bethlehem, W. H. Hodges, 27; Cane Creek, W. J. Kirkland, 20; Centre Hill, J. D. Doyle, 141; Elon, same pastor, 55; El Paso, same pastor, 206; Garner, L. F. Taylor, 12; Hepsibah, W. H. Hodges, 32; Higginson, R. J. Coleman, 13; Judsonia, B. F. Bartles, 116; Kensett, J. M. Davis, 38; Kentucky Valley, J. A. Chamblee, 39; Liberty, J. M. Davis, 112; Plateau, John Stephens, 26; Rose Bud, M. T. Webb, 78; Searcy, 137; Shiloh, W. J. Kirkland, 76; South Antioch, J. A. Chamblee, 57; Wake Forest, W. J. Kirkland, 13; West Point, J. M. Davis, 54. All of these belong to the Caroline Baptist Association, from the last published proceedings of which the above information has mostly been taken. Since then some changes may have been made in pastors, and the memberships may have increased. The aggregate membership as above given is 1,386.

There are two Presbyterian Church organizations within the county, one at Searcy, Rev. Richard B. Willis, pastor, with a membership of 53, and one near Centre Hill, Rev. W. S. Willbanks, pastor, and a membership of 14.

Below is the list of Cumberland Presbyterian Church organizations in White County, together with names of pastors and membership of each annexed: Beebe, Finis Wylie, 60; Stony Point, J. A. Pemberton, 40; Antioch, same pastor, 86; Pleasant Grove, same pastor, 40; Gum Spring, Finis Wylie, 60; New Hope, J. C. Forbus, 40; Good Springs, Rev. Barlow, 60; aggregating a closely estimated membership of 386.

Of the Christian Church there are Beebe, Clear Water, Garner and Bald Knob. The first has a membership of 70, and the others have a fair membership. Elder J. B. Marshall is pastor of the Beebe organization, and Elder Brown of Clear Water and Garner.

There are also a number of church organizations among the colored people, at Searcy, Beebe, Judsonia and other places. Sunday-schools are taught with much success in connection with most of the churches, and all in all much is accomplished in the cause of Christianity.

Saloons for the selling of intoxicating drinks are not allowed in the county.

The people are generally moral and law-abiding, and cheerfully extend the hand of welcome to all honest and industrious newcomers.

H. K. Adams, merchant at El Paso, Ark., and one of the leading citizens of that city, was born in Rockingham County, N. C., January 29, 1846, being the son of Samuel and Francis (Reid) Adams. Samuel Adams was a farmer by occupation, and a native of Virginia, but most of his life was passed in North Carolina. He was married in that State (where he had a fine farm), and died there in 1870, at the age of sixty-three years. He was magistrate for a number of years, and an energetic, enterprising citizen, and in whatever place he resided that locality might well consider itself the better for his citizenship. His wife died in 1854. She was a sister of Ex-Gov. Reid, of North Carolina, and her mother was a lady of national fame, who had near relatives on the supreme bench of Florida. H. K. Adams is the fifth in a family of eight children, five of whom are now living: Fanny B. (wife of J. W. Thompson, teacher in the Edinburgh High School, in Cleburne County, Ark.), Henrietta (wife of W. P. Watson, a farmer of Monroe County, Ark.), Reuben (a teacher in Prattsville) and Frank R. (a printer, married, and residing in Texas.) Those deceased are: Samuel F. (who lost his life at the hands of raiders, in 1865), David R. (died in college at Madison, N. C., aged eighteen) and Annie E. (who died in infancy.) H. K. Adams was reared on a farm, receiving a good common-school education at the district schools, and at the age of twenty-one launched his bark and began life for himself. He had nothing with which to cope with the world but a stout heart and his wit, and though it was rather discouraging, he never lost heart, and as a natural result was successful. He began first as a clerk in a country store at Boyd's Mill, N. C. A year later he enlisted in Company E, Forty-fifth North Carolina Regiment, and served until the surrender, in May, 1865, participating in the battle of the Wilderness and numerous other skirmishes, but through his entire career was never wounded. At the battle of Spottsylvania he was taken prisoner and held at Point Lookout and Elmira, in all about six months. He was again captured on the retreat from Petersburg, a few days before the surrender of Gen. Lee, and carried to Point Lookout, and remained in prison six weeks after the close of the war. After this Mr. Adams returned to his native State and engaged in farming until 1869, then coming to Arkansas (St. Francis County) where he resided two years. His next move was to El Paso, and after tilling the soil some two years he was engaged as clerk for W. H. Grisard, a prosperous merchant, for several years. For two years he was with C. P. Warren, and at the end of that time (1884) formed a partnership with J. T. Phelps and J. C. Harkrider, under the firm name of Adams, Phelps & Co. A short time later Mr. Phelps sold his interest to the other gentlemen, the firm name becoming Adams & Harkrider. Mr. Adams eventually purchased the entire stock, and after a time formed a partnership with B. A. Neal, whose interest he bought, and then Mr. J. T. Booth purchased an interest, and since that time the firm has been known as Adams & Booth. They are doing a splendid business, and carry a well-assorted stock of general merchandise. Being wide-awake merchants and eminently responsible they command the respect of the entire community. Mr. Adams was united in marriage June 7, 1874, to Miss Florence Harkrider, a native of Alabama and a daughter of W. H. Harkrider, a farmer and mechanic of White County. Their union has been blessed with ten children, six of them now living: Martha F. (born in April, 1875), William S. (born in July, 1876, died in August, 1883), Hugh K., Jr. (born in March, 1878, and died in September, 1879), David C. (born in November, 1879), Dean (born in May, 1881, died in August, 1883), Eva E. (born in November, 1882), Horace E. (born in July, 1884), Sarah Florence (born in November, 1885, died in July, 1886), Myrtle I. (born in January, 1887), and Grace (born in February, 1889). Mr. Adams is giving his children all the advantages of good schools, and is determined that they shall have every opportunity for an education, regardless of expense. Himself and wife are members of the El Paso Methodist Episcopal Church, and Mr. Adams is at present a member of the school board and a notary public. He has served his township as bailiff for a number of years. In addition to his mercantile business he owns a small farm, which is carefully cultivated and yields excellent crops. In his political views he is a Democrat, but not an enthusiast.

James H. Adkins, a man of good repute and thoroughly respected in his community, is a Tennessean by birth and is the son of Elcaney N. and Elizabeth (Hughes) Adkins. The mother of the subject of this sketch was a daughter of Harden and Sarah Hughes, of Tennessee. Mr. Adkins followed farming in Tennessee, and in 1845 immigrated to White County, Ark., and died shortly after his removal to this county, leaving three children: James H., William and Visey. James H. was born in 1844, and enlisted in the cavalry service when eighteen years old, in the Confederate army, and saw some hard fighting from the time of his enlistment, in 1864, until peace was declared. After the war he returned to this county and bought eighty acres of land and commenced to farm for himself. He now owns 140 acres, with over one-half of it in a good state of cultivation, and he vouches that his farm will produce almost everything. Mr. Adkins was married, in 1866, to Frances E. Woodle, a daughter of Turner and Catharine (Matthews) Woodle. Mrs. Adkins died September 3, 1867, leaving one daughter, Sceprobney B. Mr. Adkins took unto himself a second wife (their marriage being solemnized in 1876), Mary F. Cullum, a daughter of Matthew and Mar-

garet C. (Childers) Cullum, natives of Tennessee. Mr. and Mrs. Adkins are the parents of eight children: Dora A., Martha A. (deceased), William O. (deceased), Henry B., James S., Cynthia L. (deceased), Robert C. and Ella A. Himself and wife are members of the Methodist Episcopal Church, South. Mr. Adkins is an A. F. & A. M., belonging to the Mount Pisgah lodge No. 242. He takes a prominent part and is deeply interested in all work beneficial to the community.

Hon. John M. Allen, well and favorably known in this vicinity as a prosperous farmer, and, indeed, throughout this portion of the State, was born in Tennessee, in 1839, being one of two children born to the marriage of Thomas J. and Anna E. (Black) Allen, the father a native of Tennessee, born about 1812, and a son of Daniel Allen, who was a descendant of the famous Ethan Allen. Thomas J. was reared and married in his native State, the latter event taking place about 1834, and there he reared the following family of children: William, John, Neal S., Richard J., Allie, Mary and Hall B., who is deceased. Mr. Allen was a farmer throughout life, and is now living in Arkansas with his son John, and is about eighty years of age. He is a member of the Agricultural Wheel, and he and his wife, who died in 1872, were members of the Baptist Church. John M. Allen received excellent educational advantages in Tennessee, and completed his education in Pulaski College, after which he (in 1856) started out to fight the battle of life for himself and engaged in farming, and this occupation has received his attention up to the present time. In 1859 he married Emma Sparkman, a daughter of William Sparkman, of Tennessee, but in 1877 he was called upon to mourn the death of his wife, she having borne him a family of five children: William (who is married and resides in Beebe), Lizzie (Mrs. Hubbard, residing in Dogwood Township), Arch, Claude and Eugene. Later Mr. Allen wedded Mrs. Hannah (Walker) Seawell, and by her has three children: Adella, Eula and Lonnie. In 1860 Mr. Allen moved with his family to Butler, Mo., and from there, in 1861, enlisted in Company B, Col. Lowe's regiment, as captain, and was shortly promoted to the rank of major. After the battle of Belmont his company was disorganized and his regiment transferred to the Army of the Tennessee and was in nearly all the principal battles of the war from that time until the close. He returned to Missouri after peace was declared and engaged in farming and the mercantile business, but becoming dissatisfied with his location he came to White County, Ark., in 1880, and a year later purchased the farm of 320 acres now belonging to him in Dogwood Township. He has 150 acres under cultivation, but, as his home is in Beebe, he only goes to his farm to attend to the gathering of his crops. He has always been found ready to assist worthy enterprises, and for years past has given much of his attention to politics, and is a member of the Farmers' and Laborers' Union of America, and is the present representative of that party in the State legislature from White County, Ark. He belongs to the State executive committee and is a Mason, holding a demit from Faithful Lodge No. 304. He and wife are members of the Baptist Church. Through his grandmother he is a distant relative of Chief Justice Hale.

Thomas Smith Anderson, a prosperous merchant and cotton dealer, of El Paso, Ark., was born in Madison County, Tenn., August 2, 1832, and is a son of Samuel Lindsay Anderson, who is of Scotch-Irish descent and was born in the "Palmetto State." His ancestors, as well as his wife's (Eliza Braden), came to this country while it was still subject to the British crown and fought in the Revolutionary War. The paternal grandparents were married in Newberry District, S. C., and removed to Tennessee between 1800 and 1812, their son, Samuel L., being born in 1800, and died May 22, 1884, his wife dying in Tennessee in 1847. A great uncle, Joshua Anderson, was under the jurisdiction of Gen. Jackson during the War of 1812, and took part in the battle of New Orleans. In 1858 our subject came to Arkansas and located in Pulaski County (now Faulkner), where, in company with his brother, James A. Anderson, he purchased 420 acres of land, and at the time of his brother's death, in June, 1885, had cleared about 100 acres. In July, 1861, Thomas S. Anderson

enlisted in Company B, Tenth Arkansas Infantry, Confederate States army, and served as second sergeant until the fall of 1862, when he was promoted to brevet second lieutenant, remaining such until the summer of 1865. He was at the battle of Shiloh in charge of the commissary department of his regiment. He was captured at Port Hudson, La., and was a prisoner of war for twenty-one months, being confined at Johnson's Island, Lake Erie, Point Lookout (Md.), and then transferred to Fort Delaware, about forty miles from Philadelphia. He was exchanged at Richmond, Va., and started to rejoin his command at Marshall, Tex., but in his attempt to regain his regiment he was compelled to endure many hardships, and, owing to exposure, he contracted rheumatism, but finally managed to reach Shreveport, that garrison being under command of Gen. Kirby Smith, and with him surrendered. He arrived at home the middle of June, and again, in company with his brother, who had also been in the Confederate army, took up farming. On May 12, 1868, he was united in marriage to Miss Margaret Ann Laws, of Haywood County, Tenn., origin, and a daughter of J. P. and Minerva (Leathers) Laws, who were born in North Carolina. In 1878 Mr. Anderson purchased a stock of general merchandise and opened a store at El Paso, where he has successfully conducted business ever since, and, in connection with this, keeps a line of such furniture as is demanded in his community. He is also an extensive dealer in cotton, and his annual sales for this commodity amount to $10,000 to $12,000. Mr. Anderson votes with the Democratic party, and while a resident of Faulkner County, and since the war, he has served as justice of the peace. He is a Mason, having been initiated into that society in 1859; was secretary of El Paso Lodge for several years, but has been demitted to Velonia Lodge, being its Master one year. He and wife are members of the Methodist Episcopal Church, South.

Moses E. Andrews has been actively and successfully engaged in farming in White County since twenty-one years of age. He was born in Lincoln County, Tenn., in 1844, to the union of Samuel and Marion (Adking) Andrews, natives of

Virginia and Tennessee, respectively. They were married in Lincoln County, Tenn., and there remained until 1851, when they removed to Arkansas, and located in White County, near the place upon which the village of Judsonia is now located. This was then in the woods, but Mr. Andrews cleared up a good farm and made a home. He was a prominent Democrat, and served as justice of the peace for several years, and died May 20, 1867, at the age of fifty-six. Mrs. Andrews died in 1864, leaving a family of seven children, two of whom only are living: Moses E. (our subject) and Joseph D. (who is a farmer of White County.) Moses E. Andrews was married in 1873 to Elizabeth Eaton, a daughter of E. S. Eaton, an old settler of White County. She was born in 1851. They are the parents of two children: Benjamin W. and Rosella. Mrs. Andrews is a member of the Missionary Baptist Church. Mr. Andrews is a prominent Democrat and a leading citizen.

Moses Morgan Aunsspaugh, farmer and stock raiser of Little Red, Ark., is one of the much respected and esteemed residents of Denmark Township, where he has made his home for many years. He is the son of Benjamin and Ruhama (Hartley) Aunsspaugh, the former of German descent and a native of Pennsylvania. George Aunsspaugh, the great-grandfather of the subject of this sketch, came from Germany at an early day, located in Pennsylvania, and served in the Colonial army from that State in the capacity of drum-major in Gen. Washington's immediate command. The great-grandfather Hartley was a native born Englishman, came to America before the Revolution, settled in Pennsylvania, and served as a private soldier. Grandfather Aunsspaugh was a soldier in the War of 1812, and arrived in New Orleans the day after the battle, having served with the Ohio State troops. Benjamin Aunsspaugh came to Arkansas in 1833, in company with John Hartley and his family, and located in Jefferson County, of that State, all having traveled from Zanesville, Ohio, on a keel-boat, leaving that point in the early part of the fall of 1833, and arriving in the above county in December of the same year. Benjamin married Miss Ruhama

Hartley in Jefferson County, Ark., and the following children were born to this union: Jobe (born 1834), Moses Morgan (born 1835), John (born 1837), George (born 1839) and Amoa (born 1840). The mother of these children died in the last of June, 1845, in White County, Ark., whither Benjamin Aunsspaugh had moved with his family in October of the previous year, and here the father also died in 1876. In this county Jobe, Moses and John grew to manhood. Moses Morgan Aunsspaugh was born on the keel-boat, upon which his father and the Hartley family journeyed from Ohio, on April 12, 1835. He attended school about three weeks and had got as far as "baker" in his spelling book when his school days suddenly terminated. He learned the blacksmith trade with his father and followed this occupation for a number of years. On January 17, 1858, he was wedded to Miss Sarah Winford, a native of Tennessee, and the daughter of Samuel and Martha (Morris) Winford, who came to Arkansas in 1844, settled in Poinsett County, where the father died the same year. The Winford family consisted of these children: Margaret (married Thomas Anderson and became the mother of eight children; she died in 1859), Jane (married Dave Ellster, and has one child) and Sarah. To Mr. and Mrs. Aunsspaugh were born three children: Martha Ann Ruhama (born November 4, 1858), Samuel Benjamin Franklin (born August 31, 1862) and George Washington (born April 25, 1872). Martha Ann Ruhama married Albert M. Bryant on August 4, 1874, and became the mother of four children: John Thomas, Lindsay E., Oliver and Mary Ella. Samuel B. F. married Miss Martha Porter on March 4, 1879, and became the father of three children. He, his wife and all his children are deceased. Benjamin Aunsspaugh bought eighty acres of land in White County, improved it, and in 1846 moved to Searcy, where he carried on his trade as blacksmith. He and his son Moses ironed the first wagon sent out of White County to California in 1849. In 1851 he returned to the neighborhood of his old home, and there bought 160 acres of land, subsequently adding to this until he at one time owned 320 acres. At the time of his death he owned 240 acres, with thirty acres under cultivation, and in connection with tilling the soil he also carried on the blacksmith trade up to that time. Benjamin Aunsspaugh was married the second time in 1853 to Mrs. Jane McDonald, a native of Alabama, and these children were the result: William (born 1854), twins (born 1855), James and an infant who died unnamed and another infant died unnamed. James W. married Mrs. Jennie Copeland, who bore him three children, two living. He resides on a farm in White County. Moses M. Aunsspaugh made his first purchase of land in 1858, paying 50 cents an acre for eighty acres. In 1862, much against his will, he was conscripted by the Confederates, and served three years in that army, participating in the battle of Helena, but did not fire a gun. He served his company in the capacity of cook, and returned home in 1864. He sold his first purchase of land in 1860, and in 1861 purchased 160 acres near Searcy, which was partly improved. He then cleared twelve acres, erected a log-house 16x16 feet and lived there for eight years, two and a half years of which time he rendered Union service in the Confederate army. In 1869 he sold his farm and moved to his present property, where he has since made his home. He first purchased 170 acres, but afterward added to this eighty acres, and soon had fifteen acres under cultivation, and resided in a log-house for six years. In 1875 he erected his present comfortable house, and there he has since resided. The same year he noticed a peculiar looking stone on his place, picked it up, called the attention of an experienced geologist to it, and it was pronounced gold quartz. Mr. and Mrs. Aunsspaugh are members of the Cumberland Presbyterian Church, and their daughter Martha D. and her husband are members of the United Baptist Church. Mr. Aunsspaugh is a member of the Agricultural Wheel No. 176.

William C. Barclay, postmaster and merchant of Russell, Ark., of Jackson County, Ala., nativity, and whose birth occurred January 28, 1858, is the son of James C. and Melinda (Wright) Barclay, natives of Alabama. James C. Barclay is still a citizen of Alabama, and follows farming for a livelihood. The wife of James C. died in November, 1864, having borne him eight children: Anna, Penelope, Tommie, John P., James P., William L., Jane and Sarah, all living. Mr. Barclay again married, choosing for his second wife Miss Ransom of Jackson County, Ala., and the result of this marriage is one child, Wiley F. Barclay, born in 1868. In February, 1875, Mr. Barclay was married the third time to Miss Galbreath of De Kalb County, Ala., and to them has been given one child. The grandparents of William C. came direct from Ireland to Alabama. Our subject was reared in Jackson County. His advantages for learning were limited in his youth by reason of the Civil War and its attendant and subsequent hardships. But by constant study and close observation, he is well informed on the important events of the day. Mr. Barclay began for himself in July, 1870, as a farm hand, then as a salesman in a general merchant mill in Alabama. In 1877 he moved to Arkansas, settling in White County, and engaging in farming followed it for two years. At the expiration of the two years he accepted a position as salesman in Russell, but soon after accepting this he was appointed railroad and express agent of that city, which office he filled for one year. Mr. Barclay then started a general merchandise business, in this meeting with flattering success. He carries a good stock, which is valued at $2,500 to $3,000, and by his courteous manner and upright dealing has obtained a liberal patronage from the surrounding community. Mr. Barclay was united in matrimony, December 23, 1880, to Miss Fannie N. Watson, a daughter of Hiram B. and Henrietta (Bankston) Watson, of Columbus County, Ga. By this marriage two children have been born: Fred B. (born August, 1881, now deceased), and Frank Carlton (born November 23, 1884). Mr. Barclay received the appointment of postmaster at Russell in 1881, holding that position until 1885, when he was re-elected, and is still filling the office, discharging the duties that devolve upon him in a manner that is entirely satisfactory to all and commendatory to one in that responsible position. He is president of the school board, and takes an active part in all educational interests; contributes liberally to the relief of the poor, and is a thorough worker in all public enterprises. He is a Democrat in his political views and a Methodist in religious belief, though not a member of the church. Mr. Barclay is a Master Mason in good standing, also belongs to the Triple Alliance, a mutual benefit association.

John M. Bartlett is the son of George Bartlett, who was born in Kentucky in 1811, being married in Illinois, about 1830, to Mahala Gowens. She was brought up among the Indians and had Indian blood in her veins, her mother being a half Cherokee. Mr. Bartlett after his marriage settled in Illinois, where he remained three years. He then moved to Kentucky and remained there until his death, which occurred in May, 1864, his wife also dying within a few days. They were the parents of six children: Martha J., William, Thomas J., John M., Dudley and Elizabeth P. Thomas and Dudley are deceased. John M. Bartlett was born in Fulton County, Ky., in 1843. At the outbreak of the war, inspired by patriotism, he enlisted, May 1861, in the Fifth Tennessee Infantry and participated in the battle of Shiloh and in a number of skirmishes. After his term of service had expired he returned home before the close of the war and engaged in farming, and married, in 1864, Miss Josephine Baldridge, a daughter of one of the early pioneers of Kentucky. Following his union Mr. Bartlett immigrated to Arkansas, and settled in Van Buren County and three years later, came to White County, where he has since made his home. He has a fine farm of 120 acres, seventy-five of which are under cultivation. Mrs. Bartlett was a Free Will Baptist, and died in 1883, leaving four children: George (deceased), Jennie, Ida and Josephine. Mr. Bartlett was married the second time to Mrs. Sutton, a widow. By his second marriage he has one boy: Edgar. Mr. Bartlett is a member of the Christian Church, and is a member and the vice-president of the County Wheel. His influence in the affairs of this community has been of decided good.

Judge J. J. Bell, the present efficient clerk of

9

the circuit court and recorder of White County, is a native of Arkansas and a son of Robert S. and Louisa (Jacobs) Bell, natives of Kentucky and Vermont, respectively. Robert S. Bell was born in 1805, and when a young man moved to Arkansas and located in Monroe County, being one of the early settlers of that locality. In 1850 he became settled in White County, where he was engaged in his work as a Presbyterian minister, also serving as county clerk for four years. While in Monroe County he served as county clerk, and besides occupied the office of county judge for several years. He remained in White County ten years, but subsequently removed to the Chickasaw Nation, going there as a missionary and a teacher to that tribe. In their midst he remained until his death, which occurred in 1880. He was a son of James Bell, of Irish descent, who was a missionary Baptist minister, and died in White County. Louisa Jacobs was a daughter of Joseph Jacobs, of Vermont, who came to Monroe County at an early day, being one of the early settlers, and where he died. Mrs. Bell died in 1848, after which Mr. Bell married Arvilla A. Waterman, who is still living. By his first marriage he was the father of six children, our subject being the only one living. By his second marriage there are two children: Robert S., Jr. (who is a resident of the Indian nation), and Albert G. J. J. Bell first saw the light of day in Monroe County December 11, 1841, but accompanied his parents to White County when nine years of age. When sixteen years old he commenced farming for himself, at which he was occupied until the breaking out of the war, when he enlisted in the Eighth Arkansas Infantry, serving as second lieutenant of Company K, and participating in the battles of Murfreesboro, Chickamauga, Missionary Ridge, Atlanta, and a number of others. He was captured at Jonesboro, Ga., September 1, 1864, and was held twenty-one days when he was exchanged and rejoined his regiment. At the battle of Murfreesboro he was wounded by a gunshot in the forehead, and at the battle of Nashville he was again slightly wounded in the head. After the war he went to Tyler, Tex., then to Ouachita County, Ark., and in 1870 returned to White County, when he again turned his attention to farming. In 1880 Mr. Bell was elected clerk of the circuit court, which office he held for four years. In 1887 he was elected to fill the unexpired term in the office of county judge, and in 1888 was again elected clerk of the circuit court. His official duties have been discharged in a manner above reproach, and to the satisfaction of all and his own credit. Mr. Bell was married May 22, 1865, to Miss Sarah A. Banks, who was born in Alabama August, 1846. She came to White County with her parents when a child. Mr. and Mrs. Bell became the parents of eleven children, eight of whom are still living; William H., George H., Franklin, Charles E., Joseph T., Richard L., Sarah A., and Katie. Mr. Bell is a member of the Agricultural Wheel and is a strong Democrat. He and his wife are also associated with the Cumberland Presbyterian Church.

John W. Benton has been worthily identified with White County's affairs for a long period. His parents, William and Malinda E. (Wilson), were natives of Virginia and Georgia, respectively. The former was born in 1803, and was a son of John Wilson, who moved from Virginia to Georgia when the father of our subject was a boy. William Wilson married in 1824, and was engaged in the milling business all of his life. He became the father of eight children; Willis R., James W., Catharine, William M., Lucinda, John W., Steven and Martha. Mr. Benton died in 1887, and his wife in 1843. John W. Benton's birth occurred in Georgia in 1839, he spending his early life in the mill of his father. In 1858 he was married to Rachel Burket, a daughter of William and Rachel (Hughs) Burket, in White County, Ark., whither he had moved some two years before. Mr. and Mrs. Benton are the parents of thirteen children: Linda E. (who married David Volenteer), Francis B. (who married Frances Nipper), John Steven (married to Katie Coffey), James W. (married to Emma Horton), William M. (who married Etta Scruggs), Willie R. (married Jennie Copper), Jessie A., David H., Fannie S., Elneo L., Charley W., Mamie L. and Henry V. Mr. Benton enlisted during the war (in 1863) in Capt. Thompson's company, and took part in the Missouri raid, being captured at Van Buren and taken to Little Rock. Mr. Benton has a fine farm of 160 acres, with over half of it cleared. Himself and wife are members of the Presbyterian Church, Mr. Benton being one of the elders. He is a Democrat in politics, and an esteemed citizen.

T. B. Bobbitt, M. D., is one of the most worthy men engaged in the practice of medicine in White County, and is much esteemed and respected by all his medical brethren. He was born in Gibson County, Tenn., November 8, 1849, and while assisting his father on the farm, he attended school at every opportunity, and by applying himself closely to his books he, at the age of twenty years, had a much better education than the average farmer's boy. Not being satisfied with the education thus acquired, he entered the high school at Gibson, Tenn., and formed while there a desire to enter the medical profession. In 1872 he entered the Nashville Medical College, graduated in the class of 1873 and the following year engaged in selling drugs. He next farmed one year and in 1876 began the practice of medicine in Madison County, Tenn., continuing there until 1879, when he settled in White County, at Antioch Church, and in 1886 came to Beebe. Since his residence here he has practiced his profession, kept a drug store and has farmed, and in all these enterprises has been successful, being now the owner of 500 acres of good farming land, lying in several different farms, and has 200 acres under cultivation. In 1873 he was united in marriage to Miss Eddie James, a daughter of Edward James, a native of Tennessee. They have four children: Nora (born March 1, 1875), Pinkie (born in 1879), Lawson (born in 1881) and Edgar (born in 1886). The Doctor is a member of the A. F. & A. M. and was a member of the K. of L. He and his wife and eldest daughter are members of the Cumberland Presbyterian Church. His parents, T. J. and Elizabeth (Wallace) Bobbitt, were born in South Carolina and Tennessee, respectively, and the former at the age of seven years was taken to Tennessee by his father, James Bobbitt, who had previously been an influential planter of South Carolina. They were married in Gibson County,

Tenn., in 1835, and reared the following family: William H. (a lawyer of Humboldt, Tenn.), Caroline (wife of W. F. Lawson, at present mayor of Eureka Springs, Ark.), James (a carriage and wagon maker of Joplin, Mo.), Mattie (who died at the age of twenty at Eureka Springs, Ark.), Ellen (wife of H. M. Brimm, a druggist at Eureka Springs), Mollie (wife of William Boyd, an editor of Seneca, Mo.) and Lena (who died in infancy). Both parents are living in retirement at Eureka Springs and are members of the Cumberland Presbyterian Church, the former a Mason and a member of the Union Labor party. J. N. Wallace, the maternal grandfather of our subject, was a soldier in the War of 1812, was a farmer and one of the pioneers of Tennessee.

Robert I. Boggs, a leading planter and stock raiser of White County owes his nativity to the State of Mississippi, and was born in June, 1843, being the son of John W. Boggs, of South Carolina. The former was born in 1815 and received his education in Yorktown, S. C., immigrating to Mississippi in 1840, where he married Catherine J. Smith in 1841. Mrs. Boggs was a daughter of John and Martha Smith, and a devout member of the Methodist Church. Her death occurred in 1889. Mr. and Mrs. Boggs were the parents of fifteen children: Mandy, Joseph W. (deceased), Robert I., James P., Newton J. (deceased), John (deceased), Martha (deceased), Lucy and Sarah (died at the ages of twenty-five and twenty-three, respectively), Franklin L. George P., Charley W., Margaret M., Addie E. and Harrison B. Mr. Boggs was a Democrat, and a man who manifested a great interest in all church and educational matters. He helped to organize the first church at Mount Pisgah, Mount Pleasant and Oak Grove, and has acted as class-leader in the Methodist Episcopal Church for fifty years. He is a member of the Wheel and also the Grange, and is enjoying good health, though passed his seventy-fourth year. Robert I. received his education in the county schools of White County near Searcy, and there married November 12, 1867, Miss Eliza J. Whisenant, of Mississippi, and a daughter of Nicholson and Nancy Whisenant, natives of South Carolina. To the union of Mr. and Mrs. Boggs six children have been born: Ida M., James M., Edward, Robert C., Annie J. and John W. Ida and Edward are deceased; the rest reside at home. Mr. Boggs owns about 150 acres of good land, sixty in cultivation, and well stocked with all that is requisite to successfully operate a farm of that size. He is a member of the Wheel, in which he has held the office of president and vice-president, discharging in a highly commendable manner the duties of that office. He served in the late war on the Confederate side and entered in October, 1862, returning home in 1863, but again enlisted, remaining only a short time. In 1864 he enlisted again under Gen. Dobbins, his first hard fight being at DeVall's Bluff. He was wounded in the Big Blue Fight by a ball which struck him in the left cheek, but did not prove serious. Mr. Boggs received an honorable discharge and at once returned home, engaging in farming, which has been his occupation ever since, and proving very successful. He is a member of twenty years' standing in the Methodist Episcopal Church, and his wife has held a membership in the Cumberland Presbyterian Church for twenty-three years.

M. Love Booth, retired farmer and merchant, was born in Middle Tennessee, Bedford County, in 1819, but owing to his father's early removal to Haywood County, he was reared there. The parents, James and Mary (Lofton) Booth, were both Virginians, and after residing in Tennessee for many years they removed to White County, Ark., and died at the home of their son in 1861. He was a member of the Baptist Church, a Mason, a lifelong Democrat, and was for years sheriff of Bedford County. After his wife's death, which occurred in 1851, he married again and came to Arkansas. M. Love Booth is the third of their six children, four now living: John (deceased, who was a farmer in Tennessee), William (a farmer of West Tennessee), Samira (deceased), M. Love, Susan (the wife of Henry Bacon, of Mississippi) and Louisa (who is the wife of a Tennessee farmer). Our subject has been familiar with farm work from his earliest boyhood, but his early advantages for acquiring an education were not so good. At the age of twenty he was a farm hand, later a trader and stock breeder, and after his marriage to Miss Elizabeth Budrell he became an overseer, and successfully followed that-occupation for forty years. He then gave up that work and built a livery stable in Brownsville, his establishment there being the largest of the kind in the State. In 1858 he came to Arkansas and purchased 320 acres of land near El Paso, seventy acres of which he cleared the first year. He was signally successful until the war broke out, when all his personal property was lost. He did not espouse either cause, and was not molested during those turbulent times. When he came to El Paso there were only two farms open here, but now the greater part of the land is in a high state of cultivation. After the war he, with Thomas Warren, built a large mill, which was destroyed by fire, when he returned to his farm, which he again began to till. He became the possessor of 1,000 acres, and has cleared over 300 acres, and since giving each of his children a farm he still holds 310 acres. His wife died October 1, 1887, and since that time he has made his home with his children, and is at present living with J. T. Phelps, his son-in-law, in El Paso, where he has an interest in the store of M. L. Phelps & Co. Mr. Booth was the first man to build a store in El Paso after the war, and is now managing a livery stable in that place, and, although he has attained the age of seventy years, he is an excellent business manager and is very active. Although quiet in his habits of life, he has always been interested in the public affairs of the county, and has done his full share in making the county what it is. He joined the Masons while in Tennessee, and he as well as his children are members of the Baptist Church. His children's names are here given: Nancy (is the wife of Monroe Oakley, a prosperous farmer of White County), Rebecca (is the wife of John C. Harkness, a farmer of El Paso), Elizabeth L. (is the wife of Thomas K. Noland, a farmer of the county), Narcissus (is the wife of John Russ, a farmer and president of the State Wheel), Martha A. (is the wife of J. T. Phelps, a merchant of El Paso), Mosella B. (deceased) and three infants, deceased.

Gilliam Harper Booth, known to the citizens of White County as one of its wide-awake, energetic, ever-pushing men, is of Tennessee nativity, and a son of William A. and Delia Jane (Leathers) Booth, who claim Virginia and North Carolina, respectively, as the land of their birth. William A., the father of our subject, was born in 1811, and when a young man came with his parents to Mississippi, and later on removed to Fayette County, Tenn., and thence to Haywood County. He was married in Fayette County. In 1856, after the election of James Buchanan to the presidency of the United States, they removed to Arkansas. He was an emphatic Democrat, casting his vote with that party, and a member of the Methodist Episcopal Church, South. William A. Booth was a son of Harper Booth, a Revolutionary War veteran, who served in that memorable conflict, and who died in 1859 at an extreme old age. The grandfather was a Virginian by birth, and a descendant of the Harper family from whom Harper's Ferry derives its name. Delia Jane Leathers was born in 1817, and was taken to Tennessee by her mother when a child of seven years. Mr. and Mrs. Booth were the parents of twelve children, four of whom are still living: Isabella J. (the wife of Dr. W. P. Lawton), Martha Ann (the wife of Capt. Rayburn, deceased), Gilliam H. (our subject) and Charles L. Gilliam H. Booth received his education at the public schools of West Point and at Judsonia University. His birth occurred August 26, 1850, in Haywood County, Tenn. He has been actively engaged in teaching school, clerking and farming, and owns a fine farm of 356 acres, with 150 under cultivation. In religion he is a member of the Methodist Episcopal Church, South, and a Prohibitionist, but, being a radical free trader, inclines toward the Democratic party, voting that ticket. In the community in which he lives he is regarded as a highly respected citizen.

William F. Bradley is a traveling salesman for a Lynchburg (Va.) tobacco firm, and is a gentleman who enjoys the respect and esteem of the people of White County. He was born in Caldwell County, N. C., June 6, 1847, and is a son of Jackson and Martha (Ferguson) Bradley, who were born, reared and married in that State, the latter event taking place in 1841. Mrs. Bradley was born in 1825, was of Scotch descent, her grandfather having emigrated from Scotland to North Carolina before it became a State, and took part in the Revolutionary War, being in sympathy with the cause of the Americans. Jackson Bradley was born in 1818, and was of Welsh descent, his ancestors having come to America long before the Revolution. After his marriage he was engaged in farming in his native state until 1855, and after residing successively in Mississippi, Georgia, and Missouri, he came to Arkansas in 1861, and to White County in 1875. He resided on a farm two miles east of Beebe till his death in March, 1887, his wife preceding him to the grave by ten years. Both worshiped in the Missionary Baptist Church. William F. Bradley was the third in a family of seventeen children, the following of whom are living: Madelia (Mrs. Thomas), Amelia (Mrs. Mosier), Susan (Mrs. Bailey), Burton and William F. The latter received his education in the various States in which his father lived, and after attaining his twenty-first year, he worked as a farm hand for two years, then attended school at Butlerville, Lonoke County, for ten months. After teaching one term of school he engaged as a clerk at Beebe, at the end of six years engaging in the same business in partnership with J. T. Coradine, under the firm name of Bradley & Coradine. At the end of two years they took a Mr. Burton into the business, the firm then becoming Bradley, Coradine & Co., continuing such one year. Mr. Bradley then sold his interest, and became associated with Richard S. Bradley under the firm name of W. F. & R. S. Bradley, general merchants; but a few months later they made an assignment, losing all their goods. After this misfortune Mr. Bradley began working as a salesman, then secured a position as traveling salesman for Charles G. Peper & Co. of St. Louis, but at the end of a few months was compelled to give up this position on account of poor health. After recovering he worked for some time as a railroad clerk, then resumed clerking, continuing until May 1, 1889, when he accepted his present position with

J. W. West & Co., tobacco manufacturers of Lynchburg, Va. He is nicely situated in the town of Beebe, and has a pleasant and comfortable home, and socially is a member of Beebe Lodge No. 145, of the A. F. & A. M. He has belonged to the city board of aldermen, and he and wife, who was a Miss Emma S. Dement, and whom he married November 4, 1874, are members of the Missionary Baptist Church. They have a charming young daughter, Maud E., who was born October 26, 1876, and is attending the schools of Beebe. Mrs. Bradley is a native of De Soto County, Miss., and is a daughter of James T. and Ellen (Binge) Dement, the former of Alabama, and the latter of Tennessee. Mr. Dement was a farmer, and in 1872 came with his family to White County, dying there a year later, at the age of forty-five years. His wife survives him, and lives with Mrs. McIntosh in Beebe. The following are her children: Betty J. (born in 1857, the wife of Dr. McIntosh, the leading physician of Beebe), Emma S. (Mrs. Bradley, born June 24, 1859), Ella (born 1861, wife of A. M. Burton, a prosperous merchant of Beebe), Jennie (wife of Maxwell Welty, a railroad agent at Beebe), and James T. (who was born in February, 1874, and is attending the high school at Beebe).

William Sackville Brewer. Ever since his connection with the agricultural affairs of White County, Ark., Mr. Brewer has displayed those sterling characteristics—industry, perseverance and integrity, that have resulted in awarding him a representative place in matters pertaining to this community. The paternal ancestors came to America prior to the Revolutionary War and settled in Virginia, the grandfather, Barrett Brewer, an Englishman, participating in that struggle. He married Malinda Pollard, and by her became the father of four children: Martha (Mrs. Sanders), Sarah (who first married a Mr. Harder, and afterward a Mr. Scott), Benjamin and John Pollard (the father of our biographical subject). The maternal ancestors were also English, and came to America while it was still subject to the crown. The maternal grandmother was a Sackville, belonging to the distinguished English family of that name. John Pollard Brewer was married to Susan Jefferson Townsend September 1, 1833, and to them the following children were born: William Sackville (born June 10, 1834), Martha M. (born July 18, 1836), James M. (born July 3, 1838), Pollard J. (born October 24, 1840), Sarah W. (born March 5, 1843), Andrew T. (born November 19, 1845), Benjamin A. (born May 19, 1848), John B. (born January 22, 1851), Mary E. (born September 19, 1853) and Karilla W. (born July 2, 1855). The father and mother of these children were born October 15, 1812, and March 14, 1817, respectively, the latter being of German descent, and a daughter of Andrew Criswell and Elizabeth (Barnett) Townsend. The father was one of the early settlers of Alabama, and represented Pike County in the State legislature. William Sackville Brewer was born in Pike County, Ala., and was educated in the subscription schools and reared on a farm. At the age of nineteen years he left home and united his fortunes with those of Miss Eliza H. Clayton, their union taking place October 10, 1852. She was born in Fayette County, Ga., June 6, 1834, and is a daughter of Richard and Jane (Carter) Clayton, the paternal ancestors being emigrants from Ireland to America prior to the Revolution. Mr. and Mrs. Brewer have a family of ten children: Susan E. (born September 6, 1853, became the wife of W. J. Turner in 1872, and died in 1883, leaving two children), Howell C. (born December 8, 1855, and died September 3, 1863), John William (born January 8, 1858), Ara Anna (born March 30, 1860, and died September 12, 1864), James R. (born September 18, 1862), Lela Lewis (born January 8, 1865, married D. A. King in 1882 and became the mother of two children), Henry W. (born September 1, 1867, and died June 8, 1871), Minnie Lee (born August 4, 1870), Robert B. (born March 23, 1872) and Richard J. (born December 24, 1874). Mr. Brewer has been a resident of Arkansas since 1873, and for two years farmed on rented land near Searcy. He continued to farm rented land until 1878, when he bought the farm of 129 acres where he now lives, of which about thirty-five acres are under cultivation. The buildings on the place were badly dilapidated, but Mr. Brewer now has all the buildings in excellent repair and his farm otherwise well improved. Mr. Brewer and his wife are professors of religion, and he at one time belonged to the Masonic fraternity, and is now a member of the Agricultural Wheel.

Charles Brown, M. D., was a native of Virginia, and was born May 3, 1783. He was the son of Bernard and Elizabeth (Dancy) Brown. He received his early education in Virginia, and later attended the Jefferson Medical College at Philadelphia, from which he graduated about 1807, subsequently settling in Charlotteville, Albemarle County, Va., and commenced the practice of medicine. Mr. Brown was married April 1, 1813, to Mary Brown, a daughter of Bezakel and Mary (Thompson) Brown, originally of Virginia, who was born April 24, 1790. They were the parents of the following children: Bernard O. (deceased), Elvira (deceased), Elizabeth D. (now Mrs. Jones, of Virginia), Bezaleel T. (deceased), Charles T., Algerion R. and Ezra M. Mr. Brown held the office of high sheriff of his county for two terms. His death occurred in 1879, at the age of ninety-six years; at the time of his death he was still a strong man with a wonderful memory. Algerion R. Brown was born in Albemarle County, Va., March 5, 1831. He attended the University of Virginia and in 1850 left it and studied medicine with his father a short time, and in 1852 went to Marshall County, Mississippi, where he engaged in the mercantile business until the war broke out. Mr. Brown was married January 26, 1855, to Mary F. Williams, a daughter of Alexander and Martha (Delote) Williams, of North Carolina nativity. Mrs. Brown was a native of Tennessee. Mr. Brown enlisted in 1861 for three years or during the war, in Company F, of the Thirty-fourth Mississippi Infantry in the Army of Tennessee. During the first twelve months he was first lieutenant, afterward was on staff of "general inspector," and after the battle of Lookout Mountain he went back to his regiment and was placed in command of three companies for some time and was then promoted to captain of the engineer department of staff duty, filling this position till the time of surrender. He participated in the battles of Shiloh, Murfreesboro, Chickamauga, Lookout Mountain, Missionary Ridge, and nearly all of the principal battles during the terrible conflict. Mr. Brown removed from Mississippi to Tennessee in 1881, remaining there four years, then moved to White County, Ark., settling in Cane Township on eighty acres of land, where he now has about thirty acres under cultivation. Mr. and Mrs. Brown have a family of five children and one deceased: Martha E. (deceased), Mary W., Susan W., Charles E., Samuel H., Walter L. Himself and wife are members of the Methodist Episcopal Church, South. Mr. Brown has served as delegate to the district and annual conferences, and is one of the stewards of the church. He is an energetic and well-educated man, and a fine talker, and takes an interest in all school and religious work. He was one of the committee from Mississippi to the New Orleans fair in 1883.

Dr. R. L. Browning, physician and surgeon, Judsonia, Ark. Prominent among the comparatively young men of White County, whose career thus far has been both honorable and successful, is the subject of the present sketch. His father, R. C. Browning was a native of Kentucky, and while attending school in Indiana, met and married the mother of the Doctor, her maiden name being Miss Eliza Frady. She was born in North Carolina, but was reared in Indiana. After their marriage the parents settled in Kentucky, and here the father followed teaching until 1849, when he moved to Sac County, Iowa, where he followed agricultural pursuits for a means of livelihood. He took an active part in politics, was county treasurer of Sac County one term, and in the fall of 1870 moved to Judsonia, where he continued tilling the soil. In 1877 he engaged in merchandising and still continues in that business. He and wife reside in Judsonia. Their family consisted of the following children: J. H. (married and living in Judsonia), W. C. (married and residing in Kirksville, Mo., engaged in merchandising), R. L., Maggie (now Mrs. Marsh, of Judsonia), Viola (now Mrs. Drake, of Judsonia). Dr. R. L. Browning was born in Sac County, Iowa, in 1859, assisted his father on the farm, and received

his education in the Judsonia University, one of the best schools of the county. He commenced reading medicine in Judsonia in 1877, and in 1878-79 took a course of lectures at the Cincinnati Eclectic Medical Institute, Cincinnati, Ohio, graduating in the class of 1882. He then came back and commenced the practice of medicine, where he was reared, and continued the same until the summer of 1882, having met with success and built up a big practice. He was married in Judsonia, Ark., on November 27, 1882, to Miss Emily B. Ellis, a native of New York, and the daughter of John Ellis, of English origin. Mr. Ellis came to this country, settled in New York, was civil engineer, and also engaged in horticulture. He came to Judsonia, Ark., in 1882, and died the same year in San Francisco, Cal., the mother dying in New York in 1872. To the union of Mr. and Mrs. Browning were born two children (only one now living): Harry R. (who was born in 1887), and Carroll Ellis (who died in 1884, at the age of eight months and twelve days). Dr. Browning is not very enthusiastic in regard to politics, but his vote is cast with the Republican party. Socially he is a member of Judsonia Lodge No. 45, I. O. O. F., at Judsonia, and has been Noble Grand of the order. He belongs to the Missionary Baptist Church and Mrs. Browning to the Episcopal Church. The Doctor is secretary of the Building Association, also of the board of Judsonia University, and is one of the first men of the county. He has been unusually successful in his practice and has won the confidence and esteem of all.

Prof. Augustine W. Bumpass, a prominent citizen and teacher of White County, is a native of Madison County, West Tenn., where he was born, near Jackson, on January 22, 1851. He is the eldest son of Dr. E. L. and Lucinda E. (Young) Bumpass. His father was a native of Giles County, Tenn., where he was born April 15, 1816, being reared in Lauderdale County, Ala., and there educated both in literature and medicine. Graduating at the Louisville Medical College, in the class of 1841-42, with the highest honors, he was for many years a prominent physician in Alabama, but removed to Madison County, Tenn., in the latter part of 1850, where he resided until 1856, at which time he removed to Arkansas and settled in Prairie (now Lonoke) County. Here, in a wild and unsettled country, he purchased land and opened up a farm, which he conducted in connection with his practice until his death, December 3, 1883. He was a man of generous and humane impulses, a warm-hearted and devoted Christian, and a member of the Christian Church. He was a Master Mason and a member of the I. O. O. F., standing high in both of those societies. An old line Whig until the dissolution of that party, he then affiliated with the Democratic party until his death. The mother of our subject, Lucinda E. (Young) Bumpass, was a native of Alabama, where she was reared, educated and married. She was the daughter of Elder James Young, a prominent minister of the Christian Church in Alabama. He died in 1852. Mrs. Bumpass died on December 5, 1881, aged fifty-nine years, eight months and nine days. Dr. Gabriel Bumpass, grandfather of Augustine W., was a native of North Carolina and died in Lauderdale County, Ala., in 1875, aged one hundred and seventeen years. He was the oldest physician in America, if not in the world, having practiced medicine for more than eighty years. He was a remarkable man in many respects, and as physician, farmer or merchant, was very successful. Our subject's parents were married in Lauderdale County, Ala., on May 18, 1845. To their marriage seven children were born, five sons and two daughters, five of whom are living, as follows: Mary E. (at Pine Bluff, Ark.), Augustine W. (near Searcy, in White County, Ark.), Samuel J. (at Lonoke, (Ark.), Edward K. and Ross H. (at Pine Bluff, Ark.). The two last named are mechanics and buggy and carriage manufacturers; Samuel J. is a farmer, stock-raiser and trader. Romelia C., the eldest, a daughter, and Robert W., the fourth child, are dead. A. W. Bumpass was reared in Tennessee to the age of five years, and from that time in Arkansas, where he was educated, obtaining a good academic instruction and preparing himself for the profession of law. However, he began teaching early in life and has paid but little attention to the law, except in the lower courts.

Commencing for himself at the age of eighteen as a teacher in the public schools of his State, he has been occupied in teaching more or less for twenty years, gaining an enviable reputation in many counties where he has been engaged in the public and private schools and academies. He is a politician of some note, and represented his county (Lonoke) in the legislature, in 1879 and 1880, taking always an active interest in the campaigns of his party, Democratic. He was married in Lonoke County, Ark., on April 25, 1875, to Miss Virginia C. Kirk, a native of Marshall County, Miss., born April 11, 1856, a daughter of Richard L. and Virginia (Hayes) Kirk. Her father is dead, but her mother is a resident of White County, at the home of her daughter. Prof. Bumpass and wife have five children, four sons and one daughter: Edward W., Herbert R., Robert H., Prentice and Mary Moyner. The Professor is a member of the Christian Church and takes an active interest in church and Sunday-school matters. He has been Sunday-school superintendent for many years, was notary public from 1885 until 1889 in White County, and is a highly educated, intelligent gentleman, having the respect and confidence of those with whom he comes in contact. Generous to a fault, he aids all worthy enterprises to the extent of his time and means.

Patrick Burns was the second settler in White County, and for this reason, if for no other, deserves prominent mention in the present volume. Now the oldest resident of the county, he came here in 1844 and located some land, having to make the journey from Springfield on foot and passing about fifteen days en route. His arrival was in September and he remained in the wilderness country until the following February, when he returned on foot to Sangamon County, Ill., going thence to Ohio in the same manner. After about one year's stay in the Buckeye State he again came to White County and was engaged in farming until 1863. Going to Missouri he worked there at farm labor also, and in 1865 settled permanently on the farm where he now lives. His career since that time has been one of which he need not feel ashamed. Mr. Burns was born in

Washington, D. C., in 1814, being a son of Thomas and Katie (Larner) Burns, of Irish descent. Thomas Burns was a laborer, and after marriage settled in Washington, where he died from the cholera, in 1833. His wife had preceded him a few years. Patrick was reared up to ten years of age in Washington, and then passed his time on a farm in Virginia, attending the subscription schools of that State. He went to Ohio in 1835, but one year later removed to Morgan County, Ill. Three years following he became settled in Sangamon County, Ill., his home until 1844. His subsequent travels have been noticed. Mr. Burns first opened up a farm of 120 acres here, which he has given to Mr. Sparrow, his father-in-law. Mr. Burns was married in 1850, in Pulaski County, to Edith Sparrow, a native of North Carolina. He was formerly a member of the Grange, and is now connected with the Agricultural Wheel.

George T. Burton, like so many agriculturists of White County, Ark., is also engaged in fruit culture, and has been exceptionally successful in these occupations. His birth occurred in Indiana, in 1849, and he is one of nine children born to Eli and Mahala (Conley) Burton, the father having been born in North Carolina in 1812, the youngest child of John P. and Mary Burton, who were born in the "Old North State." After living in his native State until he reached manhood, he moved to Indiana, settling in Lawrence County, where he followed farming and coopering and was married in 1834, his wife being a daughter of John Conley, who was born in North Carolina and came to Indiana at an early day. They reared a large family of children: Simpson, Wiley G., Catherine, Rebecca, Isom, John W., William H., George T. and Milton P. The father is a Republican in politics, and has held many public offices in the State of Indiana, and is still living. His wife died in 1852. George T. Burton received his education in the State University of Indiana, and in 1872, started out in life for himself, following the occupations of farming and fruit growing, which callings have received his attention up to the present time. After his marriage, in 1877, to Miss Mary E. Bundy, a daughter of William and Sarah (Cob-bell) Bundy, of that State, he came to White County, Ark., and bought a farm of 160 acres, seventy-five acres of which he devotes to corn and fruit of various kinds, being especially successful in the cultivation of strawberries and grapes. He takes a deep interest in all matters pertaining to the good of the county and is agricultural reporter of White County for the Government. He is an earnest member of the Baptist Church and politically is a Republican. His children are: Eli N., Morton, Ethel B. and Benjamin H. Mr. Burton is a Mason and is a demitted member of the Grand Lodge of the State.

Robert W. Canada, a well-to-do farmer and stockman, residing near Beebe, Ark., has been a resident of White County for a period of time. He was born in Madison County, Tenn., April 3, 1829, and is a son of Hugh and Melissa R. (Duckworth) Canada, who were born in North Carolina, in 1808 and 1810, respectively. They were married in 1828, and in 1832 removed from Madison to Haywood County, Tenn., and here the father's death occurred in 1856. Their children are Robert W., Catherine (born January 1, 1831, and died at the age of four years), William J. (was born on May 16, 1833, and lost his life in the Confederate service, being killed in the battle of Atlanta, in 1864, and is now filling an unknown grave), Joseph V. (was born April 16, 1835, and died February 17, 1879, a farmer of White County), James R. (was born July 27, 1837, and died at El Paso in December, 1879, a merchant by occupation), John F. (who was born February 8, 1840, and died at Okolona, Miss., in 1863, being a soldier in the Confederate army), Alpha C. (was born April 16, 1842, and died August 8, 1881, the wife of A. L. Fisher, a farmer of Union Township), Mary E. (was born February 21, 1844, and is the wife of Richard Hill, a farmer of El Paso, Ark.) and Miles C. (who was born on September 20, 1846, and is now a farmer near Stony Point). Robert W. Canada spent his youth on his father's farm and attended the old subscription schools of his youth. At the age of twenty-one he began life for himself, and spent the first few years of his freedom as an overseer. This he followed in connection with farming until coming to White County, Ark., and a few months later entered 160 acres of land three miles east of El Paso, which he began to develop. Four years later he sold this farm and bought eighty acres near Beebe, but after residing here a term of four years he went to Illinois, and there made his home during 1865. In 1867 he made the purchase of his present farm of 100 acres, and by good management has increased his acreage to 500, and has 200 acres under cultivation, his land being well adapted to raising corn, cotton and fruits. Small grain does well also, and strawberries grow to perfection and are one of his most profitable crops. Since his residence in the State he has cleared over 200 acres of land and has built more good barns than any other man in the section of White County. Although his principal occupation has been farming he has been engaged in other occupations at different times, and in 1873 erected a livery stable in Beebe, the first establishment of the kind ever erected there. He managed this a few months and at the same time acted as constable, and later served as justice of the peace for eight years. In 1882 he kept a grocery in Beebe and during this time, and for three subsequent years, he acted in the capacity of postmaster of the town, having received his appointment in 1881. He has been a Republican since that party has been in existence, but he has never been an office seeker. He is a member of Beebe Lodge No. 145, of the A. F. & A. M., and has held all the offices of his lodge with the exception of Senior Warden. He is a member of the Agricultural Wheel, and is one of the influential men of the county, and although he differs from the most of the citizens in his political views, yet he is highly esteemed and his opinions respected. When Gen. Grant was elected to the presidency Mr. Canada was the only man in Union Township who voted for him. He has always been an advocate of schools and has contributed liberally to the building of churches, school-houses and to the general improvement of the county. October 28, 1851, he was married to Miss Mahala Hendrix, a native of Hardeman County, Tenn., born October 24, 1838, a daughter of William and Nancy

(Clements) Hendrix, who removed from their native State of South Carolina to Tennessee in 1856, and were among the pioneer settlers of White County. The children of Mr. and Mrs. Canada are Sonora E. (born October 27, 1852, and died December 7, 1856), Almeda (born November 10, 1855, and died June 3, 1857), William R. (born April 26, 1858; is a merchant in business with C. A. Price, of Beebe), Joseph B. (was born September 17, 1860, and is a farmer of Union Township), Martha A. (was born October 15, 1869, and is a school teacher, residing with her parents) and Mary M. (who was born September 24, 1874, and died August 29, 1876). Mr. Canada has given all his children good educational advantages, and he and his family attend the Methodist Episcopal Church, South, he having been a steward in that church for the past thirteen years. Mr. Canada's mother still lives and makes her home with him.

R. W. Carnes, sheriff, Searcy, Ark. This gentleman was elected to his present office in September, 1888, and has filled that position in a capable and efficient manner ever since. He owes his origin to Carroll County, Tenn., where his birth occurred in 1849, and is the second in a family of five children born to John D. and Sarah (Dunn) Carnes, natives of Tennessee. The father was a physician and surgeon and died in Tennessee in 1857. He took quite an active part in politics in the early history of the country. The mother came to White County, Ark., in 1868, settled on a farm near Searcy, and here her death occurred in 1885. Of their family five are now living: R. W., Barbara A. and Alice (now Mrs. Magness), still residing in White County. R. W. Carnes passed his early life in duties upon the farm and in securing an education in the common schools of Tennessee. In 1868 he came to White County, following farming until 1882, when he engaged in general merchandising at Centre Hill, White County, and there continued for three years. In 1885 he embarked in the same business at Searcy, and continued at that for some time. He is not very active in politics, but votes independently and for the best man in the county, and in national affairs votes with the Democratic party. He is also deeply interested in educational affairs and is a member of the school board. Socially he is a member of Searcy Lodge No. 49, A. F. & A. M., and has been Worshipful Master of the lodge. He was married in White County in 1875 to Miss Anna Montgomery, a native of White County and daughter of J. W. and Ophelia A. (West) Montgomery, the former of North Carolina and the latter of Monroe County, Ark. The father is now deceased. Mrs. Montgomery resides on a farm. Mr. Carnes lost his wife in 1880 and was left with two children: Anna Belle and John D. His second marriage took place in White County in 1884, to Miss Elnora Neelly, a native of White County and daughter of Samuel D. and Sally (Montgomery) Neelly, natives of Tennessee and North Carolina, respectively. Her parents came to White County in 1855, and there their deaths occurred a number of years ago, the mother in about 1874, and the father in 1885. They were the parents of three children: Sally Mattie, Neelly and an infant. Mr. Carnes has seen many changes in the country since coming here in 1868, and has always taken an interest in the country. He is one of the prominent and representative men of the county.

William H. Carodine, known to be reliable and honorable, is a liveryman and planter of White County, and a native of Mississippi, being born October 3, 1843, in De Soto County. His father, William Carodine, was born in Tennessee, but immigrated to Mississippi, where he married Miss Emily Hall, also of Tennessee. Soon after their marriage they came to Arkansas (in 1860) and settled first in White County, but subsequently moved six miles west of Beebe, and in 1873 moved two miles south of this town, where the remainder of their life was spent. William H. was reared on a farm and passed his boyhood days in the pioneer schools, obtaining a good education there and in the common schools of Mississippi and Arkansas. In 1862 he started out in this world for himself, their first venture from home being to enlist in the Confederate army, under Col. Glenn McCoy's brigade, in which he served four years. He was in the battles of Prairie Grove, Pilot Knob, Jefferson City, Boonville, Lexington, Independence,

and at Wilson's Creek, in Missouri. He was with Price on his raid through Missouri, and also at the battle of Helena, where he was slightly wounded, but during his entire service in the war he was never once captured. At the time of the final surrender he was home on a furlough. At the close of the struggle Mr. Carodine rented a farm and began working it with nothing but his own exertion to depend on, yet it is not strange that he succeeded, for with his great determination of purpose, the lack of "filthy lucre" would not prevent him at least from making an attempt to cope with the many hardships incident to his start in life. In October, 1867, he was married to Miss Elizabeth Massey, a native of Tennessee, but whose parents came to Arkansas in 1858. To their union three children have been born, two of them now living: Mary Jane, William (deceased) and Jones D. Shortly after his marriage Mr. Carodine purchased his father's homestead and conducted that place for several years, but in 1878 he traded his farm for town property in Indiana, which he still owns. It consists of a lot and good residence in Bainbridge, Putman County, Ind. In 1878 he bought what is known as the Massey place (160 acres) and took up his residence at that place, remaining there until the fall of 1888. He then purchased the rolling stock in the livery business, which he is now successfully conducting. In connection with his other property he now owns eighty acres of land, two miles east of Beebe, and of that farm fifty acres are cultivated. The farm is in an excellent locality, and is adapted to all kinds of crops. Since his residence in White County he has opened over 160 acres of land, and has done his full share in developing the country round him, and it is to his credit, be it said, that very few have done as much. In 1875 Mr. and Mrs. Carodine took an extended trip through Texas, for the latter's health, and after an absence of a year they returned, her health being greatly improved. Mr. Carodine thought Texas a very fair country, but concluded that, as far as he had been able to judge, Arkansas had no superior. He is a member of Beebe Lodge No. 146, A. F. & A. M., also at one time was a Wheeler. In his political views he sides with the Democratic party. He has been a member of the school board for a number of years, and with his family worships at the Beebe Methodist Episcopal Church.

W. B. Carter, Searcy, Ark. Among the most skilled and reliable druggists of Searcy may be classed Mr. Carter, who is a member of the well-known firm of Carter & Son. This firm is doing a good business and carries a full line of drugs, chemicals and everything kept in a first-class drug store. He came to Searcy in 1851, engaged in the dry goods and boot and shoe business, where the Perry Block is building, then purchased a frame building across the street, and later moved to the north side of the public square, where he erected the second brick building in Searcy. At this time the firm title was Carter, McCanley & Co., under which it continued until some time during the war. From 1861 to 1865 Mr. Carter was out of business, and in 1867 he engaged in general merchandising under the firm name of J. C. McCanley & Co. He continued with him until 1873, when he embarked in his present business on the north side of the square, and in 1884 moved to his present location. Mr. Carter was born in Prince William County, Va., in 1822, and was the eldest in a family of six children born to James P. and E. J. (Davis) Carter, natives of the Old Dominion. The father was a planter and opened up a large farm in Virginia, where he remained until 1838 and then moved to Independence County, Ark., where he entered land and there passed his last days. His death occurred in about 1860. His wife died in 1876. Of their family these children are now living: W. B. (subject) and T. E. Carter (who is married and resides on a farm near Sulphur Rock, Ark.). W. B. Carter was early initiated into the duties of farm life, and received his education in the schools of Virginia. He moved to Pike County, Mo., in 1837, engaged in farm labor, and in 1838 moved to Independence County, Ark., where he engaged in agricultural pursuits. He purchased land in that county, but sold it and in 1851 came to Searcy, then a very small rough place, but soon after a class of settlers moved in and the town was soon built up. Mr. Carter was an enrolling officer

for some months during 1863, was taken prisoner and held during the winter of 1863 and 1864 at Johnstown Island. He was paroled in March of the last-mentioned year and taken to Point Lookout, thence to Richmond, and finally went on foot from Mississippi across the swamps to Southern Ark., where he joined the army. After the surrender he returned to Searcy. In 1867 he engaged in business continuously for thirty-four years, and is one of the oldest and most reliable merchants in Searcy. He is not active in politics but votes with the Democratic party, and held the office of justice of the peace for about four years. He was appointed postmaster under President Buchanan and served four years. He was married in White County in 1853 to Miss E. J. McCanley, a native of Tennessee, and the daughter of James and Mary (Fletcher) McCanley, natives of North Carolina. Her parents immigrated at an early day to Tennessee, and in 1851 came to White County, Ark., where both passed their last days. Four children were born to Mr. and Mrs. Carter: Ella (now Mrs. Patterson, of Little Rock), and W. F. (who is married and resides in Searcy) and two deceased. Mr. and Mrs. Carter are members of the Methodist Episcopal Church, South, and socially Mr. Carter is a member of the Searcy Lodge No. 49, A. F. & A. M., of which he has been secretary and warden for many years. He is a member of Tillman Chapter No. 19, R. A. M., of which he is King. He is also a member of the council, and has been for some time.

Alfred T. Carter, a leading citizen and of an old and highly respected family, was a native of Mississippi, and was a son of Alfred and Drucilla (Willkins) Carter, of Tennessee nativity. Alfred Carter first saw the light of day in 1812, and lived in Tennessee (where he was married) until 1830, when he moved to Panola County, Miss., and in 1859 came to Arkansas, locating in White County, where his wife died in 1871, at the age of fifty-nine. He then married a Mrs. Conner, a widow, who is still living. The senior Carter was the father of seven children by his first wife, three of whom are still living: S. R. (a farmer of Logan County, Ark.), Alfred T. (our subject) and

Sarah (the wife of W. H. Bailey). By his second marriage he became the parent of two children, both living: Fannie and Alfred. Mr. Carter belongs to the Methodist Episcopal Church, as did also his first wife. He died in 1878. Alfred T. Carter was born in Panola County, Miss., on February 3, 1851, but has resided in Arkansas since eight years of age. At the age of twenty he commenced farming for himself, and in the fall of 1870, bought forty acres of land in the woods, and began clearing it. He now is the owner of 280 acres, with ninety under cultivation, which he has made by hard work and economy. On August 28, 1870, he was married to Miss Emma Ward, also a native of Panola County, Miss., and who was born April 22, 1854. They are the parents of eleven children, six of whom are still living: Ella J., Sallie M., Albert J., George O., John T. and Penina. Mr. Carter is a prominent Democrat, and was elected to the office of constable in 1882, which office he held for six years. Mr. and Mrs. Carter belong to the Methodist Episcopal Church, South, of which he is trustee, and officiated as class leader for several years.

J. M. Cathcart, one of the members of the popular and well-known Enterprise Basket and Box Company, manufacturers of fruit and vegetable boxes, etc., was born in Elkhart County, Ind., in 1844, and was the youngest of three children born to B. F. and Joanna (Calkins) Cathcart, the former having been born in that State in 1818, his youthful days being also there. His children are Royal (who died in infancy) and Harrison (who served in Company K, Ninth Indiana Regiment, and was killed at the battle of Shiloh). The mother of these children, who was a daughter of Caleb Calkins, died in 1845, and the father married again, his second wife being a Mrs. Mary (Newell) Ireland, daughter of John and Mary (Crockett) Newell, a native of Kentucky. She bore him one child, J. F., who resides in Arkansas, and is in business with our subject, J. M. Cathcart. After her death he wedded Sarah J. Calkins, an aunt of his first wife, the children of this marriage being Anna and Royal W. and Rosa (twins). Mr. Cathcart is still living, but his par-

ents, James and Paulina, have long been dead. J. M. Cathcart's youth was spent in following the plow on his father's farm in Indiana, and in attending the district schools, but these sober pursuits he put aside upon the opening of the Rebellion, and at the age of seventeen years he enlisted in Company C, Ninth Indiana Regiment, and after participating in a number of engagements he was captured and confined in the county jail at Stanton, Va., one month and in Libby two months. After being paroled he went back to Indiana, and was married there, in 1872, to Miss Anna Snyder, a daughter of William and Lavina (Knight) Snyder, natives of Pennsylvania. Mr. Cathcart was in the railroad business for about thirteen years, as clerk and station agent on the Lake Shore & Michigan Southern Railroad. Resigning his position as agent in 1881, he engaged in the manufacturing business with his brother, J. F., at Bristol, Ind. In 1885 they moved their machinery to White County, Ark., and established the Enterprise Basket and Box Company, known as the Cathcart Bros. They employ on an average about thirty hands, and during the fruit season have a much larger force. Mr. Cathcart is a member of the G. A. R., a Republican in his political views and is one of the aldermen of Judsonia. The junior partner of the firm, J. F. Cathcart, married Miss Flora Boyer, by whom he had two sons, John and James, born in 1880 and 1884, in Indiana. John F. spent his youthful days on a farm raising fruit and in attending the public schools of Indiana. He engaged in the manufacturing business while still a resident of his native State, and after coming to Arkansas in 1885, engaged in the same calling. He is the inventor of the Cathcart's ventilated berry case, which has proved a decided success. His wife, who is a member of the Methodist Episcopal Church, is a daughter of John and Hannah Boyer, the former a Pennsylvanian. Mr. Cathcart is an excellent musician and is the leader of the band in Judsonia.

R. W. Chrisp, farmer, Searcy, Ark. This prominent agriculturist owes his nativity to Gibson County, Tenn., where his birth occurred in 1835, and is the ninth of seventeen children born to the union of William and Mary J. (Elder) Chrisp, natives of the Old Dominion. The father was a tiller of the soil, and moved to Rutherford County, Tenn., entered land, and there remained until 1831. He then settled in Gibson County, Tenn., and made that county his home until his death, which occurred in 1863. He was in the War of 1812, and took quite an active part in politics. His wife died in Searcy in October, 1884. Of their family the following children are now living: R. W., Frances W. (now Mrs. Lane, of Gibson County, Tenn.), Horace (married, and resides in Higginson Township) and L. M. (who is married, and resides on a farm in the last-named township). One son, John W., enlisted in the army from Gibson County, Tenn., was Gen. Pillow's commissary, and died of pneumonia in 1863, at Memphis, Tenn. Another son, William B., was a member of the One Hundred and Eleventh Tennessee Infantry, and after the war was a cotton factor of Memphis. His death occurred in 1870. Two other sons, Henry and Starks, were in Gen. Forrest's cavalry, and both died in 1883. R. W. Chrisp was early taught the duties of farm life, and received his education in the subscription schools of Tennessee. In 1857 he came to White County, Ark., then being a single man, and taught the Gum Spring schools during 1858–59. He was married in White County in the last-named year, to Miss Sarah F. Neavill, a native of Jackson County, Ala., and the daughter of Elihu and Margaret (Jones) Neavill, natives of Alabama. Her father was in the Florida War, came to White County in 1844, and was for many years engaged in farming and in the tannery business, becoming quite wealthy. His death occurred in 1851 and the mother's in 1887. They resided in White County for over forty years. After marriage Mr. Chrisp settled in Gray Township on a timber tract of land, which he rented for a few years, and then, in 1867, purchased 240 acres, partly improved. This he sold, and bought forty acres in the timber which he immediately commenced clearing, erecting buildings, and added to this land from time to time until he now has 280 acres, with 100 acres under cultivation, besides a home farm of twenty acres just outside the corpora-

tion. Mr. Chrisp lost his excellent wife, October 9, 1887. The result of this union was the birth of the following children: William H. (married, and resides on the subject's farm), Vinnie R. (at home, attending Galway College), James Everett, Henry Beecher and Benjamin Clark. July 4, 1861, Mr. Chrisp was elected second lieutenant of Company K, but held first position in the Seventh Arkansas Infantry, commanded by Robert Shaver. He was in the battle of Shiloh, after which the company was reorganized, and he came to Searcy to recruit for the Trans-Mississippi Department. He then entered the ranks as private in the cavalry, and was temporarily promoted to the rank of lieutenant-colonel in front of Helena. He was in the Missouri raid, participated in the battles of Pilot Knob, Ironton, Jefferson City, Newtonia and Mine Creek. He returned to White County, Ark., from Fayetteville, and engaged in farming, but later was occupied for about a year in merchandising in Searcy. He has taken an active part in politics, and although originally a Whig, votes with the Democratic party. He has taken an active interest in schools and has been a member of the school board for twenty years. In 1883 he was sergeant-at-arms for the State of Arkansas. He received the nomination for representative, but was declared disfranchised in the reconstruction days. Mr. Chrisp is a member of Searcy Lodge No. 49, A. F. & A. M., and is also a member of Tillman Lodge No. 19. He has been Worshipful Master of Searcy Lodge, and has held office in Chapter. He is practically a self-made man and all his property is the result of his own industry. Although fifty-five years of age he has never drank a drop of liquor.

Arthur Smith Claiborn, eminently fitted and well worthy to be numbered among the successful farmers and stockmen of White County, Ark., is a son of John B. and Perlina E. (Thomason) Claiborn, the former a Tennesseean of Irish descent and the latter a native of North Carolina. They were married in Tennessee, and in 1859 moved to Kansas, purchasing a partly improved farm, consisting of 160 acres, in Prairie County. After considerably improving this land they moved to White

County, settling on a tract of railroad land, where the father died seven years later, September 17, 1874, his wife having died October 16, 1870. Their children are as follows: Mary Jane (who became the consort of L. D. Hendrickson, deceased, and is living in Kentucky with her five children), Millie C. (married Jasper Scott, and in 1856 moved to Illinois; her husband was killed at the battle of Nashville, in 1865, leaving her with six children), W. B. (was killed at Franklin, Ky., while a member of the Eighth Tennessee Regiment), Mary F. (was married to R. H. Ferguson, but died after having borne two children), John H. (residing in Texas, and by his wife, who was Miss Mary Ware, is the father of six children), Perlila C. (was wedded to John Hodges, and upon her death left two children), Pleasant T. (died at Jackson, Miss., while serving in the Confederate army), Arthur Smith (our subject), Thomas J. and Samuel B. Arthur Smith Claiborn was born in De Kalb County, Tenn., February 3, 1847, and was educated in the subscription schools of his native county, but it must be acknowledged that his advantages were very meager, and at the time he had attained his twenty-first birthday he had only received three months' schooling. He immediately began business for himself upon attaining his majority, and for two years raised crops of cotton and corn on shares, and at the end of this time was married to Miss Martha J. Hale, a native of Mississippi and daughter of Francis J. and Louisa (White) Hale, who were among the old settlers of Arkansas, having come to the State in 1859. Their marriage took place December 2, 1869, and of eight children born to their union seven are living: Elnora (born October 7, 1870), William B. (born August 20, 1872), James (born July 25, 1874), Mattie J. (born in September, 1876, and died in August, 1877), Annie (born October 16, 1878), Alcora (born March 28, 1882), Arthur S. (born February 27, 1885) and Aver A. (born February 26, 1886). After their marriage Mr. and Mrs. Claiborn settled on eighty acres of land belonging to the latter, and in 1876 Mr. Claiborn became able to purchase 116 acres of wild land, which he has improved and to which he has added

eighty acres. He now has seventy-five acres under cultivation, a good frame house, good barns and one tenant house. He rented his land on shares until this year (1889) but now rents for cash. Mr. and Mrs. Claiborn and two of their children, Elnora and William, hold memberships in the Methodist Episcopal Church, South, and Mr. Claiborn is a Democrat in his political views. He has always been a liberal contributor to the advancement of religious, social and educational institutions, and has also given generously to all enterprises which he deemed worthy of support.

Green B. Clay is a well-to-do farmer and stock raiser of Cadron Township, and was the youngest in a family of ten children of John and Diallia (Morris) Clay. Mr. Clay was a native of North Carolina. His family consisted of the following children: Nancy, Harriet, Louisa, Jackson M., Emily, Sarah, Susan, William H., Martha and Green B. (our subject.) He was reared on a farm in Tennessee, where he was born in 1827, and started out in life when he was sixteen years of age. In 1851 he was married to Mary W. Mizzells, a daughter of Miles and Elizabeth (Rooks) Mizzells. In 1868 Mr. Clay bought a farm in Tennessee. He subsequently sold it and moved to Arkansas, settling in White County, where he bought a farm of 560 acres, clearing about seventy-three acres. Mrs. Clay was the mother of eighteen children, eight of whom are still living: John M., Joseph H., Zacariah M., Francis M., James N., George A., Charles C. and Albert A. He was married the second time to Nancy E. Burton (nee Neal), a widow. To them have been given five children: Walter L., Nathan B., Stephen M., Neoma Parlee and an infant which is not named. Mr. and Mrs. Clay are members of the Missionary Baptist Church. He is a strong Democrat and a member of the County Wheel. He is deeply interested in all work for the good of the church, school or any public enterprise.

J. C. Cleveland, M. D., was born in Independence County, November 19, 1852, and is the son of Joseph and Elizabeth (Butcher) Cleveland, natives of Georgia and Alabama, respectively. Mr.

Joseph Cleveland moved to Alabama when a young man, where he was married and in 1852, he removed to Independence County, Ark. He served his county a number of times in an official capacity, and in 1873 he represented his county in the legislature. He served eighteen months in the Confederate army, during which time he was taken prisoner and held at Fortress Monroe eight months before he was exchanged. He was with Gen. Price in his raid through Missouri and Kansas. He was a Republican and belonged to the Masonic fraternity, in which he had taken the Royal Arch degree. He died in the early part of the year 1887, at Newport, Ark., at the age of sixty-one. Mrs. Cleveland is still living and a resident of Newport, Ark., and is the mother of eleven children, nine of whom still survive: Martha E. (wife of J. W. Kennedy), J. C. (our subject), Henry P. (a lawyer by profession), Mary A. (wife of J. D. Cantrell), Susan A. T. (wife of L. D. Bownds), James F., Charles E., Samuel and Edward. Dr. J. C. Cleveland began his career as a school-teacher in his nineteenth year, following that profession till 1883, when he began the study of medicine. He graduated from the Missouri Medical College in 1888, first having taken lectures at the Kentucky School of Medicine, Louisville. Dr. Cleveland was married, November 7, 1875, to Miss Nancy E. Vick, a daughter of Dr. T. A. Vick. She died in 1885, having had three children, only one of whom survives, Lavina E., who is still living with her father. Dr. Cleveland was again married, in 1886, to Miss Nannie F. Goad, who is the mother of one daughter: Susan Estella. Mrs. Cleveland is a member of the Methodist Episcopal Church, South. The Doctor is a member of the Masonic fraternity and a strong Republican. He is now a resident of Bald Knob, where he has built up a large and successful practice, and is an enterprising and highly respected citizen.

John D. Coffey is a well-known citizen of White County and was born in Macon, Fayette County, Tenn., June 19, 1838. His father, David P. Coffey, was a Presbyterian clergyman, and first saw the light of this world in Tennessee in November,

1805. He was given all the advantages for an education to be had at that time, and applied himself so assiduously to his studies, that he became an accomplished and finely educated gentleman. He was married in his native State November 12, 1835, to Miss Mary C. Cogville, a daughter of Charlie and Pollie Cogville, and to their union fourteen children were born, of which John D. is the second child and the oldest son. Of that family seven are now living, six residing in this State. The Rev. Coffey immigrated from Tennessee, in 1854, and located near Searcy, where he died in 1883, his good wife surviving him but two years. He was a member of the Masonic lodge, and also a Royal Arch Mason, and was the originator of the first church that was ever organized in Stony Point, the denomination being the Cumberland Presbyterian. This township, where John D. Coffey now resides, derived its title from his father, in whose honor it was named. John D. served in the late war on the Confederate side, and enlisted in 1861, in Douglas County, in Brown's Tennessee Regiment. His first hard fight was at the battle of Shiloh, and he also engaged in numerous other engagements. He was captured at Port Edson, but was soon after paroled, and at once returned home to claim his promised bride, Miss Malicia G. Harris. After his marriage Mr. Coffey returned to the war and accompanied Price on his raid through Missouri, and received his final discharge from service in 1865. To Mr. and Mrs. Coffey have been born a family of eight children: John H., Mary, Josephus, Lucy E., David P., Hugh, James S., Minnie C. Mr. Coffey has a good farm of forty acres, finely stocked, and with all the conveniences and modern improvements to make the home comfortable. Himself and wife are members of the Presbyterian Church, and highly respected by every one.

John Reed Coffey is a prominent farmer and miller of White County, Ark., and owes his nativity to the State of Tennessee, the date of his birth being December 19, 1856. His father, Wiley D. Coffey, was born in Bedford County, Tenn., October 6, 1827, where he received his education, and there married Narcissa A. Muse, August 5, 1850.

Mrs. Coffey is a daughter of Richard and Margaret Muse, and a very estimable lady. To their union eight children were born, five of them now living: Mary C., John R., Richard H., Sarah H., Joseph H. The other three died in infancy. Mr. Coffey is a teacher and minister, and owns 286 acres of good land with 100 in cultivation. He immigrated from Texas to Arkansas in 1871, locating in White County, which has been his home ever since. When he came to this county his worldly possessions consisted of a team of horses and a wagon, but he is now worth $5,000, and a farm well supplied with all the necessary stock for its successful operation. Mr. Coffey has educated three of his children for teachers. He has held a membership in the I. O. O. F. and in the Wheel, but has severed his connection with the latter order. He served in the Confederate War, enlisting in 1862, in Company A, Forty-fourth Regiment, and received his discharge in the same year. J. Reed Coffey acquired his education at home by the aid of the fire light, and when twenty-one years old began life for himself, working for two years, then returned home and worked with his father to pay a debt that hung like the sword of Damocles over the old homestead. At the age of twenty-eight years he was married to Sarah A. Harriss, their marriage occurring in October, 1885. She was a native of Illinois, and a daughter of Johnson and Keziah Harriss. They are the parents of two children: Clifton B. and Robert L. He owns 400 acres of good land, which lies southeast of Bald Knob and is well stocked with all the necessary appurtenances required to operate a farm. He is a Democrat politically, and as might be supposed by his home surroundings of English descent. Mrs. Coffey is a member of the Baptist Church, and a favorite in her wide circle of acquaintances. Mr. Coffey richly merits the reward which has attended his efforts during life. Active, industrious and prudent, he enjoys wide respect.

William R. Cook, a man of no little prominence throughout White County, Ark., is a wealthy farmer, stockman and fruit grower, residing near Judsonia, and, although born in Tennessee in 1836, he has been a resident of Arkansas since 1848, al-

though he first resided in Independence County. He was the eldest of six children, born to John and Ann (Anderson) Cook, the former of whom was born in that state in 1814, and was educated as a Methodist minister, being a son of William and Margaret Cook. He was married in Tennessee in 1835 and followed farming there until his removal to Arkansas, his wife bearing him in the meantime these children: William R., Mary, Eliza, Lavinia, Arkansas and Andrew. They took up land in Arkansas and here the father died in 1879, and the mother in 1872. The maternal grandparents were Anderson and Dorcas Clark, Kentuckians, who came to Tennessee at an early day. William R. spent his youth in Tennessee but received the most of his education in Arkansas, and in the year 1860 started out in life for himself. A year later he joined Company B, Seventh Arkansas Infantry, First Arkansas Brigade, and took part in the battles of Shiloh, Perryville, Murfreesboro, Big Creek, and was with Price on his raid through Missouri, and with Bragg in Kentucky. He received his discharge in 1865 and after coming home was married (in 1866) to Albina, a daughter of Thomas and Margaret (Price) Bownds, and by her became the father of four children: Ida, Ella, Maggie and John (the latter dying in 1881). Mr. Cook was the owner of 240 acres of land in Independence County, but sold this and removed to White County, purchasing 460 acres near Judsonia, of which he now has 225 acres under cultivation. He is a steward in the Methodist Episcopal Church, of which his wife is also a member. He belongs to Anchor Lodge No. 384, of the A. F. & A. M., and is Deputy Grand Lecturer of his district. In his political views he is a Democrat. In 1879 he was called upon to mourn the death of his wife, and he afterward espoused Isabel Sisco, a daughter of Zedichire and Thurza Sisco, the father a native of Alabama and the mother of Middle Tennessee. They came to Arkansas about 1838, and here Mrs. Cook was born. The father died in 1858 and the mother in 1862. Mr. Cook and his present wife have had two children, both of whom are now deceased: Reuben P. and Sterling, the former's death occurring in 1881 and the latter's in 1883.

10

Joshua J. Crow was attending school in this county at the time of the outbreak of the war, when he laid down his books, left family and friends to join the Confederate Army. He enlisted in Taylor's regiment of Texas troops, and later in the Second Trans-Mississippi Department, in the Second Arkansas Cavalry; also took part in the battles of Jenkins' Ferry, Helena, Poison Springs, Little Rock, and a number of other battles and skirmishes. After peace was once more declared he went to West Point and engaged in the mercantile business, remaining there until 1870, when he removed to Searcy and subsequently filled the position of traveling salesman for a wholesale grocery house at St. Louis, Mo., for the next six years. In 1876 he started in the saw-mill business which he still follows. In 1877 he was married to Miss Emma J. Jones, a daughter of B. F. and J. C. Jones, and is the mother of three children: Frank F., Norman and Norton B. Mr. Crow owes his nativity to Mississippi (being born in Marshall County, June, 1844) and is the son of Joshua B. and Lavinia (West) Crow, natives of Alabama. Mr. Crow, Sr., was born in 1810, and when a young man removed with his parents to Northern Alabama, where he resided until his marriage when he immigrated to Marshall County, Miss., and lived there until 1847, then came to De Soto County, same State, and in February, 1849, came to Arkansas, locating in White County. He was a passenger on the second steamboat which came up Red River. He was a Democrat in politics, a member of the Masonic order, and in religious faith belonged to the Missionary Baptist Church, as did also his wife, and was one of the best-posted men in regard to real estate in his county. His death occurred in 1866 and his wife's in the same year, at the age of fifty-three. They were the parents of eleven children, seven of whom are still living: Mrs. J. N. Cypert, Mrs. T. D. Hardy (of this county), Mrs. T. P. Boon (of Los Angeles, Cal.), Joshua J. (our subject), M. C. (of West Point), Mrs. J. R. Hardy (of Mississippi) and Miss Ella Crow (of West Point). The mother of our subject was a descendant of Gen. Israel Putnam, of Revolutionary fame. Himself and wife are connected with the Missionary Baptist Church, in

which they take an active part. He owns 1,400 acres of fine farming land, and is a prominent Democrat in his county.

Jesse N. Cypert, is an attorney, at Searcy, Ark. Among the leading firms of attorneys in this city is the well-known one of Messrs. Cypert & Cypert, of which Jesse N. Cypert is the senior member. This gentleman is one of the pioneer settlers of Searcy, Ark., and was born in Wayne County, Tenn., in December, 1823, being one of eleven children, the result of the union of Jesse and Jemimah (Warthen) Cypert, the father a native of North Carolina, born 1781, and the mother of Pennsylvania, born 1783. The grandparents on the mother's side were of Welsh descent, and at an early day moved to North Carolina. Jesse Cypert, Sr., was married in 1802, then moved to Knox County, Tenn., where he farmed and resided until 1819, after which he moved to Wayne County, of the same State, and there his death occurred in 1858. He was a private in the War of 1812, Tennessee Volunteer, Carroll's brigade, and was in the battle of New Orleans under Gen. Jackson. He was sheriff and collector one term, and justice of the peace and member of the county court for a number of years. The mother died in 1857. Jesse N. Cypert's time in early life was divided between working on the farm, clearing and developing the home place, and in attending the subscription schools of Wayne County, Tenn., in a log-cabin with dirt floor, etc. Later he attended the district schools of that State. He then studied law in the office of Judge L. L. Mack, of Wayne County, and was admitted to the bar at Waynesboro, Tenn., in 1849. Subsequently he went to Walker County, Ga., engaged as clerk, and in May, 1858, came to Crittenden County, Ark., and began practicing at Marion. Here he remained for eight months, and in February, 1851, came to Searcy, Ark., where he began the practice of law and this has continued successfully ever since. In connection with this he also carries on farming. During the war, or in October, 1861, he served as captain of the Confederate army, Fifth Arkansas Battalion, and on the organization of the battalion at Pocahontas, Randolph County, Ark., in October, Mr. Cypert was elected major. He was east of the Mississippi River, and after the battle of Shiloh he resigned and came home on account of health. Later he entered the commissary department, purchasing supplies for the troops, and was thus engaged until after the surrender of Little Rock. He was taken prisoner in October, 1863, detained at Little Rock about three weeks, and paroled as citizen the same month. He was in the convention that passed the ordinance of secession in 1861, and was a delegate to both conventions. He continued the practice of law after the war, and this has continued ever since. He has taken quite an active part in politics, votes with the Democratic party, and was a delegate to the convention that voted the State into the union in 1868. He was also in the convention in 1874 that furnished the constitution that the State is under now. Mr. Cypert was elected judge of the circuit court in September, 1874, and served eight years, two terms. Socially he is a member of Searcy Lodge No. 49, A. F. & A. M., Tillman Chapter No. 19, R. A. M. He was married in White County, in February, 1855, to Miss Sarah Harlan Crow, a native of Alabama, and the daughter of Joshua B. and Lavinia (West) Crow, natives of South Carolina. Her parents moved to White County, Ark., in 1849, settled on a farm near the present town of Kensett, and here the mother died in April, 1866, and the father in August of the same year. To Mr. and Mrs. Cypert were born three children, two living: Florence (now Mrs. W. M. Watkins, of Searcy) and Eugene (a partner in the firm of Cypert & Cypert, he having read law in the office of his father, and was admitted to the bar in 1884). The other child, Mary Alice, married H. A. Smith, a merchant of West Point. She died in February, 1886, and left one child, Eugene Austin, and the subject of this sketch is rearing this child. Mr. Cypert takes an active interest in all that pertains to the good of the county, and is one of the pioneers of the temperance cause. He ran for the legislature in 1854, on the temperance question and received a good number of votes. He was the first president of the Temperance Alliance, and served in that capacity

for two years. He is a member of the Methodist Episcopal Church, South, and Mrs. Cypert is a member of the Missionary Baptist Church.

J. W. Darden, the efficient and popular lumber manufacturer and flour-mill operator of Rosebud, is engaged in manufacturing all grades of lumber of oak and pine. He commenced this enterprise in 1861 within one mile of where he is now doing business. In connection with this business he is engaged in operating a flouring-mill, his establishment being the second of the kind erected in White County and the first one in this vicinity. He has been a resident of Arkansas since 1860, and since that date has been a resident of Kentucky Township, removing thither from his native State of Tennessee. He was born in Warren County in 1833 and was the fourth in a family of seven children born to Robert and Elizabeth (Woten) Darden, who were also of Warren County, and were there married. In 1855 they moved to Greene County, Mo., where Mr. Darden had a blacksmith shop for some years, and in 1864 they came to White County, Ark., where Mr. Darden followed the same calling and also that of farming, occupying himself with these callings until his death, in 1886, his wife's death occurring some two years previous. The following are the names of the surviving children: J. W., Elizabeth (now Mrs. Clymer, of Taney County, Mo.), Mattie (unmarried and a resident of Faulkner County) and Sarah (now Mrs. Williams, a widow, residing in Faulkner County). J. W. was educated in the schools of his native county and commenced life for himself by trading in stock. He remained with his father for one year after the latter's removal to Missouri, then returned to Tennessee and was married there in 1856 to Miss Nancy Layne, who was a native resident of that State. Her father, George Layne, was a farmer, and died in Tennessee in 1848, his wife, who was a Miss Aramintie Dickerson, removing with her daughter, Mrs. Darden, to Arkansas, and dying in White County in 1867. Upon the beginning of the Civil War J. W. Darden was detailed by the Confederate Government to operate his mill, and in this work he has continued for nearly thirty years. After purchasing land he began improving it, and now owns in this and adjoining counties 2,000 acres, with something over 100 acres under cultivation. He is rapidly converting his timber into lumber, and, although he lost about $10,000 by fire in 1875, he has retrieved this loss in a great measure and is now doing well. In politics he casts his vote with the Democratic party, yet is not an active politician. Socially he is an A. F. & A. M., belonging to St. Mary's Lodge No. 170. He also belongs to Tillman Chapter and Searcy Council. His wife is a member of the Baptist Church. To the union of Mr. and Mrs. Darden have been born four children: Allie (now Mrs. Dr. Moon, of Rosebud), William, Elzie and Lula.

Dr. James M. Davie, an able and learned physician, but now retired from the active practice of his profession, is engaged in farming and stock raising on his farm, which comprises 1,000 acres, about one mile southeast of Beebe. He has something like 400 acres under cultivation and a number of acres that is yet in its wild state and very heavily covered with timber. The soil is good and is well adapted to raising all kinds of grain, and besides this property he has about 1,000 acres of equally as good land in Prairie County. He was born in Pearson County, N. C., December 13, 1830, but in 1836 came with his parents to Madison County, Tenn., and there made his home until 1856, at which time he took up his abode in Arkansas. His father, Dr. George N. Davie, was born in North Carolina of Scotch-Irish descent, his wife, Sarah Coldman, a native of North Carolina, being of Welsh lineage. The paternal grandparents, Edward and Margaret A. (Yarbrough) Davie, the former a native of Scotland and the latter of England, eloped from England to America, coming to North Carolina, and were married here. On the Davie side the family are lineal descendants of Sir Humphrey Davy. Dr. George N. Davie was born in 1800, his wife in 1805, their marriage taking place in 1829 and their deaths in 1836 and 1883, respectively, Both were finely educated, and the father was a physician and surgeon of considerable prominence, and his early death left our subject an orphan at the age of six years. His early childhood was spent on a farm and in attending the country schools, later entering higher schools, and at the age of twenty years was a pupil of the school at Huntsville, Tenn., having for a room-mate Dr. A. M. Westlake, of New York, who induced him to take up the study of medicine. They entered Jefferson Medical College, of Philadelphia, Penn., and after an attendance of two years in that institution, graduated in the class of 1854. The two following years Dr. Davie spent in traveling over the States of Arkansas and Texas, and in 1856 located in Hickory Plains, Prairie County, Ark., and there practiced his profession one year. In 1857 he purchased his present farm in White County, but in 1861 gave up farm work to organize a company of 125 men for the State service, and was chosen captain of the same. In 1862, seeing the need of the general army, he disbanded and reorganized his company, and became connected with the regular Confederate service. He was promoted several times, and when the war closed was colonel of the Thirty-sixth Arkansas Infantry. He was badly wounded in the battle of Helena, was slightly wounded at Prairie Grove, and for several months was on post duty at Camden, and with this exception participated in all the engagements of his command. Upon hearing of Lee's surrender he stacked arms, in Texas, and started for home, and in the latter part of July, 1865, was paroled at Little Rock. He resumed the practice of his profession, regained what he had lost during the war, and until 1874 was a successful practitioner of the county, since which time he has devoted his attention to farming with the above results. He is a Democrat on general principles, but is an independent voter, and although often solicited by his friends to run for office, has always refused to do so. He is a demitted member of Beebe Lodge No. 145, of the A. F. & A. M., and also belongs to the I. O. O. F., and was connected with the Agricultural Wheel. In October, 1859, he was married to Miss Emma Z. Bowling, a native of Tennessee, their union taking place in Obion County, but her death occurred in July, 1872, she having borne four children: George C. (an intelligent and well-educated young farmer of the county), Mattie (who died in infancy), Isom (who also died in infancy) and John C. On April 2, 1874, Mr. Davie led to the altar Caroline M. Bowling, a sister of his first wife, but on December 26, 1881, she died of that dread disease, consumption. His third union, on December 9, 1885, was to a Mrs. Hinson, a daughter of Major Thomas, one of the early settlers of Prairie County, Ark.

J. C. R. Davis is a prosperous general merchant of Rosebud, where he has been engaged in business since 1875. His store building, which he erected in 1885, is a substantial frame building, 22x60 feet, and in addition to handling merchandise, he buys and ships cotton. He has been a resident of White County, Ark., since 1874, coming from his native county of Barbour, Ala., being born in 1852. He was the youngest of nine children given to John and Mary (Mooney) Davis, the former of whom was born in North Carolina, and the latter in Georgia. Their wedding took place in the latter state in 1827, and later on they moved to Alabama (1846), and the father opened up a plantation. He died in 1871 and his wife in 1878. He and his father-in-law, Jacob Mooney, were participants in the Indian War of 1836, the latter being killed in battle. J. C. R., our subject, was reared to farm life and was educated in the schools of Alabama, being married there January 6, 1875, to Eugenie Stevens, whom he brought with him to Arkansas. By exercising judgment and ingenuity and prudence he has become the owner of 800 acres of land, lying in White, Cleburne and Faulkner Counties, and has about 200 under cultivation. Although he affiliates with the Democratic party he is not an active politician, but being the people's choice for the office of constable, he filled that position during 1877 and 1878. He is a Mason. In religion he and wife are members of the Missionary Baptist Church. Their union has been blessed with six children, five of whom are living: John Green (who died in 1877 aged eleven months), Tay B., Ora O., Hattie C., Grover C. and M. E. Mrs. Davis is a daughter of Green and Margarette (McRae) Stevens. The father was a planter and in 1871 came to White County, Ark. Here he spent the remainder of his life, dying in 1885. His wife died in Alabama.

James D. Davis is a well-known farmer and stock raiser of Bald Knob, and came to Arkansas, locating in the woods of White County in 1871, when but nineteen years of age. The first four years he lived with J. H. Ford, while he was clearing up his farm, after which his marriage to Miss Delanie Watters was solemnized. She was born in Perry County, Ala., May 23, 1854, and is the mother of three children, two of whom are still living: William D. and Susie H. Mr. Davis first saw the light of day in Perry County, Ala., on November 26, 1852, and is the son of Huriah and Tobitha (Morris) Davis, who were also natives of Alabama, and married in that State, residing there until after the war. He enlisted in the Confederate army in 1861, in the Eighth Alabama Infantry, and died on the battlefield. Mrs. Davis then removed in 1873 with her children to Mississippi, where they remained several years, subsequently coming to Arkansas and locating in White County, where they made their home with James D., who had preceded them several years. In 1888 she went to live with a daughter at Springfield, Mo., where she now resides. She was the mother of nine children, six of whom are still living: Frances (now Mrs. Goodnight, of Mississippi), William C. (of Logan County), Caroline (wife of William Green, of Logan County), James D. (our subject), Nancy (wife of James Finney, of Springfield, Mo.) and Thomas H. (a farmer of Pope County.) Mr. and Mrs. James Davis are members of the Missionary Baptist Church, as were also his parents. In politics he is a Democrat, and also belongs to the Agricultural Wheel. He has been a very successful farmer and stock raiser, and deals in all kinds of live stock.

John D. DeBois is a distinguished attorney at law and real-estate dealer of Judsonia, Ark., of which place he has been a resident since 1871, coming from Henry County, Tenn., where he was born in 1848. He was the elder of two children born to John and Mary C. (Guinn) DeBois, the former a native of West Virginia and the latter of North Carolina. The father was reared in the "Buckeye State" and was married in Tennessee, the latter State continuing to be his home until his death in 1851, he having been a harness-maker by trade, and after marriage directed his attention to farming. His wife died in June, 1888, at Judsonia, Ark. John D. DeBois spent his early life on a farm and received his education in the academy of Henry, Tenn., and in the schools of Lebanon, Ohio. Upon his removal to White County, Ark., in 1871 he engaged in the mercantile business at West Point and in 1872 came to Judsonia and for some time was associated with Dr. J. S. Eastland in the drug business. During this time he began the study of law under the preceptorship of Coody & McRae, and in July, 1878, was admitted to the White County bar and has practiced continuously ever since. Since 1880 he has been in the real-estate business and now owns about 1,000 acres of land, comprising six farms, and has from 350 to 400 acres under cultivation. Mr. DeBois is a Democrat and has been a member of the State and County Conventions at different times. Socially he is a member of the Anchor Lodge No. 384, of the A. F. & A. M. In December, 1872, he was married to Miss Mollie V. Hicks, a daughter of John T. and Martha W. (Heigh) Hicks, originally from North Carolina, who came to White County, Ark., in 1854, settling in Judsonia. Mr. Hicks was a physician and surgeon of many years' standing, and while serving in the Confederate army during the late conflict between the North and South, he received a gunshot wound in the knee (in 1863) from the effects of which he died. His wife survives him, making her home in Wylie, Tex. The children born to this marriage are James Tatum, Flora Blanche, Mary Martin, Iola Opal, Duke Howard (who died in January, 1887, at the age of twenty-two months), and Pattie. Mr. DeBois has taken an active interest in school matters and has served as a member of the school board. He belongs to the Methodist Episcopal Church, South, while his wife worships with the Missionary Baptist Church, being a member of that church.

John J. Deener is a native of Virginia, and is a son of John Jacob and Tobitha (Hamolen) Deener, natives of Virginia. Mr. John Deener, Sr., was born February 25, 1790, and learned the millwright's trade when a boy, and lived in Vir-

ginia, where he married, until 1836, when they removed to Fayette County, Tenn. He then engaged in farming, in which he was very successful. Mr. Deener died in 1867, and his wife in 1849 at the age of forty-four. They were members of the Methodist Episcopal Church, South, and were the parents of seven children, three of whom are still living: Martha Ann (wife of William A. Old, deceased), John J. (our subject) and James B. The paternal grandfather of our subject was John Jacob Deener, and a native of England, and came to this country during the Revolutionary War in which he took an active part, on the side of the Americans, and served under Gen. Washington and under Gen. Francis Marion. After the war he settled in Virginia, where he died, leaving three sons: George, John Jacob and William. The Deener family as a race are of small stature. John J. Deener, our subject, was born April 22, 1830, and received his education at the Macon Masonic College, and when nineteen years of age he left school and worked on a farm, and also engaged in clerking in a store. During the war he was occupied in teaching school. After the war he went into partnership with Samuel E. Garther, of Williston, Tenn., in the mercantile business, where he remained about six years, then removing to Arkansas and locating on the farm where he has since resided. In 1883 he was elected assessor of the county, and held the office four years, also officiated as justice of the peace for twelve years while in Tennessee. Mr. Deener was married on November 13, 1851, to Miss Sarah A. Gober, who was born in Franklin County, Ga., in 1832. They were the parents of four children: Eliza Hamblin (wife of George W. Dobbins), Lula A. (wife of S. S. Putty), Richard S. (a Methodist Episcopal minister) and John J. Mr. and Mrs. Deener are members of the Methodist Episcopal Church, South, in which they take an active part. Mr. Deener also belongs to the Masonic order, and is a strong Democrat.

G. W. Dobbins, county assessor, Searcy, Ark. Every life has a history of its own; and although in appearance it may seem to possess very little to distinguish it from others, yet Mr. Dobbins' career as a farmer and stock raiser, as well as his experience in the political affairs of the community have contributed to give him a wide and popular acquaintance with nearly every citizen of White County—if not personally, then by name—and serves to make his career a more than ordinary one. His birth occurred in Monroe County, Ark., in 1851, and was the second in a family of three children born to A. M. C. and Frances Ann (Carlton) Dobbins, natives of North Carolina. The father was a prominent physician and surgeon, and after his marriage, which occurred in his native State, he immigrated to Tennessee, and there followed his practice until about 1850. He then moved to Monroe County, Ark., settled at Clarendon, followed his profession there until 1857, when he went to Izard County and settled at Evening Shade. He remained there until March, 1860, when he moved to North Carolina. His wife died in Izard County, Ark., on January 1, 1860, and in the fall of 1861 he enlisted in the Thirteenth North Carolina Regiment and participated in the battle of Seven Pines, where he received a gunshot wound. He was taken prisoner at the second battle of Fredericksburg and confined at Rock Island, Ill., and was also confined at Johnstown Island, where he was paroled in June, 1865. He then returned to North Carolina, remained there until 1867, and then moved to Fayette County, Tenn., where he engaged in his practice. His death was caused by yellow fever in 1878. He was a strong temperance man. His children were named as follows: Frances Ann (now Mrs. Baxter, of Gray Township), G. W. and John M. (married and resides in Marion Township, White County). G. W. Dobbins was educated in the schools of North Carolina, and commenced for himself as a clerk in a store, where he remained two years with a salary of $8 per month. In 1869 he attended the Olin College, in Iredell County, N. C., and in 1870 went to Fayette County, Tenn., where he again engaged in clerking. This he followed until 1875 when, in that and the following year, he, in partnership with J. J. Deener, engaged in the mercantile business, thus continuing for nearly two years. He then followed farming in 1877, and

the same year came to White County, Ark., where he purchased and improved a farm of 180 acres, and now has sixty-five acres under cultivation. He is raising considerable stock. He is not very active in politics but votes with the Democratic party, also with the Wheel or County Alliance, and is a member of the Agricultural Wheel. He was elected county assessor in September, 1888, and has been deputy tax collector twice, in 1885 and 1886. He has also been deputy tax assessor two terms, in 1885 and 1888. He has been a member of the school board four years, and takes an active interest in educational affairs. He was married in Fayette County, Tenn., on August 26, 1873, to Miss Eliza H. Deener, a native of Tennessee, and the daughter of J. J. and Sarah A. (Gober) Deener, natives of Virginia and Georgia, respectively. Both are living at the present time, and reside in White County, whither they moved in 1877. To Mr. and Mrs. Dobbins were born these children: Lula Alma, Jessie Eva, Samuel Harold, George Milas, Mary Sadie, Shelly Gober and an infant. Mr. and Mrs. Dobbins are members of the Methodist Episcopal Church, and he has been church secretary since 1878. He takes a deep interest in church affairs.

Charles L. Douthat received his education at Buchanan, Botetourt County, Va., and when eighteen years old, was employed as salesman for nearly two years, and then worked at the tinners' trade for about three years. He then went to Memphis, Tenn., where he was employed as salesman in a wholesale grocery house, until 1859, when he came to West Point and started in the mercantile business, with a capital of a few hundred dollars, which he had saved out of his salary. In 1861 he enlisted in the Confederate army, in the First Arkansas State Troops, but which soon after disbanded, when he then joined Ben McCullock's First Arkansas Mounted Rifles, and was with that command until the close of the war. He was elected to take an official position, but preferred remaining in the ranks as a private. On coming out of the army, Mr. Douthat was financially broken, and again returned to Memphis, and was employed by a wholesale grocery house as sales-

man, where he remained about two years, then returned to West Point, and entered into business
with W. C. West, and afterward with A. T. Jones,
with whom he was engaged for three years, then
running the business alone. He has built up a
large trade, and carries a fine stock of goods. Mr.
Douthat was born in Rockbridge County, Va., in
1831, and was the son of William H. and Susan
(Lewis) Douthat, natives of Richmond, Va., and
of Irish descent, the ancestors coming to this
country before the Revolutionary War. Robert
Douthat, the paternal grandfather of our subject,
was the owner of the Rock bridge, or Natural
bridge, and was the proprietor and builder of a
large woolen mill, and brought many workmen
from Ireland. William H. Douthat was a prominent Mason of Virginia, and died in 1858, his
wife surviving him till 1883, at the age of seventy-
two years. They were the parents of twelve children, nine of whom are still living: Mary J., Robert R., Charles L. (our subject), Henry C., Susan,
Fielding (now a stock raiser in Montana), Warner
L. (in California), Sarah and Annie (who still lives
in Virginia). In 1866 C. L. Douthat was married to Mary C. Whitney, who was born in Fayette
County, Tenn., in 1842. They are the parents of
three children: Effie L., Alma and Charles W.,
all of whom are at home. Mr. Douthat and family are members of the Methodist Episcopal Church,
South. He is a strong Democrat, and a prominent
citizen of West Point.

William T. Dowdy, a sharpshooter in the late
war, came to White County in 1855 with his
father, who bought 320 acres of wild land and
commenced improving it, and cleared up forty or
fifty acres before the war. His father, Andrew
J. Dowdy, was a native of North Carolina and
came to Tennessee when he was a young man,
where he was married, in 1835, to Sarah Sutherland, of Tennessee origin, and a daughter of
Thomas Sutherland. After his marriage he was
employed as overseer on a plantation for thirteen
years. He was the father of three children:
Anna E. (afterward Mrs. Barger), William T.
(our subject) and James S. (deceased). William
T. owes his nativity to Western Tennessee, being

born in 1839, and spending his younger days in
that State. He was married in White County, in
1860, to Emeline E. Barger, a native of Tennessee, and who died on December 10, 1860. He
was married the second time on April 17, 1866, to
Elizabeth Sessums, also of Tennessee. They are
the parents of four children, two of whom are
still living: Richard A. (editor of the Economist
at Searcy, Ark.) and James A. Mr. Dowdy enlisted in 1861 for twelve months, and afterward
for four years or during the war, in Company D,
of the Thirty-first Arkansas Infantry, and was one
of the Confederate sharpshooters who did such
valuable service for the Confederate cause. He
took an active part in the battles of Corinth, Stone
River, Chickamauga and a number of others, and
was taken prisoner on July 22, 1864, near Atlanta,
Ga., and then to Camp Chase, Ohio, when he was
released on parole, February 12, 1865, and went
to Richmond, where he received a furlough. He
then went to Western Tennessee, where he remained until the close of the war. He then returned home and has since engaged in farming.
He owns a farm of 200 acres, with sixty-five acres
under cultivation. Mr. and Mrs. Dowdy are members of the Methodist Episcopal Church, South.
Mr. Dowdy is also connected with the County
Wheel, of which he has been chaplain since first
entering the society. He is also a constituent of
the Centre Hill Lodge No. 114, of the Masonic
order. Mrs. Dowdy was a daughter of Richard J.
and Rachel (Little) Sessums. Mr. Sessums was
born in North Carolina in 1805 and died in 1863.
He was married in 1833, and was the father of
five children.

R. A. Dowdy is editor and publisher of The
Arkansas Economist, the official journal of the
Farmers' and Laborers' Union of Arkansas, Searcy,
Ark. Mr. Dowdy has had charge of the paper
since its name was so called, or during 1889. It
was made the official organ July 26, 1889, at Hot
Springs, and it has quite a circulation and is
building up a good State circulation. Prior to
the above-mentioned date it was a local paper.
Mr. Dowdy took charge of the paper in May, 1888;
was partner until April 1 of the following year,

when he purchased the full interest in it. The paper was organized in October. 1887, under the name of "White County Wheel," and remained thus until after the meeting at Hot Springs, when it was issued under the present name in August, 1889. Mr. Dowdy was born in Des Arc Township, White County, Ark., in 1868 and is the eldest in a family of four children born to the marriage of William T. and C. E. (Sessums) Dowdy, natives of Tennessee and Kentucky, respectively. The father came to White County, Ark., in 1859, settled in Des Arc Township, and here met and married Miss Sessums. Both are now living and reside in White County. R. A. Dowdy received his education in the district schools, and then took a course in Quitman College in 1885. After leaving college he engaged in teaching in Cleburne County for a few terms but later engaged in editorial work on his present paper. Socially, Mr. Dowdy is a member of the Farmers' and Laborers' Union, and takes a deep interest in all things pertaining to the good of the county.

T. A. Duncan enjoys the reputation of being not only a substantial and progressive farmer, but an intelligent and thoroughly posted man on all matters of public interest. In his dealings with his fellow-men he has been upright and honorable, and his character will stand any investigation which may be given it. His native birthplace was Jackson County, Ala., where he first saw the light of day in 1830, he being the eldest of eight children born to Jesse and Nancy E. (White) Duncan, who were Tennesseeans, the father reared at Nashville and the mother near Winchester. They were married in Tennessee and at an early day removed to Alabama, and here Jesse Duncan followed the occupation of millwrighting and erected one of the first mills in the county, also opening a large plantation. He died in 1884 and his wife in 1883. Their children are: T. A. (living in White County, Ark.), W. R. (who is married and resides in Texas), James H. (married and living in Alabama), J. C. (married and living in Kansas), Mary (Mrs. Selby, living near Iuka, Miss.) and Elizabeth (who also resides at Iuka). T. A. Duncan's early life was like the majority of farmers' boys, and he assisted

his father in clearing up the home farm and began that work for himself at the age of nineteen in Alabama. He was married in Jackson County, of that State, in January, 1849, to S. B. Pace, and upon the opening of the war he enlisted from Jackson County in the Confederate army, for three years, or during the war, becoming a member of Berry's artillery. He was in the battle of Peach Orchard Gap (Ga.), Jackson (Miss.), Resaca, and was taken prisoner at Spanish Fort and sent to Ship Island and afterward to Vicksburg. Upon being paroled in 1865 he returned to Jackson County, Ala., and in 1872 came to White County, Ark., and bought a timber tract of 180 acres which he began clearing and upon which he erected good buildings. He has 110 acres of his 400-acre farm under cultivation, all of which he has cleared since coming to the county. He is a Democrat, has been magistrate nine years, and taken an interest in the finance of the county, which was in bad shape at that time, and succeeded in settling affairs. He is also a member of the school board, and has always taken a deep interest in school matters. He and wife are the parents of the following children: William F. (who is married and resides in White County, Ark.), Cassie (who died in 1885 at the age of twenty-eight years, was married to Mr. Holleman), B. E. (who is married and lives in the county), J. J. (married and living in Cleburne County), Minta (who married A. J. Holleman after the death of Cassie, and lives in White County, Ark.), Nancy (Mrs. J. F. Lawrence), C. A. (who married F. W. Raney, and also lives in White County), Mila and Jo (still with their parents). Mrs. Duncan's parents, William and Elizabeth (Wininger) Pace, were both members of old Virginia families, and moved to Alabama about the year 1827, being among the earliest to enter land in that State. The father died in 1870 and his wife one year later.

James Dupriest is a farmer and ginner of Marshall Township, and owns 850 acres of land, of which 300 acres are under fence, 200 in pasture, and 100 acres under cultivation. He is a native of Georgia, his birth occurring in 1821. His father, Martin Dupriest, was also of Georgia origin, where he was educated and subsequently married, and to this union was born a family of eight children. James D. was a twin, being sixth in order of birth and a prosperous boy. He lived in Georgia until 1840, when he moved to Alabama with his father, locating in Coosa County and there remained seventeen years. He was married to Sarah Malcolm and moved to Arkansas in 1856, and by her had two children who died in infancy. His wife died in 1864 and in 1865 was married to his second wife, Mrs. Louisa Henry, and to this union has been born a family of seven children: Ebbie, Burton, Thomas, Cathron, Cullen, McFerrin, Joseph. His second wife had one son by her first marriage, Fenton Henry, he being a thoroughly and highly educated man. James Dupriest honors the Democrats with his vote and takes quite an interest in politics though not an enthusiast; he is also a Mason, belonging to the Blue Lodge. Himself and wife worship with the Methodist Church to which they belong.

Dr. J. S. Eastland is one of the foremost physicians and surgeons of White County, Ark., and his practice lies among the wealthiest and most intelligent people of the county. He has been a resident of Judsonia since March, 1872, having, prior to this, been a resident of Richland County, Wis. He was born in Hinds County, Miss., December 18, 1844, and was the second of a family of ten children born to David J. and Mary E. (Cameron) Eastland, the father born in Genesee County, N. Y., and the mother in Hinds County, Miss. When a young man the father went to the vicinity of Schoolcraft, Mich., and at the age of twenty years removed to Mississippi, and was engaged in teaching school in an academy at Cayuga, and was married there about the year 1841. From 1852 until the present time he has been engaged in milling in Richmond County, and is making his home on a large farm which he purchased near Sextonville. Dr. J. S. Eastland was about eight years old when he was taken to Wisconsin, and he received his education in the schools of Richland County. In 1863 he enlisted at Madison, Wis., in Company H, Seventeenth Wisconsin Infantry, and was assigned to the Army of the Tennessee. He

was a participant in the engagements at Chattanooga, Resaca, Buzzard's Roost, Kenesaw Mountain, and was with Sherman in his memorable march to the sea, and in the Carolina campaign. He was at the grand review at Washington, D. C., but received his discharge at Madison, Wis., in June, 1865. After returning home he began reading medicine, and took a course in the Eclectic Medical Institute during the winter of 1869–70. The following year he entered Blakely Hospital of Philadelphia, Penn., and after graduating the same year he came to Arkansas, taking up his abode in Randolph County, but only remained there until 1872, since which time he has been a resident of White County. In September, 1886, he opened a fine drug store at Judsonia, which is in a flourishing condition, and in addition to managing this establishment and practicing his profession, he is employed as surveyor of the Iron Mountain Railroad. He is a Democrat, a member of the board of medical examiners of White County, and socially is a member of Anchor Lodge No. 384, of the A. F. & A. M., and was Worshipful Master of the lodge for some years. He was married in White County, in 1873, to Miss Samantha W. Boatwright, a native of White County, and a daughter of Charles W. and Virginia (Subbaugh) Boatwright, who were natives of Virginia. In 1856 they settled at West Point, White County, Ark., but Mr. Boatwright is now residing at Jonesboro, Ark. The mother died in 1889. When Dr. Eastland first came to White County the country was, in a great measure, unsettled, and there was a great deal of sickness among the settlers, but it is now much healthier. Mrs. Eastland is a member of the Baptist Church.

J. W. Edie. Among the early settlers of Judsonia will be found the name of J. W. Edie, who came from Buchanan County, Iowa, and settled in the town in 1873. After following the lumber business for some twelve years he began making a specialty of sash, doors and blinds, and does an extensive business. He was born in Harrison County, Ohio, December 6, 1834, and is the eldest of two children born to Thomas and Levina (Palmer) Edie, who were born in the "Keystone

State." They immigrated to Ohio with their parents in 1819 and 1821, respectively, and were married in that State in February, 1834. The father was a farmer, and followed that occupation both in Ohio and after removing to Iowa in 1853, in the latter State paying much of his attention to the manufacture of lumber also. These occupations received his attention until his removal to Judsonia in 1877, and from that time until his death, in February, 1883, he lived a retired life. His wife survives him. The paternal grandparents, James and Mary (Ward) Edie, were born in Pennsylvania and England, respectively, and settled in the State of Ohio, in 1819; the great-grandfather was a Scotchman. The maternal grandparents, James and Margaret (Arnold) Palmer, were born in Maryland, and moved to Ohio in 1821, from which State they removed to Iowa in 1853, making the latter their home until his death in 1857, at the age of eighty-one years. He was a soldier in the War of 1812. His wife died, in 1868, at the age of eighty-three years. The children of Thomas and Levina Edie are: Margaret (now Mrs. Wagner, of Judsonia, whose husband is in the Government employ) and our subject (who was reared on his father's farm and received his education in the schools of Ohio. After his removal to Iowa with his parents, he resided there until 1856, when he was married, in Buchanan County, to Miss Rebecca J., a daughter of Joseph and Mary (Garner) Chitester, of Pennsylvania. The father was a millwright, and in 1845 moved to Shawneetown, Ill., and, in 1850, to Iowa. Since 1885 they have resided in Judsonia, Ark., and have passed the sixtieth milestone of their wedded life. After his marriage, Mr. Edie made his home in Iowa until 1873, then came to Judsonia and engaged in business as mentioned above. He is not an active politician, but votes the Democratic ticket, and has been mayor of the town in which he lives three terms, and has also been a member of the city school board. Socially he is a member of Anchor Lodge No. 384, of the A. F. & A. M., and has been Worshipful Master of his order. He belongs to Tillman Chapter No. 19, and Occidental Council No. 1. Mr. and Mrs. Edie are worthy members of the Baptist Church, and their union has been blessed in the birth of eight children, seven being now alive: Silas A. (died in 1878, at the age of twenty-two years), C. F. (is unmarried, and is an engineer on the Denver & Rio Grande Railroad), Ida (now Mrs. McDearman, lives in Judsonia), T. M. (is married, and lives in the town; a carpenter and joiner by trade), Ada Aletha (Mrs. Sims), A. J. (a resident of Little Rock), Eva (Mrs. Croy, of Darke County, Ohio) and Stella. Mr. Edie is public-spirited, and is a member of the board of directors of the Judsonia University.

William H. Edwards. Among the many old settlers of White County, Ark., there is none more highly esteemed than the subject of this sketch, for in his walk through life he has been honest and upright in every particular. He was born in Madison County, Tenn., August 7, 1811, and is a son of Sanford and Mary (Thetford) Edwards, both of whom were born in Greenville District, S. C., the former in 1787 and the latter in 1805. They were married in Tennessee, reared their family in the western portion of that State and there spent their lives, the father's death occurring in 1874 and the mother's in 1869. They were members of the Methodist Episcopal Church and he was a soldier in the War of 1812, and in his political views was an old line Whig, but was not an enthusiast in politics, being one of those quiet men whose life was without reproach. Their family was as follows: Nancy (deceased, was born in 1806 and became the wife of a Mr. Fussell), Anderson (deceased, was born in 1808), William H. (the subject of this memoir), James F. (deceased, was born in 1814 and died in May, 1889, a farmer of White County), Rebecca (deceased, was born in 1817, and was the wife of James Stowbuck, a blacksmith of Tennessee), Ina (deceased, was born in 1819), Joseph (was born in 1822, and is a farmer of White County), Elizabeth (was born in 1823 and is the wife of Enoch Terry, of Texas), Sophronia (deceased, was born in 1828 and is the wife of William Tedford), and Sanford (who was born in 1831 and is a farmer of Tennessee). William H. Edwards received very poor chances for acquiring an education, owing to the newness of the country during his youth and to the fact that his services were required on the home farm. On June 4, 1835, he was married to Miss Lucinda Dockins, and to them were born the following children: James M. (a farmer of White County, born in 1836), William L. (born in 1837), George W. (born in 1839) and Mary E. and Rebecca J. (twins, born in 1841, Rebecca being the widow of James Powers). Mrs. Edwards died in 1844 and January 28, 1846, Mr. Edwards married Lucinda Wilson, daughter of James Wilson. She was born in Tennessee in 1825 and by Mr. Edwards became the mother of four children: Sarah Ann (born in 1847 and died the same year), Joseph M. (residing near his father, was born in December, 1848), Susan A. (was born September 26, 1851, and died August 1, 1852), an infant (died, unnamed) and Noah A. (who was born November 15, 1854, and is a farmer of this county). After his marriage Mr. Edwards worked for his father two years and then began tilling his father's farm for himself, continuing until 1852, when he purchased a farm of his own, on which he resided for seven years. Since that date he has resided in White County, and in 1860 purchased the farm of 160 acres where he now lives. He has seventy acres under cultivation and his farm is well adapted to raising all kinds of farm produce. He was reared a Whig, but since the war, in which he served on the Confederate side three years, he has been a Democrat. He became a Mason at Stony Point twenty-six years ago, but is at present a member of Beebe Lodge No. 145, A. F. & A. M., and has held every office in that order. He is also a valued member of the Agricultural Wheel and has always taken hold of every movement that had for its object the social or educational welfare of the community in which he resided. He has ever lived in peace and harmony with his neighbors and he and family are worthy members of the Methodist Episcopal Church.

Thomas J. Edwards. Hayden S. Edwards, the esteemed father of the subject of this memoir, was born in Shelby County, Ky., on April 2, 1811, and was a son of Rev. James P. Edwards, one of the first Baptist ministers that came to the State of Arkansas. He was also a surveyor and came to this State to assist a corps of engineers, and was over a large part of the State. Hayden S. was married to Miss Mary Lumkins, a native of Knox County, Tenn., on January 26, 1832, and in 1853 removed to Arkansas, locating in White County, on the farm now owned by his son, Thomas J., who took charge of the farm and cared for his parents the latter years of their lives. Hayden Edwards was a school-teacher in his younger days, and also served in the Mexican War as wagon master. He was a strong Democrat and a member of the Masonic order, and was connected with the Missionary Baptist Church, as was also his wife. He died in 1887. His wife was born in 1815, and died in 1882, leaving a family of six children, Thomas J., the principal of this sketch, being the only one living. He was born in Ballard County, Ky., on April 17, 1841. In 1861 he enlisted in the Confederate army, under Col. Patterson, and took part in all of the battles in the Missouri raid. He was wounded at Little Rock, and was taken prisoner but soon escaped. After the close of hostilities he returned home and found his family stripped of every thing of value, and as he was without means he was obliged to start from the beginning, but with a will that overcame all obstacles has risen to an eminence of success, and is now the owner of 280 acres of land in the old homestead and eighty south of Bald Knob, and has about 130 under cultivation. In 1884 he was married to Miss Ida N. Maxwell, a daughter of Joseph Maxwell, and who is the mother of one daughter, Mary Stokes, who was born February 5, 1885. Mrs. Edwards is a member of the Methodist Church. Mr. Edwards is a Democrat and a prominent citizen of White County.

James H. Edwards, one of White County's leading citizens, is a son of James and Eliza (Simmon) Edwards, natives of Haywood County, Tenn., who moved to Arkansas in 1850, and located in White County, and later moved to Cleburne County, where Mr. Edwards, Sr., still lives, in his sixty-eighth year. He is a member of the Missionary Baptist Church, and also of the Masonic order. He is still engaged in farming, and owns 460 acres of fine land. His wife died on August 26, 1889, at the age of sixty-two. They were the parents of fourteen children, ten of whom are still living: John F., Thomas H., Tennie (wife of J. W. Blasingim), James H. (our subject), Mary J. (wife of J. R. Fortner), Martha Ann (wife of Frank Epps), Ann Eliza (wife of Richard Davis), Nannie, Benjamin and Henry. James H. Edwards claims White County as his birthplace, his birth occurring on April 26, 1854, and remained on his father's farm until twenty-seven years of age, though part of the time was spent in farming for himself. He married Miss Emma Fortner, a daughter of J. E. and Mary C. Fortner, and who was born in White County, in 1861. Joseph E. Fortner was born in Wayne County, N. C., December 4, 1812, and died in White County, Ark., July 5, 1888. In 1832 he was genuinely and soundly converted to God and joined the Presbyterian Church. After a few years of devotion to that branch of God's church he joined the Methodist Church, in which he kept his membership until God called him home. From North Carolina he moved to Tennessee, and from there to Arkansas, where he lived for thirty-four years, being among the pioneers of this country. He was the father of fifteen children. His seat was never vacant at church, unless sickness kept him away. Mr. and Mrs. Edwards are the parents of two children: Adga May and Hollice Taylor. He owns a fine farm which is well under cultivation, and has been a very successful and highly respected citizen. Himself and wife are members of the Methodist Episcopal Church. Politically he is a prominent Democrat, and also belongs to the County Wheel.

Thomas B. Ellis. Benjamin Ellis was a native of the Old Dominion, where he was married to Mary Malone, also of that State. They removed to Kentucky in 1807 or 1808, and the following year moved to Alabama, where they made their home until their death, Mrs. Ellis passing away in 1853 and Mr. Ellis in the following year. They were the parents of eleven children: Benjamin R. (married and residing in Shelby County, Tenn.), Sallie M. (Harris), Nancy H. (Norris), Mary H. (deceased), Thomas B. (the subject of this sketch),

James B. and William T. (both deceased), Joseph F. and John W. (residents of Alabama). Thomas B. Ellis was born in Madison County, Ala., in 1820, where he resided for over thirty years, and where he was married to Judith A. Critz, of Alabama, who died in 1850, leaving two children: Mary E. (now Mrs. Hussey, of Searcy, White County) and Olivia C. (now Mrs. Goodlow, also of that place). Mr. Ellis was married the second time, in 1851, to Mary A. Corrington, of Marshall County, Miss., who died in 1860, leaving three daughters: Sarah A. (Mrs. Menus, residing near Nashville, Tenn.), Martha E. (now Mrs. Lanier, of Searcy), Roberta A. (now Mrs. Dickey, residing near the old homestead). His third and present wife, was Mary A. Montgomery, a daughter of Edward and Tobitha Montgomery, of White County, Ark., to whom he was married in 1860. They are the parents of four children: Virgil B., Nora, Thomas B. and John E. (deceased). Mr. Ellis came to Arkansas in 1856, settling in Des Arc Township, White County, where he bought a farm of 560 acres with 110 cleared, and on which he still lives. He enlisted in 1861 as a forager, in which capacity he served a short time, and was then given an honorable discharge on account of age. He returned to his farm, which he found in a state of decay and dilapidation. He has since resided on the farm and been very successful as a farmer, remaining here until the last year, when he removed to Centre Hill and started in the grocery business. Mr. Ellis is a member of the Masonic order, and belongs to Centre Hill Lodge No. 114, and is Master of his lodge. Mr. Ellis and family are members of the Methodist Episcopal Church. Mr. Ellis is a prominent Democrat, and held the office of constable shortly after the war.

James Figg was born in Gates County, N. C., January 31, 1804, and received a practical education in the schools of his native State. He was married March 19, 1829, to Miss Margaret Lewis of North Carolina, who was born March 19, 1809. To their union ten children were given: Mary J. (deceased), Sophia A. (Mrs. W. H. Hallford), F. C. (Mrs. Samuel Gray, deceased), John L. (now residing in Alabama), one child who died in infancy (unnamed), Martha R. (who married F. M. Rice), George A. (deceased), Emma J. (Mrs. L. Byrd), Joseph J. and Mary E.   Mr. Figg was a man who took an active interest in political affairs, being a Whig up to the time of the war, and a strong secessionist. A farmer and mechanic by occupation, he owned 120 acres of land highly cultivated at the date of his demise.   He was a Master Mason and had held office as Tyler in Newton Lodge No. 224, in Alabama, and was a member of Mount Pisgah Lodge No. 242 in Arkansas at the time of his death, which occurred February 10, 1873.   He and wife were members of the Methodist Church, South, and he was one of the prominent factors in organizing the church in the neighborhood where he lived; ever taking an active interest in all church and educational matters.   Joseph J. Figg received his education in Alabama, and at the age of twenty-one immigrated to Arkansas and settled in White County, where he is now residing. Reaching an age where he realized that it was not good for man to be alone, he selected for his life's companion Miss Mary F. Andrews, who was born February 16, 1853, a daughter of Benjamin and Elizabeth Andrews.   Their marriage was consummated January 13, 1875, and five children have blessed their union: Lelia V. (born May 20, 1877), James L. (born February 2, 1879), Robert G. (born June 20, 1881), Maggie E. (born November 22, 1883), and one who died in infancy.   Mr. Figg is a farmer and school-teacher, and owns 120 acres of hill and bottom land, with twenty-five acres under cultivation.   He is Master Mason, and has held office as Junior Deacon for one term in Mount Pisgah Lodge No. 242; he was also formerly a member of the Wheel, but has recently resigned.   During his connection with that order he acted as secretary of the lodge; he has held the office of justice of the peace for three consecutive terms in the township in which he resides, serving in an acceptable manner.   Mrs. Figg is a consistent member and an earnest worker of the Baptist Church.

W. E. Fisher.   It has long been acknowledged that, no matter what a man's occupation in life may be if his energies are directed toward advancing the interests of the community in which he resides, he is a useful and respected and prominent man. W. E.'s early life was surrounded with many hardships and privations, and his early education was acquired by reading at night by the flickering light of a brush fire after his day's work was done. Upon commencing life for himself the occupation he had been taught when young naturally became his by adoption, and he now owns 353 acres with about 155 acres under cultivation.   Mr. Fisher was born in Wilson County, Tenn., November 25, 1819, and on August 11, 1840, he was married to Miss Martha Adkinson, her death occurring on September 19, 1852, after having borne a family of seven children: Anderson L. (born August 23, 1841, was married to Miss Martha Canada, became the father of six children, and is a farmer of White County), David (born in 1843 and died in infancy), David L. (born September 19, 1844), Cordelia M. (was born December 23, 1846; first married John Winford, by whom she became the mother of three children, and after his death she wedded John Drenon), Amanda J. (was born February 14, 1849, and married Thomas Martin, a farmer of Pope County, becoming the mother of seven children), Eliza J. (was born February 16, 1851, and married Paton Burris, who left her a widow with one child, and she afterward married Frank Massey, a farmer of Searcy County).   In January, 1855, Mr. Fisher wedded Mrs. Susan Brown, of Carroll County, but she too died on May 31 of the following year.   He espoused his third wife, Miss Harriet Agours, of Fayette County, Tenn., June 24, 1857, and their children are as follows: Mary E. (born June 30, 1863, is the wife of S. J. Crabtree, editor of the Arkansaw Hub at Beebe, by whom she has one child living and two children deceased), Martha E. (was born April 2, 1858, and is the wife of James Martin, who keeps a meat market in Brinkley), Laura E. (was born February 23, 1865, and wedded John Watson, and they also have one child living and one deceased), Harriett A. (was born October 25, 1867, and is the wife of John Shelton, only one of their two children being now alive), George W. (born September 27, 1859), Joseph E. (born

April 7, 1861), Maggie (deceased), Sallie (born November 13, 1871) and Jimmie (born July 16, 1873). All Mr. Fisher's children have received good school advantages and are intelligent young people. Our subject removed with his family to Arkansas on November 23, 1860, and located about three-quarters of a mile west of the farm on which he is now living, where he purchased 162 acres of land, and after making his home here for about nine years he bought the farm on which he is now residing. Mr. Fisher affiliated with the Democrat party until 1885, when he united with the Agricultural Wheel, and has been a member of the State Deputy Organization and has also served faithfully and well in the capacity of State lecturer. At the present time he is chairman of the State Central Committee. He is a man who has always taken a deep interest in public affairs, and is well informed in all matters pertaining to county, State and national matters, taking that side in politics which he deemed best calculated to promote the interests of the people. He has served his county in the State legislature and filled this position to the entire satisfaction of his constituents. He holds membership in Beebe Lodge No. 144, of the A. F. & A. M., and has served as Senior Warden and is a Royal Arch Mason of El Paso Lodge. He and wife are members of the Methodist Episcopal Church, South, as are also eleven of their children. Mr. Fisher is a son of Anderson Fisher and Sinie Johnson, the former of English ancestry, his people having come from England prior to the Revolutionary War. Anderson Fisher was a scout under Gen. Jackson in the War of 1812, and for a few years prior to his death drew a pension, although he had refused to do so up to that time. He died in 1876 at the age of eighty-three years, four months and six days. He was the father of ten children: Jeremiah, Eliza, Sarah, James, W. E., Leonard B., Elizabeth, John H., Anderson M., Lucinda A., and Cordelia, who died in infancy, the remainder of the family growing to manhood and womanhood.

J. B. Foreman is a successful planter of South Carolina nativity, and has been a resident of White County, Ark., since 1859. He was born in York District, in 1836, and was the third in a family of seven children born to the marriage of James T. and Elizabeth Luraney (Rowell) Foreman, who were also born in York District, S. C., and were there married. The father was a planter and the year following his wife's death, which occurred in South Carolina, October 6, 1859, he removed to White County, Ark., where he became the owner of 620 acres of timber land. He died on this farm March 26, 1873, and left three children to mourn his loss: William Rowell (who is married and resides in Howard County, Ark.), Elizabeth L. (who is a Mrs. Mann and lives in the county) and J. B. The latter left South Carolina, a young man, and came direct to White County and purchased 160 acres of land on credit, but before getting it in shape to be tilled was compelled to rent land. In 1862 he joined Company B, Gen. McRae's regiment, and was in the battles of Helena, Prairie Grove, Little Rock and Cache River, and then joined the cavalry under Col. A. R. Witt, and was in the Missouri raid, taking part in the battles of Pilot Knob, Jefferson City, Independence, Kansas City and thence to Fayetteville. Upon his return home he resumed farming, and has opened up sixty acres of land. He is a Democrat, a member of the Agricultural Wheel, a Mason, belonging to St. Mary's Lodge No. 170 of the A. F. & A. M., and he and his wife are members of the Methodist Episcopal Church, South. He was married in White County, in October, 1860, to Martha Ellen, a daughter of Valentine and Alice (Carr) Harlan, who were born in Georgia, the father a farmer and carpenter by trade. He came to White County, Ark., in 1857, and here died in 1873, his wife dying November 18, 1877. Mr. and Mrs. Foreman have these children: James V. (a resident of Kentucky), William Edward (in Kentucky), Ann H., Martha E., Wade H., Bernie P. and Alice E. Mary E. died August 30, 1886, when nearly five years old.

John C. Fussell, farmer and stock raiser. The life of this gentleman affords an example which might well be imitated by the young men of the present day, for his capital on commencing life for himself was limited, and throughout his career he has been industrious and frugal. He was born in Madison County, Tenn., February 23, 1845, and was brought to Arkansas by his parents in 1859, they having been married in 1840. They first settled on railroad land in White County, but later pre-empted 160 acres of wild land and began building a home, but traded this in 1876 for eighty acres where our subject, John C., now lives. Wyatt Fussell, the father, prior to coming to Arkansas, was a business man of Jackson, Tenn., and kept one of the best livery stables in the place. He was marshal of the town for several years, and in his political views was an old line Whig. He and wife, whose maiden name was Elizabeth Mattox, were members of the Baptist Church, and their deaths occurred in Arkansas, August 12, 1889, and Tennessee, in 1853, respectively. Of six children born to them four lived to be grown: William N. (who is a physician of Denmark, Tenn.), John C., Elmira (deceased, the wife of J. J. Rogers, a farmer of Lonoke County) and Mary E. (the wife of J. B. Shelton, of White County). John C. Fussell was reared to a farm life, and although his facilities for acquiring an education were very poor, he acquired a thorough knowledge of the three R's. Until twenty-five years of age he worked for his father and sisters, then was married to Miss Mary E. Powers, a daughter of A. M. Powers, a farmer of Tennessee, who came to Arkansas in 1860. Their union resulted in the birth of three children, two of whom are living: James W. (a young man residing with his father) and Betty O. Jennie died in childhood. Mr. Fussell is a man who has always been interested in the welfare of his county, and always supports enterprises which tend to benefit the same. He is a member of Stony Point Lodge No. 20, of the Agricultural Wheel. His wife is a daughter of A. M. and Eliza (Moore) Powers, who were Tennesseeans, and as above stated came to Arkansas in 1860, locating near Beebe, where he became the owner of a large number of slaves, and resided for fourteen years. He and his wife reared a family of eight children to manhood and womanhood, their names being as follows: Mary E. (Mrs. Fus-

sell), Robert (a mechanic), Nancy (wife of William L. Edwards, a farmer of White County), Martha (wife of James Edwards, also a farmer), Jennie (widow of William Hartbrooks), William (a farmer of Beebe) and Sophia (is wife of John Lestie, of Lonoke County).

Uriah E. Gentry is a native of South Carolina and a son of Cornelius and Mary (Johnson) Gentry, also natives of that State, where they lived until after their marriage, removing thence to Georgia when our subject was a child. Later they became located in Tennessee, and in 1836 in Alabama, where the father died in 1842 at the age of thirty-nine. After this unhappy event Mrs. Gentry went to Mississippi with her family and located on the head waters of the Tom Bigbee River, going in 1856 to Texas, and remaining until 1868 when they came to Arkansas, settling in Independence County. The family consisted of nine children the following being the only ones living at this time: Susanah (now Mrs. Provence), Thomas, Uriah E., M. V. and Parthenia (wife of Elisha Bass). Uriah E. Gentry was born in Spartanburg, S. C., on July 12, 1830, and continued with his mother until twenty-two years of age when he commenced for himself as a farmer. In 1863 he enlisted in the Confederate army, in the Twenty-ninth Texas Cavalry, in which he served only a short time, having received a wound; after this he was put on detached duty. Upon the close of the war he rented a farm in Texas for two years, but coming to Independence County, Ark., here bought a farm and remained until 1874 when he sold out and located in White County. He now owns a farm of 200 acres with a large portion of it under cultivation, and has also helped his boys in getting a substantial start in life. Mr. Gentry was married after reaching manhood to Mary Davis, who died in 1864, leaving a family of children, two of whom only are living: Robert C. (a farmer of this county) and Louisa (the wife of a Mr. Saulefor, of Independence County). In 1865 he was married to Miss Winnie Bass, who died in 1868, having borne two children: Thomas R. and Jerry L., both farmers of this county. In 1869 Miss Elizabeth Thomas became Mr. Gentry's third wife. She died in 1872. In 1873 his fourth matrimonial venture resulted in his marriage to Miss Estelle Churchwell. They are the parents of six children: Carrie L., Mary T., Sallie, Jessie B., Ora B. and Mattie J. Mr. and Mrs. Gentry are members of the Methodist Episcopal Church, South. The former belongs to the Masonic order, and is a prominent Democrat. He is recognized as one of the leading men of his township and enjoys a well-deserved popularity.

M. N. Gentry, groceryman, Searcy, Ark. The family grocery trade of Searcy is well represented by honorable commercial men, who are full of enterprise. Among those who hold a leading position in this line is Mr. Gentry, firmly established in his business and enjoying an excellent trade. He carries a full line of queensware, groceries, etc., and started his house in 1876. In April, 1882, he was burned out, and in the same year erected a good one-story brick building, 100x25 feet. Mr. Gentry moved to Independence County, Ark., in 1868, remained a short time, and in the same year moved to West Point, White County, where he resided until 1869. He then moved to Gray Township and followed farming. He owes his nativity to Tishomingo County, Miss., where he was born in 1856, being the third in a family of four children, the result of the union of N. J. and Jane (Eaton) Gentry, natives of South Carolina and Alabama, respectively. The father when a boy moved to Alabama, was married in that State, and followed agricultural pursuits for a livelihood. In 1856 he moved to Red River County, Tex., remained there until 1866, then moved to McLennan County, where he resided until 1868. He then moved to Independence County, Ark., and later to White County, purchased land, improved it, and in 1876 engaged in business under the firm name of Ward & Gentry, which title continued until 1878, after which it was changed to Gentry & Son, remaining so until 1887. The father died in June of that year. Socially he was a member of Searcy Lodge No. 49, A. F. & A. M. The mother is still living, and resides at Searcy. Since 1887 the firm title has been M. N. Gentry. The children of the above-mentioned couple are named as follows: W. C. (married, and resides in Navarro County, Tex., engaged in farm-

.ing), J. T. (married, residing at Hillside, Tex., and is a railroad agent), M. N. and Mary (who resides in Searcy). Mr. Gentry was reared to farm life, and received his education in the schools of Texas, and in White County, Ark., attending one year in Searcy. He assisted his father in clearing and developing the home place, and remained on the farm until he engaged in business in 1876. Socially he is a member of Searcy Lodge No. 49, A. F. & A. M., and served as Junior Warden for six years, Senior Warden for one year, and Worshipful Master for two years. He is at present one of the masters of ceremonies. He served four years as a member of the city council, one of which was known as the Dade council, and during that year sheds were erected over the springs. Mr. Gentry takes an active interest in everything for the good of the county. He aids in all enterprises for the public good, and is one of the substantial citizens.

C. S. George, clerk of the county and probate court, Searcy, Ark., is well known to the residents of White County, as one, who, in all his relations to the public, has proven himself faithful to the trusts committed to him. Whether in his private or official capacity no taint of dishonor can be found. He was born in Coahoma County, Miss., in January, 1853, being the fourth of eight children, born to C. L. and Catherine M. (McDermott) George, natives of Kentucky and Ohio, respectively. The parents were married at Helena, Ark., and later settled in Mississippi, where the father followed agricultural pursuits. His father took an active part in politics, was clerk of Phillips County, Ark., was also assessor in the early history of the county, and county judge of Coahoma County, Miss., and in 1867 moved to Lawrence County, Ark., where he purchased an improved farm. From there he moved to Searcy, in 1876, lived a retired life, and there died in November, 1881. His excellent wife still survives and resides in Searcy. C. S. George was reared to the arduous duties of the farm, and received a fair education in the schools of Mississippi and Arkansas. He commenced for himself as deputy clerk of Lawrence County, Ark., in 1871, served two years and moved to White County, Ark., in 1876, locating at Searcy. He then entered the office as deputy county clerk in 1880, served eight years, and in 1888 he was elected clerk of the county, having the honor of being the only one elected on the Democratic ticket. He has been connected with the records of White County longer than any one else now living. He is a member of the Masonic Fraternity, Searcy Lodge No. 49, is also a member of Tillman Chapter No. 19, R. A. M. Mr. George was married in Searcy, in February, 1880, to M. B. Isbell, a native of White County, and two children living are the fruits of this union: Herbert L. and Leland S. Those deceased were named: Lillie (who died in 1882) and Charley (who died in 1884). Mr. George is a member of the school board, and takes an active interest in all that pertains to the good of the community. Mrs. George is a member of the Methodist Episcopal Church.

Robert N. Gill, though one of the younger citizens of the county, has risen to a worthy place among its farmers and merchants. He was born in Tennessee in the year 1855, and is the oldest in a family of five children in the family of W. F. and Ollie A. (McDowell) Gill. The former was a native of Tennessee, and spent his life in farming, which occupation proved very successful to him. Moving to Marshall Township, White County, Ark., in 1853, he purchased 300 acres of land, and at once proceeded to carefully cultivate this property. His wife died in Arkansas in 1875, leaving five children: Robert, James N., Ellen, Molly, and Georgia A. Mr. Gill subsequently married again and reared a family of four children; he was called to his final home in 1889. Robert N. passed his early life on a farm, and received a good education in the schools of Arkansas. He was married in 1874 to Miss Johanna Thompson, daughter of Henry Thompson, and a native of Arkansas. To their union six children have been born: Frank M., Ora B., Olie E., Johnie M., Jessie Lee and Elmer. Mr. Gill is an expert mechanic, and has built many houses in the country, which are excellent specimens of his skill. In 1887 he embarked in merchandising business in Romance, where he carries a large and carefully

selected stock, and is building up a substantial and lucrative trade, also owning a fine farm of 120 acres, of which seventy-five acres are under cultivation. He has observed a very great change in the country since taking up his residence here, and in the general growth and advancement has borne a faithful share. In politics Mr. Gill is a Democrat, and with his wife worships at the Methodist Episcopal Church, South.

Emmet O. Gilliam was the fifth son in a family of six children, of William and Mary (Spencer) Gilliam, natives of Virginia and North Carolina, respectively. William Gilliam was at one time a resident of Mississippi, and later became settled in Tennessee, finally coming to White County, Ark., where he opened up a farm of 160 acres, in Gray Township. After remaining here for three years, he sold out and moved to Des Arc Township. The children of himself and wife were named: Albert A., William S., Robert H., Leona L. (deceased), Emmet O. (our subject) and Edward C. Emmet O. Gilliam was born February 8, 1860, in White County, on the farm where he now lives. Consequently he is numbered among the community's younger citizens. In 1880 he took charge of the old homestead, consisting of 160 acres, of which 100 acres are under a high state of cultivation. Mr. Gilliam is a strong Democrat, and although a young man in years, takes an active and influential interest in politics. His energy and determination promise to render him one of the leading men of his county.

James Monroe Gist, M. D., medical practitioner and a resident of Beebe, Ark., was born December 31, 1833, in Carroll County, Tenn., being a son of Joseph B. and Dorcas (Mitchell) Gist, the former of English descent. In 1739 the Gists first came to America and Dr. Gist can trace his ancestry back five generations. Grandfather Mitchell was a participant in the battle of New Orleans and in 1858 came to White County, Ark. He was united in marriage to Miss Sarah Scott in 1812, while a resident of Kentucky. Dr. James M. Gist received his early education in the private schools of his native county and began his medical studies under Dr. J. W. McCall, of Carroll County, and took his first course of medical lectures in the medical department of the University of Tennessee at Nashville, during the winter of 1857-58 and 1859-60, graduating in the latter year. In 1858 he had removed to Arkansas and after his graduation he returned here and settled at Austin, Prairie County. In the spring of 1860 he moved to Stony Point, White County, being there united in marriage June 5, 1861, to Miss Mary Eleanor Thomas, a native of Marshall County, Miss., a daughter of John Franklin and Nancy Thomas, both of whom were of English descent, the former a native of North Carolina and the latter of Mississippi. To the Doctor and his wife two children were born: Nancy Dorcas (born January 10, 1867, was married to J. E. Fisher in 1885 and died, July 9, 1887, at her home in Texas, of cardiac rheumatism, having given birth to a daughter, Myron Gist Fisher, December 6, 1886), Minnie Laura (the younger daughter, was born October 22, 1869). When Dr. Gist first came to Arkansas game was very abundant, the country being very wild and unsettled. There were two log school-houses in the southern part of the county in which religious services were often held, but the morals of the people were at a very low ebb. In the summer of 1862 the Doctor joined the Confederate army as a private in Col. Dandridge McRae's regiment, but was detached from his company and assigned duty in the hospital serving in the Trans-Mississippi Department, in which service he remained for a period of eight months, being discharged by reason of disability. He returned to his home at Stony Point where he was living at the time of his enlistment, and again engaged in the practice of his profession. In 1865 he embarked in mercantile pursuits with H. B. Strange at Stony Point, carrying a general stock of goods, but the firm dissolved partnership in 1872. Dr. Gist then engaged in the drug business for about eight years. In 1873 he was elected by the Democratic voters of his county to represent them in the State legislature, serving two terms in the regular session and in the extra session called by Gov. Baxter in 1884. In the spring election of 1876 he was chosen mayor of Beebe and has served at different times two or

three terms. The Doctor has held a membership in the Masonic fraternity for a number of years, and has attained the Chapter order. He and wife are members of the Christian Church and are charitable and hospitable.

George W. Goad, planter and stock raiser of Denmark, Ark. This enterprising agriculturist is a son of John and Elizabeth (Hardin) Goad, natives of Kentucky, born 1806 and 1809, respectively. The father was of English descent, and his ancestors came to America prior to the Revolutionary War. They first settled in Virginia, but as the country developed moved farther west, and were among the first settlers of Tennessee. Benjamin Hardin, the great-grandfather of the subject of this sketch, was a participant in the War for Independence. John Goad and Elizabeth Hardin were married in Graves County, Ky., in the year 1826, and to their union were born the following children: Susan (born August, 1827), George W. (born July 21, 1830), Mary (born 1833), Nancy (born 1836), Sarah Ann (born 1839), John (born 1841), James J. (born 1844), Elizabeth (born 1847), an infant (died unnamed) and Louisa S. (who was born in 1853). Seven of these children grew to maturity. Elizabeth died in the spring of 1852, John died in 1861, Louisa died in 1864 and Mary died in 1853. John Goad left his home in Kentucky to move to Arkansas, and located in Denmark, White County, of that State, on February 3, 1846, after a tedious journey overland of two months. His was the first family to settle in that part of White County. In 1847 he took a claim of 320 acres, improved it and resided upon the same until 1875, when he sold out. He then settled upon Section 31, Denmark Township, and after the death of Mrs. Goad, which occurred in the fall of 1875, he married a lady by the name of Miss Clarissa Pinegar, and resided in Denmark Township until his death, which occurred on December 3, 1887. Five of his children are still living and all married. Susan is now living with her second husband, G. C. Caruthers, and is now residing in Independence County. She had eight children by her first husband, Steven Whilton. Nancy, married Nicholas Lovell and became the mother of seven children. Sarah Ann, married George Swick (deceased), became the mother of five children (one living) and is now living with her second husband, Wiley Westmoreland. James J. Goad married Miss Quintilliss Barnes, resides in Jackson County and has one child living. George W. Goad received a limited education in the common schools of Kentucky and at the fireside at home. He was reared principally to the arduous duties of the farm, but also learned the tanner's trade with his father, which business the latter carried on, both in Kentucky and Arkansas. George W. Goad selected for his wife Miss Elizabeth J. Riddle, a native of Tennessee, supposed to be of Irish descent, and the wedding took place on December 25, 1851. Ten children were born to this marriage, six now living: James E. (born September 19, 1852), William (born January 16, 1854, and died March 29, 1864), Mary J. (born February 10, 1855), Harmon M. (born April 23, 1856), Stephen (born May 29, 1857), John (born December 29, 1858, and died April 6, 1864), Lewis W. (born June 16, 1860), an infant (born and died in 1862), Andrew (born February 2, 1863,) and Elizabeth T. (born November 15, 1866, and died August 28, 1868). Mrs. Goad died on November 15, 1866, and Mr. Goad took for his second wife Mrs. Julia A. Wilson, whom he married on August 1, 1867. The following children were the result of this marriage: Margaret (born May 20, 1868), Gabrey (born February 22, 1870), George H. (born January 18, 1872), Jacob (born November 25, 1875), Susie (born August 6, 1880). Of the first children, Mary married William Morgan on December 25, 1873, and has seven children; James married Miss Virginia McCauley, and became the father of seven children; Stephen married Miss Mollie Yarbrough, and has three children; Harmon married Miss Jane Wagoner, in 1882, and has five children; Lewis married Miss Florence Wagoner, in 1883, and has two living children. And of the second marriage, Margaret married Roy M. Hodges, on January 27, 1889, and has one child. Mr. Goad was in the Federal army during the war, served about one year in Col. Baxter's regiment, which was organized at Batesville in the latter part of

1863 and fore part of 1864. The regiment participated in a number of severe skirmishes. Mr. Goad made his first purchase of land in 1855, buying forty acres, upon which he has since made his home. By subsequent purchase he added to the original tract until he owned 480 acres, but now owns 340 acres, with 100 acres under cultivation. He gave his children a liberal portion of land. Mr. Goad is a Republican in politics, is a member of the Agricultural Wheel, and he and wife are members of the Regular Baptist Church.

Joseph H. Grammer is a native of Virginia, and was the eldest in a family of five children, born to P. W. and Mary B. (Tyus) Grammer, both of whom were also Virginians by birth. P. W. Grammer was reared on a farm in the Old Dominion, and in 1836 moved to Haywood County, Tenn., where he died in 1853, his wife preceding him one year. They were the parents of the following named children: Joseph H., Rebecca, Edmond W., B. F., and one whose name is not given. Joseph H., the subject of this sketch, first saw the light of day in Petersburg, Va., in 1829, removing to Tennessee with his parents when seven years of age. He commenced farming for himself in 1851, and in 1853 was married to Miss Josephine W. Pettey, a native of Alabama, and a daughter of G. G. and Elizabeth (Capell) Pettey, of Virginia birth. Two years after his marriage Mr. Grammer came to Arkansas and settled in Des Arc Township, White County, where he bought 320 acres of land, near the present site of Centre Hill. To himself and wife eight children have been born, three being deceased: William Henry (deceased), Emmett L., William N., Nora, Fannie E., Hattie Lee, Jennie B. (deceased) and Jennie D. (also deceased). They also have three grandchildren. Mr. Grammer is a strong Democrat, and has been called upon to serve in various official capacities. He held the position of deputy sheriff of White County, was postmaster of Centre Hill for a number of years, and was appointed postmaster of Mount Pisgah, in April, 1889, by President Harrison. Mr. and Mrs. Grammer and children are members of the Methodist Episcopal Church, South. The former has been engaged in farming all his life, and in connection therewith has given his attention to the mercantile business for a number of years, commencing that branch of trade in 1872, at Centre Hill, and in 1889 at Mount Pisgah; his family, however, still residing on the farm. Mr. Grammer is a member of the Masonic order, and belongs to Centre Hill Lodge No. 114, and to Chapter No. 19. He has been instrumental in aiding many worthy movements hereabouts and helped to build the first church and first schoolhouse in White County.

B. F. Grammer, a Tennesseean by birth, a farmer by occupation, a Methodist in his religious preferences, a Democrat in politics and a veteran of the Civil War, has been a resident of White County since December, 1856, a period of sufficient length to render him well and favorably known. His parents were P. W. and Mary B. (Tyus) Grammer, both natives of Virginia, as were also their parents. B. F. Grammer was united in marriage in January, 1861, to Miss Sarah J. Neal, who was born in Fayette County, Tenn., a daughter of James and Mary (Smith) Neal, also of Tennessee origin, and who came to Arkansas in about 1852. Mr. Grammer enlisted in 1862 for three years' service during the war in the Thirty-sixth Arkansas Infantry, and participated in the battles of Oak Grove and Pleasant Hill, whither his regiment was sent as reinforcement to Gen. Dick Taylor who had been in a siege of eighty-three days. His next engagement was at the ford of the Saline River, after which he was sent to Marshall, Texas, on garrison duty. Upon the close of the war he returned home and again engaged in farming. Mr. and Mrs. Grammer are the parents of seven children, all boys: John B. (married, and resides at Centre Hill), James H. (attending school), Elmer, Horace, Edwin L., Marvin F. and Tyus C. Mr. Grammer has a farm of 125 acres, which he has cleared himself, besides some timber land. Himself and wife and three oldest sons are members of the Methodist Episcopal Church, South. His acquaintance throughout this territory is a wide one and he enjoys universal esteem and respect.

Philip Yancey Graves. The estate upon which Mr. Graves now resides, and to which he has given

such close attention in its cultivation, embraces 520 acres, a well-improved farm, substantial and convenient buildings being a leading feature of these improvements. He is a son of John and Mark (Yancey) Graves, the former a native of North Carolina, and the latter of Tennessee, their marriage taking place in the latter State, where the father died in 1841. Philip Y., his son, inherits Scotch blood from his paternal ancestry, and was born in the State of Tennessee, on October 8, 1830, and after his father's death, being the eldest of the children, the support of his widowed mother and three younger children devolved almost entirely upon him. He worked out by the day and month, and at the age of fifteen years, began working on a tract of timber land, on which his father had held a claim, and which was partly improved. He began clearing off the timber and making it into shingles and clapboards, for which he found a market at Somerville, Macon, Moscow and other places. After clearing off the timber from about five acres, and erecting thereon a good log-house, he was compelled to give up all claim to the land, as others had a clearer title than he. In 1855, in company with Joseph Hollis, he purchased some cypress timber near La Grange, Tenn., and this was made into shingles and sold at that place for the academy and college, which were in process of erection at that time. He followed this occupation in Shelby and Hardeman Counties, but in 1857 he gave this up and moved to Tippah County, Miss., where he rented land and engaged in general farming. About one year later he removed to Arkansas, and was married in Mississippi County, of this State, to Mrs. Elizabeth Hollis (nee Tingle), the widow of Joseph Hollis, his former partner. In the fall of 1859 he returned to Mississippi, but owing to rheumatism contracted from exposure while pursuing the shingle business, he was compelled to give up work for about four years. From 1861 to 1865 he farmed in Marshall County, then returned to Arkansas and purchased 160 acres of land, four miles north of Beebe, upon which were some log buildings and other improvements, twenty acres being under cultivation. He now has 150 acres under the plow, and seven acres in an orchard consisting of peach, apple and plum trees. He finds a market for his fruit at Beebe, his peaches averaging about 50 cents per bushel, and the apples 60 cents. He also ships to St. Louis. His land is well adapted to raising any kind of grain or grasses, and he has raised as high as twenty-two bushels of wheat to the acre. Mr. Graves is a Democrat, a member of the Agricultural Wheel, and he and family are members of the Cumberland Presbyterian Church, at Antioch, Ark. Mrs. Graves had five children by her first husband, two of whom are now living: Arminta (married in 1866, R. W. Bell) and Caroline (who became the wife of S. S. Hayney in 1868, and is now Mrs. F. W. Rodgers). The children of Mrs. Graves' second marriage are: Penelope (born March 22, 1859, is the wife of N. M. Parker, who has a farm near Beebe, but works at the carpenter's trade. They have three children: Fred D., John W. and Gertrude). Ella was married to John H. Pendleton, a native of Tennessee, in 1881, and has two children: James D. (born March 6, 1884) and Bettie Estelle (born November 13, 1885).

Alfred Greer enjoys a deserved reputation as a prominent planter of White County. Born in Davidson County, Tenn., February 22, 1820, he received his education in Alabama, near La Fayette. His father, Elijah Greer, was a Virginian by birth and when about twenty-two years old immigrated to Kentucky, where he married Miss Mary Acors, of that State. To them a family of fourteen children were born, twelve of whom grew to maturity, Alfred being the thirteenth child. Elijah Greer manifested a great interest in politics, and served in the War of 1812 as a fife-major. He was a farmer by occupation, and moved from Kentucky to Tennessee in 1810, going in 1830 to Georgia, and settling in Pike County. He resided in that State until his death, in 1841, his wife surviving him only three years. Alfred was married October 13, 1839, in Alabama, to Miss Elizabeth J. Waters, a daughter of William and Feriberry Waters, and their union has been blessed by the birth of ten children, three boys and seven girls: William V., Elisha J., Hiram A., Mary F., Nancy, Feribey, Lucinda, Susan F., Georgia F. and

Margaret E. who died in 1846. Mr. Greer owns 160 acres of land, with seventy-five under cultivation. He is a member of the Wheel, in which he has held the office of chaplain for three months. He served in the late war, and enlisted in 1864 under Capt. Choshea, as a home guard, and at the final surrender, returned at once and resumed his occupation of farming, which he has continued with good results since that time. Mr. Greer and wife are members of the Baptist Church, in which the former has acted as deacon. He was one of twenty-four who organized Mount Olive Church, and many other enterprises, which have proven of substantial worth, may be attributed in a large degree to his energy and support.

James E. Gregory. There are a number of men prominently identified with the agricultural affairs of White County, but none among them are more deserving of mention than Mr. Gregory, who was born in Rutherford County, Tenn., on September 5, 1837. He was reared in his native county, and after attending the common schools until nineteen years of age, he took a one-year's course in Bethel College, Carroll County, Tenn. After entering on the active duties of life, he clerked one year for Woods & Herrell, of Bell Station, Tenn., and in 1859 came to Arkansas, and spent nearly one year in this section of the State, hunting and enjoying himself in his own way. Upon returning to the State of his birth, he again clerked several months, then returned to Arkansas for the purpose of purchasing land for his friends, but before they could make a settlement the war came up and Mr. Gregory enlisted, November 4, 1861, in the Seventh Tennessee Cavalry, and served three years as second lieutenant of Company F, known as Fork Deer Rangers, being under that intrepid soldier, Gen. Forrest, and with him participated in many battles. He was captured three times, first at Brays Station, Tenn., January 18, 1863, and for four months was kept a prisoner at Alton, Camp Chase and Fort Delaware, and was exchanged at City Point, Va., May 4, 1863. His second capture was in November at Corinth, Miss. After the battle of Harrisburg he returned home and never rejoined the army. From that time until the present, with the exception of 1865, 1866 and 1867, when he was engaged in milling, he has followed farming as an occupation. In 1872 he came to White County, Ark., and purchased 214 acres of land, two miles west of Beebe, on the Iron Mountain Railroad, and after living the life of a bachelor for one year he was married, March 17, 1873, on his father's birthday (he being sixty-one years old), to Miss Mary Burns, and by her became the father of the following family: Maud Lee (deceased), Odem S., Richard, Isabella and Elena. On February 6, 1882, he was called upon to mourn the death of his wife, and after remaining a widower until November 7, 1888, he led to the altar Mrs. Henrietta McClelland, the widow of Newton McClelland, of Crockett County, Tenn. Since locating on his present farm he has cleared about ninety acres of land, and in all has 140 acres under cultivation, his farm comprising 260 acres of exceedingly fertile land. He is a member of the Agricultural Wheel, the I. O. O. F. and the K. of H., and being interested in the cause of education, he is a member of the school board of his district. His parents, Madison and Julia E. (Mason) Gregory, were born in Rutherford County, Tenn., March 17, 1812, and May 2, 1817, respectively, and were married in their native county about 1835, remaining there until 1846, when they removed to Haywood County, making their home there until their respective deaths. The father was an extensive planter and slave holder, and at the time of the Civil War was the owner of thirteen negroes. His plantation comprised 480 acres, and 300 were under cultivation. He and wife were Methodists, and he died at the home of our subject on August 15, 1881, his wife preceding him to the "Silent Land" July 18, 1880. Their children are as follows: James E., Mary F. (deceased), Sarah E. A. (wife of Young Wortham, a farmer of White County), the next in order of birth was an infant who died unnamed, Isabella (wife of James H. Hubbard, a farmer of Parker City, Tex.), Susan P. (deceased, was the wife of James Hart, a farmer of Crockett County, Tenn.), Emeline (wife of John Blades, a druggist of Pet-

tey, Lamar County, Tex.), Mosella (wife of Henry Graves, a farmer of Pettey, Lamar County, Tex.), Madison (a farmer, residing near Alamo, Tenn.) and Joseph H. (a farmer of Johnson County, Tex.). Edwin Gregory, the paternal grandfather, was a Virginian, and was one of the early settlers of Rutherford County, Tenn., whither he moved in 1808, there following the occupation of farming. The maternal grandfather was Joseph Mason, a Revolutionary soldier, and a native of Tennessee. He was for many years a planter, and also kept a tavern, his establishment being midway between Nashville and Murfreesboro. He educated himself after having children large enough to go to school, all attending the sessions together. He filled the office of esquire forty-nine years in succession; all cases stood as he rendered judgment, but one. He freed sixty-seven slaves, and owned 1,500 acres of land. His father was one of the first settlers of Nashville, Tenn. He raised eight children: Elizar, Julia, Polley, Allen, Rinier, Martin, Susan and Isabellar, all lived to be grown and have families. Joseph died in November, 1868.

Dr. Albert Griffin, physician and surgeon, of El Paso, and a graduate of Shelby Medical College of Nashville, Tenn., is a native of Louisiana, and was born in Assumption Parish September 6, 1836, the son of Solomon and Charlotte T. (Edney) Griffin, originally from North Carolina. They were married in West Tennessee in 1834, and the same year moved to Louisiana, where Mr. Griffin engaged in the sugar business, owning a large refinery and plantation. His death occurred in 1837 at the hands of some slaves. Immediately after her husband's demise Mrs. Griffin returned to Williamson County, Tenn., and resided there until 1840, when she was married to Dr. Bruce, a native of North Carolina, but who had been for years a resident of Tennessee. She accompanied him to his home in Haywood County, and died there in 1872. Dr. Bruce was a prominent physician, and his record is one that will be an honor to his children and their offspring. By her last marriage Mrs. Griffin-Bruce was the mother of seven children, five of them now living. Albert Griffin, the subject of this sketch, was the only child of his mother's first marriage. He received his primary education in the schools of Brownsville, Tenn., supplementing this course by an attendance at Andrew College at Trenton, Gibson County, Tenn. He then took one year's course in the Emory and Henry College, in Washington County, Va., leaving that school at the age of twenty years with an excellent English training. In the spring of 1857 young Griffin began the study of medicine under the efficient tutelage of his step-father, Dr. Bruce, with whom he continued for one year, adding to this one year's instruction with Drs. Taliaferro & Turner. In the fall he entered Shelby College, from which he graduated in 1859, as before intimated. The year 1860 witnessed his marriage to Miss Mary E. Laws, a native of Tennessee, and a daughter of James P. Laws, of White County. Dr. Griffin enlisted in Carroll's Partisan Ranger Regiment during the war, but was detailed to attend the sick at home by the request of the people of his county. He has been a member of his school board for years, and Mrs. Griffin belongs to and is an active worker in the Methodist Episcopal Church. Dr. Griffin has a beautiful little home in the suburbs of El Paso, which is made cheerful with carefully attended flowers and shrubs. He is a Democrat, and exerts no little influence in local politics, having held various positions on committees in his party. He takes an active interest in schools, churches, etc., is an enterprising citizen and a valuable acquisition to any place.

Elijah Guise has been a resident of White County, Ark., since 1868, and his example of industry and earnest and sincere endeavor to succeed in life, especially in the occupation of farming, is well worthy of imitation. He was born in Hardeman County, Tenn., in 1846, and was the youngest of a family of seven children born to Enoch and Nancy (Patterson) Guise, both of whom were born in the State of Alabama. They were reared and married, however, in Tennessee, and were engaged in farming there until their respective deaths, in 1863 and 1866. Enoch Guise was a minister of the United Baptist Church, and in his early days of labor for the cause of the Master, he was compelled to take long rides in order to preach at his different appointments. His children are: Gann (living in White County), Rebecca (Mrs. J. H. Sellers), Alvira (Mrs. Daniel Campbell), J. L. (residing in White County), Rachel (Mrs. James Sellers) and Elijah. The latter, after remaining with his father until he was eighteen years of age, began farming for himself, in his native county. He was married, in Shelby County, Tenn., in 1866, to Miss Lenora Ann Singleton, a native of De Soto County, Miss., and a daughter of Dr. A. J. and Margaret L. (Guinn) Singleton, both of whom were born in Georgia and Tennessee, respectively. They were married in Mississippi, moved to Tennessee and thence to Arkansas, in 1859, settling in Izard County, from which county he enlisted, in 1861, in the Eighth Arkansas Regiment, Infantry, Company A, and afterward took part in the following battles: Greenville, Corinth, Iuka, Chattanooga, Murfreesboro, Lookout Mountain and siege of Vicksburg. He was one time taken prisoner, but shortly afterward exchanged, and rejoined his family in Mississippi, and in the latter part of 1865 went to Memphis and was in business in that city for one year. He then farmed near there until 1868, when he purchased land in Big Creek Township, Van Buren County, Ark., and there erected a mill. In 1869 he removed to Cleburne County and there died, in 1882, still survived by his wife, who is a resident of White County. A. J. Singleton was also a minister of the Primitive Baptist and a physician of repute. After coming to Arkansas, in 1868, Mr. Guise bought a partly improved farm of 160 acres, and this farm has greatly improved in the way of buildings and in the amount of land he has cleared, having now forty acres under cultivation. He is a Democrat in politics and has held a number of local offices, and is a member of the Primitive Baptist Church. He and wife have had three children: Joseph Andrew, Lillie Ann (who died at the age of two months, in 1867) and Emma Florence (who died in 1874, when five years of age).

John M. Hacker is a farmer and fruit grower of Harrison Township, White County, Ark., and was born in the "Hoosier State" in 1831, being the third in a family of eight children born to John and Cynthia (Becler) Hacker. The father was born in the State of Tennessee and inherited Irish and Scotch blood from his ancestors. He was the second of five children and after spending his younger days in Tennessee he moved to Indiana, going thither after the celebration of his marriage, which occurred in 1827. The children born to him in his adopted State are as follows: Malinda, Joseph D., George W., Margaret A., Mary E., Conrad D., James K. and John M. In 1832 the family moved from Indiana to Illinois, settling on a farm in the southern part of the State, and at a still later period moved to St. Louis, where the father engaged in the mercantile business until 1843, when he moved to Jefferson County, of the same State, where he died four years later. He was survived by his wife until February, 1888, when she, too, died. The early childhood of John M. Hacker was spent in Illinois and Missouri, but his education was received principally in the latter State. Being of an enterprising disposition, he determined to start out in life and seek his own fortune, and accordingly, in 1853, went west to California and spent some time in mining in Eldorado County, becoming thoroughly familiar with western life and the hardships and privations which the miners were compelled to undergo in those days. After his return to Franklin County, Mo., he engaged in farming and in 1862 was married to Martha F. Johnson, daughter of Thomas J. and Mary F. (Falweele) Johnson, who were Virginians, the grandparents having been early settlers of that State. The paternal grandfather was in the War of 1812, and Gen. Joseph E. Johnston was an uncle of Mr. Hacker. Mr. and Mrs. Hacker have a little daughter, born in August, 1881. They are quite well-to-do and own 112 acres of good farming land in Missouri, 130 acres in Harrison County, Ark. (which is under fruit culture), and the farm on which he now lives, comprising 130 acres, seventeen of which he devotes to strawberries. He has an orchard of about 4,000 trees and he has just purchased a farm of forty acres in Fulton County, on which he expects to raise fruit. He is a member of Anchor Lodge No. 384, A. F. & A. M., and he is deeply interested in churches and schools, he

and wife being members of the Missionary Baptist Church.

James William Hall was born in Calhoun County, Miss., on January 12, 1850, and is a son of Hiram and Sarah (Holifield) Hall, natives of Madison and Gibson Counties, Tenn., respectively, the former of English birth. The father moved to Chickasaw County, Miss., in 1844, and engaged in farming and cotton ginning there until January, 1869, when he sold out and moved to De Soto County, and eventually became the owner of large tracts of land in that county. Here he died on January 17, 1888, his wife having departed this life in 1859. Of seven children born to them four are living: John Calvin (who was captured in the battle of Fort Donelson in 1862, and died in prison at Indianapolis, Ind., in the same year), Samuel H. (living), Henry T. (deceased), James William, Sarah S., Senath A. (who became the wife of John W. Wynn, and the mother of two children; she died in 1876 at the birth of her second child, who died at the same time as the mother). The first child, Virginia, is living in Crawford County, Ark., and Hiram E. James William Hall followed the life of the farmer's boy, and received a fair education in the subscription schools. May 8, 1870, he was married to Margaret A., a daughter of G. W. McKinney, of Monroe County, Miss., and for a number of years after he and a brother operated and managed a mill which their father had erected, our subject having an interest in the business, which was fairly successful. On October 7, 1872, he removed to Arkansas and located upon the farm on which he is now living, his worldly possessions at that time consisting of $200 in cash, two mules, a wagon and some household furniture. His original purchase of land comprised 160 acres in a wild state, but he has now 440 acres and 100 acres under cultivation. His children are: Beulah Ann (born March 5, 1871, and died June 22, 1872), Sarah Cornelia (born December 24, 1872), Hiram Luther (born on December 3, 1875, and died November 12, 1886), Helen Caroline (born May 24, 1878) and Georgia Etta (born January 12, 1886).

Jacob Alah Hammons, planter and stockman, Hammonsville, Ark. Among the many successful agriculturists of White County, none are more worthy of mention than the subject of this sketch, who owes his nativity to Autauga County, Ala., where his birth occurred on March 7, 1822. His parents, John and Hannah (Dodson) Hammons were honored and respected citizens in the community in which they lived, and the father was a native of Virginia, his birth occurring in that State in 1784. The paternal ancestors came to America prior to the Revolutionary War, and some of them were soldiers in that world-renowned struggle. Grandfather Dodson was a native of England, and came to America before the Revolutionary War. Grandmother Dodson was a native of Germany. John Hammons was a soldier in the War of 1812. Jacob Alah Hammons received a limited education in the subscription schools of Cherokee County, Ala., and was one of eleven children born to his parents: John W. (born in 1817), Elizabeth (born 1820), Jacob A. (born 1822), Jane (born 1824), Martha (born 1826), Luzella (born 1828), Lavina (born 1830), Mary and Susan (twins, born 1832), William P. (born 1835) and Thomas. Luzella died in 1868. In 1846 Jacob A. Hammons went to Cherokee County, Ga., where he assisted in erecting a mill which he afterward operated. In 1847 he returned to Cherokee County, Ala., purchased a tract of eighty acres of land, about ten acres of which was under cultivation, but with no other improvements, and there remained until 1849. He then came to Arkansas, followed agricultural pursuits, and in 1852 was united in marriage to Miss Jane Goodman, a native of Cherokee County, Ala., born on May 18, 1837. Two children were born to this union: John W. (born July 19, 1855) and Minerva L. (born October 6, 1858). In 1856 Mr. Hammons purchased a tract of land with about four acres under cultivation, and a small log-hut being the only improvement on the place excepting the fencing. Mr. Hammons erected a log house, 16x16, in which he lived for about a year, and then erected another log house, 18x18, in which he resided until 1870. He then erected the fine frame house which is such an ornament to his farm, and in which he has resided since that time. One hundred and twenty acres of

the first purchase are under cultivation, and he is now the owner of 320 acres of land. Some of his land has been under cultivation for thirty-five years, and although it has never been fertilized, it produces fine crops. In 1864 he enlisted as a private in a company of Col. McRae's regiment, and served one year, participating in the Missouri raid under Gen. Price. Mr. Hammons is a member of the Masonic fraternity, and he and wife are members of the Methodist Episcopal Church, South.

John William Hammons, merchant and farmer, Hammonsville, Ark. For a number of years past the town of Hammonsville has been noted far and wide for its excellent mercantile establishments, and particularly that of Mr. Hammons, who is one of the representative business men of the place. Aside from this he is also engaged in farming, and is the owner of 106 acres of land. He was born in Van Buren County, Ark., on July 19, 1855, and is the son of Jacob D. and Jane (Goodman) Hammons. In 1857 the father moved to White County, Ark., and there reared a large family of children, seven now living. John W. Hammons was reared in White County, Ark., and received his education in the private schools of that county. He assisted his father on the farm for some time, and then commenced business for himself by teaching school, which profession he followed for some time. In 1874 he made a prospecting tour through California and Oregon, in which States he sojourned for nearly three years, and while there followed various lines of industries, viz.: mining, farming, saw-milling, teaming, etc., obtaining some knowledge of farming and mining as conducted in those States. In 1877 he returned to Arkansas, and there resumed the profession of teaching, organizing a school at Hammons' Chapel, near what is now the village of Hammonsville. This he conducted for two years, during which time he also followed agricultural pursuits, having purchased 160 acres, which he hired help to clear and improve. On January 28, 1878, he was united in marriage to Miss Mattie Nelson, daughter of George Nelson, and her death occurred in 1878. In 1879 Mr. Hammons married Miss Mollie J. Nelson, of White County, Ark., and a sister of his former wife. By this marriage six children were born: Edgar L. (born June 13, 1880), John R. (born November 4, 1882), Eva (born in 1883), Grover Cleveland (born March 2, 1885), Troy M. (born November 23, 1886) and an infant son (born in August, 1889). Edgar died in November, 1881, and Eva in 1884. In 1879 Mr. Hammons moved to his farm, followed tilling the soil, and also speculated in patent rights. He also ran a well-auger. In 1885, in partnership with J. T. Phelps, he erected a store building at Hammonsville, and engaged in merchandising under the firm title of Phelps & Hammons. The partnership lasted but a short time, and in 1887, in company with Messrs. Moore & Rollon, at Quitman, Cleburne County, Ark., he again engaged in merchandising. In 1888 he bought the interest of his partners, and located at Hammonsville, where he has since remained. About September Mr. Hammons completed the building in which he now does business, and it is a large, commodious structure. His stock of goods consists of a good line of dry goods, boots and shoes, clothing, groceries, drugs and plantation supplies. In politics he is a stanch Democrat, and has held the office of justice of the peace. At present he is the postmaster at Hammonsville.

Abraham Hancock. John Hancock was a native of North Carolina, and was born July 26, 1804, and was married in 1828 to Miss Martha Harrington, who was born in North Carolina June 10, 1809. In 1836 he moved to Madison County, Tenn., and there engaged in his trade of blacksmithing until 1858, and after a residence of several years in Van Buren County came to White County, where he now resides with his aged wife. Mr. Hancock is of Irish descent and an own cousin of Gen. W. S. Hancock. He has held the office of sheriff in Van Buren County, but has never aspired to office. His wife is of English descent, and both are adherents of the Baptist faith. To them have been born a family of nine children, all living, in which Abraham, the subject of this sketch, is the eldest. He is a native of North Carolina, and was born November 22, 1830. He was reared on a farm and learned the saddle and harness-maker's trade, which has been his principal work, but is also a good carpenter. He was given a good education in the common schools of his native State, and at the age of twenty-one began life for himself, first as office boy in a bank and later as clerk for a cotton ginner. He was married on March 20, 1851, to Miss Leana C. Jones, and to their union one child was born, Martha R. (now the wife of J. J. Martin, a farmer of Faulkner County, Ark.) Mrs. Hancock died in September, 1857, and in March, 1858, Mr. Hancock was united in marriage to Miss Rebecca A. Bertram, a native of Tennessee. To this union five children have been born, two of whom are now living: John S. (a farmer of White County, and who married Elizabeth Landers, a daughter of Thomas Landers, of White County) and Vera A. (born March 14, 1883). Those deceased are William H., Paralea A. and Lena. In May, 1861, Mr. Hancock enlisted in Company B, Twelfth Tennessee Infantry, and served until the surrender in 1865. He participated in the battles of Belmont (Mo.), Shiloh (Tenn.), Richmond (Ky.), Murfreesboro (Tenn.), Chickamauga (Ga.), Missionary Ridge, and at the latter place was wounded by a gunshot, and was helpless for one year. At the battle of Shiloh, he was shot through the hip, and from that wound he still suffers. The last engagement that he took part in was the encounter at Franklin, where he was injured, and which disabled him for some time. During the entire war Mr. Hancock served as orderly-sergeant, his military record being one without a blemish. He received his parole in 1865, and at once returned home; here he resumed his trade of harness making until 1871. He then came to White County and purchased a farm of sixty acres. One year later he moved to El Paso and worked at his trade there, and has since been engaged at farming and carpentering up to the present time. Mr. Hancock has erected some twelve or fourteen gin-powers in White County alone, and there are many marks of his handiwork in different parts of the country. He is a Democrat in his political views, but is an independent voter. He has held the office of constable and deputy sheriff in Tennessee, and in 1885 was elected to the position of justice of the peace of Royal Township, which office he is at present filling. Mr. Hancock is an honorary member of El Paso Lodge No. 65, A. F. & A. M., and was secretary of said lodge for eight years; he is also a member of Lodge No. 6, and is E. S. W. P. of that lodge. Mr. and Mrs. Hancock are members of the El Paso Baptist Church, and the former always gives his support to all laudable enterprises for the public good. Mr. Hancock is a member of New Hope Wheel No. 32, in which he was the efficient secretary for years, and is an ardent worker for his order.

Edward Harper, an influential citizen of Romance, is the son of the late Edward Harper, Sr., who was born in North Carolina in 1774, and was an only son of Samuel Harper. His parents died when he was a small boy and he was left with an uncle. He married, in about 1801, Elender Scallorn, a native of Maryland, after which he moved to Alabama, where he engaged in farming, thence moving to Tennessee and in 1855 came to Arkansas, settling in Prairie County, where he died three years later. His wife died in 1862, leaving a family of eleven children: Overton W., Jefferson B., Andrew J., Durinda, Edia, Malinda, Pomelia, Edward (our subject), Joseph A., William A. and Sarah A. Edward, Jr., was born in Alabama in 1821, and spent his early life in Western Tennessee, where he received a good common-school education. He taught school in Tennessee for a number of years, and was married in 1851 to Mary Kyle, who was a daughter of Marvin and Sarah (Dement) Kyle, originally of Alabama and Virginia, respectively. To this marriage the following children were given: Martha S. (now Mrs. J. B. Matthews), William K., Edward L., Julia T., James H., Ellen O. (deceased), Jefferson D., Sidney K., Marvin A., John F. and Adolphus. In 1856 Mr. Harper came to White County, Ark., where he purchased 240 acres of land, and now has nearly 100 acres cleared and under cultivation. Himself and wife are members of the Methodist Church. Mr. Harper belongs to the Masonic order, affiliating with Mount Veran Lodge No. 54, and has taken the degree of Royal Arch Mason. Mr. Harper is a highly respected citizen, and has

held the office of justice of the peace for twelve years.

Rev. Henry F. Harvey, one of the leading planters and a popular minister of White County, Ark., is a native of Tennessee, and was born in 1842. His father, Jesse F. Harvey, was born in Alabama, in 1818, where he received his education, and afterward immigrated to Mississippi with his parents, there marrying Miss Mary C. Wyatt, in 1841. To their union was born a family of twelve children, of which Henry F. is the oldest. Jesse Harvey and his estimable wife were respected members of the Church (Methodist), and always manifested a great interest in all worthy enterprises. Henry F. was educated in Mississippi, and moved from that State to Arkansas with his parents in 1869. His marriage with Miss Sarah J. McCleskey was consummated on November 26, 1867. Mrs. Harvey was the daughter of John and Nancy McCleskey, and was born in 1849. To their union eight children have been born, six boys and two girls, seven of whom are now living: John F., Mary Ida, Luther B., William P., Eugene B., Walter W., Samuel J. and Mattie M. Mr. Harvey owns 232 acres of land, with 125 cultivated. He is a member of the Masonic Lodge, and has held the office of secretary of Lodge Chapter, Centre Hill No. 45, also affiliates with the Wheel, in which he held the office of State Chaplain for one year. He has been a member of the council for twelve years. He served in the late war on the Confederate side, and enlisted in 1861, under Gen. Buckner of Kentucky. His first hard fight was at Fort Donelson, where he was captured and carried to Camp Morton, Indianapolis, and imprisoned for seven months. He was then exchanged and again captured in Virginia, near Petersburg, and taken to Point Lookout, Md., and incarcerated for seven months, then exchanged at Richmond, where he received his parole. After the war he returned home at once and began teaching school, which he continued for one year, and then commenced farming and preaching, his present occupation. He is an eloquent and brilliant speaker, and makes many converts to his faith (Methodist), to which he and wife belong.

Richard D. Harris, familiarly known as "Uncle

Dick" Harris, was the eldest son in a family of thirteen children born to Newton and Nancy (Spencer)' Harris, natives of North Carolina. Newton Harris, the father, was born in 1801, and married in 1821; he was the son of a soldier in the Revolutionary War. He was the father of the following children: Richard D. (our subject), D. C., Louisa, Roland (deceased), Victoria M. (deceased), Milton, M. D., Newton (deceased), Wesley (deceased), Sidney (deceased), Steven D. and Dolly. Richard D. Harris first saw the light of this world in Tennessee in 1824, and was married October 20, 1846, to Arcissie Bowman, a daughter of Maj. William and Cassander (Wade), who were of Maryland nativity. Mr. Harris settled on a farm in Tennessee after his marriage, and in 1862 enlisted in Company C, of the Forty-seventh Tennessee Cavalry, and participated in the battles of Corinth, Richmond (Ky.), Perrysville, Murfreesboro, Chickamauga, Kenesaw Mountain and Franklin. He received his discharge in 1863, on account of deafness and a weakness in the back. He then entered the cavalry under Forrest, but served only a short time when he returned home badly disabled. He had eight brothers in the Confederate army, one of whom, Leven, only was wounded. His first wife died October 2, 1858. She was the mother of nine children: Cassander (deceased), Ella (now Mrs. John Banks, of Tennessee), Molly (now Mrs. Reid), John D., E. A., Abbilow (McDinworthy), Decksy (Turnage) and Effie. Mr. Harris came to Arkansas, settling in White County, in 1871, where he purchased a quarter section of land, of which there were about sixty acres cleared. He was married the second time in 1881 to Elizabeth McDougald, a daughter of Alexander and Ellen (Wade) McDougald. Mr. Harris is a strong Democrat, and cast his first presidential vote for James K. Polk. Mr. and Mrs. Harris are members of the Presbyterian Church, but most of his children are Methodists.

Hubbard P. Heard, a most successful agriculturist and stock raiser, of White County, received his education in this county, where he grew to manhood, and remained at home until the organization of the Third Arkansas Confederate Cavalry, in the early part of 1861. His regiment took part in sixty-five engagements, and of the 104 men which started out, only eight returned, and he had many narrow escapes. He was in the siege of Corinth, at Beauregard's retreat into the river, at the battles of Shiloh, Thomas' Station (where three flag bearers and the colonel of his regiment were killed), Missionary Ridge; also at the capture of Knoxville, and many others, including those in the Georgia campaign, where he was in constant fighting for sixty days. He was taken prisoner near Holly Springs, and carried to Cairo, Ill., where he was kept for nearly three months; then he was exchanged with 1,100 Confederate soldiers. After peace was declared he returned home, and at the death of his father commenced farming, and in 1880 he engaged in the saw-mill business, which occupation he followed for five years, since which time he has given his attention exclusively to farming and stock raising, and owns 400 acres of land, with 150 under cultivation. Our subject was born in Heard County, Ga., August 1, 1840, and is the son of Hubbard P. and Mary (Ware) Heard. The paternal grandfather of Hubbard P., Jr., Thomas Heard, was a soldier in the Revolutionary War, and also in the War of 1812, and was county judge of Heard County, which was named in honor of him. Hubbard Heard, Sr., was born in 1800, and was married in Georgia, and came to Arkansas and located within ten miles of Augusta, Woodruff County, in 1840, and in 1849 removed to White County, where he was engaged in farming and stock raising the rest of his life. He was a prominent Democrat and a constituent of the Masonic order, and both he and his wife were members of the Methodist Episcopal Church, South. Mrs. Heard died in February, 1862, at the age of sixty-one, leaving six children, five of whom are now living: Eliza (widow of John Griffin), Sophia (widow of John Wesley), Amanda (widow of James Asque), Martha (widow of David Duke) and Hubbard P. (the principal of this sketch). After the death of his first wife Mr. Heard married Mrs. Sarah Pierce, who is now deceased. The senior Heard died in White County in 1866, and was highly respected by all who knew him, and had been a very successful farmer, but met with heavy losses financially during the war. Hubbard P. Heard was married in 1870 to Miss Jennie Martin, a native of Tennessee, and who was the mother of five children, four of whom are still living: Dora V., Joseph W., Hubbard, Jr., and James H. He was married to his second wife, Olive B. Markham, in 1884, who lived but three years after their marriage, and was the mother of one daughter, who died soon after her mother. Mr. Heard is a Democrat in politics and in secret societies belongs to the Masons.

Col. V. H. Henderson, Searcy, Ark. In preparation of this brief outline of the history of one of the most influential citizens of White County, appear facts which are greatly to his credit. His intelligence, enterprise, integrity and many estimable qualities, have acquired for him a popularity not derived from any factitious circumstance, but a permanent and spontaneous tribute to his merit. He is at present proprietor and manager of Searcy College and is also actively engaged in the real-estate business. He owes his nativity to Haywood County, West Tenn., where his birth occurred in 1833, and is the fourth in a family of nine children born to the union of T. C. and Eunice (Haraldson) Henderson, both natives of South Carolina. The parents moved to Tennessee at an early day, thence to St. Francis County, Ark., in 1849 and located in what is now Woodruff County, where the father followed agricultural pursuits. He died in Mississippi in 1844, and the mother afterward came to Arkansas and thence to Texas in 1858. Col. V. H. Henderson came to Arkansas at the age of sixteen years, engaged in merchandising in Cotton Plant in 1857 and continued at that until the beginning of the war. In that year he enlisted at the above-mentioned place in Capt. Stephen's company, was elected second lieutenant, but served only a short time when he was discharged on account of ill health. He then engaged in the pursuit of farming on a large scale, and in connection carries on merchandising extensively at Cotton Plant. He came to White County in 1884 for the purpose of recruiting his health, which had become impaired, and purchased a farm of 240 acres, which he improved and which is now known as the

Griffin Springs, a great watering place. He also raises some fine stock and is extensively engaged in the real-estate business. He has been active in building up the town and is deeply interested in educational matters. Socially, he is a member of the Masonic fraternity, and in politics, although not active, votes with the Democratic party. He selected for his companion in life Miss Sarah J. Simpson, a native of Mississippi, and was married to her in Woodruff (then St. Francis) County, Ark., in 1857. Her death occurred in 1871, leaving one child as the result of this union: Robert C., who is now married and resides at Cotton Plant. Col. Henderson was married to his second wife, Miss Martha A. Davies, a native of North Carolina, in 1872, and the fruits of this union are four children: Freddie Davis, Mary Virgie, Carl C. and Ross K. Col. and Mrs. Henderson are members of the Presbyterian Church.

John T. Hicks, attorney, Arkansas. This gentleman is the junior member of the well-known law firm of House & Hicks, and practices in this and adjoining counties. He was born in Searcy, Ark., on July 21, 1861, and was the second in the family of six children born to William and Martha A. (Lytle) Hicks, natives of North Carolina, born near Hillsboro. The father, when about eighteen years of age, came to Searcy, Ark., read law at that place, and was admitted to the bar. He then began practicing and followed this during life. He took an active part in politics and was senator from this district in 1866. Prior to that he was county judge. He was a prominent Mason, was a Chapter member of Searcy Lodge No. 49, and was a member of Tillman Chapter No. 19. He met the mother of the subject of this sketch while attending college, and was married to her in Fayette County, Tenn., in 1857. Six children were the result of this union, two of whom are living: John T. and Willie (who resides in Searcy). The father was a progressive man and took an active part in building up the town and county. He was also deeply interested in educational matters, and as a man, well and favorably known. He was a member of the Episcopal Church. During the late war, or rather at the beginning of the late war, Mr.

Hicks had strong Union proclivities, but after the State seceded, he joined with the State, recruited a company, and was promoted to the rank of colonel. He was in the battle of "Whiting Landing," was wounded by a shell at Helena, and was with Gen. Price on his raid through Missouri. After the war he returned to Searcy, resumed his practice, and died August 13, 1869, at the age of forty-one years. He was the son of Howell T. and Sally (Roberts) Hicks, natives of North Carolina, who came to Searcy in 1846, settled in Gray Township, and engaged in tilling the soil. The grandfather died in 1858, and the grandmother in 1881. The maternal grandparents of the subject of this sketch, John C. and Sarah (Graham) Lytle, were natives of North Carolina. At an early day they moved to Tennessee, where the father followed farming, but also continued the trade of a mechanic. The grandmother died in Tennessee, and her husband came to Searcy (1870), where he is now residing. John T. Hicks was liberally educated in the schools at Searcy and at Fayetteville, Ark., after which he took a course at the University of Virginia. After this he took a law course in 1881-82 and was admitted to the bar in 1883, after which he commenced practicing. He was married at Searcy in 1883, to Miss Minnie Snipes, a native of White County and the daughter of Dr. J. A. and Elizabeth (Murphy) Snipes, natives of North Carolina and Virginia, respectively. Both are residing at Searcy. Mr. and Mrs. Hicks have two children: Everette B. and Willie B. Mr. Hicks takes an active part in politics and was mayor of Searcy from 1884 to 1887. Socially, he is a member of Searcy Lodge No. 49, Masonic fraternity, and is Junior Warden in that order. He is a member of Tillman Chapter No. 19, R. A. M. He is a member of the Episcopal, and she of the Methodist Episcopal Church, South.

N. B. Hilger, a native of this county, is a son of John and Catharine (Yenglan) Hilger. John Hilger was born in Monhan, Germany, on the Rhine, in 1802, and spent his school-days in that country and was married there. A few years after his marriage he emigrated to America with his family, locating in White County, Ark., where he entered a quarter section of land, and at the time of his death, in 1853, owned 900 acres of land. His wife was born in 1807 and died in 1878, leaving thirteen children: John, Bardoia, Philip and Shibastas (who were born in Germany) and Elizabeth, Catharine, Louisa, Louie, Minerva, Nancy, Mary, N. B. (our subject) and Margaret (who were born in this county). N. B. Hilger was married, in 1868, to Frances Elliott, who died the following year, leaving one child, also deceased. In 1873, he married Lucy A. Crump, a native of Alabama, and who is the mother of three children, two of whom are living: Noah and Laurie. He owns the old homestead on which he lived when a boy, and has 440 acres of land, about half of which is under cultivation and which he helped to clear. Socially, he is a member of the Masonic order and is school director of his district, and is a successful farmer and raises good stock, and is well and favorably known throughout the township.

Rev. William H. Hodges. The father of our subject was James L. Hodges, a native of South Carolina, where he was born about 1787, and was the son of William and Elizabeth Hodges, also of South Carolina. Mr. Hodges, Sr., was married, in about 1810, to Sarah Comings, and they were the parents of eleven children: Francis, Nancy, Thomas, Elizabeth, William H., Sarah, Margaret, James, Mary, Martha and Benjamin F. William H. was born in South Carolina on March 22, 1822, and came to Mississippi with his parents when but eight years of age, where he was reared on a farm. He was married, in 1844, to Sarah F. Roseman, a daughter of Samuel and Frances (Hill) Roseman. After his marriage he settled on a farm, where he resided until 1869. As the result of this union the following children were born: James S., Casandria E. (deceased), Thomas H., John F., William A., Benjamin F. (deceased), Marshall L., Sarah F., Archie N. (deceased), Emmett L. and Joseph T. They also have twenty-seven grandchildren. Mr. Hodges commenced preaching the Gospel in Choctaw County, Miss., in 1863. In 1869 he came to Arkansas and settled in White County and in Cane Township, on 240 acres of land, of which he now has about 100 acres under cultivation. Mr.

Hodges is pastor of the Bethlehem Missionary Baptist Church. He has been a very active worker in his labors and has organized four churches in this neighborhood.

John G. Holland, one of the editors and proprietors of the Beacon, owes his nativity to Wake County, N. C., where his birth occurred on December 10, 1845. He is the son of Willis B. and Lucinda (Barbee) Holland, natives of Wake County, N. C., the former born in 1818 and died in 1869, and the latter born in 1814 and died in 1888. The parents moved from North Carolina to Henderson County, Tenn., in 1851, and nearly two years later to White County, Ark., where the father followed several different avocations—farming, surveying and civil engineering. He was also deputy county surveyor for several years. Both he and wife were members of the Missionary Baptist Church; he was a Royal Arch Mason, and of the Council degrees, and in his political views affiliated with the Democratic party. Of the five children born to this union, John G. Holland is fourth in number of birth. He received a liberal education in the schools of White County, and during the late war served a few months in the Confederate army in the capacity of private. At the age of twenty-one years he turned his attention to the reading of law under Judge Cypert, and in 1867 was admitted to the bar. He practiced his profession until 1882, when he turned his attention to the newspaper business. He was associate editor of the Arkansas Beacon, and in 1883 became partner. In December of the same year John R. Jobe became a partner in the paper, and they have so continued ever since. In 1877 he was mayor of the city of Searcy, continuing in that capacity one year. In 1885–86 he was justice of the peace. He is at present president of the school board of Searcy. In 1877 he was elected assistant clerk of the lower house of the General Assembly, and in 1879 was elected to the position of chief clerk in the same; in 1881 he was elected secretary of the senate, and has served in that capacity ever since. On January 14, 1879, he married Miss Ella M. Henley, daughter of B. F. and Mary J. Henley, and she died in April, 1889, leaving five children: Lillie C., Della,

Percy, Bessie and Lewis F. Mr. Holland is a member of the Missionary Baptist Church at Searcy, and is clerk of the same. He is a Council Mason, is a member of the K. & L. of H., and in his political views affiliates with the Democratic party.

W. G. Holland, M. D. In recording the names of the prominent citizens of White County, the name of W. G. Holland, M. D., is given an enviable position. He was a faithful student in his chosen profession, and truly merits the prominence accorded him in the medical fraternity, as well as the confidence and respect shown him by the entire community. He owes his nativity to Tennessee, and was born in Henderson County, April 6, 1847. His father, Dr. James C. Holland, was born in Wayne County, N. C., December 12, 1807, and he received his education in his native State, and in 1833 he was united in marriage to Rebecca, daughter of Frederick and Lucy Collier, and by her became the father of six children: Julia F., Eliza, Maria R. (deceased), Charles E. (deceased), W. G. and his twin brother (who died in infancy). Mrs. Holland died at Searcy, May 10, 1861, and for his second wife, Dr. Holland chose Miss Ellen Kirby of Tennessee. Dr. Holland was both physician and silversmith by occupation for over fifty years. He immigrated to Arkansas from Tennessee in 1853, and located in Searcy, where he resided until his death in 1887. He was a man of considerable influence, and a politician to some extent. He was a devout member of the Methodist Church, as was also his wife. He held a membership in the Masonic lodge for over forty years, being a member of Searcy Lodge No. 49, and Tillman Chapter No. 19, where he discharged the duties of secretary and treasurer up to the date of his death. W. G. Holland received a good practical education in the schools of Searcy, but obtained his medical knowledge in the University of Louisville, Ky., during the years 1869–71. After his graduation Dr. Holland returned to his home and built the foundation of his present large and lucrative practice. He was married December 8, 1872, to Annie Goad, a daughter of Henry and Mary Goad, and their union has been blessed with three children: Mary E., William E. (deceased), and an infant, who died unnamed. Mrs. Holland died August 10, 1887, and in 1889 Dr. Holland was united in marriage to Rachel V. Fancette, their marriage occurring September 1. Dr. W. G. Holland served in the late war, entering in 1864 under Gen. Shelby. He was wounded at Pilot Knob, September 28, 1864, and also captured and taken prisoner to Alton, thence to Rock Island and Richmond, Va., where he was exchanged in March, 1865, receiving his parole at that point. He at once returned home and entered the literary school for three years, and began the study of medicine in spring of 1868. Dr. and Mrs. Holland are members in high standing of the Methodist Church.

A. B. House is accounted a prosperous farmer and stockman of Red River Township, and like the majority of native Tennesseeans, he is progressive in his views and of an energetic temperament. He was born in Maury County, in 1822, and is the youngest in a family of nine children born to Joseph and Alcy (Bedwell) House, the former of whom is a native of North Carolina, born in 1775. When a lad he was taken to Tennessee, and about the year 1800, was married in that State and engaged in farming and raising stock, his land amounting to 200 acres. He died in 1862, and his wife in 1845, both having been earnest and consistent members of the Cumberland Presbyterian Church. Their children are: Mary (deceased), Reuben (who is married and lives in White County, Ark.), John (married and lives in Tennessee), Patience (Mrs. Haines, now deceased), Charlotte (the wife of John Myers, is also dead), William (and his wife, formerly a Miss Bedwock, are deceased), Marcenie (is the wife of Mr. Brazele and resides in West Tennessee), Jane (and her husband, D. House, are both dead) and A. B. (the subject of this memoir). The paternal grandfather was John House, and the mother's father was Reuben Bedwell, a native of Tennessee. A. B. House resided in his native State until he arrived to manhood, then came to White County, Ark. He reared his family in his native State, and with the assistance of his wife, Eliza Wilkes, whom he married

12

in 1840, he succeeded in giving them good educations. Their names are: Thomas (who married Mary Minifee, by whom he has two children, resides in Arkansas), Joseph (who married Ina Dowdy and lives at Little Rock, the father of four children), James P. (married Lou Parcell, but is now a widower and lives in Augusta with his one child) and Mary (who married Mr. Harville. She died, leaving one child, who was reared by his grandfather). Mrs. House died after their removal to Arkansas, in 1884. She was a daughter of Thomas and Ruth Wilkes, and was one of a family of thirteen children. After coming to Arkansas Mr. House settled on a woodland farm of 140 acres, and now has eighty acres under cultivation. He raises some of the finest stock in the county and many of his animals have won first premiums at the county fairs. He is a Democrat and a member of the Masonic order and he and his present wife, who was Martha McMillan and whom he married in 1884, are members of the Cumberland Presbyterian Church, his first wife being also a member of this church.

Andrew J. Hughs is the son of Harden Hughs, a highly respected man who was born in Tennessee, in 1791, and took a prominent part in the French and Indian Wars of 1813 and following. He was married in 1813 to Miss Sallie Jones, and they were the parents of eight children: Thomas, Katie, Polly, Betty, Andrew J. (the principal of this biography), Marian, Louisa and Harding. The senior Hughs immigrated to Arkansas and settled in White County, in 1842, where he purchased a quarter section of land and on which he lived until his death, which occurred in 1858, his wife surviving him until 1871. Andrew J. owes his nativity to Tennessee, his birth occurring in 1828, and was fourteen years of age when his parents came to Arkansas. He was married on January 30, 1850, to Miss Sarah Marsh, who was born in Tennessee, January 7, 1831, and was the daughter of Roland and Sarah (Webb) Marsh. Her parents both died in Tennessee, in 1835, and she then came to Arkansas with her brothers, John and Harvey Marsh, who located in White County. Mr. and Mrs. Hughs were the parents of eleven children, four of whom are deceased: Francis M. Mary M. (deceased), Thomas F., Harden M., Martha (now Mrs. Asia Buchanan), Sarah Jane (now Mrs. Woodell), John A. (deceased), Ulysses M., Rachel A., Cymantha and Emma. They are also the grandparents of sixteen children. Mr. Hughs has 300 acres of land, with 180 acres under cultivation, which he and his father before him have farmed for the past forty-five years, and which Mr. Hughs says is as fine a piece of land as there is in the State. He and his wife have been members of the Methodist Church for over thirty-five years, and take a very active part in all church work. He also belongs to the County Wheel. He takes an active interest in all public matters, and was on the Review in 1866 and helped to reconstruct the State.

D. W. Holiman is a citizen in good standing, and is held in high esteem by his associates. He was left an orphan at the age of four years, and cared for and reared by his older brothers and sisters, on a farm in Mississippi. At the age of twenty-one he started out for himself, and came to Arkansas, and located in Van Buren County, and four years after removed to White County. In 1876 he married Lucinda Bouliand, a daughter of J. W. and Martha A. (Harvey) Bouliand, originally of Kentucky, and who came to Arkansas at an early day, and settled in White County. His nearest town and market at that time was Little Rock. Mr. Holiman was the youngest son in a family of ten children, born to Willis and Eliza (Virnan) Holiman, natives of South Carolina, and parents of the following children (and two others deceased, whose names are not given): James P., Malinda, William H., John, Martha, Bell, Willis and D. W. (our subject, who was born in Mississippi in 1849). D. W. Holiman and wife are the parents of four children: Martha J., Willis W., Eddie Lee, Hettie J., all of whom are at home. He has a farm of 258 acres, with fifty under cultivation. In religious belief, he and his wife are members of the Baptist Church, in which they take an active part. He is also a member of the County Wheel. Mrs. Holiman has seen a great change in White County during her lifetime, having been born and reared in this county. Mr. Holiman is a strong Democrat, and a good citizen.

George Irwin is a general farmer and fruit grower of Harrison Township, White County, Ark., and although a native of Kentucky, born in 1822, he has been a resident of this State for the past thirteen years. His father, Joseph Irwin, born in Kentucky in 1782 in a small neighborhood stockade, called Fort Hamilton, in the western part of Nelson County, was of Scotch-Irish descent, being one of a family of nine children born to John Irwin, who came from Ireland before the Revolutionary War. Joseph spent his youthful days on a farm, and on March 30, 1808, was married in Kentucky to Sarah Thompson, and by her became the father of the following sons: Hardin, James, Joseph, George, John and Benjamin. In 1828 he moved to Indiana, and died in Knox County, in 1858, having been a member of the Whig party, and he and wife members of the Baptist Church. His wife's death occurred in Parke County, Ind., in 1862. George Irwin acquired a fair education in the subscription schools of his native county, but at the age of seventeen years he left home and went to the pineries of Wisconsin, and until the spring of 1850 followed the lumbering business. In 1850 he resolved to seek his fortune in California, and after reaching the "Eldorado of the West," he engaged in mining, and succeeded far beyond his expectations. At the end of two years he returned to Indiana, and settled down to the peaceful pursuit of farming, and there, in 1854, was united in the bonds of matrimony to Catherine Black, a daughter of Thomas and Lavina (Dudley) Black, of Sullivan County, Ind. After remaining in Indiana some ten years, Mr. Irwin immigrated to Dallas County, Iowa, and twelve years later came to White County, Ark., buying, almost as soon as he reached the county, 160 acres of land where he now lives. He has sixty acres under cultivation, and owing to the attention which he gives to the minutest details of his work he is doing well. He belongs to the Agricultural Wheel, and although formerly a Republican in his political views, he is now a Prohibitionist. He and wife are members of the Baptist Church, and are the parents of these children: May (Mrs.

Charles Briggs, residing in White County), Broughan (who died in 1887), Dudley, and Grace, the youngest, who was eighteen years old in March, 1889.

James M. Jackson, of Russell, Ark., was born in Perry County, Ala., February 18, 1853, and is the son of Lorenzo D. Jackson, of North Carolina. The former's birth occurred in 1811, and at the age of twenty-two years he moved from North Carolina to Alabama, where he was residing at the time of his death, in 1865, when fifty-four years old. He was a farmer by occupation, and quite successful in his chosen profession. In his party views he sided with the Democrats, though not a political enthusiast. He was a member of the Baptist Church and a zealous worker in religious and all charitable enterprises. His wife, Anna (Winston) Jackson, was a daughter of James Winston, and a native of North Carolina. Her marriage with Lorenzo D. Jackson was consummated in 1833, and after her husband's demise she resided with her son, James M., until her death in 1886. To Mr. and Mrs. Jackson a family of eight children were born, three sons and five daughters, four of whom are now living: Anna (wife of L. D. N. Huff, of White County, Ark.), Fannie (first married to Britt Perry, now the wife of Henry C. Strange, of White County), Mary S. (Mrs. John Huff), James M. (the subject of this sketch) and Lacy J. (wife of Reuben Bennett, now deceased). William L. died in the Confederate army, and was one of the first volunteers of the war. Thomas was killed at the battle of Sharpsburg, in the Confederate army, and Martha died in Alabama. James M. received his education in the common schools of his native State, and at the age of eighteen came from Alabama to White County, Ark., where he launched his own canoe, and began life for himself. His choice of an occupation was farming, to which he had been carefully drilled by his father. Mr. Jackson now owns 160 acres of good land in a fair state of cultivation, divided into two farms. He is also interested in a large grist-mill and cotton-gin at Russell. Active, energetic and industrious in his efforts, he is on the high road to prosperity. He was first married, January 10, 1877, to Miss Nannie, daughter of William and Emily Plant. Mr. Plant is a native of Tennessee, but moved to Arkansas in 1859, his being one of the oldest families in this county. Mrs. Jackson died November 20, 1877, leaving one child, William D. In 1886 Mr. Jackson was united in marriage with Miss Virginia L. Shelton, of Arkansas, and at that time a resident of Jackson County. To this union two children have been born: Robert L. and Frank Earl. Mr. Jackson served as township bailiff and deputy sheriff for two and a half years, discharging the duties of that office faithfully and to the entire satisfaction of all concerned. He is a Democrat in politics, and a member of the Baptist Church at Russell, Ark. In societies he is identified with the Masonic order, is a Knight of Honor and a member of the Triple Alliance Mutual Benefit Association. He is a liberal contributor to his church, and the needy are never sent from his door empty-handed. Indeed too much praise can not be accorded Mr. Jackson for his upright course, for he is noble-minded, generous, and of that caliber of men who build up a community to places of thrift and enterprise.

J. R. Jobe, who is one of the editors and proprietors of the Beacon, owned by Holland & Jobe, became connected with the paper in December, 1884, and has continued with it ever since that time. He was born at Ringgold, Ga., on August 24, 1855, and was the fifth in a family of thirteen children born to David and Sarah (Hardin) Jobe, natives of East Tennessee and Georgia, respectively. The father was a farmer by occupation and came to Columbia County, Ark., in 1857, settled on a farm, remained there one year and then removed to Des Arc, Prairie County, Ark., where he followed mercantile pursuits until 1861. He then moved to Pope County, Ark, remained there until 1863, when he moved to White County and settled in Union Township, where he followed agricultural pursuits until his death, which occurred in May, 1888. His excellent wife, still living, resides at Russellville, Pope County. J. R. Jobe's early life was divided between assisting on the farm and in attending the district schools of White County, although he greatly improved his education by personal application in later years. He started out on the highway of life at the age of twenty years, engaged in farming until he was elected county clerk in 1882, and in October moved to Searcy, where he filled the above-mentioned office to the satisfaction of all for two years. He then purchased the interest of the Beacon from Rev. Z. T. Bennett, who was the founder of the paper in 1878, and has been connected with it ever since. He is active in politics and votes with the Democratic party. He was married in White County in November, 1878, to Miss Cora E. Harris, a native of Tennessee, and the daughter of Dr. D. C. and Susan E. Harris, natives of Tennessee, who came to White County, Ark., in 1874. Her mother died in 1879, but her father resides at Beebe, and aside from being a practicing physician is also engaged in mercantile pursuits. By his marriage Mr. Jobe became the father of three children: Edgar Wilmett, John Bertram and Lucille. Mr. Jobe was elected in January, 1886, to fill an unexpired term of city recorder and ex-officio treasurer, and has filled that position satisfactorily since that time. He is also corresponding secretary of the Arkansas Press Association, and is now serving the second term.

Wiley A. Johnson, the senior member of the well-known and representative firm of W. A. Johnson & Son, wagon manufacturers of Beebe, Ark., was born in Indiana, October 12, 1832, being the son of Daniel S. and Nancy (Parker) Johnson, natives of New York and Pennsylvania, respectively. Daniel Johnson's younger days were spent in the State of his birth, but when grown to manhood he went to Indiana and there married in 1822. He was a tailor by trade, and a few years before his death served as county clerk of the county in which he resided, in Tennessee. His demise occurred in 1833, at the age of thirty years, Wiley A. Johnson at that time being only one year old. After his father's death the latter moved to Weakley County, Tenn., with his mother, who remained in her widowed state for sixteen years, at the end of which time she was united in marriage with Mr. George Winston, but only lived one year after that event. The parents were members of the Methodist Episcopal Church, and were held in high esteem by all who knew them. Wiley A. Johnson was educated in the schools of Dresden, Tenn., proving a bright and intelligent scholar, and when seventeen years old became an apprentice to a blacksmith. After completing his apprenticeship, at the age of twenty, he at once went to work for himself, and for several years was employed in different shops all over Western Tennessee. In 1856, settling at Union City, Obion County, he was there married to Nanny Curlin, a native of that county, on October 14, 1856, and to them one child has been born, William W. Following his marriage, Mr. Johnson settled in Union City, and carried on his business of blacksmithing and wagon-making for nine years, moving thence to Trenton, Gibson County, where he remained for three years. After living in Verona, Miss., and Sulphur Rock, Ark., he came to Beebe in 1885 and formed the present firm, now having a large and substantial trade. Mr. Johnson and son are among the leading business men of this section, and enjoy the respect of all, both as business and social factors. They are public-spirited and lend their support to those enterprises that are intended for the good or growth of the country. In his religious belief, Mr. Johnson clings to the Methodist faith, of which church his wife is also a devout member. The paternal grandfather of the subject of this sketch, Collert Johnson, was probably a native of Pennsylvania, and a wealthy planter of Indiana. He had several sons who figured prominently in the early wars, and when last heard from were residing in Southern Indiana. Included in Mr. Johnson's maternal relations, of whom he knows but little, were two uncles, Lorenza and Gideon Parker, both holding high offices in the Florida War.

Thomas P. Jones, a distinguished citizen of White County, and a native of South Carolina (his birth occurring in Abbeville District, October 13, 1830), is the son of Clayton and Nancy (Miford) Jones, natives of the same State and district. Clayton Jones was of Welsh descent, and first saw the light of day July 11, 1802. He honored the Democratic party with his vote, and in his religious belief was a member of the Baptist Church. He was a farmer, and quite successful in the accumulation of wealth, and a very prominent citizen, contributing liberally to all church and charitable works. In short, he was a good man in all that the term implies. He died February 2, 1885, at the age of eighty-three years, sincerely mourned by his many friends and acquaintances. Mrs. Jones received her education in South Carolina, and from an early age was a consistent member of the Missionary Baptist Church. She was a faithful wife and an indulgent mother, loved by all who knew her, and at the time of her death (in her fifty-fourth year) was residing in South Carolina. To the union of Mr. and Mrs. Jones five children were born: Elizabeth (wife of Jackson Clements, deceased, and now residing in Anderson District, S. C.), T. P. Jones (living in White County, and the subject of this sketch), Samuel C. (who died in South Carolina), James S. (deceased in Mississippi) and Clayton W. (died in Virginia). Thomas P. Jones received the limited advantages for an education that the schools of the period afforded, and began for himself at the age of twenty-four, being employed as a farmer in his native state. In June, 1854, he was united in marriage to Margaret A. Tribble, of South Carolina, and a daughter of John and Essa Tribble, of Welsh and Irish descent, respectively. The result of their marriage was eleven children, ten of whom are now living: James M. (a farmer of Cross County, Ark.), Thomas C. (also of Cross County), Martha J. (wife of Thomas J. Futrell, a prosperous farmer of Cross County), Christopher E., William N., Emma J., Laura T., Dixie A., Leona A., Samvann and George A. (killed by machinery in 1877). Mr. Jones moved from South Carolina to Georgia in 1854, whence, after a residence of two years, he returned to Pickens District. At the end of two years he came to Jefferson County, Ala., and there resided until the opening of the Civil War. His family returned to South Carolina at the commencement of hostilities, and remained there until joined by Mr. Jones at the final surrender. Removing from South Carolina to Cross County, Ark., in 1868, and thence to White County,

in 1882, where he is at present residing, he now owns a farm well improved and very productive, besides 240 acres of woodland, in two farms. Mr. Jones' second marriage was to Mrs. Tabitha Berry, the widow of Fenwick Berry (deceased), of Cross County, Ark. Mr. Jones enlisted in the Confederate army in December of 1861, in Blount's Battalion, Alabama Volunteers. He participated in the battles of Shiloh, Lookout Mountain, Missionary Ridge, the battles around Corinth, and other engagements of minor importance; was captured at Missionary Ridge and taken to Rock Island, where, for nineteen months, he endured all the horrors and privations of prison life. He was exchanged at the mouth of Big Red River, in May of 1865, the last exchange of prisoners during the war. He was a gallant soldier, nobly espousing the cause, and truly merited the many marks of commendation and praise that he received from his superior officers. At the close of hostilities he returned home and came to Arkansas, as above stated. Mr. Jones is a stanch Democrat, though not an enthusiast in political matters. He is a Master Mason and a Knight of Honor, and a prominent and influential member of the Missionary Baptist Church. A leader, and not a follower, in worthy enterprises, he contributes liberally to all charitable objects, and enjoys the confidence and respect of his fellow-men.

H. C. Jones, M. D., was a son of H. C. and Nancy (Akin) Jones, natives of North Carolina and Alabama, respectfully. The father went to Alabama from his native State, where he married, and in 1846 moved to Mississippi. Himself and wife were the parents of the following children: Silas S. (deceased), Rufus C., Happach (now Mrs. Braddock, of Texas), Josephine (now Mrs. Maddox), H. C. (our subject), Perry Q., Nancy and Adel J. (now Mrs. Leppard). Mr. Jones died in February, 1868, but his widow still survives him and lives in Mississippi. H. C. Jones, Jr., was born in Itawamba County, Miss., at old Correllville, now Baldwyn, where he resided until 1871, when he removed to Arkansas and settled in White County. Having previously obtained a good medical training, he commenced practicing here in 1873, and has met with that success which close attention to business and careful, painstaking effort always merit. Dr. Jones, was married in 1869 to Sarah Q. Alford, a daughter of Thomas and Sarah Alford, of St. Clair County, Ala. They have a family of three children: Angie, Mark P. and Irena, all of whom are at home. Mr. Jones is an active Democrat; his wife and family are members of the Baptist Church. Dr. Jones is a very successful physician, and enjoys an extensive practice. He is also an excellent school worker, taking the lead in his township in all school enterprises, and is a local politician of some note.

Arthur Clifford Jordan, M. D. Among the younger members of the medical profession in White County, Ark., is he whose name heads this sketch, already well established as a physician of merit and true worth, and regarded with favor by those older in years and experience. He was born March 10, 1860, and is a son of John B. and Ella (Emmons) Jordan, of Scotch and English descent, born in Alabama and New York, respectively. They were married at Blackhawk, Miss., in 1858, and became the parents of three children: Arthur C., John Preston (born February 19, 1865, is a bookkeeper in the city of Memphis), Lena Lee (born in 1870, lives with her mother who is now widowed, her husband having died in October 1885). Dr. Arthur Clifford Jordan was reared in his native county (Holmes County, Miss.), and acquired a fair education in the Yazoo District high school. At the age of sixteen years he matriculated in the Literary Department of the University of Nashville, Tenn., and after attending school there for two years he began the study of medicine, being guided in his studies by his father, who was an able practitioner at Blackhawk. After holding the position of principal of the Masonic Male Academy, of Carrollton, Miss., for two terms, and teaching in the public schools of Holmes and Carroll Counties, he (in 1884) entered the Medical Department of the Vanderbilt University, and was graduated as an M. D. in 1886. In March of that year he returned to his home in Mississippi, and completed his preparations for his removal to Arkansas. He settled in Beebe in May of that year, commenced practic-

ing, and has continued it with such success that an unusually brilliant future is predicted for him. He has performed many of the intricate operations which pertain to major and minor surgery. The Doctor is a Democrat and has served as alderman of Beebe, and is a member of the board of school directors. January 12, 1888, he was married to Miss Florence Merrill, who was born in Michigan October 25, 1871, and by her has one child, Mable Clare (born July 27, 1889). The Doctor and his wife belong to the Methodist Episcopal Church, South, and are among the honored residents of Beebe. His maternal grandfather was a major in the Revolutionary war.

J. S. Kelley, retired, Judsonia, Ark. Not very far from the allotted age of three-score years and ten, Mr. Kelley has so lived that no word or reproach against his character as a man has ever been heard; for his whole ambition has been to do his duty in every capacity, as a father, husband, citizen or friend. Progressive in all matters, he has kept outside of the political arena, though a Republican in politics. Like many of the older inhabitants of this community Mr. Kelley is a native of Vermont, his birth occurring in 1822, and is the son of Daniel and Mary (Ballard) Kelly. The father was born in Rhode Island, but when a boy immigrated to Vermont with his parents, and was reared in that grand old mother of States. Later he moved with parents to Vermont, and there met and married Miss Ballard, the daughter of David Ballard, a native of the last-mentioned State. After his marriage Mr. Kelley settled near Rutland, followed farming and there reared to maturity the following children: David, Erastus, Alonzo, Smith, Daniel, Julia, J. S., Moses and Elisha. The father died in Vermont in 1859, and his widow followed him to the grave in 1865. J. S. Kelley was taught the principles of farm life when young and secured a fair education in the district schools of Vermont. He was married in that State in 1846 to Miss Mary Hall, a daughter of David and Esther (Wheaton) Hall, natives of Pittsford, Vt., and two children were the fruits of this union: Emma A. and Ella A. (twins). The former is now deceased, but the latter is the wife of Rev. James Tompkins, of Galesburg, Ill., and now resides in Chicago. She is the mother of four children. J. S. Kelley left Vermont in 1854 and settled near Wheaton, Du Page County, Ill., where he followed agricultural pursuits until 1872. He then moved to Judsonia, White County, Ark., and in 1875 his wife died at Hot Springs. In 1876 he was married to Miss Willie Key, daughter of James and Elizabeth (Brown) Key, who settled in White County, Ark., in 1859. Mrs. Kelley was second in a family of nine children, who were named as follows: Cassie M., Willie P., Alpha B., George F., Etoils S., Benjamin F., Harriet C., Lena G. and Maud M. The parents of these children are still living and reside in Judsonia. By his marriage Mr. Kelley became the father of four interesting children: Fannie J., James C., Elmer L. and Ira W. Elmer died at the age of eighteen months. Mr. Kelley was a member of the Masonic lodge and also of the I. O. O. F. lodge in Illinois. When first coming to White County he engaged in the milling business, but later engaged in the livery business, which he continued for a number of years. He is now living a retired life. Mrs. Kelley is an honored and much-esteemed member of the Methodist Episcopal Church.

James M. Key, retired farmer, Judsonia, Ark. This much-esteemed citizen owes his nativity to the Old Dominion, where his birth occurred in 1814, and is the youngest in a family of fourteen children born to the marriage of John and Elizabeth (Watson) Key, natives also of Virginia, the father's birth occurring in 1760. James M. Key was early taught the principles of farm life, and when twelve years of age went to Philadelphia, where for six years he attended school, there and at Burlington, N. J. In about 1833 he went to Alabama, and after remaining there a short time, removed to Tennessee, where he was married, in 1836, to Miss Mary Scruggs, a native of Virginia, and daughter of Robert and Mary Scruggs, who were also natives of that State. To the marriage of Mr. Key were born the following children: Hettie, John, Sidney, Mary A., Myra A., James R., Fannie W. and Floyd B. Mr. Key lost his

wife in 1848, and was married again, in 1854, to Miss Elizabeth M. Brown, daughter of Colonel William R. and Sarah P. Brown. The result of this union were the following children: Sarah M., Willie P., Alfred B., Sallie E., Benjamin F., Harriet C., Lena (deceased), Maud and May. Mr. Key settled in White County, Ark., in 1858, followed agricultural pursuits on a farm consisting of from 300 to 400 acres, and there remained twelve years. He then moved and purchased a farm of 160 acres, seven miles from Judsonia, where he remained until 1888. He then retired from active pursuits and moved to Judsonia, where he expects to spend his declining years. He has seen many changes in the country since residing here, and is one of the county's most respected and honored citizens. He votes the Democratic ticket; is a member of the Methodist Episcopal Church, South; has been magistrate and takes great interest in all that pertains to the good of the county, schools, churches, etc., having helped to found the first churches in this part of the country. In early days Mr. Key took great interest in hunting and was quite a marksman. He had two sons in the late war. His wife is a member of the Missionary Baptist Church.

Blount Stanley King, farmer and stock raiser, Little Red, Ark. The entire life of Mr. King has been one without any material change from the ordinary pursuits of farm toil, and yet not devoid of substantial results as an agriculturist. He is a native-born citizen of White County, his birth occuring in October, 1845, and is one of seven children born to the union of James and Susan (James) King, the father a native of East Tennessee, and probably of German descent. The ancestors came to America prior to the Revolutionary War, and the grandfather participated in that world-renowned struggle. Mrs. Susan (James) King was a native of North Carolina. The parents came to Arkansas on January 6, 1829, and settled in Caldwell Township, White County, Ark., where Blount S. King received a limited education in the common schools. He was reared to agricultural pursuits, and has followed that calling all his life, meeting with substantial results. On June 4, 1871, he was united in marriage to Miss Sarah Pinegar, and the fruits of this union were three children. Jerome L. was born April 1, 1874, but the other children died in infancy. Mrs. King died on September 5, 1875. On December 24, 1876, Mr. King took for his second wife, Miss Caroline Virginia Clark, a native of Kentucky, born May 10, 1855, and whose parents came to Arkansas from Kentucky, in 1856. This second union resulted in the birth of the following children: Noah Lot (born October 13, 1877, and died August 31, 1886), Austin Ward (born August 22, 1881), Willia M. (born October 7, 1883), Daniel D. (born July 31, 1885, and died April 23, 1888), and Florence Orenia (born on August 14, 1888). Mr. King came into possession of his farm by will from his father, eighty acres, with about eighteen under cultivation, and well adapted to agriculture or horticulture. He takes an interest in all matters relating to the good of the county, and his children are having as good educational advantages as his means will admit. He is a member of the Agricultural Wheel, and he and his wife are members of the United Baptist Church.

John Thomas King, planter and stock raiser, Little Red, Ark. A lifetime devoted with perseverance and energy to the pursuit of agriculture, have contributed very materially to the success which has attended the efforts of Mr. King, a man of substantial and established worth. He was born in 1849, and is the son of James and Louisa (James) King whose marriage took place in 1846. This union resulted in the birth of six children: Newton (born in 1847), John Thomas (born in 1849), Pinkney McDonald (born in 1851), Joseph (born in 1853), Jesse (born in 1855) and William (born in 1857). Previous to this James King married a sister of his second wife, Miss Susan James, in 1829, and by her became the father of seven children: Sophia (born in 1830), Richard (born in 1832), Jasper (born in 1834), Robert (born in 1837), Marion (born in 1839), Allen (born in 1842) and Blount S. (born in 1845). John Thomas King owes his nativity to White County, Ark., and his education was obtained in the subscription schools of that county. He was reared to agricultural pursuits, and when grown was united in marriage to Miss Mary Jane Pinegar, a native of Tennessee, born in 1848, and the daughter of William and Clarissa (Redmond) Pinegar. The wedding of our subject took place July 17, 1864, and ten children were born to them: Jesse (born in 1866), James (born in 1868), Eliza (born in 1870), LaFayette (born in 1872), Frances (born in 1874), Laura (born in 1876), Rosa (born in 1878), Viola (twin, born in 1880), Minnie (born in 1882) and David (born in 1884). Viola's twin sister died at birth. John T. King received by deed from his father eighty acres of land in Jackson Township, which he began to improve. In 1879 he purchased the old homestead which adjoined his eighty acres, and made the purchase just prior to the death of his father, receiving a deed from the latter and a dowery from his step-mother, she being his father's fourth wife. The father died on November 4, 1879, at the age of seventy-seven years. Our subject lived on the old home place, consisting of eighty-five acres, until 1886, when he moved to his present home in Denmark Township, where he now owns 275 acres of land with 100 acres under cultivation. His eldest son, Jesse King, was married to Miss Louisa Turley, a native of Arkansas, and the daughter of Samson and Mary Jane (Howell) Turley, and the result of this union has been two children: Commodore (born in 1886) and Fred (born in 1888). His son James was married November 21, to Miss Laura E. Middleton, daughter of Dr. P. A. and Amanda (Moseley) Middleton. Mr. and Mrs. John T. King are members in good standing in the United Baptist Church and are much respected by all acquainted with them. Mr. King is a member of the Agricultural Wheel No. 76. He is giving his children good educations and takes a deep interest in all school matters. His son Jesse is a professor of penmanship and LaFayette is well advanced in the English branches and is taking a commercial course at the Commercial College at Batesville, Ark., the present winter.

E. C. Kinney, editor and proprietor of the Judsonian Advance, is a newspaper man of experience, and his connection with this paper dates from 1880, he being its organizer. He managed the paper until 1885, then sold out to B. W. Briggs, and then engaged in the general mercantile business, selling out in the fall of 1889. September 18 of that year he again resumed control of the Judsonian Advance, and its advance under his management has been more noteworthy and rapid than formerly. At the present time it is recognized as a journal of decided merit, its editorials being written with a clearness and force which indicate a writer of ability. He was born in Livingston County, N. Y., in 1843, and is the eleventh of twelve children, born to Ezra and Louise (Clough) Kinney, the former a native of Connecticut, and a minister of the Methodist Episcopal Church. In 1817, during the early history of Livingston County, N. Y., he became one of its settlers, and experienced many of the hardships and inconveniences which are incident to early pioneer life. He died in 1855, and his wife in Walworth County, Wis., in 1868. E. C. Kinney was reared in Mount Morris, N. Y., and in youth learned the harness-maker's trade, and followed it some ten years. Upon the breaking out of the Rebellion he enlisted at Rochester, N. Y., in the Fifty-eighth New York Infantry, Company E, as a private, and was promoted to corporal-sergeant, and in 1862 to second lieutenant. After participating in the battle of Manassas, he was on detached duty for some time, but was taken sick, and after remaining in the hospital at Annapolis, Md., about six months, he, in 1863 returned to Mount Morris, N. Y., and began following his trade. In 1865 he removed to Painsville, Ohio, and was married there in 1866, to Miss Anna R. Abbott, a native of Salem, Mass. Becoming dissatisfied with his location in Ohio, he determined to push westward, and in 1868 settled in Independence, Buchanan County, Iowa. Two years later he became connected with a circus, and was thus enabled to travel over the greater part of the United States. In 1870 he became connected with Sprague, Warner & Griswold, and later with Kinney & Co., and when with the latter company, traveled with a team from Chicago to New York City, making every town on the route selling goods. In 1878 he left Iowa and went overland to Davidson County, Dak., and homesteaded land, remaining there a sufficient length of time to see the full growth of

Mitchell and Alexandria. In 1880 he came overland to White County, Ark., arriving here on May 17, and engaged in the hotel business. He has followed horticulture ever since his arrival in the county, and owns two fruit farms adjoining Judsonia, also one near Little Rock. He is an active Republican, and was president of the first Republican convention ever held in White County. He is the present mayor of the town, and has held other offices of public trust. Socially he is a member of Anchor Lodge No. 384, of the A. F. & A. M., and has been secretary of his order. His children are: George (a printer), Myrtie, Earl and Carlie.

Hon. H. C. Knowlton. If industry united with a strong and determined perseverance can accomplish the desired ends, Mr. Knowlton should be, and is one of the well-to-do planters of the county. He came to the county in 1870, from the State of Tennessee, but was born in Vermont in 1825, being the youngest in a family of three children born to James and Lydia (Cheney) Knowlton, who were natives of the Bay State. They were married in that State in 1813, afterward settling in Vermont, where he worked at the blacksmith's trade until about 1829, at which time he moved to Lenawee County, Mich., and settled on a farm between Adrian and Tecumseh. He was one of the pioneers of this county, and became one of its wealthiest farmers. In 1842 he went to Anderson, Ind., and made that his home, and here his death occurred in 1847, his wife's death following his in 1860, her demise occurring in Tennessee. H. C. Knowlton learned the trade of a general mechanic in his youth, and after moving to Hardeman County, Tenn., in 1845, followed his trade until the opening of the war. He was married in Hardeman County, four years after his arrival in the State, to Miss Mary Agnes Stone, a native of Fayette County, Tenn., and a daughter of William H. and B. P. (Johnson) Stone, the former a Virginian, and the latter a native of North Carolina. At the age of eighteen the father went to Missouri, and assisted in surveying that State, then went to North Carolina, and was married there in 1818, after which he moved to Tennessee and engaged in farming, making this his calling until his death in 1866. His wife died in 1877. In 1870 Mr. Knowlton came to White County, Ark., and purchased an improved farm of 200 acres, and at the present time has sixty acres under the plow. Although not an active politician, he supported the Democratic party until he affiliated with the Labor party in 1884, and in 1887 was elected on that ticket to the State legislature, serving one term. He is a strict temperance man, a member of the Agricultural Wheel, and socially is a member of Mount Pisgah Lodge No. 242, of the A. F. & A. M., and is treasurer of his order. The following are the children born to himself and wife: Mary C. (Mrs. Dr. Wells, of Marion Township), Horace C. (a farmer of the township), R. S. (a resident of Oregon), C. M. (who died in 1886), E. E. (who is married and lives in the township), J. D. (married and living in Big Creek Township), W. H. (married and living in the township), Lelia F. (Mrs. Cate) and W. B. (who died in 1875). Mr. and Mrs. Knowlton are members of the Methodist Episcopal Church, South.

Enoch Langley, who is an able representative of the ginning interests of the county as well as the agricultural class, is of Georgian nativity, being born March 31, 1847, and was the third of seven children born to Enoch and Elizabeth (Stone) Langley, who were also of Georgia, and whose births occurred in the years 1824 and 1828. They were united in the holy bonds of marriage in 1843, and as a result of this union seven children came to gladden their hearts: Nancy, Oswell, Enoch (our subject), William B., Mary, Jepha and Kattie. Enoch Langley, heeding the call of his country, enlisted in 1864, in the Thirty-fifth Georgia Infantry and participated in the battles of Cross Junction and the battle of the Wilderness. After the close of the Rebellion he returned to Georgia and, in 1868, was married to Josephine Hopper, who was born July 5, 1852, and a daughter of Thomas C. and Martha (Hendrix) Hopper. Soon after this event Mr. Langley settled in Floyd County, Ga., and farmed for awhile, but in 1874 immigrated to Arkansas and settled in Des Arc Township, White County, and in 1880 bought 235 acres of land in Cadron Township, which he commenced to improve, and he now has 120 acres in a high state of cultivation. Nine children call Mr. and Mrs. Langley father and mother: John M. (born January 9, 1869), James T. (born November 26, 1870), Martha E. (May 30, 1874), Larah B. (January 10, 1878), Luther C. (April 27, 1878), Alice I. (July 18, 1882), Enoch P. (November 28, 1884), Isam I. (December 9, 1887), Oscar B. (April 13, 1889). Mr. Langley is giving the ginning business, in which he has been very successful, his most watchful and careful attention. He is a member of the Agricultural Wheel, and politically a strong and stanch Democrat, and anything relating to his adopted county or to any public enterprise receives his most hearty support.

Rev. Isom P. Langley, pastor of the First Baptist Church of Beebe, owes his nativity to Arkansas, and was born in Clark County, September 2, 1851. His parents, Samuel S. and Mary J. (Browning) Langley, were natives of Arkansas and Alabama, respectively. Samuel S. Langley was born October 29, 1831, in Clark County, and is the son of Miles L. and Sally (Butler) Langley, natives of North Carolina, who came to Arkansas in 1818, and were married in this State in 1819. The maternal grandfather, Francis J. Browning, was a native of Georgia, and was born in 1800. His wife was a native of Alabama, and they were of English descent. The maternal ancestors were all finely educated, and figured as prominent men during their life. Francis J. Browning was a teacher and farmer, also a great and earnest worker in the Baptist Church, having served as a delegate to the first Baptist association that ever met south of the Arkansas River. This meeting was held at Spring Creek Church, near Benton, Saline County, August 12, 1835, and he was also one of the originators of Mount Bethel Church, six miles west of Arkadelphia, in 1835. At the time of his death, and for a number of years before it, he had been occupied as a teacher. He died in 1884, his wife having been called to her final home in 1879. Miles L. Langley died in 1831, and his wife in 1848. They were among the first settlers of Clark County, and endured all of the privations and hardships incident to that time. To them a family of seven children were born: John (was in the Mexican War, also in California during the gold excitement, and is now a prosperous farmer of Clark County, Ark.), Joseph (deceased, was a leading farmer of Clark County, where his family now live; his death occurred in 1882.), William (deceased, was a farmer, and lost his life by a tree falling on him, 1864, and at the time a soldier in the Confederate army), Miles L. (deceased, a very prominent Baptist minister. He was a member of the State Constitutional Conventions of 1864 and 1868, and was a chaplain in the State Senate. He died December 27, 1888.), Isom P. (is a prosperous farmer of Clark County, Ark.), Jensey (deceased) and Samuel S. (the father of the subject of this memoir, who is still living, and is a prosperous farmer of Pike County, Ark. He served four years in the Confederate army as second lieutenant, and was prisoner of war for nineteen months at Johnson's Island. He was also captain, and was acting commander at Helena. He and his estimable wife are earnest workers of the Baptist Church, and he is a Master Mason of considerable note). Rev. Isom P. is the eldest in a family of thirteen, ten of whom are now living: Thomas (deceased), Porter (deceased), Mary C., Andrew V., Permelia G., Abi (deceased), Samuel S., Jr., Annie, infant not named, Sallie, Robert, Penn and Frank. Our subject was reared to farm life, and spent his school-days in the schools of his county, and later took up the study of physiology and phrenology, under the tutorship of Miles L. Langley, his paternal uncle, and a man of very fine attainments; at the same time, and under the same teacher, he studied the English language. At the age of twenty-two he began the study of law under Gen. H. W. McMillan, of Arkadelphia, and Judges M. P. Dobey and H. H. Coleman. He completed his law course, and was admitted to the bar in 1875, and practiced his profession at Arkadelphia and Hot Springs until 1885, when he was obliged to discontinue it on account of throat disease. He joined the Baptist Church at the age of sixteen years, was licensed to preach in 1868, and ordained in 1869, since which time he has been engaged in the work of the min-

istry. He has filled the pulpits of Arkadelphia, Hot Springs, and that of the First Baptist Church of Little Rock, but a large share of his time has been devoted to churches where there was no regular pastorate. In 1880 he formed a partnership with Capt. J. W. and J. N. Miller, the firm name being Miller, Langley & Miller, editors of the Arkadelphia Signal, conducting the same with marked success until 1881. Mr. Langley then withdrew from the firm, and started the Arkansas Clipper, in 1882, a Greenback Labor paper, of which he was sole owner. This he published until 1883, then sold it and went to Hot Springs, and in company with a Mr. Allard founded and edited the Daily and Weekly Hot Springs News. In 1886 he became the editor of the Industrial Liberator, the official organ of the Knights of Labor, and made that paper a decided success, in the meantime having sold the Hot Springs News. He resigned his position in June, 1886, and engaged in the insurance business. He also purchased a controlling interest in the National Wheel Enterprise, acting as its editor until December 17, 1888, when he retired from the newspaper business, and in doing so deprived the literary and newspaper world of one of its brightest lights. In 1885 Mr. Langley became a member of the Local Assembly 2419, K. of L., at Hot Springs, the first assembly ever organized in the State, acting at present as one of the national organizers of that order. He is a member of Union Lodge 31, A. W., and was a delegate to the State convention that met at Litchfield in 1886. While at that convention he was elected as one of the delegates to the National Wheel, which met at the same time and place, and was its acting secretary. It was at this assembly that he wrote the constitution for the National Wheel, and at this same meeting was elected National Lecturer, and in that capacity wrote the demands of the National Wheel that were adopted at McKinzie, Tenn., November, 1887, and in all the conventions he has taken a very prominent part, and in behalf of the National Wheel made the response to Senator Walker's address of welcome at Meridian, Miss., December 5, 1888. That speech which elicited such favorable comment from the press.

was the crowning effort of his life, and placed him at the head of the list of deep thinkers and eloquent speakers in the labor ranks. On October 20, 1887, he became President of the Famous Life Association, of Little Rock, and served one year, managing its affairs with extraordinary ability. In 1886 he was nominated by a labor convention as a candidate for Congress against Judge J. H. Rogers, of the Fourth Congressional District, and polled more than twice the labor votes of his district. As a stump speaker he has no superior in the State. He has always figured prominently in schools, and was the secretary of the board that reorganized the splendid school system of Arkadelphia. Mr. Langley has done all kinds of work, from the hoeing of cotton to the highest calling man can perform, and is one of the best posted men in the State. In August, of 1870, he was married to Miss Martha A. Freeman, a native of Arkansas, and a daughter of Thomas J. Freeman. He was born in Little Rock, 1821, and settled in Clark County in 1840, where Mrs. Langley was born in 1851. To these parents have been born a family of five children, all living: Florence R., Charles E., Ada J., Katie and Lessie. Father, mother, and the three oldest children are members of the Baptist Church. Socially Mr. Langley affiliates with the I. O. O. F., and has filled all the offices of that order. He is a typical Arkansan, and perhaps is without his peer in public value in the State, considering his age.

Fayette T. Laster, well known to the residents of Russell, Ark., is a native of West Tennessee, his birth occurring in Decatur County, May 27, 1866. His father, William W. Laster, also of Tennessee, was born in 1837, and there married in 1860 to Sinthey A. Wright, of Tennessee, her birth occurring in 1840. Soon after their marriage they came to Arkansas and settled in White County, where they remained until their respective deaths. Mr. Laster was claimed by the grim destroyer, Death, 1886, and his faithful wife only survived him a few months, less than a year. To the union of Mr. and Mrs. Laster three sons were born, of whom only one, Fayette T. (the subject of this memoir) is now living. Albert and John both

died in Tennessee. Mr. Laster was a farmer, a hard-working and law-abiding citizen, and by his unostentatious manner gained many friends. At the date of his demise he had succeeded in amassing quite a comfortable amount of property and money. Fayette T. moved with his parents, when quite a boy, to Arkansas, where he grew to manhood with nothing but the monotonous routine of the pioneer's life to occupy his attention. His educational advantages were from necessity limited, as the schools at that time were far from satisfactory. He started out for himself at the age of twenty-one and began farming and stock raising, in which he is still engaged, and is meeting with very fair success. He now owns 200 acres of excellent bottomland, well improved and in a high state of cultivation. On September 28, Mr. Laster was united in matrimony with Ida (Lee) Mote, adopted daughter of John and Hattie Mote, and own daughter of Arcy and Martha C. Lee. To Mr. and Mrs. Laster's union two children have been born: Elva Theola (born September 10, 1878, and died December 6, 1888) and Belle Alrietia (born November 4, 1889). Mr. Laster is independent in his political views, casting his vote for the best interests of himself and the country at large. He is a prosperous young farmer, of industrious and frugal habits, and has gained the good will of his fellow-citizens.

Winfield Scott Lay is a native Arkansan, his birthplace being Van Buren County, where he received his education. He enlisted at the age of seventeen in the Confederate Cavalry (Twenty-seventh Arkansas), in which he served until the close of the war, being with Gen. Price on his raid through Missouri. Subsequently he attended school, remaining two years, and in 1868 came to Searcy, where he engaged as a clerk in a store and followed this for three years, then commenced business for himself on a capital of $600, and is now one of the leading business men in Searcy. In 1884 he was burned out, losing several thousand dollars worth of goods, but immediately built up again; and the following year did the largest business he has done before or since, selling $52,000 worth of goods. He was born on November 24, 1846, and is a son of William H. and

WHITE COUNTY, ARKANSAS.

Polly (Bacon) Lay, natives of Virginia and Tennessee, respectively. William H. Lay went to Knox County, Tenn., when a young man, where he was married and resided until 1839, when he came to Arkansas and located in what was then Van Buren County, but which is now Cleburne County, where he farmed until his death. In his political views he was a strong Democrat, and while in Tennessee served several years as deputy sheriff, and afterward as sheriff. The Lay family is of English descent, the paternal grandfather of our subject coming to this country from old England. Mr. and Mrs. Lay were members of the Methodist Episcopal Church, South. They were the parents of eight children, seven of whom are still living: Allen S., Elizabeth Witt, Emma Simmons, Sarah Fulko, Mattie Manus, Winfield Scott (who heads this sketch), and W. L. (now a resident of South America). W. S. Lay was married in Searcy on September 13, 1870, to Miss Nannie Stevenson, a daughter of the Rev. Alexander Stevenson, pastor of the Cumberland Presbyterian Church, at Searcy, and who was born in White County in 1853. Mr. Lay is one of eight stockholders in the Searcy and West Point Railroad, of which he is also a director and secretary. He is a strong Democrat, and a wide-awake business man, and has one of the largest trades in his line in Searcy.

Hon. F. P. Laws, president of the local board of immigration at Beebe, Ark., also engaged in selling wagons, buggies and farming implements, has probably done more to develop the resources of White County than any other one person, and is a very popular man wherever he is known. He is a native of Missouri, and was born in what is now Benton County May 10, 1840. His father, Joel J., was a native of North Carolina, and was born February 17, 1812, in Wilkes County, and was considered one of the best farmers of his section. His wife, the mother of the subject of this sketch, was also of North Carolina nativity, her birth occurring about 1814. Her name was Martha Grissum, and was of English ancestry, as was also her husband. She was a bright and highly cultured lady. Mr. and Mrs. Laws were married in North Carolina

in 1838, and the same week left for Missouri, settling in what is now Benton County, and there lived for about two years. They then moved to Farmington, St. Francis County, but at the time of Mr. Laws' death, in 1848, they were residing in Ste. Genevieve County. He was a life-long Democrat, though not an active politician. In his religious faith he was not identified with any particular church, but was a man of high moral character, honor, and strict integrity, and one who always left a pleasant impression and a desire to enlarge acquaintance with him. After her husband's death Mrs. Laws married again, her second marriage taking place in 1850 to Mr. Harvill Shepherd, a farmer of Ste. Genevieve County, and by him became the mother of four children. She was left a widow in 1858, and is at present living with her third husband, Mr. Humphfrey, a farmer of Miller County. Hon. F. P. Laws is the oldest in a family of four children as follows: Hon. F. P., Jane (Mrs. A. J. Humphfreys of Crawford County), Mary (married, living in Miller County, Mo.), Marion J. (married, and a well-to-do farmer). F. P. was reared to farm life, and received such advantages for an education as the schools of that period afforded. At the age of seventeen he left his step-father's home and started out to make his fortune, facing the world with nothing to back him but his courage and determination to succeed. He went first to Franklin County, Mo., and engaged in the lumber business for about four years, and was very successful. In 1861 he enlisted in the Confederate army, and served for one year. He then returned to Washington, Mo., and resumed his work in the lumber business, and while there fell in with his friend, Mr. Morris, of New Orleans, and from him secured the contract to furnish the heavy square timbers for the first grain elevator ever erected in the city of St. Louis. This contract was successfully carried out, and was the means of his securing lucrative employment in the way of large contracts. During the years 1872–73 he built sixty miles of fence for the 'Frisco Railroad, but the panic of 1873, in which so many were financially embarrassed, left him without regular work until 1875. He next traded for a tract of land fourteen miles north of Beebe, Ark., and moved to Beebe at once, but the same year sold the saw-mill and land, continuing the timber business in Beebe, also building several houses there. Ever since his residence in White County he has been interested in all movements for the good of the county, and is a liberal contributor to all worthy enterprises. He engaged in the real-estate business in 1888, and when the Beebe Board of Immigration was organized he was elected president, and has since given his time and attention to that work. In September, 1883, Hon. F. P. Laws was elected on the Democratic ticket as a Prohibitionist to the office of county and probate judge, and in that capacity did more for the county in the way of internal improvements than had ever been done before by any one county judge. He built a good fire-proof jail on the latest improved plans, bettered the condition of the county farm by erecting three new and comfortable houses, and took special care of the county poor. He repaired all the existing bridges, and built five new ones in different parts of the county, where they were greatly needed, also bought a copy of the field notes of the county and placed them on file in the county clerk's office. At the expiration of his term of office he left the county without a saloon in it. Judge Laws organized the Beebe Artesian Well Company, in August, 1889, and is acting president of the same, and fills the same position in the Southern Building & Loan Association. October 17, 1864, witnessed Judge Laws' marriage with Miss Lorinda J. Johns, a native of Missouri and a daughter of one of the oldest families of Franklin County. To their union six children have been born, only one now living: Nellie, a charming young lady of fourteen. Mamie, Eddie, Charlie, Jennie and Bessie are deceased. Judge Laws was made a Mason in Pacific Lodge No. 159, A. F. & A. M., in 1864, at Pacific Mo., and with his wife and daughter is a member of the Methodist Episcopal Church, South. He was a lay delegate to the general conference of the Methodist Episcopal Church, South, which met at Richmond, Va., in 1866, and was a delegate to the annual conference which met at Searcy December 11, 1889.

George W. Leggett, the well-known dry-goods merchant, of Floyd, has been engaged in the mercantile business since 1878, first in Mount Pisgah, and two years later in Floyd, where he is at present engaged. He was born in Hardeman County, Tenn., in 1849, and was a son of E. S. and Polly (Whitford) Leggett. E. S. Leggett owes his nativity to Tennessee, being born in that State in 1811, and is son of Daniel Leggett, who settled in Tennessee at an early day. He engaged in the mercantile business in Tennessee in 1849, and later came to White County, Ark., where he still continues in business. Mrs. Leggett was a daughter of David Whitford, of Tennessee, and died in White County in 1885. George W. was married in 1875 to Lue Bailey, who died in 1885, leaving one child, also deceased. Mr. Leggett was married the second time to Miss Vincie Greer (a daughter of O. and Coraline Greer, of this county). They are the parents of two children: Vincie Pearl and Henry L. Mr. Leggett was appointed postmaster under President Garfield, and has held the position ever since. He carries a large stock of general merchandise, and does the largest business in his line in the place, having a trade of about $1,500 to $25,000 per year. He also owns a farm of 140 acres, eighty of which are under cultivation. In politics Mr. Leggett is a strong Democrat.

Dr. John L. Leggett, known to be one of the most progressive farmers in his township, and well qualified to discharge the trust reposed in him by the people, commenced the study of medicine shortly after the war, under Dr. M. F. Dumas, and upon obtaining his certificate in 1876, located at Little Red, White County, and commenced practicing. On coming out of the army he was without means, but taking up the study of medicine he became very proficient and very successful as a physician, but in 1883 he turned his attention to the mercantile business and to farming, and now owns a fine farm of 250 acres on the Red River, mostly bottom land, with 150 acres under cultivation, and is one of the most extensive farmers in Jackson Township. The Doctor was born in Madison County, Tenn., October 9, 1844, and is a son of E. S. and Polly (Whitford) Leggett, natives of North Carolina and Tennessee, respectively. E. S. Leggett came to Madison County, Tenn., when a boy with his parents, and after his marriage was engaged in farming in that State until 1860, when he removed to Arkansas, locating in White County. He has filled the office of justice of the peace for a number of years, is a Democrat and belongs to the Baptist Church, as did also his wife, who died in 1876, being the mother of ten children, five of whom are still living: F. M., J. B., George, Martha (now Mrs. Rushing) and John L. (our subject). The senior Leggett is still a resident of White County, and is eighty years of age. Dr. Leggett enlisted in the Confederate service, in 1861, in the Eighth Arkansas Infantry, in which he served one year. He then came home and joined the Tenth Missouri Cavalry, and took part in the memorable Missouri raid, and also in a number of hard-fought battles. In 1866 he was married to Miss Bettie Martin, a native of Alabama. They were the parents of ten children, eight of whom are still living: Mary (wife of D. C. Middleton, a farmer of this county), William L., Lewis T., Icy, Ida, Charles, Lida and Isaac. Mrs. Leggett is a member of the Missionary Baptist Church. Dr. Leggett is one of the most enterprising men of his community, and a leading Democrat, and has served as postmaster at Little Red since 1876.

John H. Leib. Near the little town of Lancaster, Ohio, on November 13, 1836, John H. Leib first saw the light of day, being one of ten children born to the marriage of John and Elizabeth Leib. John Leib, Sr., was born in York, Penn., in the year 1800, and his wife was born the same year in Juniata County, Penn. They were united in marriage in Bremen, Fairfield County, Ohio, in 1823, and spent fifty-seven years in happy wedded life. Mr. Leib died in 1883, at the age of eighty-three years, and at the time of his death was in Russell, Ark. His wife had gone to her final rest in the year 1880, aged eighty years. They resided in the States of Ohio, Indiana and Illinois, and were quite successful in the accumulation of wealth, being quiet, industrious people. For many years Mr. Leib was an old line Whig, but at the

dissolution of that party he united with the Republican, though was not active in party measures or campaigns. In their family of ten children only five are now living: James (a farmer of Lagrange County, Ind.), Benjamin (farmer, resident of Crawford County, Ind.), John H. (the subject of this sketch), Anna E. (living in White County, Ark., and Mary J. (Mrs. William Poindexter, of Crawford County, Ind.). Lydia, John and Augustus were born and died at Bremen, Ohio. Hamilton deceased at Russell, and George S. died at Chauncey, Ill. John H. resided at Bremen, Ohio, until sixteen years of age, at that date removing with his parents to Lagrange County, Ind. His education was limited to the common schools of the period, and though they were far from satisfactory, he managed to acquire a thorough knowledge of business, and is now a well-informed man. In November of 1861 Mr. Leib entered the United States army as a volunteer in the Forty-eighth Indiana Infantry, in Col. Eddy's regiment. He enlisted as a private, but was soon promoted to the office of first lieutenant in Capt. Mann's Company G. His ability was recognized and commented on by his superior officers, and in 1865 he was given the title of captain, commanding a company until the close of the war. He participated in the siege of Corinth, Vicksburg, and in the battles of Iuka, Corinth, Raymond, Champion's Hill, Jackson and Black River Bridge in the State of Mississippi, Altoona and Bentonville in Georgia, also in Chattanooga, Tenn. He was with Gen. Sherman on his famous march to the sea. After the close of hostilities, Mr. or rather Capt. Leib returned home and engaged in farming and stock raising, which is still his occupation. He is a Royal Arch Mason, having reached the seventh degree, and is a liberal contributor to schools, churches and all public enterprises.

Benjamin W. Lewis. David and Elvira (Hagler) Lewis, the parents of the subject of this sketch, were natives of North Carolina and settled in Tennessee at an early day, rearing a family of thirteen children: Benjamin W., Nancy F., J. L., Elizabeth, Lucy, Polly, Lucinda, John L., Elvira, Sarah, William, Richard (also a resident of Kane Township, White County) and Martha. Mr. Lewis died in Tennessee in 1870, and his wife in 1852. B. W. was born in Western Tennessee, where he grew up on a farm and was educated in the common schools. He was married on January 2, 1851, to Mary E. Hastings, a daughter of John M. C. and Elizabeth (Sexton) Hastings, of North Carolina nativity, and who immigrated to Tennessee at an early day. After his marriage Mr. Lewis settled on a farm in Henry County, Tenn., where he lived until 1870, when he removed to Western Tennessee, and settled in Gray Township, White County, and three years later bought a farm of 160 acres in Cane Township, where his home now is. He enlisted in the fall of 1862 in the Forty-sixth Tennessee Infantry, commanded by Col. J. M. Clark, and was in the service five months. Mr. and Mrs. Lewis have a family of eight children, all of whom were born in Tennessee: Nancy J. (now Mrs. Osborn), John D. (lives in this township), William L., James W. (deceased), L. D., Henry W., Elvira (wife of Dr. V. W. Ware, of this township) and Benjamin F. In politics he is an active Democrat, and takes a strong interest in all work for public improvement, and has been school director for the past five years. Himself and wife are members of the Methodist Episcopal Church, of which Mr. Lewis is one of the trustees.

Jefferson Pinkney Linder is one of the enterprising and industrious agriculturists of this region, and is a son of Abraham W. and Itea (Templeman) Linder, the former of whom was born in Spartanburg District, S. C. He was of English descent, his grandfather having emigrated from England to America before the outbreak of the Revolutionary War, and took an active part in that struggle on the side of the Colonists. He settled in North Carolina, and there reared his family, his son John, the grandfather of our subject, being born there. He was married in that State and at an early day removed to South Carolina, where his son Abraham W. was educated and grew to manhood. He was also married there and eight of his children were born there prior to the year 1844, after which they moved to Alabama and settled in Benton County, where four more children were given them. Their names are as follows: John A. (born July 18, 1823), Calvin D. (born July 1, 1825), Elizabeth Ann (born July 10, 1827), Delilah E. (born September 9, 1829), James Templeman (born April 17, 1832), Lewis M. (born October 24, 1834), Austin A. (born March 17, 1837), Jefferson Pinkney (born August 10, 1839), Mary A. (born October 6, 1841), Arcena S. (born March 21, 1844), Virgil Taylor (born June 3, 1848) and Martha C. (born on March 8, 1851). The father and mother of these children were born on September 23, 1803, and February 27, 1807, respectively, and in 1857 they came to Arkansas. Abraham Linder and his sons were opposed to secession, but Lewis M. and Austin A. espoused the Confederate cause after the ordinance of secession had been passed, and served as members in a company of Arkansas Volunteer Infantry. Lewis M. died of measles while at home on a sick furlough, and Austin was mortally wounded at the battle of Helena, Ark., on July 4, 1863, and was taken from the field where he fell by the Federals to a hospital at Memphis and there died. Jefferson Pinkney Linder (our subject) was reared to farm life and received his education principally in the subscription schools of Alabama, whither his father had moved from South Carolina. He embraced religion at the age of twenty-one years, and is now a member of the Presbyterian Church. On December 4, 1861, he was married to Miss Lucinda Jane Shelton, a daughter of John F. and Martha Payne (Milam) Shelton, of Shelby County, Tenn., her birth occurring in that county on May 8, 1846. The names of their children are here given: Thomas Jefferson (born March 28, 1863), Laura Eudora (born August 24, 1865), Margaret Itea (born December 26, 1867), John Robert (born January 6, 1870), Charles Henry (was born on February 1, 1873, and died August 1, 1875), McWilliam (was born on August 4, 1875,) Oscar B. (was born on September 5, 1877), Albert Lee (born February 8, 1880), Mertie Velmer (born March 23, 1882, and died October 9, 1884), Vida May (born June 16, 1884, and died August 3, 1886), Burrillah (born on February 14, 1887). Thomas J. was married to Miss Fannie Dennis, of Henderson County, Tex., on December 23, 1886, and is now farming in Monroe County, Ark. Laura E. became the wife of S. N. Trotter, and lives in Monroe County, Ark. Margaret Itea bore one child by her husband, J. W. Acree, but is now separated from him by mutual consent. Mr. Linder has been noted for his industry and thrift, and on commencing life these constituted his capital stock and well he has made use of them, being now the owner of 360 acres of land, his first purchase being only eighty acres. He has 100 acres under cultivation and makes a specialty of stock raising, his mules being of a fine grade, and he also has some very fine horses of the Tone Hal breed. Mr. Linder was troubled for some time with a scrofulous white swelling on one of his legs which finally resulted in the loss of that member, the operation being performed in 1879. He is a man possessing a fund of useful information and is a Democrat in his political views. Himself and wife and four children are members of the Baptist Church.

Elder Benjamin H. Lumpkin, a prominent Baptist minister of White County, is a son of Robert and Jane (Harden) Lumpkin, and owes his nativity to Arkansas, his birth occurring May 2, 1849. Robert Lumpkin was a native of Georgia, and his wife of Ballard County, Ky. They were married in the latter State and came to White County in February, 1835, settling near Denmark, said county, where Mr. Lumpkin died in 1855. He was a Universalist in belief and a farmer by occupation. Mrs. Lumpkin was a member of the Methodist Episcopal Church for many years, and closed her eyes to the trials and tribulations of this world in 1857. Mr. Lumpkin in his political views was a Democrat, and manifested an active interest in party campaigns. To the marriage of Mr. and Mrs. Lumpkin eight children were born, three sons and five daughters: Louisa (wife of Elder J. M. Butler, a Baptist missionary to the Cherokee Indians), Susan M. (Mrs. Ramer, of Shelby County, Tenn.), Sophia E. (now Mrs. J. F. Burket, residing in Northern Arkansas), Benjamin H. (subject of this sketch), John (died while in the Rebel army at Bowling Green, Ky.), Noah (deceased in boyhood, in White County), Charity (wife of Thomas Simmons, a farmer of Fulton

County, Ark.) and Rebecca (died in White County, Ark., in 1868). Benjamin H. passed his early life near Denmark, Ark., and received but meager advantages for an education in his youth, but is now a well-read gentleman, and conversant on all important subjects of the day. He began preaching at the age of twenty-nine years, and by his earnest and eloquent expounding, has made many converts to his faith. He began farming at the age of fifteen years, which he continued until he reached the age of thirty. In 1883 Mr. Lumpkin embarked in the mercantile business in connection with his preaching, and has been very successful in that departure. He carries a stock of carefully selected groceries, valued at $15,000. Mr. Lumpkin was married July 19, 1870, to Rachel F. Ruminor, of White County, and a daughter of James Ruminor. By this marriage five children have been born, two sons and three daughters: Allie F., Hayden A., Maggie A., Benjamin T. and Lena Rivers (deceased). Mr. Lumpkin was elected justice of the peace in September of 1888, for a period of two years, and is discharging the duties of that office in a manner that proves beyond a doubt his ability to satisfactorily fill that position. He is a member of the Missionary Baptist Church in his religious belief, and a stanch Democrat in politics. Mr. Lumpkin contributes liberally to all worthy enterprises, and lends his valuable support to all church, school and charitable movements. In societies he is identified with the Masonic order, in which he is a member in high standing.

Dr. J. F. McAdams, physician and surgeon, Searcy, Ark. There are few men of the present day whom the world acknowledges as successful more worthy of honorable mention or whose life-history affords a better example of what may be accomplished by a determined will and perseverance than that of Dr. J. F. McAdams. This gentleman was born in Shelby County, Ala., in 1830, and was the fourth of seven children, the result of the marriage of James and Sarah (Foreman) McAdams, natives, respectively, of South Carolina and Tennessee. The father was a planter, and when a young man went to Alabama, where he married

Miss Foreman and settled on a farm within five miles of Columbiana, where he lived for over fifty years. His death occurred in 1867, and his wife died in February, 1889. Of their family the following children are living: Isaac F. (resides in Dallas, Tex.), J. F., Elizabeth (now Mrs. Edwards, of Shelby County, Ala.), Sarah (now Mrs. Horton, resides in Shelby County, Ala.), and Dr. Henry Clay (who is married and resides in Shelby County, Ala.). Dr. J. F. McAdams was reared to plantation life and secured a good practical education in the schools of Shelby County, Ala., subsequently taking a three-years' course in Talladega, Ala. After leaving school he engaged in teaching, and at the same time commenced reading medicine at the Mobile Medical Institute, graduating in the class of 1861. After this he practiced some and in the spring of 1862 came to Searcy. He was the leading physician of the county during the war, and remained at home by request. He was married in Perry County, Ala., in 1859, to Miss Sarah J. Crow, a native of Perry County, Ala., and daughter of Joseph W. and Elizabeth (Hopper) Crow, natives of Alabama. Her father was a successful agriculturist and his death occurred in 1865. His wife died in 1876. When coming to Searcy in 1862 Dr. McAdams found the town very small, and where fine business streets now are was then undergrowth. The Doctor opened his office in the public square and began practicing, which he continued all through the war without molestation. He is not very active in politics, but votes with the Democratic party. Socially, he is a member of Searcy Lodge No. 49, A. F. & A. M. To his marriage was born one child, Frank Waldo, who is book-keeper for F. Lippman, at Olyphant, Ark. Dr. McAdams has seen many changes since first residing here, both from an educational and moral standpoint. The customs of the people have also changed. He and Mrs. McAdams are members of the Baptist Church.

Maj. John C. McCauley, Searcy, Ark., is one of the well-known and esteemed pioneer residents of this county, having come to White County in 1851. He was born in Orange County, N. C., February 24, 1834, and was the second in a family of nine children born to James and Mary A. (Freeland) McCauley, both natives of North Carolina. The father grew to manhood near Chapel Hill, N. C., settled on a plantation and made that his home until 1836, when he moved to Tennessee. He first settled in Fayette County, then Tipton County, and kept a hotel at Concordia, Tenn., in 1851. Later than this he came to White County, settled in Gray Township, speculated in land (being also a contractor), and erected a great many houses in Searcy. He there closed his eyes to the scenes of this world in December, 1888, at the age of seventy-nine years. His excellent wife died in 1883. The father was a member of Searcy Lodge No. 49, A. F. & A. M., and was charter member of the same. Of their family, seven children are now living: E. J. (now Mrs. E. J. Carter, who resides in Searcy), Maj. John C., Mary A. (now Mrs. William T. Holloway, of Searcy), Martha E. (now Mrs. Joseph R. Hall, resides in Tipton County, Tenn., near the old homestead), James (is married, and resides on the father's homestead near Judsonia), Catherine B. (now Mrs. John D. Sprigg, resides at Searcy), and George C. (who married Miss Emma Black, resides at West Point, White County). The paternal great-grandfather, John McCauley, was a captain under Gen. Marion in the War of the Revolution. He was at Antrim Island in the war against England, retreated and took secret passage on a Colonial vessel, in which he safely crossed the ocean to America. He landed in North Carolina, and made that State his home. Grandfather John McCauley was a soldier in the War of 1812, and held the rank of colonel. He represented Orange County, N. C., in the legislature for many years, and his death occurred in that State. On the mother's side, the family was of Scotch descent. Maj. John C. McCauley was nearly seventeen years of age when he came to White County, and received his education under the tutelage of Dr. James Holmes, an able educator. After coming to Arkansas he commenced studying law under Scott McConaughey, but in 1852 engaged in merchandising, which business he has since continued, with the exception of four years during the war (1861–65). He has had different partners, the present firm being McCauley & Son, which has continued since 1865, and carry everything to be found in a general store. In 1861 Mr. McCauley raised Company K, First State Guards, and entered the State's service January 1, 1861. Later he was transferred to the Seventh Arkansas Infantry, and remained there during the war. He was in the bombardment of Columbus, Ky., and was at Bowling Green and Shiloh; was twice wounded, and was confined in the hospital at Tupelo, Miss., and Blount Springs, Ala. After the battle of Shiloh the company was reorganized, and the subject of this sketch was the only one of the company re-elected, and he was promoted to the position of major. He was in Farmington, took the battery and then rejoined Gen. Bragg in his invasion of Kentucky. After the battle of Chickamauga, Ga., he was promoted to the rank of lieutenant-colonel, and after the battle of Missionary Ridge he was detailed and put in charge of a company to recruit men. He was captured by the Third Missouri Cavalry near Batesville and taken to the military prison at Little Rock, where he was paroled by Col. Chandler at the house of Mrs. Green, remained two months, and was then taken to Johnston Island, where he was exchanged on January 9, 1865. He surrendered on May 9, 1865, after which he returned to White County and engaged in merchandising. He has taken quite an active part in politics, and votes with the Democratic party. He was deputy postmaster for many years before the war, and was postmaster under President Hayes, filled the same position under President Cleveland, and occupies that position at the present time. He has been Master of the Masonic Lodge No. 49, Searcy, for six years, is a member of Tillman Chapter No. 19, and has been High Priest and King; is also a member of the Council, having been Thrice Illustrious. Maj. McCauley was married in Tipton County, Tenn., in 1855, to Miss Eliza J. Hall, a native of Tennessee, and the daughter of Thomas S. and Mary Hall, natives of North Carolina. Her father was a farmer and tanner, and both he and wife died in Tennessee. They were related by marriage to Stonewall Jack-

son. To Mr. and Mrs. McCauley were born four living children: Aurora (now Mrs. Fancette, resides in Searcy), Charles E. (widower, and is postal clerk on the Iron Mountain Railroad between St. Louis and Little Rock), Ernest J. and James Thomas. Mr. McCauley and wife are members of the Old School Presbyterian Church, and he is deacon and Bible-class teacher in the same.

James A. McCauley, farmer and ginner, White County, Ark. Permanent success in any calling in life is largely dependent upon the energy, perseverance and enterprise of an individual, and this, together with honest, upright dealing, will eventually bring him to the front. Mr. McCauley was originally from Tipton County, Tenn., where his birth occurred in 1842, and was the fifth of seven children, the result of the union of James and Mary (Freeland) McCauley, natives of Orange County, N. C. The parents were married in Chapel Hill, N. C., and in 1836 moved to Tipton County, Tenn., where the father tilled the soil until 1851. He then came to White County, settled at Prospect Bluff, now Judsonia, and in connection with his former pursuit, ran a steam saw-mill, one of the first in the county, and doing the grinding for several counties. In 1885 he moved to West Point, White County, and there his death occurred on December 15, 1888. His wife received her final summons in Searcy, in 1882. James A. McCauley attained his growth on the farm, received his education in the schools of Searcy, and on April 13, 1861, he enlisted in Company K, Seventh Arkansas Infantry, as a private, for one year. He was in the battle of Shiloh, and after this disastrous engagement he re-enlisted for three years or during service, in the same company and regiment. He was in the battles of Perryville and Murfreesboro, and at the reorganization of the company he was promoted to the rank of second lieutenant. This was after the last-named battle. The regiment was consolidated with the Sixth Arkansas Infantry, and Mr. McCauley was transferred to Gen. Kirby Smith. He was put in Turnbull Camp, Washington, Hempstead County, for four months, drilling troops, and was then transferred to Dobbin's brigade, McGee's regular cavalry. He was with

Gen. Price on the Missouri raid and was paroled at Jacksonport, Ark., in 1865, after which he returned to White County. Mr. McCauley then embarked in mercantile pursuits in Searcy, in 1866, but the following year sold out and returned to the farm. His marriage occurred in White County, on December 13, 1865, to Miss Nancy A. Bond, a native of White County, and the daughter of John W. and Emily (Smith) Bond, natives of North Carolina and Georgia, respectively. The father moved to Arkansas Territory in 1836, and was residing there when it was admitted into the Union. He was the first county clerk of White County, was one of the prominent and first merchants of Searcy, and started his store in the woods. His death occurred in 1887. His wife died in 1869. Mr. McCauley settled where he now resides in 1856, and in 1874 he purchased 715 acres of land, and now has 315 under cultivation. He raises grain and cotton. Mr. McCauley has been running a cotton-gin ever since he settled on the farm, and has been quite successful. In his political views he is a cotton-mouth Democrat. To his marriage were born ten children: James Walton, Emma, Holmes, Stonewall, Lee, Hardee, Pat Cleburne, Jeff Davis, Allen and Mary. Mr. and Mrs. McCauley are members of the Presbyterian Church.

George C. McCauley is not unknown to the many readers of the present volume. He learned the miller's trade when a boy, and operated a gristmill and cotton-gin at Judsonia for six years, after which he engaged in farming on the old Beeler place, where he remained nine years. Moving thence to West Point, he engaged in farming and in the cotton-gin business, in which he is still engaged, enjoying the confidence and liberal patronage of his many acquaintances. On October 24, 1877, he was married to Miss Emma Black, a daughter of W. G. Black, who was born in 1860, in Searcy. They became the parents of three children, two of whom are still living: Mattie May and Maud E. Mr. McCauley is a strong Democrat, and a liberal donator to all enterprises for the benefit of church or educational work. He was born in Tipton County, Tenn., on February 5, 1851, being the son of James and Mary Ann Mc-

Cauley, natives of North Carolina, who were reared near Raleigh, where they were married and made their home for some time. After residing awhile in Tennessee and Missouri, they finally came to Arkansas in 1851, settling in White County. Mr. McCauley was one of the most successful farmers that ever found a home in Arkansas, being the owner of 1,200 acres of land at the time of his death, which occurred in December, 1888, at the age of seventy-seven years; his wife had died in 1882, in her seventy-second year. Both were members of the Presbyterian Church, and were the parents of ten children, seven of whom are still living: Elizabeth (the wife of W. B. Carter, of Searcy), John C. (the present postmaster of Searcy), Mary (wife of W. T. Holloway), Martha (wife of J. R. Hall), James A. (farmer of this county), Catharine B. (wife of Capt. J. D. Spriggs, now deceased) and George C. (our subject).

R. H. McCulloch, farmer and stock raiser, Searcy, Ark. In reviewing the lives of those individuals mentioned in this volume no adequate idea of the agricultural affairs of White County, or of its substantial citizens, would be complete, which failed to make mention of Mr. McCulloch, or of the substantial property which he owns. Originally from Murfreesboro, Rutherford County, Tenn., his birth occurred August 26, 1849, he passing his boyhood days and early manhood in Tennessee. He was educated in Andrew College of that State, and after leaving school began the study of pharmacy, subsequently going to Giles County, Tenn., where he was engaged in agricultural pursuits from 1870 to 1871. The next year he became book-keeper at Plum Bayou, in Jefferson Township, on the Arkansas River. In March, 1873, he came to Gray Township, White County, and finally locating at Beebe, entered the employ of Strange & Ward as book-keeper, with whom he remained for two years. Deciding to settle in Union Township, he purchased a farm of 120 acres, with sixty-five under cultivation, and now has eighty-five acres of it improved. On October 27, 1884, Mr. McCulloch moved to Searcy, having the previous September been elected clerk of the circuit and chancery court, and also recorder, and served efficiently in that capacity until October 30, 1888, when he was engaged as traveling salesman for Mitchell & Bettis, of Little Rock, continuing on the road until March 1, 1889. He then moved to his present farm, having bought in 1887 eighty acres, with thirty acres under cultivation. He now owns a good place of 200 acres, with 115 acres under substantial improvement, besides a timber tract of 169 acres. Mr. McCulloch is the eldest in a family of five children born to Dr. P. D. and Lucy V. McCulloch, both being natives of Tennessee. The father was a physician and surgeon by profession, and in 1876 moved to Hot Springs, Ark., where he still resides. He has been active in the Masonic order, having just retired as Grand Knight of the Grand Templars of the State. He represented the Grand Lodge of Tennessee in all its various offices. The mother of R. H. McCulloch died in July, 1865, in Gibson County, Tenn. In their family were the following children: R. H., P. D. (married, and resides in Lee County; is an attorney and an extensive planter), E. A. (married, and an attorney in Lee County) and Lydia B. (now Mrs. J. T. Hogg; resides in Trenton, Tenn.; her husband is traveling salesman for a Memphis firm). R. H. McCulloch was married in White County, Ark., November 25, 1874, to Miss Anna E. Cobb, a native of Tennessee (Haywood County), and the daughter of T. T. and Mary (Rose) Cobb, of North Carolina origin, who immigrated from that State in 1832 and 1833, respectively, to Tennessee. In 1858 they came to White County, Ark., settling in Union Township, and there the father's death occurred in 1881. The mother died about 1860. Mr. McCulloch lost his excellent wife in 1876, and was married again in White County, June 30, 1878, to Mattie L. Cobb, a Tennesseean by birth, and the daughter of S. P. and Eliza (Rose) Cobb, originally from North Carolina. The parents moved to Tennessee in 1832, coming thence to White County, Ark., in 1870, and settling near Beebe, where the father followed agricultural pursuits. Both parents are now living. To Mr. and Mrs. McCulloch were born five children: Samuel R., Philip D., Bertha C., Maggie and R. H., Jr. Mr. McCulloch is a member of Searcy Lodge No. 49, A. F. & A. M.;

was Worshipful Master of Beebe Lodge No. 145 for about ten years; is a member of Tillman Chapter No. 19, R. A. M., and belongs to Searcy Lodge, K. of H., at Searcy. He has been for a number of years a member of the Grand Lodge, and for the past three years has been secretary and treasurer, and chairman for two years.

Miles C. McDowell, actively occupied as a farmer and stock raiser, of Marshall Township, White County, Ark., is the son of Harvey and Ruth (Walker) McDowell, and was born in Tennessee in 1854. Harvey McDowell, also a native of Tennessee, dates his existence from July, 1806, as a son of Joseph and Olive McDowell. He spent his younger days on a plantation, and in the schools of Tennessee, and was married in April, 1834, to Ruth Walker, becoming by her the father of the following family: Ollie (Mrs. W. F. Gill, now deceased), Parthena (Mrs. L. Jones, also deceased), Louisa (widow of Mr. Greegs), William (married), Gideon, Robert, John, Harriet C. and Miles C. (the subject of this memoir). Harvey McDowell died soon after the war, his last days being spent in Missouri, where he had moved with his family from Tennessee. After his father's demise, Miles C. came to Arkansas in company with his mother, and purchased land in White County which he soon after sold, and subsequently acquired another 120 acres in the same township, one mile south of Romance. This farm he bought in 1888, and now has forty acres in an excellent state of cultivation. His farm is well and carefully stocked, and in many respects is the equal of any in the country. His mother, who is residing with him, is an estimable lady, and is hale and hearty for a person of her age. Mr. McDowell takes decided interest in all those movements which promise good to the county, and never fails to give his support to any worthy cause.

George W. McKinney is one of the most enterprising and progressive farmers of White County and one who has done a great deal in changing the country from a dense wilderness to what is now a prosperous and thrifty community. Born on May 9, 1826, in Monroe County, Miss., he came to Arkansas in 1870, and settled on the farm that he now owns, buying 120 acres on which was a small log-cabin and about ten acres cleared, but shortly after he purchased 200 acres more, and erected a good house, barns, fences, etc., having here 135 acres under successful cultivation, and all the necessary improvements of the present day. Mr. McKinney is a model farmer, as everything around his place indicates; negligence and degeneracy being traits unknown about his home. He is the son of John and Rosanna (Land) McKinney, natives of North Carolina and Tennessee, respectively, who were married in the latter State and shortly afterward moved to Mississippi, there becoming engaged in farming. Mr. McKinney was a Democrat, and soldier in the War of 1812, also serving as magistrate of his county for several years. His death occurred in 1832, his wife surviving him until 1872. They were the parents of nine children, five now living. The oldest son, J. G., is a prosperous farmer in Texas. Susan C. (Mrs. Chesley Malone, at present resides in Calhoun County, Miss.), Andrew J. (is a farmer of Chickasaw County, Miss.), and one daughter (Mrs. R. E. Brewer). George W. was reared to farm life, and received a good education in the common schools of the period. He cared for his aged mother until her death, giving her all the comforts necessary to her declining years, and in his twenty-fourth year was married to Miss Helen C. Gibbs of Mississippi birth, by whom he became the father of eight children, six now surviving: W. T. (a farmer of Royal Township, White County), John M. (also a farmer in Royal Township, White County), George W. (at home), T. A. (a farmer of Royal Township, White County), Margaret A. (wife of James W. Hall, a prominent farmer of Royal Township), J. R. and Julia E. (now Mrs. Thomas S. Kitchen). Mrs. McKinney died in 1889, and Mr. McKinney chose for his second and present wife, Mrs. M. E. Malone, a native of Mississippi. At the time of the war Mr. McKinney was justice of the peace and consequently did not enter the service until 1863, when he enlisted in Col. Duff's regiment, remaining until the final surrender. He was in McCullough's brigade in the cavalry service, and participated in several brisk skirmishes, but was never wounded.

He was ordered to Mobile with Col. Duff, and advised by that colonel to go to his family. While in Mississippi Mr. McKinney held the office of justice of the peace and overseer of roads and men. He is a member of El Paso Lodge No. 65, A. F. & A. M., and was made a Mason in 1865, also belonging at this time to New Hope Agricultural Wheel No. 32, T. A., and is treasurer of the Wheel. He is at present a member of his school board, and takes an active interest in schools, churches, and gives his influence and help to all public enterprises. In his political views Mr. McKinney is a Democrat, but casts his vote irrespective of party and where he considers it will do the most good, supporting always the best man for the position.

D. L. McLeod, who, though comparatively young in years, has had an experience such as but few men enjoy, is now a prosperous planter and fruit grower of White County. When only fourteen years of age he became a "sailor boy," and in 1869 received the honor of being made captain in the merchant service. He was born in Prince Edward's Island, Canada, April 27, 1841, and is the son of Donald McLeod, also a native of Canada, who there married Miss Annie Henderson, her birth also occurring on Prince Edward's Island. A family of six children blessed this union, five of whom are still living. Donald McLeod was principally engaged in agricultural pursuits during life, in which he was very successful. Himself and wife were members of the Presbyterian Church, in which he had been deacon for a number of years, rigidly upholding the tenets of his belief. His wife died some years previous to his demise, which occurred in 1886. From January, 1864, D. L. McLeod served as chief quartermaster in the United States navy, receiving honorable recognition for the manner in which he discharged his duties. His term of service in the navy expired in May, 1867, but he at once returned to the sea and engaged in the merchant service continuing until 1879. One noteworthy event marks his career during this time: A beautiful marine telescope was presented to him in 1873, awarded by the King of Norway for a brave and noble deed in rescuing a

Norwegian crew, on the Atlantic Ocean. Mr. McLeod was married, in 1874, to Susie K. Kitchen, a daughter of William and Jane Kitchen, and a native of Ontario, Canada. To this union two children have been born: Lillie J. (born in Akyobe, India, April, 1875, and died in 1880), William (born in February, 1877, and died at sea May, 1878, and is buried at Belfast, Ireland) and Arthur R. (who is now seven years old). In 1880 Mr. McLeod became a resident of Iowa, where he remained for three years engaged in fine stock raising, in Fayette County, but in 1883 he moved to Arkansas and located at Judsonia, White County, where he still lives, successfully occupied in fruit growing. He owns 240 acres of excellent land, and has a fine residence, which he has erected during his abode here. He is a Master Mason in good standing and is also president of the Arkansas Fruit Growers' Union, which was organized in 1886. Besides this he is first vice-president of the State Horticultural Society, and, with his wife, belongs to the Baptist Church.

Dandridge McRae, attorney at law. Searcy, Ark., has every reason to be proud of both its law courts and the members of the bar who support them. Among the leading firms of attorneys in Searcy, is the well-known one of Messrs. McRae, Rives & Rives, who are notable representatives of the learned profession. Mr. McRae has also been expert for the United States treasury department, appointed in 1889, and this business is to gather statistics for that department. He was born in Baldwin County, Ala., on October 10, 1829, and the eldest in a family of eleven children born to the union of D. R. W. and Margaret (Braey) McRae, the father of West Florida Parish, Miss., and the mother of South Carolina. The parents were married in Alabama in 1828, and were the owners of a large plantation, which he carried on although he was a lawyer by profession. He took quite an active part in politics, was sheriff of Clark County, and represented that county in the legislature. His death occurred in March, 1849. After the death of her husband and the same year, Mrs. McRae came to White County, Ark., settled in Little Red River Township, entered land, improved it, bought several claims, and in 1859 moved to Pulaski County, near Little Rock, and made that her home until 1861. After this she visited the Lone Star State, but returned, and her death occurred at the home of her son, Dandridge McRae, in Searcy in 1867. Those members of the family living are: Dandridge, Rebecca (Mrs. Col. G. F. Bancum, of Little Rock), Ann (wife of A. T. Jones, near West Point, White County, Ark.) and Mrs. Mona Rawles (at Perryville, Perry County). Dandridge McRae was early trained to the arduous duties of the farm, received his education at home under a private tutor, and later entered the University of South Carolina, from which institution he graduated in the class of 1849. He then aided in opening up the farm in Red River Township, but in 1853 moved to Searcy, and there commenced reading law. He was admitted to the bar by Justice C. C. Scott, of the supreme court, in 1854, and commenced the practice of law immediately afterward. In 1856 he was elected county and circuit clerk of the county, and served six years. In 1861 he was actively engaged in organizing troops for the State, and in the same year was sent by the military board to muster Gen. N. P. Pierce, brigadier of State troops, while even at that time the Missourians were driven from the State by the Federal Generals Lyon and Siegel. Gen. Ben. McCulloch in command of the Arkansas and Indian Territory, issued a proclamation to the people of Arkansas to go to the border and repel invaders. Many companies organized reported to Mr. McRae, and at the request of the General, the former took command and moved into Missouri, toward Springfield, to make a diversion, while the General moved to Carthage to relieve Gen. Parsons of the Missouri State Guards. Upon his return to Arkansas Mr. McRae organized a regiment under the direction of Gen. McCulloch, and was made colonel of the same. He served until 1862, was with Gen. McCulloch at Wilson's Creek, Pea Ridge and Corinth. He returned to Arkansas in 1862, raised another regiment by June, and was assigned by Gen. Hindman the command of a brigade. This brigade served until 1862, when Mr. McRae was promoted in December, to the rank of brigadier-general, and served in that capacity until the close of the war. He was in the battle of Helena, captured the only fort taken, also Jenkins' Ferry, Prairie Grove, and returned to Searcy, White County, in 1865. He engaged in the practice of law until 1881, and was then deputy secretary of State for four years. In 1885 he was acting commissioner for Arkansas, at the World's Fair at New Orleans, and in 1886 was the commissioner. Mr. McRae was appointed expert on December 26, 1888, by United States treasury department for gathering information. He was vice-president of the bureau of emigration of Arkansas in 1887. Socially, he is a member of Searcy Lodge No. 49, A. F. & A. M., and was Worshipful Master of the same; is a member of Tillman Chapter No. 19, and a member of the Council. Mr. McRae was married in De Soto County, Miss., on January 10, 1855, to Miss Angie Lewis, a native of Mississippi, who bore her husband two children: Annie (now Mrs. Neeley, residing in Searcy) and Minnie (now Mrs. J. F. Rives, Jr., residing in Searcy).

Thomas Jefferson Malone, planter and stock raiser at Pleasant Plains, Ark., is the son of Stephen and Sarah (Parks) Malone, natives of North Carolina, being born December 16, 1816, in Henry County, Tenn. He was reared in the arduous duties of the farm, received his education in his native county, and on December 20, 1846, he was married in Fayette County, Tenn., to Miss Pinie E. Ozier, a native of North Carolina, where she partly received her education. In about 1848 Mr. Malone purchased a tract of land, consisting of 160 acres of unimproved land, and this he went to work to improve. After clearing about twenty-five acres and erecting good buildings, he sold this property and came to Arkansas. To his marriage were born six children, four of whom are now living: Sarah Frances (born in 1847), William Thomas (born in 1849, and died in 1857), Alice Jane (born in 1858), an infant (died unnamed), Charles Calvin (born May 7, 1861) and Lititia (born in 1863). Sarah Frances married W. Yarbrough, a native of Tennessee, is the mother of three children, and now resides in

White County. Calvin C. married Miss Ella Boen, a native of Alabama, and now resides with parents. Martha Ann married James Kilo, a native of Arkansas, and has one child. They also reside with the parents. Mr. Malone came to Arkansas in 1856, located in Independence County, and there made their home for one year, he engaged in tilling the soil. In 1857 he came to White County, located on his present farm, and there he has since made his home. The original tract contained about 194 acres, which were uncultivated at that time. Mr. Malone has purchased other tracts at various times and has always sold to advantage. He has put all the improvements on his place and has about fifty-three acres under fence. The soil is of good quality and furnishes nearly all the necessaries of life, corn and cotton being the principal crops. Vegetables of all kinds grow in abundance, and he also raises some tobacco which is of good quality. Mr. and Mrs. Malone are members of the Methodist Episcopal Church, and have held membership since 1843. They live true Christian lives and have the love and esteem of a large circle of friends. Mr. Malone is a member of Cedar Grove Lodge, A. F. & A. M., and is also a member of the Agricultural Wheel No. 88. The parents of Mr. Malone were natives of North Carolina, and were married in that State. They were of Scotch-German descent and their ancestors on both sides came to the United States prior to the Revolutionary War. Grandfather Malone served seven years in the Colonial War and drew a pension for some years previous to his death, which occurred at the age of eighty-one years. Grandfather Parks also participated in that war, serving in the capacity of colonel, and died about 1804. To Stephen and Sarah (Parks) Malone were born thirteen children, all of whom grew to maturity.

Mrs. Malinda J. Malone, proprietress of a well-kept hotel at Auvergne, Ark., is a daughter of Henry R. and Mary E. (Follis) Bray, the former a Baptist minister and a native of Virginia, and the latter born in the "Palmetto State." They were married in Alabama in 1832, and shortly afterward moved to Lynnville, Tenn., where they made their home for twelve years, Mr. Bray being engaged in conducting a large woodyard, blacksmith's shop and also attended to his ministerial duties. In 1850 Rev. Bray removed with his family to Alabama, where he followed the occupation of farming and preaching until 1860, when he settled in Madison County, Ark., and two years later moved to Cotton Plant, in Phillips County, where he resided five years. In the fall of 1867, he came to Jackson County, and purchased 250 acres of land and was here residing at the time of his death in July, 1870, his wife's death occuring five years later. Mrs. Bray was a daughter of William and Mary (Dickinson) Follis who were natives of South Carolina, and removed to Alabama at an early day. The father's ancestors were Virginians and of Irish descent. Mrs. Malone is the eldest of a family of nine children and is the only one now living, her birth occurring on November 23, 1837. The remainder of the family were: William R. (born March 14, 1839; he was twice married and died January 3, 1888, two children and his last wife surviving him), Mary E. (was born August 1, 1841, and was married to Gabriel Couch of Jackson County, Ark., and died in 1871), Sarah A. (was born in 1843, and was the wife of G. C. Harrison, by him becoming the mother of three sons; she died in 1882), Charity E. (was born 1845 and was twice married, her first husband being William Johnson and her last Newton Bleakley; she died in 1880, leaving two sons, Charley W., who resides with Mrs. Malone and William, who lives in New Mexico), Iradel (was a farmer of Texas, but in 1881 moved to Jackson County, Ark., and died the same year), Martha (was the wife of Levi Blakely and died in 1871 leaving no issue), Boldon (died in 1877 at the age of eighteen years) and a little sister, Katie (died in infancy). Mrs. Malone was reared in Lynnville and in that town and in Rogersville, Ala., received her education. In 1854 she was married to B. T. Malone, she at that time being only fourteen and a half years of age and he nineteen. Their children are named as follows: John T. (a miller at Athens, Ala., has a wife and two children, Charlie and Dollie), Henry E. (a man of Thornton, Miller County, Ark.; is married and has had five children but now has only three, Emmet, aged nine; Lulu, aged seven, and Lucile, aged five), Emma (is a young lady at home), Mollie L. (was born in 1863 and is the wife of J. A. Canada, a merchant of Beebe; she died in 1885 and her husband and one child survive her), Dollie (was born August 1, 1872, and died May 7, 1886), Mattie (was born August 2, 1866, and died August 6, 1877), Linnie (was born January 1, 1877 and died April 1, 1879), James W. (was born August 3, 1858 and died June 2, 1859) and Charles (born August 2, 1876, and died in infancy). After their marriage Mr. and Mrs. Malone resided in Tennessee until 1859 and after a short residence in Northern Alabama they settled in Mississippi and there made their home for ten years. In 1869 they removed to and purchased a large plantation in Jackson County, Ark., and there also managed a mercantile establishment up to 1877, when they sold their land and moved to Beebe, purchasing considerable town property at that place on which they erected good buildings. Mr. Malone was also engaged in merchandising; in his political views was an active Democrat and held the offices of magistrate and notary public for a considerable length of time. He was a leading member of the Baptist Church and was a member in good standing of the Masonic fraternity. Mr. Malone died in 1884 and his widow immediately put her shoulder to the wheel, increased her stock of dry goods and carried on the business at Beebe, and also erected a store at Auvergne which she put in charge of her son Henry E., her eldest son conducting the business at Beebe. In 1877 Mrs. Malone located in Auvergne and took charge of the Auvergne academy and for one year filled the office of matron of that institution. In September, 1888, she opened a hotel which she is at present successfully conducting and since the death of her husband she has so successfully conducted the property he left that it has greatly increased in value. She is a lady of great force of character and more than ordinary powers of mind and has reared her family in such a manner as to win the respect of all with whom she comes in contact. She is a member of the Missionary Baptist Church and her family are also church members.

Jeremiah E. Manasco. The Manasco family,

or rather that branch to which the subject of this sketch belongs, were early settlers of Arkansas, having originally come from Alabama, and were in all probability of French descent. Mr. Manasco, our subject, was born in Tipton County, Tenn., in 1833 or 1834, and is a son of James and Ruby E. (Crawford) Manasco, both of whom died about the year 1841, and although he was the youngest of a family of nine children, he was left to shift for himself, and became a bound boy to his brother John, and was reared by him to manhood on a farm. He suffered the trials of the orphan, and although his school advantages were very limited, and he was compelled to work very hard, he remained faithful to his bondsman till he reached his twenty-first year, when he drifted out into the world to try his own powers. He first engaged as a farm hand, doing all kinds of heavy work, becoming in the meantime thoroughly familiar with the details of farm work. In 1857 he was married to Miss Mary J. Flanagan, a native of Tennessee, and by her became the father of six children, three of whom lived to be grown: John F. (a railroad man of Little Rock), William J. (a resident of Tennessee), Preston V. (deceased), Amandeville W. (living) and twin girls, Emily and Martha (who died in infancy). The mother of these children died in September, 1869, in full communion with the Methodist Episcopal Church. After remaining a widower two years, Mr. Manasco married Miss Virginia P. Wooten, a native of Tennessee, and of their large family of ten children all are living: Nellie Naomi, May L., George W., Calla D., Bedford F., Reuben B., Fanny, Helen, Bertha and Leonora M. In 1864 Mr. Manasco joined the Twelfth Tennessee Cavalry, but owing to weak eyes soon left the service. Before the war and afterward till January, 1872, Mr. Manasco carried on farming in his native State, and in this calling succeeded far beyond his expectations, but sold his property in December, 1871, and in 1872 removed to Prairie County, Ark., where he rented land and farmed for three years. Since that time he has resided in White County, and in 1875 purchased 160 acres of land, on which were erected some log-cabins on fifty acres of cleared land. He set ener-

getically to work to improve his property, and soon had one of the finest homes in White County. In June, 1885, he had the misfortune to lose his residence and nearly all its contents by fire, but he has since rebuilt, and now has one of the most substantial residences in the county. By subsequent purchases he has increased his lands to 245 acres, and has 100 acres under cultivation. The land is well adapted to raising all kinds of grain, but his principal crops are corn, cotton and oats. Mr. Manasco is public-spirited and enterprising, and has always favored worthy movements. He is a member of El Paso Lodge No. 65 of the A. F. & A. M.

John S. Marsh, one of the well-known farmers and stock raisers of White County, is the son of Roland and Sarah (Webb) Marsh, his birth occurring in Warren County, Tenn., July 28, 1825. Roland Marsh was born and educated in North Carolina, emigrating when quite young to Tennessee in company with his parents, where he met and married Miss Webb, also of North Carolina nativity, and the daughter of Elisha and Sarah Webb. To the union of Mr. and Mrs. Marsh five children were born, four of them now living, and residents of Arkansas. They are Harry, Pollie, Sarah, Rachel and John S. Mr. Marsh was a farmer, and quite successful in the accumulation of wealth. He died in 1835, and his estimable wife only survived him about a year. Both were members of the Baptist Church. John S. passed his boyhood days in the schools of Warren County, Tenn., and in 1845 was united in the bands of matrimony to Annie Potter, also of Tennessee. Ten children blessed their marriage: Rollin, Tillman, Sarah J., Thomas M., Jackson R., Martha, William H., Martina and Martisia (twins) and Johnnie. Mrs. Marsh died in 1873, and in 1879, Mr. Marsh chose for his second wife Sarah Gordon, a resident and native of Tennessee. In 1849, when the subject of this sketch immigrated to Arkansas from Tennessee (locating in White County), he found himself the possessor of a single wagon and a yoke of oxen, the two comprising his worldly all. He now owns 120 acres of land well culti-vated, and having exercised great care in the selection of his stock, has some excellent animals. His farm, though not as large as some in the county, is perfectly complete in all its appointments, and its general appearance is indicative of peace and prosperity. Mr. Marsh takes a great interest in all educational matters, and is determined that his children shall be deprived of nothing that tends to advance their intellectual training. He is one of the organizers of the first church established in Mount Pisgah, and is an influential member. His wife and entire family are all members of the Methodist Church. He belongs to Lodge No. 460 of the Masonic order, in which he has held the office of treasurer.

John W. Matthews was the eldest son in the family of Robert and Annie (Howard) Matthews, the former of whom came upon the stage of life's action in Alabama, in 1802. His parents were Walter and Rachel Matthews, of South Carolina origin, but who moved to Alabama at an early day. Robert Matthews was married about 1830, and followed the occupation of a farmer all his life. Coming to Arkansas in 1836 (his family following him in 1852), he settled in White County; his wife had died shortly before his removal. Mr. Matthews enlisted as a soldier during the Civil War in 1863, and served until his death, which occurred at Rock Port in 1864. Himself and wife had a family of three children: John W., Sarah J. and Delia F. John W., the only surviving member, was born in Alabama in 1832, and was married in 1858 to Nancy Brady, daughter of William and Mirah (Cordal) Brady. Mr. and Mrs. Matthews are the parents of nine children: Mirah Ann (now Mrs. Pruett), Mary Jane (married S. M. West), James C., William R., John W., Joseph E., Benjamin F., Ester A. and Nancy N. Mr. Matthews enlisted in 1861 in Morse's company, Fourth Battalion, Arkansas Infantry, and took part in the battles of Cotton Plant, Ark.; Columbus, Ky., and a number of other engagements. He now owns a fine farm of 313 acres of land, 175 acres of which are under cultivation. Mrs. Matthews is a member of the Baptist Church. Mr. Matthews is treasurer of the County Wheel, and is an influential and highly respected citizen.

Burwill M. Merrill is a member of the go-ahead, enterprising firm of Merrill & Reed, dealers in real estate in Beebe, Ark., a native of the "Empire State." He was born in Chautauqua County in 1835, as the son of George and Eliza (Millard) Merrill, natives of Massachusetts and Canada, respectively. George Merrill was born in 1809, and died in 1884, his wife, who was also born at an early date, dying at Burwill's birth. The latter, the only child of his father's first marriage, when about five years old, moved to Michigan with his parent, who became a very successful farmer in the "Wolverine State," giving his careful and undivided attention to that occupation. By his second marriage Mr. Merrill became the father of two children, only one now living: Letitia (wife of John Gordon, a farmer of Floyd County, Iowa). Burwill M. Merrill was given such advantages for obtaining an education as the excellent schools of Michigan afforded, and at the age of twenty-one assumed the responsibility of his father's farm, the care of which he continued until the latter's death in 1884. In 1854 he was married to Miss Lydia Wilson, a native of Canada, and to their union two children were born: Letitia (the wife of J. C. Covert, manufacturer of store fronts and other building materials, at Belmont, Iowa) and De Forest (a mechanic at Detroit). Mrs. Merrill died in 1867, having been a devoted wife and mother, and a member of the Baptist Church. Mr. Merrill chose for his second wife Miss Alviria Cross, who also died in Clinton County, Mich., in 1884, having become the father of two children: George W. (who died at the age of eighteen, unmarried) and Florence L. (now the wife of Dr. A. C. Jordon, a prominent physician of Beebe, Ark., with which daughter Mr. Merrill now resides). He came to Arkansas in 1885, that he might find a home in a more genial climate, also desiring to try small fruit raising in this favored section. Purchasing sixty acres in White County, one mile west of Beebe, he at once turned his attention to the cultivation of small fruits and grasses. Mr. Merrill has tried all kinds of grasses, and is thoroughly convinced that the soil of White County will produce liberally any of the various kinds grown so bountifully in the

East and North. Red clover, three feet in length, was raised on his farm one season, which was something of a curiosity. He is now successfully raising regular crops of clover and timothy. Strawberries and root crops yield immensely. Garden vegetables are especially productive, sweet potatoes yielding 350 bushels per acre. Mr. Merrill is a member of Beebe Lodge No. 47, I. O. O. F., and has passed all the chairs in the subordinate lodge. He has been a member of the Methodist Episcopal Church for many years, and is a public-spirited, enterprising man, giving his hearty support to all movements that betoken the good or growth of the county.

Christian Miller is a farmer and fruit grower of White County, Ark. This gentleman was born on Bornholm Island, Hasley, Denmark, in 1842, and is the second in a family of ten children, the result of the union of John and Elizabeth Miller, natives, also, of Denmark, and who died in their native land. Their children were named as follows: Mary, Christian, Sena, John, Petra, Lena, Otto Line (deceased), Andrew, James and Julyno. Four of these children came to this country, two of whom reside in Wyoming. Andrew and the subject of this sketch came to Arkansas and settled in White County. The latter spent his youth in his native country, was educated there and came to America in 1865, but first settled in New York. Later he moved to Illinois, remained there until 1871, and then, as stated above, came to White County, Ark., and settled in Harrison Township. He purchased eighty acres of timber land, improved it, and has added to the original tract until he now owns 240 acres, with 130 acres cleared and 100 acres devoted to horticulture. Mr. Miller was married in Illinois in 1871 to Miss Mary Hahn, daughter of Saro Hanson and Eline Christian Hahn, natives of Denmark. Mary Hahn came to America in 1861, first settling in Illinois. Mrs. Mary Hahn's marriage to Christian Miller was in 1871. After his marriage Mr. Miller moved to Arkansas, where he has remained ever since. He has about sixteen acres of land devoted to the raising of strawberries, ten acres in raspberries, and an extensive peach orchard of sixty acres. He is one of the most extensive shippers in Judsonia. He is also the owner of a good town property in Judsonia. Socially, he is a member of Anchor Lodge No. 384, A. F. & A. M., and he and wife are members of the Missionary Baptist Church, of which he is a deacon. He is active in church and educational matters, and, in fact, takes a decided interest in all enterprises for the good of the county.

John S. Mitchell, M. D., whose professional career is one in which he may take just pride, is a son of a veteran of the Mexican War, James S. Mitchell, and has been a resident of White County since 1858. James S. Mitchell was born in Monroe County, Ky., on August 14, 1793, and was married shortly after his return from the War of 1812, in which he was actively engaged, to Miss Sarah Scott, a Tennesseean by birth, born January 18, 1795. They were the parents of seven children: Dorcas (afterward Mrs. Gist), Frances (Wilson), Mary (Dies), Matilda (Barger), John S. (our subject) and Louis B. (who is also a physician of Monroe County. Mrs. Mitchell's family were also originally from Tennessee. The Mitchells were connected with the celebrated Boone family of Kentucky. John S. was born in Kentucky November 14, 1824, growing to manhood on a farm, and accompanying his father to Henderson County, Tenn., when a boy. He was married December 30, 1849, to Miss Sarah J. Dotson, daughter of Thomas and Charlotte (Pipkin) Dotson, who were married in 1815, and became the parents of four children. After his marriage, Dr. Mitchell returned to Tennessee, living there nine years. In the spring of 1858 he came to White County, where he bought a farm of two hundred acres of unimproved land, clearing the same himself, and placing over half of it under cultivation. Himself and wife have been blessed with seven children, five of whom are living: Irena F. (Swinford), James B., William B., John T. (deceased), Albert G., Sally A. and Virgil. Dr. Mitchell also has ten grandchildren. He is a strong Democrat, and served as justice of the peace during the war and until the reconstruction. A Master Mason, he belongs to Centre Hill Lodge No. 114, and to Centre Hill Chapter. Dr. Mitchell and wife are connected with the Christian Church.

Two of their children only are living at home at the present time.

Nathaniel Lee Mitchell. The entire life of Mr. Mitchell has been passed in an industious manner, and not without substantial evidences of success, as will be seen from a glance at his present possessions. His birth occurred on April 11, 1828, and he is a son of Charles B. and Nancy (Miller) Mitchell and a native of Boonville, Cooper County, Mo. His paternal ancestors came to America in 1760, and the paternal grandfather, Thomas Mitchell, was born in the State of Virginia. The Millers came to America prior to the Revolution, probably about 1750. Owing to war troubles Great-grandfather Miller was forced from his home, and without his family, which consisted of his wife and infant, he was compelled to flee elsewhere for protection. Grandfather Miller was born in North Carolina, about 1780. Nathaniel Lee Mitchell received his early education in the district schools of his native county, and afterward entered the high school of Boonville, his school-days ending in the State University at Columbia, Mo., in 1850. In 1850 he crossed the plains to the gold region of California, and there worked in different mines for about one and a half years, his labors being attended with fair results, and he then returned to his home in Missouri, and the following year became second assistant of Solomon Houck, who was engaged in freighting goods between Kansas City, Mo., and Santa Fe, N. M., making one trip which required about eight months' time. In 1853 he again crossed the plains to California, via Salt Lake City, Utah, and as before only met with moderate success. At the end of two years he engaged in the butcher's business, and in 1857 bought a farm in Yolo County, consisting of 160 acres of improved land. In addition to managing this farm, he engaged in teaching, but in 1859 concluded to return home, so sold his property, and after returning home, engaged in collecting notes, and in 1861 rented a farm near Sedalia. The troubles incident to the war coming up at this time, he left his farm and enlisted in Company G, Second Missouri Volunteer Cavalry, Confederate States Army, under Gen. Price, who was at that time commanding the Confederate army in Southwest Missouri. Almost immediately after joining he was called to duty in the commissary department, and was given the rank of captain. After holding this position two years he resigned, and returned to duty with his company as a private soldier, and was at various times under the famous cavalry leaders : Price, Forrest, Chalmers and Armstrong. He surrendered with his command at East Port, Tenn., and was paroled at Columbus, settling soon after at Panola, Miss., where he became acquainted with Miss Susan A. Hall, to whom he was unifed in marriage on November 30, 1865. She is a Mississippian by birth, and is a daughter of Porter and Mary Hall (the father of Scotch-Irish descent, and a native of South Carolina). Some of his ancestors were soldiers in the Continental army during Revolutionary times. After their marriage Mr. and Mrs. Mitchell rented and farmed land for one year, and in 1866 immigrated to Missouri, and took up their abode on a farm near Kansas City, on which they resided three years. In 1870 they came to White County, but eleven years later moved to Washington County, where they purchased a forty-acre tract of land. Since 1884 they have resided on their present farm. Their children are: Mary M. (born August 30, 1866, and died in September, 1872), Charles Porter (born May 18, 1868, and is now studying medicine under the tutelage of Dr. McIntosh, of Beebe. He was married November 15, 1888, to Miss Mattie Byram, a native of Arkansas, and a daughter of William W. and Margaret (Williams) Byram), and William Nathaniel Mitchell (born January 6, 1871). These children have received good educational advantages, and are a credit to their parents. Mr. Mitchell is a Democrat, serving his party for years as justice of the peace, and he and his wife, and their son Charles and wife, are members of the Methodist Episcopal Church, South. Mr. Mitchell is favorable to educational and religious advancement and in fact all worthy movements. He became a Mason in 1859, joining Cooper Lodge No. 36, and now holds a demit from that lodge, bearing date January 23, 1886.

Josiah J. Moncrief, M. D., Hammonsville, Ark.

This able and successful practitioner owes his nativity to Harris County, Ga., where his birth occurred on April 13, 1858, as the son of George W. and Emily A. (Calhoun) Moncrief. The father is a native of Georgia, and of French descent, his ancestors having emigrated to America prior to 1770, and settled in Georgia. The grandfather, Lebanon Moncrief, was a soldier under Gen. Jackson, and was at the battle of New Orleans in 1812. The maternal ancestors were of Irish descent. Dr. J. J. Moncrief moved with his parents to Alabama in 1857, acquired a good English education, and in 1881 entered the office of D. Dunlap, M. D., where he commenced the study of medicine in St. Clair County, of that State. In 1887 he attended a course of lectures in the Medical Department of the University of Arkansas, situated at Little Rock, and later located at Tupelo, Jackson County, Ark., where he practiced medicine for a short time. In April of 1889, he came to Hammonsville, where he located, and where he contemplates making his home. The Doctor is a member and secretary of Hammonsville Lodge of the A. F. & A. M. He also holds membership in the Methodist Episcopal Church, South.

William Bird Moon, M. D., is a native of Georgia; born June 12, 1821. He was reared and educated in his native State, receiving his medical education in Louisville Medical Institute, now the Medical University of Kentucky, following which he began practicing physic in 1845. After having remained in Georgia eight years he moved to Alabama and continued in active practice for nineteen years, coming thence to White County, Ark., in 1872, where he purchased real estate, upon which he now lives. Dr. Moon was married October 19, 1845, to Roena Cathrine Spratlen, daughter of Henry and Mary Spratlen, natives of Georgia. The Doctor and his wife are the parents of eleven children: Mary Caroline (born August 15, 1846, married S. S. Pearson in 1867, and died January 27, 1878), Francis L. (born April 21, 1848, married H. M. Ware, died March 26, 1876), Jacob Oliver (born July 31, 1856, died October 31, 1877), Susan C. (born June 20, 1854, married D. G. Copeland, and died March 27, 1888), James Calhoun (born October 8, 1864, died August 27, 1865), Theodosia Earnest (born May 31, 1866, died October 6, 1873), William David (born February 11, 1850, married Allie E. Darden), Ana P. (born April 19, 1852, married H. McKay), Emma Wilkinson (born September 6, 1858, married W. E. Powel), Robert Urial (born July 22, 1860, married G. H. Neely), and Alice Virginia (born September 5, 1862, married G. C. Layne). Dr. Moon is a son of Jacob and Mary Ann (Staples) Moon, who were also of Georgia nativity. Their ancestors came originally from Virginia. Jacob Moon was born September 28, 1795, and died August 13, 1877, and his wife, whose natal day was December 6, 1799, died November 16, 1876. Dr. Moon's brothers and sisters are: Lavina (born December 28, 1817, died in 1840), David Staples (born November 16, 1819), John Chapel (born August 15, 1824, died April 9, 1855), Thomas (born February 24, 1827, died March 21, 1852), Mary Ann (born February 18, 1829), Susan E. (born July 9, 1841). Dr. Moon is a devoted Democrat. He and his wife are members of Missionary Baptist Church, and take active interest in all laudable enterprises. He is deacon of his church.

William D. Moon, M. D., is a worthy son of one of the most esteemed residents of this county. His parents were Dr. William B. and Roena C. (Spratlen) Moon, natives of Georgia, who moved to Alabama in 1853, as stated in the biography which immediately precedes this. William D. Moon first saw the light of day in 1850, improving to the utmost the advantages enjoyed for receiving an education in the common schools of Alabama. In 1877 he attended the medical college at Louisville, where his father had studied, and in 1878 commenced practicing in White County, Ark., which locality has been his parents' home for some years. His later career has been an encouraging and highly satisfactory one. Dr. Moon was married in the fall of 1872, to Allie E. Darden, daughter of J. W. and Nancy H. Darden. They have a family of four children: Robert E. Lee (deceased), Lena L., Yandell and William Darden. Dr. Moon and wife are members of the Missionary Baptist Church. The former is a Democrat in politics and is a highly respected citizen. Yandell is named after the Yandells in Louisville, Ky., who were fellow-students and teachers of the Doctor's grandfather, and several of them belonged to the medical faculty when the father was attending medical lectures in 1877.

Moore & Lyon are proprietors of the largest livery, sale and feed stables at Searcy. The senior member of the firm, James L. Moore, is a son of Robert W. and Sally (Carter) Moore, natives of North Carolina and Tennessee, respectively. In 1858 the father moved to Arkansas and settled in White County, where he died March 24, 1884. His wife still survives him and resides in Cleburne County with her daughter and younger children. James L. Moore came originally from Tennessee, where his birth occurred July 27, 1857. A year after this event his parents moved to White County, Ark., where he has since made his home, gaining by his upright course a wide and honorable acquaintance. He was engaged in farming until 1887, when he moved to Searcy and embarked in the livery business, the patronage accorded this establishment being liberal and of increasing dimensions. Jack F. Lyon, associated with Mr. Moore in the conduct of the stables referred to, was born in Mississippi, on September 5, 1858, as one of a family of William and Lydia (Arnold) Lyman, of Alabama origin. Mr. and Mrs. Lyman moved to Tennessee in 1864, where the former engaged in farming and remained until 1883, then becoming located in Cross County, Ark. Here he died three years later. Jack F. Lyon removed to White County in 1881, and was occupied in stock raising for the following six years. In 1887 he settled at Searcy and entered into the livery business in company with Mr. Moore. Mr. Lyon has two brothers similiarly occupied in Wayne, Cross County, and another brother is engaged in farming in Cross County. Messrs. Moore & Lyman are doing the largest business, in their line, of any firm in Searcy, and are very popular, being affable and obliging in their intercourse with the public.

M. M. Morris, proprietor of cotton-gin, grist-mill and planing-mill, Searcy, Ark. There are few men of the present day whom the world ac-

knowledges as successful, more worthy of honorable mention, or whose history affords a better illustration of what may be accomplished by a determined will and perseverance, than Mr. Morris. He owes his nativity to Kanawha County, W. Va., where his birth occurred February 25, 1828, and is the third in a family of nine children born to the union of P. H. and Ann (Summers) Morris, natives of West Virginia. The father was a miller by trade, but in connection carried on farming, and became the owner of a large plantation. His death occurred in 1842. The mother is still living, makes her home in West Virginia, and is in perfect health, although eighty-three years of age. Their children were named as follows: Floyd W. (married, and resides in West Virginia), Henry (was killed in White County, by a mule, in 1868), M. M. (subject of this sketch), F. T. J. (married, and resides in Garner, White County, Ark.), F. F. (married, and resides in West Virginia), Nancy Jane (now Mrs. Poindexter, of West Virginia), William (married, and resides in West Virginia), George L. (married, and resides near Searcy) and Harriet Ann (now Mrs. Crisp, resides in the Lone Star State). M. M. Morris was reared in a town in West Virginia, received his education in the subscription schools of that State, and there learned the blacksmith trade. On January 13, 1850, he came to Searcy, engaged in blacksmithing in front of the Gill House, and continued there a number of years. Later he erected the first steam-mill in White County, on Red River, near Searcy, and one year later, or in 1851, at Searcy Landing. Mr. Morris ran the mill over one year, and then sold it. He next engaged in cutting wood, and the same year erected a mill and went to work. He was married on October 22, 1852, to Miss M. J. Story, a native of Tennessee, and the daughter of Henry and Annie (Moore) Story, who were originally from Tennessee. Her parents came to Independence County, Ark., settled in Batesville, in 1844, and here the father followed merchandising the principal part of his life. His death occurred in 1845 or 1846, but his wife survived him many years, and made her home with her son, M. M. Morris. She died in 1868. To Mr. and Mrs.

Morris were born seven children: M. G. (married to Miss Pruitt, and is the father of five children), T. J., W. F., Mary Ellen (widow of Andrew Mc-Ginnis), George L., Henry (died in 1875), Charley and Hattie. Mr. Morris lost his excellent wife in April, 1885. He has been continuously in business for nearly forty years, and, although starting with little or no means, he is now one of the successful and progressive men of the county. He owns sixty-eight acres of land joining Searcy; has about 400 acres under cultivation, and has some fine buildings on his farms, one costing $3,300. He has all the latest machinery for running his farm, and follows agricultural pursuits more extensively than any other man in Gray Township. He is not active in politics, but votes with the Democratic party. Socially, he is a member of Searcy Lodge No. 49, A. F. & A. M. He takes an active interest in all matters relating to the good of the county, and has been a member of the Methodist Episcopal Church for many years. His wife was also a member of the same church. During the late war Mr. Morris was boss workman of a Texas Brigade shop, in Texas Brigade, Col. Taylor's regiment.

George L. Morris, one of the representative men of White County, came to this locality when nineteen years of age. When the war-cry sounded he joined the Confederate army, under Col. McRae, remaining in service until the declaration of peace, mostly on detached duty as wagon master and marshal of trains. After the war he engaged in farming, and, though financially embarrassed when leaving the army, he has, by hard work, good management and economy, become the owner of one of the best farms in White County, 800 acres of land in extent, with 400 of these thoroughly cultivated. Mr. Morris was born in Putnam County, W. Va., in 1840, and is the son of Harry and Annie (Summers) Morris, natives of Old Virginia. Mr. Morris, Sr., was a farmer, miller and distiller. He departed this life in 1840, when about forty years old. Mrs. Morris afterward married Richard Chandler, now deceased. She is still living, somewhere in the neighborhood of eighty-nine years, and has been a consistent and faithful member of

the Baptist Church for seventy-five years. Mr. and Mrs. Morris were the parents of nine children, eight of whom are still living: Floyd (a farmer of Putnam County, W. Va.), M. M. (resides in Searcy), William (an attorney of West Virginia), Ferdenand, Nancy (now Mrs. Poindexter), Harriett (now Mrs. Crisp, of Texas) and George L., our subject, who was united in marriage on May 20, 1868, to Sarah Sewell, a daughter of Frank Sewell, and was born in Tennessee on October 6, 1850. They were the parents of nine children, eight of whom are still living: M. M., John W., Eura May, George W., Minnie Lee, Eura, Kate and Henry. Mr. and Mrs. Morrison worship with the Methodist Episcopal Church, of which Mr. Morris is steward. To him this society is largely indebted for their church edifice, he furnishing the ground on which it stands, and also a part of the material. He is engaged in raising mules and cattle, which he ships to the Southern markets.

James R. Neal is a citizen of Centre Hill, popularly and well known as a prosperous farmer of White County. He is a native of Fayette County, Tenn., and was born in 1840, being the son of William D. and Mary A. J. (Parham) Neal, also of Tennessee origin. William D. Neal's birth occurred August 14, 1809, and in business was a prominent planter of Tennessee. He was married August 19, 1831. His father was also a native of Tennessee, who lived and died there. He had a family of eight children: Betsey, Ann, William D. (the father of our subject), Meredith H., James M., Polly, Nancy and John H. Our subject's maternal grandparents, Thomas and Nancy Parham, were natives of Georgia, and came to Tennessee in 1820. William D. Neal was the father of fourteen children: James T., Martha J., John W., William M., James R. (the principal of this sketch), Elica T., Samuel A., Nancy E. (now Mrs. Clay), Sarah A. (Hicks), Eunice M. (Harrison), Susan H. (deceased), David J., next an infant (who died before it was named) and Newton H. Mr. William D. Neal came to Arkansas in 1842, settling in Searcy County, and in 1853 moved to White County, where he bought a farm of 160 acres, all timbered land, and cleared about sixty of these. James R. Neal spent his early boyhood on the farm and attended the subscription schools. He was married to Mary J. Holland, a native of North Carolina, as were also her parents and grandparents on both sides. James R., his father and four of his brothers were all in the Confederate service. He enlisted on September 13, 1861, in T. H. McRae's regiment, for twelve months, at the end of which time he enlisted for three years or during the war. He participated in the battles of Prairie Grove, Helena, Little Rock and many others, and received his discharge June 5, 1865. He was married while in the service and while home on a furlough. After the war he settled on a farm in this county where he has since resided. To this union were born seven children: Alice C. (Brumlow), Kiddee S., Lucy A. (deceased), Mary J. (Harrison), John W., Ella F. and Henry W. Mr. Neal is a Mason, and belongs to Centre Hill Lodge No. 114. Himself and wife are members of the Missionary Baptist Church; he has a fine farm of 160 acres, with fifty improved and in a high state of cultivation. He is a prominent Democrat, and takes an active interest in all public improvements, or all work for the good of the community.

John H. Neal, Searcy, Ark. This much respected citizen and pioneer came to White County, Ark., in 1850, and settled in Searcy, where he followed merchandising. In 1851 he embarked in the grocery and general merchandising business, and this continued until 1854, he being one of the pioneer business men of Searcy. In 1854 he engaged as clerk in dry-goods business houses, and this continued until 1861. He was born in Maury County, Tenn., in 1830, being the youngest in a family of nine children, born to James and Sarah (Dodson) Neal, natives, respectively, of North Carolina and South Carolina. The father was a planter, and at an early day moved to Tennessee, where he died, in Fayette County, in 1845. The mother died the same year. In their family were the following children: William D. (married, and came to Arkansas in 1844, settled in Searcy County, and followed farming. He enlisted in Van Buren County, in 1861, and re-

ceived a gunshot wound through the thigh. He was taken to Camp Dennison, Ohio, remained as a prisoner until exchanged, and returned in 1863; he died in 1869), Meridith H. (came to White County, in 1852, and lost his first wife the same year. He was a Methodist Episcopal, South, preacher, and returned to Memphis in the fall of 1852, taking charge of South Memphis Church. In 1874 he returned to White County, Ark., and in 1877 went to Tennessee, where he died in 1883), James M. (married, came to White County, October, 1850, and settled in what is now Des Arc Township, where he opened up a farm. His death occurred in 1852), Nancy (married P. L. Downey and moved to Searcy County, Ark., in 1846. Her death occurred in about 1857 or 1858), Elizabeth L. (married W. R. Johnson and moved to Searcy County, Ark., in 1846. She died in Fulton County, Ark., in 1877), Mary G. (married J. J. Crouch, a Methodist minister, and came to Searcy County, Ark., in 1849. He was a pioneer preacher of that county. Her death occurred in 1850), Martha A. (now Mrs. Evans, the only surviving daughter, lives in Izard County) and an infant named Sarah. John H. Neal was reared to farm life, received his education in the schools of Fayette County, Tenn. He commenced for himself at Searcy, Ark., in business, in 1850, and continued thus employed for some time. He was married in Searcy, Ark., in 1852, to Miss Mary A. Clay, a native of Louisiana, but reared in Missouri, and the daughter of Lewis A. and Mary Clay, natives of Virginia. Her father came to White County, Ark., at an early day and died in Searcy in 1874. The mother died some years before. To Mr. and Mrs. Neal were born five children, three now living: Augustus E. (died in 1887, at the age of thirty-three years), James A. (died in 1865, at the age of ten years), John D. (is a prominent educator, and is teaching in the public school at Newport, Ark., where he has taught for six years), Henry Clay (is married and resides in Corsicana, Texas, and is engaged in commercial pursuits) and Mary A. (who is now Mrs. Hale, resides at Texarkana, Ark.). Mr. Neal lost his wife in November, 1863, and was married again, in White County, in

1864, to Mrs. Kiddy A. Neal (*nee* Holland), a native of North Carolina, and the daughter of Willis B. and Lucinda (Barbee) Holland, natives of Wake County of the same State. The father was a planter by occupation, and in February, 1851, immigrated to Henderson County, Tenn., where he continued his former pursuit, and in connection taught school. In 1852 he came to White County, Ark., resided in Gray Township for three years, and in 1854 moved to Des Arc Township, settling where Centre Hill is now located. He sent in the petition and established the postoffice at that place, and was made the first postmaster. In 1860 he moved to Van Buren County, and in 1863 returned to White County, where he remained until 1865, and then moved to Searcy. His death occurred at that place on March 7, 1869. His excellent wife survived him until January 22, 1888. The father was county surveyor, surveyed and resurveyed a great deal of the country. Socially, he was a member of Searcy Lodge No. 49, A. F. & A. M., was also a member of Tillman Chapter No. 19, R. A. M., and was High Priest of the same. He was also a member of Searcy Council No. 12, and aided in the organization of Centre Hill Lodge No. 114. He was a charter member and was Worshipful Master of that lodge. There is a lodge, Holland Lodge No. 158, in Van Buren County, which was named for him. To Mr. Neal's second marriage were born no children. Socially, Mr. Neal is a member of Searcy Lodge No. 49, A. F. & A. M., and was the second Mason initiated into that lodge, having joined in 1852. He has been a Worshipful Master of the lodge, and assisted in organizing Centre Hill Lodge No. 114, and was Worshipful Master of that. He is a member of Tillman Chapter Lodge No. 19, R. A. M., and has been High Priest in the same. He is also a member of Searcy Council No. 12, and has thrice been Illustrious Master of it. Mr. Neal is a member of the Eastern Star Chapter No. 5, and is one of the representative men of the county. Mrs. Neal is a member of the Eastern Star, has been Worthy Matron several times, and was elected First Grand Matron of the State, in 1876, and served one year. She is a member of the Baptist Church, and he a member of the Methodist Epis-

copal Church, South, and both have been members for thirty-six years. During the war Mr. Neal was postmaster and justice of the peace, and after the war (in 1871) he engaged in the undertaking business, which he has carried on successfully ever since that time.

John A. Neavill, Searcy, Ark. There are many citizens represented within the pages of this volume, but none more deserving of mention than Mr. Neavill, who is not only one of the pioneers of the county, but is universally respected by all who know him. He was born in Jackson County, Ala., in 1826, and was the eldest in a family of nine children, born to the union of Elihu and Margaret (Jones) Neavill, the father a native of Alabama, and the mother of North Carolina. Elihu Neavill was married in his native State, in about 1825, settled on a claim and followed agricultural pursuits there until 1844, when he came to White County, Ark. He settled near where his son James A. now resides, entered land, erected a tanyard, and in connection carried on farming and the tannery business until his death, which occurred April 17, 1888. He was a resident of the county for over forty years, and had the esteem and respect of all. He was in the Florida War, was orderly-sergeant and was in service twelve months. He was of French descent, and the mother of Scotch-Irish. Of their family the following children are the only ones living: James A. (subject), Elijah (married and resides in Cane Township), William H. (married, and is the marshal of Searcy) and Mary (now Mrs. F. W. Smith, of Gray Township). James A. Neavill was early taught the rudiments of farming, and received his education in the subscription schools of Alabama and White County, Ark. He was eighteen years of age when he came to Arkansas, and he was employed for a number of years in assisting his father in clearing up the farm. After this he began farming for himself near where he now resides. He was married in White County, Ark., in 1853, to Miss Smith, a native of Mississippi, who bore him two living children: John and William B. The latter is married and resides in Gray Township. Another child, Mary, was the wife of

John Gilliam, and died August 9, 1884. Mrs. Neavill died in 1856, and Mr. Neavill selected his second wife in the person of Mrs. Mary (Barkley) Britt, widow of Mr. Davis Britt, a native of Middle Tennessee, and the daughter of Andrew and Hannah C. (Walker) Barkley. The father was a native of Tennessee, and his ancestors were the earliest settlers of that State. He followed agricultural pursuits and opened up a large tract of land. His death occurred in 1862. The mother was a native of North Carolina, and died in Tennessee, Rutherford County, in 1887, at the advanced age of ninety years. To Mr. and Mrs. Neavill was born one child: Andrew A. After his marriage, which occurred in 1875, Mr. Neavill moved to his present residence, and is now the owner of a good farm of 125 acres, with about seventy acres under cultivation. He is active in politics, and votes with the Democratic party. He is a member of the Agricultural Wheel, takes an active interest in educational matters, and has been a member of the school board. He has also filled the position of constable of his township, and in a highly satisfactory manner. Mrs. Neavill is a member of the Methodist Episcopal Church, South. Grandfather Neavill was in the War of 1812, and was at the battle of New Orleans with Gen. Jackson. Mr. Neavill (subject of this sketch), came to Arkansas in 1844, and can hardly realize that it is the same country now, on account of the many and rapid changes made since that time. Searcy was in the woods, and there were but three houses between that town and Beebe. Off the main traveled roads there were no settlements, and Mr. Neavill has killed many a deer on land now under cultivation, at a distance of 175 yards. He still has in his possession his trusty gun. During the war he was with Gen. Price, in his raid through Missouri, and enlisted in Capt. Black's company, participating in the following battles: Pilot Knob, Ironton, Newtonia, Blue Gap, etc. He was with Gen. Price until reaching Fayetteville, Ark., when he returned to White County.

Charles E. Newman, farmer, fruit grower and educator of White County, Ark., was born in Madison County, Ill., on Feburary 17, 1844, and is the eldest of six children born to William E. and Martha A. (Harrison) Newman, the former a native of Madison County, Ill., the latter originally of Kentucky. William E. was also of a family of six children. His father was a native of Pennsylvania, and one of the early settlers of Illinois, locating in the territory as early as 1804. They trace their family name back five generations to Ireland. William E. Newman lived and died in the county in which he was born. His birth occurred in February, 1821, was married in 1843, and died June 17, 1886. He and his wife were members of the Cumberland Presbyterian Church, and became the parents of the following named children: Charles E. (the subject of this sketch), Eliza (now Mrs. Fields, living near the old homestead), Mary (Kimball, now deceased), Henry (still living near the old homestead), Ida (deceased) and Mattie (married October 5, 1887, now living in Montgomery County, Ill.). The mother of these children still resides at the old home, and is a daughter of William and Mary (McClure) Harrison, Virginians, who at an early day removed to Kentucky, in which State she was born, being one of four children: Maria, Martha, Elizabeth and Benjamin. Charles E. obtained his education in the common schools of Illinois, and assisted his father on the farm. August 9, 1862, he enlisted in Company D, One Hundred and Seventeenth Illinois Volunteer Infantry, under Col. R. M. Moore, and went to the front to do battle for his country, participating in a number of battles and skirmishes during his three years' service. He received his discharge June 3, 1865, and upon returning home, commenced teaching school in the same room he left three years before to wear the blue. After spending two years teaching, he took Horace Greeley's advice and went West, locating near Paola, Miami County, Kas., again engaging as a pedagogue, remaining in the same school seven years. He was married November 9, 1871, to Amanda L. Porter, daughter of John and Amanda (Hampton) Porter, people from Ohio, in which State Mrs. Amanda Newman was born June 11, 1849. Mr. Newman was engaged in horticulture in Kansas, in connection with teaching, but the grasshopper scourge of 1874 caused him to return to Illinois, where an educator received better pay and a longer school term. He followed teaching until 1884, when, September 3, of that year, he came to Arkansas, and settled at Judsonia, where he has followed farming, fruit growing and teaching. He has sixty-five acres of good second bottom land under cultivation, devoted to general farming and fruit growing. He takes an active interest in the political issues of the day. In religious faith himself and wife are Cumberland Presbyterians. They have three children: Lillian (born September 3, 1872), Edna (born September 26, 1877) and Ethel (born February 3, 1887).

Elijah B. Norvell. Although in his active career through life Mr. Norvell has not amassed the wealth which has fallen to the lot of many others, yet he is in comfortable circumstances, and has gained to an unlimited extent the confidence and esteem always awarded integrity, honor and industry. His birth occurred in Bedford County, Tenn., April 5, 1841, and is a son of David and Martha (Bomar) Norvell, who were also born in that State, and were of Scotch-Irish and Dutch descent. By occupation the father was a farmer, and for several years he served his county as bailiff and deputy sheriff. He died in the State of his birth in 1858, his wife dying at her home in White County, Ark., in 1869. Their children are: David (a physician of Johnson County), Elijah B., B. B. (a farmer of Texas), Mary (wife of Charles Devers, a farmer of Johnson County), William (a farmer of Boone County), R. H. (a mechanic of Texas) and Martha (wife of James Holiday, of Johnson County). Like the majority of farmers' boys, Elijah B. Norvell was compelled to work hard in his youth, and received very little schooling, but being possessed of a bright intellect, and through his own exertions he obtained a very good general knowledge of the world of books. In 1861, when he was in his nineteenth year, he joined the army, enlisting in Company B, Forty-fourth Tennessee Infantry, and during his service of nearly three years, he was in the battles of Shiloh, Hoover's Gap, Tullahoma and others, being wounded in the first-named engagement. After his return home he worked as a rail-

road hand for about three years, then engaged in the liquor business in Tennessee, continuing one year, and in 1866 came to Arkansas, conducting the same business at Stony Point a year longer. Since that time he has been engaged in farming, the first two years renting land, after which he purchased a farm of forty acres on Bull Creek, which he improved and four years later sold. In 1886 he purchased eighty acres of his present farm, and now has 120 acres, of which fifty-five are under cultivation. The soil is fertile, and is well adapted to raising corn, cotton, oats and all kinds of fruit. He has given considerable attention to experimental farming, trying different kinds of seeds and fertilizers, and has succeeded far beyond his expectations, and the past year had perhaps the best cotton in Union Township. In 1881 he purchased property in Beebe, and was a resident of that town for three years in order to give his children the benefit of the city schools, but farm life being more congenial to his tastes, he has since lived in the country. He has been a member of Lodge No. 35 of the Union Wheel ever since its organization, and in 1885 was a delegate to the National Wheel, which met at Little Rock, and to the State Wheel, which convened at the same time and place. Although formerly a Democrat in politics, he has been a member of the Union Labor party for the last few years. In 1869 he was married to V. A. Mossey, a native of Shelby County, Tenn., and a daughter of Jerry Mossey, a farmer and later a merchant of Beebe. Of a family of seven children born to them, four are now living: Robert H. (who is at present attending the schools of Beebe, and is in every respect an exemplary young man, was born in October, 1871), Virginia (was born in 1878), George's birth occurred in 1880, and Ruth was born in 1883. Mr. Norvell and his family worship in the Methodist Episcopal Church, and he has filled the office of steward.

T. J. Oliver, farmer and stock raiser, Searcy, Ark. A lifetime of hard, earnest endeavor in pursuing the occupation to which he now gives his attention, coupled with strict integrity, honesty of purpose and liberality in directions, have had a result to place Mr. Oliver among the truly respected and honored agriculturists of the county. To this he has continually added improvements of a high order, until now about the place everything is in excellent condition. He was born in Maury County, Tenn., in 1833, was the eleventh in a family of thirteen children born to Hezekiah and Mahala (Shumac) Oliver, natives of the Old Dominion. The father was a tiller of the soil, and in 1820 moved to Maury County, Tenn., where he entered land, and made that his home a number of years. Later he moved to West Tennessee, where his death occurred in 1867. His wife died about 1848. He was in the War of 1812. T. J. Oliver was reared to farm life, and received his education in the schools of Tennessee. When it became necessary for him to start out in life for himself, he very naturally and wisely chose the occupation to which he had been reared, and from that time to the present his success has been such as only a thorough acquaintance with his calling and years of experience might lead him to achieve. At the age of twenty-one he commenced farming in Madison County, Tenn., and purchased a timber tract, which he improved. He was married in Gibson County, Tenn., in 1860, to Miss Mary E. Scott, a native of Arkansas, born in Fayetteville, and received her education at the Memphis (Tenn.) State Female Academy. She is the daughter of Dr. Scott, who was assassinated at Memphis in 1864. After his marriage Mr. Oliver settled in Madison County, and in 1861 enlisted in the Twelfth Tennessee Infantry for twelve months, from Gibson County, Tenn., and participated in a number of skirmishes. On account of ill health he was discharged in 1862, and returned to Tennessee, where he engaged in farming. In 1883 he came to White County Ark., purchased an improved farm of 100 acres, with eighty under cultivation, and on this has many good buildings. He is not very active in politics, but votes with the Democratic party at State elections. He is a member of the I. O. O. F. He and wife are members of the Methodist Episcopal Church, South; he has been Sunday-school superintendent for six years, and is one of the progressive men of the town. To his marriage were born these children: Edgar (married, and resides at

Greer, Ark.), Benetta (now Mrs. Witt, of Conway), Roland C., Eugene, Wilber, Herbert Earl and Bertram.

William De Berry Overstreet, now residing on Section 34, Caldwell Township, White County, Ark., is a son of William and Caroline (Jumper) Overstreet, the father a native of South Carolina, and of English ancestors. His forefathers probably came to America before the War for Independence. The maternal ancestors were of English-German descent. The parents of our subject were married November 23, 1832, in Alabama, came to Arkansas in 1860, located near Little Red post-office, in Harrison Township, and there rented land and farmed until 1864, when they moved to Caldwell Township. Here they still continued to till the soil and here the father died October 28, 1882. Their family consisted of the following children: Samuel D. H., David J., Elicas S., Mary Ann, John H., Martha H. C., Eliza F., William De Berry, Dora A. and Paralee J. All the children were born in Tishomingo County, Miss., with the exception of Paralee, and all grew to maturity with the exception of her. William De Berry Overstreet comes of a long-lived race, some of his ancestors living to be over ninety years of age. He was born October 19, 1850, and his educational advantages were enjoyed in the subscription schools of White County. He attended part of a term near what is now known as Little Red Postoffice, also part of a term at Clear Water, then Clear Springs school-house, the whole time of attendance not being more than two months. Mr. Overstreet is a diligent reader, is observing, and is probably better posted on the majority of subjects than many who have had better educational advantages, having made the best use of his opportunities. At the time of the death of his father he was the only son at home, his brothers being away in the Confederate army, and the support of the family, consisting of the mother and three sisters, devolved upon his shoulders until 1865. Then his brother, John H., returned from the war and took part of the duties upon himself for about a year. By the end of that time he was married and the duties again fell upon the shoulders of William, who took care of his sisters until they were married. He is now the counsellor of the family. Mrs. Eliza F. Gordon lost her husband in 1878 and was left with four helpless children, but Mr. Overstreet again came to the assistance, and Mrs. Gordon is now living upon his farm and receives help from him. Her children are now almost large enough to contribute toward her support. October 28, 1870, Mr. Overstreet was united in marriage to Gabriella Lumpkin, a native of Jackson County, born in February, 1857, and the daughter of George W. and Sarah (Martin) Lumpkin, who died when their daughter was but a child. She was then taken by her uncle, Hoyden Edwards, with whom she lived until her marriage. To this union have been born ten children, five of whom are now living: William David (born September 13, 1871), Mary Anna (born May 1, 1873), Dora Lee (born January 7, 1875, and died September 18, 1878), Lula May (born February 20, 1877), Laura Della (born February 10, 1879), Mattie Maud (born February 22, 1881), John Marvin (born October 29, 1885) and three infants, who died unnamed. Mr. Overstreet made his first purchase of land in 1871, and this consisted of 160 acres. He has made all the improvements on his farm, and has one of the most comfortable and home-like places in the county. He has three dwellings on his farm, one occupied by his aged mother and another by Mrs. Gordon. He has good barns, cribs, sheds, etc., and is a thrifty, industrious farmer. He also has a fine peach orchard, which supplies the family with this luscious fruit, and also leaves a surplus for the market. He raises principally cotton, corn, oats and grass. He has a fine grade of cattle, being a cross between the Durham and the native stock, and is also raising some fine hogs, a cross between the Poland-China, the Berkshire and the Chester White, which experience has taught him is a very profitable venture. In politics Mr. Overstreet is a Democrat, but has never been an office seeker. In his religious belief he is a Methodist, and has been a member of that church for twenty-two years. He is a liberal supporter of schools, churches and all laudable enterprises, and is much respected by all acquainted with him. Mrs. Overstreet is also a member of the Methodist Episcopal Church.

Rev. William M. Owen, pastor of the Missionary Baptist Church, Shady Grove, one mile from Bald Knob, is a native of Tennessee, and a son of Felix and Permelia H. (Plant) Owen, of Kentucky and Alabama origin, respectively. Felix Owen came from Kentucky to Fayette County, Tenn., when a young man, and remained there until 1849, when he again moved with his family to Arkansas and located in White County, when the country was but sparsely settled, and with the aid of his family cleared up a farm, on which he lived until a few years before his death (which occurred in 1883, at the age of seventy-four), when he removed to Judsonia. Mrs. Owen is still living at this place and is the mother of eight children, six of whom are living: William M. (our subject), Sarah C. (wife of Rev. E. T. Church), Robert H. (in business in Judsonia), Green B. (a Baptist minister of this county, also engaged in farming), Elizabeth and Melinda (wife of John O. Kelley, of this county). Rev. William M. Owen was born in Fayette County, Tenn., on October 29, 1839, and was educated at the common schools and by self-study at home, and when arriving at the age of manhood (twenty-one), began life as a farmer. In June, 1861, he joined the Third Arkansas Cavalry, remaining in this company until the close of the war, having had part in the battles of Corinth (where he was taken prisoner and held captive at St. Louis and Alton, Ill., for four months), Chickamauga, Atlanta, and many others. After the war he returned home and again commenced farming, in which he has ever since been engaged. In 1867 he joined the Missionary Baptist Church, and in ten years thereafter (1877) was licensed to preach, and the following year was ordained, and since his ordination he has been faithfully engaged in preaching the Gospel, having under his charge three or four churches at a time, and has also been instrumental in organizing a number of new churches, among them the one at Bald Knob. In 1866 he was married to Miss Laura Coffman, a native of Alabama, who died in 1875. She was the mother of four children, only two surviving her: Leander and Mark. In 1877 he was married the second time, to Mrs. Edwards (*nee* Patty), a widow. They are the parents of three children: Gracie M., Willie E. and Edith M. Mrs. Owen, with her two oldest children, belongs to the Missionary Baptist Church.

Littleberry B. Parker is a prominent farmer of White County, and first saw the light of day in Northampton County, N. C., on February 8, 1831, and is a son of Saul and Miriam (Hicks) Parker. Saul Parker was born in England and came over to this country when a boy, and participated in the War of 1812 at Craney Island. He subsequently located at Norfolk, Va., and later removed to North Carolina, where he died in 1835, while yet comparatively a young man. He was a brick-mason by trade. His wife was a native of North Carolina and was the mother of seven children, four of whom are still living: Samuel (a farmer and ex-sheriff of Jasper County, Miss.), Tabitha T. (wife of Jesse Lassiter of Northampton, N. C.), Jacob J. (a farmer and brick-mason, of Lonoke County) and L. B. (our subject). After the death of her husband, Mrs. Parker removed with her family to Calloway County, Ky., subsequently to Madison County, Tenn., and in 1852 came to Arkansas locating in Lonoke County, where she died in 1881, at the age of eighty-four years, and was a member of the Methodist Episcopal Church. L. B. Parker remained with his mother until eight years of age, when he was bound out to James B. Wheeler, a cabinet-maker and farmer of Northampton County, N. C., with whom he remained until Mr. Wheeler's death, which occurred four years later, when he was hired out to a farmer for $1 per month, part of which was to be paid him in money and the balance in clothes. He remained there one year and was then (1844) hired out for a year for $10 for the year, but quit in April and joined an emigrant train and worked his way to Kentucky, where he found employment at $5 per month, and remained there until 1847 when he went to Madison County, Tenn., where he was engaged as a mail-carrier during the year 1847. He then farmed for a short time, after which he was employed on a flat-boat running to New Orleans. One year later he came to Arkansas, locating in White County. At the outbreak of the war he joined the Confederate army in the Fourth Battalion Arkansas Infantry. He served until the surrender of Island No. 10, when his battalion was the only one which escaped by wading back through the water twelve miles to the boat, which they carried to Fort Pillow. Mr. Parker becoming disabled received his discharge at Corinth. He then returned to Arkansas and located in Prairie County, but after the cessation of hostilities he came back to White County locating on the farm which he now calls home, and which was then in the woods. He is the owner of 320 acres, with 100 under cultivation. In January, 1852, he was married to Miss Hannah E. Longmire, who was born on March 22, 1839. Mr. and Mrs. Parker never had any children of their own, but have reared three orphan children: George W. and James Coleman and Mary F. (who is now the wife of William Tidwell). Mrs. Parker is a member of the Presbyterian Church. Mr. Parker has taken the Council degree in the Masonic order, and has represented his lodge in the Grand Lodge of the State several times. He is a strong Democrat and a respected and valuable citizen.

John T. Patterson is one of the well-to-do and successful agriculturists of White County, Ark., and although he has only resided here since 1881, coming from Tennessee, he has become well and favorably known. His birth occurred in Franklin County, Ala., in 1834, and he was the third of a family of nine children born to James and Catherine (Gray) Patterson, the former born in the "Old North State" and the latter in the "Keystone State." James Patterson went to Alabama when the country was new, and opened a plantation which he afterward sold, moving thereafter to Hardeman County, Tenn., with his wife, whom he married in Alabama. They settled on a farm in Tennessee in 1844, and here the father spent his declining years, his death occuring in 1873. He served in the Seminole War. His wife passed from life in 1888. Their children are: Mary Jane (Mrs. Ethridge, resides in Tennessee), William (lives in Kentucky), John T., Hugh (residing in

Conway County, Ark.), Jacob (who died in Tennessee, in 1863), Joseph (who also died in that State in the same year) and Enoch and Franklin (both residents of Tennessee). Joseph Gray, the maternal grandfather, was born in England, and served in the Revolutionary War. John T. Patterson spent his youthful days in attending school and in farm work, and after attaining his twentieth year he began working for himself. He was married in McNairy County, in 1855, to Miss Emeline Brown, a native of North Carolina, and a daughter of Isaac and Millie (Dunn) Brown, who were born, reared and married in the State of North Carolina. In 1844 they removed to McNairy County, where they settled on a farm, on which the mother died, in 1855. The father moved to Bell County, Tex., in 1858, and there is now making his home. From the time of his marriage until 1858, Mr. Patterson lived in Tennessee, then spent two years in Texas, after which he returned to McNairy County. On March 4, 1862, he enlisted in Company C, Thirty-second Illinois Infantry, United States army to defend the Constitution of the United States, but left his wife and two children in the South, with little hope of ever returning to them, but through the kind providence of God returned to them in safety. He was wounded at Shiloh on April 6, 1862, and was confined in the hospital at Savannah, Tenn., for some time, being honorably discharged on July 31, 1862, after which he returned to his home and resumed farming. Since 1881 he has been the owner of 160 acres of land in White County, Ark., and has fifty under cultivation. He is an active supporter of the Republican party, and not only has he been a prominent supporter of schools, but he is a member of the school board. Socially, he is a member of Rock Springs Lodge No. 422 of the A. F. & A. M., of which lodge he has been Worshipful Master for some years. He and his wife are members of the Missionary Baptist Church, and are the parents of the following children: Green Harrison (deceased), Melissa (Mrs. Martindale), Alice (Mrs. Holmes), Isabelle (Mrs. Stringfellow), Arca (Mrs. Langley), Elizabeth, Cordelia, Elzora, Cora Lee and Florence. Two children died in infancy.

Rev. J. A. Pemberton is an elder of the Cumberland Presbyterian Church and by occupation is a farmer, and being one of the old settlers of White County, has figured prominently in public affairs. His native county is Wilson, Tenn., where he was born on December 13, 1825, and is the only one now living of a family of five daughters and three sons born to Thomas J. and Mary (McHaney) Pemberton, who were born in Virginia in 1804 and 1800, respectively. They were married about 1822, and followed the occupation of farming, both being members of the Missionary Baptist Church. Mr. Pemberton took part in the Creek and Florida War, and assisted in the removal of the Creek and Seminole Indians to the western reserves. He died February 26, 1871, and his wife in August, 1861. The Pemberton family came to the New World prior to 1700, from their native country, England, and settled in Virginia, and the great-grandfather was one of four sons of the first settler. When the Revolutionary War came up the grandfather Pemberton was only twelve years of age, so of course did not take part in that struggle. He was one of the first settlers of Tennessee, and in this State reared his family, his son, Thomas J., being a relative of Gen. Pemberton of the Southern army, in the late Civil War. Andrew McHaney, the maternal grandfather, was born in Ireland, and as a boy joined the American army and took part in the Revolutionary War, serving from the beginning until the close. He was in Col. William Washington's command, and was present at the battle of Cowpens and witnessed the personal encounter between Washington and Tarleton, in which the latter fled with a sword gash in his hand. After the war was over he settled in Tennessee, where he became a wealthy planter, and died at the age of sixty-five years. Rev. J. A. Pemberton, our subject, attended subscription school in the old-fashioned log-houses of his day, and at the age of twenty-one years began an independent career. In 1846 he married Miss Sarah C. Harrison, and with her removed to Arkansas in 1857 and entered 160 acres of land a few miles northwest of where Beebe now is. When the war came up he, in July, 1861, enlisted in the Tenth Arkansas Infantry, and was made captain of a company which he had assisted in organizing. While in the infantry service he participated in the battle of Shiloh, but in the latter part of 1862 he became a member of the cavalry, and was at Helena, Little Rock, Pine Bluff, Pilot Knob, and was with Price until that General's command was divided at Fayetteville, in 1864. The same year he was captured at Augusta, and was held a prisoner of war until peace was declared. After his return home he continued to farm near Antioch until 1879, then came to Beebe to live. He became a member of the Cumberland Presbyterian Church in 1865, and since 1874 has been a minister of that denomination and has preached in Beebe and vicinity. He has been a very active worker for the cause of his Master and has expounded the doctrine of his denomination in nearly all the principal churches of White County. He was a member of the General Assembly that met at Bowling Green, Ky., in 1876, and for the last two years has been the representative of the Arkansas Synod. He has never been an office seeker, but since his residence in Beebe has been a member of the board of aldermen, and during the reconstruction period was a member of the board of supervisors of White County. He is a Royal Arch Mason and is a member of Beebe Lodge No. 145. He and wife have never had any children of their own, but have given homes to a number of orphan children, and have reared three from infancy. Mrs. Pemberton is a daughter of J. P. and Ann C. (Sweeney) Harrison, who were born in Virginia, the former of whom was an active soldier in the War of 1812.

Joshua W. Pence, an old settler and prominent citizen, of White County, and postmaster of Egbert, is of Tennessee nativity, and a son of George J. and Rebecca (Webb) Pence, natives of South and North Carolina, respectively. George J. Pence was born in 1802, and was married in Alabama in 1825, and remained there until 1829, when he removed to Warren County, Tenn., and six years later to Williamson County of that State. In 1839 he immigrated to Wilson County, where he died in 1852. He was a member of the Christian Church and a man of decision and strong will

power, and was an old-time Jacksonian Democrat. Mrs. Pence was born in 1806, and in 1855, after her husband's death, came to Arkansas, locating in White County, on the farm on which our subject now lives, and where she died on July 16, 1888. She was a member of the Baptist Church, and was the mother of thirteen children, three of whom are still living: Louisa (widow of William Allen), Joshua W. (the principal of this sketch) and Marion T. (a farmer of Prairie County). Joshua W. was born in Warren County, Tenn., May 18, 1830, and when twenty-two years of age, commenced farming for himself, which occupation he has since followed, and in 1855 commenced farming the place on which he still lives, his mother living with him during the last twenty years of her life. He now has a fine farm of 252 acres, with about seventy-five under cultivation. In June, 1862, he enlisted in the Eighth Arkansas Infantry, but remained only a short time, being discharged on account of disability. Upon his discharge he returned home and found his farm in a state of dilapidation. In 1866 he was elected justice of the peace, which office he held for sixteen consecutive years, and was appointed postmaster of Egbert in February, 1887, which position he is still holding. He was married in February, 1854, to Miss Damaris L. Grissom, a native of Tennessee, who died in 1874, leaving nine children, six of whom are still living: Matilda (now Mrs. Hood), George L. (farmer and justice of the peace, of Dogwood Township), Oren D., Oscar D., Ira R. and Lillie A. Those deceased are Wiley H., Joshua M. and Barbara E. In 1874 he was again married to Mrs. Freeman (nee Belton, a widow, and who died in 1883, leaving no children), and on December 19, 1888, he married his third and present wife, Mrs. Ellen M. Rimer (nee Strodder, also a widow). Mr. Pence and wife are members of the Christian Church. He is a prominent Democrat and a member of the Knights of Labor, and of the County Wheel. He joined the Freemasons in July, 1867, of which he is still a member in full fellowship, in West Point Lodge No. 24. December 23, 1873, he joined the Grange No. 137, and has since filled several prominent offices in that society, such as Master, Overseer, Chaplain, Steward, etc. He and wife also belong to the Famous Life Association of Little Rock, Ark., their policy of membership being limited to the amount of $3,000.

N. B. Pettey. Among the early settlers of White County was our subject, N. B. Pettey, who came to this county with his widowed mother in 1855. Mr. Pettey was a son of George G. and Annie E. (Chappell) Pettey, natives of South Carolina and Virginia, respectively, and was born in Limestone County, Ala., August 26, 1839. Mr. George G. Pettey settled in Alabama at an early day, and later moved to Mississippi, where he died in 1850. Five years later his widow moved to Arkansas with her family, where she died in 1861. N. B. Pettey was raised and educated in Tennessee, Mississippi and Arkansas, and at the age of sixteen went to Hickman County and engaged in clerking, where he remained two years. In 1856 he came to White County, Ark., landing at Negro Hill in September, where he worked at farm labor in the summer season and attended school in the winter. He then went to Searcy and accepted a position as clerk for W. B. Carter, where he remained until 1861, when he enlisted in July of that year in Company E of the Third Arkansas Cavalry, enlisting for three years, or during the war, as private. Mr. Pettey was in the battles of Shiloh, Murfreesboro, and was with Bragg in his invasion of Kentucky, and was in the Georgia campaign. He was captured as a prisoner November 1, 1864, and was taken with Sherman to the coast, and up to Point Lookout, where he was paroled February 21, 1865, and returned and joined his command prior to the battle of Bentonville, N. C. He arrived home at Searcy on June 7, 1865, and took up farming. In 1871 he was elected deputy sheriff, and the following year elected sheriff of the county (White), serving three successive terms. In 1879 Mr. Pettey bought an improved farm of sixty acres, near Centre Hill, and commenced farming, and also engaged in merchandising, which he followed some two or three years. He served as postmaster under President Cleveland's administration. Mr. Pettey was married on September 20, 1866, to Jennie Dannelly, a native of Mississippi, and daughter of Rev. George A. and Annie E. (West) Dannelly, originally of South Carolina and Alabama, respectively. Rev. G. A. Dannelly immigrated to Phillips County, Ark., at an early day, then to Jackson County, where he joined the Methodist Episcopal Conference at Batesville in 1856. He is now in Woodruff County. His wife died in 1865. Mr. and Mrs. Pettey are the parents of two children: George G. and Napoleon B. Mr. Pettey has seen the complete development of the county and has taken an active interest in all work for the good of the community. He is a prominent Democrat, and a member of the I. O. O. F. Mrs. Pettey is a member of the Methodist Church. Her grandfather Dannelly was a member of the Masonic order, of which he held the office of Grand Master of the Grand Lodge of the State, and was Grand Lecturer of the State some five or six years, and was District Deputy Grand Master in 1871. He was also prominently connected with the order of the I. O. O. F.

John Andrew Phelps is a merchant doing business and residing in El Paso, and to him may be applied that often much abused phrase, "self-made man," for he started out in life for himself at the early age of fifteen years, and has attained his present enviable place in business and society. He was born in Haywood County, Tenn., on January 16, 1852, and is one of two children (the other member being J. T. Phelps) born to Philip P. and Arkansas (Overton) Phelps, both of English descent, the former a native of Kentucky and the latter of Virginia. They were married in Tennessee about the year 1850, and in Hardeman County of this State; the father died eight years later. John Andrew Phelps followed various employments until the year 1875, when he began clerking in a mercantile establishment belonging to D. H. Thorn, of Jonesboro, Ark., and during a three years' stay with this gentleman became thoroughly familiar with all the details of the work. During this time Mr. Thorn was sheriff of the county, and Mr. Phelps acted as his deputy, and in this capacity rendered valuable service. Upon leaving Mr. Thorn he rented land in Craighead County of the Hon. W. H. Cate, who, taking a fancy to our subject, gave him an excellent chance and furnished him with stock to till his land. During this time he also acted as foreman of Mr. Cate's cotton-gin, and upon leaving this gentleman, took with him about $500 in money which he had earned. On April 3, 1879, he was united in marriage to Miss Avey Broadway, by whom he has one child, John Andrew, who was born on November 30, 1884. In 1879 Mr. Phelps engaged in merchandising in El Paso in company with his brother, J. T. Phelps, and M. L. Booth, under the firm name of Booth & Phelps, continuing in business with those gentlemen until 1882, at which time Mr. Booth withdrew from the firm and the two brothers continued alone under the firm name of Phelps & Bro. This partnership was dissolved in 1883, and the firm then took the name of Phelps & Co., and from 1885 to 1888 Mr. Phelps was in business alone. The firm has since been known as Warren & Phelps, and they carry a large and well-selected stock of general merchandise, and in connection they carry on a harness and saddlery shop, and in this establishment employ none but the best workmen. They are also extensive dealers in cotton, and in the year 1888 they shipped 1,330 bales to St. Louis and Memphis. In invoicing their goods in July, 1889, they found in accounts and stock on hand $40,000, their average stock amounting to $12,000. Mr. Phelps is a Democrat, a member of El Paso Lodge No. 65 of the A. F. & A. M., and in his business relations is shrewd and enterprising. He and wife are rearing a little girl named Mamie Canada, whose mother died in 1881, when she was but two weeks old. Her father is Thomas J. Canada, and her mother was a Miss Ada Booth.

Joseph T. Phelps is a prosperous merchant of El Paso, Ark., and in his relations with the public has ever proven trustworthy and reliable. By his superior management and rare business ability and efficiency he has done not a little to advance the reputation the county enjoys as a commercial center, and is well liked and esteemed by all. He was born in Hardeman County, Tenn., June 25, 1854, and is the son of Philip and Arkansas (Overton) Phelps, who were Virginians, but were married in Tennessee, and lived the lives of farm-

ers in that State. The father was an Englishman by descent and was a man who, had he lived, would have become wealthy, but he was cut down in the prime of life, in 1858, at the age of thirty-five years. In 1860 his widow married P. Rainer, a farmer of Tennessee, who came to Arkansas about 1870, and are residing in Craighead County. The mother, as well as her first husband, were members of the Old School Presbyterian Church, but she is now a member of the Methodist Episcopal Church. Joseph T. Phelps was left fatherless at the age of three years, but was reared to a farm life by his step-father, and in his youth acquired a fair education in the common schools of Tennessee and Arkansas, paying his own tuition. At the early age of fourteen years he began life on his own responsibility, and for about three worked as a farm hand, earning sufficient money to take a course in a higher grade of school. Upon leaving his step-father he could neither read nor write and had very little clothing. He made his home with an uncle, with the agreement that he should work one-half the time and go to school the remainder, but his uncle failed to live up to the contract and he left him. He next made his home with a lady who treated him kindly, and later with a Mr. Turner, who took considerable interest in him, and at the age of sixteen years, through the recommendation of this gentleman, he succeeded in obtaining a good position with a Mr. Parker, of Bolivar, Tenn., and remained with him six months, attending school and working in his store, doing chores to pay for his board. After teaching school for a short time, he obtained a situation as clerk in a dry-goods store at Bolivar at $10 per month, a position which he held for six months; then became newsboy on the Mississippi Central Railroad, continuing for three months. In the fall of 1872 he came to Craighead County and he and his brother bought a house and lot in Jonesboro, and followed the occupation of saw-logging a sufficient length of time to get enough logs to build a house, but the mill burned and their property was lost. Their next bad luck was the discovery that the title to their house and lot, for which they paid $100, was worthless, but nothing daunted, they went in debt for forty acres of land, and their first year's crop paid for the property. At the end of one year our subject sold out to his brother and began teaching a subscription school, which was a great success. He next engaged in clerking in a store in Jonesboro, but came to El Paso after a few months, and spent eight months in school at that place. After cutting cord wood for about three months, he hired to M. L. Booth as a farm hand, at $20 a month, working one year. December 21, 1876, he was married to Miss Martha Booth, a daughter of his former employer, and her birth occurred in Haywood County, Tenn. This union has been blessed with six children, four of whom are living: Roberta H. (born August 2, 1878 and died August 2, 1888), Reuben C. (born February 8, 1880), Philip L. (born June 19, 1883, and died December 20, 1884), Joseph H. (born October 15, 1884), Oklahoma (born February 6, 1887) and an infant (born March 29, 1889). After his marriage, Mr. Phelps made one crop on his father-in-law's farm, but in the fall of 1878 he began the mercantile business with a Mr. A. P. Poole, under the firm name of Poole & Phelps. This partnership lasted two years, then Mr. Phelps sold out and engaged in business with M. L. Booth, the firm name being Booth, Phelps & Co., for one year. During his business connection with Mr. Poole, he was appointed postmaster at El Paso, and served in this capacity for six years. He is now engaged in merchandising under the name of M. L. Phelps & Co. His life has been an eventful one, and notwithstanding the many difficulties which have strewn his pathway, he has been successful and is of material benefit to any community in which he resides. He and his wife are members of the Missionary Baptist Church, and he is a member of El Paso Lodge No. 65 of the A. F. & A. M., in which organization he has held all the offices with the exception of Worshipful Master.

Wiley D. Plant. Hilary Plant was born in South Carolina, July 7, 1812, and, when quite young, moved to Alabama, where he met and married Mercy Tatum, a native of Alabama. Shortly after his marriage Mr. Plant immigrated to Ken-

tucky, thence to Arkansas, where the remainder of his quiet, uneventful life was passed. Mr. Plant was a stanch Democrat, and a consistent member of the Methodist Church, South, for many years. He was a quiet, law-abiding citizen, charitable, industrious and frugal, and at the date of his death, in 1880, had amassed quite a fortune. Mrs. Plant is now a resident in White County, Ark., aged eighty-five years. To the union of Mr. and Mrs. Plant ten children were born, five sons and five daughters, four of them now living: Nance B. (widow of George Hamby, of Jackson County), Charles F. (a farmer of White County), Wiley D. (the subject of this sketch), Green L. (a planter of White County), Andrew W. (died in Woodruff County), Robert L. (died in Conway County), Mary A. (widow of George M. Smith, deceased in White County), Susan M. (died in Jackson County) and Sarah F. (wife of N. E. Kidd, died in Woodruff County). Wiley D. Plant was reared in White County, and received excellent advantages for an education, which he was not slow to improve, and is a well-informed man. He is a typical Arkansan, and a native of that State, his birth occurring in Conway (now Faulkner) County, January 19, 1847. He began for himself at the age of twenty-one years, first as a farmer, which was his occupation for a few years, but realizing that his vocation lay in another direction he turned his attention to the mercantile business, in which he has been successful. He located at Bradford, White County, where he is now one of the prominent men of the community. His stock consists of general merchandise, valued at $8,000, and by his courteous manner and straightforward dealing he has established a permanent and lucrative business. Mr. Plant is well worthy the liberal patronage bestowed on him, for he endeavors in every possible way to please his customers, considering their interests his, and the petty, disagreeable traits of so many merchants are entirely foreign to his characteristics and nature. In May of 1885 Mr. Plant led to the hymeneal altar Mrs. Sarah E. Moore, daughter of William and Prudence McKnight. To their union two bright children have been born, Bessie and William D., who, with their childish prattle, make the house bright and joyous, and gladden the hearts of their devoted parents. He is a Democrat in politics, takes an active part in the elections, and is a strong partisan. He is a believer in the Methodist faith, though not a member of any denomination. He is a leading citizen, contributes liberally to all public movements; is a prominent personage in his town and community, active and progressive.

Henry W. Pope is a prominent farmer and stock raiser of Cane Township, a native of Georgia, and a son of Micajah and Hattie (Bruce) Pope. Micajah Pope was born in Virginia, November 21, 1808, and was a son of John and Mary (Morris) Pope of Virginia origin, and was married in 1827. John Pope moved to Georgia in 1818, and settled on land where Atlanta now stands. Mrs. Pope, the mother of Henry W., was a daughter of Daniel and Sallie (Prenct) Bruce, who were the parents of eleven children. Our subject was born December 28, 1835, and was married December 27, 1855, to Mollie E. Rea, a daughter of Rev. W. T. Rea and Rhoda (Brown) Rea. Mrs. Rea was a daughter of William and Nancy Pruet. After his marriage Mr. Pope found employment in teaching, following this for several years. All of his brothers were in the Confederate army, and Henry W. was mustered in, but was unable to stand muster, and was discharged. In 1867 he removed to Jefferson County and taught school, and two years later came to White County. In March, 1878, he came to Cane Township, and commenced farming on a quarter-section of unimproved land, and, by his energy, has 100 acres of it under cultivation. To this union have been given twelve children: Sarah F. (now Mrs. Earnest, and the mother of six children), Mollie H. (now Mrs. Langforo, and the mother of two children), William H. (married, and has one child), Mamie (now Mrs. Cagle), John D. (a professor of penmanship), Horace E. (deceased), Ella (deceased), Katie B., Daniel W., Samuel T. (deceased), Albert J. and James E. Mr. Pope is a strong Democrat, and takes an active part in politics, and is now holding the office of justice of the peace of his township. Himself and family are members of the Methodist Episcopal Church, South. He always takes an active interest in the temperance movement.

Frederick R. Price, one of Gen. Price's soldiers in his raid through Missouri, Kansas and Mississippi, is the fifth son of a family of twelve children, born to Russell and Mary (Turner) Price. Russell Price was the son of Joseph Price, who died in South Carolina in 1833. Russell Price was born in 1790, and was married about 1810, and was the father of the following ten children, and two whose names are not given: Delia, Thomas, Jane, Fielding, Frederick R., Minerva, Mahaley, Joseph, Mary Ann and Nancy. He followed farming in South Carolina, and moved to White County, in 1836, taking up eighty acres of land, and where he died two years later, his wife surviving him until 1844. Frederick R. first saw the light of this world in South Carolina, March 2, 1821, and was married at the age of twenty to Lucinda Jones, a daughter of B. Jones, of Cane Township. After his marriage he commenced farming for himself. By this marriage they had eleven children: John T., Russell, Levi (deceased), Polly (deceased), William (deceased), Sarah J. (deceased), Louisa, Fielding, Lucy C. (deceased), Elizabeth and George W. (deceased). Mr. Price's first wife died in June, 1872. He was married the second time, in 1873, to Ruth J. Taylor (nee Chrisman), widow of W. H. Taylor. She was born in 1831, and was the daughter of Isaac S. and Lucinda (Allen) Chrisman, natives of Lee County, W. Va., who came to White County in 1856, both of whom are now deceased. Mr. and Mrs. Price are the parents of one child, Allie O., who was born May 29, 1874. Mr. F. R. Price moved to White County, in 1836, where he has ever since lived. Himself and family belong to the Methodist Church, of which denomination his wife has been a member since eight years of age. He is also a member of the County Wheel, and has been honored with the office of president. In his younger days he was engaged principally in hunting. He is a highly respected citizen, and always has the good of his community at heart.

Amaziah M. Price is what might be called a life resident of White County, having been born on the farm which he now calls home, and where he has always lived. It is a fine tract of 240 acres, 100 of which are under cultivation. Joseph R. Price, the father of A. M. Price, was a native of South Carolina, and was a son of Russell and Sarah (Turner) Price, both of South Carolina origin. Mr. Price was married in March, 1846, in White County, to Martha Guthery, a daughter of Joseph and Susie (Wood) Guthery, also natives of South Carolina. To their union were born seven children: Mary A. (deceased), A. M. (our subject), Arva J. (now Mrs. Chumbley), Carrel A., Rhodie J. (married James Hodges, of this county), Monroe and Susan (who married William Chumley). Mr. Price died in 1860, and his wife some ten years later. A. M. Price was born on November 13, 1849, received a common-school education, and was married in 1882 to Miss Susan M. Taylor, a daughter of James M. and Maggie J. (Barker) Taylor. Mr. Taylor is originally from Tennessee, and a son of Alexander and Margaret (Davis) Taylor. Mrs. Taylor was a daughter of Alexander and Margaret (Dodson) Barker. Mr. and Mrs. Price are the parents of two daughters: Lenna (born September 14, 1883) and Bertha (born November 21, 1885). He is a member of the Presbyterian Church, and his wife of the Baptist Church. Mr. Price is a strong Democrat, politically, and takes an active interest in all work for the good of the community.

Carroll A. Price. A glance at the notes from which this sketch has been prepared indicates at once that the mercantile career of Mr. Price has been one of ceaseless activity, and that he has been successful is well known. His parents, Joseph and Mary (Guthrie) Price, were of French and Scotch descent, and were born in North and South Carolina, respectively. After their marriage they came to Arkansas, and became farmers of White County. The father died in 1859 and the mother in 1866, their union having been blessed in the birth of seven children, all of whom grew to manhood and womanhood: Mary Ann (was born in 1846, was married to M. J. H. Jenkins, but was left a widow with six children in 1887), A. M. (was born in 1848, married Miss Susan Taylor,

a native of Tennessee, and has two children), Zennance (was born in 1850, and was married to J. M. Couch, by whom she has two children), Carroll A. (our subject, was the fourth child), Rhoda J. (was born in 1852, became the wife of J. S. Hodges, of Mississippi, and is the mother of seven children), Monroe (was born in 1856, married Nancy Gibson, a native of North Carolina, and by her has four children), Susan (born in 1858, married to W. T. Chumley, of Illinois, and has two children). The paternal great-grandfather was a soldier in the Revolutionary War. Carroll A. Price was born November 13, 1852, and was educated in the private schools of White County, and attended a male academy for two terms, paying his way through this institution with money earned by industry, perseverance and economy. In 1874 he became a salesman for his uncle, Nelson Guthrie, in Pope County, but at the end of one year returned to White County, and engaged in farming and stock dealing, which calling he continued to pursue until 1878, then came to Beebe and engaged as a clerk with D. C. Harris, with whom he remained until 1880. The following year he formed a partnership with J. M. Liles in general merchandising in the town of Beebe, and successfully conducted business at that place until 1887, when they dissolved partnership, Mr. Liles buying Mr. Price's interest. The latter invested his money in real estate, but in the spring of 1887 went east and purchased an excellent line of general merchandise, his stock being now valued at $10,000, and he controls a large share of the patronage of town and county. On September 17, 1883, he was united in marriage to Miss Mary G. Gibbs, of Arkansas, their marriage taking place in the Cumberland Presbyterian Church, in Beebe, Rev. R. T. Wylie officiating. They have two children: Cecil (born July 30, 1884) and Cuthbert A. (born December 7, 1887). In his political views Mr. Price is a liberal Democrat, and he and wife are earnest members of the Cumberland Presbyterian Church, of Beebe. He is progressive in his views, and contributes liberally to all religious, social, educational and political interests.

L. M. Pyles, a prominent fruit and vegetable-grower of Judsonia, was born in Maryland, near Washington, D. C., in 1849, and was the eldest son in a family of thirteen children given to William V. and Margaret A. (Ryan) Pyles, also owning Maryland as their native State. Mr. William V. Pyles was a son of William and Massie (Allen) Pyles, who was born in 1825 and was married in 1847 to Margaret A. Ryan, daughter of William and Sarah (Kingsburry) Ryan, of Maryland. To the union of Mr. and Mrs. Pyles were born the following children: L. M. (our subject), Anna S. (deceased), Laura V. (now Mrs. Allen), Emma J. (married Bud Ball), Maggie (now Mrs. Stewart), Fannie (married Robert Padgett), Amanda (Mrs. Middleton), Lucy (now Mrs. Langley), Jennie, William H. and Thornton. Mr. L. M. Pyles was married in 1877 to Laverna Clark, daughter of Alfred and Mary Clark, who were of Ohio origin. After his marriage Mr. Pyles moved to Cincinnati, and thence to Warren County, Ohio, where he started in business as a butcher, which he followed for seven years. His wife died in 1881, in Warren County, leaving two children: Mary M. and William L. After the death of his wife Mr. Pyles returned to Maryland, remaining in that State but a short time, and then came back to Ohio and located in Darke County, where he was married the second time, in Greenville, in 1884, to Almeda Good, daughter of Samuel and Margaret Good, of Ohio. The year following he removed to White County, Ark., and located in Judsonia, where he made the raising of fruit and vegetables a business for two years, and then opened a meat market, in which business he continued for a limited time, and again took up the employment of growing fruit and vegetables, giving his principal attention to the raising of fine strawberries, which he ships to northern markets. Mr. and Mrs. Pyles are members of the Methodist Episcopal Church. He is also connected with the I. O. O. F., holding the office of Noble Grand. Mr. Pyles is a strong Republican and a member of the town council. He owns some property in Judsonia, and is widely known and highly respected as a citizen. His father was one of the three men who were allowed to cross the Potomac on the night of President Lincoln's assassination.

Thomas Jefferson Quick. Since commencing life for himself Mr. Quick has given his attention to two callings, that of farming and stock raising, and in these enterprises has met with well merited success, for he is not only progressive in his views, but is intelligent and thoroughly posted in all public affairs. He was born February 11, 1842, and is a son of Nathan and Pency Emeline (Hubbard) Quick, the father, being in all probability, of Spanish descent, his birth occurring in the "Palmetto State." The mother was a Georgian, and her union with Mr. Quick resulted in the birth of nine children, eight attaining manhood and womanhood: Nancy Melissa (was born in 1838, and was married to W. R. T. Singleton, of Mississippi), William (was born in 1840, and died in 1852), Thomas Jefferson (the subject of this memoir), Martha Adeline (born in 1844, was married to J. M. Butler, of Mississippi, in 1865), Eliza Permelia (born in 1846, wedded to L. R. Butler, of Mississippi, in 1865), James Robert (born in 1848, espoused Miss Mary Allen, of Mississippi, and died in Arkansas, in 1882), Mercy F. (born in 1850, married James E. Timms, of Mississippi), Sarah Ellen (born in 1852, wedded Thomas Hill, also of Mississippi), Amanda R. (born in 1854, became the wife of J. H. Roberts, a Mississippian), Matthew Isom's birth occurred in 1856, and he took for his wife Miss Evaline Summons. Mr. Quick, the gentleman whose name heads this sketch, received his education in the subscription schools of his native county (La Fayette County, Miss.), and has been familiar with farm work from his earliest boyhood. This work continued to receive his attention until he had attained his seventeenth year, when, with the enthusiasm of youth, he enlisted as a private in Company F, Nineteenth Regiment Mississippi Volunteer Infantry, the first battle in which he participated being Williamsburg. On March 3, 1865, he was captured at Petersburg, Va., and taken to Hart's Island, N. Y., where he was kept in confinement for two months and a half. On being paroled he went to New York City, embarking there on a steamer for New Orleans, going from there up the Mississippi River to Memphis, from there by rail to La Fayette Station, thence on foot to Oxford, Miss., a distance of seventy miles, to his father's plantation, two miles east of that place, arriving at home May 6, 1865. He assisted his father on the farm for two years, and on January 16, 1867, wedded Miss Mary A. Callaway, of Georgia, and started out in life for himself. November 18, 1869, he came to Arkansas, and settled in White County, residing for one year on a farm he had purchased, then sold out and removed to Van Buren County, and after purchasing a saw-mill near Quitman, operated it for one year. Being dissatisfied with this location, he resolved to return to White County, and here purchased a farm, comprising 320 acres, all wild land. He resided on this until 1884, then sold it, having in the meantime made many valuable improvements, among which was the clearing and putting under cultivation of 120 acres of land. In 1884 he took up his abode in El Paso, but in 1885 purchased his present farm, consisting of 106 acres, on which was an incompleted house and fair stables. He has since completed the house, and has erected a cotton-gin, which has a capacity of six bales per day. On May 4, 1880, his wife died, and September 7, 1881, he married Sallie E. Crosby, of the State of Arkansas, and to them were born two children: Lawrence Bernard (born June 28, 1882, and died October 31, 1882), Clarence Leonard (born June 28, 1882, and died August 12, 1889). The mother of these children died October 17, 1884, and June 21, of the following year, Mr. Quick took for his third wife Mrs. Elizabeth (Arnold) Griffin, a daughter of John and Cynthia (Smith) Arnold, the father about one-fourth Cherokee Indian, and the mother of Irish descent. The following children have been born to Mr. Quick's last marriage: Thomas Fletcher (born July 16, 1886) and Quro (born October 26, 1888). At the present writing Mr. Quick owns 200 acres of land, with eighty acres under cultivation. His land has on it a fine peach and plum orchard, and a vineyard of about 100 vines. Mr. Quick is a member of the Methodist Episcopal Church, South, and also of El Paso Lodge No. 65, A. F. & A. M.

William C. Rainey is an extensive planter and cotton-ginner of Union Township, and was born in Madison County, Tenn., in 1829, being a son of Isaac and Parthena (Rainey) Rainey, who were also people of Middle Tennessee. The father was a farmer by occupation, and a son of Zebulon Rainey, a soldier in the War of 1812. Both parents were members of the Methodist Episcopal Church, and died in Middle Tennessee, after rearing a family of six children: William C., Theophilus (who died in youth), Addison Levi (a farmer of West Tennessee), Samuel (a farmer of West Tennessee), James W. (of Lauderdale County, Tenn.), Henderson A. (of Haywood County, Tenn.), Delicia F. (widow of Joseph L. Hendron, of Tenn.), Amanda (wife of W. Coffman, a merchant of Woodville, Tenn.), Elizabeth (who died at the age of four years), and Martha (who died in 1856, aged eighteen years). William C. Rainey began life for himself when twenty-two years of age, and after working one year as a farm hand and from that time up to 1858 was an overseer. In the fall of 1856 he was married to Elizabeth Coffey, a daughter of Rev. D. P. Coffey of Tennessee, and by her has had a family of eleven children, eight of whom are living: James D. (who was born November 25, 1857), Mary F. (wife of Jeff Walker, was born May 14,'1860), Leonidas E. (was born January 12, 1866), William J. (born February 29, 1868), Thomas (born October 7, 1870), Samuel (born November 30, 1872), Jesse C. (born March 4, 1874), Joseph L. (born December 27, 1879), and Eddie (born February 27, 1877). On December 20, 1854, Mr. Rainey first set foot in White County, Ark., and for two years he acted as overseer for one of the well-to-do planters of this region. After his marriage he moved to Hickory Plains, and in 1857 came to this portion of the county and settled on the land where Beebe now stands. After a one year's residence at this place he sold out and settled in the vicinity of Stony Point, and here has since made his home. His first purchase of land was 160 acres, and in 1856 he erected the first gin put up in the south part of White County, which he is still operating. Prior to 1883 the machinery was run by horse-power but since that time he has used steam. Mr. Rainey is a member of the Agricultural Wheel, and he and wife are members of the Cumberland Presbyterian Church, as are the most of their children, Mr. Rainey and his eldest son being ruling elders in that church. During the war he served in Company D, Tenth Arkansas Regiment, but after May 28, 1862, became a member of Forrest's cavalry and served under him until the close of the war, when his company was disbanded on January 9. He was at Shiloh, Corinth, the gunboat fight on the Big Sandy in Tennessee, Murfreesboro, Guntown, Franklin, and was in the various engagements in which Forrest's cavalry participated.

John F. Randall, a worthy and conscientious representative of White County, was born in Cape Girardeau County, Mo., near the city of Cape Girardeau, March 31, 1832. His father, Willam C. Randall, was born in Lexington, Ky., December 15, 1805, and died in Arkansas, February 4, 1863, aged fifty-eight years. He was a regular apprentice to the boot and shoemaker's trade, and an expert in that profession. He was an old line Whig, and manifested great interest in all party campaigns. In 1831 Mr. Randall was united in marriage with Sarah A., daughter of Anthony and Mary Randol, and a native of Missouri. She received her education in her native State, where the greater part of her life was passed, and at the date of her death, in 1854, she was residing in Stoddard County, Mo. To the union of Mr. and Mrs. Randall twelve children were born, all of whom grew to maturity. Those living are: John F., Sarah E. (wife of James Samuels, of Missouri), Orlando L. (of Hood County, Tex.), Martha J. (widow of Joseph M. Lean). Those deceased are: William O., Carrol V., Mary Z., Eliza A., Charlotte V., Rebecca L., Edward L. and Harvy C. John F. received but limited advantages for education, as the schools of his boyhood days were very few, but he received a practical knowledge of farming, which occupation he has always followed in connection with stock raising. He owns 320 acres of excellent land, highly cultivated, and everything on his farm indicates thrift and prosperity. He was first married in Calhoun County,

Ill., in 1859, to Martha J. Scott of that State, and the result of this marriage was two children, who died in infancy. His second marriage occurred in 1862 to Edna P., daughter of Andrew and Nancy Woodley, of Pike County, Ga., and by her he became the father of three children: William O. and a daughter (dead), and Edward L., now living. He also reared W. R. Randall, a nephew, born June 7, 1860, and Mattie Lee Woodley, a niece, born March 25, 1877. Mr. Randall enlisted in the Union army, July 27, 1862, in Company A, First Arkansas Mounted Rangers. This regiment was reorganized in 1863, at Benton Barracks, Mo., with John E. Phelps as colonel; the regiment afterward being known as the Second Arkansas Cavalry. He acted most of the time as recruiting officer, and in the capacity of scout and escort duty. He participated in the battles of Independence, Jefferson City, Kansas City, Big Blue and many others of minor importance. He received his discharge as first sergeant from said regiment, Company A. For twenty years Mr. Randall has acted as justice of the peace in White County, where he has lived since 1860, and is now filling said office and discharging its manifold duties in a creditable and exemplary manner. He is a Prohibitionist in politics, though not in any way a partisan. He is one of the most prominent members of the Methodist Church, South, and takes an active interest in all the affairs and work of the church, also contributing to all charitable enterprises. He is a member in high standing in the Masonic order.

James F. Ray, M. D., is a substantial and well-known practitioner of Arkansas, his first field for the practice of medicine being in Centre Hill in 1883. His early days were spent in Jackson County, where he was born in 1854, and in White County, and when nineteen years of age he commenced the study of medicine. Dr. Ray was the son of Samuel and Jane (Sorrell) Ray. Samuel Ray was born in Alabama in 1824, and was a son of Samuel M. Ray, a native of North Carolina. He moved to Arkansas in 1854, settling in Jackson County, and in 1860 came to White County, where he followed farming. He enlisted in 1862 and

15

served in the Confederate service. Mrs. Ray was born in Alabama, in 1828, and was a daughter of James F. and Flora Sorrell, and died in White County in 1869. They were the parents of three children: James F., John and William. Dr. Ray was married in 1877 to Susan E. Barnett, a daughter of Z. H. and Emiline (Stewart) Barnett, natives of Tennessee. To these parents were given seven children, four of whom are still living: Floyd S., Mary E. (deceased), Arthur Curtis (deceased), Mamie A., Samuel H. (deceased), Ethel I. and Blanch W. In 1885 Dr. Ray moved to Mount Pisgah, where he still lives and practices, and is the owner of a forty-acre tract of fine timber land. Himself and wife are members of the Missionary Baptist Church. When the Doctor first came to this county, bear, dear and wild turkey were abundant. Politically he is a strong Democrat, and although not taking an active part in politics, has held the office of bailiff of the township; he is a highly respected citizen, and enjoys a large practice extending throughout the adjoining townships.

William P. Reaves, a miller and ginner, of Cadron Township, was born in Alabama, in 1850, and was the second son in a family of eleven children of Emery G. and Elizabeth A. (Davis) Reaves, also of Alabama. Their family consisted of the following children: Emily, William P., Amandy, John T., Narsiscey, Nancy A., Sarah E., George W., Sarah J., Thomas and David. Mrs. Reaves died in 1879, and Mr. Reaves was again married, in 1881, to Susan Foster, and they are residing in Alabama, and have a family of small children. William P. Reaves, the gentleman whose name heads this sketch, was married at the age of seventeen, to Majourie O. Monk, a daughter of Silas and Nancy (Youngblood) Monk. Her father was a Primitive Baptist minister. Mrs. Reaves died in 1885, having been the mother of nine children: Tresser T. (deceased), Tulula, Mary M., William Lee, Ransom L., Caroline (deceased), Georgia (deceased), James (deceased) and Effie (deceased). Mr. Reaves came to Arkansas in 1877, and settled in this township, and in 1882 started a saw-mill and is now sawing and converting the pines of Arkansas into lumber. He was married the second time in 1887 to Anna Drain, the daughter of the Rev. William W. Drain. To this union have been born two children: Isaac E. and Jessie J. Mr. Reaves owns 160 acres of fine timber land, and has twenty acres cleared and under cultivation. He is a member of the Masonic fraternity, belonging to the Rock Springs Lodge No. 422, and also a member of the County Wheel. He is a prominent worker in all matters relative to educational and school work, and is one of the esteemed directors of School District No. 28.

J. F. Redus came with his parents to White County, in 1851, they settling in Marion Township. He was born in Alabama, in 1844, and was the second son in a family of nine children born to Joel S. and Susan J. (Gill) Redus, also of Alabama nativity. The senior Redus had a land warrant for service in the Mexican War, and on which he settled and broke land for a farm, where he lived until he died in 1858, his wife surviving him ten years. The family consisted of the following nine children: W. G. (who resides in this county, and who enlisted in Company B of Thirty-sixth Arkansas Infantry), J. F. (our subject), L. S. (who also served in the Confederate army), L. E. (now Mrs. Simmons, of Cleburne County), John C. (deceased), D. J., Joel S. (deceased), M. G. and T. J. J. F. Redus assisted his father in opening up the farm, and in 1861 enlisted in the Confederate service for twelve months, in Company K, of the Seventh Arkansas Infantry. After the reorganization of the company, he reenlisted for three years, or during the war. He participated in the battles of Shiloh, Murfreesboro, Perrysville (Ky.), Liberty Gap, Chickamauga, and in the ninety-days' fight before Dalton, also at Lookout Mountain, Atlanta and a number of others. He marched barefooted from Franklin, Tenn., to Pulaski, Tenn. Immediately after the cessation of hostilities, he returned home and again took up farming. He now owns a farm of 160 acres, with eighty-five acres under cultivation. He takes an active part in politics, and is a strong Democrat, and was candidate for county treasurer in 1889, but was defeated by combined efforts.

He and entire family are members of the Baptist Church.

Jackson V. Reynolds, a prominent farmer and fruit grower of White County, was born in Tennessee in 1844, and is a son of Samuel and Margaret (Maderis) Reynolds, natives of Alabama. Mr. Samuel Reynolds was born in 1808, and was married in 1831, after which he moved to Tennessee, and in 1851 came to Arkansas, settling in White County, where he bought a farm of 160 acres, on which he lived until his death, which occurred in 1861. His wife survived him twenty years, and was the mother of nine children, three of whom are living: Jackson V. (our subject), Samuel T. and Marquis L. Jackson V. Reynolds was reared on a farm, educated in this county, and was married, in 1866, to Margaret Thompson, a daughter of James and Martha Thompson of Tennessee origin, and who came to Arkansas at an early day. Mrs. Reynolds died in 1880, leaving five children, four of whom are still living: Edward, Minnie, Mary and Florence. After the death of his first wife, Mr. Reynolds married Mrs. Mitchell (nee McMurtry), a widow, and by this marriage became the mother of three children: Willie, Effie and Van. In 1862 he enlisted in the Confederate army, serving in Capt. Hick's regiment, but was wounded at the battle of Helena, and received his discharge. Mr. Reynolds has a farm of 237 acres, with 140 acres under cultivation, and devotes the most of his attention to fruit growing.

James P. Rheu, planter, Stevens Creek, Ark. White County, is acknowledged by all to be one of the best agricultural portions of the State, and as such its citizens are men of advanced ideas and considerable prominence. A worthy representative of this class is found in the person of Mr. James P. Rheu. He was originally from Dickson County, Tenn., where his birth occurred on November 23, 1824, and is the son of John and Margaret (Dunnegan) Rheu, natives, respectively, of North Carolina and Kentucky, and both of Scotch-Irish descent. The maternal grandparents probably came to Alabama before the Revolutionary War. John Rheu and family moved to Kentucky in about 1830, located in McCracken County, where they remained until about 1840, and then moved to Graves County. There he improved a farm, and made his home until death, which occurred in 1855. The mother died about 1827. James P. Rheu was early initiated into the duties of farm life, and received a liberal education for those days. In 1857 he came to Arkansas, located at Denmark, Jackson County, and engaged in merchandising, which he continued successfully for many years. On May 15, 1859, he was united in marriage to Miss Martha V. Edens, a native of Fayette County and the daughter of H. and Ann (Price) Edens, natives of Lincoln County, Tenn., and probably of Irish descent. The maternal great-grandfather of Mrs. Rheu was connected with the commissary department of the Colonial army, and her grandfather Price, was a soldier under Gen. Jackson, in the War of 1812, participating in the battle of New Orleans, also in the subsequent Indian Wars. To Mr. and Mrs. Rheu were born four children: Ider E. (born June 11, 1860), Lelia C. (born October 8, 1865), William F. (born February 8, 1875), and Maggie A. (born February 22, 1876). Ider E. married J. C. Meadows on November 30, 1879, and is the mother of four children: Claude L., Ollie V., Lillian M. and Homer C. Mr. Meadows is a farmer by occupation. Mr. Rheu's other children are at home. In the fall of 1862, Mr. Rheu had become nicely fixed in business, had erected a fine dwelling-house, also a store, and excellent outbuildings upon his place; was also speculating in cotton, and had about ten bales on hand, when his buildings were set on fire, and his store, his entire stock of goods and his cotton were destroyed. After this severe loss he rented land, followed farming near Denmark, and there remained until 1866, when he bought a farm in Jackson County. This tract contained eighty acres of improved land, and there he resided until 1871, when he moved to his present property, arriving there on December 20 of that year. He purchased one hundred acres, with about fifteen under cultivation, and erected their present house the same year. At present he has about thirty acres under cultivation. He is a member of Anchor Lodge No. 49, A. F. and A. M., and has served the lodge in the capacity of Senior Warden and Junior Warden, and has also been secretary for seven years of Fredonia Lodge No. 229. He holds a demit from Tillman Chapter No. 19, R. A. M., Searcy, Ark. In his political views he affiliates with the Democratic party. Mrs. Rheu, and her daughter Lelia, are members of the Methodist Episcopal Church, South, and Mrs. Ider E. Meadows is a member of the Missionary Baptist Church.

Mrs. Mary M. Rhoden is the daughter of Jacob Free Coffman (deceased), who, from an early period in the country's history, gave to Independence County (to which he came in 1851, locating on the White River) the best energies of his life as one of the most worthy and respected citizens, and to the community and all among whom he lived, the example of a life well and usefully spent, and the influence of a character without stain. In this county he bought a farm of 400 acres, on which he lived till his death in 1858. His birth occurred February 10, 1805, and he was united in marriage to Miss Catherine Young on March 17, 1826, in Lauderdale County, Tenn. He was the son of Lovell and Sallie (Greene) Coffman, the former a native of Virginia, of German descent, and whose ancestors came to America previous to the Colonial War. Sallie (Greene) Coffman was a relative of Gen. Greene of Revolutionary fame. Mrs. Catherine (Young) Coffman was the daughter of Samuel and Keziah (Hogue) Young. Samuel Young was a native of South Carolina, was of English descent, and his grandfather came to America about 1740 and located in South Carolina where Samuel was born. Keziah (Hogue) Young was a native of South Carolina, her parents being of English descent. The maternal grandfather (Doolittle) was killed by Tories in South Carolina during the Revolutionary War. Jacob Free and Catherine (Young) Coffman were the parents of these children: Sarah Ann K., Samuel Lovell, Mary Margaret, John Tillmore, Daniel A., Martha Jane, Elizabeth C., Amy Evaline, Susan Rebecca and Laura Malinda. Mary M. Coffman was the third daughter of the above-mentioned family, her birth occurring on January

25, 1832, in Franklin County, Ala., and she received a good English education in the subscription schools of her native county. There she grew to womanhood and was united in marriage to John Harrison Rhoden, a native of Alabama, on November 11, 1847, in Lawrence County. To this union were born eight children: Archie C. (born August 2, 1848), Frances Catherine (born November 3, 1849), Martha Jane (born September 6, 1851, and died in December of the same year), Rebecca Walker (born November 2, 1854, and died on September 5, 1858), Sarah E. (born January 25, 1856), Laura Sophronia (born September 6, 1858), John Breckenridge (born October 15, 1860) and Lucy Coleman (born December 20, 1862). All the children were born in Arkansas, with the exception of Archie, whose birth occurred in Alabama. Archie C. married Miss Matilda J. Means, a native of Virginia, and Frances C. married J. W. Moseley, a native of Kentucky, who is now residing in White County; Sarah E. married Lawrence Westmoreland, a native of Georgia, who is now deceased, Sophronia married William Woodall, a native of Arkansas, John B. resides in Texas, Lucy C. married Dr. Joseph H. Fillinger, a native of Virginia, and now residing in White County. The settlement of the Rhoden family in Arkansas was made in 1849 when the country was an unbroken wilderness. Mrs. Rhoden is a member of the Missionary Baptist Church, having united with that denomination in 1849. The family purchased 160 acres when they first settled in this State, and Mrs. Rhoden now owns 120 acres of that farm.

Dr. Willshire Riley is engaged in the drug business at Judsonia, Ark., and has been established there since 1880. He was born in Auglaize County, Ohio, in 1828, and in 1866 settled in White County, and after residing in Searcy one year, he moved to Red River Township, and for some years was engaged in shipping corn at Riley's Landing. He was educated in the schools of Ohio, and in 1849 was married in Mercer County, of that State, to Miss Ruth Lindsey, removing in 1854 to Toledo, where he acted as deputy collector of customs. . He also published the Toledo Daily, but in 1856 went to Perry County,

Ill., and began practicing medicine, having previously taken a course in the Cincinnati Medical College, graduating in the class of 1856. He remained in Perry County until 1866, then came to Searcy, and has been in business here since that time. He took an active part in politics during reconstruction days, and in 1870 and 1871 was senator, representing White and Pulaski Counties. He has been interested in the cause of education, and has aided all enterprises which were for the good of the community. He is a Douglas Democrat, and he and wife are members of the Methodist Episcopal Church. Of five children born to them, three are living: Horatio (who is married, and resides in Pine Bluff), Kate (Mrs. Hines, resides in Van Buren County) and Willshire (a druggist of Pine Bluff). Dr. Riley is a member of Lodge No. 384 of the A. F. & A. M., and belongs to Tillman Chapter No. 19, and Searcy Council. He is one of the family of six born to James W. and Susan (Ellis) Riley, the former a native of Connecticut, and the latter of New York, and their union took place in Ohio. Mr. Riley was a Government surveyor, and did the most of the surveying of Northwest Ohio and Indiana, but. was also a lawyer by profession. He died in January, 1876, and is still survived by his wife, who is a resident of Denver, Colo. The paternal grandfather, Capt. James Riley, was born in Middletown, Conn., and was the author of Riley's Narrative. Being appointed by President Jackson to survey the Northwestern Territory, he came to Ohio in 1819, and laid out the town of Willshire. Being a sea captain he returned to his calling, and died on the ocean while on one of his voyages in 1840.

Elbert A. Robbins, the eldest son of D. and Olivia (Shinpouch) Robbins, natives of Alabama and Mississippi, respectively, dates his existence from December 23, 1857. His father became a resident of Arkansas in 1856, settling in White County, on a farm of 160 acres of land, ten miles south of Rose Bud, where he died in 1865, shortly after returning from the war. His wife survived him nine years, leaving a family of five children: Elbert A. (the subject of this sketch), J. W. [refer-

ence to whom follows], C. D., Molly and Samuel. E. A. Robbins started out in the world for himself at the age of fifteen without means or influence. He worked on a farm for three years, with but little success, after which his time was spent in a saw-mill until in April, 1881, when he bought a saw-mill, selling it, however, in October of the same year. In 1882 he farmed, but commenced the mercantile business at Rose Bud, in January, 1883, in partnership with his brother, J. W. Robbins. This he has followed ever since, with encouraging results. Besides his only brother he has one sister, Mollie Holmes, still living. Mr. Robbins professed religion, and joined the Baptist Church in 1887. He was married, in 1878, to Miss Ida Crooms, and to them have been born six children, three of whom are living: Emma, Walter and Maudie; those deceased are Mollie, Elmer and an infant. Mrs. Robbins is also a member of the Missionary Baptist Church. He takes an active part in the Sunday-schools, and exerts his whole influence for the promotion of religious and educational institutions.

J. W. Robbins, a brother of E. A. Robbins, commenced in life on his own account at the age of fourteen, in 1883 entering into the mercantile business in White County. He was born in this county in 1860, his parents being D. and Olivia (Shinpouch) Robbins [reference to whom appears in the sketch which precedes this]. J. W. Robbins was married, in 1886, to Susan I. Thomas, a daughter of W. A. and Jane (Post) Thomas. Mr. and Mrs. Robbins are the parents of two children: Oscar (living) and Laura A. (deceased). Mr. Robbins is a strong Democrat, and takes an active interest in all work for the interest of schools or general public good.

John A. Roberson. Among the farmers and stockmen of White County, Ark., none are more prominent than our subject, who, though he is a native of Rutherford County, Tenn., born November 19, 1835, has been a resident of White County since 1870. He was reared to a farm life and his knowledge of the "Three R's" was acquired in the common schools. He was thrown on the world to fight his own way through life at the early age of sixteen years on account of the death of his father, and until his marriage on November 17, 1854, he worked as a farm hand. His wife, Angeline Redmon, was a native of Haywood County and bore Mr. Roberson eight children as follows: George (who died in infancy), a child who died unnamed, William (who is a farmer of White County), James (also a farmer), Anna (wife of Elijah Cupp, died leaving one child), Lela (is the wife of William P. Brickell, a farmer of Phillips County, Ark.), Thomas (farms in Texas) and Edgar (who was born on June 20, 1873). Mr. Roberson departed this life on July 27, 1888, an earnest member of the Methodist Episcopal Church. Mrs. Mary (Coleman) Murphy, a native of Alabama and a resident of Arkansas for about nineteen years, became his wife February 24, 1889. After his first marriage Mr. Roberson farmed and acted as overseer until 1864 when he went into the army and served until the cessation of hostilities. He then became manager of a large farm owned by a wealthy planter of Haywood County, but since 1870 has resided in White County, he being now the owner of 320 acres of land. At the time of his purchase there were sixty-five acres under cultivation, but he now has 110 acres under the plow and has added 130 acres to his original purchase. His land is well adapted to raising all necessary farm products, and for several years past he has devoted much of his time to stock raising. He has been an active worker for the cause of Christianity for many years and socially is a member of Beebe Lodge No. 145 of the A. F. & A. M. His parents, Jesse and Mary A. (Vaughn) Roberson, were born in Virginia and South Carolina in 1815 and 1810, respectively, and were married about 1834. They died in Tennessee, the former in Haywood County in 1851, and the latter in Davidson County, in 1848. Three of their eight children died in infancy: William (lived to be grown and lost his life in the battle in June, 1863, and was buried in a soldier's cemetery), Mary (is the wife of James Tatum, of Bell Station, Tenn.), Fidelia (is the wife of James Collins, an Englishman, residing in Tennessee), Eliza (is the wife of Robert Pitner, a farmer of Tennessee), and John A. (our subject).

A. T. Rodmon has ably served his county as commissioner four years, as school director six years, and also as president of the board of registration. His parents, James and Jennie (Kell) Rodmon, were natives of South Carolina, his paternal and maternal grandfathers being of Irish origin, who came to this country at the same time and settled in South Carolina. Grandfather Rodmon had a family of four children: John, Thomas, Sarah and James. James Rodmon was married in 1828 or 1829, and had a family of five children: A. T. (our subject), Mary A. (who married a man by the name of Blunt), Susan (Ballard), John C. and James C. Mr. Rodmon died on July 13, 1849, in South Carolina, to which State his family moved from South Carolina that year. A. T. Rodmon was married, after attaining manhood, in 1856 in Mississippi, to Miss Mary Williams, a daughter of P. W. and Nancy (McDowell) Williams, and of North Carolina birth. After this event Mr. Rodmon settled on a farm and devoted himself to agricultural pursuits for four years, then moving to White County, Ark., in 1859, and locating on a farm twelve miles south of Searcy. In 1862 he enlisted in the Confederate army and served on detached duty during the war. In 1873 he removed to Kane Township, where he now resides, enjoying at this time a wide and honored acquaintance. Mr. and Mrs. Rodmon have had twelve children, four of whom only are living: Alice M., Nora E., Frank and Clinton J. These are at home and attending school. In 1868 Mr. Rodmon was appointed justice of the peace, and the same year elected county commissioner, which position he held four years. In 1872 he was elected president of the board of registration, and is now school director, having discharged the official duties connected therewith for six years. He is a member of the Masonic order, and has been connected with the I. O. O. F. Himself and wife have been members of the Baptist Church for the past thirty-two years, Mr. Rodmon having held the position of church clerk for seventeen years. He has also acted as president of the County Wheel for six years, besides holding the office of district deputy for two years. Mr. Rodmon is a strong

Republican and has taken an active interest in the politics of his county. A highly respected citizen, he worthily deserves the universal esteem bestowed upon himself and family.

Benjamin Rogers, in his active career through life, has amassed considerable wealth, and is now owner of a fine farm, comprising 400 acres, 120 of which he has put under cultivation, clearing ninety acres himself. He has around him every convenience, and his buildings, fences and orchards have been placed on his property by his own hands. From his earliest remembrance he has been familiar with farm life, but his youthful advantages for acquiring an education were very limited. He came with his father to Arkansas, and made his home with him until twenty-six years old, having married, at the age of twenty-four, Miss Anna E. Bailey, a native of Tennessee, and a daughter of J. J. Bailey, a pioneer settler of White County. Mrs. Rogers died in September, 1862, and on January 15, 1865, he married Miss Hannah J. Jackson, a native of Tennessee, and a daughter of H. Jackson, a blacksmith by trade. Eleven children have been born to them, of whom ten are living: Marion F. (born February 24, 1866, and lives on his father's farm), J. M. (who was born October 13, 1868), William H. (born August 27, 1869), Robert E. (born June 23, 1871), Mary E. (born August 6, 1873, and died September 2, 1887), Minnie B. (born January 30, 1875), Bettie H. (born November 13, 1878), Benjamin D. (born February 9, 1880), Calvin J. (born January 27, 1883), Ava L. (born January 27, 1885), and Arthur L. (born April 25, 1887). Mrs. Rogers, the mother of this large family, departed this life February 7, 1889, having been a life-long member of the Missionary Baptist Church, a faithful wife and mother, and her death is not only mourned by her immediate family, but by all with whom she came in contact. In 1861 Mr. Rogers bought 160 acres of the farm where he now lives, going in debt for the same, and notwithstanding the fact that the war came up and scattered his property, he has succeeded admirably. In June, 1862, he joined Company A, Thirty-sixth Arkansas Regiment, and was in the battles of Prairie Grove, Helena, Little Rock, besides numerous skirmishes.

He was not wounded nor taken prisoner during his term of service, and was a faithful soldier to the cause he espoused. Upon his return home he found himself robbed of all his property, except the land for which he was considerably in debt, but he began devoting his entire attention to his farm, and has succeeded in putting himself and family beyond the reach of want. He is a Democrat, a member of Beebe Lodge No. 145 of the A. F. & A. M., and for the past seventeen years has been one of the most faithful members of the latter organization. He is public-spirited, and keeps thoroughly apace with the times on all matters of public interest. He was born in Haywood County, Tenn., on August 1, 1836, and is a son of William and Sarah E. (Powers) Rogers, the former born in North Carolina in 1809, and the latter in 1811. They were married in Tennessee about 1830, and in 1854 came to White County, Ark., and settled on what is well known as the Williams' farm, near where Beebe now stands. Mr. Rogers bought 400 acres of woodland, and until he could build him a log-house his family lived in a tent. Like the majority of the pioneer settlers of early times

"He cut, he logged, he cleared his lot,
And into many a dismal spot
He let the light of day."

During his lifetime he cleared over 100 acres of land, and at the time of his death (in 1871) he was one of the wealthy men of the county. In politics he was an old line Whig. His wife died in 1838, and in 1842 he married again, having by this union five children, only two now living, Rufus H. and Robert E., both farmers. His first marriage also resulted in the birth of five children, Benjamin and Elizabeth (wife of Oliver Greene) being the only ones alive.

Thomas J. Rogers, another of the prominent pioneer settlers of White County, has been located here for a period of over forty years, and has not only become well known, but the respect and honor shown him is as wide as his acquaintance. He came to White County in 1848, settled with a brother, Robert J., within three miles of Searcy, which at that time contained two small supply stores, one made of log and the other of plank, and a blacksmith shop. Mr. Rogers was born in Chatham County, N. C., in 1826, was the sixth in a family of ten children (all dead but two), born to Absalom and Hannah (Johnson) Rogers, natives of North Carolina. The parents immigrated to Tennessee at an early day and there the father carried on agricultural pursuits. He was one of the jury that convicted J. A. Merrill. His death occurred in Tennessee, in 1840, and his wife died in North Carolina. Grandfather Rodgers is buried in North Carolina, of which State the family were pioneers. Brought up as an agriculturist it would have been quite natural had Thomas J. Rogers followed in the footsteps of his father, but his tendencies inclined elsewhere, and after securing a fair education in the subscription schools of Tennessee and Arkansas, and farming one year, in 1849 he came to Searcy, where he clerked for Bond & Maxwell, general merchants. He remained with this firm until 1851, and went into partnership in a separate house with the firm, taking the management. In 1852 Mr. Rogers purchased the full control and continued in business until 1862, when he had everything taken from him, it all becoming common property. During the war he raised a company and followed guerrillas, but later he moved to Urbana, Ill., purchased property and remained until the close of the war. The people were anxious to know what he was going to do, so in 1865, he returned to Searcy, Ark., but before coming back liquidated his debts at 25 and 50 per cent with Philadelphia houses. He paid it and received their receipts in full, and later paid it in full with interest, in 1867. After this Mr. Rogers engaged in the real-estate business, in which he is now interested, and is the owner of 20,000 acres in White and Cleburne Counties. He has twenty improved farms in these counties, is renting out land and owns a fine body of timber situated on White and Red Bayou, Des Arc. Politically, Mr. Rogers is the father of the Prohibition party in this county and bought the Lever by the thousands, distributing them gratuitously through the country. He fought for the Local Option bill, was successful, and all rejoiced. He is a member of the Masonic fraternity, Searcy Lodge No. 49, and was charter

member of the same. He was married in White County, Ark., in 1859, to Miss Susie M. Lewis, a native of Mississippi, and to this union were born seven children, five now living: Thomas B., Hallie B., Angie (now Mrs. Jones, of Memphis, Tenn.), Susie M. and Naomi. The mother of these children closed her eyes to the scenes of this world in 1877. She was a member of the Methodist Episcopal Church, to which Mr. Rogers also belongs, having joined in 1840; he has been a scholar and teacher ever since. In 1852 Mr. Rogers joined the Sons of Temperance, but now considers that their work was largely in vain. In 1880 he was sent to Cleveland, Ohio, to the Prohibition National Convention, became a member of that party, and has been on the executive board ever since; was sent to the National Prohibition Convention, which met at Indianapolis, Ind., in 1888, and assisted in forming the Prohibition platform, every plank of which exactly suited him. The same year he was also delegate to the Arkansas State Convention at Little Rock, which adopted the national party platform.

Hon. John P. H. Russ is a man who needs no introduction to the readers of this volume, for he has been usefully and honorably identified with the interests of this county and with its advancement in every worthy particular for many years. His early paternal ancestors were of Scotch-Irish descent and were among the original settlers of Jamestown, Va., but the two immigrants, Vinĉent and John, spelled their name Rusk, although the old Scotch way of spelling the name was Russ, a fact which was discovered by Charles E. Russ, the father of our biographical subject, while reading Scotch history, during his attendance at Hillsboro (N. C.) College. He adopted the old way of spelling the name, and as such it has continued to the present time. Charles E. Russ and his brother, John P. H., afterward graduated from Raleigh College, Raleigh, N. C., and the latter subsequently became a prominent politician, and was honored with the office of Secretary of his native State, a position he held several terms, serving in the interests of the Democratic party. Charles E. Russ was strongly opposed to secession, and stumped the "Old North State" and Georgia in opposition to that measure. His wife, Sarah A. Parker, was a daughter of Harrison and Sarah (Parrish) Parker, the former of Scotch-Irish descent and the latter of French. Hon. John P. H. Russ was born in Floyd County, Ga., April 27, 1852, and in 1859 he was taken by his parents to Charlotte, S. C. After a residence of a few months in Florida they settled in Marengo County, Ala., remaining there until 1866, when Denmark, Tenn., became their home. Their first settlement in Arkansas was in the year 1869, when they settled at El Paso, in White County, purchasing a farm of 160 acres, twenty acres of which was heavily covered with timber. Here both father and mother died, in 1884, the former in January and the latter in June. They were members of the Methodist Episcopal Church, South, and Mr. Russ was a Mason, his wife belonging to the Eastern Star Lodge. Their family consisted of four sons and two daughters, two of whom are living besides our subject: James E. (who was married to Miss Belle Andrews, a native of Kentucky, is an attorney at law of Beebe, Ark.) and Laura J. (the wife of Thomas Midyett, a resident of El Paso Township). This couple was married in Tennessee and came to Arkansas in 1870, and are here rearing their family of three sons: Henry, Charley and Bascom. Hon. John P. H. Russ first commenced attending school in Red Mountain, Ala., but was afterward a student in the common schools of Tennessee, and finished his education in the Methodist graded school under the supervision of Prof. J. W. Thompson. June 23, 1872, he was united in marriage to Miss Narcie L. Booth, a daughter of M. L. and Elizabeth (Bushel) Booth [a sketch of whom appears on another page of this work], and their union resulted in the birth of the following family: Mary E. (born May 18, 1873, and died September 4, 1885), Samira M. (born March 14, 1875), Charles L. (born March 23, 1877), Lena Mora (born December 4, 1880, and died March 4, 1889), Walter M. (born February 9, 1882), Otey S. (born February 28, 1884), John T. (born April 2, 1886), and Laura B. (born January 21, 1888). Mr. Russ always voted with the Democrat party until 1883 and, as he says, did more for the party than his Satanic Majesty, the Devil,

ever did, but he left it in consequence of dissatisfaction with the corruption of both the Democrat and Republican parties and identified himself with the Labor movement; and at a meeting of the White County Wheel, May 7, 1884, he was elected a delegate to the State Wheel, which was held at Little Rock, on June 9, of the same year. At this meeting a full county ticket was organized and Mr. Russ, the delegate, was told to use his own judgment as to which to support—a Labor State or a Wheel ticket. The result was the nomination of the Labor State ticket, and Mr. Russ was chosen by the committee as chairman of the committee for drawing up a platform, and wrote the first four planks. He was afterward elected chairman of the State and Labor Central Committee, and when a meeting was called at Litchfield, Jackson County, on July 27, 1884, he again filled out the ticket, and Charles E. Cunning was the nominee for Governor and received 19,706 votes in twenty-three counties organized in the State, out of seventy-five. At this meeting the delegates met under the shade of a tree and nominated a ticket for Congress, their nominee, R. B. Carl Lee, receiving a small vote in the district. At a meeting of the State Wheel at Little Rock, in 1884, Mr. Russ was elected as a delegate to the Labor Convention at Cincinnati, Ohio, the meeting to be held February 2, 1885. At the meeting of the Union Labor party in White County he was chosen permanent chairman, and was a delegate to the State convention with instructions to put in the field a full State ticket, using his judgment in favor of the best man. He did so, and a vigorous canvass was carried on, the result being the election of Hon. C. M. Norwood, an ex-Confederate, one-leg soldier, as Governor, by a majority of from 8,000 to 10,000 votes. In 1886, at a meeting of the State Wheel, he was elected a member of the executive committee of that body, and was re-elected for three consecutive terms. He was also a delegate to the National Agricultural Wheel, the meeting of all Labor organizations, at Meridian, Miss., in December, 1888; was a member of the first National Cotton Committee, also at that place, and the second one, held at Atlanta, Ga. In 1886 he represented the Arkansas State Wheel, at Raleigh, N. C., and was elected by that body to the Farmers' Union to be held at Shreveport, La., in 1887. At a meeting of the State Wheel held at Little Rock, the same year, he was chosen State Lecturer, and was re-elected in 1888. The following year, at a meeting of the State Wheel at Hot Springs, he was chosen president of the State Wheel of Arkansas, and was at the same time elected a delegate to the National Farmers' and Laborers' Union, which was held in St. Louis, in December, 1889. October 19, of the same year, as president of the above-named body he issued a proclamation dissolving the State Wheel, and adopting the Farmers' and Laborers' Union of America, as agreed at the meeting of all the Labor organizations in 1888. Mr. Russ was president of the first district Wheel ever organized in White County, and filled the same position for the Twenty-seventh, the first senatorial Wheel, comprising White and Faulkner Counties. He discharged the duties of this position also for the Second Congressional Wheel, to which office he was elected in 1884, and he has been re-elected each succeeding year. He has held the office of Lecturer in the subordinate office for five years, and in this capacity has lectured in a great many counties. He is a strict temperance man, and for many years has been a member of the Methodist Episcopal Church, South, and in support of the latter, as well as in the cause of education, he has been exceedingly liberal and free-hearted. He is now acting as deputy sheriff of White County, and although repeatedly urged to run for representative of White County, he has declined, thinking he could do more good for his party off the ticket than on. In 1873 Mr. Russ purchased from the United States Government 160 acres of wild land, and by subsequent purchases has increased his land to 660 acres, of which 122 are under cultivation. His first farm was heavy timber land, but after many years of arduous labor and with the assistance of his worthy wife, who has proved to him a true helpmate, he has become one of the wealthy agriculturists of the county. In the comparatively short time which has elapsed since he commenced doing for himself, he has developed and improved

two fine farms, and has made all the property he now has by the sweat of his brow as, at the time of marriage, he only possessed $23, a horse and a gold watch. At the time of locating, he, his wife and father could carry their effects on their backs, and the furniture with which their house was provided was made of lumber from their own land. Many changes have occurred since this esteemed citizen first located here, and he has witnessed the growth, of what was once a vast wilderness, to one of the most prosperous and influential counties of the State. He and wife have hosts of warm friends, and as they look back over their past careers they can see little to regret, while the future in the life to come stands out brightly before them.

James E. Russ, an attorney at law and notary public, of Beebe, is recognized as a prominent member of the legal fraternity of White County. A native of North Carolina, he was born in Orange County, November 9, 1855, being the son of Charles E. and Sarah A. (Parker) Russ, also of North Carolina origin [a sketch of whose lives appears on a previous page, as well as a history of this illustrious family]. Charles Russ was born in 1819 and his wife in 1826. They were of Scotch-Irish and English descent, and were married in their native State in 1843, moving in 1859 to Alabama, where Mr. Russ conducted an extensive plantation, and managed a large force of slaves until after the war (in which he held the rank of major for four years). He subsequently went to Tennessee and after a residence there of four years, moved again, this time settling in El Paso, Ark., where he followed the occupation of farming until his death in 1885. He was a Universalist in his religious belief, his wife, who only survived him a few months, being a devoted member of the Methodist Episcopal Church, South. Mr. Russ was a member of high standing in the Masonic order, and Mrs. Russ of the Eastern Star. James E. was the fifth in a family of six children, as follows: Laura J. (wife of Thomas H. Midyett, a wealthy farmer of El Paso), J. P. H. Russ (farmer and president of the State Wheel of Arkansas), Charles W. (who died at the age of twenty-two, unmarried), Mary and Robert (who both died in their youth). James

E. was reared to farm life, but his opportunities for obtaining an education were very limited, three months being the extent of his entire schooling. At an early age, however, he became a careful student and constant reader at home. When twenty-one he entered upon the reading of law, at the same time managing the farm and supporting his parents. This course he continued until 1883, when he was admitted to the bar at Little Rock, having passed a critical examination before Judges W. F. Hill, T. J. Oliphant and J. M. Rose, committee, with Judge F. T. Vaughn as presiding judge. After passing this examination Mr. Russ formed a partnership with Judge Oliphant, under the firm name of Oliphant & Russ, which relation existed nearly two years. Compelled to withdraw at that time on account of ill health, he passed several months in traveling, later returning to Arkansas, and finally settled in Beebe, where he has since resided, gaining by his upright course and recognized ability, the confidence and esteem of all acquaintances. As a practictioner he has built up an enviable and lucrative clientage, having a general law business in all courts of the State. In January, 1887, he lost his residence and contents by fire, but by energy, economy and strict integrity, has recovered from that disaster almost entirely. In December, 1883, Mr. Russ was united in marriage with Miss Belle Andrews, an estimable lady, daughter of William Andrews, a lawyer of Paducah, Ky. To them have been given a family of two children: Paul Eaton (born in September, 1884) and Jane (born November 2, 1886). Mr. and Mrs. Russ are members of the Methodist Episcopal Church, South, and both are deservedly popular in society circles. The former votes the straight Democratic ticket, but has never been looked upon as an aspirant for political preferment. During the year 1888 he was a member of the real-estate firm of Merrill, Russ & Co.

Christopher N. Saunders, a farmer and stockman of Dog Wood Township, White County, Ark., was born in Virginia in 1822, and is the second child born to Wren and Mary D. (Teatroff) Saunders, who were also Virginians, the father's birth occurring in 1822. His parents, Reuben and Frances Saunders, were born in that State, and there reared their family, of which State their son Wren is still an inhabitant. He was married in 1840, his wife being a daughter of John Teatroff, and he and wife reared a family of eleven children: Columbia I., Christopher N., Jane (who was a Mrs. Hunt, and is now dead), Reuben, Daniel (who died young), Mary (also died in childhood), Ellen and Logan (both died in infancy), Millard P. (a resident of West Virginia), Artemas and Leanna D. (married). The mother of these children died in 1865, a consistent member of the Christian Church at the time of her death. Christopher N. Saunders spent his youth on a farm, and also received his early schooling in his native State. In 1862 he enlisted in Company F, Twenty-fifth Virginia Cavalry, and the first battle in which he participated was near Richmond. After the war he began farming for himself, and in 1871 was married to Malina Owen, a daughter of William and Keron Owen, natives of Virginia, both of whom are now dead. Mr. Saunders and his wife reared a family of six children: Wren, Minnie, Claudius, Keron, Clifford G. and Charles C. John W. died in childhood, and Mattie Lee died in October, 1889. In 1876 our subject removed with his family to White County, Ark., and in 1881 bought his present farm of 160 acres. He has forty acres under cultivation, and is doing well. He is a Democrat, and he and wife belong to the Christian Church.

Elihu Q. Seaton is the son of George W. Seaton, a native of Alabama, who was born near Huntsville, Madison County, N. Ala., on June 13, 1820, moving when quite young with his parents to Panola County, Miss., where he grew to manhood. In 1841 he was united in marriage to Miss Lucinda Smart, also of Alabama origin, her birth occurring in Florence, Lauderdale County, April 9, 1820. When a young girl she accompanied her parents to Mississippi. George W. Seaton was by profession a farmer, but spent a greater part of his time in teaching school, being a man of superior education and refinement. He was an exemplary member of the Missionary Baptist Church, and took an active part in all church and charitable enterprises, particularly so in his later years. In his political views he sided with the Democrats, and held many offices of trust, discharging his duties in a highly commendable manner, and winning great credit for himself and family. He was a Mason in high standing, and recognized as a prominent and influential citizen. Mrs. Seaton, though a professor of religious faith from a very early age, was not connected with any church. She and her husband were descendants of some of the oldest and best families of Northern Alabama. Removing from Mississippi to Lonoke County, Ark., in 1878, they were residing there at the time of Mr. Seaton's death in September, 1880. Mrs. Seaton then went to Texas, but soon returned to her home in Lonoke County, where she now lives. To their union nine children were born, seven of whom survive: William (a farmer of Panola, Miss.), George S. N. (a planter of Sevier County, Ark.), Sarah S. T. (the wife of J. M. Smith, of Faulkner County, Ark.), Elihu Q. (the subject of this sketch), Albertine, J. (now Mrs. J. D. McPherson, of Collins County, Tex.), Lucy A. (wife of Elias Harrell, of Prairie County, Ark.), Georgiana A. (Mrs. Frank White, a prosperous farmer of Lonoke County, Ark.), Frances H. (widow of William Mason; now the wife of Andrew Lowe), B. A. (the wife of L. J. Pardue, and died in Lonoke County in 1887). Elihu Q. Seaton's educational advantages in youth were limited to the inferior schools of the period, but by constant reading and close observation, he has obtained a good practical education. He began for himself at the age of twenty years, first as a farmer, and then as a teacher in the public schools, where for eight years he instructed the young idea, and gained an enviable local reputation as an instructor. For the last three years Mr. Seaton has been engaged in the mercantile business, and is now located at Russell, Ark. He carries a general stock valued at $2,000, and has been quite successful in this business, and in the accumulation of property. He was married January 13, 1889, to Miss Frances A. Gamble, of White County, and a Kentuckian by birth. To this marriage one child has been born, Benjamin A., on October 11, 1889. Mr. and Mrs. Seaton are mem-

bers of the Cumberland Presbyterian Church, to which they give their support. In all worthy enterprises Mr. Seaton is a leader, not a follower, and has accomplished, by his progressive spirit, many things that might otherwise still be in an embryo state. He is a conservative Democrat, and a member in high standing of the Masonic order. In 1888 he received an appointment as notary public for a term of four years.

Andrew C. Shoffner, M. D., deserves honorable mention as one of the successful practitioners of the healing art in White County, and since 1876 has been actively engaged in alleviating the sufferings of the sick and afflicted, his services being in demand among the best people of the county. He was born in Tennessee, in 1830, and is a son of Martin and Jane C. (Johnson) Shoffner, and grandson of John and Christenia Shoffner. Martin Shoffner was born in North Carolina, in 1806, and inherited German blood from his parents. He was married in 1828, and the children born to his union are as follows: Andrew C., Mary A. (Mrs. Johnson, living in Tennessee), Minerva A. (Mrs. Powell, now deceased), James H. (a resident of Mississippi), Elizabeth J. (Mrs. Howard, living in Mississippi), Susan A. (Mrs. Vick, also a resident of Mississippi), John F. (who was killed in the battle of Chickamauga), Josephine (Mrs. Curl, of Mississippi) and Francis M. (living in De Soto County, Miss.). Martin Shoffner followed the occupation of farming all his life, and spent his declining years in Marshall County, Miss., his death occurring there in 1858, his wife's death having occurred in 1851, both being members of the Cumberland Presbyterian Church. Dr. Shoffner, our subject, spent his youth on a farm in Tennessee, and completed his education at a private school. In 1862 he enlisted in the army, but was shortly after discharged on account of ill health and returned home. He was married in 1851 to Miss Julia A. Vick, a daughter of Ransom and Elizabeth Vick, the former of Virginia, and the latter a Tennesseean. Of a family of thirteen children born to the Doctor and his wife, only one is dead. Those living are: Robert L. (who married Sallie A. Walker, and resides in the county), Cordelia (Mrs.

Smith, a resident of Marshall County, Miss.), Jennie (Mrs. Walker, is a resident of Dog Wood Township), Ella (Mrs. Davis, lives in Argenta, Ark.), James M. (lives at Searcy), Laura (Mrs. Beaver, is a resident of Arkansas), Augustus F., Lucy E., Henrietta, Idonia and Addie, all single. In 1866 Dr. Shoffner came to White County, Ark., settling in Searcy Valley, but since 1874 has been a resident of Dog Wood Township, where he has a farm of 100 acres, with fifty under cultivation. He devotes his time to the practice of his profession, and leaves his sons to manage the farm. He is ever interested in all good works, and gives liberally of his means in the support of schools and churches. Politically he is a Republican, and socially, belongs to the Masonic fraternity.

Thomas Smith. Personal popularity results largely from the industry, perseverance and close attention to business which a person displays in the management of any particular branch of trade, and in the case of Mr. Smith this is most certainly true, for he has adhered closely to farming and the stock industry, and helped in so many ways to advance all worthy interests in the community, that he has won the admiration and respect of all. His parents, Matthew and Mary (McCue) Smith were born in Killeshandra Village, Ireland, and to them were given three sons: Peter (born in 1821), Thomas (born in 1822), and James (born in 1824). The father died in 1824, and his widow resided in her native county until 1831, when she with her family moved to the city of Balbriggean, County Dublin, and there lived until her demise in 1840. Seven years later Thomas Smith and his brother James emigrated to America, the elder brother, Peter, having emigrated to this country in 1845. They landed at New York, May 27, 1847, and after a few days' stay in that city they joined their brother Peter in Delaware County, Penn., he having secured work with a farmer, S. T. Walker. They were also fortunate enough to find employment, and from the time they reached Pennsylvania until three and one-half years later Thomas was engaged in farm labor. In 1850 he, with his brother James, removed to Arkansas and settled in Faulkner County (then Conway County), each be-

coming the owner of 160 acres of land, both of which are in the possession of our subject at the present time. In 1850 he was married in the Catholic Church of Old Chester, Penn., to Miss Mary Ann Collins, a native of County Donegal, Ireland, and after their removal to Arkansas they both set energetically to work to clear and improve their farm, which was a heavy timber tract inhabited by all kinds of wild game. Their capital consisted of a pair of willing hands and a determination to succeed no matter what the obstacles might be, and to say that they had been successful would not do the subject justice. The year following their arrival in the State they built them a substantial log-house, and the first letter they received after settling in their new home, was from a friend in Pennsylvania, Mr. Smith walking to the nearest postoffice, a distance of twenty miles to receive it. He has cleared 150 acres of his farm from timber, and now has some of the most fertile land of which the county can boast. Having experienced the many hardships and privations which beset a man in his journey through life, Mr. Smith never turns the more unfortunate from his door, but is always generous, charitable and hospitable. The following family was born to him and his first wife: James (born August 19, 1851), Mary Ann (born in 1853), Sarah (born in 1855), Susan (born in 1856), Thomas (born in 1857) and Edward (born in 1859), all of whom died in infancy, the mother also dying August 1, 1859. In 1861 Mr. Smith espoused his second wife, Miss Elizabeth Hogans, of Arkansas, but her death occurred in 1870, in giving birth to her son, Henry. The children of this union are: William (born January 20, 1862), Alice (born May 9, 1864), Thomas (born October 24, 1865), Hugh (born April 17, 1867), Edward (born April 27, 1867), Robert (born December 9, 1869) and Henry (born January 27, 1870). On January 18, 1871, Mr. Smith's union with his third wife took place, her name being Elizabeth Wilson. Mr. Smith and wife are members of the Catholic Church, and all their children have been baptized in that faith, but were never confirmed. Mr. Smith is a Democrat, and a member of the Agricultural Wheel No. 99.

Joel W. Smith, a prominent farmer of White

County, is a son of Alexander and Sarah (Follwell) Smith, natives of Virginia. Alexander Smith was married in 1816 or 1817, and had a family of five children: Catharine, William H., James M., Sarah A. and Joel W., our subject. Mrs. Smith died in 1828, in Alabama. Mr. Smith then married his second wife in 1830, her maiden name being Miss Margaret Ellis. They were the parents of nine children: Aaron G. (deceased), Keziah, Alyrah, Mary, George, Margery, Lottie, Victoria and Martha. Joel W. Smith was born in Limestone County, Ala., in 1826. He was reared on a farm, and received but little education, his father dying in 1852. Upon arriving at maturity he was married on November 25, 1845, to Elizabeth F. Lewis, also of Alabama nativity, and a child of William and Jane (Rogers) Lewis, being the second daughter in a family of ten children. Her birth occurred May 8, 1820. Mr. and Mrs. Smith are the parents of six children: Henrietta (Redus), John A., Edward F., Margaret J. (Yearby) Sarah F. (Alford), and Harriet A. (Sowel). Mr. Smith came to Arkansas in 1858, and settled in White County, whence he enlisted in 1862 in Company B of the Arkansas Infantry, under Capt. Critz, Col. Schofer being in command of the regiment. He was taken sick and received his discharge and returned home, but re-enlisted in 1863, under Col. Geyn. He was in the battle of Helena, and was taken prisoner and carried to Little Rock, later to Walton, Ill., and afterward to Rock Island, Ill., being confined until the close of the war. Mr. Smith has a farm of 300 acres, with over 200 under cultivation. He is a member of Centre Hill Lodge No. 114, A. F. & A. M., and himself and wife belong to the Baptist Church. Mr. Smith is a strong Democrat, and has been school director for the past six years, taking great interest in the work.

Frank W. Smith, Searcy, Ark. Another pioneer settler of the county, and a much-respected citizen is the above-mentioned gentleman who came to White County, Ark., in 1853, from Mississippi. He was born in Fayette County, Miss., in 1833, and was the eighth in a family of nine children, the result of the union of John and Rebecca Smith, natives of Tennessee. The father was a

planter, and in connection carried on merchandising at Oxford, Fayette County, Miss. In 1830 he moved to Benton County, Ark., remaining there a short time, and then returned to Mississippi in 1831, making that his home until his death which occurred at Oxford, Miss., in 1844. His widow survived him many years, came to White County in 1853, and there her death occurred in the fall of that year. Their family consisted of the following children: Harrison (married, and a farmer of De Soto County, Miss.), Benjamin (married, and resides in Gray Township), Margaret (wife of William Graves, of Howard County, Ark.), Catherine (died in White County, Ark., in 1889; she was the wife of John Boggs), Thomas (married and resides in Gray Township), William (died in White County in 1871), John (married and resides in Gray Township), Frank W. and Mary (wife of James Neavill; she died in 1858). The father of these children participated in the War of 1812. Frank W. Smith's youth in growing up was passed in attending to duties about the home place, and in the subscription schools of Mississippi. He commenced farming for himself in White County, Ark., at the age of twenty-one, and in 1855, in partnership with his brother, John, purchased 160 acres of land which he improved. Later the brothers separated, each doing for himself. F. W. Smith has erected all the buildings, and has added to his farm from time to time until he is now the owner of 400 acres, with 150 under cultivation, and 100 acres or more in pasture. He does mixed farming, raises corn and cotton and also considerable horses and cattle, and is one of the wide-awake farmers of the county. He enlisted in the army at Searcy in 1862, and for twelve months was in Capt. Davis' company, Gen. McRae's regiment. He participated in several skirmishes and later went into the State troops, where he remained but a short time. At the close of the service he returned to the farm. He was married in White County in 1855 to Miss Mary L. Neavill, a native of Alabama, and the daughter of Elihu and Margaret (Jones) Neavill, natives of Alabama. Mr. and Mrs. Neavill came to White County in 1844, settled in Gray Township, and he was one of the influential men of the county, being treasurer of the same one term. His death occurred in 1852 and the mother's in 1888. After marriage Mr. Smith settled where he now resides, and there he has since remained. Although not very active in politics he votes with the Democratic party; is a member of the Agricultural Wheel, of which organization he was steward, and he and wife are members of the Methodist Episcopal Church, South. To this union two living children were born: Sarah and Kirby (of which Kirby is married and resides with his father). Mr. Smith came to this county when all was wild and unbroken, and when game was in abundance. Now fine farms cover the country, and everything is in a prosperous condition. He is practically a self-made man; having started with little he is now very comfortably fixed, and can pass the remainder of his life in ease.

William Smith. Faulkner County is rapidly coming into a position as one of the foremost stock counties in the State, and it is but uttering a plain fact to say that to a few men in this community is due the credit for advancing stock interests here and establishing a reputation in this department which is bound to stand for years. Mr. Smith has had not a little to do toward developing the stock matters of this region and if for no other account he is accorded a worthy place in this volume. His parents, Ebenezer and Permelia (Murphy) Smith, were married in Tennessee, in 1823, but the former was born in the State of Mississippi. He was left fatherless when a small boy, his paternal parent dying in Georgia, after which his widowed mother moved with her family to Tennessee, where she died, having borne a family of five sons and two daughters. Ebenezer Smith and his wife became the parents of eleven children, who grew to manhood and womanhood, seven of whom were born in Mississippi and four in Tennessee. After the mother's death in 1855, Mr. Smith married again, his second wife being Miss Elizabeth Chambers of Mississippi, their marriage being solemnized in 1856; six children were born to this union. William Smith, our subject, was reared to a farm life and received a limited education in the subscription schools of Tishomingo County, Miss. He grew to manhood, and on April 26, 1856, was married there to Miss Melvina Dotson, the wedding taking place at the home of the bride's parents, William and Nancy (Bales) Dotson. Victoria A., their eldest child, was born March 26, 1859, and June 14, 1874, became the wife of D. A. Thornton, a farmer who resides in Faulkner County, by whom she has four children. Sidney, the youngest child, was born August 15, 1860, and died August 24, 1864. September 15, 1886, witnessed the celebration of Mr. Smith's second marriage to Mrs. Mattie E. (Tucker) Beasley, daughter of LaFayette and Jane (Knight) Tucker, who were born in Mississippi, the father being of Irish origin. At the age of twenty-one years, Mr. Smith's father made him overseer of his plantation, and for his services gave him a one-fourth interest in the profits of the farm, and at the end of one year he had accumulated sufficient property to enable him to purchase eighty acres of land, all of which was heavily covered with timber. During the six following years, he cleared thirty acres of this tract, and erected thereon a dwelling-house, and the necessary outbuildings. Owing to the turbulent state of affairs during the war he, with his wife and children and a few articles of household furniture, removed by wagon to near Union City, Ky., making their home there for about ten months, and raising one crop. They next settled in Tennessee, near Island No. 10, and here Mr. Smith left his family and went to Paducah, Ky., where he enlisted in the First Kentucky Calvary, Confederate States Army, and served six months or until the close of the war. He then returned to his family and soon after purchased 100 acres of wild land in Gibson County, and this he resided on and continued to improve until 1870, since which time he has been a resident of the State of Arkansas. The farm upon which he is now residing consists of 243 acres, the original purchase consisting of 160 acres. Only a small portion of this land had been cleared, but at the present writing seventy acres are in high state of cultivation, the soil being well adapted to the raising of cotton, corn, oats and all varieties of vegetables. Both Mr. Smith and his wife are professors of religion, the former a member of the Missionary Baptist Church, and the latter of the Methodist Episcopal Church. Mr. Smith is a supporter and member of the Agricultural Wheel, belonging to El Paso Lodge No. 158, is a man of enterprise and progress, and being hospitable and generous is a valuable addition to the county of his adoption.

Abner F. Smith received his education at the high schools of Powhattan County, Va., but left his implements of study and literary pursuits in May, 1861, to take up the instruments of war. Joining the Confederate army he entered the Powhattan Rifle Company and was in the battles of Prairie Grove, Cotton Plant, Helena, Little Rock, Jenkins' Ferry, and a number of skirmishes. After the war Mr. Smith went to Grand Glaize, Ark., and commenced farming, and in 1870 engaged in the grocery business in partnership with John Thurman. Two years later he started alone, but the credit business proved unprofitable to him and he embarked in the timber business, being engaged in getting out ties for the Iron Mountain Railroad. In 1886 he opened up a store in Bald Knob, and is now enjoying a large and lucrative patronage. Abner T. Smith was born in Chesterfield County, Va., in 1843, being the son of William S. and Elizabeth (Edwards) Smith. The former was a railroad contractor and also contractor for public works while in Virginia, but after his removal to Arkansas carried on merchandising at Grand Glaize. He was a Whig in politics, and belonged to the Masonic order at the time of his death, which occurred in 1864, when forty-eight years old. Mrs. Smith has long been a member of the Methodist Episcopal Church, South. She was born in 1815 and is still living in Bald Knob, Ark. In this family were six children, only two of whom are living: Abner F. (our subject) and Alonzo (who is in business with his brother). Mr. Smith was married February 22, 1867, to Miss Fanny Heard, daughter of Baily E. Heard. She died in 1873, leaving three children, only one of whom is living: William B., a student at Searcy College, and who intends entering a law school after graduating at Searcy. June 24, 1874, Mr. Smith married Lucy C. Patrick, who died April 20, 1871, leaving one child:

Edward A. He was married to his present wife, Adeline Allen, March 4, 1876. Mrs. Smith is a daughter of Dr. John Allen, of White County, and is the mother of one daughter: Mamie. Mr. Smith is a strong Democrat and belongs to the Masonic order, also holding membership in the Methodist Episcopal Church, South. While in Jackson County he was appointed justice of the peace by Gov. Garland.

Dr. J. A. Snipes, Searcy, Ark. The career of Dr. Snipes as a physician and surgeon has long been well and favorably known to the many who have tested his healing ability, and his popularity as a druggist is firmly established. He owns a good two-story brick business building, 100x30 feet, carries a full line of drugs, paints, oils, etc., and does a thriving trade. He first engaged in the drug business in the early part of 1885, and since then he has been thus employed. He was born in Orange County, N. C., in 1825, was the third in a family of seven children born to E. P. and Nancy (Burnett) Snipes, natives of North Carolina, the father born in 1800 and the mother in 1801, and in Orange and Chatham Counties, respectively. The parents were married in Chatham County, N. C., in 1821, and the father followed agricultural pursuits there until 1845, when he moved to Madison County, W. Tenn. After residing there until 1854 he moved to Haywood County, Tenn., purchased an improved farm, and still owns 560 acres in Jefferson County, with 350 acres under cultivation. The father is still living, and makes his home with the Doctor. He has been a very industrious, energetic man, was magistrate of several counties, and has been a member of the Methodist Episcopal Church for sixty years. The mother died in Madison County, Tenn., in 1857. The paternal grandparents, Thomas and Martha (Williams) Snipes, were natives of the Old Dominion, and moved to North Carolina when children. The maternal grandparents, Isaiah and Jane (Herndon) Burnett, were natives of North Carolina, and always made that State their home. They died many years ago. The seven children born to E. P. and Nancy (Burnett) Snipes are named as follows: Walter A. (married, and in 1856 came to

White County, locating in Marion Township, followed farming, and there remained until 1857, when he went to Jefferson County, and there continued his former occupation; his death occurred in the winter of 1884–85, and he left one child, William E., who is a machinist and resides in Jefferson County, Ark.), Eliza J. (widow of C. B. Horton, resides at the Doctor's), Dr. J. A., Farrington B. (married, resides in Madison County, Tenn., and is a lawyer and farmer), Julia A. (now Mrs. Allen, of Brownsville, Tenn.), Martha M., (now Mrs. J. T. Key, of Searcy, Ark.) and Thomas J. (who enlisted in the army in Jefferson County in 1862, and died of smallpox in Mississippi two years later). Dr. J. A. Snipes was reared to farm labor and was favored with such educational advantages as the district schools of that day afforded. After coming to Tennessee he engaged in teaching and also read medicine for about three years, subsequently attending that far-famed institution, the Jeffersonian Medical College, at Philadelphia, Penn., in 1848. In 1851 he began the practice of medicine in Dyer County, Tenn., thence in 1852 went to Madison County, Tenn., and finally in 1854 came to White County, locating in Searcy, and has practiced his profession in White County continuously for thirty-five years. He is one of the earliest practitioners and is one in whom all have confidence. Aside from his practice he has also been engaged in farming in this and Marion Townships. He resided in the last-named township from 1856 to 1868, and opened up a large farm in Big Creek. He has resided in Searcy since 1868, with the exception of three years, when he resided on his farm in the suburbs. Dr. Snipes was married in Lauderdale County, Tenn., in December, 1853, to Miss Elizabeth J. Murphy, a native of Halifax County, Va., and the daughter of Thomas and Lucy (Coleman) Murphy, natives of Virginia. Her father died in that State, and the mother afterward immigrated to Tennessee (1842), thence to Searcy in 1854, and made her home with the Doctor until 1867, when she was killed in the memorable cyclone of May 27 of that year. By this union five children were born, three now living: Anna B. (now Mrs. W. H. Lightle, of Searcy),

16

Minnie (now Mrs. John T. Hicks, of Searcy) and Emmett (a pharmacist in the drug store of the Doctor). Mrs. Lightle has four children: Minnie H., Edward J., Bettie K. and Julian. Mrs. Hicks has two children: Everett B. and Willie Burnett. The Doctor's deceased children are named as follows: Everett (died, in 1876, at the age of eighteen years, and Camillus (died, in 1874, at the age of fourteen years). Socially, the Doctor is a member of Searcy Lodge No. 49, A. F. & A. M., and is a member of Tillman Chapter No. 19, R. A. M. He is also a member of the I. O. O. F. Lodge at Searcy. Dr. Snipes has seen the full growth and development of Searcy during the many years of his residence here. What is now Mrs. Chambless' hotel was the court house at that time, and many and great have been the changes. He took an active interest in working for the location of the State University that was finally located at Fayetteville, but union not existing in Searcy, that city failed to get it. The Doctor, his wife and all the family are members of the Methodist Episcopal Church. Dr. Snipes has always been deeply interested in educational matters.

Omal H. Stanley is the eldest son of a family of eight children born to John H. and Elizabeth (Yancey) Stanley. John H. Stanley, born in about 1800, was a native of Halifax, Va., and a carriage-maker by trade, his marriage occurring in 1829. He afterward moved to Jackson, Tenn., where he went into the carriage business, and there he died in 1848, his wife following in 1873. O. H. Stanley learned the carriage-maker's trade of his father when a boy, and upon reaching manhood was married, in Jackson, Tenn., in 1852, to Jane M. Lauffort, originally from Madison County, Tenn., born in 1835. Her father held the office of county clerk in 1848 and for four years following, and in 1852 was elected county treasurer, occupying this official position for two years. In 1856 he moved to Arkansas, where he died in 1862. After his marriage, Mr. Stanley started a carriage shop at Jackson, remaining until 1860, when he removed to Austin, Prairie County, Ark., and carried on business there until 1864, excepting one year, while serving in the Confederate army, in Glenn's regiment; he was in the quartermaster's department. Upon receiving his discharge, in 1864, he went to Perry County, Ill., but thirteen months after, or in September, 1865, came back to Arkansas, and settled at Devall's Bluff, where he took charge of the Government shops. Four years later he started a shop in Searcy, tarried two years, then moved to a farm on Dead River, where he remained four years, and in 1874 came to Cane Township, White County, purchasing 160 acres of wild land. This he has partially cleared (about sixty acres), and on it has erected a good house and other buildings. Mr. and Mrs. Stanley were the parents of ten children, nine of whom are still living: Edgar H. (deceased), James R., Jason C., Mary E. (now Mrs. Smith), Elanora, Willie B., Oscar L., Gertrude, Emma L. and Charles W. Mr. and Mrs. Stanley are members of the Methodist Episcopal Church, Mr. Stanley being chairman of the board of trustees. He is a strong Democrat in his political preferences, and takes an active interest in all movements for the good of the community.

J. W. Starkey is a representative and wideawake farmer of White County, Ark., having been a resident in this county since 1870. He first saw the light of this world in Tuscaloosa County, Ala., in 1853, and was the second in a family of twelve children given to John B. and Nancy (Weaver) Starkey, the former born in North Carolina and the latter in Alabama. They married in the latter State in 1851, and after clearing and living on a farm there until 1866, he immigrated to Itawamba County, Miss. Four years later he settled in White County, Ark.; here he purchased a partially improved farm of 160 acres, and now has 100 under the plow. In 1862 he enlisted from Alabama in the Confederate army, and served three years. His death occurred in White County, January 14, 1889, and at the time of his demise was counted one of the members of the Wheel organization. His wife still lives, and resides on the old homestead. Their children are: Martha A. (Mrs. Weeks), John W. (the subject of this sketch), D. A. (a resident of the county), E. J. (Mrs. Worthen, of Kentucky Township), N. B. (Mrs. Troxell, of

the same township), M. F. (Mrs. Rissell, of the same township), R. C., Ellen, George Robert, Robert Bruce, William Bedford and Ollie B. John W. Starkey learned the carpenter's trade in his youth, in addition to becoming familiar with farm work, and received the greater part of his education in the schools of Mississippi. At the age of twenty-four he began farming for himself, and was married to Mattie Jones, a native of Georgia, purchasing soon after a timber tract of eighty acres, and now has fifty-five cleared and improved. He gives considerable attention to raising stock, and is succeeding in his enterprises. In politics he is a Democrat, and he, with his wife, worships with the Missionary Baptist Church, to which they belong. They are the parents of five children: John T., Alwilda, Nancy Jane, Grover Cleveland and Bersada. Mrs. Starkey is a daughter of Thomas F. and Nancy (Kilpatrick) Jones, who were native Georgians, the father a boot and shoe maker by trade. In 1870 he settled in Brownsville, Prairie County, Ark., but a year later removed to Searcy, White County, and, in 1885, to Texas, where he now resides. His wife died in Searcy, in 1873.

Hon. Lee Thomas Stewart, a man who has held public office every year since he was twenty-one years old, of Beebe, Ark., was born in the county in which he is now residing on April 16, 1863, and is one of seven surviving members of a family of thirteen children born to Robert M. and Catherine (Walker) Stewart, from whom he inherits Scotch-Irish blood. The father and mother were born in North and South Carolina, respectively, and were among the early immigrants to White County, Ark., settling about ten miles from Searcy on the Searcy and Des Arc road. Here Mr. Stewart improved a farm and at the time of his death, in 1868, owned considerable land, of which seventy-five acres were under the plow. When the war broke out he owned fifteen slaves, but of course they were all lost during the Rebellion. R. M. Stewart moved to this State in 1856. He was a member of the Presbyterian Church, and a Mason, standing high in this order and was buried with Masonic honors. He also helped build the first church and schoolhouse in the southern part of White County. The following are the members of his family: Joseph (was born in 1842 and died during the war while in the hospital in Little Rock), Adaline (who was born in 1844 and became the wife of Isaac Chrisman, a farmer residing on the Arkansas River in Lonoke County), J. G. (who was born in 1846, and wedded Mrs. Nancy Carter *nee* Myrick; he is a school-teacher and farmer near Pine Bluff), Bettie (born in 1848, became the wife of Edward Barnes, a farmer and stockman of Texas, and died in November, 1882), D. M. (was born in 1850, he being also a farmer and stock trader, and he was married to Miss Allie Allen), Susan (was born in 1852 and died at the age of twenty-two), Robert G. (was born in 1854, and by occupation is a druggist being now a resident of the town of Dayton, Ark.), W. C. (was born in 1856, and he is a practitioner of dentistry at Dripping Springs, Tex.), Mollie (was born in 1858, and is the wife of Dr. J. D. Harris, of Butlersville, Ark.), Dora and Cora (were born in 1860, and are both deceased, Cora dying in infancy and Dora at the age of twelve years). The next in order of birth is Lee Thomas (our subject) and Rena (who was born in 1865, and died in infancy). Lee Thomas Stewart remained on his father's farm until about fifteen years of age and received the greater portion of his early education in the schools of Searcy, being an attendant at the high school for two years. After returning to the neighborhood in which he was reared he taught a subscription school for three months and the three following years worked as a tiller of the soil. After coming to Beebe he clerked in the general mercantile establishment of D. C. Harris for about eighteen months and then devoted the entire year of 1883 to the study of telegraphy, after which he went to Hoxie, on the Iron Mountain Railroad, where he hèld the position of telegraph operator for some time. In the winter of 1883 he returned to Beebe and resumed clerking in Dr. Harris' store, but the following year engaged in the same business with T. S. Neylon. This connection lasted for two years, then Mr. Stewart sold his interest and the next six months acted as book-keeper for J. M. Liles, after which he spent six months in the study of law. In Jan-

uary, 1888, he began clerking in the drug store of Dr. Ennis, but in the spring of 1889 was elected to the office of mayor of Beebe over his competitor, a popular gentleman, and is at the present time the incumbent of that office. He was elected by the Democrats to the position of alderman when only twenty-one years of age and served two terms. Mr. Stewart is progressive in his views, liberal in his opinions and labors and contributes willingly to the advancement of the county and State and is an ardent advocate of education. Though thoroughly democratic in his views politically, he respects very highly the opinions of others who differ with him in matters generally.

A. L. Stowell was born, reared and educated in Bureau County, Ill., the former event taking place August 8, 1841. Just after commencing his apprenticeship as a carpenter, the war broke out and Mr. Stowell, full of youthful enthusiasm, joined his destines with the cause of the Union, enlisting in Company B, First Battalion of Yeats' Sharpshooters, and served in Mississippi, being present at the battles of Corinth and New Madrid (Mo.). He was stationed one year at Glendale, near Corinth, after which his regiment returned to Illinois and was reorganized, or rather veteranized, into the Sixty-fourth Illinois Infantry. While serving in this capacity he was with Sherman on his march to the sea, and was at the siege of Atlanta, where he was under fire for sixty days. He carried his knapsack to Washington, D. C., and was present at the grand review. He was as well acquainted with the face of Gen. Sherman as that of a brother, and when the latter came to part with his command, on July 4, 1865, he made the division that Mr. Stowell was in a special speech and wept like a child, so warm a place had these veterans gained in his heart. The company was mustered out of service at Louisville, Ky., and was disbanded at Chicago, Ill., and for three years Mr. Stowell was president of the reunion of this command. He is now vice-commander of his post of G. A. R. After his return from the war he resumed the carpenter's trade, which had been so suddenly broken off, and continued this occupation at McComb, Ill., until 1883, at which time he settled in Beebe,

Ark., and engaged in fruit growing, making strawberries a specialty. In order to save his fruit he commenced making his strawberries into wine, some five years since, and in this enterprise has established a remunerative business. Mr. Stowell is a member of the I. O. O. F. and in his political views is a Republican. He was married March 19, 1867, to Miss Sarah B. Kissinger, who was born in Pennsylvania in 1843. The earliest facts known in the history of the Stowell family is that they were originally Normans, and removed to England with William the Conqueror, and were there knighted. Two brothers came from that country to the United States, one settling in California and the other in the eastern part of the United States, and all the Stowells in this country are their descendants. The parents of our biographical subject are Joshua and Amanda (Harrington) Stowell, the father being born in the Green Mountains of Vermont. He was a harness-maker by trade, and after residing for many years in Princeton, Ill., he removed to Chicago, where he is now living. The Harringtons were of German descent.

Henry Beverly Strange is a general merchant and farmer, of Beebe, Ark., and is well known throughout the county as a business man of honor and integrity. Like many other prominent men of the county he is a Tennesseean, his birth having occurred in Maury County, September 29, 1830, where he was also reared and educated. At the age of twenty years he started out in life for himself as a book agent, and for two years sold "The Southern Family Physician" and other books, meeting with signal success in this undertaking. In 1859 he came to White County, Ark., and engaged in business at Old Stony Point until 1872, when the Iron Mountain Railway reached Beebe, and in order to get a station at this point Mr. Strange built a depot and gave it to the company. He then moved his goods here and has since done a prosperous general merchandise business, being particularly successful in house furnishing. He has the largest business of any firm in the town, and his residence property is the finest in the place. He also has a store at Ward which nets a good income. He was first married in 1859 to Miss E. Ward, a native of North Carolina and a daughter of Whitman Ward, who was one of the prosperous farmers of Tennessee. Mrs. Strange died in 1870, leaving one child, Florence, wife of John Walker, five other children she bore having died in infancy. Mr. Strange married Sallie Apple in 1872, she having come from North Carolina to Arkansas at an early date, and their union resulted in the birth of three children, two of whom are living: Hubert (a youth of fourteen) and Vida (about sixteen years of age). Mrs. Strange is a member of the Methodist Episcopal Church, South, and he belongs to Beebe Lodge No. 145, A. F. & A. M., and also to the K. of H. and the A. L. of H. He is vice-president of the American Building, Loan & Savings Association, and is one of the public-spirited men of Beebe and takes an interest in all movements designed for the public good. He is a son of Beverly and Susanna (Martin) Strange, who were Virginians, and removed from that State to Tennessee shortly after marriage, and there engaged in farming. At the time of their deaths both were worthy members of the Methodist Episcopal Church, South.

William H. Strayhorn is a worthy descendant of Gilbert Strayhorn, who was a native of North Carolina, and was engaged in farming all his life. He died about 1835, having been the father of six children: John D., William James, J. K., Margaret and Rebecca. John D., the eldest, was born in Tennessee, in 1800, and was also a farmer by occupation. He married in 1829, Mary A. Stevenson, a Tennesseean by birth, and a daughter of Henry and Ann (Robinson) Stevenson. John D. Strayhorn was familiarly called major on account of being, as a general thing, the commanding officer on celebration days. He was a member of the Old School Presbyterian Church. To himself and wife only one child, a son, William H., was born. William H. Strayhorn first made his appearance upon the scenes of this world in Tennessee, in 1833. He moved to Arkansas, in 1850, with his grandfather Stevenson, who settled in White County; his father died and his mother marrying the second time, in 1840, W. R. Fortner. Mr. Strayhorn, in 1854, took for his wife Mary J. Burket, daughter of William and Rachel (Hughs) Burket, natives of Tennessee, who moved to White County, Ark., in 1848. They have become the parents of eleven children (two of whom are deceased): Josiah, William H., John D., Samuel W., Alexander, Poney, Benjamin, Mary A., Rachel E., Elvira (deceased) and Elizabeth (deceased). Mr. and Mrs. Strayhorn are members of the Cumberland Presbyterian Church. The former settled on the farm upon which he now resides, July 14, 1856, having a place of 230 acres, 150 being under cultivation. He is a strong Democrat, and although not taking an active part in politics he has held the office of justice of the peace for two years, Mr. Strayhorn says he can raise any crop here that can be grown at all, and thinks Arkansas is the State of the Union.

Alfred B. Sutton's war experience is perhaps similar to that of many other soldiers, mentioned in this volume, but they are all interesting, and give the present generation some idea of the hardships and perils endured by the gallant and brave boys, thousands of whom now fill an unknown grave. In 1861 Alfred Sutton entered the Confederate service, and fought under Col. McCarver. His first serious engagement was at the battle of Corinth, Miss., from which he escaped serious injury. He was captured at Vicksburg, Miss., and taken to Indianapolis, where he remained for three months, then being removed to Port Delaware, and from there to Point Lookout on the Chesapeake Bay. In the latter place he was incarcerated for nine months and nine days, receiving his parole in December, 1864. He was in several engagements and skirmishes, but escaped serious wounds. After receiving his parole he returned to Camden to his command, and in 1865 was discharged, and at once returned to his home, resuming his former occupation of farming, which he has followed principally ever since. His father, Jesse Sutton, was born in Wilson County, Tenn., in 1817, where he received his education, there marrying Elizabeth Hight, of the same State. Their union was blessed with a family of nine children, of whom Alfred B. is the second, his birth occurring in 1840. He was a farmer by oc-

cupation, owning 500 acres of excellent land at the time of his removal from Tennessee to Arkansas, in 1848. He located in Cleburne County, and there resided until his death in 1887, his wife having preceded him a few years. Mr. Sutton and his estimable companion were devout members of the Christian Church, and he was a man who took a great interest in all enterprises, especially those of an educational nature. Alfred B. received a common-school education in the schools of Arkansas, and in February of 1867 was united in marriage with Miss Sarah Bailey, daughter of Henry and Frances Bailey. To their union have been born a family of three children: Henry, Jesse L. and Nora L. Mr. Sutton is a prosperous farmer, and owns 160 acres in White County, and 200 acres in Cleburne County; of this amount 100 acres are in a high state of cultivation. He is Past Master of the Masonic lodge, and has represented that order in the Grand Lodge two different times, besides having held various other offices. He has served as school director for twelve years, and is a man respected and esteemed by the entire community.

Rev. J. M. Talkington, pastor of the Methodist Episcopal Church, South, at Searcy, took charge of the church at that place in December, 1888, but prior to that time, from 1885 to 1888, was presiding elder in the White River district, embracing about seven counties. He joined the White River Conference at Mount Zion in 1870, and was located in the Searcy circuit, consisting of several pastoral charges adjacent to Searcy and in White County. He remained on that work from 1871 to 1873, after which he received a call to West Point, and after remaining there some time, moved to the El Paso charge, where he was given the presiding eldership one year. He subsequently left the Searcy circuit, went to Lebanon circuit, then returned to El Paso circuit, thence to Helena district, then to the pastoral charge· in Beebe in 1884, where he remained two years. From there he went to the Searcy district, remained there until 1888, and in that year received a call to the pastorate of Searcy Church. Mr. Talkington is a native of Jackson County, Ala., where his birth occurred in 1835, and was the oldest in a family of nine children, the result of the union of Andrew Jackson and Mary Ann (Isbell) Talkington, natives of Alabama. The father was a farmer by occupation, opened up a plantation and remained on the same until his death, which occurred in 1856. The mother's death occurred in 1889, at the advanced age of seventy-three years. The father was a soldier in the Florida War. Their children were named as follows: J. M. (the subject of this sketch), Henry F. (married and resides in Union Township), Jane (died in Lonoke County, Ark., in 1887), Elizabeth (died in 1857, in Alabama), Margaret (wife of Joseph Pace, of Alabama), William T. (died in Alabama, in 1857), John (married, and is farming in Alabama), Vincent (died in 1855, in Alabama) and Mary S. (who died in Alabama, in 1855). Rev. J. M. Talkington was educated in the schools of Jackson County, Ala., and came to White County, Ark., at the age of nineteen, where he engaged as clerk for Isbell & Co., general merchants, and remained with them some time. In 1855 he engaged in teaching in Searcy, and followed this profession in White County for ten years. He was married in that county in 1856 to Miss Sarah A. Wright, a native of Independence County, Ark., and the fruits of this union have been eight children: Mary Ann (now Mrs. Arnold, in Gray Township), Julia (now Mrs. Sherrod, resides in Gray Township), Pearl Josephine, Virginia, James M., William Pierce, Cora Ann and John Wesley. While teaching school Mr. Talkington was also engaged in agricultural pursuits, and in 1867 was licensed to preach. From that date up to 1870 he did local work, and in 1877 he purchased a partly improved farm of 170 acres. This he has since improved, and has ninety acres under cultivation, with forty-five acres in fruit. He is deeply interested in horticulture, and now has one of the best fruit farms in the county, raising all variety of fruit that does well in this climate. Mr. Talkington was made a Mason in Searcy Lodge No. 49, A. F. & A. M.; is also a Mason of Tillman Chapter No. 19, R. A. M. In his pastoral work Mr. Talkington has organized many churches in the county,

and has organized some of the principal churches in this and adjoining counties. He has seen a vast change in the county since living here, and the greatest is from a moral standpoint.

Andrew B. Tate, a prominent citizen of Gray Township, is a native of South Carolina, and was born in Chester District, March 21, 1840, being the son of Samuel and Mary J. (Collins) Tate. Samuel Tate was also of South Carolina origin, as was his wife; they were married in Chester District, and moved to Lincoln County, Tenn., in 1841, where the remainder of their lives were passed. They were members in good standing of the Presbyterian Church, and held in high regard by all who knew them. Andrew's grandfather came to America from the Emerald Isle, at the age of twenty-seven and located in Chester District, S. C., where he was recognized as an influential and enterprising citizen. Mrs. Tate's people came from England. To the union of Mr. and Mrs. Tate the following children were given them: William V., Andrew B. (the subject of this memoir), Agnes J., Sarah M., Robert J., Caroline and Tirzah A.; Lavenia G. and James L. (deceased). Samuel Tate died at the age of forty-nine, and his wife in 1866, at the age of sixty-three. The early days of Andrew B. Tate were spent in Lincoln County, Tenn., but when quite young began for himself as a farmer, which has been his principal avocation ever since. His home was in Lincoln County until 1877, when he decided that there was a better opening in Arkansas, to which place he came, locating in White County, and has never had cause to regret the change. He was married on February 6, 1879, to Miss Emma N. Wortham, a daughter of Young Wortham, and to their union two children have been born: Anna B. (born April 18, 1880) and Hettie B. (born April 26, 1885). Mr. and Mrs. Tate, in their religious sympathies, are with the Methodist Episcopal Church, South. Mr. Tate, in his political views is an uncompromising Democrat, and served in the late war, enlisting in the Confederate service in April, 1862, in Col. Stanton's regiment of Tennessee Infantry. On account of disability he was honorably discharged after three months' active service. In social fraternities he is identified with the Masonic order.

A. Byron Tapscott, M. D., although a young man, is one of the leading physicians of West Point, and has a large practice, enjoying a reputation of which many older in the professional experience might well be proud. Dr. Tapscott is a native of Tennessee, and a son of Ira and Mary (Jones) Tapscott, natives of North Carolina and Tennessee, respectively. Ira Byron was also a physician, and a graduate of the Medical College of Richmond, Va. He was a surgeon in Forrest's cavalry, in the late war, and after that struggle practiced in Tennessee until 1872, when he removed to Arkansas, continued his professional duties at West Point. He was a strong Democrat, a member of the Methodist Episcopal Church, and also of the I. O. O. F., and died in January, 1887, at the age of fifty-one years. Mrs. Tapscott is still living in West Point, and is the mother of five children, all living: A. Byron (our subject), Charles V. (an attorney), Emma J., Mary G. and Samuel F. At the age of fifteen Byron Tapscott commenced the study of medicine under his father's instruction, and in 1887 and 1888 attended the Missouri Medical College, at St. Louis. After graduating, he returned to West Point and embarked upon a career as a physician, also opening up a drug store, which he continued until October, 1889. Then he sold out, and has since devoted his whole attention to his rapidly increasing practice. He is firmly Democratic in his preferences, and a member of the Methodist Episcopal Church, South.

Thomas P. Taylor is a prosperous agriculturist and fruit grower of White County, Ark., and was born in Carroll County, Tenn., being the only child of Hiram A. and E. A. (Moore) Taylor, the former a native of North Carolina, and one of a family of six children born to Peter Taylor and wife. In 1848 he moved to Tennessee, and was married there in 1852, his wife being a daughter of Wesley Moore, also of North Carolina. Hiram A. Taylor was a contractor by occupation, held the highest rank in the Masonic order, and he and his wife were members of the Methodist Episcopal Church. He died in Tennessee. Thomas P. Taylor has always resided on a farm, but since seven years of age has resided in White County, Ark., making his home with his mother, who died in 1878, being the wife of A. V. Van Meter. He received fair educational advantages, and in 1882 he was married to Miss Mattie Sharp, a daughter of T. H. Sharp of this State, who died at an early day, his wife's death occurring in 1880. After his marriage Mr. Taylor settled one and a half miles from Judsonia, and has 140 acres of his 700-acre farm under cultivation. He was at one time quite extensively engaged in the stock business, but now only raises enough for his own use. He has seen the county develop in a remarkable manner since his early location here, and has done his share in aiding in this development. He is independent in his political views, and votes for the man rather than the party. Mrs. Taylor is a member of the Methodist Episcopal Church, South, and by Mr. Taylor has become the mother of two children: Irma (who died at the age of three years) and a boy by the name of James.

W. J. H. Taylor is a prominent farmer and stock raiser in Coffey Township, and a son of Newton W. and Ellen (Hickman) Taylor, natives of Alabama and Tennessee, respectively. Newton W. Taylor was born in Alabama in 1820, and was married in 1846, subsequently engaging in farming. In 1860 he moved to White County, Ark., and bought a quarter section of land, on which he resided until his death, in about 1879 or 1880. W. J. H. Taylor came upon the stage of action in Tennessee in 1848. He was married in 1870 to Miss Jennie Madith, of White County, and to them an interesting family of six children has been given: Maggie, Emmett, Albie, Wesley, Pearl and Newton. Since his marriage Mr. Taylor has farmed several different places, but is now located in Coffey Township, whither he came in 1885. He has a farm of eighty acres, with about fifty acres under cultivation, and in connection with farming has operated a cotton-gin until recently. Mr. and Mrs. Taylor are members of the Methodist Episcopal Church, South. The former is a Democrat, and actively interested in schools, having long been school director of his district.

Manuel Teer is a representative citizen and a large tax payer of White County, owning over 1,000 acres of land, his fine home farm of 200 acres being under excellent cultivation. He enlisted in the Confederate army in 1862, and served throughout the war, taking part in Price's raid through Missouri from beginning to end. He was born in North Carolina on December 29, 1826, and was a son of Ludwick and Mary (Sheppard) Teer. The former's birth occurred in South Carolina in 1790; he was married in 1820, and died in his native State in 1858, a family of four children having blessed the union of himself and wife: Haywood S., Manuel, Francis E. and Susan J. (the widow of the late W. W. Horn). Manuel Teer came to Arkansas in 1857, and settled in White County, where he bought a farm. He was married in 1846 to Miss Martha J. Craig, of North Carolina origin, and a daughter of Abraham and Jane (Steel) Craig, who came to Arkansas in 1857, purchasing an improved farm of 160 acres in White County. Mr. Teer lost his esteemed wife on August 15, 1880. She had been a member of the Methodist Episcopal Church, South, since thirteen years of age. Mr. Teer is connected with the Masonic order, and is a highly respected citizen, having always taken a great interest in the improvement and prosperity of the county. He has been a liberal donator to all religious and charitable institutions during his residence here, keeping thoroughly apace with the progress of the times. Mr. Teer has now retired from active life, and as he has been an industrious, energetic farmer all his life, can now rest in the consciousness of a career well and usefully spent.

Prof. W. H. Tharp, president of Searcy College, Searcy, Ark. A glance at the lives of many representative men whose names appear in this volume will reveal sketches of some honored, influential citizens, but none more worthy or deserving of mention than Prof. W. H. Tharp. This gentleman was born in Fayette County, Tenn., on November 21, 1853, and was the eldest in a family of eight children, three now living, who blessed the union of Dr. W. H. and Susan Payne (Whitmore) Tharp, natives, respectively, of North Carolina and Tennessee. The father was a prominent physician and surgeon, was married in Fayette County, Tenn., and there died, in 1869. The mother died in 1874. She was cousin to Bishop Payne. Grandfather W. H. Tharp was one of the leading and deservedly popular men of Fayette County, Tenn., and was chairman of the county court for many years. He moved from North Carolina when quite a young man. Though young, he was very prominent in his native county, and was a member of the General Assembly of the State. He was, repeatedly, strongly urged to become a candidate for a similar position in his adopted State, but always declined. Prof. W. H. Tharp graduated at Macon Masonic College, in 1871, and, the same year, was in school at Lexington, Ky. In 1872 he entered the U. C. College, at Toronto, Can., and from this college was called in 1873, by the declining health of his mother, whose death, in 1874, made it necessary for him to take charge of the farm and look after his younger brothers, both minors. Here he remained till 1879. While residing on the farm he was, for three years, principal of the Union Hill Academy. In 1879 he was engaged as president of the Male College at Somerville, Tenn. At the end of his year's work he was elected president of Female College, at Somerville, Tenn., where he remained until 1883, and then came to Searcy, Ark. While occupied in teaching at Somerville, he had charge of a county paper called The Falcon, which became very popular throughout the county, but he sold his interest on coming to Searcy, in 1883. Prof. Tharp was married in Tennessee, in 1874, to Miss Lizzie Joe Cocke, a native of Fayette County, Tenn., and the daughter of Thomas R. and Laura (Winston) Cocke, also of Tennessee origin. Her father was a statute lawyer of fine ability, and was county judge for many years, never being defeated. His death occurred in 1886. The mother is still living and resides in Somerville, Tenn. Mrs. Tharp received her education in Somerville Female Institute and Columbia Institute. She is a member of the Ladies' State Central Committee, editor of the children's column of the Arkansas Baptist, and is a smooth and clear writer. She has always been a very valuable assistant to Prof. Tharp in his school work. For the past six years Prof. Tharp has given his time and energies to Searcy College, which he projected, and, together with Prof. Conger, founded in 1883. No institution in the State has more character for thorough work than Searcy College. Prof. Tharp is a man of progressive ideas, and has always taken a deep interest in educational matters. That his work and ability have gained recognition in the State of his adoption is evidenced by the fact that he is at present the president of both the State Teachers' Associations and the Arkansas Summer Normal School. He is also managing editor of the Arkansas Educational Journal, a live and progressive monthly. To his marriage were born two children: William J. and Kathleen. Prof. Tharp and wife are members of the Baptist Church.

J. C. C. Thomas has been from earliest boyhood familiar with the duties of farm work, and is now also extensively engaged in ginning cotton. He was born in Richmond County, N. C., in 1834, and in 1869 came to Arkansas and settled in Independence County, and after farming there one year, came to White County. He acquired a good education in his youth, and after attending the common schools of his native county, he entered Rockingham Academy, which he attended three years. After commencing the battle of life for himself, he removed to Louisiana in 1856, locating near Monroe, and there bought land. From this State he enlisted in the Confederate army the first year of the war, being a member of Company B, Fourth Louisiana Battalion, and served by re-enlistment until the close of the war, participating in the battles of Chattanooga, Missionary Ridge, Lookout Mountain and others. After his return home he spent two years in raising crops, then spent one year in Independence County, and has since resided in White County. He was married here in March, 1875, to Susan L. Watkins, a native of Alabama, and by her has four children living: Sarah A., Grover C., Carlyle and Clifton B. Although Mr. Thomas votes the Democrat ticket, he is not an active politician. His wife is a member of the Baptist Church, and he is a believer in the doctrine of that denomination. In 1876 he purchased a farm comprising 204 acres of land, but now 360, and has 160 acres under cultivation. He also owns one of the oldest cotton-gin stands in the county, and does quite an extensive business in that line. He is one of eight children born to William C. and Sarah A. (Williams) Thomas, the former born in North Carolina, and the latter in Cumberland Island, Ga. Their union took place in the former State, and the father was well known in the community in which he lived, as a successful planter. He was also a millwright and erected the first cotton-gin in Richmond County, N. C. He died in North Carolina in 1852, preceded by his wife in 1848. Grandfather Thomas was an Englishman, and was a soldier in the Revolutionary War. The maternal grandfather was born in Wales and was a Tory during the Revolution.

John A. Thome, M. D., numbered among the rapidly rising practitioners of White County, received his education in this county, and at Union Academy in Gibson County, Ind., after which he worked on his father's farm until twenty-three years of age. During this period he studied medicine at home, and in 1877–79 attended lectures at Evansville Medical College from which he graduated February 27, 1879. Returning thence to West Point he commenced at once the active practice of his profession, which he has continued with such success as stamps him undoubtedly one of the thorough, capable, professional men of the community. Dr. Thome was born in Gibson County, Ind., November 29, 1854, being the son of Jacob and Isabella (Hayhurst) Thome. The former came originally from Prussia (near Berlin) where his birth occurred on March 26, 1818; he emigrated to this country by way of New Orleans, in 1848, first locating in Evansville, Ind., but in 1865 removed to Arkansas and settled near West Point, on a farm on which he resided until his death on February 26, 1888. Mrs. Thome was born near Troy, Ohio, on January 8, 1833, and is still living in this county with some of her children. They were the parents of nine children, five of whom survive: John A. (our subject), David C., Alice (wife of C. W. Davis), Nathallia (wife of J. R. Riner) and Naomi (wife of James Thomas). Dr. Thome was united in marriage on June 22, 1882, with Miss Fouzine McCallister, who was born at West Point November 2, 1864. They have two daughters: Evia I. and Vera B. Dr. Thome is a strong Democrat, and as popular socially as he is in professional circles.

James Wair has been a farmer all of his life and has harvested his fiftieth crop, thirty-one of which have been raised in this county. This experience has given him a wide and thorough knowledge of the affairs of agricultural life. Born in Western Tennessee on December 20, 1814, he was the seventh son of H. and Jane (Ware) Wair. After reaching manhood Mr. Wair was married in June, 1844, to a Miss Bobson, who died in 1858 leaving five children: William, Mary, Martha, Margaret and Tennessee. Following this event he moved to Arkansas in the fall of 1858, and settled in White County, where he bought a quarter section of land. Mr. Wair's second marriage occurred in 1860, Mrs. Elizabeth Low, a widow, and a daughter of Edwin Perergrew, of Georgia, becoming his wife. She departed this life in 1873, leaving six children: James E., Frank B., Lucy V., Ellen T., George H. and Lawrence V. Mr. Wair and each wife were members of the Presbyterian Church. He is a Democrat in politics and a highly respected citizen.

Capt. Calvin Calkins Waldo is a successful gardener and fruit grower, residing in White County, Ark., and like the majority of people who claim New York as the State of their nativity, he is enterprising, intelligent and thrifty. He was born in Genesee County, January 16, 1829, and is a son of Samuel and Mercy (Calkins) Waldo, the former of French descent and a native of Oneida County, N. Y., where he was born in 1794. The family belong to the ancient and honored Waldenses family, and first became represented in America in 1650. Robert and Benjamin Waldo were private soldiers in a Connecticut regiment during the Revolution, and in the battle of Brandywine Robert was killed by a Hessian ball. The maternal ancestors were of Scotch-Irish descent, and were members of the Primitive Baptist Church

and were represented in the Revolutionary War by the maternal great-grandfather of our subject, Joshua Calkins, who served as commissary in Gen. Washington's immediate army from 1775 to 1783. He died in 1838, at the advanced age of ninety-two years. Daniel Calkins, the paternal grandfather, commanded a company in the War of 1812, and served six months, but afterward died of disease contracted while in the service, at the age of fifty-seven years. The parents of our subject were married about 1827, and became the parents of six children: Calvin C., Minerva S. (born March 31, 1831, married Joseph Cooper, of Wyoming County, N. Y.), Permelia (born in 1833, and was married to Moses H. Tyler, of Utica, Ind.), Daniel S. (born in 1835, and married Mrs. Julia Gardner, of Jonesville, Mich.), Lloyd Garrison (born in 1837 and died at the age of four years) and Maria (born in 1839, and married Samuel Cooper, a brother of Joseph Cooper). Capt. Waldo (our subject) received the education and rearing which is accorded the majority of farmers' boys, and after attending the common schools he entered the Perry Center Academy for one year, and at the age of twenty-three years graduated from Middlebury Academy, a normal school of good standing. During the winter of 1851–52, previous to graduating, he taught the district school at La Grange, N. Y., and he afterward taught a four-months' term at Leroy. During the winters of 1853–54 and 1854–55 he taught school at Elyria, Ohio, and in 1856 immigrated to Jeffersonville, Ind., and in February of that year was united in marriage to Miss Polly Jane Raymond, a native of Columbia County, N. Y., and a graduate of Mrs. Willard's Female College of Troy, N. Y. In her girlhood she was a pupil of Mrs. Lyons, at Mount Holyoke, Mass., and was a teacher in the Methodist school at Bardstown, Ky., at the time she formed Mr. Waldo's acquaintance, having previously taught in a female seminary at Murfreesboro, Tenn. After their marriage they engaged in teaching a select subscription school in Jeffersonville, Ind., continuing two years. Mr. Waldo having for some time spent his leisure moments in the study of law was admitted to the bar of Charleston, Ind., moving the same year to Utica of that State, where he again began teaching, holding the position of principal of the schools for the period of one year. In 1859 he opened a female boarding and day school, of which his wife became principal, but deeming the facilities for practicing law much better at the county seat, he removed to Charleston, where he followed the practice of law until the spring of 1861. Upon hearing of the bombardment of Fort Sumter he and others began immediately to raise a company for the three months' service, and Mr. Waldo was elected orderly-sergeant and reported with his company to Gov. Morton, but in consequence of the quota of Indiana being full they were disbanded. Later Mr. Waldo assisted in raising a company for the Twenty-second Indiana Regiment, then assisted Capt. Ferguson in raising a company for the Twenty-third Indiana Regiment. For the money expended and the service rendered in his patriotic and successful efforts to serve his country in her dire need he has never received one cent in compensation, or even a favorable notice. In July, 1861, he, with the assistance of Cyrus T. Nixon, of Charleston, Ind., raised sixty men for Company F, Thirty-eighth Regiment Indiana Infantry, and owing to Mr. Nixon's illness reported in person to Adj.-Gen. Noble, of Indianapolis, who assigned him and his company to camp duty at New Albany, Ind. Here he was elected captain of his company, known as Company, F; Thirty-eighth Regiment Indiana Volunteer Infantry, commanded by Col. B. F. Scribner, but through the latter's instrumentality he was deposed and a favorite, Wesley Connor, put in his stead. Owing to the dissatisfaction caused by these proceedings about two-thirds of the commissioned officers left the regiment, among whom were Judge Gresham, who was at that time lieutenant-colonel of the regiment. Many private soldiers also left the company, the Hon. Lee Clow, now of Hempstead County, Ark., being among the number. After leaving his command Mr. Waldo returned to Charleston, and during the remainder of 1861 and the summer of 1862 he was engaged in the practice of law, but in the latter year was also engaged in assisting the Hon. W. H. Eng-

lish in recruiting a regiment, which afterward became the Ninety-fifth Indiana Infantry. He was commissioned first lieutenant, but relinquished his position to one of the aspirants of the regiment for promotion, and then began assisting in raising another company, known as Company I, Eighth Regiment Indiana Legion, and was chosen orderly-sergeant. The only important service rendered by this regiment was in repelling Morgan in his raid of 1863, after which it was disbanded and Mr. Waldo removed with his family to his native State (New York). Here, after a short time, he enlisted as a private in Company F, Second New York Veteran Cavalry, was commissioned captain of provost guard, and was on duty at Lockport, N. Y. In November he reported to his company, at Geisboro Point, D. C., and February 1, 1864, the regiment embarked on a steamer for New Orleans, La., where they arrived the same month, being five days over due, on account of a severe storm. He was with Gen. Banks in the disastrous Red River campaign, and was seriously injured while making a cavalry charge by his horse stumbling and falling on him, and as a result, was confined to the hospital at New Orleans for thirty days, after which he again joined his regiment, and in February, of the following year, he embarked with his regiment, at Lake Ponchertrain, for Mobile, and while marching overland from Barancas Island to that city, they met Gen. Clerndon, of the Confederate service, whom they defeated, wounded and captured. After assisting in the reduction of Fort Blakely and Spanish Fort, they routed and captured a Confederate cavalry force, which had annoyed them during the siege of Mobile. After the capture of the latter city the regiment was ordered to Talladega, Ala., where Capt. Waldo was detached from his company and sent to Jacksonville, Ala., as quartermaster's clerk, remaining until September, 1865. He was mustered out of service at Talladega, Ala., November 8, 1865, went to Mobile, and there doffed his suit of blue and donned citizen's clothes once more. He returned to Utica, Ind., to which place his family had previously returned. Here his wife suddenly died, as did also a little son, four years old, leaving his home desolate indeed. During the succeeding three years he followed teaching and such other occupations as his impaired health would permit, but his health grew no better, and thinking that a change of climate might prove beneficial, he removed to Jo Daviess County, Ill., in the spring of 1869, where he followed teaching and prospected for lead. In 1872 he went to Osceola, Iowa, and was employed by the Sioux City & St. Paul Railroad Company, in detecting and bringing to justice county swindlers, in which he was successful. In the latter part of the same year he returned to Illinois, where he again engaged in teaching school. The following year he went to Salem, Iowa, and was there united in marriage to Miss Elvira Garretson, and in September of that year he removed to Council Bluffs, Iowa, where he purchased a farm adjoining the corporation, and began market gardening and fruit raising. This occupation received his attention for about six years, with the exception of one year which he spent traveling in the interests of the Howe Truss Company, being present at the Centennial Exhibition in 1876. Three years later he again settled in Salem, and in consequence of ill health, again took up teaching as an occupation, and was also engaged in canvassing for a book. In 1882 he became a resident of Ravenden and Eureka Springs in search of health, but returned to Salem in April, 1882, where he was called upon to mourn the death of his wife, June 3, after an illness of about three weeks. She left two children: Grace (born in June, 1874) and Frank S. (born in February, 1876). Since March, 1884, Mr. Waldo has been a resident of Beebe, Ark., and has confined his attention to market gardening and fruit growing. He has been a member of several secret societies, but through indifference, is not an active member of any at the present time. He is a Republican, and holds a membership in the Missionary Baptist Church.

J. T. Walker is a merchant and farmer of Dog Wood Township, and in his relations with the public has won the respect and esteem of all, for he is honest, upright and attends strictly to his business. His birth occurred in Rutherford Coun-

ty, Tenn., and he was the third child born to George and Anna E. (Barkley) Walker, the former a native of Virginia, born in 1807. His early life was spent in his native State, but when still quite young he was taken to Tennessee, and there the nuptials of his marriage to Miss Rebecca Keilouct were celebrated. She died after they had been married only a short time, and in 1842 Mr. Walker espoused Anna E. Barkley, a daughter of Andrew J. and Hannah Barkley, who were Virginians. Mrs. Walker was born in Tennessee, and the following are the children born to her union with Mr. Walker: William B., Andrew J., Henry B., Hannah C. (Mrs. Allen, living in White County), Martha J. (Mrs. Crisp, also residing in White County), Sallie A. (Mrs. Shoffner, a resident of the county), George R. and Mary E. (Mrs. Ferrell, who is now deceased). In 1850 Mr. Walker moved to White County, Ark., and at the time of his death, in 1872, was the owner of about 1,000 acres of land, of which 125 were under cultivation. He was a Republican, and died in the faith of the Presbyterian Church. His widow survives him, and resides in White County with her children. Up to the age of thirteen years J. T. Walker resided in the State of Tennessee, but after coming to Arkansas he acquired a good education in the common schools, and in 1867 started out in life for himself. He opened up a farm, and in December, 1872, was married to Jennie C. Shoffner, a daughter of Dr. A. C. and Julia A. Shoffner, who removed from Mississippi to White County, Ark., in 1870. Mr. Walker and his wife have five children who are living, and one, Daisy, who died at the age of seventeen months: Evelina, Louella, James D., Lorambla and Maxie are those living. Mr. Walker is a Democrat, and in 1878 was elected to the office of magistrate, and held the position four years. He and wife belong to the Baptist Church, and he is deeply interested in the cause of education, and has held the position of school director of his district for about twelve years. He owns about 500 acres of land, with 200 acres well improved, and for some time has been engaged in merchandising at Walker's Store, the place taking its name from him. He is doing well in both enterprises, and fully deserves the success which has attended his efforts. He is a grandson of Bird Walker.

Walker & Ford. This firm comprises one of the prominent and reliable business houses of Beebe, and is composed of Robert C. Walker and J. A. Ford, two of the honorable and upright men of the county. The senior member of the house, Mr. Walker, was born in Marshall County, Miss., March 16, 1850, his parents, Rev. Charles B. and Jane O. (Jelton) Walker, having been born in Virginia and Tennessee, respectively. The father was born May 26, 1811, and moved with his parents to Rutherford County, Tenn., in 1818, where he embraced religion in December, 1829, becoming a member of the Baptist Church the following year. He was ordained a minister of that denomination on November 17, 1839, and on October 4, 1841, was married to Miss Jelton, and with her removed to Arkansas in 1858, locating at Stony Point, where he engaged in general merchandising. Later he followed the same occupation at Beebe, and was here residing at the time of his death, in 1872, his wife's death occurring three years later. The latter was a daughter of Isaac and Anna Jelton, of Rutherford County, Tenn., and for three years after her marriage lived in Lamar County of that State, then made her home in Marshall County, Miss., until 1858, after which they removed to White County. They were abundantly blessed with worldly goods, and Mr. Walker showed excellent judgment in selecting land, and was very prosperous in his mercantile enterprise. Their son, Robert C. Walker, spent his early life in Mississippi, attending school there and in Arkansas, but after becoming thoroughly familiar with the common branches he entered Hickory Plains Institute, attending one year (1868). After teaching a three months' term of school he entered the State University of Fayetteville, as a beneficiary for White County, but at the end of nine months was called home by the death of his father, and did not again enter school, but remained at home to care for his mother, which he continued to do until her death. He was married in 1875 to Miss Sallie Percy, a native of Jackson, Tenn., and to them were born

two children: James (born August 29, 1877) and Ollie (born October 12, 1879), the mother's death following the birth of the latter, October 24. She was a member of the Methodist Episcopal Church, a faithful wife, mother and friend, and her death was deeply lamented by all. In January, 1881, Mr. Walker espoused Miss Mattie L. Scott, of Arkansas, whose father, John Scott, was a farmer of Mississippi and later of Arkansas, but died at Selma, Ala., in 1862. This union resulted in the birth of four children: Sallie (born February 11, 1885), Minnie and Winnie (twins, born July 28, 1886, and died August 2, 1886), and Viola (born October 7, 1887). The first experience Mr. Walker had was in settling his father's estate, he being one of the executors. He was afterward associated in business with Mr. Westbrooks, continuing with him until 1875, following farming from that time till February, 1888. At that date he and Mr. Ford purchased their present stock of goods, and, owing to their genial dispositions and excellent business qualifications, their union has prospered. He and wife are members of the Baptist Church. Mr. Ford, the junior member of the firm, was born in Georgia, December 4, 1851, his native county being Whitfield. His parents, Joseph R. and Palmyra (Cowan) Ford, were also natives of Georgia, and until the war the father was a wealthy merchant of Dalton, and wielded a wide influence in the politics of the State. He was for a long time collector of his county, and represented the same one term in the legislature. He served as orderly-sergeant in the Confederate army during the war, and upon being taken captive was imprisoned for fifteen months at Camp Chase, Ohio. He and his wife are members of the Baptist Church, and are residing at Bellevue, Tex. J. A. Ford is the second of their eight children, the other members of the family being as follows: George (who is circuit and county clerk of Clay County, Tex.), Marion (who is a conductor on the Alabama & Chattanooga Railroad), Edward (a salesman at Poplar Bluff, Mo.), Joseph (a ranchman near Bellevue, Tex.), and Robert L. and Lawrence (who reside with their parents in Texas), Ava (the only sister, is the wife of Robert Miller, a stockman at Gainesville, Tex.). J. A. Ford received his education at Dalton, Ga., and Flint Springs, Tenn. At the age of nineteen years he began life for himself, and after teaching school for several years he clerked one year, embarking in business on his own account in 1873, doing a general business. Owing to failing health, he was compelled to give up this work for awhile, and accordingly sold his goods and returned to Georgia, where he was engaged in farming until 1876, at which time he came to Arkansas. After farming three years in Conway County, he came to Judsonia, agriculture receiving his attention here also, and in the fall of 1883 bought a farm near Beebe. In 1886 he became associated with Mr. Campbell in the mercantile business, and until February, 1888, the firm was L. Campbell & Co., since which time it has been Walker & Ford. January 31, 1879, Mr. Ford was married to Miss Lane, a native of Georgia. She was reared in Missouri, and is a daughter of John F. Lane, a prominent attorney at law of Poplar Bluff, Mo. He and wife have four children: George L. (born December 4, 1870), Samuel E. (born September 14, 1881), Joseph Lee (born November 8, 1883) and Palmyra (born August 16, 1887). Mr. and Mrs. Ford are members of the Baptist Church, and he belongs to Beebe Lodge No. 145, A. F. & A. M., and has been a member of the I. O. G. T. He has the interest of the county at heart, and supports all movements tending to promote the public good.

W. T. Wallis has been a resident of White County since 1856, acquiring during this time an enviable reputation as a citizen of energy and enterprise, and a man honest and conscientious in his walk and transactions. A native of Tennessee, he is a son of John and Mary (Bird) Wallis, originally from North Carolina, who had a family of eleven children: John B., Mary, Elizabeth, Myas, Rebecca, Josiah, Nancy, Doctern, Catharine, W. T. (the principal of this sketch) and three whose names are not given, and who were older than W. T. The father of our subject died when he was only two years old, the mother following six months later. W. T. Wallis was born in 1829, and spent his early days in Tennessee, starting out for himself, in 1851, first as a carriage-maker and then as farmer, to which occupation he has since given his attention. Removing to Mississippi, he was married there, in 1852, to Leamia E. Bromson, and in 1856 came to this county, where he entered 200 acres of land. At the beginning of the war Mr. Wallis enlisted in Col. Monroe's regiment, and served until the close of hostilities, participating in twenty-seven battles and skirmishes. His career as a soldier was honorable and effective. Mr. and Mrs. Wallis are the parents of eight children: John S., William H., Mary E., Martha A., Thomas, Patrick L., Annie E. and Lucinda V., all married and living in Arkansas, and most of them in this county. Mr. Wallis and wife belong to the Missionary Baptist Church, the former owns 1,000 acres of land, and has about 150 acres under cultivation, his stock numbering some two or three hundred head of cattle.

Caleb Parker Warren. The connection of Mr. Warren with the interests of White County has proven to be a fortunate thing for its residents and especially for the citizens in and near El Paso, as a perusal of the sketch will testify. He is a son of Thomas and Rebecca (Wright) Warren, who were born in North Carolina, and immigrated to West Tennessee about 1820, and were there married in 1833. They came to Arkansas in the fall of 1856, and located in the country then known as Royal Colony, purchasing 160 acres of wild land, on which they erected a double log-house, this being the first of the sort in the colony. In 1861 Mr. Warren enlisted as a private soldier in Dr. F. M. Christian's company, known as the Border Rangers, remaining in that capacity and with that command for four years and ten days. He took part in a number of battles and skirmishes, one in particular being the battle of Chickamauga, in which his company dismounted and fought as infantry. He was also at Shiloh and Corinth, and was under the famous Confederate cavalry commanders: Forrest, Wheeler, Hampton and Armstrong, but a greater portion of the time was with Forrest and Wheeler. His first experience in warfare was at Lost Creek, Mo., in 1861, and he surrendered with his command at Charlotte, N. C., at which time there was a request made by the commanding officers of both armies for volunteers to go to Chesterville, S. C., to guard and serve the rations to the Confederate soldiers as they were paroled, the Government allowing the cavalry to retain their arms and horses. Mr. Warren finally arrived at home, June 15, 1865, having ridden his horse all the way. His first venture in business after his return was to invest in some cotton, making his purchase with money loaned him by a Mr. Hadley, who at that time had charge of the penitentiary at Little Rock, and his enterprise met with fair success. The next year he put in a crop on land deeded him by his father (160 acres), and to the thirty acres which were already under cultivation he improved and added ten more. These he devoted to cotton and corn in equal parts, but the second year he left his crop to be gathered by others and embarked in merchandising at El Paso, under the firm name of Warren & Son, his father furnishing the capital and receiving half the profits. At the end of eight years our subject became the sole proprietor, paying over to his father all the money he had furnished, and took into his employ O. P. Poole, and at the end of one year gave him an interest in the business. Mr. Poole's wife and three children were killed in the terrible cyclone of 1880; he and his little daughter, Martha J., being the only ones of the family to escape with their lives, but Mr. Poole was so badly injured that existence became unendurable, and in July of the following year he ended his weary life. Mr. Warren has since acted as guardian of his daughter, and has placed her in Ouachita Baptist College, Arkadelphia, Ark. Mr. Warren's wife, who was formerly a Miss Mary A. Harkrider, was born in Tennessee, and is a daughter of John and Eunice Harkrider, native Dutch. Their family are as follows: Mattie M., John Thomas, Rebecca Eunice, Mary P. and Cora V. These children have received excellent educational advantages, and the eldest has graduated from Searcy College, Arkansas, and is at present principal of the public school at El Paso, Ark. Thomas, after having spent several terms at the State University, Fayettville, Ark., took a course at Goodman & Eastman's Business College, Nashville, Tenn., and is filling the position of book-keeper for Warren & Phelps, the present style of the firm. The three youngest daughters are at Ouachita Baptist College. The family worship in the Missionary Baptist Church, and Mr. Warren is a member of the A. F. & A. M., El Paso Lodge, No. 65. He was born in Tennessee, January 21, 1840.

Thomas Warren. He whose name heads this brief sketch, is one of White County's pioneers, and is an active and enterprising agriculturist, alive to all current issues, public spirited and progressive in all matters tending to benefit the community. His life has been an active one, and by his own industry and intelligent management, has secured a substantial footing among the citizens of White County. He was born in Edgecombe, County, N. C., September 22, 1814, and about the year 1820 he removed with his father, Caleb Warren, to the State of Tennessee, and was there reared to farm life. The schools of Tennessee were not of the best at this time, and were only conspicuous for their scarcity, therefore the educational advantages which Thomas received were of the most meager description. He learned to read a little, but never did an example in arithmetic in his life. In the year 1834 he was wedded to Miss Rebecca Wright, a daughter of John Harrison and Nancy (Whitiss) Wright, and a native of North Carolina, born on June 16, 1815. Their marriage resulted in the birth of ten children, whose names are as follows: Martha Ann (born November 22, 1834; was married December 31, 1853, to William J. Canada, who was killed while serving in the army. His wife died in 1869, leaving three children: Martha J., born in November, 1855, Thomas, born in December, 1857, and Joseph, born in 1859), Sarah E. (was born September 25, 1837, married Isaac Dougan, and bore him two children, both deceased), Caleb P. (born January 22, 1840), Matilda N. (born on March 22, 1842, and married Dr. M. Costen, of El Paso), Clarissa E. (birth occurred on the 31st of August, 1844, and her marriage took place in 1861; she and her husband had two children, William P. and Barbara), Nancy C. (was born March 31, 1847, and in 1862 she was married to Joseph Grissard; she died in September, 1869), William T. (the next in order of birth, was born August 17, 1849, and died in infancy), Josiah W. (was born June 21, 1851, and died five years later), Mary K. (was born December 31, 1853, and died in December, 1856), Rebecca T. (was born April 18, 1856, was married to Rufus Blake in 1872, and became the mother of eight children, four of whom are living). Prior to leaving Tennessee, Mr. Warren purchased three slaves, paying $600 and $800 apiece for two women, and $1,000 for a man, but on coming to Arkansas in 1856, his slaves had increased to six. He located on a quarter section of land which had been deeded to him by his father, and subsequently added, by purchase, three other quarter sections of land, and at the opening of the Rebellion was the owner of large landed estates, and had fourteen slaves. At the time of his location in Arkansas the country was in a very wild and unsettled condition, but, with the energy which has ever characterized the early pioneers, he set to work and soon had a good double log-cabin erected on his land, also negro cabins and a horse cotton-gin, the latter being the first erected within a radius of twenty miles. After a few years he put up a steam cotton-gin and grist-mill, at a cost of about $3,500, and hauled his machinery from Des Arc, a distance of thirty-five miles. In 1867, he, in partnership with his son Caleb P., engaged in the mercantile business in El Paso, and the latter is now one of the wealthiest merchants of the State. Mr. and Mrs. Warren are now seventy-five and seventy-four years old, respectively, and the latter has been a member of the Missionary Baptist Church for nearly seventy years. Mr. Warren has belonged to the same church for about forty years, all their children being members of the same, and those who are deceased died in full communion with the church, and with the hope and belief of immortality. Mrs. Warren is an active member of the Ladies' Aid Society, and she and her husband are ever ready with open purse to aid the needy and afflicted, and when their Master calls will be found ready and waiting to pass "over the river." The paternal ancestors of Mr. Warren came to the United States prior to the Revolutionary War,

and took sides with the Colonists in that struggle. Of his maternal ancestors he has no knowledge.

Col. Thomas Watkins, known as a prominent early settler of White County, is a Virginian by birth, and a son of Joel and Fannie (White) Watkins, whose birthplace is found in the Old Dominion. Mr. Joel Watkins was born March 4, 1784, and was married in Virginia, removing in 1830 to Tennessee. He served in the War of 1812, was a justice of the peace in Tennessee for several years, and a member of the Missionary Baptist Church, as was also his wife. He died in 1863. He was a son of Thomas Watkins, of English descent, and an old time Virginian, who was an officer in the Revolutionary War; the latter was with Gen. Washington at the surrender at Yorktown, and represented his county in the State legislature a number of times. Fannie White, the mother of our subject, was a daughter of Thomas White, also originally from Virginia, and a captain of a company in the American troops during the Revolutionary War. To Mr. and Mrs. Watkins nine children were born, three of whom are still living: Thomas, Catharine (wife of William H. Watts) and Fannie (now Mrs. Crossett). Thomas Watkins first saw the light of day in Halifax County, Va., in January, 1820. When fourteen years of age he went to Lebanon, Tenn., where he was employed as clerk in a store, remaining there until twenty-two years old, at which time he bought a farm in De Soto County, Miss. In 1853, coming to Arkansas, he located in White County, on the farm which he still occupies, consisting of 218 acres, with 150 acres under cultivation. In 1838 he was married to Miss Moore, of Tennessee, who died in 1843, leaving three daughters, all deceased. In 1848 Miss Amanda Dowdle, a native of South Carolina became his wife, surviving until her death, in 1854; she bore two children: William M. (a merchant of Searcy) and Allen D. (a farmer of White County). Mr. Watkins' third wife was formerly Mary Walker, to whom he was united in 1856. A native of White County, she was a daughter of James Walker, and departed this life in 1857, leaving one daughter, who died when an infant. In 1863 Mr. Watkins married his fourth and present companion, Mrs. Margaret E. Stone (*nee* Core), a widow, whose birth occurred in Haywood County, Tenn., July 25, 1834. They are the parents of two children, living, and two now deceased. Those surviving are: Mary Kate and Maggie C., both at home. Mr. Watkins is a member of the Masonic order, in which he has taken the Royal Arch degree, and belongs to the Methodist Episcopal Church, South, as does his wife. He is an enterprising and highly respected man, enjoying universal esteem.

Hon. T. W. Wells, Searcy, Ark. Every community is bound to have among her citizens a few men of recognized influence and ability, who, by their systematic and careful, thorough manner of work, attain to success which is justly deserved. Among this class is Mr. Wells, a man esteemed as a prominent and substantial, as well as one of the pioneer citizens of the county. He was born in Haywood County, Tenn., May 18, 1834, and was the second of eight children, the result of the union of William Stokes and Penelope (Standley) Wells, natives of Kentucky and Tennessee, respectively, who were married February 15, 1832. When a boy William S. Wells occupied the claim where Brownsville is now located, and later traded it for a suit of clothes. He was married in Tennessee, and followed farming all his life near the city of Brownsville, Tenn. His death occurred July 20, 1867 (he was born August 2, 1807), and his wife previous to this, on April 9, 1866. Her birth was February 28, 1811. The grandfather, John Wells, was a native of Kentucky, and a pioneer of that State in the time of Daniel Boone. Grandfather William Standley was a native of Tennessee, and among the pioneers of that State. T. W. Wells was reared to farm life, and educated in the district schools of Tennessee, although the main part of his education was obtained by personal application. He left home at eighteen years of age without money, attended school at Cageville, Tenn., worked his way through by labor, but was under the tutelage of Prof. William A. Allen. After leaving college Mr. Wells engaged in teaching, and followed this profession from 1852 to 1854. On October 25 of the last-mentioned year he was

united in marriage to Miss Jeannette Edwards, a native of Tennessee, and the daughter of William and Lavinia Edwards, natives of Edgecombe County, N. C. Mr. and Mrs. Edwards settled in Tennessee in an early day, or in 1835, and here both died the same year. After marriage Mr. Wells settled in Tennessee, and was engaged in teaching and farming on the shares. During 1857 and 1858 he was engaged in the book business, but in the last-named year he moved to Avoyelles Parish, La., where he was occupied in overseeing. In May of 1859, he moved back to Tennessee, followed teaching for three months, and in the fall of that year came to Arkansas, landing at Des Arc with 15 cents and a sick wife. From there he went to El Paso, White County, Ark., and taught school for about ten months, when he and wife regained their health. After this Mr. Wells engaged in the mill business at El Paso, and in partnership with James M. Wright erected the first steam mill in that place, being connected with it until 1861, when Mr. Wells was left to conduct it alone. In 1862 he engaged in milling in Van Buren County, and in July of the following year he purchased the McCauley mill, at Prospect Bluff, and had the only fine flouring mill in White County. This he continued until 1867, when he moved to Clay Township, White County, and bought a timber tract of eighty acres. This he opened up, and has now 360 acres, with 165 under cultivation. He owns a good steam-mill and gin. He moved to Searcy in 1868, but still continued the milling and farming business. He lost his wife in 1875, and his second marriage was in 1877, December 5, in Woodruff County, to Mrs. Delilah J. Bosley, a native of Tennessee. Three children were the fruits of this union, only one now living, Thomas W., who was born on January 1, 1886. The other two were named Thomas Clarence and Felix Grundy (both of whom died with measles, April 25, 1885, at the age of two and five years, respectively). Mr. Wells takes a prominent part in politics, and is a stanch Democrat. He represented White County in the legislature in 1874, and was re-elected two years later, serving until 1878. In 1882 he represented the Twenty-seventh senatorial district, com-

17

posed of White and Faulkner Counties, and served until 1884. He is in very comfortable circumstances, and this is all the fruits of his own exertion. He is one of the honored pioneers of White County, and during the many years he has resided here, he has not only become well known, but the respect and esteem shown him is as wide as his acquaintance.

Dr. M. C. Wells, has been for years successfully engaged in the practice of medicine, but also pursues the occupation of farming. He was born in Haywood County, Tenn., in 1848, and was the youngest in a family of eight children born to W. S. and Penelope (Standley) Wells, natives, respectively, of Kentucky and Tennessee. The father was a farmer by occupation, and after settling in Tennessee, which was at an early day, he opened up a farm on which he died in 1868, his wife having died a year earlier. Dr. M. C. Wells was reared to a farm life and was educated in the schools of Haywood County, in that county also receiving his first medical knowledge. In 1869-70, and the winter of 1870-71, he attended lectures in the Washington University of Baltimore, Md. (now known as the College of Physicians and Surgeons), and later took an intermediate course at Louisville, Ky. He first settled in White County, in the year 1871, and began his practice in Des Arc Township, but since November of the same year he has been a resident of Marion Township. During his medical career of nineteen years he has won the reputation, and deservedly, of being a skillful physician, and his practice lies among the best people of the county. He keeps his own medicines and is ready to answer calls at any time. He is giving his attention to farming also, and owns a good farm of 150 acres on Big Creek Township, of which seventy are under cultivation, and all is well adapted to the raising of stock. Dr. Wells owns a handsome home in Searcy, his residence being situated near Galloway College, in a very pleasant part of the town. He has always been public spirited, and in his political preferences is a Democrat, and as he has always taken a deep interest in school matters he has served a number of years as a member of the school board. He

was married in 1872 to Miss Mary Cheney Knowlton, a native of Tennessee, and a daughter of Hon. H. C. and Mary Agnes (Stone) Knowlton, the former born in Vermont and the latter in Tennessee. In 1870 they settled in White County, Ark., and here are now residing. The Doctor and his wife are the parents of four children: Beulah S., William H., Grace Garland and Lois Lina.

George G. Wells is in every respect worthy of being classed among the successful farmers of White County, for by his own industry and good management he has become the owner of 160 acres of land, sixty of which he now has under cultivation. He assisted in tilling his father's farm in Haywood County, Tenn., there also receiving his education, and when Civil War broke out, he joined Company G, Fifteenth Tennessee Cavalry (being regimental flag bearer for that regiment for two years), under Gen. Forrest, and was at the battles of Fort Pillow, Harrisburg, Yazoo City, Corinth, Pulaski, Columbus, Mount Pleasant, Spring Hill, Franklin, Nashville and others. He was taken prisoner at Columbus and Nashville, but both times was soon retaken. He surrendered at Jonesboro, N. C., in June, 1865, and returned to his home in Tennessee, where he resumed farming. He was married in his native State in November, 1867, to Callie B. Hooks, of Kentucky, a daughter of Henry Clinton and Rebecca (Somersault) Hooks, also Kentuckians, who moved to Tennessee at an early day. The father died in April, 1865, and the mother in 1885. Mr. Wells and his wife continued to reside in Tennessee until 1872, when they sold their farm and came to White County, purchasing, in 1880, their present farm. They now have sixty-five acres under cultivation. They first bought an improved farm of 100 acres near El Paso, paying $12 per acre, but owing to defective title, they afterward lost it, and were compelled to commence anew, but owing to their frugal habits and shrewd management, they are now in good circumstances. Mr. Wells is a believer in temperance, is a Democrat, and he and wife are believers in the Christian religion. He has three children by his first wife, who died in April, 1883. Mr. Wells subsequently married M. V. Choat, widow of Stephen Choat. By her first husband she has two children: Lee and Willie. Mr. Wells is a brother of Dr. M. C. Wells, whose biography appears elsewhere in this work.

William C. West is justly conceded to be among White County's most extensive merchants, and his career as such is one which redounds to his own personal credit. A native of Alabama, he is a son of William and Mary (Howard) West, natives of North Carolina, who moved to Alabama shortly after their marriage, and in 1837 to Marshall County, Miss. After the death of his wife, in 1844, Mr. West went to Arkansas and located in White County, where his death occurred, in 1859, at the age of eighty-four years. He was a Baptist minister, in which work he had been engaged for forty years. He was the father of eleven children, two of whom only are living: R. R. West (who is a chancery clerk in De Soto County) and William C. (our subject). The latter was born in Perry County, Ala., March 14, 1828. At the age of nineteen he was employed as a clerk in a store; but, on coming to White County, started into the mercantile business for himself on a small scale, a short time after, however, entering the employ of a firm in West Point. In 1858 he resumed general merchandising, with a capital of $400 or $500. Just before the Missouri campaign he enlisted in the Confederate army and served as adjutant for Gen. Mitchell, remaining in service throughout the Missouri raid. During the war he lost all of his property, and had to start from the beginning after returning home; but by hard work, energy and perseverance he has built up an extensive patronage, and his yearly sales will now average $25,000. He also owns 1,200 acres of land, with 300 acres cleared, and a good portion under cultivation. May 27, 1856, Mr. West was married to Miss Frances Adams, a daughter of Hardin S. Adams, of Mississippi. She died in 1886, leaving four children: Charles E. (who is in business with his father), Lavenia H., Fannie H. and Mary E. Mr. West is a member of the Missionary Baptist Church, as was also his wife. He is a Democrat in politics and a member of the Masonic order. He was postmaster of this place in 1877–78.

Judge N. H. West, Searcy, Ark. This much-esteemed and representative man of the county was elected to his present responsible position in September, 1888, and has effectively conducted the affairs of the same since. He was originally from Madison County, Tenn., where his birth occurred in 1836, and was the oldest in a family of five children born to the union of Philip T. and Hurelia (Harris) West, natives of Tennessee. The father was a farmer, a local minister, and in November, 1851, he moved to White County, locating in Marion Township, where he entered land. He died there in 1853, and his excellent wife survived him until 1886. Their family consisted of these children: N. H., H. T. (married and resides in White County), Thomas N. (died in 1870), Mary A. (was the wife of R. G. Thomas, died in the county in 1888) and Martha J. (was born in White County; married W. A. Patterson and resides in Marion Township). Judge N. H. West came to White County when fifteen years of age, was early taught the duties on the farm, and received his education by his own exertions and by the aid of the pine knot, by the light of which he spent many hours poring over the pages of his books. He stood between the handles of the plow at the age of seven years, and has continued agricultural pursuits ever since. He learned the blacksmith trade and followed that pursuit for some years, but later purchased a timber tract of eighty acres, which he has since added to until he now has 191 acres, with 125 acres under cultivation. He is pleasantly situated two miles from Searcy. During the Civil War he enlisted under Capt. Critz's Company, Eighth Arkansas Infantry, Tennessee Army, and was in the battles of Corinth, Chattanooga, Murfreesboro, Chickamauga, and participated also in Bragg's invasion of Kentucky. He was paroled at Atlanta, Ga., on May 6, 1865, and returned to White County where he engaged in farming. He is active in politics, was justice of the peace for some time, and votes with the Union Labor party. He is a member of the Agricultural Wheel No. 145, and was president of the County Wheel at the time he was elected to his present office. He is a member of the Mount Pisgah Lodge No. 242, A. F. &

A. M., and was secretary of the same for about eight years. Mr. West was married in White County in 1856 to Miss Martha J. Stayton, a native of Georgia, and the fruits of this union were two children: William F. (married and resides in Clay Township, White County) and Nancy Jane (now Mrs. Mayo, resides in Marion Township). The mother of these children died in 1868. Judge West selected his second wife in the person of Miss Ellen Robinson, a native of Pope County, Ill., and was married to her in 1870. She was left an orphan at the age of two years, and she came to Arkansas with an uncle in 1853, where she grew to womanhood. By that union nine children were born, six now living: Harriet E., James T., David N., Henry Clay (died in 1887), Sarah Malvina, Lillie (died in 1888, at the age of six years), Viola, Martha Ellen (died at the age of two years) and Anna Elizabeth. Judge West has seen a great many changes in the country since his residence here. Searcy was then a small hamlet, there were no railroad facilities, and game was plentiful. He has been active in everything pertaining to the good of the county, and is one of the foremost men of the same.

A. J. West is one of the most successful of White County's farmers and stockmen, and deserves much credit for the way in which he has battled with fate and conquered, for he not only possesses large landed estates, but is extensively engaged in stock raising. He is now the owner of 2,462 acres of some of the best land in the county, 600 acres in cultivation, and his residence in West Point is surpassed by none. He was born in Mississippi in 1850, being the youngest of seven children of Adam and Mary (Jarvis) West, both Tennesseeans. The former was a son of John West. He was educated in Cannon County, Tenn., and when a young man moved to Alabama, near Tuscaloosa, where he followed farming. After his marriage, in 1833, he moved to Mississippi and settled on a farm, being the owner of a one-half section of land. His wife was one of a large family of children born to Levi Jarvis. Adam West served with distinction in the Mexican War. He and his wife were both members of the Missionary Baptist Church,

and were honored and respected wherever they made their home. They both died on the old plantation in Mississippi. Their son, William, was for many years a prosperous and influential citizen of Memphis, where he acquired considerable property, and was beloved by all. He was a Mason, belonging to St. Elmo Commandery. He died in 1885. Emily, a daughter was married to Thomas Bice. Rachel married W. C. Wooten: they are both deceased, also Caroline, who died in 1867. Mary married Patrick Smith, and in 1887 she and her son moved to White County, Ark., with A. J. West, where they now reside. A. J. spent his early life on the plantation in Mississippi, and received his schooling at Oxford University, and afterward at Murfreesboro, Tenn. After leaving college he farmed and taught school; his father and brother-in-law being dead, he devoted the best years of his life in caring for his widowed mother and sisters and their families. He was married January 15, 1888, to Miss Jessie Bramlitt, of Corinth, Miss., who was a daughter of Jessie L. and Mary (Anderson) Bramlitt. Her father was for many years a successful merchant of Jackson, Miss. He moved from there to Prentiss County, Miss., and purchased one of the most desirable farms in the county. Her mother was the only daughter of Samuel Anderson, of Pulaski, Tenn.

Samuel A. Westbrook, of Beebe, White County, Ark., was born in Maury County, Tenn., April 29, 1833. Being left a poor boy, after arriving at the age of eighteen, he followed overseeing for several years, and came to Arkansas in December, 1858, where he engaged in the mill business and farming. The former he has discontinued, and now gives his attention to farming and stock raising. He has become noted for the fine stock he raises, and especially for his Short-horn cattle and Clydesdale and Morgan horses. In addition to his land being well adapted to stock raising, it is exceedingly fertile, and all kinds of fruit and grain can be raised in abundance. Mr. Westbrook is one of the pushing men of the county, and from his mill lumber was procured with which to build nearly every church and school-house in the county. He served three months in the army, but as he was exempt, and on account of his services being required at home to operate his mill, he returned to Arkansas. He was a Whig in former times, but is now Independent in his political views. On March 30, 1865, he was married to Miss Susan A. Walker, a daughter of Rev. C. B. Walker, of Mississippi, who removed to Arkansas in 1857. Of eight children born to Mr. and Mrs. Westbrook five are living: Charles B., S. A. and W. H. (twins), Jennie, Robert T., Willie and Walker Lipsey.

Daniel W. Wheaton, son of James and Betsey A. Wheaton, was born in Pomfret, Conn., October 3, 1833, on the old Wheaton homestead, which had been in the family since the Revolutionary War, being the youngest of a family of thirteen children. His father, James Wheaton, a native of Connecticut, was born in 1790, and his mother, Betsey (Angell) Wheaton, was born in Rhode Island, in 1795. They were married about 1815, and the following are the names of their children: Marshal (who died in Rhode Island. in 1840, at the age of twenty-four years), Mason N., Angell, Seth T., Gurdon N., Monroe, Nancy L., Horatio, Henry W. and D. W. James Wheaton was a farmer all his life, and died on his old homestead in Connecticut, in 1876. He was twice married, his first wife dying in 1814, left him with two children: Warren L. and Jessie C. His second wife, the mother of our subject, died in 1857, on the old farm in Connecticut. James Wheaton, the grandfather, reared a family of five children. D. W. Wheaton, our biographical subject, remained on the home farm in his native State until he was twenty-five years of age, then came West and spent twelve years in the State of Illinois, Du Page County, and was there married to Priscilla P. Beith, a daughter of William and Mary (Allen) Beith, her birth having occurred in Illinois. Her parents were Scotch and settled in Illinois about 1844, where they became the parents of three children. Mr. Wheaton and his wife have become the parents of four children: Mary E. (wife of A. P. Moody), Julia, Clara and William. Since the year 1871, Mr. Wheaton has resided in White County, Ark., his farm, comprising 275 acres, being situated one and one-half miles from Judsonia. At the time of his purchase, the land was heavily covered with timber, but he has cleared about seventy-five acres and devoted it to the raising of fruit, for which he finds a ready sale. He and his wife are members of the Methodist Episcopal Church, he being one of its stewards, and in his political views he is a Republican. He has two brothers who are large land holders at Wheaton, Ill., the town taking its name from them.

James K. Whitney has risen to a position as one of White County's leading citizens through his own merits. A native of Tennessee, he received his education in this county, and graduated from the Bryant & Stratton Commercial College, after which he went into the mercantile business in company with C. P. Douthar, at West Point, there remaining until 1874. He then wound up his father's business, and engaged in farming and stock raising, and in 1884 commenced the breeding of Holstein cattle, the only herd of which breed he now has in White County. Mr. Whitney was born in Fayette County, Tenn., January 27, 1846, being a son of Elijah and Mary (Anderson) Whitney, of Kentucky and Tennessee nativity, respectively. Mr. Whitney, Sr., learned the machinist's trade when a young man, and was engaged for a number of years in selling cotton-spinning machinery, through Kentucky and Tennessee. After his marriage, February 22, 1842, he removed to Fayette County, Tenn., and carried on farming, in 1859 removing to Arkansas, and locating in White County, where he lived until his death, in January, 1873. He was a son of Hiram Whitney, a soldier in the War of 1812, and was with Gen. Hull on his disastrous campaign. His wife was a niece of Gen. William H. Harrison. The Whitney family are of English descent, and the Anderson family of Scotch origin. Mr. and Mrs. Whitney had a family of five children, two of whom only are living: a daughter (now Mrs. Douthar, whose husband is a merchant of White County) and James K. (our subject). In 1876 James K. Whitney was married to Miss Ella T. Black, daughter of W. D. Black. She was born in White County in 1858, and has borne six children, four of whom are still living: Leslie E.,

Floyd W., Bessie and Mary E. Mr. and Mrs. Whitney are members of the Missionary Baptist Church, in which the former is clerk and treasurer. He is one of the leading Democrats of the county, and as a citizen and neighbor enjoys wide respect.

I. J. Whitsitt is also numbered among the well-to-do farmers of Dogwood Township. He was born in Alabama in 1848, as the son of Wilson and Elizabeth (Price) Whitsitt, Kentuckians by birth. Wilson Whitsitt was born in 1808, and moved to Alabama when a boy with his father, being married in 1828 to the mother of our subject. Her birth occurred in 1812. Mr. and Mrs. Whitsitt were the parents of ten children, seven of whom are still living: Jane, Camily, Sallie, Harriett, I. J. (our subject), Katie and William. The father was a prosperous farmer and a member of the Methodist Episcopal Church, South, as was also his wife. He died in 1878, having survived his worthy companion eight years. I. J. Whitsitt passed his school days in Alabama, and commenced his occupation of a farmer in that State in 1864. In 1873 he chose for his life associate, Elizabeth Sherwood, a daughter of Thomas and Ruth (Jinkins) Sherwood, natives of Tennessee. They have a family of two children: Benjamin and Hughes. In 1876 Mr. Whitsitt moved to Texas with his family, and was engaged in farming until 1881, then coming to White County, Ark., where he bought his present farm, consisting of 160 acres of land, with fifty acres under cultivation at the present time. He is a stanch Democrat and a member of the Missionary Baptist Church, as is his wife. Mr. Whitsitt is indeed a good citizen of White County, taking an interest in all work for the benefit of the community in which he lives.

William M. Williams, a native of Randolph County, N. C., and a son of John and Ellen (Craven) Williams, also originally from the old North State, was born in 1842. John Williams was a son of James and Frances Williams, and was married between 1825 and 1830, rearing a family of seven children: Evaline, Sauliman, Robert, Susan, William M., Alexander and John. Mr. Williams died in 1846. William M. started in life for himself, in 1868, at farming, and, in 1871, came to Arkansas, settling on a farm in White County, which he rented. A short time afterward he bought 320 acres of land, and now has eighty acres under cultivation. During the war he enlisted in the Confederate army, in the Forty-sixth North Carolina Infantry, and was engaged in the battles of Seven Pines, Oak Grove, Sharpsburg, Fredericksburg and the battle of Plank Road and others, serving until the close of the war, and being present when Lee surrendered under the famous old apple tree at Appomattox. Mr. Williams was married in 1872 to Miss Frances Tote, a daughter of Andrew and Mary (Tees) Tote, natives of North Carolina. Himself and wife are members of the Methodist Episcopal Church, South. Mr. Williams says the soil of Arkansas will raise anything that can be grown elsewhere. He has been very prosperous in the nineteen years of his residence here and counts his friends by the score.

Dr. F. M. Winborn, one of the most prominent physicians of White County, is a native of Alabama, and was born in Florence, February 27, 1835, being one of nine children in the family of William and Mary (May) Winborn. The former's birth occurred in North Carolina, July 5, 1800. He was educated in the schools of Alabama, and immigrated from the latter State in 1816 to Tennessee, whence, after a residence of two years in Tennessee, he returned to Alabama and was married, there passing the rest of his life. His wife, Mary May, was a daughter of John and Elizabeth May, of Alabama. Mr. Winborn's demise occurred in December, 1875, his wife having been called to her final home some years before. The grandfather, William Winborn, was of North Carolina nativity and a soldier in the War of the Revolution. He died in Alabama in 1832. The maternal grandfather, John May, was originally from Georgia, and served in the War of 1812. His death occurred in 1854. His father was born in England, his mother being a native of Ireland. F. M. Winborn was educated at the Diasburg Academy, Tennessee, and received his medical education at the University of Mississippi, graduating with honors from that institution. He was married in November, 1858, to Miss Amorett

Doyle, a daughter of Sarah and David Doyle. Dr. and Mrs. Winborn are the parents of nine children, four boys and five girls: William G., Robert L., Lemuel H., John B., Ida, Edgar V., Dock, Louella and Olla A. Dr. Winborn moved from Mississippi to Arkansas in 1878, and settled in Lonoke, where he practiced his profession successfully for three years. Thinking, however, that White County offered better inducements as a place of residence he came here, and has established an enviable reputation as a careful, able practitioner. He is almost constantly at the bedside of the sick, and is invariably given the most hearty welcome, for his coming means the alleviation of their suffering. But though his attention is so taken up in the pursuance of his chosen profession, he aids and supports all enterprises of a worthy character. He is a member of the Masonic order, and has held the office of magistrate for two years. He served in the late war, and enlisted in 1861 under Gen. Polk, Preston Smith's Brigade, Forty-seventh Tennessee Regiment, being wounded at the battle of Shiloh by a ball passing through the calf of his left leg. The Doctor also held the office of first lieutenant in the Kentucky campaign, a position which he filled with honor. The company was known as the Miller Guards of Richmond, Ky.

Robert J. Winn is a Buckeye by birth, and during the period of the Civil War served in the Federal army, enlisting in the Second Ohio Infantry, August 16, 1861. He was in the battles of Stone River, Chickamauga, Missionary Ridge, Mill Creek Gap, Buzzard's Roost, Peach Tree Creek, Atlanta and a number of others, and was captured at Pulaski, Tenn., May 30, 1862, by Morgan, but was exchanged and received his discharge, October 11, 1864. March 7, 1866, Miss Alma Wymer became his wife, a daughter of John and Rebecca (Gormer) Wymer, originally from Pennsylvania. Robert J. Winn was born in Muskingum County, Ohio, in 1837, and was a son of Adolphus and Rebecca (Jordon) Winn. Adolphus Winn was a Virginian by birth, his existence dating from 1810, and he was one of a family of twelve children born to William and Rebecca (Russel) Winn, also of the Old Dominion. He

was married in 1836 and moved to Ohio, where he bought a farm of 500 acres, there residing until his death in 1885. Mrs. Winn, the mother of Robert J., was a daughter of Cabot and Rachel Jordon, natives of Maryland, and who went to Ohio in 1825, where Rebecca was born. Her parents lived to an advanced age, her father dying when seventy-six years old, and her mother at the age of seventy-eight. Mr. and Mrs. Adolphus Winn were the parents of thirteen children: Robert J., Martha R., Nancy J. (deceased), Caleb J. (deceased), Elizabeth and Margaret (twins), Fennan S., John A., Albert J., Mariah, Hattie, Harmon S. and Simeon S. Mrs. Winn is still living. To the subject of this sketch, and wife, six children have been given: Lillie C., Herbert H., Edith R., Louis A., Mable O. and Clarence A. Mr. Winn moved to this State in 1875 and settled in Judsonia, White County, where he bought a farm of eighty acres, and is engaged principally in raising fruit and vegetables for market. He also owns considerable town property and an interest in the Judsonia Canning Company, of which he is president, being also president of the board of trustees of the Judsonia University, and is a member of the board of trustees of the Building Association. Besides he is secretary of the Arkansas Fruit Growers' and Shippers' Union. Mr. Winn is a member of Judsonia Lodge No. 54, I. O. O. F., and of the Grand Lodge of the State. He and his wife and eldest daughter belong to the Baptist Church, and take an active part in all religious work. The former has been engaged in teaching school for a number of years.

John W. Womack is the son of Jacob and Nancy (Bates) Womack, and was born in Meigs County, Tenn., February 16, 1833. Jacob Womack was a Virginian by birth, his natal day being in 1797. His youth was passed in the Old Dominion and in 1822 he was united in marriage with Miss Bates, also a native of Virginia. One year after this event Mr. Womack moved to East Tennessee and died there in 1863, his wife surviving until 1865. He was a successful farmer and a quiet, law-abiding citizen. In his political views he sided with the Democrats, and was a Primitive

Baptist in his religious belief. Mr. and Mrs. Womack became the parents of eight children, three of whom are now living: John W., Martha J. (Mrs. J. N. Brown, of East Tennessee), and Elizabeth (widow of James Masner, of Independence County, Ark.). Those deceased are: David, Sarah (Mrs. Heard), Daniel, Mary A. (Mrs. W. C. Grubbs) and Susana (wife of Thomas Bonner). John W. Womack was reared in Meigs County, Tenn., and received such advantages for an education as the schools of the period afforded. Remaining on the farm with his parents until thirty years of age, at the expiration of that time he branched out for himself, engaging in farming and stock raising, which is his present occupation. In 1867 he removed to Arkansas and settled on his farm where he now resides. The farm consists of 240 acres of valuable land, highly cultivated and his stock is of various kinds, all of the finest breeds. Mr. Womack was married in 1867, in Meigs County, Tenn., to Miss Ellen B., daughter of Uriah and Mary Denton, of Virginia, and to them a family of five children have been born, four living: Daniel U., Mary A., John and Sabinus. Mr. Womack served in the Confederate army, in Col. McKenzie's Third East Tennessee Cavalry during the war, and was mostly on scout duty in various skirmishes and fights, but in no regular battles of any prominence. He was captured while ill, in 1865, being released just before the final surrender. Mr. Womack is an influential member of the school board, a stanch Democrat in politics, and has been a Master Mason for over twenty years.

Alfonsus A. Wood might well be called a self-made man. His father, Joseph P. Wood, a native of Weakley County, Tenn., was a farmer by profession, and very successful in that calling. He was united in marriage, in 1836, in Weakley County, Tenn., to Mary E. Freeman, of Virginia. In 1870 they moved to Arkansas, and settled in Jackson County, where Mr. Wood was residing at the date of his death, in 1872, though he was in Tennessee when he died, having been called there on business. His belief was with the Methodist Episcopal Church, South. Mr. and Mrs. Wood were the parents of eleven children, five of whom are now living: Fannie (wife of T. M. Thompkins, of Carroll County, Tenn.), Mary F. (Mrs. W. B. Gamble, of White County, Ark.), Emma B. (Mrs. H. S. McKnight, residing in White County, Ark.), Alfonsus A. and Portia S. (wife of B. F. Whitley). Mrs. Wood makes her home at this time with her son in White County, and notwithstanding that she has reached the age of three-score years and ten, is still active in all church and charity work, and a liberal contributor to these enterprises. Alfonsus A. began for himself at the age of eighteen, choosing his father's occupation, which he has successfully conducted ever since. He owns eighty acres of excellent land in White County, and a half interest in a large steam grist-mill and cotton-gin, at Russell, Ark., where he is now residing. Mr. Wood was married in White County, on December 16, 1875, to Miss Lucinda F. Plant, a daughter of William and Emily Plant, old settlers of White County. By this marriage one child was born, who died in infancy. Mrs. Wood died November 18, 1876, and in 1881 Mr. Wood was united in marriage to Margaret L. Drenan, whose parents, A. R. and Mary Drenan, natives of Tennessee, are now residing in Russell. Mrs. Wood died in February, 1884, leaving two children: Tennie and Alvis A. Mr. Wood is a Democrat in his political views, though not an enthusiast. He is an earnest worker and a member of many years' standing in the Methodist Episcopal Church, also belonging to the Triple Alliance, a secret mutual benefit association. He is a man of quiet habits, charitable, and very popular in the society of his little town, being respected by all.

Daniel T. Woodson was the eldest son of James M. and Pauline L. (Gregory) Woodson; the former was a native of Virginia and went to Western Tennessee in 1845, removing in 1858 to Arkansas, and settling in White County. Daniel T. Woodson first saw the light in Virginia, on October 19, 1839. He accompanied his parents to Arkansas at the age of nineteen, where he was married at the age of twenty-one years to a Miss Park, of Tennessee nativity, and who came to White County four years previous to the Woodsons. Daniel T. enlisted during the war, in May, 1862, in the Confederate army, first in the cavalry and afterward in the infantry service, being a member of a foraging force throughout the war. Foraging was a dangerous occupation at that time, and he had many narrow escapes from capture. After the cessation of hostilities Mr. Woodson bought a place of 160 acres in White County, on which he resided until 1877, when he sold his farm and purchased another of 211 acres in the same township, near Centre Hill. In 1882 he bought a mill and cotton-gin, in which business he has been very successful. Mr. Woodson's wife died in 1870, leaving two sons, James M. and Joseph Y. He was married the second time in November of that year to N. L. Dollar, by which marriage five children have been born: Phillip C., Mary L., Bula L., Zula B. and Bertha D. Mr. Woodson is a member of the Masonic order, to which he has belonged since 1862; his membership is now in Centre Hill Lodge No. 114, where he has held an office for the last fifteen years. He is a decided Democrat, politically, and held the office of justice of the peace in his township in 1887–88. Mr. and Mrs. Woodson belong to the Missionary Baptist Church, of which they have been members nearly all their lives. In the organization where they worship, Mr. Woodson is leader in the choir and also superintendent in the Sunday-school.

James R. Woodson. There is generally more or less similarity in the sketches of those who have for the most part been engaged in agricultural pursuits from boyhood, but Mr. Woodson's career has been sufficiently diversified as to render him well posted with different affairs, people, etc. The State of his nativity is West Virginia, where he was born in 1841, being the second of a family of ten children born to James M. and Paulina (Gregory) Woodson, both of whom were Virginians, the former's birth occurring in 1813. They were married in 1838, and their union resulted in the birth of the following children: Daniel T., James R., Elizah, John L., William J., Martha J., George W. D., Clements and Bettie. James R. Woodson removed to Tennessee with his father in 1843, and after residing there twelve years came with him to White County, Ark., but the latter's death occurred in Memphis, Tenn., in 1862. James R. Woodson gave his attention to farm work until the outbreak of the war, then enlisted in Company A, Seventh Battalion, under Col. D. Shay, and took part in the following engagements: Perryville, Dalton, Spring Hill, Franklin, Nashville (Tenn.) and Atlanta, and in the last-named engagement received a gunshot wound in the thigh, and thirty-six bullet holes in his clothes. At the time of the surrender he was filling the position of teamster. He came to Arkansas, and in 1866 was married to Amanda Goad, a daughter of Henry and Mary (Sowell) Goad, natives of Tennessee. He now owns a farm of 120 acres, and has fifty acres under cultivation, all his property being acquired by hard and persistent labor. The children of this marriage are: Mary L. (the wife of Monroe Henderson and the mother of one child, Julia E), Docia A. (the wife of William Elded and the mother of one child, Martha J.), Emma G. (was married to Thomas Baker, by whom she has one child, Elmer J.), Martha F., James H., Alice M., William E., George E., Lula E., John S. and Joel F. Mrs. Woodson died February 2, 1889, her infant son, Aaron, also dying. Mr. and Mrs. Woodson held memberships in the Methodist Episcopal Church, South, and he has always been an active worker for schools as well as churches. He is a member of Mount Pisgah Lodge No. 242 of the A. F. & A. M., and has been an officer of the same.

James Maury Wright ranks among the most prosperous of White County's agriculturists, and enjoys the reputation of being not only a substantial and progressive farmer, but an intelligent and thoroughly posted man on all public affairs. He first saw the light of day August 12, 1834, in Madison County, Tenn., and through his paternal ancestor, James Wright, has inherited Irish blood, his grandfather having come from Ireland to America about the year 1780, and took up his abode in Franklin County, N. C., where he engaged in farming and died at an advanced age. James Wright was married in North Carolina in the year 1818 to Miss Patsey Stigall, and after they had become the parents of five children they removed to Gibson County, Tenn., where their family was increased to eleven children. James Maury Wright was born in the latter State, and was the tenth of the family in order of birth. His early education was confined to the subscription schools, and he was reared to the duties of farm life on his father's plantation. September 11, 1856, his nuptials with Miss Martha R. Vann were celebrated, she being also a native of Tennessee. Their children were as follows: Elizabeth (born June 14, 1857, was married to William G. Ross in 1878, and has five children), Mary (born in January, 1858, died February of the same year), Martha (born May 15, 1859, was married to Thomas Burns in 1878, and bore one child. Both she and her husband are now dead, the former dying in 1884, and the latter in 1879), James Henry (was born on January 31, 1860), William N. (born January 31, 1863, and is now a salesman in the mercantile house of Messrs. Warren & Phelps of El Paso, Ark.), Charles T. (born May 19, 1867), John R. (born August 27, 1869), Nettie (born in July, 1871), and Hattie (born in June, 1874). The mother of these children died in July, 1880, an earnest member of the Missionary Baptist Church, and two years later Mr. Wright wedded Miss Minerva Hendricks. In 1857 the family came to Arkansas, and Mr Wright began to make improvements on a tract of railroad land, but one year later moved to El Paso, where he began working at the carpenter's trade having served an apprenticeship under his father, but also continued his farming operations on a tract of land containing forty acres adjoining the town. In 1860, in company with T. W. Wells, now of Searcy, he erected the first grist-mill in the vicinity of El Paso, a need which had been long felt by the people of the community. Peach Orchard (now El Paso) at time of Mr. Wright's location only consisted of a double log-house, but in the fall of 1859 and the winter of 1860, there were three business houses erected. Wild game was plentiful in the surrounding woods, and many a deer was brought low by the unerring aim of Mr. Wright's rifle. In 1861 he sold his land and purchased two acres in the town upon which he erected a dwelling house and other buildings, oc-

casionally working at his trade in connection with his milling operations. After purchasing a farm of 160 acres in Conway County, in 1862, he settled his family there, and June 20 of the same year he enlisted in Company A, Col. Glenn's regiment, and was on detached duty in Arkansas for about a month as teamster, and was afterward promoted to the position of wagon master, in which capacity he served until January, 1864. While at home on furlough the Federal troops got possession of the State of Arkansas, and Mr. Wright was cut off from his command, and did not again enter service. In 1864 he bought an interest in a large flouring mill, which was known as the Peach Orchard Tap Mill, but sold out two years later, and, in 1869 purchased the farm where he is now residing, and since 1870 has also operated the Warren & Davis flour, grist and cotton-gin mill, following the latter occupation in El Paso from 1872 to 1886. He has been very successful and at one time owned 240 acres of land, but at the present time has in his possession 160 acres with about 100 acres under cultivation. Mr. Wright and his wife belong to the Missionary Baptist Church, and in his political views he is a Democrat. He belongs to El Paso Lodge No. 65 of the A. F. & A. M., and has attained the Chapter degree. He has taken an active interest in the advancement of education in his county, and was one of the few who voted for the special school tax. He has also contributed liberally to schools.

James A. Wright, postmaster and express agent at Higgins, grew to manhood in Alabama, and in Independence County, Ark., receiving a good education. In 1861 he joined the Confederate army, in the Eighth Arkansas Infantry, and served the first year east of the Mississippi, afterward being transferred to the Trans-Mississppi Department, and undergoing capture as a prisoner of war, at Little Rock, though he was only retained only six weeks. He was in Price's raid through Missouri, and participated in the battles of Prairie Grove, Helena, Pilot Knob and a number of skirmishes, and was accidentally wounded, losing his right leg. After being discharged in the latter part of 1864, he went to Searcy and engaged in farming and the mercantile business, and in August, 1874, moved to his present location where he has since been selling goods with flattering success. Mr. Wright was born in Jackson County, Ala., February 21, 1842, to the union of N. A. and Martha (Byranny) Wright, natives of Alabama. The former was a Methodist minister, and upon his removal from Alabama to Arkansas, located in Independence County in 1858, ten years later coming to Searcy. After one year here he went to Red River County, Tex., and died there October 2, 1877, at the age of sixty-two years, his wife preceding him two months; she was a member of the Methodist Episcopal Church. They were the parents of nine children, six of whom are living: James A. (our subject), Lovenia (wife Mr. Gideon, of Alabama), Malinda (now Mrs. Malden, of Texas), Amanda (also Mrs. Malden, residing in Texas), Mary (Mrs. Taylor, of St. Francis County), and Ellen (widow of a Mr. Malden). In connection with his other business Mr. Wright held the position of agent of the Iron Mountain Railroad at Higgins, from 1875 until July, 1889, also being appointed postmaster of Higgins, in March, 1875, which office he still occupies. May 15, 1864 he was married to Mary A. Ellis, who was born in Carroll County, Tenn., in 1846. They have a family of nine children: Mattie (wife of W. H. Chrisp), W. H., Maud L., Tommie, P. H., George D., Ollie and Willie. Mrs. Wright is a member of the Methodist Episcopal Church, South. Mr. Wright belongs to the I. O. O. F., is a decided Democrat and is one of the founders of the village of Higgins. As an esteemed citizen he is widely known.

CHAPTER XVI.

WOODRUFF COUNTY—PERIOD OF SETTLEMENT—FIRST PIONEERS—COUNTY FORMATION—SEAT OF JUSTICE
—BUILDINGS FOR PUBLIC USE—JUDICIAL HISTORY—LEGAL BAR—POLITICAL STATUS—DIREC-
TORY OF OFFICIALS—MILITARY AFFAIRS—GEOGRAPHICAL SITUATION—BOUNDARY
AND AREA—TOPOGRAPHY—PHYSICAL DESCRIPTION—RESOURCES—CEN-
SUS STATISTICS—VALUATION AND TAXATION—TRANSPORTA-
TION—POPULATION—EDUCATIONAL AND RELIGIOUS
FACILITIES—SOCIETY—COMMERCIAL CENTERS.

Look forward what's to come, and back what's past;
Thy life will be with praise and prudence graced;
What loss or gain may follow thou may'st guess,
Then wilt thou be secure of the success.

BEFORE the settlement of Arkansas by the Americans began, the Chickasaw Indians occupied the eastern part, and the Quawpaws were located on and along the Arkansas River in the western part. In visiting each other these tribes crossed White River at the point where Augusta is now located. Hence long before Augusta was established its site was called Chickasaw Crossing. The first white settler of the territory composing Woodruff County was a Mr. Hamilton, who, about the year 1820, landed at Chickasaw Crossing, and "squatted" upon the present site of Augusta. Soon thereafter—say some time between 1822 and 1826—Rolla Gray, with his family and others, came up the river in a small boat from a former settlement made near Indian Bay, or mouth of Cache River, near the present town of Clarendon,

and landed at Chickasaw Crossing. Mr. Gray then bought the right, "good-will or possession," of Mr. Hamilton, became a permanent settler, and lived here until his death. The sons of Mr. Gray, who came and settled with him, were John, Jesse, Daniel, Samuel and Jacob, all of whom afterward made individual settlements. John Gray and two of his brothers settled in that part of the county now known as the Point, in the southern part of the county. John became a stock raiser, and succeeded so well that in 1840, he owned "upward of 100 horses," and in 1841 he drove "400 or 500" head of cattle to Jacksonport, and there shipped them to New Orleans. The two brothers built the first mill in the Point, on Bayou Cache. These three constituted the entire settlement of that section until 1843, when Durant H. Bell, of Tennessee, came and settled there. Others then followed in rapid succession until the Point was

*In the compilation of the history of Woodruff County, acknowledgments are due to Thomas E. Erwin and wife, Dr. F. D. Dale, writer of the pamphlet entitled "Woodruff County," and others for valuable information furnished.

Yours Truly

Jas B Dent

WOODRUFF COUNTY, ARKANSAS.

fully settled. Daniel Gray is said to have been a great bear hunter.

In 1827 John Dennis, a son-in-law of Rolla Gray, settled about three miles south of Chickasaw Crossing, and near the same time two brothers, Michael and Joseph Haggerdon, settled in the vicinity of the Crossing. Redding Stokes and his two sons, George Hatch and Samuel Taylor, were the first settlers on Taylor's Bay, it being named after the latter. Dudley Glass and John Teague settled the O'Neal place, four miles north of Augusta. Teague Lake was named after the latter. In 1835 Maj. John Roddy and his brother, Elias B., natives of South Carolina, settled in the vicinity about three miles northeast of Chickasaw Crossing. In the latter part of 1840, or early in 1841, James Barnes, an eccentric pioneer, founded the Jennie Colony between Cache River and Bayou De View, now De View Township. He named it in honor of his wife, whose first name was Jennie. Thomas Arnold, Absalom Arnold and his son Jerry, were the next settlers of the Jennie Colony. The fame of this colony "spread round about," and it soon became more fully settled. Perhaps the most noted pioneer settler, though not the first, was Thomas Hough, the founder of Augusta. His work as a public man will be mentioned further on. Among what may properly be called the second early settlers, were Thomas E. Erwin, J. L. Murphy and Lieut. L. M. Sawyer, all of whom are living. Mr. Erwin settled in the territory composing Woodruff County, on Taylor's Bay, in 1840, and is now the oldest surviving settler. Mr. Lewis settled ten miles south of Augusta, in 1846. [For further mention of pioneer settlers see Biographical Department.]

Inasmuch as the territory composing this county was nearly all taken from Jackson, it is proper here to mention the formation of that county. Jackson County was organized in accordance with an act of the legislature of the Territory of Arkansas, approved November 5, 1829, and early in 1830 the first courts were held at the house of Thomas Wideman, where Erwin Station* is now situated,

on the Batesville & Brinkley Railroad. The courts were continued to be held there until 1832, when the seat of justice was established at the town of Litchfield, which was located on Village Creek, at the crossing of the Jacksonport and Augusta wagon road. The county seat remained at this place until 1839, when it was removed to Elizabeth, on White River, midway between the present towns of Jacksonport and Newport, on the same river. Here it remained until 1852, when it was removed to Augusta (the present county seat of Woodruff County). The following year it was removed to Jacksonport, where it has ever since remained.

The assertion that the county seat of Jackson County was held at Augusta in 1852 and 1853 has been strenuously disputed by certain later citizens of that place, but the statement is made upon the authority of personal examination of the county records; additional conclusive proof of this avowal is seen by the following letter from the present clerk of Jackson County:

Jacksonport, Ark., July 15, 1889.
SIR: The record here shows that the county court of the county was held from April, 1852, to October, 1853, at Augusta. The opening order for the April term, 1852, reads as follows: "At a county court begun and held for the county of Jackson, at the court house in the town of Augusta, on Monday the 12th day of April, 1852, present Hon. John H. T. Webb, presiding judge." The circuit, chancery and probate courts were also held at Augusta.
Respectfully yours, J. J. WALKER, *clerk.*
Per E. L. BOYCE, *D. C.*

Certainly this *record evidence* is all that is necessary to settle the question, as the county court and all the other courts of Jackson County would not have been held at Augusta if it had not been the county seat.

Woodruff County was created by a vote of the people in pursuance to ordinance of the State Convention of 1861, and was organized in 1862. It was named in honor of William E. Woodruff, editor of the first paper published in Arkansas, the Arkansas Gazette, first published at Arkansas Post, in 1819. He was one of the most distinguished pioneers of the State, and died recently, at Little

---

*This was the oldest cleared place in Jackson County, having been cleared by the Indians over 100 years ago.

It was the site of the old Shawnee Indian village, but abandoned as such when Mr. Wideman settled thereon.

Rock, at a very advanced age. It being during the war period, the organization of the county was not fully and permanently completed until 1865, the end of that period. The county court record prior to September, 1865, seems not to have been preserved, at least it does not appear on file in the clerk's office.

Immediately upon the organization of the county, the seat of justice was established at Augusta, where it has ever since remained. The first court house erected at Augusta was a one-story frame building, which is still standing on the west side of Second Street, on Lots 11 and 12, in Block 8, according to the original plat of the town. The second court house was a residence with two rooms (frame), and stood on the northwest corner of Block 22. It was purchased by the county, but used only a short time, until the present court house was occupied. This latter house was built just before the Civil War, by Thomas Hough, for a residence, and was used as such by his family, through the war period and later. On April 21, 1870, Mr. Hough, for the consideration of $28,000, conveyed the realty on which this house stands, consisting of a full block of ground, according to the plat of that part of the town, to the county for a court house and public square. The building is a large, two-story brick structure, and, though built for a residence, it answers very well for a court house. It stands in the northern suburbs of the town.

Soon after this property was purchased, a stone jail was erected on the southeast corner of the square, and was afterward set on fire by prisoners and destroyed. The present jail is in a brick building, which was erected by Mr. Hough near his residence for the occupancy of his servants. The county owns a "poor farm," with fair average buildings thereon, for the home of its paupers. This farm lies in Section 16, Township 8 north, Range 3 west.

The courts of the county consist of the county, probate and circuit. The regular terms of the former begin on the first Mondays of January, April, July and October of each year, and the regular terms of the probate court on the fourth Monday of the same months. The regular terms of the circuit court convene the third Mondays of February and August. The first term of this court, as appears of record, was held in October, 1865, by Hon. William R. Cain, judge presiding. The grand jury selected and empaneled at this term consisted of the following-named gentlemen: James P. Ferguson (foreman), Edmond N. Shelton, William Kemble, Andrew J. Henry, Y. B. Brantley, Littleberry G. Wilkerson, Thomas B. Roddy, Thomas H. Penn, Gabriel Couch, Gabriel M. Couch, George Mayfield, Henry W. Linthicum, Jesse H. Wolf, Samuel Whitcomb, William B. Tilmon and Oliver O'Neal. The Woodruff Circuit Court belongs to the First judicial district, composed of the counties of Phillips, Lee, St. Francis, Prairie, Woodruff, White and Monroe. The present judge is M. T. Sanders, of Helena, and the prosecuting attorney is S. Brundidge, of Searcy. The local legal bar of this county consists of: T. E. Stanley and D. D. Leach, of Augusta, and A. F. Maberry and Will T. Trice, of Cotton Plant. It is evident from the small number of attorneys that there is but little litigation carried on in the county.

To show the political aspect of Woodruff County, the votes cast for the candidates for Governor and for President at the late elections is here given: For Governor at the September election, 1888, James P. Eagle (Dem.), 1,548; C. N. Norwood (Com. Opp.), 1,375; for President, at the November election, 1888, Cleveland (Dem.), 1,236; Harrison (Rep.), 1,021; Streeter (U. L.), 192; Fiske (Pro.), 2.

The following is a list of the names of the county officers of Woodruff County, with date of terms of service annexed, from the time of organization:

Judges: I. McCurdy, 1862–64; E. T. Jones, 1864–65; R. W. Martin, 1865–66; E. T. Jones, 1866–68; A. D. Blanchard, 1868–72; L. M. Ramsaur, 1874–76; E. T. Jones, 1876–82; J. B. Dent, 1882–88; W. T. Trice, present incumbent, elected in 1888.

Clerks: V. L. Walters, 1862–64; D. H. Johnson, 1864–66; W. P. Campbell, 1866–68; D. H.

Johnson, 1868–74; W. P. Campbell, 1874–82; A. W. Jones, 1882–86; W. E. Ferguson, present incumbent, first elected in 1886.

Sheriffs: J. R. Jelks, 1862–64; John Thorp, 1864–66; J. R. Jelks, 1866–68; J. N. Bosley, 1868–74; J. R. Jelks, 1874–76; A. W. Jones, 1876–78; Ed. Roddy, 1878–80; A. W. Jones, 1880–82; W. E. Ferguson, 1882–86; Ed. Roddy, present incumbent, first elected in 1886.

Treasurers: James Smock, 1862–64; T. E. Erwin, 1864–66; R. L. Barnes, 1866–68; W. M. Reynolds, 1868–71; E. H. Shelton, 1871–72; T. E. Erwin, 1872–74; C. T. Petit, 1874–82; Warren Sale, 1882–84; J. W. Sallee, 1884–86; Warren Sale, present incumbent, first elected in 1886.

Coroners: James Crawford, 1862–64; William Cornelius, 1864–66; W. H. Dickinson, 1866–68; Edwin Wilson, 1868–72; J. A. Hamlet, 1874–76, B. F. Hawkins, 1876–78; N. J. Barbee, 1878–80; William Elsberry, 1880–82; C. H. Devain, 1882–84; R. W. Stokes, 1884–86; H. D. Spivey, 1886–88; W. A. Harper, present incumbent, elected in 1888.

Surveyors: C. S. Cabler, 1862–64; R. H. Cotney, 1864–68; G. D. F. Malone, 1868–72; C. W. Montague, 1872–74; R. T. Cotney, 1874–78; R. K. Fitzhugh, 1878–82; W. F. Fesperman, 1882–84; E. S. Freeman, 1884–86; L. H. Weed, 1886–88; R. K. Fitzhugh, present incumbent, elected in 1888.

Assessors: W. P. Anderson, 1868–72; J. H. Johnson, 1872 to May, 1874; James B. Dent, from May, 1874; W. W. Garland, 1874–80; W. E. Ferguson, 1880–82; G. W. Gordon, 1882–86; J. P. Hobbs, 1886–88; J. W. Sallee, present incumbent, elected in 1888.

Delegates in State Conventions: W. H. Gray was elected to represent the county in the State convention held January 7 to February 18, 1868, but did not attend. William J. Thompson represented the county in the State convention held July 14 to October 31, 1874.

Upon the approach of the Civil War of 1861–65, many of the citizens of the territory now embraced in Woodruff County, were opposed to secession, but when actual operations of a warlike nature began, they generally cast their lot with the proposed Southern Confederacy, and did what they could to help establish it. In May, 1861, Capt. Charles Matlock organized a company of State troops at Augusta, and in July following, it was mustered into the Confederate service at Mazzard Prairie near Fort Smith, and became a part of Col. Churchill's regiment—the First Arkansas Mounted Rifles. Capt. James H. Patterson raised the second company at Augusta, in July, 1861, "The Independent Jackson Rangers," as they were called, and soon after this company moved to Mammoth Springs in Fulton County, and there joined Col. Snavell's battalion of Missouri Cavalry. Later, in 1861, Capt. Robert Anthony, Jr., raised a company, mostly in what is now the northern part of Woodruff County, and it joined and became a part of the Eighth Arkansas Infantry. Afterward, in May, 1862, Capt. Ed. T. Jones raised a company at Augusta, and, moving to Little Rock, it joined Col. Pleasant's regiment of the Trans-Mississippi Department. Subsequently Capt. John Bland raised a company, or part of a company, in the territory now composing Woodruff County. This company was composed largely of deserters from the army and conscripts.

All of these companies served in the Confederate army, and acquitted themselves as gallant soldiers. No troops were raised within what is now the limits of the county for the Federal army. In the spring of 1864, Gen. Davidson came up the river in a boat or boats with the Third Minnesota Infantry, landed at Augusta and sent out a company of about ninety men to reconnoiter. On or near the Fitz Hugh farm about six miles northeast of Augusta, this company encountered several hundred Confederate soldiers under command of Gen. McRae. A fight ensued and the Federals fell back in good order to Augusta, suffering a small loss in killed and wounded. Capt. John Bland of the Confederate force and a few of his men were killed. It is said that he and his men did most of the fighting in this engagement, on the part of the Confederates. This was the only skirmish of note that occurred during the war in what is now Woodruff County.

In moving southward, Gen. Steele, commanding a portion of the Union Army, stopped and spent the first week in July, 1862, at Augusta, making his headquarters at the residence of Thomas Hough, now the court house. The General pitched his tent on the lawn near the house, and near where lay a large pile of earth (probably thrown from the cellar). Presently a party of soldiers came and began to dig into the earth pile, but the General stopped them and demanded to know what they expected to find; he was informed that a "nigger," one of Mr. Hough's servants had informed them that a keg of currant wine was buried there. The General at once put an end to further pursuit for the wine, and informed Mr. Hough that he had better remove it. The latter was a Union man but would not fight against his neighbors. Gen. Steele and his staff boarded at Mr. Hough's table. The wine was removed from its hiding place, and there is no doubt about the knowledge that the General and his staff had of its quality. Mr. Hough (now deceased) was very liberal, and the wine was free.

Steele's army then moved on toward Helena, and afterward, in the winter of 1864–65, a small force of Federal troops occupied Augusta for a short time. A portion of Gen. Price's Confederate army passed through Augusta on the occasion of his last raid into Missouri, and some of Gen. Joe Shelby's men passed through it frequently. It was never occupied as a military post by either of the contending armies.

The county of Woodruff, in Eastern Arkansas, is bounded north by Jackson, east by Cross and St. Francis, south by St. Francis and Monroe, and west by Prairie and White Counties. It lies mostly in the 36° of north latitude, and between the fifth principal meridian of the United States surveys, and longitude 14° 21' west from Washington. It comprises an area of 590 square miles, of which less than one-fifth is under cultivation.

Its boundary lines are as follows: Beginning on the fifth principal meridian, where the line between Townships 8 and 9 north, crosses it; thence south on said meridian line to the line dividing Townships 4 and 5 north; thence west on the township line to the southwest corner of Section 32, Township 5 north, Range 2 west; thence south to the southeast corner of Section 6, Township 4 north, Range 2 west; thence west to the southwest corner of Section 2, Township 4 north, Range 3 west; thence south on section lines to the line dividing Townships 3 and 4 north; thence west on the township line to the line dividing Ranges 3 and 4 west; thence north on the range line to the line dividing Townships 4 and 5 north; thence west on the township line to the line dividing Ranges 4 and 5 west; thence north on the range line to White River; thence up White River following its meanders to the line dividing Townships 7 and 8 north; thence west on the township line to the southwest corner of Section 35, Township 8 north, Range 4 west; thence north on section lines until White River is again intersected; thence up White River, following its meanders to the line dividing Townships 9 and 10 north; thence east on the township line to the line dividing Ranges 2 and 3 west; thence south on the range line to the line dividing Townships 8 and 9 north; thence east on the township line to the place of beginning.

Of the area of the county, the St. Louis, Iron Mountain & Southern Railway Company, owns between 2,000 and 3,000 acres, and between 30,000 and 40,000 acres is public property, and the balance is owned by individuals.

Its meteorology for the past forty years gives no record of cyclones or other character of violent storms. The annual mean of barometer officially given for the county is $30\frac{0718}{1000}°$. The rain fall is from 44 to 49 inches annually. The mean temperature for the year is 60°. The isothermal belt crossing the county is that which includes the vicinity of Norfolk, Va., Raleigh, N. C., Atlanta, Ga., Nashville, Tenn., Fort Smith, Ark., and El Paso, N. M.

Woodruff County is a part of the vast scope of lowland farm country, lying between White River, below its confluence with the Black and the Mississippi. There are no hills in the county. The surface is comparatively level, its uplands comprising above five-eighths of the whole area, ranging from one to fifteen feet above high water mark. White River, as has been shown, runs nearly all the way along the western boundary of the county. Cache River, a confluent of the White, enters the county from the north, near the middle of Range 2 west, and flows thence in a general direction a little west of south, and leaves the county near the southwest corner of Township 4 north, Range 3 west, its average distance from the White being between eight and nine miles. Bayou De View, another confluent of the White, enters the county from the north about two miles west of the northeast corner, and flows southward in nearly the same direction as that of Cache River, leaving the county near the middle of Range 2 west, its average distance east from the Cache being between seven and eight miles. Eastward from this latter stream, the country rises gently to the summit of the ridge between it and L'Anguile River, which flows in a southerly direction through the western part of Cross and St. Francis Counties. Nearly all the natural drainage of the county is through White and Cache Rivers, Bayou De View and their tributaries.

The longitudinal course of these streams has the effect of dividing the county into three great bodies, viz.: that portion lying between White and Cache Rivers, and that lying between Cache River and Bayou De View, and that lying east of the latter. These again are subdivided into small bodies or slight ridges by the smaller streams. The bottom lands along the large water courses, comprising perhaps nearly three-eighths of the area of the county, and known as the "slashes," are more or less subject to overflow. The major part of these lands, however, can be reclaimed and made tillable by levees and a proper system of drainage. The lands thus far cleared and occupied are on the ridges between the streams. The soil of the entire county is very rich and fertile. It has two grades known as the "gum lands and the white oak lands," the former being the strongest and most productive. The soil of the uplands is a rich, dark, sandy loam, quick and generous, deep and durable; that of the lowlands is more tenacious. The soil in general is composed of vegetable mold, clay and sand, and much of it is of the alluvial deposits.

18

The territory of Woodruff County was originally an unbroken forest of timber, large and dense, and it is estimated that over five-eighths of its area is yet covered with timber. The remaining forests as yet are mostly unbroken, and throughout the uplands are accessible at all times of the year. The varieties of timber are white, red, black, over-cup, burr and swamp oak, gum, cypress, ash, walnut, hickory, etc. A number of saw-mills and an extensive stave factory are now in operation in the county, cutting the timber into lumber and staves for shipping purposes, and much of it is thus going to distant markets. A large amount of timber is also floated down the streams in the log.

There are but few, if any, valuable springs in Woodruff County, but well water of an unexcelled quality, is everywhere obtainable at a depth varying from twenty to forty feet, without digging or boring through any solid rock. Driven wells are in general use, and they can be easily put in and at a cost comparatively low. Some cisterns are found, though driven wells are preferable, as from them a fresh and pure supply of water can always be had. From the sources named, an abundant supply of water for all purposes is obtained. No minerals have been found to exist here.

At present, and for some time to come, there is and will be, a considerable income from the timber resources of the county, but this can not always continue, for the supply will sooner or later become exhausted. Agriculture, horticulture and the raising of live stock are the principal resources, and these will be permanent. The soil is well adapted to the growing of cotton, corn, oats, millet, clover, the tame grasses, and all kinds of vegetables. With proper cultivation it will yield, in fair seasons, from 1,000 to 1,500 pounds of seed cotton to the acre, forty to sixty bushels of corn, thirty to fifty bushels of oats, from 200 to 300 bushels of Irish or sweet potatoes, and other things in proportion. Wheat sometimes does well, but it can not be claimed as a good wheat-producing country. Immense quantities of hay can be produced, but as yet the farmers have not turned their attention, to any considerable extent, to its production. Clover and the tame grasses are but little cultivated. The soil has continued to produce so well that cotton and corn have been raised from year to year, on some lands for half a century, without returning anything to the land to refertilize it. Fertilizing matter is seldom gathered and returned to the soil. Clover has not been grown at all as a fertilizer. A better and more economical system of farming should be adopted. The price of improved lands varies, according to quality, from $10 to $40 per acre, and unimproved lands from $2 to $10. ''Cotton is King,'' but still a great amount of corn is produced.

According to the United States census of 1880, there were 934 farms in Woodruff County, and the amount of improved land was 40,671 acres, and from these the estimated value of all farm products raised in the year 1879, was $684,059. Following are the number of bushels, pounds, etc., of the cereal and vegetable productions of the county for that year: Indian corn, 229,962 bushels; oats, 9,908 bushels; wheat, 1,867 bushels; hay, 124 tons; cotton, 12,311 bales; Irish potatoes, 3,691; sweet potatoes, 6,960 bushels; tobacco, 2,435 pounds. The products of the present year, 1889, will be given in the next United States census reports, and will be interesting to compare with the products here given for the year 1879. In the last ten years the area of improved land has been largely increased, and the productions in proportion. In 1880 there were 1,455 horses, 1,038 mules and asses, 7,720 neat cattle, 1,107 sheep and 10,539 hogs in the county, and in 1888, according to the assessor's reports, 2,135 horses, 1,755 mules and asses, 8,941 neat cattle, 403 sheep and 6,356 hogs, a large increase in horses, mules and asses and neat cattle, but a material decrease in the number of sheep and hogs. The decrease in the number of sheep is probably due, largely, to the reduction in the price of wool, while the decrease in the number of hogs is wholly due to the fact that the number shown on the assessment rolls is only the number that was ''on hand'' when the assessment was taken, and did not, as did the census report of 1880, include those slaughtered, sold or otherwise disposed of during the previous year. When these figures are compared with the forthcoming census

of 1890, a large increase in the number of all, excepting, perhaps, sheep, will appear. Woodruff County is well adapted to the raising of live stock, on account of the productiveness of its soil, the mildness of its climate and its abundant supply of water. But little feed is required, except for a short season in the winter, and costly buildings for shelter are not required at all. Cheap buildings with good roofs, and single board walls are all sufficient for wintering stock here. Horticulture has not yet been developed, except for the home supply of fruits. Apples, pears and cherries do not succeed so well as in the more elevated portions of the State, but peaches and plums thrive well, and the smaller fruits and berries can be raised in unlimited quantities, the soil and climate being so well adapted for them. For strawberries the soil is unsurpassed. The market facilities by rail to the city markets being so good, the county must eventually become largely a garden of small fruits and berries.

In 1880, the real estate of Woodruff County was assessed for taxation at $898,316, the personal property $330,121; thus making a total of $1,228,437; and the total taxes charged thereon were $31,278. In 1888 the real estate of the county was assessed for taxation at $1,337,297, and the personal property at $582,402, making a total of $1,919,699, and the total amount of taxes charged thereon was $30,-170.64. By comparison it will be seen that during the eight years the taxable wealth of the county increased to the amount of $691,262, or 56 per cent, while the amount of taxes slightly decreased.

Woodruff is traversed by three railroads. The St. Louis, Arkansas & Texas Railroad (the Cotton Belt) enters on the fifth principal meridian, near the middle of Township 7 north, and runs thence in a southwesterly direction, leaving it near the southwest corner of Township 5 north, Range 1 west, the length of its line within the county being sixteen miles. The Batesville & Brinkley Railroad runs north and south through the center of the county, the length of its line through these limits being twenty-four miles. The Bald Knob & Memphis branch of the St. Louis, Iron Mountain & Southern Railway, crosses Woodruff

County east and west, near the line dividing Townships 7 and 8 north, thus leaving about one-fourth of the area to the north and three-fourths to the south. The length of its line here is twenty miles. This makes the combined length of railroads in the county sixty miles, and for the year 1888 they were assessed for taxation at $310,470. The railroad property constitutes a large proportion of the county's taxable wealth, and, accordingly, pays a large percentage of the several taxes.

The population of Woodruff County was, in 1870, white, 4,205, colored, 2,686, total, 6,891; in 1880, white, 4,163, colored, 4,483, total, 8,648. The increase since 1880, on account of the large immigration, has been so great that the population is now estimated at 14,000; the late immigrants being mostly white has caused the white population to exceed the colored by several hundred.

The educational facilities of Woodruff County consist of the free schools, with now and then a private school. The following statistics pertaining to the free schools of the county are taken from the report of the State Superintendent of Public Instruction for the year ending, June 30, 1888: Scholastic population : white, males, 975, females, 835, total, 1,810; colored, males, 1,185, females, 1,173, total, 2,358; total, white and colored, 4,165. Number of pupils taught in the public schools : white, males, 641, females, 516, total, 1,157; colored, males, 845, females, 790, total, 1,635; aggregate, 2,792. Number of school districts, 25; number reporting enrollment, 18; number voting tax, 15. Number of teachers employed, males, 45, females, 30, total, 75. Average monthly salaries paid teachers: first grade, males, $45, females, $35; second grade, males, $40, females, $40; third grade, males, $35. Amount expended for the support of the schools, all purposes, $10,318.79.

By comparing the above figures it will be seen that only 64 per cent of the white, and only 70 per cent of the colored scholastic population were taught in the public schools. In most of counties a greater per cent of the white than of the colored children are taught in the public schools. That the reverse of this is true in Woodruff County,

speaks well for the system, as it shows that the authorities have provided ample facilities for the education of the colored, as well as for the white children. It will also be observed that a less per cent of the white than of the colored children were taught in the free schools. This is accounted for by the fact that some of the white children were taught in private schools at home, and in colleges or schools abroad. The public school at Augusta is graded, and upon the whole Woodruff is fully up with other counties in sustaining the free school system. A teachers' institute was held at Augusta, beginning July 30, 1888, with only a small number of teachers present.

Of the various religious denominations, it seems that the Methodist Episcopal Church, South, has Woodruff County as an almost exclusive field of labor. Early in the 50's Mr. Thomas Hough, of Augusta, built at that place a substantial two-story frame edifice, at a cost of about $6,000, and donated it to the religious denominations and the Masonic fraternity, the lower story to be used as a church and the upper as a lodge hall. The church was dedicated for union religious services in June, 1854, by Rev. Joshua F. Green, a Presbyterian minister at Little Rock. The denominations that occupied it were the Methodists and Presbyterians. In the course of time the latter retired; and for a consideration, conveyed their interest in the property to the former, and finally the Methodists became the sole owners thereof. During the month of July, 1889, they removed the upper story, elevated the lower, and remodeled the building entirely and made a complete church edifice of it. This was the first church house erected in what is now Woodruff County.

On retiring from this building, the Presbyterians received by donation from the hands of Mr. Hough, a beautiful site upon which to erect a separate church edifice, and with the able assistance of the liberal donor and his estimable wife, they erected, in 1876, the present large and handsome brick church. This was the only Presbyterian Church erected in the county, and unfortunately the Presbyterian society has become, in a measure, disorganized and regular preaching has been dispensed with. A site was also donated by Mr. Hough to the Baptists, on which they built a frame church edifice, prospered for a few years and then disorganizing sold the property to the colored people who now use it for religious purposes. White Church, in the northern part of the county, is owned by the Baptists, but the latter are scattered throughout the county and are not generally organized.

Of the Methodist Episcopal Church, South, there is Augusta Station, Rev. N. B. Fizer, pastor, membership 132; De View Circuit, consisting of five appointments, Rev. Thomas Whittaker, pastor, membership 327; Howell Circuit, with four appointments, Rev. M. U. Umstead, pastor, membership 168; Union and Revel Circuit, with four appointments, Rev. G. A. Dannelly, pastor, membership 142, and a part of the Weldon Circuit, located mostly in Jackson County. Augusta Station and Union and Revel Circuit belong to the Searcy District; De View and Howell Circuits to the Helena District, and all belong to the White River Conference.

The people of Woodruff county, excepting those born there, are from many different parts of the Union, and a few are from "foreign lands." In the language of Dr. Dale, "Society is well organized, but without any cliques or 'sets' to set their faces against any lady or gentleman who is entitled to recognition; the people are not distant toward strangers, but, on the contrary, cordial and hospitable, and the lines of their lives having been in pleasant places, their visions of the world are not hedged by State or county boundaries."

Augusta, the county seat of Woodruff County, is situated on the east bank of White River, a mile and a quarter north of the Bald Knob & Memphis Branch of the St. Louis, Iron Mountain & Southern Railroad, and is connected with the latter by means of a street-car railway. As elsewhere stated, the place was originally called Chickasaw Crossing, and here, in the spring of 1847, John R. Elliott, from Philadelphia, Penn., in partnership with William Polite, opened the first store in the town, at the point where the printing office now stands, at the west end of Main Street. Elliott soon

retired from the business, and his partner, Polite, entered a piece of land adjacent, and moved the store thereto. Thomas Hough then began business in the building first occupied by Elliott & Polite. In March, 1848, the town was surveyed and laid out by Thomas S. Carter, of Independence County, for Thomas Hough, its proprietor and founder, who named it Augusta in honor of his favorite cousin, Miss Augusta, daughter of S. B. T. Cald, of Virginia, where Mr. Hough formerly resided.

The town has a beautiful site, and is well laid out, with streets crossing at right angles and running east and west and north and south. The site is at least ten feet above high-water mark, and there is a good river landing. After the town was laid out the second business house on the site proper was erected on the opposite side of the street from the first one, and from thenceforward the place began to grow, and at the beginning of the Civil War it had attained a population of about 600. During the war the town was almost entirely destroyed. On the approach of the Federal army, in 1862, the citizens generally fled and abandoned their houses, which were then torn down by the soldiers, who used the material to build shanties in their camps. At the close of the war many of the citizens who had fled returned, and together with those who had remained and some newcomers, began to rebuild the town, which, having the advantages of a good navigable river, and, there being no railroads through the adjacent territory to interfere with or draw its trade away, it soon recovered and became prosperous, doing a good business and an immense amount of shipping by river communication. It reached its climax early in the decade of the seventies, when it had a population of about 1,000. Since that time three railroads, the Iron Mountain, Batesville & Brinkley, and the Bald Knob & Memphis have been constructed, all missing the town except the latter, which is a mile and a quarter distant. On these railroads villages have sprung up all around Augusta, and compelled it to divide its former trade with them, and consequently it has declined so that its population is now estimated by the best-informed citizens, at about 700 to 800. However, having the advantages of one railroad, a navigable river and the county seat, it will continue to be a good trading point and a desirable place in which to live. It has many handsome residences, with beautiful and well kept lawns. White River is navigable to this point for large vessels, at all seasons of the year, and at low water it is the point at which the freight bulk is broken for steamers which ply the upper White and Black Rivers.

Augusta has suffered great loss by fire, but it has been rebuilt, and now contains six general, two drug, six grocery, one harness and saddle, one confectionery and two furniture stores, four hotels (including boarding houses), a restaurant, two meat markets, a jewelry store, two livery stables, a complement of mechanics' shops, a saw-mill, four church edifices (two each for the white and the colored people), two public school-houses (one for the white and one for the colored people), three physicians, two lawyers, etc. Also Augusta Lodge No. 45, A. F. & A. M., Augusta Chapter No. 37, Augusta Council No. 22, Augusta Lodge, K. of H., No. 1122 and Chickasaw Lodge No. 244, K. & L. of H. The Augusta and White River Street Railway connects the town with the Bald Knob & Memphis Railroad at Augusta Station. The "Chickasaw" steamboat, during the summer months, makes one trip per week between Augusta and Memphis, and during the cotton-shipping season other boats also ply the river regularly. Augusta is incorporated and has a full line of corporate officers. E. E. Blackman was mayor at the time of compilation (July, 1889). The town consists almost wholly of wooden buildings.

The Woodruff County Vidette, now in its twelfth volume, is published weekly at Augusta, by W. W. Folsom, editor and proprietor. It is an eight-column folio, is neatly printed and ably edited, and is Democratic in politics. The first newspaper published in Augusta was The Augusta Sentinel, established about the year 1860, by Maurice Lewis, and printed on a press owned by Thomas Hough. The press was destroyed by Federal soldiers, and the editor, Mr. Lewis, was killed in the Confederate army in front of Atlanta, Ga.

Dr. F. D. Dale, in his pamphlet on "Woodruff County," says: "Cotton Plant is located in Cotton Plant Township, in the southern portion of the County, on the Batesville & Brinkley Railroad. Its shipments per annum are from 1,500 to 2,000 tons of cotton seed and from 4,000 to 7,000 bales of cotton. The directory of the place gives seven cotton buyers and general merchants, one mill, two druggists, four grocers, one cabinet-maker and undertaker, one carpenter, one blacksmith, one wheelwright, two physicians, two lawyers, two hotels, one restaurant, one butcher shop, one livery stable, one steam saw and grist mill, with gin attached. The population numbers from 500 to 600. According to size it is one of the busiest hives of industry in Eastern Arkansas. It is the natural center for all the trade of Freeman, Cotton Plant and Cane Townships." Since this sketch of Dr. Dale was written there has been much additional improvement in the town, and being situated, as it is, in a representative cotton-growing district, it is destined to continue a prosperous and substantial town. It has been wholly built since the construction of the Batesville & Brinkley Railroad.

De View is an old village situated two miles south of McCrory, containing two general stores, a drug store, blacksmith and wood shop, a church edifice, and a school-house, with a Masonic hall in the second story. It has only a few families, and its business is being absorbed by the neighboring towns on the railroads.

Gray's Station, on the Batesville & Brinkley Railroad, two and a half miles south of its crossing with the Bald Knob & Memphis Railroad, contains two general stores, a "temperance saloon," a boarding house, restaurant, school-house and church combined, a blacksmith shop and a livery stable.

Howell Station, also on the Batesville & Brinkley Railroad, about eight miles farther south, contains three general stores, a blacksmith shop, church edifice, etc.

McCrory, on the Bald Knob & Memphis Railroad, two miles east of its crossing with the Batesville & Brinkley Railroad, is only two years old and contains seven general stores, two grocery stores, a hardware and furniture store, a complement of mechanics' shops, one of the largest stave factories in the State, a hotel, livery stable, two restaurants, two frame church edifices (one for the white and one for the colored people), a public school-house, two physicians and from 250 to 300 people. It was named after its founder, Wade McCrory, the owner of its site. It has a beautiful location, and being near the railroad crossing is the most accessible town from all parts of the county, and is, therefore, a prospective candidate for the subsequent location of the county seat, which in due time it will make an effort to secure. The town is well laid out, the streets running north and south and east and west, and being of good width. It is also easy of access by important wagon roads. It has a large area of excellent farming country tributary to it.

Riverside, located on the Batesville & Brinkley Railroad, two miles north of its crossing with the Bald Knob & Memphis Railroad, contains three general, a drug and a grocery store, a "temperance saloon," hotel, livery stable, blacksmith shop, a steam saw-mill, a church and school-house combined, three physicians, etc.

The intersection of the two railroads above named is called Martin Crossing, and there is nothing there but a depot and a small dwelling house near by. All the towns named above, that are situated on railroads, have each a railroad depot and a postoffice, and all do their proportion of shipping products. The county has a few other post hamlets or villages, consisting of a postoffice, store, etc.

I. T. Andrews, planter, of Cotton Plant, Ark., is one of the leading planters of Woodruff County, and was born in Limestone County, Ala., in 1837, being the son of Daniel and Mary (Morris) Andrews, natives of Virginia and North Carolina, and born in 1814 and 1815, respectively. The parents were married in 1836, and to their union were born two children, a son and daughter: I. T. and Dionitia, wife of T. L. Westmoreland. Daniel Andrews died in 1841, and Mrs. Andrews was married the second time in 1843 to J. H. Deaver. By this union she became the mother of five children:

Mary A. (wife of Dr. J. W. Westmoreland), Thomas H., Martha J. (widow of Saul Slinger), Bettie (wife of H. C. McLawrence) and D. J. (wife of J. B. Whitfield). J. H. Deaver died in 1853, and Mrs. Deaver, who survived her husband, now lives with her widowed daughter, Mrs. Slinger, at Cotton Plant. She is and has been for many years a consistent member of the Methodist Episcopal Church, South. I. T. Andrews started into business for himself in 1858, by farming his mother's land in Tennessee, but left that State and immigrated to Arkansas in 1860, locating in Poinsett County. His mother purchased 240 acres of land, which he farmed until the breaking out of the war when he enlisted in the infantry under Capt. Westmoreland, and served until July 9, 1863. He was then captured at Port Hudson, taken to Johnson's Island and there held until February 9, 1864, when he was transferred to Point Lookout; there retained until March 3, when he was sent to City Point and was there paroled. After the war he resumed farming, also operated a cotton-gin in Woodruff County. He selected as his companion in life, Miss Martha Westmoreland, daughter of Mr. and Mrs. Thomas Westmoreland, and was united in marriage to her in 1858. This union has been blessed by the birth of three children, but only one is now living: Samuel, who married a Miss C. Keath, and resides on a farm in this county. The children deceased were named: Edione and Minnie. Mrs. Andrews was born in Giles County, Tenn., in 1836. Her father died in 1865, and her mother in 1887, both members of the Methodist Episcopal Church. Mr. Andrews is a member of the I. O. O. F., Lodge No. 76, and he and wife have been members of the Methodist Episcopal Church for seventeen years. Mr. Andrews is one of the enterprising farmers of the county, is the owner of 230 acres of land in Woodruff County, Ark., with 120 acres under cultivation and his principal crops are corn and cotton.

Dr. L. L. Battle, a man of remarkable ability and great prominence in the profession, is numbered among the leading members of the medical fraternity in Woodruff County, Ark., and originally came from Wake County, N. C., where he was born March 20, 1828. He was reared in

Shelby County, Tenn., whither his parents, William and Chloe (Body) Battle, moved from their native State of North Carolina, both dying in Memphis, Tenn., and here our subject received a liberal education. He began the study of medicine when eighteen years of age, and having chosen this profession as his life's vocation, he graduated from the Memphis Medical College in 1849, and in 1851 from the Jefferson Medical College, of Philadelphia, Penn. Thus becoming thoroughly fitted to successfully pursue his calling, he settled in Shelby County, Tenn., but at the end of two years came to Mississippi County, Ark., and in 1855 returned to his first location. Here he remained until 1885, then came to Riverside, where he has since successfully practiced, and is now a member of the Woodruff County Medical Association, and is vice-president of the Trio-State Medical Society of Memphis. He is a Royal Arch Mason, and since 1854 has been a married man, his first wife being Miss Martha B. Chester, a daughter of Robert I. Chester, of Jackson, Tenn., by whom he has the following children: Dr. William B., Mrs. Dr. J. W. Jones, Mrs. L. P. Cooper, Jr., Mrs. John Cunningham and Miss Patsey C. Dr. Battle's second wife was a Mrs. Preston, who bore him one son, Preston, and for his third wife he took Mrs. M. W. Riley. The Doctor is one of the wealthy men of the county, and owns about 1,500 acres of land, of which 375 acres are under cultivation. In 1849 he was appointed surgeon of a company of men on their way to California to dig gold, but before reaching their destination thirteen men starved to death and the Doctor was reduced in flesh thirty-five pounds. His expedition suffered many hardships and privations, and met with many thrilling adventures, too numerous to be given to this volume. During the hostilities between the foreigners and Americans in South California, in the winter of 1849 and 1850, he was appointed surgeon of the latter's forces.

John B. Beard, a prosperous and well-known farmer and ginner of Howell Station, is a native of Arkansas and was born in 1851, being the son of Samuel and Eliza (Beauy) Beard. Samuel Beard came to Arkansas from Mississippi, at an early day,

and settled in Woodruff County. He was an industrious, enterprising farmer and citizen, and his death, which occurred in 1857, was mourned by many. His excellent wife survived him about fifteen years. Of a family of seven children, John B. and one other are the only surviving members, he being the younger. He was reared by his widowed mother, and as the school facilities of his boyhood were few, his education was of necessity neglected, but by constant reading and his keen sense of observation he has become a well-informed man. In 1881 Mr. Beard was married to Mollie, daughter of Thomas and Esther Berry. Mrs. Beard is a native of Arkansas, her birth occurring in Woodruff County, where her aged father is now residing, her mother having died some years ago. Mr. Berry was one of the early settlers of this portion of the country, and relates many interesting episodes of the first experience of the pioneers, what they were obliged to submit to, their privations and inconveniences without number; these now seem almost improbable. To Mr. and Mrs Beard a family of four children have been born, three sons and one daughter. He has 600 acres of land with 300 under cultivation, and in connection with the substantial buildings of his farm he owns a fine town residence. His farm is only three miles from town, which of course makes it very much more valuable. He certainly is justified in feeling proud of his possessions, for they are his only by personal efforts and hard work. He is a Democrat and voted for Greeley in 1872. He is a liberal contributor, and lends his support to all worthy movements for the good or growth of the county. Mrs. Beard is a member of the Methodist Episcopal Church.

John W. Becton, planter and ginner of Cotton Plant, owes his nativity to North Carolina, his birth occurring in that State in 1834, and he is the son of Thomas and Nancy M. (White) Becton, also of North Carolina origin, born in the year 1814. Mr. Becton was a prosperous planter, and at the time of the war was worth $100,000, but, like many others, lost all he had during that disastrous period. He was a well-educated gentleman, a Universalist in his religious belief, and a great Bible reader, oftentimes being able to speak fluently on subjects at a better advantage than those who professed a clearer knowledge of the same. His death, which occurred in 1867, was regretted by his many friends and acquaintances. His father, John B. Becton, a wealthy planter, was born and died in North Carolina, the date of his birth being in the year 1777. His father was one Michael Becton. Mrs. Becton, the wife of Thomas Becton, died in 1869. Her father, Reuben White, was a native of North Carolina, and a man of unusual attainments and business qualifications. John W. Becton, the subject of this sketch, is the eldest of four sons and daughters: Corie (now the wife of ex-Gov. James Robinson, now of Kentucky, and one of the war Governors of that State), Mary E. (the wife of Rev. B. F. Mills. Mr. Mills was an ex-Federal officer in the Civil War, married during that time, and is now residing in Michigan), Sarah A. (Mrs. West, of Durham, N. C.), Olie (Mrs. Kornezy, of Kingston, N. C.), Edward G. (holding a prominent position as teacher in Texas), Fred B. (a merchant of Kingston, N. C.) and William R. (died in 1878). John W. Becton was given the advantages of a good common-school education, and these facilities he was not slow to improve, being to-day a well-educated man. He was married in 1859 to Miss Sallie, daughter of James and Pearcy Nunn, of North Carolina, where Mr. Nunn died in 1861. Mrs. Nunn survives her husband, and though at quite an advanced age enjoys ordinary health. Mrs. Becton was born in North Carolina, and died May 5, 1886, having borne twelve children, all of them deceased. She was a member, in excellent standing, of the Methodist Episcopal Church, and respected by her many friends and acquaintances. On December 15, 1886, Mr. Becton was united in marriage to Miss Alice Foy, daughter of James H. and Catherine Foy, who resided in North Carolina the greater portion of their lives. Mr. and Mrs. Becton are the parents of two children, only one now living. In January of 1860 Mr. Becton moved to Prairie County, Ark., and after a residence of seven years came to Woodruff, having lived on his present farm for seventeen years. His plantation is among the

best in the county, consisting of 720 acres, with 225 under cultivation. Among the improvements, which are numerous, he owns and operates a good gin. One of the finest fruit and grain farms in the State is the property of Mr. Becton, situated in Boone County. He also raises and deals in stock quite extensively, being considered a superior judge of all breeds. He served in the late war, enlisting in Company G, Twenty-first Arkansas Infantry, and remained in Tennessee until the fall of Vicksburg. There he was captured, but soon after paroled, returning at once to Arkansas. He accompanied Gen. Price on his raid through Missouri and Kansas, and surrendered at Devall's Bluff. At the close of hostilities Mr. Becton found himself almost destitute, with a wife and three children dependent on him, but, nothing daunted, he never lost courage, and by his untiring energy and great ambition stands to-day one of the wealthy and influential men of the county. He served as justice of the peace two years in Woodruff County, and since the war has been a stanch Republican, though formerly a Whig. His first vote was cast for President Fillmore. Mr. and Mrs. Becton are held in high esteem by their many friends. The latter is a member of the Methodist Episcopal Church.

Eli Burkett, an enterprising planter, blacksmith and wood workman, first saw the light of day in Upson County, Ga., January 28, 1828, being the son of John and Celia (Ethridge) Burkett. John Burkett was born September 10, 1805, in Marlborough District, S. C., and was reared to farm life, which occupation he followed the remainder of his years. He was married to Miss Ethridge, in Wilkinson County, Ga., August 4, 1826, and by her became the father of eight children, four of them now living: Enoch V., William L., Mary (the wife of J. A. Baley) and Eli. Mr. Burkett was a member of the Baptist Church, as was also his wife; his death occurred December 29, 1869. Mrs. Burkett was born in Cumberland County, N. C., August 5, 1803, and died in 1885. Her parents were natives of North Carolina. Eli Burkett's early life was passed on the farm helping his father, and attending school a few months in the year. He was married to Miss Rosanah Gilbert, the daughter of Mr. and Mrs. Jabez Gilbert, of Butts County, Ga. Their marriage was solemnized June 4, 1850, and to them were born seven children: John, Jabez, Margaret (the wife of J. B. McMurtrie), Drewry, Thomas, Davis and Lee. Mr. Burkett immigrated from Georgia to Arkansas, in 1869, locating in Woodruff County, where he bought 140 acres of land, with sixty under cultivation. In connection with his farming, Mr. Burkett owns and operates a blacksmith and wood shop, which he established in 1873. He manufactures wagons, buggies and farming implements; he has built up a good trade, of which he is well deserving, being an industrious, hardworking man, and respected by all. In societies he is identified with A. F. & A. M., Colony Lodge No. 190, and of the I. O. O. F., De View Lodge No. 71. At the breaking out of the late war, Mr. Burkett enlisted in January, 1862, in the Thirty-second Georgia Infantry, Company I, where he served as a private, until November, 1864, when he was promoted to second lieutenant, and commanded his company on that memorable day, March 19, 1865, at Bentonville, N. C., in which eight of his company was killed and thirteen wounded, he receiving a wound in this battle, which disabled him until April 16, when he was discharged at the hospital at Thomasville, N. C. Mrs. Burkett is a native of Butts County, Ga., this county being the place of her birth, which occurred April 15, 1825. Her parents were residing in Georgia at the time of her demise, Mr. Gilbert dying February 4, 1864, his wife surviving him until April 29, 1888.

J. W. Buster & Bro. Throughout Woodruff County and vicinity there is probably no more favorably known business firm than that of Buster Bros., which has been established since 1877. They are careful and painstaking buyers, and are thrifty merchants, strictly attending to business, thereby gaining a large share of the county's patronage. They established the postoffice at Riverside, and kept it in charge for two years. Conjointly the members of the firm own 500 acres of land, with about 270 under cultivation. Their parents, Samuel and Emily K. (Lewis) Buster, were of Virginia and Alabama, respectively, and were married in Germantown, Shelby County, Tenn. In 1850 they came to Arkansas, and located in Woodruff County, where the father purchased a farm, cultivating and living on it until his death, which occurred in 1852, that of his wife occurring in 1880. To the father and mother was born a family of eight children, three now living: John W., Lucy and Thomas M. The latter was born in Shelby County, Tenn., January 4, 1844, but was principally reared in the home of his parents' adoption (Woodruff County), and from his earliest youth has given much of his attention and time to farming, and in connection with his duties at the store assists his brother in the management of their extensive plantation. Thomas M. was married, in 1872, to Miss Rebecca Bellington, who departed this life in 1879, leaving two children: Fannie and Rebecca. He and his brother are Masons, having been initiated into the secrets and sworn allegiance to this society; they also belong to the K. of H. J. W. Buster came into this world in 1834, and like his brother, spent most of his boyhood and received his education in the State of Tennessee. During the war he enrolled himself with the Fifth Arkansas Regiment, was wounded by a gunshot at Mark's Mills, and was captured at Decatur, Ala., but managed to make his escape. He served until the surrender, which sounded the bugle-note of peace, then returned home. He is unmarried.

N. D. Byrd, a prominent merchant of De View Township, who, by his pleasing and affable manner and keen sense of honor, has won many friends, is the son of Bryan and Sallie (Ross) Byrd, of Henry County, Tenn., nativity, being born in 1826. Bryan Byrd, N. D.'s father, was born in Chester County, S. C., and reared to farm life; was a carpenter by trade, and eventually became a minister of the Baptist Church. He immigrated from Tennessee to Arkansas in 1855, locating in Yell County. His marriage with Miss Ross was solemnized in North Carolina and by her became the father of twelve children; only one of that large family is now living, N. D., the subject of this sketch. The senior Byrd was a soldier in the Revolutionary War, and died in Yell County in 1856, his wife surviving him until 1864. He and his wife were connected with the Baptist Church. N. D. Byrd started out in the world for himself in 1847, his first venture was farming on rented land in Tennessee in which he was quite successful. On December 30, 1847, he was united in holy matrimony with Miss Frances J. True, and to them were born six children, four boys and two girls, three of them now living: Josephine (the wife of L. B. Smith), Leonidas and Thomas C. Mrs. Byrd died in 1855 in full faith of the Methodist Episcopal Church. Mr. Byrd remained a widower until 1865, then married Miss Alice Crook, the daughter of Mr. and Mrs. James Crook, of Marshall County, Miss. Mr. Byrd came to Arkansas from Tennessee in 1870, locating in Van Buren, Crawford County, residing here one year, then came to this place where he engaged in farming until 1886. Since 1886 he has been occupied in the mercantile business and has established a most lucrative trade. He served in the late war, enlisting in the cavalry in 1863, and received his discharge after one year of brave and chivalrous service. Mr. and Mrs. Byrd are members of the Cumberland Presbyterian Church, and are highly esteemed by all who are fortunate in knowing them.

James H. Campbell, merchant, Augusta, Ark. This successful and enterprising business man owes his nativity to Mecklenburg County, Ky., where his birth occurred in November, 1843, and is one of six children, three now living: William P., James H. and Mrs. R. D. Hopkins, born to the union of Alexander and Sallie W. (Kenchelve) Campbell, the father a native of Ireland, and the mother of Kentucky. The father died in the last-named State, but the mother died in Woodruff County, Ark. James H. Campbell attained his growth and received his education in Kentucky. In 1861 he came to Augusta, and the same year he enlisted in Company A, First Kentucky Cavalry, and served until the surrender. He was wounded through the right shoulder-blade by a gunshot at a railroad fight under Gen. Forrest, and was in the principal engagements of his regiment. At the close of service he returned to Kentucky, and there remained until 1870, when he came back to Augusta, where he has since resided. The firm of W. P. Campbell & Bros. was organized in 1872, and still continues. They carry a large stock of goods and general merchandise, and handle a great deal of cotton each season. They are also interested in considerable real estate. Mr. Campbell is secretary and treasurer of the White River Hedge Company, which has sold over 100 miles this season. He was married, in 1872, to Miss Eliza Hopkins, of Kentucky, and a daughter of Dr. H. H. Hopkins. To this union were born two children: Tilman and Alex. H. Mr. Campbell is a member of the Knights of Honor, and has been recorder of same since the organization, in 1878. He has been mayor for several years.

R. Cariker. In numerating the names of the prominent planters of Woodruff County, the name of R. Cariker should not be omitted. He is a native of Tennessee and was born in Hardeman County in 1853, as the son of G. M. and Elizabeth (Gray) Cariker. G. M. Cariker owes his nativity to Middle Tennessee, having been born in that State in 1829. He immigrated to Arkansas in 1859, locating in Woodruff County, where he purchased 440 acres of land, and was married to Miss Grey, of Tennessee, in 1852. To this union a family of six children have been given: Thomas J., Lycurgus, Levina (the wife of E. H. Arnold), Fuller (deceased), Cynthia E. (now Mrs. B. F. Doughty) and R. Cariker (the subject of this sketch). Himself and wife were members of good standing in the Methodist Episcopal Church, and enjoyed a large circle of friends and acquaintances. He died in this State, in 1878, his wife having "gone before" in the year 1857. R. Cariker was married in 1875 to Miss Tululae Sears, a native of Georgia, and born in 1858, and whose parents were also natives of Georgia. R. Cariker is a farmer by occupation, and is an A. F. & A. M., belonging to Augusta Lodge. He owns 170 acres of excellent land, with about ninety under cultivation, the principal crop being corn and cotton. Mr. Cariker is a prosperous agriculturist, favors all public improvements, such as churches, schools, etc., and is a man held in high esteem by the entire community.

A. C. Carter, a leading and long-established merchant of Cotton Plant, and who is known the county over, having settled himself in business in that town in 1871, is a native of Rowan County, N. C., and was born in 1840, the son of Thomas and Eliza L. (Johnson) Carter, of North and South Carolina origin, respectively. Thomas Carter was of Scotch-Irish descent, a well-to-do farmer, and was married in North Carolina, where he died when A. C. was about twelve years old. His wife is living at the age of seventy-six, a devout member of the Presbyterian Church. She was twice married, her second husband dying during the war. A. C. Carter is the third in a family of four sons and two daughters, and received all the education to be had at that period. He left the parental roof at the age of sixteen, and worked as a farm hand until 1861, when he enlisted in the war and joined Company K, Fourth North Carolina Infantry in Lee's army, participating in nearly all the battles of that army. He was wounded in June, 1862, at Cold Harbor, and was sent home on furlough for some time. In April, 1864, he surrendered with Lee, and shortly after returned to his home, Rowan County, N. C., and engaged in farming till the spring of 1870, when he came to Arkansas and farmed till the fall of 1872; after which he embarked in the mercantile business with one Robert Holt, their capital consisting of only a few hundred dollars. Notwithstanding that the financial start was very modest, he stands to-day among the best-known firms of the town. Mr. Carter has a fine farm of 212 acres in Monroe County, with 170 under cultivation, and on which farm is a good residence. A fine block in the town erected by him is another mark of his ambition and enterprise, all the work of perseverance and economy. He was married in 1872 to Miss Emma Gideon, of Mississippi nativity, who came to Arkansas with her parents when small, and left an orphan when quite young. Two children have been born to this union, one son and one daughter. Mr. Carter, believing that education is the foundation stone to future success, spares no pains or expense to give his children every advantage to be had. In his political views

Mr. Carter is a stanch Democrat, voting for Greeley in 1872. He affiliates with the Knights of Honor and Knights and Ladies of Honor at Cotton Plant, and has held various offices in these lodges, quite recently holding the office of Assistant Dictator in the former lodge, and that of Treasurer in the latter. He was formerly a member of I. O. O. F., and wherever he goes is greeted with a royal welcome and a hearty hand-shake, all going to show that he is far from unpopular. He and wife are both members of the Methodist Church, and in all church and educational matters, he is a ready and liberal contributor.

Capt. William A. Chaney, prominently identified with the mercantile interests of Cotton Plant, and one of the leading planters of the county, is a native of Tennessee, his birth occurring in Tipton County, in 1838, as the son of Capt. Joseph E. and Nancy (Shelton) Chaney. They were natives of Virginia, and born in Petersburg, where they were reared and married, but in an early day moved to West Tennessee. They died in Tipton County, Tenn., Mr. Chaney passing away when William was only three or four years old; Mrs. Chaney's death occurred in 1870, at the age of seventy years. Both were members of the Missionary Baptist Church, and he served in the War of 1812, with Jackson at New Orleans, wearing the title of captain. He was of Irish descent, and possessed of great educational attainments. Grandfather Thomas Shelton was a native of Virginia, one of the early settlers of Tennessee, and moved from there to Brandon, Miss., where he died very wealthy. Capt. William A. Chaney, the youngest of eleven children, and the only one now living, remained with his mother until grown to maturity, and received liberal advantages for an education, all of which he was careful to improve. In March, 1858, he was married to Ann J. Versur, a daughter of Dr. William Versur, of Tennessee (who died in Lonoke, Ark., having come to that place in 1858). Subsequently removing to Arkansas he settled in Lonoke, where his wife died in 1859. In 1861 he joined a company of the First Arkansas Cavalry of Fagan's army, and gave his efficient service until the close of the war, being in Arkansas, Missouri,

Texas and Kansas, in various ranks. He was mustered out as captain, and served in nearly all the engagements with great credit. In March, 1865, Capt. Chaney was united in marriage with Miss Emma, daughter of J. K. Crossett, a prominent physician in White County. There he died in 1887, having made it his home from 1858. Mrs. Chaney was born in Mississippi. To their union have been given seven children, three daughters and two sons now living. Soon after the war the Captain returned to Tipton County, Tenn., where he farmed until 1871, and then came to Cotton Plant, since being engaged in farming and merchandising. He owns a large amount of property (improved) in Tennessee and Arkansas, and a very nice residence in town. He is a Democrat and voted for Bell in 1870. The K. of H. Lodge at Cotton Plant counts him as a member, and he was formerly an Odd Fellow. Capt. Chaney is sparing no pains or expense to educate his children, and is giving them every opportunity to become accomplished. His wife is an earnest worker and member of the Methodist Church.

L. D. Cole, a wealthy farmer and ginner of Barnes Township, is a native of Georgia, and was born in Cass County in 1851, the son of Jacob W. and Laura (Banks) Cole. Jacob W. Cole was a Virginian by birth, and when a young man immigrated to Georgia, where he was married and resided until his death in 1880. He served in the Confederate army in the First Georgia Infantry as captain, but was discharged after two years on account of disability. His father, Plum Cole, also a native of Virginia, died in Gilmer County, Ga., at the age of one hundred and twelve. He was a Presbyterian in his religious faith, and his wife, who died when one hundred and thirteen years of age, was also of the same belief. Plum Cole was of Irish descent, and served in the War of 1812 with Jackson. Mrs. Cole, the mother of the subject of this sketch, is now residing in Texas, a devout member of the Baptist Church. Her father, William Banks was born in the Old World, but is at this time a resident of Georgia, at the age of nearly one hundred years. Mr. Banks has always been a farmer and miner, enjoying fair prosperity, and

the respect of all who know him. L. D. Cole, the third child in a family of six sons and three daughters, received his primary education in the schools of his native State, and also spent four years at Stilesborough (Ga.) College. In 1870 he came to Cross County and worked for one year as a farm hand, also putting in a crop one season for himself. He was married in 1873 in Cross County to Tolly, daughter of John and Lucinda Clark. Mr. Clark was married in South Carolina, and in 1849 came to what is now Cross County. At that time it was a perfect wilderness, but by his unceasing labors he soon raised his place from its embryo state to that of high and successful cultivation. Himself and wife were members of the Presbyterian Church, and died in 1858 and 1863, respectively. Mrs. Cole was born in South Carolina, and was one of five children, two sons and three daughters. The year of Mr. Cole's marriage, he came to Woodruff County and settled in the woods in Barnes Township, where he improved a farm and resided until 1885. He then came to his present farm, which was at that time entirely unimproved, but through energy and persevering labor he now has a home of 360 acres in two farms with 200 acres under cultivation. It is all his own property, and the result of his industry, which considering the inconveniences and hardships endured by all pioneers at that time is truly commendable. Mr. Cole trades in cattle and hogs, and for two years has been running one of the best steam gin and corn mills in the county. He was court and deputy sheriff of Barnes Township for four years, and is an active worker in all educational purposes. He is a Democrat, and voted for Greeley in 1872. Mrs. Cole is a member in good standing of the Methodist Church, to which her husband liberally contributes.

D. R. Compton. There is no sketch within the Biographical Department of this work which presents a better example of the rise of young men from a lowly place to a position of honor and respect, than appears in these few lines, for, at the age of nineteen years, Mr. Compton started out in life for himself, and is now the owner of 370 acres of land, of which 150 acres are under cultivation.

He was born in Pittsylvania County, Va., October 16, 1830, and is the oldest child born to Reuben and Nancy (Farmer) Compton, who were also Virginians. He was reared and educated in his native county, and upon first leaving home, went to West Tennessee, where he was engaged in farming for about nine years. In 1860 he took up his permanent abode in Woodruff County, Ark., and was for a short time located near Augusta. From 1862 until the close of the war, he has served in Company E, Twenty-second Arkansas Infantry, and since the war he has been engaged in conducting his farm, his efforts in this direction being attended with the best results. In 1853 his marriage with Miss Tabitha Lax was celebrated, and of six children born to them, only two are living: David and Edward. His marriage to his present wife, whose maiden name was Berna Neill, took place in 1882, and their union has been blessed in the birth of three children: Reuben H., Virginia B. and Columbus N.

B. B. Conner, a so-to-speak pioneer of Woodruff County, and a man who, by courage and a firm determination to overcome the obstacles encountered in making a home in a new country, was born in Giles County, Tenn., on March 29, 1829, and is a son of Lewis and Nancy (Preston) Conner, the former a Kentuckian and the latter a native of Tennessee. They were married in Tennessee and lived and died in Giles County, where the father made the occupation of tanning and farming a means of livelihood. Four of their eight children born to this marriage, are now living: James H., Bolivar B., John C. and Mrs. Carter. Bolivar B. Conner was a pupil in the common schools of Giles County in his youth, and learned the art of agriculture on his father's farm, which occupation he continued to follow after coming to Woodruff County, in 1851. He purchased a quarter section of land, with twenty-one acres cleared, on which was a little log-cabin in which he settled and set himself energetically to work to clear his land, and that he has been successful will be clearly shown when the fact is stated that he now owns 1,000 acres of as good land as there is in Woodruff County, and has some 600 acres under the plow. His farm is one of the finest and most valuable in the State and is admirably adapted to the raising of all kinds of cereals. He has a handsome residence, fitted up in modern style, and is so situated financially that he can now enjoy life. He was married, in 1854, to Eliza L. Hall, a native of Virginia, and by her he has had a family of seven children, five of whom now live: Mrs. Stacy, Emerson H., Mrs. Cora McDonald, Minnie L. and John L. Mr. Conner is a Mason.

E. J. Crossett, a leading merchant and a very prominent citizen of De View, was born in Carroll County, Tenn., in 1845. J. K. Crossett, his father, was born in South Carolina, in 1815, and was reared and educated to farm life, which occupation he never departed from. In 1836 Mr. Crossett led to the hymeneal altar, Miss Elizabeth Cupp, of Carroll County, Tenn., originally from South Carolina, her parents being from that State. To Mr. Crossett's marriage a family of eight children was born, six of them now living: W. R., J. J., R. B., C. M., Emma (the wife of W. A. Chaney) and E. J. They immigrated from Tennessee to De Soto County, Miss., in 1845, thence to Arkansas in 1853, locating in this county. Mr. Crossett purchased 160 acres of land, which he brought to a successful state of cultivation. Mrs. Crossett died in 1860, a consistent Christian and an earnest worker in the Methodist Episcopal Church, of which she was a member. In 1861 Mr. Crossett was married to Mrs. Elizabeth Corley, of St. Francis County, Ark., and to their union two children were born: Addie and Ida (the wife of J. D. Parttow). Mr. Crossett was a constituent of the I. O. O. F., and died in 1887, at his home in this county. E. J. began life for himself in 1865. His war record, though not a brilliant one, will always be remembered by him as one on which there is not a blemish, and he has the satisfaction of knowing that he was earnest in the discharge of his duties. He enlisted under Capt. Wilson, in the Twenty-second Arkansas Cavalry Regiment (B), entering service in 1863, remaining until the surrender in 1865, at Wittsburg, Ark. He then returned home, and for one year farmed, at the end of which time he learned and became skilled in the carpenter's trade, which occupation he followed until 1871. Subsequently dropping his trade, he again resumed the tilling of the soil, continuing in this up to the year 1878, at which time he embarked in the mercantile business in De View, remaining in this place ever since. Mr. Crossett was united in marriage with Miss Mattie McMurtry in 1870, and to their union four children were born. Mrs. Crossett was born in Tennessee, in 1853, and came with her parents, Mr. and Mrs. Moses McMurtry, to this county when about two years old. Mr. McMurtry was a native of Ohio, and his wife was born in Mississippi. Both died in 1878, in full communion with the Methodist Episcopal Church. In politics Mr. Crossett votes with the Democratic party. Himself and wife belong to the Methodist Episcopal Church. He is a courteous, hospitable gentleman, making numerous friends, few if any enemies, and enjoys with his estimable wife, the respect of all.

Dr. F. D. Dale, physician and surgeon, of Augusta, Ark. Few men have attained more prominence in Woodruff County in a social as well as a professional point of view, than Dr. Dale, who is courteous and pleasant in all his relations to the public. He owes his nativity to Jefferson County, Ky., where his birth occurred on February 14, 1847, and was reared on a farm until eighteen years of age, receiving the rudiments of an education in the common schools, but supplementing the same by a course at St. Mary's College, at Lebanon, Ky. At an early age he began the study of medicine and graduated at the University of Louisiana, in 1869. The same year he commenced practicing in Augusta, Ark., and there he has remained ever since, his time being entirely devoted to the relief of suffering humanity. He has built up an extensive practice and is one of the first-class physicians of the town. He has one of the finest residences in Augusta, and his surroundings show him to be an energetic citizen. He has done much toward building up the country. He is president of the Woodruff County Medical Association and a member of the Railway Medical Association of Surgeons of the United States. He was a member of the town council two years. His marriage occurred in

1872 to Miss Ida Hamblet, of Augusta, and the fruits of this union are three children: Hamblet, Ruth and Pat. The Doctor is a member of the Masonic order, K. T., K. of H. and K. & L. of H. He is the fourth in order of birth of eight children, six sons and two daughters, born to the union of Delancey and Ruth (Caruthers) Dale, natives of Spencer County, Ky. The paternal grandfather was a native of Virginia, and of Irish origin, while the maternal grandfather was of German origin. Delancey Dale followed the occupation of a farmer and lived and died in his native county. The mother is yet living.

Hon. J. B. Dent, widely and officially known throughout Wood County, and a prominent citizen of Augusta, is a native of Monongalia County, W. Va., being born May 10, 1831, and is a son of James and Dorcas (Berkshire) Dent, the former a Virginian and the mother from Cumberland, Md., the marriage of the parents taking place in the former State. The paternal grandfather, John Dent, was the first sheriff of Monongalia County, W. Va., and was a captain in the Revolutionary War, his father-in-law, Col. Evans, by his bravery, also won his title in that struggle. John Dent died in Virginia, having been known throughout his entire life as a man of active and energetic habits, retaining these even in his old age. The maternal grandfather, William Berkshire, was a Baptist minister, and his son Ralph was chief justice of West Virginia for several years. James Dent was captain of a company of militia in his young days, and in 1835 moved with his family to Putnam County, Ill., where he made his home until his death, in 1883, his wife dying in 1878. Six of their eleven children are now living: Mrs. McCoy, Mrs. Parrett, Hon. J. B., Mrs. Douglass (of Iowa), Mrs. Taylor (of Kansas) and S. E. J. B. Dent was put to school at an early day, and after acquiring a fair knowledge of the English branches, he entered Judson College, remaining here for two years. Upon starting out in life for himself he accepted a position as salesman in a wholesale house of Chicago, filling this position for two years; later was in business in Galena, where he remained also two years, and afterward spent some time in Cairo. In 1861 he enlisted in Company A, First Illinois Cavalry, and was commissioned second lieutenant, but at the end of one year he joined the Fourteenth Illinois and was made captain of Company C. When mustered out of service was major of his regiment. He was in the battles of Lexington, Buffington's Island, Knoxville, Cumberland Gap, and was in all the battles from Dalton to Atlanta, and during his war career was thrice captured, once at Lexington, in 1861, and again in 1864, while with Stoneman on his raid on Macon, and was put under fire of his own batteries at Charleston, S. C., but remained uninjured. When captured the third time he was on a train going from Charleston to Cincinnati, and was taken back and put in Libby prison. After being held in this dungeon for two months was exchanged. In the fall of 1865 he came to Arkansas and located in Woodruff County where he met friends and decided to permanently locate. Although his finances were at a very low ebb he bought a farm, and is now one of the largest real-estate owners in the county, his lands amounting to about 5,000 acres, 2,500 of which are wild land, and the remainder of very fertile soil. He officiated as county assessor in 1874, and for three terms held the position of county and probate judge. In 1888 he was elected on the Democrat ticket to the State legislature, and is now filling the duties of that position in a manner highly satisfactory to his townsmen who honored him with their votes. He was a delegate to the National Convention that nominated Cleveland for the presidency, which met in St. Louis. He was one of the men who defended Gov. Baxter and replaced him in office, acting as lieutenant from Augusta during the Brooks-Baxter trouble. During the Ku-Klux and militia times he fearlessly expressed his opinion, defended himself against both parties and assisted in protecting his neighbors from the depredations of these lawless men. The Major is a whole-souled and honorable man, and is ever ready to defend his country, friend or neighbor. He has taken the degree of Knight Templar in the order of Masons, and takes great pride in his lodge.

Capt. S. E. Dent, merchant, Riverside, Ark. This prominent and highly esteemed business man owes his nativity to Putman County, Ill., where his birth occurred, in September, 1843, and is the son of James and Dorcas (Berkshire) Dent, she a sister of Judge Berkshire, of the Old Dominion. Both parents were natives of Virginia, and were married in Monongalia County, W. Va., where they remained until 1833. Then they immigrated to Illinois, and located in Putman County, where they passed their declining years, both dying since the war. They had a family of ten children, six now living: Mrs. Nancy McCoy (in Illinois), Mrs. Emily Parrett (widow of Judge Parrett), Margaret (deceased), Mrs. Lucinda Douglass (in Johnson County, Iowa), Mrs. Gilla Taylor (in Red Cloud, Neb.), Judge J. B. and S. E. (who is the youngest of the family). The last named was principally reared and educated in Illinois, and his principal occupation in boyhood was in attending the common schools and in assisting on the farm. He remained under the parental roof until the breaking out of the war, and, although quite young at that time, he determined to enlist. Through the influence of his brother, Judge J. B. Dent, he was successful, and enlisted first in the First Illinois Cavalry. He was captured at Lexington, Mo., and about a year later the regiment was mustered out. He went to Nashville in the Sixth United States Infantry, and served until the surrender. He was captain of Company F, Sixth Regiment, at the time of the battle of Nashville. He was an intrepid and fearless young man, and fought his way with vigor. After being mustered out he went home, and in March, 1867, came to Woodruff County, Ark., located on a farm, and has since been engaged in tilling the soil. In September, 1885, he embarked in mercantile pursuits at Riverside, carries a large and select stock of goods, and also buys and sells cotton and cotton seed. He will handle about 1,000 bales of cotton this season. His marriage occurred in 1873 to Miss Ella K. Darling, by whom he has two children living: Emma and Robert both attending school in Illinois. Capt. Dent was married the second time, June 1, 1885, to Miss Blanche Bancroft, a daughter of

Judge Bancroft, and the result of this union was two children: Major and Olga. Mr. Dent is a member of the Masonic order, K. T., K. of H. and K. & L. of H. The Dent family are relatives of the Grant family. Capt. Dent has always been a Democrat in politics, and, although not an aspirant to any political office, he takes a deep interest in the political welfare of the country. He organized the first Democratic club of Woodruff, in the campaign of 1888, and the club is still in existence. He is a prosperous and influential citizen of the county.

J. H. Douglas, the genial and ever-popular superintendent of the F. G. Oxley Stave Company, of McCrory, owes his nativity to Wisconsin, his birth occurring in Jackson County in the year 1851. His father, Thomas Douglas, was born in Donfreece, Scotland, in 1819, and at an early age learned the lumber business, which occupation he has followed all his life. He was married to Miss Caroline S. Tyler in 1849, and they became the parents of five children, only two of whom arrived to the age of manhood and womanhood: Ruby Amanda (the wife of Dr. R. Rodgers) and James Henry (the subject of this sketch). Mr. Douglas emigrated from Scotland to Wisconsin in 1836, and engaged in the lumber business, which he carried on successfully for twenty-five years, subsequently going to St. Louis, where he engaged in the same business, and thence to Walnut Ridge, Ark., still following this pursuit. He then went to San Diego, Cal., where his death occurred in 1888. His wife, who survives him, is a native of Connecticut, and was born in 1851. She is a member of the Congregational Church, as was also her husband. J. H. was married in Walnut Ridge, Ark., in 1876, to Miss Amanda J. Snow, and the result of this marriage is six boys, only three living: Bertrun Bruce, Charles Hirun and Arthur Henry. Miss Snow was the daughter of Mr. and Mrs. George Snow, natives of Chattanooga, Tenn., her birth occurring in 1858. Mr. Douglas received his education in St. Louis, and commenced life for himself at the early age of sixteen years. He has represented the public corporations ever since he has been in the employ of the

F. G. Oxley Stave Company, which is one of the most extensive manufacturing companies in the United States. He was first paymaster and general purchasing agent of the firm. In societies he belongs to the A. F. & A. M., and is a Knight Templar, being a member of Hugh De Payne Commandery, also belongs to Little Rock and Walnut Ridge Chapter No. 86, and affiliates with the K. of P., Douglas Lodge No. 56, and I. O. O. F., Janesville Lodge, Ark. Mr. Douglas is a man of fine business qualifications, and is universally esteemed. He is of pleasing address, hospitable and courteous, enjoying with his wife a wide circle of friends and acquaintances.

William T. Echols, one of the leading cotton dealers in Woodruff County, and a member of the firm of Henderson, Echols & Co., dealers in farm implements, wagons and general merchandise, of Cotton Plant, first saw the light of this world in De Soto County, Miss., in 1844, and is a son of J. M. and Mary E. (Henderson) Echols. Mr. J. M. Echols was of French origin and was born in Virginia, coming to St. Francis County in 1848, where he followed the pursuits of farming and real estate. His wife died in 1862. In religion she was a Baptist, having belonged to this church for a number of years. William T. enlisted in the Confederate army, in the Second Arkansas Cavalry, and served with Gen. Price in his raid throughout Missouri and Kansas. After the war he returned to Woodruff County, where he again took up farming, following this until 1869, when he moved to Cross Roads, near Cotton Plant. He was married in 1871 to Isabella Davies (a native of Virginia, and who died in 1877, leaving two children, now deceased). He was married the second time in 1880 to Mrs. Mattie Blakemore (originally of Mississippi). Mr. Echols entered into business with the present firm of Henderson, Echols & Co. in 1875, at Cross Roads, and in 1879 removed to Cotton Plant, where they are now doing a large business, and have a capital stock of $12,000. Mr. Echols is one among the largest land owners in Woodruff County, having over 1,000 acres, with about 600 under cultivation, all of which he owes to his own industry. Politically he is a strong Democrat, and was appointed postmaster of Cotton Plant, holding this office four years. Mr. and Mrs. Echols are members of the Presbyterian Church.

Rolfe Eldridge, a prosperous planter of Point Township, of keen perception, prompt in business and thoroughly alive to the interests of the county, is of Tennessee nativity and was born in Shelby County, in January, 1842. His father, Rolfe Eldridge, Sr., was born in Virginia in 1806, and immigrated from Virginia to Tennessee in 1830, and thence to Arkansas in 1850, locating in what is now Woodruff County. In 1820 he was married to Miss Carolina Hall, a native of Virginia, as were also her parents. Mr. and Mrs. Eldridge reared a family of nine children, six girls and three boys: Elizabeth (deceased), Harriett, Carolina (Mrs. Eldridge), Laura, Lucy (wife of Mr. F. E. Pope), John T., Robert and Rolfe. Mr. Eldridge, Sr., was justice of the peace for a number of years in this county and was a devout member of the Methodist Episcopal Church. His wife, belonging to the same denomination, died in 1880. Rolfe, Jr., was married in 1869 to Miss Ella Watson, originally of De Soto County, Miss., and this union has been blessed with five children: Sammie, Rolfe, Robert, John, and Ella (deceased). Mrs. Eldridge died in 1880, and Mr. Eldridge was again married in 1887 to Miss Mollie Dawson, the daughter of Mr. and Mrs. Jacob Dawson, of Arkansas. To them one child has been given, Cora, a bright little lady. In response to the call to arms in defense of his country Mr. Eldridge entered the army under the command of Col. Gause. He enlisted in February, 1862, and first was in the cavalry under Capt. Hooker, participating in the battles of Prairie Grove, Helena and Pleasant Hill, and in all the principal engagements during his service. After the war he resumed the cultivation of his farm, which consisted at that time of 200 acres, since which time he has added to it until he now owns 1,500 acres, with 1,000 under cultivation, and finely improved, the most important crops grown being corn and cotton. He is interested in the finest cotton-gin in the State, which now has four plants running with all the improved machinery. Mr. Eldridge is one of the most suc-

cessful and energetic farmers in the State, and his elegant and commodious residence, fine grounds and outbuildings all show that thrift, enterprise and refinement predominate. Himself and wife are members of the Methodist Episcopal Church, and he belongs to the Masonic lodge and Knights of Honor.

Dr. G. B. Fakes, a prominent citizen, retired physician and surgeon, and considered one of the wealthiest planters in Woodruff County, making his home in Barnes Township, is a native of Wilson County, Tenn., and was born in 1840. His father, William C., first saw the light of day in Kentucky about 1813, and his mother was born in Wilson County, Tenn., in 1816. Mr. Fakes was a well-to-do farmer, and he and wife were connected with the Cumberland Presbyterian Church. His wife resides in Wilson County, where the greater part of her life has been spent. Grandfather John Fakes is a Scotchman by birth and emigrated to America when a young man, settling in Kentucky where he married and passed the remainder of his life, working at his trade, that of a hatter. The maternal grandfather was a native of Virginia, where he married and lived for a number of years after, but his death occurred in Tennessee. Dr. Fakes is the third in a family of eleven children, and with them was reared on a farm, receiving all the advantages of the schools of that period. In 1860 he came to Woodruff County, where he took up the study of medicine, but was interrupted by the outbreak of the Rebellion. He cast aside the dry and musty volumes of medical lore, and joined the First Arkansas Mounted Riflemen as a private soldier and was appointed assistant-surgeon, serving as such for two years. After the war he continued his practice with marked success for some years, but retired later on, after gaining an enviable reputation as a son of Æsculapius. He was married in 1863 to Miss Eleanor J., daughter of William and Mary Edmonds, natives of Alabama, but after their marriage came to Woodruff County in 1849, settling in woods which soon became an improved farm. Mr. Edmonds was an influential and very wealthy citizen, and his death, which occurred in 1868, was regretted by the entire com-

19

munity. His wife survived him some twenty-four years, and still lives in the faith of the Methodist Church. The Doctor's marriage has been blessed with two children, only one of them living, a son. He has a farm of 1,000 acres, with about 400 under cultivation. A large portion of this farm was inherited by Mrs. Fakes, and is without doubt one of, if not the finest farm in the county, and by the careful management of Dr. Fakes it has been doubly increased in value. The county recognizes in Dr. Fakes one of the most popular and enterprising citizens, and well worthy the respect and confidence reposed in him. He is now engaged in the manufacture of lumber and shingles, supplying the long-felt want of a mill of that kind in the county, and was also at one time the proprietor of a store opened on the old homestead of Mr. Edmonds, and which was well patronized by the surrounding residents. Dr. Fakes is a Democrat, and is connected with several secret societies, being a member of the Seymour Lodge No. 1,268, A. F. & A. M., Augusta Lodge, also belongs to the Royal Arch Chapter at Augusta. The K. of H., De View Lodge, count him as one of its members, and the K. of L. find him well qualified to discharge the duties of Protector of the lodge. Himself and wife are members in good standing in the Methodist Church.

James Felker, a farmer of prominence, also stock raiser and ginner of Pumpkin Bend Township, is the son of Peter and Nancy (Eaves) Felker, and was born in Tennessee, in 1822. Peter Felker (his father) was born in Tennessee, and his wife in Abbeville District, S. C. They were married in South Carolina, and soon after settled in Tennessee, but when James was a boy they changed their location to Cherokee Purchase, near Chattanooga, and there spent the remainder of their lives. After a happy marriage of nearly eighty years, Mr. Felker passed away in 1877, aged one hundred and three years, his wife surviving him until 1883, dying at the age of ninety-seven. Mr. Felker was a very successful farmer, and amassed a large fortune, but during the war became financially embarrassed. He was one of the early settlers in Southeast Tennessee, and carried the mails at an early period. He was the son of William Felker, a soldier in the Revolutionary War, and while en route for home with his wife, or after getting home, was assassinated by British soldiers. Grandfather Eaves was of English descent, a farmer, and at the time of his death was living in Abbeville District, S. C. James Felker was the third in a family of four sons, all of them living as follows: William (a merchant of Franklin County, Ark.), Stephen (a farmer of Missouri) and Jesse (farmer and merchant of Georgia). They are all enterprising men, and have accumulated very comfortable fortunes. James received a limited education, as the schools of Tennessee at that date were inferior in quality and few in number. He was married in Hamilton County, Tenn., in 1847, to Caroline, daughter of William and Polly Brewster. Mrs. Felker was born in Tennessee, and died in 1867, having borne a family of seven children, four now living: Misnier (wife of Ensley Ball), Margaret (wife of Hughey Gilluly), Jesse and Louisa. Mr. Felker was again married in 1872 to Mrs. Charlotte Guest, a native of Georgia, and born in 1833, who died in 1878, and in 1882 Mr. Felker was wedded to his present wife. She was Mrs. Adrain Hawkins, a native of Mississippi, and born in 1848, the daughter of William Worthington. Mr. Felker's first home in Arkansas was in St. Francis County, where he resided until the year 1869, then came to Pumpkin Bend, and settled in an almost complete wilderness. Of this he owned 830 acres, and has 130 cultivated, all the result of his own labor, with little or no assistance. He raises a great many cattle, horses and hogs, and for nearly fifteen years has run a gin and corn mill, and for a short time had a good steam saw-mill attached. For some years Augusta was the nearest postoffice and market, which made it quite a long distance to go, the journey being contemplated and talked of a long time before its execution. Mr. Felker enlisted and served about three years in the Confederate army, in Company C, with Col. McGee of Price's army. He participated in the battle of Helena, Fitz Hugh, Wallace's Ferry, Little Rock and all through the Missouri raid. He served as lieutenant most of this time, and surrendered at Wittsburg. Mr. Felker is a strong and thorough Democrat, and voted for Polk, in 1844, and every Democratic candidate since, with the exception of the war period. His financial condition is based on a solid foundation, which is all due to hard work, perseverance and close attention to business. He is one of the most prosperous of Pumpkin Bend citizens, and enjoys the respect of the entire community. Although he has lived thirty years in the bottom lands, he has always had very good health, and is still well able to stand and endure the varying changes of weather. He comes of a long-lived race, and bids fair to carry the record of his ancestors. Mrs. Felker is a member of and in high standing in the Cumberland Presbyterian Church.

W. E. Ferguson is not only known as a popular and worthy citizen, but as county and circuit clerk of Augusta, Ark. Though claiming Coahoma County, Miss., as his place of birth, which occurred on September 10, 1851, Mr. Ferguson was reared in Woodruff County, Ark. His parents, James P. and Maria L. (Alcorn) Ferguson, originally from Kentucky, immigrated to Woodruff County in 1850, when W. E. was but eight years of age, and after moving to this county settled in Augusta Township, where the father purchased a tract of land from Dave Johnson, one of the early pioneers of the county. Some of this land he found improved, and a portion was in its wild and natural state. In 1861, Mr. Ferguson moved to Augusta, making his home there ever since. He was a Union man in principle, and opposed the secession of the States, but the first Confederate company that was raised in his adopted county, through courtesy, made him lieutenant. He resigned, and in way of acknowledging the compliment thus shown him, presented the boys in gray with blankets. He has been a farmer and land speculator, and, although the owner of an extensive tract of land, he is practically living a retired life. Hon. James L. Alcorn, one of Mississippi's distinguished senators, is a brother of Mrs. Ferguson. There are five children now living born to the union of Mr. and Mrs. Ferguson: William E., Mary M. (widow of Anderson O'Neil), Minnie T., Bettie T. and Alcorn. W.

E. Ferguson's younger days were passed principally in Woodruff County, and being placed in the common schools to be educated, he remained in there until fifteen years of age, when he entered the Emory and Henry College of Emory, Washington County, Va., to complete his studies, but only remained through the sophomore year. After leaving this institution, he returned home, staying but two years, and acting as deputy sheriff, then, 1873, entered the Lebanon Law School, from which he graduated the following year. He was admitted to the bar at Augusta the same year, after which he practiced his profession until October, 1874, when he found that he would be compelled to take up his father's business in the farming interest in order to save the business, the employes of his father having involved him to a considerable amount. W. E. then assumed charge of affairs, and superintended the place, buying and weighing and ginning cotton. He worked diligently for two years, straightened things out, and then went to Dardanelle, where he found employment as a clerk. He remained in this position until September, 1878, when he returned to Augusta, and clerked for L. Rosen, continuing with him until 1880, when he was elected to the office of assessor. In 1882 he was elected sheriff and collector, and re-elected in 1884 without opposition in his own party. In 1886 he was elected to his present office (that of county and circuit clerk), and re-elected in 1888. Mr. Ferguson is one of the prominent political leaders of Woodruff County, and has a host of friends, his affability and thorough education qualifying him for any position of trust the people may confer upon him. He was married in May, 1884, to Miss Mary E. Douglass, a native of Iowa, who bore him two children: Louise and Ruby. Mr. Ferguson is a member of the Masonic fraternity, also a Chapter Mason and Knight of Honor and Knight of Pythias. In 1870 he entered the commercial school of Evansville, Ind., remaining at this institution of learning one term.

R. K. Fitzhugh, Jr. In making mention of the subject of this memoir, it is not an injustice to him when it is said that he is foremost in agricultural pursuits, and as a planter is exceedingly successful. He is a native of Virginia, his birth occurring in Greene County in 1854. He is a son of Rufus K., Sr., and H. E. (Baytop) Fitzhugh, the former of King George County origin and the latter of Gloucester County, Va. In 1859 Mr. Fitzhugh came to Arkansas, purchased a tract of land, and in 1866 moved his family to this place, and being an extensive slave holder in his native State, brought with him a large number of negroes. He became an extensive land owner, his place being known as "Walnut Woods," and at the time of his death he had about 550 acres under cultivation. He died in 1888, his wife and ten children surviving him. R. K. Fitzhugh is next to the oldest of the family, and although principally reared in Arkansas, he received his education in the Agricultural and Mechanical College of Auburn, Ala., graduating from this institution in 1874. Since his graduation he has turned his attention to farming, and has 800 acres of land in his home place, near Augusta, with 600 acres under cultivation. On this farm is a large cotton-gin, having a capacity of ten bales per day. He has held the office of county surveyor for three terms, being first elected in 1880, and socially is a member of the Masonic fraternity.

Dr. B. A. Fletcher, physician and surgeon, Augusta, Ark. This prominent practitioner was born in Fayette County, Miss., October 14, 1862, and, quite naturally perhaps, early formed a determination to follow the practice of medicine, for his father, Dr. John P. Fletcher, is a physician and a graduate of the New Orleans Medical College. The father, a native of Tennessee, married Miss Mary A. Cooper, a native of Mississippi, and in 1871 they moved to Arkansas and located in Lonoke County, where the father still lives, practicing his profession in Mississippi and Arkansas. The mother died in 1873. Dr. B. A. Fletcher, the youngest in a family of ten children, was but eight years of age when he came with his parents to Arkansas. His early scholastic advantages as he grew up tended to increase the natural desire which he possessed to follow the medical profession, and quite early in life began the study of medicine. He attended the session of 1883–84,

graduating from Bellevue Medical College of New York City. He then began practicing in Lonoke County, and there remained until 1885, when he came to Augusta, and has since been engaged in the practice of his profession at that place. He has met with flattering success for a young physician, and his future prospects are bright. His brother, J. J. Fletcher, who established a drug store in Augusta, died in 1885, and the Doctor came to this place to settle the estate. He concluded to remain, and is now building up a good practice. He was married in December, 1884, to Miss Mary A. Baker, of Virginia, who has borne two children, only one of whom is living: Mary A. The Doctor is director of the County Medical Association and secretary of the Woodruff County Board of Medical Examiners and also of the county society.

W. W. Folsom, who has been editor of the Woodruff County Vidette for the past ten years, was born in Charlotte, N. C., on August 23, 1836. At the age of twelve years he entered the office of the Columbia (Tenn.) Record, where he served a time at the printing business. Leaving Columbia in the year 1860, he became a citizen of Jackson, Tenn., from which point he went into the Southern army, in the Sixth Tennessee Infantry, and served to the close of the war in Gen. Cheatham's division. At the close of the war he came home like many others, penniless, but went to work to build up his own and the fortunes of his bright Southland, as a citizen of Mississippi, engaging in a mercantile and farming life. In 1875 he became a citizen of Arkansas, and since that time he has been laboring to build up every interest of his adopted State. In 1879 he became the editor of the Brinkley Times, the office of which was burned in November of that year when he became the editor and proprietor of the Vidette. In that capacity he has given his every energy to the advancement of the State, and particularly to the pushing forward of Woodruff County, and by his untiring energy and perseverance has succeeded in giving prominence to his paper, among his brethern of the press, both in and out of the State. In 1888 he was made president of his State Press Association, and is now serving his second term as a member of the executive committee of the National Editorial Association. He is still devoting himself to the advancement and development of Woodruff County, and will take pleasure in giving information to any person wishing to know the advantages of this beautiful and fertile region.

George W. Gordon, a conscientious and upright citizen, known and respected by all for the ability and faithfulness with which he discharges all duties imposed upon him, is a wealthy planter residing near Riverside, Ark., and born in Giles County, Tenn., July 4, 1847, and is a son of J. P. W. D. and Martha (Anderson) Gordon who were also Tennesseeans. The Gordon family were early settlers of the State and before the war the father was an extensive trader in negroes and owned a large plantation. He was also the owner of an hotel and livery stable at Pulaski, and died at this place in 1863, his wife having died in 1853. To these parents were born four sons and three daughters, of whom their son, George W., was the youngest boy. His boyhood days were spent in Pulaski, Tenn., and he there received his early schooling, but upon reaching a suitable age he began farming, continuing in this occupation for a number of years. On December 24, 1873, he took up his abode in Woodruff County, Ark., where he has since been engaged in the duties of farm work. He owns 535 acres on Taylor's Bay. In 1880 he was elected to the office of constable, serving two years, also filling the position of deputy sheriff, and in 1882 was chosen county assessor, remaining in this appointment four years. In 1886 was defeated for sheriff by a small majority in the primary Democratic election. He is a worthy constituent of the Masonic fraternity, and he and wife, whom he married in 1873, and whose maiden name was Kate Shell, are the parents of three children: Clarence, Lelia and Fannie. Mrs. Gordon was born in Woodruff County. Himself and wife are worshipers of the Methodist Episcopal Church. He taught two private and three public schools near Riverside, also served as Sunday-school superintendent for three years.

Dr. E. O. Grigsby, the trusted and tried friend of suffering humanity, the center of a host of friends, is a prominent physician and citizen of this (Woodruff) county, was born in Madison County, Miss., on March 18, 1835, the son of John R. Grigsby, of Scotch descent. His father, John R. Grigsby, was born in Rockbridge County, Va., in 1781, and was reared and educated to farm life. When quite young he immigrated from his native State to Henderson County, Ky., where he married, and after losing this companion he then went to Mississippi, where he was again married to Mrs. Elizabeth Sanders (maiden name Briggs) in 1833. To this marriage three children were born, two boys and a girl: E. O., M. R. and Eliza (deceased). Mr. John R. Grigsby served in the War of 1812, and was called to his final home in 1847. Mrs. Elizabeth Grigsby was born near Natchez, Miss., in 1805, and died in 1841. Dr. Grigsby's career as a man and physician dates from 1857. He attended lectures at St. Louis Medical College at that time, and graduated from this institution. He first practiced medicine in Madison County, Miss., locating in sight of the county school-house he attended when a boy, and in the neighborhood where he was reared an orphan, and there he remained until the late war between the States, and when Mississippi passed the ordinance secession, his Southern pride bade him go, and he enlisted at once in a company then forming and known as the Madison Rifles, afterward Company I, in the Tenth Mississippi Regiment, where he served twelve months as a private, though frequently detailed as medical assistant for special duties. At the expiration of his twelve months of service as a private, he was commissioned as assistant-surgeon, and assigned to duty with the Tenth Mississippi Regiment, the same in which he had served as a private soldier. In 1864 he was promoted to full surgeon, ordered to report to Gen. Forrest, who assigned him to duty with the Seventh Alabama Cavalry, under the command of Col. Colvin, where he remained until the close of the war, when returning to Mississippi and finding himself unable to live the life of former days, he immigrated to Arkansas, and in 1867 located in De View, where he has been engaged in the successful practice of his profession ever since, with the good-will of a host of friends around him, and always true to his trust and generous to a fault, and not lacking in those qualities which go to make up the courteous and affable gentleman. Dr. Grigsby was married to Mrs. Eliza Brigham in 1868, and by her became the father of two children: Nettie O. and John R. (deceased). Mrs. Grigsby's maiden name was Norrell, and was born in Tennessee in 1836, and came with her parents to Mississippi when quite small, and from Mississippi to Arkansas in 1851. Her father was married in Alabama, and was the parent of seven children, two of whom are now living: Eliza and Amanda (the wife of Mr. James Crawford, of Walnut Springs, Tex.). Mr. Norrell served in the War of 1812, and was a devout and earnest Christian, belonging to the Baptist Church, and died in 1853, his wife surviving him but eight years and was a member of the Methodist Episcopal Church. The only association to which Dr. Grigsby belongs is the Knights of Honor and the society of true honorable men. He is now engaged in the drug and grocery business, in connection with his practice, and has been for the past six years.

J. T. Hamblet, merchant, Augusta, Ark. In the list of industries of the city of Augusta that of merchandising takes a prominent position, and among the houses engaged in this branch of business that of Mr. Hamblet is entitled to due notice and recognition. Mr. Hamblet was originally from Dinwiddie County, Va., where his birth occurred in 1825, and is the eldest child born to the marriage of G. B. and Joannah Hamblet, natives of the Old Dominion. The parents immigrated to Tennessee, and there resided until the death of the father, which occurred in 1841. The mother died in Woodruff County, Ark. J. T. Hamblet was principally reared in Tennessee, and his early scholastic advantages were enjoyed in that State. He began clerking in a store in Memphis in 1843, and there remained until 1848, when he came to Augusta, Ark., and engaged in the mercantile business, which he has since continued. He is the oldest merchant in the county, and does a general furnishing business, carrying a large and select stock of goods, and is one of the leading merchants in the county. He has always attended strictly to business, and this in some measure accounts for success. He is also the owner of considerable real estate. Mr. Hamblet chose for his companion in life Miss Cordelia P. Penn, and was united in marriage to her in 1850. They have three children living: Mrs. Josie Harry, Ida Dale and Georgie Elsberry. Mr. Hamblet has been a member of the Masonic fraternity for forty years, and is one of the first-class citizens of the county.

Dr. T. A. Hightower has attained to an established reputation as a physician of ability. A resident of McCrory, his birth occurred in Limestone County, Ala., June 5, 1850, he being the son of James Hightower, a prosperous farmer. The latter, who was of Virginia nativity, was born in 1817 and accompanied his parents to Kentucky from the Old Dominion, and then to Alabama when quite a young man. Concluding that it was not good for man to be alone, he selected for his helpmate, Miss Lucy Westmoreland, their marriage occuring in 1846. Their union was blessed with a family of nine children: John C., James L., William E., Lou C. (Mrs. R. R. Riley), Robert L., Bettie (the wife of Mr. Gilbert), India, Martha and T. A. Mr. Hightower was a member of the Methodist Episcopal Church, and a man respected by all. His death occurred in Limestone County, Ala., in 1879. His wife, who was born in Giles County, Tenn., in 1831, is now residing in Alabama. Dr. Hightower was married in 1875 to Miss Emma Simpson, in Lawrence County, Ala. She is the daughter of Mr. and Mrs. Isaac Simpson, and was born in 1858. Dr. and Mrs. Hightower are the parents of five children: Isaac, Pearl, James, Katie and Thomas. The Doctor was educated in Tennessee, and attended medical lectures at the University of Nashville, Tenn., in 1870–73. He first practiced medicine in Town Creek, Ala., in 1873, but immigrated from Alabama to Tennessee in 1878, and that year came to Arkansas, locating in this county, where he has since resided, enjoying, as he well deserves, a large and lucrative practice. Dr. Hightower is identified with the following orders: K. of P., Douglass Lodge No. 56, K. of H. and A. F.

& A. M., belonging to the Blue Lodge, Chapter, and Commandery No. 1. Mrs. Hightower is a member in high standing of the Methodist Episcopal Church, and a general favorite in society.

J. P. House, merchant, Augusta, Ark. To be successful in any calling in life a man must be honest, industrious and saving, and with these essential qualities he can not fail to accumulate property, and at the same time hold the respect and esteem of his fellow-men. Mr. House was originally from Hardeman County, Tenn., and is the son of A. B. House, a native of Tennessee, and a planter, who is still residing in White County, Ark. The maiden name of the mother was Eliza Wilkes, who was also a native of Tennessee. J. P. House was in his eighth year when he came to White County with his parents, in 1858. He received a fair education in the common schools, and early in life was taught the duties of farm life. He left the parental roof at the age of eighteen years, and clerked in a store for three years. He then studied law, and was admitted to the bar in White County, where he practiced his profession for four years in that and Woodruff Counties. He established the Vidette in 1877, and ran it until 1879, when he gave it up. After this he began keeping books for Hamblet & Penn, and held this position until 1884, when he engaged in mercantile pursuits with a partner, E. H. Conner, the firm title still continuing House & Conner. They carry a general line of merchandise, and are doing a successful business. Mr. House selected his wife in the person of Miss L. Purssell, and was united in marriage to her in 1880. She died in 1886, leaving one child, John. W. Mr. House is a member of the Masonic fraternity, Knights & Ladies of Honor, and Knights of Pythias, and a Knight Templar and Knight of Honor.

Joseph L. Howell. Mr. and Mrs. David Howell, of North Carolina, the former a prosperous farmer of that State, were the parents of nine children, as follows: James L., Eliza (wife of Nedy Hyatt), Mary (now Mrs. H. C. McCraken), C. J. (Mrs. J. I. Jaredd), N. E. (Mrs. Morgan Osborn), Adaline (Mrs. George Butler), Joseph L. (the subject of this sketch) and two sons deceased.

Mr. Howell was claimed by the dread destroyer, Death, in 1864, his wife having preceded him in the year 1848. They were earnest workers and members of the Methodist Episcopal Church. Joseph L. began life for himself in 1852, as traveling agent of musical instruments, and also taught music until 1861. During the war he went to Texas, and freighted cotton from Waco to San Antonia for the Government. After the close of hostilities, Mr. Howell came to Arkansas and settled in this county, engaging in farming, which occupation he has since followed, being to-day one of the wealthiest planters of the county. He owns between 5,000 and 6,000 acres of land, about 1,200 in a fine state of cultivation. A good gin is one of the many improvements made by him, which was rebuilt during the year 1889, enabling the ginning of from fifteen to twenty bales per day. Mr. Howell was married to Miss Fannie Butler, the daughter of Mr. and Mrs. Joel J. Butler, of Georgia, and their marriage resulted in a family of five children, three girls and two boys: Martha (the wife of Dr. Mewborn), Effie (Mrs. Richard Izard), Eddie, Joseph and Fannie (deceased). Mrs. Howell was born in 1838, owing her nativity to Georgia, where her parents were life-long residents. Mr. Butler died in 1864, and his wife two years before. Mr. Howell has erected a very fine residence in Howell Station, and is the founder of that place. He is foremost in all enterprises relative to the welfare of town and county, many of which owe their origin and successful completion to his ever ready support and to his spirit of progression. His wealth enables him to contribute largely to all charitable purposes, and in performing many good works he follows the Bible injunction, "Let not thy left hand know what thy right hand doeth."

S. L. Ingalls, real-estate and insurance agent, Augusta, Ark. In a country like Arkansas, with so much land still unoccupied or not built upon, the office of the real-estate agent is an important one, and exercises considerable bearing upon the welfare of the community. He is an instrument for the building up of the country and making the wilderness to blossom as the rose, figuratively speaking. Among those largely interested in this line of business is Mr. S. L. Ingalls, who is also an insurance agent, one of the most important branches of business in any community. Mr. Ingalls was born in Boston, Mass., in 1846, and is a son of Elias T. and Eliza (Chase) Ingalls, natives also of Massachusetts. This family was early settlers of the New England States, and the Great-grandfather Ingalls was the founder of the city of Lynn. Elias T. Ingalls was a shoe manufacturer, and followed this pursuit up to the breaking out of the war, after which he was the buyer for his son, R. M. Ingalls, of Louisville. He is still living at his home in Massachusetts. S. L. Ingalls, the youngest son of seven children, five sons and two daughters, received his education in his native State, and in 1861 went to Louisville, Ky., where he remained with his brother in the shoe business until 1865. He then returned home and was book-keeper in Boston until 1870, when he came to Arkansas, located at Jacksonport, and was also book-keeper here for E. L. Watson for some time. In 1876 he came to Augusta and was book-keeper for Hamblet & Penn for two years, after which he was made deputy county and circuit clerk, filling this position for eight years. In 1884 he embarked in his present business, represents twelve fire-insurance companies and is a large real-estate dealer, both in town and country. He owns one of the finest residences in Augusta. By his marriage, which occurred in 1871, to Miss Kate H. Weiss, of Louisville, Ky., he became the father of two children, both deceased. Mr. Ingalls is justice of the peace of Augusta Township. He is a brother of Senator Ingalls, of Kansas. He is a member of the Masonic fraternity, Chapter, K. of H. and K. & L. of H. He is also a member of the K. of P.

Richard T. Jett, one of the most prominent and influential citizens in the vicinity of Gregory, was born in Kentucky (Barren County) in 1834. His father, R. H. V. Jett, was a native of Virginia, born in 1806. He followed the occupation of milling, and in 1828 was married to Miss Elizabeth Bradley, of Maryland, by which union were born ten children, eight boys and two girls, seven now living, viz.: Mary J. (wife of Gabe Corn), Rich-

ard T., Catherine (wife of William Langstay), Albert N., J. S., James F. and G. W. Mr. Jett was a member of the Christian Church, and died in 1872. Richard T. Jett immigrated from Kentucky to Arkansas in 1870, locating in Woodruff County. He turned his attention to the improvement of land and now cultivates some 300 acres, the principal crops being cotton and corn. He has erected a good residence, and enjoys the acquaintance of many residents about Gregory, in the southern portion of the county. The year 1858 witnessed his nuptials with Margaret A. Haden, daughter of Mr. and Mrs. John Haden, of Kentucky. To their marriage three children have been given, two girls and one boy: Carrie (wife of Lawrence Richey), Josie (now Mrs. James Snodgrass) and Albert C. Mr. Jett is an expert machinist and followed that business for several years. From 1861 till 1866 he engaged in steamboating, and now has an interest in a large saw-mill, also in partnership with W. J. and E. G. Thompson, Minor Gregory and R. Eldridge in the possession of a gin, the style of the firm being Mill & Gin Co. They run four stands and have the latest improved plans. Mr. Jett possesses any amount of energy, and his having an interest in anything means the successful termination of that enterprise. His refined surroundings and hospitable board ensure for him the respect and esteem of all who know him.

F. B. Jones is a member of the general mercantile firm of S. M. Jones & Co., of Riverside, and was born in Limestone County, Ala., in the year 1851, and is a son of I. H. W. and Mary Jones, who were natives of the State of Alabama. They removed to Woodruff County, Ark., in November, 1861, and located four miles east of Augusta, and here both died on a farm which they had purchased. At the time of the father's death he owned 480 acres of land, about 200 of which was under cultivation. Of the seven children born to them two are now living: F. B. and S. M. F. B. Jones was in his ninth year when brought to this State, and here he grew to manhood, receiving his education in the St. John's Masonic School of Little Rock. He also graduated from the Eastman Business College of Poughkeepsie, N. Y., in 1874, and after clerking for his uncle in Searcy for some time, the present firm was established (in 1885), and has since continued under very favorable auspices. They carry a general line of merchandise, and also handle large quantities of cotton and produce. F. B. Jones has land to the extent of 420 acres, and has 150 acres under cultivation, and in addition to giving much of his attention to his farm, he raises considerable stock. He has served as constable one term, and he and his brother have charge of the postoffice, which was established in 1884, S. M. Jones being appointed postmaster one year later. Mr. Jones was married in 1883 to Miss Claudia H. Jelks, by whom he had one child, now deceased.

S. M. Jones, of the general mercantile firm of S. M. Jones & Co., of Riverside, is an Alabamian, who was brought to Arkansas by his parents when an infant, and until ten years old was a resident and attendant of the schools of Woodruff County. The next fifteen years were spent in White County, and since then he has resided at his present place of abode. In the spring of 1884 he engaged in the mercantile business, but gives the most of his attention to the conducting of his farm, which comprises a tract of 430 acres, with 200 acres under cultivation. He is a member of the Masonic fraternity, and is an intelligent and enterprising young man. May 3, 1887, he was married to Miss Mary B. Word, a native of Arkansas. Maj. B. M. Jones is a merchant and proprietor of a hotel at Riverside. He was born in Limestone County, Ala., March 24, 1830, and is a son of John J. and Martha (Wilburn) Jones who were born in Virginia. They removed to Northern Alabama at an early day and there resided until their respective deaths, the father being an energetic tiller of the soil. Maj. B. M. Jones was reared and educated in Alabama, and in 1858 came to White County, Ark., and located at Searcy, where he carried on the mercantile business for several years. In 1862 he enlisted in Company E, Thirty-sixth Arkansas Infantry as first lieutenant, was promoted to captain, and at the time of the surrender was mustered out as major, and returned to his

home at Searcy, where he remained until 1884. Since that time he has been a resident of Riverside, engaged in merchandising, and also buys cotton very extensively. To his marriage with Susan Greene in 1860 one child was born, who is now deceased, and by his present wife, who was a Miss Elizabeth A. Dismukes, he has three children: Henry, Lizzie and Fannie.

Maj. D. D. Leach is one of the few men who fully recognize that a thorough education is absolutely necessary if a man wishes to become eminent in the practice of law, and he is also cognizant of the fact that a systematic course of reading gives variety to thought and a clearer perception to the motives of men. The Major is a prominent attorney of Augusta, and was born in Homer, Mich., March 29, 1841, being a son of R. T. and L. M. (Calhoun) Leach, the former a native of New York and the latter of Pennsylvania. After their marriage they removed to Michigan (about 1846), and a few years later settled in Wisconsin, and in 1871 removed to Arkansas, locating in Augusta where the father died in 1875. His widow still survives him. He was deputy sheriff, constable and city marshal for some years, and by trade was a millwright, at which he worked for years. D. D. Leach was reared principally in Waukesha, Wis., receiving his education in Carroll College. After studying law in Waukesha for some time he removed to Colorado, and while in Central City, in 1864, passed a legal examination, and was admitted to the bar. Prior to this, he had enlisted in the Twenty-eighth Wisconsin Infantry (in 1862), and was an able soldier of the Union until the close of the war. For bravery and good conduct he was advanced in the rank of officers to that of major. In 1868 he came to Augusta, Ark., and established himself as a lawyer, continuing in this profession ever since, winning for himself an excellent reputation as a pleader, his speeches being eloquent and to the point. He held the office of prosecuting attorney for ten years, and in 1886, was a candidate for Congress on the Republican ticket, but owing to the large Democratic majority in his district he was defeated. The Major is a member of the Masonic fraternity and the K. of H., being Past Grand Dictator of the latter lodge and is Deputy Supreme Protector of the K. & L. of H., and has also been Thrice Illustrious Grand Master of the Grand Council of the State of Arkansas. In 1864 he was united in marriage to Miss Dora Smith, a native of Wisconsin, and by her is the father of three children, Calhoun D. surviving.

A. C. Lewis is known as a worthy son of John Lewis, a native of Missouri, who was born in 1800, and educated to farm life, but when quite young he left his father's home and operated a steamferry on the Mississippi River at St. Louis. He was married, in 1822, to Miss Nancy M. Curry, and by her became the father of the following family: Harvey, Robert O., Elizabeth (the wife of William S. Halloway) and A. C. (the subject of this sketch). Mr. Lewis was a gallant soldier in the Indian War, and at the time of his death, in 1848, was residing in St. Louis County, Mo. Mrs. Lewis died in the same county in 1863, a member of the Methodist Episcopal Church, as was also her husband. A. C. Lewis first saw the light of day in St. Francis County, Mo., in 1835, and commenced life on his own responsibility at the age of eighteen years. After managing his mother's farm until the war, he laid down the implements of peace to take up those of a soldier, and enlisted in the artillery service under Capt. Emmett McDonald. In 1861 he was captured and taken to Vicksburg. During his career he participated in the battles of Wilson's Creek, Pea Ridge and the skirmishes at Corinth, the battles of Iuka, Baker's Creek and the siege of Vicksburg, serving as second lieutenant in the battery for a short time, just before the closing of hostilities. In 1866 Mr. Lewis was married to Miss Barbara Edmond, daughter of William Edmond and wife, of Alabama. Mrs. Lewis was born in Tennessee, and died in 1869, leaving three children: Fletcher, Eleanor (the wife of Joseph Grant) and one child not named. Mr. Lewis chose for his second wife Miss Lena Jelks, and to them five children have been given: Ada, Letitia, John, Austin and Gracie. Mr. Lewis owns and operates a cotton-gin and grist-mill, which is second to none in the county. His farm consists of 780 acres of land, with 300 acres under cultivation, the principal crop being cotton and corn. He and wife are members of the Methodist Episcopal Church, and he is a public-spirited man, supporting all educational and religious enterprises; a good financier, he is also a practical farmer and excellent business man, well worthy the respect and esteem in which he is held by all who are so fortunate as to know him.

Thomas T. Locke, planter, ginner and merchant, and one of the representative men of Cotton Plant Township, is originally from Rowan County, N. C., being born in 1825, and one of six children given to J. Richard and Margaret (Gheen) Locke. Richard Locke and wife were of North Carolina nativity, and died in that State in 1836 and 1849, respectively. He was a prosperous farmer, and his father, Alex. Locke, was also of North Carolina, his birth and death occurring in that State. The maternal grandfather, Joseph Gheen, was of Dutch descent, a native of North Carolina, and died in Kentucky. Thomas T. Locke is the only member of his father's family living. He was educated in the common schools of his home, and in 1851 was married to Margaret A., daughter of Daniel and Hethey Harris, who were natives and life-long residents of North Carolina. To Mr. and Mrs. Locke seven children have been born, two of them now living: Thomas A. and Ida L. (wife of Frank P. Hill). Mr. Locke came to Woodruff County in 1858, settling on his present farm, which is five miles north of Cotton Plant. It is, without doubt, one of the finest farms in the county, consisting of 640 acres, with over 450 under a careful state of cultivation. On his daughter's marriage he presented her with 200 acres, which in itself is a very fine farm, and the two farms combined make a very fine plantation. Mr. Locke operates a plantation store and a gin, which has been in successful operation since his residence in Arkansas. It would seem that with so much on his mind something would have to be neglected, but Mr. Locke manages his farm, gin and mercantile business in a way that demonstrates his perfect efficiency to complete anything he undertakes. Mrs. Locke died in 1868, while in Mississippi, where she had gone for her health, and in 1876 Mr. Locke again married, this time to Mrs. Mary E. Linthicum, of Arkansas, and a daughter of the Hon. Parley P. Hill, who was among the first settlers in Woodruff County, and one of its most prominent citizens in an early day. He was a member of the legislature from Woodruff County from 1848 to 1849, and a wealthy planter. His death occurred in 1866. Mr. Locke served in the war a short time, under Capt. Cauley, in 1864. Previous to the war he was a Whig, voting for Taylor in 1848, but since that time has been a stanch Democrat. He has been connected with the Cotton Plant Presbyterian Church since 1864, and has presided as an elder since 1877. Mrs. Locke has been a member of the Presbyterian Church for a great many years, and is known and respected by every one. Mr. Locke is a good citizen, lending his support to all worthy movements, and is of the character of men who help to build the villages into towns and the towns into cities.

Robert C. Lynch is the youngest of the children of William D. and Eliza J. (Mann) Lynch. The former, of Irish descent, was born in Mississippi in 1819, and in 1846 moved to what is now Woodruff County, becoming engaged in the mercantile business in Cotton Plant, where he built the first store, and was largely the means of making the town what it is at this time. When Mr. Lynch moved here his nearest postoffice was Des Arc. He entered a large amount of Government land in the township, and made it his home until his death, which occurred in 1876. He was a Mason. Robert C. Lynch was born in Cotton Plant in 1855, and received a good education, graduating from the Mound City Commercial College of St. Louis in 1874, after which he embarked in the mercantile business with his father. Upon the demise of the latter he took the old homestead (which he still owns and on which he was born, consisting of 320 acres), and other land in the county, having over 300 acres under cultivation. He carried on farming with good success. Mr. Lynch was married in 1876 to Augusta J. Woods, a daughter of Daniel and Jane Woods, natives of North Carolina. He is now occupied as bookkeeper for Alexander Salinger, of Cotton Plant, in connection with his agricultural duties. Mr. Lynch is a member of the Knights of Pythias, in which he holds the office of Keeper of Records and Seals; is also a member of the A. F. & A. M., of the K. of H., and of the K. and L. of H., in the last-named lodge filling the office of Past Dictator. Mrs. Lynch is a member of the Presbyterian Church. Her husband is a highly respected citizen, and one of the leading men of Cotton Plant, having the finest residence in the place.

John J. McDonald. Perhaps the most important of Mr. McDonald's history is his war record, which is without a blemish, and though not characterized by any special act of prominence, it is one to which he can refer with pardonable pride, and that may be read by those who are to come after him with a sense of honor. He enlisted in the Confederate army in 1861, and joined the Sixth Georgia Infantry, his service extending over the States of Virginia, North and South Carolina. During this time he participated in the battles of Seven Pines, Chancellorsville, Fredericksburg, Second Manassas, battle of the Wilderness, and the seven days' fight around Richmond, besides many minor engagements. He was with Stonewall Jackson when that great general was killed, but was never himself wounded or captured. Early in 1865 he was sent South, and was under Johnston at his surrender. His two older brothers (twins) William and John, were in the same war, both receiving severe injuries in the seven days' fight. After they were all at home he in company with his father and one sister came to White County, but about a year later his father returned to his native State. Mr. McDonald is a native of Jones County, Ga., and was born in 1842, the son of John and Wealthy (Clifton) McDonald, originally from North Carolina and Georgia, respectively. They were married in Georgia and reared a family of eight children, of whom John J. is the fourth in order of birth. Mrs. McDonald died in 1854. Mr. McDonald married again, and with the exception of a few years spent in Arkansas, as before stated, resided in Georgia all his life, his death occurring there in 1874. He served in one of the Indian wars. His father, Henry McDonald, a Scotchman by birth and a soldier in the Revolutionary War, died in North Carolina. John J. McDonald was married in 1870 to Miss Mary, daughter of William Thompson. She was born in Georgia and died after nine years of wedded life. For his second wife Mr. McDonald chose Victoria Turner, whose parents, Stephen and Susan Turner, were married in North Carolina and from there moved to Jackson County, Ark., where the former died, but Mrs. Turner is still living. Mrs. McDonald was born in Jackson County and died in 1889, a member of the Christian Church. She bore five children: John L., William H., Walter H. Eugene and Rufus. In 1869 Mr. McDonald moved to White County, and since 1880 has resided on his present place, consisting of 600 acres with 125 in a successful state of cultivation. The farm at the time of his purchase was nearly all woods, but it is now second to none in the county, as far as careful cultivation is concerned, all brought to this condition by the individual efforts of Mr. McDonald. He is an enterprising farmer and citizen, lending his support to all worthy movements for the good and growth of the county, and enjoys the esteem and respect of those who know him. He has been school trustee for many years, and many a successful termination of some enterprise owes its existence to a large degree to his quick judgment and keen penetration. He has been a Democrat during life, and voted for Greeley in 1868. The Colony Lodge No. 190, A. F. & A. M., find in him one of its best members.

Ransford P. McGregor, a man looked up to and held in the highest esteem by his fellow-citizens, also a wealthy planter of Cotton Plant, is a native of Tennessee, and was born in Rutherford County, in 1848, being the son of Ransford and Isabella (Henderson) McGregor. The senior McGregor was probably born in Davidson County, Tenn., in 1801, and his wife in Rutherford County. They were married in the latter State, where their entire lives were passed. Mrs. McGregor was called to her final home in 1849, and her husband died in 1882. He was a justice of the peace and a leading farmer at the time of his demise. His father was of Scotch-Irish descent, and among the early settlers of Davidson County, Tenn., his death occurring in Wilson County. His grandfather, Col. James Henderson, was killed at the battle of New Orleans, January 8, 1815. He was colonel of a Tennessee regiment, and a man of considerable prominence. Ransford P. was the youngest of seven children, five sons and two daughters. He is the only one married, and the only one living out of their native State. His education was greatly interfered with by the war, but notwithstanding he is a well-read, intelligent gentleman. At the age of twenty-seven he left his home and went to Alabama, where he engaged in farming for a few years, and in 1878 came to Cotton Plant, where he was married in the year 1879. His wife was Sallie, daughter of William Cooper, of South Carolina. She was left an orphan when quite small, but was reared and educated by Dr. T. D. Chunn. To Mr. McGregor's marriage seven children were born, four sons and three daughters, all of whom are being educated by a private tutor at home. He resided on a farm one mile east of his present home, till 1889, then came to the town, where he has recently built a very fine residence. His farm is second to none in the county, consisting of 3,000 acres with about 1,000 under a high state of cultivation, also a good school-house and yard in connection with his property in town. Mr. McGregor is one of the principal land holders of the county, rising from the possessor of a few hundreds to one of the wealthy and influential men of the county. He has a good steam gin, which has been in successful operation since his residence here, and is now ginning twenty bales per day, and he will produce about 600 bales of cotton from his land this year. Mr. McGregor is a stanch Democrat, and voted for Greeley in 1872. He is known far and wide for his charities and liberal contributions, doing many of his kind acts and generous deeds, which never reach the ears of the outside world. Mrs. McGregor is a member in good standing of the Presbyterian Church.

Andrew J. Marsh. I. M. and Jane M. (Walker) Marsh, the esteemed parents of our subject, were natives of North Carolina and Tennessee, respectively, their marriage occurring in the latter State, and in 1858 they moved to Arkansas, settling in Woodruff County, four miles from the present site of Howell Station. Here the senior Marsh improved a large farm, residing on it until 1867, at which time he returned to Tipton County, Tenn., where he lived for several years, but while visiting in Arkansas, in the year 1869, was claimed by Death. His wife died from injuries received from a vicious mule at her home in Tipton County, Tenn., in 1870. They were both members of the Presbyterian Church. To their marriage a family of thirteen children were born, Andrew J. being the ninth in order of birth. His education was from necessity very limited, as the schools in the days of his youth were not many. He was thoroughly drilled in the management and successful operation of the farm, and has proved himself a worthy example of the sons of the soil. Since his twelfth year Mr. Marsh has resided in Arkansas, and is an ardent admirer of the land of his adoption. In 1871 he settled on his present farm (it then being in the woods), three miles northeast of Howell Station, and is now the owner of 400 acres of excellent land, with 125 under cultivation, all the result of hard work and good management. With the exception of two years in Colona, where he engaged in the merchandising business, Mr. Marsh has always followed the occupation of farming. In 1864 he enlisted in Company C, Third Missouri Cavalry, operating in Indian Territory, Missouri and Kansas; also participated in numerous skirmishes in Arkansas. He was with Gen. Price on his famous raid through Missouri, Kansas and Indian Territory, surrendering at Shreveport, La., June 7, 1865. After the war he returned to his home. Mr. Marsh has been married three times, his first marriage being in 1869 to Miss Sarah A. Sanders, who bore him two children. She died in 1872, leaving an infant twenty-four hours old. Mrs. Marsh was born in Mississippi, and came with her mother and step-father (Mr. Collins) to this State, settling in Woodruff County. Her mother is now residing in Texas. In 1873 he was again married, to Mary Tubbs, of Humphreys County, Tenn., she being the mother of two sons. This wife dying in 1882, in 1885 he married Julia

Joyner. He has met with many accidents, narrowly escaping death at times, one accident in particular being the fall of a nail-keg filled with mud. This keg fell thirty-two feet striking him on the head, fracturing it and breaking his arm and shoulder. Politically he is a Democrat, his first vote being for Seymour, in 1868. He was formerly allied with the lodge of K. of H. at Cotton Plant, and, with the exception of his sister, is the only member of his family residing in Woodruff County. Mr. Marsh, his wife and two children belong to the Methodist Episcopal Church, of which he is steward.

Robert T. Martin. Among the leading planters of Cadee Township the name of Robert T. Martin is well known. This name is synonymous of all that is honorable and upright, and is a guarantee that the confidence reposed in him will not be betrayed. He was born in Spartanburg District, S. C., in 1846, and is the son of Thomas Jefferson and Louisa M. (Dodd) Martin. Thomas J. Martin and wife were natives of South Carolina, and in 1850 came to Cass County, Ga., thence to Mississippi, where his death occurred in 1858. He was a major in the South Carolina militia at an early day. His father, Thomas Martin, was also of South Carolina nativity, though of Scotch-Irish descent, and during his life was a very prominent planter. His wife was of French origin. To Thomas J. and wife a family of five children were born, of which Robert T. is the oldest. After her husband's demise, Mrs. Martin and her family moved to Arkansas, settling in what is now Woodruff County, where she died May 3, 1866. She was the daughter of Thomas Dodd, a native of South Carolina, but who resided in Georgia, also Mississippi, and finally ended his days in Arkansas, in 1865. He was of Scotch-Irish descent, and at the time of his death was a successful planter of St. Francis County. Robert T. Martin has called Arkansas his home since his thirteenth year; though the facilities for schooling were far from satisfactory in his early youth, he has, by constant reading, become conversant with the events of the times. In 1862 Mr. Martin joined Company G, Eighteenth Arkansas Infantry, and was in service east of the Mississippi till the siege of Port Hudson. He participated in the fights of Farmington, Corinth, Big Creek, Ironton, and all through the raid of Gen. Price in Missouri, Kansas, Indian Territory, etc. He surrendered at Helena, June, 1865, and was held prisoner for about eight days after the capture of Port Hudson. After the close of the great struggle Mr. Martin resumed his occupation of farming, and in July, 1867, he married Mattie E. Robertson, a native of Georgia, and a daughter of Elijah and Sarah (Miliner) Robertson. Mr. and Mrs. Robertson resided in Georgia for a number of years, then moved to Florida, thence to Cape Girardeau, Mo., and during the war they came to Arkansas. After a short residence in Arkansas they moved to Mississippi, and then again to Alabama, where Mrs. Robertson now lives, her husband having died in Alabama a number of years ago. He was at one time a farmer and merchant, and later a contractor and builder. To the marriage of Mr. and Mrs. Martin eleven children have been born, two sons and one daughter now living, and all enjoying excellent educational advantages, no expense nor pains being spared. Mr. Martin lived near Cotton Plant, engaged in farming until 1883, then came to Howell Township, where he is now residing. While in Howell he engaged in the mercantile business, which he successfully carried on for three years in connection with his farming. He is one of the leading land holders of Woodruff County, owning 1,300 acres of land, 600 of which are under cultivation, and on this farm is erected one of the most magnificent residences in this county, all the result of good management and careful attention to every detail of business, however trifling or insignificant. He has met with several severe reverses, in 1867 and 1869 lost all, but after a short absence in Mississippi, he returned, and went to farming on shares till 1873. Subsequently he purchased 164 acres near Howell, this being his first land, since which time he has constantly added to his possessions until obtaining the present amount of land, which he calls his own, and all through his own exertions. He has served in the official position of court deputy, sheriff, etc. In his

political views Mr. Martin has been a life-long Democrat, voting for Greeley in 1872. He is a member of A. F. & A. M. Lodge, at Cotton Plant, of Richmond Lodge, and was once secretary of I. O. O. F., at Cotton Plant, now disbanded; also a member of Augusta Lodge No. 1122, K. of H., and he, with his wife, belongs to the Methodist Episcopal Church.

Rufus J. Martin is one of the many successful planters residing near Snapps, Ark., and, like the majority of them, has worked his way up to his present position through his own endeavors. He has given his attention to farming all his life, and to say that he has been merely successful would but mildly express the results which have attended his endeavors. He owns excellent farming land to the amount of 480 acres, and has 230 acres under cultivation, all his land being well improved with good buildings, fences, etc. Mr. Martin was born in Lawrence County, Ark., December 22, 1854, and is a son of Rufus and Ann (Hickerson) Martin, of North Carolina, who immigrated to Arkansas at at early day, settling in Lawrence County. About 1855 they removed to Woodruff County, and in 1873 settled in Little Rock, where they now live. The father followed farming for nearly fifteen years, and was a very extensive land holder in the State. He is president and a large stockholder of the Batesville & Brinkley Railroad, and is now in the broker, banking and real-estate business. The following are their children: Rufus, Anna, Jessie, Gustave, Susie and Raymond. Rufus J. Martin was reared in his Woodruff County, and after attending the common schools he completed his education at a well-known collegiate institute in North Carolina. Since 1880 he has been married to Florence Shish, by whom he has three children: Katie, Winfield and Willie. Mr. Martin is an intelligent and thrifty farmer, and socially is a Mason.

Dr. William J. Mathis, of the firm of Mathis & Baker, physicians and surgeons at Cotton Plant, is a native of Paris, Tenn., and was born September 7, 1851, the son of Josiah and Angelina (Paynter) Mathis, who were Kentuckians by birth. Josiah Mathis dates his existence to the year 1816, his wife having been born in 1826, but when very young they moved to Henry County, Tenn., were there married, and spent the remainder of their life. Mr. Mathis was a member of the Baptist Church, and his wife of the Methodist. Their death occurred in 1863 and 1880, respectively. Josiah Mathis was the son of Jesse Mathis, and at the time of his death enjoyed the distinction of being a prosperous farmer. Jesse Mathis, who died in Henry County, Tenn., was born on the ocean; he died in 1875, having been in the War of 1812, and with Jackson at New Orleans. His father, William Mathis, came originally from France, and died in Kentucky. Grandfather William Paynter, of Irish descent, first saw the light in the Blue Grass State, and died in Henry County, Tenn. The father of our subject was twice married, his last wife being the mother of William J. He was the oldest of six children born to their union. Educated at Caledonia Academy, in Henry County, Tenn., at the age of nineteen he began the study of medicine, and took a course of lectures in 1872 and 1873 at Nashville University, graduating from that institution in 1879. After practicing in Henry County until 1881, he came to St. Francis County, and in 1887 located in Cotton Plant, where he has since resided, continuing his practice with marked success. In November, 1875, Dr. Mathis was united in marriage with Miss Emma W., daughter of Harry Wyms, of Houston County, Tenn. Six children have blessed this union, only two now living, a son and daughter. Dr. Mathis is conservative in politics, and voted for Tilden in 1876. He is a member of a Masonic Lodge in St. Francis County, and is Medical Examiner in the K. of H. and K. & L. of H.

R. W. Murray is one of the pioneers of the early history of Arkansas, and one who has been largely instrumental in the rapid and steady growth of his adopted county. Mr. Murray is a Tennesseean by birth, being born in Hardeman County, July 18, 1831. His parents, James and Eliza (Beazel) Murray, were also Tennesseeans, and about 1845 came to the State of Arkansas, settling in Woodruff County, and resided there until their respective deaths in 1863 and 1866.

Their family was a large one, but only seven children are now living. R. W. Murray was about eight years of age when brought to Arkansas, and here he grew to mature years and received such education as the schools of that day afforded. He became familiar with the duties of farm life at a very early date, but when the war broke out he dropped all work to take up arms, and enlisted in Company A, Eighth Arkansas Regiment, serving about three years. After the cessation of hostilities he returned home and again took up the duties of the farm, and has made agriculture his calling ever since. Owing to his early removal to this State he has witnessed the development of Woodruff County into a very prosperous county. He was married in 1861 to Miss Mary M. Walker, by whom he had eight children, only three of whom are now living: Lee, Addie and Stella. His second marriage took place in 1882, his wife being Miss Sallie E. Campbell, and is the mother of two children: Elmo and Edith.

W. J. O'Shields. In the township in which the subject of this sketch lives there is not to be found a more attractive farm than his, and which calls forth the admiration of all who see it. His residence, barns, outbuildings, and, in fact, all necessary conveniences, bespeak of prosperity and show that he is a thrifty farmer, and of the 500 acres of excellent farming land which he possesses there are about 225 under cultivation. This he devotes to the raising of cotton and corn, and he also raises the necessary stock for the successful conducting of his farm. He was born in Jackson County, Ga., July 23, 1833, and is a son of Jethro and Polly (Boyce) O'Shields, the father a native of South Carolina and the mother of Georgia. They were married in the latter State, and at the time of the late conflict resided at Resaca. In 1867 he and his family came to Woodruff County, Ark., and here he departed this life during the following year, his wife's death having occurred in Georgia prior to his coming to Arkansas. W. J. O'Shields is one of the three surviving members of a family of seven children, and was reared and educated in the State of Georgia. In 1862 he enlisted in Capt. Keith's Company and was on active duty during the entire war, coming out of the army with no wound or mishap of any sort. He came with his father overland to Arkansas and in December, 1869, he purchased the farm where he is now living. He was married January 1, 1876, to Paralie Amelia Thompson.

J. P. Penn, one of the foremost in the ranks of Augusta's prominent and enterprising business men, and a citizen of good repute, was born in Maury County, Tenn., October 8, 1833, and from his earliest youth has been familiar with farm work, and by his own pluck and indomitable will has acquired the property he now owns, being one of the largest real-estate holders in the county. He was sixteen years old when he came to the State of Arkansas, receiving the larger portion of his education in his native State. Upon his arrival in this county his sole possessions consisted of the trunk which contained his clothes. He immediately sought employment and hiring out to a farmer worked on a farm for some years. By strict economy he soon laid by some money, and in 1852 he began clerking for Hamblet & Penn, his brother being a member of this firm. After remaining with them two years he began clerking for Purssell & Bro., and upon this firm selling out he continued in the employ of their successor one year. He and his brother, Thomas H., then became proprietors of the establishment and the business continued under the firm name of T. H. Penn & Bro. until the breaking out of the Rebellion. In 1861 J. P. enlisted in the service and served the cause he espoused faithfully until the final surrender. He clerked one year after his return home and then formed a partnership with John T. Hamblet in the mercantile business, remaining in the firm until 1882, when he sold out and engaged in the real-estate business. He was first married to Lucy Bland, by whom he had three children, all deceased. Again he was married, taking for his second wife, Martha H. Hall. He is a member of the Masonic fraternity. His parents, Philip and Louisa (Brisco) Penn, were born in Prince Edward County, Va., and removed to Tennessee during the early history of that State. Here the father's death occurred, but the mother died in Woodruff County. To this couple were given ten children, five of whom are now living.

Capt. D. F. Price, a well-to-do planter residing near Snapps, was born in Prince Edward County, Va., November 21, 1841, and is a son of Nathaniel and Mary (Compton) Price, also Virginians of English-Irish descent, respectively, who spent their lives in their native State. The father was a tobacconist and farmer, and was a man who possessed sterling traits of character well worthy the emulation of all. His father was born in Ireland, but at an early day came to America, and took part in the War of 1812, rising to the rank of captain. Capt. D. F. Price was one of eight children, only four of whom are now living: Harry, D. F., Josie and Cora. The subject of this memoir was reared and educated in Virginia, and remained with his father until the latter's death. Upon reaching the age of eighteen years he left home and went to Memphis, Tenn., and worked for a cotton firm in that city until 1861, when he dropped his work and enlisted in Company A, Fourth Tennessee Infantry, and served until the surrender, holding the rank of captain of his company after the battle of Smithville, N. C. At the battle of Shiloh he was wounded in the right leg by a gunshot, but fully recovered after a short furlough home. He received two other slight wounds which were of not much importance, and after the war he returned to Tennessee, and commenced farming in Gibson County, continuing until 1869, at which time he went to Fayette County, where he followed the same occupation for two years. In January, 1871, he came to Woodruff County, Ark., and now owns an excellent farm of 120 acres, with seventy-five acres under cultivation, which he devotes to the cultivation of cotton and corn. Miss A. F. Corley (a daughter of C. C. Corley), became his wife in 1872, and by her he has a family of four children: Corley G., Arthur, Cora and Otis. Mrs. Price is a consistent member of the Methodist Episcopal Church.

W. A. Reed, prosperous and exceedingly popular, takes his place in the corps of Woodruff County's most eminent business men as one of the oldest merchants of Lone Grove. He is a native of Tennessee, being born in Murfreesboro in 1856. His father, John W. Reed, was of Scotch descent, born about 1831. He was of Virginia origin, but at the time of his death, in 1861, was a prosperous mechanic in Tennessee. In 1854 he was married to Miss Annie E. Alexander, and to them two children were born: W. A. and Ada W. (now deceased). Mrs. Reed was again married in 1863 to J. W. Bruster, of Nashville. Mrs. Bruster was a member of the Methodist Episcopal Church, and died in 1883. W. A. Reed, the subject of this memoir, immigrated from Tennessee to this State in 1871, locating in this county. For the first four years he rented land and farmed, meeting with great success. His next business venture was a clerkship for four years with B. F. Hall, at the end of which time he formed a partnership with Mr. Hall, the firm being known as Hall & Reed. After a few years (about four) Mr. Reed purchased Mr. Hall's interest, and since then has conducted the business on his own responsibility. His trade is a very good one, his yearly sales amounting to quite a snug sum. In the year of 1879 Mr. Reed was married to Miss Ellen M. Land, a daughter of Mr. and Mrs. Abram Land, of this county. To this marriage four children have been born: Florence M., Kenneth A., William Logan and Douglass A. (deceased). In secret societies Mr. Reed affiliates with the K. of H., and although a young man is counted among the foremost and is one of the most successful merchants in the village. He advocates and donates liberally to all public enterprises, such as schools, churches, etc., and is respected and esteemed by all. He has a fine residence, and the sociability of himself and wife make his home a favorite place of entertainment in the community.

John W. Revel, conceded to be a very popular and prosperous planter, and one of, if not the best in the county of his adoption, was born in Northampton County, N. C., February 1, 1832, and is a son of Louis and Martha (Outland) Revel, who were of English-Dutch descent, and natives of North Carolina. They immigrated to the State of Tennessee about the year 1844, and located in Shelby County, living here until their deaths, the

mother dying in 1868 and the father in 1870. John W. is the eldest son of eleven children, and from the time he was twelve years of age was a resident of Tennessee. When at the outbreak of the Rebellion he, with all the ardor and enthusiasm of youth, espoused the Southern cause and enlisted in Company A, Eighteenth Mississippi Cavalry, but was subsequently captured, and taken to Alton, thence to Fort Delaware, being confined in prison some twenty months. After being discharged, he came home, and in December, 1865, determined to seek his fortune, turned his face farther westward and accordingly settled in Woodruff County, Ark., where he rented land for three years, and tilled the soil. In 1869 he purchased a portion of the farm which he now owns, and which then had but few improvements; adding to this from time to time, he now owns 1,200 acres, having about 550 of these cultivated and fairly improved. He has labored hard to make his farm one of the best in the county, and judging from its appearance and the amount realized from it every year, he has admirably succeeded. His land is exceedingly fertile, and about 400 acres is devoted entirely to the cultivation of cotton. He has been married three times. In 1868 he married Abbie Brown, having by her one child, now deceased, and in 1873 he wedded Katie Didlake, she being the mother of one child, also deceased. He married his third wife, Mary L. Miller, in 1882, and by her has a son, John W., Jr. Mrs. Revel is a member of the Methodist Episcopal Church, and in his political views Mr. Revel is a Democrat.

Edmond Roddy, sheriff and collector, Augusta, Ark. Mr. Roddy is now filling his third term as sheriff and collector of Woodruff County, and no man ever held the position who was better fitted to discharge the duties connected with it than he. He was born in this county (then Jackson) on November 11, 1850, and is the son of Thomas B. and Elizabeth R. (Erwin) Roddy, the father a native of Spartanburg District, S. C., born in 1821, and the mother a native of North Carolina. The parents were married in Jackson County, Ark. Thomas B. Roddy was left an orphan when very young, both his parents dying the same day of

20

some malignant disease, and he came with an uncle to Tennessee from his native State. In 1833 he came to Jackson County, Ark., located about four miles east of Augusta, entered a tract of land in the woods and cut and hewed logs to make a cabin. Here he opened a farm and tilled the soil for a number of years. He then purchased a second farm in the woods, three miles north of Augusta, cleared it and resided there until May, 1887, when his death occurred. The mother died in 1858. There are only two children of this marriage: Edmond and Morgan A. The subject of our sketch was reared to agricultural pursuits, and received his education in the log school-house of pioneer times. He remained on the farm until 1874, when he hired to W. P. Campbell, then clerk of the circuit court, now clerk of the supreme court of the State, and remained with him until his election to the office of sheriff in 1878. He served one term and was defeated on a second run. He purchased a farm, moved on it, and there remained for three years. In 1886 he was re-elected to the office of sheriff and again elected in 1888. He owns 500 acres of land, and has 300 acres under cultivation. He also ownes a homestead of twenty-five acres in Augusta. He was married on February 12, 1877, to Miss Beatrice Skinner. Mr. Roddy is a prominent political worker, and is a first-class citizen. He is a member of Knights of Honor, and Mrs. Roddy is a member of the Methodist Episcopal Church. Mr. Roddy spent one year at the Gulf of Mexico, on account of a slight misunderstanding between himself and Powell Clayton's militia, occurring in 1868 and 1869.

Ed. Scales, a successful merchant of McCrory, is a native of Tennessee, having been born in Tipton County, in 1855. His father, Dr. James Scales, was also of Tennessee origin, a prominent physician in that State. He attended medical lectures in Louisville, Ky., and Philadelphia, Penn., and after graduating, was recognized as one of the shining lights of his profession. In 1860 he immigrated to Arkansas, locating in Woodruff County, where he met with great success, building up a large and esteemed practice. In 1854 Dr. Scales

was married to Miss Jennie Whitner, and by her became the father of six children: Ed., Alice (wife of Dr. James, of Cotton Plant), Pleasant, Walter, Cornelius and Augustus. Dr. Scales purchased 160 acres of land on his arrival in the county, which has been increased to 1,200 acres. He is a member in high standing of the Masonic order, and an influential, enterprising citizen. Mrs. Scales died in 1878. Ed. Scales began life for himself in 1878, at that time engaging in mercantile business, in De View, but is now located at McCrory, in the same branch of trade, the firm name being Crosby & Scales. They have a liberal patronage, and enjoy an average annual patronage of about $40,000. In 1881 Mr. Scales was united in marriage with Miss Rebie Johnson, the daughter of Stephen Johnson and wife, of North Mississippi. To this union two children were born: Edwin (now deceased) and James. Mr. Scales belongs to the K. of H. and Douglass Lodge No. 56, K. of P. He is deemed one of the progressive merchants and citizens of McCrory, and an affable and courteous gentleman.

John Shearer. Although America can not claim Mr. Shearer as one of her native-born citizens, De View proudly and justly claims him as one of her most prosperous merchants. He is a native of "Bonny Scotland," his birth occurring in Edinburgh in 1840. His father, John Shearer, Sr., first saw the light of day in the highlands of Scotland in the year 1815. His occupation was that of a ship carpenter, which he followed for a livelihood until his death, in 1852, on board a ship that was wrecked. He was married in 1840 to Miss Jane Heslop, and by her became the father of one child, John, Jr., the subject of this sketch. John Shearer, Jr., sailed from Scotland in 1844, landing in New York, and went from there directly to Montreal, Canada, where he remained twelve years, then traveled through several States and came to Arkansas in 1860, located in this county, and in 1870 he was united in marriage with Miss Hettie E. Brown, by whom he had five children, only one of them now living, Ruth. Mrs. Shearer was born in Lauderdale County, Ala., in 1852, and came with her parents to Arkansas, from Tennessee, in

1861. Her father, Mr. Brown, was born in North Carolina, in 1820, and her mother owes her nativity to Franklin County, Tenn., where her birth occurred in 1822. Mr. and Mrs. Brown were married in 1844, and to them a family of eight children were born: Andrew J., William, Abigail, Hettie and Lena, the others having died in infancy. Mr. Brown died in 1879, and his wife in 1865, both dying in Augusta, Ark. They were members in good standing in the Methodist Episcopal Church. When John Shearer, Jr., first came to this State, he worked for $1 per day on the White River levee, then was employed by a Mr. Allen, a blacksmith of Augusta, this county. Subsequently he worked for Dr. Leach as chore boy and errand boy, and later for James Ferguson as a farm hand on his plantation on Cache River. At the breaking out of the late war Mr. Shearer, Jr., enlisted in the artillery service, under Capt. McGowen, of Jacksonport, Ark., in 1861. He participated in all the principal engagements, serving with great bravery until the final surrender. At the close of the war he found himself penniless and almost destitute of clothing. An old boot leg served him for shoes, a crownless hat sheltered (?) his head from the weather, and the few articles that comprised his clothing were all in rags; he was indeed a picture of despair. But possessing an unbounded amount of pluck and energy he came out all right, and in the year of 1869 he was able to engage in farming on a small scale, in connection with a mercantile business at White Church. In 1873 he came to De View and again embarked in the mercantile business with a stock invoicing about $8,000, also has a store at McCrory, Ark., of about the same value. His career is an illustration of what can be accomplished by perseverance and determination of purpose. To-day he stands one of the wealthiest men in the county. He owns 880 acres of land with 260 cultivated, and owns real estate valued at $3,000, in McCrory, and $1,500 worth of property in De View. This he has accumulated by his own individual efforts, and all since the war. Mr. Shearer is a member of Lodge No. 45, F. & A. M., being initiated into that order in 1867, Chapter 37, Council 22, at Augusta, and

Hugh De Payne Commandery No. 1, at Little Rock. He also belongs to the K. of H. and K. & L. of H., of De View. Politically he is a Democrat, and though a stanch adherent to his party, is not a political enthusiast. He stands high in this community, both socially and financially, and this sketch shows him to be, what he certainly is, a shrewd financier. Mrs. Shearer is a favorite in social circles, entertains largely in her easy, graceful manner, and is an earnest worker in the Methodist Episcopal Church, to which she belongs.

D. P. Shoup, merchant, Augusta, Ark. Among the enterprising business establishments of Augusta, whose operations are worthy of record, is that of Mr. Shoup, who is not only deeply interested in mercantile pursuits, but is also one of the first-class farmers of the county. He was born in Bedford County, Penn., on August 7, 1851, and came to Woodruff County, Ark., with his parents in infancy. He was reared in Yell County of this State and received a fair education. In 1867 he went north and traveled to different points; but, finally, in 1875, located in Woodruff County, Ark., where he was engaged in agricultural pursuits for four years. In 1880 he embarked in the mercantile business and has since continued this in connection with agricultural pursuits. He owns about 1,400 acres of land, has about 700 acres under cultivation and raises a vast amount of cotton. He was married, on January 7, 1875, to Miss Elva Gulic, a native of Mississippi, and the fruits of this union are four living children: Freddie, Ida, Ruby and Charlie. Mr. Shoup is a member of the Masonic fraternity, Royal Arch, K. of H. and K. & L. of H. He has also held the position of city alderman. He is the second of three living children (William A., Daniel P. and Joseph W.) born to the union of Jonathan T. and Virginia (Pound) Shoup, natives of Pennsylvania and Mississippi, respectively. The parents were married in Pike County, Mississippi, whither the father had gone when a young man, and he died at Danville, Yell County, Ark., in 1860. His wife died in 1859. The father was a merchant and carried on this business in different places. He came to Arkansas in about 1851. He had two brothers, Abraham and Henry, who were born in the Keystone State. They removed to the State of Ohio, and since that time has lost all trace of them. They were owners of considerable property which was left them.

L. D. Snapp is one of the thoroughly reliable and upright business men of Woodruff County, and is said to be one of the largest and most successful real-estate owners in the county, he owning 3,000 acres with 1,000 acres under cultivation. On this property are thirty-five tenement houses, all occupied, and his own private residence, a very handsome structure, also a large cotton-gin which has a capacity of twenty-five bales a day. He has done more than any other one man in developing the county; and it is through his influence that a post-office has been established bearing his name, and at this place he has a general mercantile establishment which nets him a fair annual income. He is a man of exceptionally fine character, and noted for his exceeding liberality, always being ready to assist the poor and distressed. His birth occurred in Taney County, Mo., April 22, 1842, and here he received the greater part of his education and rearing. He abandoned farm work at the outbreak of the Rebellion to take up the weapons of warfare in defense of his country, and in 1861 enlisted in Company E, Third Missouri Cavalry, serving until June 27, 1865. He was promoted to the rank of first lieutenant of the company, meriting it by his bravery and was in all the engagements of the Trans-Mississippi Department. Two brothers fought with him in the army and one was killed at the battle of Glasgow. After the proclamation of peace Mr. Snapp returned to Missouri and in the fall of 1866 came to Woodruff County, Ark., where he has since made his home. He was married on March 4, 1869, to Miss Mary H. Luckenbill, by whom he has had a family of ten children, five now living: James C., Harry, Walter, Myrtle and Pearl. The parents of our subject, Harrison G. and Emily D. (Parry) Snapp, were born in East Tennessee, and in 1838 moved to Missouri, where they died. Of a large family of children born to them four only are now living.

Francis M. Spradlin is a planter of White River Township, whose operations are extensive and lucrative. Born in Coweta County, Ga., October 22, 1830, he is the son of David and Sarah (Stone) Spradlin, also natives of Georgia. In the year 1845 Mr. and Mrs. Spradlin immigrated to Arkansas, and located in what is now Woodruff County near White Church, making one of the first entries of land in this part of the State. There were no improvements whatever on the land, and they camped out until they could build, their home for many years being a little log-cabin covered with clap-boards. Of the family of eleven children born to them only four are now living: Francis M., Missouri, William I. and Susan Hariston. Mr. Spradlin was a quiet, unassuming man, and liberal in his contributions, but many of his generous deeds were never known to the outside world. His death in 1856 was lamented by all who knew him. Mrs. Spradlin only survived her husband two years. Francis M. Spradlin was fourteen years old when he came to Arkansas, and the education that he received was given him in Georgia, as there were no schools in this county at that time. His youthful days were spent in helping to clear away the forest of his parents' new home, and in 1861 he left the quiet monotony of the old homestead to enlist in Company E, Col. Gause's regiment, serving until the final surrender. He has resided on the farm where he now lives for twenty-eight years, and his recitals of the many inconveniences and privations endured years ago, and the improvements up to the present day, sound almost incredulous. In this place are 160 acres of land highly cultivated, and he also has an interest in a tract of 240 acres partially improved. In 1872 Mr. Spradlin erected a cotton-gin, which was run with horse-power until 1885, after which he has put in an eighteen-horse-power engine, and has successfully conducted it since that time. Mr. Spradlin was first married in 1857 to Miss Amanda Hubbard, and the second time to Josephine Scott, in 1863. His third wife was Miss Martha Thomas, by whom he has one child living, Columbus. Mr. Spradlin was married in 1872 to Miss Sarah Childress, and to their union two children were born: Norella and Wyatt. Mr. Spradlin is a member of the Baptist Church, and has served as magistrate for fourteen years. He is a prosperous and well-to-do farmer, and is worthy the respect and esteem shown him by the entire community.

Hon. T. E. Stanley, attorney at law, Augusta, Ark. Every life has a history of its own, and, although in appearance it may seem to possess little to distinguish it from others, yet the political career and experience of Mr. Stanley, as well as his popularity in his profession, have contributed to give him a wide and popular acquaintance with nearly every individual of Woodruff County and throughout the State, if not personally, then by name. Mr. Stanley was born in Lawrence County, Ala., on October 15, 1844, and is a son of Joseph H. and Maria L. (Hill) Stanley, the former a native of North Carolina and the latter of Virginia, and both of Scotch origin. The father was a planter and immigrated from North Carolina to Alabama in about 1823. He died in Courtland, that State, in 1852, and his wife died in 1871. The paternal grandfather, Jonathan Stanley, was killed near Corinth, Miss., by a robber. Hon. T. E. Stanley is the only one living of three children born to his parents. He was reared and educated in his native State, and there. remained until the breaking out of the war when, in June, 1861, he enlisted in the Sixteenth Alabama Infantry, and served until May, 1865. Previous to the war he attended school at La Grange Military Academy, and was but sixteen years of age when he enlisted. Although he entered the army as a private he left the ranks as a lieutenant. On the retreat from Corinth in May, 1862, he was wounded by a gunshot through the left hand, was wounded the second time at Murfreesboro in the hip, and received a third wound at Chickamauga, where his right foot was almost crushed to pieces. He was a boy of great nerve and will-power, hardly knew what it was to fear, and his career as a soldier is one of honor and renown. He was in all the principal engagements of the Western army, and at the close of the war he returned home, where he followed agricultural pursuits until 1869. In 1870 he entered Cumberland University, at Lebanon, Tenn., and after passing a strict examination, graduated from the Law Department in 1872. The same year he came to Augusta, opened an office, and in 1876 was elected to the legislature, serving three consecutive terms. He was also a delegate to the Cincinnati convention which nominated Hancock and English, and was brought into the race before the Democratic convention for Governor in 1882. He is a prominent man and a bright ornament to the legal profession. He is the owner of about 1,400 acres of land in Woodruff County, with about 900 acres under cultivation; also owning some real estate in Alabama. Mr. Stanley was married in May, 1873, to Miss Laura McCurdy, a native of Augusta, Ark., and the fruits of this union have been three living children: Louise, Thomas E., Jr., and Joseph H.

Capt. James A. Stoker, pre-eminent among the farmers of Barnes Township, was born in Stanly County, N. C., in 1831, and is the son of David H. and Sarah (Coleman) Stoker. Mr. Stoker and wife were natives of North Carolina, where he spent his life, and was killed in that State in 1864. He was a wealthy farmer, sheriff for fourteen years, and captain of State militia for a number of years. He organized a regiment for the Mexican War, but was not actively engaged in it himself. He was a son of Allen Stoker, who was born in Rowan County, and died in Davie County, same State, a farmer, as well as a soldier in one of the early wars. His father was a native of the "Emerald Isle." Mrs. Allen Stoker was a sister of Wade Hampton (Senator), thus making Capt. James Stoker a cousin of Senator Wade Hampton, United States senator from South Carolina. Grandfather Coleman was a farmer of Irish descent, and died in Stanly County, N. C. Mrs. Stoker, mother of James A. (Captain), died in Sebastian County, Ark., in 1868, a devoted member of the Baptist Church. Capt. James A. was the first in a family of five children, and was educated in the common schools of his native State. At the age of eighteen he went to Texas, but in 1849 took passage on a steamer at New York for California, here spending four years as an employe in the mines of that State. He then returned to North Carolina, and in 1853 was united in marriage with Frances, daughter of Akrela and Lucinda Griffin, of North Carolina. To this union five children were born: Robert W., Ira, Albert, Hattie (deceased) and Della. Capt. Stoker moved to Newton County, Mo., in 1856, and there formed the first company of Confederate troops of regulars, organized in that county (Company A). He was in command of the company about eighteen months, and fought in numerous battles, among them being Oak Hill, Richwoods, Lexington, Pea Ridge, etc. At the battle of Oak Hill he entered the fray with 118 men, but after the fighting ceased, found only eleven were left of that gallant 118. After eighteen months of service, and one without a blemish on his record as a soldier, he resigned, and subsequently joined Col. Tom Livingston's Partisan Rangers. He served as a member of this staff until the death of the Colonel, which occurred in Missouri in the latter part of 1864. Capt. Stoker then returned to Arkansas, but soon after Gen. Price made the request that he act as special guide for his advance guard, during his raid through Missouri and Kansas, which he did and surrendered 200 men at Forsyth, Mo., at the close of the war. His family were living in Arkansas during the hostilities, but in 1865 he moved to Jackson County, and in 1867 moved to Central America. A short residence in the latter place proved to the Captain that Arkansas was more to his taste, so he returned to this State, settling in Woodruff County, where he has since resided. He has a fine farm of 400 acres, with 140 under the plow, and keeps himself well posted on all subjects relative to the improvments of the day, and is in every respect a wide-awake, enterprising farmer and citizen. In his political views Capt. Stoker is a Democrat, and voted for Buchanan. Mrs. Stoker is a member of good standing in the Christian Church, and is respected and esteemed by all who know her, as is also her husband. One episode worthy of mention in the Captain's life, and which will be of interest to his numerous friends, is that of the Pool expedition, in 1857. He in company with 135 men, all, except himself, from Newton County, Mo., under command of J. P. Ogden, and Mr. Pool acting as guide, started out to explore the west and northwest of the Wichita Mountains in search of the golden treasures supposed to be hidden in these

mountains. Going in the vicinity of the Bluestone Park, they went southwest until they reached the Pigist River, then went down into New Mexico. While en route the guide related to the company that, while lost in the vicinity of these mountains, in 1854, he discovered large deposits of gold. He was lost eight months, but was never able to find his way back to where he supposed he had discovered the vein. He had on his person some nuggets of gold. This party was out sixty or seventy days.

E. G. Thompson, of the firm of Thompson & Gregory, general merchants, Augusta, Ark. Prominent among the mercantile resources of the town of Augusta is the dry-goods trade. It is thoroughly representative in its character, being conducted with much ability and success. Foremost among those engaged in it here are Messrs. Thompson & Gregory, who have won the confidence and respect of the public by their honest, upright dealing. Mr. Thompson is a native of Lewis County, Mo., born September 1, 1850, and is the son of A. M. and Helen (Waters) Thompson, natives of the "Old Dominion." The father was a tiller of the soil, and immigrated to Missouri with his parents at quite an early day, and died on the old homestead in Lewis County. The mother is still living on the home place. E. G. Thompson is the youngest of four sons born to his parents. When seventeen years of age he entered La Grange College, Missouri, and graduated from that institution in the class of 1871. In October of the same year he came to Augusta, Ark., studied law and was admitted to the bar in 1872, but never practiced. One year later he engaged in the real-estate and banker's business, which he has since carried on. He is agent for a great deal of land besides being the owner of about 15,000 acres of his own, with a vast amount under cultivation. He entered the mercantile business in 1883, under the present title, and has since continued. They carry an immense stock of goods and do a heavy business at all their stores, it being probably the largest business firm in Woodruff County. Mr. Thompson is a thorough business man, as is also his partner. They do a considerable cotton trade, and besides their store at Augusta also have establishments at Grays and Lone Grove. Mr. Thompson was married in 1872 to Miss Fannie Gregory, a sister of his partner. They have three living children: Leah C., Helen M. and Lottie L. Two children are deceased. Mr. Thompson is a member of the Masonic fraternity and the K. of H. and is a very prominent man.

Judge William T. Trice is a man well versed in the lore of his chosen profession, and fully competent to discharge the duties to which he has been elected, that of judge of county and probate court of Woodruff County. He is a native of Arkansas, and first saw the light of day in Woodruff County, May 17, 1859, being the son of Judge Tazewell W. and Martha A. (Dunlap) Trice. Judge Trice, Sr., was born in Virginia in 1812, and his wife in Limestone County, Ala., in 1827. They were married in Mississippi in 1854, and came to Woodruff County in 1858, settling in Freeman Township, on unimproved land, where the remainder of Mr. Trice's life was spent. He was a man of an excellent English education, and began practicing as an attorney at twenty-five years of age. He was a probate judge in Alabama four years, and in 1872 was elected county and probate judge; but this election did not amount to anything, he being counted out with the rest of the ticket. He was a man of many accomplishments, and well qualified to fill the positions that he did so successfully. He owned a fine farm of 600 acres, on which he was residing at the time of his death, in December, 1873. The A. F. & A. M., Richmond Lodge, at Cotton Plant, counted him as one of its members for many years. He was the son of William A. Trice, who was born in England, and came to America when a young man, first locating in Virginia, but afterward immigrated to Alabama, where he was living at the time of his death as a successful farmer. Mrs. Trice was a daughter of John Dunlap, a prosperous farmer, who died in Alabama. His parents were born in Ireland. Mrs. Trice is now living, and for a great many years has been a member of the Methodist Church. Judge William T. Trice, the subject of this sketch, is the fourth in a family

of six children, all residing in Woodruff County, and, with the exception of one, all married. Judge William T. was reared to farm life, receiving a good common-school education, and at the age of eighteen began the study of law, and as the result of his untiring efforts in that direction was his admission to the bar, in 1882, by Judge J. N. Cypert, since which time he has practiced with great success, being now a successful attorney of Woodruff County. In January, 1884, Judge Trice was united in marriage with Minnie C., daughter of Capt. John R. and Elizabeth Shelton. Mr. Shelton was born in Tennessee, but came to Arkansas (Woodruff County) in 1854, where he occupied himself with farming. He was a soldier in the Confederate army, and received the title of captain, his death occurring in 1881. Mrs. Shelton is still living, and belongs to the Methodist Church, as did her husband. Mrs. Trice was born in 1864. To Judge and Mrs. Trice two sons have been born, both still living. Judge Trice lived on a farm until 1887, then came to Cotton Plant, where he has a fine residence. His farm in Freeman Township is second to none of its size in the county. Its extent is 180 acres, with 100 under cultivation. This farm was obtained largely by his own efforts, but partially by inheritance. Judge Trice was justice of the peace two years, from 1884 to 1886, and in 1888 was elected county and probate judge, which position he filled with honor and distinction. He is a member of the K. & L. of H., Aurora Lodge, at Cotton Plant, No. 1314, in which he is present Protector, and of the K. of P., at Cotton Plant, Lodge No. 94, is Master of Finance. He is a strong Democrat, and voted for Hancock in 1880. Himself and wife belong to the Methodist Church, in which he is steward.

P. A. Vaughan, of Howell, Woodruff County, Ark., is a native of Virginia, his birth occurring in Petersburg, in 1825. He is one of thirteen children born to Thomas and Martha P. (Rivers) Vaughan, only five of whom survive: P. A., John F., Virginia (the wife of S. Gardner, of Memphis, Tenn.), Minerva and Robert. Mr. Vaughan served in the War of 1812, and died in Fayette County, Tenn., in 1838, his wife surviving him until 1843.

P. A. Vaughan was united in matrimony with Miss Mary Whitmore, of Fayette County, Tenn., in 1849. She died in 1864, having borne seven children only two now living: John T. and Charles E. In 1866 Mr. Vaughan was married to Miss Sallie Clark, daughter of Mr. and Mrs. Robert P. Clark, of Louisiana, and eight children have blessed this happy marriage, four boys and four girls, five of whom are alive: Roberta (now Mrs. Joel York), Augusta C., Minnie, Peter A., Jr. and Martha P. Mr. Vaughan served in the late war under Capt. W. F. Cody, enlisting in 1862, and remaining on the field of action until the final surrender. After the cessation of hostilities he returned home and engaged in farming, which occupation he is still pursuing. The life of this worthy citizen presents an excellent example of what may be accomplished by energetic application and determination, for he started with comparatively nothing, and is now the possessor of 1,500 acres of land, with 500 under cultivation, being to-day one of the "solid" men, financially, of the county. He immigrated from Tennessee to this State in 1850, and purchased a small, insignificant tract of land lying in the heart of a forest, built a log-house, and began clearing what is now one of the finest farms in the county. Mr. Vaughan owns the only brick farmhouse here, the bricks for which were burned by him, so he knows and can appreciate the labor requisite in that work. It is certainly an elegant home, and what is better, a hospitable one, the friend or stranger alike receiving a hearty welcome by Mr. Vaughan and his estimable wife. The latter is a member of the Methodist Episcopal Church.

William S. Waide, an agriculturist and stock raiser of considerable prominence, is the son of William and Mary (Ray) Waide, of Hickman County, Ky., nativity, being born in 1845, and one of four children (one son and three daughters). William Waide, Sr., was born in Virginia and his wife in Kentucky. Their deaths occurred in 1846 and 1863, respectively. After Mr. Waide's death in Kentucky, the family came to Woodruff County, and here Mrs. Waide ended her days, after a widowhood of seventeen years. The subject of this sketch received but a meager education, as the schools in his early boyhood days were very limited; sometimes a few weeks only would be the extent of his schooling for the year. Mr. Waide and a sister are the only surviving members of the family, and since 1861 Woodruff County has been his home. In 1862 he joined Company G, Eighteenth Arkansas Infantry, which was stationed east of the Mississippi river until the fall of Port Hudson, when he was captured and held a prisoner for eight days. He was then paroled, came home and finished his war career in Arkansas and Missouri, being with Price in his raid through Missouri, Kansas, etc., and finally surrendered at Wittsburg, in May, 1865. After the war he resumed his occupation of farming, and in March, 1871, he was united in marriage to Miss Emma Riddle, who was born in North Carolina, and the daughter of John and Cely Riddle. Mrs. Waide's parents came to what is now Woodruff County when she was only six months old (1850). Mr. Riddle was a justice of the peace some years, and a soldier in the Confederate army, being captured and dying a prisoner in Alton, Ill., during the war. Mrs. Riddle died in 1853, and was a life-long member of the Methodist Church. To Mr. Waide's marriage four children have been born, three sons and one daughter. In 1875 he settled in the woods on 360 acres of land, three miles east of Howell's Station, and since clearing the land has got one of the finest farms in that portion of the county, and all due to his own efforts. Mr. Waide is largely engaged in stock raising, and is a hard-working, ambitious farmer and citizen, lending his hearty support to all worthy movements for the advancement of the country. He is a Democrat in his political views, voting the Seymour ticket in 1868. He is a member of the I. O. O. F. and K. of H. at Augusta. Mrs. Waide is a communicant of the Baptist Church.

Dr. J. W. Westmoreland, in his connection with the professional affairs of White County, as a practicing physician and surgeon, located at Cotton Plant, has attained to well-deserved prominence. He is a native of Tennessee, and was born in Giles County, in 1838, being the son of Laborne and Nancy (Neale) Westmoreland. The birth of these individuals occurred in Virginia in 1812, and South Carolina in 1807, respectively, and they were married in Giles County, Tenn., where their lives were spent, with the exception of two years in Mississippi. Mr. Westmoreland died in 1860, his wife surviving him four years. He was the son of Reuben Westmoreland, from Virginia, originally, and one of the early settlers of Tennessee, where he was residing at the time of his decease. He was a descendant of the family of Westmorelands who were numbered among the Virginia colonists from England. Grandfather Neale was born in Ireland, but came to America when a young man, and followed the occupation of farming, living at the time of his death in Giles County, Tenn. J. W. Westmoreland, the seventh in a family of twelve children, was reared with them to farm life, receiving such educational advantages as were to be had in that day. He began the study of medicine at the age of nineteen, and in 1859 was graduated from the University of Nashville, Tenn. Subsequent to his graduation he practiced in Giles County, for two years, moving thence to Woodruff County, Ark., from which locality, after a residence of seven years, he went to Alabama. In 1883 the Doctor returned to Arkansas, settling in Cotton Plant, where he has since lived. In 1862 he joined Hooper's Second Company of Arkansas Troops as quartermaster, but soon after was detailed to furnish supplies until the close of the war. In March of 1859, Dr. Westmoreland was united in marriage with Mary A. Deaver, a daughter of James M. and Mary S. Deaver, of Giles County. Her father died in Giles County, Tenn., but his wife is now living in Woodruff County. To the Doctor's union two bright children have been born, which inherit the love of study from their father, and the charming disposition of the mother. Dr. Westmoreland owns 160 acres of land seven miles from Cotton Plant, which is in a fine state of cultivation. For some years he was engaged in the mercantile business in Alabama, and for several years in the drug business at Cotton Plant. In his political views he sides with the Democrats, having voted for Breckenridge in 1860. He is a member of Lodge

No. 3367, K. of H. at Cotton Plant, and also the I. O. O. F. The Doctor has met with several reverses, which resulted in financial losses, but by his untiring determination and perseverance, it is easy to see that he is not one to be discouraged or kept down.

J. C. Widener is a prosperous planter living near Augusta, and is the owner of a fine farm of 200 acres, which have been carefully tilled, and all the buildings put in good repair. This farm has been his home for the past thirty years, and he now has 100 acres of land under cultivation, which is devoted principally to the raising of such commodities as cotton and corn. Our subject was born in Gwinnett County, Ga., March 30, 1840, and is a son of Littleton and Nancy (House) Widener, both of whom were born in the "Palmetto State." In the year 1857 they immigrated to Woodruff County, Ark., and here spent their declining years. The father was a blacksmith and wagon maker by trade. To these parents were given eight children, three of whom are now living, J. C. Widener being the eldest. He was reared in Gordon County, Ga., and came with his parents to Arkansas, enlisting from this State in 1861, in Company B, Eighth Arkansas Infantry, and was but a short time in service. After learning the mechanic's trade he worked in machine shops for five years, assisting in making supplies for the army. Since the termination of the great struggle he has resided in Woodruff County, excepting the six years spent in Texas. He was married in 1866, to Lucinda C. Harris, a native of Georgia, and by her has had two children, both of whom are deceased. During the past fall Death claimed his estimable wife.

Dr. J. E. Woods, physician and surgeon, Augusta, Ark. Dr. Woods owes his nativity to Livingston County, Ky., where his birth occurred March 5, 1843, and is the son of Henry W. and Nellie (Hodge) Woods, both natives of Kentucky. The grandparents were from Virginia, and were early settlers of Kentucky. Mr. and Mrs. Woods passed their last days in their native State. The father was a successful agriculturist, and this vocation followed up to the time of his death. Of their large family of children, seven are now living, and Dr. J. E. Woods is the third eldest child living. He was reared and received a fair education in Livingston County, remained on the farm until eighteen years of age, and then began the study of medicine at Marion, Ky. He then entered the University of Louisville Medical College, and attended first course of lectures at that institution in 1863. He then graduated at Long Island College, Brooklyn, N. Y., in 1864, after which he began practicing at his home in Kentucky. In September, 1865, he came to Augusta, Ark., began practicing, and is the oldest practitioner in that place. He is a very successful physician; is of pleasing address and most agreeable manners, possessed of a mind clear, penetrating and comprehensive, thoroughly posted in his profession, and a practitioner of decided merit. He has been president of the Woodruff County Medical Society and delegate of the National American Medical Convention from Arkansas. He is a member of the board of examining physicians of the county, and a prominent citizen. He was married April 24, 1866, to Miss Clara T. McCurdy, a native of St. Francis County, Ark., where she was reared. Four children were the result of this union: Nellie, Harry M., Kitty and Roscoe. Dr. Woods is an Odd Fellow and a Knight of Honor. Mrs. Woods is a member of the Presbyterian Church. Her father, Samuel M. McCurdy, was a very brilliant and prominent attorney in his day, and occupied positions of influence.

CHAPTER XVII.

CROSS COUNTY—ACT OF FORMATION—EARLY AND SUBSEQUENT SETTLEMENTS—NAMES OF PIONEERS—
ORIGIN OF COUNTY NAME—SEATS OF JUSTICE—JUDICIAL TRANSACTIONS—BUILDINGS FOR PUBLIC
USE—SITUATION, BOUNDARY AND AREA—SURFACE DESCRIPTION—MUNICIPALITIES—COURT
AFFAIRS AND BENCH AND BAR—NOTED CASES—ECCLESIASTICAL HISTORY—SCHOOLS
—LIST OF OFFICIALS—SECRET SOCIETIES—POLITICAL STATUS—RAIL-
ROADS—GENERAL DEVELOPMENT—FAMILY RECORD.

When the summer harvest was gather'd in,
And the sheaf of the gleaner grew white and thin,
And the ploughshare was in its furrow left,
Where the stubble land had been lately cleft.—*Longfellow.*

CROSS County, Ark., traces its beginning to an act of the General Assembly passed in November, 1862, entitled, "An act to establish the county of Cross."

Section 2 of that act reads as follows: "All that portion of the counties of Poinsett, St. Francis and Crittenden embraced within the following boundaries, viz.: Beginning at the northwest corner of Township 9 north, of Range 1 east; thence east to the northeast corner of Township 9 north, of Range 6 east; thence south to the southeast corner of Township 9 north, of Range 6 east; thence south to the southeast corner of Section 7, in Township 6 north, of Range 1 east; and thence north to the beginning, shall be and.the same is hereby created and established a separate county, called the county of Cross. The temporary seat of justice of said county of Cross, and until the same may be permanently located, shall be at Wittsburg in said county."

Thus was formed Cross County; and its history, though extending over but comparatively a few years, has been one of substantial growth and material advancement and progress.

The settlement of any locality is always of interest. What is now Cross County, then forming a part of Poinsett, Woodruff and Crittenden, was early settled by an exceptionally sterling class of citizens; in most cases men of means, who came to this section because here was offered an opportunity to secure sufficiently large tracts of fertile land, which promised to make a happy home, and independent fortune for the owners.

Among the earliest of known pioneers were the McCallisters, who settled near the present village of Vanndale; the Searcys, Tyers, Greenwoods, Hydricks, Neeleys, Halks and Stacys; all living here prior to 1840.

Since then the Hares, McClarans, Hintons, Crumps, Cross, Perrys, Shavers and Hamiltons, Warrens, Lewellens, Levesques, Jones, Magetts, Vanns, Barnes, Blocks, Deadarick, McFarrans, Applewhites, and the Rev. W. C. Malone have become permanent residents. Later others came to this section mostly between 1850 and 1860, and the numerous descendants of most of them are living in this county at the present day.

Samuel Filligan was unquestionably the earliest white settler in the present territory of Cross. He located on the waters of Cooper's Creek, about two miles northwest from Wittsburg and now five miles east of Wynne, on the Memphis branch of the St. Louis, Iron Mountain & Southern Railroad, as early as 1798. There he was living when N. Rightor located the following Spanish grants for William Russell in the year 1813: No. 494, 495, 498, 2379, 2382, 2383, 2374, 2375 and 2387. After Mr. Russell had completed his surveys, Mr. Filligan purchased eighty-four acres from the southwest part of Spanish grant No. 498, to complete his farm; this deed bears date July 25, 1820.

All these Spanish grants have been cleared and improved, and now comprise some of the finest farms in Cross County. Upon the authority of William M. Block, real-estate agent and abstractor of Cross County, it is learned that William Russell was choosing valuable lands to locate as early as 1808. All the property that he selected proved to be very valuable, and on one grant, 2379, Wittsburg was afterward built.

In 1851 Thomas P. Hare, then some twenty-four years of age, settled at about the center of Cross County, half a mile south of where Vanndale stands. This was wild and dense timber, and he cleared the land on which is a part of the village of Vanndale. His wife, who was a Miss Turbeville, and two children, accompanied him to this new home. On the day that they took possession a wild turkey sat in a tree immediately at hand, and watched, as if with apparent interest, the proceedings of these strange comers. Mr. Hare lived here thirty-two years, cleared over 200 acres of land, and died full of years and honors, in February, 1883.

Col. David C. Cross was for a long time a leading citizen of Cross County, having come from Western Tennessee to this locality about 1850. He bought a large tract of land in Cross' present limits, became a large land speculator, and at the outbreak of the civil strife owned some 85,000 acres

in Poinsett and what is now Cross County. When the mutterings of war were heard he was elected colonel of the Fifth Arkansas Regiment, but saw very little actual service, and on account of ill health soon returned to Cross County. In 1862 when the county of Cross was organized, it was given the name of Cross in his honor. The first seat of justice was located at a point on his land, he donating some fifty-three acres for a town site. This place was named Cleburne. Mr. Cross was a generous-spirited, influential gentleman of the old school, possessing exalted ideas, and is remembered by the citizens of the county which bears his name with pride.

Rev. R. G. Brittain, was born in Buncombe County, N. C., in 1826, and was reared to farm labor, till the age of eighteen years. During this time he attended the common schools and later at Washington College, near Jonesboro, Tenn., which school he left at the age of twenty-one years, and volunteered in the Mexican War. Serving for one year, he was in a battle fought near Saltillo, in 1846, and at the close of the war, returned and settled in Arkansas. He at once entered the ministry, and has been preaching in this State ever since, at the present time being in charge of the Harrisburg and Vanndale station. He was married in 1849, to Miss Sarah A. Bland, who died in 1863, leaving two children: James Henry and Mary Elizabeth. Mr. Brittain was married the second time in 1867, to Miss Mary K. Kellum, of Searcy, White County. To this union was born one child, John Thomas.

The county court, soon after the organization, ordered an election, to appoint commissioners to select a suitable location for the permanent seat of justice of the county. The election was held in the winter of 1862, and resulted in the choice of John Applewhite, William H. Barnes and John McElroy. The Civil War then raging so demoralized affairs generally in this region, that these commissioners made no report till July, 1865. Their accepted report, as spread upon the minutes of the county court record of July, 1865, is as follows:

"The commissioners, etc., have proceeded to

select a suitable site for the said county seat, and have located the same immediately in the center of said county of Cross, on a portion of the northeast quarter of Section 34, and a portion of the northwest quarter of Section 35, in Township 8 north, Range 3 east, of the fifth principal meridian; said lands being donated to this county, by one David C. Cross, as is hereinafter described, and it further appearing that said commissioners have proceeded to lay off the site so selected by them, into the form of a town, the same being divided into blocks, lots, streets and alleys; which town said commissioners have designated by the name of the town of Cleburne. And it further appearing to the court, that there is contained within, in the limits of said town, about fifty-two acres of land, and that the center block in said town, including the improvements thereon, and containing about one and three-fifths acres of land has been donated to the county by said Cross, as a public square, whereon may be erected a court house, and that the buildings now situated on the same are very suitable to be used as a court house and clerk's office for the time being, and it further appearing that said Cross has also donated to the county, in addition thereto, one-half of the remaining lots and blocks in said town, to be used and appropriated by the court in assisting to raise funds for the erection of permanent public buildings, etc.''

Cleburne soon became the seat of justice of Cross County, but the fond dream of building a town here was never realized. No public buildings were erected; the county clerk had his office at the residence of Col. Cross, and the various courts held their sessions in a tenant house upon the farm. It is literally a deserted village now, a few huts occupied by negroes, being all that is left to mark the place, where once Cross County transacted its judicial business and administered its laws.

At the May term of the county court in 1868, a petition signed by a majority of the taxable inhabitants of the county, praying the removal of the seat of justice of the county of Cross, and asking the court to order an election for the pur-

pose of electing three commissioners to decide a suitable site for the same, was presented and approved. The election which was ordered and held on Saturday, June 6, 1868, resulted in choosing J. M. Levesque, Louin Chappell and J. M. Landron as a committee to locate a site for the county seat. The report of this committee is spread upon the minutes of the August term, 1868, of the county court, and is substantially as follows: '' That the seat of justice, of the county of Cross, be at the town of Wittsburg, and that the deed of donation by Caroline M. Austell to said commissioners of Lots No. 201, 202, 205, 206, 299, 300, 301 and 302, in said town of Wittsburg, as a site for the court house of said county is accepted by the court, and ordered to be filed for record, and it is further ordered, that the contract and agreement of certain citizens of said town of Wittsburg, donating to the county the use and enjoyment of the new church and school-house, now in course of erection in Wittsburg as a court house, during the sittings of the terms of the various courts, until such time, as the county may erect a court house proper, be also accepted by this court, and filed and recorded; and said building is declared to be the court house of this county, and shall be the lawful place for the holding of said courts, until further ordered by this court.''

It will be seen that the citizens of Wittsburg contributed for the county's use a church and school-house. These structures served their purpose as public buildings during the entire time that Wittsburg was the seat of justice, as no court house was ever erected there.

On the completion of the Helena branch of the St. Louis, Iron Mountain & Southern Railroad through Cross County, Wittsburg began rapidly to decline as a place of importance, and it was soon thought advisable to again change the location of the county seat. Accordingly, at an election held in September, 1884, Vanndale was chosen by the people as the proper judicial center, and after being contested by Wynne, was formally declared to be the county seat in April, 1886.

During the twenty-seven years that has intervened since the formation of Cross County there has always been decided opposition to the various places in which the seat of justice has been located; consequently, the people have not been disposed to invest very extensively in permanent improvements. For this reason no court house was erected either at Cleburne or Wittsburg; but when the county seat was finally located at Vanndale, in 1884, it was done so under such flattering conditions that the people at once concluded that its infancy was over. Actions for the erection of a court house affording ample accommodation for the present, with a view also to the rapidly accumulating demands, were at once begun. County Judge S. S. Hare, in 1887, appointed Thomas B. Smith as building commissioner, who soon employed B. J. Bartlett as architect, and from his plans and designs an advertisement was published soliciting sealed proposals for the building's completion.

The lowest bid received was from Slagh & Powers, well-known contractors of Little Rock, to turn the completed building over to Cross County for $13,700. Upon proper bond being given, this bid was accepted, and in September, 1887, work was commenced. On the early date of May 24, 1888, the building was completed, and accepted by the commissioner, and Cross County at last had a court house in which it may justly take no little pride.

Occupying a large open space in the center of the town, its beautiful proportions and symmetrical lines at once attract the observer. It is a two-story structure, with high basement, and a commanding tower built of brick, with stone trimmings, and in size is 50x58 feet. The lower floor is devoted to offices for the various county officials; these rooms are large and commodious, and fitted and furnished with all necessary appointments. On this floor also is a fire-proof vault, for the reception of the county books and records. The upper story is wholly appropriated to court uses, the large court room being conveniently and tastily furnished and trimmed, with everything that its purpose may require. Indeed, a personal examination shows nothing wanting in any essential detail throughout the building.

Few counties in Arkansas can boast of a better

or more convenient court house; none of one more economically and honestly constructed.

The county will always be under great obligation to Judge Hare for frugality, and to Commissioner Smith for business perception and close attention to details, while the architect's work stands as a lasting memento to his profession, and the completed edifice a credit to the builder's skill.

The county also owns a jail, situated at Wittsburg. It was erected several years ago, but is now in bad repair. To the credit of Cross County, however, be it said that but little use is manifested for this building, and it stands almost a wreck of other times—lonely, tenantless and forsaken.

Cross County is located in the eastern part of the State, and is bounded on the north by Poinsett, east by Crittenden, south by St. Francis and west by Woodruff and Jackson Counties. It contains an area of 600 square miles, or 384,000 acres, of which about one-thirtieth is in a state of cultivation. The St. Francis River runs from north to south through the eastern part, and is navigable about nine months in the year. The L'Anguille River runs through the western part of the county.

The surface of the county in the eastern part, owing to its low and flat condition, is subject to overflow from the St. Francis River. Through the middle portion runs, from north to south, a ridge of the Ozark chain of mountains, known as Crowley's Ridge, which begins at Cape Girardeau, in Missouri, and ends abruptly at the Mississippi River, at Helena. This is the great water-shed of the county, the country east draining in the St. Francis and west in the L'Anguille. West of this ridge are some excellent table lands, rolling enough for drainage, and watered by many springs of never-failing water, which break forth along the ridge; this land is better adapted to grasses and grains than to the growth of cotton. On the east side the soil is a sandy loam, rich and fertile, and adapted to the cultivation of any crop.

Along the summit of the ridge the lands are somewhat thin, though good farms are found, in a high state of cultivation.

Cross County has its usual complement of towns and villages.

Cherry Valley is a thriving village, situated in about the center of Mitchell Township, and twelve miles north of Wynne, on the Knobel branch of the Iron Mountain Railroad.

Mr. G. W. Stacy, who lived about a mile from the present village, had for some time held a commission as postmaster, and kept the office in his residence on his farm. This office derived its name from a large grove of wild cherry trees, on Cooper's Creek, in the vicinity.

On the completion of the railroad, in 1882, Mr. Stacy erected a hotel at the railroad, and on the completion of this (which was the first building in the place), removed the postoffice there also; the name of Cherry Valley was retained, and from that time the village grew rapidly, being now (1889) the third largest place in Cross County.

Its business interests consist of two general stores, conducted by Mitchell & Stacy and Clampitt Bros.; one drug store, by Dr. C. P. Jones; two saw-mills, A. Jordan and R. H. Wade & Son, proprietors; one stave factory, by the Cherry Valley Stave and Heading Company; carpenters, Smith Bros. and W. M. Taylor; blacksmith, George Hydrich; cotton-gin, M. W. Riley; lawyer, J. H. Gunning, and justice, A. H. Brown. Cherry Valley Hotel is conducted by G. W. Stacy; two churches are found, Methodist and Baptist; one school; the physicians are C. P. Jones and J. G. Wright. The population of Cherry Valley is about 200; S. L. Clampitt, postmaster. The most important enterprises in this vicinity at the present time; are its valuable timber resources; as the timber is being cut away the land is rapidly being reduced to a state of cultivation and the soil of this entire township is generally conceded to be the best in the county. The health of this immediate region is excellent; Dr. Jones reports but two deaths in his entire practice during the past year. The territory adjacent to Cherry Valley and throughout Mitchell Township offers flattering inducements to settlers; good land can be secured at reasonable prices, and a cordial welcome awaits all industrious and enterprising immigrants.

Vanndale, the county seat of Cross County, is a flourishing little city, six miles north of the crossing of the Bald Knob and Knobel branches of the Iron Mountain Railroad, in Searcy Township, situated very near the center of the county, at the western base of Crowley's Ridge; it has a population of about 300.

A long time ago a postoffice was established on a farm southeast of the present town site, where J. M. Vann was postmaster for many years; the office was called Vanndale in his honor, and on the completion of the Knobel branch of the Iron Mountain Railroad through Cross County, he moved his store and the postoffice to a point on the railroad, and that location continued, or retained, the old name of Vanndale.

Here soon sprang up a very busy little town. J. P. May erected the first residence in 1882, and later started a store. This place soon attracted the merchants from Wittsburg, who from time to time moved to the new town, and Wittsburg soon became a village of small proportions. In 1884, as stated, the seat of justice was located here, and its subsequent growth has been steady and rapid. In addition to its commanding court house erected in 1887-88, at an expense of $13,700, it has a commodious school, costing $1,000, a Methodist Episcopal Church with parsonage, two hotels and a stave factory.

The following firms and business men compose the commercial interests of the town: General stores, R. Block, Killough & Erwin, Applewhite & Co., J. M. Vann and W. R. Foote; grocery stores, J. T. Rolfe and F. M. McClaran; drug stores, May & Malone and T. D. Hare; stave factories, Applewhite & Co.; saw-mills and cotton-gin, J. T. Lewellen; blacksmiths, W. J. Woolf and 'Squire Oliver; livery stables, G. W. Griffin, carpenters, William Davis, D. E. Whitney and D. J. Randal; hotels, Vanndale Hotel, T. Rolfe, proprietor, and Johnson House, J. W. Killough, proprietor; physicians, Drs. J. D. McKie, J. B. Scarborough, T. D. Hare and J. L. Hare; real-estate agent, William Block; lawyers, T. E. Hare and O. N. Killbrough.

The people of Vanndale are enterprising, clever

and hospitable, ready to extend a sincere welcome to strangers and to encourage new enterprises that promise to reflect credit on the community. Among the business men of the town are to be found several of the most substantial and solid firms in Eastern Arkansas.

The timber and agricultural resources surrounding the place are rich and varied, and, in fact, Vanndale is an admirable point for people seeking new homes. One can not do better than to investigate the inducements its surroundings offer as a place of settlement.

The city of Wynne is located near the center of Cross County, at the junction of the Helena and Memphis branches of the Iron Mountain Railway. Where this thriving city now stands was a wilderness six years ago. The first house was built in 1883. In June of the same year B. B. Merryman started the first store, and soon after Mr. Austell received the commission as first postmaster of the place. The town has a beautiful situation on an elevated plateau at the western base of Crowley's Ridge. The surrounding plain receives ample drainage from the L'Anguille River, the land gradually declining to the valley of that stream. An examination of its situation gives abundant evidence that it is, as reported, one of the healthiest locations in Eastern Arkansas.

Its citizens are people of activity and enterprise, who have in the short space of six years, cleared the timber from the land and built their town. Its streets are lined with many neat and tasty residences, some of which would be a credit to a much older and larger town.

There are three church organizations here, Methodist, Presbyterian and Baptist, with one good church edifice; a public school, with an attendance of about 150 pupils.

The business interests are represented by the following firms: General stores, Smith, Graham & Jones, Johnson & Hamilton, Daltroff, Sparks & Oliver, Goodman & Potlitzer, and Martin & Neeley; groceries, John Cobb, Landers & Mitchell, W. L. Lancaster, William Ivy, W. J. Pardew, H. Davis, B. F. Stanley and Poe Bros.; drug stores, T. A. Bedford and J. W. Hazelwood & Co.;

jeweler, Harry Vaughn; hotels, E. J. Commercial Traveler, J. Badinelli, proprietor, Wynne Hotel, B. F. Stanley, proprietor; livery stables, James Lyon and Martin & Kirby; physicians, William D. Allen, C. H. Montgomery and Paul Gargaro; blacksmiths, Lipscomb & Snowden; lawyer, J. R. Robertson; gents' furnishing goods, R. G. Oliver; saloons, Robert Orr and Brusch & Hamilton; barbers, C. Stewart and Dillard & Johnson; meat markets, John Greene & Co. and J. H. Chappelle.

The city of Wynne was incorporated by an act of the county court May 28, 1888. An election held July 10 of the same year resulted in the election of the following city officers: Thomas L. Thompson, mayor; Charles M. Mebane, recorder; Shields Daltroff, Robert M. Smith, C. M. Harris, W. M. Johnson, S. A. Martin, aldermen.

At that time it had a population of 400. It now has about 1,000 inhabitants, and is rapidly growing. In commercial importance it ranks among the first of Eastern Arkansas towns, and numbers among its merchants some of the soundest firms in the State. It is surrounded by a more than ordinary rich farming country which, however, is not yet very extensively cleared, and rich timber land within a mile or so of town await the advent of the husbandman.

A disastrous fire on the night of September 2, 1887, destroyed over two-thirds of the business portion of the town, entailing a loss of upward of $200,000. Since then the burned district has been rebuilt with a better class of buildings, so that what appeared to be a calamity at the time is now looked upon as a real blessing.

Wittsburg is not a town of the present, but of the past. Situated at the head of navigation of the St. Francis River, it was at one time the distributing and shipping point for nearly all Northeastern Arkansas. With this immense tributary country, its volume of trade was for many years simply marvelous, shipping, it is said, 30,000 bales of cotton annually, with several business firms doing a business of from $100,000 to $300,000 per year.

The completion of the railroad through the eastern part of the State gave markets and shipping points to the country that supported Wittsburg, so that from the advent of the iron horse its fall was rapid. It was the county seat of Cross County from 1868 to 1884, but prior to the latter date a great many of the merchants had forsaken the town and removed to Vanndale or Wynne. Most of the merchants of both of these places either started their business in Wittsburg or served their apprenticeship as clerks for some of the large firms there.

To-day it is a wreck and ruin of its former greatness. Large logs and timbers show where warehouses and stores occupied its streets. A few large stores are standing yet, but they are rapidly falling beneath the action of destroying time, and in a few years more the last of them will have disappeared. It still contains a church, school-house and one store, carried on by Mr. Casbeer, who is also the postmaster.

At the organization of the county, in 1862, provision was made for the county and probate court. In 1873 this was abolished and a board of supervisors, composed of three men, who had control of county matters alone, established in its stead. Probate matters were referred to the circuit judge, sitting in chancery. This state of affairs continued until the adoption of the new State constitution, October 13, 1874, and by that constitution was provided the holding of county and probate court by the same judge, who is styled county and probate judge. The criminal law and chancery courts are condensed and known as the circuit court, and presided over by the circuit judge, who holds all three courts during one term, criminal cases taking precedence.

The first attorneys to locate in Cross County were William Neeley, Samuel L. Austell, James G. Frierson, Earl C. Bronaugh, Martin L. Clardy, J. S. Brookfield and Charles S. Cameron; these men settled here during and immediately after the war. Some of these men were noted for their intellectual and legal acquirements, notably James G. Frierson, E. C. Bronaugh and Charles S. Cameron.

Mr. Frierson was afterward elected State senator from Cross County, and Mr. Cameron became noted for his eloquence and oratorical ability.

In 1868 he was the Democratic nominee for representative in Congress, was elected, but unquestionably counted out through fraud. He is now practicing law in Chicago.

In 1869 George H. Sanders was licensed to practice law in this county; he lived here about three years after, and during that time made a very enviable reputation for his legal ability; he is now located in Little Rock. From 1880 to 1885 Mr. N. W. Norton was one of the legal lights of this community.

The personnel of the bar of the county, at the present time, consists of Hon. T. E. Hare, who represented the county in the State legislature from 1878 to 1882; Hon. J. D. Block, at present prosecuting attorney for the Second judicial circuit; O. N. Killough, J. R. Robertson and J. H. Gunning.

In 1878 William Nesbitt, aged twenty-three, procured a license to marry Mrs. H. M. Hammett, a widow of forty-six years of age. The proposed marriage was so distasteful to the family of Mrs. Hammett, that her two sons, David L. and "Dock," vowed that the marriage should never take place. So on the evening preceding the day appointed for the ceremony they went to her house where Nesbitt was, and shot him through the window. Mrs. Hammett grasping a gun, ran to the door and shot at her fleeing sons, but with no effect. Mr. Nesbitt died in the course of an hour. "Dock" was soon captured, but the next day attempting to make his escape, was killed by the deputy sheriff, W. T. Levesque. His brother, David L., was caught in Brinkley by J. D. Block, was brought to Cross County, tried and convicted, and sentenced to a term of five years in the State prison. He served but a few months of this term, being pardoned by Gov. T. J. Churchill.

During the term of Sheriff Levesque he executed Charles Carr, who had been sentenced to be hanged for rape. He previously escaped by breaking jail, but was captured in Missouri, returned and executed at Wittsburg, in October, 1878. This was the first legal execution in Cross County.

In 1882 a negro, named Abraham Sublett, was executed by Sheriff L. T. Head for wife murder.

21

For several years a noted desperado, Martin Mitchell, made the swamps in the eastern part of Cross and adjoining counties his resort. As early as 1877 he killed a man in Mississippi County, for which he was compelled to leave the country. In 1882 he killed J. T. Greer, a clerk in a store at Byhalia, Miss., for which crime a reward was offered for his capture, and he came to the swamps of the St. Francis River, in Cross and adjacent counties. Here he held forth for some time, defying the authorities and resisting capture, till three brothers, John, "Dock" and "Woodie" Hammett, citizens of Cross County, determined to hunt him down. They found him with several choice spirits of a similar desperate character, in the swamps of Craighead County, where a pitched battle was at once fought, and as the Hammett boys killed one of his companions he immediately shot John Hammett dead.

It seems that no further attempt to capture him was made at that time, but in 1885 he was arrested for selling whisky; he was confined in the jail at Wittsburg, and from this, however, he soon made his escape. One Irvin, an old companion of his, who for some cause had become his enemy, attempted his capture. They met accidentally while out hunting, when on sight a duel, with rifles, was fought. Mitchell was slightly wounded, but Irvin was killed on the spot.

Mitchell made the swamps of Cross County his stronghold for several years following, hunting, trapping, and even working in the timber and rafting some, till in 1887, while in St. Francis County, he became involved in a difficulty with Charley Conway, who, it was supposed, shot at him through a window, as he sat beside a fire. The shot was fatal, and as he died all Eastern Arkansas felt relieved at being rid of one of its most desperate and dangerous outlaws.

Religious movements have obtained throughout Cross County from an early day. Among the Methodists, Cherry Valley Church was organized in 1885 with about fifteen members, J. F. Jernigan being their first pastor. The original members were Joseph Taylor, Eliza Taylor, Eva Stacy, Glen Mitchell, Marshal Brooks, William Taylor,

Mrs. Emma Taylor, Mrs. Martha Bowns, J. W. Bogard, Mrs. Ada Jordan, Sanders Cagle, Mrs. Amanda Cagle, Mrs. Rebecca Stacy, John Taylor and James Taylor. The membership now numbers about thirty-six.

Cherry Valley Baptist Church was organized as the New Salem Baptist Church, a long time ago at a point about one mile southeast of the present village of Cherry Valley. In 1885 the old church was torn down and a new edifice erected at the latter place. It is in a flourishing condition, with a present membership of about twenty-five.

Mount Zion Methodist Episcopal Church, South, was constituted and organized about 1848 at a point one and a half miles southeast from the present village of Vanndale. Some of the original members were S. S. Hare, Rev. Thomas P. Hare, Rev. Jacob Hare, Jacob S. Hare, Rev. John Hare, David Hare, Rev. Rensalier Vann, Col. David C. Cross, T. N. Deadrick, Charles Magett, John D. Magett, James Lewellen, William Barnes, Dr. B. D. McClaran and John Sullivan.

Mount Zion was a great religious center in the early days of this country, and the White River annual conference was organized by Bishop Keener, within the walls of this old country church in 1870. During protracted meetings, crowds of people came to this church from long distances, and it was often presided over by ministers of noted intelligence and education.

In 1885 the church was moved to the village of Vanndale, where the ladies of the Ladies' Aid Society had erected a fine church edifice. It is at present in a very flourishing condition, and in good growing order; it has a membership of about 115, and is presided over by the Rev. R. G. Brittain. Mr. Brittain was also pastor of this church in 1856, thirty-three years ago; was then transferred to work in other sections of the State, and returned here again for two years in 1866. He is now preaching on the last year of his appointment here.

Around this old church, in days gone by, the old settlers, as they passed away from this world, were laid to rest. Here, upon the summit of Crowley's Ridge, beneath the shade of forest trees, which stand as sentinels to guard their silent home, they sleep in peace; here, half a century and more ago, they labored strong with the hope of youth, and an indomitable ambition to reduce this wilderness of nature to broad and smiling tracts of cultivated fields, to found their fortunes and to build their homes. Here, forty years ago, they met beneath these trees to organize a church, and here, when that old church was built, have they returned, but borne by sorrowing friends, to find an everlasting rest, as Death, from year to year, has called them home.

Another generation now worships in another church built for them, and many changes mark the progress of Time; yet as one stands amid these graves and reads the names of these old pioneers, upon the stones which mark their resting place, it is easy to realize how appropriate is this place, founded and consecrated by themselves to God, in which to rest, till the everlasting trumpet proclaims the resurrection morn.

The First Presbyterian Church at Wynne was organized in 1887, with the following members: George F. Dixon, Mrs. L. M. Koonce, Mrs. John Graham, Miss Mary Graham, Miss Mary Dixon, Mrs. George F. Dixon, Robert H. Mebane and Dr. W. T. Mebane. Since the date of formation, the membership has gradually increased, and is now in a very flourishing condition. Rev. S. T. Reid is pastor.

The Wynne Methodist Episcopal Church, South, was organized at Wynne by the Rev. J. F. Jernigan, in 1885, with the following original members: J. S. Brookfield, William Standley and wife, R. S. Martin and wife, W. S. Martin and wife, David Tyer and wife, and William Head and wife.

In 188– this organization erected an attractive church edifice, the only one in Wynne. It now has a membership of about forty, and is progressing with encouraging success. Rev. A. C. Griffin is pastor.

The public schools of Cross County are financially in a flattering condition, there being an abundance of reserve money in the treasury to guarantee good salaries to teachers, and consequently good service can be secured. The county is fairly well supplied with school buildings, and the county examiner reports great advancement in better buildings and a higher grade of teachers. In 1887 the enumeration was: White, 1,424; colored, 860; making the total number of children of school age, 2,284. The examiner's report of 1888 shows a slight falling off, probably from incomplete returns.

In 1887 there was $6,030 expended for teachers' salaries and for building, and in that year there was a surplus left in the hands of the county treasurer of over $6,500.

In 1888 there was nearly $8,000 expended for the same purposes, and the county still had a reserve fund of over $5,000 on hand.

There are twenty-six districts in the county, mostly supplied with good school buildings. The school-house at Vanndale is a fine building, erected in 1877 at a cost of $1,000. Its dimensions are 24x48, one-story frame. It is situated in a fine park of six acres. At Wynne is a high school employing three teachers.

The present county officials are: County judge, W. F. Robinson; clerk, J. M. Levesque; sheriff, J. B. Hamilton; treasurer, Eli Bailes; coroner, A. Phillips; surveyor, J. W. McElroy; assessor, T. W. May.

Since the formation of Cross County the various offices have been filled by the following named:

County judges: S. L. Austell, W. A. Lee, H. B. Robertson, L. N. Rhodes, J. C. McElroy, S. S. Hare and W. F. Robinson.

Clerks: B. D. McClaran, James Levesque, W. K. Stokes, B. Rolleson, T. O. Fitzpatrick, J. N. Dobson, L. C. Chappelle and R. E. Dobson. The present clerk, J. M. Levesque, has served six terms or twelve years.

Sheriffs: J. N. Dobson, L. Chappelle, W. H. Cole, J. M. Levesque (Mr. Levesque served from 1874 to 1880, six consecutive years), J. H. Legg, L. T. Head, J. W. Killough and J. B. Hamilton.

Treasurers: Robert Meek, W. F. Gray, G. N. Legg, A. J. Harrell, G. W. Griffin (served two terms), J. M. Simmons (three terms), J. A. Sadler and Eli Bailes.

Coroners: K. B. Pledger, J. Fountain, David Fitzpatrick, J. T. Rolfe, J. H. Legg, J. Applewhite, L. N. Block, P. A. Warren, Perry Warren (four terms), J. H. Brinkley, J. T. Rolfe and A. Phillips.

Surveyors: M. Halk, G. Jones, Henry Cummins, H. Bond, T. O. Fitzpatrick, William M. Block, H. Newsom, B. Rolleson and J. W. McElroy (four terms, eight years).

Assessors: J. E. Gailey, L. N. Rhodes, R. M. Spain, J. H. Legg, W. P. Brown (four terms, eight years), H. C. Winters and T. W. May.

J. D. Block of Wynne, Cross County, was elected, in the fall of 1888, prosecuting attorney of the Second circuit, comprising Mississippi, Crittenden, Cross, Poinsett, Craighead, Greene and Clay Counties. The first representative to the State legislature from Cross County was David Fitzpatrick. In 1868–74, J. A. Houghton; 1874–76, G. M. Sharp; 1876–78, B. Rolleson; 1878–82, T. E. Hare; 1882–84, W. C. Malone; 1884–86, N. W. Norton; 1886–88, J. D. Block, and 1888–90, J. F. Patterson.

In 1871, Mr. J. G. Frierson, of Cross County, represented this, the First senatorial district, in the State senate. The present senator for the First district, Mr. R. Pope, is, too, a citizen of Cross County.

J. G. Frierson was also a delegate to the State constitutional convention, in 1874. In the fall of 1888 he was elected circuit judge, and died in 1884.

Hon. T. E. Hare was a member of the Democratic National Convention at Chicago in 1884.

Secret societies seem to thrive as well in Cross County as elsewhere. Arcadia Lodge No. 183, A. F. & A. M., was organized in 1865, at Cleburne, with the following charter members: R. Vann, W. M.; W. H. Robins, S. W.; W. H. Barnes, J. W.; E. J. Williams, Treas.; W. A. Lee, Sec.; W. D. Peterson, S. D.; J. H. McFarran, J. D.; C. J. Searcy, Tyler; J. M. Levesque, William Taylor, J. C. McElroy, A. S. Graves and M. S. Fielder.

This lodge is now located at Vanndale, and has a membership of twenty-five. The following were the officers during the year 1889: G. W. Griffin,

W. M.; William Taylor, S. W.; W. E. Fountain, J. W.; J. E. Buchannon, Treas.; S. S. Hare, Sec.; Isom Julian, S. D.; Z. Couch, J. D., and Robert Lawrence, Tyler.

In former years this was one of the brightest lodges in the State. It still numbers among its members many who are noted for their knowledge in Masonic matters. It is in a flourishing and good working condition.

Wittsburg Lodge No. 606, K. of H., was organized at Wittsburg October 19, 1877, with the following charter members: Louin Chappelle, James Applewhite, L. N. Block, John W. Killough, Alvis L. Malone, Robert E. Dobson, John Q. Thomas, Shields Daltroff, James M. Levesque, R. Block, George M. Arnold and Ann Reddick Pope. The lodge was removed to Vanndale in 1886, and its present standing is all that could be desired, the insurance feature offering attractive inducements to members. The present officers are: J. M. Simmons, D.; J. E. Erwin, V. D.; J. Q. Thomas, A. D.; James Applewhite, Treas.; J. P. May, Guide; J. W. Killough, P. D.; S. M. McKenzie, G.; J. W. Lewellen, S.; O. N. Killough, R.; R. Pope, F. R.; J. W. Killough, Rep. to the G. L., and J. B. Scarborough, Med. Ex. The lodge has a membership of fifty-four.

Pearl Lodge No. 175, K. & L. of H., organized at Wittsburg on September 15, 1879, was moved to Vanndale in 1886, and consolidated with a lodge already in existence there. The object of this order is social and beneficial, its membership numbering about seventy-five. The charter members were G. M. Arnold, I. M. Deadrick, S. W. Thornton, J. M. Levesque, L. N. Block, S. Daltroff, W. C. Malone, J. M. Simmons, J. W. Killough, R. Pope, A. S. Casbeer, J. Q. Thomas, H. H. Ross, P. Van Patten, Walter Gorman, J. E. Erwin, Ike Block, Ben Block, A. L. Malone, R. Block, L. Chappelle, G. W. Griffin, A. J. Harrall, W. H. Gardner, E. W. Simmons, Lola Thornton, Fannie J. Block, J. M. Arnold, Nannie Levesque, M. V. Deadrick, Mary A. Simmons, Josie Thomas, Delana Kisbeer, M. E. Killough, Cora Gorman, Roselle Erwin, Fannie Block, Mollie Simmons, Hester Block, Emma Chappelle, M. E. Griffin, M.

A. Gardner and Anna Block. The present officers are: J. M. Simmons, Protector; Mrs. Josie C. Thomas, Vice-Protector; Mrs. R. Erwin, Chaplain; J. M. Vann, Treasurer; T. E. Hare, Secretary and Financial Secretary; J. P. May, Guide; J. E. Erwin, Guardian; S. A. McKenze, Sentinel; J. Q. Thomas, District Deputy Supreme Protector; J. W. Killough, J. E. Erwin and John Thomas are Trustees.

Vanndale Lodge No. 677, K. & L. of H. was organized May 29, 1883, with the following charter members: Joseph Samuels, Ida H. Vann, W. R. Foot, H. H. Roberts, E. M. Rolleson, T. E. Hare, F. M. Hare, J. T. Rolfe, F. M. Applewhite, John P. Hilburn, Mollie Head, L. H. McKie, James D. McKie and James T. Lewellen. This lodge increased in membership and carried on a separate existence until January 28, 1886, when Harland P. Gage, Supreme Protector, granted a dispensation for the consolidation of the two lodges, Pearl of Wittsburg No. 175, and Vanndale No. 677. The two lodges were united February 23, 1886, retaining the name of Pearl Lodge No. 175.

The Vanndale branch of the American Building, Loan & Tontine Saving Association (parent office at Memphis, Tenn.), was organized in Vanndale in September. The stockholders who organized this branch are: J. M. Levesque, J. W. Killough, R. Block, W. M. Block, T. E. Hare, C. M. Gardner, O. N. Killough, J. T. Lewellen, R. L. Block, J. T. Rolfe, O. A. Hamilton, C. W. McClaran and D. J. Randal. The establishment of this association in Vanndale will unquestionably prove of value to the community, as it affords the investment of small sums by all, and is, in its nature, virtually a savings bank. The present officers are: T. E. Hare, president; C. M. Gardner, vice-president; R. L. Block, secretary and treasurer; O. N. Killough, attorney.

On May 16, 1889, Levesque Lodge No. 52, K. of P., was established at Wynne, with a membership of about thirty-five; following were elected officers: S. Daltroff, C. C.; C. M. Mebane, V. C.; W. J. Brusch, P.; S. A. Miller, K. of P. & S.; G. N. Sparks, M. of F.; C. D. Oliver, M. of E.; J. K. Hancock, M. at A., and G. W. Brown, P. C.

The Ladies' Aid Society of Vanndale was organized in April, 1883, by Mrs. Hattie Marshall, Mrs. Dr. McKie, secretary, and Mrs. Ida H. Vann, treasurer. The principal object of this society was to build a Methodist Church. To these ladies much praise is due, for now the church is an accomplished fact, having been erected at an expense of $1,500 and a parsonage which cost $350. This money was mostly raised by suppers and entertainments given by the association. The present officers are: Mrs. J. L. Thomas, president; Mrs. Roselle Erwin, treasurer, and Mrs. Ida H. Vann, secretary.

Among the enterprises of Cross County worthy of mention is the Wynne Ripsaw, published by D. J. Burks, which was established at Wynne October 1, 1888. It is the official organ of Cross and Poinsett Counties and is ably conducted, the publisher, by his earnest efforts, doing much to advance the condition of the people in social and moral matters. Seeing the prospects of the future in this section, it invites with liberal-spirited cordiality, immigration from overcrowded neighborhoods to the rich and fertile bottom lands of this county.

As the county of Cross was not organized at the time of the beginning of the Civil War, most of the soldiers from the county's present limits are credited to Poinsett. However, this county raised five companies and sent some 500 men into the field.

The first company was organized in the spring of 1861, under the command of Capt. Will H. Trader. They were attached to the Fifth Arkansas Infantry. For the first year this company saw but little fighting, but in the latter part of the struggle was in many important battles and surrendered with Gen. Joseph Johnston, in North Carolina, in May, 1865. Also, in the spring of 1861, Company C, of the Thirteenth Arkansas Regiment, was organized in Poinsett County, with a good many men from the limits of Cross in its ranks. This company was immediately sent to the front and took part in the battles of Belmont, Shiloh and Corinth. After the latter battle the regiment was reorganized and Lieut. J. M. Levesque was elected captain. The company then passed through the Kentucky campaign, participating in the battles of Perryville, Richmond and Murfreesboro. At a reorganization of the regiment, after the latter battle, Capt. Levesque was detached from this company, when he returned to Cross County and raised a company of cavalry. This company operated in Eastern Arkansas till 1864, when it joined Price on the Missouri raid. On account of illness Capt. Levesque did not accompany it on this campaign. The company surrendered at Wittsburg in May, 1865. In 1862 Capt. Tom Westmoreland raised a company, and in 1864 a company under the command of Capt. T. N. Deadrick was sent into the field.

More than one-half of the men forming these five companies were either killed in battle or died from wounds or sickness, and their vacant places at the family hearth have been mourned for many years.

There were no engagements between troops in Cross County, yet the armies of both sides often passed up and down along Crowley's Ridge, annoying the citizens and often interrupting their farming operations and other pursuits.

The political status of Cross County is Democratic. Out of a vote of 1,900 about two-thirds vote the Democratic ticket in State and National issues. In county affairs the Republicans vote for whom they consider the best man, not being recognized as a county organization, and, consequently, never placing a ticket in the field.

Cross County is well supplied with railroads, being traversed north and south twice, and east and west once by different lines. These roads afford excellent facilities for shipping produce and supplies, and have helped amazingly to bring Cross County to the position of prosperity which it at present enjoys.

The Helena branch of the St. Louis, Iron Mountain & Southern Railroad has 28.85 miles of main track in this county which cross the entire breadth, nearly through the center, from north to south. It was constructed in 1882.

The St. Louis, Arkansas & Texas has a length of 16.85 miles, and crosses the county north and south along its western line. It was also constructed in 1882.

The Memphis branch of the St. Louis, Iron Mountain & Southern passes through Cross County east and west, and has a length within these limits of thirty-one miles. Ground was broken and construction began on the road in 1886. It was completed and open for travel in June, 1888.

During the years between 1850 and 1860 the value of realty in Cross County was held very high. About this time the section was attracting the attention of rich and enterprising planters from the east and south who emigrated here and improved large tracts of land, which soon became valuable and productive plantations. At the outbreak of the war farming on a large scale was practically suspended, and the industries of the country paralyzed. The close of hostilities found the people impoverished and all lands greatly reduced in value. The people at once began to overcome this state of things by renewed perseverance and labor, and just as the future seemed to give them flattering hopes for a return of prosperity, the period of reconstruction followed, lasting from 1868 to 1874. During this time industries suffered more than from the effects of the war. Property of all kinds declined in value, while the rate of taxation was greatly increased till Cross County became nearly bankrupt. After this time all industries took on a healthy growth; labor became settled and the country prospered, large areas of land being placed again in cultivation which had been lying idle since the war. The construction of the various lines of railroads through this county has developed many enterprises and established the timber interests which are scarcely equaled by any county in the State.

Saw-mills and stave factories dot the three lines of railways that pass through this county, and manufacture vast quantities of fine timber into merchantable lumber and staves, which are shipped to all markets of the United States.

The St. Francis River is a means of transportation of hundreds of thousands of logs rafted to the mills on the lower waters.

Crowley's Ridge, passing through the center of the county, is especially adapted to the growth of fruits, berries and vegetables. This industry is slightly developed at the present time, yet there is an inviting field for hundreds to engage in these pursuits.

Stock raising may be made a source of immense wealth, as the range of Cross County is almost absolutely unsurpassed for pasturage. The western portion is dotted with prairies, comprising from 100 to 10,000 acres, which afford the finest spring and summer grazing grass, while the bottoms of the St. Francis basin furnish grass and corn, on which the cattle feed and fatten during the entire winter, without attention.

While cotton, that king of agriculture, is the principal product of the planter, yet cereals of every description grow abundantly, and it is easy to see that, with a diversity of crops, the farming interests would be improved and their value enhanced.

The experiments with grasses and clover have proved very satisfactory, and show that they will grow as well here as in any part of Tennessee or Kentucky.

After reviewing the resources of Cross County, with its various interests—its railroad facilities, fertile soil and salubrious climate—one may safely assert that this county is destined with such advantages as to become in the near future one of the foremost in Eastern Arkansas.

Dr. William D. Allen, of Wynne, Ark., has been a successful practitioner of Cross County, Ark., for forty years, and is ever to be found at the bedside of the sick and afflicted. His birth occurred in Baton Rouge, La., in 1823, and he was the fifth of a family of ten children, the result of the union of William and Clementine J. (Quillin) Allen, natives of Tennessee. Both Mr. and Mrs. Allen removed with their parents to Louisiana when children, and there attained their growth. William Allen was a farmer by occupation, also carried on stock raising, and remained in Louisiana until 1836, when in the spring of that year he came to Arkansas. He settled about six miles southeast of the present village of Wynne, in what was then Phillips County, Ark., and when there were about forty families living along Crowley's Ridge, a distance of about sixty miles. Here Mr. Allen, Sr., bought about 4,000 acres of land, on which he at once began making improvements, clearing land, erecting buildings, etc., and he brought with him a large number of negroes, who, with his family, numbered fifty-six souls. He chartered a small steamboat to transport his family and slaves to Arkansas, and landed at a point called Andrew's Landing. This boat was the second one up the St. Francis River. He then went to work and cleared about 400 acres, and resided on the same until his death, which occurred in 1846. The mother lived until 1880, and died at the age of seventy-eight years. Dr. William D. Allen was twelve years of age at the time his father moved to Arkansas, and prior to that time had attended school in his native State. After moving to Arkansas his father engaged a private teacher for his family and other children in the vicinity, and the Doctor received instruction in this manner for three years; then as new settlers came in they had permanently established subscription schools. At the age of twenty-one years Dr. Allen went to Lexington, Ky., and entered the Transylvania University, where he took a literary course of three years. There were attending, at that time, Gen. Morgan, William Walker, Gen. Buckner, Col. Pickett, and a number of others, who have since become known in history. From there Dr. Allen went to Louisville, where he took a year's course in medicine, and then went to the University of Pennsylvania, where he graduated after a strict examination, in May, 1849. He then returned to Arkansas, and at once began the practice of his profession in the country surrounding his father's homestead. The Doctor has been in the constant practice of his profession since that time, and in the immediate vicinity of the place. In 1852, Dr. Allen was united in marriage to Miss Eliza Oliver, a granddaughter of John Johnson, who came to Arkansas in 1812, settling in Phillips, now St. Francis County, where he cleared a large tract of land, and there died about 1830. Many of his descendants are still living in this section, prosperous and well-to-do. After marriage Dr. Allen continued his practice, and in connection speculated considerably in land, making large sums on some of their sales, and on some tracts making extensive improvements. In 1884 he came to Wynne, a station on the railroad, that had just been named, and at that time there was but one shanty in the place. His office was a small log-cabin. In 1886 he erected an office which was destroyed in the fire that year. The Doctor is a member of the Masonic fraternity, Forrest City Lodge No. 34, and he and family are members of the Methodist Episcopal Church. To his marriage were born four children: Willie, John, Walter and Emmett. The first three are living in St. Francis County, where they own fine farms, and the last is attending medical lectures in New Orleans.

S. L. Austell, farmer, Wittsburg, Ark. This successful agriculturist owes his nativity to Cross County, Ark., where his birth occurred in 1848, and is the son of Samuel and Mabel Caroline (Wofford) Austell, natives of South Carolina, but who came to Arkansas at an early date. The Woffords were early pioneers, and Grandfather Isaac Wofford built the first house in Wittsburg. He opened a large farm, and there passed his last days, his death occurring in 1849. Samuel L. Austell at first settled on Crowley's Ridge, near the present city of Wynne, but removed to the bottoms, about one mile from Wittsburg, where he cleared about 100 acres. Mr. Austell was for many years one of the leading spirits of that section. He took a prominent part in politics, and was elected the first county judge of Cross County. He was also quite prominently spoken of as Governor of Arkansas. He died in 1866, and the mother in 1870. At one time he owned nearly all the land around Wynne, and speculated largely in real estate. S. L. Austell was reared principally to farm labor, and received his education in the public schools. After the death of his father, he, with his brothers, managed the farm until 1880, when he bought out the only remaining heir. This farm consists of about 1,100 acres, with 140 under cultivation. Mr. Austell also owns about 100 acres near Wittsburg, and in 1884 he bought the old home of the widow of Maurice Block, at Wittsburg. Mr. Austell owns, aside from this, 500 acres on Crowley's Ridge, 175 of which are under cultivation. This land he rents out, but farms the principal part of the balance himself. In 1860 his father built a cotton-gin, and this our subject still runs. In the early days of the country, Grandfather Wofford started a ferry across the St. Francis River, at Wittsburg, and this descended by inheritance to S. L. Austell, having been in the family for many years, as may be seen. In 1877 Mr. Austell married Miss Page Johnson, a daughter of Thomas Johnson, who moved to Cross County, Ark., in 1864, and here followed farming until his death, which occurred in 1875. The mother is still living. Mr. and Mrs. Austell became the parents of five children, three of whom are deceased: Blanche (deceased), Samuel (deceased), Pearl and Thomas (living) and Clay (deceased). The family are members of the Methodist Episcopal Church at Wittsburg. Mr. Austell is only moderately active in politics, but takes a deep interest in school matters, being at present one of the directors. He is an active, energetic citizen.

Eli Bailes, farmer and treasurer of Cross County, is prominent among the comparatively young men of Cross County, whose career thus far has been both honorable and successful. Well-informed on the general topics of the day, he can not but impart to those with whom he comes in contact something of the truths with which his mind is stored. He was born in York County, S. C., in 1850, and was the youngest of a family of seven children born to Eli and Mary A. (Alexander) Bailes, natives, respectively, of South Carolina and North Carolina. The father was a tiller of the soil and died in his native State in 1886. The mother died in 1887. Eli Bailes was reared in South Carolina and his time was divided in early life between assisting on the home place and in getting a limited education in the common schools. During the war his father and two brothers were in the Confederate army and one brother was killed. Eli Bailes came to Arkansas in 1867, located in St. Francis, bought a farm of 110 acres, erected buildings, cleared land and remained there until

1877, when he came to Cross County and located on the Bay Ridge farm. He remained there for four years and then removed to the McCrae farm, where from overflow and several bad speculations he met with temporary financial embarrassment. He remained on this farm until 1885, and then came to Deadrick, now known as Levesque, where he farmed about 450 acres. On this farm he has a store, mostly intended for his own plantation supplies, but has a fair stock of goods and is doing a good business. On December 1, 1888, he was appointed postmaster at Levesque and on the first of the following year, at a special election, he was made treasurer of Cross County. He has always taken a deep interest in politics and is known as one of the hardest workers for the Democratic party. He has been married twice, first in March, 1869, to Miss Dovie Lembler, a native of South Carolina, but who was reared in St. Francis County. She died in September, 1875, and left two children, a son and daughter: Charles Edward and Dovie Ethel. His second marriage took place on January 19, 1877, to Miss Maggie Wood, who was born and reared in St. Francis County. The fruits of this union were four children, two of whom are living: Robert H. and Lucile. Those deceased were unnamed. Mr. Bailes is a good farmer and a respectable citizen.

R. B. Bamson, one of the prominent citizens of Bedford Township, was born in Devonshire, England, in 1838, being a son of William and Sarah (Louis) Bamson, also natives of England, who became the parents of four children: William, Mary, John (who served twelve years in the English army, and was taken with dropsy and died at Canton, China, in 1864) and R. B. (our subject.) Mr. and Mrs. Bamson both died in 1874, in their seventy-second year, having never been outside of their native county. R. B. Bamson was apprenticed to a gunsmith at the age of fourteen, with whom he worked seven years, after which he followed his trade in England until twenty-seven years of age. Coming thence to America, and landing in New York September 1, 1860, he worked in a machine shop on Fifty-second Street for $5.50 per day, and the following year went to Savannah, Ga., where

he was employed in a carriage shop at $6 per day, there remaining until May, 1862, when he joined the Confederate army, in the Fulton Dragoons, commanded by Capt. Waley. He served until May, 6, 1865 (when he was paroled), most of the time acting as a sharpshooter and scout, and was one of the "boys" who captured Gen. Crittenden, and was the possessor of that officer's pistols. After the war Mr. Bamson returned to Georgia and settled in Decatur, where he was married in 1866 to Mrs. S. T. Puitte, nee Moore. After his marriage he opened a shop and was engaged in the repair and manufacture of guns. In 1870 Mr. Bamson came to Arkansas, and bought a farm in Cross County, where he resided for three years, then removing to Douglas County, Mo., buying a farm there. He sold out two years later and went to Baxter County, where he was engaged in farming and also opened up a shop. Four years afterward he settled at Rome, Ga., resumed farming, and also ran a grist-mill and saw-mill three years. In 1879 Mr. Bamson returned to this county and purchased a farm, also opening a gunsmith shop, in which business he is still engaged. He owns a farm of eighty acres, with thirty acres under cultivation. In addition to farming and his gunsmith business Mr. Bamson owns a one-third interest in a steam-gin, which turns out annually 375 bales of cotton. Himself and wife are the parents of four children, three of whom are still living: W. B. and M. E. (twins) and Neoma. Mr. and Mrs. Bamson are members of the Methodist Episcopal Church, South. The former is also a member of the County Wheel, and is an enterprising citizen, lending his aid to all work for the public welfare, and extending a welcome to anyone seeking a home in this community.

T. A. Bedford, druggist, Wynne, Ark. A very reliable as well as popular drug store is that of Mr. Bedford, who engaged in the drug business in Wynne, in February, 1889, and who has every requisite and convenience in this line. He is a native of Middle Tennessee, where his birth occurred in 1842, and is the second of four children born to John H. and Lizzie (Allen) Bedford, natives of Tennessee, where the father was for many years engaged in farming, manufacturing tobacco and merchandising. In 1849 he and family moved to West Tennessee, nine miles from Memphis, and there he engaged in the cultivation of cotton, continuing at this until his death, in 1851. After this his widow moved with the family to Columbia, Tenn., where she remained for three years for the purpose of educating her children. They were then sent to Lebanon to complete their education. The mother died in 1870. T. A. Bedford attended school until the end of 1860, when he came to Arkansas and purchased a farm in what is now Cross County, about five miles west of Wynne, bought about thirty negroes and embarked in the cotton raising business. After making one crop he went to Tennessee to visit his mother, and while there enlisted in the Confederate army, Company K, Fourth Tennessee Cavalry, commanded by Col. Paul Anderson, and was assigned to duty in Gen. Bragg's army. He was in the battles of Murfreesboro, Chickamauga, Perryville, Dalton and Resaca, and was captured in May, 1864, while bearing a dispatch from Gen. Hood, would not take the oath and was sent as a prisoner to Alton, Ill. There he remained until peace was declared. In 1866 he returned to Arkansas to look after the property he had left there, and found his slaves, mules and horses gone and the plantation overgrown with underbrush. He settled here, however, and returned to agricultural pursuits. In January, 1868, he married Miss Mary Rebecca Cogbill, a native of Tennessee and a daughter of George Cogbill, who came to Arkansas, in 1860, settled in Cross County, and followed farming until his death, in 1867. Mr. Bedford also tilled the soil until the death of his wife, in 1882, and in the following year he went to Wittsburg, and was in the drug business at that place for some time. He was then in the warehouse and shipping business, which occupation he still continues. To his marriage were born three children: Thomas A. J. (is at present postal clerk on the Memphis & Bald Knob Railroad), Mattie R. (is a graduate of Shelbyville, Tenn., in the class of 1889), and Mamie (is attending school at Nashville, with the same teacher under whom the elder sister graduated). In 1886 Mr. Bedford was appointed postmaster of Wittsburg, and opened the office in his drug store. He remained at Wittsburg until 1888, when he resigned the postoffice (having sold the drug store in 1887) and went to Wynne, where he purchased the drug stock of Bunch & Hamilton. He now has as fine a drug store as can be found in Eastern Arkansas, and carries a complete line of pure drugs and chemicals, toilet articles, paints and oils and the usual druggists' sundries. For compounding and putting up prescriptions he has the assistance of S. A. Miller, a graduate of the Pennsylvania School of Pharmacy, at Philadelphia and York (Penn.) School of Sciences. This assistant has a complete chemical outfit and is thus prepared to analyze water, mineral ores and chemical compounds. Mr. Bedford owns a farm one and a half miles east of Wynne.

Alonzo A. Berry, M. D., numbered among the rising young medical practitioners in this portion of Arkansas, is a worthy son of Bartlett A. and Elmira (Hennasu) Berry, natives of North Carolina. The former, now in his fifty-seventh year, has held a public office since twenty-one years of age. He was first sheriff of his county (Burke), which position he held during the war, and was again elected in 1887, discharging his duties of trust at the present time. He was a representative to the State legislature two terms in the Lower House, and also represented his district in the State senate from 1880 to 1884. Mr. and Mrs. Berry are members of the Methodist Episcopal Church, and the parents of ten children: Lenore, Letitia (wife of Dr. Flow, of North Carolina), Alonzo A. (our subject), Clara E. (wife of Dave Berry, of North Carolina), Robert B., Lillie P., Bartlett A., Jethroe W., Forrest C. and Marvin G. A. A. Berry was born in North Carolina in 1865, and was educated in the common schools of his county, attending also Rutherford College, and Finley High School, at Lenoir, N. C., from which he graduated at the age of eighteen years. Following his literary course, he entered the Louisville Medical College, and the Kentucky School of Medicine, at Louisville, Ky., graduating in 1887. He then returned to North Carolina, where he commenced practicing, but remained only a short time, coming the same year to Arkansas, and locating in Bay Village, Cross County, where he now enjoys a large and lucrative practice. He is rapidly becoming one of the leading physicians of the community.

Maurice Block, deceased, was for many years a leading merchant in what is now Cross County. He was born in Germany in 1819, and spent his youth until fifteen years of age at home with his father, who was a merchant, and in attending school. At the above mentioned age his father wished him to learn the baker's trade, but this not proving satisfactory to Maurice, the latter left home and went to Paris, where he worked in a clock factory, doing the fine ornamental brass work and putting on the finishing touches. He worked at this until twenty-two years of age. The year previous he wedded Miss Bettie Bloon, a native of Paris. In 1842 he came to the United States, landing at New Orleans, where he started out by selling goods through the country, and remained in that city for four or five years. While there Mrs. Block was stricken with the yellow fever and died, leaving two sons: Losso (who died in St. Louis in 1849) and Nathan (who is a merchant in Memphis). Soon after the loss of his wife, Mr. Block took his children and removed to Memphis, Tenn., where he continued his business of selling goods through the country for nearly a year. On May 17, 1849, he married Miss Anna Woubilman, also a native of Germany, and in July of the same year they moved to St. Louis, where they resided for two years. In 1851 they moved to Arkansas, settled in Bolivar, the old county seat of Poinsett County, and here made their home for little more than a year. After this they removed to the Cold Water Spring, and here Mr. Block began clerking for David Block (a man of the same name but no relation), and remained in that capacity for two years, when he became a partner in the business, doing the largest cross roads trade on Crowley's Ridge. In 1859 they shipped 700 bales of cotton and over 10,000 coon-skins. During the year 1858 this firm had the contract to furnish the city of Memphis with beef, and during that year they shipped over 2,600 head. This firm was dissolved

in 1859 by Mr. David Block retiring, and the subject of this sketch then moved to Farm Hill in 1860, and there started a store. He soon built up a large trade by his honest upright dealings, and bought a farm which promised to give good returns, but the war breaking out he was compelled to close his store in August, 1861. In the fall of that year the Confederate soldiers burned 139 bales of cotton for him and a large quantity still in the seed, amounting in all to nearly 300 bales. Mrs. Block, with the assistance of two negro women, succeeded in saving a quantity of cotton by throwing the straw out of the bed ticks and filling them with cotton. Five months later this was taken from the ticks and made into two bales which Mr. Block, with the assistance of his son Isaac, took to Island No. 37, where they sold it for $1.20 per pound. During the years of the war Mr. Block bought cotton and cattle, which he succeeded in smuggling into Memphis, and which resulted in immense profits, as he often sold calico at $1 per yard, coffee at $1 per pound and salt at $100 per barrel. Those goods and others he would buy in exchange for cattle and cotton. In 1865 Mr. Block formed a partnership with his old partner, David Block, J. J. Hamilton and A. A. Luckey, and started a large store at Wittsburg, at the head of navigation on the St. Francis River. Mr. Luckey retired after six months. This firm, known as D. Block & Co., soon became one of the largest commercial firms this section has ever known, doing over $100,000 annually, and during the last year, 1875, their sales were over $175,000. Mr. Hamilton withdrew in 1874, and the subject of this sketch died on October 14, 1875. His widow continued his interest in the business until 1878, when David Block died, and the firm was dissolved, the business being sold out to J. Hall & Co. To the union of Maurice Block and his estimable wife were born ten children, seven sons and three daughters: Adam (died in infancy), Isaac (is a retired merchant and farmer residing at Wynne), William M. (is a real-estate agent at Vanndale), Joseph (a mute, has the position of manager of the freight department for the Missouri Pacific Railroad, at Wynne), Samuel (died in 1870 at the age of thirteen years), Julia (is the wife of Ben Block, a merchant at Memphis), Jefferson Davis (a lawyer, at present prosecuting attorney from the Second judicial district of Eastern Arkansas), Callie (wife of B. T. King, real-estate agent of Springfield), Robert E. Lee (county school examiner of Cross County) and Fannie, who died at the age of ten years, in 1880. Maurice Block was long a leading merchant in this section, and was an active energetic citizen. He was the father of a family of children, all of whom are noted for their success in life, and most of whom have been the author of their own fortunes. His widow, hale and hearty, is still living and enjoying the ample means left of her husband's estate, makes her home alternately with one or the other of her children.

Sol. Block, senior member of the firm of Block & Ralph, merchants and planters, at Bay Ridge, Ark., is a native of Baden, Germany, where his birth occurred in 1827. He was educated in the common schools and under a private tutor, until about twenty-one years of age, when he came to the United States (1849). Here he engaged in business for himself in the State of Illinois, remained there until about 1860, when he moved to St. Louis and there engaged in the insurance business (life, fire and accident). After residing in that city for about ten years he removed to Memphis, where he followed the same business for about the same length of time. In 1878 he came to Forrest City, Ark., was engaged as book-keeper for two years, and then, after making a trip to Europe, returned to Chicago, where he made his home for several years and was engaged in the insurance business. Later he returned to St. Louis, where he embarked in the cigar and tobacco business, continuing at this until 1886, when he came to Cross County, Ark., and in company with J. Ralph, erected a fine storehouse on the farm, which had recently been purchased by Mr. Raphaelski, and which Block & Ralph manage. This farm embraces a tract of 1,400 acres of land and at one time was valuable property, but had been allowed to run down and needed everything in the way of improvement. They at once began to make extensive improvements, soon had 500 acres under

cultivation, some of which they cleared from the timber. They rebuilt the dwelling, erected a large brick stable and a first-class cotton-gin, saw and grist-mill. This gin and mill is the best in the county, costing about $8,000. They have an engine of sixty-five horse-power and can gin twenty-five bales of cotton, and saw 20,000 feet of lumber per day. The lumber is shipped to St. Louis. In the store they keep a full line of general merchandise, buy and ship cotton and all country produce. They carry a stock of goods valued at $6,000 and have a rapidly increasing trade. Mr. Block was married, in 1863, to Miss Amelia Raphaelski, of English and German parentage. She was born in Liverpool, England, and came to the United States with her parents in childhood. Mr. Jacob Ralph, Mr. Block's partner, was born in Memphis, is still a young man, and was in business in Chicago for a short time. He was married, in 1886, to Miss May Bronson, and the fruits of this union has been one child, a daughter named Mabel. This large farm is one of the prettiest as well as the most valuable to be found in this part of the country, and by it may be seen what can be accomplished when the right steps are taken and a proper amount of energy is brought to bear.

I. Block, one of the prominent business men and planters, of Cross County, Ark., was originally from St. Louis County, Mo., where his birth occurred in March, 1851, and is the son of Maurice and Anna (Woubilman) Block. [See sketch of Maurice Block.] I. Block attended school at Harrisburg, in Poinsett County, until the outbreak of the war, and during those troublesome times he assisted his father in many expeditions, smuggling cotton into Memphis, and goods and provisions to the people back home on his return. During those trips they met with many adventures, and endured much hardship, but with cotton at $500 per bale, and all goods that could be brought home yielding an enormous profit, they continued this business until the end of the war. In 1866 I. Block attended school for one year at Wittsburg, and during the next three years he assisted his father on the farm. During 1868 he spent another year in school at Covington, Tenn., and then his father gave him a farm, after which for five years he was engaged in cultivating the soil, "baching it" on the farm. He was quite successful, raising a great deal of cotton, corn and live-stock. In 1875 he went to Wittsburg, and engaged as clerk with his brother, L. N. Block & Co., continuing with this firm for about eight months. At that time his father dying, he entered the firm of D. Block & Co., representing his mother's interest in that business, and continued with the same for about three years, or until 1879, when the firm dissolved partnership. After this he became a member of the firm of L. N. Block & Co., and the title was changed to Block Bros. & Co. This firm immediately began to do a large trade, the first year handling $85,000 worth of cotton, dealing extensively in live-stock and machinery. This firm continued in business until the decline of Wittsburg as a trading point, when they dissolved. For about two years they ran a branch store at Wynne, under the title of Block & Co., and these two stores were connected by a Bell telephone, the only one ever used in Cross County. These stores were closed out together. In 1882 Mr. Block bought 160 acres on the Helena branch of the Iron Mountain Railroad, at Wynne, and continued to add to this tract of land until now he is the owner of 766 acres. In 1884 he built a saw-mill and ginnery at Wynne, and the saw-mill soon became valuable property, as the railroad created a large market for lumber, and during this time Mr. Block acquired the reputation of being the shrewdest saw-mill man in Cross County. They sold this mill in 1888. After clearing out the commercial interests at both Wittsburg and Wynne, Mr. Block applied himself diligently to clearing his large farm adjoining the town of Wynne. In four years time he had cleared up, and reduced to a state of perfect cultivation, 400 acres, and made improvements on the same, which have at once placed this plantation among the highest improved places in the State. This fine piece of land adjoins the town of Wynne, and extends two miles along the railroad, being enclosed for over two miles by solid plank fence. Along the front every twenty acres has a neatly constructed tenant house; each 40 acres has a double four-roomed cottage, and each house is surrounded by a plank fence. This row of cottages, extending for two miles along the road, each one painted white with red trimmings, present the appearance of a street in a town. There is no plantation in Eastern Arkansas that is better improved, or shows better taste, or business judgment in improving or erecting buildings than this. In addition to this place, Mr. Block owns over 1,000 acres in all parts of Cross County, and on those tracts there are about 150 acres under cultivation. Mr. Block now spends most of his time in looking after his extensive farms, and occupies as a residence an attractive home in the city of Wynne. This residence was constructed in 1884 and 1885, and is furnished with taste and care. He was married in 1878, to Mrs. Fannie Puryear, a widow and daughter of J. M. Levesque [see sketch], and his wife, with her many social graces, is a true helpmate to her husband, and his home-life is a pattern of domestic peace. Mr. Block has also built in Wynne a large two-story brick house, with a hall for exhibitions, and the store rooms are elegantly fitted up, and are very attractive. He has also built a number of the houses in the town and several small stores. He is a member of the Masonic fraternity and the Odd Fellows Lodge.

Raphael Block is a leading merchant of Vanndale, was born in the town of Tremblade, Alsace, France, in May, 1852, and was the fourth in a family of five children, born to Herman and Rebecca Block, the father a successful business man of the old country. Raphael remained at home attending schools, until thirteen years of age, and in 1871 determined to seek his fortune in America, and came to Wittsburg, Cross County, Ark., and engaged as a clerk for D. Block & Co., but about two years later, became an employe of G. M. Arnold & Co., general merchants of the same place. In 1874 he engaged in general merchandising at Wittsburg, being associated with B. Block, and they immediately began doing an extensive trade, the largest in all probability that has ever been done by any one firm in Cross County. This partnership was dissolved in 1886, and our subject became sole proprietor, and in 1887 he bought the interest of J. W. Killough, of that well-known mercantile firm of Killough & Erwin, of Vanndale, and since January 1, 1889, has been sole proprietor of this establishment also. He has a large and well-selected stock of general merchandise, amounting to about $10,000, and he commands a large and constantly improving trade. He is quite extensively engaged in buying and shipping cotton, and is an enterprising and wonderfully successful young business man, and is courteous, pleasant and cheerful, a leading spirit in the commercial affairs of the county. He is quite an active politician, and is always found at the polls on election day. Socially he belongs to Arcadia Lodge No. 183, of the A. F. & A. M., at Vanndale, and he also belongs to the K. of H. and the K. & L. of H. December 28, 1874, he was married to Mrs. Hester C. (Hamilton) Perry, a daughter of J. G. Hamilton, a member of the firm of D. Block & Co. They have had five children: Herman (attending school at the Christian Brothers' College of Memphis), Felix, Nina, David and Mary (who died in infancy).

Joseph Block, freight agent for the Missouri Pacific Railroad, is a son of Maurice and Anna Block, his birth occurring in Poinsett County, Ark., in 1853. He is unfortunately a deaf mute, but has a bright mind, and is perfectly capable of filling the position of responsibility conferred upon him by the railroad company. He entered the Little Rock Deaf and Dumb Asylum at the age of fourteen years, and continued in this institution until eighteen years of age, when he began to learn the saddler's trade, serving an apprenticeship of three years at Memphis. He then worked at his trade a short time as journeyman, and received very good wages. After this he engaged in business for himself at Wittsburg as a saddler, but soon began and conducted a saloon under the firm title of Joseph Block & Co. for two years at the above mentioned place. In 1884 he secured a situation as express agent for the Southern Express Company, and held this position for one year to the universal satisfaction of the company and all its patrons. Later he became assistant freight agent, and in 1888 was promoted to general freight agent for the station of Wynne. This railroad company employs over 8,000 men, and Mr. Block is the only mute in their employ. He is exceptionally brilliant, and, but for his infirmity, would long ere this have been included among the prominent business men of this section. He is moral, reliable and temperate in all his habits.

William M. Block, the present efficient and esteemed deputy treasurer of Cross County, and real-estate dealer at Vanndale, was born on the place known as the Bond Farm, in Poinsett (now Cross) County, about eight miles northeast of Vanndale, March 9, 1853, being the third son in a family of eight children born to Maurice and Anna (Woubilman) Block. He was educated in the common schools of this county, and in 1871–72 attended the Tipton County high school, at Covington, Tenn., subsequently taking a course in 1872–73 at the University of Mississippi at Oxford. Upon his return home in September, 1873, Mr. Block was appointed deputy county clerk, under Thomas O. Fitzpatrick, which office he creditably held until the following March, when he became engaged in the livery business at Wittsburg, and the following November was again appointed deputy clerk, under James N. Dobson. In this position he served until the death of Mr. Dobson in December, 1875, at which time he was appointed deputy collector of taxes, under James M. Levesque, remaining so occupied until the following June. Mr. Block engaged in his present business as real-estate agent and abstractor of titles, in June, 1876, and has made and owns the only set of abstract books in Cross County. On May 19, 1880, he was appointed clerk of Cross County, to fill an unexpired term, and also has held office as justice of the peace for six years, having been a notary public the same length of time. The abstracts of Mr. Block's are a model of neatness, by which the transfers of title, and all liens affecting the title of any property in the county can be readily found. He owns considerable property in this and adjoining counties, and also a fine residence in Vanndale, and has no superior as a thoroughly posted man on the real-estate of this county. Mr. Block was married on December 18, 1878, to Miss Alice Austell. They are the parents of three children.

J. D. Block. To the thoughtful mind a contrast between the work of the bar of the present day, and a lawyer's life journey fifty years ago in Arkansas, is something worthy of more than passing interest. The great task necessarily performed by those faithful practitioners of years gone by, did not combine to form a smooth path of gentle declivity leading to a beautiful temple of justice, elaborately arranged with all the comforts and belongings of the present. Neither is success in the legal profession now, won by lack of energy or persevering effort, in the line of this gifted calling. Mr. Block, one of the younger attorneys of Cross County, and its present prosecutor, has attained to a front rank as a member of the bar of the Second judicial district. Born in Poinsett County, Ark., he is the son of Maurice and Anna W. Block, representative people of this county, to whom mention is made elsewhere in this volume. A thorough Arkansan by bringing up, as well as by birth, he secured a good common school education, which only served to fit him more thoroughly for the study of law, whose practice he had decided to make his life vocation. After a careful course he was admitted to the bar and at once entered upon what was destined to be a remarkable experience, for one so young in years. From his majority the field of politics seemed to offer unusual attractions for him, and at an early age he was found active in local political movements throughout Cross County. In 1886 he was elected to the State legislature, and had the distinction of being the youngest member in that important body. His term of service was marked by such decided ability and fitness for the position, that he was subsequently honored by being made prosecuting attorney of his district, receiving the largest vote given any man on the ticket. Mr. Block has also held the office of county school examiner. His public life has already been one to which he may refer with credit. Brave, candid, truthful, with decided opinion, his moral and political convictions have been strong and unwavering. His manners stamp him a gentleman, and his career thus far promises to render him one of the most distinguished of Arkansas' lawyers. Mr. Block if for no other reason would be prominently recognized on account of his connection with that well-known family of Cross County, whose name he bears.

Robert Lee Block, county school examiner, of Cross County, Ark., was born in 1866, about sixteen miles northeast of Vanndale, being the youngest child born to Maurice and Anna Block [see sketch]. At the age of six years he was taken by his parents to Wittsburg, where he received the benefits of the schools of that place for eight years. The three following years he spent in the Christian Brothers' Institute at Memphis, and, being of a studious turn of mind and very industrious, he succeeded in acquiring an excellent education, and graduated from that institution as an A. B. in June, 1884. His first start in life for himself was in the capacity of a clerk in a drug store, at Jonesboro, where he continued to remain until September 28, 1884, after which he went to Springfield, Mo., to accept a position as cashier and book-keeper for Priest & King, remaining with them until August, 1885. His next position was as bill clerk with the Springfield Grocery Company, and after continuing in their employ until May, 1886, he went to Memphis and became stock clerk for Robson, Block & Co., remaining with them until October 12, 1886, when failing health compelled him to seek change of employment. From that time until January 16, 1887, he was an employe of Buck & Trexler, at Crawfordsville, Ark., and then worked for C. O. Richards & Co., as commissary clerk on the Memphis branch of the Iron Mountain Railroad. On June 10, 1887, the work on the west end of the road was finished, and the day following he became book-keeper and clerk for William M. Block, real-estate agent at Vanndale, and with him still remains. January 12, 1889, he was appointed county school examiner, and since filling this position has striven to raise the grade of teachers and the standard of schools by recommending only those who hold the higher grade certificates, and the excellent education which he has eminently fits him for this responsible place. Being enterprising and ambitious to rise in the world, he, in partnership with E. L. Applewhite, on September 9, 1889, started a stock farm on a tract of 700 acres of land, they being joint owners of the same, which they stocked with 130 head of cattle, a one-half Norman horse, seven brood mares, four horses, two Kentucky jacks and eight mules. They have recently put up twenty-five tons of hay, for winter use, besides 1,000 bushels of corn, and, as can readily be seen, are admirably equipped to keep their stock in good condition throughout the winter. They have seventy acres planted in rye, timothy and clover, for spring pasture. Mr. Block belongs to an old and influential family of the county, and has five brothers, all prosperous and intelligent men, and, like himself, are progressive and enterprising in their views.

W. P. Brown, an old settler of Wynne Township, is a native of North Carolina and a son of Thomas and Elizabeth (Speight) Brown, who also came originally from that State. He has been a resident of this county since fifteen years of age. Thomas Brown was numbered among the prominent physicians of Colerain, Bertie County, N. C., and was also proprietor of one of the leading hotels of that place. He came to Arkansas when a boy, but only remained a short time, when he attended the medical school at Philadelphia, from which he graduated, subsequently settling in Colerain, Bertie County, and commencing his practice. He remained there until his death, in February, 1861. He was twice married, first to the mother of our subject, who bore ten children, two still living: W. P. and T. H. Mrs. Brown died in 1855, and in 1858 Dr. Brown was married to Miss Harriet Riddick. Dr. Brown was a member of the A. F. & A. M., and also of the I. O. O. F., and was a man of considerable means. His father owned 100 slaves and gave each of his four children twenty-five negroes. The Doctor was the owner of a saddle belonging to Gen. Zachary Taylor, and which he used during the Mexican War. W. P. Brown was born in 1846, and passed his early days in North Carolina, until fifteen years of age, when he came to Arkansas, residing with an uncle's family in this county. At the age of seventeen years he enlisted in the Confederate service and served two years in McGee's regiment. After the war Mr. Brown commenced farming his aunt's place, where he remained until 1867, later returning to North Carolina and settling up his father's business. Coming again to this county in December of that year, he rented a farm and remained upon it until 1871, when he was married to Miss Laura Jenkins. After his marriage he bought a farm of eighty acres, which had some clearing, but no buildings. In 1884 Mr. Brown traded this farm for his present place, consisting of eighty acres, which was unimproved, with the exception of a house, and of this amount he now has about fifty acres under cultivation. Himself and wife are the parents of six children, all at home: Thomas, Oline, Mattie, Hattie, Paul and Porter. Mr. Brown was elected assessor of this county in 1876, in which capacity he served eight years. Mr. and Mrs. Brown are members of the Methodist Episcopal Church. The former belongs to the Knights of Honor, and is a man who favors all public enterprises.

John B. Bruner was born in Springfield, Ohio, in 1844, and is the fourth of nine children, born to Daniel and Eunice (Bond) Bruner, the father a native of Ohio, and the mother the first female child born in Dunkirk, N. Y. John B. Bruner was reared and attended school in Springfield, Ohio, Jamestown, N. Y. and Meadville, Penn., in all of which places his father was engaged in merchant tailoring. He acquired a good education, and at the age of sixteen years began clerking in a drug store in Dunkirk, and later served in the same capacity in Jamestown, N. Y. and Franklin, Penn. In 1860 he went to the "Hoosier State," and embarked in the lumber business, but after a year or two returned to Jamestown and resumed clerking; after a short time he became dissatisfied with his location and went to Michigan, and served in the same capacity for a grocery firm. In 1871 he went to Memphis, and became a traveling salesman for a liquor house, but discontinued this about four years later and engaged in business for himself. After remaining there about two years he began traveling for a St. Louis firm, remaining with them seven years, purchasing in the meantime, in 1881, a farm of 200 acres, one mile north of Vanndale; 160 acres are under cultivation, and is excellently adapted to raising cotton, corn, grass, etc. He has some thoroughbred Durham cattle, a high grade of Jerseys, and his hogs are a cross between the Berkshire and Poland China. On this farm, in 1887, he erected a fine residence, it being a two-story frame, 60x42 feet, containing nine rooms, ornamented by a number of handsome double porches, and presenting a handsome view from the road. He made other improvements in the way of buildings, and has a fine new barn and other substantial outbuildings. His farm is nearly all under fence, and he has recently set out over a mile of hedge. He is a thoroughgoing and thrifty farmer, who sees the advantage of raising the best of every thing for his family's use, including fruit and berries. With his introduction of blooded stock, new seed grains, different and improved methods of farming, the community will at least have an opportunity of seeing what taste and enterprise, combined with skill and industry, can accomplish. In manner he is agreeable and courteous, and his wife, whose maiden name was Bettie Mansford, and whom he married on February 1, 1875, is an educated and accomplished lady. She was born in Madison County, Tenn., and her father has for a long time been a well-known farmer of Gibson County, and is still residing there.

T. D. Bryant, pastor of the Cumberland Presbyterian Church, of Nolton, and a man thoroughly respected by his fellow-citizens, is originally from South Carolina, as were also his parents, Joab and Mary (Stewart) Bryant, of Scotch and English descent. Joab Bryant was a leading farmer of his county, and though not educated was a well-informed and a good business man. Mr. and Mrs. Bryant were married in 1831, and were the parents of twelve children, nine of whom are living: Louisa (now Mrs. Reid), F. A. (a Methodist minister of Texas), J. R. (also of Texas), Minerva (now Mrs. Hemphis), Elizabeth (who married F. L. Dullard), W. J., J. W., T. D. (our subject), M. L., B. W. (a manufacturer of Mississippi), G. W. (a resident of South America) and Joseph (a resident of this county). The grandfather (on the father's side), James Bryant, was a soldier in the War of 1812. Joab Bryant and wife were connected with the

Methodist Episcopal Church, South. The senior Bryant died in 1874, and his wife in 1889. He was a Mason. T. D. Bryant was reared to farm life. In his boyhood days the advantages for schooling were very limited, but by close application to study he has educated himself, mostly at home. At the age of fourteen Mr. Bryant enlisted in the Confederate service, joining the First Regiment of Heavy Artillery of South Carolina, which was stationed at Fort Sumter, and in 1862 joined the regular army; was in a number of hard-fought battles, and witnessed the bombardment of Fort Sumter on April 7, 1863, and was present at its capitulation. He was captured at Smithfield, but, escaping, was recaptured the same night. Mr. Bryant served as orderly and was promoted to sergeant. While in the army he was wounded four times, once in the head by a piece of shell, again, on James Island, by a bayonet thrust into the left side, which entered between the fifth and sixth rib; then again in the knee joint and also in the arm by a bayonet. After the war he returned home and the following year moved to Kentucky, where he engaged in farming in the eastern part of the State and also taught school. In 1867 he removed to Dwyer County, Tenn., where he farmed, following this for two years, then taught for two years in McNairy County, Tenn. He returned to South Carolina and busied himself with farming and teaching for twelve years. In 1882 he removed to Alabama and in 1886 immigrated to Arkansas, settling on his present property, which comprises 120 acres of land, with thirty-five under cultivation. Mr. Bryant was born in 1846. He has been twice married, first in 1866 to Miss N. J. Fitzgerald, of South Carolina, who died in 1871, and who was the mother of three children: George (a resident of this county), Edgar (a resident of South Carolina) and Elector (a teacher in South Carolina). Mr. Bryant was married the second time to Miss D. E. Fitzgerald, in 1872. They have been given seven children, all living: Lillie, Joseph, Milas, Lelier, Lulu, Thomas and Talmage. Mr. Bryant began preaching in 1885, three months before joining the presbytery, and he is the founder of the first Creek Cumberland Presbyterian Church, as well as the

22

Cumberland Presbyterian Church of Woodruff County. Mr. Bryant preaches in Cross, Woodruff, Poinsett and Jackson Counties, and is very active in all religious and educational enterprises. He is a Royal Arch Mason.

Archie S. Casbeer began life as a saloon keeper at Wittsburg in 1870. In 1874 he commenced clerking in the store, and in March, 1879, opened a general merchandise establishment, which he continued for three years, after which he conducted a saloon and grocery combined. In 1886 he started his present store, carrying a small stock of general merchandise valued at about $1,000. He also owns 587 acres of land in this county, and forty acres in St. Francis County. Mr. Casbeer was born in St. Francis County, October 13, 1844, being a son of Thomas M. and Martha A. (May). The former was born in Maury County, Tenn., on July 4, 1813, and was of German parentage. Thomas Casbeer, Sr., the grandfather of our subject, immigrated to Arkansas in 1817, and was one of the early settlers of St. Francis County. Thomas Casbeer, Sr., was a farmer, blacksmith and proprietor of a large saw-mill. He was married September 13, 1838, and died on September 25, 1872. Mrs. Casbeer first saw the light in North Carolina, September 25, 1820, and died October 2, 1867; she was the mother of thirteen children, five of whom are now living. Archie S. Casbeer enlisted in the Confederate service in a cavalry regiment during the war, in which he served one year, and was in the battles of Big Creek, near Helena, Pilot Knob, Fort Scott, and a number of skirmishes. Mr. Casbeer is a Royal Arch Mason, a member of the I. O. O. F., also of the Knights of Honor and Knights and Ladies of Honor. He is a strong Democrat, and has held the offices of constable and deputy sheriff. January 7, 1874, he was married to Delana Block, a native of this county, who died June 28, 1887, having become the mother of two children, one of whom is living. She was a member of the Methodist Episcopal Church, South. Mr. Casbeer has a gourd dated 1766, which was used as a powder-flask by his grandfather, T. M. Casbeer, Sr., at the battle of New Orleans.

William J. Cobb, Vanndale, Ark. The entire life of Mr. Cobb has been passed in an industrious manner, and not without fairly substantial results of success. He was born in Washington County, Ark., in 1846, was the second in a family of eight children born to William A. and Susan (Brodie), the father a native of North Carolina, and the mother of Tennessee. The father was reared to farm life and attended school in his native State until about twenty-one years of age, when he went to La Grange, Tenn. There he attended school for about a year, and was then ordained a minister in the Methodist Episcopal Church by the Tennessee Conference. He then began preaching on a circuit in North Alabama, and was engaged in this work about one year. In about 1838 he came to Arkansas, followed his ministerial duties in this State, and after a year or two was sent by the Conference of Arkansas to the Indian Nation, where he preached, and had charge of the mission schools of that Territory until about 1854. Prior to that time, about 1844, he had married in Washington County, Ark., the daughter of Ludwick Brodie, a pioneer from Middle Tennessee, to Northwestern Arkansas. After giving up the work in the Indian Nation, he was on the retired list for a year or so, and in 1857, he, with his family, went to Florida, where, after residing about a year, they came further north, and located at Trenton, Tenn., in order to educate their children. Here he followed farming, was also engaged in merchandising, continuing at this until 1862, when the family returned to Poinsett, now Cross County, and settled about two miles southeast of the present village of Vanndale. Here he at once took charge of the Poinsett Male and Female Academy, which educational institution he conducted during war times, the last session of this school being held in 1865–66. He then joined the conference, and was immediately placed in charge of the Harrisburg Circuit, preaching from that time until 1873, in various districts and circuits of Eastern Arkansas. About that time he retired, and soon after died from a cancer, which had troubled him for many years. W. J. Cobb was attending school at Trenton, Tenn., at the breaking out of the war, but came with his parents to Arkansas, in 1862. In 1863, at the age of sixteen years, he enlisted in the Confederate army, and was assigned duty in Eastern Arkansas, participating in his first engagement near Augusta, on White River. He was with Gen. Price on his Missouri raid, and was in every engagement of that campaign. After that he returned with his regiment to Arkansas, and on May 25, 1865, surrendered at Wittsburg. He then at once began farming in Cross County, on his father's place, and here he remained until 1878, after which he went to Northwest Arkansas, and was engaged as clerk for A. A. Brodie, a merchant at Huntsville, Madison County. Here he remained four years, when he returned to Cross County, and again followed agricultural pursuits on the old homestead. He remained there until 1887, when he moved to Vanndale, bought a lot, erected a dwelling, and has since made his home there, following the carpenter's trade. In February, 1889, he engaged with Killough & Erwin as clerk in the store at Vanndale. He was married, in 1874, to Miss Alice E. Burnett, a native of Tennessee, but who was principally reared in Arkansas, and who is a daughter of John O. Burnett. Mr. Burnett was a soldier in the Confederate army, was wounded in the battle of Prairie Grove, and died from the effects. His family are members of the Methodist Episcopal Church, South.

William H. Cole, one of the genial members of the enterprising firm of Smith, Cole & Davis, also the general manager of the three mills owned by this firm, is a Pennsylvanian by birth, being a son of Joseph and Ellen (Yost) Cole, of German descent, the paternal grandfather, Joseph Cole, was a hotel keeper and also owned an interest in a lumber business. He moved to Iowa, living in this State about four years, then in 1870 came to Mississippi County, Ark., where he busied himself in farming until his death, which occurred in 1872. To the parents were given seven children, five of whom are still living: William H., Clemenza E. (the wife of John J. Merrison), J. C., James R. and Edward F. William H. Cole (whose biography is here given) was born in 1852, and lived at home with his mother until 1875, when he started

in the mercantile business at Richardson's Landing, Tenn., which he followed for four years, losing in this business some $10,000, after which he went into the lumber business, being very successful. In October, 1888, he removed his mill and family to this county and located near Bay Village, erected a saw-mill in charge of the firm of Cole & Davis, which was moved from Tipton County, Tenn., where it had been operated six or seven years by said firm. They bought 260 acres of timber land and erected their first mill, which turns out annually about 1,500,000 feet of lumber, the capacity of this mill being 20,000 to 22,000 feet daily. In June, 1889, they bought the mill at Levesque, of John N. White, which has been improved and now turns out 2,000,000 feet annually. Messrs. Smith, Cole & Davis have now under lease another mill, which has about the same capacity as the one at Levesque. They also have a planing-mill connected with one of their mills. Mr. Cole was married on September 25, 1877, to Miss Martha Isabelle Davis, and they are the parents of four children, two of whom are living: Elizabeth and John. Mrs. Cole is a member of the Old School Presbyterian Church. Mr. Cole is one of the prominent men of his county, known and respected by all.

William H. Copland, a prominent and energetic farmer of Searcy Township, was born in Tennessee in 1827, and was the younger of two children, the result of the union of Thomas and Elizabeth (Huey) Copland, respectively of North Carolina and South Carolina origin. The father was a farmer by occupation principally, but for a long time found employment in overseeing and railroad contracting. In 1840 he was under contract to build three miles on the Georgia Railroad, and after that he followed agricultural pursuits in the last-named State, but before he had gathered the crops, sold out and in 1843 came to Arkansas. He remained in this State but a few months when he went to Memphis and there resided for one year. From there he went to Georgia, thence to Mississippi, but not finding a location to suit him he returned to Tennessee, where he bought land and remained until 1849. He then went to Memphis, and later spent a number of months in various parts of Arkansas, settling eventually in Poinsett County, where he died in 1872 at the age of seventy-three years. William H. Copland remained with his father until 1846, when he came to Arkansas and located in what is now Cross County, where he farmed for a number of years on rented land. In May, 1859, he married Mrs. Hester Stanley (*nee* Hamilton), a daughter of Theopolis and Mary Hamilton, natives of Georgia and South Carolina, respectively. Mrs. Hamilton was born in a fort which the men protected from the Indians. Mr. and Mrs. Hamilton came to Cross County, Ark., in 1836, and settled on what is now known as the Bay-Road. They were obliged to go a long way to mill and endured many hardships. Mr. Hamilton bought 160 acres of land in 1837, cleared about forty acres, erected buildings and made quite a pleasant home. He did much to improve the country, and took a great interest in politics, and in fact all that pertained to the good of the country. He died in 1849. His daughter Hester, the wife of the subject of this sketch, was married first in 1837 to Mr. George Shaver, also a descendant of one of the old pioneer families. He died in 1846 leaving his wife with three children: Obediah, Charles and Mary, all deceased and the sons dying in the army. In 1852 Mrs. Shaver married Mr. S. Stanley, who died in 1859 leaving her with two children, Nancy and Leander, both of whom died in childhood, and the father and children dying within two weeks of each other. At the time of his marriage Mr. Copland had about 100 acres under cultivation, and now has another 100 acres also under cultivation. He has made many improvements, and in 1863 planted an orchard which is still the best in the county. His fine residence was erected in 1855. In 1870 Mr. Copland erected a horse-gin, which he ran for ten years, when it was replaced with a steam-gin. This he sold in 1886. He is the owner of 440 acres of land, 200 of which are under cultivation. In 1863 he enlisted in the Confederate army, was in all the battles of Gen. Price's raid through Missouri and never received a wound. In November, 1864, he returned home, surrendering at Wittsburg in the spring of 1865. Mrs. Copland is a member of the Baptist Church, and Mr. Copland is a member of the K. of H. In 1876 he fell from a horse and hurt his leg, rendering amputation necessary, the following year. To the marriage of Mr. and Mrs. Copland has been born one child, a son, Willie, whose birth occurred in 1861. He is living at home, and has control and management of the farm. Mr. and Mrs. Copland are among the intelligent and much respected citizens of Cross County and are universally respected.

S. Daltroff, of the firm of Daltroff, Sparks & Oliver, merchants at Wynne, Ark., is an affable, pleasant gentleman, and is now at the head of one of the largest firms in Eastern Arkansas. He began his commercial life as an errand boy, and rose by rapid stages, until he occupied the highest places, and was always a trusted employe. His birth occurred in New Orleans, La., August 13, 1852, and he was the youngest in a family of six children born to the union of S. and Fannie (Seelig) Daltroff, natives of France and Germany, respectively. The parents were married in Mayence, Germany, in 1844, and immediately emigrated to the United States, landing at New Orleans early in 1845. The father started a private school of languages, teaching French, German and Hebrew, and continued this in New Orleans until 1853, when he went to Lake Providence, La. Here he started a general store, but soon discontinued, and proceeded to Vicksburg, where they remained until 1861. From there they went to Memphis, and here the mother died in 1880, and the father June 29, 1881. S. Daltroff, Sr., was very talented, and from the conclusion of the war until his death, taught languages, mostly in Memphis. While in that city, and during the war, he was foreman of the cannon molding of the Confederate army, and when Memphis fell he followed the fortunes of the Confederate cause, and was located at Meridian, Miss. Here he remained until 1864, when he returned to his family at Memphis. S. Daltroff, Jr., was reared principally in Memphis, where he attended the public schools, and later the Commercial College of Leddins, in the same city. After leaving school he began his mercantile career as errand boy, and advanced with this firm until he was made shipping and receiving clerk over the wholesale department. He remained with this firm for seven years, or until 1873, when he engaged with Lowenstein & Bros., as shipping and receiving clerk. At the outbreak of yellow fever in Memphis Mr. Daltroff left this firm, made an extensive trip through the Southern States, and in 1875 came to Wittsburg, Cross County, where he accepted a position with D. Block & Co. He only remained with this firm two months, when he was transported to the firm of L. N. Block & Co., and remained with the same until April, 1877, when he was admitted as a member of the firm. This partnership lasted until 1879, when it was dissolved, and Mr. Daltroff accepted a position as book-keeper for the firm of Block Bros. & Co., remaining with them until 1883, when he became a member of that firm, remaining in this company until 1886, when it was dissolved. He then became senior member of the present firm of Daltroff, Sparks & Oliver, the successors of Block Bros & Co. This firm almost immediately removed to Wynne, where they started a large store, but this was burned out in 1887. After this they erected a large brick building, covering 290 square feet of floor, which is the finest arranged commercial building in Eastern Arkansas. They carry a stock of goods valued at $15,000, which comprises a full line of dry goods, clothing, boots and shoes, hats and caps, groceries and general plantation supplies. Mr. Daltroff was married, in 1879, to Miss Willie Malone, a daughter of Rev. W. C. Malone, of this county. She died in 1886, leaving three children, all daughters: Frederica, Bettie M. and Willie Florence. In December, 1887, Mr. Daltroff married Miss Rosa Ackerman, a native of Pennsylvania. On his arrival at Wynne Mr. Daltroff erected a fine residence, which, after the death of his wife, in 1886, he sold to his partner, G. N. Sparks. In 1888 he erected another home, which is among the handsomest and best residences in Wynne. Mr. Daltroff is a member of the K. of P., Levesque Lodge No. 53, at Wynne, and he is Chancellor Commander of the same. He is a Royal Arch Mason, is a K. of H. and K & L. of H., belonging to John M. Hewitt and Pearl Lodges.

He is active in politics, and is a stanch Democrat.

R. J. Ellis, one of the oldest settlers of Mitchell Township, and among its leading farmers, is a native of Tennessee, and came to this county in 1856 with his father, where he purchased a farm of eighty acres, remaining upon it for three years. Then he accepted a position as overseer of a large plantation owned by Jesse Cross, D. J. Burt and Maj. Wynne, a position that he held until the breaking out of the war, when he joined the Confederate army, in Company C, of the Thirteenth Arkansas Infantry, and participated in the battles of Shiloh, Corinth, Richmond, Murfreesboro and a number of others. He was taken sick at Murfreesboro and sent to the hospital, where he received his discharge and returned home. He was also shot at the battle of Belmont in the arm, by a minie ball. Mr. Ellis sold his farm in 1865, and moved to Shelby County, Tenn., where he remained until 1871, engaged in farming one year, and the rest of the time operating a saw and gristmill. In 1871 he returned to Cross County, entered 103 acres under the homestead laws, and now has sixty-one acres under cultivation, with good buildings. Born in Carroll County, Tenn., in 1833, he is the son of William and Elizabeth (Allin) Ellis, natives of North Carolina and Tennessee, respectively, and the parents of ten children. William Ellis moved to Arkansas in 1849, and located in this county, bought a farm of eighty acres, partially improved, and remained until 1865, then returning to Tennessee, where he died the following year; his wife survived him until 1886. Both were members of the Presbyterian Church. R. J. Ellis was married, in 1856, to Miss Sophia Burks, and they became the parents of five children, two of whom are living: W. A. and Elizabeth (the wife of John Stephens). Mrs. Ellis died in 1873, and Mr. Ellis married his second wife in 1875. She was formerly Miss Mollie Airs, and lived about four years after marriage. In 1881 Mr. Ellis married Mrs. Mary Robinson (nee Mitchell). Mr. and Mrs. Ellis are members of the Seven Day Baptist Church, his first and second wives having belonged to the Missionary Baptist Church. He is a member of the County Wheel and is a strong Democrat, taking an active interest in the politics of the day.

James E. Erwin, merchant, Vanndale, Ark. In this brief outline of the life of this representative citizen of Cross County appear facts which are greatly to his credit, given as plainly as it is possible to put them, and without the intention of anything savoring of flattery. Mr. Erwin is a member of the general mercantile firm of Killough, Erwin & Co., of Vanndale, Ark., which business was established in 1889, and they carry a full stock of general merchandise, dry goods, groceries, clothing and plantation supplies. Mr. Erwin owes his nativity to Tennessee, and his birth occurred in 1849, and is the sixth of ten children born to W. F. and Lucinda (Tucker) Erwin, natives of Tennessee, where the father followed farming until 1856. He then came to Arkansas, settled in Hempstead County, where he remained until 1868, when he came to Poinsett County, and located near Harrisburg. He there purchased a farm of over 200 acres, cleared much of it, made many improvements and here died in 1872. The mother died many years previous, about 1855. James E. Erwin divided his time in youth between assisting on the farm and in attending the common schools where he received a good practical education. At the age of nineteen years he engaged as clerk after which he kept the books of a firm in Harrisburg. In the spring of 1873 he went to Wittsburg and became a book-keeper for the firm of D. Block & Co. until 1877, after which he bought an interest in the business and continued a member of the same until the firm closed out in 1879. On February 1 of the same year Mr. Erwin, with J. W. Killough, formed the firm of Killough & Erwin, and began business at Wittsburg, continuing there until February, 1884, when they moved to Vanndale. In February, 1884, Mr. Killough sold his interest to R. Block, and for two years after this the firm continued as Block & Erwin. In 1889 Mr. Erwin sold out to his partner and soon started in a new store as the present firm of Killough, Erwin & Co. This firm carries a full stock of general merchandise, dry goods, groceries, clothing and plantation supplies. Mr. Erwin was married in 1872 to Miss R. M. Wade, a native of Virginia, and the daughter of W. H. Wade, who came to Poinsett County in 1860. To the union of Mr. and Mrs. Erwin were born three children: William F. (attending school at Searcy College), Henry Gordon, and Hugh Maitland. The family are members of the Methodist Episcopal Church, South. Mr. Erwin is an enterprising business man and for years identified with the commercial interests of Cross County, and is always found at the head of all improvements of a public nature. He takes a deep interest in school matters and is at present director of Vanndale School.

J. T. Fannin was reared on a farm in Georgia, and at the age of nineteen commenced farming for himself on a rented place, on which he remained three years, then moving to Western Tennessee, his place of abode for two years. In 1875 coming to Cross County, Ark., he rented for two years, when he bought his present farm, consisting of 320 acres of fine bottom land, with thirty-five acres under cultivation. He now has 120 acres improved, and on it has erected a fine residence, having lost his former dwelling, furniture and household goods by fire in March, 1889. J. T. Fannin was born in Georgia in 1844, the son of John and Eliza (Thomas) Fannin, natives of North Carolina. Mr. Fannin, Sr., was a farmer by occupation, rented land in North Carolina for awhile, and shortly after his marriage moved to Georgia, then, in 1862, going to Kentucky, where he remained for two years. Returning thence to Georgia, in 1874 he went to Western Tennessee and settled in Fayette County, where he made his home for some eight or ten years, or until coming to Arkansas in 1885, and locating in Cross County, where he still lives at the age of seventy-five years. Mr. Fannin took part in the Indian War of 1836, and in the Mexican War, and during the late war served in the Home Guards in the Confederate service. Mr. Fannin has been twice married, first to the mother of our subject, by which marriage he was the father of eleven children, seven of whom are still living: William (resides in Georgia), Martha (wife of A. Wadkins), Lafayette, Wylie A., J. T. (our subject), Alfred B. and J. A. (a resident of Western Tennessee). Mrs. Fannin was a member of the Baptist Church, and died in 1883. Mr. Fannin was married the second time in 1885 to Elizabeth Thomas, who bore four children. J. T. Fannin was married in 1868 to Mrs. Harriet Daugherty (*nee* Garrin). This union resulted in the birth of seven children, six of whom are living: Thomas, Amanda, Emma, John, F. V. and Alice. Mrs. Fannin died April 16, 1885. Mr. Fannin was married the second time in December, 1888, to Miss Bettie Spillman. They are members of the Methodist Episcopal Church. Mr. Fannin belongs to the K. of H., and is a liberal contributor to all enterprises for the good of the community in which he lives.

W. A. Faulkner is a son of William and Permelia (Mullins) Faulkner. William Faulkner, Sr., was born and reared near London, England, and emigrated to this country some time in the 40's, locating in Mississippi, and followed his trade, that of brick-mason and plasterer, until 1869, when he removed to Arkansas, settling in this county, where he entered land under the pre-emption laws. During the Rebellion, he served in the Confederate army for two years. Mrs. Faulkner died in 1859, leaving two children: W. A. (our subject) and James T. She was a member of the Methodist Episcopal Church. Mr. Faulkner was married the second time in 1861, to Mary Jackson, who died in 1871, leaving one child, now deceased, and in 1872 he married his third wife, Mrs. Lou Smith (*nee* Ellis), who is still living. To this union were given four children, three of whom still live: Robert, Lillie and Edward. He and wife belong to the Methodist Episcopal Church. W. A. was born in Mississippi, in 1855, where he spent his younger days, coming to this county with his father when fourteen years of age. At the age of twenty-one he rented a farm which he worked for three years. He then bought his present farm of 240 acres, which he works, besides one of 160 acres belonging to his wife. His farm is considered among the finest in the county, having good buildings upon it, a large orchard of some seven or eight acres and good stock. He was married, in 1879, to Mrs. Sarah Bowers (*nee* Auldrigh). They are the parents of two children:

I. H. and N. B. His wife has been married three times, her first husband being James Stephenson, her second Jacob Bowen, who lived only one month after their marriage, and the third, Mr. Faulkner. Mr. Faulkner is an enterprising and industrious farmer and highly respected by all who know him.

William Fountain, one of the oldest and most respected farmers in Cross County, was born in 1829 to the union of Cary and Sarah (Powers) Fountain, natives of North Carolina and of English descent, the paternal grandfather of our subject coming to this country from England. Cary Fountain was a farmer by occupation, and a slave owner. The paternal grandfather served in the Revolutionary War after emigrating to this country, and the maternal grandfather served in the American Navy. Cary Fountain was the father of six children, two of whom only are living: Maria (wife of Wyatt Earp, of North Carolina) and William (our subject). The latter was reared on a farm in North Carolina, his native State, and at the age of fourteen engaged in teaming, hauling turpentine, in which occupation he was engaged for two or three years. He was afterward occupied in clerking in a dry-goods store for some years, and then learned the carpenter's trade, at which he worked for about twenty years. Mr. Fountain has been married three times; first to Martha A. Cutchins, who died in 1855, leaving four children, one now surviving, George A., who resides in this county. His second wife was Clara A. Parker, a native of Tennessee; she was a member of the Methodist Church, and died in 1880, leaving one child now deceased. In 1880 Mr. Fountain was married to his third and present wife, Mrs. Charlotte T. Martin (*nee* Shaver). They are the parents of two children: Cary E. and Ernest R. In 1849 he left North Carolina for Tennessee, and remained there until 1860, when he came to Cross County, Ark., locating on the place on which he now resides. This then consisted of 140 acres, upon it there being a log-cabin, with ten or twelve acres of land under cultivation. He now owns 827 acres, 100 under cultivation, and raises a large amount of stock, which costs but little to keep through the winter. Mr. Fountain is a member of the Masonic lodge, and holds the office of Junior Warden. He was formerly a notary public of Cross County, and has held the office of constable for about six years, serving as school director for some twenty years. He is also president of the County Wheel, and is one of the prominent Democrats of the county.

Alexander Futrell, farmer and stock raiser of Vanndale, Ark. Among the influential and respected citizens of Cross County, Ark., there is no one more justly entitled to representation in this work than Alexander Futrell. He was born in Northampton County, N. C., in 1830; was taught the duties of farm life when quite young and received his education in the common schools. At the age of twenty-one he came to Arkansas, settled in Poinsett County, where he was engaged as overseer until the outbreak of the war. He then enlisted in Company A, Fifth Arkansas Regiment Infantry, and was in the battles of Shiloh, Perryville, Murfreesboro, Chickamauga, Nashville and Franklin, and was in ten other of the principal engagements, besides many skirmishes. He was in the battle of Raleigh, N. C., and two days later surrendered at Greensboro, N. C. He then made a visit to his old home, where he spent three months, then returned to Cross County, Ark., settling on a tract of 160 acres of wild land, one mile west of the present city of Vanndale. In 1868 he married Miss Isabella F. Lewellen, daughter of James A. and Nancy E. Lewellen, after which he removed to his new home, erected buildings and made many improvements. At the end of four years he had eighty acres under cultivation and has a pleasant and comfortable home. He raises a variety of crops and can make three-fourths of a bale of cotton to the acre and forty bushels of corn. By his marriage Mr. Futrell became the father of these children: Eddie E. (died at the age of seven years), John Lewellen, James A., Blanchard W., Mary B., Gordon C., Emma M., Ernest H., Pearl. Gordon C. died at the age of six years; Ernest H. at the age of six months. The family are members of the Methodist Episcopal Church, South. Mr. Futrell is one of the most progressive

and enterprising farmers of the county; is honest, industrious and a man who has the respect of all. He is the youngest son born to John and Charity Futrell, and was left fatherless when a child. The father was also a farmer and was born, reared and passed his last days in the same county.

William Ganley was a son of James Ganley, who was born in Ireland and emigrated to this country soon after his marriage, locating in New Jersey, about five miles below Trenton, on the Delaware River; afterward he moved to Philadelphia, where he died about 1833. His wife, formerly Bridget Doane, died in St. Louis from the cholera, as did also several of the children. They reared a family of eleven children, of whom William, our subject, was the seventh. The latter was born in New Jersey, March 17, 1827, and was reared in that State until about eighteen years of age, when he left home and came west, engaging in rafting lumber down the Mississippi from Minnesota to St. Louis. In this occupation he continued for eleven years, being the first man to take a raft of pine lumber from Minnesota to that city between the points mentioned, an industry that has now grown to one of considerable proportions. He then started for California, but passing through Cross County, Ark., became interested in the beauty of the country and stopped here, and has since made it his home. When first coming to this county Mr. Ganley embarked in the lumber business and afterward went to farming, in which he is still interested. He was married about 1852, to Martha Miles, a native of Alabama, who died in 1862, leaving five children, one of whom only is living, Bridget, still at home. Mr. Ganley now owns 600 acres of land, with 100 acres under cultivation, located near the Tyronza River; he has good buildings and a large orchard. He is a Catholic in religion and a Democrat in politics.

Cassius M. Gardner is a progressive farmer and stockman of Cross County, and was born about three miles east of the present village of Vanndale, in 1858, and was the eldest of seven children born to William H. and Martha A. (Malone) Gardner, who were natives of Virginia and Tennessee, respectively. The former, with his father, was among the early pioneers of the State of Tennessee, and there received the most of his rearing. In 1854 he came to Arkansas and settled in what is now Cross County, and here he was married in 1856 to Miss Martha Malone, a daughter of Samuel Malone, one of the pioneers of Arkansas. Mr. Gardner purchased land for a farm and soon opened a store at a place called Pineville, and here held forth for a short time, being one of the first merchants of the place. In 1885 he sold his farm to locate in the village of Vanndale, and here he has since lived in retirement. His son, Cassius M., attended the district schools of Cross County until he was seventeen years of age, and then for a short time was an attendant of the schools of Forrest City and Wittsburg. After clerking in the postoffice of the former place for a short time he, in 1878, settled in Wittsburg and became an employe of Block Bros. & Co. and remained with them for nearly four years. He then returned to the farm, having previously purchased 240 acres, and here built a nice dwelling-house and made many other valuable improvements, clearing forty acres, and now has ninety acres in an excellent state of cultivation. In 1887 he bought forty acres adjoining Vanndale, on which he erected a handsome cottage the following year, and in the winter moved to his new home. He has a fine property and is rapidly making improvements, and, being enterprising and possessing ideas aside from the beaten track, his labors are always attended with good results. In 1885 he was married to Miss Helen Halk, a daughter of Nathan and Amelia Halk, the former of whom died in 1887. The latter still lives on her fine farm on the Cherry Valley Road. To Mr. and Mrs. Gardner have been born two children: Bertram F. (who died at the age of eighteen months) and Olive V. (who died when seven months old). Mr. Gardner belongs to Pearl Lodge of the K. & L. of H. of Vanndale.

John Graham, a very successful farmer and a member of the firm of Smith, Graham & Jones, merchants at Wynne, owes his nativity to North Carolina, where his birth occurred in 1847, and is the eldest in a family of five children, born to C. C. and Mary E. (Mebane) Graham, both natives of North Carolina. The father conducted an iron furnace and owned iron mines in his native State, but sold his interest and moved to Arkansas in 1854. He bought a large tract of land, 1,100 acres in all, southeast of the present village of Wynne, which was a dense wilderness at the time, and immediately proceeded to clear the land, erect buildings and to make other improvements. The house now on the place was partially erected in 1854, and the modern two-story frame in 1860. As early as 1855 Mr. Graham erected a horse-power cotton-gin, the only one at that time within ten miles. During the war Mr. Graham remained at home, followed farming to some extent, but was often interrupted by raids from Federal soldiers. At the close of the war he engaged in merchandising at Wittsburg under the title of Knight, Graham & Co. Knight withdrew and the name was changed to Graham, Thomas & Co. This firm did an extensive business, and the partners made considerable money. In 1870 Mr. Graham withdrew from the business and soon went to Memphis, where he engaged in the commission business under the firm name of Rutland, Graham & Co. After two years Mr. Graham withdrew and was soon elected president of the Mechanic and Trader's Bank in Memphis. He was in this office for about four years when he resigned and engaged in the brokerage business. During his residence in Memphis he erected a number of dwellings, also some business houses and was an active business man up to the time of his death, which occurred August 18, 1886. In Mr. Graham's life we can trace the active and successful business man. In fact, few men in the early history of our country have shown a greater knowledge of how to carve their fortune from the rough elements of the times. He was esteemed as one of the most progressive, intelligent and energetic business men of the community, and was in every way a worthy man and citizen.

"'Tis ever wrong to say a good man dies".

He always lived a correct life and was one of the leading members of the Second Presbyterian Church in Memphis. John Graham was reared to farm labor and attended the common schools at home until 1858, when he attended school at Greensboro, N. C. Subsequently he was under the instruction of a teacher at a private school and remained there until the breaking out of the late war. In 1863, when only sixteen years of age, he enlisted in Company A, McGee's regiment cavalry, and for a year operated in Eastern Arkansas. In 1864 he joined Gen. Price in his Missouri raid, was in the battle of Pilot Knob and in all the battles until West Port, when, holding the field until Price could escape with the wagon train, our subject was captured, taken to Kansas City and later to Fort Leavenworth, where he was held in captivity, and after some time was removed to Camp Morton, Ind., and here retained until the close of the war, being released about June 1. He immediately started for home and made the journey from Memphis on foot. He at once took charge of his father's farm. In 1866 he went to Mebaneville school, remained there one year and then came home, residing with his parents for one year. From there he removed to the bottoms, engaged in agricultural pursuits for himself and there remained three years. Following this he took charge of the old homestead, while his father went to Memphis, and tilled the soil for five years, after which his father gave him an interest in the place, on which he erected a dwelling and there resided. At the time of the father's death he bought out the heirs and moved back to the old homestead. Since then he has cleared about sixty acres and now has 500 in a fine state of cultivation, and on another tract near by he has sixty acres under cultivation. He moved his gin to the home place, has a good dwelling, orchard and is considered one of the best farmers in the county. He is quite extensively engaged in stock raising, principally mules, and has been very successful at this, raising some of the largest and finest mules ever seen in the State, and as good as any from Kentucky or in fact, any State. He seeds down a large part of his farm to improve and fertilize the soil. He raises large crops of cotton and corn and is a practical, as well as a scientific farmer. His farm embraces about 600 acres under cultivation, lying on the west slope of Crowley's Ridge, and presents a

magnificent view, for, from his residence, nearly every acre is spread out like a picture before the eye. He was married in December, 1870, to Miss Jennie Allen, a daughter of Abijah Allen, one of the early settlers and prominent farmers of St. Francis County. Eight children were the result of this union: Mary C., Charles C. (died at the age of three years), John M., Abijah Allen (died at the age of three weeks), Jennie Clay, Willie Vernon (died at the age of three years), Carey Osceola and James Franklin. Mrs. Graham is a member of the Presbyterian Church. In 1888 Mr. Graham joined with his partners in the large mercantile firm at Wynne. He is the leading spirit in all movements pertaining to the good of the country, and is not only a leading farmer, but is a member of the leading commercial firm in Cross County.

G. W. Griffin is a successful farmer, and is the proprietor of the Vanndale livery stable. He was born in Georgia in 1839, and was the eldest in a family of six children born to Tilam M. and Elizabeth (Raspberry) Griffin, the former a blacksmith by trade, who, in 1854, came to Arkansas, and settled one mile east of the present village of Vanndale, where he began following his trade, his establishment being the first of the kind in this section of the country. Here he died in 1856, his wife's death having occurred in Alabama, prior to the coming of the family to Arkansas. G. W. Griffin acquired a fair knowledge of the English branches in Tennessee and Alabama, and after his father's death, when only eighteen years of age, he took charge of the blacksmith shop, and continued this business without a break until the opening of the war. He enlisted in Capt. Martin's Company, Fifth Arkansas Regiment, Trans-Mississippi Department, and was in the battles of Greenville, Prairie Grove, Jenkins' Ferry, and Pleasant Hill, and also in a number of minor engagements, serving in the cavalry for some time. After his return from the war he farmed for one year, then opened the shop at the old stand continuing there until the spring of 1882, when he moved to the village of Vanndale, and engaged in business there. In 1860 he bought a small tract of land comprising five acres, added five more in 1867, and two years later bought fifty-five acres, all of which was wild land. He has since had it all cleared, and has continued to purchase from time to time, until he now owns 331 acres, and has 100 acres under tillage. His dwelling-house and barns are in good condition, and his fences are kept in excellent repair, in fact he is a thoroughgoing and thrifty farmer, as can easily be seen in giving a glance at his farm. He is Worshipful Master of Arcadia Lodge No. 183, A. F. & A. M. Mr. Griffin was elected to the office of county treasurer, and served two terms by re-election. He has also held the office of justice of the peace for three years. In 1861 he was married to Miss Mary E. Snowden, a native of Fayette County, Tenn., who came with her father, W. H. Snowden, to Arkansas in 1858. This gentleman was also a blacksmith, and died in 1881. To Mr. and Mrs. Griffin was born the following family of children: Silas W. (who lived to be twenty-seven years of age, and died April 10, 1889), Susan C. (who was married, died in 1886), Sarah Irene, Nannie Izoarah, Annie, Mollie Virginia, Mattie, Charles George, Frank Lee, Hugh and one that died unnamed. Mr. Griffin is a member of the Methodist Episcopal Church, South.

James O. Halk is a son of M. T. and Permelia (Stacy) Halk, who came to Arkansas from Georgia, and settled in what was then Poinsett (now Cross) County, in 1843, entering 200 acres of land in the locality known as "Crowley's Ridge." As part of his first crop he put in six acres of cotton, which was considered a large amount in that section of the country at the time. He afterward sold his farm and bought a place containing 400 acres on the west side of the ridge, where he lived at the time of his death, in 1887, at the age of sixty-three. Mr. Halk enlisted in the Confederate army during the war, and served as a private on Price's raid through Missouri. In his three years' service he was not permitted to fire a gun. Himself and wife were members of the Methodist Church; they had a family of ten children, eight of whom are still living: James O., Flora (wife of W. L. Neal), Bettie (wife of J. N. Ables), Helen (wife of C. M. Gardner), John, Robert, Gussie and Elsie. The last four children are at home with their mother, who lives on the old homestead. When James O. Halk was twenty years old he was presented by his father with eighty acres of fine farming land, upon which he engaged in agricultural pursuits and stock raising for himself, and now has some seventy-six acres under cultivation, with a good house, buildings and fences, and considerable stock, mostly cattle, mules and horses. Mr. Halk was married in his twenty-first year to Miss Julia Shaver, of this county. They are the parents of five children, three living: Annie, Zemmie and Sheton. James O. Halk was born in this county in 1857, and is one of the leading young Democrats of the community. His wife is a member of the Methodist Episcopal Church.

John J. Hamilton (deceased) is a son of Theophilus Hamilton, one of the pioneers of this section, and who came to Arkansas in his childhood. The family came to Middle Tennessee, settled on what is now called the Bay Road in Cross County, and here John J. Hamilton spent his youth in farming pursuits, and had but limited educational advantages. When twenty-one years of age he left home and commenced working for himself as an overseer on the plantation of Col. Cross, with whom he remained two years. On April 17, 1848, he married Miss Parmesia Shaver, a daughter of Charles Shaver, who was among the very first of the pioneers of what is now Cross County. Mr. Shaver came to this State, perhaps as early as 1815, settled on Sugar Creek where he cleared up a good farm, and erected the first mill in this section. Soon after his arrival the Indians stole nearly all his stock. He lived on the original place, now known as Bay Village, until his death. After the conclusion of his contract with Col. Cross, Mr. Hamilton purchased a small tract of land on Otter Creek, in the northern part of Cross County, where he and his young wife moved, and began clearing up a place for a home. They remained there three years, and during that time Mr. Hamilton cleared about thirty acres. They then moved to a tract of 480 acres, and later bought near the first settlement. Here they remained for about ten years, during which time Mr. Hamilton cleared about 100 acres.   In 1866 the commercial firm of D. Block & Co., of Wittsburg was formed, consisting of David and Maurice Block, and the subject of this sketch.   This firm soon began to do an astonishing business for this section, their business yielding annually from $100,000 to $300,000.   The partners in this business died, Mr. Maurice Block first and John J. Hamilton May 3, 1878.   The latter, a few years previous to his death, withdrew from the firm, and removed to the old home at Bay Village.   Here he built a cotton-gin, opened a general store and drug store, and thus was practically the first business enterprise started in the place.   He lived but one year after moving back. His success in business enabled him to leave a fortune to his heirs and widow, consisting mostly of real estate in Cross County.   He was very public spirited, and very active politically.   He was self-made, carved his way to fortune, and mainly educated himself after marriage.   The result of his union with Miss Shaver resulted in the birth of ten children: Hester C. (wife of R. Block), William Boone (died at the age of twenty-four years), Obediah A., Charles M. (merchant at Wynne), David H. (died at the age of twenty-seven years), J. B. (at present sheriff of Cross County), A. P. (died at the age of six years), Forest (merchant at Wynne), Effie (wife of Willis Levesque, of Cross County) and Edward (clerk at railroad office).

C. M. Hamilton, merchant, Wynne, Ark.   This prominent business man, of the firm of Johnson & Hamilton, first saw the light of day near Wittsburg in 1855, and was the fourth of nine children born to the union of J. H. and P. (Shaver) Hamilton. [See sketch of J. J. Hamilton.]   C. M. Hamilton was taught the duties of farm life when young, attended the common schools until twenty years of age, when he engaged in the drug business at Wittsburg in partnership with R. M. Smith, and continued at this for eight years.   Also during this time he had an interest in a similar store at Forrest City.   In 1879 he opened a general store, and for several years conducted the two establishments. In 1885 he sold the drug store, and turned his attention to the general store, which business is conducted under the firm name of Hamilton, Smith

& Co. · He was very successful, and during the year 1887, he shipped about 700 bales of cotton. This firm dissolved partnership in the same year, and in July, 1888, Mr. Hamilton formed a partnership with W. M. Johnson, and opened an extensive general store at Wynne.   They carry a stock valued at $6,000, buy everything a farmer has to sell, and have everything he wishes to buy. Mr. Hamilton has been married twice, first in 1878, to Miss Spraggins, a native of Arkansas, and daughter of D. Spraggins, who was a pioneer of this section, a merchant at Wittsburg for a number of years, and also an extensive farmer.   She died in January, 1887, and left two children: Charley and Floy.   His second marriage occurred in October, 1888, and the same year he built a neat cottage in Wynne, where he now has a pleasant home.   Aside from this he has two other residences which he rents, and also a residence in Forrest City.   He is somewhat active in politics, and votes with the Democratic party.   Socially he is a K. of P., Lodge No. 52, and a K. of H., and belongs to the K. & L. of H.   He is a good and an enterprising citizen.

J. B. Hamilton, sheriff, Cross County, Ark. Were one to ask the leading characteristics of Mr. Hamilton as a man, the answer would come almost involuntary that he is brave and fearless, honest, but unpretending, and a man who has been tried, but not found wanting, and one capable of discharging his official and private duties with competency.   J. B. Hamilton was born in Cross County, Ark., in 1862, and is the son of John and Parmesia (Shaver) Hamilton.   [For further particulars see sketch of father.]   He passed his boyhood days in assisting on the farm and in attending the common schools, finishing his education by a course in the Commercial College at Memphis, Tenn.   In 1880 he went to Poinsett County, where he was in business in Harrisburg for two years. In 1885 he started a livery stable at Wittsburg, but in 1886 moved his business to Wynne, and continued to follow this occupation in that city until in June, 1889, when he sold out.   Mr. Hamilton has always taken a deep interest in politics, served as deputy sheriff for two years under Sheriff J. W. Killough, and in 1888 was elected sheriff and collector of Cross County. At the time of his election he was just twenty-seven years of age, and is the youngest sheriff ever elected to that office in Arkansas. Mr. Hamiliton was married December 19, 1888, to Miss Rena Cogbill, a native of Cross County, and the daughter of W. H. Cogbill, who has been a citizen of Cross County for some time. Mr. Hamilton is a member of the K. of P., and is one of the brightest young men of the county. He is pleasant and courteous, and his abilities have been recognized by the people as may be seen from the office to which they have elected him. To his marriage has been born one child, a daughter, Margery.

B. F. Hamilton, Wynne, Ark. Prominent among the very successful business men of Wynne, stands the name of B. F. Hamilton, who is gentlemanly and courteous in all his relations with the public, and whose popularity is established. He was born in Cross County, Ark., in 1866, and is the eighth of ten children born to John G. and Parmesia (Shaver) Hamilton, old settlers of this county. The father died in 1879, but the mother is still living. B. F. Hamilton passed his boyhood days in assisting on the farm and in attending the common schools until eighteen years of age, when he engaged as drug clerk for Hamilton & Norton, at Wittsburg. After remaining in that capacity for a year and a half, he changed to a position in the same business for M. C. Collins at the same place. One year later, in partnership with T. A. Bedford, he began business for himself at Wittsburg, continuing there for two years, when Mr. Bedford withdrew, and the same business was continued with the present partner. In 1887 they removed to Wynne, and started a store in the same business. In February of 1889, they sold out, and under the same firm name are continuing in business at Wynne. Mr. Hamilton, though still a young man, is at present treasurer of the city of Wynne; is quite active politically, and always takes a deep interest in all things that tend to the upbuilding of the county or town. He is one of the successful and well-known citizens of the town, and comes of an old and honored family.

F. M. Hare, one of the most prominent farm-ers of Cross County and among its old settlers, is a son of Jacob and Emma M. (Wheeler) Hare, the former of whom was a native of North Carolina, being married about 1826. His wife came originally from New Brunswick. Removing from North Carolina in 1832, they settled in Fayette County, Tenn., thirty-two miles east of Memphis, where Mr. Hare bought a large tract of land (some 6,000 or 8,000 acres), mostly under cultivation, and also owned about seventy negroes. He was a minister of the Methodist Church for nearly twenty-five years. Previous to leaving North Carolina (near 1830) Mr. Hare represented his county and three adjoining counties in the State senate one term. Upon locating in Tennessee he engaged in farming and the prosecution of his ministerial duties. Later, or in 1854, he moved to Arkansas and settled in Cross County, where he bought about 2,000 acres of land, and where he died in 1859. He was one of the best-educated men of the county, having acquired his learning in the leading schools of North Carolina. Mrs. Hare died in 1873, leaving a family of ten children, only two of whom are now living: F. M. (our subject) and Bettie (the widow of the late Dr. Crump, who resides in Jonesboro, Ark.). F. M. Hare was employed as overseer of his father's slaves for a number of years, and in 1861 organized a company for the army, joining the Fifth Arkansas Infantry; he was appointed first lieutenant. The regiment was commanded first by Col. Cross, but afterward was put under command of Col. Murray, of Pine Bluff, a graduate of West Point, being with Morgan in his raid through Ohio, during which Mr. Hare was captured at Buffington Island, on July 19, 1863. He was taken to Johnson's Island and kept nine months, and then transferred to Point Lookout and afterward to Fort Delaware, from which place he was exchanged and rejoined his regiment. After the war he returned home and found the farm dilapidated, the negroes set at liberty and fences burned. Mrs. Hare, the mother of our subject, had succeeded in fencing up some forty acres and had a small crop of corn. Mr. Hare took hold of the old place on his return from the army and remained upon it for two years, when he was married, in 1867, to Miss Lizzie Reid, a native of Fayette County, Tenn., and daughter of William and Eda (Brown) Reid, of North Carolina origin. Two years later he bought the farm on which he now lives, a fine place, well under cultivation. Mr. and Mrs. Hare are the parents of ten children, nine still surviving: Pearl, Eda, Emma, Nellie, Birdie, Francis, Sallie B., Thomas R. and Frederick. Mr. Hare was born in Fayette County, Tenn., in 1838, is a member of the A. F. and A. M., and also of the K. of H. He is a Democrat politically, but does not take a very active part in politics. He has a fine farm of 220 acres, with eighty-five acres under cultivation and is one of the leading farmers of the township.

Hon. T. E. Hare is an eminent lawyer of Cross County, and by virtue of his ability as a jurist and his victories at the bar is eminently worthy a prominent place among the leading members of the legal fraternity. He is systematic and exact in all things and counts as worthless, all knowledge that is not accurate, and in his defense of the right is bold and unyielding. He was born on land now occupied by the village of Vanndale and was the third in a family of five children born to Thomas P. and Olivia B. (Turbeville) Hare, natives, respectively, of North Carolina and Virginia. In 1851 they came to Arkansas and settled on a large tract of land, comprising 1,000 acres, in Cross County, all of which was in a wild condition but this he began immediately to improve and clear, and proceeded to build him a home in the then almost wilderness. He succeeded in clearing about 200 acres of land and put it under cultivation and in addition to his farm work his time was considerably occupied in preaching the Gospel, becoming well known in both capacities. His death occurred February 23, 1883, his estimable wife still surviving him, a well-preserved and intelligent old lady. T. E. Hare, their son, spent his youth on his father's woodland farm and in addition to receiving the advantages of the common schools he entered and graduated from the University of Mississippi, at Oxford, leaving that institution in 1873, he being only nineteen years old at the time, the youngest of his class. After teaching

one term of school he began practicing law in Cross and other counties, becoming so well and favorably known that, in 1878, he was elected to the legislature from Cross County and was re-elected in 1880. While a member of this body, he introduced a railroad bill extending the charter of the Helena & Iron Mountain Railway soon after the road was built from Knobel to Helena. He was a member of the Judiciary committee during this time and was the youngest member of the house. In 1884, he was a delegate to the Democratic National Convention at Chicago, and was the youngest of this body also. In connection with his practice of law, he makes loans of foreign capital, of which he invests about $1,000 to $5,000 per month, and in every enterprise in which he engages he meets with splendid success. He owns an excellent farm of 120 acres, of which seventy-five are under cultivation, and is president of the Vanndale branch of the American Building & Loan Association. October 28, 1880, he was married to Miss Mary D. Shelton, of Haywood County, Tenn., and by her has one child, Thomas Shelton, born June 15, 1883. Mr. Hare belongs to the society of the K. & L. of H.

Edward Harris, one of Smith Township's successful farmers, is a native of the State of Georgia, and a son of W. M. and Lucinda Scaggin, also originally from that State. W. M. Harris moved to Mississippi in 1840 and in 1859 to Crittenden County, Ark. Three years later he came to this county, where he died in 1876. His wife survived until 1879, leaving at her death eight children, three of whom are living. Edward Harris was born in 1832 and remained with his parents until their demise, passing his youth in a manner similar to the early days of other boys. In 1881 he was married to Miss Mary Anderson, daughter of William and Timby Anderson, all natives of Alabama. Mr. Harris enlisted in the Confederate army, in 1862, in the Twenty-third Arkansas Infantry and served throughout the war, his career as a soldier being one to which he may refer with pride. Himself and wife are the parents of two children. Mr. Harris owns a fine farm of 222 acres, with about thirty acres under cultivation.

He is a member of the Masonic order. His wife belongs to the Baptist Church.

Augustus W. Hinton, who came to Cross County in 1852, is a son of Samuel H. and Mary M. (Walton) Hinton, natives of North Carolina. The former became engaged in the mercantile business at the age of twenty-one, and in 1834 moved to Fayette County, Tenn., where he bought land and commenced farming. In the fall of 1835 he was married, eleven children being born to himself and wife, five of whom are still living: A. W. (our subject), Almira J. (the wife of Edward Hare), Samuel G., G. W. H. and Ella (wife of W. P. Beard). In 1852 Mr. Hinton took up his residence in this county and bought a quarter section of land in Mitchell Township, with 100 acres under cultivation, upon which he resided until called away by death, December 25, 1866, at the age of fifty-two years. He had held the office of justice of the peace in Tennessee, and discharged the duties of county judge of Poinsett County before the division of that and Cross County. Mrs. Hinton died in July, 1887. They were both members of the Methodist Episcopal Church. A. W. Hinton was born in 1837, and was fifteen years of age on coming to Arkansas. He returned to Macon, Fayette County, Tenn., in 1854, and attended school, and three years later entered Andrew College, at Gibson County, Tenn. Coming home the following year, he was married to Miss Mary E. Akins, daughter of William and Sarah C. (Kimble) Akins, natives of Alabama, and who were the parents of twelve children, four now surviving: Mary E. (who was born in March, 1836), Isabella (the wife of Samuel G. Hinton, a brother of A. W.), Ervin P. and Lettie W. (wife of S. G. Cunningham). M. Akin was a member of the "S. T. & H. M.," and both he and his wife belonged to the Methodist Episcopal Church. The former was quite a successful farmer, and was the owner of some twenty or twenty-five slaves. He died in 1859, and his wife in 1866. Samuel Hinton possessed about seventy-five or one hundred negroes at the time of the war. A. W. Hinton joined the Confederate army in 1862, in the Twenty-third Arkansas Infantry, and afterward joined the cavalry under Col. McGee. He was taken prisoner at Port Hudson, on July 12, then walked home, a distance of 700 miles, and was paroled a short time after, subsequently joining McGee's regiment of Arkansas Cavalry, and serving until the cessation of hostilities. Upon returning home, in June, 1865, he found his family in very destitute circumstances. He then resumed farming on his mother-in-law's land, and worked a part of it for three years, until his father's death, when he took charge of the old homestead, in 1881, purchasing his present farm of 160 acres, with seventy-five acres under cultivation. Mr. and Mrs. Hinton are the parents of nine children: Almira A. (deceased), W. T., S. W. I. (deceased) and Sarah M. W. (twins, Sarah is wife of J. B. Bullard), Helen H. O., Mary E. (deceased), Susan C. (deceased), Solomon R. and Robert E. (also deceased). Mr. Hinton is a very successful farmer, and has one of the best arranged farms for stock of any one in the county. He has been a school director for the last thirteen years. Mr. and Mrs. Hinton and family are members of the Methodist Episcopal Church; the former also belongs to the County Wheel, and is a leading Democrat of the county.

Rowland R. Hodges, though comparatively a newcomer in Cross County, is conceded to be one of its prominent farmers. He was born in Kentucky in 1845, and is a son of Edward and Lourena (Mullens) Hodges, also Kentuckians by birth, the family having come originally from Virginia. Edward Hodges owned a large plantation in Kentucky and one-third of twenty or more negroes. He was born in 1812 and was married in 1838. A strong Republican, he was a member of the Baptist Church, and died in November, 1888, in the same county in which he was born. Mrs. Hodges' birth occurred in 1822; she died in 1886, having become the mother of eight children, seven of whom are now living: R. R. (our subject), Rebecca (wife of John Taylor), Joshua, Stephen, John, Caleph and Sarah A. (wife of John Sturgill). Rowland R. was reared and educated in the "Blue Grass" State, and at the age of twenty-one commenced farming for himself on rented land. The following year he purchased 130 acres of land, where he remained until 1876, then removing to within fifteen miles of Louisville and engaging in the saw-mill business, which he continued for two years. He then became associated with a man by the name of Vickers, as foreman, in the manufacture of wagons, but the business did not prove successful, and in 1881 he entered the employ of a firm in the manufacture of wagons at Owensboro, Ky., where he continued four years also as foreman. Previous to this he had come to Arkansas in 1880 and entered 160 acres of land in Craighead County, whither he moved his family. In 1885, resigning his position at Owensboro, he joined his family and then moved to Cross County, purchasing the grist-mill and cotton-gin which he still owns, and is also operating a saw-mill started about the same time. Mr. Hodges was married in 1867 to Mrs. Martha M. McHargue (nee Miller). They are the parents of five children: Hiram H., James S., E. R., David E. and Nannie B. In 1863 Mr. Hodges joined the Federal army and enlisted in the Thirteenth Tennessee Cavalry, serving to the close of the war in Gen. Burnside's command. He participated in the battles of Strawberry Plains, Perryville (Ky.), and a number of skirmishes. Himself and wife are members of the Methodist Episcopal Church. Mr. Hodges belongs to the I. O. O. F., is an enterprising citizen, and highly respected.

O. J. Hodge, an agriculturist of prominence and a man thoroughly alive to the interests of his county, started out in life at the age of twenty-five years with $500, which was given him by his father, and which he invested in a small farm in Georgia, his native State, where he remained until 1883, when he removed to Alabama and bought a farm in Marshall County. In 1886 Mr. Hodge again moved, this time to Cross County, Ark., where he purchased his present farm, consisting of 570 acres, with 225 acres under cultivation, for which he paid about $5,500 and which is now said to estimate some $7,000 or $8,000. The subject of this sketch was born in Georgia September 20, 1850, and was the son of S. M. and Martha Hodge, originally of Georgia. Mr. Hodge was a farmer by occupation, and in connection with his

farm owned a grist-mill. He enlisted in the Federal army in the late war and was married in 1844. He was a Democrat in politics and belonged to the society of the A. F. & A. M. His death occurred in 1888, at the age of sixty-five years. His wife still survives him and lives at the old homestead. They were the parents of seven children, five of whom are still living: Josephine (widow of H. C. Christian, of Georgia), Samuel A., O. J. (our subject), Martha (wife of Robert Gordon), Annie (wife of T. E. Zellmer). O. J. Hodge was married December 28, 1873, to Miss Mary E. Harkins. They are the parents of eight children, five living: Nora Addie, S. J. T. (deceased), O. J., Mattie, Ida, T. J. and R. G. Himself and wife belong to the Missionary Baptist Church. Mr. Hodge has 170 acres of land in one field, which is now all under cultivation, and a depot or shipping station on his property of the Iron Mountain & St. Louis Railroad, which runs on the west line of his farm. Mr. Hodge is a self-made man, having made all that he is worth, except the $500 given him by his father. He belongs to the A. F. & A. M., and is a member of Sincerity Lodge No. 116, of Clinton, Ga.

Newton P. Johnson, an energetic young farmer, and a native resident of Cross County, is a son of Lemuel Johnson who was born in Alabama, near Tuscaloosa. The latter, upon immigrating to Arkansas, settled in St. Francis County, and later moved to Cross County, where his death occurred in 1867. He was married twice, his second wife, Mary Ruminor, being the mother of Newton P. Mrs. Johnson was of German and Irish descent, her father having been born in Germany and her mother in Ireland. She died in 1875, leaving nine children, two of whom are living. Newton P. Johnson came upon the stage of action in Cross County on January 23, 1853, and lived with his mother until her death. He was married in 1879 to Miss Rozella Ferguson, whose birth occurred in Shelby County, Tenn., in 1861. Her father, William Ferguson, was a native of Tennessee and a hardware merchant of Memphis. Mr. and Mrs. Johnson are the parents of two children: Charles F. and Lola F. The former owns 450 acres of land, sixty acres comprising the farm on which he lives, and he has over 100 acres under cultivation. He also has three shares in the old homestead. In connection with farming he is occupied in the timber business quite extensively. Mr. Johnson is a strong Democrat. His wife is a member of the Baptist Church.

William W. Johnson, member of the firm of Johnson & Hamilton, merchants, Wynne, Ark. As a man of business Mr. Johnson's name is co-extensive with Cross County and the surrounding country. He owes his nativity to Holly Springs, Miss., where his birth occurred in 1858. He passed his youthful days among relatives, attending school at Neophigan College, near Spring Falls, Tenn. but left this school in 1872 to attend Bethel College, McKenzie, Tenn. He left this school in 1876 and then engaged with Clark, Johnson & Co., merchants at Memphis, remaining with this firm at their stores at Clarkson, Crittenden County, Ark., for thirteen years, at first as clerk, then book-keeper and for the last five years as manager of the entire estate of 4,700 acres, all under cultivation. Mr. Johnson left this firm in 1855, came to Wynne, Ark., and here opened a general store, as Johnson & Williams, which continued one year, after which the title was changed to W. W. Johnson & Co., which was succeeded in 1888 by the present firm of Johnson & Hamilton. This firm carries a stock of goods valued at $7,000 and do nearly a cash business. Mr. Johnson was married in 1881 to Miss Hattie B. Forgey, a native of Tennessee, and they have three children: Julia, William and Charles. Mr. Johnson is a Knight of Pythias (belonging to Lodge No. 52) and also a member of Memphis Lodge K. of H. He is the youngest of three children born to the marriage of M. J. and Fannie S. (Cole) Johnson, natives of North Carolina and Louisiana, respectively. The maternal grandfather, L. H. Cole, during all his business life was engaged in slave trading. He was also extensively engaged in farming, owning large tracts of land in Louisiana, Mississippi and Arkansas. M. J. Johnson moved from North Carolina to Tennessee in 1848, and he and his father started a carriage factory, the first in Memphis.

23

He, in connection with a brother, ran a stage line, in those early days from Memphis to Jackson, Tenn., and they also built the first hotel, which they named the Boone Hotel. This building is still standing. The paternal grandmother, Mary B. Boone, was a granddaughter of the celebrated Daniel Boone. M. J. Johnson moved to Arkansas in 1859, as agent for his father-in-law, who was speculating in land, and started to open a large plantation about seven miles south of Crittenden County at the breaking out of the war. They then left Crittenden County and did not return for several years. During the war they purchased a large plantation known as Rosborough Island, for which they gave $16,000, there being 1,320 acres there, and which, owing to a defective title, was wholly lost. In 1874 they returned to the old place, which was then running wild, and this he practically recleared. They now have about 300 acres under cultivation in a tract of 450 acres. This all belongs to William W. Johnson, but is occupied by his parents at the present time.

C. P. Jones, M. D. Prominent among the names of the leading physicians of Cross County, and, indeed, of Eastern Arkansas, appears that of Dr. C. P. Jones, of Cherry Valley, who was born, reared and educated in Northern Mississippi, and during his boyhood days worked on his father's farm. In 1879 he entered the Medical Department of the Vanderbilt University, at Nashville, subsequently returning to this county, where he had been teaching school for two years, previous to starting upon his collegiate course. Commencing at once his practice, he continued until 1882, when he entered the Memphis Hospital and Medical College, and graduated the following year, later locating at Cherry Valley. He has since been very successful in his career as a practitioner, building up an enviable patronage. Dr. Jones was married, in 1882, to Miss Nannie C. Stafford, daughter of W. B. and Mattie (Bowers) Stafford, of Tennessee nativity, both of whom are living in Poinsett County. Dr. and Mrs. Jones are the parents of three children, but one is deceased; Heber and Zellmer survive. Dr. Jones commenced in the drug business in 1886, in which he is still engaged in connection with his practice. A stanch Democrat, he is very much interested in politics. Mrs. Jones is a member of the Methodist Episcopal Church. The Doctor was born in Mississippi in 1851, being the son of Harden and Mary C. (Caruthers) Jones, who came originally from Tennessee and South Carolina, respectively, and who were married in the former State about 1836. Mr. Jones moved to Marshall County, Miss., at an early day, and from there to Pontotoc County, where he lived for twenty-nine years, dying in 1885, at the age of seventy-two years. Himself and wife became the parents of eight children: C. P. (our subject), A. J., Taylor, D. D., James N., Frances C. (wife of James Johnson), Clementine B. and Evilee. Mr. Jones served in the Florida and Indian Wars in 1836.

W. A. Jones, merchant, Wynne, Ark. Among the prominent business houses of Wynne, one deserving of special mention in connection with the dry goods and grocery line, is the firm of Smith, Graham & Jones. This firm has assumed a position in the mercantile community creditable to themselves, and of benefit to the city. Mr. Jones was born on his father's farm, known of old as the William Strong Place, a fine farm in the southern part of Cross County, on the St. Francis River, in 1854, and is the only living member of a family of six children born to William A. and Mary J. (Granbery) Jones, natives of Virginia and North Carolina, respectively. The father came to Tennessee in youth, clerked for a few years, and then bought an interest in the same store. He continued at this business until perhaps thirty-six years of age, when he moved to a farm near Memphis, and tilled the soil for a few years, then, with the proceeds of the sale of this farm, he bought a fine piece of property partly in each St. Francis and Cross Counties, on the St. Francis River, and consisting of about 1,200 acres. This is one of the historic places of this neighborhood, being situated on the old military road running from Memphis to Little Rock, and was conducted as an hotel by Mr. Strong. At the time of Mr. Jones' purchase, Mr. Strong had about completed a large house, which Mr. Jones

immediately proceeded to finish, and it stands to-day as one of the best houses in the county. Early in the settlement of the place, Mr. Strong had conducted a large store, and for some time it was the county seat of St. Francis, while Arkansas was still a Territory. Mr. Strong was the first postmaster, and this was the only postoffice for miles around. Mr. Jones purchased this place in 1848, and immediately instituted extensive improvements in the way of clearing land and farming. At the time of his death, which occurred in December, 1860, he was the owner of about 500 acres under cultivation, over 300 of which he had cleared himself. Mr. Jones was a member of the legislature, from St. Francis County, and a member of the State senate from this district, at the time of his death. He introduced a bill to form a new county; this was passed, the new county was added and named Craighead, while the county seat was named Jonesboro in his honor. While a citizen of Tennessee he was also a member of the legislature of that State, and after becoming a resident of Arkansas he was one of that State's worthy and esteemed citizens. He was a self-made man, and, although his educational advantages were limited, he carved his way to social and political eminence, and leaves a name and memory that is revered by all. His son, W. A. Jones, passed his youth on the farm, attending country schools, until about sixteen years of age, when he went to Tennessee, where he attended school for eighteen months. After this he returned and assumed the management of the farm, which he conducted successfully until 1886. The mother died in 1887. His sister, Mollie C. (Jones), wife of L. N. Rhodes, had been living with him, and died in 1883. Mr. Jones left the farm in 1887 and engaged with Hamilton, Smith & Co., at Wittsburg, for the benefit of the experience to be derived. On January 1, 1888, the firm of Smith, Graham & Jones was formed, and in February they moved their business to Wynne. This firm carries a large stock, and has a well-assorted class of goods, with a rapidly increasing business. Mr. Jones is a member of the K. of H. and Levesque Lodge No. 52, K. of P. His life is another example of the self-made men of this section; his father dying when he was young, and the demoralizing effect of the war, through which he passed his youth, it would certainly seem to have some influence over his future; but when he assumed charge of the large farm and the heavy incumbrance that he paid off in two years is the first exhibition of his inherited business qualifications. Since that time his life has been one of success, and now, sound and substantial, he takes his place among the leading merchants of the county.

James A. Jones, one of the self-made men of Cross County, and an enterprising and rising young agriculturist, is a son of Newton and Sarah (King) Jones, natives of Virginia and North Carolina. They were the parents of twelve children, six of whom are living: Zilphia (wife of J. A. Campbell), J. A. (our subject), Mary E. (the wife of M. A. Merriman), Martin, Henry and John. Mr. Jones died in 1863. His wife still survives him, and lives with her son, John, in Woodruff County. James A. Jones was reared to farm life in Mississippi, and at the age of twenty-four commenced farming for himself in Cross County, where he had moved with his mother in 1873, to a farm which he rented. In 1878 he bought his present farm, consisting of 160 acres, which had at that time about forty acres cleared, but by improving and cultivating has over eighty acres in a good condition. Mr. Jones was married in 1876 to Lora Ann Pearson, who died in 1878, leaving one child, Washtella. In November, 1878, Mr. Jones was married to his second wife, Sarah A. Bryant, who died in 1884 and was the mother of three children, two of whom are still living: Newton and Jerome. Mr. Jones was married to his third and present wife, Missouri Griffin, on August 23, 1884. They are the parents of two children, who are still living: James T. and Lessie. On coming to Arkansas Mr. Jones had nothing. Now he owns his fine farm with good buildings and stock, and is one of the most industrious and energetic young farmers in the township.

A. Jordan was reared and educated in Williamson County, Tenn., and supplemented his early training by attendance at the Bedford County University, between the ages of ten and fifteen. The war breaking out the university was closed, and in 1866 young Jordan was a student at the college at College Grove, Williamson County, for eighteen months. He then commenced farming the old homestead, and in 1870 moved to Western Tennessee, where he remained until the following spring, coming thence to Arkansas, and locating in Crittenden County. In 1874 Mr. Jordan became a resident of Cross County, and bought an improved farm of 420 acres, where he resided some twelve years, after which he sold this place and purchased some 500 acres of timbered land, with sixty or seventy acres under cultivation. Mr. Jordan was born in Tennessee, in 1849, as a son of Williamson and Sarah (Davis) Jordan, natives of Virginia. Williamson Jordan went to Tennessee when a boy with his father, and settled in Williamson County, where he was married in 1844, being engaged in farming on an extensive scale and owning quite a number of slaves. There he lived until his death, in 1861. He had been twice married; first in Wilson County, Tenn., by which union he had three children, one now living. He was married the second time in 1844, to Miss Sarah Davis, who bore nine children; of these five survive: John M., Powhattan (deceased), Adelbert (our subject), Catherine (now Mrs. Cooper, of Nashville), Addie (deceased), Samuel G. and Lizzie (now Mrs. Capley). Adelbert Jordan has also been twice married. In 1868 Miss Ellen Gilliland, daughter of Samuel and Viola (Logan) Gilliland, became his wife, by which marriage he was the father of two children: Willie (deceased) and Ella V. Mrs. Jordan, who was a member of the Methodist Church, died in 1868. Mr. Jordan was married the second time, in 1879, to Miss Ada Jelks, daughter of Dr. John A. Jelks. They have had four children: Blanch I., Pearl, John A. and Robert M. Mrs. Jordan is a member of the Methodist Church. Mr. Jordan is an outspoken Democrat, and in 1875 was elected justice of the peace of this township, which office he held for fourteen years. In 1863 he joined the Confederate army, and was in a company consisting of about 100 men. At the close of the war there were only six of the company remaining. In March, 1889, Mr. Jordan purchased his present mill, and is now engaged in the saw-mill business in connection with farming, enjoying a large patronage.

I. S. Julian, who holds prominent citizenship among the residents of Brushy Lake Township, is a well-to-do farmer and a native of Tennessee, being the eldest son of John and Sarah (Murphey) Julian, of French and Irish parentage, and also natives of Tennessee. John Julian was engaged in farming in that State until 1858–59, when he removed to Alabama, where he still lives. Himself and wife were the parents of eight children, five still living: I. S. (our subject), James M., George H., Mary J. (now Mrs. Carter, of Alabama) and J. P.; all reside in Alabama excepting our subject. Mrs. Julian died in 1854, and two years later Mr. Julian married Miss Jane Wilson, who is the mother of one son, Samuel. Mr. and Mrs. Julian are connected with the Methodist Episcopal Church, as' was also the first wife. I. S. Julian was reared to farm life, and educated in the common schools of Tennessee, later attending the academy at Harrison, Tenn. At the age of twenty he entered upon a career as farmer, and also worked for a railroad company for two years, and on January 8, 1871, moved to this county, where he bought a farm of 160 acres of unimproved land; since then he has purchased 330 acres additional, and has 100 acres under cultivation, though having given his children most of his land. In 1863 Julian entered the Confederate service, but remained only a short time as his health failed, at which he furnished a substitute. Mr. Julian was born in 1834, and has been twice married; first, in 1854 to Miss Rebecca J. Henderson of Georgia, and a daughter of John and Eda (Brooks) Henderson, Mrs. Julian died in June, 1856, leaving one daughter, Georgia A. (now the wife of Phelix House). February 14, 1858, Mr. Julian was married to Miss Rebecca J. Sherrill, of Tennessee origin. They became the parents of eight children, five still living: John M. (a Methodist minister of Texas), James A. (a resident of this county), Elizabeth (the widow of the late George M. Gailey), Isham, Jr., and William A. Mrs. Julian died September 4, 1889, leaving a

large family and devoted husband to mourn her loss. She was a consistent member of the Methodist Episcopal Church, South, and is much missed by her many friends and acquaintances. Mr. Julian has been a member of the Methodist Episcopal Church (as was also his first wife) for the last sixteen years; he is also connected with the A. F. & A. M.

John W. Killough, an exemplary citizen, a prominent merchant and stock raiser of Vanndale, was born in St. Francis County in 1840, and was the youngest son of John G. and Fannie P. Killough. His parents died within one month of each other when our subject was but a child. His father was a school-teacher and also engaged in stock raising. After the death of his parents Mr. Killough was adopted in the family of Dr. John P. Mardis, of Poinsett County, remaining with him until twenty years of age. He then engaged in farm labor until the breaking out of the war, when he enlisted in the Confederate army, in the Twenty-third Arkansas Infantry, and participated in the battles of Iuka, Mississippi, Corinth, Pocahontas (Tenn.), and at the siege of Port Hudson, and many skirmishes. After the seizure of Port Hudson he was paroled and returned home, and after his exchange assisted to organize a company, in which he was commissioned second lieutenant, and served principally in Eastern Arkansas. At the close of hostilities Mr. Killough again commenced farming, following this till 1869, when he engaged in the mercantile business in Poinsett County, remaining here until 1873, then removed to Wittsburg, Cross County, and in 1879 entered into a partnership with a Mr. Erwin, and in 1884 they moved their stock to Vanndale, where they opened a store, retaining the firm name of Killough & Erwin till 1887. Mr. Killough here erected a fine hotel, and a number of residences. He was married in 1861 to Miss Mary E. Rooks, a native of Tennessee. They were the parents of five children, three of whom are still living: Oliver N. (a lawyer of Vanndale), Ida Estella (wife of George P. Gardner, of Mammoth Spring) and John Wesley, Jr. (who is clerking at Mammoth Spring). Mr. Killough has served as justice of the peace two years; was county judge in 1880, and was sheriff of Cross County three years, filling these offices with satisfaction to the citizens and credit to himself. Mr. Killough owns 4,000 acres of land, and has about 400 acres under cultivation, one-third of which he cleared himself. He is also engaged in raising fine stock, mules, Poland-China hogs, etc., making a specialty of short-horn cattle. Mr. Killough is a member of the Masonic order, also of the K. of H. and the K. & L. of H., and is one of the leading citizens of Cross County, always foremost in all work for the improvement of the county, and has made a worthy county official and a good business man.

Oliver N. Killough, a rising young lawyer of Vanndale, was born in Poinsett County of this State, on February 18, 1865, being the eldest living son of J. W. and M. E. Killough. [See sketch.] He attended the common schools near his home until he was fifteen years of age, then entered the University of Mississippi, at Oxford, from which he graduated as an A. B., in 1885, and soon after returned to Vanndale, where he taught one term of school. He next began clerking for Smith & Killough, at Harrisburg, serving in this capacity for some time, then became deputy sheriff of Cross County under his father. During all this time he had been desirous of studying law, and in 1887 he entered the Law Department of the University of Virginia, and after taking a one year's course he returned to Cross County and was admitted to the bar on December 20, 1888, at Jonesboro. Since that time he has been actively engaged in the practice of his profession at Vanndale and was associated with N. W. Norton, but since July, 1889, he has been by himself, and although quite a young man he has become well known throughout the county as a leading member of the legal fraternity. He belongs to Lodge No. 52, K. of P. at Wynne, also Lodge No. 606, K. of H., at Vanndale, and Beta Beta Chapter of Beta Theta Si college fraternity.

W. L. Lancaster, postmaster and merchant, at Wynne, owes his nativity to Giles County, Tenn., where his birth occurred August 15, 1844, the eldest in a family of eleven children born to the union of Elisha and Malinda (Kerr) Lancaster, natives also of Tennessee. The grandparents on both sides were early pioneers of Maury County, Tenn., coming from Virginia at a very early date. Elisha died in 1880, and his wife many years previous to that. W. L. Lancaster was early taught the duties of farm life, and attended the common schools of that section until about sixteen years of age, when, at the breaking out of the late war, he flung aside the implements of peace and took up the weapons of warfare. He enlisted in the Confederate army, Company F, Forty-eighth Tennessee Infantry, and participated in the battles of Richmond, Perryville, Chickamauga, and was captured June 4, 1863, at Kenesaw Mountain, being retained from that time until the close of the war. After being released he returned home and was for two years engaged in buying cattle. In 1869 he came to Arkansas, settled in St. Francis County, where he purchased a farm and followed agricultural pursuits until 1873, but was also for some time engaged in mercantile pursuits in Forrest City, and was jailor of that county. He then came to Wynne and opened a general store, there being at that time but two other stores in the place. He purchased a lot, erected a store building, and had a good business which was rapidly increasing, until September, 1887, when half the town, including his store, was destroyed by fire. In less than two weeks he was again in business, selling from a tent, but in a few months moved into a store. September 1, 1889, he was appointed postmaster at Wynne. He was married in 1874 to Miss Fannie Speer, a native of Tennessee, and the fruits of this union have been two children: Dot and Normer. In 1883 Mrs. Lancaster was called to her final home. She was a member of the Methodist Episcopal Church. Mr. Lancaster is a member of the Masonic fraternity, the Knights of Honor, and is also a Knight of Labor.

John W. Lewellen, the subject of this sketch, is recognized among his town's-people as one who has been instrumental in the upbuilding of the town in which he is a resident. He was born three miles south of the present village of Vanndale January 13, 1850, his father and mother having moved from Northampton County, N. C., to Arkansas in that year. They were farmers, and Mr. Lewellen was one of the representative men of this section. He died in August, 1888, at the age of seventy-four years. John W. Lewellen received in his youth such education as Cross County afforded, and was an attendant of the common schools, until he attained his majority. In 1871 he purchased 160 acres of land from his father, on which slight improvements had been made, and with the energy and perseverance which has ever characterized his efforts, he has made much more extended improvements, and in addition to farming his own land, farms some rented land. He at one time owned 320 acres, but sold 160, and now has seventy-five acres of his land under cultivation. When the town of Vanndale was located, about one-half of it was laid out on his farm, and he donated five acres to the railroad, and four acres to the county, and on the latter, the court house of Cross County has since been built. In 1873 he built a fine residence in the town, but in 1885 sold it to Mr. R. Block. He has been one of the leading spirits in the school work of Vanndale, serving six years as director, and he has also been interested in the political matters of the county, but has not been an office seeker. He was married in January, 1876, to Miss Annie Stanley, a native of Cross County, and a daughter of Thomas Stanley, an old pioneer and sheriff of this county, and later a merchant of Wittsburg, who died in April, 1877. To Mr. and Mrs. Lewellen six children have been born: Gracie A., John T., William E. (who died when about a year and a half old), James F., Norma E., and Joseph H. Mrs. Lewellen is a member of the Methodist Episcopal Church, South.

J. T. Lewellen is a prominent mill man and also operates a cotton-gin at Vanndale. He is a native of the county, born in 1858, and was the fifth of six children born to James A. and Nancy E. (Gardner) Lewellen, who were natives of the "Old North State," and came to Arkansas at an early day, settling in what is now Cross County, where they entered a tract of land comprising 320 acres. By industry and good management they soon had 150 acres under cultivation, and in time he became one

of the most successful and best-known farmers in the county, and his death, which occurred at his daughter's, three miles from Vanndale, in 1888, was lamented by his many warm personal friends. J. T. Lewellen attended the common schools until 1879, when he rented his father's farm and began energetically to till the soil on his own account. He lived on the old homestead until the winter of 1882 and was then married to Miss Mollie Block, a daughter of David Block, of Wittsburg. [See sketch.] After his marriage he removed to Vanndale and erected a grist-mill and cotton-gin, his brother being associated with him in business for two years, then he became sole proprietor, added a saw-mill, and is now managing a grist and saw mill and cotton-gin. In 1888 he ginned 852 bales of cotton, and his saw-mill supplies all the local trade besides what he ships to other points. His land now amounts to 420 acres in various tracts, and he has about eighty acres under cultivation. In 1883 he erected a fine residence in Vanndale, and has now one of the pleasantest homes in that village. His marriage has been blessed in the birth of two children: James Adelbert and an infant daughter (unnamed). He is a member of the K. & L. of H.

Capt. J. M. Levesque, the worthy and esteemed county clerk of Cross County, enlisted at the outbreak of the Civil War, in Company C of the Thirteenth Arkansas Infantry, the first regiment organized in that part of the State, Cross County, and was immediately elected orderly-sergeant of his company. The regiment was sent to Fort Pillow, and thence to Kentucky, and was also in the battle of Belmont, Mo., November 7, 1861, evacuating at Columbus, Ky., in March, 1862. At the battle of Shiloh, April 6, 1862, Lieut. Joe Hall was wounded, and Mr. Levesque was chosen to fill his place as second lieutenant. Shortly after this the first lieutenant was wounded and discharged, and our subject was elected to his position, and at the reorganization of the regiment at Corinth, in April, 1862, he was elected captain, and served through the Alabama and Kentucky campaign, also participating in the battles of Richmond, Ky., under Kirby Smith, at Perryville,

Yours Truly
J. M. Levesque

Ky., and Murfreesboro, Tenn. At the reorganization of the army, he was sent to the Trans-Mississippi Department, and there engaged in recruiting a company of cavalry, mostly from Cross County; was in a number of skirmishes, but not in any important battles, his company going on the Missouri raid under Gen. Price. At the close of the war, he took up farming as an occupation, buying a farm of 336 acres, near Vanndale, but in 1866 he was elected circuit and county clerk of Cross County, which office he held until the reconstruction of the county, when he was disfranchised for having held office at the beginning of the war, and in participating in the Rebellion. He then again engaged in farming, in which he continued until 1874, during which time he improved his farm, and adding to it, till in 1878, he was the owner of 2,000 acres of land. In 1874 he was elected sheriff of Cross County, and was re-elected in 1876, and again in 1878. In 1880 he was elected circuit and county clerk, and was also re-elected to that office in 1882, 1884, 1886 and 1888, and is the present incumbent of this office, and that he has given satisfaction is shown by the fact of his having been elected to the same office for four terms in succession. In 1868 he was selected as one of the three men on a locating committee, to choose a site for the county seat, which was then changed to Wittsburg, and in 1885 was appointed one of the committee which located the seat of justice in Vanndale. Mr. Levesque was born in Fayette County, Tenn., in 1834, and was the son of James and Elizabeth (Arnett) Levesque, natives of Tennessee and Mississippi, respectively. His father was a farmer by occupation, and died when our subject was five years old. His mother dying when he was the age of thirteen, he then went to live with an uncle, the Rev. William Levesque, of Alabama, remaining with him until he was sixteen years of age, when he then returned to Fayette County, and was employed as a farm overseer until 1854. In this year he was married to Miss Nannie Willis, of Tennessee origin, and in the fall of that year he removed to Arkansas, settling in Cross County, in what was then a part of Poinsett County. Here he was again employed as a farm overseer, until 1860, when he was elected constable of Mitchell Township, and which office he held till the breaking out of the Rebellion, and the call for men for the Confederate service, to which he responded so readily. He has been a delegate to the Democratic State Convention every year since 1876, and has the unbounded confidence of his party, which he has never betrayed, and is so wholly depended upon that he goes uninstructed and uses his own judgment in the convention. The results of this marriage are five children, three of whom are still living: Elizabeth (wife of Thomas B. Smith, of Cold Water Township), Fannie (wife of Isaac Block, of Wynne), Willie T. (married and resides in Cold Water Township), James Cheatham (deceased) and John Phillip (deceased). Capt. Levesque owns considerable property in different places throughout the county, and owns some 2,000 acres of land, of which there are 800 under cultivation. His farm, on which his son resides, is a field of 500 acres, which is as level as a floor, and on which are good buildings, mills, gins, barns, etc., in fact everything needed to carry on a well-equipped farm. When the Bald Knob Railroad was built through Cross County, the company named a station in honor of our subject, and Levesque Lodge No. 52, K. of P., is also named after him. Capt. Levesque has been connected with the Masonic fraternity since 1861, and a member of the Chapter since 1872, and became a Knight Templar in 1889. He also belongs to the K. of P., K. of H. and the K. & L. of H., and I. O. O. F. The Captain is one of the most influential politicians of the county, and a highly respected man, and one of the county's self-made men, having come to it as a laborer, and is now a wealthy man, all due to his own efforts and honest industry.

W. T. Levesque, one of the prominent young farmers of Cold Water Township, is a worthy son of J. M. and Nannie (Willis) Levesque [a sketch of whose lives immediately precedes this]. Born in Cross County in 1860, he was reared on a farm, and at the age of seventeen was appointed deputy sheriff of the county, his father being sheriff at that time, serving under him for four years; he was also called upon to act in a similar capacity the next two years under Sheriff Legg. At the age of twenty-three Mr. Levesque commenced farming on his father's land, in which occupation he is still interested, also operating a saw-mill and cotton-gin. He was married in 1884 to Miss Effie Hamilton, of this county, a daughter of J. G. and Permesia (Shaver) Hamilton. Mr. and Mrs. Hamilton are the parents of ten children (seven living in this county): Hester C. (wife of R. Block), W. B., O. A., D. H., C. M., J. B., P., B. F., Effie and Edward. Mr. Levesque is a member of the K. of H., and of the K. & L. of H. He is enjoying a large business in his mill and gin and is justly recognized as among the county's leading young men.

Philip B. Littlefield, a farmer of no mean ability, and one highly respected, is originally from Mississippi, but attained his manhood in St. Francis County, where [he lived until 1879; then going into Cross County occupied himself with farming. In 1872 his marriage to Miss Ann McDonnell (also of this State), was solemnized, and who died in 1876, the mother of two children, now deceased. He was again married to Mrs. Ollie Rose (nee Johnson) of Tennessee nativity, and a daughter of Thomas Johnson, who came to Arkansas in 1864 from Missouri. By his second wife he became the father of one child, deceased. Philip B. Littlefield (our subject) was born in Panola County, Miss., in 1852, and is a son of Andrew J. and Elizabeth (Beliew) Littlefield, of Alabama and Tennessee origin, respectively. Andrew J. Littlefield came to Panola County, Miss., where he remained until 1858, then coming to Arkansas he settled in St. Francis County and entered a tract of land which he has converted into a good farm, and on which he made his home until his death in 1880. He and wife were members of the Baptist Church. Mrs. Littlefield is still living, and is the mother of ten children, four of whom are deceased: Flemming M. (a soldier during the Rebellion was killed at Cumberland Gap), Shelton (who served in the Confederate army and died in 1877), John S. (also in the late war, died in 1887), and an infant now deceased. Those living are: Zachariah, George W., Mattie C.,

Sarah E., Jennie and Philip B. Philip B. Littlefield is numbered among the Knights of Honor and is a strong Democrat politically, He owns valuable property and has about 125 acres under cultivation. Mrs. Littlefield is a member of the Methodist Episcopal Church.

J. W. Logan, one of the early and prominent settlers of this county, is a Kentuckian by birth and a son of J. R. and Emeline (Wright) Logan, also natives of the Blue Grass State. The paternal grandfather, J. R. Logan, Sr., was a soldier in the Revolutionary War, during which he was captured by the Indians, and for two weeks had his thumbs tied together with sinews of deer, at night being suspended to a branch of a tree. At the end of three weeks, while under the care of one Indian, he managed to escape. J. R. Logan, Jr., the father of the subject of this sketch, served a short time in the Mexican War. He and his wife were members of the Methodist Episcopal Church, South, and were the parents of seven children, three of whom are still living: J. W., Mattie C. (wife of J. Pryor, of Henry County, Ky.), and Mary F. (the widow of J. A. Patterson, and resides in Louisville, Ky.). J. W. Logan was born in Henry County, Ky., in 1840, and at the age of twenty-one commenced farming for himself on rented land in Kentucky, continuing until 1860, going thence to Canada, remained some five or six years and during that time traveled over a large part of British America, including Nova Scotia, New Brunswick, and Eastern and Western Canada. He returned in 1865 to Kentucky, but a year later started out again, and traveled over the Eastern and Northern States, and back to Canada. In 1874, Mr. Logan was married to Miss Florence M. Garr, of Jefferson County, Ky., after which he settled down to farming near Louisville, also carrying on the dairy business until January, 1880; removing to Arkansas he settled within two miles of his present farm, bought 260 acres of land and in 1887 purchased his present farm on which he lives, now owning altogether 1,531 acres, with 300 acres under cultivation. Mr. Logan has considerable stock and raises hay, corn, etc., being considered one of the most prosperous farmers in the county. Himself and wife were the parents of six children (two of whom are deceased, the others are at home): James E., Mamie, Virgie, George, Willie (deceased) and Jessie (also deceased). Mr. and Mrs. Logan are members of the Methodist Episcopal Church, South.

J. L. Lyon is the son of W. D. and Lydia (Arnold) Lyon, and was one of a family of thirteen children, eight of whom are still living: Elizabeth (wife of J. L. Robinson), P. L. (a resident of St. Francis County), Mattie (wife of G. W. Dallas), Nannie (wife of G. W. Timuel), Catharine, J. F., J. L. and B. A. J. L. Lyon was born in Mississippi in 1863, and at the age of twenty came to Arkansas with his father. For three years previous to this he had been clerking in a store in Memphis, Tenn. Subsequently he took charge of his father's business for eight years, and in June, 1889, bought the livery stable of J. B. Hamilton, which he has until recently owned and conducted. Mr. Lyon has enjoyed a large and lucrative business, and is one of the representative men of Wynne. W. D. Lyon was a native of Alabama, and upon moving to Mississippi settled in Chickasaw County, where he engaged in farming, there remaining until 1864. During this time he served as sheriff of the county for several years, and later was appointed county clerk to fill an unexpired term. In 1864 Mr. Lyon moved to Shelby County, Tenn., where he was occupied in farming for nineteen years, and in 1883 came to Arkansas, locating in St. Francis County. In 1886 he became a resident of Cross County and rented a farm in Searcy Township, where he died in June of the same year, at the age of seventy-five years. Mr. Lyon belonged to the Methodist Episcopal Church. He served in the war with Mexico, and was a member of the A. F. & A. M., and of the I. O. O. F. During the last eight years of his life he was afflicted with blindness. Mrs. Lyon is connected with the Old School Presbyterian Church.

J. C. McElroy, the subject of this sketch and prominent in the affairs of his county and known to all as a law-abiding citizen, was born in the State of Georgia in 1827, as the son of John and M. S. (Belk) McElroy. Mr. McElroy was reared on a farm, and removed with his father, John McElroy, to Arkansas in the year 1848, and the following year married Miss Sara C. Lantroupe. Then settling an adjoining farm to his father, he has since lived there. Mr. McElroy was put on detached duty by the Confederate Government during the war, and had charge of the Government tanyards; also served in the postal service during that conflict. He was justice of the peace for several years, and also acted as county judge from 1868 till 1874, since which time he has taken no active part in politics. Mr. and Mrs. McElroy are the parents of nine children, three of whom are still living: John W., Sallie (wife of James A. Sadler) and Emmet L. (all residents of this county). Mr. and Mrs. McElroy are strict members of the Methodist Episcopal Church. The former is also a member of the A. F. & A. M. He is one of the prominent farmers of Bedford Township and a highly respected citizen. John W. McElroy, the oldest son, has been county surveyor of Cross County for six years.

A. J. McElroy served four years in the Confederate service during the late war as a member of Company B, McRae's Regiment, and participated in the battles of Helena, Red River, Prairie Grove and a number of other battles and skirmishes, remaining in the field of duty until the surrender in 1865. Leaving home at the age of twenty-six he engaged in farming on 160 acres of land which he had bought in this county, and where he still resides. He now has upward of 100 acres under cultivation, with good buildings and good stock. Mr. McElroy was born in Georgia in 1833, as the son of John and Mary (Stephenson) McElroy, natives of South Carolina. Soon after the latter's marriage he came to Georgia, remaining until 1848, when he moved to Arkansas, settling in this county, where he entered 480 acres of land. Here he lived until his death in 1866, at the age of sixty-eight years. He was four times married. His first wife, Miss Shy, became the mother of one child, now deceased. By his second wife (Miss Belk) he had five children, only one of whom survives: J. C. (of this county). After her death Mr. McElroy was married to Mary Stephenson, who died in 1859 leaving nine children. Two only of these are living: A. J. (our subject) and Elizabeth. Mr. McElroy's fourth and last wife was Rachel McDuffie. The union of A. J. McElroy to Miss Rebecca J. Lantroupe, of Tennessee, was consummated in 1853, she being a daughter of William and Charity Lantroupe. Mrs. McElroy departed this life in 1880, having been the mother of eight children, four living: Robert (in this county), George, James and Parlee (now Mrs. Weeden, who resides in Wynne). Mr. McElroy is a member of the Methodist Episcopal Church, as was also his wife. He is a leading and respected farmer in this township.

Mrs. Cora H. McKie. Many of the younger citizens of Vanndale, hold sacred the memory, and all respect the name of W. P. McKie, a former citizen of Vanndale, who came to this village in 1872, and engaged in teaching school. Mr. McKie was born in Lafayette County, Miss., on October 12, 1847, and was a son of James M. and Juliette (Fondren) McKie, natives of Mississippi. He was reared and educated in Mississippi, and was married to Miss Cora H. Hare in 1873. [For sketch of the parents of Mrs. McKie see that of T. E. Hare, in this work.] To. Mr. and Mrs. McKie were born three children: Thomas W., James M. and Juliette B. Mr. McKie died on October 8, 1882, after a short illness. He was very popular in his community, and his death was deeply felt and much regretted by his large circle of friends. Mrs. McKee was born on November 3, 1857, her family being one of the oldest in the county, coming here in 1840. She is a member of the Methodist Episcopal Church, as was also her husband. He also belonged to the society of the Knights and Ladies of Honor. Mrs. McKie is a generous and hospitable lady, very popular, and a leading spirit in all church and charitable works.

James D. McKie, a prominent physician of Vanndale, and a graduate of the Medical University of Louisville, Ky., is a native of Mississippi, and a son of James M. and Juliette (Fondren) McKie, who were also of Mississippi origin. The father died in 1861, and his wife in 1888, in Lafayette County, Miss. James D. McKie received his literary education at the University of Mississippi, before entering the Medical University of Louisville, from which latter he graduated in March, 1876. Following this he began his practice at his home in Mississippi, and the succeeding October came to Arkansas, settling in Vanndale, Cross County, where he has built up a large and influential practice, in fact more than he can well attend to. Dr. McKie was married in 1879 to Miss Lula Lea, originally from Tennessee. They are the parents of one child, Willie H. The Doctor and wife are members of the Methodist Episcopal Church, South, and are also connected with the Knights and Ladies of Honor. He owns a fine residence in Vanndale, and also a farm of 320 acres, with sixty-five acres under cultivation, having a fine orchard; he is somewhat engaged in stock-raising, and has about twenty head of horses. Dr. McKie is a highly educated gentleman, and a leading citizen of this section.

John K. Malone, at present occupying the responsible position as deputy county clerk of Cross County, was born in Poinsett County, and is a son of William C. and E. M. (Gardner) Malone, natives of North Carolina and Virginia, respectively. William C. Malone came to this State with his father in 1854, settling near the present site of Vanndale. He was a minister of the Methodist Episcopal Church, South, and a man of considerable importance in the county. In 1868 he was elected county clerk of Poinsett County, served one term, and in 1882 he was elected to the legislature to represent his county (Cross) and was made the chairman of the committees of education, agriculture, and temperance. In connection with his farming, Mr. Malone was engaged in the mercantile business in Wittsburg, and later at Vanndale, where he died in November, 1885. At that time there were but very few men surviving, who had been here at the first settlement of this county. Mrs. Malone is still living at Vanndale. Our subject was born in 1862, and was educated in the common schools of this county, and finished his schooling at Little Rock. In 1885 Mr. Malone was appointed deputy county clerk, which office he still holds, discharging his duties with great credit to himself. Mr. Malone is a strong Democrat, and takes an active part in politics. He is a young man of ability and promise, and a son of a noted and highly respected man, and is rapidly rising into a citizen of note and prominence.

Thomas L. Martin is not unknown to the many residents of Cross County. A native of Alabama, he is a son of Joseph and Sallie (Fitzgerald) Martin, who came originally from North Carolina, Joseph Martin having moved to Tennessee when a boy. At the age of twenty-one he went to Alabama and settled in Lawrence County, where he engaged in farming, being the owner of several negroes. In 1858 he came to Arkansas and settled in this township, and entered 120 acres of land. Mr. Martin was twice married; first, to Miss Ruttidge, by whom he had four children, all now deceased. His second wife was the mother of our subject. Mr. Martin was a member of the Cumberland Presbyterian Church, and died in 1863, at the age of seventy-six years. Thomas L. Martin was born in Lawrence County, Ala., in 1841, and was reared to farm life, coming to this county with his father in 1858. In 1861 he joined the Confederate army, serving as one of the celebrated "Walker Grays," for a short time, and in February, 1862, he became connected with the Fifth Arkansas Provisional Regiment, known as the Walker Regiment, in which he served until the surrender of Island No. 10, in 1862; there he was captured and sent to Camp Douglas, being held until the following September. He rejoined his command in December, at Port Hudson, was again captured in the following May and sent to New Orleans, and afterward to Fortress Monroe, where he was paroled. Returning home, he walked a distance of 500 miles in fourteen days and a half, reaching his destination in August, 1863. In the following April he started for Kirby Smith's headquarters, but did not again go into active service, being engaged in getting together Government cotton. After the war Mr. Martin resumed his farming operations and rented land until 1876, when he bought his present place, consisting of 100 acres, which at that time had only four acres under cultivation. He now owns another farm of 200 acres, and has about 100 under cultivation. He is a member of the K. of H. and of the Agricultural Wheel. Mr.

and Mrs. Martin are members of the Methodist Episcopal Church. The former is one of the leading farmers in Bedford Township, and is respected by all who know him. He has been twice married; first, to Elizabeth Wigby, on February 1, 1866, by whom he had three children: Maggie Emma (born September 28, 1869), Thomas Jefferson (born December 17, 1870) and Kittie Ellen (born November 17, 1873). Mrs. Martin died September 30, 1881, and Mr. Martin subsequently married on December 6, 1882, having four children by his second wife (she was a widow, Mrs. Mollie F. Everet): Wesley Hargus (born March 1, 1884), Eliza Dolphus (born March 6, 1885), Edgar Shuford (born December 15, 1887) and Porter Featherston (born October 7, 1889).

John P. May, druggist, Vanndale, Ark. This successful and enterprising business man is a native Tennesseean, born in Madison County, in the year 1844, and at present is a member of the well-known firm of May & Malone. He is a son of John May, and a grandson of John May, Sr., who was a native of the Old Dominion, but who was one of the pioneers of Eastern Tennessee. He was an extensive planter, and was working about 100 hands at the time of his death, which occurred about 1846. John May, father of our subject, was a native of Tennessee, and also became very extensively engaged in farming, in Mississippi, going to that State in 1845. He resided in La Fayette County until 1860, and then came to Arkansas, and settled in what is now Cross County. Here he purchased 2,000 acres of land, on the Memphis & Jacksonport dirt road, on L'Anguille River, known as Shaver's Bridge, and opened up about 400 acres of land, erected buildings, and made a comfortable home for his family. While on a trip to Memphis, in 1863, he was taken sick, and died at Marion, Crittenden County, Ark., November 23, of that year. His wife (the mother of the subject of this sketch), whose maiden name was Miss Cynthia M. Cook, was born in North Carolina, and after the death of her husband continued to live on the farm until November, 1867, when the place was sold, and she has since made her home with her son, John P. May. The latter attended school at College Hill, Miss., and at Memphis, Tenn., until sixteen years of age, or until 1860. Two years later he enlisted in Company D, Thirtieth Arkansas Regiment Infantry, and was elected corporal of Company D, and in January, 1863, was promoted to orderly-sergeant, and filled that office till 1864, when the Thirtieth regiment was consolidated with the Thirty-second Arkansas. Shortly afterward he was promoted special courier in the Trans-Mississippi Department. He participated in the battles of Greenville, Mo., Prairie Grove, Ark.; was at the evacuation of Little Rock; was at Mansfield, La., Pleasant Hill, La., Camden, Ark., and Jenkins' Ferry, Ark. He was also in a number of skirmishes on the different campaigns, and was made special courier in October, 1864, for Gen. John S. Roane, serving in that capacity until the close of the war, or until May, 1865. His command was disbanded at Marshall, Tex., and he surrendered at Little Rock. After being paroled at Memphis, June 6, 1865, he returned home, and immediately engaged in farming; left the old homestead in 1867, and farmed on rented land for one year, after which he went to Mississippi, where he remained one year on account of his mother's health. He then returned to Arkansas, and in November, of 1869, bought a farm about one mile south of Walnut Camp, known as the Mitchell farm. Here he remained until 1879, and during that time he cleared about fifty acres, erected buildings, and made many other improvements. At that date he sold out and bought a farm of 160 acres adjoining the old homestead, on the west side of Crowley's Ridge, where he remained two years. In 1880 he moved to Wittsburg, and engaged in hauling, which he continued until November 15, 1882, when he came to Vanndale, and erected the first residence at that station. He opened a restaurant and confectionery store in December of that year, it being the third place of business started in Vanndale, and after a short time he converted his business into a drug store, and in 1885 admitted Mr. W. C. Malone as a partner. The latter died November 26, 1885, and his interest succeeded to his wife. This firm now carries a full and complete line of drugs, paints, oils, notions, toilet articles, stationery, school books, tobacco, cigars and con-

fectionery. Mr. May is a member of the K. of H., and K. & L. of H., of the Masonic fraternity, and is also one of the Building & Loan Association, of Vanndale. He was married February 14, 1871, to Miss Sallie E. Applewhite, a daughter of John and Nancy J. Applewhite, who came to Arkansas in 1859, and the father became extensively engaged in farming operations, which he continued up to the time of his death, in 1883. Mrs. Applewhite still resides on the old homestead, about three miles north of Vanndale. To the union of Mr. and Mrs. May were born six children, three of whom are deceased: Lena Burton (died in 1881, at the age of nine years), Fletcher Garland, Harry (died at the age of two years) and an infant daughter, Helen. The eldest child died in infancy, and unnamed. Mr. May is one of the first-class business men of the place, is an exemplary citizen, and was a brave and fearless soldier.

Thomas W. May is justly recognized as one of the prominent farmers of this community. He has also attained to great esteem as a faithful public official of Cross County, now serving as county assessor. A native of Mississippi, he is a son of Thomas W. and Mary A. (Taylor) May, who came originally from Alabama and settled in Mississippi shortly after their marriage, locating in 1871 in Cross County, Ark. Here the senior May bought a farm of 320 acres, near Cherry Valley, which had about seventy acres under cultivation. Shortly after coming to this county he died, and the home place was then divided, and a portion of it sold. Mrs. May still resides on the remainder. Thomas W. May, Jr., our subject, was born in Mississippi in 1859, and until 1879 helped his mother carry on the farm after his father's death. In that year he was married to Miss Agnes Bowers, of this county, and daughter of Jacob Bowers, a well-known citizen of Cross County. Mrs. May died in August, 1888, leaving four children: Ada, Edna, Effie and Pearl. Mr. May was married the second time on March 26, 1889, to Miss Georgia Jackson, also of Cross County birth. Mr. May has held some public office here for the past eight years. In 1881 he was appointed constable of Mitchell Township, to fill an unexpired term, and was afterward elected to that position, serving two terms. In 1888 he was elected county assessor, which office he still holds. Mr. May bought a farm of 160 acres, in 1885, near Cherry Valley, having about forty acres under cultivation, and has cleared as much more since owning it. He has since bought out the interest of the heirs of his first wife's parents to a large and valuable estate. An enterprising young man, he is very popular in the community in which he lives.

Dr. William T. Mebane, physician and farmer, Wynne, came originally from Greensboro, N. C., where his birth occurred in 1825. Dr. William T. Mebane was the son of Dr. John A. Mebane, who was a native of North Carolina. The father was for a long time a prominent physician in North Carolina and also a soldier in the War of 1812. He died July 11, 1864, at the age of seventy-three years. The mother (whose maiden name was Celia A. Sutton) was also a native of North Carolina. The paternal grandfather, Alexander Mebane, was a brigadier-general in the Continental army during the Revolutionary War. He was one of the founders of the University of North Carolina and served in the Congress of the United States up to the time of his death. Dr. William T. Mebane began attending school before he was five years of age and in 1846 graduated at the University of North Carolina and in 1851 from the Medical Department of the University of Pennsylvania. He then received a commission in the United States Navy but unqualified. Instead he returned to Greensboro and soon removed to a plantation given him by his father in Mississippi. In December, 1851, he settled on the western base of Crowley's Ridge in St. Francis (now Cross) County, and here he purchased 730 acres, all wild land. He then began an extensive scale of clearing and improving and soon had a large tract under cultivation. In 1853 he was appointed postmaster and held the office (which was called Eureka) in his house until about 1876, when the name was changed to Mebaneville. Dr. Mebane has been the only postmaster in Cross County and is, therefore, the oldest postmaster in Eastern Arkansas. He at once began practicing medicine, which pro-

fession he has kept up through all these years; still rides some and does an extensive office practice. He has a good farm with 180 acres under cultivation and during all these years he has been an old landmark for Cross County. He was married in 1854 to Miss Lucy Antoinette Magette (daughter of Charles G. Magette, one of the old settlers in this section). The fruits of this union were seven children: Lucy S. (widow of J. W. Koonce), Charles M., Mary (wife of R. M. Smith), William Thomas (died April 11, 1884, at the age of twenty-four years), John Alexander (died October 14, 1866, at the age of three years), Robert Henry (died August 2, 1888, at the age of twenty-two years) and an infant daughter, unnamed. Dr. Mebane has practiced his profession in that State for many years, is educated and refined and has been a close student for forty years.

Charles Neely is a member of the firm of Martin & Neely, who are doing a large business at Wynne, carrying a complete and well-assorted stock of general merchandise. A native of this State he was born in 1860, being a son of W. A. and M. J. (Deadnam) Neely, originally from South Carolina and Arkansas, respectively. W. A. Neely was an attorney by profession, and practiced at Batesville and different places in Eastern Arkansas, afterward moving to a farm in this county, where he died in 1866. He was a prominent man in the politics of the community and enlisted in the Confederate service during the war, toward the close of which he served as an enrolling officer. Mrs. Neely was a member of the Methodist Episcopal Church, and died in December, 1865, just one month before her husband. Charles Neely was born in what is now Cross County, being educated in the common schools of this county, and at the age of eighteen engaged as a farm laborer, in which capacity he remained occupied for six years. In 1886 he embarked in the grocery business in this place, and gave his attention to that branch of trade until June, 1888, when he went into partnership with J. A. Martin. They are now doing a general mercantile business, amounting to about $15,000 annually. Mr. Neely also owns his residence in Wynne, and about ten acres of land under cultivation outside the town limits. He is a thorough business man, and is bound to succeed, also being a popular citizen of Wynne. He is the only living representative of his family.

Charles D. Oliver, merchant, Wynne, Ark. The well-known business firm of Daltroff, Sparks & Oliver was organized in 1887, and since that time has been doing a rapidly increasing business. Mr. Oliver owes his nativity to St. Francis County, Ark., where his birth occurred in 1862, and is one of eight children, the result of the union of R. G. and Luginia R. (Palmer) Oliver, natives of Arkansas, and one of the Carolinas, respectively. The father was a successful agriculturist. Charles D. Oliver was left an orphan when quite young, and as he only attended school until eleven years of age, his education in consequence was rather limited. He began working for James Fussell & Co., merchants at Forrest City, and there remained for nine years, during which time he secured a good schooling in matters of business. In 1881 he left this firm and went to Wittsburg, where he was in the employ of Block Bros. & Co. for about three years. During this time he had started a grocery store at Wynne, and thinking it needed his attention he gave up his employment at Wittsburg and came to Wynne. He conducted his business until January 1, 1887, and during 1886 it had proved very profitable, Mr. Oliver being so fortunate as to make considerable money out of it. In the beginning of 1887 he entered the firm of Daltroff & Sparks, general merchants, under the firm title of Daltroff, Sparks & Oliver, which title continues at the present time. This firm is doing a good business, having won the confidence of the public by honest, upright dealing. Mr. Oliver was married in 1884 to Miss Etta Block (daughter of David Block, who was for a long time one of the leading merchants and one of the wealthiest men of Cross County). To the union of Mr. and Mrs. Oliver were born two sons: Charles Edward and John David. Mr. Oliver is a member of the K. of P., Lodge No. 52, and is a Knight of Honor. After the death of his parents he took charge of all the younger members of the family, educated his sisters and made a home for the youngest, who was

an infant at the time of the parents' death. The family have always looked to him for advice and assistance and never failed to get both. The younger brothers are in business for themselves and have good situations. The youngest, John P., is traveling salesman for Malone, Chapman & Elder at Memphis, and is a bright, capable business man. Charles D. Oliver owns the old homestead in St. Francis County, a good farm of 220 acres with 125 under cultivation, and has a fine residence on the same place. He also own 580 acres in various tracts in Cross County, and 175 acres of this are cultivated. He owns a block in the city of Wynne which is partially covered with buildings which yield about $400 annually for rent. Charles D. Oliver has always been successful in all his business enterprises and is pre-eminently a self-made man.

R. G. Oliver, merchant, Wynne, Ark. By his excellent business qualifications, and by his social and polite treatment of the public, Mr. Oliver, although a young man, has became one of the leading business men in his particular line in Eastern Arkansas. He owes his nativity to St. Francis County, Ark., where his birth occurred in 1864, and is the fifth of eight children born to the union of R. G. and Luginia R. (Palmer) Oliver. The parents are natives of Georgia and South Carolina, respectively. The father came to Arkansas at an early day and followed farming and stock raising in St. Francis County, until his death in 1876. The mother's death occurred in 1879. R. G. Oliver was early taught the duties on the farm, and attended the public schools of Forrest City, until about fourteen years of age, when he went to Memphis, and engaged as a clerk for Zellner & Co., shoe dealers. He remained with this firm for about seven years, and then went to Crawfordsville, Crittenden County, where he engaged with Buck & Trexler, continuing with them for about two years. He then began business for himself in the same place, opening a store of general merchandise and plantation supplies, but continued in business but a short time, when he sold out to his partner, and in 1888 came to Wynne. He here established a store of clothing, boots and shoes and gents' furnishing goods. He carries a stock of goods valued at about $10,000. Last January (1889) he moved into a fine brick store, which he has fitted up, and this is now one of the largest stores in Eastern Arkansas. Mr. Oliver was married January 2, 1889, to Miss May Kelley, a native of Arkansas, and daughter of John Kelley, an old settler of Lee County. Mr. Oliver has recently purchased a lot in Wynne, on which he expects to erect a residence ere long. In his political views, he has always affiliated with the Democratic party. Socially he is a member of the K. of P., Levesque Lodge No. 52, at Wynne, and is also a K. of H. at that place.

R. W. Orr, Wynne, Ark. Prominent among the business men of Wynne stands the name of Mr. Orr, who has been established in business at this place for about four years, and has become one of the permanent and enterprising residents of the town. His birth occurred in Middletown, Butler County, Ohio, in 1850, and he was left fatherless at a very early period of his existence. On this account his educational advantages were limited, and he was compelled to apply himself to his books when grown in order to fit himself for business. When about seven years of age he began to work for himself on the Miami Canal of Ohio, and followed this for about eight years, after which he was engaged in various occupations, dealing in lumber, etc., for some time. In 1882 he came to Arkansas, worked on the Cotton Belt Railroad for two years, and then in 1884 settled in Jonesboro, where he opened a restaurant. This he conducted for one year, and then moved to Wynne, where he started another restaurant, investing all he had in his small stock. From that time he rapidly built up a large business, and by his honesty and attention to his patrons, became highly esteemed in the community. January 1, 1889, Mr. Orr opened a saloon. Since living here he has purchased three business lots on the main streets of Wynne, on which he is now erecting a new brick building, 24x96 feet and one story. He will occupy all this large store-room for his business, which he proposes to fit up and run as a first-class sample room. He also owns a neat cot-

tage which he bought in 1889. He was married July 6, 1864, to Miss Catherine Brown, a native of Indiana, and three children have been the result of this union: Lulie May, Charles and Miles. Mr. Orr is the youngest in a family of eleven children born to William and Lucinda (Macy) Orr, natives of Ohio.

Anderson Phillips, one of the most prominent colored farmers in Searcy township, was born a slave of David H. Walker, of Carroll County, Mo., in 1843. His father, Carter Phillips, died in 1889. His mother at last accounts was in Nebraska. Mr. Walker had crossed the plains with his slaves, and left the mother of our subject in the West, and she never returned. After the Emancipation Proclamation, Anderson Phillips came north and joined the Federal army, and served until October, 1865, when he received his discharge, then coming to Phillips County, Ark., where he remained seven years. In 1874 he bought his present property, consisting of 240 acres in Cross County. He first purchased 660 acres, but has given a portion to his children, and now has 130 acres under cultivation. Mr. Phillips was married first in 1866 to Charlotte Smith, who died in 1874, leaving three children: G. A., James H. and Glenn A. (wife of Jeff Ham, a resident of this county). His second marriage was to Alice Ham (who was killed in a railroad accident in 1879). They became the parents of four children, all of whom are deceased. Mr. Phillips' present wife was formerly Martha E. Davis, whom he married in 1880. They have one boy, Anderson. Mr. and Mrs. Phillips are members of the Independent Order of the Immaculate, and are connected with the Baptist Church. The former is a strong Republican, and takes an active part in politics, having held the office of coroner of the county two terms.

William M. Pierce is a son of James Pierce, who was born in Indiana, where he was reared, but coming to Arkansas when a young man, he located in Pope County, and there married Susan Davidson. She first saw the light in St. Charles County, Mo., and died in Pope County in 1868. Her father was a soldier in the War of 1812. William Pierce, the second son in a family of three children, and the only one now living, was born in Pope County, December 24, 1855, and came to Cross County when fourteen years of age, the year after his mother died, his father having died when he was a small boy. He was married in 1875, to Miss Fannie Staner, a native of Illinois (born about 1858), who departed this life in June, 1888, leaving four children: Willie and Anna (twin daughters), Edgar and Samuel. Mr. Pierce moved to his present farm on the St. Francis River in 1875, and now has a fine place of 120 acres, with forty acres under cultivation. He is a decided Democrat, and a good citizen.

Maj. Riddick Pope, a prosperous agriculturist and citizen, was reared on a farm in Southampton County, Va., gaining his mental knowledge in the common schools of that county, remaining in these until nineteen years of age, after which he accepted the position of clerk in a dry goods store at Drewryville, Va. Two years later he went to Memphis, Tenn., and again engaged as clerk in his former trade, where he remained two years. In 1854 he formed a partnership with his brothers, Oswald and Madison, and started in the dry goods business, and about this time they bought 700 acres of land, in what is now Cold Water Township, Cross County, but was then Poinsett County, and after putting 100 under improvement, they closed out the business in 1859, removed to this farm. In 1861 Mr. Pope enlisted in the Confederate service, in Company A, of the Fifth Arkansas Infantry, in which he was appointed third lieutenant, and served throughout the war. He was later made major, which position he held until after the battle of Shiloh, when he was then transferred to Price's command, and took part in that never-to-be forgotten raid through Missouri: In this he officiated as brigade-quartermaster, being in McCray's Brigade. After the war Mr. Pope came home and engaged in farming for the next nine years. Then followed a period of nine years in which he held a position in the largest dry goods house in Wittsburg. In 1885, after his return home, he was elected to the State senate, which office he still fills. Maj. Pope was born in Virginia, in 1830, and was a son of Nathan and Annie (Stephenson) Pope, na-

tives of Virginia. Nathan Pope was a planter, and one of the largest slave-owners in Virginia, and was a soldier in the War of 1812. His father was a participant in the Revolutionary War, and was present at the surrender of Lord Cornwallis. Nathan Pope was in the battle of Parkersfield at the time of the insurrection of the negroes in 1831, during which he was unhorsed and slightly wounded, but was rescued by six of his companions from some sixty or seventy infuriated negroes. He was twice married, first to a Miss Joyner, by which marriage he was the father of two children. After his first wife's death, Mr. Pope married Mrs. Annie (Stephenson) Barrett (the mother of our subject), who became the mother of eight children, Riddick, being the only child living. Mr. Pope was a member of the English Church, and Mrs. Pope a member of the Methodist Church. He died in 1841. Maj. Riddick Pope was married in December, 1865, to Miss Virginia Mosby, a daughter of J. H. and Maria (McClain) Mosby, natives of Virginia and Tennessee, respectively, and the parents of eight children. Mr. and Mrs. Pope are the parents of five children, all of whom (with Mrs. Pope) are deceased. Himself and wife were members of the Methodist Episcopal Church. He affiliates with the K. of H., the K. & L. of H. the A. F. & A. M., being a Knight Templar, a member of the I. H., and is connected with the County Wheel. He is one of the leading politicians of his county, and very popular, as is shown by the overwhelming majority given him at the polls when elected to the senate, and which confidence has been more than justified by the way in which he has discharged his duties.

Albert M. Pope, a prominent citizen of Cross County, was born near where the village of Vanndale is now situated, and in what was then (1861) Poinsett County, and is the only child of Madison and Julia F. (McClaran) Pope. Madison Pope was a native of Southampton County, Va., where he spent his youth and where he received his education. In 1852 Mr. Pope immigrated to Arkansas, and with his two brothers, Oswald and Riddick, bought and entered lands to the amount of 2,000 acres, after which they formed a partnership in the mercantile business in Memphis, which they continued until 1860, doing a large business. At that time the war coming on, and attendant circumstances, freed their slaves and left them with nothing but land. Mr. Pope was married in 1858, to Julia F. McClaran, of Macon, Fayette County, Tenn., a lady of education, who has taught school in the immediate neighborhood of Vanndale, for over the space of twenty years. Mr. Pope died in 1862, leaving to his widow and infant son a large tract of land, and the much better legacy—a good name. He was one of those men whose deeds live, after they have departed this life. His brother Oswald, senior partner of the firm, died in 1879, while Riddick survives, and is an honorable member of the State senate. Mrs. Julia F. Pope, after remaining a widow for twelve years, was married in 1874, to J. C. Brookfield, her present husband, with whom she now resides in the town of Jonesboro, Craighead County. A. M. Pope remained on the farm with his mother, till about eighteen years of age. He then clerked, respectively, in the towns of Wittsburg and Harrisburg, for about three years, after which he returned home and engaged in farming and stock-raising, till the removal of his mother to Jonesboro, when he built a neat and substantial residence in Vanndale, where he now resides, engaged in the drug business with Dr. T. D. Hare.

Napoleon B. Raulston, postmaster at Tyronza, is a native of Georgia, and a son of William Evander Raulston, also of Georgia birth, who is now living in Crittenden County. The latter was married in Georgia, before coming to this State, to Mary Tate, who died in 1855 in Prairie County, to which he first moved, leaving two children, of whom Napoleon was the eldest. The subject of this sketch was born July 24, 1853, and was reared in this State from the age of two to thirteen years. At the latter period he went to Tennessee and remained a number of years, being married in November, 1878, to Miss Alice Robins, who was born in Shelby County, Tenn., in 1861. They then moved to Arkansas, and have been residents of Cross County since 1884, having moved here from St. Francis County at that time. They are the

parents of three children: Willie G., Howard E. and Thomas B. Mr. Raulston has held the office of justice of the peace, and is now postmaster of this place. He has no land of his own but has control of the farm on which he lives. He always voted the Democratic ticket, and cast his first presidential vote for Samuel J. Tilden in 1876.

M. A. Riley, well known among the business circles as proprietor of one of the largest cotton-gins and grist-mills in Cross County, was reared on a farm in Shelby County, Tenn., and subsequently farmed for himself in his native county, until 1869, when he removed with his family to this county, and purchased his present farm of 100 acres, then in a wild state. He now has fifty acres under cultivation, with a good house, barn and buildings. M. A. was the son of L. C. and Eliza C. (Wiley) Riley, of North Carolina origin. His parents were married in North Carolina, and came to Tennessee in 1836, where his father purchased 320 acres of land. Mr. Riley, Sr., was a member of the Cumberland Presbyterian Church, and died in 1846, his wife dying in 1881 at the age of sixty-two years. To these parents were given five children, three of whom are still living: William, John and M. A., all residents of this county. In 1885 M. A. Riley moved to Cherry Valley, where he purchased four acres of land, and erected one of the finest residences to be found in the village, and also erected a large steam cotton-gin and grist-mill, and has a large custom throughout the surrounding territory. Mr. Riley was married in 1868 to Miss Rebecca A. Wiley, a native of Tennessee, and a daughter of Macaney and Nannie (Lovel) Wiley, also of Tennessee. They are the parents of five children, two of whom are deceased: Luella (deceased), Etta, Laura, Robert (deceased) and Walter. Politically Mr. Riley is a Democrat. He and his wife are connected with the Baptist Church.

William Henry Roberts is, not without merit, conceded to be one of the substantial farmers of Smith Township. His father, Zachariah Roberts, was a native of Virginia, and leaving that State in 1827 moved to Tennessee, where he married Sarah Fly. She still lives, and resides with William Henry, our subject, who is the only child of the family living. In 1850 Mr. Roberts settled in Cross County, Ark., and resided here about three years, then returning to Virginia, where his death occurred a short time after. William Henry Roberts was born in Gibson County, Tenn., August 6, 1835. He was reared on a farm, being denied the privileges of an education, and was married in 1861, to Eliza J. Thomas, who has borne seven children: William S., Georgia, Robert L., Mary L., James H., Nannie L. and Fannie D. Mr. Roberts enlisted in 1862 in the Fifth Arkansas Infantry and served about two years, when he was wounded at the battle of Helena, by a minie-ball, in the left shoulder. This disabled him, and he returned home. In 1865 he purchased the farm on which he now resides, then containing eighty acres, and has at this time 120 acres, with forty-five acres under cultivation. Mr. Roberts is a Democrat in his political preferences, and an esteemed resident of the community.

Judge W. F. Robinson, an esteemed member of the bench, was reared on a farm in North Carolina and at the age of nineteen, commenced farming for himself, but four years later he entered the Peabody School of Pigeon Gap, N. C., but remained in this institution for a short time only, when in the fall of 1873 he came to Arkansas, locating in Cross County and renting a farm in Searcy Township until 1888, when he purchased his present farm, which consists of eighty acres of timbered land. The Judge was born in Haywood County, N. C., on November 22, 1849, and was a son of John P. and Jane M. (Clark) Robinson, of North Carolina nativity. Mr. John P. Robinson (the father) was a farmer by occupation. Hearing his country call for volunteers during the Civil War, he enlisted in the Sixteenth North Carolina Infantry. He is still a resident of Haywood County. Mr. and Mrs. Robinson were blessed with ten children, five of whom are still living: W. F. (our subject), I. M., Dovie L. (wife of James Rinehart), John B. and Lorah J. Mr. and Mrs. Robinson are members of the Methodist Episcopal Church. He is a worthy member of the A. F. & A. M. Judge Robinson has been twice married. First to Miss

Mary E. Shaver, on August 5, 1880, and who died the following March. She was a member of the Methodist Episcopal Church. He was married the second time on March 28, 1889, to Miss Mary Baker, of this county. In 1876 the Judge was elected justice of the peace of Searcy Township, which office he held eight years, resigning it to accept that of county and probate judge, to which he had been elected, and is now serving his second term, with satisfaction to the people who honored him with their votes and confidence, and with great credit to himself.

Reuben R. Rogers, is also numbered among the representative agriculturists of Cross County. A native of Louisiana, he was born November 24, 1852, being the son of James and Huldah (Armstrong) Rogers, both originally from Mississippi. James Rogers moved to Louisiana when a young man and engaged in farming and stock raising, in which occupation he was interested until his death in 1860. His wife died in this county, in 1879 at the age of forty-nine, leaving three children. Reuben Rogers was reared on the home farm in Louisiana, until about five years after his father's death, when the widow removed with her family to Cross County, the subject of this sketch being at that time thirteen years of age. He lived with his mother up to twenty-two years of age, when he was married December 27, 1874, to Miss Alice Stanley, a native of Crittenden County, Ark., and a daughter of John Stanley. Though of Mississippi origin, he became one of the early pioneers of Crittenden County. Mr. and Mrs. Rogers are the parents of eight children, four now living: Leslie T., Irwin E., Lewin C., and Fannie G. Mr. Rogers has a fine farm of 255 acres, with about 100 acres under cultivation, situated some three miles from the mouth of the Tyronza River, at the place formerly known as Robinson Ferry. He also owns a farm of 160 acres, three-fourths of a mile east of home place, and located on the same river, of which upward of sixty acres are under cultivation. Mr. Rogers is an energetic and enterprising young farmer and is making a success of his business, being well known and highly respected by all.

J. T. Rolfe, proprietor of the Vanndale Hotel, if for no other reason, deserves especial mention as a direct descendant of the famous John Rolfe and Pocahontas; this is undisputed and reliable, as the traditions for many generations point directly to those illustrious characters as the founders of the family. Mr. Rolfe was born in Mecklenburgh County, Va., in 1834, being a son of Samuel D. and Susan (Stone) Rolfe. He attained his majority in the "Old Dominion," and became engaged in mercantile pursuits at the age of sixteen. Coming, in 1857, to Arkansas and settling in Poinsett (now Cross) County, where he resumed his interests of merchandising at a town called Pineville. This place has now disappeared. Here Mr. Rolfe remained until 1862, when he enlisted in the Confederate army, in McGee's company. After the war he took up farming and gave his attention to it until 1882, also serving as constable and deputy sheriff for two years during that time. In 1882 he moved to Vanndale and built a hotel and has been engaged in the hotel business since that time, with very successful results. The hotel building is a large, two-story structure 28x60 feet, and erected at a cost of $1,200. Mr. Rolfe was married, in 1860, to Miss Lizzie Rose, who died in 1864, leaving one child, Mary Susan (now Mrs. Rodgers). He was subsequently married to Mrs. Mary V. Rolfe, the widow of his brother Alexander. Mr. and Mrs. Rolfe are the parents of one son, Samuel A. The family are members of the Methodist Episcopal and Baptist Churches, and also of the K. & L. of H. In addition to his hotel, Mr. Rolfe owns a store in Vanndale, in which a large and steadily increasing business is being carried on.

Eli E. Sigman (deceased). Among the many estimable citizens of Cross County, who have passed to their long home, but who, from an early day were intimately and prominently associated with the county's development, the name of Eli E. Sigman can not be omitted. He was born in Catawba County, N. C., in 1835, and was the son of Barnet Sigman, who was a farmer in his native State. Eli E. Sigman remained at home and attended the common schools, supplementing the same by a course at Newton, N. C., after which he began the carpenter's trade and followed this in his native State until 1858, when he came to Arkansas and settled in what is now Cross County. Here he followed his trade and erected most of the frame houses from that time up to the beginning of the war. He then volunteered in Company A, Fifth Arkansas Regiment, was elected second lieutenant and later promoted to the rank of first lieutenant, serving with distinguished bravery in the battles of Shiloh, Perryville, Chickamauga, Nashville, Murfreesboro, Franklin and many other minor engagements. He surrendered in North Carolina soon after the battle of Raleigh. On his return in 1865 he soon married Miss Marie J. Lewellen, a native of Tennessee, who came to this State with her parents in 1850. Previous to the war Mr. Sigman bought a farm of 320 acres, about one and a fourth miles west of the present village of Vanndale, and when peace was declared he moved to this farm, on which there was but slight improvement, and at once began to clear up. He soon erected a neat residence, cleared about fifty acres of land and made a pleasant home. Mr. Sigman raised a variety of crops and was also engaged in the rearing of stock. To his marriage were born these children: Henry J., Willie E., M. Luther and N. Jervel. One infant died unnamed. Mr. Sigman joined the Lutheran Church in his youth but on his arrival in Cross County he connected himself with the Methodist Episcopal Church, South, and was class leader, steward and Sunday-school superintendent for a long time. Mr. Sigman departed this life on December 8, 1879, from pneumonia, and his death was lamented by a large circle of relatives and friends. The community, the church, the Sabbath school, all felt the loss of a good and wise man. Mrs. Sigman is a daughter of James Lewellen, who came to this county in 1850 and who was one of the pioneers and most highly respected citizens of the community. He reared a large family of children and up to 1881 they with their parents were all living within the vicinity of Vanndale. Since then the parents have died, also two of the children, but still a number are yet living in the community and are among Cross County's most respected citizens. Mrs. Sigman has a very pleasant home which she makes more attractive by the cultivation of innumerable flowers. With the assistance of her sons she manages and cultivates her valuable farm.

W. H. Slocum. One of the leading farmers and old settlers of Cross County is W. H. Slocum, who is a native of North Carolina, and the eldest son of G. C. and Sarah (Griphith) Slocum, also of North Carolina birth. Mr. G. C. Slocum was a blacksmith by trade, and moved to Tennessee in 1844, where he died in 1849, and his wife in 1879, leaving nine children, three of whom are now living: Mary (the wife of E. Robins, of this county), Joseph D. and W. H., all residing in this township. The subject of this sketch dates his existence from January 6, 1828. He received only five months' education in youth, his father needing his help in the blacksmith shop, in which he worked from the time he was able to swing a sledge until twenty-three years of age. In 1844 he accompanied his father to Tennessee, and in 1851 was married to Elizabeth Roberts, after which he moved to Arkansas and settled in this county (then Poinsett), where he rented a farm for two years. In 1853 he made entry of a quarter section, on which he now resides, and afterward bought 960 acres, about 500 of which he has given to his children. When Mr. Slocum first moved to Brushy Lake Township, in February, 1861, there were but three families for a distance of ten miles north or south. When he entered his land there were no clearings on it, and he erected a shanty in which he lived by himself until a log house was built. In 1874 he constructed the first steam mill and gin in the township, at that time the woods abounding in game, including bear, deer, and wild turkey. Mr. and Mrs. Slocum are the parents of nine children, eight living: Benjamin, Preston, Rebecca (now Mrs. Ott), Lovenia (wife of B. Burns), Samuel, Charles and Virg. Mr. Slocum joined the Confederate army in 1863, and served until the close of the war. He was taken prisoner south of Little Rock on July 4, 1863, and removed to Little Rock, from which he was paroled, and afterward rejoined the army, serving throughout the war. Upon the close of hostilities he returned home and engaged in farm-

ing and stock raising, in which he has been very successful. Mr. and Mrs. Slocum are members of the Methodist Episcopal Church, and take an active part in its affairs.

R. M. Smith, senior member of the firm of Smith, Graham & Jones, merchants at Wynne, owes his nativity to Batesville, Independence County, Ark., where his birth occurred in 1849. His parents, William and Mary (Miller) Smith, were also natives of Arkansas, and the father died when his son, R. M., was quite young. The paternal grandfather, Robert Smith, was a native of Maryland and came to Arkansas in about 1835, settling at Batesville where he followed farming for many years. He owned a fine tract of land on the opposite side of the river from the town. He moved to Springfield, Mo., in 1878, and there he died a few years later at the age of seventy-eight years. The maternal grandfather, John Miller, moved to Independence County, Ark., in 1817, bought a large tract of land near the site of the present city of Batesville and was a very successful farmer, accumulating a very large fortune. He died in 1886 at the advanced age of ninety-seven years. R. M. Smith passed his youth in Batesville and in 1866 went to Little Rock, where he entered St. John's College, and there remained for four years. After this he engaged in the retail grocery business in Little Rock, remaining there until 1871, when he sold his business and went back to Batesville. Going to Wittsburg in 1875 he started a drug store, which he carried on until 1881 when the firm title was changed to Hamilton, Smith & Co., continuing thus until January, 1888. That partnership was then dissolved and the firm of Smith, Graham & Jones was formed, which in February, 1888, opened business in the brick block known as the Commercial Hotel, at Wynne. Here they carry an average stock of $20,000 and are doing a good business. Mr. Smith was married in 1881 to Miss Mary Mebane (a native of Cross County and daughter of W. T. Mebane). To the union of Mr. and Mrs. Smith have been born two children: Bertie and Willie. Mrs. Smith is a member of the Presbyterian Church. Mr. Smith owns two farms comprising 475 acres, with fifty under cultivation and another tract three miles southeast of Wynne with 125 acres under cultivation. He is at present building an elegant new cottage with the hall and ceilings finished in natural wood and the rooms planned and designed by Mrs. Smith.

T. B. Smith, of the firm of Smith, Cole & Davis, of Cross County, is a native of Northern Alabama, a son of W. H. and Minerva (Levesque) Smith, who also came originally from that State. The father moved to Arkansas in 1854 and located in Poinsett (now Cross) County, where he bought and entered a farm of 640 acres. He served in the Indian War of 1836 for a short time, and was married in 1842–43, being the father of ten children, five of whom are still living: W. A., T. B. (our subject), Ophelia (wife of J. W. Perkins, of Jonesboro), Ala (wife of R. P. Fulenwider, of Jackson, Mo.), and Laura (wife of J. M. Puryear, of Jonesboro). Mrs. Smith was a member of the Methodist Church, and died in 1879, her husband surviving until 1884. He was a very popular man and served in several local offices. T. B. Smith was reared on a farm and educated in the subscription schools of this county, also attending the school of Covington, Tenn. He afterward engaged in farming on his father's land and also on a rented farm until 1876, when he bought a place containing 240 acres. This original amount has been increased until he now owns some 2,000 acres, having about 400 acres under cultivation. Mr. Smith was married in 1874 to Miss Bettie Levesque, daughter of Capt. J. M. Levesque [whose sketch appears elsewhere in this work]. They are the parents of three children (two living): Nannie B., Rufus (deceased) and Morris. Mr. Smith is the largest farmer in the county, cultivating over 1,000 acres, and is also extensively engaged in the sawmill business, having an interest in two mills with Messrs. Cole and Davis. Their output will be some 2,000,000 feet yearly from each of the two mills. He is also interested in a steam-gin, in connection with one of his saw-mills. His brother-in-law, Mr. W. T. Levesque, is associated with him in the gin. Mr. Smith has served as a member of the county court, and is at present county commissioner, and it was under his management that the present court house was built. For this attractive and useful public structure he deserves great praise. Mr. Smith is a member of the A. F. & A. M. His connection with the affairs of Cross County has caused him to become widely known, and the faithful manner in which he has deported himself in the discharge of public duties has redounded greatly to his own credit and the benefit of the community.

R. M. Spain enjoys extensive acquaintance as one of the oldest settlers of the county. He is also a farmer of Wynne Township. A native of Virginia he is the son of N. G. and Martha (Hall) Spain, originally from Virginia and South Carolina, respectively, the former of whom, in 1840, moved to Maury County, Tenn., where he engaged in farming, and where his wife died in 1847. After that event Mr. Spain married Mrs. L. D. Benderman (nee Matthews). By his first marriage he was the father of eight children, two of whom are living: Addison H. and R. M. By his second union there were three daughters: Lenora (wife of John Thomas), Samuella and Lieusha (twins, the latter the wife of Thomas English). R. M. Spain was born in 1834, and was reared to agricultural pursuits in Maury County, Tenn., from the ages of eighteen to twenty-three being employed as a farm laborer. In 1856 he was married to Miss Margaret E. Benderman, and for two years after lived with his father-in-law. He then rented for a short time, and in 1859 came to this county, buying his present farm, consisting of 297 acres, to which he has added some eighty-six acres, and has now 125 acres under cultivation. Mr. and Mrs. Spain are the parents of ten children, four of whom survive: Emma E. (wife of J. W. Moore), Ozni, Lenora E. and John A. In 1862 Mr. Spain joined the Confederate army in McNeil's regiment and served until July 4, 1863, when he was wounded at the battle of Helena, and was taken prisoner, being removed to the Memphis hospital, where he was kept until October of that year; then he was confined at Alton, Ill., and in August, 1864, he was removed to Camp Douglas, from which he was paroled in 1865. When he returned home his family were in much better circumstances than he expected to find them. His negroes were still on the farm, and had it in good order and crops growing. In 1874 Mr. Spain was elected assessor, acceptably discharging the duties of that position for two years. Mrs. Spain is a member of the Cumberland Presbyterian Church. He belongs to the A. F. & A. M., and is a public-spirited and enterprising man, enjoying the respect of all who know him.

G. N. Sparks, of the firm of Daltroff, Sparks & Oliver, merchants at Wynne, is one of the most enterprising business men of the place. ·He owes his nativity to McMinnville, Tenn., where his birth occurred in 1853, and is the youngest of ten children born to the union of Thomas and Mary L. (Boothe) Sparks, both natives of the Old Dominion. The father was a tiller of the soil and followed this occupation in Tennessee until 1859, when he moved to Arkansas, and settled at Jonesboro, Craighead County, where he purchased 320 acres of land, only slightly improved. Mr. Sparks immediately began erecting good buildings, clearing land, and soon bought other tracts in the vicinity. He gave all of his children homes at the time of their majority and was a man whose shrewd business tact is remembered by old settlers. He became one of the best-known men in several counties, and died in 1878. The mother's death occurred two years later, and both were seventy-four years of age. G. N. Sparks early in life became familiar with the duties of the farm and attended the schools of Craighead County until fifteen years of age. Later he took a commercial course at Leddin's College at Memphis, and when seventeen years of age he left the parental roof, went to Forrest City, where he engaged as clerk in the dry goods store of N. O. Rhodes & Co., and remained with this firm for two years. Subsequently he began work for his brother, who was a member of the firm of Sparks & Rolloage, and continued with this firm until 1874, when he was united in marriage to Miss Jennie Cobbs, a native of Arkansas, and the daughter of C. H. Cobbs, a pioneer of St. Francis County. After his marriage Mr. Sparks removed to the old homestead, where

his father had settled on his arrival in Arkansas, and which was given to G. N. Sparks at that time. Here he was engaged in farming and teaching school for four years, and in 1880 he engaged as book-keeper for Killough & Erwin at Wittsburg. After five years he changed to a similar position with Block & Co., who had opened a branch store at Wynne. In January, 1886, that firm was bought out by Daltroff, Sparks & Oliver, who opened a fine large store in Wynne. Mr. Sparks owns a fine residence in that city, is also the owner of real estate in Forrest City and 160 acres of good land in Craighead County. He is a member of the K. of P., Levesque Lodge No. 52, at Wynne, and is also a member of the K. & L. of H., Pearl Lodge. Mrs. Sparks is a member of the Methodist Episcopal Church. To the union of Mr. and Mrs. Sparks were born two children: Lena May and Annie Blanche. Mr. Sparks is a young man of cordial and generous disposition, is a member of a large firm and is well thought of by all. He remembers distinctly that at their first settlement in Craighead County, there was but one shanty where the city of Jonesboro now stands, and this was used as a saloon and kept by a man by the name of Pollard.

G. W. Stacy, known throughout the county as an upright and thorough-going citizen, was thrown upon his own resources when very young. At the age of sixteen he took charge of his mother's farm and bought out the other heirs interested in this farm. The old homestead consisted of 200 acres, located in this county, with forty-five cultivated. He sold this place a few years since, and bought the eighty acres of land on which he now lives, this lying near to the corporation of what is now Cherry Valley, yet was not surveyed at the time he purchased this tract. He has since sold thirty acres of this land for building purposes. Mr. Stacy engaged in the mercantile business in 1877, at this place, carrying a stock of general merchandise worth between $4,000 and $5,000 and built up a large trade, doing a business which averages about $20,000 per year. Mr. Stacy was born in this county in 1853, and was the son of Miles and Rebecca (Duke) Stacy, natives of Arkansas and

Tennessee, respectively. The senior Stacy was a farmer and machinist by trade, living in this State until his thirteenth year, when he went to New Orleans, remaining there until twenty-seven years of age, when he returned to this State. He was married in Mississippi in 1834. In 1844 he came to Cross County, where he purchased some 400 acres of land. He held the office of county judge for five years, holding this up to the time of his death, which occurred April 18, 1853. He was the father of fourteen children, five of whom are living: Amelia, Louisa, C. M., R. M. and G. W. (our subject). Mrs. Stacy is still living in her seventy-third year, and resides with G. W. The latter was married in June, 1875,· to Miss Eva (McCall) Beadle, a daughter of B. G. and Evaline (Wilson) Beadle, originally of Indiana and North Carolina, respectively. Mr. Beadle was a first-cousin of Abraham Lincoln, and served during the late conflict in the United States frigate, "Annie." Mr. Beadle was engaged in the manufacture of cotton-gins, and died in 1876. Mr. and Mrs. Stacy are the parents of six children: C. M., Lena and Ester (who are away at school) and Miles, Henry and Glenn (at home). Mr. Stacy is a Democrat in politics, and has officiated as the postmaster of Cherry Valley for a number of years.

John Stoner, M. D., a retired physician of Tyronza, has been closely identified with professional affairs during an active and busy life. He graduated from the Jefferson Medical College, of Philadelphia, in 1851, after which he commenced the practice of his adopted calling in Pennsylvania, remaining there for three years. While in that State he was married, in 1842, to Louisa Bixler, who died in 1866, leaving five children, two still living: Robley D. and Mary (the wife of Mr. Simcox). Dr. Stoner married, in 1867, his second wife, formerly Miss Kate Huxtable, of New York State. They are the parents of two children: Frank and Ida. Dr. Stoner was born in York County, Penn., October 17, 1822, and was a son of Samuel S. Stoner, originally from Germany, and Mary Brubaker, of Pennsylvania nativity. About 1871 Dr. Stoner moved to Arkansas, and settled in Cross County, where he now lives, having been engaged in farming and stock raising since that time. He has a fine place of 320 acres on the St. Francis River. Dr. Stoner served in the Union army for three years, as assistant surgeon in the Seventy-seventh Illinois Infantry. Himself and wife are members of the Methodist Episcopal Church, South. He also belongs to the I. O. O. F., and is recognized as a citizen of influence and worth.

Joseph Taylor is one of the oldest settlers in Cross County, and was born in Kentucky in January, 1809, being the son of Peter and Elizabeth (Dawson) Taylor, natives of Kentucky and Georgia, respectively. Peter Taylor, whose parents were Chapman Taylor and Rachel Taylor, was married in 1806, and became the father of twelve children, five still living: Joseph (the second one of the family), Daniel (in Colorado), Peter (in Texas) Elizabeth (now Mrs. Hodges, of Illinois), and Rachel (now Mrs. Williams, of Texas). Mr. Taylor died in 1825. Joseph Taylor has been twice married: first, to Susan Levesque, in 1830, who died in 1866, leaving seven children, five of whom survive: William, James (who resides in Augusta, Ark.), Ellen (the widow of J. J. Fields, an old settler of this county), Elizabeth (now Mrs. McKey, of Texas) and Mary. Mr. Taylor was married to his second wife in February, 1872, she being Miss Louisa Stafford. They are the parents of one child, now deceased. Joseph Taylor came to what was then a part of Poinsett (now Cross) County, in 1857, where he purchased 200 acres of land, with about sixty acres under cultivation, to this he has since added some forty acres; in 1886 moved to Cherry Valley, where he bought a house and lot, and now has one of the finest homes in the village. Mr. and Mrs. Taylor are members of the Methodist Episcopal Church, as was also his first wife. He belongs to the A. F. & A. M. Mr. Taylor is a Democrat, politically, but never took an active part in politics, and never favored slavery.

William Taylor, in his association with the affairs of this county, has come to be recognized as one of the prominent farmers. Born in Alabama, in 1830, he is a son of Joseph and Susan (Levesque) Taylor, and growing up was reared principally in

Alabama, receiving a good education, for the times, in the common schools. At the age of twenty he commenced farming for himself on rented land, and in 1852, removed with his father to Western Tennessee, where he remained only one year, then going to Panola County, Miss. He worked at the carpenter trade for a few years in that county, and in 1859, came to Cross County (then Poinsett County), Ark., locating in what is now Mitchell Township. At first renting land until 1866, he then bought eighty acres on Crowley's Ridge, but in 1871, he sold this place, and bought his present estate, consisting of 160 acres, with twenty-five acres under cultivation. He has also cleared up some seventy-five acres of fine bottom land, and has a splendid frame house close to the village of Cherry Valley. Besides his farming interests he is in the carpentering trade. In 1861 Mr. Taylor enlisted on the side of the Confederacy, in the Thirteenth Arkansas Infantry, serving in the Tennessee Division. He acted as wagon-master for some time, and took part in the battles of Murfreesboro, Chickamauga, Missionary Ridge and Dalton, Ga. After this last battle he came west and joined Gen. Price's command as first lieutenant in a cavalry regiment, remaining with him on his raid through Missouri, in 1864 and 1865. Mr. Taylor has been married twice; first, in 1851, to Mary C. Murphy, a native of Alabama, who died in 1871, leaving five children (three now living): Julia O. (wife of P. C. Crumpton), Frederick P. (deceased), W. C. (deceased), John M. (clerk in the Commercial Hotel of St. Louis) and James P. (deceased, who was killed in a storm while riding through the woods, by a tree falling on and killing him). Mr. Taylor was married the second time in 1872, to Mrs. Emma C. Brinkley (nee Stevens), daughter of James and Rachel (Stovall) Stevens, of Tennessee nativity. By this union there are five children, (four living): Robert N., Charles (deceased), Rachel, Maud and Lillie (twins). Mr. and Mrs. Taylor are members of the Methodist Episcopal Church, as was also the first wife. He is a Royal Arch Mason, and belongs to Arcada Lodge No. 183, in which he holds the office of Senior Warden. Mr. Taylor is also connected with the I. O. O. F., and the K. of H. A strong Democrat, he is a liberal donator to all church, educational and charitable objects.

J. H. Taylor commenced life as a farmer at the age of twenty, on a farm in this county, which he rented for about five years, when he purchased forty acres some three miles east of Wynne. In 1878 he traded this for the land on which he now lives, consisting of 160 acres with ten acres under cultivation. At this time he has forty acres under cultivation, with a good residence and orchard containing about fifty or sixty fine apple trees, all in good order. In 1862, Mr. Taylor embraced the principles which he believed right, enlisting in the Twenty-third Arkansas Infantry in which he served only eighteen months, being captured at Port Hudson, then he was paroled and never exchanged. He has been married twice: first in October, 1864, to Miss L. C. Pulley, who died in May, 1887, having been the mother of nine children, four of whom are still living: Mary I. (wife of A. May, a resident of St. Francis County), A. S., A. M. and George (who are at home.) Mr. Taylor was married the second time in 1888, to Mrs. Ellen Ramsey (nee Griffin). She is a member of the Methodist Episcopal Church, as was also Mr. Taylor's first wife. Mr. Taylor belongs to the A. F. & A. M. and is a popular citizen of Wynne Township. His parents, Adolford and Martha A. (Brown) Taylor, were natives of Tennessee, the former of whom moved to this State in 1842 and first settled in Jackson County, where he remained two years, then finding a home in St. Francis County. After two or three years there he came to Cross County and settled at the foot of Crowley's Ridge, where he rented a farm. In 1847 Mr. Taylor entered a quarter section of land, one mile from where the town of Wynne is now located. Afterward selling out, in 1854 he bought the farm on which he resided until his death, in March, 1881, having survived his wife twenty-two years. They were members of the Methodist Church, and were the parents of nine children, two of whom are living.

John Toole, roadmaster of the Helena branch of the Iron Mountain Railroad, from Knott to Helena, was born in Brooklyn, N. Y., in 1847, and is the son of John and Mary Toole. The parents moved to St. Louis in 1856, and here John Toole, Jr., received his education. He remained in school until about fifteen years of age, and then commenced railroading on the Iron Mountain road, beginning as brakesman, and after a time being promoted to conductor. He ran on the road in the latter capacity for about eight years, and was then appointed roadmaster on the main line between St. Louis and Little Rock. In May, 1888, he was put in charge of the Helena branch, and has since made his headquarters at Wynne. Mr. Toole selected his companion for life in the person of Miss Conley, a native of St. Louis, Mo., and the wedding took place in 1869. To this union were born three children, a son and two daughters: John, Kate and Alice. Mr. Toole is a member of Lodge No. 52 of the K. of P., and is one of the much respected citizens of the county. He has discharged every duty incumbent upon him in his positions of trust with accuracy and dispatch, and has the confidence of the public.

Samuel Tyer, Wynne, Ark. This venerable man has been a resident of Arkansas since 1817 and this of itself is sufficient to give him an extensive acquaintance, even if his personal characteristics were not such as to draw around him many friends. He was born in Tennessee in 1812, and in 1815 the family moved to Cape Girardeau County, Mo., where his father, Wright Tyer, made one crop and then, not liking the country very well, he went down to the present State of Arkansas and made one crop in what is now Smith Township, Cross County. The next year (1817) he brought his family to this section and there lived for two years on vacant land. In 1820 he bought eighty acres of land from William Russell, of St. Louis, who had been buying up most of the valuable land in this section. The father died in 1831. On this farm Samuel Tyer spent his youth, helping to cultivate the farm. In those early days they experienced many hardships and endured many privations. At the time of their settlement, in 1817, there were but six families between Ben Crowley's, in Green County, and the Jones place, then called Cherokee Village, on the southern border of the county.

Here they lived, and as an occasional settler joined them the population increased. In 1838 Mr. Tyer married Miss Nancy Newton, a native of Wayne County, Tenn., whose father came to Arkansas in 1836 and started a blacksmith shop, but subsequently moved to Independence County, where he died at Sulphur Rock. After marriage Mr. Tyer bought a farm three miles north of the present village of Wynne, cleared about twenty-five acres and then sold out and moved to the Lone Star State, making the trip of 1,600 miles overland in six months. Not liking the country or the people he soon returned to Arkansas, satisfied that this country was good enough for him. On his return in 1862 he bought the place on which he still resides, a farm of 160 acres, which was almost wild land. This he immediately began to improve and at the present time has about forty acres under cultivation. He and wife are living all alone in a little house which has been their home for many years, and during that time they have witnessed the gradual development of the country. Their family consisted of eleven children, all now deceased but three: Josephus and Monroe (who are living on the old place) and Melinda Jane (who resides in Poinsett County). Mrs. Tyer spun and wove the goods from which their clothes were made and she had not bought any domestic until a few years ago. Mr. Tyer has lived in what is now Cross County, Ark., longer than any one now living, and in the vicinity of Copper's Creek, where his father first settled, there were over thirty panthers killed in two years. This old and much-respected couple have lived for fifty-one years a happy married life and have had their share of the hardships incident to the early pioneers. They raised all their provisions and made their own clothing. Mr. Tyer still farms and has a good crop of corn this year. This worthy couple have a set of knives and forks, still in a good state of preservation, which they have used through all their married life.

D. A. Tyer was born in St. Francis County, Ark., shortly after his parents came to this State. Curtis Tyer, the father, was a blacksmith by trade and a native of Tennessee, who removed here in 1840, settling in St. Francis County, where he was married to Elizabeth Sparks, who was also of Tennessee origin. Mr. and Mrs. Tyer were the parents of eight children, four of whom are living: D. A., Mattie (wife of R. Harrell, of this township), T. C. (also of this township) and Sallie (wife of W. H. Newsom, a resident of Wynne). Mr. Tyer died in 1866, and his wife, who was a member of the Baptist Church, in 1873. D. A., the subject of this sketch, was born in 1846, and was reared on a farm, being educated in the subscription schools of the county. At the age of twenty-one he commenced farming for himself, and also ran a blacksmith shop, having learned that trade in his father's shop. In 1864 he joined the army, in defense of the Southern cause, and was in Price's raid through Missouri, in which he served until the close of the war. Mr. Tyer was married in 1866 to Miss Mary F. Lindley. Their union has been blessed by eight children: Ida (wife of T. N. Holt), Cora, Willie, Robert, Allen, Sallie, Stephen and Grove M. In 1868 Mr. Tyer bought forty acres of land, to which he has since added another eighty, now having about sixty acres under cultivation, with a good dwelling; he also raises some stock. A public-spirited man he is a liberal donator to all enterprises for the good of the community in which he lives.

John M. Vann, merchant and postmaster, Vanndale, Ark. Ever since his connection with the affairs of Cross County, Mr. Vann has displayed those sterling qualities, industry, perseverance and integrity, that have resulted in awarding him a representative place in matters pertaining to this community. He owes his nativity to Fayette County, Tenn., where his birth occurred in 1845, and is the eldest in a family of seven children born to Renselear and Emily M. (Maget) Vann, natives of North Carolina. The father was a farmer and came to Arkansas, in 1850, settling in St. Francis (now Cross) County, about three miles south of the present town of Vanndale. In the same year he erected a cotton-gin and grist-mill, which was the first mill and gin in this section. He bought 640 acres of land on which he made many improvements, clearing about 200 acres, erecting buildings, etc., and made a good home for his family. He

was well known as a thrifty and enterprising citizen, and was for a long time postmaster at Mill Ridge, the only postoffice in that section for a long time. He was also justice of the peace for a number of years. His death occurred on April 30, 1887, at the age of sixty-nine years. His estimable wife had died two years previous. John M. Vann remained at home until his twentieth year and attended the common schools of the section. He was preparing to go away to school when the breaking out of the war caused him to throw aside all thoughts of books. In 1867 he engaged as clerk for J. Q. Thomas & Co., at Wittsburg, with whom he continued for one year, and after which he began business for himself at Cleburne, at that time the county seat. He continued in this business until 1879, when he moved to his farm and there erected a store, where he continued business until 1882. In October of that year he came to a place on the Iron Mountain Railroad that had just been named in his honor, Vanndale, and here he erected a store and dwelling. He has since been increasing his business and now carries a full line of general merchandise, and has a stock of goods valued at $5,000. In 1870 he was appointed postmaster at Cleburne and has continued as such at that place and Vanndale ever since, being the only one ever at the latter place. Mr. Vann owns 440 acres of good tillable land, 100 acres of which is under cultivation and the balance mostly covered with good timber. He was married in 1870 to Miss Ida Hare a native of Tennessee and the daughter of Rev. Thomas P. Hare, a pioneer preacher of this section. Three children were the result of this union: Claude (at present publishing the Register at Forrest City), Thomas and Bessie. The family are members of the Methodist Episcopal Church, South. Mr. Vann is a member of the Knights and Ladies of Honor. He has served as school director for ten years and takes a deep interest in educational matters.

Mrs. Ella Warren. Among the early and most prominent farmers of this county some twenty-five years ago, was James W. Warren, who came to this State in 1852. He was the son of Jesse and Rebecca (Boon) Warren, who were the parents of seven children, all of whom are now dead. James Warren was married to Ella Futrell in Tennessee, in 1847, both natives of North Carolina. After his marriage Mr. Warren moved to this State, settling in what is now Cross County, but at the time of his settlement Poinsett County, where he purchased a section of land, part of which is now the village of Vanndale. He also owned a number of negroes, and carried on a large plantation previous to the war. At the time of the rebellious outbreak Mr. Warren was in poor health, and so did not take any part in the Confederate service, and died soon after the war closed, in 1868. He was very active in politics, and was one of the leading men of his community, besides being one of the largest land owners in the county. He left his widow in good circumstances at the time of his death, and she has proven herself thoroughly capable of taking care of the property left her. Mr. and Mrs. Warren were the parents of seven children, two of whom are now living: Jefferson (who is married and carries on the farm for his mother) and James (also at home). Mrs. Warren's parents were very wealthy. They moved from North Carolina to Tennessee when she was but a child. To these parents were born eight children, five of whom still live: Ella (our subject), Sarah, Martha A. (now Mrs. Outland), Mary L. and James G. Mr. Futrell (our subject's father) died in 1883, and his wife in 1868. Mrs. Futrell was a member of the Baptist Church. Mrs. Warren is an enterprising and accomplished lady, and highly respected.

John N. White, proprietor of the cotton-gin at Levesque, Smith Township, Cross County, Ark., first saw the light of day in Michigan, in 1848, and was the second of six children born to the marriage of James and Jane (Williams) White, natives of England and New York, respectively. The father went to California in 1849, and after returning followed agricultural pursuits in Michigan at an early day. Both parents are living at the present time. John N. White attended the public schools and the college at Hillsdale, until twenty-one years of age, when he engaged in the hardware business for himself in that town, and this continued for some time. In 1873 he moved to Missouri, located in Cole County, and engaged in the timber business, which he continued for three years. He then came to Arkansas and engaged in the same business on White River. In 1884 he came to Cross County, settled at Cherry Valley, erected a saw-mill and there remained about a year in partnership with D. J. Burks. They moved the mill in 1885, continuing at this new location until the fall of 1886, and then bought a mill on the bay, where they were engaged in cutting timber for the railroad during 1886 and 1887. They then built a gin and saw-mill on the railroad, at a point now named Levesque, and soon after erected and opened the first store at that place. This store was soon sold to O. A. Hamilton, and in 1887 the gin was burned down. Mr. White then bought his partner out and, in 1888, put up a new steam-gin with a capacity of twelve bales daily. In 1889 he sold the saw-mill to Smith, Cole & Davis. At present Mr. White is engaged in the logging business in the St. Francis bottom and in his gin at Levesque. He is a prominent saw-mill and timber man, is active and energetic, and although of Northern birth, finds Arkansas good enough for him. He was married, in 1884, to Miss Alice Cartright, of Pine Bluff, and to this union has been born one child, a son named Elmer.

W. P. Wilkins was partly reared to farm life in Tennessee, where he was born, and also in Kentucky, his parents having removed to the Blue Grass State when he was twelve years of age. In 1847 he came to Arkansas and located in what was then St. Francis (now Cross) County, within two miles of his present place of residence, and was engaged for the next five years as a farm laborer. In 1852 he purchased a quarter section of land, since which time he has added forty acres more, now having over 100 acres under cultivation, with a good house, buildings and orchard, etc. In 1861 Mr. Wilkins joined the Confederate service in Mc-Gee's regiment, in which he served until the close of the war, participating in the battles of Big Creek, Ironton (Mo.), Wittsburg, and a number of skirmishes. Mr. Wilkins was born in Tennessee, in 1827, as a son of William and Nancy J. (Sutfin) Wilkins. The father was a prominent Tennessee farmer, and in 1839 moved to Kentucky and settled in Jackson County, remaining there until the year 1845, when his wife died. Returning thence to Marshall County, Tenn., he also died, at the age of ninety-six years. Mr. Wilkins served in the Revolutionary War, and was present at the surrender of Cornwallis. He was always blessed with good health, and was never known to call a doctor in his life. He had been twice married; first, to a Miss Ellison, who was the mother of four children, all now deceased, and after her death to the mother of our subject, who bore eleven children, three living: Isabella (the widow of William Trout), B. F. (a resident of Yell County, Ark.) and W. P. The latter was married in 1849 to Miss Mollie Eldridge. They have a family of ten children, seven of whom survive: P. P. (a resident of Wynne), Isabella (wife of P. Anderson), N. J., John, Mollie L. (the wife of James Halk), Rufus C. and R. G. Mr. and Mrs. Wilkins are members of the Methodist Episcopal Church, South. He is connected with the A. F. & A. M., and is a member of the school board. Mr. Wilkins is a prominent man hereabouts, and takes an active part in politics, having served as constable of the township.

H. C. Winters is widely remembered as an old settler of Bedford Township. A native of Alabama, he is the eldest son of Henry and Sarah (Rinfrow) Winters, who came originally from North Carolina and Tennessee, respectively. Henry Winters went to Alabama in 1828 and settled in Morgan County, where he remained five years, going thence to Tippah County, Miss. He was twice married, and by his first wife had two boys. one of whom is living: Aaron, a resident of Pope County, Ark. Mr. Winters was married to the mother of our subject in 1828. They were the parents of six children, all of whom are still living: H. C., J. J. Thomas, William C., Mary E. (now Mrs. Harbinger) and Sarah J. (Mrs. Vandover), all living in Texas excepting the first named. Mr. Winters was a soldier in the War of 1812, and died in 1852. Mrs. Winters was a member of the Methodist Episcopal Church, and died in 1880. H. C. Winters was born in Morgan County, Ala., in 1829, and was reared on a farm in Tippah County,

Miss., remaining at home until twenty-six years of age, when he came to St. Francis County, Ark., and was an overseer for some five years on a plantation. In 1861 he enlisted in the Confederate service, Fourth Arkansas Infantry, and served in the Trans-Mississippi Department, being wounded at the battle of Jenkins' Ferry, and having the thumb shot from his left hand. After the war Mr. Winters returned home and engaged in farming on his own land, which he had bought in 1859, consisting of 160 acres. In 1880 he purchased the interests of the heirs of his father-in-law to his farm on which he now lives. It is a fine place, consisting of 240 acres of land, of which some sixty acres are under cultivation, and he also owns 600 acres besides, with forty acres improved. Mr. Winters has been married twice; first, to Miss Mary E. Meek in 1866, who died in 1886, after having reared eight children; five of these are still living: H. L., R. M., W. T., J. E. and G. M. In December, 1886, Mr. Winters was married to Mrs. Ada Edwards (nee DeKey). She is a member of the Baptist Church, his first wife being a member of the Christian Church as he himself is. Mr. Winters belongs to the A. F. & A. M., and is a charter member of Levesque Lodge No. 227; he is also a member of the I. O. O. F.

J. G. Wright, M. D., one of the prominent physicians and surgeons of Cross County, is a native of Illinois and was born in 1830, as the son of T. J. and Mary (Griffin) Wright, originally from Virginia, and of English descent. The father moved to Illinois in 1829, and settled in Edgar County, where he remained until 1855, then going to Worth County, Mo. Buying a farm he resided until his death which occurred in 1866, at the age of fifty-four years. Mr. Wright served as justice of the peace four years in Missouri. Mrs. Wright still survives him and lives in Worth County, and though eighty years of age, she enjoys the best of health. They had in their family five children (two of whom are living): J. G., Martha (the widow of Samuel Adams, late of Missouri), C. C., Ester (deceased) and Elizabeth (deceased). Mrs. Wright is a member of the Cumberland Presbyterian Church. Dr. J. G. Wright joined the United States army at the age of sixteen, and served in the war with Mexico, participating in the siege of Vera Cruz, and a number of other prominent battles. After the engagement at Vera Cruz he received his discharge and returned home. During his time of service in that war he marched 500 miles on foot, and was disabled and laid up for eight weeks at the hospital at Matamoras. After coming home he entered upon the study of medicine at the age of eighteen in the office of Dr. Lenbrook, of Paris, Ill., a graduate of the Jefferson College of Medicine at Philadelphia. In 1849–50 Mr. Wright attended the Rush Medical College at Chicago, and in 1850 began his career as practitioner under his former instructor, where he remained for six years, then going to Worth County, Mo. Locating at Oxford, he continued the practice of his profession until 1886 and also served as county justice for two years, and was postmaster of Oxford for eight years. He then moved to Ottawa, Kan., but after six months came to this county. Dr. Wright was married in 1851 to Miss Julia Daugherty, of Ohio. They are the parents of five children: Florence E. (wife of W. D. Sharp, of Ottawa, Kas.), Alice D. (wife of J. W. Cubine, of Coffeeville, Kas.), C. J. C. and T. J. (both at home) and Mary M. (now Mrs. J. M. Tinson, of Kansas City, Mo.). Mrs. Wright is a member of the Baptist Church. Dr. Wright is a very decided Democrat, but does not take an active part in politics. He has a large and extensive practice as the constant demands made upon his time amply indicate, and his kindly manner makes him welcome in the sick room.

CHAPTER XVIII.

CRITTENDEN COUNTY—ACT OF ORGANIZATION—THE NAME—EARLY SETTLEMENTS AND LAND ENTRIES—
TRIBUNAL CENTERS—PUBLIC EDIFICES—MATERIAL ADVANCEMENT AND PROGRESS—THE CRIT-
TENDEN OF TO-DAY—ITS DESIRABILITY AS A PLACE OF RESIDENCE—RESOURCES,
LOCATION AND TOPOGRAPHY—MILITARY AFFAIRS—OFFICIAL DIREC-
TORY—MILITARY ROAD—RAILROADS—SCHOOL MATTERS—
RELIGIOUS CONDITION—NEWSPAPER PRESS—TOWNS
AND VILLAGES—BIOGRAPHY.

> On the overwork'd soil
> Of this planet enjoyment is sharpen'd by toil;
> And one seems, by the pain of ascending the height,
> To have conquered a claim of that wonderful sight.—*Meredith.*

PROPERLY speaking, the history of any definite locality commences with its formation. The county of Crittenden was formed by an act of the Territorial legislature of the territory of Arkansas, in 1825. It embraced a large part of what is now Cross, St. Francis and Lee Counties and portions have been cut off from time to time as those various counties were formed. It now comprises less than half of its original area. This county was named in honor of Robert Crittenden, who was appointed first secretary of Arkansas Territory, and served in that office from 1819 to 1829.

The earliest record of land entries in Crittenden County are forty Spanish claim grants. Some of these grants are now located in other counties, as they were formed from parts of this. The first entry is dated 1828, and is by John J. Bowie, the patentee of the Bowie knife. In 1829 land was entered by Charles Kelley, Francis Duvall, W. D. Ferguson, Antoine Bearvis and Richard Searcy. The first entries of United States lands were in 1829: eighty acres by Joseph Hudson; eighty acres by Weldon Vanwinkle in 1831; eighty acres by Robert Larkin in 1832. In 1833 land was entered by Michael Elsberry, William Hagins and Preston Yeatman; in 1834 by James Erwin, James Shelby and Isaac Bledsoe; in 1835 by James Erwin, Isaac Bledsoe, Jonathan Hand, Robert Larkin, Daniel Harkelwood, Preston Yeatman, Robert Larkins, Jonathan Hann and John J. Walton. In 1836, the year in which Arkansas was admitted as a State, there are too many to enumerate. In 1826 John Grace deeded a tract of 220 arpents to Nancy Procter. On the record book of this county there is on record a freedman's certificate given by William Williams, a notary public of New York, to John Brown, a negro, dated May 13, 1812.

Benjamin Flooy was perhaps the earliest settler in Crittenden County. He was military commandant at the Spanish post or fort of Camp of Hope, on the Mississippi River, opposite Memphis, now known as Hopefield. When this country was sold to France, by Spain, and his office was abolished, he remained at the old post and began farming. Here was made the first clearing, and here he lived and died and left children who lived here for many years after him. The old house which he built was standing till 1858, when the land on which it stood caved into the river, and this old landmark was destroyed.

Augustine Grandee came to what is now Crittenden County, as a Spanish officer, about 1801. Upon the sale of this country to France, he, like Commandant Flooy, concluded to remain and make this fertile land his home. He settled about four miles west of the Mississippi River, on a lake that has since borne his name, and near where the town of Marion is now built. He died on his plantation and left six children, of whom many descendants are still living in Eastern Arkansas.

Gen. Bradley settled on the Mississippi River, eighteen miles above Memphis, at an early day. He opened up a large plantation and became one of the prosperous planters in the pioneer period of Crittenden County.

A member of the State Confederate Convention, which met at Little Rock in 1861, he opposed the secession of the State with all power, and when he died it was with the same sentiment, though he was highly esteemed by all who knew him; he was the soul of honor, and while his course aroused the animosity of most Confederates, they soon promoted him to a command of a regiment, but on account of old age and feeble health he afterward resigned.

Some of the oldest settlers in this county were the Harklerodes, Burgetts, Foglemans, P. G. Pollock, E. Garrett, B. F. Allen and Maj. J. B. Lyles, who settled at Marion in 1841; at that time he bought and ran the old hotel which still stands in the village.

The Territorial legislature placed the seat of justice of Crittenden County, temporarily, at Greenock. This place was soon selected as the permanent county seat, and the first court was held here, in the house of William Lloyd in June, 1826.

The old record of deeds of this county shows that on June 13, 1827, H. N. Ferguson transferred to the county of Crittenden, a tract of land for county purposes. This place remained as the seat of justice for ten years, when it was permanently removed to Marion. The site of old Greenock has long since been washed away by the Mississippi River.

In 1837 the county court appointed J. R. James and John Owens commissioners to select a site for the county seat, as the people of the county had petitioned for a change. They chose a point fourteen miles northeast of Memphis, and four miles west of Oldham. On the records is found that on June 25, 1837, a deed was given to these commissioners in trust for the county of Crittenden for county purposes, by Marion Tolbert and wife, Temperance, for one-half of the lots in twenty acres. A town was here laid out, and, in honor of Mr. Tolbert, was named Marion.

The first court of Crittenden County was held in the house of William Lloyd, and it is not positively known whether a court house was ever erected at Greenock or not. Mr. A. H. Ferguson remembers seeing the old jail at that place, but the site of this old town disappeared beneath the waves of the Mississippi River so long ago, that no one now remembers whether there was a court house there or not; it is probable, however, that one was erected there.

Soon after the seat of justice was removed to Marion, the county erected a frame court house; this was destroyed by a cyclone, and thus for many years court was held in various buildings, in old churches or vacant store-houses, till 1873, when the new brick building was constructed. The contract for this building and the jail was let at $60,000, and county bonds were issued for that sum to pay the bill. For two years no work of any kind was done, but the county was required to pay the interest on the bonds. The building was completed in 1873–74, but before the indebtedness was canceled it cost the county over $100,-000. It is, however, a neat, two-story brick building, commodious and thoroughly satisfactory for all purposes.

From the first settlement of Crittenden, early in the nineteenth century, the productiveness of its lands have been phenomenal. With a climate mild and genial, admitting of outdoor labor almost every day of the year, and a soil that will yield abundantly every variety of plant or vine, and in addition that king of vegetable products— cotton, Crittenden soon began to secure a class of active, enterprising and wealth-acquiring citizens. During the latter part of the decade of 1840, and all through 1850, this county enjoyed unparalleled prosperity. By this time immense areas had been reduced to cultivation, and wild land was selling at from $10 to $35 per acre. The change in the current of affairs at the outbreak of the Civil War in 1861, settled like a blight upon the fair fields of Crittenden, compelling a cessation of all farming operations, and this in an agricultural district, meant poverty and ruin. Most of the able-bodied men also enlisting in their country's service, left the land without protection or support. As a great part of the planters' wealth consisted in slaves, the close of the war found many ruined, while the homes of nearly all were despoiled, fences destroyed, and the land run to brush and bramble. Notwithstanding all these drawbacks the people began life after the war, under the changed condition of things, with hope and promise. Then followed the days of reconstruction, which proved for Crittenden County a far worse evil than the war. The people look back upon those times with horror, and speak about them with indignation. Nearly all the county offices were held by negroes, who, in the main, were both ignorant and incompetent. The State militia, mostly negroes, were quartered in the county for the better part of two years, during which time constant strife, many murders, and other crimes were constantly being committed. Taxation rose till it reached the limit of legal interest, while the county scrip depreciated to a value of 5 per cent on the dollar.

In 1874, under the adoption of the new State constitution, the county passed out of this crucifying period, and the prosperity of the people since has only been interrupted by the general overflows from the Mississippi in 1882–83.

Land is being rapidly cleared and improved in every township in the county, and the general condition of the people now is better than at any period of its past history. Under the wise administration of county and local affairs, taxation has been reduced to thirteen mills on the dollar, while the annual assessments are being constantly reduced.

The lands, both cultivated and in the timber, are rapidly rising in value, and, with the construction of a levee to protect the country from overflow, will in all cases advance at least 100 per cent more. The completion of this levee, which will unquestionably be an accomplished fact in a few years, will make hundreds and thousands of acres accessible to the farmer, and increase the county's wealth almost beyond belief; for these overflowed lands are the richest and most productive in the Mississippi basin, and will annually yield from one to one and a half bales of cotton per acre; practically inexhaustible, it may safely be said that for a hundred years their fertility would scarcely be impaired.

The erection of the Memphis bridge will bring new lines of railroads through Crittenden County, adding to her already favorable market facilities, while at its western terminus in this county, West Memphis, a large town will be apt some day to rise.

The county is well supplied with schools and churches and a condition of peace and tranquility, indicating continued prosperity for all, is apparent. Some of the grandest plantations to be found in the South, are situated in Wappanocca, Jasper, Jackson and Proctor Townships of this county, whose individual excellencies it would require too much space to record. Suffice it to say, that the owners of many of these places came here poor, and are actually self-made men, the wonderful fertility of the soil making it possible to accumulate a fortune here by farming operations in a few years. It is safe to assert that few localities in the United States can offer to the husbandman advantages like this.

Wild lands in Crittenden County are still to be bought at from $1 to $10 per acre, on which in many cases, the timber can be sold for an ample sum to pay the cost of clearing and preparing for the plow. This land may now be valued at from $40 to $100 per acre, and, with the most ordinary improvements in the way of buildings, will rent for cash at a price per acre which will yield a profitable investment for the latter sum, or even at $6 per acre, yielding an annual return of 6 per cent on $100. This is no exceptional instance, but is the general rule throughout the entire county. That this state of things should exist so near the thickly populated districts of the North and East, without more people from those sections taking advantage of the wonderful opportunities, can only be accounted for by the fact that Eastern Arkansas has long rested under the odium of prejudicial and falsifying reports.

It is true that for ten years following the war the condition of the State was most critical. During that period the eyes of the rest of the Union were intently gazing upon its various phases of life and action while passing through a most trying social and political ordeal. Hearsay evidence was often employed and political capital manufactured by the press out of the most ordinary occurrences of civil life. Anarchists in Pennsylvania and Illinois might murder citizens by the dozen in defiance of State authorities; railroad employes in Ohio might band together and obstruct general travel, to the danger of the lives of thousands of people; mobs might gather in New York and Massachusetts, demanding bread or work in menacing terms; anything else of a like nature and worse character might transpire in any Northern city without attracting special attention from the news agents, but the moment any trivial offense of law happened in Arkansas the whole country must be aroused to gaze upon the evil times in this unlucky State. But whatever hopes or fears may have been the secret of this unfortunate condition of affairs, they no longer exist, and no community in the land enjoys more absolute obedience and respect for the civil law, than the people of Crittenden County. There also exists abroad a very wrong opinion as to the healthfulness of Eastern Arkansas. Reports were circulated in the pioneer period of the county's

25

history, based, perhaps, on reports from hunters, trappers, wood-choppers, etc., people whose exposed occupations would tell upon the strongest constitutions. At the present time, however, one may find, by six months' constant travel through Eastern Arkansas, as favorable a condition of health among its people, as could be expected in any new country; many of the citizens here report cases of continual good health among all the members of their families for many years. The leading physicians state that, as the land is being cleared, cultivated and drained, the proportion of sickness is materially decreasing. To all who contemplate removing to Crittenden County, or to Eastern Arkansas, it is not improper to state that no fear need be anticipated of serious ill health; the only requisite being to conduct one's self and live as people in a somewhat colder climate are compelled to do, and this will be found as healthy a locality as any section of the Mississippi Valley.

With all these advantages to attract immigration the citizens of Crittenden cordially invite and warmly welcome all worthy and enterprising settlers. This county is capable of supporting ten times its present population. Farm hands here, at the present time, are scarce, and a thousand laborers might secure employment the year round, such help being earnestly sought for and gladly employed.

To the actual settler who comes here with his family and buys his farm, need only be shown the many cases of the county's self-made men as convincing proof that success is sure and fortune certain.

Crittenden is purely an agricultural county, and as such ranks among the very first in Eastern Arkansas. While the staple product is cotton, almost any plant, vegetable or grain that thrives in a similar latitude can be produced here. Until recent years it was scarcely thought to be possible to raise domestic grasses, but it has now been demonstrated that no soil can raise better clover, timothy, orchard grass and red top. Vegetables of nearly every known kind grow here, planted as early as February. Fertilization is practically unknown, yet Irish potatoes yield on an average seventy-five bushels to the acre, sweet potatoes from 150 to 200 bushels, turnips 250 bushels. Watermelons, muskmelons and pumpkins are of famous growth. Cabbage, peas, beans, lettuce and spinach do well.

A good variety of domestic and wild fruits is found: Apples, peaches, pears, cherries, plums and the several berries. Of apples, early varieties do best; of peaches, the medium and late; of plums, wild goose and other native plums; of the berries, strawberries and blackberries are the best, and requiring but little cultivation grow abundantly. At the New Orleans International Exposition, held in 1885, and at the California Exposition held in 1887, at San Francisco, Arkansas apples and other fruits took the first prizes. It must be remembered that though Crittenden County possesses great natural adaptability to produce all the above they are in almost every case made subsidiary to the one great crop—cotton; the majority of the people scarcely raising enough for their own use, and none producing any for market. It will thus be seen that as the field is wholly unoccupied in the production of these articles their cultivation would be attended with profitable results from the beginning; even corn, a great and never-failing crop, is seldom raised in sufficient abundance to supply the home demand.

Of cotton, that grand agricultural product, immense quantities are annually procured. It is the only money-making crop which the people of this county handle at the present time, while the peculiar adaptability of the soil (a rich alluvial deposit of sand and sandy loam) makes it highly profitable. As scarcely one twentieth of the available land is under cultivation the capacity of the county is susceptible of a vast increase.

The luxuriant vegetation of natural grasses affords excellent grazing for horses, cattle and sheep. Corn, which thrives throughout the county, affords a nutritious food for stock. So far there are not many regularly established stock farms, but the business is beginning to develop. The mildness of the climate saves the great expense of costly stables, which falls so heavily on farmers of the North and East. At the same time stables sufficient to protect against the rain and spells of comparatively cold weather are not to be dispensed with by wise farmers. Raising hogs is also profitable, but there are not nearly enough raised to supply the home demands.

The value of the lumber-producing trees of Crittenden County is extensive and almost incalculable. This source of wealth remains to-day almost untouched, and only awaits the introduction of saw-mills and means of transportation to place hundreds of millions of feet of valuable lumber on the markets of the world. There are, throughout all sections of this locality, large areas of forests of cypress, oak of many kinds, ash, pecan, hickory, cottonwood, sycamore and many others that may be profitably employed in various articles of manufacture and commerce. There are yet but few saw-mills in this county, and still fewer stave and bucket factories, while there is an abundance of the best timber in the world for use for those purposes.

The rich and fertile county of Crittenden is situated in the eastern part of the State of Arkansas, and is bounded on the north by Poinsett and Mississippi Counties, on the east by the Mississippi River, which separates it from Tennessee and Mississippi, on the south by the Mississippi River and on the west by Lee, St. Francis and Cross Counties. It extends for seventy miles north and south along the river, and has an area of 660 square miles. The country is of an alluvial deposit and stretches a solid expanse of rich bottom land. There are many ridges that are above overflow, but by far the greater part of the county is subject to inundation from the annual river floods. Tyronza Bayou, in the northwestern part, is a navigable stream, and Lake Grandee, which communicates with the Mississippi at Mound City, is plied by small steamboats during periods of high water.

Reference has already been made, in a general way, to the county's share in the results following the war of 1861-65. During that conflict, in proportion to its population, Crittenden sent more men to the field, perhaps, than any other county in Arkansas, while among these soldiers were many who won distinction for their valor on the battlefield, and shed glory on their name at home; also giving an enviable distinction to their county in the annals of the Confederate cause.

Maj. J. F. Earle, early in 1861, raised a cavalry company of State troops. After a short time this company was turned over to the Confederate Government and attached to the army of Gen. Hardee, at Pocahontas. This company was in the Hardee division all through the war, and was in many severe battles.

O. P. Lyles enlisted in this company, but was detached after three months; he then returned to Crittenden County, and raised a company, known as Lyles company. This company joined the Twenty-third Arkansas Regiment, Infantry. This company was in the battles of Corinth, Iuka, Davis' Bridge, Plaines Store (La.), siege of Port Hudson, and many minor engagements and important campaigns.

At Tupelo, the company was reorganized, and attached to Maury's division. Here its captain, O. P. Lyles, was made colonel, serving as such for two months, and was then put in command of a brigade, and sent to Louisiana to aid Gen. Villipig. The General died soon after Lyle's arrival, and Gen. Bealle was put in command of all the troops. The boys were then called the Fourth Arkansas Brigade. Bealle was succeeded by Gen. Gordon, and soon after that began the siege of Port Hudson, which continued fifty-one days and nights.

Capt. John B. Baxter, who commanded a company from Monroe County, was also in this fort during the siege. On one occasion he was directed by Col. O. P. Lyles to hold a point called the citadel, and informed by the Colonel that the enemy had already tunneled under him for eighty feet, and might at any time explode the mine beneath him. Having warned him of the danger, he elected to go himself, saying he "might as well brook danger as any of his men." He held the position that night, and the next night the surrender occurred. Col. Lyles was informed by the Federals that they were to have exploded the mine at 12 o'clock the next night, but he (Lyles) had planted a barrel of powder to have blown them up at 10 o'clock.

After the surrender the officers were sent to New Orleans and Johnson's Island, in Lake Erie, while the privates were allowed to return home on parole.

Capt. Crump, of Crittenden County, did good work at Belmont, where he was wounded, and deserves special mention. [A fuller account will be found in his biography.] Various other companies secured troops from this county, operating mostly on police duty and home defense. Of the men who so nobly and promptly responded to the call for troops from Crittenden County, about one-half fell in battle, or died in the hospital, or upon the march. The county officers of Crittenden County, at the present time, (1889), are: Judge, S. A. Martin; county clerk, Samuel Keel; sheriff, W. F. Werner; treasurer, A. H. Ferguson; coroner, C. E. Rasberry; surveyor, Ed. Cheatham; assessor, W. J. Harden; representative in the State legislature, Asa Hodges. Some of the former county officers are also here appended.

County judges: D. H. Harrig, Charles Blackmore, A. B. Hubbins, H. O. Oders, W. C. Trice, T. M. Collins (4), W. B. Hay, A. Mensinger, John Thorn, B. C. Crump, J. A. Alexander, W. P. Farnum, William Rives, G. W. Duke, J. F. Barton, Asa Hodges, A. B. Gatlin, T. L. Daugherty, R. B. Barton, J. H. Williams, Daniel W. Lewis and S. A. Martin.

Clerks: J. Livingston, S. R. Cherry, J. H. Wathen, J. Broadenax, W. Armistead, W. P. Cherry (5), S. T. Gilbert, J. J. Lyles, O. P. Lyles, J. F. Earl, J. Swepston, D. W. Lewis, T. W. Gibbs, A. H. Ferguson, David Ferguson and Sam Keel.

Sheriffs: W. D. Ferguson (served for twelve years), J. S. Neely, F. B. Read, C. Stubble, G. W. Underhill, C. J. Bernard, B. C. Crump (served for ten years), J. G. Berry, J. S. Halloway, J. T. Grooms, W. D. Hardin, E. B. Lewis, W. F. Beattie, J. Swepston (14) and W. F. Werner.

Treasurers: A. B. Hubbard (1), F. B. Read, G. S. Fogleman (served for twenty years), R. C. Wallace, B. Westmoreland, ·W. D. Hardin, Samuel Floyd, W. F. Werner and A. H. Ferguson.

Surveyors: S. A. Cherry, F. B. Read, R.

Wallace, R. R. Williams, J. Bayless, J. Earle, A. Jones, J. C. Duncan, W. Fullwood, Q. M. Bellows, E. T. Wimpey, L. B. Hardin, R. Mosely, J. Brown, R. Henderson (12), A. Martin, S. A. Martin, Russ Davis and Edward Cheatham.

Coroners: W. Goshen, William Cherry, O. Wallace, John Tory, J. Withworth, H. Bacon, G. McMullen, J. B. Lewis (2), Joshua Hicks, T. M. Peak, John Peak, J. Markham, Wm. Maggerson, P. H. Berry, R. Hood, J. A. Lyles, J. W. Jones, P. Houston, M. L. Johnson, Jeff Rives, S. N. W. Whitting (6), B. Westmoreland, John Terry, S. R. Rushing (11), Shipp Cobb, J. Smith, D. Sumrell (15), C. E. Rasberry and Eli Jackson.

Assessors: B. C. Crump, A. J. Haynes (7), W. L. Copeland, Jubilee Adams, G. W. Oglesby, L. P. Berry, J. Wofford, H. Waterford, R. Y. Logan, J. R. Rooks and W. J. Harden.

In the Territorial legislature Crittenden County was represented by the following named: In 1827, John Johnson; 1829, W. D. Ferguson; 1831, James Livingston. In the council during these years, G. C. Barfield, E. H. Bridges and W. W. Elliot served.

In 1836 the Territory of Arkansas was admitted to the Union of States, and Crittenden, since that time has sent the following members to the General Assembly:

Senate: In 1836–40, W. D. Ferguson; 1842–44, A. G. Greer; 1844–45, P. G. Rives; 1846–53, G. W. Underhill; 1854–61, Thomas B. Craighead; 1865, T. Lamberson; 1866–67, O. P. Lyles; 1873, Asa Hodges; 1874–75, J. M. Pollard and C. L. Sullivan; 1879–81, R. G. Williams; 1883–85, R. F. Crittenden; 1887–89, Riddick Pope.

House: In 1837–38, C. N. Blackmore and J. N. Calvert; 1838, W. C. Trice and L. H. Bedford; 1840, T. M. Collins and A. J. Greer; 1842–43, Thomas M. Collins and P. G. Rives; 1844–49, Thomas M. Collins; 1852–53, J. A. Lovejoy; 1854–55, James F. Barton; 1856–57, Henry B. Edmonson; 1858–59, O. P. Lyles; 1860–61, B. L. Armstrong; 1864–65, F. Thrusby; 1866–67, R. C. Jones; 1868–69, Asa Hodges; 1871–73, Adam Johnson; 1874, S. P. Swepston and J. F. Smith; 1875, W. L. Copeland; 1877, James Wofford; 1879, A.

C. Brewer; 1881, R. F. Crittenden; 1883, Daniel Lewis; 1885, Asa Hodges; 1887, S. S. Odom; 1889, Asa Hodges.

Many of the men who have served Crittenden County in these various official capacities, whether in State or in county positions, have been men of rare personal attainments and ability, highly educated and intelligent, some absolutely self-made, as Asa Hodges, who, from youth has been the architect of his own fortune. He served in the house of the General Assembly in 1868–69, was elected to the State senate in 1873 and while still a member of that body, was elected to the National Congress. Few men with brighter minds than Mr. Hodges are found in any land, none with a more patriotic devotion to his country. Conservative in his views, he is never blinded by trifles which float in the atmosphere of party strife, but always seeks with the mildest measures harmonious adjustment for the good of all. In his declining years his powerful mind still retains the activity of younger days, and Crittenden County had no better man than he to return to the General Assembly in 1888, at which election he received a large majority of votes, and the earnest support of the county's best citizens.

In 1832 the United States Government constructed a road west from Memphis to Little Rock, over which they moved the Indians from the States east of the Mississippi River. It passes west through Crittenden County a length of twenty-six miles, and immediately after its construction became the grand highway for emigration to all western points. This was the only passage through the Wilderness, as the Mississippi bottoms were called at that time, and Texas received its flood of pioneers from over this highway, as did Kansas, Nebraska and Western Missouri; so from the time of its completion till 1860 there was hardly a day of any month in all those years, but what, from any point along its path, long trains of wagons could be seen slowly wending their way beneath the overhanging trees, and through the swamps that often lay for many miles along their track.

Crittenden County is well supplied with railroads, having in the aggregate about seventy-one miles of track belonging to three different lines of roads, all passing through its territory and terminating at the river opposite Memphis.

The first road constructed through the county was the Memphis & Little Rock. It is nineteen miles long, passing southwest from Hopefield through Mound City and Proctor Township.

The Kansas City, Fort Scott & Memphis Railroad, completed in 1883, passes from West Memphis northwest through Mound City, Jasper, Wappanocca and Fogleman Townships, and has a length in this county of twenty-six miles.

The Memphis or Bald Knob branch of the Iron Mountain Railroad was completed through Crittenden County in 1888; it also has a length here of twenty-six miles, and traverses west from West Memphis, through Mound City, Jasper and Jackson Townships.

These various lines of railroads represent in value about one-half of the taxable property of the county.

In Crittenden County there are twenty-one school districts, in all of which school is held during several months of the year.

The county examiner's report of 1888 shows a total enrollment of 3,570 children of school age.

To employ teachers for the education of this large school population the county has abundant funds, for while the amount expended for teachers' salaries in 1888 was $9,874 the income from various sources was $16,934, leaving a balance in the hands of the county treasurer of over $7,000. With this large sum, and with the interest that the people of the county are taking in educational matters, it will be plainly seen that Crittenden County will soon have as good schools as any county in the State.

The Methodist Church of Marion was organized many years ago by some of the old pioneers of this section. In 1879 a fire in the town destroyed this church, soon after which the ladies of Marion, taking the matter in hand, were instrumental in raising funds for the erection of another edifice. The new building was completed a year or so later; it is a tasty and ornamental structure, costing about $800. Mr. Smith and Dr. Whitsitt,

superintended the work, and lent such assistance as was needed from time to time.

In May, 1889, Col. J. F. Smith, and others started the Marion Reform, a weekly newspaper, whose purpose was to improve and elevate the morals of the citizens, and improve the intellectual condition of the people generally. A paper published by the colored people at Marion, called the Marion Headlight, had been in circulation for about two years, and was outspoken, and strenuous in inciting the colored people to discontent and discord. The promoters of the reform advocated a practice of fair and just dealing, showing the colored people, that as peace was their everlasting hope, its preservation was equally essential to all, both white and black. Mr. W. M. Holmes, the present publisher, has had it in charge but a short time, yet he is building his publication into a creditable county newspaper, and one that is destined to wield decided influence.

There are no towns in Crittenden County that can be properly so called except Marion, the county seat. This village is situated fourteen miles northeast of Memphis, and five miles directly west from the Mississippi River. The settlement near here was made early in the nineteenth century by Augustine Grandee, who settled on a lake that still bears his name. Around this old Spaniard's settlement soon clustered others, seeking favorable situations for a home, till, in 1826, when the commissioners appointed by the county court to select a site for the seat of justice for the county, chose this point; so on the banks of Lake Grandee, which is navigable in high water, the town of the future seat of justice was laid out. The alternate lots of twenty acres were deeded to Crittenden County by Marion Tolbert and wife, Temperance, and the name Marion given to the town was likely bestowed in honor of Mr. Tolbert. A postoffice was soon established, and the first postmaster was (upon the authority of Mr. William Vance) Sam Gilbert. Among the early merchants was Capt. McAlister.

The principal industries now in the place are represented by the following: General stores, James Bassett, William M. Bingham, Lewis & Newman, Raymond Henderson, A. F. Ferguson, Samuel D.

Bassett, J. R. Chase, T. Ankrun and J. F. Smith; lawyers, L. P. Berry, R. F. Crittenden; physicians, W. M. Bingham, T. O. Bridgforth, W. R. Barton; blacksmith, G. W. Hunter; cotton-gins, Asa Hodges, J. F. Smith, S. C. Cox, R. H. Weaver, Sam Keel and John Burns. There is one white and one colored Methodist Episcopal Church, and three Baptist colored Churches in the place. C. L. Lewis is postmaster. The city officers elected in April, 1889, were: L. D. Blann, mayor; C. L. Lewis, recorder; L. P. Berry, James Bassett, James Brooks, A. W. Mathews, J. S. Smith, aldermen; John Painter, marshal, Frank Forrest, deputy marshal.

Marion is surrounded by a magnificent stretch of cultivated land, thousands of acres surrounding it on every side, while along the military road the plantations extend unbroken to the river, or for more than five miles. In the immediate vicinity are some of the largest and finest cotton plantations to be found in the South.

Marion Lodge No. 3114, K. of H., was organized by the Rev. Mr. Futrell, about 1885. Some of the original members were: C. L. Lewis, A. S. Grigsby, Sam Bassett, James Bassett, A. H. Ferguson, J. R. Chase and J. H. Smith.

In 1883 the Kansas City, Fort Scott & Galveston Railroad was completed to the bank of the Mississippi River opposite Memphis. The company at once built a station and made railroad yards, to which Gen. Nettleton gave the name of West Memphis.

In 1870 Robert and Hope Vance settled on about 600 acres that had been bought by their father, William Vance, for his children. This was all wild land, and the Vance boys built a log-cabin in which they "bached."

In 1875 Robert built a neat frame residence, which now stands opposite the railroad station. Up to the completion of the railroad these were the only houses at this point.

In 1884 Robert, Frank and Arthur Vance conceived the idea of laying out a town here. All the buildings erected there have been built on this site or on the land of Hope Vance, which has been laid out as an addition to the town.

In 1888 the Memphis branch of the Iron Mountain Railroad was completed to West Memphis, and the trains cross on the Kansas City transfer boats.

There are three stores there now, conducted by Winchester Bros., Richard Bros. and C. B. Gwin.

The St. Louis Wood & Willow Factory have just completed their large manufacturing establishment here, and in the near future will give employment to a large force of hands.

In 1885 a postoffice was established and Robert Vance was appointed first postmaster; he has since held the commission and had charge of the office.

The present population is about 200, but on the completion of the Memphis bridge, now in the course of erection, it will offer great opportunities for business investment.

In the early history of this county Mound City was one of its important points. It was located on the Mississippi, a few miles above Memphis, and was made the terminus of the military road. Early in 1850 and 1860 there were several stores here, and immediately after the war they did an extensive trade, it being the distributing point for all the interior country. There were several large hotels, only one of which is standing now, and that is a ruin. In 1865 the steamboat Sultana, crowded with discharged Federal soldiers returning home, blew up in the channel in front of Mound City. It was a horrible accident, in which it is estimated that 2,000 people lost their lives. The boat sank in the channel, and around the old hull a bar soon began to form. It enlarged from year to year, and soon changed the channel of the river. The bar thus formed about the sunken hull is now an island of considerable size, and completely shuts off Mound City from the river. So, as it has no river trade, and the railroads taking the freight to the interior, it is now nothing more than the barest remembrance of what it used to be. There is one store here, kept by John Malone, who is also postmaster. Several large and fertile plantations are around this old place.

The village of Crawfordsville is situated in the eastern part of Jackson Township, in the western part of Crittenden County. It is in the center of a farming district that was settled many years ago, and surrounded by some of the choicest and most productive lands in the State. It is a great cotton-producing section, and since the completion of the Memphis branch of the Iron Mountain Railway it is rapidly growing into an active business center.

There is a larger area of arable land about Crawfordsville than in any other part of the county.

The business interests consist of four general stores, conducted by A. R. Strong, J. H. Williams & Bro., Arthur Blann and R. G. Logan; one saloon by A. M. Gibson; two steam cotton-gins by Mrs. Jenkins and Mr. Swepston.

A white Methodist Episcopal Church, South, and several churches for the colored people are found, besides two schools for the colored children and one for the white. B. M. Williams is the postmaster, and the village has a population of about 200 souls.

Edmond M. Apperson, Jr., an enterprising citizen of Proctor Township, owes his nativity to the State of Kentucky, where he was born, in Shelby County, August 25, 1858, being the son of J. W. and Margaret A. (Thomas) Apperson, natives of Tennessee and Kentucky, respectively. J. W. Apperson was connected with the business house of E. M. Apperson, Sr., at Memphis, Tenn., prominent wholesale grocers, cotton factors and commission merchants, and met his death at the battle of Shiloh. Mrs. Apperson continued to reside in Memphis after her husband's demise, and gave her children liberal advantages for obtaining an education. By her union with Mr. Apperson she became the mother of three children: Edmond M., Jr., Bertha (wife of C. H. Bond, of Cuero, Tex.) and John W. (traveling salesman). Edmond M., Jr., passed his boyhood days in the schools of Memphis, and at the age of fifteen entered the college at Lexington, Va., a well-known and popular military institution. At the expiration of three years he accepted a position as shipping clerk in the firm of E. M. Apperson & Co. In 1886 he was united in matrimony with Miss E. D.

Jeffies, and to their union two children have been born: William J. and Edmond M. (who died in 1888). Mr. Apperson and Mr. Jeffies are the owners of 240 acres of valuable land, as mentioned in the sketch of Mr. Jeffies. Politically the former is a Democrat and exerts considerable influence in the county during election. He comes from one of the oldest families to settle in Memphis, and is a man whom it is a pleasure to meet. Popular in business and social circles, he is well worthy the confidence and esteem reposed in him by the entire community.

Maj. James F. Barton (deceased), whose portrait appears in this volume, was one of the most prominent citizens of this county as well as of the State. The Barton family is one that is well known in connection with the history of Arkansas, and is of English-Irish lineage. The first history that we have of them is a Barton, whose given name is unknown, that came to this country and settled in Charlotte County, Va., long before the Revolutionary War, where his son, James Barton, is supposed to have been born, and he is known to have immigrated to Abbeville District, S. C. He also had a son, James, who was born February 22, 1772, in Charlotte County, Va. He left his native State in 1784, going to South Carolina with his father, where he remained for ten years, when he married and went to Mercer County in 1794; in 1796 to Barren County, where he died September 24, 1846. He was a self-made man, having started with little but his hands, and a determined mind to make his fortune, which he did, for he was very wealthy when he died. He was an earnest worker in the Christian Baptist Church, very charitable, of a pushing and energetic turn of mind. James Barton, son of the above, was born July 5, 1794, in Mercer County, Ky., and in 1823 he moved to Henry County, Tenn., where he remained till 1835, when he moved to Tipton County, Tenn., where he died March 5, 1852. James Forbes Barton, son of the above and subject of our sketch, was born in Henry County Tenn., December 7, 1824. He went to Barren County, Ky., where he reached his majority, and received the last years of his educational training. While in this county he was married

December 7, 1847, to Frances B. Edmunds, who was born December 7, 1831. In 1850 they moved to Texas, but at the request of his father returned in 1852, and settled in Crittenden County, where he purchased large tracts of land, on which he made many valuable improvements. He also engaged in steamboating, and having become very prominent in politics was elected to the legislature and was afterward county and probate judge. At the outbreak of the Civil War he was a sympathizer of the Union, but when the South seceded, he took sides with his State and joined the Confederate army, and after casting his lot with the South, he took active part and served with great credit. He organized a company in Crittenden County, of which he was made captain of the rank of major. He was assistant quartermaster under the then chief quartermaster of the Trans-Mississippi Department, Maj. John D. Adams, of Little Rock, Ark. He held the position of collector of cotton-tax till 1863, when he was recommissioned to organize a battalion in the Confederate States. Going into the service as a captain in Col. Dobbin's regiment, he was commissioned by the department to go into Georgia to secure arms for the soldiers. After making four trips, he secured enough arms to equip nearly all of Gen. Price's army, previous to the last raid through Missouri, Kansas and Indian Territory. Near the close of the war he was made major, which office he filled till the close, when he surrendered at Mound City, this county, in 1865. During the war the Federal troops burned his home, leaving his family in very destitute circumstances, having neither food nor clothing. The war ended, he returned to his family and took active part in righting the wrongs brought on by the long contest. He held the office of county judge till the reconstruction, when he was disqualified. He then moved to Memphis, Tenn., where he owned considerable property, and lived there till his death, which occurred October 11, 1873, of yellow fever. While in Memphis he became very prominently engaged in the manufacture of cotton-seed oil, and was the cause of the establishing of the second cotton-seed-oil mill in the city of Memphis, and at the time of his death was super-intendent of the Memphis Cotton Seed Oil Company. He never raised a bale of cotton in his life, but was mostly engaged in buying and selling real estate, and before the war owned quite a number of slaves; he also owned the ferry-boats that ran between Memphis and Arkansas from 1857 to 1860 and after the war for several years. He was always foremost in any movement to develop the county, was liberal and charitable to a fault, and was an active member of the church, having joined the Methodist Episcopal Church, South, at Louisville, and upon his arrival at Memphis united with the First Methodist Episcopal Church, South, at that place, and was later made steward of the same. Maj. Barton had a family of eight children, seven of whom lived to be grown, and five are still living, as follows: William Edmunds, James T., Charles F., Richard (deceased), H. F. (deceased in his twenty-fourth year), Dr. Robert W., John F. (who died at the age of twenty-two years) and Lee. After the death of the Major, his wife was married to Col. A. M. Hardin, of Marshall County, Miss. She visited, in 1888, her childhood's home in Barren County, Ky., hoping to be restored to health. While there surrounded by relatives, including three of her sons, she died expressing complete faith in Christ. She was for forty-four years a devout Christian and a member of the Methodist Episcopal Church, South. She was an estimable lady and loving wife, and co-operated with Maj. Barton during the adverse as well as the favorable circumstances of his life.

Frank H. Barton (deceased), remembered as among the leading influential residents of this community, was born in Henry County, Tenn., February 22, 1832, and died August 30, 1884. He was reared in Tipton County, Tenn., and came to Crittenden County from Memphis in 1852, locating on an island near Marion, where he had only fourteen acres of land under cultivation. In the fall of 1859 he built the handsome residence in which his family still lives. From the small place of fourteen acres, under his energetic and careful management, grew the large farm that consisted of over 1,000 acres, with 500 acres in an excellent state of cultivation at the time of his death. He

JAMES F. BARTON.

(DECEASED)

CRITTENDEN COUNTY, ARKANSAS.

was elected treasurer of Crittenden County before the war, when he took an active part in political, school and church matters, and joined the Christian Church of Memphis in 1872. He joined the Confederate army near the close of the late war, and did active service till the close of the war. Mr. Barton was first married to Alice E. Fogleman, who was born November 22, 1842, in this county, where she was reared and where she died December 26, 1865. She was the daughter of John and Elizabeth A. (Trice) Fogleman, and was the mother of one child, Frank G., who is unmarried and living on the home place. Mr. Barton was a second time married January 8, 1867, his wife being Lizzie Edmunds, a native of Barren County, Ky., and the daughter of Charles P. and Elizabeth (Eubank) Edmunds, who came from Virginia to Barren County. The father was born in 1811, and died in his seventy-second year; his wife was also born in 1811, and died November 24, 1881. They were both members of the Christian Church, of which he was also an elder. They reared a family of ten children to be grown, of whom Mrs. Barton is the sixth. She attained womanhood in Kentucky, where she was married to the subject of this sketch. This couple were the parents of eight children, of whom five are still living, viz.: Mamie B. (now the wife of G. A. Fogleman), Louis W., Charles G., Perry A. and Richard B.; those deceased are Charles E., James C. and Robert E. Most people are familiar with the history of the great disaster that occurred opposite Mound City, March 27, 1885, by the explosion of a boiler on the steamer Mark Twain. There were five white ladies on the boat, among whom was Mrs. Barton; there were two white men killed, both of whom were from Kentucky; seven colored men were also killed in the wreck. The names of the officers were as follows: Captain, G. A. Fogleman; pilot, J. E. Pennell; engineer, Henry Gayham, and the bar-keeper was Frank Huxtable. Capt. McLone, who had charge of the boat only a short time before, had his leg broken, and Capt. Fogleman had his leg broken in two places, and the pilot escaped without injury. Mrs. Barton's daughter and niece were also on board, but none

of the ladies were injured. When the Sultana sank just below this place, in 1865, Mrs. Barton's people were the instruments in saving many of the doomed soldiers. The Barton family stands among the most prominent and best-liked people of Crittenden County. They are noted for their public-spirited and liberal-minded disposition, and have done much to advance the development of their county.

R. B. Barton, a prominent citizen of Crittenden County, was born in Tipton County, Tenn., in 1839, and is the youngest of eleven children, born to James and Elizabeth W. (Hardin) Barton, who were natives of Kentucky. The father was a farmer by occupation, and died in Tennessee in 1851. The maternal grandfather was a major in the Revolutionary War, and fought in the battle of Cowpens. After the father's death, the family moved to Crittenden County, Ark., and settled on Rosebrough farm, in 1852. R. B. Barton lived with his brothers, J. F. and F. H., till 1865, when they moved to Mound City, where they bought 200 acres of unimproved land, of which R. B. cleared sixty acres up to the outbreak of the war. In 1861 he enlisted in a cavalry company, known as the Crittenden Rangers, which went to Kentucky, and was in Hardin's division, which took part in the battle of Shiloh. Then the regiment was reorganized, and Mr. Barton returned to Crittenden County, where, in company with Col. McGee, he raised a company of which he was elected first lieutenant. This company was engaged in scouting and police duty, and during the war captured three steamboats. Lieut. Barton was captured in 1863, and was placed in prison at Memphis for two months, when he was removed to Johnson's Island for eleven months. He returned home in 1864, and commenced the planting and timber business. In 1868 he went on a farm of thirty-five acres, at Mound City, and in 1885, when he had improved it till it was worth $14,000, he sold it. In 1888 he bought eight acres on the Bald Knob Railroad, where he built a station, and has put about $10,000 worth of improvements, consisting of a cotton-gin, with all modern improvements, at a cost of $3,000, a store, livery stable, hotel, and, in fact, he owns everything at the station. Mr. Barton was married in 1865, to Miss Fannie K. Fogleman, a daughter of John Fogleman, one of the pioneers of this county. Mr. and Mrs. Barton are the parents of three children, of whom two are dead, Lizzie (died at the age of fifteen years, while attending school at Fayetteville), Mary Alice (who is now attending school at Memphis) and Gussie (who died at the age of twelve years). Mr. Barton moved to Memphis in 1885, and has since resided there. He is a progressive and energetic business man, and has done very much toward the improvement of Crittenden County.

James T. Barton is justly numbered in the list of Crittenden County's most prominent farmers. A native of Tipton County, Tenn., he is the second child in order of birth born to the union of James F. and Frances (Edmonds) Barton, natives of Kentucky. [See sketch of J. F. Barton.] James T. received his education in Memphis, Tenn., and at Louisville, Ky., where he attended the graded schools, obtaining thorough and practical instruction. At the age of eighteen he went in company with his father to Memphis, and engaged with him in the Cotton Seed Oil Company., in which he held the position of foreman for some time. When twenty-six years old he came to this county, and embarked in farming and merchandising. During the war Mr. Barton was three times a prisoner before he had reached his thirteenth year, once in the Union Block, at Memphis. He has been twice married: first, in 1877, to Miss Lizzie B. Hardin, a daughter of Col. A. M. Hardin, of Mississippi, and by her became the father of four children, one now living, James A. (at home). Mrs. Barton died in 1882, and in 1888 he was united in marriage with Miss Vara M. Hoblitzell, of Baltimore, Md., whose parents, William and Henrietta (Gephardt) Hoblitzell, were natives of Maryland. They had a family of ten children, five of whom survive: Oliver, Fetter S., Lottie V. (wife of G. M. Wolf), Sue G. (now Mrs. J. C. Zimmerman) and Vara M. (Mrs. Barton). In 1877 Mr. Barton settled on lands purchased by himself, but at the present time is leasing some 2,000 acres, 1,300 of which he controls individually, and in addition 900, in

which he has a partner. He raises about 1,000 bales of cotton on the two places, and is one of, if not the largest, land leasers in the county. It would be difficult to find a man more popular, or one who enjoys the undivided esteem and respect of all to a greater extent than Mr. Barton; always courteous, a perfect gentleman, jolly, quick at repartee, he never wounds a friend, and his mirth harbors no sting nor bitterness. He was appointed sheriff of this county, pending an election, to fill the unexpired term of Henry Ward, in 1873, and in the same year was elected to the office, which he filled with entire satisfaction. He also acted as county collector, and during that time the acting sheriff died, and Mr. Barton was again appointed to fill the latter position. He has served as justice of the peace of his township, and has been one of the associate justices of this county. He is a Knight of Honor, belonging to Crawfordville Lodge No. 3110, and is a member of the A. F. & A. M. Politically he is a Democrat. Both Mr. and Mrs. Barton are members of high standing, in the Methodist Episcopal Church, South, and are very popular in society.

Robert W. Barton, M.D., considered among the profession as one of the leading physicans, and an upright and honest citizen of Crittenden County, was born in this county, March 17, 1860, to the union of James F. and Frances (Edmonds) Barton. [See sketch.] Robert W. Barton spent most of his youth in Memphis, Tenn., and was educated in the common schools of Louisville, Ky., and the Lincoln public school of St. Louis, Mo. In 1876, during the big strike in St. Louis, he volunteered as a soldier and served throughout that affray in that city, the youngest of 3,000 volunteers, and did active and honorable service for eleven days while quelling the riot. He was requested and urged by his officers to become a West Point cadet at large from Missouri, but owing to the fact that he was a son of a Confederate soldier he could not be appointed, although endorsed by Capt. Elerby, Lieut. Barlow and other officers, and quite a number of prominent men of both Nashville and Memphis, Tenn. In 1879 he entered the State University of Tennessee, and owing to his ill health remained for only two years, and commenced the study of medicine in Memphis with Dr. Rogers as his preceptor, in 1882, and later he assisted R. D. Murray, United States army surgeon for four months. In 1883, he was appointed interne in the city hospital of Physicians and Surgeons of Baltimore, Md., from which school he graduated in 1884, and returned to Memphis, Tenn., where he commenced the practice of his profession. In July of that year he came to this county, where he has since practiced. While in Memphis he was a member of the State Medical Association of Tennessee, and is now of the Tri-State Medical Society of Mississippi, Arkansas and Tennessee, and president of the board of medical examiners of this county. Dr. Barton was married to Miss Mamie G. Grasty, who was born in Danville, Va., and was reared in Baltimore, Md., where she graduated from the Western Female High School, taking the Peabody medal. She then graduated from the Maryland Musical Institute, under Prof. May. Mrs. Barton is a very highly educated lady and is in every way an estimable woman. She is the mother of two children: Phebe Housen and Francis Edmunds. She is an active and prominent member of the Second Presbyterian Church of Memphis, Tenn.

James Bassett, merchant and farmer of Marion, was born in Vicksburg, Miss., in 1845, and is the son of Samuel and Lydia (French) Bassett, who are natives of England. They came to the United States before their marriage and were united at Vicksburg, making their home there, whence he went into the Mexican War. Soon after his return from the war he died of yellow fever, and after his death the mother and family remained at Vicksburg where Mrs. Bassett was married to David McClure, a native of Mississippi. In 1856 Mr. and Mrs. McClure moved to Memphis, and in the following year to Crittenden County, Ark., where the aged mother still lives, her husband having died in 1871. To her first marriage were born two sons, James and Samuel D., and by the second marriage was born one child (now deceased). Before the war James Bassett made his home in Memphis most of the time and at the commencement of the war joined the Confederate army as a private in the Twenty-first Tennessee Regiment, under Col. Pickett. He served three years and was not in any battles of note; was in Memphis when that city was besieged. After the war he returned to Crittenden County, where he has since lived and has been engaged in farming, and in 1883 embarked in the merchandising business at Marion, and to-day is one of the most prominent citizens of that place. He was married to Mary A. Fox, who was born in Memphis and reared in Arkansas, and a daughter of John H. and Eva (Echeiner) Fox, natives of Germany. The mother died in 1889 at a very old age. To Mr. and Mrs. Bassett have been born four children: Lydia E., Mary E. (who is the wife of Dr. T. O. Bridgeforth), Samuel C. and Virginia M. Politically, Mr. Bassett is a Democrat and is a member of the Knights of Honor, Lodge No. 3114 of Marion. This family is composed of fine-looking people and has been noted for some time for its remarkable health. Mr. Bassett in many ways is a typical western man, imbued with that vim, enterprise and push so characteristic of the free sons of the West, and has done much for the advancement of his county.

Samuel D. Bassett, a merchant and farmer of Marion, was born in Vicksburg, Miss., in 1846, and is the son of Samuel and Lydia (French) Bassett. [See sketch preceding.] When a small boy Samuel Bassett moved to Memphis with his mother, and from here they soon came to Crittenden County, Ark. During the war the mother and her two children went to Cincinnati, and after staying there a few months, Samuel returned to this county, and in 1864 attended the Christian Brothers' College, at St. Louis. After leaving college in 1865, he returned to this county, where he has lived ever since, except two years (1870 and 1871) that he spent in Texas and Kansas. He commenced business for himself at the age of twenty-one years, and has since been engaged in farming and merchandising. He first put in a stock of general merchandise, which he sold in 1878, and has since been doing a general business. He now has a stock of goods at Marion, and one at Gavin Station, where he had an establishment several years before the station was founded. This station is on the old place that was first settled by his people, and on which his mother still lives. Mr. Bassett was married in 1875 to Miss Love Swepston, who was born in Ohio, and is a daughter of John Swepston. This union was blessed by one child (Musetta) in 1876. Mr. Bassett has always taken an active part in educational matters, and his prominence in these affairs has given him a position as director on the school board; he is also postmaster at Gavin Station. He is a Democrat in politics, and a member of Lodge No. 3114, K. of H., of Marion. He and his wife are members of the Methodist Episcopal Church, and are good Christian people, well liked by all.

William Matthews Bigham, M. D., a merchant and druggist, of Marion, Ark., is one of its most prominent business men. He is of Irish descent and was born in Shelby County, Tenn., in 1859, being the only survivor of a family of three children born to William M. and Mary F. (Winston) Bigham. The paternal grandparents were born in Ireland and came to America about the time of their son's (William M.) birth, which occurred in 1816. William M. Bigham was reared in North Carolina and moved to Mississippi and from there to Tennessee in 1850. In Mississippi he was engaged in farming and milling, and while here he met and married a Mrs. Matthews in Tennessee. The wife accompanied her parents to that State in 1832, when she was nine years of age. Here she attained her womanhood and was married to M. S. Matthews, a native of North Carolina, who died in Shelby County, Tenn., nine years after his marriage, leaving a wife and four children, two of whom are still living: Adolphus and Virginia. After Mr. Bigham was married to this lady he sold out his business in Mississippi and moved to Shelby County, Tenn., where he remained for one year, and in January of 1860 moved across the river into Crittenden County, Ark., living here until his death which occurred two years later. Mr. Bigham was a member of the Presbyterian Church and his wife of the Baptist Church. Mrs. Bigham is now sixty-six years of age and resides with her son William M. In 1865 the family returned to Tennessee, where William M. Bigham reached

his majority. He had but poor advantage for an early education, and with the desire for a complete literary knowledge he commenced the study of medicine with his half brother, B. A. Matthews, who was a physician and graduate of the Old University of Nashville. Dr. Bigham remained here till he was nineteen years old, when he entered the Vanderbilt University of Nashville, and one year later went to St. Louis, where he graduated in March, 1881. After his graduation he returned to Shelby County, Tenn., where he practiced his profession for two years, then moving to Arkansas; he has since lived here and practiced medicine, being engaged also in merchandising and the drug business. The Doctor married Mary E. Brown, who was born in this county, a daughter of James and Katie Brown, also among the native residents of Crittenden. Mrs. Bigham is a member of the Methodist Episcopal Church, South, and is an estimable lady in every respect. Dr. Bigham is a Democrat politically and a member of the Baptist Church. He is an honest, upright and worthy citizen, having by his short time in business placed himself in a worthy position in the hearts of his fellow-citizens.

L. D. Blann is a young farmer and broker at Marion, Crittenden County. Born in De Soto County, Miss., in 1860, he is the oldest of a family of five boys of J. C. and Mary Jane Blann. The father was a farmer by occupation and came to this county in 1876, living here till his death, which occurred in 1885. His wife died while L. D. was a child. The latter spent his youth on his father's farm in Mississippi where he attended the free schools, and after his father came to Arkansas he was a student at the college at La Grange, Tenn., until 1881. Upon leaving college, Mr. Blann returned to Crawfordsville and engaged in buying cotton seed until 1884, when he moved to Marion, since giving his attention to buying cotton, cotton seed, cattle, etc. He has also been extensively interested in farming, and the past year, 1889, had in a crop of 100 acres of cotton. Mr. Blann was married to Miss Julia B. Johnson, January 9, 1885. He is a member of the Masonic fraternity, belonging to Lodge No. 375, at Crawfordsville, and is an industrious, energetic citizen.

A. D. Blann is recognized as an energetic and enterprising young merchant at Crawfordsville. He was born in 1865, being the son of J. C. Blann, a native of Tennessee. [See sketch.] Mr. Blann reached his majority in Arkansas, having come to this county in 1875, and has since lived here. He was educated in the high schools of Memphis, Tenn., and commenced for himself in 1883 as a stock dealer, soon afterward entering into general merchandising at the above place. In a short time he closed out this business and entered the employ of E. Buck & Co., remaining from 1883 to 1887, when he resumed his former business at a place called Needmore. One year later he opened up the business at Crawfordsville. Mr. Blann is one of the most promising young men of this county, and is now enjoying a trade of about $60,000 per year. He conducts a general supply business, dealing also in cotton and cotton seed. He was married March 1, 1889, to Winnie Spicer, a native of Shelby County, Tenn., and the daughter of R. S. Spicer, one of the leading farmers of that county. Mr. and Mrs. Blann have an elegant home built in 1889. They are both social young people and are much respected by their host of acquaintances.

Levi Barton Boon, the present efficient and popular postmaster and a dealer in general merchandise at Gilmore, was born in Yates County, N. Y., June 24, 1841, and is the son of Eli Alonzo Hogaboom, a native of Germany, who came to New York when a young man, and lived there till his death. He was married to Miss Margaret Wells, who was born in New York, and is now living in Tioga County, Penn. To Mr. and Mrs. Hogaboom were born eight children, of whom the subject of our sketch is the fourth child. The mother was afterward married to a Mr. Boon, from whom L. B. Boon takes his name. L. B. was reared in New York, and never received a day's schooling in his life. In 1861 he enlisted in the Fourth Regiment of Ohio Cavalry, and did active service throughout the war, being discharged at Nashville, Tenn., July 20, 1865. During the civil strife he fought in the severe battles of Chickamauga, Murfreesboro, Lookout Mountain, Stone River, Atlanta, Ringgold, and was in Wilson's raid from Eastport, Miss., to Macon, Ga. He was wounded four different times, once by a spent-ball hitting him between the eyes, a scar of which he will carry to his grave; and once by being shot below the knee, besides two other slight wounds. After his discharge he remained in Nashville until 1868, when he went to Burning Springs, Va., in the oil regions, and went from there to Kentucky the following year. He went from Kentucky to Jackson, Tenn., where he was married January 12, 1873, to Miss Charlotte Emaline Stock, who was born in Union County, N. C., in June, 1861. She is the mother of seven children: Amos Alonzo, Emma (deceased), Levi Barton (deceased), Margaret (deceased), John T., Nellie G. and Edwin. Mr. Boon commenced railroading at Jackson, Tenn., and followed this occupation till 1883, when he came to Gilmore in the fall of the same year. He opened the first street in the village of Gilmore, where he carries a stock of goods worth $1,500. He also has a livery stable and a farm of about 200 acres in cultivation. In 1883 he built the first cotton-gin in this part of the county at a cost of about $1,500. He has been a Democrat since casting his first vote, which was for McClellan. He is a Master Mason, and a member of Frenchman Bayou Lodge No. 251, in which he is Steward. He also belongs to the K. of H. Lodge at Marion. Mr. Boon is one of the most energetic business men in the county, and it is from his efforts that the village of Gilmore now exists. He was justice of the peace in the township for two years, and is at present serving his second term as notary public, having also been the same four years in Tennessee, appointed by the Governor.

William D. Brooks, a leading farmer and stock raiser of Crittenden County, was born in Shelby County, Tenn., October 5, 1856, and is the first of four children born to Hugh M. and Mattie J. (Scott) Brooks. The father was born in Nashville, Tenn., September 20, 1835. He was the son of Isaac Winston Brooks, who was born in Virginia and died in Tennessee. Mrs. Brooks was a daughter of Eli Scott, and was born in Shelby County, Tenn., October 17, 1840. She was the mother of four children now living and four deceased; those living are William D., Hugh L., John M. and Frank S. Hugh M. Brooks, the father, was a prominent man who immigrated to this county from Shelby County, Tenn., January 7, 1861, and located on 320 acres of land, which he purchased near where William D. now lives. He served three years in the Confederate army, and was appointed judge of this county by the Governor at one time. He was filling the office of justice of the peace at the time of his death, which occurred March 9, 1889. William D. Brooks was reared in Shelby County, Tenn., and received his education at the La Grange College of Tennessee, and was married October 20, 1880, to Birdie E. Shepard, who was born in Yazoo City, Miss., March 8, 1864, and is the daughter of C. D. and Bettie (Hottiman) Shepard. Mr. and Mrs. Brooks are the parents of two children, both living. Mr. Brooks now resides on the old homestead that his father purchased when he came to this county. He is a member of the Masonic order and is Master of the lodge to which he belongs; is also a member of the K. of H. He is a Democrat in politics, and cast his first presidential vote for Tilden. Mr. and Mrs. Brooks, as his parents were, are prominent members of the Methodist Episcopal Church, South. They are prominent in their county, and enjoy the respect of their acquaintances.

William H. Brown, an enterprising farmer of Wappanocca Township, was born in Hardeman County, Tenn., May 10, 1834, and is the son of John Brown, whose birth occurred in Williamson County, Tenn., in 1806. He always resided in that State, following the calling of a farmer and merchant. He was married to Rachel Hamor, also of Tennessee nativity, and to them were born nine children, of whom William H. was the sixth. The father was a son of William Brown, of Irish descent; he died in 1875, and his wife followed four years later. William H. was reared in his native State, where he received a limited education, and was married to Mary N. Craig in 1859. She was also born there in 1840 and is the daughter of David and Nancy Craig, of Tennessee. Mr. and Mrs. Brown are the parents of twelve children, of whom

the following eight are now living: James W., Robert H., Charles F., Samuel F., M. Ellen, Alice, Minnie P. and Lester, all at home. In 1874 Mr. Brown emigrated from Lauderdale County, Tenn., to where he now lives, and in the following year purchased a farm of 160 acres, with sixty acres under cultivation. He now has one of the finest places in Crittenden County, there being about 125 acres under cultivation. In 1881 he erected a cotton-gin, which he has run very successfully ever since, and in 1889 attached a shingle-machine. The entire plant runs by steam, and cost about $2,000. Mr. and Mrs. Brown are active members of the Methodist Episcopal Church, South, and are good, honest citizens, being held in the highest esteem by all that know them. The former is a Democrat in politics, and cast his first vote for Buchanan.

Albert H. Campbell, one of the oldest settlers of Tyronza Township, was born on the farm on which he lives, in 1852, being the only child resulting from the union of Hiram and Julia Marriman (nee Richards) Campbell. Mr. Campbell had been previously married, and was the father of four children by his first wife, of whom Steve and John are the survivors. He came to this State in 1834, and was one of the earliest settlers in this county, having come here before there was any thing in the way of a farm in this section. He only took up 220 acres of land, where he farmed and run a store and also had a ferry on the Tyronza. He raised a great deal of stock and was one of the leading merchants of this county at the time of his death, which occurred in 1852. Hiram Campbell was born and reared in New York, going from there to Illinois in 1821, and thence to Arkansas by way of the Mississippi River to Wappanocca Lake. Proceeding down that body of water to Big Creek, he floated down the Tyronza River and settled on the bank of the stream in the present Crittenden County. Mrs. Campbell died June 18, 1883, at the age of sixty-three years. Although coming to this State when there was much game, such as bear, elk, deer, turkey, etc., he did not spend much time hunting, but devoted most of his attention to his farms and in rafting logs. A.

H. Campbell was reared to farm life and educated in this county, and at the age of sixteen years took charge of his mother's affairs, which he continued until 1885, when the farm was divided. Young Albert got 110 acres of land with seventy-five acres in cultivation, on the home place, and since that time he has added forty acres of wild and twenty acres of cultivated land. Like most farmers in this county he raises considerable cotton, though plenty of corn, hay, etc., is also grown, and he devotes a great portion of his time to cattle and horses in the bottoms, making a specialty of the former. In 1887 Mr. Campbell was united in wedlock to Miss Bettie, daughter of R. C. and Mary E. (May) Hampton, natives of Virginia and Arkansas. Mr. and Mrs. Hampton are the parents of five children, with four still living: Richard, Bettie, Thomas D., J. F. and L. L. (deceased). Mr. Hampton died in 1867 and his wife survived him eight years. Mr. and Mrs. Campbell are the parents of two children: Nancy S. and Charles A. Being quite an enterprising young man and a native of this State, Mr. Campbell appreciates the advantages derived from education and emigration, therefore he favors these as an opportunity to develop the excellent qualities of his life-long home.

Thomas Cashion (deceased) was born in Bullitt County, Ky., in May, 1858, and died December 3, 1888, in Crittenden County, Ark. When a boy he went from his birthplace to the State of Texas, where he was married to Miss Nannie E. Rives, January 11, 1880. She was born April 27, 1860, in this county, and is the daughter of Samuel D. Rives, who was born in Kentucky and died here on April 16, 1865. He came from the Blue Grass State, with his parents, when he was a boy. Mrs. Cashion's father was a well-to-do farmer; her mother was born and raised in this county, where she died December 31, 1879, having had four children of whom two are still living: Nannie E. and Edna (who resides in Galveston, Tex.). Mrs. Cashion, the second child, moved from Crittenden County to Texas with her mother, and received her education in the district schools of Collin County, afterward attending the high school in McKinney.

She has borne three children: John P. (born October 12, 1880), Mary J. (born April 3, 1882), and Thomas E. (born October 4, 1884). Thomas Cashion, Sr., was an employe of the Houston & Texas Railroad, while in Texas, and remained in that position for nine years. Discontinuing railroading in 1884 he farmed in Texas one year, when he came to this county and located on the farm now owned by his widow, formerly the property of Mr. Rives. This contains 800 acres, with 375 acres in cultivation, and is located on the Mississippi River bottoms. The farm now belongs to Nannie and her sister and never has been divided. Mr. Cashion was a member of the Masonic and Knights of Honor fraternities, and was a good citizen and highly respected. His widow rents all her land, but lives on her farm. Her grandfather, Peter G. Rives, was one of the first settlers of this county, having come here before Pierce was president. He was a large land owner, and cleared most of the land south of West Memphis, and was a prominent and useful citizen.

Anthony M. Clement (deceased) was a son of William and Mary E. (Brassfield) Clement, natives of North Carolina. He was born January 9, 1826, and was the twelfth child and seventh son of seventeen children, of whom Mary (widow of James Leach, residing near Beebe, Ark.) is the only surviving child. A. M. Clement was born in Tennessee, reared and educated in Gibson County, and at the age of twenty-one engaged in business for himself, principally merchandising, near Humboldt. In 1852 he was married to Mary Catherine, daughter of R. N. and Margaret (Froenabager) Patrick, natives of South Carolina and North Carolina, respectively, but at that time living in Gibson County. They were the parents of eleven children, of whom Mary Catherine was the eldest. During the war of the Rebellion Mr. Clement resided near Humboldt, but took no part in the contest. In the spring of 1867 he moved with his family to Crittenden County, Ark., locating on the Mississippi River, near Bradley's Landing, and in 1869 purchased the tract of land on which his widow now resides. He was of English descent, his grandfather (father of William Clement) having come from England many years before the revolt of the colonies, settling in North Carolina. From the beginning of the Revolution he and his sons took an active part, he being surgeon and his sons soldiers in the American army. They were in the battle of King's Mountain, one son being killed. At the age of ninety he married a second wife, who was quite young (mother of William Clement) and lived to see a young family growing up around him. Mr. Clement and wife (parents of the subject of our sketch), were active members in the Methodist Episcopal Church. Mr. Clement died in 1867, aged eighty-nine, leaving a second wife, his first wife having died many years before. Anthony M. Clement and wife became the parents of eight children, five of whom are now living. They are: Matilda (who is the second time a widow), Josie M., Robert E. Lee and Benjamin C. (the youngest), all at home with their mother. Lillian, the sixth child and fourth daughter, was married September 13, 1888, to S. S. James, of Jericho, this county. Mr. Clement was a member of the Methodist Episcopal Church, in Gibson County, Tenn., and a member of the A. F. & A. M., and at the time of his death was justice of the peace in his township. He was kind-hearted, genial, generous to a fault; though quick to resent an insult, ready to forgive an injury—a typical Southern gentleman. He died November 24, 1888, being sixty-two years of age. Mrs. Clement is a good, Christain lady, and a member of the Cumberland Presbyterian Church.

Seth C. Cocks has attained a prominence and merited reputation as one of the leading farmers of this county. Born at the Gayosa Hotel of Memphis, in 1860, while his parents were on their way from Mississippi to Crittenden County, Ark., he was a son of Philip A. Cocks, of Kentucky nativity, who moved from there to Mississippi, where he was married (in Washington County) to Miss Anna C. Egg, a native of that State. Mr. Cocks moved to Arkansas in 1860 and located on the farm he had purchased the previous year. He was an energetic and prosperous farmer and died February 5, 1869, on the place he settled, and on which his family still lives. Mrs. Cocks, his

widow, survived him till 1878. They were the parents of three children, of whom Minnie was burned to death at the age of three years, in Crittenden County, Ark.; Seth C., our subject, and Blanche D., an artist of talent, is the widow of Charles L. Lyles, son of Col. Lyles, now of Memphis. [See sketch.] Mr. and Mrs. Lyles gave birth to one son, Philip Lyles. Seth C. Cocks attained his majority in this State, having continued to live on the place settled by his parents in 1860. He is a man of great energy and business ability and one of the successes of his career is seen in the position he now occupies, as the owner of a large farm. His parents having died while he was very young, he has, by his own vim and push, kept up the old place. He attended school in Memphis for two years, and then after spending four years at the Frankfort Military Academy of Kentucky, returned to the home farm and was married to a very estimable lady, Miss Mary Belle Lyles, daughter of Col. Lyles, one of the old and prominent settlers, and for many years clerk of this county, now numbered among the leading lawyers of Memphis. Mrs. Cocks is a very highly educated lady and an excellent conversationalist, and is in every way a woman to be admired. She and her husband are the parents of three children: Amy, Blanche and an infant girl. Mrs. Cocks is a prominent member of the Episcopal Church. Politically, Mr. Cocks is a Democrat. He owns a large farm under cultivation bearing all the latest improvements.

Robert F. Collins, a prosperous planter of Proctor Township, is a native of this county, born December 16, 1843, and the son of Thomas M. Collins, who was born in Virginia, in 1813, and died in Memphis, in 1853. His parents moved from Virginia to Tennessee in an early day, and Thomas came to this State while yet single, marrying, in this county, Miss Virginia W. Hulbert, a native of Pennsylvania. After Mr. Collins' death she was married, in 1857, to W. E. Scanlan, and died in 1878. She was a sister of Henry T. Hulbert, who was a great literary man and a prominent lawyer of Memphis. Thomas M. Collins was one of the early settlers of this county, and a prominent man, being popular as a politician; he was a member of the State legislature from an early day until nearly the time of his death, and could have been Governor had he been a Democrat instead of a Whig. He was a large owner of real estate, and was a prominent Mason; was very charitable, and educated many children with his own means. Noted for his integrity, he was mail contractor from Memphis to Little Rock for a number of years. Mr. and Mrs. Collins were the parents of eight children, of whom three sons are the only survivors. Robert F. Collins was reared in this county, and was educated in St. Joseph's College, of Kentucky, his brothers attending St. Mary's College of Kentucky. He lived with his mother and step-father till twenty-one years of age, when he commenced life for himself as a farmer, which he has followed up to the present time. He and his two brothers jointly own 205 acres of land, with 150 acres under cultivation. Mr. Collins was married January 5, 1870, to Miss Julia Wood, who was born in Brownsville, Tenn., September 4, 1847, and is a daughter of William P. and Ara A. (Leanard) Wood, natives of North Carolina and Tennessee, respectively; both died in Brownsville. To Mr. and Mrs. Collins have been given two children: Robert A. and Sadie W. Mr. Collins is a Democrat in politics, and cast his first vote for Hancock. He is a member of the K. of H., and he and his wife are members of the Catholic Church, and are good citizens, and highly respected.

Richard Stephen Combs (deceased), who was an enterprising farmer of Tyronza Township, was born in Carroll County, Va., October 25, 1853, and died October 15, 1889. His parents were both Virginians by birth and came to this county in 1876, locating where the widow of the subject of this sketch now lives. R. S. Combs was married October 23, 1883, to Mrs. Julia F. Cloar, who was born in this county October 11, 1856, the widow of Y. Y. Cloar and daughter of Joseph A. and Julia (Richards) Lyles. Mr. Lyles was born in Obion County, Tenn., and immigrated to Crittenden County, Ark., at an early day. He and his wife both died in this county, the former in 1862 and Mrs. Lyles in 1883. Mrs. Combs lives on the

farm that she inherited from her father. It consists of 225 acres, with 125 in cultivation, upon which is a fine young orchard and good buildings. A part of her land is located on the Tryonza River. Mrs. Combs is the mother of one child, Mary Lyles Combs. She is an estimable lady, and is respected by all who know her. She is a sister of Albert H. Campbell, a sketch of whom appears on a previous page.

Baxter C. Crump (deceased), one of the old and much-esteemed citizens of this county and who for many years was sheriff before and after the late war, was a native of Virginia, born in 1822, and died in 1874. He came to Arkansas some time previous to 1840, and when a young man held the office of county judge, also representing this county in the legislature, being a very prominent politician. He was a Union man at the outbreak of the Civil War, but deeming it his duty to stand by his people he raised three companies, of the second of which he was captain. He was slightly wounded in the ankle at the battle of Belmont, where all of his company but three men deserted him, whereupon he returned home and organized another company being made its captain. He was again wounded at the battle of Helena, Ark., and was afterward quartermaster, doing active service till the close of the war, when he surrendered with his regiment in Arkansas. At the cessation of hostilities he returned home to his family of small children, his wife, formerly Miss Lucy McPeak, having died in 1861, leaving five small children, two of whom are still living, namely: Mrs. Alice Geaurant, at Barton, Ark., and Mrs. Dellan Swepston, in Nashville, Tenn. Mr. Crump was subsequently married to Mrs. Mary E. (Butler) Higgs, a native of North Carolina and daughter of William C. and Courtney R. (Green) Butler, who were also of North Carolina origin, moving to Georgia in 1844. In Floyd County, Ga., Mrs. Crump attained her womanhood and was married to Marcus A. Higgs, formerly from North Carolina. Mr. and Mrs. Higgs moved to Memphis, Tenn., in 1856, where he practiced law, having studied and been admitted to the bar in Georgia. He remained in Memphis

26

until the fall of 1859, when he came to Crittenden County, Ark., and followed his profession, until the war broke out, when he joined the Confederate army and was killed in September, 1863. He and his wife were active members of the Methodist Episcopal Church. Of five children given them three lived to be grown, and of these Mrs. M. Aurelia Morgan, of Tennessee, is the only survivor. Paul C. and Randolph E. who attained their manhood and were promising young men are now deceased. Mrs. Crump's mother, Mrs. Butler, is still living and is making her home with her daughter; she is seventy-three years of age and is active and healthy. Her husband was a Master Mason, and was buried by that order with the highest honors. They were members of the Methodist Episcopal Church and reared a family of six children to be grown, of whom the following three still survive: Mrs. Kate Ritche (who lives in Florida), Mr. L. W. Butler and Mrs. Crump.

Carlile Daniels is a substantial farmer of Wappanocca Township, and the son of Bevley and Charlotta (Measles) Daniels, having been born in this county, January 4, 1846. Bevley Daniels was a Virginian by birth, and came from North Carolina to this county, where he remained till his death, which occurred when our subject was a child. He and his wife were the parents of seven children, one daughter and six sons, three of whom are living, two in this county and one in Baxter County. After the death of Bevley Daniels, his wife was married twice; she died August 20, 1887. Carlile Daniels received his limited education in this county, and October 8, 1877, married Mrs. Alice A. Daniels, of Greenville, Miss., a daughter of Samuel Truley. Four children blessed this union, two of whom are now living, viz.: Walter C. and Horace W. Mrs. Daniels died May 28, 1887. Mr. Daniels and his brother, William B., own 300 acres of valuable land on the Mississippi River, about twenty miles above Memphis. About 100 acres of this are in cultivation, and under the skillful management of these gentlemen it produces a bountiful crop each year. Carlile Daniels served six months in the Confederate army near the close of the war. He is and

has been a perfect Democrat since he cast his first vote, which was for Seymour. He is a member of the County Wheel, and has served very efficiently as school director for six successive years in School Districts No. 9 and 10. He, along with his mother and wife, has for a long time been a working member of the Methodist Episcopal Church, South.

Peter G. Daugherty, a well-to-do and enterprising farmer of Jackson Township, was born in Northern Alabama, in 1849, to the union of Noble and Judith (Gassett) Daugherty, natives of Virginia and Kentucky. The father moved to the Blue Grass State when a young man and remained there several years, then moving back to Alabama, where he was married. When Peter G. was but a child, both he and his wife died, leaving a family of seven children, of whom our subject is the fourth child; of that number three are still living. Peter G. Daugherty grew to maturity in Alabama, where, having been left upon his own resources, he commenced to earn his livelihood at the age of fifteen years, as an overseer on his uncle's plantation. There he remained for three years and then came to Arkansas, settling in Crittenden County, where he rented land for several years. Later purchasing a tract of wild land four miles from Crawfordsville, he settled upon and commenced to clear it. In 1876 he moved on another place and remained there till 1884, when he moved to the estate on which he now lives, where he has over 200 acres of land under cultivation, all the result of his own labor. He started in the world with nothing, and when he came to this State had only about $800 with him, which he took as a foundation; and today it has grown to be 320 acres of this county's best land. Mr. Daugherty served in Johnson's regiment from Alabama, during the latter part of the war, and was captured at Selma, Ala., being held prisoner for eleven days, when he made his escape and returned to his regiment; soon afterward he surrendered, with his regiment, at Mount Hope, Ala., in May, 1865. He takes but little part in political matters, but at all times votes the Democratic ticket. He has held some of the minor offices of the township, and is a hearty advocate of schools and a liberal contributor to any movement that he deems worthy of support.

Samuel K. Davis has for some time been occupied as a planter and merchant of Bartonville. A native of Maryland, he was born in Hartford County in 1842, being the son of Philip and Louisa B. (King) Davis, both also of Maryland nativity. They moved to Vermilion County, Ill., in 1854, and remained till 1867, when they went to Missouri, locating in Barry County. Four years later Kingman, Kas., became their home, where the mother still lives. The father was born in 1811 and died in 1888; the mother was born in 1821. She is a good Christian lady and takes an active part in church and Sunday-school matters; she is a member of the Baptist Church and is superintendent of a Sunday-school. Mr. Davis was a member of the I. O. O. F. for many years before his death; was a Democrat in politics, and manifested a great interest in school matters and anything that would promote the welfare of the public. Himself and wife were the parents of ten children, of whom two died before leaving Maryland; one from a fall and one by drowning. The others lived to be grown and six are still living. Samuel K. Davis, the second born, attained his majority in Illinois, and moved to Memphis in 1862, entering the service of the Adams Express Company and remaining with them four years. He then commenced farming in Phillips County, Ark. (now Lee County), and in company with his brother Reece he tilled about 1,000 acres till 1874, and in 1875 he commenced merchandising. He was married in February, 1874, to Miss Augusta Holt, a native of Tennessee. Mr. Davis was engaged in merchandising at Phillips Bayou for several years, when he moved to Hot Springs, Ark., the year of the big fire at that place, and bought out Mr. King's interest in the firm of Gordon & King. The trade was made on Thursday and on Monday the establishment was in ashes. The morning after the fire his possessions consisted of but $6.15 upon which to again commence. His wife owned a house and lot, however, so he worked and sold goods for about six years, when he came to Crittenden County and started a store at Needmore, where he remained in business till he moved to Bartonville. He is now running a store with good success and a farm of 400 acres. Upon moving to this county from Hot Springs he had $800 and now owns a fine farm well equipped. Mr. and Mrs. Davis are the parents of two daughters and three sons: Fannie K., Florence Lee, Samuel K., and Claudie W. and Clarence W. (twins); one child is deceased, Effie May. Mrs. Davis is an active member of the Baptist Church, and her husband is a member of the Masonic fraternity, of which he has held several offices. He is a Democrat in politics, but takes little part in any party movement, giving his whole attention to his store and farm. Mr. Davis has been very successful in business and is a man of enterprise and decided business ability.

Alexander H. Ferguson, the present efficient and popular treasurer of Crittenden County and also a merchant at Marion, was born at Greenock, on the Mississippi River, in this county, March 17, 1839, and is the son of Horatio N. and Jane G. (Proctor) Ferguson, natives of Tennessee and Arkansas. The Grandfather Ferguson went from Greenock, Scotland, to Virginia, while a young man, moving from there to Tennessee, where he lived until his death. He was the father of three children: William D., Allen McL. and Horatio N. (all now deceased). The boys came to Arkansas in 1820 and settled at Greenock, a Scottish town named after the town in which their father was born. William D. was the first sheriff of Crittenden County, holding the office from 1825 to 1835, and died at Memphis, Tenn., in 1866. He fought in the battle of New Orleans, January 8, 1815; was a member of the I. O. O. F. fraternity and belonged to the Presbyterian Church. He took active part in the development of this county and filled the office of deputy surveyor for several years. Allen McL. served as postmaster of Oldman, now Greenock, and was justice of the peace for several years. He died in Sharp County, Ark., in 1872. Horatio N. the father of our subject, came to this State when a young man, married upon attaining his maturity, and settled at what was afterward called Greenock, remaining here until 1835. Then he moved to a place lower down the river. He was an extensive farmer and owned large tracts of land which he acquired after coming to Arkansas. He died in 1841 at Frankfort, Ky., where he had gone for his health. Jane G. Proctor, his wife, was also an Arkansan by birth, her parents having emigrated here about the beginning of the nineteenth century, settling below Memphis on the river. Mrs. Ferguson was a member of the Presbyterian Church and remained a widow till her death, which occurred in 1871. She was the mother of six children, two sons and four daughters, of whom three are now living: Mrs. Kate A. Brown (who lives at Marion), Mrs. Nancy E. Lyon (in this county) and Alexander H. (the youngest). The latter was reared in this county where he has always lived. As school advantages were not very good hereabouts in his youth he attended school at Memphis until the death of his brother, when he had to return home and assume charge of affairs. In that position he remained up to the death of his mother, when he was married to Miss Kate Ritchie, of Memphis. In 1884 he located at Marion and has since been engaged in merchandising. In 1880 Mr. Ferguson was elected county clerk, and discharged the duties of that office until elected treasurer in 1884, in which position he is now serving his third term. He has always taken a great interest in the advancement of education and is also a hard worker in the Democratic party. He was married January 19, 1882, and after the brief space of eight months was left a widower. His wife was a true Christian lady and devoted wife, and was a member of the Baptist Church. Alexander Ferguson entered the Confederate army in August, 1862, and had served but a short time when he was wounded at the battle of Corinth, being several times hit in the body by grape-shot from a cannon. He was taken from the battlefield to a hospital at Iuka, where he had his leg amputated between the knee and ankle. He started home as soon as able to travel, coming to Memphis in a buggy, his sister, Sarah J., and Thomas Baldwin, having gone after him to the field of action. Mr. Ferguson is a competent officer for the place which he fills and is in every way worthy of the trust reposed in him.

Capt. LeRoy Fogleman, deceased, is remembered as a prosperous planter of Crittenden County, whose association with its material affairs proves of decided benefit to the community. He was born in this county October 7, 1847, and lived here till his death, December 24, 1879. John Fogleman, his father, was also a native of Arkansas, having been born April 29, 1813, and he lived to be over seventy years of age. [See sketch of G. A. Fogleman.] LeRoy was reared and received his education in the common schools of Crittenden County, where he tilled a farm, and was for a number of years captain of the steamer John Overton. After arriving at maturity he was married to Miss Sallie F. Barton, who was born and reared near Russellville, Logan County, Ky. She came to Arkansas with her husband in February, 1868. They are the parents of three children living and two dead. Those living are: Alice E., Carrie Lee, and John LeRoy. Fannie B., one of the sweetest of little girls, was killed by a cotton-gin when she was twelve years old and Sallie Hall died at the age of two years. Mrs. Fogleman is the third daughter of eleven children, of whom seven survive, born to John and Carrie (Edmonds) Barton, numbered among the oldest and most respected families of Kentucky, and who are still living at Union City, Tenn. Mrs. Fogleman was reared and educated in the State of Kentucky, and is not only a woman well esteemed, but one who commands the respect of all her acquaintances. She had never known what hardship and misfortune meant till the death of her beautiful little daughter, and the subsequent loss of her husband left her with a family of small children to care for. She has done most nobly, however, having kept up a large farm and educated those of her children that are old enough, and one daughter is a teacher in the Memphis high school, she having graduated at the Clara Conway School with the highest honors. Mrs. Fogleman has an excellent family of whom she is justly proud, and to whom she is a devoted mother. They are all active members of the Methodist Episcopal Church of Memphis.

Capt. G. A. Fogleman has become thoroughly identified with Crittenden County's interests, and is now conceded to be a well-to-do planter. Born October 21, 1852, in this county, he is the son of John Fogleman, whose birth also occurred here, April 13, 1813. His father, George Fogleman, was a native of Europe, where he lived till about middle age, then coming to the United States and locating in Arkansas, where the village of Hopefield now stands. Here he remained but a short time, when he moved to the place where the subject of this sketch lives. He improved a small farm, and, on account of the newness of the country, there being more red men than white in those days, built a huge log-house to protect himself and family from danger. He was a very brave man and knew no such thing as fear. A family of five children blessed his union, of whom George, the second child, was born at what is now Hopefield, being reared on the place where his son, G. A., now lives. His father having died when he was thirteen years of age, he had to work for the small sum of 25 cents per day to support his mother and two sisters, but by diligent perseverance and economy he laid the foundation upon which he afterward erected his fortune, consisting of 2,500 acres of land and many negro slaves. He dealt largely in timber, selling logs at the mills and rafting them to New Orleans. In 1865, when the steamer Sultana, loaded with about 1,700 Union soldiers, sunk opposite his place, he, with his family and friends, rescued and saved the lives of some seventy-five men. Although a stanch Confederate, he did all in his power to assist the perishing soldiers of the opposite faction. He did not himself serve in the late war, but took active part in contributing of his means and supplies to the Confederate forces. He delighted in telling the tale of having walked to Memphis on dry land from his place, which is five miles distant, and on the other side of the river. By the change in the channel of the river he did actually accomplish this feat, though it took him over twenty years to do it. Mr. Fogleman married Miss Elisabeth Trice, who was born of a most excellent family, February 28, 1821, in Kentucky, in which State she was reared. Her parents came to this State in 1842. When the late war broke out he moved to Mound City, where he died. Elisabeth was an earnest and true Christian lady, and was devoted to her family, which consisted of eight children, and of whom two are still living, viz.: Gustavus A. and Fannie K. (now wife of R. B. Barton, living in Memphis). The mother died February 26, 1858. Capt. G. A. Fogleman, the only son now surviving, has always lived in this county. About seventeen years of his life were spent on the river as captain of the John Overton and the Mark Twain, which, after it was rebuilt, was called the Alace; he was pilot on the same boats for a number of years, commencing when he was but a boy and continuing till February 1, 1889. He has a large farm, with 500 acres in a good state of cultivation, and this now receives his personal attention. Capt. Fogleman was first married to Anna Dickey, January 23, 1878; she died August 2, 1881, when twenty-one years of age, leaving one child, LeRoy, who was born December 1, 1878, and died September 25, 1887. Capt. Fogleman was married January 15, 1889, to Mamie T. Barton, an estimable lady. [See sketch of F. G. Barton.]

John Gilmore (deceased) was, during life, the largest stock raiser in Crittenden County, having lived near Gilmore, which was named in his honor. He was born in Virginia, in 1831, and died while visiting in Texas, in 1883. His parents moved from Virginia to Missouri when he was a small boy, and he was mostly reared in the latter State, coming to this county when yet single. In 1860 he was married to Miss Sarah A. Mooring, who was born in Lexington, Tenn., in 1839, the daughter of Dr. John E. and Matilda (Johns) Mooring. They also immigrated to Crittenden County in pioneer days. Dr. Mooring was born in North Carolina, and his wife, Miss Matilda Johns, in Tennessee. The former died in Texas, the latter in Tennessee. John Gilmore was a pioneer settler in this county in early days. A successful raftsman, a famous bear hunter, a prosperous and prominent man, whom every body liked, he was the largest stock raiser in this county, a man of sterling integrity, who did all that he could to promote the interest of his country and the community in which he lived. He was a loving husband, an indulgent father, and a kind and considerate neighbor. His father. James Gilmore, spent the latter part of his life with his son at his Arkansas home. At the time of Mr. Gilmore's death he owned about 2,500 acres of land and 800 head of cattle. Mrs. Gilmore has now about the same amount of land and stock. She resides on the old homestead, at Gilmore, a station on the Kansas City, Fort Scott & Missouri Railway, with her two children: John Q. (a young man of sterling worth and Kimmie (a beautiful and accomplished daughter). Mrs. Gilmore is a true Christian woman, and a member of the Methodist Episcopal Church, South.

John P. Hackler. In giving the biographies of the prominent men of Crittenden County, that of J. P. Hackler should not be omitted. A native of Arkansas he was born in Phillips County, July 17, 1859, being the oldest child which blessed the union of John G. and Verturia (Harkelroad) Hackler, also of Arkansas origin. John G. Hackler's father came to Arkansas in 1836 and settled in Phillips County. He (John G.) served in the late war on the Confederate side, under Gen. Hindman, and while home on furlough was captured and taken to Memphis, then to Alton, Ill., and from there to Richmond, Va., where he was paroled in 1865. Returning home he resumed farming in Phillips County, but in 1874 moved to Crittenden County and was renting land until 1878. At that time John P. bought the farm where he now resides, and for one year Mr. Hackler made his home with his son, but at the date of his death, November 6, 1885, was living with his daughter, Mrs. Conlan. John P. and his sister, Mrs. Conlan, are the surviving members of their father's family. Mrs. Hackler had been married previous to her union with Mr. Hackler, her first husband being Mr. Thrailkill, and by him became the mother of five children, only one living: Emma (Mrs. Langston, residing in Tate County, Miss). Mrs. Hackler died in 1863, a member of many years' standing in the Cumberland Presbyterian Church. John P. Hackler attended the schools of Phillips County in youth and received a practical education, being a care-

ful student, and applied himself diligently to his studies. In February, 1881, he was united in marriage to Miss Annie Walker. Mr. Hackler owns 800 acres of fine bottom land with 175 under cultivation, and raises about eighty bales of cotton per annum. He also has engaged quite extensively in stock raising, in which he has met with fair success. He was elected justice of the peace, of Lucas Township in 1886; was re-elected in 1888, and is also postmaster, having held the latter office with creditable distinction for the past four years. In his political views he is a stanch Democrat, and a supporter of all worthy enterprises, that indicate the growth of the county, and especially favors immigration.

William J. Hardin is favorably known as the present assessor of Crittenden County, as well as one of its most energetic young men. Born in what is now Lonoke County, near Carlisle, Ark., in 1855, he is the son of John and Nascissa (Percefull) Hardin, natives of Mississippi and Arkansas, respectively. The Percefull family were among the first settlers in the section of country near Carlisle, and Uncle Johnie Percefull is now one of the oldest citizens living in Lonoke County. John Hardin died while his son, William J., was an infant in Lonoke (then Prairie) County. The mother died in the same county, in 1882, at the age of forty-two years. William J. Hardin lived with his mother until grown and came to Crittenden County in 1878, where he followed farming and clerking, until being appointed deputy sheriff in 1884, which office he held to the satisfaction of all for a term of four years. In 1888 he was put forward by the Democratic party for assessor and was elected, and now occupies that responsible position. He is a man of rare abilities, and has a bright future before him, being recognized as a leader in the Democratic party in Crittenden County.

Hon. Asa Hodges. The great men of our time are self-made. Born in the ordinary walks of life, with no especial advantage above their fellows, and forced in early youth to labor for their daily bread, they have risen above the common level by dint of personal effort, working their way up the hill "difficulty," the true road to fame. The secret of their success is industry, perseverance and integrity. Firmness of purpose, rectitude of intention, and persistence in effort are their stock in trade, to which is very seldom added the jewel genius, the uncertain brilliancy of which too often dazzles, but to mislead. Its place is, however, supplied by a stock of that very uncommon article—common sense. A clear head, a quick eye, an accurate judgment, willing hands and self-reliance, are the true essentials to success. The great man is noted for his deeds of endurance; the man of power is known by his influence. While but a small proportion of the human family attain to positions of prominence, fewer still exhibit the ability to lead the masses. To achieve the greatness of power, one needs the ability to grasp, group and generalize the facts and ideas of the times in advance of the mass, to reason out the solution of the ever recurrent social problem, and make it patent to the popular mind, pointing out the path of improvement, mental, social, or physical, and inducing the people to travel therein, not by the force of fire and steel, but through the high and loftier process of enlightenment. He who at once informs and impels is the true hero, the king among his fellow-men. Such a man is the subject of this sketch, such his sphere of action, such his influence, and it is indeed a pleasure to the historian of the present day to refer to a life so filled with usefulness, so encouraging to struggling youth, and so worthy of emulation by them. Asa Hodges was born in Lawrence County, Ala., January 22, 1822. His father was Hon. William Hodges, a brave son of North Carolina, who, smarting under the would-be tyranny of the mother country, bore with his father an active share in the colonies' struggle for independence. Great-grandfather Hodges was of sturdy Scottish birth, possessed of those sterling characteristics of honesty, uprightness and energy, that stamped him a man among men; and these noble traits have come down in a marked degree to his descendants. William Hodges, it almost goes without saying, was endowed with unusual vigor of character, and decided natural ability. A blacksmith in early life, he was

held in universal esteem as a citizen, and in 1828 and 1829 was called upon to represent his native county in the General Assembly of the State, serving with a faithfulness and distinction that won for him permanent reputation. He was united in marriage with Miss Jeannette Daugherty, of Tennessee nativity, though her parents came originally from Nova Scotia. She attained to womanhood in the State of her birth, being married in Smith County, after which she accompanied her husband to Alabama, and there died in 1832. Firm in character and gentle in disposition, she was greatly beloved, the influence of her thorough training producing lasting impression upon the minds of her children. Of the original family of five sons and four daughters, two sons and two daughters survive. Of these Col. Fleming Hodges makes his home in Mississippi; Mrs. Townsend is a resident of Shelby County, Tenn., and Mrs. Phillips lives in Memphis. By the death of his father, in 1837, Asa Hodges was thrown upon his own personal resources at the age of seventeen. The family estate having been left in an embarrassed condition, he found himself face to face with the stern realities of life, never knowing much about the real pleasures of boyhood, but the very obstacles and struggles, which his self-dependent circumstances obliged him to undergo, served to develop those intellectual and moral characteristics which in after life made him a man of influence and mark among his associates. With praiseworthy ambition he set about to acquire an education. To a young man possessing no means this was not an easy thing to do, but great determination and a "keeping-everlastingly-at-it" spirit overcame the serious difficulties which earlier surrounded him, and he passed the later years of his student life in attendance at La Grange College, an institution of wide repute at that day, conducted under the auspices of the Methodist Episcopal Church. It was, perhaps, not strange that young Hodges should have turned almost intuitively to the legal profession as a field offering the greatest inducements for his talents; at any rate he became a student of law in the office of Hon. L. P. Walker, of Florence, one of the most able and successful practitioners in Northern Alabama, under whose instruction he pursued a thorough course of study until qualified for admission to the bar. Upon receiving his diploma in 1848, as a regularly licensed attorney, he entered into partnership with the eminent Thomas M. Peters, afterward chief justice of the supreme court of Alabama, which relation proved mutually beneficial, and more than ordinarily lucrative until dissolved by the loud mutterings of civil war. Some years before Mr. Hodges had met and formed a pleasant acquaintance with Mrs. Caroline Chick, an estimable lady, whom he married April 17, 1853, Mrs. Hodges bringing to this union the culture, influence and wealth of a prominent family of South Carolina. Subsequently, and previous to the breaking out of the Rebellion, he purchased and settled upon a large and valuable plantation in Crittenden County, Ark., which he still owns. After locating here he was made judge of probate, the duties of which position he discharged with peculiar care and fidelity, winning unbounded commendation from his fellow-citizens, who soon transferred him to a seat in the State constitutional convention as a delegate under the reconstruction act of 1867. Following the adoption of the constitution he was elected to the General Assembly in 1868, and in 1870 was the choice of the people of his district as State senator, in which body he served as a member for a term of four years. While holding the latter position, Mr. Hodges was sent as a Republican to represent Arkansas in the XLIII Congress. Here, also, a loyal, consistent adherence to the best interests of those whom he represented attended his career. While there may have been no occasion for especial brilliancy of oratorical powers, or momentary manifestation of personal aggrandizement, there was always about him that quiet, thoughtful, dignified demeanor which is never without its influence. Indeed, it is well known that Congressman Hodges was a man able to do his own thinking and act upon a judgment rarely, if ever, at fault. Public service, honorably discharged, stands as a lasting monument to any man, and no words that might here be added could carry with them more power, or a greater appreciation of Mr. Hodges' public efforts than the verdict

accorded him, "Well done, good and faithful servant." In his private life he is all that his national reputation would indicate him to be. Considerate, thoughtful, and always courteous, is it any wonder that he is so generally beloved? The large means given him have not been misused, as the many recipients of his open-handed charity stand ready to testify. His pecuniary success is well known. His immense plantation in this county, 3,000 acres in extent, laid out into highly cultivated fields, is a present reminder of his industry and labor, for when he moved upon it only seventy acres were cleared. Several other tracts in various parts of Crittenden are included in his possessions, some 2,000 acres of which are also worked. A 350-acre plantation in Bolivar County, Miss. (yielding a bale of cotton to the acre annually), another 1,000 tract in Monroe County, Miss., and city property in Memphis also comprise a part of his wealth, a single block in the latter city being valued at $40,000. The opinion gathered by ninety-nine out of every 100 individuals, from a survey of his appearance, would be that he is a man of good, sound, sterling, practical common sense; not afraid of work, persistent in effort, quick in perception and temper, straightforward, sincere, a fast friend, a man with a large heart, clear head, quick eye, and honest intentions. His character is this and more. There is nothing of the hypocrite about him, and he detests hypocrisy in others. As a friend to progress he is especially liberal, and it is his great desire to see this favored section become rapidly appreciated by the outside world. The accompanying excellent portrait of Mr. Hodges is reproduced from a photograph taken while he was a Congressman, and though twenty years have spread the mantle of declining years and left their silvery imprint on his hair, they have not dimmed the honest candor of his eye, obliterated the intellectual cast of his facial features, dulled the activity of his mind, nor quenched the milk of human kindness that has forever flowed from his generous heart. Here, in the meridian of life, happy in his domestic relations, he resides, enjoying the sincere respect of all who are favored with his acquaintance.

Eng. by J.R. Rice & Sons, Phila.

A. Hodges

Ralph Hathaway, a prosperous planter and saw-mill man of Crittenden County, is a native of North Carolina, born in 1836, and is the fifth of six children born to John and Lucy (May) Hathaway, natives of North Carolina, who moved to Shelby County, Tenn., about 1845, where they lived till their death. They were both earnest Christian workers, and members of the Baptist Church. Ralph Hathaway reached his majority in Shelby County, Tenn., and in 1856 commenced business for himself on a farm in that county, where he remained for four years, coming to Crittenden County in the spring of 1860. Here he purchased a lot of wood land and made improvements on it for two years, when he sold it, and for four years tilled a rented farm on the river in the same county. In 1867 he purchased land and commenced to open it up, and in 1872 commenced merchandising at Mound City. He sold his farm in 1876, and when he went out of the merchandising business two years later, he purchased the farm upon which he how lives, consisting of a good body of land in an excellent state of cultivation; also a gin and saw-mill attachments. He makes his home on his farm, but his family lives near Barton, Tenn. He served in the Confederate army during 1863 and 1864, and when the war ended he returned to his farm work. He was married to Eveline Carlton, a native of Tennessee, in 1856, and by this union were born seven children, four of whom are still living: Viola, Laura, Lelia and Wellington. Viola is the wife of W. O. Christie, of Dyersburg, Tenn. Mrs. Hathaway is a member of the Methodist Episcopal Church. Mr. Hathaway is a member of the A. F. & A. M., and is a Democrat in politics.

John D. Hodges was born in Lawrence County, Ala., in 1842, as the son of Milton and Emiline E. (McCamey) Hodges, who were natives of South Carolina and Alabama, respectively. When John D. was six years of age, his parents moved to Pontotoc County, Miss., and settled on a large plantation. Here he was reared, enjoying the advantages of good public school facilities, and when the Civil War broke out, he was attending the Union University of Murfreesboro, Tenn. In Au-

gust, 1861, he joined the Confederate army, in Company A, Forty-first Mississippi, and served four years and two months, under Col. W. F. Tucker, who was soon promoted to brigadier-general, LaFayette Hodges being captain. Mr. Hodges was wounded at the battle of Perryville, Ky., by a shot in the left ear. He was taken prisoner at Selma, Ala., in the Wilson raid, and was paroled at Montgomery, in 1865. Going thence to his home, he remained for two years, when he moved to Arkansas and purchased the farm upon which he now lives. In the following year, 1868, his parents came to Arkansas, and remained for two years, moving later to Memphis, where they lived till their death, which occurred in 1878, of yellow fever. Mr. Hodges' wife was formerly Miss Ella Kennedy, who was born in Cadiz, Ky., in 1845; she is the mother of seven children, of whom the following five still survive: Grace E., Dudley T., Jesse T., Nellie A. and Annie E.; those deceased are: Mary Ellen (who died an infant) and John M. (who died at the age of three years and nine months). Mr. Hodges is a member of the Baptist Church, and his wife of the Christian Church. He is a Democrat in politics, and a member of Lodge No. 3114, K. of H. He owns a farm of 160 acres, most of which is under cultivation, and by his judicious management it yields an abundant crop annually.

James F. Hodges in his association with the plantation interests of Lucas Township, has come to be very favorably known. He was born in North Carolina, September 29, 1846, being a son of Davis W. Hodges, a native of South Carolina, born April 10, 1825, whose father was John Hodges, a soldier in the War of 1812. Davis W. Hodges was married in South Carolina to Miss Susan J Davis, she having first seen the light of day in North Carolina in 1838. They are still living in South Carolina, where they follow farming for an occupation, and are the parents of six sons and one daughter, all living. James F. Hodges is the oldest son and he and his brother Milton are the only members of the family in Arkansas. He was reared and educated in the common schools of South Carolina and lived at home till he reached his majority. In 1863, enlisting in Company I, of the Hampton Legion of the Confederate army, he served up to near the close of the war when he returned to his native State, remaining there till 1875, the time of his removal to this county. In 1879 he returned to his native State and was there married October 15, 1879, to Miss Lulu Archer, of South Carolina, born October 30, 1852. Mr. and Mrs. Hodges have a family of four children: Walter D., Eva S., Harry G. and Freddie. Mr. Hodges now controls 2,000 acres of land, acquired since 1876, and upon which he has lived since 1883. A Democrat in politics, himself and wife are earnest workers in the cause of Christianity, belonging to the Methodist Episcopal Church, South. Mr. Hodges raises from 750 to 1,000 bales of cotton per year. He is an honest, upright and hard-working man whom everybody respects.

J. L. Holloway is a prominent and wealthy planter of Lucas Township, who was born in Monroe County, Miss., September 14, 1843, being one of ten children that blessed the union of Samuel and Sophia (Mitchiel) Holloway, natives of Edgefield District, S. C. Samuel Holloway was reared and educated in South Carolina, and at the age of seventeen accepted the position of manager of his uncle's business, which he successfully conducted until his twentieth year. He then moved to Tuscaloosa, Ala., and there married, and immediately took the management of his mother-in-law's estate. He afterward bought a farm in Tuscaloosa County, and though quite a young man, received the election of sheriff of that county, which office he filled with entire satisfaction to all concerned, for many years. In 1843 he moved to Monroe County, Miss., from there to Aberdeen, Miss., and in 1854 took his family to the latter place, where he had purchased a large plantation, and there remained until the close of the war. In 1848 Mr. Holloway bought a farm in Monroe County, Ark., which consisted of 400 acres in cultivation; this was owned by the family until 1862; and in 1858 he purchased a large piece of land in De Soto County, Miss., on the Mississippi River, consisting of 1,212 acres, 400 acres improved and highly cultivated. This is the family homestead, and now contains some 1,100

acres of the best of improved land, with good residences, barns, etc. Mr. Holloway died at age of fifty-seven, his excellent wife surviving him thirty-one years; her death occurred in 1889. He was a leading member of the Baptist Church, in which he was a deacon many years. His wife was connected for sixty-five years with the same church. J. L. Holloway passed his youth in Monroe County, Miss., receiving his education in the schools in the village of Aberdeen, and at the breaking out of the war was about to enter college. Notwithstanding that he had made every preparation and studied diligently, and passed critical examinations, he gave up the idea, and in 1861 joined Company B, Twentieth Mississippi Infantry as a private. He was soon after promoted to the office of assistant of commissary of Stewart's corps, and held that position until the close of the war. He participated in seventeen pitched battles, the first being on Gauly River, W. Va., at Fort Donelson, where he was taken prisoner and sent to Camp Douglas, Chicago, there being retained for nine months; he was exchanged at Vicksburg in 1862. His regiment was reorganized at Clinton, Miss., and engaged in various skirmishes from Jackson to Vicksburg, the hardest fight being at Champion's Hill, and it captured over 300 prisoners from Raymond back to Vicksburg, and held them until the surrender of that place. The regiment was not engaged in the city, but on the outskirts, and after the surrender of that place was dismounted and sent to Jackson, and afterward to Canton, Miss., for winter quarters, where it remained until the following spring. Being ordered to Resaca it participated in that famous battle, and in all the engagements around Atlanta, Ga., up to the time Gen. Hood took command. After his (Hood's) defeat, Mr. Holloway returned to Tupelo, Miss., and there the troops were furloughed for ten days. At the expiration Joseph E. Johnston was reinstated to the command, and Mr. Holloway rejoined the regiment at Raleigh, N. C., remaining with Gen. Johnston until the final surrender in 1865, after which he received his parole and arrived home in May of the same year. Upon the close of the war he found to his dismay that his worldly possessions were almost nothing, but not discouraged he set out resolutely, determined to succeed, and he has, for the word "fail" was unknown to him. He commenced farming, and as he had never done any manual labor, of course he encountered many obstacles, and a man of less determined purpose might have failed utterly. After farming rented land for some time, he returned to the homestead which now belongs to himself and the other heirs, only three of whom are living out of the large family of ten children: Ira G. (residing in Oxford, Miss., and a member of the State senate), Samuella (wife of Dr. George A. Cairns, of Oxford, Miss.), and J. L. (the subject of this sketch). Mr. Holloway was married at Clinton, Miss., in 1863, to Miss Jerusha E. Mosby, daughter of John and Nancy (Smith) Mosby, natives of Tennessee. Mr. Mosby was a colonel in the War of 1812, and retained the title so gallantly won, during his entire life. Himself and wife were the parents of nine children, five surviving: Mrs. William Priestly (of Canton, Miss.), Matthew A., Jerusha E. (Mrs. Holloway), Mrs. Augusta Coleman and William J. (druggist of Canton, Miss.). Mr. Mosby died in 1841, and his wife in 1861. To the union of Mr. and Mrs. Holloway three children have been given: Willie (Mrs. Young of this county), Miss Elise and Corinne (Mrs. Richards of Crawford, Miss). Mr. Holloway has control of 6,800 acres of land on the Arkansas side of the Mississippi River, 725 of which are under cultivation, the rest being leased. He raises from his individual labor 100 bales of cotton, and corn sufficient to supply the Arkansas side of the farm. He receives for his rented land on the Arkansas side $1,325, and on the Mississippi side $800. Mr. Holloway is public spirited and progressive, and is a liberal supporter of all laudable enterprises, well deserving the confidence reposed in him by his fellow-citizens. He is a Democrat in his political views, a member of Indian Creek Lodge No. 2383, K. of H., and with his eldest daughter, a member of the Cumberland Presbyterian Church. Mrs. Holloway and youngest daughter belong to the Presbyterian Church.

William M. Holmes, editor and publisher of the Marion Reform, was born in Memphis, Tenn., May 29, 1865, and is the son of George C. Holmes whose birth occurred in Georgia in 1834. The latter is a son of George L. Holmes, born in Massachusetts, of English descent. George C. Holmes was reared in Memphis from the time he was one year old, and was married in that city to Miss Ann Frances James, daughter of James C. and Sarah (Winkford) James, originally from Tennessee and Kentucky, respectively, the former of whom was at one time Governor and United States senator of his native State. Gov. James was a self-made man and an old line Whig and died in Tennessee in 1859. Mr. Holmes died in Memphis February 21, 1884, and his widow still resides in that city. William M. Holmes, the fifth in a family of eight children, of whom five are still living, was brought up and educated in Memphis, where he learned the printer's trade, mostly in the Avalanche office. He worked at his adopted calling for about nine years before commencing for himself and during that time rose from the lowest position to the highest in the Avalanche office, first being office boy, and then, respectively, apprentice, compositor, proof-reader, assistant foreman, local reporter and lastly, commercial editor. In August, 1889, he came to Marion from Memphis and started the Reform, which is a splendid success as a local newspaper, published in a manner to win the commendation of all. In 1885 Mr. Holmes was married in Memphis to Miss Ruby Burrow, born in Humboldt, Tenn., July 20, 1868. She is a daughter of John Burrow. Mr. and Mrs. Holmes are the happy parents of two children: Frank E. and Eunice. Mrs. Holmes is an earnest worker in the Cumberland Presbyterian Church, to which she belongs. Her husband is connected with the Typographical Union of Memphis, and has been a stanch Democrat since casting his first vote, which was for Cleveland. He is a man of intellect and deep thought, and the Reform promises to become a reforming power under the brilliant management of its present editor.

Sterling Hood deserves special mention as one of the oldest citizens of Tyronza Township. He was born in Limestone County, Ala, in 1818, being the second child of a family of three children given to the union of Frederick and Elizabeth (Moseley) Hood, natives of Virginia, as were the grandparents. The paternal grandfather, Sterling Hood, was a soldier in the War for Independence and the maternal grandfather was Captain William Moseley of Revolutionary fame, who went to the war from near Halifax, Virginia; he died in Alabama about 1830. Frederick Hood went to Alabama when quite a small boy and was with General Jackson in the War of 1812. He .was sick at the time of the battle of New Orleans, and died in Alabama in 1836 at the age of forty years; he had been twice married, first to the mother of our subject from which union resulted three children, Sterling, William (deceased) and Robert (deceased). After the death of Mrs. Hood, in 1822, Mr. Hood was married to Betsie Bowlin, and by her was the father of five children, two of whom are still living. Sterling Hood, reared to farm life, was educated in Alabama, and at the age of eighteen years he commenced life for himself as an apprentice to a brick mason, for whom he worked three years in Decatur, Ala. He helped do the brick work on the freight house of the Memphis and Charleston railroad and was present in 1836, when the first boat landed at Decatur. After learning his trade he left Decatur and went to Yalobusha County, Miss., where he manufactured and laid brick, but only stayed there a short time, going thence to Coahoma County, Miss., where he followed overseeing for Dr. Hobson and his son and son-in-law for two years. Later he went to Carroll County for a short time, but in the fall of 1839 settled in Brazoria County, Texas on the Brazos River, where he engaged in keel boating cotton from the upper Brazos to Brazoria. He then was occupied as captain of a sailing vessel from the mouth of the Brazos River to Galveston, and after remaining on the vessel for some time returned to his former occupation, overseeing, on the plantation of the Widow Whorton, close to the Brazos River. After staying here for eighteen months he left Texas in 1843 and started back to Mississippi by way of New Orleans. From that State he went to Memphis, resumed his trade and helped to build the navy yard (which was never completed), assisting also in erecting the first house in that city, built under the hill, by Enoch Davis for a tavern; the building has since been washed away by the river. He could have purchased one acre of land near where the Gayosa Hotel now stands, for $75, but thought it a poor investment. In 1840 Mr. Hood came to this county and two or three years later bought the land upon which he now lives, consisting of 120 acres of unimproved land, now having seventy-five acres improved. Since coming here he has devoted his whole attention to his land and the raising of stock. He was nearly ruined by the high inundations of the rivers in 1882 and 1883, losing over 100 head of cattle. When Mr. Hood first settled here there were but five or six families living on the Tyronza for a distance of fifty miles and no road to Memphis except a trail. What few people lived here were prosperous and happy and most of them depended on trapping for support. Many Indians still roamed the woods and the chiefs, Moonshine and Cornmeal, came with their tribes and hunted during the winter, but went west in summer. Also when first coming to this State Mr. Hood saw a number of the men that belonged to the Merrill clan. He was married in 1849 to Rhoda Richards of this State and a native of North Carolina, who came to Arkansas in 1839, settling where she and her husband now live. Mr. and Mrs. Hood are the parents of seven children, of whom five are living, viz.: J. W. (who resides in this county), Nancy (wife of B. F. Bush), Robert, Laura (wife of Thomas Wilkins, in Phillip's County) and Eddie at home. Mr. Hood was constable and deputy sheriff for twenty years and until he was too old to serve any longer. He is a member of the Methodist Episcopal Church and takes great interest in public schools, churches, etc., favoring all public improvement and extending a welcome to all white emigration, from whatever country they may come to this, the land of prosperity and plenty. The early settlers of this county were compelled to go to a horse mill at Crawfordsville, and Mr. Hood erected a band mill, two rawhide bands being attached to levers and pulleys and run by horse power. He, Hood, is still able to ride through the bottoms to look after his land and stock, and is active as most men of forty-five or fifty years. He has taken very few doses of medicine and scarcely knows what sickness means either in himself or family.

W. P. Jeffries is one of the leading young farmers of Proctor Township, and owes his nativity to Mississippi, his birth occurring in Marshall County, in 1858. W. A. and Sallie M. (Moore) Jeffries, his parents, came originally from Alabama and Pennsylvania, respectively. The former was reared to farm life, and when a young man purchased land in Marshall County, Miss., where he resided for many years. In 1880 he came to Crittenden County, Ark., and settled in this immediate vicinity, purchasing the property where Mr. W. P. Jeffries now resides. It consisted of 160 acres, with very little improvement, though 125 acres were cleared ready for the plow. It is nearly all cleared at the present time, and under a high state of cultivation; a good frame residence and numerous outbuildings are among the recent improvements. Mr. and Mrs. Jeffries became the parents of seven children, only two now living: W. P. and E. D. (the wife of E. M. Apperson, Jr.). Mr. Jeffries died in 1887, and Mrs. Jeffries is residing with her son, W. P. The latter was reared and educated in Marshall County, Miss., and always resided with his parents. Since his father's death he has managed his mother's estate, and has proven himself a man of unusual business aptitude and qualifications. He raises some eighty-five bales of cotton annually on his farm, and in company with E. M. Apperson, Jr., has bought a farm of 240 acres, adjoining his own homestead. About 180 acres of this farm are improved, in a moderate manner. On this plantation the yearly products are estimated at 125 bales per annum. Mr. Jeffries is a member of the A. F. & A. M. Mrs. Jeffries belongs to the ladies' department of the same order, and is a devout member of the Episcopal Church. He is always in favor of public improvements, being a liberal supporter of every laudable enterprise, and is "a man esteemed among men."

M. J. Johnson has long been considered one of the most prominent and respected citizens of this county. Born in North Carolina in 1827 he is the son of Devrick Johnson, a native of Wake County, N. C., who was married to Mary, daughter of Henry Boone, a brother of the noted Daniel Boone. In about 1836 Mr. Johnson, in company with his wife and son, M. J., his brother, Dudley Johnson and his family, with all of their slaves came to Memphis and settled. The father of our subject was a carriage manufacturer, and purchased a large gin-house and mill in Memphis, where he placed his factory. He had a family of four children, all sons, who lived to be grown; those surviving are M. J. and Thomas B. (who is living in Memphis). Thaddeus B. died in 1871, from disease contracted in the Confederate service, and Charles H. died in 1873 of yellow fever. While a boy M. J. Johnson served a six years' apprenticeship with Meraman & Clark, jewelers, going after he left them to Holly Springs, Miss.; where he engaged in the jewelry business and four years later added a stock of merchandise. He remained here for ten years, and was married to Miss Fannie Cole, a native of Mississippi, and daughter of Lemuel H. Cole, of North Carolina. Mrs. Johnson died at her father's home in 1850, leaving two children: Julia B. (wife of L. D. Blann) and William M. (now living at Wynne). Coming to Arkansas with his wife and father-in-law, Mr. Johnson purchased over 2,500 acres of land, on a part of which he now lives, and continued on this plantation till 1884, when he moved his family to Randolph County; one year later, however, he returned to the plantation. He was a second time married, this wife's maiden name being Miss Sally A. Torian. She was a Kentuckian by birth, but raised in Nashville by an uncle. By this marriage there are eight sons, four now living: Trice, Jacob, Mat and Boyd; those deceased are: Charles W., Thomas, Aca and Daniel B. Mr. Johnson is very active and a strong advocate of a better school system, and is one of the county's best citizens. He was wealthy before the war, and owned large and valuable tracts of land and over 100 negroes; now he has about 200 acres of land in cultivation on which are a good residence, cotton-gin, good outbuildings and all other modern improvements. He is a Democrat in politics, and he and his wife are active members of the Methodist Episcopal Church. He is a very reliable man, and is admired by all who know him.

Minos C. Jordan, as a leading physician of Proctor Township, deserves especial mention. He is a native of Rutherford County, Tenn., born March 27, 1843, and is the son of William Jordan, who came upon the stage of action in Williamson County, Tenn., March 4, 1801, and died October 17, 1867, in Rutherford County. The Jordan family is of English lineage, and their advent into this country was made by two brothers, one of whom settled in New York, and the other in Virginia. The father of William Jordan, Johnson Jordan by name, was born in Virginia. William Jordan married Miss Sarah J. Wood, also a native of Williamson County, Tenn., born in 1819, who is now living in Rutherford County. She is the mother of ten children, of whom only five are living, three having died in infancy, and one son was killed in the late war. Minos C. Jordan, the second child in this family, was reared and educated in Williamson and Rutherford Counties, Tenn., and after attending the common schools for a number of years, entered the College Grove School of Williamson County. When within ten months of his graduation the Civil War broke out, and on May 27, 1861, he enlisted in Company D of the Twentieth Regiment, Tennessee Infantry, Confederate States Army, being relieved from duty May 30, 1864, on account of disability, having been wounded by a ball in the right leg at that time; the bone was fractured, and he is now a cripple from the effects of that injury. He was acting as sharpshooter near Dallas, Ga., at the time he was wounded. During his service he was engaged in the following important battles: Shiloh, Fishing Creek, Murfreesboro, Chickamauga, Hoover's Gap, Mission Ridge, and various skirmishes of less note from Chattanooga to Dallas, Ga. After being wounded he was sent to a hospital and remained there till Lee's surrender, when he returned to Tennessee, and in 1866 taught a term of school. In 1868 he kept books for Miles & McKinley, of Murfreesforo, Tenn., and in 1869 commenced farm-

ing, which he continued for one year. Going to Texas, he was engaged in the cattle business for a few years. In 1874 he went to Alabama and commenced the study of medicine under Dr. A. C. Ashford, where he remained for one year, taking a course of lectures at the Medical University of Louisville, Ky. He then practiced for one year, and returned to the university, from which he graduated in 1878. From April, 1876, to January, 1879, he practiced in Lauderdale County, Tenn., whence he moved to Cottonwood Point, in Southeast Missouri, and followed his profession until December 11, 1881. Then he found a location in Crittenden County, Ark., and has since resided here, enjoying a practice that brings him an annual return of $1,500 or $2,000. On January 20, 1880, the Doctor was married to Miss A. D. Martin, of Holly Springs, Miss. She was born in Pemiscot County, Mo., December 5, 1853, and is now the mother of two children: Goston M. and William A. Dr. Jordan owns a house and lot at James' Landing, on the Mississippi. He is a thorough Democrat, and has been since casting his first vote, which was for the separation and representation of the State of Tennessee in the Southern Confederacy. His second vote was for Jefferson Davis, for President of the Confederate States of America. He is a jovial, good-natured man, and is liked by all of his neighbors.

Samuel Keel, though occupied with his present duties as clerk of the Circuit Court of Crittenden County but for a short time, has ably demonstrated his fitness for the position. He was born in Memphis, Tenn., in 1847, and is the third of a family of eight children born to E. T. and Louisa C. (Grace) Keel. The father was a native of North Carolina who moved to Tennessee in 1830, settling in Memphis, where he worked in a saw-mill for a time. In 1840 he formed a partnership with I. T. Gibson and embarked in the saw-mill business which he continued for several years. About 1850 he started a soap factory, and in 1852 opened a grocery store, this receiving his attention till he died at the age of sixty-one years, of yellow fever, in 1879. The Graces, of whom Samuel Keel's mother is a descendant, settled in this county when it was first opened, and are of Spanish origin. A Mr. Grandee who was living here at the beginning of the nineteenth century, and who was a Spanish officer, is one of her ancestors. Lake Grandee, which lies beside Marion, is named after this old settler. Samuel Keel was brought up and educated in Memphis, and at the age of eighteen years commenced to clerk in his father's store, and later he was engaged with Arbuckle, Richardson & Co. In 1880 he came to Crittenden County and began planting on a farm inherited from his father, and which is situated one mile north of another very fine place of 375 acres, 200 being under cultivation. Since he took charge of this farm he has made many valuable improvements, among others a fine house that cost him about $1,700, a large and modern barn, and has cleared over 100 acres. Mr. Keel has been married three times; first, to Miss Mary Avery, a native of Tennessee, who died in 1873 of yellow fever, having borne one child, also deceased. He was married to his present wife, Miss Mary Moffett, a native of New York, in 1882. Mr. Keel has taken considerable interest in politics, and was elected clerk in 1888. He is a gentleman of winning manners and pleasant address, and all who know him are profited by the acquaintance of a worthy and honorable gentleman., He owns one of the finest and most productive farms in this county, which has become such by his skillful management. He is therefore prominent as a farmer, a citizen and a county official.

Fredrick Koser, an extensive planter of Wappanocca Township, first saw the light of day in Germany, September 3, 1835, and is the son of Gotlep Koser, who was born and died in Germany. Our subject was left motherless when an infant, and he was reared and educated under his father's care. At the age of seventeen, having decided to try his fortune in the West, he sailed for the United States, and located at Sandusky, Ohio. In 1857 Mr. Koser was married in Tennessee to Permelia J. Nokes, a native of Mississippi. They are the parents of four children, of whom Thomas F., who resides in Memphis, Tenn., is the only survivor. Mr. Koser is now living with his third wife, who is the mother of one child, Charles C. On

Christmas day, 1867, Mr. Koser landed in this county from Shelby County, Tenn., and purchased forty acres of land, where he now lives, of which there were thirty acres in cultivation. Having every characteristic of a German he commenced to increase his possessions till he now owns 530 acres of unimproved land, and 350 acres of land under cultivation in Crittenden County; also a farm and a house and lot in Randolph County, Ark. Politically Mr. Koser is a Democrat, and cast his first presidential vote for Buchanan. He is a member of the Knights of Honor, and his wife and some of his children belong to the Methodist Episcopal Church, South. He is the framer of his own fortune, and by his strict attention to business has made himself a comfortable income for life. He is a public-spirited man and an honest and honored citizen.

J. T. Lambeth is a respected resident of Fogleman Township, and a man whose superior education and display of public enterprise have linked his name to the affairs of Crittenden County in such a way that he is admired and honored by all who know him. His birth occurred in Wilson County, Tenn., in 1847, and he is the son of J. T. and Susan (Wall) Lambeth, also natives of Tennessee. J. T. Lambeth, Sr., was a school-teacher by profession and was principal and one-half owner of the Clinton College. He sold his interest in the college before the war and moved to his plantation, on which he lived till his death, which occurred in Smith County, Tenn., November 6, 1857, when he was thirty-nine years of age. He was a man of considerable literary talent and wrote a book on biblical subjects, entitled "Number Seven;" also a work on temperance, called "Happiness and Wealth," beside a number of poems which were published in the different periodicals of the day. Mr. Lambeth was the father of three sons: J. T. and Warner (twins), being the first born. W. E. resides in Golddust, Tenn. Warner died on the 23d of August, 1889, at Golddust, Tenn., where he was engaged extensively in the mercantile business, now owned and operated by his brothers. Mrs. Lambeth has lived with her son, J. T., most of the time since her husband's death. J. T. Lambeth was educated principally in Illinois, where his mother moved in 1858 and lived for twelve years. During his stay in Illinois he and his brothers purchased some town property in Weston, Crittenden County, Ky., also buying a saw-mill and carrying on the mercantile and saw-mill business under the firm name of Lambeth Brothers. In 1875 these enterprising men built a saw-mill and tow-boat which they called the Tidal Wave, and placed on the trade between Evansville and Memphis. In 1880 they bought the tract of land where J. T. now lives, consisting of 400 acres of timbered land for their saw-mills and seventy-five acres of improved land on which they have a cotton-gin and all other modern improvements. At this writing they have moved their saw-mills to replace them with a larger and more improved concern. In 1885 the Lambeth Brothers embarked in the mercantile and saw-mill business on a large scale at Golddust, Tenn., and in 1887 bought a farm of 1,200 acres, of which about 450 are improved, raising annually upon this tract about 400 bales of cotton. In addition to the amount ginned for themselves, they gin for others some 600 bales, making their capacity 1,000 bales of cotton. W. E. Lambeth was married, in 1883, to Miss Mattie Graham, of Illinois. Like his brother, he is noted for his business ability. J. T. Lambeth takes considerable interest in the political issues of the day, although he has no desire for public office. He is still unmarried and lives with and cares for his mother. Our subject and brother have spent considerable time on board of steam-boats, and have filled the positions of captain and pilot of the same. J. T. Lambeth is practically a self-made man and can point with pardonable pride to the property he has amassed by his careful and intelligent business management.

Capt. John G. Lewis, a planter, merchant and deputy postmaster of Marion, was born in Hardin County, Ky., in 1827, and is the son of Coleman and Winneford (Nall) Lewis, of Virginia and Kentucky origin, respectively. William Lewis, the grandfather of our subject, was a native Virginian, being an extensive and prosperous planter in Culpeper County. He was a soldier in the Revolutionary War, enlisting when he was seventeen or eighteen years of age, and for his faithful service he was promoted to the rank of major, retaining and carrying this title with him to the close of the great struggle for liberty. He raised a family of fourteen sons, and one or two daughters, all of whom lived to be grown. Some of the sons of this family went to Kentucky, settling close together, and others went to Indiana, and the rest to Alabama. Coleman Lewis attained his majority in Virginia, then moved to Kentucky, where he was married and lived for several years; coming to a place called West Point, he opened a hotel and in connection with this did a commission business. He and several of his brothers fought in the War of 1812. He died in this county in 1845, at the age of fifty years. After the death of her husband, Mrs. Lewis moved to Mississippi where she died. Six children were born to these parents, of whom three are still living, two older sisters and Capt. Lewis. After the death of his father, in 1850, Capt. John commenced life for himself by taking an overland route to California, his means of conveyance being a mule which he rode. He remained in this State four years, and by pluck made clear of expense $3,000, then returning to his Kentucky home by way of the Isthmus of Panama and New Orleans. After spending about three years in Kentucky he went to Arkansas in 1857, locating in Crittenden County, on the little river Tyronza, where he has since lived and reared his family. He joined the Confederate army just before the fall of Vicksburg, enlisting in Company E, First Arkansas Cavalry, Dobbins' regiment. In the fall of the year of his enlistment he was promoted from the rank of sergeant to that of captain. He was in the battles of Helena, Ark., Big Creek, Phillips County, Nealy's Ferry on St. Francis River, Cross County, one in Prairie County, also at Little Rock, and was with Price on his last raid through Missouri, Kansas and Indian Territory. After his eventful career in the army he returned home and resumed his former occupation. He was first married to Camilla Lansdale, she being born in Kentucky in 1831, and died in Arkansas in 1874. She was the mother of six children, three sons and three daughters, of whom three are still living: Charles L. (who is a merchant and postmaster at Marion), Louisiana (now the widow of C. J. Powell and lives with her father), Lena C. (who is unmarried and at home. Mr. Lewis was a second time married, his second wife being Mrs. Jennie (Young) Gatlin; she dying in 1887. Mr. Lewis and family are living in Marion, and his business is that of general merchandising. In religion Mr. Lewis is a firm Methodist, he belonging to the Methodist Episcopal Church of his town. His son Charles is a worthy constituent of the K. of H., and is also secretary of that society. As a family they are held in high esteem by all who know them, and they are all imbued with that spirit of enterprise that makes them popular.

Mrs. Mary Lloyd, who lives three miles north of Marion, on a farm of 160 acres, of which she cultivates over 100, was born in Mississippi to the union of Mr. and Mrs. John Coble, natives of that State. When she was an infant her father died, and the mother was married, after five years of widowhood, to Henry Butler, who was also a native of Mississippi. Soon after his marriage he moved to Marion, Ark., and followed blacksmithing for a livelihood, and afterward moved to Poinsett County, where he resided till his death. The subject of this sketch was married August 9, 1867, to James Lloyd, who came originally from Mississippi County, Ark. He served as a soldier in the Confederate army, and after the war returned to Marion, Ark., where he engaged in farming, trading and trapping. He was an excellent farmer and business man. Mr. Lloyd died on April 3, 1881, leaving a wife and five children: Sophia, Willie, Belle, Le Roy and Robert Lee (deceased). Sophia is the wife of P. A. Bobbitt, who lives in this county. The other three are at home. Mrs. Lloyd owns two tracts of land besides the one on which she resides. She is industrious and enterprising, and keeps her property in good condition. She is a good true Christian lady and a member of the Methodist Episcopal Church, South.

D. C. Louder is the son of Louis and Mary (Lawrence) Louder, and was born in 1854. Louis Louder, a farmer by occupation, was in moderate circumstances. He served in the War of 1812, and participated in the battle of New Orleans. He was twice married, by his first union becoming the father of seven children, only one now living, Minerva, wife of E. J. Lawrence, of Gibson County, Tenn. His last wife was the mother of D. C. Louder (the subject of this memoir), and the following family resulted from this marriage: Mrs. S. A. Harris (wife of Rev. Mr. Harris), Corretta (wife of Jones Evans, residing in Gibson County, Tenn.), Willie (now Mrs. James Evans, also of Gibson County), and E. J. (a well-known resident of the same locality). Mr. Louder died in 1865, his wife having been called to her final home just previous to the war. D. C. Louder was reared in Gibson County, Tenn., and at the age of eighteen began for himself as a farmer in that county, continuing until 1869, at which time he came to Arkansas, locating in Crittenden County and in this township. He has since followed the occupation of an agriculturist, mostly on rented land, and usually rents from 200 to 400 acres, proving beyond a doubt that he is the right man in the right place, for the number of small details of farming which many are wont to overlook, are to him as important in their way as the larger ones. Mr. Louder was married in 1875 to Miss Allicia Lowrance, of Memphis, Tenn., and by her is the father of four children, two of them now living: Fannie A. and Mamie B., both at Memphis, attending school. The home, which was so happy, was robbed of the devoted wife and mother in 1884, after a short illness. Mr. Louder is a successful farmer, and is rapidly accumulating a competence. He is extensively engaged in raising cotton, and is recognized as one of the principal cotton growers of the county. He is a member of Fountain Lodge No. 296, K. of H., at Memphis, Tenn., and is held in high esteem by all.

Col. O. P. Lyles, the extent of whose reputation is by no means confined to the immediate limits of Memphis, his present place of residence, has been so closely and worthily identified with the affairs of Crittenden County, both in an official capacity and as a private citizen, in the more humble but not less important walks of life, that an

27

omission of a brief sketch of his life from the present volume would be greatly to be regretted. A Tennesseean by birth and bringing up, he first saw the light of day in the month of November, 1829. From an early age he found it very necessary to exercise a firm determination to fit himself for the responsibilities of after-life. His first remunerative efforts were as clerk on a river trading-boat, an occupation to which he devoted himself until about 1844, when he located at Marion, Ark. Self-educated and taught by hard experience the value of self-reliance, he rapidly demonstrated his worth and ability in his new home, and in 1850 was elected clerk of the circuit court, a position that he ably filled some eight years. During this time he began the study of law, and applied himself closely to an insight into the legal profession, being admitted to the bar in 1857. In 1858–59 he was representative from this county in the State legislature, and in 1861, when the threatening war cloud burst in all its fury, he became identified with that section to which his interests were so closely allied. Enlisting as a private, upon the reorganization of the army, he was unanimously elected colonel of the Twenty-third Arkansas Infantry Regiment, and participated in the hard-fought battles of Corinth, Davis' Bridge, siege of Port Hudson, and various skirmishes, his career as a soldier being more severe and fraught with harder service than characterized the experiences of many noble "boys in gray." On July 9, 1863, he was taken prisoner after the siege of fifty-one days, and suffered the tortures of prison life for some time. During his military service he was in command of one or another of the wings of the army, and it is a matter of record that a recommendation was made to Jeff. Davis to bestow upon Col. Lyles a commission as major-general; a brigadier's commission was offered him, but this well-deserved honor he declined. At the expiration of the war the Colonel was sent to the senate, and while a member of that body was elected to the United States Congress, but was not allowed to take his seat. During the troublous period of reconstruction his life was often threatened; his personal bravery and firmness of position seeming to aggra-

vate, especially, the bitter hostility of unscrupulous citizens. In 1868 he received a positive warning that the members of the Loyal League intended taking his life upon a certain night. Immediately removing to Memphis with his family, he awaited on the night of the intended attack the assault to be made, when at a certain hour a knock was heard, to which Mrs. Lyles responded by opening the door; immediately two ruffians brushed roughly by her, but being confronted by a gun in the hands of Col. Lyles quickly withdrew. From the time of residence in Memphis he has followed closely the practice of his profession, the result of which has placed him in a most desirable pecuniary position. He still claims Crittenden County as his home, where he has considerable property interests. His record as a public servant redounds greatly to his credit, and for the assistance which he has rendered this community, all refer to him in terms of the highest praise. Col. Lyles was married, August 13, 1848, to his present wife, Miss Jane McClung, daughter of James and Margaret McClung. Five children have blessed this union, three sons and two daughters: William L. (married and a resident of Texas), Charles L. (died in 1884), George W., Mary Bell (wife of Seth Cox) and Olive Blanche. The family are numbered among the active, influential members of the Methodist Church. As a man, Col. Lyles is possessed of sterling and irreproachable traits of character, enjoying in a high degree, the esteem and respect which those qualities create. Generous to a fault, kind and affectionate as a husband and father, he is alike admired in social and professional circles.

Benjamin Franklin McConnell (deceased) was born in Lexington, Ky., October 10, 1841, and died in this county December 16, 1887. He was a son of Francis McConnell, of Irish descent, who was the father of three sons and one daughter. The latter died in infancy and the two sons now reside in Lexington, Ky. The father departed this life in 1880, in his sixty-fourth year, at the home of his son James, in Arkansas. Benjamin F. was first married after reaching manhood to Mrs. Mary A. (Montgomery) Jones, who died in 1875, leaving one son, Lewis F., now living with his step-mother. After her death Mr. McConnell was united in matrimony to Ella G. (Goff) Rives, who was born in Memphis in September, 1850, a daughter of James D. and Phoraty W. (McCoy) Goff. Mr. Goff was a Virginian by birth, and was killed in this county in 1866 by a man named Lake. Along in the fifties he was the largest merchant in the city of Memphis and at one time was worth about $500,-000, besides having made and lost several other fortunes. He was an extensive planter in this county at the time of his death. Mrs. Goff died in Memphis in 1852. She was the mother of three sons and two daughters, of whom there are still living: George B. and Ella G. Ella G., the youngest child, was brought up and attended school in Memphis up to her sixteenth year, when she went to an educational institution at Nazareth, Ky., and remained for two years. She was first married May 18, 1870, to John G. Rives, whose birth occurred in Nashville, Tenn.; he died July 31, 1875. They were the parents of two children both now dead. He had two children by his first wife, and of these, one is still living, Florence H. (wife of James C. Hubert). Mrs. McConnell has four children by her second husband, viz.: Brodnax F., Ella G., John G. and Bennie. Mrs. McConnell resides on the farm left her by her husband which he purchased in 1882, containing 820 acres with about 200 under cultivation; this is located twelve miles south of Memphis on the Mississippi River. She rents her land for cash and it usually yields from 125 to 150 bales of cotton.

John C. Mann is practically a self-made man, having risen from a position without means to be a prosperous planter of Jasper Township. Born in North Carolina, in 1821, he is the son of John and Elizabeth (Cleves) Mann, who were also natives of North Carolina, and were planters in that State. John C. Mann attained his majority in North Carolina, and in 1844, in company with a body of immigrants, made his way into Mississippi, stopping in Marshall County, while en route, where he worked as a laborer and overseer for some time. In 1845, going to De Soto County, Miss., he remained for two years, and thence to Yazoo County, where he spent four years. Settling in Bolivar County, at a town called Lake Bolivar, he continued there and in adjoining neighborhood till he went to Arkansas, in 1879. Upon arriving in this State he located on a farm, about three and one-half miles northwest of Marion, where he still lives, having a place of 360 acres, most of which is under cultivation. Besides this farm he has tracts of land in other parts of the county, most of it also being under cultivation, from the effects of his own supervision. Mr. Mann was first married January 24, 1850, to Indiana Hamberlin, a native of Mississippi; she died September 6, 1851, leaving one child, who also died, at the age of one year, five months and four days. On July 22, 1852, Mr. Mann was married to Miss Mary M. Yarborough, of Mississippi origin, having been born in Bolivar County, October 14, 1833. Mr. and Mrs. Mann are the parents of two children: Amelia Ann (married William F. Loring, and became the mother of two children; after his death she was married to Robert A. Rolland, and by him had four children) and Mary Emma (married to James H. Mann, and lives on the home place with her parents, and is the mother of two children; one died in infancy; Eddie still lives). John C. Mann and family are prominent members in the Methodist Episcopal Church, South, and he has acted as steward in that church for a number of years. Politically a Democrat, he is one of the most prominent men in his township. He came here without a dollar, and by his own hard work, amassed a fortune of $15,000, which he lost during the late war; but by good management, so characteristic of him, he has made what he now has—one of the finest farms in Crittenden County, containing all the latest improvements, among which is a large gin, placed there in 1881. He and his family are good Christian people, and are ornaments to the society in which they move.

Archibald C. May deserves mention as a leading farmer and stock raiser of Tyronza Township, Crittenden County. He was born in St. Francis County, Ark., March 1, 1843, as the son of Archibald May, whose birth occurred in North Carolina in 1808, he dying in St. Francis County in 1854.

His parents immigrated from North Carolina to Arkansas when he was a boy, and were among the first settlers of St. Francis County. They came to this State on sleds when Memphis had but one store. The father of the subject of this sketch was married to Miss May Casbeer, of Tennessee, the daughter of Thomas Casbeer, who moved from Tennessee to St. Francis County, Ark., with all his worldly possessions on horseback; he was one of the earliest pioneers of that county. Archibald C. May, the sixth child of a family of nine children, of whom four are still living, was reared in St. Francis County, there receiving his education in the common schools. Moving to Cross County he was married in 1863, his wife being formerly Miss Mollie Pigram, who was born in Tennessee, January 2, 1844. She died December 1, 1884, being the mother of five children, of whom the following three are still living: Archibald B., Joseph M. and Berry P. Mr. May was married to Ida Pickett, July 10, 1886. By this union two children have been born, Jimanna and an infant unnamed. Mr. May has lived in Crittenden County since 1877, and has a farm of 200 acres, with twenty acres in cultivation, located in the Tyronza River bottoms. He enlisted in the Confederate army June 16, 1862, in McGee's company, and served very efficiently till December 19, 1862, when he was accidentally shot in the shoulder and discharged on account of his disability. He was constable in his township in St. Francis County for four years. Politically, he has been a Democrat since casting his first vote, which was for Seymour.

G. F. Morris, a descendant of the well-known pioneer settlers of this county, whose name he bears, was born in 1857, and is the oldest of a family of three children born to the union of C. F. and Mississippi H. (Fogleman) Morris. His maternal grandfather, G. S. Fogleman, came to this county in a keel-boat from Ohio, about 1824, when land that is now worth from $6 to $8 per acre could have been purchased for ten cents. After locating here he followed the occupation of a wood chopper, and, not being able to buy a team, he and his wife carried the wood on their backs to the boat landing.

After laboring in this manner for some time he bought a team, and from such an humble start was enabled before long to hire hands and contract on a larger scale, and he finally commenced buying negroes, at the time of his death owning sixty-five negro men besides a number of women and children. He was also the owner of twenty-one miles front on the Mississippi River, consisting of over 20,000 acres. He died in 1865 and his wife in 1857 or 1858. C. F. Morris and wife were married in 1856, at Fogleman's Landing, on board the steamer Kate Frisbey. Mr. Morris, at that time, was a steamboat man at Memphis, Tenn. His father, W. B. Morris, and grandfather were among the early settlers of Sumner County, Tenn., and were manufacturers of paper. W. B. Morris moved to Memphis when it was a village of only a few hundred inhabitants, and engaged in the mercantile business, remaining there till his death. His son, C. F. Morris, was the first steamboat agent at Memphis, and was clerk on the first boat built at that place, which was run in the Memphis and White River trade. Mr. Morris followed steamboating for twenty years, discontinuing it just before the commencement of the late civil strife. After the war he engaged in farming, his wife having inherited about 17,000 acres of land. He also followed the wood business till the boats began to burn coal. Mr. and Mrs. Morris were the parents of four children of whom two are still living; they are: G. F., Calvin M. (deceased), Cynthia (deceased), Lazinka E. (wife of A. M. Morrow). G. F. Morris was reared in this county and received his education in Memphis, being married, in 1880, to Miss Mary Speck, daughter of Lawrence Speck. Mr. and Mrs. Morris have a family of two children: Oliver W. and Frank K. When the former reached the age of fourteen years he embarked in life for himself in the wood business, which he followed till 1880, then starting as a farmer. This he continued for only a short time and soon secured a position on the Phil. Allen, serving many years as pilot on this boat and the G. W. Cheek. Since leaving the river he has been occupied in the mercantile and saloon business.

W. P. Phillips (deceased), whose name occupies a substantial place in the memory of his many former acquaintances, was born in Tennessee, though reared in Alabama, having gone there when a child. He was a grandson of Col. John Phillips who fought in the War of 1812, and a son of John Phillips, a Kentuckian by birth. The subject of this sketch reached his manhood in Alabama, and there followed merchandising and farming, being very successful before the war. He was married to Miss Ann H. Stewart, also of Alabama nativity, and the daughter of William and Mary (Hogins) Stewart, originally from North Carolina. They were reared in Tennessee, where they were married, and later moved back to Alabama, where they were well-to-do farmers. The father died when Mrs. Phillips was but a little girl. She was the only daughter and remained with her parents till her marriage, which occurred in 1846. Mr. Phillips was a prominent and influential farmer and merchant, and during the war served in the commissary department till the close of the struggle, spending most of his time in Georgia. He lost very heavily in that conflict, but at its close resumed his farming and merchandising pursuits. In 1869 he moved with his family to Hale County, Ala., where he manufactured the Avery cotton-gin. He went to Memphis, Tenn., in 1873, having purchased large tracts of land in Crittenden County, Ark., in 1871, with the intention of opening a farm there, but he died before his plans were consummated. Mr. and Mrs. Phillips were the parents of four children, of whom three are yet living, namely: Mrs. Virginia Avery, Mrs. Alice Quinn and Mrs. Willie Cheatham. Minnie died of yellow fever in 1878. Mr. Phillips died December 31, 1874. He was an excellent man, a Master Mason, a firm believer in Christianity and the Bible, and was admired by all who knew him. Mrs. Phillips lived in Memphis till 1884, when she moved to Crittenden County on the land that her husband had intended to open, and where she has a good farm of 160 acres. She is an estimable Christian lady, and enjoys the universal respect of her neighbors and acquaintances.

La Fayette Pickett, by occupation a farmer and blacksmith, was born in Jefferson County, Ill., July 28, 1851, being the son of Benjamin Pickett, a native of Wayne County, Tenn., who was murdered in Ballard County, Ky., May 10, 1861. His father, James Pickett, was a Virginian by birth, and moved to Tennessee with his parents, being among the early settlers of that State. La Fayette Pickett came to Crittenden County with his mother and step-father in 1868. There were four children in the family, of whom only Mary E., besides the subject of our sketch, is living, and she is the wife of Dr. Martine. La Fayette Pickett lived in Kentucky till he was fifteen years of age, then coming to this county, where he received most of his limited education in the common schools. He was married in 1872, to Miss Sarah E. Goad, daughter of William and Amanda M. Goad, early settlers here, having located in the neighborhood in 1856. This was their home until called away by death. Mr. and Mrs. Pickett are the parents of five children: John H., Le Roy, Della, Cora and Alice. They have lived in their present place of residence, since 1881, and have 170 acres of land, with sixty acres in cultivation; upon it is an orchard of 120 trees and a blacksmith shop for his own work, in which he also does the custom work for his vicinity. Mr. Pickett is a member of the County Wheel, and is a Democrat in politics, having cast his first vote for Tilden. His wife is a member of the Methodist Episcopal Church, and is a good Christian lady. Mr. Pickett is a hard-working, industrious and enterprising citizen.

John F. Rhodes, merchant of Earle and among the substantial citizens of Tyronza Township, was born in Tipton County, Tenn., in 1862, being the first child to bless the union of J. C. and Margaret E. (Fleming) Rhodes, natives of Tennessee. J. C. Rhodes is a trader and now lives in Mississippi. He has been twice married: first to Miss Townsend, of Tennessee, by whom he was the father of seven children, only two now living, Belle (wife of J. W. Clove, of Australia, Miss.), and W. H. (who resides at Frazier, Tenn.). In 1860 Mr. Rhodes married the mother of John F., and by her has had four children, all deceased except John F. He has again been left a widower, his wife having died in 1875. He is a member of the A. F. & A. M. and R. A. John F. Rhodes was reared and educated in Tipton County, Tenn., and since 1875 has supported himself, having been cast upon the cold charity of the world at the age of twelve years. He has given himself a good business education, spending his thirteenth and fourteenth years in Texas as a farm hand, his fifteenth and sixteenth years in Tennessee at the same occupation, and his seventeenth, eighteenth and nineteenth years in Mississippi. In 1883 Mr. Rhodes came to Lee County, Ark., and entered a dry goods and grocery store at Bledsoe, where he remained for twenty months, when he commenced the grocery business at Memphis, Tenn. After one year there he returned to Bledsoe and associated himself with W. M. Taylor, buying one-third interest in the business of general merchandising. He continued with Mr. Taylor till January, 1889, when the firm dissolved, and he established his present business in April of that year, transacting $20,000 or $25,000 worth of business the past year. He runs a general country store, and has a large trade, employing two clerks besides himself. Mr. Rhodes is a pushing young man and his present business is due solely to his own efforts; he has the prospect for a bright and prosperous life.

James E. Richards, one of the oldest native citizens of Crittenden County, was born in 1856, and is the eldest child of a family of three children born to the union of W. A. and Sophroney (Gilmore) Richards, originally of South Carolina and Kentucky, respectively. When Mr. Richards came to this State there were but few roads in this part of the county, and only a few claims staked out, with from two to five acres in cultivation. People that lived here then spent most of their time hunting and rafting logs down the Tyronza River, and in raising stock. It cost nothing to raise cattle, and the timber which was rafted was close to the streams and could be had without expense, save the labor of cutting and rafting, which was mostly to New Orleans. Mr. Richards bought land and opened one of the first farms of any size in this section of the country, and devoted his time to farming and stock raising, which he continued

until his death, January 10, 1875. To himself and wife three children were born, of whom two are still living: James E. and W. A. Mrs. Richards died in 1864, and in 1866 Mr. Richards was married to Mrs. Sarah (Rose) Vernon, becoming by her the father of four children; three of these survive: Addie, Meda and Katie. After the death of Mr. Richards, Mrs. Richards was married to Thomas Eskridge, who died in 1879; she subsequently married Mr. Davis, of Mississippi County, Ark., where she still resides. Mr. Richards held the office of justice of the peace in this county for a number of years, and during the Civil War, in which he took no part. James E. Richards was reared to farm life, and at the age of eighteen years commenced life for himself (or at the time of his father's death). He engaged in the timber business for some years and was later employed in the dry goods and grocery store of C. J. Powell, at Crawfordsville. At the age of twenty-two he was married to Miss Fannie Brown, of this county, the daughter of E. D. and Della (McGee) Brown, natives of Kentucky and Arkansas, respectively, who were the parents of two children: Richard and Fannie. Mr. Brown came to this State in an early day, and died in 1874; his wife died in 1864. To Mr. and Mrs. Richards have been born six children (of whom four are still living); the following are their names in order of birth: Della (deceased), Willie (deceased), Carrie, James C. and R. E. and Arthur (twins). Mr. Richards is principally occupied with his brother in rafting logs and the farming of 100 acres on the old home place. He has the largest interest in a 196-acre tract of land, with 100 acres in cultivation, and his wife owns a farm near Crawfordsville, consisting of 109 acres, with fifty acres in cultivation. Mr. Richards is a member of Lone Star Lodge No. 375, A. F. & A. M. of Crawfordsville, and takes great interest in educational and church matters; his desire to promote educational facilities has placed him on the board of school directors for his district for a number of years.

Capt. J. G. Sands, a farmer by occupation, and a man admired by all for his untiring efforts to promote the best interests of the county in which he lives, was born in Tennessee in 1829, and was the fourth and youngest child of John and Jane (Reid) Sands, natives of Illinois. John Sands had been previously married, and had reared two children, Susan and Martha, who are now dead. When our subject was only six days old his mother died. The father then married Mrs. Betsie Pounds, who died in 1841, and after her death he again married, Miss Sarah Summers becoming his wife. This union was blessed by three children, all now deceased. Mr. Sands moved to this county in 1843, and settled here while it was almost a wilderness. He followed overseeing, and rented land for his children to cultivate; was a brave soldier in the bloody Black Hawk War, and died in 1849. When Capt. Sands was three years old his father moved to Illinois, where he lived till coming to this county. At the age of sixteen he commenced business for himself in rafting logs, together with running a store and steamboats on the Mississippi River till 1861. His store-boats were floating general stores, and three steamboats ran from Mound City to Memphis, Hatchie River to Memphis, Osceola to Memphis, and on the St. Francis River to Memphis. At one time he owned an interest in seven flat-boats and store-boats. In 1861 he enlisted in Company F, of the First Regiment, Arkansas Cavalry, which was stationed west of the Mississippi River throughout the war. Capt. Sands fought in the battle of Helena, besides a number of smaller battles and skirmishes, and was captured in 1863. His captors started with him to Alton, but at the head of Island No. 40 he jumped from the boat and escaped to his home, although he broke his thigh in the fall, after which he never did any regular service. He, with twenty-seven of his company, out of eighty-six original members, surrendered at Memphis, Tenn. At the close of the war Capt. Sands returned home, and commenced farming and land trading, and in 1867 he moved to Mound City, where he engaged in the mercantile business, which he continues to the present day. He also has about 500 acres of good land in cultivation, 300 acres of which he rents; besides this he owns 2,100 acres in all of wild and improved land, of which about 500 acres could be cultivated without draining. At the close of the war Capt. Sands' possessions were valued at $100, and in 1868, when he was again getting a start, he was robbed of his mules and cattle, and his store was rummaged, leaving him in the same condition that he was at the close of the war. By his untiring efforts, however, he has made a fortune for himself, and has gained a prominence among his fellows in Crittenden County worthy of emulation. Mr. Sands was first married to Miss Casandra James, who was the mother of four children, all of whom died while young. Mrs. Sands was an ardent member of the Methodist Episcopal Church. She died in November of 1860. Mr. Sands was the third time married to Mrs. Mattie (Wallace) Osborn, and they were the parents of only one child, who is now dead; the mother died in 1864. In 1865 he was married to Miss Mary C. West, and by her was the father of three children, of whom one is now living, Gertrude Lyon (wife of John Stevens), residing with her father. Mrs. Sands died in 1879, and in the same year the Captain was married to Mrs. Sue (Kirbie) Dennis, to whom has been born one child, deceased. Capt. Sands is a member of Lone Star Masonic Lodge of Crawfordsville, Ark. He is a Democrat in politics, and favors all public improvement and white emigration. He has ever been a leading citizen, and is foremost in every movement for the upbuilding of the locality in which he lives.

George W. Scott justly deserves his present position as one of the well-to-do farmers and stock raisers of Tyronza Township. A native of Tennessee, he was born in Madison County, January 17, 1831, and is the son of Cyrus and Cyntha (Davis) Scott, natives of New York and Connecticut, respectively. The former immigrated from New York to Tennessee and from there to Missouri, where he resided about two years, moving thence to Illinois which was his home till death. Mrs. Scott survived her husband for a few years. She was the mother of seven children, of whom George W. is the fifth. He grew to manhood in Illinois, being educated in the common schools of Madison County, and upon reaching his majority went to Goodhue County, Minn., where he engaged in farming for four years.

Then moving across the Mississippi River, he bought an interest in a saw-mill and after a short time bought his partner out, and ran the mill alone till 1862, when he enlisted in Company G of the Fifth Minnesota Infantry Regiment, serving till the close of the war. He was wounded in the battle of Corinth, May 22, 1862, by being shot in the forehead with buckshot, after which he was sent to a hospital and was occupied on detached duty most of the time afterward. He was in the battle of Pleasant Hill in 1864. He was discharged at Memphis, Tenn., and after spending about one month in Illinois, Minnesota and Wisconsin he came to Crittenden County, Ark., where he has since resided. Mr. Scott has lived at his present home since 1875; here he has a farm of 240 acres with about 120 in an excellent state of cultivation. He has in another place 640 acres, of which 140 are in cultivation. His home farm is on the Tyronza River and has upon it a good orchard and it is a fine stock farm. Mr. Scott was married in 1874 to Mrs. M. C. Thorn, who was born in St. Francis County, September 21, 1833, and had two children, a girl and a boy, by her first husband. Mr. Scott was justice of the peace for sixteen years in this township; was notary public for four years and postmaster of Blackfish postoffice for seven years. He cast his first vote for Pierce and has since been an ardent Democrat. He is one of Crittenden County's best farmers and an industrious and wide-awake man. Mrs. Scott is a sister of Archibald C. May. [See sketch.]

Capt. H. W. Sebree. Prominent among the farmers of Crittenden County, is Capt. Sebree, who was born in Kentucky, in 1817, being the son of Reuben and Jane (Watts) Sebree, natives of Virginia. Their parents were also Virginians by birth, the father of Reuben Sebree, Richard Sebree, being a very prominent and wealthy planter, who lived to be over ninety years of age, and died while our subject was a small boy. Reuben reached his majority in the Old Dominion, where he was married, and one child had been born to himself and wife, when he moved to Kentucky, and settled in Boone County. There he engaged in farming till his death. He was a well-to-do man and took an active part in the War of 1812. Some of his comrades were captains in the war, but owing to his age, he could not be admitted as a soldier. He was an old time Whig, and died in his seventy-third year, having been an upright, moral man, and well-liked, commanding the respect of all who knew him. His wife died several years afterward, being seventy-seven years of age. To this union were born six children, five sons and one daughter. All but one lived to be grown: Oner, one of the sons, fell in a well and was drowned at the age of four years. Only two of the children, Norman (an engineer living in Cincinnati) and Capt. H. W. (the fourth child) survive. At the age of twenty years, the latter went on the Hartford City, a towboat running between Pittsburg and New Orleans, of which he soon afterward became pilot, then captain, and the principal owner. He owned the Star, Argus, Rockford and several other boats, and was on the river from 1859 to 1876, holding positions on various boats, and had three boats destroyed during the Civil War, the Queen of Memphis, Hartford and Star. Purchasing a fruit farm in Crittenden County, he lived at Mound City for a short time, when he moved to his farm on which he has since made his home. Here he has 350 acres of good land under cultivation, though only seventy-five were improved when he bought the place; he owns other lands that are unimproved. While living in Kentucky, he took an active part in political matters, and represented Boone County in the legislature, in 1856, also holding the office of sheriff, magistrate and several minor offices. He was a Whig till the war, and then a Democrat, but now gives his whole attention to his farms. Capt. Sebree was married to Elizabeth Wingate, a native of Kentucky, and a daughter of William Wingate, a wealthy planter of Boone County, who lived to be very old. Mrs. Sebree died November 4, 1888, in her sixty-ninth year. She was a good Christian lady, and one of the best women that the world has ever produced. She was the mother of eight children, the following two of whom are still living: Sarah J. (the wife of Moses Corey, living in Pennsylvania) and Katy Cole (wife of J. W. Cole, who lives on the home place with her parents; they

have one son, Howard W.). Mr. Sebree has been
a very active, and is yet one of the most energetic
men in the county. He is wide awake and pushing, and has done much toward the advancement
of the locality in which he lives.

Otto Seyppel, a planter and merchant of Lucas
Township, was born in Germany June 18, 1854,
being the son of Achilles and Mina (Jacobs) Seyppel, also natives of Germany. The father was a
magistrate by profession and died in his native
land in March, 1860. Mrs. Seyppel was born in
Germany about 1838 and died in Memphis in 1878,
of yellow fever. She and her husband were the
parents of two children: Alexander (who died of
yellow fever at Holly Springs, Miss., in 1878) and
Otto. Our subject, the second child, was raised
in his native land till he was eleven years of age,
and there received most of his education. He
came with his mother to this country, and after
spending a few months in New York went to Memphis, Tenn., in 1865, living with the mother's
brother till sixteen years old, when he commenced
life for himself in the wood-yard business, which
he continued for one year. He then entered a
grocery store as a clerk, remained so occupied for
two years, when he clerked for a coal firm for three
years, and after leaving this firm was manager of
the McCormick Ice Company of Memphis for four
years. He then invested in steamboat stock and
run a tow-boat from Memphis to New Orleans for
eight months. While he was with the McCormick
Ice Company he was married, February 13, 1878,
to Mrs. Minnie (McCue) Burgett, who was born in
Memphis September 25, 1854, being the daughter
of John and Mary (McWilliams) McCue. Her first
husband was waylaid and killed after they had
been married but three weeks. Mr. Seyppel is a
member of Germania Lodge No. 369, K. of H., of
Memphis, and of the Knights of Pythias Lodge of
the same city, as well as the German Bruder Bund
Lodge of Memphis. He is an extensive farmer
and owns 350 acres of land with 200 in a good
state of cultivation, on which he raises annually
from eighty to 100 bales of cotton. This farm is
located twenty-nine miles south of Memphis and
sixty miles north of Helena, and is known as the

Burgett farm. He is postmaster of Seyppel postoffice, which was established in 1888. Mrs. Seyppel's father, Mr. McCue, was born in Stark
County, Ohio, and is now living in California. He
was married to Miss Mary McWilliams, who was
born near Tuscumbia, Ala., in 1833, and died in
Hernando, De Soto County, Miss., in 1871. Minnie was the only child born to this union. She
was reared in Memphis till fifteen years of age
and received most of her education in that city.
At the age of fifteen she went with her mother to
Hernando, Miss., where she remained until her
marriage, in 1873, to Peter M. Burgett, who was
born on the farm on which Mr. Seyppel now lives.
He was a large planter and left a farm of 2,800
acres, situated on the Mississippi River, to his wife.
His father, Isaac Burgett, settled the farm where
our subject now resides, and was one of the early
settlers in this section. He was born in Perry
County, Mo., November 20, 1801, and died in this
county December 18, 1865, at time of his death
being the county's oldest citizen. He was a man
of sterling good sense, great enterprise and un-
bending integrity, and at his death left a very
large estate. He had six children, viz.: John C.,
Peter M., William L., Isaac W., Henry E., Bettie
B. and Nannie P.

Albert Sinclair, a planter and carpenter of Jasper Township, and one of its oldest and most respected citizens, was born in Rutherford County,
Tenn., in 1833. His parents having died while he
was but an infant, he was reared by James and
Rachel Cunningham, farmers, who came to Arkansas in 1844, and settled near Marion, where
they lived till their death. Mr. Cunningham was
a soldier in the War of 1812. Mr. Sinclair remained with this family until 1851, when he commenced life for himself as a laborer, and in 1859
was married, and leased a farm, on which he lived
till after the war. At the commencement of the
Civil War he joined the Confederate army, and
hired a substitute, who served in his stead for one
year, after which he took his place and served in
Dobbins' regiment till the close of the war. He
was taken prisoner below Marion, Ark., and kept
at Hope Field for a time, when he made his escape

and returned to his company. After the close of hostilities he returned to his farm work, and in 1866 purchased land near Marion, on which he lived till 1882, when he moved to a farm that he had bought in 1874. This consists of 160 acres of splendid land, with a part under cultivation, upon which he has a good residence, gin and all modern improvements. He has occasionally worked at his trade, since the war, and has built several horse-power gins, and some of the fine residences that adorn this portion of the country. His possessions are wholly the result of his own labors, and he can say without boasting that he is a self-made man, for he commenced with nothing, and to-day is in very comfortable circumstances. His first wife was Mrs. Catherine M. (Lloyd) Garrett, who was born and reared in this county; they were the parents of three children, all girls, two of whom died, three hours apart, while small. The oldest daughter, Sarah C., is the widow of James R. Keel, and has two children, Floyd Atwilda and James A. L. Mrs. Sinclair was a member of the Methodist Episcopal Church, and died in 1887, at the age of fifty years. After her death Mr. Sinclair was married to Fannie E. Everton, who was born in Mississippi, and came to this State in 1887. Mr. Sinclair and his daughter are members of the Methodist Episcopal Church. He is a Democrat in politics, and takes great interest in schools, churches, and in fact anything that will increase the morality and the business interests and prosperity of the county in which he lives.

J. F. Smith. The lives of noble men who have built up and fostered the interests of Arkansas are always read with pleasure, not only by their friends, but by a grateful people, who have watched its industrial, agricultural and moral development from year to year under the skillful management of those men who had the ingenuity and enterprise to cultivate its resources. Mr. Smith was born in Tennessee in the year 1834, and was the only child of William and Catherine (Mc-Crimmon) Smith. His parents died when he was young, and at the age of seventeen he took his place in the world's great struggle and sought to carve for himself a name in the temple of fame.

His first venture was to find employment, which he succeeded in obtaining in a store near his native place, remaining here until the outbreak of the Civil War. He responded promptly to the call of his country and began to make preparations to enlist, and at the option of the company which was being formed in the town of his birth, was elected to the rank of first lieutenant, and at the organization of the regiment (Thirty-first Tennessee Infantry) was appointed major. During his war career he took part in the battles of Columbus (Ky.), Fort Pillow, Corinth (Miss.), Harrisburg (Miss.), and several others. When the army was reorganized he was detached, but immediately formed a company of cavalry and was elected colonel of the Second Mississippi Cavalry, to which the company had allied themselves. In this capacity Col. Smith remained until the end of the war, fighting for the cause he so gloriously undertook, with all his heart and soul, even up to the final bitter moment when defeat at last crushed his hopes and the stars and bars of the Confederacy lay trampled in the dust. In 1866 Col. Smith came to Arkansas and located at Marion. Here he purchased a small farm of thirty-four acres, from which he cleared the timber and put it under cultivation, and now, what better evidence of his determined will and tireless energy can be found than to look over his broad acres, numbering over 2,000, and view with admiration the 800 that he has placed under cultivation. Col. Smith was married in 1857 to Miss Paralee Derryberry, but death entered his home in February, 1861, and took from it his estimable wife, leaving one son, Lee, who resides at Marion and is engaged in farming. His second marriage occurred in 1863 to Miss Martha J. Gidden, by whom he has had five children: Emma (now the wife of Thomas Koser), Willie S., Frank G., Mary G. and Charles Edgar. Col. Smith's plantation is without doubt one of the finest in Crittenden County, and the most of it he has placed under cultivation himself. In appearance he is a typical Southerner, of a tall and commanding figure, dark complexion, with prominent features and an eye that is piercing in its glance, and withal a courteous gentleman. As an army officer, Col. Smith stands without a peer in his rank, as his splendid record through the dark days of rebellion will show, when his courage and gallantry commanded the admiration of both friend and foe. Possessed in a strong degree with journalistic qualities, Col. Smith saw the need of a paper in Crittenden County, and was one of the leading promoters of the Marion Reform, which advocates those missions that will unquestionably be beneficial to both white and colored citizens. He held the office of mayor of Marion and during his administration made many improvements in the town, especially in laying the sidewalks, and was also one of the leading spirits in building schools for both white and colored children and the Methodist Church in Marion. He was also one of the principal advocates of prohibition in Marion, which was secured in 1885. During 1889 Col. Smith was levee commissioner, and an earnest advocate of levee protection. In his dealings with tenants on his plantation he is scrupulously exact that they shall have to the last penny their share, and as an evidence of the esteem in which he is held, some of his tenants have been with him since the war. In politics Col. Smith is one of the prominent men of his county, and in 1874 was sent to the State legislature. He is a director of the Memphis bridge now being built from a point in this county to Memphis, and in other affairs that tend to push forward the progress of Crittenden County he is always ready and generous with his assistance in every way possible. His name is an authority on many matters of public interest and he holds a place in the hearts of his fellow-citizens that will never be banished.

J. L. Smith could hardly be other than one of the leading and prosperous citizens of Crittenden County, because he is a son of Col. J. F. Smith, a worthy resident of this community. Born in McNairy County, Tenn., in 1863, he lived in that State till twelve years of age, when he came to Arkansas with his parents and has since remained here. Most of his education was received in the common schools, and in 1881 he commenced business for himself as a merchant at Marion, and in 1884 began farming on the island where he now lives. He was married to Miss Lillian Brooks, who was born in Tipton County, Tenn., in 1888, the daughter of James and Matilda Brooks, the father being deceased, but the mother is still living. To this young couple has been born one child, named Brooks Franklin. Mrs. Smith is a member of the Methodist Episcopal Church. Mr. Smith cultivates about 550 acres of land. Politically he is a Democrat, and is a young man of rare abilities. At the rate in which he has so far progressed he will have amassed a large fortune before he passes out of his prime.

J. W. Stewart is a shining light in and a credit to the medical fraternity. A native of Tennessee, his birth occurred in 1867, he being the fourth in a family of five children born to James R. and Ellen J. (Thomas) Stewart, natives of Tennessee and Mississippi, respectively. James R. Stewart was a merchant of Shelby Depot, now Brunswick, Tenn., and for many years was identified with prominent business houses of that place. Previous to his mercantile career he engaged in farming in the same county, and was quite successful. His death, in 1878, was sincerely mourned by his numerous friends and acquaintances. Mrs. Stewart is now residing in Brunswick, Tenn., with her daughter, Addah, the wife of E. E. Beaty; E. N. also resides in Brunswick; and besides these children there are Ana F., James W. (subject) and Lulla. Mr. and Mrs. Stewart are of English descent. Mrs. Stewart traces her ancestry back to the Lords of England. Her maternal Grandfather McCullough was a lord of no slight prominence in England. James W. Stewart was reared and educated in Shelby County, Tenn., until eighteen years of age, leaving home at that time to enter the Memphis Medical Hospital and College. He graduated from that institution in 1887, commencing his practice the same year in this county. His modest little sign would scarcely have attracted the passer-by, but his reputation as a physician and surgeon preceded him, as his brilliant college career and the commendation from the faculty were his passport to his present lucrative practice. His success is truly phenomenal, and would compare favorably with others who have practiced for years. Dr. Stewart purchased an interest in the firm of Williford &

Whitaker, in 1889, that establishment now being known as Stewart & Co. The business amounts to $8,000 annually, and is rapidly increasing.

Mrs. Margie Strong. Among the enterprising and extensive farmers and fruit growers of Crittenden County will appear the name of Mrs. Strong, who is the wife of J. L. Strong, and daughter of William and Elizabeth (Barton) Dickson, all of Alabama. Mr. Dickson was one of the prominent men of Alabama before the late war and deeply interested in the progress and prosperity of this State. He was connected with Brinkley, Greenlaw, Tate and others, the original projectors of the Memphis & Little Rock Railroad, and with these gentlemen he purchased large tracts of land in this and adjoining counties, doing as much or more to advance the interest of the county and State in which he lived than any other man; and he is remembered with the kindest esteem for the industries that he put on foot, and which will live as monuments to his public-spirited efforts. Among the finest and most productive of the many farms owned by Mr. Dickson is the one upon which his daughter now lives and does business. Mrs. Strong was married to J. L. Strong in 1863 and in 1867 they moved to Tulare County, Cal., where they remained for thirteen years. Mrs. Strong has one brother, Barton, residing at Dickson, Ala., on the old homestead and one sister, Loutie, now Mrs. T. H. Ward, of Memphis, Tenn. Mrs. Strong's farm consists of 1,200 acres of land, of which there are 500 acres in cultivation. She is greatly interested in the culture of fruit, especially peaches and pears, of the former of which she has an orchard of fifty acres and an extensive orchard of the latter. From a statement by Mrs. Strong concerning the profits of fruit culture on Holly Grove farm, as her place is called, valuable information is gained. Besides the peaches and pears spoken of she has quite an extensive apple orchard, but does not find this branch of business as profitable as peaches, which she says can be grown more successfully here than in any other country in which she has been, with the exception, perhaps, of California. The profits of peach culture are certain and large. The orchards of Holly Grove

farm have been bearing only three years. The net receipts for the first year were $159.34 per acre, the second year $103 per acre and the third year $136 per acre. Mrs. Strong gives valuable facts from her experience as to the relative benefits of budded and seedling trees. She finds the "Beatrice" the most profitable early peach on account of its uniform size and freedom from rot; also that all budded fruit bears fitfully, some years bearing heavy crops and some light; that they are also subject to rot. Her experience demonstrates seedling fruit to produce the best returns, because they are healthier and bear uniform crops, gradually increase and do not rot. The profits from seedling trees in 1889 was $232.36 per acre after deducting every conceivable expense. Mrs. Strong is the largest individual shipper to the Memphis markets and when the people there want the choicest fruit they seek out the package that bears the label "Holly Grove Farm." She is also a large shipper to the New Orleans market. The trees are grown and now ready to extend her peach orchard to 100 acres and the pear orchard to ten acres. She finds pear culture profitable also. She plants only the Leconte and Keiffer pear and they net $170 to $400 per acre. Mrs. Strong has originated twenty-four varieties of peaches on her farms and she will plant the entire increase with these, with the exception of the "Early Crawfords." She deserves the greatest praise for the large business which has sprung up under her own supervision. If one-half the men were as enterprising and energetic the world would be enriched and improved many fold.

A. R. Strong, one of Crittenden County's young men of note, and a merchant at Crawfordsville, is a native of Louisiana, born in 1859, and the son of A. R. and Elizabeth (Shaw) Strong, originally from New Jersey and Louisiana, respectively. The father went South when a young man and commenced dealing in timber, having gone South for his health from New York, where he had been keeping books. At the time of his death, which occurred in December, 1858, he had been a farmer for ten years. Three months after his death his wife gave birth to A. R. Strong, our subject, who attained his majority in Louisiana, where he received his education in the common-schools. In 1876 he commenced business for himself on a farm in Mississippi, and continued for two years, returning to Louisiana, and taking up the same occupation there. Since 1881 he has been occupied in merchandising, going into business for himself in 1886, at Kilbourne, La., and following it till he came to Arkansas in January, 1889. He is enjoying a substantial trade at Crawfordsville, aggregating upward of $15,000 the past year, besides having a large business at his old place in Louisiana. Mr. Strong was married to Miss Mary Hill, a native of Chicot County, Ark.; they are the parents of three children: Merrietta, Julia and Creola. Mr. and Mrs. Strong are members of the Baptist Church, and he belongs to the K. of H. of this place. Mr. Strong's short acquaintance in this county has made him many warm friends, who will share with him in the success which is inevitable if he pursues his present course.

George T. Stull, M. D. Prominent among the citizens and the well-read and educated men of Crittenden County appears the name of Dr. Stull, who was born at Nashville, Tenn., in 1820. He is the son of Samuel and Rachel (Mathias) Stull. The grandfather, Zachariah Stull, was one of three brothers, of German descent, that came from Maryland, being among the first settlers of Marengo when Nashville was but a stockade, in about 1780. Soon after this two of the brothers were killed by the Indians. Zachariah Stull was an industrious farmer, and died near the place of his settlement, leaving two children: Samuel and George; the former of whom died in 1826, the latter in 1851. These two sons followed farming for an occupation, and Samuel was a surveyor and did considerable work on the government surveys of Alabama and Tennessee. He was a great lover of home, and was devoted to his fireside. His motto was, "Pay as you go," to which he adhered very rigidly and never went in debt. He was strict, but honest in all his dealings, and it is said that if he owed a dime he was not easy till it was paid. The mother was connected with the Cumberland Presbyterian Church, and was a devoted Christian. She died

in 1844, leaving four children, two sons and two daughters: Isaiah (the youngest of the children, was killed at the battle of Atlanta), Mrs. Charlotte Scott (died at Nashville, in the winter of 1888), Mrs. Elizabeth Ledbetter (died at Nashville, in 1871), George T. Stull (the subject of this sketch) is the oldest of the family and is the only male member now living. He grew to manhood in Tennessee, where he graduated from the Nashville University, in 1842, and later cultivated a farm from the time of his graduation till 1848, when he went to the Philadelphia Medical College. After his graduation from this college he practiced in New Orleans for four years. Going from New Orleans to Fayette County, Tenn., he gave his attention to the profession till the close of the late war, when he moved to Memphis, where he engaged in buying notes, bonds, building, etc.; he remained in that city till 1883, then came to Crittenden County, Ark., and settled on the place where he now lives, adjoining Crawfordsville. Dr. Stull was first married to Elizabeth Williams, of New Orleans, who died in Fayette County, Tenn., on New Year's day of 1856, leaving one child, a girl, now deceased. In 1861 the Doctor was married to Sally Goode, of Giles County, Tenn., who died in 1870, leaving one daughter, Parmelia G., now the wife of W. S. Graham, of Forrest City, Ark., where he is engaged in general merchandising. Dr. Stull was married to his present wife, Mrs. Addie B. Pamphlin, of Memphis, Tenn., in 1880. He has entirely given up his profession since moving to Memphis, and devotes his time to his land, which he rents. He is a man of extensive travels, and is one of the best read men in the county. He spends his winters in the South and his summers in the North. He takes great interest in his gardens, orchards and vineyards.

Wilsie W. Swepston, a leading planter and ginner of Crawfordsville, was born February 9, 1848, in Vinton, Ohio, and is the son of John and Asenath (Darby) Swepston, originally of Virginia and North Carolina, respectfully. They came to Arkansas April 1, 1859, when our subject was eleven years old, and located at the Fifteen-mile Bayou in this county. Here the father ran a saw and grist-mill, and was engaged in that business at intervals till 1868, when he was elected county clerk, and held this office for four years, and officiated in the same capacity several times afterward, and was holding the office of county sheriff at the time of his death. He took an active part in political matters in Ohio, as well as in Arkansas. He was not in favor of the secession of the States, so did not participate in the war. He filled some position of responsibility and trust most of the time after the reconstruction till his death; he was a conservative Republican in politics. His wife worshiped with the Christian Church, to which she belonged, and died in 1868, being the mother of ten children, of whom seven lived to be grown and six are still living. Wilsie W. Swepston is the second son, and attained his majority in this county, where he commenced life for himself by raising a crop on shares, on the Donegan Island, and in 1877, opened a general store at Marion and remained in this business for two years, when he came to Crawfordsville and followed merchandising till 1882. He has since been occupied in cultivating his farms, of which he has several, all in a good state of cultivation. In 1888 he built a gin on the Bald Knob Railroad, with the capacity of twenty-five bales per day, which is the largest and best equiped custom gin in the county; he uses the Thomas press and the Sailor system of elevating. He also has plenty of storage-room for cotton and cotton seed in connection with his gin. He was elected justice of the peace in 1888, getting every vote in his township, and has held this office for two years, and has never paid any attention to politics, but has given his time exclusively to his farms and gin. Mr. Swepston was first married in 1880 to Miss Ida H. Haley, of Memphis, Tenn., who died the same year. In October, 1882, he was again married to Mary W. Denton, a native of this county. The fruits of this marriage were four children: Edith, Pierre, Lee St. Clair and Io. Mr. Swepston is a very energetic worker in educational matters, and has been a live and active member of the school board for the past nine years, being elected on this board when the town had neither funds nor buildings, and by close and strict adherance to business they now have two nice

school buildings, and a good corps of teachers. He is a member of the A. F. & A. M., and the K. of H. He always votes the straight Democratic ticket and is opposed to the sale of intoxicating liquors.

Lafayette Swoope, M. D., needs no formal introduction to the many readers of this volume, but in compiling the biographies of the principal citizens of Crittenden County, his name should not be omitted. Born in Augusta County, Va., in 1835, he is the son of Washington and Eliza (Trent) Swoope, natives of Virginia. Washington Swoope was a prosperous farmer, and came from one of the F. F. V's. He and his wife reared a family of nine children, seven of whom are now living: Dr. W. M. (living at Buckingham Court House, Va.), Mary M. (wife of Col. Forbes, of Virginia), Eliza M. (Mrs. William Carr), Sarah A. (Mrs. Col. G. W. Hull, of Virginia), Mariah A. (wife of Gen. Edward C. Cornington, residing in Virginia), Francis M., Bowling R. and Lafayette. Mr. Swoope died in 1870 and his wife in 1873. Lafayette was educated in the schools of Virginia, and at the age of eleven years entered the high school of Stanton, Va., attending when fourteen years old the high school at Lexington, Va. When fifteen he took a course at the Baptist College, at Richmond, Va., and about four years later became a student of the University of Virginia, at Charlottesville. He then took up the study of medicine, and subsequently entered the Richmond Medical College, from which he was graduated with honors. He embarked upon the prosecution of his chosen profession at Richmond, and at the time of his removal to Courtland, Ala., in 1860, had built up a comfortable practice. After one year's residence in Courtland, he moved to De Soto County, Miss., and located where Star Landing now is, then called Old De Soto Front. In 1861 Dr. Swoope joined the Confederate service, as lieutenant in Company I, Sixteenth Alabama Regiment (Wood's Brigade). After the battle of Mills Springs he was promoted to a captaincy, participating in the battles of Shiloh, Perryville, Murfreesboro and numerous engagements of minor importance. He received his discharge at the battle of Murfreesboro, on account of inability to serve, caused by exposure and a wound received at Shiloh. Returning to Virginia, he remained out of the army twelve months, at the end of which time his health had sufficiently improved to admit of his serving again, so he entered the cavalry, and continued on the field until 1863. In August, 1863, he was captured on the Weldon Railroad, near the Yellow Tavern, and remained in prison at Point Lookout, Md., until the final surrender. After receiving his parole he returned to Virginia, but on Christmas day, 1865, started up Mississippi, and settled in De Soto County, resuming the practice which he had established previous to the war. In 1882 Dr. Swoope came to Crittenden County, Ark., and purchased a quantity of wild land, and at this time has about 150 acres improved, on which he produces annually about forty-five bales of cotton. He also devotes a large portion of his farm to the raising of corn and peas, owning besides this farm the southeast quarter of Section 5, which is wild land. Dr. Swoope in addition to being a prominent physician is very popular as a citizen. He is courteous, obliging, and one of the shining lights of society, and while not taking any active part in the politics of the day, is a strong supporter of the Democratic party and a liberal contributor and friend to all laudable enterprises.

Dr. James C. Throgmorton, a practicing physician of Tyronza Township, living near Earle, was born in Wayne County, Tenn., August 30, 1841, and is the son of Edward B. Throgmorton, who first saw the light in Halifax County, Va., in 1811, and died in this county, June 30, 1884. His parents were Robert and Mrs. (Crittendon) Throgmorton, they moving from Virginia to North Carolina when Edward B. was a child, and remaining there till he was twelve years old. Then they went to Bedford County, Tenn., and died there at a very old age. The Throgmortons are of English descent, three brothers having first come to this country from England, and two of them settled west and one east of Blue Ridge, Va. Edward B. Throgmorton was married in Bedford County, Tenn., to Patience West Jones, born in Tennessee in 1812, and is now living in Wayne County. Her parents were natives of North Carolina, and were of Irish origin. She is the mother of eight children,

all of whom lived to be grown, and three daughters and the subject of this sketch are still living. Dr. James C. Throgmorton was brought up in Wayne County, Tenn., and received his literary education at the Clifton Masonic Academy. He began reading medicine in 1866, under Dr. Cicero Buchanan, at Waynesboro, Wayne County, and was with him until 1869, when he commenced practicing the same year. In July, 1872, he came near where he now lives, and was married March 6, 1873, to Miss Mary E. Pickett, originally of Jefferson County, Ill. In 1874 the Doctor moved to Southern Illinois, practiced there for about two years, and then returned to Crawfordsville, this county. To himself and wife have been born six children: Eudora, Ada, Clifford, Hayden, Jimmie C. and Walter E. In the fall of 1862 Dr. Throgmorton enlisted in Company G of the Seventh Tennessee Regiment, Confederate States Army, as a private; was captured at Fort Donelson and taken to Paducah, Ky., and made his escape from the Campbell Hotel on the night of April 6, while the battle of Shiloh was in progress. He then went to Corinth and again joined the command. He was in the Farmington fight, also the engagements at Jackson Lane, Meridian Station, Corinth, Spring Hill and Franklin, and was on the ground when Gen. Vandorn was killed; also taking part in many skirmishes of less note. He has been a stanch Democrat since casting his first vote, which was for Horace Greeley. He is a Master Mason and belongs to Lodge No. 375, at Crawfordsville, of which he has been Worshipful Master for four years. Dr. Throgmorton is a believer in Universalism, and is a good citizen. He is a well-to-do man and commands a practice that occupies his undivided attention.

Emmett B. Tolleson, a substantial planter and merchant of Lucas Township, whose postoffice is at Pinckney, is a native of this State, born at Helena, March 14, 1842, and is the son of William P. Tolleson, originally from Spartansburg, S. C., who died about 1845. He immigrated from South Carolina to Helena, Ark., near the year 1830, and was one of the early settlers of that portion of the State. A lawyer by profession and circuit judge of the Helena judicial district for several terms, he was an influential citizen, and as a Democrat in politics, was one of the electors of Polk and Dallas. He was married in Helena in 1836 to Miss Nancy Elliot Williams (then the widow West) who was born in Lexington, Ky., in 1809. She died in her native town in 1885, being the mother of one child by Mr. West and three by Mr. Tolleson: W. P. (deceased), Margaret W. McConnell (who resides at Lexington, Ky.) and Emmett B. The latter, the youngest child, grew up in Phillips County, Ark., receiving his education at the private schools of Helena. He lived with his mother till he was grown and then commenced for himself as a planter in the county where he now lives. He was married in Memphis, Tenn., to Miss Annie Elise Harris, September 29, 1874. Miss Harris was born in this county in 1853 and is a daughter of James Harris, of Columbia, Tenn. He was for a time book-keeper in Memphis and afterward became an extensive planter in Arkansas. His wife was Martha Arnold of Tennessee origin, where she died. Her father, Gen. William Arnold, was a graduate of West Point and a brigadier-general in the United States army, and died in Texas about 1836, owning vast landed estates. To Mr. and Mrs. Tolleson have been born five children, all living except one, viz: Martha E., Annie Imogene, Emmett B. and Marguerite A. Mr. and Mrs. Tolleson own two plantations, 675 acres of good land, with 350 in a fine state of cultivation, upon which are usually raised 200 bales of cotton. These are superior farms, located on the Mississippi River sixty miles north of Helena and thirty miles south of Memphis, and upon one Mr. Tolleson has resided since 1852. In 1861 he joined the Confederate army, enlisting in Company E of the Third Arkansas Cavalry. He served till near the close of the war and participated in the following noted battles: Jonesboro, Ga., Chickamauga and was with Longstreet at Knoxville. He was captured at Island No. 40, near Memphis, in January, 1865, and was immediately paroled, returning to his home. He is a stanch Democrat and cast his first vote for Seymour. Mr. and Mrs. Tolleson are members of the Episcopal Church and are highly respected.

William Vance, Jr. This much-esteemed and influential citizen is one of the most distinguished and prominent residents of West Memphis, and is of Irish birth. Born in Belfast, Ireland, in 1823, he is the son of William and Mary (Small) Vance, also of Ireland nativity, who came to the United States in 1827 or 1828, locating in New Orleans. He was a linen draper and bleacher, and lived in New Orleans till 1840, then moving back to Belfast, where he died. William Vance, Jr., was left at Belfast to be educated, after which he emigrated to New Orleans in the latter part of 1838, and commenced clerking in a wholesale grocery house. He remained with this firm for several years, then left them, and for five years kept books for one of the largest commission cotton houses in New Orleans. Locating at Memphis he was similarly occupied for the Planters' Bank a little more than a year. He then crossed the river and settled on and commenced farming his father-in-law's farm until 1856, when, the latter having died, he was made executor of the estate, and still remains as such. Mr. Vance purchased over 600 acres of land in what is now known as West Memphis, in 1869, and laid out the town of that name in 1870. He married Frances Winchester, a native of Tennessee, who died in 1867 at the age of forty years. To this union were born ten children, of whom the following seven are still living, viz.: Robert, Hopefield, Agnes (who is the wife of H. L. Bugg), Frank E., May (who is the wife of John C. Dunlap), Arthur and Stonewall J. The deceased are Lucy (wife of C. P. Williams, died in 1869, leaving two children, who died soon afterward); William (who died at the age of two years), and one infant unnamed. All the children are living in West Memphis except Agnes, who lives in Black Rock, Ark., and Arthur, in Memphis, Tenn. Robert and Hopefield were educated in Toronto, Canada; his three daughters were educated in Memphis, Tenn., and the other son, at home. The entire family are adherents to the Presbyterian Church, but at present are not members. Mr. Vance has received several prominent appointments from the Governor, among which are those of assessor, auditor, and circuit court clerk, all since the war. Politically, he was an old line Whig before the civil strife, but since then he has voted for the best man. In 1871 he made a general division of his property among his children, and in 1881 presented them with deeds for the same. Hopefield Vance is married to Bettie Sweeney, a native of Virginia, and is the father of three children: Leslie, Ralph and Hope. Robert Vance is married to Miss Lula Franklin, a native of Tennessee, and has four children: Walter, Robert, Nellie and Lottie.

R. N. Wallace, prominently identified with the mercantile affairs of Bartonville, was born in Weakley County, Tenn., in 1840, being the son of James Wallace, originally from Barren County, Ky., who came to Tennessee about 1820 with his parents when eight years of age. He grew to manhood in Weakley County, and engaged in farming there, becoming married to Miss Mary E. Goldsby, a Kentuckian by birth, who went to Tennessee with her parents in 1852 when she was a child. After they were married Mr. and Mrs. Wallace moved back to their native State, and lived there till their death. They were both members of the Baptist Church, and the parents of three sons and three daughters, of whom three sons and one daughter lived to be grown. J. G. Wallace, the youngest of the children, was reared by his grandfather, and is now a practicing lawyer in Russellville, Ark. R. N. Wallace, the oldest son, was left on his own resources at the age of sixteen, his father having died at that time, and he came to Arkansas in 1856, and to Crittenden County in 1859, where he has since lived. During his stay here he has spent two years in Tennessee attending school, and after his return he was occupied in teaching. At the breaking out of the late war he enlisted with the Crittenden County Rangers, Joe Earl's company, and later joined the Second and Third Arkansas as a private. He was captured near Dalton, Ga., in 1864, and taken to Camp Chase, Ohio, from which he was paroled after being kept for five months. Returning to his command he was again taken prisoner the day before the surrender of Joseph E. Johnston, and was paroled from Chester Court House, S. C., and came back home on horseback. After his arrival he resumed farm-

28

ing till 1869, when he entered the firm of R. C. Wallace & Co., and opened the first store at Crawfordsville. A. F. Crawford, a member of the above firm, was the first postmaster at Crawfordsville, in 1870, the first postoffice established west of Marion. Mr. Wallace remained with this company for two years, when they sold to Anderson & Allen. He then carried on farming till the spring of 1887, when he opened and conducted a store for one year at Needmore, and after going out of business at Needmore, embarked in merchandising at Bartonville, where he continued till October, 1889. Then he sold to H. F. Avery, and has since given his attention to his farm which consists of 300 acres under cultivation, besides small tracts of wild land. Mr. Wallace was married to Mrs. Sarah A. Chambers, nee Graham, daughter of H. Graham, one of the old settlers in this county. Mrs. Graham is still living, and is seventy-nine years of age. Mrs. Wallace died in January, 1888. She was an active and earnest member of the Methodist Episcopal Church, and was the mother of one child, John G., who was born August 26, 1874. Mr. Wallace is a Master Mason, and stands high among the prominent citizens of Crittenden County.

Charles A. Walter, a farmer and stock raiser of Fogleman Township, is a native of Germany, born March 19, 1847, and is the fourth child of a family of seven children born to the union of Frederick and Caroline (Wittersburg) Walter, both born in Germany, who died there at a very old age. Charles A. received his education in his native country, and came to the United States in 1868, locating in Wisconsin, where he worked in a brewery till coming to this county the first time, in 1871. He now has 240 acres of land, with 110 in a good state of cultivation, and has made this his home since 1880. He has cleared all his land himself, and the past year had seventy-five acres of cotton, which produced a heavy crop. His farm is located one and one half miles from Gilmore Station, west of the railroad, and is splendid for stock purposes, on which are raised a number of cattle, hogs, mules and horses. Mr. Walter is the only one of his family now in this country. He is a Democrat in politics, and cast his first presidential vote for Tilden. A good honest citizen, he possesses the chief characteristics of a true son of Germany, which make that people so prosperous as a nation.

C. T. and I. O. West, brothers, and jointly associated in farming and stock raising, stand among the most prominent in their line in Wappanocca Township. C. T. West was born in Virginia in 1856, and his brother in this county in 1861. They are sons of Levi and Lucy C. (Barnard) West, both Virginians by birth. The father was a farmer and moved to this county in 1858, renting a farm in this township till 1879, when he purchased an unimproved bottom farm of eighty acres, of which he cleared some fifteen acres and built a comfortable residence. The father and mother of our subjects were the parents of three children: C. T., I. O. and Ida, wife of W. J. Mann, who is now living with her brothers. The father had previously been married to Mary Barnard, sister of his last wife, who was the mother of seven children, all now deceased. C. T. West was reared on a farm in this county and received a fair education at Miller and Caruther's graded school, in Shelby County, Tenn. At the age of twenty-two years he rented a farm and has since followed his chosen vocation with the greatest success. Like his brother, I. O. West was brought up to a knowledge of agricultural pursuits, and received his education in the public schools of Shelby County, Tenn. When he reached the age of nineteen he commenced business for himself on his father's farm, on which he has since lived and tended to its cultivation. Ida also attended school in Shelby County, Tenn., where her father had moved at the close of the war to educate his children. She was married to W. J. Mann, and to their union have been given five children. The three now living are: Willie, James T., and an infant unnamed. Mr. Mann, who came to this county in 1878, is the only son of William and Martha (Wilson, nee Bracy) Mann, the latter of whom died in 1859, after which he was married to Cherry Futrell, and Dallas M. (deceased) was the only child born to this union. Mr. Mann's first wife was a Miss Outland, and they were the parents

of five children, two now living: James H. (in this county) and Martha T. (wife of James Fennett), residing in North Hamilton County, N. C. The three gentlemen mentioned in this sketch, are all public spirited and progressive, and extend a welcome to all thrifty white emigrants, from whatever country they may come. They live together on the old farm cultivated by their father till his death in 1880, and by their spirit of enterprise and their careful business attention have developed, from the Mississippi wilderness, one of the most beautiful and productive farms that adorn Crittenden County.

John C. Williams, like many other prominent citizens of Lucas Township, is worthily occupied as a planter. He was born in Hardeman County Tenn., March 7, 1827, as the son of Nathan Williams, a native of Rockingham County, N. C., born in 1788. He was married in North Carolina, and immigrated to Alabama about 1822, and after residing there for about four years, moved to Western Tennessee, where he remained till 1834, the time of his location in Northern Mississippi: he was the first white man to take his family into that part of the State, and at the time the red man was frequently seen. He remained there till his death, in October, 1850, on the farm that he opened—the first in that section of the country. He was of Scotch-Irish descent, and the son of John Williams, who is supposed to have been born in Ireland. His wife was Miss Nancy L. Carr, of North Carolina origin, born in 1800, who died while visiting her son, John C., in Austin, Miss., in 1876. Mr. and Mrs. Williams were the parents of nine children, only two of whom are alive: John C. and a brother, Dr. W. G. (living in Texas). The subject of this sketch, the fifth child, was raised in Mississippi after he was seven years of age, receiving his education in the common schools of Benton County. In 1849 he was married in Mississippi to Miss Nancy Terry, who was born in South Carolina, in 1827, and died in Benton County, Miss., in 1856, being the mother of two children: Emma (deceased, the wife of Mr. Knight) and Louisa C. (wife of William Phillips, who lives on a farm in this county). Mr. Williams was married a second time in 1859, his wife being Sarah C. Jarrett, then the widow of a Mr. Knight. She was born in Petersburg, Va., in 1827, and had two sons by Mr. Knight; none were born of the last union. Mr. and Mrs. Williams have reared several children, among whom are her two children and his by his first wife, Sally and Lillie Redus (daughters of his deceased sister), Lycurgus War (a relative of his present wife), two children, by the names of Jennie and Edward Rupe (children of his sister) and two grandchildren, Mary and Henry Knight, are now with him. All but three of the children that he has brought up are now married and doing well. Mr. Williams immigrated from De Soto County, Miss., in 1885, to where he now lives, having 1,600 acres of land, with 200 in cultivation, on which he raises from 100 to 150 bales of cotton annually. He enlisted in the Confederate army with the scout, Thomas Henderson, and served in this capacity from Mississippi to New Orleans, until he was paroled, June 19, 1865. Politically he has been a stanch Democrat, since casting his first vote, which was for James K. Polk. Mrs. Williams is a member of the Methodist Episcopal Church, South, and her husband is a believer in Universalism. Mr. Williams is a good, moral man, and is not addicted to playing cards or any other gambling devices, and has not taken any intoxicating drinks for twelve years. He first went to Memphis in 1838, when that city was a village, and it has been his home market ever since.

Judge John H. Williams, a farmer and stock raiser of prominence, of Wappanocca Township, was born in Shelby County, Tenn., in 1841, and is the twelfth child of Robert and Elizabeth (Beasley) Williams. The parents of the Judge were of Middle Tennessee nativity, who moved to Shelby County, Tenn., in 1840. Here the father bought a farm, living on it till his death in 1885. He was elected sheriff of Shelby County, Tenn., before the war. By his first wife, who died in 1858, he was the father of twelve children: Mary (wife of Ben Wilson), Martha (wife of John Mathews), Jones (deceased), Peter (of Jerico), Charles (of Shelby County, Tenn.), Benjamin (of Crawfordsville), J. H. (our subject) and Willie (deceased). In 1860

Robert Williams was married to Octavious Williams, and to this union was born one child, Nettie (wife of James Hall). Mr. Williams was closely allied to the A. F. & A. M., and was respected by all who knew him, as an honest and honorable citizen. J. H. Williams was reared to farm life, receiving his education in Shelby County, Tenn., and when at the age of twenty, during the outbreak of the Rebellion he joined Company B, Thirteenth Tennessee Infantry, and fought in the battles of Murfreesboro, Belmont and Shiloh, where he was struck twice by a spent ball. At Murfreesboro he was captured and sent to Camp Morton, Ind., being kept here for three months, when he was exchanged and went home. Abandoning the army for all time he commenced farming in Shelby County, Tenn., remaining here till 1869, when he moved to this county in February of that year. He then rented land in this county till 1872, when he purchased land that he cultivated till 1880, when he exchanged it for another farm. He now has 150 acres in his homestead, and is the owner of 160 acres, with ninety acres improved, in another section of the county. When Mr. Williams came to the county in 1869 he was in very poor circumstances, but by close economy and strict attention to business, backed by a superior business ability, he has in a few years accumulated considerable property. In 1869 he was married to Miss Fannie Wallace, and to them have been given six children: Iola (deceased), E. R. (at home), Vesta E., R. B. (deceased), Ethel H. (deceased) and Hubert A. Mrs. Williams is a member of the Methodist Episcopal Church, and Mr. Williams is an A. F. & A. M., belonging to the Lone Star Lodge No. 375, and to the K. of H., No. 3110. He served as justice of the peace from 1874 to 1880, and in 1882 was elected county and probate judge, which office he filled, with satisfaction to all, for a term of two years.

Edwin J. Williams, prominent as one of the younger farmers of Jasper Township, was born in Shelby County, Tenn., in 1854, to the union of Jesse and Mary (Watson) Williams, natives, respectively, of Kentucky and Georgia. When an infant the father went to Tennessee with his parents and located in Maury County. Here he attained his majority and was educated for the Methodist ministry, which he followed for a profession. He preached in Tennessee, Georgia and Kentucky and was a faithful worker in the church till his death, in 1877, when he was seventy years of age. He located in Shelby County on a farm when about thirty-five years of age, and lived there till called to a home above. He was a member of the Masonic lodge. The mother is still living in the same neighborhood, and is above seventy years of age, active and hearty; she is a faithful member of the Methodist Episcopal Church, and is a devoted and active Christian, doing much to advance the interests of her chosen denomination. Mr. and Mrs. Williams are the parents of eight children, seven now living. Eugene O., the youngest child, is deceased. Edwin J., who is the fifth of the family, was reared in Shelby County, Tenn., and received his education in the common schools of that vicinity. Coming to Arkansas in 1879 he remained for three years, when he moved to Fayette County, Tenn., and after spending four years there returned to this county and located on Rosebrough Island, where he is still living, engaged in farming. In connection with James T. Barton, under the firm name of Barton & Williams, he is also occupied in buying cotton seed at Gavin. Mr. Williams was married to Miss Lena Finch, who was born in Macon, Tenn., the daughter of Alphonso and Sally Finch, natives of Tennessee. He is a Democrat in politics, and he and his wife are members of the Methodist Episcopal Church, South. They have two children: Valcour F. and Annie V. Mr. Williams is of a philanthropic disposition and is always eager to take hold of and push anything that will advance the interests of the public.

J. F. Williamson, one of Crittenden County's prosperous young planters, has reached a prominence and popularity that would do credit to many of more advanced years and wider experience. He owes his nativity to Mississippi, his birth occurring in De Soto County, in 1863, he being the third in order of birth in a family of nine children born to F. H. and Mary E. (McGraw) Williamson, of whom

only six are now living: Mary E. (wife of Dr. W. P. Conner, residing in Mississippi), J. F., Artinatia T., Robert M., Ellen and Hal. F. H. Williamson went to Memphis, Tenn., from Virginia, in 1840, and engaged in merchandising, the firm name being Franseoli & Williamson, dealers in queensware. After successfully conducting that business for twenty years, he moved to De Soto County, and there carried on farming, but in 1886 he returned to Memphis, and has retired from active business life. He served as captain of a company in the late war (on the Confederate side) from 1861 to 1865, and participated in a number of important battles, among them being that of Shiloh. While in Mississippi he received a severe wound in the shoulder, and was taken prisoner at Memphis, but only retained a short time. Though Mr. Williamson is in his seventy-first year he enjoys excellent health and takes an active interest in the progressive ideas of the day. Mrs. Williamson is fifty-two years of age, and a member of the Baptist Church. J. F. was reared and educated in De Soto County, Miss., and when twenty-five years old accepted the position as manager in the mercantile house of Conner Bros., at Scanlan's Landing. At the expiration of one year he was made a member of that firm. In 1888 Mr. Williamson led to the hymeneal altar Miss Louisia Earle, daughter of J. F. and L. R. (Richards) Earle, natives of Arkansas. After his marriage he assumed the management of his mother-in-law's plantation, which consists of 600 acres. He raises about 400 bales of cotton, and does all his own ginning, having a steam-gin on his farm. He is one of the most successful farmers of this county, and takes great interest in and lends his support to all public improvements for the good and benefit of the county and its residents. Mrs. Williamson's father, J. F. Earle, came to this portion of the county with his parents when about fourteen years old. They were from England, and the paternal great-grandfather was lost at sea. The grandfather was a sea captain, and controlled an interest in a line of steamships. Mr. Earle suffered considerable loss through disasters at sea, having owned at one time a large estate in this county. He was a soldier in the War with

Mexico, and a major in the Confederate States service, serving through the entire war, and later, held with distinction the offices of circuit and county clerk. Subsequent to the war he served as county and circuit clerk of this county, and was one of its progressive and influential citizens. When Mr. Earle came here he had very little on which to build a fortune, but at the date of his demise, was the owner of 1,600 acres of valuable land, with 600 acres under cultivation, which, as before stated, is now under the efficient management of Mr. Williamson. Mrs. Earle's father (Mr. Richards) was one of the first settlers of Crittenden County, and his brother was city register for about thirty years of the city of Memphis, Tenn., holding and discharging the duties of that office with entire satisfaction to all concerned.

Solomon P. Williford, of Crittenden County, was born December 31, 1848, in Shelby County, Tenn., and is the sixth in a family of nine children, which blessed the union of Solomon F. and Susan A. (Andrews) Williford, natives of North Carolina. Solomon Williford came to Tennessee, in 1830, and settled in Shelby County, where he purchased a large tract of land, making farming his special delectation. Here he reared and educated his children, and previous to the war owned a number of slaves. The children were as follows: B. F. (resides in Tennessee), Agnes T. (wife of A. C. Douglass, deceased, and with her family resides in Tennessee), Joseph H. (killed in the battle of Franklin), R. A. (passed through the war under Gen. Forrest), James M. (deceased, and left a family who reside in Tennessee), Piney (deceased), Annie L. (deceased, wife of A. M. Bledsoe, of Tennessee), Bernie (deceased, wife of R. W. Bledsoe, of Tennessee) and S. P. (subject of this sketch). Mr. Williford was killed in 1862, by United States troops, at Bartlett, Tenn. Mrs. Williford died in 1875 or 1876, a member of the Baptist Church, as was also her husband. Solomon P. Williford attended the common schools of Shelby County, and also took a course in a prominent college of Madison County, Tenn. At the age of twenty he started out to make his fortune, and began farming, having purchased a fine tract

of land in Shelby County, and after a residence of several years on that farm, or until 1881, he disposed of his property and came to Arkansas, following his adopted occupation of farming, on what is now called the McConnoll Place. This place is situated at the head of Cat Island, and embraces 180 acres. Mr. Williford also cultivates 500 acres, on which he raises a great deal of stock, such as cattle, hogs, etc., having discovered that they can be handled with comparatively little expense, and yield excellent returns. In 1877 Mr. Williford was united in holy matrimony with Miss Bettie Massey, a daughter of Crawford and Sarah P. (Bledsoe) Massey. Mr. and Mrs. Massey were the parents of six children, five of whom are now living: Bettie E. (Mrs. Williford), Mary (now Mrs. Oglesbey), Charles J., Sallie A. (the wife of Mr. Walker) and Katie (at home). Mrs. Massey died July 6, 1875. Mr. Massey is a prosperous farmer, and a member of the Farmers' Alliance. The paternal grandfather of Mrs. Williford served with great distinction in the War for Independence. To the union of Mr. and Mrs. Williford five children have been born: Ethel G., Joseph C. (deceased), Lith P., Emmet P. and Daisy M. Mr. Williford is one of the most successful farmers in this portion of the county, and owes his prosperity to no one but himself, all being secured by hard labor and constant application. He takes an active part in political affairs, and is an ardent admirer of the principles of the Democratic party. A member of the K. of P., K. of H. and I. O. O. F., he is a man of whom the citizens of Crittenden County have just cause to be proud.

William H. Williford, an auspicious planter of Jasper Township, was born in Shelby County, Tenn., in 1856, and is the son of Henry and Celia (Taylor) Williford, who were reared and married in North Carolina. The father located in Shelby County, Tenn., in 1851, and followed farming for an occupation. He furnished a substitute during the late war, who was killed at the battle of Franklin, Tenn. Mr. and Mrs. Williford were members of the Baptist Church. The former died in 1880, and his wife in 1868. They were the parents of eleven children, of whom four lived to be grown, and of these William H. was the fifth child, and is now the only survivor. The father was married the second time in December, 1869, to Miss Pain. They have two boys, living in Memphis at present. William H. was reared and educated in the common schools of Shelby County, where he assisted his father on the farm and attained his majority. He commenced life for himself in 1878 by coming to Arkansas, and settled on a farm that was owned by his father and near the Lyon place, on which he lives at the present time. Mr. Williford was married to Miss Katie E. Lyons, who was born in this county in 1859, and is the daughter of Dr. T. B. and Elizabeth (Ferguson) Lyon. Dr. Lyon is a native of Ohio, having graduated there at a medical college, and upon coming to this State located in Mississippi County, but later moved to Crittenden County. Here he was married and followed his profession, which greatly injured his health, and from the effects of which he died in 1886, at the age of sixty-three. He was a member of the Methodist Episcopal Church, and was well liked by all who knew him. His widow lives on the old home place with Mr. and Mrs. Williford. She is a member of the Presbyterian Church. To Mr. and Mrs. Lyon were born three children, of whom one died when quite small; Katie E. and Hattie J. still survive. Mr. and Mrs. Williford are the parents of four children, as follows: Myrtle, Thomas H. and Willie Lee living, and one died in infancy. Mr. Williford is a member of the Baptist Church, and his wife of the Methodist Episcopal Church. He is a Democrat in politics, and is a worthy and

enterprising citizen. He has an elegant farm of 130 acres in cultivation and 190 acres still unimproved.

William R. Young, like others mentioned in the present volume, an energetic planter of Lucas Township, was born in Crenshaw County, Ala., May 10, 1856, and is a son of Richard W. Young, who dates his existence from 1842, in South Carolina. He now resides in Mississippi. Richard W. Young was married to Miss Susan Clyburn, who was reared in South Carolina, where she was also born about 1845; she is living at Huntsville, Ala. They are the parents of twelve children, of whom ten survive, and of these William R. is the second child. When the latter was but eleven years old his parents moved from South Carolina to Huntsville, Ala., where he received his education. He commenced life for himself at about seventeen years of age, working for wages in a store and on a farm, and was married December 7, 1886, to Miss Willie Holloway, born in Madison County, Miss., October 15, 1866, and brought up in De Soto County. She is a daughter of J. L. Holloway. [See sketch.] Mr. and Mrs. Young have one child. They moved from De Soto County to where they now live in 1885. Mr. Young cultivates 450 acres of land, on which he usually raises from 200 to 250 bales of cotton annually, requiring eighteen mules to do the work. His wife is an active member of the Presbyterian Church. Mr. Young has been a Democrat since casting his first vote for Tilden; he is an enterprising and energetic business man, and deserves much praise for his untiring efforts to make things comfortable for himself and his neighbors.

CHAPTER XIX.

St. Francis County—Its Advantageous Location—Area and Boundary—Streams—Population—
Navigation—Period of Entry—First Settlers—Mound Builders—First Building and
County Seat—William Strong—Soil—Climate and Production—Stock Raising
—Growth and Material Progress—Valuation—Organization—
Court Affairs—Prominent Cases—War Record—Sketch
of Forrest City—Political History and Di-
rectory of Officers — Summary—
Biographical.

Neither locks had they to their doors, nor bar to their windows;
But their dwellings were open as day, and the hearts of the owners;
There the richest were poor, and the poorest lived in abundance.—*Anon.*

ST. FRANCIS COUNTY, near the center of the eastern tier of counties in Arkansas, is bounded on the north by Crittenden and Cross, on the east by Crittenden, on the south by Lee, and on the west by the counties of Monroe and Woodruff. It contains an area of 615 square miles, or 393,600 acres, and is divided into ten municipal townships, viz.: Griggs, Johnson, Telico, L'Anguille, Blackfish, Franks, Prairie, Goodwin, Madison and Wheatley.

The St. Francis and L'Anguille Rivers cross the county from north to south, dividing it into three nearly equal divisions, which topographically have each their distinctive features; that lying east of the St. Francis River being generally level, sloping gradually toward the Mississippi River. The central division, between the St. Francis and L'Anguille, is divided by Crowley's Ridge, which is nearly equi-distant between the two rivers, having an average altitude of 300 feet above sea level. The country west of the L'Anguille is slightly undulating.

The seat of justice and principal town in St. Francis County is Forrest City, though numerous other smaller places exist in various convenient localities, the most important of which are Madison, Palestine, Goodwin and Wheatley, on the Little Rock & Memphis Railroad; Colt, Caldwell, Bonair and Bucklin on the Iron Mountain Railway.

The county's population by the census of 1880 was 8,389; white, 4,923, colored, 3,467. This has very materially increased, so that now it is safe to estimate the present population at from 12,000 to 15,000.

The principal rivers of the county are the St. Francis and the L'Anguille, which traverse the territory from north to south, with their numerous tributaries fed by perennial springs, furnishing a never-failing and abundant water supply. The St.

Francis is navigable for small boats its entire length in the county, and in early days, before the advent of railroads, no inconsiderable trade was carried on by keel-boats. The first steamboat to ply on the St. Francis within these present limits was an old "stern-wheeler" called the Wheeling, owned by Col. J. C. Johnson. This made only a few trips, then being transferred to the Arkansas River, and, shortly after having run upon a snag, was sunk in that river near the present site of the city of Little Rock.

The most familiar names connected with the early steamboat navigation of the St. Francis River, and names that will forever be favorably associated with events of the past, are those of "Capt." Thomas R. Bowman and wife, Pauline (familiarly known as "Auntie" Bowman). Capt. Bowman is still living in Memphis, having been the pioneer of steamboating on the St. Francis. His first venture was with a small concern called the Plow Boy, which was soon replaced by a larger boat, and this in turn succeeded by one still larger, called respectively St. Francis Nos. 1 and 2. The latter he ran till the breaking out of the war when his boat was taken into the Confederate service and burned at the fall of Little Rock. After the war Capt. Bowman resumed his business in a boat called the Mollie Hambleton. Supposing that the demands of the trade would require a larger and more commodious craft, he built the St. Francis, which was a model for beauty and would compare favorably with any of the Mississippi boats in equipment and furnishings. The trade, however, failing to meet his expectations, he was forced to sell, not being able to meet all demands against him. The boat was run on the river by Capt. Samson Basket until 1875, when it was sunk in the St. Francis near Madison, thus ending any important navigation of the river. At certain seasons of the year the river is still navigable by a few small steamers.

The first permanent settlement of this county began about the year 1819, immigrants entering from the States of Tennessee and Kentucky. At that time, as the country was a comparative wilderness and occupied by the Indians, settlers located principally on the eastern slope of Crowley's Ridge.

Additions to these settlements from time to time were made, but no general influx was apparent until the opening of the old military road, in 1836. This road was located and cut through the county from the eastern to the western border, by the United States Government, to aid in the removal of the Indians from the States east of the Mississippi River to the Indian Territory, which latter had been given them as a permanent home. The highway was 300 feet in width, and was after its completion the generally traveled thoroughfare of immigrants from the east, many of whom, attracted by the fertility of the soil and the genial climate, settled near the road. From these points as a center, the population radiated to different portions of the county. Among the pioneers were the Strongs, Lewises, Moseleys, Pattersons, Hughes, Evans, Castiles, Prewetts, Roys, Joneses, Mays, Seaborns, Williams, McDaniels, Hargraves, Curls, Myrics, Whitsits, Izards, Davises, Hodges, Mallorys, Coles, Fitzpatrics. The early history of these settlers is but the repetition of pioneer experiences anywhere. Log rollings, cotton pickings, corn huskings, bear hunts, etc., made up the yearly routine of their work and enjoyments, and occasionally a murder relieved the monotony, and added interest to general gossip.

A noble, generous and adventurous band of pioneers, inured to the hardships, trials and privations of a life far removed from the conveniences and amenities of the settled portion of the continent, they were men, self-reliant and determined, well fitted by nature and training for the niche they filled in the development and reclamation of this western wilderness. Fearlessly they blazed the way for advancing civilization, with no conception of the magnificent empire, whose foundations their toils and privations were laying.

All over the county one found the evidences that indicate the presence at a remote period of the Mound builders. These are more numerous in the eastern portion, where may be seen innumerable mounds of different shapes and sizes, evidently built for different purposes. Some are from fifteen to 200 feet in diameter, and from twelve to twenty-five feet in height, and may be classified, according to their uses, into residence, burial, sacrificial, defensive and observatory mounds. The implements found therein, though rude, would indicate that the builders were of an agricultural class.

The pottery which has been unearthed constitutes the most interesting relics. This is found in abundance and embraces every size and form, manifesting the exercise of wonderful skill in its manufacture. The material used is, as a rule, an aluminous clay mixed with pounded shells. Some of the vessels are plain, the majority, however, being ornamented in devious ways. A few bear representations of animals, such as coons, bears, birds and fishes.

Here is an extended field for the painstaking archæologist; here, 'neath the shadow of these wonderful mounds, the monuments of a prehistoric race, may he muse and speculate and devolve theory as to their origin and disappearance, giving to the world for its profit and help the benefit of his deliberations.

On the old military road, about twelve miles north of Forrest City, stands a building worthy of note, not alone for its antiquity (having been built, from the most reliable data obtainable, about the year 1827), but for its beauty of design and immense proportions. The building is four stories high and contains twenty rooms, with a veranda extending entirely around it, supported by red cedar posts, eight inches in diameter, which, it is said, were brought here from East Tennessee, having been floated down the Tennessee River to the Ohio, down this river to the Mississippi River, and thence to the mouth of the St. Francis, and finally to their destination. This structure is in a remarkable state of preservation, scarcely a square yard of the plastering being missed from the various rooms. It has only been roofed twice, the second roof having been replaced about thirty-nine years ago. Unquestionably this strong house is the most costly and best-preserved residence in the county. Its design and erection at the time and under the circumstances have occasioned considerable comment. The building's site was once the site of an Indian village, a trail leading from this point to Arkansas Post, one of the early trading points hereabouts.

William Strong, the builder, came to this county at a very early day. A shadow of mystery seemed to hang over most of his transactions from the first, frequently causing his neighbors to suspicion that his saintly guise covered many dark and hidden crimes. That he practically controlled the affairs of his section was more than once verified; even the magistrates through fear or mercenary motives were wont to do his bidding. On one occasion a gentleman whose appearance indicated a person of wealth passing through the country stopped with Mr. Strong over night. While eating breakfast the visitor's saddlebags which he had left in his room were opened and part of the contents removed and replaced by a coverlid taken from the bed. After settling his bill the stranger mounted his horse and resumed his journey but had not gone far when he was overtaken by Strong and a posse of men who accused him of stealing the coverlid. This, he of course denied and readily consented to allow his saddlebags searched. The evidence of his accused guilt was found; he was arrested, carried back to Strong's and given a mock trial, which resulted in his being robbed of all that he had, not excepting his horse. Large tracts of land came into the possession of Strong by purchase and otherwise, which he mortgaged to the old Real Estate Bank, and in later years considerable confusion and litigation resulted over titles to these lands, embracing some of the finest tracts in the county. Among these was the Spanish grant upon which the town of Wittsburg in Cross County stands.

Strong was also one of the contractors for cutting and locating the old military road before referred to. The soil in that section of country lying between the St. Francis River and the east boundary of the county is an alluvial sandy loam, a portion of the great Mississippi bottom, being the richest land on the continent. Unfortunately, however, most of this is subject at times to overflow. The soil of the central portion of the county between the St. Francis and the L'Anguille Rivers is somewhat alluvial, but the greater part includes Crowley's Ridge, which is rolling and is not surpassed in fertility by any uplands in the State.

In the county's western territory is a loamy soil with clay subsoil mostly covered with a growth of black jack. A portion of Grand prairie extends into this county, having a width in the southwest corner of six miles and coming to a point near the northwest corner. Lands improved range from $18 to $40 per acre and unimproved from $5 to $12 per acre. The soil is of a warm nature and of easy cultivation. Here fruit grows in its greatest perfection. Apples, peaches, pears and plums have been successfully raised and small fruits and berries yield to perfection. In addition to the excellent agricultural feature presented the locality is widely known as a grazing region, being well adapted to this and dairying purposes.

No finer timber is found anywhere and the quantity is practically inexhaustible, consisting principally of poplar, and the different kinds of oak, walnut, hickory, etc. It is rather strange that no poplar timber is found west of the line of the L'Anguille River in this State.

The principal crops are cotton and corn. At present only about one-third of the county is under cultivation, but the proportion of land not susceptible of cultivation is comparatively insignificant. The average yield of cotton on the lowlands is one bale to the acre and sixty-five bushels of corn, the uplands produce three-fourths of a bale per acre and thirty bushels of corn.

The climate is temperate, and the winters short and mild, the mean annual temperature being 60°. The rainfall averages forty-five inches. Snow rarely covers the ground for one continuous week, and the atmosphere is healthful for man and beast, and unusually favorable for the increase of the latter. Cattle uniformly graze until Christmas, and with the exception of those kept for dairying purposes remain out through the entire winter, subsisting on the cane. The putting up of hay on the prairie in the western part of the county is fast developing as an industry, being baled and shipped by carloads to distant markets.

The yield of timothy and red top per acre is about 3,000 pounds, clover and millet 4,000 pounds and hungarian some 3,000 pounds.

The raising of cattle is becoming one of the leading sources of income in this portion of the country. Large tracts of prairie are being inclosed by wire fences and turned into cattle ranches. Notably among these is "Prairie Grove" ranch owned by a prominent Northern man, which is well stocked with blooded cattle and horses.

The growth of St. Francis County was materially retarded by the war, but has since been rapid and steady, and the influx of newcomers has been of a desirable and substantial character.

The great obstacle to the increase of population in the lowlands, heretofore, has been the immense amount of timber necessary to be cleared and put aside before a farm could be opened; but this timber once a hindrance to progress is now becoming most valuable, and saw-mills are found in every neighborhood. Large bodies of these forests have been opened by the St. Louis, Iron Mountain & Southern Railway, affording an outlet for the great varieties and vast quantities of timber of this region. The great rush of homeless humanity to the Oklahoma country would seem to be evidence that most of the desirable Government land, the great wealth of the nation, has been taken up. The truth is, however, and the same has been a matter of comment with persons familiar with western emigration, that the great body of emigrants in their eagerness pass over sections where they could procure partially improved and more productive land, situated with every advantage for schools and churches and many other of the conveniences and luxuries of a thickly settled country, at a less sum than would have been demanded for the farming communities toward which they are hastening.

The property value hereabouts has kept pace with the county's increased population. The last assessed value of the real and personal property amounted to $2,519,000 or a little over $300 per capita, and this assessment really represents only about forty per cent of the actual valuation. The county is practically out of debt, owing only a few thousand dollars of railroad bonds which have not yet matured.

There is a mammoth saw, planing and shingle mill at Madison, with a capital of $50,000, in addition to which there have been built six new mills in the county within the past eighteen months. The immense amount of lumber shipped also adds materially to the general wealth.

St. Francis County was organized October 13, 1827, at which time it contained a considerably larger area than its present limits. The site for the seat of justice was first located at William Strong's house on the military road in the north part of the present limits, remaining there until about the year 1841, when it was moved to the town of Madison, in Madison Township. Near 1855 it was again removed, this time to Mt. Vernon, whence shortly after it was returned to Madison, and in 1874 became permanently located at Forrest City. The county has not as yet erected a court house, and the sessions of the courts are held in a frame building purchased for that purpose. The jail is a frame structure with steel cells. The old public buildings at Madison, formerly owned by the county and used by the court while located at that place, were sold, and are now in the hands of private parties.

It is very difficult to learn anything of the early courts of St. Francis, the records having been twice destroyed, the first time in 1862 during the war. They were moved to an old house surrounded by woods for safety, but the woods catching fire, and no one being apprised of the whereabouts of these valuable papers, save the parties who had removed them, and who were not on hand at the time, the house and contents were entirely destroyed. Again, in 1874, the same agency again wrought devastation.

Among the early judges on this circuit was J. C. P. Tollison, W. K. Sebastian, J. T. Jones, T. B. Hanley, Chas. W. Adams, Geo. W. Beazley, M. W. Alexander and E. C. Bronaugh. Since the war, J. M. Hanks, William Storey, W. C. Hazeltine, John W. Fox, H. N. Hutton, Jesse Cypert and N. T. Sanders have served in this capacity.

Among the first important cases of a criminal character noted was the killing of William S. Moseley. William Allen was accused of the crime, but, the evidence being only circumstantial, he was acquitted. The name of Hi Dunn also occupies a conspicuous place in the early criminal records.

He lived on an island in Rose Lake, was a very desperate man and a member of the famous outlaw band of John A. Murrell.

Another murder that attracted the attention of the people at the time was the killing of James Whitsit by Hugh Castile, both of whom had been living on the same land (and occupying the same house), working together. After a time Whitsit went to Little Rock, and upon his return informed Castile that he had entered the land. This so enraged the latter that he seized a butcher-knife and dispatched Whitsit. The murderer then left the country and was lost sight of.

Among the more recent crimes the killing of Fox by Aldridge, which happened in Forrest City about 1874, deserves mention. The circumstances of this affair briefly stated are these: Aldridge on one occasion was sent to jail for contempt by Fox, who was presiding judge of the circuit court. Aldridge keenly felt the disgrace, and, after the adjournment of court, and when both had returned to their home in Forrest City, on the first appearance of Fox on the streets Aldridge met him, and, without warning, shot him down with a double-barreled shotgun which he had concealed in a convenient drug store. Aldridge was arrested and placed under $10,000 bond, but died before the convening of court.

At the breaking out of the war, though this county was very sparsely settled, the sentiment and sympathies of the people were almost without exception, in behalf of the Southern cause. There were raised here five companies, the first by Poindexter Dun, who afterward represented this Congressional district in the United States Congress for five consecutive terms. The second company was raised by the well-known commander Frisk. These companies were attached to Cross' regiment, known as the Fifth Confederate regiment. The third company was recruited by Capt. J. McGee, and the fourth by Capt. F. M. Prewett, now a leading merchant of Forrest City, and the oldest business man in the place. The fifth company was raised by Paul M. Cobbs, now State land commissioner. The last three mentioned were attached to Col. McNeil's regiment in the Fifth Arkansas

Cavalry. The gallantry of these companies is attested by the few members who survived at the close of the war, the number returning not exceeding 100, out of an aggregate of 600 who enlisted. It is worthy of note that Jack Cheney, of Paul M. Cobbs' company of the Fifth Arkansas, was the first man to mount the breastworks in the charge made by the Confederate troops at the battle of Helena.

There were no battles of importance fought within the limits of this county during the war, though a couple of cavalry engagements gave thrilling evidence of war, one near the present town of Forrest City, at what is known as Stewart's Springs, and one at the crossing L'Anguille River, within fourteen miles of Forrest City.

Forrest City, the county seat and principal commercial center of St. Francis County, is located on the western slope of Crowley's Ridge, near the county's geographical center, and at the crossing of the Memphis & Little Rock and the Iron Mountain Railroads. The town was first laid off March 1, 1869, by J. C. Hill, at that time county surveyor; the land on which it stands having belonged at that time to the Izards and Prewetts. The first store was opened under the firm name of Izard Bros. & Prewett. Capt. F. M. Prewett was the first person to settle and build upon the present town site, which then was covered by a heavy growth of poplar timber. The name was bestowed upon the village after the celebrated Confederate general, N. B. Forrest, who was the contractor for grading the Memphis & Little Rock Railroad through this portion of country.

The first mayor of Forrest City was J. W. Grogan, chosen at the first municipal election held shortly after the incorporation of the town, May 11, 1871. At present the population numbers 1,500, of which about 150 are colored.

The Avery Hotel, a large three-story brick building, is the finest structure in the city, and a magnificent monument to the enterprise and thrift of the citizens, having been built by a stock company composed of representative men. It contains forty commodious and well furnished rooms. The cuisine of this house is all that can be desired.

Mr. J. H. Avery, the proprietor, is a genial and courteous gentleman, thoroughly versed in matters pertaining to the conduct of a first-class hotel, and is a general favorite with the traveling public.

There are in addition to the Avery several smaller well-kept hotels and boarding houses.

Society here is cultured and refined, and religion is fostered in a becoming manner, the Methodists, Baptists, Presbyterians, all having large and substantial houses of worship. The Catholics also have a good church edifice. The colored people are principally connected with the Baptist and Methodist denominations, and have four comfortable church buildings, two belonging to each organization.

Educational facilities are ample and complete. The school buildings, both for white and colored pupils, are attractive, large, light and airy, and supplied with all the modern conveniences and helps. The white graded school has an efficient principal and three assistants, with an enrollment of nearly 200 pupils. The colored school, conducted separately, has a good enrollment, and able and competent instructors.

The professions are well represented, and among the members of both the legal and medical branches are found individuals whose fame and well-deserved reputation extends beyond the limits of the State.

There are two principal newspapers published here, the Forrest City Times and the Forrest City Register, each of which has an encouraging circulation, and enjoys a liberal advertising patronage. Faithful to the interests of their adopted locality, they exercise commendable influence in the moral elevation of their readers.

The Enterprise, published by the colored people and devoted entirely to the upbuilding and wants of this class, is a bright, newsy little sheet, conservative and neatly printed.

All branches of trade are embodied in the industries of Forrest City, and the business houses are generally large two-story bricks, which will compare favorably with those of any other town of like size. Some ten stores carry stocks of general merchandise, ranging from $10,000 to $30,000, six large grocery stores are found, three drug stores and two jewelry stores, besides numerous small provision, meat and confectionery establishments. The Bank of Eastern Arkansas, with a capital of $50,000, is in a flourishing condition, and does a general banking business. The trade of the town amounts annually to about $600,000. There was shipped from this point in 1888, 12,000 bales of cotton and several thousand tons of cotton seed. The transportation facilities are unsurpassed, direct communications being furnished with St. Louis and Texas, by way of the Iron Mountain Railroad, and the same with Memphis and the east, over the Little Rock & Memphis Railroad.

Forrest City is favorably situated to become one of the leading commercial cities of the State, being fortunate in its location, with such a large and fertile region, tributary to it. This is fast becoming settled and will in a few years pour into its lap the wealth of all productions. Successful in the past the city has still before her a more prosperous future.

Secret societies of the Masons, Odd Fellows, Knights of Pythias, Knights of Honor and the Agricultural Wheel, sustain a devoted membership, and thrive in a satisfactory manner.

The residence portion of the town is beautifully adorned with numerous shade trees and flower gardens, and many of the homes in their construction and beauty evidence the taste and refinement of the citizens. Most of the buildings are planned on the modern style of architecture, but not a few represent the typical Southern home. Everything indicates quiet and true domesticity, and if home comforts can exist anywhere it is here.

That the people of this county are pre-eminently a Christian people is shown by the fact that three-fourths of the adult population, both white and colored, are members of one or another of the leading religious denominations, the principal of which are the Methodists, Baptists and Presbyterians. In every section of the county, churches of more or less pretentions obtain always of a substantial character, and the court records indicate a very small proportion of crime, mostly misdemeanors.

The political parties are nearly equally divided in the county. At the last presidential election, Cleveland received 838 votes, Harrison, 923; Streeter, 248, and Fisk, 10. The county is in the First Congressional district, commonly known as the "Shoe String" district, taking as it does the whole eastern tier of counties from the north to the south boundary of the State. It is also included in the First judicial district.

The circuit court meets the eighth Monday after the third Monday in August and February, the term in each case being two weeks. The county courts convene quarterly the first Monday in January, April, July and October, the sessions being regulated in the length of their continuance by the business to be disposed of, generally, however, lasting only a few days.

Since the organization of the county the following county officers have served:

Judges: John Johnson, William Strong, William Enos, R. H. Hargrave, E. Franks, W. M. Fulkerson, J. C. Johnson, P. Littell, J. M. Griggs, Sr., J. M. Griggs, Jr., W. J. Jones, E. Mallory, T. Pearce, G. W. Laughinghouse, L. Finley, R. T. Scott, W. H. Coffey.

County Clerks: Andrew Roane, S. Crouch, Isaac Mitchell, R. H. Hargrave, J. M. Parrott, G. B. Michie, H. Halbert, W. Becker, W. H. Wills, H. C. Davis, J. M. Stewart, T. O. Fitzpatrick.

Sheriffs: William Strong, T. J. Curl, J. M. Halbert, William Dunn, G. V. C. Johnson, G. B. Michie, G. W. Seaborn, J. R. Gurley, John Parham, W. J. Matthews and D. M. Wilson.

The school system here is on a firm basis and the means for acquiring good common-school instruction are within reach of all, white and colored. There are in the county thirty-one organized school districts, two schools being conducted in each district, one for the white and one for the colored children. The value of school property exclusive of real estate is $15,000, and the amount expended for the employment of teachers for the past year reaches to about $16,635.06. The total school population last year was 4,871. Each district votes the full amount allowed by law for school purposes and there is an increasing interest manifested by all in the cause of education. There are now twenty-eight good commodious schoolhouses in the county.

In concluding this reference to St. Francis it is well to add that in the destruction of the records containing the official history serious disadvantages have been met with in the compilation of this sketch, rendering it necessary to depend almost wholly on personal recollections and reminiscences. These, of course, are more or less faulty and conflicting, human memory varying with the lapse of years. Intercourse with the people has been of the most agreeable and satisfactory nature and all have been ready and willing to impart such information as they possessed. The undeveloped wealth of this county, with its many other natural advantages, combine to offer a most favorable field for individuals contemplating a change of residence.

John J. Ables, proprietor of one of the leading groceries of Colt, is a native of this county, and when a boy worked on his father's farm, attending school at intervals; although not regular in attendance, he being a bright scholar and willing to learn, received a fair common-school education. In May, 1861, at the age of seventeen, he entered the Confederate service, enlisting in Company B, Fifth Arkansas Regiment, Govan's brigade, Pat Cleburne's division, Hardee's and Cheatham's corps of the Army of the Tennessee, commanded by Beauregard, Albert Sidney Johnston, Braxton Bragg, Joseph E. Johnston and J. B. Hood, of Texas. Mr. Able's career as a soldier led him through many different battles—Chickamauga, Murfreesboro, Franklin, from Bowling Green, Ky., to Bentonville, N. C., via Nashville, Chattanooga and Dalton down the railroad and State line to Atlanta, thence to Jonesboro via Augusta, Ga., back to Bentonville. He fought the last battle under Johnston at that place, that famous general then falling back to Greensboro, N. C., where he surrendered. Mr. Ables took his chances for his home in Arkansas, and was in all the engagements of that march, soldiering through East Tennessee, around Knoxville, on Clinch River, at Clinton, with Bragg through Cumberland Gap to Kentucky. He was wounded in the right hand, losing his little finger, which, though a small and seemingly unimportant member, necessitated his absence from active duty for three months. He served throughout the war, and took an active part in every battle of his division in the Mississippi Valley, with the exception of those during the three months of his disability. Returning home in May, 1865, Mr. Ables was married the following August to Miss Mary A. Stutts. They are the parents of eight children, all of whom are living: Cora Belle, John W., Willis R., Anna C., Micager C., Samuel, James D. and Emma Lou. Following his matrimonial venture Mr. Ables engaged in farming, and now has a nicely improved farm of 160 acres. He was born in 1844, being the son of M. C. and Jane C. (Moore) Ables, natives of Tennessee and Alabama, respectively. M. C. Ables came to Arkansas in 1828, and settled in this county at a time when there were but few families in the locality. Here he bought a farm of 320 acres, on which he lived until the time of his death, with the exception of a year or two during his residence in Wittsburg, and also while in the Mexican War. In 1887 our subject sold out his farming interests and came to Colt Station, embarking in the grocery business, in which he is still engaged. In this he has been very successful. He held the office of constable of his township before moving to Colt, and was also justice of the peace for ten years, and has now a commission as notary public. Mr. Ables is a stanch Democrat and a member of the I. O. O. F. and Knights of Honor.

J. L. Adare, a native of Northern Alabama, is a son of Samuel W. and Mary J. (Freeze) Adare, who also came originally from that State, the father being of French descent, and the mother of Irish ancestry. J. L. Adare assisted his father on the farm until twenty years of age, when he was engaged in clerking for about four years. In 1879 he came to Arkansas and located in St. Francis County, gave his attention to farming the first year, and the following year entered the employ of Mr. Vital Lesca, as clerk, and is now at the head of the business. Mr. Adare was born in Madison County, Ala., on December 27, 1850, and was married on September 8, 1889, to Mrs. Delia Lesca, widow of his former employer, and a daughter of Stephen Snowden, a native of Tennessee. Mr. Adare is a member of the K. of H., and is a well-known citizen and highly respected.

William E. Allen, active in the agricultural affairs of this county, was born in St. Francis County, Ark., being the son of William and Eliza L. (Oliver) Allen, natives of Louisiana, and Arkansas, respectively. The former began life for himself at the age of twenty-one years, and now owns 261 acres of valuable land, with 100 acres carefully improved and cultivated. Aside from his many farming interests, he is engaged in stock raising, making a success of that branch as with everything else. In 1877 Mr. Allen was married to Miss Flora L. Beazley, who died in 1884, leaving one child, Mary A. In 1888 Miss Ella E. Gray, a daughter of William F. and Sarah E. Gray, became his present wife. To their union one child has been born, Willie L. Mr. and Mrs. Allen are members in high standing of the Methodist Episcopal Church, South, and the former is a Democrat in his political views. He contributes liberally to all public enterprises, and is held in high esteem by the entire community.

W. H. Alley, M. D., in his connection with the professional affairs of this community has attained a well-deserved prominence. Born in Mississippi, in 1861, he passed his boyhood days in the common schools of that State, obtaining a practical education, and manifesting at an early age an unusually bright mind. At the age of fourteen he was at the head of classes in which the majority were many years his senior. When seventeen years old he commenced the study of medicine under a tutor, and in 1879, entering the Vanderbilt University, was graduated from the Medical Department of that institution in March, 1881. He first located in his home, in Mississippi, where he practiced with success for two years, but later became located at Lewisburg, Miss., for one year, and then in Bellevue, Miss., where he remained until 1888. Dr. Alley then came to Arkansas and settled in Forrest City, and though only a few years have elapsed since his entrance, he has built up a practice of which others of more advanced years and experience might well feel proud. Dr. Alley's wife was formerly Miss Emma L. Cobbs, daughter of Paul M. Cobbs, State and land commissioner of Arkansas. To their union one interesting little daughter has been born, Mary. The Doctor owns an attractive home, which is furnished in excellent taste, and three valuable farms. He is a Democrat in his political views, a member of the K. of P. and prominently identified with the County Medical Society. J. H. and Ophelia (McCombs) Alley, his parents, were natives of Tennessee. The father followed merchandising in Byhalia, Miss., nearly all his life, but in 1884 came to Arkansas and is now engaged in operating a large plantation. Mrs. Alley is still living, and is of Scotch and Irish descent. The paternal grandfather was born in Virginia and the maternal grandfather, N. H. McCombs, came originally from North Carolina, spending the greater portion of his life in Mississippi, where he died at the age of seventy-three years. The maternal grandmother's name was Reid; she was directly descended from the Scotch and Irish.

Mrs. Margret E. Anderson. On the first day of January, 1839, was born in St. Francis County the subject of this sketch. Her father, Alfred K. Houston, first saw the light of this world in South Carolina, December 21, 1814, and came to Arkansas with his parents at the age of five years, who settled in St. Francis County, Ark., where he was reared, and followed the occupation of a farmer, dying in this county in March, 1879. He was married to Miss Sallie Evans, of North Carolina origin, who came to Arkansas when a girl, and who departed this life in 1860. The issue of this union was seven children, four of whom are living: Margret E. (the principal of this sketch), Wellman C. (a farmer of this county), Hiram (living in this county, whose sketch is given elsewhere), Francis M. (also a resident of this county). Mrs. Anderson has been twice married, and is now a widow, her second husband dying some ten years ago. Her first marriage, on June 20, 1855, was to Aaron M. Hughes, of Georgian birth, and who died May

18, 1862; by this marriage were two sons, only one of whom is living, Wellman T., born November 15, 1860. She married again on June 20, 1867, to Robert Anderson, of South Carolina, and a son of Robert and Lucy (Beazley) Anderson, who died February 20, 1879. Four children were given to them, three of whom are still living: Sarah L., Robert K. and Nancy E. Of her husbands it can be said they were honest, industrious farmers, who succeeded in life and laid up some property for those who were dependent on them, and merited the great respect shown them. Mrs. Anderson is now living on her magnificent farm, situated on the banks of the St. Francis River, and in connection with this, owns a half-interest in 560 acres of valuable land, also the homestead, 115 acres. Her son, William T. Hughes, a model and rising young farmer, has the affairs of the farm under his supervision, and is making a decided success of it, and they have a happy home, wherein dwells ease, comfort and plenty. Mrs. Anderson is a member of and worships with the Methodist Episcopal Church. William T. Hughes is a member of the Knights of Honor.

Samuel D. Apperson, the present popular and capable assessor of St. Francis County, was born in Marshall County, Miss., near Holly Springs, February 22, 1853, being the son of W. T. and Martha (Howes) Apperson, originally from Virginia and Tennessee, respectively. The parents had a family of six children, three now living, of whom Samuel D. is the third in order of birth. The latter accompanied his parents to Arkansas when quite young, and having settled near Forrest City before the present site was located, can justly be deemed a pioneer of the community. He remained here until 1873, attending the schools of the county, and then drove stock over the States of Tennessee, Indiana and Mississippi. In 1875 he returned home and came to Forrest City, where he conducted a general freight and dray business until 1880. His fitness for the position becoming recognized, he was elected marshal of Forrest City and served two terms of one year each. In 1886 he accepted the superintendency of trestle work on the Bald Knob Railroad from Bald Knob to Memphis, receiving a salary of $115 per month. Returning to Forrest City he found employment awaiting him as farm superintendent, which position he held for one year. Mr. Apperson was then elected county assessor to fill a vacancy, and is now discharging the manifold duties of that office in a highly creditable manner. He is a member of the K. of H. and I. O. O. F. fraternities, and a Democrat in his political views. He is of French descent, his grandfather having been a native of France. Mr. Apperson is progressive in his ideas, and many improvements in the city owe their existence to his liberal support and hearty co-operation.

Edward Bonner was born in Spartanburg District, S. C., in 1841, being the son of Andrew and Louisa Bonner, also natives of that State. Young Edward remained in the vicinity of his birthplace until grown to manhood, receiving but limited advantages for an education, and attending school only a portion of each year. When nineteen years of age he assumed charge of his father's farm, and after the latter's death remained with his mother, conducting her business in a most satisfactory manner. When twenty years old he enlisted in the Confederate army in Company G, Fifth South Carolina Regiment, under Capt. Carpenter, commanded by Col. Jenkins, and participated in the first battle of Manassas, but being taken ill shortly after, he was detailed to manage the Magnetic iron works, located at Cherokee Ford, S. C. This was one of the most important branches of industry in connection with the Southern cause. Mr. Bonner remained in this position until the close of the war, after which he commenced business as a merchant at Limestone Springs, S. C. After one year, at his mother's earnest solicitation, he returned to her home and resumed control of her extensive business. In 1869 he was married to Miss Julia G., daughter of Elijah and Julia (Ray) Harris, and their marriage has been blessed with three interesting children: Edward L., Carl Ray and Erma. The oldest child, Edward, is a promising young man, and bids fair to be a leader among men, standing intellectually far above the average, a young man whose example is worthy of imitation. Mr. Bonner moved to St. Francis County in 1874, locating in Forrest City, and four years later was appointed postmaster at that place, serving in that capacity for five years, and also as agent for the Southern Express Company. The change of administration in 1883, or President Garfield's reign, caused his removal from the position of postmaster. Since leaving the office Mr. Bonner has been merchandising, and is at present managing the co-operative store at Forrest City inaugurated by the people for their benefit. The stock is valued at $45,000 and under his efficient control is rapidly increasing in value, and is one of the city's leading enterprises. In politics our subject is a Democrat, and in religious faith a Baptist, as is also his wife. Mr. Bonner is a liberal contributor to all charitable movements, and, in fact, every act that betokens the good or growth of the county finds him a stanch supporter. Previous to the war his parents were quite wealthy, but the ravages incident to that period robbed them of nearly everything, their land being about all they possessed. The paternal grandfather was a native of Virginia, born near Petersburg, but afterward moving to South Carolina, died there at the age of sixty-three. The maternal grandfather was Joseph Camp, of South Carolina nativity, who was called to his final home at a very advanced age. Mrs. Bonner's father was Rev. Elijah Ray, a Baptist minister of South Carolina. Her mother's father, Col. William Washington Harris, a native of North Carolina, was a soldier in the War of 1812, serving as colonel in the volunteer service, and died at the age of eighty-eight years. He was one of the first settlers of Spartanburg, S. C.

Calvin N. Bynum, an extensive stock raiser and tiller of the soil. Born in Hickman County, Tenn., in 1838, he is the son of James and Rebecca Bynum, natives of Virginia, who moved to St. Francis County, Ark., in 1848; Mrs. Bynum only living a few months after their arrival. Mr. Bynum died the year following. Calvin N. began life on his own responsibility at the age of eleven, and in 1861 settled his present farm, which consists of 326 acres, with 225 under cultivation. From this land he receives excellent crops, and is also extensively engaged in stock raising. He enlisted during the war,

29

in 1863, in Company G, Hart's regiment, serving until the final surrender. Mr. Bynum has been married three times; first, in 1865 to Miss Emeline Price, who bore him three children: James H., Laura A. and Josephine. Mrs. Bynum died in 1870, and Mr. Bynum was again married, his second choice being Miss Louise Price. By this union there were five children, two now living: Sinah E. and Martha E. In 1877 Mrs. Bynum was called to her final home, and his third and present wife was formerly Lucy J. Price. To them seven children have been given, five surviving: Sara I., Francis C., William H., Charlie and John C. In politics Mr. Bynum is a Democrat and in his religious faith a Presbyterian. He contributes liberally to all public enterprises, and is regarded as one of the representative men of the county.

James L. Caldwell is a native of Tennessee and a son of William and Amanda (Christan) Caldwell, who came originally from South Carolina and Tennessee, respectively. William Caldwell was born in 1811 and was reared on a farm, removing to Bedford County, Tenn., when a young man, where he was married in 1844 to the mother of our subject. In 1861 they came to this county, and here the father engaged in farming and also in the milling business, in which he was occupied until his death, in 1865. He was a prominent citizen of his county, a member of the Masonic order and of the I. O. O. F., and belonged to the Cumberland Presbyterian Church, and at one time, while a resident of Bedford County, Tenn., represented that county in the State legislature. Mrs. Caldwell was born in Bedford County, Tenn., in February, 1816, and died in April, 1888. James L. Caldwell also first saw the light in Bedford County, his natal day being March 23, 1846, and when a young man he took charge of his father's mill, continuing it until 1864. Then he enlisted in a company raised by C. M. Biscoe, which formed a part of McGee's regiment (the Fifth Arkansas Cavalry), was elected second lieutenant, and a short time after promoted first lieutenant. After the war he returned home and engaged in merchandising for over a year, subsequently entering into the saw-mill business, which he followed in this and Cross Counties until selling out to his brother in 1887. He erected a mill two miles west of Caldwell, and also took a contract for building ten miles of the Bald Knob Railroad which he completed in that year. Mr. Caldwell has built and owned fourteen different mills in St. Francis and Crittenden Counties, and now owns the mill near Caldwell and a half interest in a mill in the last-named county; besides this he has and operates several farms in these two counties and Cross County, in all about 1,800 acres, with over 100 acres under cultivation, the rest being fine timber land. He aided largely in putting in most of the bridges in St. Francis and Crittenden Counties, and now has taken the contract for the erection of the buildings for the Little Rock Oil Company. He was married November 20, 1874, to Miss Annie Halbert, a daughter of John Halbert, a native of Missouri. They are the parents of six children: Willie J., Lillie A., Mary Ann, Henry H., Tennie and James L. Mr. Caldwell was justice of the peace of Johnson Township for six years, and is one of the prominent men of his county. He is a member of the Masonic order, and belongs to the County Wheel, being made vice-president at its organization here.

William Thomas Clifton, an active carpenter of Forrest City, was born in Elerton, Jefferson County, Ala., near Birmingham, March 23, 1823, being a son of Amza H. and Adelissa (Goode) Clifton, natives of Virginia and North Carolina, respectively. The paternal grandfather of our subject, William Clifton, was a Scotchman by birth and came to America about the close of the Revolutionary war, settling in North Carolina, where he married a Miss Martha Rice, daughter of John Rice. Mr. Rice was in the employ of the United States Government as a surveyor under President Monroe, and assisted in moving the Indians west, receiving 5,000 acres of land for his services, part of which tract is the land on which Memphis is now situated, and to this day it is known as the Rice grant. The father of Adelissa Goode (Thomas Goode), was a soldier and served seven years in the Revolutionary War, and was commissioned colonel in Gen. Washington's body guard, and his grandson, Thomas Goode Clark,

was a soldier in the late war, and fell at the battle of Gettysburg, together with his son; the pine boards which marked their resting place are now among the relics at the Libby Prison War Museum. Mr. Amza H. Clifton was born in Caswell County, N. C., and was married in 1821 at Hopkinsville, Ky. He settled in Jefferson County, Ala., moved to Tennessee in 1828 and located in Covington, where he lived about ten years, and then moved to Mississippi in 1837. In 1840 going to Memphis, Tenn., he resided there and worked at his trade as carpenter, until his death in 1849. William T. Clifton gave his attention to the carpenter's trade under his father's instruction until of age, and in 1845 came to Arkansas, but remained only a short time, in 1847 making another trip. In 1848 he was married to Miss Araminta Cathey, and settled in Mount Vernon near the present site of Forrest City, where he has since lived. He and wife are the parents of three children: Mattie C. (wife of Joseph M. Davis, of this city), William A. (a confectioner of Morrillton, Ark.), and Mollie, now Mrs. Ritter of the same place. Mr. and Mrs. Clifton are members of the Baptist Church. He is a strong Democrat and a prominent citizen.

Judge W. H. Coffey, an eminent lawyer of St. Francis County, widely known and highly esteemed by his associates on the bench, is originally of Fayette County, Tenn., but was taken by his parents when an infant, to De Soto County, Miss., in which State his father died two years later. His mother then returned to her father's home in Hardeman County, Tenn., and afterward married John Coates, of that county. In 1861 Mr. Coffey enlisted in the Fourth Tennessee Infantry, taking an active part in the battles of Shiloh, Murfreesboro, Missionary Ridge, Chickamauga, and a number of others. He was captured and taken prisoner at the battle of Missionary Ridge, thence conveyed to Camp Morton, Ind., held in captivity for nine months, when he was exchanged, and receiving a furlough turned his face toward his native land, walking over 225 miles, and reaching home a short time before the surrender. He then took up farming for his livelihood, and in 1869 was married to Miss Mary E. Harris, who died in 1870, leaving one son, James W. In 1872 Mr. Coffey removed to Arkansas, and settled in St. Francis County, on a farm nine miles from Forrest City, purchasing first 160 acres of land, to which he has added from time to time, until he now owns 1,120 acres, and besides these he has his home farm, 225 acres, which are cleared and under cultivation. Two years after his removal to this county, he was elected justice of the peace, holding this office until 1886, when he was elected county judge, and was again elected to this office in 1888, and is now finishing his second term. In December, 1873, he was again married to Mary A. Houston, a daughter of James M. Houston. They are the parents of eight children, five of whom are still living: Mary E., Martha T., Noma, Nora Belle and Clarence Elbert. Mr. Coffey affiliates with the Masonic fraternity, in which order he has taken the degree of Royal Arch, and in the thirteen years of membership, he has not missed but four regular meetings. He is also a member of the County Wheel, being one of the charter members of this lodge, and was its first president.

J. H. Cole. In passing through Eastern Arkansas it would be impossible to meet a gentleman of more marked characteristics than J. H. Cole, the subject of this sketch. He is a typical Tennesseean, and a man of more than ordinary physical strength and activity, and the observer needs to be no expert to recognize in him a person of unyielding determination and will. He still stands erect and walks with the agility of a man of forty years, although three score years and two have passed their mantle upon him, his birth occurring in 1827. He spent his boyhood days in Stewart and Humphries Counties, Tenn., but the monotony of his quiet life made him restless and the opening of the Mexican War gave him an opportunity to see life in its most exciting phase. Eagerly embracing the opportunity, he enlisted in 1846, and followed the fortunes of the war until its close, participating in the famous battles of Monterey and Buena Vista At the close of hostilities he went to New Orleans, and for two years engaged in the drug business. Returning thence to Tennessee, shortly after he was married in Carroll County to Miss May Math-

ews, and moved to Hickman, Ky., where he accepted a position as marshal and wharfmaster. He then came to Madison, the old county seat of Arkansas, landing there in September of 1857, having made the journey from Helena in a dugout or canoe. In Madison he opened a livery business, acting as agent for the line to Hot Springs, and contractor for the lines from Helena to Cherokee Bluff. At the breaking out of the war he joined the Fifth Arkansas State Troops, under Ristor, but when they joined the Confederate army he left and took charge of Hardee's wagon train for Missouri. He was suddenly taken ill, and obliged to come home, but afterward reported to Col. Walker, and was with him in the fight at Helena. He was taken prisoner by Powell Clayton, a short time after receiving his parole; and was once charged with the burning of a boat, and on trial for his life, but Clayton proved him in his hands as a prisoner at the time, which act saved his life. As soon as the war closed he opened at Madison the first store in St. Francis County, under the firm name of Cole & Prewett. He received all the goods with which to conduct it from New Orleans on credit, through the influence of friends, and from that departure made a fortune. The firm continued till the Governor of the State called for civil instead of marshal law. A committee was appointed to select some reliable man to go and secure the commission from the Governor, but, although various parties were appointed, no one would undertake the venture; accordingly Mr. Cole—always fearless as he was shrewd—started without telling any one of his intention. He went on horseback to Memphis, and from there by boat to Little Rock, where he secured an interview with the Governor, and received the commission. He then returned home and immediately called together some of the most reliable men of the county, appointing them to the various offices. Then in a field close to an old court house, he organized the first county court after the war. The records had been buried there during the war. The commissioner of the post came and ordered him to jail, but he read him the commission from the Governor, showing him that his time of service had expired the day before.

Mr. Cole was not in favor of secession, but went with his State when it seceded. A man by the name of Inge was sent from Mississippi before the war for the purpose of preaching secession. Mr. Cole made the remark to Judge Pierce of the county, that it would have been better if South Carolina had slipped into the sea than to have slipped out of the Union. The secessionist procured a pistol and cowhide, and began to whip Mr. Cole. A fight ensued, in which Mr. Inge was killed. Our subject was afterward wholly exonerated by the court. When Forrest City became the county seat of St. Francis County, Mr. Cole closed up his business and came here. At this place Hugh H., the only child, died. He was a rising young attorney of the place, and a graduate of Lebanon Law School. Since his death Mr. Cole and wife have been disconsolate, and have tried to forget their sorrow in traveling. They have gone as far North as possible, visiting every point of interest mentionable. They were for a period abroad, spending some time in Dublin, Ireland. Mr. Cole recently united with the church, a large audience congregating to hear his experience. He is beloved by all who know him, and is well worthy the respect and deference paid him, for though he is perhaps a trifle eccentric, a mean act is something he has yet to do. He is a favorite in society and business circles, and though witty and quick at repartee, he never wounds a friend and there is no sting in his mirth. He, with his honored wife enjoys that which is so much to be desired—an unsullied name, and the sincere love of a host of friends. His grandfather was a native of Virginia and the third settler of Nashville, Tenn.

William A. Council. The village of Council Bend was named after Redwick Council, who built the first house in that locality, and who was the grandfather of the subject of this biography. His son, Simeon, was born in North Carolina, in 1805, and removed to Arkansas in April, 1822, settling in Crittenden County for a short time and then removed to Walnut Bend, on the Mississippi River, being married in St. Francis County, in 1827, to Rebecca Lane, who was born in Alabama in April, 1811. He died in April, 1848, and his wife in 1879. They were the parents of eleven children, three of whom are still living: Allen (a farmer of St. Francis County), Mary J. (now Mrs. McKay, of Hood County, Tex.), and William A. The latter was reared in this county and began life for himself as a farmer at the age of nineteen. He was born here on December 28, 1847, and was married, February 22, 1874, to Miss Anna M. Smith, who died in July of that year. The following April, Miss Elizabeth Filingim became his wife, who died April 22, 1881, leaving one child, now deceased. Mr. Council's third matrimonial venture was in February, 1883, to Miss Margaret L. Hubbard, of Alabama nativity, who died two years later, having borne one child, that died in infancy. He joined the Union army at the age of sixteen, enlisting in the Twenty-fifth Wisconsin Infantry, in which he served until the close of the war, participating in the battles of Buzzard's Roost, Big Shanty, Kenesaw Mountain, Atlanta, and a number of others. After the conflict Mr. Council went to Wisconsin, and remained two years, then returning to Arkansas and settling in St. Francis County. He is now engaged in the timber business in connection with farming, and owns 160 acres on the St. Francis River, which is very fertile and well timbered.

D. W. Davis, a brother of John M. Davis, whose sketch appears in this work, and a relative of Jeff. Davis, is a son of Cornelius Davis, the latter having come to Arkansas from Kentucky, his former home, in 1828. At that time the Territory was but thinly settled, the forests were filled with bear, deer, wild turkey and other game, and the mode of traveling was in ox carts or on horseback. Our subject was reared to farm life, but had no advantages for acquiring an education when a boy, and it is a fact that, up to his eighteenth birthday, he could neither read nor write. He was born in this county December 9, 1833. In 1851 he ran away from home, and went to Fulton County, Ill., where he attended school for three years, working for his board and enough to keep him in clothes. Then returning home he commenced teaching school, and in that way earned means to take him through college, after which he took a course in civil engineering at the McKendrie College. Subsequently he went to Leavenworth, Kan., and took part in the border warfare in Missouri and Kansas. Becoming located at Omaha, he was engaged in his profession of surveying a short time, but later returned to St. Francis County, and in 1857–58 held the position of deputy sheriff. At the breaking out of the war he enlisted in the Crittenden Rangers, the first company raised in Arkansas. A few months later he helped Marsh Walker raise his regiment, of which he was made captain and commissary. After the war Mr. Davis came home and commenced farming, and also took up the study of law, afterward entering upon his practice, but soon again abandoned the legal profession and resumed farming. This he still follows, and is also engaged in surveying, in addition being timber inspector of the Third district, comprising St. Francis, Cross and Poinsett Counties. He has the credit of sending in more money than any other inspector in the State. He has a fine farm, with over 100 acres under cultivation, upon which are good buildings and a fine orchard. His principal crop is cotton, but does not confine himself to that one product as do some. He has also tried introducing thoroughbred short-horned cattle, but the country is not yet educated up to seeing the value of fancy stock. Mr. Davis was married in 1863 to Mrs. McClintock. They are the parents of five children: Blanche (wife of James W. Steward, who was superintendent of the public schools for ten years), De Witt (nineteen years of age and who is studying surveying, of which he has a practical knowledge, having at the State Fair at Little Rock competed and taken the prize for the best plat of a thirty-two sided farm and architectural drawings), Annie, David and Mabel. Mr. Davis and wife are members of the Episcopal Church. He is also a member of the Knights of Honor, and is a strong Democrat.

Anthony D. Davis, also actively engaged in agricultural pursuits, was born in 1836 near the present site of Corinth, Miss., made historic during the war by one of the most famous battles of that period. His parents were Arthur and Elizabeth E. (Smith) Davis, natives of North Carolina. An-

thony Davis did not receive many advantages for an education in youth, a few months passed in a neighboring school during the winter months, comprising the whole amount of his literary instruction. His first venture on his own account was at the age of nineteen, when he accepted a position as manager of a large plantation, discharging the manifold duties connected therewith in a most satisfactory manner. Soon becoming tired of this employment, and wishing to own land of his own, he resigned his position, much to the regret of his employers, and went to De Soto County, Miss. Not long after his arrival at that point the war broke out, which, of course, destroyed all his plans, for the time, at least. He enlisted September 15, 1861, in Company G, Thirty-first Tennessee Regiment, Capt. Baker's company and Col. Bradford's regiment, and participated in the battles of Belmont, Chickamauga, Perryville, etc. At the close of the war Mr. Davis removed to St. Francis County, purchasing a farm of 240 acres, of which he has cleared and has in a good state of cultivation 140 acres. His improvements are such as would do credit to any country, and his beautiful residence, furnished in such excellent taste, gives evidence of culture and refinement. In addition to his farming operations he is an extensive stock raiser. In 1865 Mr. Davis was married to Miss Maria Prewett, and to them a family of four children were born: Daisy and Arthur now living, and Cheatham and William (deceased). In politics Mr. Davis is a Democrat, and in religious faith a Methodist. His wife is a Baptist, and a lady of many excellent traits and characteristics. Mr. Davis is a liberal contributor to all worthy enterprises, but many of his generous acts never reach the ears of the outside world.

John M. Davis is numbered among the well-known farmers and stock raisers of Franks Township. He was born on the farm on which he still lives, in 1845. His parents Cornelius and Eliza (Holbert) Davis, were natives of Kentucky. The former came to Arkansas in 1828, and remained one year, then returning to Kentucky, where he was married in 1832, moving permanently to this county, and engaging in farming. At that time the country was very thinly settled, the nearest market being Helena. He first entered 160 acres of land, but at the time of his death, in 1868, at the age of sixty-three years, owned 600 or 700 acres. John M. Davis grew to manhood on his father's farm, his early educational opportunities being limited, as the senior Davis was one of those men who believed in acquiring a competency before spending it. When eighteen years old John went to Kentucky, and attended school for about two years. After the war, in which he did not take part on account of poor health, he returned to Arkansas and resumed farming, and is now conducting the old homestead which his father entered and improved on coming to this State, and where he was born. Mr. Davis has been twice united in the bonds of matrimony. First, in 1868, to Mary C. Folbre, who died in 1871, leaving one son, Thomas C., who was killed in a railroad wreck in 1887. Mr. Davis took for his second wife Miss Hester A. Davis, in January, 1874, a daughter of Rev. Arthur Davis, of Western Tennessee. They are the parents of ten children: Benjamin, Arthur W., Mattie P., Drucilla, John, Susie, Eliza, Myrtle, Claudia and Elizabeth. Mr. Davis is one of the most prominent Democrats of this locality, and is now the efficient sheriff of St. Francis County, and a man whose name is a terror to law breakers. He and wife are members of the Methodist Episcopal Church, South. Mr. Davis is also connected with the Masonic order.

H. P. Dooley. Among those who have contributed liberally to the numerous enterprises of Forrest City, and are recognized as leading citizens, the name of H. P. Dooley, dentist, is a familiar one. He is a native of Tennessee, his birth occurring in Maury County in 1847, being the son of W. A. and Sarah (Joyce) Dooley. W. A. Dooley was born in 1820, participated in the Civil War and died in 1877. The grandfather came originally from North Carolina and raised the first company of soldiers in Tennessee for the Creek War. He entered the service as captain, but came out as colonel, dying a few years afterward. The great-grandfather was of Ireland origin, and the great-grandmother from Scotland. H. P. Dooley,

the subject of this sketch, received his literary education in the schools of his native State, afterward entering a seminary near Memphis, where the breaking out of the war found him. Putting away his books, despite his ambition to obtain a good education, he joined McDonald's Company of Tennessee Cavalry, serving in the Confederate army two and a half years. He was twice wounded, first receiving a severe wound in the leg, and the second time his arm was broken. Eighteen of his company were shot down, and a ball, which passed through his arm, knocked the mounting from his gun and injured him quite seriously. After recovering sufficiently to admit of his again entering the service, he returned and remained until the final surrender. The first year after the war Mr. Dooley engaged in farming, but attended school the winter of 1866, subsequently commencing the study of his profession under the tutelage of R. G. Edwards and next with one W. F. Southern. After one year spent in traveling in Northern Mississippi he came here, locating in Forrest City in 1870. When he began he had but very little, except undaunted courage and a determination to succeed, which is doubtless the secret of his present prosperity. He has amassed quite a fortune, and owns one of the most attractive residences in the city. He takes much interest in fine stock, paying careful attention to raising the same, and is trying to get the people interested generally in this industry. Mr. Dooley was married in Forrest City to Miss R. H. Johnson, a native of Arkansas and a daughter of G. V. C. Johnson. He was sheriff of this county at the time of his death. His father, John C. Johnson, was representative of St. Francis County for several years. Mr. Dooley has traveled quite extensively, and is a genial, courteous gentleman, one who makes friends wherever he may go. His business takes him in various parts of the State, and his reputation as an efficient dentist is an enviable one. He became a member of the Masonic lodge when it could boast of only seven members, and to him the lodge owes its present prosperous state. He was Worshipful Master four years, but recently refused to act any longer, though prevailed upon to accept the secretaryship; he has held an office ever since becoming identified with the order in 1872, in which year he was made Master Mason.

O. E. Dorriss, one of the oldest and most prominent of the early settlers of St. Francis County, was born in Jackson County, Ill., in the year 1819, being the son of James S. and Catherine Dorriss, of English and Irish descent, respectively. James Dorriss was a soldier in the War of 1812, and his father was chaplain to Andrew Jackson during the Creek War, participating in the famous battle of Horseshoe. Hamlet F., a brother of O. E. Dorriss, served in the war between Mexico and Texas, taking an active part in all the engagements of note, and was present at the capture of Gen. Santa Anna at Santa Jacinto. O. E. Dorriss' advantages for an education were extremely limited, but his constant reading and keen sense of observation have made him a well-informed man, conversant on all the important topics of the past and present. At the age of fourteen he left home, starting out to make his own fortune. In 1834 he came to Arkansas on a trading expedition, going southwest, and upon reaching the Saline River, in the southwest part of the State, he was suddenly taken ill, which put a quietus to his business prospects for some time. After recovering he discovered to his horror that his partner had absconded with all the finances. This left him entirely destitute and among strangers, but in time he made his way to Little Rock, suffering many privations during his long journey. At this point he was met by his father, who had come to him in response to an appeal, written in a trembling hand during his convalescence. He returned to his home in Missouri, but soon after returned to St. Francis County, arriving here in 1835, and locating on a farm of 320 acres, which he improved and has since made his home. Mr. Dorriss ran among the first steamboats that ever plied up the St. Francis River, in the years 1844–45. In 1847 he was married to Miss Julia Hanson, of Morgan County, Ga., and to their union nine children were born: Josephine, Georgia A., Lugene, Franklin, Jenette, Julia, Sallie Vick, Lou Kate and Lee, of whom four are now living. In March, 1865, Mrs. Dorriss died, and in 1866 Mr. Dorriss married Miss Ann T. Ellis, who bore him six

children: James, Mary, Ada, Willmorth, George and Thomas; of these three are deceased. Mr. Dorriss was a member of the Fifth Arkansas Regiment, Confederate army, during the war, and represented his county in the legislature of 1866. for ten years he was justice of the peace, discharging the duties of that office in a highly commendable manner, and during his entire term of office, from 1856 to 1866, only one of his decisions were taken to a higher court. He filled the office of sheriff by appointment for several years, and in this, as in everything else, gave entire satisfaction. In his political opinion he favors the Democratic party, but is not an enthusiast. Mr. Dorriss assisted in the removal of the Indians to their present home in the Indian Territory, and also gave his valuable support in laying out and opening up the old military road in this county in 1835–36. In addition to Esquire Dorriss' many enterprises he is running a fine steam-gin, with a capacity of eighteen bales per day, and a self-acting, or automatic, press of the latest improvement. He is a liberal contributor to all movements that have for their object the advancement of educational and religious matters. Mrs. Dorriss is a consistent member of the Methodist Episcopal Church, South.

John E. Douglas has attained to a position of credit as a farmer and surveyor of St. Francis County. A native of Tennessee, he is the son of John E. and Elizabeth (Sparks) Douglas, who came originally from Alabama and Tennessee, respectively. The principal of this sketch was born on January 18, 1837. His father died when he was less than two years old and his mother then came to Arkansas and settled in St. Francis County where she was shortly after married to Curtis G. Tyer. Young John lived with his mother after her second marriage, and had the advantages of a good education in the subscription schools of the county, at the age of seventeen engaging in teaching in order to raise money enough to enable him to continue his studies, as he was very desirous of taking a thorough course in civil engineering. Three years later he was offered the position of assistant teacher in St. Francis Academy, where he completed his education, acquiring a superior knowledge of surveying, in both its theoretical and practical phases. Following this he resumed teaching until the breaking out of the war, when he enlisted in the Twenty-third Arkansas Infantry and served in Price's famous raid through Missouri. After the war Mr. Douglas again turned his attention to the instruction of the young, continuing it until 1868, when he bought 120 acres of land and commenced farming. He was married on March 7, 1866, to Miss Mary A. Casbeer. They are the parents of six children: Charles M., Thomas E., Nathaniel E., Effie D., Lucy A. and Leta J. Mr. Douglas owns a fine farm with good buildings, his large orchard containing all kinds of choice fruit, and also owns forty acres of desirable land in Cross County. In 1880 he was elected census enumerator, and the same year was made county surveyor, which position he has held since that time with a faithfulness and ability which have redounded largely to his personal esteem and worth. Mr. Douglas is a member of the Knights of Honor and is an enterprising citizen, contributing liberally toward those enterprises which tend to the development or improvement of the community, physically, morally or intellectually.

William Elliott. Prominently identified with the prosperous and influential citizens of St. Francis County is William Elliott, who is a native of Alabama, his birth occurring in Huntsville, in 1826. He was the son of Allen and Jane Elliott, originally from the same State. When William was one year of age his parents moved to Arkansas, settling in St. Francis County, where his early boyhood days were passed in assisting his father on the farm. At the age of twenty-one years he homesteaded the place on which he now resides. This farm consists of 200 acres, with 125 acres under cultivation. Mr. Elliott is, aside from his many farming interests, quite extensively engaged in stock raising, and also has an interest in a good steam-gin, with a capacity of ten bales per day. He was united in marriage in 1851 to Miss Sarah Styres, and by her became the father of three children: John A., Sarah and Jane (all deceased). Mrs. Elliott died in 1854, and for his second wife Mr. Elliott chose Miss Adeline E. Adams, who

bore him three children: James H. and Benjamin F. (both deceased) and William H. In 1861 Mr. Elliott enlisted in the Fifth Arkansas Regiment, Company A, and participated in several of the most important battles of the war, among them being Paducah, Tupelo, Prairie Grove and Union City. In 1863 he was married to Melissa J. Adams, and their union has been blessed by five children: Robert L., Elisha T. (deceased), Mary E. (deceased), Martha and Mary. Mr. Elliott is a Democrat, and with his wife is a member of the Baptist Church. He has held the office of magistrate, coroner and deputy sheriff in his township, serving acceptably in these various positions. He is one of the public-spirited citizens of the community.

William T. Ellis, another enterprising farmer of St. Francis County, was born in North Carolina in 1853, as the son of James G. and Christiana Ellis, both also natives of the same State. The father enlisted in the Second North Carolina Infantry during the late war, but being wounded in the battle of Petersburg, Va., received his discharge and returned home. In 1871 William T. removed to Cross County, Ark., with his parents, with whom he remained until twenty-six years of age. However he had been married during this time to Miss Martha C. Hall, who lived only a short time after her marriage. In 1883 he was married to Melinda C. Hall, and by this union four children have been born: Mattie S., Mollie A., Thomas J. and James L. Mr. Ellis owns a farm of 123 acres, with thirty-two acres under cultivation, being engaged principally in stock raising. He is a stanch Democrat and a member of the County Wheel, and he and his wife belong to the Methodist Episcopal Church, South. Mr. Ellis is justice of the peace of his township, which office he has held for the past twelve years. He is well known throughout this part of the county, and is generally liked and respected, lending his aid and influence to all public movements for the good of the order.

J. J. Evans, of the prominent and substantial firm of H. Evans & Co., druggists of Forrest City, was born in this county in 1864, being the son of H. and Eliza (Ragsdale) Evans, also natives of

Arkansas. Mr. Evans is now one the wealthiest planters of St. Francis County, and has the satisfaction of knowing that his fortune has all been acquired by his own personal industry and integrity. He received limited advantages for obtaining an education in youth, but determined that his children should receive a good, practical literary instruction, and is giving them every chance to become scholars and students in whatever right direction their ambition may lie. To himself and wife a family of eleven children have been born, eight of whom are now living, our subject, the youngest. Mr. Evans is still living, and, though having reached an advanced age, is quite active in business, managing the affairs of his large plantation with a sagacity that would put to shame many men of younger years who take pride in their superior and advanced ideas. J. J. Evans finished his literary education in Louisville, Ky., graduating from Bryant & Stratton's College in the scholastic year of 1883 and 1884. He had been occupied in laboring on the farm before going to college, earning enough money to defray his expenses, and although his father was generosity itself, he preferred to pay his own way, and at the end of his career, still had some $4,000 with which to commence business. Having a great admiration for, but no experience in the drug business, Mr. Evans engaged the services of an expert pharmacist and established a store at this place, and has made his business house as good as can be found in an average city of 40,000 inhabitants. The store is 23x180, and the stock contained therein is worth about $12,000, an annual business of between $10,000 and $12,000 being accorded this firm; this necessitates the services of three clerks. Mr. Evans is not a benedict, but a sincere admirer of the fair sex. He is a member of the K. of P. and A. F. & A. M., and is a Democrat in politics.

Hon. L. B. Featherston deserves prominent mention in the present volume not only as the efficient ex-president of the County Wheel at Forrest City, but on account of his worth as a citizen. A native of Mississippi, he was reared in Tennessee, and received a thorough, common-school education, and then attending the Law School at Lebanon,

Tenn., which he was obliged to leave and give up the study of law on account of his eyesight, having lost one eye by hard study. He was then engaged in farming in Tennessee until 1881, when he removed to Arkansas and settled in St. Francis County, buying a farm, and now he owns 16,000 acres of land, with between 300 and 400 acres under cultivation. In 1886 he was elected to the State legislature from this county and served for two years. He entered politics to defeat the influence of the "American Oil Trust," and introduced into the legislature the first anti-trust bill ever presented before any legislative body in the United States. The bill passed the house by a vote of seventy-two to five, but was defeated in the senate, and not allowed to come to a vote. Mr. Featherston was the recent nominee for the United States Congress, of a convention which met at Jonesboro, having for its platform, "Fair ballot and free count for every citizen of the United States." He is a man of influence and thought and willingly assists the promotion of what he considers the best interests of his adopted section. Mr. Featherston was born in 1851, being a son of Lewis and Elizabeth (Porter) Featherston, natives of Alabama and Virginia, respectively. The former is of Scotch descent, and removed to Georgia with his father and brother at an early day, then going to Alabama and later to Mississippi; he is now a respected resident of Shelby County, Tenn. The subject of this sketch was married in 1874 to Miss White, a daughter of E. A. White, of Memphis. They are the parents of five sons: Elbert, Lewis, John D., Paul and Douglass.

William C. Ferguson, the son of Joseph L. and Bettie E. Ferguson, was born in Shelby County, Tenn., in 1848, being denied in youth even such advantages for an education that were to be obtained at that period. When eighteen years of age he began life on his own responsibility, choosing for his vocation the most independent of all callings, farming. In 1874 he came to St. Francis County, Ark., locating on his present farm, which consists of 539 acres, with 340 cleared and carefully improved. He has also a gin (steam) with self-acting press, and a capacity of twenty bales per day, ginning on an average 700 bales each year. He is also extensively engaged in stock raising, in which he has been quite successful. In 1887 Mr. Ferguson opened a store on his place, carrying a stock valued at $3,500, from which he is realizing very satisfactory returns. He was married in 1870 to Miss Bettie E. Ligon, a daughter of J. A. and Bettie A. Ligon, natives of Dixon County, Tenn. The result of this union is nine children: Emma D., William R., Annie V., Joe, Elton T., Cleveland, Blanche, Lulu M. and Cora E. (deceased). Mr. Ferguson is a Democrat in his political views, and in religious belief, a Presbyterian. Mrs. Ferguson is a member of the Missionary Baptist Church. In secret societies he is identified with the Knights of Honor. His maternal grandfather was a soldier in the War of 1812, and died at the advanced age of eighty-six years. The paternal grandfather, a native of South Carolina, reached four-score years and six.

Thomas O. Fitzpatrick, a successful resident of St. Francis County, is of Scotch-Irish descent, his great-grandfather having been obliged to come to this country from Ireland for political causes. He struck for the liberty of his countrymen. Upon arriving in the United States in the forepart of the eighteenth century, he served in the Revolutionary War. His son, Edmund Fitzpatrick, (grandfather of our subject) took part in the War of 1812, in which he held the position of captain. He had a family of nine children. David Fitzpatrick, the father of Thomas O., was born in Charlotte County, Va., on February 19, 1813. He was twice married; first to Miss Clementine Walker, a native of Virginia, and next to Permelia Hargrove who was the mother of three children: Marietta (the wife of Rev. C. H. Ford), Isabella (wife of E. H. Sanders, of Little Rock) and Thomas O. David Fitzpatrick was engaged in speculating in real estate until the panic of 1837, when he was financially ruined, after which he followed farming in Arkansas. Thomas O. was born in Lauderdale County, Tenn., in April, 1849. He spent his younger days on the farm, and attended the common and high schools of his county, and also had the advantages of a private tutor. On his return from school he was appointed county surveyor of Cross County, which position he held, also giving his attention to teaching, until 1871. He then started the Wittsburg Gazette, the first paper published in that county, which he continued to operate until he was elected clerk of the circuit court, and in this capacity remained until the adoption of the new constitution in 1874, when he was again a candidate on the Republican ticket, but was beaten by seventy votes. Coming to St. Francis County he embarked in farming, and also erected a steam-gin, which has proven a very profitable enterprise. In April, 1872, Mr. Fitzpatrick was united in marriage to Miss Sallie E. Eldridge, and they have five children: Eola, Garnett, Ernest D., Kate and Garfield. In 1883 Mr. Fitzpatrick was appointed postmaster of Forrest City, holding that office until Cleveland's administration. In September, 1886, he was elected county clerk, and still discharges the duties of that position with satisfaction to the community, and with credit to himself. He has also been a candidate on the Republican ticket for State senator. He is a member of the I. O. O. F., K. of L., K. of H. and of the County Wheel.

Andrew J. Fulkerson was born in 1855, St. Francis County, Ark., claiming the advent of his birth. He is the son of John J. and Frances E. Fulkerson, natives of Arkansas and Indiana, respectively. Mr. Fulkerson died in 1880 and his wife in 1858. Andrew J. received but limited advantages for an education, and when only nineteen years of age commenced farming on his personal responsibility. He was married in 1877 to Becky J., daughter of Mr. and Mrs. John H. Casteel, and to their marriage five children have been given: Frances E., John H., James Arthur, William A. and Charles. Mr. Fulkerson owns 563 acres of excellent land, with over ninety under cultivation, and everything on his plantation gives evidence of thrift and prosperity. He is a Democrat in his political views, and in his religious faith a Baptist. He is a member of the Wheel and the K. of L. Mrs. Fulkerson belongs to the Methodist Church.

John Gatling, an attorney of Forrest City, is of

Scotch descent, his ancestors coming to this country many years ago. He is a son of James and Mary E. Gatling, natives of North Carolina, and was born August 2, 1851, in Perquimans County, N. C. His boyhood was spent on a farm and he attended school at an academy at Hertford until 1870, when he entered the University of Virginia, remaining there two years, and taking an academic course. After graduating he returned home, and in 1875 began the study of law in Raleigh, in the office of Moore & Gatling, where he continued about six months, then entering the Law School of Harvard University, Cambridge, Mass. In January, 1877, he was examined by the supreme court of North Carolina, and admitted to the bar. He then returned to his native county and remained until 1881, when he came to St. Francis County and located at Forrest City, where he has since been engaged in the practice of his profession and enjoys a large practice. He was married in 1881 in Hertford, N. C., to Miss Elizabeth Gilliam. Mr. Gatling is a member of the K. of P., and a Democrat and now holds the position of United States commissioner. He has one of the finest libraries in this city, valued at about $1,000.

Orville J. Hall, enlisted during the Civil War, in the Confederate service, at the age of twenty-four, serving in the Sixth Kentucky Infantry, under Col. Lewis, who is now judge of the supreme bench of Kentucky. He entered as a private, but was appointed a corporal, later made third sergeant, and at the close of the war was virtually captain of his company, although he had not received his commission papers. He participated in the battles of Shiloh, Vicksburg, Baton Rouge (in which he was wounded), Murfreesboro, Chickamauga, Atlanta, Peach Tree Creek, Jonesboro and a number of minor engagements; was captured at the battle of Jonesboro and taken to Nashville, where he was held for twenty days. After his exchange he returned to his regiment, and during the latter part of the service was on detached duty, being attached to the provost-marshal's division. Following the war period, Mr. Hall returned to his home in West Point, Ky., and commenced farming on his father's old place, his mother living with him.

He was born in Hardin County, Ky., on September 3, 1837, being a son of John W. Hall, also a Kentuckian by birth, born in 1802, who removed to West Point, Ky., a short time after his marriage, and engaged in the hotel business; he was the proprietor of the well-known West Point Hotel, and and also owned considerable property at the time of his death, which occurred in 1852. His wife came upon the stage of life's action at West Point, Ky., in 1805, and is still living at that place. In their family were seven children, three of whom are living. In 1867 Orville J. Hall removed to Crittenden County, and the following year came to St. Francis County, carrying on the timber business for a year and the next year rented a farm. He was married in 1872 to Miss Margaret E. Davis, daughter of Jasper N. Davis, an old settler of this county. They are the parents of ten children, eight living: Margaret, John William, Orville Jessie, Robert Young, Samuel Davis, Henry Russel, Edwin Winchester and Hugh. Following his marriage Mr. Hall bought a farm of 200 acres, with fifty acres under cultivation, lying in the fertile valley of the St. Francis River. He is a good Democrat. Mrs. Hall is a member of the Methodist Episcopal Church, South.

William H. Higgins was born in St. Francis County, Ark., in 1844, a son of Jeremiah and Martha Higgins, natives of Indiana and Arkansas respectively. He passed his boyhood days in much the same manner as other farmer lads, receiving such advantages for an education as could be obtained from the meager facilities of the district. His father moved to Texas in 1853, but returned after a residence there of two years. Young William began fighting life's battle at the age of twenty-three, choosing the occupation of farming, which he has since continued. He was married in 1867, to Mary E. Saratt, who died in 1879, leaving seven children: Martha A., Mary J., Melissa E., Josephine, Melinda C., Auazablin and Rosie L. Mr. Higgins was married in 1883 to Martha A. Ellis, who was also called from earth three years later, having borne one child: Elsie J. For his third and present wife, Mr. Higgins married Martha J. Elliott, an estimable lady of culture and refinement. Mr. Higgins enlisted in the Confederate army in 1861, in Company H, Fortieth Tennessee Regiment, participating in the battles of Island No. 10, Dalton (Ga.), Allatoona and Resaca. At the first-named engagement he was captured and removed to Springfield (Camp Butler), Ill., and at the battle of Allatoona, again taken prisoner and sent to Camp Chase, Ohio, remaining in prison seven and a half months. He was exchanged at Richmond (Va.) and released on parole, but before this term expired the final surrender took place. After the war Mr. Higgins returned home, where he resumed his occupation of farming, and now owns 424 acres, with 110 cleared and improved. He is also successfully engaged in stock raising. He is a member of the Wheel, and Alliance. His views politically are Democratic, and in religious faith he is a Methodist. He is a leader, not a follower, in all public enterprises, to which he contributes liberally, and under his able and efficient management the success of any movement largely is assured. Mrs. Higgins is a member of the Baptist Church.

Cephas F. Hinton, a prominent druggist of Forrest City, has been a resident of this county all his life. His father, A. G. Hinton, a native of North Carolina, came to what was then considered the wilds of St. Francis County, in 1850, where he died in 1874, at the age of forty-seven years. He had a family of twelve children, six of whom are still living: M. D. (now Mrs. Gwynne, a resident of this State), Frank M. (of this city), Lucretia M., Annie G., R. E. and C. F. The latter remained on the farm until his eighteenth year, when he came to Forrest City and embarked in general merchandising with T. E. Hastings, with whom he was connected as a partner until 1874. Then selling out to his associate he commenced in the drug business, but was unfortunate in having all of his stock destroyed by fire, on which there was no insurance, and later he entered the employ of Fussell, Pollack & Co. Three years afterward he went into the grocery business, and continued it about two years, when he was seized with a desire to alleviate the sufferings of humanity, and the study of medicine occupied his attention the fol-

lowing two years, after which he again entered into the drug business. The high water at that time stopped traffic on the railroad, and the goods which he had ordered with which to commence business, were laid over at Mariana. Mr. Hinton obtained help and loaded his stock on a handcar, which was pushed by hand to Forrest City, and thus was made his second start in the drug trade. He has by strict attention to business and honest dealing, built up a large and lucrative patronage, and now carries a stock of goods valued at $4,000. He was married in 1874 to Miss Mary A. Brown, a daughter of John Brown, and a native of Mississippi. They are the parents of four children: Robert Emmet, Arthur Gordon, William W. and Mary Bertha. Mr. Hinton also owns several hundred acres of land, and is one of the most prominent citizens of the county seat of St. Francis County, having held the position of mayor for seven years in succession. He is a decided Democrat, and a member of the K. of H.

Jesse B. Hodges, one of the prominent tillers of the soil in this section, was born in Beaufort County, N. C., in 1837, being the son of John L. and Cynthia (Rodgers) Hodges, natives of North Carolina. Jesse B. came to Arkansas with his parents in 1859, settling on a farm not far from his present residence. His educational advantages were limited, his help being needed on his father's farm, but notwithstanding this fact, he is a well-informed man, having given considerable attention to reading, which, added to keen observation, has enabled him to be conversant on all the important topics of the past and present. When twenty-two years of age he accepted a position as manager of a farm, so continuing until the breaking out of the war, when he enlisted, in 1861, in the Confederate service, in Company G, Thirteenth Arkansas Regiment, participating in the battles of Shiloh, Richmond, Perryville, Murfreesboro, Liberty Gap, Chickamauga, Missionary Ridge, New Hope, Resaca, also Peach Tree Creek, Decatur, Jonesboro, Spring Hill, Franklin and Bentonville. Subsequently, or at the close of the war, his regiment surrendered to Sherman at Greensboro, N. C., on April 26, 1865. As this sketch will show, Mr. Hodges participated in all of the principal engagements of the late war, in which the Tennessee army took part. After peace was declared he returned home, resuming the occupation of farming, and in 1868 was united in marriage to Miss Mary F. Matthews, a daughter of Lawrence and Lydia A. (Crawford) Matthews. No children have been given them. Mr. Hodges owns 400 acres of excellent land, with 275 under cultivation. He has a pleasant, comfortable place, and all the improvements and conveniences that add so much to the happiness of home. He also is quite extensively occupied in stock raising, and has been very successful. His political views are Democratic. Himself and wife are members of the Baptist Church.

Hiram Houston is a native of this county, and as he was reared in a locality but thinly settled, his advantages for a schooling were somewhat limited, but these were enough to lay the foundation for his success in life as a farmer, which occupation he engaged in for himself at the age of twenty-two, and now owns 223 acres of fine bottom land on the St. Francis River, seventy-five acres of which are under a fair state of cultivation. He also owns a steam grist-mill and cotton-gin. He was married November 2, 1884, to Miss Annie L. Clark, a daughter of Thomas A. and Susan A. Clark, originally of Kentucky and Ohio, respectively. They are the parents of three children, only one of whom is living: Nannie E. (at home). Mr. and Mrs. Houston belong to the Methodist Episcopal Church, South. Alfred K. Houston, the father of our subject, was born in North Carolina in 1814 and died in St. Francis County in 1879, and was a most successful farmer. He married Sarah E. Evans, a South Carolinian by birth, and who was the mother of seven children, four of whom are still living: Margaret E. (widow of Robert Anderson, of this county), William C. (a farmer of this county), Francis M. (also a farmer of St. Francis County) and Hiram (the principal of this sketch).

John J. Hughes is the son of John J. and Mary S. (Patrick) Hughes, natives of Georgia and Alabama, respectively, who were residing in the latter State when John J. was born, his birth occurring in the year 1828. Twelve years after they moved to Arkansas and located in St. Francis County, where Mr. Hughes died four years later, his wife surviving him only one year. The subject of this sketch was married in 1855 to Miss Margaret Ross, daughter of James F. Ross, and their union has been blessed by seven children: William S., John J., James L., Robert Lee, Leona, Bertha R. and Cora E. The boys are engaged in the mercantile business at Haynes Station, Lee County, Ark. Leona and Cora are deceased. Mrs. Hughes died in 1873, and two years later Mr. Hughes was married to Miss Fannie J. Ballout, by whom he became the father of three children: Thomas S., Walter E. and Samuel T. Thomas S. is the only child surviving. The estimable wife and mother departed this life in 1885. Mr. Hughes owns 1,000 acres of land, with 550 acres under cultivation, and the numerous late improvements placed upon it indicate the owner's spirit of progress. A comfortable and pleasant home, furnished in a quiet, refined way, show that culture and good taste have not been lacking in his busy career. Mr. Hughes has a gin with a capacity of fourteen bales per day, and he is also engaged in raising stock. In his politics he is a Democrat, and in religious faith a Baptist, though not a member of any church.

Elijah C. Hughes, of St. Francis County, Ark., is too well known in this vicinity to render a formal introduction necessary, but in compiling a volume of biographical sketches of prominent men hereabouts, the omission of his biography would leave the work incomplete. His farm, which is one of the finest in the county, consists of 2,000 acres of valuable land, with 900 under a successful state of cultivation. He grows from 350 to 450 bales of cotton yearly, 4,000 bushels of corn, and is extensively engaged in stock raising. Mr. Hughes was united in marriage, in 1857, to Miss Martha M. Reddill, and by her became the father of five children, all deceased. He enlisted in the Confederate service during the war, as a member of Company B, McNeil's regiment, and participated in the battle of Cotton. He afterward employed a substitute and remained at home, running his steam-mill for the Confederate army. Mr. Hughes is a stanch Democrat, and though not a member of any church is an adherent to the Methodist doctrine, as is also his wife. His birth occurred in Marengo County, Ala., in 1837, he being the son of John and Susan Hughes. When only one year old his parents moved to Arkansas, which has been our subject's residence ever since, with the exception of eight years spent in Shelby County, Tenn. He has served as magistrate in this county for some time, discharging the duties of the office in a highly commendable manner. He is a member of no secret organization. Mr. Hughes lends his support to all movements of a worthy character, and is considered one of the most responsible and influential men of the county, winning by his courteous manner and honesty in all business details, the respect of those who know him.

Joseph L. Ingram owes his nativity to North Carolina, and is a son of Thomas and Ellen (Covington) Ingram, who also came originally from that State. Thomas Ingram in 1849 removed to Northern Mississippi, where he resided until his death, reaching the age of seventy-five years. His grandfather, whose name he bears, was a Virginian by birth and a wealthy planter of the old Dominion, subsequently removing to North Carolina where he lived until his final summons in 1825, when about eighty-five years old. Joseph L. Ingram was born in North Carolina in 1830. At the age of twenty-seven he commenced business for himself, and the following year was married to Martha Young, daughter of Tandy K. Young. They were the parents of four children: W. C., Martha Y., Eben J. and Lady. Mr. Ingram was engaged in farming in Mississippi from 1848 to 1885. He then removed to Arkansas and located in St. Francis County, where he purchased a farm and is still employed in planting. He joined the Confederate army in 1862 and served two years, then returning to his plantation, which he found in a bad state of delapidation, the crops and stock having been confiscated by both armies. He was justice of the peace for several years while in Mississippi, and also served on the board of county supervisors for

a term of years. Mrs. Ingram died in 1888 at the age of fifty. Mr. Ingram is a member of the Methodist Episcopal Church, South, and of the A. F. & A. M. and also the Knights of Honor.

M. W. Izard & Co. are the owners and operators of the largest saw and grist mills and cotton-gin in St. Francis County, located near Colt Station. The firm is composed of M. W. Izard and John N. Cotton, both representative, active young business men, and thoroughly worthy of the position to which they have attained. Mr. Izard was born in Fayette County, Tenn., on March 3, 1855, being a son of F. J. and Sarah E. (Whittaker) Izard. Reared in this county, he attended public and private schools and received a good education, and at the age of seventeen was employed as a clerk, which occupation received his attention for about ten years. Subsequently he went into business for himself as a butcher, and two years afterward entered in the saw-mill business, later forming a partnership with his father-in-law, John N. Cotton, in the grist-mill and cotton-gin business. He also owns a large farm of 190 acres of land, with sixty-five acres under cultivation, having good improvements, a small orchard, etc. Mr. Izard was married June 12, 1879, to Miss Emma Cotton, daughter of J. N. Cotton, his partner in business. They are the parents of two boys: John and Mark W. Mr. Izard is an outspoken Democrat, and he and wife are members of the K. & L. of H. John N. Cotton owes his nativity to Western Tennessee, where his birth occurred March 2, 1834. His parents, John and Easter (Nelson) Cotton, were natives of Virginia and of English descent, their ancestors coming to this country in colonial days and taking part in the great struggle for liberty. Mr. and Mrs. Cotton moved from Virginia to Kentucky, and in 1834 to Arkansas, settling on a farm in this county, where they both died within two years after their arrival. John N. worked on a farm, and attended school three months during the first seventeen years of his life, improving his spare moments and finding opportunity to prosecute his studies for a few terms after reaching that age. Thus he acquired a good common-school education. He was then engaged in clerking in a grocery at

Taylor's Creek, now Colt, until the breaking out of the war, when he enlisted in the Twenty-third Arkansas Infantry and served as first lieutenant until the close of hostilities. After peace was restored he embarked in the general mercantile business in Forrest City, followed it for ten or twelve years, and then entered into the tie and timber business in company with his son-in-law, M. W. Izard. Mr. Cotton was married on June 20, 1861, to Miss Taylor, who died in 1865, leaving one daughter, Emma, the wife of Mr. Izard. He was married the second time, September 2, 1867, to Mrs. Gullett. They are the parents of three children: Edna, Guy and Willie. Mr. Cotton has held several important offices since living in Forrest City, among them chief magistrate of the city, and deputy sheriff of the county. His family are members of the Methodist Episcopal Church. He is a member of the Masonic and I. O. O. F. fraternities and of the County Wheel, belonging, too, to the K. & L. of H. He is also a thorough Knight of Labor.

Col. V. B. Izard, whose name is identified with only that which is good and noble, and who has attained an enviable position in the hearts of the citizens of Eastern Arkansas, owes his nativity to St. Francis County, Ark., where he was born in 1837, being the son of Mark N. and Permelia (Sharkelford) Izard. The genealogy of the Izard family is traced to Scotland, whence at an early day the great-grandfather of our subject emigrated to the New England States. Three of his sons afterward settled in South Carolina, and some time subsequent the grandfather of Col. V. B. Izard separated from his two brothers, and located permanently in Lexington, Ky. His occupation was that of a farmer, and he was a gallant soldier in the War of 1812. His son, Gov. Mark W., was born in Lexington, Ky., in 1800, removing from his native State to St. Francis County, Ark., in 1824. Here he was successfully engaged in mercantile pursuits for some years, and also opened one of the first farms or plantations in the county. Mark N. Izard was not a man who attained high intellectuality as the result of a collegiate education, for he had scarcely more than ordinary literary attainments. Something besides scholarly accomplishments drew around him hosts of friends in the pioneer days of Eastern Arkansas, it may have been his inborn worth, and intuitive genius. He entered the political field with no other qualifications to recommend, or guide him, than his own broad sense, untiring energy and clear judgment. First elected to the Territorial legislature, he served as a member of the Constitutional Convention, distinguishing himself in both cases, and to the credit of his county. He afterward served in both branches of the Arkansas State legislature (two or more times each), assisting first as speaker of the house, and later as president of the senate. While still actively engaged in the affairs of his own State, a candidate for another term in the State senate, an incident occurred which changed the field of his political labors from the State of Arkansas to the then Territory of Nebraska. This was his appointment as United States marshal of the Territory mentioned, by President Franklin Pierce, the first to hold that office. The demise of Gov. Burt, the incumbent of that position when Gov. Izard was serving as marshal, made it necessary that another Governor should be appointed. There were, of course, many aspirants for the place, but Gov. Izard with his usual characteristic originality of method, carried the official news of Gov. Burt's death to the President, and solicited the influence of the then two senators of Arkansas, W. K. Sebastan and R. M. Johnson, to have him made Governor, but they thought action on their part useless. This rebuff, however, did not daunt him. Going in person to President Pierce, after a clear statement of his ideas, he received the appointment to the coveted office. Upon leaving the president he again sought the senators to learn if they had used their influence in his behalf; they responded in the negative, whereupon he produced his commission before their astonished gaze, with the remark that he was glad to succeed without their help. He then started on his perilous trip to Nebraska, though the mild winter greatly modified the exposure incident to the journey. On February 20, 1854, he reached Omaha, his arrival being formally announced to both houses. The house appointed a committee of reception to wait upon him, and with the council proceeded in a body to the house, Acting-Gov. Cunning presenting him to the legislature in a brief address. Gov. Izard responded in his usual courtly and entertaining way, and on the 23d took the oath of office, entering at once on the discharge of his manifold duties, his son James Izard acting as secretary. On February 27, 1855, Gov. Izard was duly inaugurated, and delivered his first formal message. The house being assembled in joint session, it was arranged that his colored servant should announce his presence at the door. That dignitary received his instructions to say, "Mr. Speaker, the Governor is now approaching," but he changed the phraseology to a vernacular peculiar to himself, saying, "Mr. Speaker, the Gubner done come." Greeted by shouts of applause the "Gubner" proceeded to deliver his annual address, after which, the citizens in order to celebrate the event in a suitable manner gave a brilliant ball or reception, in which His Excellency and son James were cordially welcomed, the only ball of the kind ever given in Omaha. On the 28th of the same month the legislature proceeded with its duties, and for a period extending over the most eventful era in history, Gov. Izard presided over the Territory of Nebraska. He met the perplexing questions of the times, face to face, always displaying an executive ability, equal to the emergency. He was in sympathy with the South at time of secession, but believed the rights of the people could best be obtained under the constitution. Gov. Izard was also in favor of popular sovereignty, and gave his opinion on this subject in a clear, concise way, in his introductory address of February 22, where he said: "The enemies of the law for organization of this Territory, the enemies of popular sovereignty are looking with anxiety for an opportunity to taunt us with breaking up in a row. Let wisdom and moderation govern all your actions. I feel that there is wisdom and integrity enough here to lay the foundation for a government, the blessings of which are soon to be enjoyed by a population unparalleled in the settlement of any country; a population which

will vie in point of numbers and intelligence with any country, new or old. We have the experience of those who have gone before us—let us profit by their example. Let us show the world we adhere to and adopt the principles of popular sovereignty." The second Territorial legislature met Tuesday, December 18, 1885, and when all was in readiness, a committee waited on the Governor stating their desire to receive any communications. Gov. Izard appeared and proceeded to deliver his annual speech. His personal appearance was commanding, and his popularity unquestioned, the people knowing that their confidence was not misplaced. He had the interests of the new settlement at heart, and his message of that date was devoted principally to the improvements of the Territory and the protection of the people. Under his governorship the State prospered, in spite of the times. Vast public improvements were made, among which was the building of the State capitol, under his personal direction, and his career as Governor was one which reflected honor upon Nebraska, and redounded with credit to himself. He was once requested to go to Kansas and quiet the troubles there, afterward receiving a request from President Buchanan to receive the governorship of Kansas. His answer was that his Territory was in good condition, and at peace with all the world, and that he did not care for further gubernatorial honors. He resigned the governorship of Nebraska in 1858, his resignation being at first repealed, but his desire to return to his family despite the strongest solicitations, secured at last his release from an office in the State which undoubtedly owes its present prosperity largely to his earnest efforts of long ago. His return to St. Francis County was more than cordially welcomed by all, and here among his friends and in the association of his early pioneer companions, he spent his declining years, closing his eyes to worldly scenes in 1866, leaving a name and memory that will never fade from his descendants, or the world at large, whose appreciation of the works of a good man can not decrease. The son of Gov. Izard, Col. V. B. Izard, has been a life-long resident of St. Francis County, with the exception of the period of his father's office in Nebraska,

CRITTENDEN COUNTY, ARKANSAS.

where he was employed as teller in the Western Exchange Bank, and afterward in the land agency business. He was married in Oxford, Miss., January 28, 1848, to Miss Mary T. Fondren, and by her is the father of four children: Lena P., Richard J., Katie and V. B., Jr. After his marriage Col. Izard engaged in farming on a large plantation which is part of the present site of Forrest City. He entered the Confederate service in 1862, in the Trans-Mississippi Department, and served until the close of the war, when returning home he resumed agricultural pursuits, and subsequently embarked in merchandising, his avocation since that time. Col. Izard has always held a prominent place among the citizens of the county, and while never having made politics a profession—as did his father—he has frequently been sent as delegate to various conventions, for the purpose of soliciting candidates for State affairs. He is a member in high standing of the Baptist Church, to which he lends his liberal support, and is also a Royal Arch Mason.

R. J. Izard, one of Forrest City's most prominent attorneys at law, was born in St. Francis County in 1865, being the son of Col. V. B. and Mary T. (Fondren) Izard. [See sketch of Col. Izard.] R. J. was educated at Jackson, Tenn., and after being prepared at that school for the study of law (which had been the ambition of his youth) he entered the office of R. J. Williams, of Forrest City. Subsequently he attended the Law Department of the University at Lebanon, Tenn., and was graduated with honors from that institution in June, 1887, at once returning to the office of Mr. Williams, where his career has been a creditable one. He is now city attorney, having been elected to that position in April, 1889. In August, 1889, Mr. Izard was united in matrimony to Miss Effie Howell, a daughter of Capt. J. L. Howell, in whose honor the town of Howell, Ark., was named. Although young in years, Mr. Izard has attained a prominence that would compare favorably with others of maturer years and wider experience. He is loyal to his profession and clients, and numerous personal characteristics of worth have endeared him in the hearts of many friends and acquaint-

30

ances, a confidence and respect which he will not do aught to misplace.

William Jolly was born in Beaufort County, N. C., in 1844, being the son of Isaiah and Senia (Williams) Jolly, natives of the same State. He came to Arkansas with his parents in 1852, locating in the eastern part of St. Francis County. His schooling was limited to a few months in the district school, as he was obliged to assist his father on the farm, and when twenty-two years old he purchased a farm near the home place in 1867, being married to Miss Mattie Cummings, a daughter of Sam and Martha Cummings, of Tennessee. Mr. Cummings was among the early settlers of the county. To Mr. Jolly's marriage five children were born: Samuel E., Katie Sliza, Lee A., Georgia Beulah and Julius H. He enlisted in 1862 in Company A, McNeil's regiment, of the Confederate army, participating in the engagements of Jenkins' Ferry, Helena, Little Rock, Mansfield and Prairie Grove. At the battle of Helena he received a wound, but which did not prove serious. He surrendered at Marshall, Tex., and returned to his home, resuming his occupation of farming, and accepting the results of the war, as a final adjustment of the difficulties between the North and South, Mr. Jolly cheerfully turned his attention to the recovery of his lost fortune, though his entire stock in trade consisted of $1.25, which he obtained from a Yankee in exchange for Confederate money. His success was swift and sure, and in 1868 he located on his present farm, numbering 125 acres, cleared and in a fine state of cultivation. A beautiful residence with all the modern improvements, gives evidence of his spirit of progress and prosperity. He is a member of the Masonic order, and a Knight of Honor, a Democrat in his political views, and with his wife a member of the Baptist Church. Mr. Jolly contributes most generously to all public movements, and is one of the representative men of the county, commanding the respect of the entire community.

Nathaniel M. Jones came to St. Francis County with his father in 1832, when nine years of age, the country at that time being a comparative wilderness. He remained with his father until his death, which occurred in 1851, and in 1856 was married to Martha A. Agerton, who has borne five children: Mary C., Nancy, James P., Cleopatra and Senoth. Mr. Jones was born in Lawrence County, Ala., in 1823, to the union of Branch and and Nancy Jones, natives of Virginia and Tennessee, respectively. Mr. N. M. Jones owns a farm of 146 acres, with sixty acres under cultivation, and is extensively engaged in stock raising. He is a Democrat in politics, and was a firm adherent to the Southern cause during the late war, serving in the Confederate army throughout that conflict. He is a member of the Baptist Church (as are also all of his family, with the exception of one of the children), in which he has been an active worker. Few men have led a more honorable life or contributed more liberally to the support of religious and educational enterprises than Mr. Jones.

Philander Littell, attorney at law of Forrest City, first saw the light of day in Chicot County, Ark., being the son of Philander and Martha Littell. He received his literary education in the schools of Arkansas, and in the Lebanon University of Tennessee, and commenced the study of law at Helena, Ark., under the prominent and able Supreme Judge Hanty. At the breaking out of the war he joined the First Arkansas Regiment, serving until the final surrender. He was aid-de-camp to Gen. Walker after the battle of Shiloh, in which battle he was badly wounded, and at the time of his duel with Marmaduke was sent by Gen. Sterling Price around the Federal army to carry the news of the wounding of Gen. Walker to his family, also to bring his wife to see him. This he did, but Walker had died of his wounds before her arrival. Mr. Littell being financially embarrassed by the war, read privately and taught school for several years, and began the practice of his profession in this city, receiving the license to practice law in any State in the year 1869. He followed farming here from the time of his admission till entering upon the prosecution of his chosen profession in Forrest City, owning several considerable plantations, and is now opening a large stock farm. His father was a native of Kentucky, and an attorney for many years, afterward practicing medicine. He

died in this county in 1864. The name Littell, as would be imagined, is decidedly French. Philander Littell is a Democrat in his political views, and a man noted for his thorough knowledge of law, and is perhaps better versed in land matters and titles than any other man in this part of the State. While he has a vast amount of land devoted to the growing of cotton, he takes decided interest in stock raising, in which he has been quite successful. Mr. Littell is conservative on all questions, and a man whose judgment is seldom biased. He believes that the race question could be solved without difficulty if it were not for local politicians, whose zeal for county offices rushes them into the perpetration of many blunders, irrespective of party. Mr. Littell was united in marriage with Miss Annie Seaborn, of this county, their marriage being solemnized in 1883.

George W. Littlefield is the son of Andrew J. and Betsy Littlefield, his birth occurring in Gibson County, Tenn., in 1844. His boyhood years were passed in Panola County, Miss., and in 1861 he came to St. Francis County, and purchased a farm of 120 acres, fifty acres of which are in a good state of cultivation. He is also engaged in raising stock, and at this occupation has been quite successful. Mr. Littlefield enlisted in 1861, in Company C, Twenty-third Arkansas Regiment, participating in the battles of Corinth, Iuka, Ripley and Port Hudson, La., and served until the final surrender. He was married in 1866, to Miss Druecillar Halbert, and by her is the father of three children: John, Maggie and George. In his political views he is a Democrat, and socially is identified with the Knights of Honor. Mr. and Mrs. Littlefield are members of the Baptist Church, and while not wealthy in the possession of this world's goods, they have that which is more to be desired—an unsullied name, and the love of a host of friends.

John F. Lynch first saw the light of day in St. Francis County, Ark., August 7, 1828, being the son of John and Pollie (Barnes) Lynch, natives of North Carolina and Tennessee, respectively. The father moved to Arkansas in 1817, some time before it was made a State, and saw it rise from an insignificant territory to a community of wealth and affluence in the sisterhood of the Union. His father, a native of North Carolina, was a resident here for many years, dying in his sixty-eighth year; he was the first man buried in the county. John F. (the subject of this sketch) began farming for himself at the age of eighteen, but at the breaking out of the war, laid aside the inoffensive implements of the farm, to take up those that robbed the country of so many of her sons. He enlisted in Company B, Capt. McNeil's regiment, and received his discharge just before the final surrender. Upon his return home he found he had suffered serious losses, in fact everything being gone but his land. Mr. Lynch was married in 1853 to Miss Lizzie Davis, a daughter of Cornelius and Eliza Davis, who came to Arkansas from their native State (Kentucky) in 1828. To his marriage with Miss Davis three children were born: Albert Sidney, Kate and Bessie. Albert is residing with his father; Kate was married in 1882 to Perry Minor, living at Phœnix, Ariz., engaged in the manufacture of ice, and Bessie, the youngest, is attending school at Lebanon, Tenn. Mr. Lynch owns 220 acres, with 150 carefully cultivated, and is also engaged in stock raising. He has amassed quite a large fortune, and is considered one of the representative men of the county, his success not having made him penurious, as is so often the case. He is always ready to assist in worthy enterprises, aiding in many movements having for their aim the growth of the country. The needy ever find in him a sympathetic listener, and many of his acts of charity never reach the ears of the outside world. He has passed his sixty-second year, and his whole life has been one of upright and honorable principles. The respect and esteem accorded him is as wide as his acquaintance.

William H. McDaniel. The father of this respected citizen, John McDaniel, of Scotch origin, was born near Lexington, Ky., January 25, 1799, but grew to manhood in Virginia, where he married Miss Nancy Calvert, of Welsh descent. Soon after that event they decided to move, the tales related of the rich valley beyond the "Father of Waters," inspiring them to seek a home in the then new territory of Arkansas, coming of ancestors who were used to conflicts with the Indians, and the hardships of pioneer life, they did not hesitate to start for this new land of promise. Their trip was made by boat to a point several miles above the mouth of L'Anguille River, where they landed in 1824, and set ashore their worldly goods, consisting of one pony, two cows, and what household goods the pony could haul on a sled, and 12½ cents in money. With his family, which then consisted of his wife and two children, and with no guide but the compass, Mr. DcDaniel struck out through the forest and staked off the farm now owned and occupied by the principal of this sketch. At that time there were not more than twelve families within the limits of the present St. Francis County. Upon the breaking out of the war, Mr. McDaniel was worth over $75,000 in lands, negroes and stock, all accumulated in a little over thirty years, in a wild and unsettled country, and upon a start of only one shilling; such a record is marvelous, and shows the latent force and energy, which was lying dormant in the character of John McDaniel when coming to this locality. Mr. McDaniel lived to a ripe old age, and died October 31, 1869, his wife surviving him only four years. She died September 15, 1873, aged seventy-four years and six months. Ten years after their arrival here, January 17, 1834, was born William H. McDaniel, who, together with his brother, John L., are the only survivors of this pioneer family. The early life of William H. was spent on the farm, helping his father clear up the land which he had settled when coming to Arkansas; the outbreak of the war found him still on the old homestead, but with the enthusiasm of a patriot, and the love of his native State burning in his breast, he enlisted in the Thirteenth Arkansas Volunteer Infantry. Entering as a private, his bravery and good conduct were soon rewarded by his being promoted, first to the position of orderly-sergeant, then first lieutenant, and after the battle of Shiloh to the rank of captain. He participated in the battles of Belmont, Shiloh, Richmond and Murfreesboro (where he was wounded and disabled for a short time, also being wounded at Chickamauga) then at Missionary Ridge, and a number of other hard-fought battles, among which was the battle of Atlanta, July 22, 1864. In August, 1864, the Captain was sent west of the Mississippi, to gather up recruits for the service, and while on duty, in October of that year, was captured and taken to Chicago, and then to Johnson's Island, where he was held until the close of the war. Then returning home, he has since been engaged in farming in this county, with substantial success, and now owns 1,480 acres in one tract, having 900 under cultivation. His principal crop is cotton, and he owns his own cotton-gin and saw-mill, and a supply store to furnish goods for his tenants. On January 24, 1867, Mr. McDaniel married Miss Mollie E. Fondrew, of Tennessee. They are the parents of three daughters: Willie, Nannie and Ada. Several years ago Mr. McDaniel moved his family to Forrest City, where he has since lived, and has been a member of the city council for a number of years; also a member of the school board, and at one time was coroner of the county.

James P. McDonald was born in Kingston, Canada, in the year 1830, and is of Scotch-Irish descent. When quite a young man he left the parental roof, engaging in the lumber business, some little distance from home, and afterward worked on the Erie Canal, in 1854 going to sea. He next went to New Orleans, and having commenced boating on the Mississippi, followed that occupation until 1857, only discontinuing to accompany Albert S. Johnston to Salt Lake City. After sojourning in the land of the "Mormons" for a while the spring of 1859 found him in California. Later he went to Leavenworth, Kas., and from there to Hagerstown, Md., where he accepted the position of wagon master in the Federal service, gaining the approbation of his superior officers for his faithful attention to every detail of his business. In 1864 Mr. McDonald moved to Memphis, Tenn., and remained until 1866, leaving to take up his permanent abode in St. Francis County, Ark. In 1870 he was united in marriage with Mrs. Williams, who died two years later. In 1874 Miss Lucy Halbert became his wife, and by her he had two children, who have

since died: Rosie A. and Sallie Baker. Mrs. McDonald closed her eyes to the scenes of this world in 1876, and in 1881 Mr. McDonald was united in matrimony with Mrs. Lane, his present wife. Mrs. McDonald is a very estimable lady, and enjoys the respect of a wide circle of acquaintances and friends. In secret organizations Mr. McDonald is identified with the Masonic order, and is also a member of the Wheel. In politics he votes the union labor ticket, and with his wife attends the Baptist Church, in which they have been members of many years standing.

Joseph McGowen, a native of North Carolina, was left an orphan at the age of seven years, his mother having died in 1836 and his father four years later. He was then bound out to a Mr. Turnage, with whom he remained until his seventeenth year, when he commenced working for himself at common farm labor in Shelby County, Tenn., and in 1852 purchased a farm in Tipton County. He was married November 19, 1854, to Cordelia A. Joyce, a native of Tennessee. They were the parents of thirteen children, seven of whom are still living: William Oliver (born January 15, 1856), Eugenia H. (born September 6, 1857) and Thomas Martin (born April 26, 1862), who are married; Edward G. (born October 1, 1860), Annie Eliza (born January 10, 1867), Mary Frances (born December 25, 1868) and James Taylor (born June 28, 1872). Eugenia H. was married to William Williams March 4, 1875; William Oliver was married to M. J. English December 28, 1881; Thomas Martin was married to Gertrude Tennant December 21, 1887. Mr. McGowen remained in Tipton County until 1878 when he removed to Lee County, Ark., but after one year there, came to St. Francis County, where he still resides. He owns a quarter section of land with all but twenty acres under cultivation. Mr. McGowen has always been an active Democrat, and is a strong advocate of the public school system.

Jesse W. Mahaffey, though a native of Georgia, was brought to Arkansas by his parents when nine years of age, and was reared on a farm in St. Francis County, growing up here when there were but few settlers, with schools and churches few and far between, and no society or companions excepting his family, consequently he had but a limited advantage for receiving an education, starting out in life as a common farm laborer at the age of sixteen. In the fall of 1849 he went into the timber business and has been engaged in getting out timber from the forest and rafting it down the St. Francis River since that time in connection with farming. He owns a fine farm on the river bottoms of 520 acres, well adapted to the growing of corn and cotton, and has ninety acres under cultivation, the remainder being timber. This land lies partly in this county, and in Cross and the balance in Crittenden County. Mr. Mahaffey was born in Georgia on March 15, 1831, being a son of John and Lucinda (Wright) Mahaffey, natives of Eastern Tennessee. John Mahaffey was born near Knoxville in 1804, and was married on January 9, 1825, soon after which he removed to Georgia, and in 1840 came to St. Francis County, Ark., living here until his death in 1859. He was a member of the Christian Church in his latter days and took an active interest in all religious matters, his chief object being to train his children in the fear of God. He was the father of seven children: Jesse Woods (the principal of this article), Elizabeth P., William R., Lutishia, Belinda, Winnie and David R. The subject of this sketch is the only one of the family living. He has been twice married; first to Sarah Duncan, in 1854, a native of Tennessee, who died the following year, leaving one daughter. The latter also died when five years old. He married his second wife on May 19, 1857; she was formerly America E. Dixon, a daughter of Thomas Dixon, and a native of Tennessee. They were the parents of eight children, five of whom are living: James W., Jesse W., Thomas F., Lucinda and Mary E. Mr. Mahaffey is a Democrat in politics, though formerly an old line Whig. He is an upright Christian gentleman and a liberal donator to all charitable objects.

John W. Mallory was born in Petersburg, Va., in the vicinity of which he resided with his mother until the year 1842, when she moved to Fayette County, Tenn. Leaving home in 1843, when fifteen years old, John went to Memphis, Tenn., and became engaged in clerking in a dry-goods store, continuing at that business until 1849. During his stay in Memphis he enlisted in a company fitting out for service in Mexico, but as their services were not needed it was soon disbanded. In the winter of 1848 he returned to Fayette County and in the January following was married. In 1852, moving to St. Francis County, Ark., he engaged in the mercantile business at Mount Vernon, at that time the county seat. To Mr. Mallory's marriage nine children were born: Etta, Cora, Emmett, Bessie, Eddie, John, Roger, Robert and Neeley. He now resides on his farm where he has made his home for thirty-seven years. He is a Mason, having passed the Blue Lodge to the Chapter, and thence to the Knight Templar degree. He is also a member of the I. O. O. F. and K. of H. Mr. Mallory's father was a native of Louisa County, Va. He was of Scotch descent and his mother of French, descended from the Huguenots who fled to America on account of religious persecution. At an early age he moved to Petersburg, Va., and engaged in business, subsequently enlisting in the War of 1812 as a member of the Petersburg Blues, and served in Canada under Gen. William Henry Harrison. He was present at the principal engagements of that war, among others the battle of the Thames, in which the celebrated chief, Tecumseh, was slain, and he was only a short distance from him when he fell. He secured his tomahawk, which is still in the possession of the family. It is a piece of wonderfully unique and grotesquely finished workmanship. After the close of the war he was elected high sheriff of Petersburg, which office he held until his death in 1830. In commemoration of his untiring energy and devotion to his office the city council presented him with a silver cup, bearing the date of his birth, March 10, 1790. It is now in the possession of his son, the subject of this sketch.

Lowry Mallory is a native of Alabama, and grew to manhood in his native State, supplementing his primary education by an attendance at Oxford College. Upon leaving school he came to Arkansas, locating on White River, in Jackson County, where he opened up a farm and remained for twelve years, improving his land; but overwork impaired his health, and he was obliged to travel for a few years. Thus were spent all the savings which he had made during that time in seeking restoration to his former condition, and he had only about $50 remaining. He then went to West Point, and was engaged in the real-estate business until 1884, when he entered the employ of the Little Rock Oil Company, and for four years was occupied as general purchasing agent of the company, employed in buying cotton seed. Mr. Mallory's marriage was to Miss Bessie Mallay, who was born in St. Francis County. She died in 1886, leaving three children: Walter E., J. W. and Bessie. William Mallory, the father of our subject, is a Virginian by birth, and moved to Alabama at an early date, being one of the pioneers of that part of the State. He was there married to Miss E. J. Blackwood. He was a son of a soldier in the Revolutionary War, and was of Irish descent.

William Manning was born near the city of Cork, Ireland, on August 12, 1835. In 1844 his father and mother emigrated to the United States, and located in Dutchess County, N. Y., the subject of this sketch, with the other children, following in 1845. The family remained in New York, engaged in the nursery business and farming, until 1856, when all moved to Will County, Ill., and settled on a farm. There our subject continued till 1866, the time of his removal to Jasper County, Iowa, where he was engaged in the nursery business until 1874. Selling his nursery, he returned to Illinois, and remained on the homestead until 1876, when he moved to his present location in St. Francis County, Ark. He was married on April 8, 1863, to Miss A. D. Harrah, a native of Pennsylvania. In September, 1861, Mr. Manning enlisted in the band of the Thirty-seventh Illinois Volunteer Infantry, and was discharged in June, 1862, when the band was mustered out of service. While in Illinois he served one term as commissioner of highways, and one year as collector of taxes. In 1888 he was elected representative from St. Francis County on the Fusion ticket. He is a Democrat in politics, but not of the ballot-box stuffing variety. In the legislature

he upheld every measure that was in the interest of progress and development, and supported every local temperance measure, and was largely instrumental in securing the passage of the native wine bill. His family consists of seven boys and one girl, ranging in age from four to twenty-five years. Since coming to Arkansas Mr. Manning has been engaged in farming and stock raising, and has been fairly successful.

W. J. Matthews, M. D., a popular physician of Forrest City and a credit to the medical fraternity, was born in Maury County, Tenn., May 28, 1831, being one of eight children born to James W. and S. K. (Dooley) Matthews, natives of North Carolina and Tennessee, respectively. James W. Matthews was a pioneer of Tennessee, a farmer by occupation, and surveyor of Maury County for many years. He died in his eighty-third year, his wife having gone before in her sixty-fourth year. The paternal grandfather was born in North Carolina, and came to Tennessee when James W. was a small boy, dying in Tennessee at a very old age. The maternal grandfather also owed his nativity to Tennessee, and served in some of the Indian wars, and was given the euphonious title of "Old Capt. Dooley." The great-grandmother was killed by Indians while holding the grandmother (a baby at the time), and engaged in spinning flax. W. J. Matthews passed his early life in the schools of Maury County, Tenn., afterward becoming enrolled as a pupil of Erskine College, South Carolina, remaining away from home for three years. On the completion of his literary education he returned home and began the study of medicine under A. T. Boyd and J. M. Buldridge of Maury County, Tenn., and after having graduated from the Medical Department of the College at Nashville, Tenn., 1860, went immediately to Taylor's Creek, St. Francis County, Ark. In June, 1861, he entered the Confederate army as a private, this company being commanded by Hon. Poindexter Dunn. After three months Dr. Matthews was promoted to the position of surgeon of the Third Confederate Regiment, and served in that company in the same capacity till the close of the war. Of a company of 100 men from this neighborhood, all were unmarried, with the exception of the captain. They were in the Army of the Tennessee, and participated in the hard-fought battles of Shiloh, Murfreesboro, Missionary Ridge, Chickamauga, Kenesaw Mountain, Ringgold Gap, Golgotha Church, Jonesboro, Franklin and Perryville. Pat. Cleburne was the major-general, and Dr. Matthews was on the field when he met his death. Twenty-one men of the original number (100) returned home, and nine of them are now living. At the close of the war Dr. Matthews resumed his former practice, which he had established a year previous to the war at Taylor's Creek, and though he voted against secession, he went with his State when it seceded. Coming to Forrest City, in 1871, he has since been actively engaged in the practice of his profession, and has attained an enviable position, both in social circles and as a competent physician. Dr. Matthews was married in 1866 to Miss Ella Eastham, of Summerville, Tenn., but death claimed her in 1871, she having borne two children, now deceased. His second wife was Mrs. Carrie Prewitt, of Saulsbury, Tenn., and to them one child was born, Leta B. Mrs. Matthews died, and his third and present wife was Miss C. M. Gray. Dr. Matthews is a member of the State Medical Association, secretary of St. Francis County Medical Society, and a member of the A. F. & A. M., I. O. O. F., K. of H., and K. & L. of H. He is also an earnest worker in the Presbyterian Church.

Archibald S. May, a well-known farmer of St. Francis County and numbered among its younger citizens, was born in that county in 1854, being the son of R. A. and L. C. May, natives of North Carolina and Georgia, respectively. With the exception of a few months spent in Texas he has passed his entire life in Arkansas. Mr. May was not fortunate in receiving a liberal education, the advantages at the period of his boyhood being far from satisfactory, but by constant and close application to study of late years he is conversant with many topics of importance of the past and present. He was married in December, 1888, to Miss Mollie Taylor, a daughter of James H. and Lucinda C. Taylor of Arkansas. Mr. May is a member of the Methodist Episcopal Church, South, and also of

the Wheel. His principal business is that of stock raising, and he is a man who stands high in his community—possessing true worth and integrity and being a liberal supporter of all public enterprises.

Thomas I. Mohler, M. D., who occupies a position of prominence in the medical affairs of Eastern Arkansas, was ushered into the world on March 10, 1844, in the State of North Carolina, but was reared in Kentucky, spending his boyhood in a tobacco factory. At the age of eighteen he went to Illinois and the following January enlisted in the Thirty-first Illinois Infantry as a private, before the close of the war being promoted to the position of second lieutenant. He served in Sherman's "march to the sea," and participated in all of the battles in that campaign. After the war going to Johnstown, Mr. Mohler bought a farm, and in April, 1866, was married to Miss Judy S. Lawrence, who died in January, 1878, leaving six children. He was engaged in farming for four years, after which he went into partnership with his brother in the manufacture of tobacco and cigars. Following the death of his wife he commenced the study of medicine and attended lectures at the St. Joe Medical College, subsequently traveling over Missouri, Iowa, Utah, California and all of the Western States. In 1887 he located at Palestine, Ark., and commenced the practice of medicine, and has built up an extensive patronage. He is a Republican in politics and a member of the K. of P.

Irving R. Nail owns one of the carefully cultivated farms of St. Francis County, Ark., it consisting of 120 acres, a greater portion of it being under the plow, and the general impression of the observer, is that thrift and prosperity prevail. He owes his success to no one, being thrown on his own resources at the age of thirteen, and though the prospect was not one to encourage one, he never grew despondent, but kept bravely on, with what success is already known. He was born in Tennessee in the year 1825, being the son of Andrew and Lucy, natives of Virginia and Kentucky, respectively. Mr. Nail came to St. Francis County in 1838 where he breathed his last a few years later. Irving R. Nail enlisted in the Confederate army in 1861 in Johnston's Company, Thirteenth Arkansas Regiment, participating in the battle of Belmont. He was shortly after discharged on account of illness, this ending his war career. He was married in 1863 to Amanda Raney, a daughter of Thomas and Jane Raney. The result of this union was four children: Martha J., William R., Dorinda and John C. Mrs. Nail died in August, 1877, and Mr. Nail remained a widower until January, 1881, when he took for his second wife Miss Nancy Cobb, whose father, W. M. Cobb, immigrated from South Carolina to Arkansas in 1855, having been born in 1825. Mr. and Mrs. Nail are members in high standing of the Baptist Church, to which the former lends his hearty support and influence. He is a Democrat politically.

John M. Parrott, a retired lawyer of Forrest City, is native of Tennessee. His father, John Parrott, moved to that State at a very early day in its history, where he engaged in the saddlery business, serving as a soldier in the War of 1812. He died in 1845, his wife surviving him twenty years. They were the parents of a large family, of whom John M., our subject, who was born in Jefferson County, Tenn., in October, 1814, is the only survivor. He lived at his native town, Dandridge, attending the academy at that place, until seventeen years of age, when his father moved upon a farm in the vicinity. In 1836 he commenced life for himself at Blountsville, Ala., going into the mercantile business, and three years later came to St. Francis County, continuing the same business at Madison. In 1840 he was appointed deputy clerk by Isaac Mitchel, then clerk of the St. Francis circuit court, and in 1842 was elected circuit clerk, which office he filled with such satisfaction to the citizens that he was made his own successor for fourteen years in succession; during this time he applied himself closely to the study of law, and in 1856 he was admitted to the bar and commenced practicing, which he followed until within a few years, when he retired from active professional life. In 1864 Mr. Parrott was elected to the legislature, but did not serve the term, owing to the fact of there being no session that year. In 1874 he was a delegate to the constitutional convention. He was a candidate for nomination for the office of auditor of State in 1876, but was beaten by John Crawford. During the war he entered the Confederate service and acted as assistant adjutant, though being in no engagements. Mr. Parrott has been twice married; first, in 1841, to Rhoda Johnson, who died in 1858. His second union, in 1859, was to Mrs. Johnson (nee Witter). They are the parents of six children, three of whom are still living: Kate C. (now Mrs. Martin), Ida Lee (now Mrs. Miller) and Mattie A., all residing in this county. Mr. Parrott has been a member of the Methodist Episcopal Church, South, for the past forty-five years. He is also connected with the Masonic order.

Rev. W. H. Paslay, prominently associated with the Baptist Church of Forrest City, first saw the light of day in South Carolina, December 18, 1831, being the son of H. W. and Mary (Wright) Paslay, born in South Carolina, in 1803 and 1802, respectively. H. W. Paslay was a graduate from the Medical Institute of Charleston, and also a minister of the Baptist Church. He was recognized as a gentleman of unusual attainments, both in his practice of medicine, and as a minister of the Gospel. He immigrated to Arkansas in 1857, where his death occurred in 1872. To himself and wife a family of eight children were born. The mother of Mr. Paslay closed her eyes to the scenes of this world in 1873. W. H. Paslay received his education in the schools of his native State, afterward taking a full course in the well-known Furman University of South Carolina, graduating therefrom in the year 1855. He then taught school for several years, and was ordained in Alabama, where for fifteen years he was engaged in preaching and teaching. Coming to Arkansas in the fall of 1872, he located in Monroe County, and has endeared himself to many friends and acquaintances by his conscientious and faithful work in the church, as well as by his efficient discharge of the manifold duties of teacher in the schools. He has been occupied in preaching (as at present) in St. Francis, Lee, Monroe and Phillips Counties, his work covering a period of over thirty-one years. During the Civil War he was prevailed upon by many soldiers, who went into active service, to remain at home to look after their families, they feeling that his watchful care would keep them from all harm, so his work in the war covered only a short time. Mr. Paslay was first married to Miss Geraldine Rupum, of Alabama, who left four daughters, viz.: Mary Tula, Ora Lana, Alna Mona and Etta Leta. He was next married to Miss Julia Prince of Alabama, who died leaving one child, Estelle. His third and present wife was formerly Miss Ann Dozier of Jasper County, Ga., and by her he became the father of three sons: W. H., Woode D. and Rob E. Mr. Paslay in connection with his many other duties, carefully cultivates a farm of 320 acres of valuable land. He is a Mason in the Blue Lodge and Chapter, and also a Knight of Honor.

G. W. Pearson, deputy circuit and county clerk of St. Francis County, was born in Mississippi December 25, 1830, being the third in a family of nine children born to John A. and Nancy (Nichols) Pearson. They were natives of North Carolina (near Fair Bluff), and married there, moving to Southern Mississippi in 1829. At the date of their deaths they lived near Brandon, Miss. John A. Pearson was a Methodist Episcopal minister, and had preached from the earliest recollections of his son until his death, in 1842. Of their large family of children, G. W. is the only one now living. Everett died at Nashville, Tenn., in the Confederate army, in the Sixth Mississippi Regiment; John was waylaid and shot by a negro; the sisters married and all died after the war. G. W. has in his possession a cane which was made by his grandfather (a native of North Carolina) when a young man. He was a carpenter and natural mechanic, and died in his seventy-third year. G. W. Pearson received his education in the schools of Mississippi, and selected farming as his occupation, in which he was actively engaged until coming to Arkansas, in 1872. He was married in Mississippi to M. A. Taylor, and their union was blessed by two children: William Atkins and Annie Everett. Mr. Pearson owns a residence in town. He was agent for the Memphis & Little Rock Railroad for nine years, subsequently being appointed magistrate, and has been filling the position of deputy county clerk since May, 1889, dis-

charging the duties of his office in a highly creditable manner. The grandfather of Mr. Pearson and two brothers were taken captives by Indians and carried far back into the interior of the country, after which the savages held a council to determine the best way to dispose of their captives. The brothers were lashed to the ground to await their terrible death, but an Indian maiden became enamored of one of them—a very handsome man—and went to his relief, cutting the lashes that bound him, and telling him at the same time to flee for his life, which injunction he was not slow to follow. He released his brothers, and after running nearly all night, they crawled into a large log, whose capacity was sufficient to hold them all. The Indians followed in hot pursuit, and were close upon them when a herd of deer crossed their path, thereby destroying the trail. The redskins gave up the chase, and actually seated themselves on the log in which the brothers were secreted, and in which they remained until night. They had been without food for three days, and when an opossum crossed their path they killed and devoured it without waiting to have it broiled, their intense hunger making them forget that it was raw. They made their way to a white settlement, and then on to their old home, where they were welcomed by their relatives and friends, who had despaired of ever seeing them again. Mr. Pearson has not been particularly fortunate in amassing property, but he and his honored wife enjoy that which is of far more consequence—an unsullied name and the sincere love of a host of friends. He is a Royal Arch Mason and a member of the Missionary Baptist Church, his wife also being connected with the same church.

Hon. R. W. Peevey, farmer, stock raiser, and one of the prominent old settlers of St. Francis County, owes his nativity to Alabama, being a son of W. H. and J. A. (Childers) Peevey, originally from Georgia and Tennessee, respectively, and of Irish descent. The parental grandparents of our subject came to this country shortly after the Revolutionary War. R. W. Peevey was born January 8, 1827, and was the fourth son in a family of seven children. He spent his boyhood days on his father's farm, and before his twentieth birthday was married to Miss Nellie A. Collier, who died in 1850, leaving three children, two still living: James J. and Emma J. (wife of W. H. Fogg), both in this county. In 1862 Mr. Peevey enlisted in the Confederate army and served in Col. Robinson's regiment, being elected captain of his company at starting out, and in May, 1863, he was promoted to major. He participated in the battles of Vicksburg, Baton Rouge, Corinth and a number of others. After the war he engaged in farming in Madison County, Ala., until 1873, when he came to Arkansas and located in St. Francis County, where he bought his present farm. In October, 1859, he married Miss Louisa Curry. She died in August, 1878, having borne seven children, and of these four survive: Thomas Elbert, Robert H., William H. and Luther B. Mr. Peevey married his third wife, Mary J. Dew, in January, 1880. He is a prominent Democrat, and has ably served his county in the State legislature, to which he was elected in 1876. He also held the office of justice of the peace for several terms, and is still filling that position. A member of the Methodist Episcopal Church, he is also connected with the Masonic fraternity.

Frank M. Prewett, one of the oldest and most respected merchants of Forrest City, was born in Bedford County, Tenn., November 4, 1827, and at the age of sixteen went to Texas and volunteered in the Mexican War, under Capt. James Arnold and Col. Albert Sidney Johnston. He participated in the battles of Monterey and Buena Vista, receiving an honorable discharge at the end of two years. On his way home he stopped at Mount Vernon, and then and there became ensnared in cupid's toils, yielding up his affections to the charms of Miss N. E. Izard. Ten days after they met she wore his engagement ring, and eight months later they were married. Mr. Prewett located at Mount Vernon and engaged in the grocery business, and, notwithstanding that he started with very little capital, he possessed at the breaking out of the war, a large plantation and twenty-nine slaves. He enlisted in Capt. Mallory's company as first lieutenant during the civil strife, and was

promoted while at Cotton Plant to the office of captain. His health giving way necessitated his resignation, which took place in the northern part of Arkansas, inflammatory rheumatism, caused by exposure, rapidly making inroads upon his usual health. At the close of the war he found his fortune all gone, and many debts previously contracted staring him in the face. His slaves remained with him, but the expense of keeping them was much more than they could possibly liquidate. One morning Uncle Frank (as he is familiarly called) was viewing his gloomy situation, naturally becoming more and more despondent, when he was accosted by Mr. J. H. Cole, an acquaintance of many years, who proposed that they go to Madison and enter into business, Mr. Prewett not to furnish any capital. The result was the establishing of a mercantile establishment under the name of Cole & Prewett. After a few months Mr. Prewett discovered something which he considered more profitable, and desired a dissolution of partnership, his share of the profits being $1,900. Mr. Cole presented him with a fine horse and saddle, which he traded for a small box house, the first house erected on the present site of Forrest City, and since converted into a saloon. Here, in connection with Col. Izard, he amassed a fortune in the grocery business, while the Little Rock & Memphis was being built. They afterward failed for $45,000, and were obliged to dispose of a large amount of real estate in order to cancel their indebtedness. Mr. Prewett went out of the business and resumed farming for ten years, at the expiration of that time coming back into the same business, where he is to be found at present. Mrs. Prewett, who died in her fifty-fourth year, was a faithful worker and member of the Baptist Church, and a most exemplary lady, being thoroughly beloved by all who knew her. By her marriage with Mr. Prewett she became the mother of eleven children, seven now living: John M. (attorney at law of Forrest City), Mark W. (mail clerk from Helena to Knobel), Thomas E. (city marshal of Forrest City), Blanche (wife of T. L. Briscoe, of Helena), Oscar (a railroad man), Mary E. and George Emma (at home). Mr. Prewett is a son of P. H. and Judy (Whittaker) Prewett. His father was born in Bedford County, Tenn., and in 1854 immigrated to Texas, breathing his last in the latter State, in 1866, at the age of seventy-two. Mr. Prewett is a Royal Arch Mason, an Odd Fellow and a member of the Baptist Church.

George C. and Frank E. Prewitt are now prominent young farmers of this county, though natives of Missouri. They removed to St. Francis County, Ark., in 1886, and settled on the St. Francis River, a section noted for its fertility and productiveness. Their father, Joseph E. Prewitt, was a native of Scott County, Ky., where he was reared and married, Miss Naomi M. Nash, a native of Covington, Ky., becoming his wife. She was a daughter of William and Elizabeth Nash, and died in 1879, leaving six children: Robert C. (M. D.), William L. (a teacher in Missouri), Bettie A. (wife of George W. Watts), George C. and Frank E., and Mattie C. (now Mrs. Clifford, of Missouri). Mr. Prewitt died in 1874 at the age of sixty-five. George C. Prewitt was born on May 20, 1850, and received a good education, being instructed in the rudiments of farm work by his father, who was an agriculturist of advanced ideas. At the age of twenty he commenced farming for himself. Frank E. was born in Pike County, Mo., June 18, 1859, and started out in life as a tiller of the soil at the age of nineteen, in 1886 becoming associated with his brother George. They are industrious and enterprising young farmers, and are turning their attention to that most lucrative branch of agricultural pursuits, as well as that most beneficial to the community, the breeding of fine stock, in which they will undoubtedly make a decided success. They are Democrats in politics and liberal donators to all charitable and worthy enterprises.

Hon. Otto B. Rollwage, mayor of Forrest City, and a member of the firm of Rollwage & Co., one of the leading mercantile houses in Forrest City, was born in Cincinnati, Ohio, in 1854, being reared and educated in that city. At the age of twenty years he came to Forrest City, and engaged as salesman in a store in this city for three months, after which he entered into the mercantile business with his brother Louis. They commenced on a small scale, but by close attention to business and strict economy, enjoy a very extensive trade, employing eight salesmen in their store. They own five business houses besides the one they occupy. Mr. Rollwage was a member of the board of aldermen for some time, and so efficient were his services in that capacity, and so diligently did he attend to the duties devolving on him that he was complimented with a nomination for mayor of Forrest City, while away from home, and without his knowledge. His administration has been very beneficial to the city, he having enforced the many ordinances that were before a dead letter on the status, and especially has he been vigorous in the prosecution of all parties violating the whisky laws; as a result there is now no better regulated city in the State. In his domestic relations Mr. Rollwage is not less happily situated than in business circles. He married Miss Jennie Anderson, of Monroe County, a graduate of a female college in Tennessee, and a highly educated and refined lady. She is a leader in the society of Forrest City, and is one of the prominent members of the W. C. T. U. in Arkansas, having been a State delegate to the National Convention held at Nashville in 1887. This worthy couple are the parents of five children: Norma, Otto, Tolise, De Velling and Madeleine. Mr. R. is a son of Frederick and Mina (Kuker) Rollwage, both natives of Germany. Frederick Rollwage is still living and resides in Cincinnati, but spends about half of his time with his son, our subject.

George M. Rowland, a prominent farmer of Utica Township, is a native of Mississippi, and a son of Charles and Mary (Lewis) Rowland, who were Virginians by birth. In 1830 they left the Old Dominion for Marshall County, Miss., then a new part of the State, and from which the Indians had just been moved. Here the father lived on a farm which he entered until 1840, then going to Benton County, where he made his home until called away by death, in 1863. His wife survived him until 1876. They were the parents of six boys, three of whom are still living: W. L. (on the old place), J. E. (a resident of St. Francis County), and George M. The latter was born in Marshall

County, Miss., February 22, 1850. His father, like a number of other Southerners, was a Union man until Virginia attempted to withdraw from the Union, when he announced his allegiance to his native State, and gave three of his sons to the Southern cause. After the battle of Shiloh the brothers returned home on a furlough, and were surprised by the Federals, but would not have been captured had it not been for the treachery of a companion. The three boys and also their father were taken prisoners, and carried to Cairo, Ill., afterward being exchanged, but the father died within eight days after his return, from exposure while coming down the river. George M. Rowland remained at home during the war, being too young to enter the service, though he heard bullets whistle on more than one occasion. In 1868 he went to Gibson County, Tenn., was engaged in teaming for a man by the name of Davis, and the following year took charge of a large farm in Hardeman County, belonging to the same party, where he remained until 1875. Going home on a visit, the month of January, 1876, found him en route for Arkansas, in charge of stock for J. D. Reans, of Forrest City, for whom he clerked the rest of the year. The next year he rented a farm, and has since been occupied in that occupation, now owning two farms, one of 214 acres, and one 185 acres in extent, with over seventy-five acres under cultivation. Mr. Rowland has been twice married, first, in 1879, to Miss Mollie V. Jeth, who died in 1881. His second wife was Mrs. Allie S. Johnson (nee Hill). They are the parents of one child, Charlie Pike, born in 1887. Mr. Rowland is an influential Democrat, and has served as justice of the peace two years. He is a member of the Knights of Honor, and at one time belonged to the County Wheel.

John L. Roy, active in the agricultural affairs of Utica Township, is a native of Tennessee, and a son of James and Mary Roy, originally from Virginia and Tennessee, respectively. John L. came to St. Francis County, Ark., with his father in 1828, being at that time only one year old. Though not having been consulted as to this change of residence, he has never regretted being a citizen of the State of Arkansas, as he is entirely satisfied with the country and people. He grew up to farm life, and while living in the country in a day when it was but thinly settled, received a good education, attending school regularly until he grew to manhood. At the age of twenty-one he commenced life for himself as book-keeper at a store in Helena, but resigned that position in a short time to take charge of a trading boat on the Mississippi River. Two years later he went to New Orleans, and resumed clerking in a dry goods and grocery house for two years, after which he returned home, and has since been occupied in farming. Mr. Roy was married in 1853, to Miss Lucy E. Dallor, daughter of James and Mary Dallor, natives of North Carolina. They are the parents of nine children: Mary E., Thomas J., Mark G., Martha J., Sarah F., William E., Nettie A., Richard L. and John A., the last two being twins. He owns a fine farm of 160 acres, with sixty-five acres under cultivation, and is engaged in raising stock and farming, principally. He is a member of the Masonic order, and of the Knights of Honor, and also of the County Wheel, and he and his family belong to the Baptist Church. In the early days when the parents of our subject first came to this country, and for a number of years after, game was plentiful, and John L. had many exciting bear hunts. At one time, while his father and William Stags were out hunting, their dog was in danger of being killed by a bear, whereupon the former caught the wild animal by the ears, and held him until Mr. Stags shot him; this exploit gained him quite a reputation as a bear hunter.

R. H. Sparkman, M. D., one of Forrest City's enterprising citizens, was born in North Carolina, May 10, 1828, being the son of John and Nancy (Wooten) Sparkman. John Sparkman owed his nativity to North Carolina, but moved to Tennessee when the subject of this sketch was quite small, locating in Shelby County, Tenn., where his death occurred in his fifty-ninth year. Mrs. Sparkman was also of North Carolina origin and by her union with Mr. Sparkman became the mother of five children, R. H. being the only one now living. The name Sparkman, as might be supposed, is Irish, the ancestors of the family coming at an early day from the Emerald Isle. The grandfather was a soldier in the War of the Revolution, and the maternal grandfather served in the War of 1812. Dr. Sparkman received a good common education in the schools of Shelby County, and afterward attended his first course of medical lectures in Cincinnati, his early ambition having been to be a physician, and by his determination and diligent application to his studies he became a credit to that most noble of all professions. He graduated with honors from the Medical School at Memphis in 1857, and immediately began practice in Shelby County, but a year afterward, in 1858, making a trip to Arkansas became convinced that that State promised a better opening, so located on the Helena road, five miles from Forrest City. At the breaking out of the war he had built up an enviable practice. He joined the Confederate army, McGee's company, McNeil's regiment, afterward becoming surgeon of that regiment. The company was soon made independent and reported to Col. Dobbins, Dr. Sparkman remaining in the service about two years. He returned to Arkansas and practiced until 1875, but succeeded in collecting only about half of his bills, some of them of long standing. He has since retired from active practice, and is now engaged in farming, owning 450 acres of valuable land. Dr. Sparkman was united in marriage on December 23, 1859, to Mrs. Liza (Purvis) Daniel, of North Carolina. Dr. and Mrs. Sparkman are members of the Baptist Church, and the former is a member of A. F. & A. M.

G. W. Seaborn, deputy sheriff of St. Francis County, is well known to the residents of that section of Arkansas, and enjoys the esteem of all, except from those whose disregard of law compels him to discharge the duties of his office in an impartial manner; at such a time he would scarcely be recognized as a jovial companion or the perpetrator of many amusing jokes. Mr. Seaborn was born in St. Francis County in 1853, being the son of G. W. and Frankie (Casteel) Seaborn. The former, of Tennessee nativity, came to Arkansas when about nineteen years of age, locating in St. Francis County, and being the first man to bring

a flat-boat load of merchandise up the St. Francis River. He purchased the goods in New Orleans, and established an extensive business near Mount Vernon, when that was the county seat. He was the first sheriff of the county, holding that office for twelve years, and subsequently served in the State legislature, and was a member of that body at the breaking out of the late war. In 1863 he moved to Tennessee, and upon the close of hostilities opened a mercantile establishment at Jefferson, Texas. In 1872 he returned to St. Francis County, and died in 1875 at the age of sixty-three years. Mrs. Seaborn accompanied her parents from Tennessee to Arkansas when quite small, and has resided in this county ever since. She was married in St. Francis County and became the mother of two children, G. W. being the youngest. Annie, his sister, is now the wife of B. F. Elington of Atlanta, Ga. Mrs. Seaborn owns a large farm, but resides with her children. G. W. Seaborn grew to manhood in St. Francis County, receiving his education in Texas, where the facilities afforded him were unusually liberal. After finishing his schooling, he came back to his old home and engaged in farming for four years, and with the exception of four years spent in the livery business at Forrest City, has made agricultural pursuits his principal avocation. He now owns about 600 acres in this and adjoining counties. Mr. Seaborn was married in 1876 to Miss Mattie Cabbs, a daughter of Dr. J. H. Cabbs, brother of the present land commissioner. Dr. Cabbs' mother is living in this county at the advanced age of ninety-three years. To the union of Mr. and Mrs. Seaborn three children were born. Mrs. Seaborn died in 1883, leaving many friends to mourn her death. In his political views he sides with the Democratic party.

James W. Skinner was born in Fleming County, Ky., in 1842, as the son of Benjamin F. and Lucinda Skinner. His early life was passed in the schools of his native State, from which he received a superior education, and at the age of nineteen he began in business on his own responsibility in New Orleans, making many friends both in social and business circles during his stay in that city. In 1861, going to Memphis, Tenn., he enlisted in the Confederate service, where he remained for one year and then commenced steamboating on the Mississippi River, following this business until the Federals gained control of the river. In 1868 he came to St. Francis County, Ark., and embarked in the manufacture of staves. Two years later he settled his present farm, which is well improved and gives evidence of thrift and prosperity. Mr. Skinner is a believer in the Christian Church, and in his political views is a Democrat. He is liberal in his support to all worthy enterprises, and a man generally esteemed by the entire community. His ancestors came from Ireland, having emigrated to America previous to the Revolution, in which conflict his grandfather was a gallant soldier.

Stephen F. Snowden was born in Gibson County, Tenn., in 1844. His father and mother immigrated from North Carolina at an early day and when he was about two years old the father died. At the age of ten years his mother moved to Memphis, Tenn., where she still resides. Stephen's first work in Memphis was in a butcher shop, where he remained about three years. He then went on the Mississippi River as cabin boy, continuing for some time in this and other capacities, or, till about 1863, when he entered the employ of the Memphis & Charleston Railroad as brakeman. He remained at this business about one year. In 1864 Mr. Snowden farmed and cut cord wood on Island Forty in the Mississippi River eighteen miles above Memphis. In 1865-66-67 he was employed on a tug plying the Mississippi River above and below Memphis. His last work on the water was acting as mate on a steamer running up and down White and Black Rivers in 1868. On the second day of March, 1869, he landed in St. Francis County, Ark., where he still resides. He has been occupied in farming since his arrival and now owns 250 acres of land, seventy acres of which are in a high state of cultivation. W. Snowden's father dying when he was quite young and leaving his mother in indigent circumstances caused him to be raised without any education. Consequently he had to depend on mother

wit'alone, but to his credit be it said he is in better circumstances than many who have had the advantage of a good schooling. Mr. Snowden was married in 1871 to Miss Temperance M. Claiborn, daughter of Thomas and Laura A. Claiborn. To Mr. and Mrs. Snowden have been born four children: Johnie (born May 18, 1873, and died October 6, 1875), Vital (born January 1, 1876), Delia (born August 14, 1878) and Mildred (born November 2, 1882). Mr. Snowden is a Democrat of the first water, and with his wife belongs to the Methodist Episcopal Church, South. He is a member in high standing of the Knights of Honor and enjoys the respect of all who know him. He is a liberal supporter of all worthy objects that indicate the growth and prosperity of the country.

D. H. Stayton, M. D., was born and reared in Phillips County, Ark. His father, Thomas N. Stayton, made his advent into the world in Delaware, in 1809, and landed in Arkansas on February 14, 1829, settling in Helena, which was at that time only a village numbering but seven families. Mr. Stayton painted the first house in that present city. His father, Hill D. Stayton, was employed as State surveyor at the time, and helped to lay out the section lines of those counties. Pioneers of such early days depended largely on their rifles for subsistence, as the farms were small and not cleared, but their children are the large land owners and prosperous farmers of the present. Mr. Stayton was married after coming to Arkansas to Miss Easter Harris, a daughter of William R. Harris, who moved to this State in 1833. They were the parents of five children, three of whom are still living: John W. (a lawyer of Jackson County and at one time judge of the court), Ruth (now the wife of Dr. Hearing, of Brinkley, Ark.) and D. H. (the subject of this sketch). The latter was born on September 13, 1837, being reared on the farm in Phillips County. His first absence from home was to attend the University of Louisville (Ky.) Medical Department. After taking his first course he served four years as assistant surgeon in the Confederate army. At the close of the war he practiced in Lee County until 1870, when he returned to the University and completed his course, which hostilities had interfered with, and graduated in the spring of 1871, afterward resuming his practice at his old home. In 1887 he came to and located in St. Francis County, at Palestine, where he has since been engaged in attending to the prosecution of his chosen profession, his practice being large and steadily increasing. Dr. Stayton was married May 9, 1862, to Mrs. Caroline Bowden (nee Lockart), a daughter of Thomas Lockart, of North Carolina. They have a family of three children: David H. (who is married and lives near Palestine), Thomas L. and Lelia C. Dr. Stayton was once president of the board of medical examiners of Lee County, and is medical examiner of the Royal Arcanum; he is also a member of the United States board of pension examining surgeons for this locality, and examiner of the K. of H. and of the K. & L. of H. Besides being a member of the three lodges named he belongs to the Masonic order, in which he has occupied all of the positions of honor. He is a Democrat in politics, and he and his wife are members of the Cumberland Presbyterian Church. He is now lord mayor of the incorporated town of Palestine, Ark.

Capt. J. G. Stern's first trip south was an unwelcome one, but he remained for some time, boarding at Libby Prison and Belle-Isle. After his exchange he was again taken prisoner at the siege of Petersburg. Preferring death to that of prison life, he took the desperate chances and left his captors on the field of battle; this being done in daylight on the run. He was given a parting salute by a volley of musketry. The patriotic enthusiasm with which it was given was shown by a bullet hole through his equipage and one through his coat. Although given such a hearty farewell he stopped not until he reached his regiment, the Eighty-fourth Pennsylvania Infantry. He participated in a number of battles, among the principal ones were Fredericksburg, Chancellorsville, Wilderness, Appomattox Court House, through the siege of Petersburg, and was present at the surrender of Gen. Lee. He was born April 17, 1844, in the State of Pennsylvania. At the close of the war he followed his parents to the State of Illinois, where he completed his education, which

was very limited up to that time. During the latter years of his residence in that State he was employed in teaching school. In 1872 he went south a second time and located in Arkansaw, Phillips County, at the mouth of St. Francis River, where he worked as a laborer in a saw-mill. He soon engaged in business on his own account, getting out logs and staves. A few years later he accepted a position as agent for the Helena Lumber Company, and purchased a half interest in a boat running on the St. Francis and Mississippi Rivers, of which he was captain and pilot. Selling out his interest in the boat about seven years ago, he came to Madison, where he is now engaged in the timber and shingle business. He leased a shingle-mill about five years ago with a capacity of from 8,000,000 to 10,000,000 shingles per year. He owns a number of thousand of acres of timber land, located near his mill and to which he is connected by a tramway, operated by steam-power and leading into the woods for several miles. His parents are both living in the State of Illinois, his father at the age of seventy-one, and his mother one year younger. They were the parents of nine children, six of whom are living.

James M. Stewart, of the representative firm of Stewart & Taylor, abstract, loan and general insurance agents of Forrest City, was born at Collierville, in Shelby County, Tenn., in 1842. In 1859 he came to Arkansas, locating at the old county seat of Madison, in St. Francis County, where for two years he was engaged as clerk and book-keeper by an establishment at that point. When the war between the States was declared he went to Kentucky to join the cavalry service, but the delicate condition of his health caused him to be rejected, much to his chagrin. Giving his supplies to a companion who had been more fortunate in being accepted, he returned to Arkansas and joined the Fifth Arkansas (Hart's) Regiment as a private of Company A; he was afterward adjutant of his regiment, and at the close of the war was commanding Company A, in the Trans-Mississippi Department. He served for four years, and participated in all the principal engagements of the State. When peace had been declared Mr. Stewart accepted a position of trust with a firm at Memphis, Tenn., where he remained until 1868, leaving at that time to return to St. Francis County to fill a position as clerk and book-keeper. In 1879 he was elected clerk of the circuit court, in which capacity he served for four consecutive terms, in a manner eliciting the satisfaction and admiration of all concerned. Mr. Stewart then ceased to be an aspirant for office, and at that time was more popular with the people of the county than he had ever been before. By this prudent and all-wise step he still remains one of the most esteemed and influential men in the community. Soon after leaving the clerk's office he, in company with Mr. Taylor, formed the present real-estate firm, which is one of the most widely known and substantial establishments of this branch of business in this section of the State, they owning over 10,000 acres of valuable land. In societies Mr. Stewart is identified with the F. & A. M., K. T., K. of H. and K. & L. of H. Washington G. and Sarah W. (Griggs) Stewart, his parents, were natives of South Carolina and Tennessee, respectively, he being the fourth of a family of nine children born to their union. Washington Stewart was a millwright by trade, and enjoyed an extensive business in Tennessee and Mississippi. He executed a greater part of the work on the plank road out of Memphis, Tenn., through Mississippi, on Big Creek Plank Road, and many other public highways. He was a man of prominence and influence, and was one of the first mayors of Madison, the old county seat of St. Francis County. He died in 1868. J. M. Stewart was married, in 1866, to Miss Ollie E. Colson, of Paducah, Ky., and by her became the father of three children: James H., Elbert and Mary E. Mr. Stewart, besides his other interests, is a stockholder in and one of the incorporators of the Forrest City Hotel Company. He was elected secretary of that company at its organization, serving as such until forced by ill health to vacate in the winter of 1888. He is also a stockholder in and one of the original incorporators of the Bank of Eastern Arkansas, located at Forrest City. A member of the city council of the town of Forrest City and chairman of the finance committee, he was also twice elected

a member of the school board of the special school district of Forrest City, and as such took an active interest in educational affairs. He served as Master of the Masonic Lodge here several terms and was Grand Marshal of the Grand Lodge of this State, also Dictator of the Lodge of K. of H. at same place, several consecutive terms.

J. E. Stone, M. D., has reached an eminence in his profession which renders his name almost a household word throughout Forrest City, and the surrounding locality. He received his literary education in Tennessee, and commenced the study of medicine under a tutor in Arkansas, afterward entering the Missouri Medical College (known then as the old McDowell College, and situated in St. Louis), where he was graduated with honors. Entering the Confederate army in May, 1861, in Company B, First Arkansas Mounted Rifles, he served over four years, participating in the battles of Oak Hill (where he was severely wounded) and Pea Ridge, and was then transferred across to the Army of Tennessee, just after the battle of Corinth. He also took an active part at Jackson (Miss.), Chickamauga, Duggers' Gap, New Hope Church, Atlanta, Jonesboro, Franklin, and several other engagements of minor importance. After the war Dr. Stone located in Van Buren County, Ark., where he actively followed the practice of his chosen profession for five years, then going to Memphis, and thence to Walnut Bend, Ark. In 1883 he came to Forrest City, and still enjoys an extensive patronage, besides a large livery business, also owning considerable land, both here and in Lee County. He is one of Forrest City's most enterprising and influential citizens, and has done much in his own peculiar way toward the present advancement and prosperity of the place. The Doctor has been twice married, his first union occurring in Tennessee, and the second in Arkansas. He was born in Virginia in 1839, and is the son of M. G. and Martha (Stovall) Stone, also originally from the Old Dominion. Dr. Stone is a member in high standing of the various Masonic lodges of this place.

Capt. J. W. Stout enlisted in the Rebel army, in 1862, in the First Battalion, Arkansas Cavalry,

Gen. Price commanding. He was captured at the battle of Big Black Bridge, Miss., May 17, 1863, and sent to military prison on Johnson's Island, in Lake Erie, where he was kept till February, 1865. After the collapse of the Confederacy, he returned to his family, and subsequently removed to Cross County, Ark., remaining there till 1871. Coming to St. Francis County, he purchased a home of 200 acres of land, and has since followed farming regularly and successfully, also serving the public as a mill and gin proprietor. Capt. Stout was born in McMinn County, E. Tenn., in 1829, and is of German descent, being a son of Daniel and Elisabeth Stout. His father was born in Virginia, and his mother in Kentucky. Her maiden name was Franklin. The senior Stout was a professional school-teacher in McMinn County, E. Tenn., for a series of years, and taught ten years in succession in the same academy. J. W.'s boyhood was spent in Tennessee, in attending school, and in 1851 he moved with his father to Walker County, Ga., following farming for about one year. Then he was engaged as salesman with Parham & Lee, in the mercantile business, till December, 1854. He was married December 26, to Mrs. Elizabeth B. Brooks, daughter of Benjamin C. Hardin, who had one daughter. They have had nine children born to them, four of whom are dead, three sons and one daughter. Five children are living, two sons and three daughters: Minnie (the wife of Rev. W. W. Hendrix), Hollace W., Flora (wife of Dr. A. A. Berry), Thomas J. and Ophelia. Georgie A., the daughter of Mrs. Stout, is the wife of A. C. Shaver. Capt. Stout and wife, and all the children are members of the Methodist Episcopal Church, South. He also belongs to the Masonic order and the Knights of Honor. His wife is a member of the K. & L. of H. He is Democratic politically.

George P. Taylor enjoys the friendship of, perhaps, a larger number of personal acquaintances than any man in Eastern Arkansas. Of magnificent physical proportions, standing over six feet high and weighing above 195 pounds, he attracts attention in any gathering. He was born in Cooper County, Mo., October 13, 1850, and traces

his ancestry back four generations to John Taylor, of Scotch and Irish descent, who was the founder of that branch of the family on this side of the continent. He came to America before the great "Stamp Act" and "Boston Tea Party" occurred, and settled among the colonists of South Carolina. He was loyal to the country of his adoption when the great conflict began which announced the birth of the greatest nation on the face of the globe, and gave one of his sons to the cause of freedom. Early in the history of Kentucky John Taylor emigrated to this new territory, and here was born and reared his son, upon whom was conferred the family name of John. He grew to manhood in a locality even then thinly settled, but being lured by the tales of the new region across the Mississippi, followed the train of emigrants westward, and among the prominent names in the early history of Cooper County, Mo., appears that of John Taylor. He was there married to Miss Cochrell. After remaining in that county until the breaking out of the war he moved to St. Louis. George P. Taylor spent his early life in his native State, and attended school at Boonville, conducted by the renowned Dr. Kemper. He was fourteen years of age when his father removed to St. Louis, and in 1867 removed to Arkansas, settling in Lee County, on a plantation, where he remained until 1873. Then he came to Forrest City and died here in 1879 of yellow fever, his wife preceding him about one year. George P. Taylor located as a citizen of St. Francis County in 1870, where he was engaged in farming, being married in February, 1873, to Miss Alice Koonce, a native of this county. She is the mother of six children: Edgar P., Walter R., Alva J., Alice N., Nannie and George P., Jr. In 1874, after the reconstruction act, Mr. Taylor was elected representative from St. Francis County, though at that time only twenty-four years of age; he was re-elected in 1878, and in 1880 was appointed county collector. In 1880 he entered into the real-estate business at Forrest City. In 1885 the "Forrest City Manufacturing Company" was formed, with Mr. Taylor as president, but a $5,000 fire shortly after caused the dissolution of the company. In 1884–85

31

he formed a partnership with Hatcher & Mann in the mercantile business, this remaining for two years. December, 1886, he was associated with James M. Stewart, as real-estate agents and brokers, then the only firm of the kind in the county. He is one of the organizers and is secretary of the Forrest City Hotel Company, a corporation with a capital stock of $24,000, and is also a stockholder and director of the Bank of Eastern Arkansas, located at Forrest City, which has a capital stock of $50,000. Both enterprises yield good returns, and their stock is quoted above par. Mr. Taylor also owns several large plantations in this county, and is conceded to be one of its most prominent citizens, especially having the esteem and confidence of the Democracy of this locality, as is shown by the fact that for eight consecutive years he has been chairman of the County Central Committee, and was a delegate to the National Democratic Convention of 1888. He was also a delegate to the National Farmers' Congress, held at Montgomery, Ala., in November, 1889. Mr. Taylor is a member of the Masonic order, in which he holds the office of Master, also belonging to the order of Knights of Pythias. Besides these he is a member of the I. O. O. F., and of the Knights and Ladies of Honor. Mrs. Taylor is a member of the Baptist Church. Their home in Forrest City is one of the finest here, elegantly furnished, and contains one of the largest and best-selected libraries in the county, embracing the leading authors in poetry, science, history and fiction.

Thomas L. Taylor, a prominent planter of St. Francis County, is a native of Missouri, and a son of John and Mary Elizabeth (Cockrell) Taylor, originally from Virginia. John Taylor and wife came to Arkansas in 1866, where he engaged in farming (in this county), during his life. Thomas L. received a good education at the public schools of this township, and later attended college in Clay County, Mo., supplementing this by an attendance at the Kemper School of Boonville. He left this institution in the fall of 1861 to join the Confederate army, in which he served until taken prisoner in 1863, being confined eight months, after which he was paroled. His health having suffered

by close confinement he went to California, but returned in 1866 by wagon train, as the cholera which was prevalent along the rivers prevented a passage by boat. Mr. Taylor was married in August, 1874, in Shelby County, Tenn., to Miss Sallie A. Jarman, but she lived only a few months. He owns a fine farm of 120 acres, with a large part of it under cultivation, having good improvements, etc. He is a prominent Democrat of the Jeffersonian type.

E. L. Vadakin, the popular editor of the Forrest City Times, owes his nativity to the State of Illinois, having first seen the light of day near the little town of Sullivan in 1864, as the son of H. F. and A. (Clements) Vadakin. H. F. Vadakin was born in Vermont, but when quite young immigrated to Illinois, settling near Sullivan, where he became well known to the citizens for many miles around as an efficient and courteous druggist. His business was of many years' standing, and his death in 1888 was sincerely mourned, both by his personal friends and those who knew him through reputation. Mrs. Vadakin died when E. L. was a little child. At the age of fourteen, the subject of this sketch entered a printing office and there laid the foundation of his future career. After a few months his brother-in-law purchased the paper, which was located at Stewardson, Ill., but soon sold it. Mr. Vadakin remained with the successor, receiving $10 per month for his services. His next move was to Tower Hill, Ill., where, as no other employment presented itself, he worked for three months on a farm. About this time a campaign paper was started in the town, and afforded work for our subject for some time, but unfortunately it was short-lived, and as it sunk into obscurity, the editor also failed to materialize, having neglected to give Mr. Vadakin any compensation for his labor. The latter, as might be supposed, found himself in rather straightened circumstances, but at this juncture, a railroad advertising agent stopped in the village, and taking a fancy to Mr. Vadakin, induced him to accompany him to Cincinnati, Ohio, promising to use his utmost endeavors to secure for him a good position in some one of the printing offices of that city. This he was unable to do, but he did furnish him a home for some time. Eager to become self-reliant, and not dependent on the bounty of his friends, Mr. Vadakin returned to his old home in Illinois, and accepted the position in one of the printing offices for the sum of $2 per week, and board. An uncle, who was a member of the Union Printing Company at Little Rock, then came to his assistance, and secured him work in an office in that city, where he remained for three years. At one time, while serving his apprenticeship, he had charge of the Union Job Office at Little Rock. Though his promotion was gradual, it was none the less sure, and he is to-day one of the expert printers in Arkansas. After working on the Democrat, at Lonoke, Ark., for some time, the proprietor purchased the Times at Forrest City, appointing Mr. Vadakin the manager, he to receive half of the net profits. The paper had almost died out, having become exceedingly unpopular from the effects of a newspaper controversy, but Mr. Vadakin brought it to the front, and it is now one of the best county papers in the State, besides being the leading publication of St. Francis County. In May, 1886, Mr. Vadakin was united in marriage with Miss Lillie B. Landvoigh, and to their union one child has been born, Dora Annette. Mr. Vadakin and his father-in-law bought the Times, and own it in partnership. He is a member of the Episcopal Church, and in politics a Democrat.

Claude H. Vann, editor and proprietor of the Forrest City Register, was born in Cross County, Ark., April 17, 1871, being the son of J. M. and Ida H. (Hare) Vann, well-known and highly esteemed residents of Cross County. Claude H. received his education in the schools of the county, and served an apprenticeship to the newspaper business in the office of the Cross County Chronicle. Having proved an able assistant in the office, at the expiration of his time he was given an opportunity to remain, but as better inducements were offered him by the Morrill Bros. Printing Company of New York as a traveling salesman, he accepted that position, and demonstrated his ability as a commercial traveler, being considered a valuable acquisition to the force of that house. He subsequently was occupied as solicitor of the Forrest

City Times, and in September of 1889 purchased the Register of that city. It had become considerably run down at the time he took it in hand, but though only a few months have intervened since then, he is making rapid strides in its up-building, and success is the sure future of his earnest endeavors. Mr. Vann is a young man, eighteen years of age, and only recently located at Forrest City, but the prominence he has attained, the esteem in which he is held, and his position in business and social circles, concede him to be a prominent factor in the county.

"Philip Van Patten, M. D." So reads the sign that noisily swings to and fro on its rusty hinges, attracting the passers-by on one of the principal streets of Forrest City. The busy little notice is given only a momentary thought by its many readers, but the reputation of him whom it represents, an efficient and popular physician, will survive him many years. Born in Schenectady County, N. Y., in 1827, Dr. Van Patten's boyhood days were passed in carving his name in wonderful designs on his desk and making pictures, much to the delight of his schoolmates, but aside from all his fun, he was a good scholar, and won the approbation and affection of his teachers. When only thirteen years old he was deprived of his father's love and protection, death claiming him while on business in Michigan. Philip then moved with his mother to Iowa, the mother afterward going to Denver, Colo., where she passed away in 1885, at the age of eighty-six years. His literary education was received in Iowa, he taking a classical course, under the able instruction of Father Pelamargues, a Catholic priest, of Paris, France. His studies extended to a course in Latin, Greek and Hebrew, the former being so thoroughly instilled in his mind, that he read Cæsar some four years ago without consulting his Lexicon but six times. He made it a rule to regularly demonstrate a certain number of mathematical problems every morning, and now devotes a half hour daily to the study of classics. Entering the Medical University of Iowa when twenty-one, he graduated with honors in 1853, and first announced himself competent to alleviate the sufferings to which flesh is heir, in

DeWitt, Iowa, where he practiced for one year in association with Dr. Asa Morgan. During the year 1861 he choose for the partner of his joys and sorrows the daughter of Col. John Miller, of Batesville, Ark., father of the late Gov. Miller. One child, Hattie L., born to Dr. and Mrs. Van Patten alone survives. She is now a student of art in Memphis, Tenn. During the war between the States, Dr. Van Patten was surgeon of the Thirteenth Arkansas Volunteer Infantry, Col. Tappen in command. He was afterward promoted to brigade-surgeon, and subsequently to the position of division-surgeon. For a short period he served as brigade-surgeon for Old Frank Cheatam, and was for two years in the Trans-Mississippi Department, under Gen. L. Polk, in Tennessee, Kentucky, Missouri and Mississippi, also being surgeon of Fort Pillow, in 1861. He was present at the battle of Shiloh, and was made division-surgeon by Gen. Polk on the battlefield, in the presence of Albert Sidney Johnston and Beauregard. He was obliged to resign before the war closed, on account of nervous prostration. In 1858 Dr. Van Patten was elected to the State senate, but was kept out of the office by fraud, perpetrated in the clerk's office in Poinsett County. In 1860 he was elected county representative from Poinsett County, and afterward State senator of the Thirteenth district. He was also acting surgeon of the United States army, of the Sixteenth United States Infantry, at Little Rock for a short time. Upon the close of hostilities he resumed his practice in his old county, and then went to Little Rock, where he acted as secretary of the board of health, and was also physician and surgeon for the State penitentiary. In February of 1885, the Doctor came to Forrest City, and formed a partnership with Dr. J. B. Cummings. He has been United States pension agent and president of the board of health here for two years. In societies he is associated with the A. F. & A. M. and the K. & L. of H. A genial companion, the essential characteristics of Dr. Van Patten as a gentleman and scholar mark his demeanor, and his numerous noble acts, though perhaps a trifle philanthropic in his way, only serve to endear him in the heart of his many friends and

acquaintances. When on the battlefield, with men more experienced and older in years, he was heard to remark to one of them, that he felt more like a son to a father, than a superior officer to his subjects. His father's (John P. Van Patten) immediate ancestors came direct from Holland and settled on Manhattan Island. The paternal grandfather and maternal grandfather were private soldiers under George Washington in the Revolutionary War. A grand uncle was a colonel, and took charge of the prisoners at the surrender of Burgoyne. Dr. Van Patten's children have inherited his own studious propensities, and have been endowed by nature with unusual capabilities. Eva Lillian graduated in higher mathematics at the age of fourteen years, under Prof. D. L. Thompson, of Wittsburg, the course extending through Calculus. After thus having her reasoning powers developed far beyond the height attained by even some of the most brilliant women of our country, in order to give her that proficiency in language, literature and the fine arts, which she had already attained in mathematics, and understanding that a harmonious development of all the faculties is requisite to attain perfect personal and intellectual culture, Dr. Van Patten wisely sent her to Notre Dame, Ind., to the female school there, made famous the world over by the Sisters of Mercy. After having well improved the opportunities afforded her she again returned to her home an even more devoted student than before. During her leisure hours she was found poring over the works of Tyndall, Huxley and Darwin, drinking in the many good things in their writings and criticising contradictory statements appearing on different pages. In mathematics, literature, language, art and every other branch, her mind searched eagerly for knowledge, and she daily meditated on many of the great questions which have from remote ages vexed and perplexed the minds of our greatest thinkers. She was the constant companion of her father, and with him discussed all questions. Her greatness of heart was unlimited, and she had charity for the faults of all. Such women are priceless gems, but her physical constitution could not stand the draft on

P. Van Pattru

her intellect, and paralysis of the brain caused her death. Such an affliction is certainly to be lamented by more than her family, and it is to be hoped her young soul, freed from its incumbrance of clay, can see, without effort into all the mysteries she was continually investigating here. Hattie L., now the wife of Eugene Parrish, of Paragould, Ark., was on the point of graduating from Notre Dame, when the breaking out of diphtheria caused her sudden return home, and prevented her receiving a diploma. Her paintings and her music show the touch of an artist. She paints from nature with absolute perfection, and her portrait gems, which have been examined by many, are pronounced worthy of an artist of national reputation. She is an excellent English scholar, and proficient in Latin, French and German. She was married November 2, 1889.

Wade Webb, a farmer by occupation, owes his nativity to the State of North Carolina, his birth occurring in Edgecombe County in 1841. John and Esther Webb, his parents, were natives of the same State. The ancestors came from England before the Revolutionary War, settling near Jones River in Virginia. Wade Webb passed his youthful days in the schools of North Carolina, and upon coming to St. Francis County, Ark., in 1853, began farming. He now owns 200 acres, with 120 under a successful state of cultivation. He was married in July, 1866, to Matilda V., daughter of Absalom and Matilda Barker, and to their union seven children were given, five living: John Lee, Remington P., Willie W., James R. and Elbert. Mr. Webb enlisted during the war in the Confederate army, in Company B of the Fifth Arkansas Regiment, serving until the final surrender. He participated in the battles of Murfreesboro, Jonesboro, Stone River, Perryville, Missionary Ridge and Cumberland Gap. At the battle of Murfreesboro he received a severe wound. Mr. Webb is an enterprising, energetic farmer and citizen, and contributes liberally to those movements which betoken the good or growth of the county.

John M. Widener first saw the light of day May 25, 1834, in a farm house situated in the wilds of St. Francis County. He grew to manhood in that locality with no companions save his brothers and sisters, and without the advantages of schools and churches which his children now enjoy. After remaining in this county until 1862, he went to Shelby County, Tenn., but three years later moved to Saline County, Ill., returning home in about a year. Mr. Widener owns, at this time, some eighty acres of land on the St. Francis River bottoms, and in connection with farming is successfully engaged in stock raising and in the timber business, his earnest efforts and industry having yielded substantial returns. His father, Samuel Widener, was born in North Carolina, in 1798, and lived there for a number of years, then removing to Alabama, where he remained for a short time. His home was Tennessee for a while, from which State he came to Arkansas, settling in the wilderness of St. Francis County. Here he resided until his death, which occurred in 1842. His wife, Margaret (Evans) Widener, died in 1838, leaving a family of ten children, John M., our subject being the only one living. The latter has been twice married; first, in 1858, to Miss Lavina Land, a native of this State, who died in 1877, leaving four children, two of these survive: Mary J. (wife of Samuel A. Mead, a farmer of St. Francis County) and Samuel A. (living at home). Mr. Widener was married the second time, in June, 1885, to Mrs. Mary McGuffey, daughter of John Halbert, of Missouri birth. Mr. and Mrs. Widener are members of the Methodist Episcopal Church, South, in which they take an active part, Mr. Widener being steward. He is of German descent, and a prominent Democrat, and a leading citizen of this county.

N. G. Williams is a descendant of a Revolutionary hero, and it was only natural that his patriotism should demonstrate itself at the outburst of civil strife in 1861. His paternal grandfather was one of the early settlers of North Carolina, and a soldier in the War of the Revolution, serving under Gen. Greene. His parents, Hardin and Martha (Tanner) Williams, were both natives of Tennessee, and had a family of three children, two of whom are living: Jane A. (widow of Samuel I.

Sutton, of Phillips County) and N. G. The latter was born in Maury County, Tenn., on April 27, 1832. He spent his boyhood on the old home farm in that State, receiving a good education in the common schools of his county, after which he attended the University at Lebanon, Tenn. Two years before becoming of age he commenced farming for himself in Maury County, and in November, 1855, moved to Arkansas, locating in St. Francis County, where he was engaged in tilling the soil on the St. Francis River bottom lands, until the breaking out of the war. Then he entered the Confederate forces in the Fifth Arkansas Infantry, but was in only a few engagements, as he held the office of commissary of his regiment. After peace was declared he settled down to farming again at Taylor's Creek, and in 1883 opened up a stock of merchandise, since which time he has carried on the mercantile business in connection with farming. His stock of goods will invoice about $1,500, and he enjoys a good trade. Mr. Williams was married in 1854 to Mary Lee Wortham, who died thirteen years later, leaving one son, Lawrence E. He was married to his second wife, Martha H. Mosley, in 1869. They are the parents of three children: M. E. Williams, N. G. and M. J., all at home. Mr. Williams now owns 500 acres of land, with 131 acres under cultivation. His life illustrates what pluck and energy can accomplish in connection with good common sense, for success is bound to follow persistent effort.

R. J. Williams, attorney at law of Forrest City, made his first appeal for his rights in Winchester, Tenn., September 23, 1848. His literary education was received in the schools of that State, and afterward he entered one of the prominent universities of the South, commencing the study of Blackstone under the efficient tutelage of Walker J. Brooks, of South Carolina, in the class of 1869–70. Finally he graduated from a law school in Virginia, and commenced the practice of his chosen profession in this place in 1873, having taught school for two years after finishing his college career, to liquidate the expenses of that course. His clientage has gradually increased, and he is, without exception, now conceded to be one of the most able practitioners of the county. He represented the Seventh senatorial district in 1878, and served until 1881, with an ability and efficiency that not only satisfied his Democratic constituents, but the people at large. Mr. Williams owns some 400 acres of land, and has the finest residence in Forrest City. He was married in Summerville, Tenn., in 1872, to Miss Sallie T. Wainright, and by her is the father of two children: Lucy and Addie. Mr. Williams is the son of J. W. and Mary (McNabb) Williams, natives of Virginia. The former, a mechanic by trade, was for many years established in Winchester. He was judge of Franklin County during the civil war, and held a similar position for twenty years in Winchester. He is now residing in the latter place at the advanced age of seventy years. Mrs. Williams died in 1863. She and her husband had a family of six children, all of them living. Mr. Williams has attained an enviable reputation in his profession, but his popularity does not end there, for he is also a favorite in social circles. Cordiality and a pleasant word for all are among his many noble attributes, and though ready at repartee and jesting, there is no occasion to regret the word spoken. He is a member of the Blue Lodge of the Masonic order, and is High Priest of the Royal Arch Chapter, also belonging to Commandery No. 11, K. T.

Eugene Wilson, proprietor of one of the largest bakeries and confectionery establishments in Forrest City, was born in St. Francis County, in 1870, and is a son of S. C. and Mary (Beck) Wilson, also residents of that city. Mr. Wilson and his partner, John Reno, do a large business in their line, their trade amounting to an average of $200 per week. The latter is a baker by trade, besides whom they also employ an experienced baker to meet the demands of a large trade, having, in connection with the bakery, an ice-cream parlor (that is liberally patronized), and the finest delivery wagon in the city. S. C. Wilson was born in Trumbull County, Ohio, in 1825, but was reared in Pennsylvania, where his parents moved when he was a small boy, settling on a farm, on which he worked when not attending school until sixteen years of age. At that time he was apprenticed to learn the carpenter's trade, serving three years in Lowell County, Ohio. After familiarizing himself with its varied details, he worked two years in New Castle, and then went South, locating in Blackhawk, Miss., in 1846, where he remained about ten years, following his adopted calling. Subsequently he was engaged in the saw-mill business until the war broke out, when he joined the Confederate army, serving in Stevenford's battery until the close of the war. He was captured at the battle Missionary Ridge, and taken to a Federal prison, being confined six months. He participated in the battles of Missionary Ridge, Chickamauga, Murfreesboro, and a number of skirmishes. After the war, returning to Mississippi, he was employed by J. H. Pait in his saw-mill until 1869, at which time he came to Arkansas, and located in St. Francis County, about three miles north of Forrest City. He erected a new saw-mill and operated it in connection with a grist-mill, until removing to the city, in 1881, since which time he has been occupied in the mercantile business, with substantial success. He has acquired some property, owning six houses in the city, besides other possessions. Mr. and Mrs. Wilson are the parents of three children, all residents of this county: Mary E. (wife of William M. Hannah), Charles M. and Eugene (the principal of this sketch). S. C. Wilson is the son of Dr. Andrew and Mary (Simpson) Wilson. His paternal grandfather was of Irish parentage, and his maternal grandfather was born and reared in England, running away from home when a young man in order to marry the girl of his choice, an Irish lady, and a sister of Thomas Nugent, the noted warrior. They eloped and came to America, and were married in New York City, after which they settled in Pennsylvannia, where he engaged in farming. Mrs. Wilson died in March, 1889, and was a prominent member of the Baptist Church, to which she had belonged for over thirty years. Mr. Wilson is a prominent resident of Forrest City, and is the present deputy United States marshal of this district. He is Grand Master of the I. O. O. F. He is the patentee and inventor of the "patent car coupler," of which he is the sole owner.

H. W. Winthrop, one of the representative cit-izens of Forrest City, was born in New England (Vermont) in 1839, being the son of William and Ann (Herron) Winthrop. William Winthrop owed his nativity to England, and was of English and Scotch descent. When quite young he came to America, and became prominently identified with politics, serving as a member of the legislature, and at the date of his death, in his eightieth year, was holding the position of county judge, having acted in that capacity for twelve years. His wife was born in Ireland, but married in Vermont, and by her marriage with Mr. Winthrop became the mother of five children. She is now living with her son, H. W. Winthrop, having passed her eighty-eighth birthday. Grandfather Herron came originally from Ireland, and after losing his first wife there, emigrated to America about the year 1800, attaining a place as one of the richest men in Vermont. He left seventy-two grandchildren, all well-fixed, and the monument erected to his memory in Vermont is one of the largest in the State. The mother of H. W. (the subject of this sketch) is his daughter by the first wife. H. W. Winthrop ran away from home when a boy, but was found in Boston and brought back by his father. He then concluded that the locality in which he was settled did not suit him, so went West, and at the date of the war was in Massachusetts. Joining the Federal army, Company N, Fifty-third Massachusetts Regiment, he served three years, having been promoted first lieutenant, though not commissioned, and he did not go to his regiment. Resigning his position he went into the sutler's department, and was brigade-sutler over the Eleventh New Jersey Cavalry, Second Iowa and Third United States, finding himself at the close of the war in Memphis, Tenn. He purchased a steamboat at that place with the intention of doing a trading business on the St. Francis River, but after making one trip, and landing at Madison, this county, he was accosted by familiar faces, who inquired if he did not recognize them, and whether he was not the man who had captured them, while serving in an official capacity during the Civil War. He first hesitated in replying, but finally admitted the soft impeachment, though not without some fear of results. He indeed was the man, and immediately was at the mercy of several of his former prisoners. Long before, when he captured them, his men, though all Federal soldiers, had given their rations to the Confederates, who were half famished, and gone without themselves. The act was never forgotton. Mr. Winthrop was entertained in a royally hospitable manner by his ex-Confederate captives, who were gratified in having an opportunity to extend favors to one who had so nobly rendered them assistance in a time of distress. This partly led to his disposing of the boat and locating at Madison, where he enterd the grocery business in the firm of Cole & Prewett, Mr. Cole being one of the leading men of the soldiers, whom Mr. Winthrop had captured as a rebel. From the moment of this second meeting a strong friendship grew up between the two, and many years of business and social relations have failed to sever the bond. Mr. Winthrop again served an appointment soon after the war, when he was appointed chief clerk of the United States Bureau, and has filled many official positions since that time. He has been United States assessor of the Eastern District of Arkansas, United States collector of the same district, and collector of St. Francis County for six years. In 1872 he was elected sheriff of the county, but a change of political administration caused him to decline the election. He discharged the manifold duties of postmaster in a highly commendable manner for several years, and was deputy United States marshal for a long period. His experience as marshal would make an interesting volume within itself, as his honesty and justice in dealing with men caused them to regard him more as a friend than an enemy or officer of the law, though he was never derelict in duty. Fortune has smiled on Mr. Winthrop in a most generous way, he now owning the city opera house, erected by himself, and other valuable property, exclusive of which he has 8,000 acres of very valuable land. His marriage with Miss Georgia Johnson has proved a most happy one. Two children have blessed their union: Mary and Fannie. In societies he is identified with the I. O. O. F. and A. F. & A. M., and in politics is a Republican. He is a direct descendant of Gov. Winthrop, of Massachusetts.

Thomas Jefferson Withers came to this county with his father at the age of five years, and remained on the home farm until the father's death, which occurred in 1876. He then purchased a tract of land and commenced farming for himself, also being engaged in teaching school for three years. In 1881 Miss Mary E. Ratton became his wife. She was a daughter of William Ratton, of Kentucky nativity, and is now the mother of one son, Clarence W. Mr. Withers was born in Kentucky, March 26, 1862, as the son of Thomas Upton Withers, who was engaged in farming in the Blue Grass State (Kentucky), and after moving here was occupied in furnishing the Mississippi steamers with wood. At this calling he was making a good income, until 1858, when, during the high water he lost several hundred cords of wood, which financially crippled him. He then came to St. Francis County, where he resided until his death in 1867, at the age of fifty-nine. His wife, who was born here, survived him eleven years. Mr. Withers owns a farm of 185 acres, of which over 100 acres are under cultivation. He is engaged in stock raising principally, and is one of the most successful farmers in Griggs Township, although a young man not yet twenty-eight years of age. He is also a leading Democrat, and having served three years as justice of the peace, and at this time holds the office of school director, and supervisor of roads of his township, being a prominent member of the County Wheel. Mrs. Withers belongs to the Methodist Episcopal Church, South.

O. P. Wolff. In 1848 O. P. Wolff, Sr., and his wife, Anne E. (Russell) Wolff, came to Arkansas from Philadelphia, their native home, and settled on the present site of the town of Colt, which he purchased from W. M. Taylor, consisting of 160 acres, with four acres of it cleared. Mr. Wolff improved the rest and bought adjoining lands, and in 1870, at the time of his death, was the owner of some 600 or 700 acres. Soon after arriving here he opened up a stock of general merchandise, and as settlements were few and far between he had a large trade and enjoyed a profitable patronage, which he continued for some years after the war. The place was then known as Taylor's Creek, by which name it was called until 1882, then being changed to Colt, after the railroad contractor who built the railroad through. Mr. Wolff was twice married. By his first union he was the father of two children, our subject being the only one living; and by his second marriage there were three children: Fisk B., Cornelia W. and Sallie J. (wife of J. H. Hancock, of Wynne). Oscar P. Wolff, the subject of this sketch, was born in St. Francis County, May 8, 1852, and up to the time of the death of his father enjoyed the advantages of being able to attend the subscription schools of his neighborhood. After the senior Wolff's demise he went to Texas and was engaged for the following five years as a "cowboy," on the western plains. Returning home he entered into farming on the old homestead for seven years, but in 1882 was employed by Mr. Lesca as book-keeper and clerk. In 1883 he was appointed station agent at Colt for the Iron Mountain Railroad, which position he still holds. November 10, 1880, Mr. Wolff married Mrs. Fannie Gurley. They are the parents of two children: Annie E. and Edward P. Mr. Wolff is a member of the Knights of Pythias and also of the Knights of Honor. He is a Democrat in politics, and a well-known citizen of Colt.

Daniel Wylds, the son of David and Mary Wylds, natives of Georgia and Tennessee, respectively, was born in St. Francis County, Ark., in 1846. David Wylds, when eighteen years of age, enlisted in the War of 1812, serving through the entire period as orderly-sergeant of his company. About the year 1821 he moved to Arkansas, locating in St. Francis County, where he died at the age of seventy-four years, and it can be truly said that no resident of the county ever passed away who was more sincerely mourned than he. A genial and courteous gentleman, he was one whom it was a pleasure to meet, and his absence in business and social circles was always regretted. He was broad shouldered, well proportioned, with a shrewd, kindly face that was more remarkable for its intelligence and keenness than for its beauty of features. He was a sympathetic listener to the sorrows and ills of the poor and needy, and no one ever told his tale in vain, or went from his home empty-handed. At the time of his removal to Arkansas it was almost a wilderness, and had not then reached the dignity of being a State. He began opening a farm, working under difficulties incident to that period, such as few, if any, of the present generation realize. They had to put up bear meat in winter to do them through the summer. It required a man of nerve and indomitable courage to undertake the work that he did, and his thrift and perseverance formed a foundation for the home of beauty and plenty that Daniel Wylds now enjoys. It should be added in this connection, however, that the wealth and accumulation of property was not all inherited by the son, for he began for himself at the age of twenty years. Possessing in a large degree his father's ambition and energy, he chose for his profession that most independent of all vocations—farming, and has continued it ever since. He has been remarkably successful in amassing property, and now owns large landed estates of over 1,168 acres, aside from being an extensive stock raiser. He is considered one of the wealthiest men in the county. When seventeen years of age, Mr. Wylds enlisted in Company K, Dobbin's regiment, Confederate States army, participating in several battles, and receiving a wound at the battle of Jefferson City, Mo.; he was taken prisoner to Illinois, remaining there until March of 1865, when he was exchanged at Richmond, Va., and again captured in April, 1865, following, then receiving his parole. After the war he started for home, but was obliged to make more than two-thirds of this distance on foot. Mr. Wylds was married in 1872 to Virginia I. Thompson, a daughter of William and Mahala J. Thompson, natives of Virginia. To their union five children were born: Charles A., Wilmoth O., Mary E. (deceased), Daniel T. and Allen G. Mr. Wylds' mother, who was a lovely woman, came to St. Francis County in 1816, when only eight years old, and made it her home until she died, at the age of sixty-six, a Christian and philanthropist. In politics our subject is a Democrat, and in secret societies is identified with the Knights of Honor. In religious faith he is a Presbyterian. Mrs. Wylds is a member of the Baptist Church. He has always been a consistent and liberal contributor to the cause of religious and educational movements, and his private charities are numerous and judicious. He has worthily followed in the footsteps of his honored father, whose favorite text was, "God loves the cheerful giver." His ideas of charity are indeed broad.

CHAPTER XX.

—————

Monroe County—Transportation Facilities—Taxation, Valuation, Etc.—Bonded Indebtedness—
Productions—Live Stock—Horticulture—Location—Topography—Variety of Soil—
Drainage—Streams, Etc.—Timber—Original Occupancy—Pioneer Settlers
and First Homes—County Organization—Seat of Justice and
Public Buildings—List of Officials—Political Aspect
—Population—Court Affairs—Civil War—
Towns and Villages—Schools and
Churches — Private
Memoirs.

—————

Ill fares the land, to hastening ill a prey,
Where wealth accumulates and men decay.—*Campbell.*

ONROE COUNTY has better shipping facilities than any other county in the State. The St. Louis, Arkansas & Texas Railway enters it from the north and runs thence in a southerly direction, bearing a little westward for a distance of thirty-two miles, passing via Brinkley and Clarendon. The Little Rock & Memphis Railroad crosses the northern portion of the county, its length therein being fifteen miles. The Batesville & Brinkley Railroad commences at Brinkley, and runs in a northerly direction to Newport, its length of line here being about eight miles. The Arkansas Midland Railroad commences at Clarendon and traverses the county a distance of seventeen or eighteen miles in the direction of Helena, its eastern terminus. The Brinkley, Indian Bay & Helena Railroad is com-pleted from Brinkley south to Pine City on the Arkansas Midland, a distance of twenty-five miles, and will have several miles more in the county when finished through. There are now nearly 100 miles of finished railroad within these limits. Aside from the shipping facilities by rail, Monroe has the advantages of the navigation of White River, a most excellent outlet for heavy products.

In 1880 the real estate of the county was valued for taxation at $836,130, and the personal property at $299,612, making a total of $1,135,-742; and the total taxes charged thereon for all purposes were $36,002. In 1888 the real estate was assessed for taxation at $870,497, and the personal at $858,254, making a total of $1,728,751. This shows that of the real estate the assessed valuation was not much increased from 1880 to 1888, but the value of the personal property nearly thribbled, and the aggregate taxable wealth increased over fifty-two per cent. The total taxes levied in 1888 were $59,222.59. With the personal property of the latter year, the railroads were assessed as follows: St. Louis, Arkansas & Texas,

$261,570; the Batesville & Brinkley, $29,505; Little Rock & Memphis, $119,390; the Arkansas Midland, $63,020, making a total of $473,485. The assessment of the Brinkley, Indian Bay & Helena line when completed will add largely to the value of railroad property. The property of the Western Union Telegraph Company was assessed for taxation at $2,600.

In accordance with a decision of the people, expressed at a special election held May 23, 1871, the county subscribed $100,000 to the capital stock of the Arkansas Central Railway Company, and bonds to that amount were afterward issued. This has been a burden to the tax payers of Monroe County, but the bonds are mostly paid. The total indebtedness of the county as shown by report for the year ending July 6, 1889, was $53,800.07, and the assets in the treasury amounted to $18,468.81, thus leaving a net indebtedness of $35,331.26. A part of the bonded indebtedness is payable by Lee County, a portion of that county having been embraced in Monroe when the bonds were issued. The Arkansas Central Railway was the former name of the present Arkansas Midland.

In 1880 the census showed Monroe County to have 952 farms and 51,238 acres of improved lands. The value of the farm products for the year 1879 amounted to $783,470, the yield of certain products having been as follows: Cotton, 14,106 bales; Indian corn, 208,667 bushels; oats, 13,995 bushels; wheat, 200 bushels; orchard products, $50.20; hay, 511 tons; Irish potatoes, 6,193 bushels; sweet potatoes, 14,128 bushels; tobacco, 2,590 pounds. These figures show that cotton was then, as now, the staple product, and corn the next in order; also, that but very little attention was then paid to the growing of wheat. This is not surprising, for it is not prudent to try to raise wheat in a country not adapted to its cultivation. These figures will be interesting to compare with the census of 1890, which will show the products of the present year, 1889, and the great increase over those of 1879. With proper cultivation the lands of Monroe County will yield from 1,000 to 1,500 pounds of seed cotton, forty to sixty bushels

of corn or oats, Irish or sweet potatoes from 200 to 300 bushels, and turnips 300 bushels per acre. Wheat may occasionally yield from twelve to fifteen bushels per acre, but it is not a certain crop, and would not pay at these figures. Carrots and rutabagas, the best of feed for live stock through the winter months, would "surprise the natives," if sown, with their abundant yield in the rich alluvial soil. Improved farms can be purchased at from $10 to $50 per acre, and unimproved lands at from $1 to $15 per acre, according to location and quality.

In 1880 the county had the following live animals: Horses, 1,459; mules and asses, 1,024; cattle, 8,470; sheep, 405; hogs, 13,318. The number of these animals in the county as assessed for taxation in 1888 were as follows: Horses, 2,222; mules and asses, 1,464; cattle, 8,345; sheep, 708; hogs, 6,749. This shows a large increase in horses, mules and sheep, and a decrease in the number of the other animals, the latter being more apparent than real. To get a more truthful comparison, compare the figures given here for 1880, with those of the forthcoming census of 1890. The raising of live stock for profit has not been developed in Monroe County, but certainly for this industry its advantages are equal to those of any other county in Eastern Arkansas.

Monroe County can produce all the fruits common to its latitude, but not with as good success as locations of higher altitudes. The small fruits and berries, especially strawberries, do exceedingly well. Not much attention is given, however, to horticulture. Cotton is the king which demands and receives the principal attention of the farmers and business men.

Monroe County, in East Central Arkansas, is bounded on the north by Woodruff and St. Francis Counties, east by Lee and Phillips Counties, southwest by Arkansas and Prairie Counties. The base line of the public survey of lands runs east and west through, or near the center of the county, and the fifth principal meridian passes through the southeastern portion thereof. The greatest distance across the county from east to west is twenty-two miles, and from its extreme northern to southern boundary is forty-seven miles. It lies partly in the 91st°, but mostly in the 92d° of west longitude. The area of the county is 642 square miles or 410,880 acres, of which about one-eighth is improved and cultivated. Nearly 30,000 acres belong to the State, all of which is subject to donation to actual settlers. The Little Rock & Memphis Railroad Company also owns a large amount. White River touches the county at or near the point where the line between Ranges 3 and 4 west, crosses the base line, and flows thence southeasterly to the southern extremity thereof, forming for many miles the southwestern boundary. Cache River flows through a portion of the northwestern part of the county and empties into the White just above Clarendon. White River is navigable the year round, and the Cache is navigable to points north when the water is high. Big Creek flows southeasterly across the northeast corner and returns into the county in Township 3 south, flowing thence in a southwesterly direction to its junction with White River in Township 5 south. These streams and their tributaries furnish all the drainage for the county. The natural surface is generally level, but sufficiently undulating to furnish good drainage. At no point is it elevated more than forty feet above the water level of White River. Good well water, mostly soft, is obtained at an average depth of twenty-five feet.

Nearly all the land of the county is of alluvial formation, and, with the exception of about fifteen square miles of prairie in the southeastern part, they are covered with timber. The soil is generally a dark loam composed of sand, vegetable mold, etc., and has a substratum of clay, at a depth of from two to three feet. It is very rich and productive, and is especially well adapted to the raising of cotton, corn, oats, clover, timothy, other tame grasses and all kinds of root crops. Clover has been introduced and raised to a limited extent, but the tame grasses, so essential to successful farming, by way of keeping the soil in good condition, have as yet, received but little attention.

In the eastern part of the county there are about 100 square miles covered with excellent pine timber; the bottoms along the streams abound with cypress, sweet gum, sycamore, elm, etc., the cypress being very abundant, and the more elevated lands are covered with nearly all kinds of oak, the white oak being large, thrifty and valuable for lumber. A few factories and several saw-mills have been established, which are cutting the timber, but as yet they have scarcely made an impression upon the native forests.

The settlement of the county, or of the territory composing it, began soon after the beginning of the nineteenth century, and the central and southern portion was settled first. Dedrick Pike settled in the vicinity where Clarendon now stands, about the year 1816, and subsequent pioneer settlers in that neighborhood were: William, John A. and N. T. Harvick, brothers, Alfred Mullens, Henry C. Toms, Samuel Martin and Col. James Harris. Isaiah Walker from Illinois settled about the year 1831 on the Walker Cypress, on the Helena road, and in October, 1855, John W. Kerr, father of B. F. Kerr, now of Clarendon, came from Missouri and settled in Jackson Township, on the Helena road, being the first settler in that vicinity. William J. Edwards, who was one of the first settlers in the Indian Bay country in the southern part of the county, is still living, and over eighty years of age, hale and active, and still hunts and traps. Dr. Duncan was the first settler of the Duncan Prairie settlement, a few miles south, bearing a little east from Clarendon. Other pioneer settlers of this neighborhood were William Pride, from Alabama, John Smith, from South Carolina, William McBride, also Oliver H. Oates, a subsequent secretary of State. Thomas and John Pledger, James F. McLaughlin and Henry F. Overton, from Alabama, were the first settlers of the Pledger settlement, about ten miles south of the present town of Brinkley.

In what is now Montgomery Township, Indian Bay country, James R. and Robert Jackson, Robert Smalley, Thomas Jackson, Major Johnson, G. W. Baldwin, John Carnagee and George Washington were the pioneer settlers. The first settlers in the vicinity of old Lawrenceville, on Maddox Bay, were Thomas Maddox, F. P. Redmond, a large planter who worked from 300 to 400 slaves, Lawrence Mayo, Elijah Kinzie, Simon P. Hughes (since Governor), John Simmons, H. W. Hays, James G. Gay and Clement C. Clark. The latter recently drew $15,000 from the Louisiana Lottery, but now is deceased.

The Daniels' settlement, northeast of Clarendon, was settled by William Daniels, S. P. Jolly and William H. H. Fellows. Capt. Andrew Park and his family, consisting of himself and wife and sons James, William, M. B., Reuben and Andrew, Jr., with three daughters, and H. A. Carter, the latter now of Brinkley, came from Mississippi in 1856, and settled what it known as the Park settlement, about six miles east of Clarendon. Three of the sons and all the daughters of this family are living now (fall of 1889). David Fancher and Thomas J. Brown, from Alabama, were early settlers in this neighborhood. Moses Guthrie was the pioneer settler in the vicinity of Brinkley. William Munn, Alexander White and a Mr. Buchanan were the pioneers of the Munn settlement north of Brinkley. The large planters began to settle in the county early in the fifties. Prior, thereto, the settlement was very slow, but little land was cleared and wild game had continued almost as plentiful as it had ever been. There is still plenty of game, though the deer have become scarce. A few bear linger in the cane brakes along White River.

The county of Monroe was organized under an act of the legislature of Arkansas Territory, approved November 2, 1829. The first section of the act provided: "That all that portion of the country bounded and described as follows: Beginning where the eastern boundary line of Range 1 east, strikes the boundary line between Phillips and Arkansas Counties; thence west on said county line to White River; thence up said river to the mouth of Rock Roe; thence west to the western boundary line of Range 4 west; thence north on said range line to the northern boundary line of Township 3 north; thence with the St. Francis County line to its intersection with the eastern boundary line of Range 1 east; thence south with said range line to the beginning, be laid off and erected into a new county, to be known and called

by the name of Monroe." The act also provided that the temporary seat of justice for the county should be at the house of the widow of the late Thomas Maddox, until otherwise provided by law.

By reference to the original boundary lines it will be seen that when created, the county contained territory that has since been cut off and attached to surrounding counties, thus reducing it considerably below its original size.

The original county seat was located at Lawrenceville, on Maddox Bay, a point on White River several miles below the town of Clarendon, and there a small frame court house and a log jail were erected. The seat of justice remained at this place until 1857, when it was removed to Clarendon, where it has ever since remained. Here the walls of a brick court house were erected on the same foundation on which the present one stands, and the building was covered, when the Civil War began and stopped its completion. After the Federal army took possession of this part of the State, the soldiers took the building down and shipped the brick up the river to De Vall's Bluff and there used them in erecting fire-places and chimneys, etc., for their own comfort. Immediately after the close of the war a one-story frame court house, 18x36 feet in size and divided into two rooms, was erected on a corner of the public square at Clarendon, to be used until a more commodious house could be built. It was built by contractors Moses D. Cheek and Henry D. Green.

In February, 1870, the county court appropriated $12,000 for the purpose of building a new court house, and appointed W. S. Whitley commissioner to let the contract and superintend its construction. In July following another thousand dollars was appropriated. The house was finished in 1872 at a cost to the county of a little over $13,000. It is a plain two-story brick structure, with a hall and offices on the first floor and court room on the second, and stands in the center of the public square at Clarendon. On the southeast corner of this square stands the county jail, a common two-story wooden building.

Following is a list of the names of the officers of Monroe County, with dates of service annexed:

Judges: William Ingram, 1829–32; James Carlton, 1832–36; R. S. Bell, 1836–40; J. B. Lambert, 1840–44; D. D. Ewing, 1844–46; William Harvick, 1846–48; J. R. Dye, 1848–50; William Harvick, 1850–52; E. Black, 1852–54; J. G. Gray, 1854–56; H. D. Green, 1856–58; W. W. Wilkins, 1858–62; P. O. Thweatt, 1862–64; E. Black, 1864–65; W. D. Kerr, 1865–68; Peter Jolly, 1868–72; B. F. Lightle, 1874–76; S. P. Jolly, 1876–80; T. W. Hooper, 1880–84; H. B. Bateman, present incumbent, first elected in 1884.

Clerks: J. C. Montgomery, 1829–32; M. Mitchell, 1832–33; R. S. Bell, 1833–36; W. B. Ezell, 1836–38; Philip Costar, 1838–40; R. S. Bell, 1840–48; H. H. Hays, 1848–50; E. W. Vann, 1850–54; N. T. Harvick, 1854–56; J. P. Vann, 1856–58; J. A. Harvick, 1858–65; D. D. Smellgrove, 1865–66; P. C. Ewan, 1866–68; A. A. Bryan, 1868–72; F. P. Wilson, 1872–74; W. S. Dunlop, 1874–86; C. B. Mills, present clerk elected in 1886 and re-elected in 1888.

Sheriffs: James Eagan, 1829–30; James Carlton, 1830–32; J. R. Dye, 1832–36; W. Walker, 1836–38; J. Dye, 1838–40; Philip Costar, 1840–46; D. L. Jackson, 1846–48; J. A. Harvick, 1848–54; S. P. Hughes (now ex-Governor), 1854–56; George Washington, 1856–60; W. B. Meeks, 1860–62; H. P. Richardson, 1862–66; R. C. Carlton, 1866–68; E. P. Wilson, 1868–72; A. Galligher, 1872–73; Frank Galligher, 1873–74; C. J. Harris, 1874–76; B. N. D. Tannehill, 1876–78; A. McMurtry, 1878–84; J. W. Walker, 1884–86; J. W. B. Robinson, present incumbent, first elected in 1886.

Treasurers: J. Jacobs, 1836–38; S. B. Goodwin, 1838–48; H. D. Green, 1848–52; T. D. Johnson, 1852–56; I. Walker, 1856–60; D. Pike, 1860–72; A. W. Harris, 1872–76; J. A. Garrett, 1876–78; A. W. Harris, 1878–86; R. N. Counts, 1886–88; H. D. Green, present incumbent, elected in 1888.

Coroners: John Maddox, 1829–32; William Ingram, 1832–36; A. D. Nance, 1836–38; E. Frazier, 1838–40; W. B. Fail, 1840–42; W. Walker, 1842–44; D. L. Jackson, 1844–46; H. Watterman, 1846–48; J. S. Danby, 1848–50; V. Vanslyke, 1850–52; Peter Jolly, 1852–54; J. W. Garrett,

1854–56; John Dalvell, 1856–58; W. E. Moore, 1858–60; J. Brown, 1860–62; W. R. Elkins, 1862–64; E. Hennigan, 1864–66; R. F. Kerr, 1866–68; T. Pledger, 1868–72; J. H. Hillman, 1872–74; W. T. Stafford, 1874–76; W. H. Odem, 1876–78; Ed Kelley, 1878–80; W. J. Capps, 1880–82; R. F. Tyler, 1882–84; M. B. Dyer, 1884–86; W. J. Hall, 1886–88; A. J. Smith, present officer, elected in 1888.

Surveyors: Lafayette Jones, 1829–30; J. Jacobs, 1832–38; D. D. Ewing, 1838–44; L. D. Maddox, 1844–46; J. B. McPherson, 1848–50; M. Kelly, 1850–52; D. E. Pointer, 1852–56; H. Garretson, 1856–58; H. P. Richardson, 1858–62; R. T. Shaw, 1862–64; P. W. Halloran, 1864–66; A. A. Bryan, 1866–68; Henry Bonner, 1868–69; A. A. Bryan, 1872–74; John C. Hill, 1874–76; A. J. Houser, 1876–78; W. M. Walker, 1878–80; H. N. Allen, 1880–84; John C. Hill, 1884–88; A. A. Bryan, present incumbent, elected in 1888.

Assessors: H. C. Edrington, 1868–72; P. Mitchell, 1872–73; John Rainey, 1873–74; L. Ward, 1874–76; D. D. Dickson, 1876–78; W. M. Speed, 1878–80; J. A. Lovewell, 1880–82; J. R. Riggins, 1882–86; B. L. Hill, present incumbent, first elected in 1886.

Delegates in State conventions: 1836, Thomas J. Lacy; 1861, William N. Hays; 1868, A. H. Evans; 1874, Simon P. Hughes.

Representatives in legislature: Isaac Taylor, 1836–38; L. D. Maddox, 1838–40; Isaac Taylor, 1840–42; John C. Johnson, 1842–44; J. B. Lambert, 1844–46; Lewis B. Tully, 1846–48; Philip Costar, 1848–50; R. Pyburn, 1850–52; Francis P. Redmond, 1854–56; Oliver H. Oates, 1856–60; Z. P. H. Farr, 1860–62; E. Wilds, 1864–66; S. P. Hughes, 1866–68; F. W. Robinson, 1874–76; J. K. Whitson, 1876–78; Lecil Bobo, 1878–80; J. K. Whitson, 1880–82; John B. Baxter, 1882–86; W. J. Blackwell, 1886–88.

The vote cast in Monroe County for the candidates for Governor at the September election, 1888, and for President at the succeeding November election was as follows: For Governor, James P. Eagle (Dem.), 965; C. M. Norwood (Com. Opp.), 1,732; for President, Cleveland (Dem.), 784; Harrison

(Rep.), 1,167; Streeter (U. L.), 15; Fisk (Pro.), 6.

The population of Monroe County, in 1860, was 3,431 white and 2,226 colored, making a total of 5,657; in 1870, 5,135 white and 3,200 colored, making a total of 8,335; in 1880, 4,365 white and 5,209 colored, making a total of 9,574. The population in 1830 was, in the aggregate, 461; in 1840, 936; in 1850, 2,049.

During a portion of the war period, from 1861 to 1865, the courts of Monroe County were suspended. No term of the county court was held after April, 1862, until July, 1865. All other courts were suspended about the same length of time. The several courts convene now in regular session on the following dates: County, first Monday of January, April, July and October of each year; probate, on the second, and common pleas on the fourth Monday of the same months; the circuit on the fourth Monday after the third Monday in February and August. The following named attorneys constitute the legal bar of the county: Grant Green, S. J. Price, J. P. Roberts, M. J. Manning, J. S. Thomas, P. C. Ewan, J. C. Palmer, H. A. Parker, C. W. Brickell, W. J. Mayo, R. E. Johnson, R. C. Lansford and W. T. Tucker.

Upon the approach of the Civil War many citizens of Monroe held out for the Union until the first gun was fired at Charleston, S. C.; then they became solidly united and cast their lot with the proposed Southern Confederacy. In the spring of 1861 the first company of soldiers was organized and commanded by Capt. James T. Harris, of Clarendon, a brother of Senator Isham G. Harris, of Tennessee. This company was called the "Harris Guards." The next company organized, the "Monroe County Blues," was under the charge of Capt. G. W. Baldwin; another company, the "Arkansas Toothpicks," was commanded by Capt. L. Featherstone. Another company was commanded by Capt. Oliver H. Oates. These were all raised in 1861, and in 1862 two other companies were raised and commanded, respectively, by Capts. George Washington and W. J. F. Jones. In the battle of Shiloh the "Harris Guards" and the "Monroe County Blues" suffered very

great loss, and soon thereafter they were reorganized and consolidated into one company, of which Parker C. Ewan became the captain. Capt. Harris was killed at that battle. The soldiers furnished by Monroe County, like their comrades in general, fought with great desperation and determination, and many fell to rise no more on earth.

The Federal forces, under Gen. Steele, took possession of Clarendon, in August, 1863, and camped there for some time, and then moved on and took Little Rock on September 10, following. Prior to this the county had not suffered much from the ravishes of war, but now it became foraging ground for the United States army possessing it. On one occasion, in 1864, Gen. Joe Shelby, with a Confederate force, captured the crews of two gunboats in White River, at Clarendon, and sunk the vessels. The next day a detachment of the Federal army went down from De Vall's Bluff, and drove Shelby's forces several miles out on the Helena road to a point from which they made their escape. The Union soldiers then returned to the Bluff. Aside from this fight there was only a few slight skirmishes in the county between guerrillas and scouting parties. However, the county suffered greatly from the ravishes of the war in general. 'Tis over, and one would gladly forget its painful incidents.

Lawrenceville, though for many years the site of the county seat, never gained much size nor importance. The town disappeared long ago, and the site thereof is now in farm lands.

Clarendon, the county seat of Monroe County, is situated on the eastern bank of White River, near the center of the county north and south. Prominent among the settlers of this place was Samuel Martin, who opened the first store and kept the ferry across the river, and erected the first steam saw-mill. The ferry was established about the year 1836. The next store was opened by Henry M. Couch, who came from Tennessee, and in 1856 it was the only one in the town. Martin died prior to the latter date, and his widow opened and kept the first hotel in the place. Col. James Harris, of Tennessee, brother of Senator Isham G.

Harris, of that State, settled at Clarendon in 1856, married the widow Martin, finished the new hotel she was then building, and with her continued the business. Harris had the town surveyed and laid out in 1857, the same year it became the county seat. The next merchants were William Granberry and Jesse Brown. Prior to the removal of the county seat to Clarendon, the place was known only by the name of "Mouth of Cache." The next year, 1858, the town took on a more rapid growth, and when the Civil War began it did a large amount of business. During the war the town was entirely destroyed, not a building was left, and at the close of that struggle, the site was completely covered with weeds. Immediately after the war the town began to be rebuilt, and soon became a great cotton market, shipping from 4,000 to 5,000 bales yearly. It now ships from 8,000 to 9,000 bales per year. It contains fourteen general stores, three groceries, two drug stores, a meat market, an undertaking shop, two blacksmith and wagon shops, an extensive feed and farm implement store, where wagons are also kept for sale, two cotton-gins, a grist-mill and machine shop, a large stave factory, run by the White River Stave Company, which was erected in 1888, and where from seventy-five to 100 men are employed, a lumber yard, three hotels and a hotel kept by and for colored folks, several boarding houses, three churches (Methodist, Presbyterian and Cumberland Presbyterian) for the whites, and two churches (Methodist and Baptist) for the blacks, a very large frame school-house for the white people, and a comfortable one for the colored people. In addition to the foregoing, there are the county buildings, railroad depots, express and telegraph offices and several other important places of business.

Of the benevolent orders there are a lodge, Chapter and Council of Masons, and a lodge each of the Knights of Honor, Knights of Pythias and American Legion of Honor. There are seven physicians, and the same number of lawyers, and a population of 800 to 1,000.

The Monroe County Sun, published at Clarendon, was established in 1876 by Capt. P. C. Ewan.

It is a seven-column folio, now published by the Sun Printing Company, and edited by W. E. Spencer. Politically it is Democratic.

The principal shipments from Clarendon consist of cotton, cotton-seed, lumber and staves. The town is not incorporated.

Brinkley is situated in the northern part of the county, at the crossing of the St. Louis, Arkansas & Texas and the Little Rock & Memphis Railroads, and at the southern terminus of the Batesville & Brinkley Railroad, and the northern terminus of the Brinkley, Indian Bay & Helena Railroad. It was laid out in the winter of 1869–70, on lands belonging to the Little Rock & Memphis Railroad Company, and the first general sale of lots took place in August of the latter year. M. B. Park and H. A. Carter, under the firm name of M. B. Park & Co., opened the first store (it being also in 1870). Baxter & Dillard established the second store (also in the same year). The town assumed a gradual and substantial growth, but has never had a boom. For the last two years, however, its growth has been more rapid than at any time before. The first brick buildings in the place were erected in 1887, and now there are six brick blocks, containing altogether fourteen large store-rooms on the first floor.

It now consists of the Monroe County Bank, seven general, six grocery, three drug and two jewelry and notion stores, a boot and shoe shop, a furniture and undertaker's store, a millinery store, bakery, feed store, billiard hall, four hotels, a hotel and restaurant kept by colored people, a meat market, a meat market and restaurant, two blacksmith and two barber shops, a pool hall and temperance saloon, the machine and car shops of the Batesville & Brinkley Railroad, two livery stables, two brick-yards, a grist-mill, cotton-gin, Niffen's foundry, the Union Wood Turning Works, Brinkley Oil Mill (employing from fifty to seventy-five men), the Brinkley Car and Manufacturing Works (employing about 200 men), three churches (Methodist, Baptist and Cumberland Presbyterian), also three Baptist churches and one Methodist for the colored people, a public school-house for the whites (the school for colored children being taught in one

32

of the church edifices). In addition to the foregoing, there is a lodge, each, of Masons, Knights of
Pythias, Knights of Honor, Knights and Ladies of
Honor, and two Building & Loan Associations.
The town is incorporated, and in August, 1889,
the school board took an actual census of the inhabitants within the corporate limits, and found a
population of 1,498, and there is said to be several
hundred outside of these limits. Brinkley is a
railroad center, a good cotton market, and its shipments are extensive.

The Brinkley Argus, a neat seven-column folio
newspaper, is now in its seventh volume and is
published every Thursday by W. H. Peterson.

Holly Grove, situated on the Arkansas Midland
Railroad about ten miles southeast of Clarendon,
was laid out and established in 1872, by John
Smith and James Kerr. D. B. Renfro opened the
first store, and Kerr, Robley & Co. opened the
second one. The village now contains one drug
and seven general stores, a grocery and restaurant,
an undertaker's shop, livery stable, a steam cotton-
gin and grist-mill, a mechanic's shop, two churches
(Methodist and Presbyterian) for the whites and
churches also for the colored people, a two-story
frame school-house, a Masonic lodge, two physicians, and a population of about 300. It is
situated in the best cotton growing district in the
county and ships a large quantity of that commodity.

Indian Bay, a small village in the southern
part of the county, contains three general stores,
two cotton-gins, grist and saw mills, and a small
population.

Pine City, a station on the Arkansas Midland
Railroad, a few miles east of Holly Grove consists
of a large saw-mill, where extensive quantities of
pine timber is cut into lumber. There are a few
small residences.

The following statistics given in the last published report of the State superintendent of public
instruction will serve to show the progress of the
free school system in Monroe County. Scholastic
population: White, males, 999, females, 892, total
1,891; colored, males, 1,449, females, 1,384, total
2,833; number taught in the public schools, white,

males, 487, females, 424, total, 911; colored, males,
853, females, 803, total, 1,656. School districts,
38, of which only 26 made any report. Teachers employed: Males, 45, females, 13, total, 58.
Amount expended during the year to support
the schools: Teachers' salaries, $8,401.50, building
and repairing, $2,718.97, purchasing apparatus,
$79.55, treasurer's commissions, $112.55, other
purposes, $200.65, total, $11,513.22. By comparing the scholastic population with the number reported attending the schools, it will appear that a
very large percentage of the children of school age
did not attend, but a greater percentage than shown
by the figures undoubtedly attended, as twelve of
the districts failed to make report.

Of the Methodist Episcopal Church, South,
there is the Clarendon and Brinkley Station, with
a membership, as shown by the last Conference
minutes, of 166, with Rev. S. L. Cochran as pastor;
the Brinkley Circuit, with a membership of 172,
and W. W. Hendrix, pastor; the Holly Grove Circuit, with a membership of 111, and N. E. Skinner, pastor; the Cypress Ridge Circuit, with a
membership of 228, and T. Rawlings, pastor; the
Howell and Cotton Plant Circuit, with a membership of 168, and M. B. Umstead, pastor. About
one half of the latter circuit lies in Woodruff
County. All of these belong to the Helena District of the White River Conference.

The Baptist Churches of Monroe County, as
shown by the minutes of the session of the Mount
Vernon Baptist Association, held at Salem Church
in Phillips County, in October, 1888, are as follows with their respective pastors and memberships:
Clarendon, G. C. Goodwin, pastor, 45; Mount
Gilead, M. A. Thompson, pastor, 23; Brinkley,
R. G. Hewlett, pastor, 52; Lone Chapel, G. C.
Goodwin, pastor, 35; Ash Grove, S. D. Johns,
pastor, 52, and Philadelphia, G. C. Goodwin, pastor, 78.

The Cumberland Presbyterians have four church
organizations within the county, one at Brinkley,
with a membership of 25, and Rev. A. B. Forbess,
pastor; one at Clarendon, membership 50, and
Rev. R. V. Cavot, pastor; one at Valley Grove in
the southern part of the county, membership 75,

and Rev. Cavot, pastor; the other on Cypress Ridge about twelve miles southeast of Brinkley, membership about 50, and Rev. Stewart, pastor. The organization at Brinkley has a new $2,500 brick church edifice, and the one at Clarendon has a fine frame building with the Masonic hall on the upper floor.

The Presbyterians (Old School) have an organization at Clarendon with a membership of about 70, and Rev. W. C. Hagan, pastor; another at Holly Grove with a membership of about 25, and Rev. Hagan, pastor; also an organization at Brinkley with a small membership, Rev. S. I. Reid, of Lonoke, pastor.

The churches in the towns in general have Sunday-schools connected with them, and some of the country churches also conduct Sunday-schools. There is a large Catholic Church with a strong membership at Brinkley; Father McGill is the priest. The people of the county are moral and hospitable, and persons seeking new homes will do well to visit this section of country.

J. T. Andrews, planter at Cotton Plant, is one of the leading planters of Monroe County. Born in Limestone County, Ala., in 1837, he is the son of Daniel and Mary (Morris) Andrews, natives of Virginia and North Carolina, and born in 1814 and 1815, respectively. The parents were married in 1836 and to their union were born two children, a son and daughter: J. T. and Dionitia F. (wife of T. L. Westmoreland). Daniel Andrews died in 1841 and Mrs. Andrews was married the second time in 1843 to J. H. Deaver. By this union she became the mother of five children: Mary A. (wife of Dr. J. W. Westmoreland), Thomas A., Martha J. (widow of Saul Salinger), Bettie M. (wife of H. C. McLaurine) and D. J. (wife of J. R. Whitfield). J. H. Deaver died in 1853, and Mrs. Deaver, who survives her husband, now lives with her widowed daughter, Mrs. Salinger, at Cotton Plant. She is, and has been for many years, a consistent member of the Methodist Episcopal Church, South. J. T. Andrews started in business for himself in 1858 by farming his mother's land in Tennessee,

but left that State and immigrated to Arkansas in 1860, locating in Poinsett County. His mother purchased 240 acres of land, which he farmed until the breaking out of the war, when he enlisted in the infantry under Capt. Westmoreland and served until July 9, 1863. He was then captured at Port Hudson, taken to Johnson's Island, and there held until February 9, 1864, when he was transferred to Point Lookout. He was there retained until March 3, when he was sent to City Point and was there paroled. After the war he resumed farming and also operated a cotton-gin in Woodruff County. He selected as his companion in life, Miss Martha A. Westmoreland, daughter of Mr. and Mrs. Thomas A. Westmoreland, and was united in marriage to her in 1858. This union has been blessed by the birth of three children, but only one now living: Sam (who married a Miss Cattie Keath and resides on a farm in this county). The children deceased were named: Edward and Minnie. Mrs. Andrews was born in Giles County, Tenn., in 1836. Her father died in 1865 and her mother in 1887, both members of the Methodist Episcopal Church. Mr. Andrews is a member of the I. O. O. F. Lodge No. 76, and he and wife have been members of the Methodist Episcopal Church for seventeen years. Mr. Andrews is one of the enterprising farmers of the county, and is the owner of 230 acres of land in Woodruff County, Ark., with 120 acres under cultivation and his principal crops are corn and cotton.

Judge H. B. Bateman, judge of the county and probate and of the court of common pleas of Monroe County, Ark., has been a resident of the county all his life, having been born one and one-half miles from Clarendon, in 1857, and is a worthy descendant of an old and highly respected family. His parents, Baker H. and Jane E. (Harvick), Bateman, were born in North Carolina, but owing to their early removal to Arkansas, they were married in Monroe County. The father died in this county in 1861, aged about forty years, and the mother's death occurred in 1874, aged forty-eight years. She was married three times, Mr. Bateman being her third husband, and by him she became the mother of two sons: H. B. and Thomas T., the latter being the present deputy sheriff of Monroe County. After passing many of the important years of his life on a farm, and in attending the common schools and the schools of Searcy, Judge H. B. Bateman began clerking in a country store, continuing one year, and in .1879 established a drug store in connection with J. B. Chapline, at Clarendon, the firm continuing business until 1889, under the title of Bateman & Chapline, at which time G. A. Franklin succeeded Mr. Chapline, and the firm is now Bateman & Franklin. Their stock of drugs is valued at $900, and their labors in this direction have met with substantial results, as they have the reputation of being safe, thorough and reliable business men. Judge Bateman has a fair share of this world's goods, and in addition to owning a fine farm of 350 acres, the most of which is under cultivation, he has a fine brick business block in Clarendon. His first presidential vote was cast for Hancock in 1880, and for some years he has been quite prominent in local political matters, and, besides being justice of the peace for about six years, he was elected to his present office in 1884, and has held it by re-election up to the present time. He has made a very efficient officer, and is respected and esteemed for his sterling integrity, sound judgment, broad intelligence and liberal progressive ideas. He is a man whose decisions are not made without careful and painstaking study of the evidence, and all feel that his judgment can be relied upon. He belongs to Cache Lodge No. 235, of the A. F. & A. M., and he is also a member of the Chapter and Council of Clarendon.

Maj. John B. Baxter is a real estate and insurance agent at Brinkley. In all business communities the matter of insurance holds a prominent place and deservedly so, for it is a means of stability to all commercial transactions, and is a mainstay against disaster should devastation by fire sweep property away. He was born in Wilson County, Tenn., in 1839, and is a son of George W. and Rebecca A. (Hooker) Baxter, who were born in North Carolina and Tennessee, respectively, and were married in the latter State, their union taking place in Wilson County, about 1833, when the father was nineteen years of age and the mother fifteen. They remained in Wilson County until after the birth of our subject, then removed to La Grange, Tenn., and here the father died May 25, 1844, having been a farmer throughout life. George Baxter, the maternal grandfather, was of Scotch-Irish descent, and was born in North Carolina, but died in Tennessee. Joshua Hooker, the maternal grandfather, was also born in North Carolina, but after residing many years in Wilson County, Tenn., he removed in 1840 to Fayette County, Tenn., and in 1851 he came to Monroe County, Ark., where he died of small-pox in 1866. He was the father of a large family, a farmer by occupation, and was a soldier in the War of 1812, and was with Jackson at New Orleans. Our subject came with his mother to Monroe County, Ark., in 1851, but soon after removed to Des Arc, where they resided until the opening of the war, then returned to Memphis, where the mother's death occurred in July, 1867, she being in full communion with the Methodist Church at that time. Maj. John B. Baxter is the fourth of six children, and only he and his youngest brother, Hon. George W. Baxter, of Hot Springs, Ark., are now living. The former received his education in the common schools of Tennessee and Arkansas, and upon the opening of the war in 1861, he joined Company K, Fifth Arkansas Infantry, and operated in Kentucky. He soon after assisted in organizing Company F of the Twenty-third Arkansas Infantry, of which he remained a member until the fall of Port Hudson, when he was captured and imprisoned at Johnson's Island, Point Lookout, Fort Delaware, Morris' Island off Charleston, Fort Pulaski off Savannah, Ga., and was returned to Fort Delaware just before the close of the war. He was released in June, 1865, and at once went to Memphis, Tenn., where his mother was still living. In 1866 he traveled in Arkansas for a Memphis cotton and wholesale grocery house, but before his marriage, in April, 1866, to Josephine, daughter of William A. and Mary Pickens, he removed to Cotton Plant, Ark., but removed shortly afterward to Clarendon, from which place he entered the army, where he followed mercantile pursuits. He next engaged in farming near Cotton Plant, but since 1872 he has lived at Brinkley, and until 1882 was engaged in the practice of law, having prepared himself for this profession prior to the war. He has been a prominent politician since his residence here and served several terms as sergeant-at-arms of the lower house of the State legislature, and in 1882 was elected to represent Monroe County in that body, and was reelected in 1884, serving four years. He has been mayor of Brinkley several terms, and in 1887 was chosen sergeant-at-arms of the State senate, being elected by the Democratic party to his various official positions. His first presidential vote was cast for Breckenridge. He is Worshipful Master of Brinkley Lodge No. 295, A. F. & A. M., and is Dictator of Brinkley Lodge No. 3127, K. of H., being also a member of the K. & L. of H. Maj. Baxter is one of only three of the original settlers of Brinkley, who are now residing in the town. His wife was born in Mississippi, but her parents were Tennesseeans who moved to that State, and in 1859 came to Cotton Plant, Ark. They both died here during the war.

William L. Benton is a farmer and blacksmith, of Pine Ridge Township, but was born in Jackson County, Ga., in 1834. His parents, Thomas and Sarah (Norman) Benton, were Virginians, spending most of their life in Georgia, in which State Mr. Benton died, September 1, 1889, at the age of eighty-six years, his wife's death occurring in 1872 or 1873, when sixty-seven years old. They were farmers, and of Irish descent. The paternal grandfather, Reason R. Benton, died in Georgia before the war, aged eighty-seven years, and the maternal grandfather's (Joseph Norman) death occurred in the State of Mississippi. William L. Benton is the sixth of fourteen children, and although his educational advantages were of a very limited description, he became a well-informed young man, and when twenty-two years of age went to Mississippi. He was married there in 1857, to Catherine Eavenson, but her death occurred in 1863, after having borne two children, only one now living, named Andrew. His second marriage took place in December, 1865, his wife

being a Miss Eliza Latimer, but he was called upon to mourn her loss by death in 1878, she having borne him three sons and three daughters. Mr. Benton's third marriage was consummated June 14, 1884, his wife being a Mrs. Catherine (Aldridge) Graham, by whom he has one son. Mr. Benton resided in Mississippi until 1870, when he came to Monroe County, and in 1872 purchased a woodland farm, comprising 160 acres, of which seventy-five acres are in a state of cultivation. In 1862 he joined Company H, First Mississippi Partisan Rangers, and operated with his command in Mississippi, Tennessee, Alabama and Georgia, and participated in nearly all the leading battles of those States, among others the battles of Shiloh, Franklin, Nashville, and was all through the Georgia campaign, and in the siege of Vicksburg, and during his entire service was never captured or wounded, surrendering at Selma, Ala. He is a conservative Democrat in his political views, and his first presidential vote was cast for Buchanan, in 1856. He belongs to Clarendon Lodge No. 2328, of K. of H., and was formerly Vice Dictator in Oak Grove Lodge. He and wife belong to the Christian Church.

Samuel Langley Black, planter, Indian Bay, Ark. Of that sturdy and independent class, the planters of Arkansas, none are possessed of more genuine merit and a stronger character than he, whose name stands at the head of this sketch; he has risen to a more than ordinary degree of success in his calling of an agriculturist, and wherever known he is conceded to be an energetic and progressive tiller of the soil, imbued with all these qualities of go-aheadativeness which have characterized his ancestors. Mr. Black is the son of John D. and Susan (Langley) Black, the father a native of Virginia and of English descent, and the mother a native of Kentucky. Samuel L. Black owes his nativity to Fayette County, Tenn., where his birth occurred March 22, 1842, and received his education in the high schools of that county, finishing at Bethel College, McLemoresville, Tenn. At the age of eighteen years he commenced the study of law at Clarendon, Ark., in the office of Oates, Cocke & Wilburn, there remaining until

1861, when he enlisted in Capt. James T. Harris' company, organized at Clarendon, this being the first company organized in this county, and served in the capacity of junior lieutenant in Patrick R. Cleburne's regiment. This regiment was the first one organized in the State for the War of the Rebellion, but through error of the officer, the services of the regiment were tendered to the State service instead of the Confederate State Government, thereby losing the opportunity of being credited with being the first regiment of Arkansas organized in that State, Gen. Fagan's regiment securing that distinction. At Bowling Green, Ky., Mr. Black was made captain of his company in 1861, and his first battle was the famous battle of Shiloh, where, by his bravery and meritorious conduct, he won his spurs. He was immediately elected to the office of lieutenant-colonel of the regiment, and was appointed to the staff of Lieut.-Col. Hardee as inspector-general of his corps, in which capacity he served the balance of the war. He participated in Gen. Bragg's invasion in Kentucky, which culminated in his retreat to Knoxville, Tenn.; was at the surrender of the Federal force at Munfordsville and the battle of Perryville. He took a leading part in the battle of Murfreesboro, and was with the Army of Tennessee until its retreat to Chattanooga. He went from there to Enterprise and Meridian, Miss., and served for a time upon the staff of Gen. Joseph E. Johnston. He was ordered back to the Army of Tennessee after the battle of Chickamauga, participated in the battle of Missionary Ridge and the retreat to Dalton, and was in all the fights and skirmishes of the Army of Tennessee from Dalton to Atlanta, including the battles around Atlanta and Jonestown. After Hood took command of the Army of Tennessee, he was released with Gen. Hardee and went with him to Charleston, S. C. He was in front of Gen. Sherman in his march from Savannah through the Carolinas; was captured by a squad of his cavalry, but escaped after a few hours by a bold ride. He participated in the battle of Bentonville and soon after surrendered with the balance of the army at Greensboro, N. C., in May, 1865. He returned home on July 4 of the same year, went to work for a firm in Memphis, Tenn., and subsequently was united in marriage to Miss Rosa E. Beasley, daughter of John P. and Eveline T. Beasley. Only one child, John S., was the result of this union, his birth occurring on September 28, 1866. Mr. Black has been constantly engaged in agricultural pursuits since, and was also a member of the firm of Martin & Black from February 1, 1882, to February 1, 1889, when he sold out. Mrs. Black died on June 1, 1886. He has never held any civil office, but at one time was a candidate for the office of secretary of State.

Mrs. Bena Black, widow of the late Maj. William Black, of Brinkley, was born in the State of New York in 1843, and her parents, John and Matelina (Leanhart) Colless, were natives of Germany. They were married in their native country, and three daughters were the result of this union: Catherine (wife of George Guisler), Julia (wife of John Bowers, of New Orleans), and the subject of this sketch. John Colless died in New Orleans in about 1847, and his wife afterward married a Mr. Frederick Buck, of New Orleans, and became the mother of five children, two sons and three daughters, all of whom are living in New Orleans. Maj. Black was born in Toronto, Canada, November 22, 1836, came to Memphis, Tenn., in 1856, and worked at ship carpentering for awhile, after which he went into the grocery business on Jefferson Street. He carried this on successfully, but subsequently disposed of this business and built a sawmill just south of Brinkley, which business increased so rapidly that a more suitable and convenient place for handling lumber had to be selected, hence the mill was moved to what is now known as "Old Mill," east of town. Again it was located on the site it now occupies, and the present corporation formed, The Brinkley Car Works & Manufacturing Company, which, in the meantime, owing to its excellent business management, has developed into the largest manufacturing concern of its kind in the State, and one of the largest in the South. It at several times had large railroad contracts, building about twenty-five miles of the Little Rock & Memphis Railroad, and about forty miles of the St. Louis, Arkansas & Texas Railroad.

He built what is known as the W. & B. R. V. Railroad as far as Tupelo, Ark. He built the Brinkley & Helena Railroad, and at the time of his death was busily engaged in extending the road through to Indian Bay, about twenty miles of which was ready for iron. He was a director and stockholder in the Little Rock & Memphis Railroad, was president and principal owner of the Brinkley Car Works & Manufacturing Company, president of the Monroe County Bank, vice-president of the Brinkley Oil Mill Company, and principal owner of the business of T. H. Jackson & Co., the largest mercantile firm in Eastern Arkansas. About five years ago, through his great business sagacity, he saw an opportunity to start a lumber business in Memphis, and as a result, owned the Brinkley Lumber Company of that city, which is, without doubt, the leading lumber establishment of Memphis, receiving and selling more lumber and doing through his extensive and extensive business. Maj. Black served through the war with distinction, participating in all the battles in and around Memphis. Soon after the war he moved to what is now known as Brinkley, then a dense forest. At that time he had to walk twenty miles to the nearest railroad, which was the Memphis & Little Rock, at Palestine, while now, by his indomitable energy, Brinkley can boast of four railroads. Maj. Black was fifty-three years, nine months and twenty-six days old when he returned from Waukesha Springs, and looked the picture of health and vigorous manhood, with the exception of a large carbuncle on the back of his neck near the base of the brain, which caused much uneasiness among his friends, but were met with hopeful assurance from the friends of the family. There were in attendance the most eminent surgeons of Memphis and Little Rock in consultation with local physicians, and all felt hopeful until the fatal day, September 18, 1889, when at the close of a surgical operation, at about 1 P. M., he breathed his last. When the sad news spread among the people that Maj. Black was dead, a hush fell upon the town that will long be remembered. Business houses were closed, a Sabbath-like calmness rested upon the streets and in the dwellings, as if each one paused in the busy walks of life to commune with himself on the uncertainty of life and the awful change, death. On Thursday, September 19, the obsequies took place, and seemingly the whole city followed in mourning to the cemetery where they carried this honored and much-respected citizen. The funeral services took place at the Catholic Church, and were conducted by Rev. Father McGill, after which the K. of H. lodge took charge of the burial ceremonies. A procession was formed at the church, headed by members of the K. of H., followed by the carriages of the family and immediate friends; next came the employes from the mill, numbering about 100, and as the procession reached the school-houses it was joined by the teachers and pupils from both schools, numbering about 200. After them came numberless carriages and many on foot, variously estimated at from 600 to 1,000 persons. The ceremonies at the grave were impressive, and at their close the school children were each permitted to place a handful of flowers on the coffin—a most touching tribute. Those most intimably acquainted with Maj. Black knew best his noble traits of character, for, though possessed of wonderful business acumen, yet he was modest and retiring to an unusual degree. Though so active, he never neglected those delicate courtesies which beautify life, but paid the strictest deference to the feelings of all his business associates, instances of which will be kindly remembered by them in years to come. He never took a very active part in politics, although at one time he represented this senatorial district in the State Assembly. He was the founder and leader, as it were, of this flourishing city, and his death produced a shock on every side, making all feel, in the presence of such a calamity, as if the ordinary pursuits of life were vain. When his death was announced at a meeting of the Memphis Lumber Exchange, remarks of profound regret were made, and resolutions of sympathy adopted and sent to the bereaved family—commending his many virtues and his noble life as an example to those whom he left behind. He was the father of twelve children, eight of whom are living at the present time, two sons and six daughters: Lena (wife of T. H.

Jackson), Katie (wife of H. H. Myers), Anna (wife of Charles Labell), Maggie, Nellie, Garland, Sarah and Willie. Mrs. Black still resides in Brinkley, and is a most estimable lady.

A. T. Blaine is another successful merchant of Indian Bay, and since 1882 has been established at his present place of business, the average value of his stock of goods amounting to $2,000. He was born in Worcester County, Md., in 1849, his parents, Thomas J. and Sarah G. (Burnett) Blaine, having been born in Somerset and Worcester Counties, in 1829 and 1833, respectively. They spent their lives in their native State, and the father at the time of his death, in 1884, was engaged in the boot and shoe business. He was a church member, as was his wife, and was a son of James Blaine, a native of Ireland, who came to the United States after becoming grown, and made his home in Maryland. Rixam Burnett, the maternal grandfather, was also born in Ireland, and after coming to the United States, settled in the west of Maryland. He had one son who was a ship carpenter and sailor for many years, on the vessel Ohio, and served in the United States navy during the war, the most of his time being spent on the Mississippi River. A. T. Blaine is the eldest of nine brothers, four of whom are living, and is the only one residing in Monroe County. He was educated in Pocomoke City, Md., attending both the private and public schools, but in 1871 he came to Indian Bay, Ark., and was engaged in clerking until 1882, when he again began business for himself, and as above stated, has done well. He is a Democrat, casting his first vote for Greeley, in 1872, and belongs to Indian Bay Lodge No. 249, A. F. & A. M., in which order he held the positions of Junior Warden and Secretary, and he is also a member of Advance Lodge No. 2491, K. of H., and is now filling the position of Past Dictator. In 1876 he was married to Jennie Rainbolt, who died in 1885, having borne one son and two daughters, and in 1887 he wedded Mrs. Emma (Erwin) Clark, a native of Tennessee, and a member of the Presbyterian Church. He owns 1,000 acres of land, with 500 under cultivation, and since 1885 has been postmaster of Indian Bay.

William H. Boyce is a planter and cotton ginner of Montgomery Township, and has been a prominent and enterprising resident of Monroe County, Ark., since 1866. He was born in Jackson, Tenn, July 19, 1847, and is a son of Isham and Elizabeth (Tharpe) Boyce, natives respectively of South Carolina and North Carolina. Both removed to Tennessee with their parents when young and were married in Paris of that State, but afterward became residents of Jackson. Mr. Boyce died at Brownsville, Tenn., in 1866, at the age of fifty-four years, and his wife in 1853, aged thirty-four years. After the death of his wife Mr. Boyce married again. William H. is the youngest of seven children born to his first union and received his early education in the common schools of his native State. When the war opened he joined Company L, Sixth Tennessee Infantry, and for some time was with Gen. Bragg in Kentucky and Tennessee, participating with that general in the battles of Perryville, Shiloh and Corinth. Just before the battle of Murfreesboro he was transferred to Company G, Ninth Tennessee Cavalry, and was at the battle of Chickamauga and in many skirmishes. He was captured at Panther Springs, Tenn., January 24, 1864, and was kept a prisoner at Ball's Island until just before the close of the war when he was released and rejoined his command and surrendered with it at Gainesville, Ala. Mr. Boyce has been very successful in his farming ventures and has an excellent lot of land, comprising 1,400 acres, lying seven miles northeast of Indian Bay. His land was almost wholly covered with timber, but with the energy and push which have ever characterized his efforts, he began energetically to clear his property and now has about 500 acres under cultivation. He keeps his cotton-gin running almost the year round and finds this a lucrative business. In 1869 he was married to Laura, a daughter of Capt. William M. Mayo, whose sketch will be found in this work, and by her became the father of ten children, three daughters only now living. Mr. Boyce is a Democrat, and his wife is a member in good standing of the Cumberland Presbyterian Church. He has one sister living, Georgia, the wife of John W. Gates, of Jackson, Tenn. William A. Tharpe, the maternal grandfather, was born in North Carolina, and died near Paris, Tenn.

W. F. Branch, merchant, Holly Grove, Ark. There are in every community some persons who, on account of their industry and practical management of the affairs which fall to their lot, deserve special credit; and such is Mr. Branch. He was originally from Wilson County, Tenn., where his birth occurred in 1849, and is the son of James Branch, who is also a native Tennesseean, born 1817. The elder Mr. Branch was a farmer by occupation, and was married to Miss Eleanor Neele, by whom he had seven children, two of whom only are living: W. F. and Sallie (wife of J. W. Walker, of Clarendon). The father moved from Tennessee to Arkansas in 1859, located in Monroe County, and there his death occurred in 1867. The mother died in 1885. W. F. Branch was married to Miss Ella Walls in 1874, and four children blessed this union, two of whom are living: Bessie and Addie. Mrs. Branch died in 1886. She was a member of the Methodist Episcopal Church. In 1888 Mr. Branch took for his second wife Miss Ada Peete, a native of Tennessee, a very estimable lady, and the daughter of Dr. and Mrs. Peete, of Memphis. Mr. Branch is a prosperous merchant, and the firm title is Branch & Wall. He opened business in Holly Grove, in 1887, and is doing well. He also owns 600 acres of land. He is a member of the K. of H., and he and wife are members of the Presbyterian Church.

Rev. Thomas J. Brickell. No calling in which a man can engage is so truly noble and unselfish as that of the man who devotes his life to the saving of souls, and although Mr. Brickell is a local minister, he has been instrumental in bringing many erring ones to the feet of the Master. He has been established in business in Brinkley since 1885, and deals in furniture and undertaker's goods, his stock being valued at from $1,500 to $2,000. He is a Georgian by birth, born in Palmetto, Coweta County, in 1849, and is a son of Nicholas and Martha J. (Sanders) Brickell, natives of North Carolina, their nuptials being celebrated at Palmetto, Ga. Since 1870 they have resided in Phillips County,

Ark., and are there still living, both having been members of the Methodist Church, South, many years. The father, the oldest of a family of four sons and one daughter, was born May 11, 1824. About 1844 he went to Rockford, Surry County, N. C., living with an uncle, J. F. Harrison, and in 1846 moved to Palmetto, Ga. His wife's mother was formerly Fannie Harris. Mr. Brickell upon leaving Palmetto, was located at Franklin several years, and in 1870 moved to Trenton, Phillips County, Ark. He now lives at Poplar Grove in the same county. He served the Confederate cause for three years during the Civil War, as a mechanic in the saltpetre works, being in Georgia most of the time. He belongs to the A. F. & A. M., and is a grandson of John B. Brickell, a Frenchman who came to the United States with Gen. La Fayette during the Revolutionary War. After that conflict he settled in the lower part of North Carolina, subsequently going to Union District, where he died. His wife, Frances Gregory, a Virginian by birth, went to Surry County, N. C., and reared a large family. At that place our subject's grandparents were married. Rev. Thomas J. Brickell is the eldest of nine children, and in addition to attending the common schools in his youth, he worked in his father's cabinet shop. He began for himself as a clerk in 1869, in Atlanta, Ga., but a short time afterward he came to Arkansas, and taught school and farmed for a few years. In 1873 he joined the White River Annual Conference, and for five years was an itinerant preacher of the Methodist Church. On account of his wife's health he then located at Poplar Grove, and was there a partner with his father in business until his removal to Brinkley, where he has established a good home and a profitable business. He owns eighty-five acres of timber land, four miles from Brinkley, together with six town lots, all his property being acquired by his own exertions. He was for some time a member of the Methodist Episcopal Church, South, joining when sixteen years of age, and at the age of twenty, upon removing to Arkansas, united with the Congregational Methodist Church, and was licensed to preach. Some three years after he returned to the Methodist Episcopal Church, and now preaches the doctrine of that denomination as a local minister. His wife, whom he married in 1872, and who was born in Alabama, April 16, 1853, was a Miss Martha J. Morriss, a daughter of William D. and Harriet A. (Curry) Morris. She was reared principally in Phillips County, Ark. Her father was born in Lawrence County, Ala., November 23, 1820, subsequently moving to Phillips County, Ark. His wife was born in Maury County, Tenn., September 17, 1823. Mr. Morris died May 21, 1888, but his widow still survives him. Our subject and his wife have one son, now sixteen years of age.

Elijah C. Brown has passed his entire life in an industrious manner and his efforts have not been without substantial evidences of success, as will be seen from a glance at his present possessions. He was born in Fayette County, Tenn., in 1851, and is the third of four children born to Thomas J. and Frances (Branch) Brown, natives respectively of South Carolina and Tennessee. They were married in Fayette County, of the latter State, where Mrs. Brown was reared from infancy, and there their home continued to be until 1859, when they settled in Monroe County, Ark. They opened a farm in what is now Pine Ridge Township, and here Mr. Brown's life expired on January 6, 1866, his wife following him to his long home August 22, 1874. The maternal grandfather, Benjamin Branch, was born in Tennessee and spent his entire life in Fayette County, having served in the capacity of sheriff and clerk. His wife was a native of the Blue Grass State, and died in Tennessee also. Elijah C. Brown has one brother and two sisters: Sarah (wife of Dr. William Parks), Thomas M. and Eva Lillian (wife of E. T. Dyer). Elijah C. started out in life for himself with a limited education, but after the war he determined to remedy this defect and accordingly entered Hickory Withe Academy of Fayette County, Tenn., and upon leaving this institution was much better prepared to fight the battle of life. He followed the slow but sure way of making money by farming until 1874, then spent two years in Clarendon, engaged in clerking, after which he returned to his farm and he and a brother opened a store and put

up a steam cotton-gin, successfully operating both until 1883, when our subject sold out to his brother, and in 1884 came to Brinkley. Here he has since made his home and in addition to managing his farm he trades in stock and real estate. He has 582 acres of fine land with about 300 under the plow, and he also owns considerable real estate in Brinkley. He is a Democrat, a member of the K. of H. and his wife, whom he married December 16, 1874, and whose maiden name was Jennie Davidson, is a member of the Methodist Church. They have had eight children, but three sons and four daughters are now living. Mrs. Brown is a daughter of James B. and Harriet Davidson, native Tennesseeans, born, reared and married in that State. Before the opening of the Civil War they came to Arkansas and Mr. Davidson was sheriff of Poinsett County for nine years. He was a large mail contractor and died in Cross County in March, 1862, while serving as captain of a company belonging to the Confederate States army. His wife died in Craighead County in 1873.

W. D. Burge has been a successful merchant of Indian Bay since 1876, F. J. Robinson also constituting a member of the firm until 1887, when he retired. Mr. Burge's stock of goods is valued at about $2,500, and his annual sales net him a handsome profit. His native birthplace is Rutherford County, N. C., where he was born in 1848, and he is a son of Woody and Dulcinea (McIntire) Burge, who removed to the State of Mississippi, when their son, W. D., was about two years old. Here the father died in 1877, having been a farmer throughout life, his wife's death occurring in 1865. W. D. Burge was the eighth of eleven children, and received his education in the common schools, and at the age of seventeen years he began for himself, his occupation being that of clerking. His life occupation has been merchandising and farming, and he has been successful in both occupations, and besides his store he is the owner of 400 acres of land in different tracts. He has been a resident of Indian Bay since 1871, and since 1877 has been a married man, his wife being Lila, daughter of Hon. F. M. and E. A. Robinson, a sketch of whom appears in this work. Mrs. Burge was born in the

State of Tennessee, and has borne Mr. Burge a son and a daughter. Mr. Burge is a Democrat and cast his first presidential vote for Horace Greeley in 1872. He belongs to Advance Lodge No. 2491, K. of H., and has held the office of Past Dictator in that order. His wife is a member of the Cumberland Presbyterian Church.

Capt. Hilliard A. Carter is a planter and a retired merchant of Brinkley and was born in Wilcox County, Ala., in 1833, being one of seven surviving members of a family of fourteen children born to Aaron B. and Elizabeth (Lee) Carter, both of whom were born, reared and married in Fairfield District, S. C., removing in 1825 to Alabama and in 1835 to La Fayette County, Miss. In 1865 they removed to Hopkins County, Tex., and the following year Mr. Carter died. His wife's death occurred in Lamar County, Tex., in 1877, at the age of seventy-five years, both having been members of the Presbyterian Church for many years. The father was a successful planter and socially was a member of the A. F. & A. M. The paternal grandfather, John Carter, was a planter and a blacksmith and spent all his life in South Carolina. He served in the Revolutionary War. His parents were born in Ireland and were among the first settlers of South Carolina. The maternal grandfather, John Lee, being also one of the early settlers of that State and a Revolutionary soldier. Capt. Hilliard A. Carter is the only one of his family residing in Monroe County, Ark., and although he received little early schooling he became versed with the world's ways at an early day and was intelligent and well posted on all current topics. In 1856 he came to Monroe County, and until the opening of the war acted in the capacity of an overseer, but gave up this work and in 1862 joined Company E, A. W. Johnson's Regiment of Infantry and held the positions of sergeant and lieutenant until 1863, when he was made captain of his company. About a year later he and fourteen other men were detailed to look up absentees, and after securing sufficient men he and his followers were called Company C. He afterward raised another company, which he commanded until the close of the war and surrendered at Helena with a portion of his men. After his return from the war he resumed his farming operations, but in 1868 gave this up to engage in mercantile pursuits at Clarendon, which he continued until 1870, then came to Brinkley where he was in business until September, 1887, at which time his property was destroyed by fire and has never rebuilt, but has given his attention to his real estate, being the owner of about 1,000 acres. He has over 400 acres under cultivation, besides valuable property in Brinkley, all of which is the result of his own hard work and good management, as he started in life for himself a poor boy. In his political views he has been a Democrat all his life and is also a Mason, having been a member of Brinkley Lodge No. 295 for the past twelve or fourteen years. In 1884 he was married to Elizabeth, a daughter of William and Elizabeth Hawkins, who were Mississippians and removed to Monroe County, Ark., prior to the war, the mother dying in 1864, and the father in 1876. Mrs. Carter was born in Jefferson County, Ala., her parents being also natives of that State.

James Allen Cocke, planter, Arkansas. That a life-time spent in pursuing one occupation will, in the end, result in substantial success, where energy and perseverance are applied, can not for a moment be doubted, and such is found to be the case with Mr. Cocke. He was born in Monroe County, Miss., on February 10, 1837, and is the son of Jester and Eliza C. (Atkins) Cocke, whose marriage occurred in 1828. The father was a native of Virginia, of English ancestors, who came to America prior to the Revolutionary War. To Mr. and Mrs. Cocke were born four children: Mary E., John B., James Allen and Sarah E. The father died in Monroe County, Miss., in 1841. After his death the mother married John M. Smith, and in 1845 came to Arkansas. James Allen Cocke was reared to agricultural pursuits, and received a limited education in the subscription schools of Monroe County. On November 6, 1866, he was wedded to Miss Nancy A. Youngblood, a native of Alabama, and a daughter of Ephraim A. and Mary A. (Bagby) Youngblood. The fruits of this union were three children: Jester Andrew (born June 28, 1868),

John Benjamin (born April 26, 1870) and Lucy Adaline (born October 26, 1871). Mrs. Cocke died on November 10, 1871, and on May 8, 1872, Mr. Cocke married Miss Elizabeth Virginia Hess, a native of Alabama, and the daughter of David and Louisiana (Kerr) Hess, the father a native of Holland, and the mother of Scotch-Irish descent. To this marriage six children were born: Sarah F. (born March 10, 1873), Thomas (born January 7, 1875), Ada Beulah (born December 5, 1878), Helen Bertha (born December 9, 1880), Anna Laura (born March 5, 1882) and David Hess (born October 12, 1885). During the late war Mr. Cocke enlisted in Company A, Fifteenth Regiment Arkansas Volunteer Infantry (the first company organized in Monroe County), and participated in the battles of Shiloh, Richmond, Perryville, Murfreesboro and Chickamauga. He was captured at the last-named place, on September 19, 1863; was a prisoner for about two months before finally reaching Camp Douglas, Ill., where he remained for eighteen months. On May 28, 1865, he was liberated at the landing below Vicksburg, and left on the first boat for home, where he arrived June 4, 1865, just a month from the time he left Camp Douglas. After this he rented land, and also carried on the carpenter's business until 1871. He then bought 160 acres of land, and now has forty-five acres under cultivation. He and wife, and his children, Benjamin and Sarah, hold membership in the Methodist Episcopal Church, South. Mr. Cocke is a member of Kerr Lodge No. 195, Holly Grove, A. F. & A. M.; Chapter No. 16, R. A. M.; Blakely Council No. 19, Clarendon, Monroe County, Ark. He was made a Mason in 1866, and united with the Chapter in 1869, the Council the same year, and has served his lodge as W. M., the Chapter as Capt. of H., and has also served in all the offices in the Council.

John W. Cooper. For a period now approaching forty-five years, this honored resident of Monroe County, Ark., has been identified with the agricultural interests of this region, having settled here with his parents, Benson and Delphia (Lindsey) Cooper, in 1845. He, like his father, was born in Spartanburg District, S. C., his birth occurring in

1843, and there the latter's marriage occurred, his wife having been born in Lawrence County, N. C. Upon their arrival in Arkansas they spent the first year in Crittenden County, afterward locating on a woodland farm in Monroe County. The father died on his farm, three miles below Brinkley, in 1863, his wife having also died there three years earlier. They had been members of the Baptist Church for many years, and the father was of Irish descent and a son of Matthew Cooper, who probably spent all his life in South Carolina. John W. Cooper is the fourth of seven children, and spent his youth in the wilds of Monroe County, receiving but few advantages for acquiring an education, as the schools of that day were few and far between. In 1861 he espoused the Southern cause and joined Company E, Twenty-fifth Arkansas Infantry, and operated in Mississippi, Tennessee, Alabama, Georgia, Kentucky and Virginia, and was a participant in eighteen different engagements, among which may be mentioned Shiloh, Richmond, New Hope, Peach Tree Creek, Murfreesboro, Missionary Ridge and Chickamauga, and was all through the Atlanta campaign. He returned with Hood to Tennessee and was in the engagements at Franklin and Nashville, but was captured at the last-named place and taken to Camp Chase, Ohio, where he was retained until after Lee's surrender. On being released he went to Fort Riley, Kan., but soon after returned home, and, in August, 1866, was married to Rachel, a daughter of Samuel and Rachel A. Martin, natives, respectively, of North and South Carolina. After the war they came to Faulkner County, Ark., where the mother died in 1846. Mr. Martin married again and in 1860 settled in Monroe County, where his demise occurred seven years later. He was a member of the Methodist Church, a farmer by occupation, and held the office of justice of the peace for some years prior to his death. Mrs. Cooper was born in what is now Faulkner County, in 1844, and has borne Mr. Cooper a family of nine children, three sons and two daughters now living. Mr. Cooper has resided in different parts of Brinkley Township, and has improved four good farms and is now putting in a tillable condition his fifth farm, which comprises 520 acres, 200 acres of which are under cultivation, but a considerable portion of his land is devoted to stock raising. He has been a resident of Brinkley for six years, in order to give his children the advantages of the town schools, and is considered one of the wide-awake and public-spirited citizens of the place. He is a Democrat and a member of the K. of H. and the I. O. O. F. At the time of his marriage Mr. Cooper was $75 in debt, but by many years of hard labor he is now in affluent circumstances. He and his elder brother, Dillard L., served together throughout the war, and during their entire service were never separated but eight days, and that was while our subject was in the hospital, after being wounded at the battle of Murfreesboro.

Richard N. Counts is a general merchant and cotton buyer of Clarendon, and although he has only been established in business at this place since October, 1888, he has deservedly acquired the reputation of being a safe, thorough and reliable man of business. He is a native of the State, having been born in Independence County, in 1851, and he is the youngest of eight children born to the marriage of Richard N. Counts and Mary A. Tucker, who were born, reared and married in the State of Missouri, afterward removing to Independence County, where the father followed the occupation of husbandry, and died in 1858. His wife died when our subject was about one year old, and after his father's death he was left to depend on his own resources, and from 1860 has made his home in Prairie and Monroe Counties, receiving a common-school education. For about six years he followed book-keeping and clerking for B. F. Johnson, and the following five years worked in the same capacity for J. M. Wheelock, by this means acquiring sufficient means to enable him to engage in his present business, which has proven a decided success. His property has been acquired by his own exertions, and in addition to his store he has a fine farm of 320 acres, of which 160 acres are in a good state of cultivation. He is a Democrat, casting his first vote for Tilden, in 1876, and in March, 1885, he

was elected to fill an unexpired term of county treasurer, and in 1886 was re-elected, serving in all nearly four years. He has been a member of the A. F. & A. M., Cache Lodge at Clarendon, also the K. of P. and the K. of H., and for several years has been financial reporter of the latter order. He also belongs to the A. O. U. W., and he and his wife, whom he married in 1885, and whose maiden name was Lucy Bonner, are members of the Methodist Church. They have one daughter. Mrs. Counts was born in North Carolina, and is a daughter of W. H. Bonner, a Tennesseean, who came to Monroe County, Ark., in 1859, and here died in 1888, having been an assessor and farmer, his wife's death occurring in 1881. Mr. Counts had previously married in 1873 Fannie E., a daughter of James H. and Eleanor Branch. She was born in Tennessee, and died in 1879, at Clarendon, leaving two children, a son and a daughter. Mr. Counts is of Irish descent, and has a brother and two sisters living: William A. (a hardware merchant of Little Rock), L. J. (Mrs. Meeks, of Brinkley) and Linnie (Mrs. Loving, of Pine Bluff).

Robert Craig, planter and ginner, Brinkley, Ark. There are many citizens of foreign birth represented within the pages of this volume, but none are more deserving of mention than Robert Craig, who was born in Glasgow, Scotland, in 1852. His father, John Craig, was a native also of Glasgow, Scotland, was a farmer and stock raiser for many years, and was also engaged in merchandising in Belfast for several years. He was married to Miss Ann Cruitle, of Scotland, in 1822, and they became the parents of eleven children, six sons and three daughters now living: James, Sarah, Mary (wife of John Curry, and still living in the old country), John, Annie (wife of James Hamilton), Robert, George, Thomas and Alexander. The father is still living and resides in Scotland. Robert Craig crossed the ocean to America in 1867, located in Arkansas, and was united in marriage to Miss Lou Stall in 1875. She was born in Arkansas in 1853, and her parents, George and Catharine Stall, were natives of Pennsylvania. To Mr. and Mrs. Craig were born three children: George R., Anna B. and Mary L.

Mr. Craig is the owner of 247 acres of land, with about 100 acres under cultivation, and his principal crops are cotton and corn. He erected a good cotton-gin in 1883, and has since added a corn-mill, with a capacity for forty bushels per hour. He is one of the most progressive and energetic farmers of this section, and his farm buildings are neat, commodious and substantial. He has also two tenant houses. He is a member of the Masonic fraternity, and his wife is a member of the Baptist Church.

S. W. Davis, planter, Cotton Plant, Ark. The subject of this sketch needs no introduction to the people of Monroe County, for a long residence here, and above all a career of usefulness and prominence, have given him an acquaintance which shall last for years. He was born in La Fayette County, Miss., in 1845, to the union of Chesley and Mary E. (Simpson) Davis, natives of South Carolina and Alabama, respectively. Eight children were the fruits of this union, two daughters and six sons, three of whom only are living: S. W., Mary E. (wife of Ben Glover) and R. S. Chesley Davis was reared to agricultural pursuits and this was his chief occupation during life. He immigrated from Mississippi to Arkansas in 1851, locating in St. Francis County, and there entered and traded for land until he had 380 acres. He was a member of the A. F. & A. M.; was justice of the peace for several years, and a member of the Methodist Episcopal Church and died in Woodruff County in 1859. His wife died in 1865 and was a member of the Baptist Church. S. W. Davis began life upon his own resources in 1867 and hired to work in a gin-house. In 1868 he began farming on rented land, continued at this until 1872, when he fell heir to some land from his father's estate. He was married, in 1867, to Miss Mollie C. Harbour, a native of Tennessee, born in 1851, and the daughter of   and Eliza B. Harbour, of Woodruff County, Tenn. The result of this union were eight children, six of whom are now living: E. B., Samuel T., John C., William A., Mattie and an infant not yet named. The parents of Mrs. Davis are originally from Kentucky, immigrating from that State to Tennes-

see, thence to Mississippi and finally settling in Arkansas, where they both died; E. B. died in 1861 and his wife in 1879. During the late war, or in 1864, Mr. Davis was in the Confederate cavalry, Company B, under Captain Wilson, and served until the surrender at Wittsburg, Ark., in 1865. After this he resumed farming and has followed this pursuit ever since. He is one of the prosperous and leading citizens of this township, has a fairly improved farm of 160 acres and has 109 acres under cultivation. He was justice of the peace for eight years and was appointed deputy sheriff in 1886. He erected a large gin in 1885 and this he has run ever since.

J. H. Dial, merchant and planter, Holly Grove, Ark. In the business of merchandising Mr. Dial is second to none in Duncan Township, and in connection is also extensively engaged in agricultural pursuits. A native of Greene County, Ala., he was born June 28, 1821. His father, David M. Dial, was born in South Carolina in 1785, was married to Miss Jennette Spence in 1801, and successfully tilled the soil all his life. His wife was born in Newberry District, S. C., in 1783. To them were given thirteen children, only two now living: J. H. (the subject of this sketch) and his sister, Rebecca (the wife of George Rix, of Keokuk, Iowa). David M. Dial was an elder in the Old School Presbyterian Church. His wife was a member of the same church. They immigrated from South Carolina to Greene County, Ala., in 1818, where the father died in 1834, the mother in 1855. At the age of sixteen J. H. Dial started out for himself, and began farming on a tract of land he owned in Sumter County, Ala. In the year 1853 he moved to this State and purchased land in Monroe County. When the late war broke out he enlisted in the Confederate army, Company E, Thirty-first Regiment Infantry, under Capt. O. H. Oates, and was wounded in the battle of Stone River, Tenn., December 31, 1862. He was first taken to the field hospital and remained there ten days, then being removed to Nashville in a six-horse wagon, going as fast as it could over the rough roads. There he was put in the guard house and three days later in the penitentiary, where he was kept four or five days and then taken to the hospital. It was found necessary to amputate his right arm, which operation was performed by Surgeon Massy, and he was then removed to Mr. Robinson's, a private house, where he was nursed and taken care of for three months by two noble ladies, Mrs. Cartright and Miss Mary Hadley. Being taken to Louisville (Ky.) as a prisoner, he and his companions were there robbed of all their clothes and money. Later, going to Baltimore, Md., and thence to Petersburg, he was finally released and from there went to Shelbyville, Tenn., where he received his discharge. Starting on a tramp for home he walked the entire distance from West Point, Miss. In 1864 he was again taken prisoner when at Clarendon on some business, had his wagon and mules taken from him and was put in prison at Devall's Bluff and kept for a week or ten days. Had it not been for the kindness of Mr. Steele and Mr. Phillip Trice he would have suffered, but they furnished him clothes and money and he fared sumptuously for a prisoner. Mr. Dial was married to Miss Letitia Caulfield, a daughter of Henry and Isabella (Watson) Caulfield, on November 2, 1853. She was born in Greene County, Ala., her parents being from Ireland. Her father came to this country in 1821. He was a successful and energetic farmer and died in Greene County October 16, 1867. The mother died March 15, 1870. They were the parents of six children, two daughters now being the only living members of the family: Bessie (the wife of Jere Horn, of San Marcos, Tex.) and the present Mrs. Dial. J. H. Dial and wife had a family of eight children, of whom six survive at this time: Belle (the wife of T. G. Trice, of Holly Grove, Ark.), Mary V. (widow of Dr. C. H. Boyd, of Holly Grove, Ark.), Margie (wife of W. M. Harrison of Pine Bluff, Ark.), their sons, David M., Thomas G. and Jere H., all live in Holly Grove, Ark. Mr. Dial owns a valuable farm and is a successful farmer. He and his wife are members of the Presbyterian Church.

Capt. Parker C. Ewan is a member of that substantial and successful law firm of Ewan & Thomas, of Clarendon. The senior member of the firm, Capt. Ewan, was born in New Jersey, in 1837, and is a son of John and Sylvia H. (Hankins) Ewan, who were also born in that State, the former in 1800, and the latter in 1804. After their marriage they moved to Clermont County, Ohio, in which place Mr. Ewan died of cholera, in 1849. His wife died in Cincinnati, Ohio, twenty-eight years later. He was a farmer, and was a son of Evan Ewan, a native of New Jersey, who died there, at about the age of eighty years, having been an iron manufacturer by trade. He was a captain in the Revolutionary War, and traced his ancestors back to Sir Raleigh Ewan, a Scotchman. Many of the family now in this country have changed the name to Ewing. Richard Hankins, the maternal grandfather, was of Irish extraction, a farmer by occupation, a soldier in the Revolutionary War, and spent his entire life in the State of New Jersey. The immediate subject of this biography is one of a family of ten children, all of whom are living, with the exception of one, who was killed by a train in Texas, in January, 1888, and in youth he became familiar with farm life by assisting his father. Until twelve years of age he attended the common country schools, then entered the Bantam (Ohio) High School, and two years later the College Hill Academy, near Cincinnati, but in 1854 left school and went South, and for a short time was engaged in flat-boating on the Mississippi River. In 1855 he began teaching school, in Phillips County, Ark., at which time the country was in a very wild and unsettled condition, the timber being full of wild animals, and at one time he stood in his school-house door and shot a panther. In 1857 he came to Monroe County, and taught school until the opening of the Civil War, then dropped the ferrule to take up the musket, and joined Company E, First Arkansas Infantry, afterward the Fifteenth Arkansas, commanded by Col. (afterward Gen.) Cleburne. His first experience in warfare was in the battle of Shiloh, and still later he was made captain of his company, and participated in the battles of Richmond and Perryville (Ky.) and Murfreesboro, (Tenn.), when he was again severely wounded, and was compelled to give up his command. After recovering he was placed in command of the post at

West Point, Ga., was made provost marshal, and when the news of the final surrender reached him he was on post duty at Macon, Ga. After his return to Monroe County he farmed one year, then began filling the duties of county clerk, to which position he had been elected in 1866, serving with ability for two years. His first experience in the practice of law was with Jeremiah Marston, and in 1872 the firm became Marston, Ewan & Bobo, which continued until the death of Mr. Marston, about ten years later. From that time until 1886 Mr. Ewan continued alone, and was then associated with Mr. Palmer for two years, after which Mr. Thomas became a member of the firm. Mr. Palmer withdrew in 1888, and the firm is now Ewan & Thomas, one of the strongest and most thorough law firms in Eastern Arkansas. Mr. Ewan was county attorney from 1868 to 1872, and is one of the leading members of the Democratic party in his county and State. He has been a delegate from Monroe County to nearly every Democratic State convention, and has never voted outside of Monroe County. He has been a member of the A. F. & A. M. since 1862, Cache Lodge No. 235, and he also belongs to the K. of P., Cowan Lodge No. 39. By his own indomitable energy and methodical business habits he has become one of the wealthiest men of the State, and is the owner of about 70,000 acres of land in Monroe, Phillips, Lee, Arkansas and Prairie Counties. He has thirty-five improved farms, ranging from eighty to 1,600 acres each, and also owns seven cotton-gins, two saw-mills, and one-half interest in a railroad, all of which he has earned since the war, and, unlike many wealthy men, he can truthfully say that he never intentionally wronged a man out of a dollar. That he is one of the honored and trusted men of the county can readily be seen. He owns the Monroe County Sun, a newspaper which he founded in 1876, and has since controlled. In 1865 he was united in marriage to Miss M. L. Rayston, who was born in Mississippi, and left her husband a widower in 1868, with a daughter to care for, named Carrie L., now the wife of W. N. Johnson. Mr. Ewan celebrated his second marriage in 1870, his wife

being Maggie H., a sister of his first wife, also born in Mississippi. After bearing him one child, who is now deceased, he was again left a widower, January 4, 1872. September 21, 1874, he married his third wife, Julia C., a daughter of Prof. Frank S. Connor, of Abbeville, S. C. His wife is a Methodist, and has borne him four children, Parker C., Jr., aged eleven years, being the only one living.

S. E. Fitzhugh, farmer, Brinkley, Ark. This comparatively young agriculturist is the son of a man who, during his residence here, was intimately and permanently associated with the county's interest, and whose memory is cherished by a host of those acquainted with him while living. S. H. Fitzhugh was a native of Dyer County, Tenn., born in 1815, was reared on a farm and followed tilling of the soil all his life. He was married to Miss Martha S. Christy, the daughter of Mr. and Mrs. Abisha Christy, of South Carolina, and became the father of ten children, two of whom are now living: S. E. and Susan M. (wife of G. W. Hullom, of Monroe County). Mr. Fitzhugh immigrated from Tennessee to Arkansas in 1846 or 1847, locating in Monroe County, and there purchased 160 acres of land. He built a log-cabin and improved his farm. He died in this county on May 17, 1886, and his wife died on March 18, 1883. Both had been members of the Baptist Church for many years. S. E. Fitzhugh now lives on the farm where his father first settled on coming to Monroe County. He started out to earn a living for himself, and first engaged in agricultural pursuits when nineteen years of age on his father's land. Here he remained until after the death of his father, when the land was divided by will, and he received 120 acres, with about sixty acres under cultivation. He married, in 1869, Miss Sarah F. Capolenor, a native of Phillips County, Ark., born January 8, 1842, and the daughter of John and Martha Capolenor, of Monroe County. They are the parents of six children, four daughters and two sons: Rilda J., James H., Joseph N., Tennessee F., Laura E. and Lulu. Mr. and Mrs. Fitzhugh are members of the Baptist Church. As she was quite young when her parents died, Mrs. Fitzhugh knows very little of the descent of her ancestors or of her parentage. She has a brother and sister living: T. C. (of Cotton Plant) and Martha (wife of John H. Tomlinson, also of this State). Mr. Fitzhugh is one of the leading planters of his township, and is a genial and clever gentleman.

J. M. and A. Flora. The business interests of this portion of the country are well represented by these gentlemen, who have been located in the town (since 1883) long enough to become thoroughly established. Their stock of goods is valued at some $6,500, the annual sales reach $20,000 and the establishment is conducted with ability and success. J. M. and A. Flora, the proprietors, were born in Shelby County, Tenn., in 1852 and 1861, respectively, and J. M. is a son of William and Elizabeth (Wood) Flora, the former a native of North Carolina, and the latter of Virginia. Their union was consummated in Shelby County, Tenn., and there Mrs. Flora died when her children were small. Mr. Flora afterward married Sallie E. White, by whom he became the father of A. Flora, one of the members of the above-named firm. Mr. Flora was a farmer by occupation, and died in 1864. J. M. Flora, the youngest of the four children born to his first union, was denied the privilege of more than a common-school education, but by contact with the world and close application to business he has added to his early schooling and has become thoroughly posted on the current topics of the day. In 1881 he began merchandising at Henning, Tenn., continuing until 1884, and he then became connected with his brother, A. Flora, who had established their present mercantile establishment in Brinkley in 1883. Their union has been very prosperous and their stock of goods is of excellent quality and is sold at reasonable prices. In 1888 they built a two-story brick business block, containing two store-rooms, which are well and conveniently fitted up. Both these gentlemen were reared to farm life and have acquired the greater portion of their property since 1881. J. M. Flora is a Democrat, a member of the Christian Church, and of the children born to his parents, one brother only is now living, John. A. Flora has one sister living, who is Mrs. Bettie Rogers, of Shelby County,

33

Tenn. Micager Wood, the maternal grandfather of J. M. Flora, was a pioneer farmer of West Tennessee, and died there.

J. M. Folkes is a successful real-estate and collecting agent at Brinkley, and no name is more prominently identified with this business than his. His judgment is thoroughly relied upon as to the value and nature of real estate, and he is an energetic and thorough-going man of business, and is strictly honest in all his transactions. He is a Kentuckian by birth, born in Pendleton County in 1851, his parents, Henry Harrison and Mary E. (Woodyard) Folkes, being also natives of that State and county, where they were reared, married and spent their lives. They were members of the Methodist Church of many years' standing, and the father was very successful in his farming operations, as he started in life with little or no capital and at the time of his death left an estate valued at $30,000. The grandfather, Jerome Folkes, was born in Harrison County, Ky., and there died, having been a life-long farmer. His parents were Virginians. J. M. Folkes, our immediate subject, was the third of nine children, and is the only one now living so far as he knows. His early life was spent in attending the common schools and following the plow, and upon attaining the age of fifteen years he went to Ohio, and began clerking in a store in Xenia, which occupation he continued to follow for four or five years. His education not being sufficient to satisfy him, he, during this time, attended night school and graduated therefrom. After clerking in Cincinnati, Ohio, for two years he began traveling for Frank Loeb & Block of that city, and continued thus for six years, after which he clerked for some time in different counties of Texas. He kept books for T. H. Jackson & Co., and managed a commission store for Black & Co. at Gray's Station. Mr. Folkes is quite an extensive traveler, and in 1871-72 made a trip around the world, his journey being varied by many interesting incidents. He is now settled down to hard work, and is doing a prosperous business, his home in the town of Brinkley being commodious and comfortable. He was married in Memphis November 30, 1886, to Miss

Libbie J., a daughter of John and Elizabeth Davis, of Brooklyn, N. Y., the father being a wholesale oyster dealer of that city, having succeeded his father, who was also in that business. He died in October, 1889, but his widow is still living. Mr. Folkes is a Democrat, and socially is a member of the K. of H., the K. & L. of H. and the K. of P., being Vice-Chancellor in the latter order. His wife is a finely educated and accomplished lady, and is a member of the Episcopalian Church of Brooklyn, N. Y.

Dr. J, W. Frazer is a physician of more than ordinary ability, located at Clarendon, Ark., and is engaged in farming and selling drugs at that place. From an early age he displayed an eagerness for study and desire for professional life, and after attending the common schools and laboring on a farm until eighteen years of age, he took a three years' course in the Jacksonville (Ill.) College, obtaining in this institution a thorough education. He then spent some time in farming, and during leisure moments pursued the study of medicine, beginning his practice in Union County, Ark., after having taken a course of lectures in the University of Louisville in 1848–49. In 1860 he graduated from the Medical Department of the University of Louisiana, at New Orleans, and from that time until 1887 was in the active practice of his profession at Tupelo, Miss., coming then to Clarendon, Ark., where he has since devoted his attention to the practice of medicine, selling drugs and farming. During about three years of the war he served as surgeon in Confederate hospitals in Mississippi and Alabama, and since the war has been conservative in his political views, although formerly a Whig. He is a member of the Masonic order, and since 1850 has been a member of the Presbyterian Church; his wife, whom he married in that year, and whose maiden name was Margaret A. Wiley, was also a member of the Presbyterian Church. She was born in Perry County, Ala., in 1830, and died in Tupelo, Miss., in 1887, childless. Dr. Frazer wedded his present wife in February, 1888, she being a Mrs. Lucy N. (Mullens) Youngblood, born near Clarendon in 1848, a member of the Cumberland Presbyterian Church, and

the mother of one child, about fourteen years of age, named Beulah M. Youngblood. The doctor was born in Autanga County, Ala., in 1826, and is a son of Walter and Nancy (Brann) Frazer, both of whom were born in Mecklenburg County, Va., and were there reared and married. About 1818 they removed to Alabama, where the father's death occurred in 1831, he having been a successful farmer. He was a lieutenant in the War of 1812, and was a son of Rev. James Frazer, who was born in Scotland, and came to America when a young man, marrying and settling in Virginia, but returned to his native land about the commencement of the American Revolution. He was a minister of the Presbyterian Church, and died in   His family remained in America.

Alfred J. Gannon is a son of John Porter Gannon, who was born in North Carolina in 1813, and immigrated to Tennessee in 1823 with his father, George Gannon. He was married in 1837 to Miss Elizabeth Hayes, a native of Virginia, and of English descent. The family of Gannon is of Irish ancestry. Elizabeth died in 1858, leaving seven children, four sons and three daughters: Martha A. (wife of Nathan McBroon, now of Delta County, Tex.), Alfred J., William C., John Q., Joanna (wife of William A. Sullivan), Fannie T. (wife of N. J. Mason) and James B. He was married a second time in 1859 to Miss Travis. They were the parents of three children, two of whom are still living: Isaac and Samuel L. He was a captain in the Mexican War. Capt. John P. Gannon followed farming and stock raising all his life. He was a strict member of the Christian Church, and a strong temperance advocate never allowing whisky to enter his house only in the form of medicine. His life was an exemplary one, both as a Christian gentleman and as a member of society. He died in August, 1870. Alfred J. Gannon was born in Cannon County, Tenn., on April 19, 1842, and being raised on a farm was taught farming and stock raising until the war between the States in 1861. He was among the first to enlist in his State, and joined the company known as the "Woodbury Guards," afterward called Company A, Eighteenth Regiment Tennessee Volunteers

(Joseph B. Palmer, colonel). Mr. Gannon was in the Kentucky campaign of 1861, and was captured at the fall of Fort Donelson, February 16, 1862. He was sent to Camp Butler, Springfield, Ill., and was there confined in close prison for seven months, and was then sent down the Mississippi River to Vicksburg for exchange in the transport steamer A. McDowell, Commodore Farragut's fleet. Here he was exchanged and went to Montgomery, Ala., and re-enlisted in the war. Mr. Gannon was in the battle of Murfreesboro and was one of the participants in the celebrated Breckenridge charge on the evening of January 2, 1863. He was also in the battle of Chickamauga, and here received a wound in his right arm, by reason of which he was honorably discharged from service. He had many narrow escapes during the war. He immigrated to this State in 1872, and was married to Miss Maggie L. Palmer on January 19, 1876, who was born in Phillips County on May 29, 1854. They have a family of five children: Katie L., John Hayes (who died on October 7, 1886, in the seventh year of his age), Maggie C., Alfred J., Jr., and Ellett Hewitt. His wife is the second daughter of John C. and Margret E. Palmer, of this State, and a granddaughter of Jesse J. Shell, one of the early settlers of the State. Mr. Gannon is a member of the Christian Church and his wife belongs to the Catholic Church. He owns a fine farm of 160 acres of land with good buildings, orchard, etc., and is also a breeder of fine cattle. He is a member of the I. O. O. F., and a stanch Democrat, as his father and grandfather were before him.

William H. Govan is the son of Andrew R. Govan, who was born in Orangeburg District, S. C., in 1796. His parents, Daniel and Elizabeth (Roach) Govan, were of Scotch descent. Andrew was a large planter of that State, which he represented in Congress in 1824. He was married to the mother of our subject, Miss Mary P. Jones, a daughter of J. Morgan and Sallie (Davis) Jones, in 1824. They reared a family of eight children, six of whom are still living: D. C. (a brigadier-general in the Civil War, who is now a resident of Helena), John J. (a farmer of Lee County), George M. (now sec-

retary of State of Mississippi), Sarah (the wife of John M. Billups, of Columbus, Miss.), Bettie and William H. (our subject, and the next to the oldest). Andrew R. Govan moved from North Carolina in 1831, and settled in Western Tennessee, near Summerville, going five years later to Mississippi, where he died in 1841. His wife was a native of New Berne, N. C., and was born in 1802, and died on July 12, 1888, in Mississippi. William H. Govan was born in Northampton County, N. C., in 1831. He was married in 1878 to Miss Jennie Jackson, daughter of John S. and Isabella R. (Rhodes) Jackson, natives of Tennessee and Mississippi, respectively. She was born in Louisiana, in 1834. Mr. Govan moved to Arkansas in 1858, and bought a farm in Phillips County, where he lived until the breaking out of the war, when he enlisted in the Second Arkansas Infantry, serving as quartermaster and paymaster. At the close of the conflict he embarked in the mercantile business with Maj. W. E. Moore, and the following year sold out and entered into partnership with Hon. H. L. Hawley and Oliver H. Oates, in the practice of law at Helena. The next year he returned to Phillips County, and engaged in farming, but in 1874, resumed the practice of law with Hon. John H. Huett, at Mariana, where he remained until 1878. Moving to Monroe County, he purchased a farm of 500 acres, with over 300 acres under cultivation. The house he now occupies is one of the oldest in the county, having been built by Dr. Duncan in 1834. He is a member of the A. F. & A. M., and of the K. of H. Mrs. Govan is a member of the Presbyterian Church.

Grant Green is a member of the law firm of Price & Green, of Clarendon, Ark. The profession of law is one of the most important of human callings, and he who takes upon himself the practice of it, assumes the weightiest responsibilities that his fellow-man can put upon his shoulders. As a copartnership, whose honor is above criticism, and whose ability places it among the leading law firms of the West, is the above named. Mr. Green, the junior member, was born in Monroe County, Ark., in 1850, and is the son of Dr. Henry D. and Martha H. (Lambert) Green, who were born in

Henderson County, Ky., in 1824 and 1832, respectively. In 1847 Dr. Green removed to Montgomery Point, Ark., but after a short time returned to his former home, and in 1848 came to Monroe County, Ark., where he was married in 1849, being among its early settlers, and one of its most prominent physicians for many years. He was an influential and public-spirited citizen, and did a great deal toward developing the country and improving the morality of the community in which he resided. His medical education was acquired in Louisville, and during the Rebellion he was assistant surgeon in the Confederate States army. He served as county judge of Monroe County, and filled the office of county treasurer two terms. He was a prominent Mason, a member of the Cumberland Presbyterian Church, and died in 1879. His father, John W. Green, was born in Kentucky, in all probability, and was killed while serving in the Mexican War. Dr. Green's wife bore him two sons and one daughter, and from a child she was reared in Monroe County, Ark., and left him a widower in 1857. She was a daughter of Rev. Jordan B. Lambert, who was a Kentuckian, but was one of the early settlers of Monroe County, having come here in 1839. He represented Monroe County in the State legislature, was at one time judge of the county, and was an influential citizen and a prosperous farmer. Dr. Green was married a second time, in 1859, to Miss Minnie I. Swift, in Fayette County, Tenn., who bore him four sons and two daughters, all of whom, including herself, are still living. Their eldest son is Henry D. Green, Jr., the present treasurer of Monroe County, and an energetic and successful young merchant at Clarendon. Mr. Lambert was a minister of the Cumberland Presbyterian Church. Grant Green, our immediate subject, was educated in the local schools of Monroe County and West Tennessee, and for one year was an attendant of the Jesuit School of St. Louis. At the age of nineteen years he entered the Law Department of the Cumberland University of Lebanon, Tenn., attending two terms, and after teaching school a few terms, and pursuing the study of law in the meantime, he was admitted to the bar in 1870, but did not enter actively upon his practice until two years later. Since then he has been actively engaged in practice; two years, 1875 and 1876, he was at Helena. He has been one of the leading members of the Monroe County bar for a number of years, and since 1882 has been associated with Mr. Price. He is one of the well-to-do men of the county, and is the owner of a fine farm comprising 1,000 acres, eight miles from Clarendon, of which 400 acres are under cultivation. Mr. Green voted first for Greeley in 1872, and has always been a Democrat in his political views. He is a member of the A. F. & A. M., the Knights of Honor and the Knights of Pythias, and has been presiding officer in all these orders. June 1, 1875, he was married to Miss Loula M., a daughter of Dr. Henry G. Jackson, of Monroe County, Ark., but she left him a widower in 1876. Mr. Green's second marriage was celebrated at Somerville, Tenn., in 1883, his wife being Mrs. Willie Word, a daughter of Maj. W. E. Winfield, of Fayette County, Tenn., who obtained his title while serving in the Confederate army under Gen. Johnston. Mrs. Green was born in West Tennessee, and she and Mr. Green have two children, a son and a daughter. They are members of the church, Mr. Green being a member of the Cumberland Presbyterian Church, and Mrs. Green of the Old School Presbyterian Church.

Henry D. Green, treasurer of Monroe County, Ark., is the son of Dr. H. D. Green, who was married twice, his last wife being the mother of our subject. His grandfather Swift, was a Tennesseean, who died in Fayette County. Henry D. Green was born in Monroe County, Ark., in 1863, the fifth of ten children, six sons and four daughters, and as he grew up he was daily instructed into the mysteries of farm life. Although he only attended school for about eighteen months he made the most of the advantages offered him and later by reading and contact with the business affairs of life, has become one of the well informed and intelligent young men of the county. Upon the death of his father he began the battle of life for himself, and until 1884 was engaged in tilling the soil. From that time until 1885 he clerked in a store in Clarendon, then engaged in general merchandising on his own responsibility and has a stock of goods valued at $1,000, the firm being known as H. D. Green & Co. He was notary public for four years or until 1888, then was elected to the office of treasurer of Monroe County by the Democratic party, of which he has long been a member, and is now filling the duties of this position. He is a member of the K. of H., of Clarendon Lodge No. 2328, and he and wife, whom he married in 1888, and whose maiden name was Kate Blake, are members of the Cumberland Presbyterian Church. Mrs. Green was born in Henderson County, Ky., and she and Mr. Green are the parents of a daughter. Her parents, Augustus and Gertrude Blake, were born in Henderson County, Ky.

William Jasper Hall, planter and stockman, Holly Grove, Ark. This prominent agriculturist is the son of Thomas and Mournen (Stephens) Hall, the father of Scotch-Irish and English descent. The ancestors of the Hall family came to America prior to the Revolutionary War, and the grandfather Hall, who was probably a native of North Carolina, served in this war. The maternal ancestors were of French-Scotch descent, and the parents of Mrs. Hall, Willoughby and Margaret (Littleton) Stephens, were natives of North Carolina, their ancestors having emigrated to America previous to the War of 1776. William Jasper Hall was born on January 31, 1844, in Onslow County, N. C., and received the rudiments of an education in a private school at Mill Run, Onslow County, completing his education at Jacksonville, the same county. He was early initiated into the duties of farm life and remained at home until the early part of 1862, when he enlisted in Company C, Fourth Regiment North Carolina Cavalry. The command was called up after the battle of Gettysburg to cover the retreat of the Confederate army after their defeat in that battle, and the regiment dismounting at a bridge on the Hagerstown road, were surrounded by Federal forces and were cut off from their horses and lost nearly all of them. The command remained on the north side of the Potomac for about three weeks after the battle, in consequence of the high water. They finally forded the river at Williamsport, a number being drowned in the attempt, and joined their comrades. Mr. Hall was with his command nearly all the time, except when driven out of Culpeper, and was paroled at New Berne, N. C., in April, 1865. He walked from New Berne to his home the latter part of April, and engaged in tilling the soil, which occupation he continued until 1870, when he came to Arkansas, locating near Indian Bay, Monroe County, where he worked for Samuel Pointer, whose sketch appears elsewhere in this volume. He returned to North Carolina about Christmas of the same year, and was united in marriage to Miss Sallie L. Stephens, the daughter of Enoch and Mary (Tatum) Stephens. Mr. and Mrs. Hall arrived in Arkansas on February 16, 1871, rented a farm on shares, and, after remaining there one year, moved on the John Walker farm, Jackson Township, Monroe County. He made his first purchase of land in 1879, a tract of 200 acres with no improvements, and has added to this until he now is the owner of 600 acres, 480 acres in one body and 275 acres under cultivation. He principally raises cotton, but also raises good corn, and has a good young orchard. He is quite a stockman and raises cattle and hogs. To Mr. and Mrs. Hall have been born eight children, seven now living: Florence Geraldine (born January 1, 1872), William Enoch, Samuel Norman, Beatrice Rosa, Paul Ransom (deceased), Paula E., Mary M. and Sallie Edith. Mrs. Hall died in Jackson Township, in November, 1887. Mr. Hall takes a deep interest in all educational matters, and is determined to give his children all the advantages possible in that direction. He is a member of the Masonic fraternity, Indian Bay Lodge No. 256, and also holds membership in the K. of H. Lodge No. 16, Indian Bay, and is a charter member of the L. of H. In 1886 he was elected to the office of county coroner, but never qualified, having been elected without being consulted.

William Hooker. Among the many enterprises necessary to complete the commercial resources of a town or city, none is of more importance than that of the grocer, as he is one of the main factors in the furnishing of our food supplies. Prominent in this trade is Mr. Hooker, who has been established here in business since October, 1889, his stock of goods being valued at about $1,500. He was born in Shelby County, Tenn., in 1856, and is a son of Joseph W. and Fannie A. (Jones) Hooker, the former a Tennesseean and the latter a native of South Carolina. Their marriage took place at Memphis, and prior to the war they came to Arkansas, and opened a farm on White River. During the struggle between the North and South they returned to Tennessee, coming again to Arkansas after the war had closed. From that time until his death he kept a hotel at Clarendon, and in the latter years of his life also an eating-house at Brinkley, and one at Black Fish for the Little Rock & Memphis Railroad. He met a violent death, being killed in a railroad accident in 1879. He was a soldier for three years in the Confederate army, being a member of an Arkansas regiment. His widow survives him, and is a member of the Methodist Church. William Hooker is the second of seven children, three now living, and received his early education in the city of Memphis, his higher education being acquired in Leddin Commercial College. After clerking for nine years for Walker Bros. & Co., of that city, then the largest mercantile house in the South, he became a book-keeper for Saul Alinger, of Saulsbury, with whom he remained eighteen months, then clerked for Gunn & Black, until they sold out. During 1883 he associated himself with Louis Salinger, in the general mercantile business, continuing until 1887, then began trading in real estate. Mr. Hooker is a Democrat politically, and has shown his approval of secret organizations by joining the Knights of Honor and the Knights and Ladies of Honor. On March 12, 1887, he was married to Emma, a daughter of John A. McDonald. She was born in Jackson County, Ark.

Wesley H. Hughen, farmer and stockman, Holly Grove, Ark. Mr. Hughen was born May 19, 1824, in Abbeville District, S. C., and received a limited education in Coweta County, Ga., whither his parents had moved in 1831. Later they moved to Rome, and there Wesley attended the male academy for about two years. He was early initiated into the duties of farm life, and on December 21, 1845, he was married in Floyd County, Ga., to Miss Elizabeth Mann, who was born November 14, 1825, and who was the daughter of Young and Mary A. (Garrison) Mann, natives of North Carolina and Georgia, respectively. After marrying Mr. Hughen engaged with his brother and father in farming, and the following year immigrated to Alabama. To his marriage were born these children: Martha A. (born August 6, 1847), Mary L. B. (born July 21, 1849), Sarah A. (born December 17, 1850), Robert A. (born August 22, 1853) and William R. (born August 22, 1855). The mother of these children died September 4, 1866, and was buried in Floyd County, Ga. While living in Alabama Mr. Hughen followed agricultural pursuits, and in 1855, he moved to Gordon County, Ga., where he engaged in the milling business with Mr. Mann (his father-in-law), and erected a flouring and saw mill. By a freshet, the property was badly damaged, but they rebuilt and had gotten fairly started again, when the Rebellion broke forth, and put another stop to their operations. In May, 1863, Mr. Hughen enlisted as a soldier, and was assigned to duty in the First Georgia Regiment Infantry, serving from that time until December, 1865. He participated in two engagements: Stone River, and during the siege of Fort Sumter he frequently went into the fort to witness the manner of defense. On the 5th day of December, 1864, while on duty, he was captured by the Union soldiers and taken to New York, being confined for thirteen days. He then took the oath of allegiance to the United States, and afterward went to Edgewood, Ill., where he engaged in milling, following this until the close of the war. He then returned to his home in Georgia, where he was employed for some time in endeavoring to repair the damages done during the war, and working at various occupations, until the fall of 1869, when he came to Arkansas. He rented land for three or four years, and in 1873 bought the land upon which he now lives, and where he has since made his home. The tract contains sixty-six acres of wild, woody land, upon which not an improvement had been made. At the present time Mr. Hughen has forty-seven acres under cultivation, and has good buildings, orchards, etc. On October 3, 1867, he took for his second wife Mrs. Eliza Moore, who bore him one child, Ida Lee, whose birth occurred July 9, 1868. At the present time, five of Mr. Hughen's children are living, and all are married: Martha A. (wife of Mr. Knowlis, who became the mother of four children. Her second marriage was to Mr. Bonner, of Texarkana), Mary L. B. (married Jasper Lampley. She died in 1883, and left children), Sarah (married twice, first to Zeke Meeks, by whom she had one child, and second to Mr. Fitzhugh, by whom she had four children, all deceased. She died in 1884), Robert A. (died at Little Rock, in 1885), William R. (died on December 9, 1887, and left four children, the result of his union with Miss Elizabeth Chrisp), Ida Lee (became the wife of Elihu Williams, and has one child). Mr. and Mrs. Hughen are members of the Methodist Episcopal Church, South, and Mr. Hughen has been a local preacher since 1883. He has been a member of that church for thirty-eight years. He is inclined to be Democratic in his political views. He is the son of James and Elizabeth (Anthony) Hughen, the father born and reared in South Carolina, and of Irish descent. His ancestors came to America, previous to the Revolutionary War, located in South Carolina, and the paternal grandfather, R. A. Hughen, was a commanding officer in the Revolutionary War. His uniform was seen by the subject of this sketch, in the clerk's office at Coweta, Ga., thirty years ago, at which time it was in a good state of preservation. Others of this family participated in the Florida War. James Hughen and Miss Elizabeth Anthony were married August 31, 1822, in Anderson District, S. C., and became the parents of seven children, all of whom grew to mature years. Mrs. Elizabeth (Anthony) Hughen was the daughter of Joel and Mary (Bratton) Anthony.

James Benton Hughes, planter, Lamberton, Ark. On August 8, 1841, there was born to Joshua and Nancy (Bookout) Hughes, a son, James Benton Hughes, who was one of a family of thirteen chil-

dren, the result of their union. The father was born in Tennessee in 1814, and was of English descent, his ancestors having emigrated to America previous to the Revolutionary War. The Grandfather Hughes participated in the struggle. James Benton Hughes' birth occurred in De Kalb County, Ala., and of the large family of which he was a member, only eight are now living. He was educated in the subscription schools of his native county, and subsequently attended Sulphur Springs Academy. He was reared to the arduous duties of the farm, and this has been his principal occupation during life, although for about three or four years he was engaged in rafting on the White River, between Indian Bay and New Orleans, their cargo being cypress logs. In 1859 Mr. Hughes went to Texas, where he was engaged in farming and herding for a year or two. He contracted with the Government to deliver supplies to the troops at Fort Colorado, and in March, 1862, he enlisted in Company C, Twenty-fourth Texas Cavalry, afterward the Twenty-fourth Texas Infantry, serving until the close of the war. He participated in the battle of Helena, was in the Missouri raid under Gen. Price, and at Pilot Knob, where he received a wound in the hand. He was also in a number of skirmishes previous to the Missouri raid. He went from his home to take the oath of allegiance at Jacksonport, but was not successful. In 1866 he worked on Dr. Washington's farm on shares, for one year, and then engaged in rafting as before mentioned. On March 5, 1871, he was united in marriage to Mrs. Sallie (Simmons) Stunson, the daughter of John and Jennie Simmons, who were among the first settlers of Eastern Arkansas. One child, Rosabell, was born to this union, her birth occurring on August 16, 1872, and her death on November 1, 1885. Mrs. Hughes died on April 14, 1876. Mr. Hughes made his first purchase of land, a tract comprising forty acres of wild land, in 1873, and has since added to this, until he now owns 380 acres, with about ninety acres under cultivation, his principal crops having been corn and cotton. He has a fine young apple and peach orchard, and raises as fine peaches as can be found anywhere. In his political views he coincides with the Democratic party. He officiated in the capacity of deputy sheriff for eight years by appointment, and was a capable and efficient officer. He is a member of the K. of H., Indian Bay Lodge No. 2491, and is also a member of the Cumberland Presbyterian Church.

G. W. Hurst, at the early age of fifteen, was made overseer of an extensive plantation, and had the full management of the same, in Monroe County, Miss., for over three years. After this he took charge of a large gang of negroes for James Erwin, being thus engaged until the opening of the war, when he enlisted in the Eleventh Mississippi. He was taken prisoner at the battle of Gettysburg, and removed to Ohio, where he was held for seven months, when he escaped and went to Buffalo, and a number of other cities, but was unable to join his regiment. G. W. Hurst was born in Franklin County, Ala., in 1840, being a son of Henry and Mary (Austin) Hurst, natives of Georgia and Alabama, respectively. They were the parents of nine children, five of whom are still living: G. W., Richard, Henry, William and Elizabeth (the wife of David Hooker, of Mississippi). Mr. Hurst was a member of the A. F. & A M., and of the Baptist Church, as was also his wife. He died in 1853 or 1854, and his worthy companion in 1849. At the close of the war the principal of this sketch returned to Franklin County, Ala., where he was married to Miss Mary E. Askew, daughter of Josiah and Permelia Askew, natives of that county. The following year they removed to Arkansas and located in Monroe County, and engaged in farming. They had a family of eight children, five of whom are living: Mary J. (the wife of W. H. Odon, of Ellis County, Tex.), James F., Clara J., George A. and John H. Mr. Hurst is a member of the K. of P., and his wife of the Baptist Church.

T. H. Jackson is the senior member of the general mercantile firm of T. H. Jackson & Co., of Brinkley, Ark., their stock of goods being valued at $35,000, and their annual sales reaching $120,-000, and in addition to successfully disposing of the manifold duties connected with this establishment, he is connected with the Brinkley Car Works and the Monroe County Bank and director of the Louisiana, Arkansas & Missouri Railroad. Being a native-born citizen of the State, he has ever had the interests of his State and county at heart, and has manifested his desire to witness their advancement by taking an active interest in all worthy enterprises, such as schools, churches, and the erection of public buildings of all kinds. In every walk of life he has proven himself to be a man of strict integrity and moral worth, and his influence in all public affairs has always been on the side of right. His birth occurred in Helena, Ark., in 1855, and he is a son of Jesse A. and Eliza L. (Hicks) Jackson, the former of whom is supposed to have been born in North Carolina, and the latter in Tennessee, their marriage taking place in Helena at an early day. During the war Jesse A. Jackson was a recruiting officer for Company A, but he afterward settled in Helena, Ark., of which place he was several times mayor, and councilman for some years, and was also in the United States land office, being there for some time, and afterward becoming interested in banking and mercantile business. He moved to Shreveport, La., where he died of yellow fever, in 1873. He was a member of the A. F. & A. M. His wife is still living and is sixty-two years of age. T. H. Jackson is the fourth of ten children, and received his education in the city of Helena, and spent three years in the Cumberland University of Lebanon, Tenn. Upon leaving that institution he was about sixteen years of age, and although his knowledge of the world was at that time very limited he was compelled to begin the battle of life for himself and his first work was in the capacity of clerking. He remained with one firm at Helena for seven or eight years, then became traveling salesman for William R. Moore & Co., of Memphis, but after remaining with them for a period of five years he settled at Brinkley (in 1886) and is now classed among the leading men of the county. He is a conservative Democrat in his political views, and socially is a member of Brinkley Lodge No. 3127, of the Knights of Honor, the Knights and Ladies of Honor and Knights of Pythias, being Chancellor Commander of the latter order. January 6, 1886, witnessed the celebration of his marriage to Lena A., daughter of Maj. William and Bena Black, prominent residents of the county. Mrs. Jackson was born in Memphis, Tenn., is a member of the Catholic Church, and her union with Mr. Jackson has been blessed in the birth of two bright little sons.

Capt. Benjamin F. Johnson is a member of the general mercantile firm of B. F. & G. F. Johnson, they being also engaged in cotton dealing at Clarendon. This firm is one of the most successful and enterprising in Eastern Arkansas, and the senior member of the firm, our subject, was born in La Fayette County, Miss., in 1839, being a son of Benjamin J. and Harriet T. (Owen) Johnson, the former a Georgian, born in 1802, and the latter a Virginian, born in 1818. The nuptials of their marriage were celebrated in Maury County, Tenn., and soon after they removed to La Fayette County, Miss., coming to Monroe County, Ark., in 1848, and settling near Cotton Plant. Here they improved a good farm, but becoming a little dissatisfied with his location, he, in 1859, went to Texas. He soon returned, however, to Monroe County, and here spent the rest of his days, dying in 1869, a successful planter and one of the leading pioneers of the county. For some years he was a leading commissioner of what was then St. Francis County, and, as he was enterprising in his views and honest and upright in character, he had many warm admirers and friends. He and wife were Baptists, and he was a son of Henry Johnson, a native of Ireland who, when but sixteen years of age, came with a brother to the United States. He served in the Revolutionary War and afterward made his home and was married in Virginia, moving thence to Georgia, but his death occurred in Alabama, he having settled where Decatur is now situated. The maternal grandfather, John W. Owen, was born in Scotland and being of an enterprising and adventurous disposition he emigrated to America when a young man and also participated in the American Revolution. He spent many years of his life in the Old Dominion, but his declining years were spent on a farm in Fayette County, Tenn. Capt. Benjamin F. Johnson lost his mother in 1854, and in 1858 his father

married again, having one daughter by his last wife, and three sons and two daughters by his first. Benjamin F. is the only child living born to his parents, and many of the important years of his life were spent on a farm, but although engaged in the monotonous duties of farm work he obtained a fair education in the schools near his home. September 13, 1859, witnessed his marriage to Miss Jane E., a daughter of William A. and Mary Pickens, who were born, reared and married in Tennessee, and moved from there to Mississippi, thence to Monroe County, Ark., in 1858, both parents dying here in 1860, having been farmers and worthy citizens of the county. Mrs. Johnson is a native of Tennessee, and two years after her marriage her husband left her to join Company B, First Arkansas Infantry, and during a service of about three years he was in the fights of Pea Ridge, Big Black, Richmond, Murfreesboro and many others. On account of failing health he was furloughed and remained at home about three months, but soon recovered his wonted energies, and in 1862 returned to the army, becoming one of Price's men, and was with him while on his raid through Missouri. He was paroled at Wittsburg and returned to farm life, but in 1869 also engaged in merchandising at Crockett's Bluff. Owing to the dullness of trade he moved to Clarendon in April, 1869, and began business after settling in Clarendon, continuing until 1874, when misfortunes overtook him and all his accumulations of years were swept away. He then went to Helena, Ark., where he worked for wages a few years, and by dint of economy and many self-denials he had accumulated sufficient property by 1878 to permit him to again embark in mercantile pursuits on a small scale. Owing to the many warm friends he had previously made in Clarendon and to his honesty, industry and strict attention to the details of his business, his patronage has steadily increased and he now does an annual business of about $90,000 in Clarendon, besides a business of $25,000 in Indian Bay. His nephew, G. F. Johnson, whom he has reared from a lad of thirteen years, is his partner and is an intelligent and wide-awake young business man. Mr. Johnson owns about 3,000 acres of land, with about 1,700 acres under cultivation, all of which he has earned since 1878. He is a Democrat, a member of the A. F. & A. M., the K. of H. and the I. O. O. F. He and wife are worthy members of the Presbyterian Church. They have no offspring, but have raised and educated seven orphan children, one girl and six boys, all of them steady and of good habits. One of the boys will study law, another medicine, one civil engineering and still another one will embark in stock raising out west. G. F. Johnson is his partner, and the sixth and last one, died just as he was in his eighteenth year. The names of these children are James B. Benson, Jasper W. Benson, Frank Miller, G. F. Johnson, William H. Johnson, E. B. Montgomery and Miss Mattie Lee Benson.

Capt. William J. F. Jones is a farmer and mechanic of Pine Ridge Township, Monroe County, Ark., but his birth occurred in Maury County, Tenn., in 1831, his parents being William and Penny (Skipper) Jones, natives respectively of North Carolina and Virginia. They were both taken to Maury County, Tenn., when small and were reared, educated and married in that State. Mr. Jones died when our subject was about twelve years of age, and his wife afterward married again and removed to Texas, where she died in 1883, both she and Mr. Jones having been earnest members of the Methodist Church. Mr. Jones was a farmer, as were his father and father-in-law, Joseph Skipper, and all were early settlers of the State of Tennessee. Capt. William J. F. Jones was the second of five children, and he and his elder brother, John W., were reared to a farm life and after their father's death assisted in the support of the family until they attained manhood, William J. F. being so occupied until he was twenty-four years of age. He was married in 1854 to Nancy A., a daughter of William and Louisa Malone, by whom he became the father of ten children, three sons and two daughters being now alive: William C., James T., Maggie I. (wife of John L. Barnett), Viola J. and Theodore T. After his marriage Mr. Jones resided in De Soto County, Miss. (which was Mrs. Jones' native birthplace), until 1856, since which date he has been a resident of Monroe County, Ark. His first home here was a little log-cabin among the woods, twelve miles east of Clarendon, and here, after many years of slow and disheartening labor he finds himself the owner of 680 acres of as fine land as there is in the county, and by his own efforts he has put 125 acres under the plow. At the breaking out of the war he owed $500 on his homestead of 120 acres, but during this time he paid off the debt in full, and although suit was afterward brought against him for the amount, the case was decided in his favor. The rest of his property has been made since then. In 1861 he joined Company A, Fifteenth Arkansas Infantry, as a private and became a member of the Army of the Tennessee, participating in the battle of Shiloh. On May 15, 1862, he was detailed home for recruits, and had no difficulty in raising sufficient men to form Company E, which was attached to the Sixth Arkansas Infantry, and he became its captain. He was in the engagements of Prairie Grove and Helena, but was taken captive at the latter place on July 4, 1863, and was taken to Alton, Ill., where he spent one month, and from that time until January 9, 1865, he was kept a prisoner at Johnson's Island. After being paroled he returned to his farm. His first presidential vote was cast for Pierce in 1852, but since 1874 he has been a member of the Union Labor party. He belongs to the Agricultural Wheel. His wife is a member of the Christian Church.

Benjamin F. Kerr is one of the early residents of Monroe County, and is a retired merchant and planter of Clarendon. He was born in what is now Hale County, Ala., in 1830, his parents, John W. and Margaret (Dial) Kerr, having been born in Lincoln County, Ky. and Newberry District, S. C., respectively, the former's birth occurring in 1798. Their nuptials were celebrated in Greene County, Ala., and in 1852 they came to Monroe County, but the father did not long live to enjoy his new home, as he was taken sick while en route to St. Louis, and died in that city in 1855. He was a very successful man of business, having been a planter and merchant, and at the time of his death was quite wealthy. His father, James Kerr, was born in Scotland, and when a young man came to the

United States and settled in Kentucky, where he made his home until his death. David M. Dial, the maternal grandfather, was born in the "Emerald Isle," and died in Sumter County, Ala., in 1834, having been a wealthy farmer. Benjamin F. Kerr is the second of six children, and although his youth was spent at hard labor on the farm he succeeded in acquiring a good education, and after attaining his twelfth year attended school at Bridgeport, Conn., for two years, then Middletown, Conn., two years, and spent the three following years at Danville, Ky., graduating from a school at that place in 1849. He spent the following eight years with a wholesale house of St. Louis, and in 1855 came to Monroe County, Ark., and settled at Holly Grove, where he farmed until 1875. Since then he has resided in Clarendon, and, until March, 1877, he was engaged in the mercantile business, but since that time he has been retired from the active duties of life. He is quite well off as far as worldly goods are concerned, and has a fine farm of 300 acres and a good house in town. His wife, whose maiden name was Kate May and whom he married in Sumter County, Ala., in 1851, was born in Marengo County of that State, and by Mr. Kerr is the mother of four sons and two daughters. She is a daughter of Asel and Charlotte May, natives, respectively, of Alabama and Kentucky. The former died in his native State in 1835, and the latter's death occurred in Rankin County, Miss. Mr. Kerr was a Whig prior to the war, but has since been a Democrat. He served the Confederate cause in the commissary department until 1863, and afterward went to Little Rock, where he was made recruiting officer. He was captured near Helena, in 1864, and was imprisoned at Camp Chase, Ohio, until just before the close of the war, when he was exchanged. He is a Knight Templar in the Masonic fraternity.

W. D. Kerr, manager of the firm of Isaac Halpin, was born in Jackson County, Ala., in 1832, and is the son of James Kerr, whose birth occurred in Pulaski County, Ky., in 1804. The father was a mechanic by trade, and this occupation carried on until late in life, when he began farming, continuing at this until his death. He was married to Miss

Cynthia Taylor, of Alabama, in about 1829, and they became the parents of fourteen children, seven sons and seven daughters, seven of whom are now living: Eliza J. (wife of J. T. Simms, of Texas), W. D., John M., James A., Rufus L., Emma A. (wife of W. H. Sperry, of Holly Grove), Martha E. (widow of Mr. Beever) and Charles G. James Kerr was a member of the A. F. & A. M., and was a member of the Methodist Episcopal Church, South, for over forty years, being class leader and steward in the same. He immigrated from Alabama to Arkansas in 1853, located in this county, and was the founder of the town of Holly Grove, owning part of the ground the town now stands on. He bought land when he came here and built a log-cabin, having previously lived in a tent. He died in 1881, and his wife died in this county in 1888. She was also a worthy member of the Methodist Episcopal Church, South. W. D. Kerr began life for himself in 1852, as a clerk in a book and music store of Gainesville, Ala., and there remained for a year, when he began clerking in a drug and dry goods store for J. H. & J. G. Webb, of Sumterville, Sumter County, Ala. He moved from that State to Arkansas in 1858, and located in or near Holly Grove, where he has remained ever since. He was married to Miss Elizabeth D. Nicholson, of Alabama, in 1854, and by her became the father of three children: Lillian (wife of W. B. Wellborn), Gertrude E. and Hattie N. Mr. Kerr was elected justice of the peace in 1860, and held the office two terms; was also county judge a number of years. Mrs. Kerr was a member of the Methodist Episcopal Church, and died in 1884. Mr. Kerr took for his second wife Mrs. Emma Metcalfe, a native of Union County, Ky., born in 1840, and the daughter of Mr. and Mrs. Martin Berry, of Union County, Ky. Mrs. Kerr is a member of the Presbyterian Church, but Mr. Kerr has been a member of the Methodist Episcopal Church, South, since he was sixteen years of age.

L. W. Kizer, farmer, Cypress Ridge, Ark. Mr. Kizer is a man who can appreciate the comforts of a desirable home and surroundings, and his well-improved farm and attractive residence prove an ornament to the community. His father, David Kizer, was born in Tennessee in 1810, was reared on a farm and followed agricultural pursuits as a livelihood all his life. He was married to Miss Susan Ferguson, of Tennessee, and they became the parents of seventeen children, only five of whom are now living: Thomas D., James M., Joseph F., William and L. W. Mr. Kizer died in Mississippi in 1877, and his wife died in 1835. He was a member of the Methodist Episcopal Church. L. W. Kizer was married, in 1883, to Miss Sallie Ferguson, a native of De Soto, Miss., born in 1855 and the daughter of Mr. and Mrs. James Ferguson. Four children have been the result of this marriage, three now living: Georgia E., Katie and Grover C. Mr. Kizer is the owner of 320 acres of excellent land, with 175 acres under cultivation, and he also owns and operates a large cotton-gin. He moved from Mississippi to Arkansas in 1883 and has since made his home in this county. He is one of the leading farmers and citizens in this section. Mrs. Kizer is a member of the Presbyterian Church.

Charles B. La Belle is the capable cashier of the Monroe County Bank, and is also a member of the general mercantile firm of T. H. Jackson & Co., of Brinkley. He was born in Little Rock, Ark., in 1860, and is a son of Charles and Margaret (Crudgington) La Belle, the former a Canadian, who, after traveling in different States, finally settled in Pulaski County, Ark., becoming one of its pioneer settlers. Here he was married and spent the rest of his life, dying June 26, 1888, a contractor and brick-mason and a large real-estate owner. He was a well-known citizen of Little Rock, a Democrat in his political views, and at the time of his death was in full communion with the Catholic Church. His wife died October 4, 1877, having borne two children, a son and a daughter, the latter now being Mrs. J. H. Laster, of Little Rock. Charles B. La Belle attended the public schools of his native town, and later graduated from the Little Rock Commercial College, after which he became book-keeper for T. S. Diffey & Co., of that city until 1883, when he came to Brinkley and spent the first three years as a clerk

for M. Kelley. He also filled the position of clerk and book-keeper for T. H. Jackson & Co., and in the month of May, 1888, was made a member of that well-known and enterprising firm. Although young in years he ranks among the leading business men of the place and in every respect deserves success, which has attended his career. In politics he is a Democrat and his first presidential vote was cast for Cleveland in 1884. He has served one year as alderman of Brinkley, and socially is a member of Brinkley Lodge of the Knights of Pythias, and also belongs to the Knights of Honor. October 3, 1888, he was married to Miss Anna, a daughter of the late Maj. William Black, whose history is given in this work. Mr. La Belle and his wife have one son, whom they expect to rear in the Catholic faith.

B. J. Lambert, merchant and farmer, Lamberton, Ark. Among the most important industries of any community are those which deal in the necessaries of life, and nothing is more necessary than bread and meat. Lamberton at least has one first-class establishment doing business in this line, which is successfully conducted by Mr. Lambert and son, who handle nothing but the best and freshest goods. This gentleman owes his nativity to Tennessee, his birth occurring in Madison County, in 1838, and is the son of Jordan B. and Judith W. (Key) Lambert, the father a native of the Old Dominion, born in 1797, and the mother of North Carolina, born in 1799. They were married in Henderson County, Ky., and later moved from there to Madison County, Tenn., where they resided for seventeen years. In 1839 they came to Monroe County, located near Indian Bay, among a wild and immoral class of people, who were opposed to culture or refinement, and rather disposed to riot and turmoil. Such a class of people was very obnoxious to the cultured and refined taste of Mr. Lambert, who put forth every effort to effect a change in that direction, and his exertions were eventually crowned with success. Here he passed the closing scenes of his life, his death occurring in January, 1860. He was a prominent Cumberland Presbyterian minister for many years, and was one of seven brothers, six of whom were ministers in that church. He was the only one to reside in Monroe County, where he was one of the prominent pioneers. In 1844 he served in the Arkansas legislature, and afterward was judge of the county and probate court. He probably did more toward moralizing the people and advancing the general interest of the country than any other one man. He was a member of the A. F. & A. M. His father, Joel Lambert, was a native Virginian, of English descent, and died in Kentucky, Mrs. Lambert (mother of the subject of this sketch) died in 1868. She was the daughter of Chesley Key, who was a native of North Carolina and who died in Kentucky. B. J. Lambert was next to the youngest of ten children, eight sons and two daughters, seven of whom lived to be grown, but only two of whom are now living: B. J. and S. T. The former received his education in the common schools and attended two and a half years at Princeton, Ky., and one year at McLemoresville, Tenn. He then engaged in agricultural pursuits and continued at this until the opening of the war. He served two and a half years in the Confederate army, in different companies, and was first with his brother, Capt. Robert Lambert, who was killed at the battle of Shiloh. Afterward he was in McCrea's brigade and operated in Arkansas. He was captured in Monroe County, April 10, 1864, and was imprisoned at Camp Chase, Ohio, until the close of hostilities, and then returned home. He was married March 20, 1861, to Miss Fannie A. Beasley, a native of Tennessee, and the daughter of Maj. John P. and Evaline T. Beasley, who came from West Tennessee to Monroe County, Ark., in 1859. There Mrs. Beasley still resides, but Mr. Beasley was murdered in Texas, December 14, 1865, whither he had gone after stock. He and wife were natives of Alabama, and both were church members, he of the Methodist and she of the Baptist. To Mr. and Mrs. Lambert were born eleven children, three sons and two daughters now living, and since 1871 Mr. Lambert and family have resided at Lamberton, where he purchased 1,500 acres of land, and has about 500 acres under cultivation. Since 1883 he has conducted the plantation store. He has been postmaster at Lamberton since the establishment of that office, and in 1872 was elected sheriff of Monroe County, but was counted out and the matter was not settled for three years. In politics he was formerly a Whig, but is now a Democrat, and his first presidential vote was cast for Bell in 1860. He is a member of the Masonic fraternity, Indian Bay Lodge No. 256, and Forest Home Chapter No. 16, at Clarendon. He and wife are members in good standing in the Cumberland Presbyterian Church.

Henry A. McGill began life for himself at the early age of twelve years, by learning the painter's trade. Six years later he went to Mason County, Ill., where he worked at his trade until the breaking out of the war, then enlisting in the Twenty-eighth Illinois Infantry, and participating in all the principal engagements of his division. He received his discharge in April, 1865, when he returned to Illinois, and engaged in farming until 1867, the time of his removal to Arkansas. Then he located in Monroe County, where he again took up his trade of painting. Four years later he bought a farm of 180 acres, with 130 acres under cultivation, and now owns a cotton-gin and grist-mill, built in 1883, which he operates in addition to his farm. Mr. McGill was born in Madison County, Tenn., in 1845, and is a son of William McGill, a native of the same county. The latter was born in 1824, and was married, in 1849, to Miss Adaline Gustin. They were the parents of three sons: Henry A. (our subject), John and William, deceased. He immigrated from Tennessee to Arkansas in 1849, and there died, having been a planter and overseer all of his life. Mr. Henry McGill was married in 1877 to Miss Annie S. Hallum, who was born in Poinsett County, in 1855. They were the parents of seven children, three of whom only are living: Volency H., Harrold and Julius. Mr. McGill is a member of the K. of H., and he and wife belong to the Baptist Church. He is a strong Democrat, and a well-known and respected citizen.

M. J. Manning is a member of one of the leading law firms of the State of Arkansas, that of Roberts & Manning. He was born in De Soto County, Miss., in 1861, and is a son of Hon. T. P.

and K. A. (Barbee) Manning, natives, respectively, of North Carolina and Tennessee, who were married in De Soto County, Miss., where the mother died in 1882. Mr. Manning was a very successful lawyer of that State for twenty years and made his home in the above-named county until 1884, since which time he has resided in Paris, Ark., and the reputation he has acquired as a lawyer has been gained through his own efforts and at the expense of diligent study and hard practical experience. He is of Scotch-Irish descent, and during the late Civil War commanded a company of men from Mississippi, Confederate States army, and on many occasions showed marked ability as a commander and achieved considerable distinction. In 1874 the people of De Soto County showed their appreciation of his ability, by electing him to the State legislature of Mississippi, and he served in that body with credit to himself and to the satisfaction of all concerned. M. J. Manning, whose name heads this sketch, was the second of nine children and after acquiring an excellent education in the schools of his native county he entered the Law Department of the Mississippi University at Oxford and upon graduating, in 1883, came immediately to Clarendon, and in September of the same year was admitted to the Monroe County bar and has already risen to distinction in his profession, and notwithstanding the fact that he is young in years he has already attained prominence in his calling. He is a Democrat in his political views, an active member of the K. of P. and the K. of H., also the American Legion of Honor. In 1885, Miss Jessie, a daughter of Major William E. Winfield, of Tennessee, who was a soldier in the Confederate army, a farmer by occupation and who died in 1878, became his wife. She was born in Tennessee and by Mr. Manning is the mother of two daughters. She belongs to the Episcopal Church and he to the Baptist.

M. D. Martin is a member of the general mercantile firm of Martin, Black & Co., of Indian Bay, Ark., the business being established on February 1, 1877, the average value of the stock being about $10,000, and their annual sales amounting from $40,000 to $80,000. In connection with their dry-goods establishment they own and operate a good steam cotton-gin and saw-mill. Mr. Martin was born in Atlanta, Ga., in 1840, and was a son of Joseph J. and Jane (Thurmond) Martin, who were born in South Carolina and Atlanta, Ga., in 1811 and 1820, respectively. They were married in the mother's native birthplace, but in the year 1852 removed to Tilton, at which place the mother's death occurred in 1867, and the father's in 1886. He was an extensive planter, and a prominent man, and both he and his wife were members of the Baptist Church. The paternal grandfather, William G. Martin, was born in Virginia, and died in Atlanta, Ga., but a number of the years of his life were spent in Abbeville District, S. C. He was colonel of a regiment of militia during the War of 1812, but did not see much service. His father was a Virginian, the first one of the family born in America, as his father was a native-born Englishman. M. D. Martin, our immediate biographical subject, is the eldest of a family of eleven children, eight now living, and his early education was acquired in the high school of Atlanta, Ga., and in the schools of Dalton. He next studied under a private tutor, and afterward read law with Judge John G. Stewart, and was admitted to the bar just at the breaking out of the late Civil War. He immediately joined the Second Georgia Battalion, and served in the Army of Virginia, until after the battle of Gettysburg, at which time he was captured. From that time until April, 1864, he was kept a prisoner at Fort Delaware and Point Lookout, and was then paroled. After spending a short time in New York City he came to Memphis, and was engaged in the timber business in that city until 1869. Since that time he has resided in Indian Bay, and after following the same business here for a few years he began keeping books, and a year later in connection with this work engaged in farming. From 1877 to 1882, he was engaged in merchandising for himself, but at the latter date he formed a partnership with Maj. S. L. Black, who sold his interest to his son, John L. Black and J. W. Martin, a brother of our subject and they now constitute the present firm. In 1872 M. D. Martin was married to Sarah E., a daughter of William Radman, formerly of Indiana, who died in Monroe County, Ark. Mrs. Martin was born in Indiana, and she and Mr. Martin have become the parents of six children, two sons and one daughter living. By push and energy Mr. Martin has become a well-to-do man, and his farm of 332 acres, near Indian Bay, is the result of his own industry. He is a Democrat, his first presidential vote being cast for Greeley in 1868, and he belongs to Indian Bay Lodge No. 256, A. F. & A. M., and has filled nearly all the chairs of this order. He also belongs to Advance Lodge No. 2491, K. of H., at Indian Bay, and the American Legion of Honor, Warsaw Lodge, at Indian Bay. He and wife are Methodists.

William Montgomery Mayo, planter and stockman, Indian Bay, Ark. There are many incidents of peculiar interest presented in the career of Mr. Mayo, which can not be given in the space allotted to this article. Known over a large region of country tributary to Indian Bay, his reputation is that of a man honorable and reliable in every walk of life. He is the son of James and Sarah Eliza (Cokely) Mayo. [For family history see sketches of John W. and Laurence S. Mayo, elsewhere in this volume.] Capt. William M. Mayo was born September 26, 1822, in Martin County, N. C. He was early initiated into the details of farm life, and received a liberal education in an academy established by his father, the latter being the prime mover in securing its establishment. William moved with his parents to Tennessee, in 1837, and finished his education in the public academy in Fayette County, taught by Hartwell Rollins, near La Grange, Tenn. Afterward this school was taught by him for one year, but his principal occupation during life has been tilling the soil. On Christmas eve of the year 1844 he was united in marriage to Miss Jane Elizabeth Anderson, daughter of Major Joel and Sallie (Younger) Anderson, both natives of Virginia, and whose ancestors on both sides probably came to America about 1765. Jane E. Anderson was born April 27, 1829, and is one of three children born to her parents: John Anthony, Lucinda Thomas and Mrs. Mayo. The latter was educated at the same school in Tennes-

see with her husband, was almost reared with him, their parents living on adjoining farms, and was a pupil of her husband during the year he taught school near La Grange. To Mr. and Mrs. Mayo have been born eleven children: Frederick Anthony (born March 31, 1846, now resides in Somerville, and an attorney at law at Somerville, Tenn. He married Miss Laura Cocke and became the father of seven children), Leauna Melvina (was born June 10, 1848, and died August, 19, 1849), Richard Dale (was born November 5, 1850, married Miss Willie Pointer, and has one daughter and four sons), Laura Montgomery (was born December 29, 1851, and became the wife of W. H. Boyce, a native of Tennessee, who is now residing near her parents; they had ten children, three now living), William Thomas (was born December 20, 1853, and died August 5, 1854), Nannie Jane (was born July 28, 1859, and married Sidney S. Bond, of Jackson, Tenn., January 14, 1879; has one child now living), William James (was born June 23, 1861, graduated in B. A. course and B. L., at the University of Mississippi in class of 1884, now an attorney at Clarendon, Ark.), Gaston Baldwin (was born September 26, 1863, and died November 28, 1865), Fannie Lula (born June 4, 1866), Lillie Lina (born August 11, 1868) and Walter Lee (born June 28, 1871, and died April 30, 1877). Fannie Lula married Samuel W. Hargis, on February 11, 1885. Her husband died on September 10, 1886, and in 1888 she was married to Major S. L. Black, Indian Bay, Ark. William James married Miss Annie C. Lake, of Oxford, Miss.; she died at Clarendon, Ark., October 10, 1886. Lillian L. Mayo married John S. Black and resides at Indian Bay; they have one child. Capt. Mayo came to Arkansas in 1853, bought a tract of 2,400 acres, with a few acres cultivated, and he now has 1,200 acres under cultivation. In 1859 the Captain completed a story and a half log-house, 18x52 feet, and the same year added to that a two-story frame, 20x52, the two constituting the house in which he has since made his home, and in which his children received the principal part of their schooling. In 1862 he enlisted in the Confederate army as a private in the company known as the

Monroe Rebels of the Twenty-fifth Arkansas Infantry. In August of the same year he received a commission as captain with orders to return and report to the command of the Trans-Mississippi Department. He then raised what is known as Partisan Company to operate in the Eastern portion of Arkansas. The company afterward became Company C of the Forty-fifth Arkansas Cavalry, operating under Gen. Shelby, at Clarendon, Ark. At or near the last-named place, in 1864, he commanded two companies in a battle near Clarendon, Ark., with a detachment of the Eighth Missouri Cavalry, which he defeated; was then in a battle at Miller's Creek under Gen. Thomas McRae, was then at Brownsville under Gen. Shelby, Ironton Mountain under Gen. Price, and at the last-named place received a wound in the shoulder and was left on the field for dead. He was afterward assisted from the field by members of his company, and although his wound rendered him unfit for duty he remained with the command through the Missouri raid and until the end of the war, being in the recruiting service near his home at that time. In politics Capt. Mayo is a Democrat, and his first presidential vote was for Henry Clay. He was a member of the convention when Arkansas seceded from the Union. He holds membership in Indian Bay Lodge, No. 256, F. & A. M., and also holds membership in the Chapter and Council at Clarendon. He and wife and all their family are members of the Cumberland Presbyterian Church.

Lawrence Sherod Mayo, planter and stockman, Lamberton, Ark. This much-esteemed citizen is the son of James and Sarah (Cokely) Mayo, of Irish and English descent, respectively. The parents were married in Edgecomb County, N. C., and the father was a successful agriculturist. His ancestors came to America previous to the Revolutionary War. To Mr. and Mrs. James Mayo were born a family of twelve children as follows, the years representing their births: 'Catherine, 1816; John W., 1818; Mary Eliza, 1820; William Montgomery, 1822; Harriet Ann, 1824; Benjamin Cokely, 1826; Sarah Louisa, 1828; Lawrence Sherod, March 13, 1830; Nancy Jane, 1832; Nathan, 1834; Olivia, who died in childhood, and

James M., who was born in 1838. The children were all natives of Martin County, with the exception of James, whose birth occurred in Fayette County, Tenn. Lawrence Sherod Mayo, with his brothers and sisters (excepting the two youngest), received his education at home under an instructor employed by the father, and never attended any other school. He commenced life as a farmer at the age of twenty-one years, and on December 18, 1850, he was united in marriage to Miss Mary Elizabeth Terrell, a native of Edgecomb County, N. C. The same year he bought a farm in Fayette County, Tenn., and tilled the soil for three years. In 1852 he sold his farm and came to Arkansas, locating in Jackson Township, then Lawrence County, and there he bought land. There he remained until 1857, when he sold out and moved to his present property. He at one time owned 1,000 acres of land, but now has about 600 acres, with about 200 acres under cultivation. He owned at one time about thirty slaves. His wife, Mrs. Mayo, was the daughter of Nathan and Alice (Redmond) Terrill, both natives of North Carolina, and of English descent. The father was a farmer and carriage dealer by occupation. To Mr. and Mrs. Mayo were born these children: Daniel Redmond (born September 28, 1854), Sherod Dale (born May 28, 1856, and died February 16, 1875), Lawrence Montgomery (born September 20, 1859, and died February 16, 1875), James (born July 26, 1861), Nannie (born April 11, 1865), Alice (born January 10, 1867, and died September 10, 1870), Patrick C. (born June 7, 1879), Henry Jackson (born March 24, 1871, and died April 24, 1881), and Mary Lawrence (born October 24, 1877). Daniel Redmond was married to Miss Annie Swift, and became the father of two children. He is now merchandising at Knoxville, Tenn. Nannie became the wife of Martin C. Bond, a farmer of Phillips County, Ark. They have three children. Mr. and Mrs. Mayo are members in the Cumberland Presbyterian Church, as are also their children, Daniel R., Nannie and Mary L. Mr. Mayo is a Democrat, and his first presidential vote was cast for James K. Polk.

John William Mayo, a farmer and stockman of

Monroe County, now residing with Wiley T. Washington, his son-in-law, on Section 24 of Jackson Township, is a son of James and Sarah Eliza (Cokely) Mayo. The founder of this branch of the Mayo family came o America in 1730, as far as is known, and the Cokely family also emigrated from England, probably before the Revolutionary War. Benjamin Cokely, John W.'s maternal grandfather, married a sister of Com. Dale. Sarah E. (Cokely) Mayo had two brothers: Benjamin and William. The subject of this sketch was married to Miss Emma Ann Winston, on February 8, 1842, at the home of the bride's parents near La Grange, Fayette County, Tenn. She was a daughter of Thomas J. and Elvira (Jones) Winston, of Fayette County. In 1850 Mr. Mayo removed to Arkansas, and located in Monroe County, where he bought a farm of 160 acres, engaging in the occupation to which he had been reared. He located on Section 30, Jackson Township, in 1859, and now owns 355 acres, with 140 acres under cultivation, upon which are five tenant houses, and his land is in a high state of improvement. Mrs. Mayo died December 2, 1888, having borne a family of children as follows: Laura C. (born February 22, 1843, married Wiley F. Washington, October 16, 1860, and died January 18, 1887, leaving eight children, three living), Winston (born March 5, 1846), Sarah Olivia (born March 27, 1848, married Oran Washington February 18, 1874, who died January 2, 1875; their only child, Oran, Jr., was born January 3, 1875. She became the wife of W. F. Washington, December 25, 1887, and has one child by this union, Lawrence, born August 4, 1889), John J. (born December 19, 1849, married Miss Lou Walker, who bore one child, John W., January 1, 1876; after her death Miss Elam became his wife in 1878, and they have four children: Alice Vivian, Sarah Olivia, Emily and Bettie), William Jones (born January 24, 1852), Mary Louisa (born October 13, 1854, died October 10, 1859), Henry (died in infancy), Harriett Ann (born October 20, 1856, died September 27, 1871), Nathan (born February 12, 1862 (deceased), and Lucy. Mr. Mayo is a prominent Democrat, though he cast his first presidential vote for William H. Harrison. He is a member of the

Cumberland Presbyterian Church, as are also all of the grown children, and some of his grandchildren, he having belonged since 1865. He had a fairly good education in youth, and is a popular man and a good citizen.

James M. Miles is a native of this county, and a son of Charles J. and Mary A. (Montgomery) Miles, originally from Tennessee, who were born in 1811 and 1816, and of Irish and English descent, respectively. They were the parents of nine children, two of whom are now living: James M. (our subject) and Richard. Mr. Miles removed to Arkansas in 1830, and settled in what is now Monroe County, where he entered three quarter sections of land, and engaged in farming and in rafting on the Mississippi. His land lay in the woods, where he erected a loghouse, living in it for a number of years. He died in 1863, preceded by his wife some nine years. He was a soldier in the Indian Wars of 1836. James M. was born April 6, 1843, and lived on his father's farm, helping clear it up, until his death. He was married August 4, 1864, to Salinda A. Spardlin, who died in 1874, leaving four children, one of whom, Richard, is now living. He was married to his second wife, Miss Louisa Crisp, June 5, 1876, who died in 1884, having been the mother of four children, one of whom, Emma, is now living. He was married February 18, 1886, to his present wife, Annie I. Olison, of this county. They have a family of two sons: Bart and Grover M. Mr. Miles enlisted in the late war in 1861, and served until he was captured in 1864, and taken to Louisville (Ky.), where he was held for over a month, when he escaped and returned home. He owns a fine farm of 280 acres, over half of which is under cultivation. He is a strong Democrat and a prominent citizen of Monroe County. Mrs. Miles is a member of the Methodist Episcopal Church.

Charles B. Mills is the efficient circuit court clerk of Monroe County, Ark., and was born in Ralls County, Mo., in 1839, being the eldest of five children born to James M. and Mary (Kelly) Mills, who were born in the State of Tennessee about 1816. They were married in Missouri and

34

made that State their home until 1866, when they came to Monroe County, Ark., where Mr. Mills died in 1878 and Mrs. Mills in 1872, both being consistent members of the Cumberland Presbyterian Church. Mr. Mills was a cabinet maker by trade, but at the time of his death he was engaged in farming and stock raising. He served a short time in the Confederate States army, and socially was a member of the A. F. & A. M. His father, James Lee Mills, was born in Maryland and died in Ralls County, Mo., a farmer and of Welsh descent. Charles B. Mills, the immediate subject of this sketch, was educated in the schools of Hannibal, Mo. In 1861 he left the school-room to join Grimshaw's command of Missouri State Troops, and operated with him until the winter of 1861–62, when he joined the First Missouri Regiment, Confederate States army, afterward designated as the Second Missouri Infantry, and served until he lost his left arm at the battle of Corinth. He was soon after placed in the commissary department under Maj. John S. Mellon, and remained thus employed until the close of the war, when he returned home. In 1866 he came to Monroe County, Ark., and was engaged in merchandising and stock dealing at Aberdeen, which place, having been cut off by change in county lines, is now in Prairie County. From 1874 to 1882 he served as circuit clerk of that county. In 1883 he was again cut off into Monroe County, of which he has since been a resident, and here he was engaged in farming and stock raising until 1886, when he was elected clerk of the county and re-elected in 1888, being chosen by the Democrat party, of which he has been a member since the death of the Whig party. He is Treasurer of Clarendon Lodge of the K. of H. and was a charter member of Des Arc Lodge, of which he was Dictator two terms. In 1870 he was united in marriage to Miss T. W. Gean, a daughter of John and Nancy Gean, who were born, reared and married in Chatham County, N. C., and in an early day removed to Hardeman County, Tenn., where their daughter, Mrs. Mills, was born. In 1859 they came to Arkansas, the father dying in Monroe County and the mother in Prairie County. Mrs. Mills belongs to the Methodist Church, and she and

Mr. Mills are the parents of one son and four daughters. Mr. Mills is a Cumberland Presbyterian in his religious preferences.

L. B. Mitchell, M. D., a practicing physician and druggist, of Brinkley, Ark., although born in Monroe County, Ky., in 1828, has been a resident of Arkansas since 1858, at which time his parents, James S. and Sarah (Scott) Mitchell, came to this State. They were born in Ohio and Tennessee, in 1793 and 1798, respectively, but were married in the Blue Grass State, and in 1836 removed to Tennessee, thence to Arkansas. They settled in what is now known as Lonoke County, and here the father died in 1862, followed to his long home by his wife in 1875, both being members of the Christian Church at the time of their deaths. Mr. Mitchell was an Irishman by descent, a farmer by occupation, and during the early history of Indiana he was a participant in a number of her Indian wars. The maternal grandfather, John Scott, was of Scotch lineage, and died in Macon County, Tenn. Dr. L. B. Mitchell is one of the three surviving members of a family of six children, and was reared on a farm, receiving his education in the common schools. Upon reaching manhood he clerked for four years, then during 1854–55 he attended college at McLemoresville, Tenn., and after making up his mind to become a physician, he entered the University of Louisville, Ky., attending during the winter of 1855–56, but did not graduate from any college until 1858, at which time he left the Nashville University as an M.D. He came immediately to Arkansas, and has successfully practiced his profession ever since, but during the war served the Confederate cause as assistant-surgeon of the Fourth Arkansas Battalion for some two and a-half years, and the two following years was with the Second Arkansas Dismounted Riflemen. Owing to his personal popularity and the respect and esteem in which he is held, he was elected in 1870 to represent Pulaski County in the State legislature, and was re-elected in 1872, being the candidate of the Democratic party, with which he has long affiliated. He was State treasurer of the Grange for about three years, and since 1855 has been a Mason, and was Master of Mount Pleasant Lodge a great many years. He resided in Austin for about thirty years, but has been a resident of Brinkley since 1888, where he has acquired a lucrative practice and trade in the drug business, this calling having previously received his attention in Austin also. He was married in 1865 to Sarah J., a daughter of Peter St. Clair, a Tennesseean, who died at Austin in 1860, a farmer and mechanic by trade. Mrs. Mitchell was born in West Tennessee, and by Dr. Mitchell became the mother of six sons and three daughters, all of whom are living. Lewis E., the eldest of the family, is now treasurer of the Famous Life Association of Little Rock. The Dr. has been a member of the Christian Church for a great many years, but his wife belongs to the Methodist Church.

Polk Montgomery is a prosperous planter of Duncan Township, and is well known to the people of Monroe County. A native of Tennessee, he was born to the union of A. H. and Hannah (Robinson) Montgomery, natives of South Carolina and Tennessee, respectively. A. H. Montgomery first saw the light of day in 1796, and was reared in his native State. In 1820 he came to Tennessee, where he was married in 1841, to Mrs. Hannah (Lady) Robinson. Mr. Montgomery was in the War of 1812, and died in 1865, and his wife in the same year. Both members of the Campbellite Church. Polk Montgomery, the only child born to their marriage, owes his nativity to Shelby County, Tenn., where his birth occurred in 1845. He was married in 1865 to Miss Anna Nicks, who was born in Cherokee County, Ga., in 1846, a daughter of Elijah and Charlotte Nicks. Mr. and Mrs. Montgomery removed from Tennessee to Arkansas, in 1868, and settled in this county, where he purchased 240 acres of land, of which 175 acres are under cultivation, lying one-half mile south of Holly Grove. He is a member of the A. F. & A. M. His wife is a member of the Presbyterian Church. During the war between the States, he served in Company C, Fourth Tennessee Infantry, Confederate States army.

Harry H. Myers is the present secretary, treasurer and director of the Brinkley Car Works & Manufacturing Co., which is one of the foremost industries of the county, and was established in 1882, the present company being the successors of Gunn & Black, who were actively engaged in the manufacture of lumber at Brinkley for about sixteen years. The present company is one of the most enterprising and extensive in Eastern Arkansas, and they have a pay role of some 260 persons, 120 of whom are employed at the saw-mill in the woods, and cut down 68,000 feet of timber per day, the rest being employed in constructing railroads and in the general car repair shop. Every facility incident to this particular industry is embraced within the works, the tools and machinery being of the most modern and improved kind, and only skillful and experienced workmen are employed. This company ships about 220 carloads of lumber, consisting of flooring, shingles, moldings, lath, pickets, doors and window sashes, per month, to Memphis, Tenn., where they have one of the leading lumber establishments in the city, it having been established through the efforts of the late Maj. Black. Prior to Mr. Black's decease, which occurred in September, 1889, he was president and director of the company, with O. M. Norman, manager, and H. H. Myers, secretary and treasurer, but after his death Mr. Norman was made president, director and manager, and Mr. Myers became secretary, treasurer and director. This company also owns the Brinkley, Helena & Indian Bay Railroad, and about 36,000 acres of land in Monroe County. Mr. Myers, a member of this company, was born in Keokuk, Iowa, in 1865, and until he was thirteen years of age, attended the schools of his native town, after which he became an employe of the Wabash Railroad Company, and for five years was telegraph operator and traveling auditor for that company. In 1883 he came to Brinkley, and was made cashier of the St. Louis, Arkansas & Texas Railroad Company, but shortly after became agent for the company at Brinkley, continuing until 1886, when he entered upon his present duties. He is also president of the Myers & Sapp Drug Company, and is prominently connected with other enterprises in Brinkley, among them as proprietor of a wholesale and retail grain produce and feed store, carrying about $5,000 to $6,000 in the business continually. All in all he is one of the foremost business men of the county, although young in years. He is also postmaster here. In April, 1887, he was married to Miss Katie R., a daughter of Maj. William Black. He is a member of the K. of P., and is Prelate of his lodge. His parents, Theodore H. and E. R. (Worster) Myers, resided in Keokuk, Iowa, before the war, but have recently moved to Kearney, Neb. The father was born in Anderson, Ind., and for many years has been a merchant. He belongs to the I. O. O. F., and the A. F. & A. M., and during the war he was captain of a company, in the Third Iowa Regiment, United States Army. His wife is a daughter of Col. Robert Worster (deceased), who was formerly one of the leading wholesale merchants of Keokuk, he being one of the founders of the Huskamp Boot & Shoe Company. He was a prominent Mason, and at one time ranked third among the Masons of the West.

Alfred Owens, planter and ginner, Cypress Ridge, Ark. This representative citizen was born in Gwinnett County, Ga., in 1826, and was the son of William Owen, who was a native of South Carolina and a farmer by occupation. The latter moved from South Carolina to Georgia, at an early day, and there resided until his death, in 1816. He had married Miss Mary Fisher and by her became the father of ten children, five of whom are now living: Tempey (wife of John Westmoreland), John, Wiley, James and Alfred. Both parents were members of the Methodist Episcopal Church, and the mother died in 1857. Alfred Owens was married to Miss Elizabeth J. Stone, in 1847, and to them were born nine children, three daughters and six sons, four only of whom are now living: W. F., Alfred L., Bryant T. and Joel M. Mr. Owens took an active part in the late war; enlisted in the infantry in 1861, under Capt. Joel Roper, and was captured in 1863, being kept a prisoner for two months. He was then paroled and after returning home was engaged in agricultural pursuits. He immigrated from Georgia to Arkansas in 1870, located in Monroe County, and is now the owner of 250 acres of land, with 160 acres under improvement. In 1883 he embarked in mercantile

pursuits, and the year following erected a gin. In 1873 he lost his wife, who was a worthy and consistent member of the Methodist Episcopal Church. In 1874 he met and afterward married Miss Harriet F. Breakefield. Both are members of the Methodist Episcopal Church. Mr. Owens raises an abundance of fine fruit: Apples, peaches, pears, etc., and is one of the wide-awake planters of the county. Mrs. Owens was born in Shelby County, Ala., in 1837, and her parents were both natives of South Carolina. The mother died in 1848, but the father is still living and is eighty-nine years of age. He has followed the occupation of a farmer all his life.

James C. Palmer, one of the leading planters of this county, was born in Phillips County, Ark., in 1860, and is a son of John C. Palmer, who came upon the stage of action in Lexington, Ky., in 1823. A lawyer by profession, he is now practicing in Helena, Ark., with substantial success. He was married in 1852 to Miss Margaret Shell, of that city, and they became the parents of seven children, six of whom are living: James C. (the principal of this sketch), Maggie (the wife of A. J. Gannon), Mamie, Sallie (widow of Capt. T. C. Hicks, of Hicksville, Ark.), Hattie (the wife of Horace Myrick) and Robert E. Mr. Palmer took part in the War with Mexico, and also in the Civil War. James C. Palmer was married in 1885 to Miss Lenora Mitchell, who was born in Phillips County, in 1862, a daughter of John and Jane Mitchell, natives of South Carolina and Arkansas, respectively. To this union were born two children: John C. and Wellman T. Mr. Palmer now lives in the old homestead, near the town of Palmer, consisting of 350 acres, with 125 acres under cultivation. This is a well-improved farm, having upon it a fine brick house that contains all of the modern improvements. He is a Democrat in politics, and is a prominent citizen of this community.

Robert W. Park was born in Lawrence District, S. C., in 1824, but since 1861 has been a resident and farmer of Monroe County, Ark. His parents, William and Jane (Word) Park, were born in the same county as himself, and there the father spent his life, his death occurring in 1828 or 1829.

He was a well-to-do farmer, and was in full communion with the Presbyterian Church at the time of his demise. His father, Andrew Park, was born in the Emerald Isle, but at an early day came to the United States, and settled in Lawrence District, S. C., where he reared a large family of sons and daughters. Thomas Word, the maternal grandfather, spent nearly all his life in the same county, but died near Gunter's Landing, Tenn., having been a carpenter by trade. Robert W. Park came with his mother to Arkansas, and her death occurred on the farm, where he now lives in 1861, she, like her husband, being a member of the Presbyterian Church. He was the youngest of five sons and one daughter, and is the only one now living; his school days were confined to about five years. In March, 1855, he was married to Charlotte, a daughter of Randall and Dorcas Ann Ramsey, who were born in Anderson County, S. C., and spent their declining years in Georgia, and they have reared, during their married life, a family of five sons and five daughters; three children died in infancy. In this State Mr. Park met his first wife, he and his mother, and her family having removed there in 1836. In 1860, as above stated, he came to Arkansas and purchased a farm of 240 acres, seven miles east of Clarendon, and by his own efforts soon had 130 acres under the plow and covered with waving grain. The country was very wild when he first came to this region, and bear, panthers and deer were very plentiful. He served all through the Civil War, being a member of Hawthorn's regiment of Arkansas Cavalry, and since that time has been a Democrat, politically. He and wife have been members of the Christian Church for many years.

James Park is one of the foremost and progressive farmers of this region and a sketch of his life is essential in this work in giving a history of its prominent men. His birth occurred in Lawrence County, S. C., November 24, 1824, and he is a son of Andrew and Isabella H. (Park) Park, both born in that county in 1797 and 1808, respectively, and were first cousins. They lived in that county until 1844, when they removed to the State of Mississippi, and soon after settled in what is now Calhoun County, but came to Monroe County, Ark., in 1856. Mr. Park was a practical and scientific planter, and owing to his progressive views and his energy he became quite wealthy. He died in 1868, and his wife in 1880, both having been members of the Presbyterian Church from early youth. The paternal grandfather, who also bore the name of Andrew, came with his only brother, James, also the grandfather of our subject on his mother's side, to America, and both were private soldiers of the American side throughout the Revolution. They settled in Lawrence County, S. C., and became extensive planters of that region, and were well known for their unimpeachable honesty and uprightness of character. They were men of exemplary habits in every respect, of religious natures, and were leaders in whatever enterprise they took an interest in. They left many descendants, who have followed in their footsteps, and all are upright and honorable citizens, some of whom became eminent in South Carolina in different professions and offices. They did much toward molding the moral and religious sentiment in the county where they lived, and were stanch members of the Presbyterian Church. Their native birthplace was County Tyrone, Ireland. Their grandson, James Park, the subject of this sketch, like the rest of their descendants, has followed their precepts and examples, and has won the respect and esteem of all with whom he has come in contact. He was the eldest of six sons and three daughters, three sons and three daughters being now alive. He received excellent educational advantages in his youth, and at the age of twenty-nine years was married at Okolona, Miss., to Catherine, a daughter of Uridge and Sarah (Smith) Whiffen, who were born, reared and married in England. After becoming the parents of two children, previous to 1832, they came to the United States, and after living in different localities in New York, they settled at Utica, where Mr. Whiffen died in 1837, at the untimely age of thirty-six years. His wife's death occurred on her farm near Carmi in the State of Illinois in 1887. Mr. Whiffin was a professor of languages and mathematics, and filled that position in both Buffalo and Utica. His wife was a teacher of music and French, and followed this occupation many years after the death of her husband in North Carolina, Mississippi, Louisiana and Illinois. Mrs. Park was born in Buffalo, N. Y., in 1835. Mr. Park came to Monroe County, Ark., in 1856, and settled on a woodland farm, and now owns 320 acres, and has 180 acres under cultivation. During 1868–69 he was engaged in merchandising in Clarendon, but since that time he has given his attention to farming. Prior to the late Civil War he was a Whig, but since that time has affiliated with the Democrat party. He is a member of the A. F. & A. M., and he and wife belong to the Christian Church.

Dr. William Park is one of Monroe County's most eminent physicians and surgeons, and was born in Lawrence District, S. C., in 1829, and is a son of Andrew and Isabella H. (Park) Park, who were first cousins. In 1844 they removed to Mississippi, and in 1856 came to Monroe County, Ark., and settled on a woodland farm six miles east of Clarendon, and here the father met with a violent death, being thrown from a buggy and killed, in 1868. His wife's death followed his in twelve years, both having been earnest members of the Presbyterian Church for many years. Andrew Park, the paternal grandfather, and James Park, the maternal grandfather, were brothers, born in Ireland, and came to America during the Revolutionary War and settled in South Carolina, James marrying an English lady and Andrew an Irish lady. Both were farmers and died in the State of their adoption. Dr. William Park is the third of six sons and three daughters, and his knowledge of the world up to manhood was only such as could be obtained on the home farm. After acquiring a good education in the common schools he concluded to engage in teaching in order to obtain means to carry on his medical education, and after two and a half years of this work, during which time he pursued his medical studies under his brother-in-law, Dr. T. F. Robinson, he entered the Medical Department of the University of Nashville (Tenn.), and at the end of two years, in 1856, graduated therefrom. He came immediately to Monroe County, Ark., whither his parents had just

moved, and entered upon his practice, and has acquired no inferior reputation as a physician and surgeon, being now the oldest resident practitioner of the county. For five years he has made his home in Clarendon, and in addition to the pleasant home which he now owns in the town, he is the owner of 320 acres of land in different farms, with 130 acres under cultivation. Although formerly a Whig in politics, casting his first presidential vote for Gen. Scott, since the late Civil War he has been a Democrat. He is a member of the A. F. & A. M., and he and his wife, whom he married in 1866, and whose maiden name was Sarah A. Brown, have long been members of the Old School Presbyterian Church. Mrs. Park was born in Fayette County, Tenn., and is the mother of two sons and one daughter. Her parents are Thomas J. and Fannie Brown, a sketch of whom appears in another part of this work.

J. T. Parker, planter, Cotton Plant, Ark. Mr. Parker is a typical Arkansas citizen, substantial, enterprising and progressive, and such a man as wields no small influence in the community where he makes his home. He came originally from St. Francis County, where his birth occurred in 1838. His parents, Archie and Mary (Adair) Parker, were natives respectively of Alabama and Kentucky and were married in St. Francis County, Ark., in 1835. Of the five children born to this marriage, only two are now living: J. T. and Prudy A., who is one of a pair of twins and who is now the wife of William Moore, of Kerr County, Texas. Archie Parker came to this State from Alabama with his parents at an early day, and became a very enterprising and substantial farmer. He was justice of the peace for a number of years and was deacon in the Baptist Church. He died in St. Francis County in 1843 and his widow afterward married William Dobkins in 1848, by whom she had three children: Samuel L., William A. and Robert P. Mrs. Dobkins died in St. Francis County in 1861 and had been a member of the Baptist Church for at least thirty years. Mr. Dobkins died in 1863. He was in the Confederate army during the late war. J. T. Parker passed his youthful days in assisting on the farm and in attending the common schools, where he received a fair education. He was married in 1861 to Miss Elizabeth Jones, a native of St. Francis County, born in 1843, and the daughter of Mrs. Richard Jones of Arkansas. Twelve children have been the result of this union, five daughters and seven sons, six of whom are still living: Nellie J., Margaret A., Sarah R., George T., Richard and Benjamin. In 1861 Mr. Parker enlisted in the infantry and served until 1864, when he was released on account of ill health. Politically he is a Democrat. After the war he bought a steam saw and grist mill in Woodruff County, Ark., and this he ran for three years, after which he resumed farming on 160 acres of land which he had purchased. He now owns 800 acres of good land, with 350 acres under cultivation and is one of the most practical and progressive farmers in the county. At the close of the war, Mr. Parker was, like many of his comrades, left without any of this world's goods, and what he has accumulated since is owing to his hard labor and good management. The parents of Mrs. Parker were natives of Tennessee and immigrated to Arkansas in 1820. Her father, Richard Jones, died in 1853 and her mother in 1884.

W. H. Peterson is the general manager of the Brinkley Argus, having successfully filled this position since December, 1888. He was born in the "Blue Grass" State in 1827, but the most of his early life was spent in the city of Philadelphia, but, notwithstanding the fact that he was in a city of schools," his early advantages for acquiring an education were very limited. At the age of fifteen years he began learning the printer's trade, which work continued to receive his attention until 1852; then, after a short residence in Illinois, he removed to Missouri, and in 1881 came to Beebe, Ark., and, as above stated, came to Brinkley in 1888. He has been in the newspaper business the greater part of his life, following his calling in different towns and cities of Missouri, and during his long career at this work he has acquired a thorough knowledge of journalism. He has always affiliated with the Democratic party, and has shown his approval of secret organizations by becoming a member of the Knights of Labor. During the Rebellion

he served for over three years in the Confederate army, being most of the time under Gen. Marmaduke. He has been married twice; first, in 1850, to Miss Ellen W. Lloyd, of Penn's Grove, N. J., who died in Missouri in 1868. His second union was consummated in 1870, his wife being a Miss Sarah Underwood, who died about 1879, leaving besides her husband two children to mourn her loss. Three children were born to the first union.

Samuel R. Pointer, a planter of Montgomery Township, Monroe County, Ark., is of English descent, and traces his ancestry back to his great-grandfather, who came with a brother to the United States, and settled in Virginia, where his son, Samuel (the grandfather of our subject), was born, his birth occurring in Halifax County. He was a soldier in the Revolutionary War. Dr. David Pointer (his son), was born and reared in Halifax County, Va., the former event taking place in 1802. After his marriage to Miss Obedience Torian, who was also born in Halifax County, her birth occurring in 1807, he removed to North Carolina, and in 1844 emigrated westward, settling in Marshall County, Miss., his death occurring at Como of that State, in 1871. He was a successful physician for a number of years, then turned planter, and in this occupation became wealthy. He was a member of the A. F. & A. M. The maternal grandfather, Torian, was born, and spent all his life in Halifax County, Va., and was also of English descent. Samuel R. Pointer was born in Caswell County, N. C., in 1828, and was the second in a family of eight children, and received his education, or the principal part of it, in the College of La Grange, Ala. In 1849, Eliza, a daughter of James and Esther (Hicks) Mooring, became his wife, she being a native of Marshall County, Miss., her parents coming to that county from their native State of North Carolina, and there dying in 1857 and 1856 respectively, both members of the Methodist Church, and the former a planter by occupation. Mrs. Pointer died at her parent's home in Mississippi, in 1856, having borne one son, who is also deceased. In 1858 Mr. Pointer espoused Susan E., a sister of his first wife, she having also been born in Marshall County, but he was called upon to mourn her death in July, 1884. Their family consisted of ten children, one son and five daughters only being alive: Willie (wife of R. D. Mayo), Susan E. (wife of L. Hall), Edwin M., Hallie, Ethel and Pearl. In 1853 Mr. Pointer came to Arkansas, and in 1856 to Monroe County, settling on a woodland farm six miles northeast of Indian Bay. His farm now comprises 800 acres, and he had about 500 acres under cultivation, all of which property he has earned by his own efforts and the help of his worthy wife. Politically he is a Democrat, and socially is a member of the A. F. & A. M., Indian Bay Lodge No. 259. He comes of a long-lived race of people, and although he has reached the age of sixty-one years, he shows but very little the ravages of time. His brothers and sisters are all living, the eldest sixty-four years of age, and the youngest forty-four. He has always been interested in the cause of education, and he has endeavored to give his children the advantages of a good education, three of whom are now attending an excellent school in Tennessee. During the war he served three years under Capt. Weatherly, who operated in Eastern Arkansas to protect the homes of the citizens, and although he furnished his own horse and ammunition he has never received any compensation.

Dr. W. D. Powell, planter and physician, Cotton Plant, Ark. Dr. W. D. Powell, the third living child born to Benjamin and Eliza (Fowler) Powell, owes his nativity to Henry County, Tenn., where his birth occurred in 1833. His father was a native of North Carolina, and was a mechanic and architect by occupation. He left his native State in 1820, journeyed to Tennessee, purchased land and followed farming for about twelve years. In 1831 he married Miss Fowler, who bore him eleven children, four sons and seven daughters, seven of whom are now living: Thomas A., Joseph D., W. D., Helen (now Mrs. John Kibble), Gurpana (wife of Allen Hill), Mollie (wife of George Bell), and Jennie A. Mrs. Powell was also a native of North Carolina and immigrated to Tennessee with her father in 1818. She was a member of the Baptist Church. Mr. Powell and family moved to Mississippi in 1854, and here he died in

Marshall County of that State, on September 15, 1889. He was a member of the Baptist Church and was a soldier in the Creek War. Dr. W. D. Powell began the practice of medicine in 1856 and the same year was united in marriage to Miss Almoina Sophner, a native of Tennessee, who bore him three children, only one, Georgiana, now living. Mrs. Powell died in 1869, and Mr. Powell was married the second time in 1881 to Miss Maria A. Hill. The fruits of this union were three children, only one of whom is now living: William Oscar. Dr. Powell was in the late war, enlisting in the cavalry, Monroe Regiment, Parson's brigade, in 1862. He served until after the surrender at Fort Smith, and then returned home, where he has since been engaged in agricultural pursuits. He immigrated from Mississippi to Arkansas in 1869, purchased 160 acres of land, and has about eighty acres under cultivation. He is progressive in his ideas, and is one of the leading farmers of this section. As above stated he began the practice of medicine in 1856, and this he has since continued in connection with farming. He is a clever, genial gentleman, and in his political views affiliates with the Democratic party.

D. B. Renfro, conceded to be among the prosperous merchants of Holly Grove, is a Tennesseean by birth, which occurred in 1843, and is a son of T. A. and Tizzie (Harrison) Renfro, natives of Kentucky and Tennessee. The senior Renfro was a prominent farmer of his county, and died in 1860, his wife dying within two hours after him. They were the parents of thirteen children, four of whom are still living: John H., T. A., Mary T. (the widow of S. H. Baulch) and D. B. (our subject). D. B. Renfro enlisted in the Confederate army, in 1861, in the Thirty-second Tennessee Infantry, and while in service was captured at Fort Donelson, and carried to Indianapolis, Ind., in February, 1862, and held until the following October, when he was exchanged. After his exchange he was again captured at Atlanta, in July, 1864, and taken to Indianapolis, where he was kept until April, 1865. At the close of hostilities he returned to Maury County, Tenn., and in 1866 immigrated to Arkansas, locating in Phillips County, where he made farming a means of gaining a livelihood. In 1871 he was married to Susan E. Smith, who was born in Monroe County, in 1849. Five children were born to this union: John W., Leroy G., D. B., Laura V. and Lizzie S. In 1872 Mr. Renfro moved to Holly Grove, and engaged in the mercantile business, and is now doing a large and lucrative trade, and carries a stock of goods which invoices about $2,000. He is the owner of a fine farm of 200 acres, with over 100 under cultivation, and also owns some real estate in the town of Holly Grove. He is numbered as a member of the A. F. & A. M., while he and his wife worship in the Presbyterian Church, to which they belong.

George A. Rich, chief engineer of the Brinkley, Helena & Indian Bay Railroad, was born in Wayne County, N. Y., in 1843, and like the majority of the native citizens of the "Empire State," he is energetic, intelligent and enterprising. He is the youngest of three sons and three daughters, and was reared on a farm in Hillsdale County, Mich., from the time he was four years old till he reached manhood, but his educational advantages were not of the best. After becoming his own man he remedied this defect by considerable self-application. In 1865 he was married to Caroline Nickerson, a native of Hillsdale County, Mich., and his second marriage was consummated in December, 1885, his wife, Jane Hanna, being a daughter of John and Ann Hanna, natives of Ireland, where they were reared and married. They afterward moved to Canada, where Mrs. Hanna died, her husband's death occurring in Michigan. Mrs. Rich was born in Canada. In 1874 Mr. Rich came to Brinkley, and was in the employ of Gunn & Black until that company was dissolved, serving them in various capacities, and cut the first ties and laid the first iron on what is now the Brinkley, Batesville Railroad. In 1881–82–83 he was in Mexico in the interests of the Mexican Central Railroad, and after a short stay in Arkansas he went to the Isthmus of Panama, where he spent one year having charge of a number of employés on the construction of the Panama Canal. Since then he has resided in Brinkley, and is connected with the Brinkley Car Works & Manufacturing

Company. Some years prior to coming West he was engaged in civil engineering in Michigan, and is a thorough master of that science. He is a conservative Republican in his political views, and is a member of the A. F. & A. M., K. of H., K. & L. of H., K. of P., and the I. O. O. F. His parents, Butler J. and Clarissa (Redfield) Rich, were born in Connecticut and Massachusetts, respectively, but their marriage took place in the State of New York. In 1847 they moved to Michigan, and here the father was engaged in farming until his death in 1865, his wife's death occurring in 1880. The paternal grandfather came from England to America with four brothers, and all were active participants in the Revolutionary War, taking part with the colonists. He died in the State of New York.

J. P. Ridout, whose prosperity and enterprise as a planter of Monroe County is well known, is a native of Tennessee, and a son of John and Lucy (Williams) Ridout, who came originally from Virginia and Tennessee, respectively. They removed to Arkansas in 1858, settling in Monroe County, Mr. Ridout being the owner, at the time of his death, in 1866, of 640 acres of land. He was a member of the A. F. & A. M. Of a family of eight children, four are still living: J. P., Martha G., Eliza (now Mrs. Hambrick) and Amanda (the wife of W. A. Roads). J. P. Ridout, the subject of this sketch, began farming for himself in 1866, after his father's demise, on rented land. In 1880 he moved to this county, and bought 240 acres of land, with seventy-five acres under cultivation. He was married in 1869 to Miss Sena Williams, whose birth occurred in Shelby County, Tenn., in 1852. They became the parents of eight children, four of whom are still living: Jennie, Luther, Joel R. and James P. Mr. and Mrs. Ridout are members of the Methodist Episcopal Church, South. He is a member of the Knights of Honor, and is a prominent factor in the Democracy of Cache Township. He owes his nativity to Fayette County, Tenn., where he was born in 1852.

James P. Roberts is a member of that well-known legal firm of Roberts & Manning, they being also abstractors and dealers in real estate. They command a large practice, and in the management of their cases show great ability and sagacity. Mr. Roberts, the senior member of the firm, is a native of Hamilton County, Tenn., born in 1851, and is a son of John and Louisa (Vaughn) Roberts, the former a native of Maryland and the latter of Tennessee. They were married in the latter State and in 1866 came to Phillips County, the father's death occurring here in 1869 and the mother's in 1870. They were prosperous tillers of the soil and Mr. Roberts was collecting officer of Hamilton County for a number of years, and during the war served as Government agent for the Confederate States. His father, James Roberts, was of English descent, born in Virginia. The maternal grandfather was Jesse Vaughn. James P. Roberts is the first of four sons and four daughters, and was reared to a farm life, receiving the advantages of the common schools, which he improved to the utmost, also making the most of his advantages while an attendant at the Savannah (Tenn.) Academy. He farmed in Phillips County, Ark., until 1875, then began the practice of law, and the same progress which marked his advancement at school has attended him in his professional career. He is a close student, well versed in law, and possesses in more than an ordinary degree the natural attributes essential to a successful career at the bar and in public. His worth and ability received a just recognition, and in 1880 he was elected to represent Phillips County in the State legislature, and was re-elected in 1884. He has been a member of several important committees, especially those pertaining to courts, and has always taken a deep interest in the political affairs of his county and State. Although his first presidential vote was cast for Grant, in 1872, he is now a Democrat in his political views. He is a member of the K. of H., the K. & L. of H., the K. of P. at Clarendon and the American Legion of Honor. His wife, whose maiden name was Lulu Boardman and whom he married in September, 1872, was born in the State of Kentucky, and is a daughter of Edward T. and Elizabeth Boardman, natives, respectively, of New York and Kentucky. They were married in Henderson, Ky., and after living some years in Indiana, came, in 1869, to Phillips County, Ark.,

where Mr. Boardman died, in 1886. His wife is living, a member of the Baptist Church. Mr. and Mrs. Roberts are the parents of four children, one son and three daughters.

F. J. Robinson's career in life, as far as its connection with industrial affairs is concerned, might be divided into two periods, that during which he was occupied in merchandising, and his more recent experience in the capacity of a farmer. In each of these callings he has had the energy and push to attain success, and he seems admirably fitted for the business in which he is now engaged. He was born in Shelby County, Tenn., in 1853, and is a son of F. M. and E. A. (Erwin) Robinson, the father being also a native of that State, born in 1828. In 1859 he came with his wife and family to Monroe County, Ark., and settled at Holly Grove, where he spent his declining years, and died in 1882, having been engaged in merchandising and farming. He and his wife (who died in 1880) were members of the Baptist Church, and he was quite a politician, and besides holding the office of justice of the peace, he represented Monroe County in the State legislature from 1874 to 1876. The maternal grandfather, John Erwin, was a farmer of Tennessee. F. J. Robinson is the eldest of six children, and in his youth received but meager educational advantages as he was obliged to assist his father in improving the home place. In 1876 he was united in marriage to Lois, daughter of D. A. L. and Anna Wilson, who were formerly from North Carolina, but died in Monroe County, Ark., and their union was blessed by the birth of four children. Mr. Robinson lived at Indian Bay from 1868 to 1882, engaged in merchandising and farming, but since the latter date has given his time and attention solely to farming, at which he has been remarkably successful. He has a fine farm of 800 acres, and has about 300 acres under cultivation, all of which he has gained since 1882. Politically he is a Democrat, and his first vote was cast for Tilden, in 1876. His wife is in communion with the Cumberland Presbyterian Church.

J. W. B. Robinson is the efficient sheriff and tax collector of Monroe County, Ark., and was born in Serepta, Miss., in 1856, being a son of Dr. Thomas F. and Nancy S. (Park) Robinson, natives of the "Palmetto" State. They were married in Mississippi in 1849, and in 1856 came to Monroe County and settled eight miles east of Clarendon, taking up their abode on a woodland farm, on which the father died the same year. On this farm his family resided until 1886, when they removed to Clarendon. Mrs. Robinson is a member of the Old School Presbyterian Church, of which the father was an elder during his lifetime. He was a very successful medical practitioner, and owing to his early death but little is known of his parents or other relatives. He left his home in South Carolina when quite young and went first to Alabama, and thence to Mississippi, where he was married. Our subject is the youngest of his four children and is now the only one living. Like so many of the substantial citizens of this county at the present time, he was initiated into the mysteries of farm life from the very first, and this continued to be his calling up to within a few years of 1886, when he was elected to the office of sheriff and county collector, and has made an efficient officer. He first voted for Hancock for the presidency in 1880, and has always affiliated with the Democratic party. The old homestead, of which he is the owner, comprises 240 acres, with about 125 acres under cultivation, and he also owns a good house and lot in Clarendon. The history of Mrs. Robinson's family will be found in a sketch of Dr. William Park, who is her brother.

W. F. Sain, a prominent planter of this township, was born in Gibson County, Tenn., in 1841, and is a son of William Sain, deceased, who was a native of North Carolina, and whose first wife was Virginia Ann Goward, of North Carolina; she being the mother of two children: Henry and Mary. He removed to Gibson County, Tenn., after his wife died, and was there married to Frances Lathan, originally of North Carolina, and who died in 1886. She was the mother of four children: Nancy J. (the wife of Josiah Cooper, of Tennessee), W. F. (the principal of this sketch), John A. and James A. Mr. Sain belonged to the Masonic lodge, and to

the Presbyterian Church. He died in 1848. W. F. Sain was a soldier in the late war, enlisting in the Thirty-fourth Mississippi Infantry, and served until his capture at Lookout Mountain, and was taken to Rock Island, Ill., where he was held until about the close of the war. He then returned to Byhalia, Miss., in 1877, and then removed to Germantown, Penn., where he remained until 1881, thence to Arkansas and located within five miles of Forrest City. In 1883 he moved to this county and bought his present farm of 160 acres. Mr. Sain was married in 1861 to Mildred Alexander, a daughter of Moses and Margaret Alexander. They were the parents of nine children, all of whom are still living: William C., J. A. S., E. A. S., Ollie B., Robert E., T. C. S., V. L. S., Mamie A. and Lelia L. S. They belong to the Presbyterian Church, of which Mr. Sain is one of the elders and an influential member.

Louis Salinger. Well directed energy and honorable dealings always tell in business, as indeed in everything else. Mr. Salinger has conducted a very prosperous business since 1871 and during the whole time that has elapsed his trade has advanced by rapid strides, until to-day he is enjoying one of the best retail trades in Brinkley. His stock of goods is well selected and will invoice at about $10,000, the sales of which will amount to $35,000 annually. Mr. Salinger was born in Prussia in 1840, and like all natives of the Fatherland, he acquired a good education. When about fourteen years of age he and an elder brother determined to seek their fortune in the New World, and after spending five years in the States of Indiana and Illinois they came to Arkansas and made their home in Woodruff and Monroe Counties. Two years later Louis Salinger joined the Fifth Arkansas Infantry and was under Gens. Hardy, Johnston and Beauregard. While on duty in Kentucky he was captured just before the fight at Perryville, but was soon after released on bond and returned North and resumed his farming operations in Arkansas. In 1866 he engaged in the mercantile business at Augusta, continuing until 1870, and in 1871 he returned to his native land and brought his mother, whose maiden name was Rebecca Cohn, with him to America, her death occurring in the city of St. Louis in 1881. The father, Saul Salinger, died during our subject's youth, having been a farmer in the old country. In 1872 Mr. Salinger was united in marriage to Miss Lena Fillman. He is one of the wealthy men of the county and, besides owning about 2,000 acres of land in Monroe County, he has a splendid brick residence in Brinkley, which was erected in 1887, and a substantial and commodious brick business block which was built in 1888. In 1882 he gave up merchandising and turned his attention to the real-estate business, but since 1887 has been following his old calling. He is a member of the A. F. & A. M., the K. of P. and the K. & L. of H.

James S. Seale. An important branch of industry is that represented by Mr. Seale, carpenter, blacksmith and general wood workman of Clarendon, and his superior work has entitled him to the distinction of a representative business man. He was born in Shelby County, Ala., in 1850, a son of Willoughby and Sarah (Ford) Seale, who were born in South Carolina and Georgia, in 1818 and 1829, respectively. They were married in Shelby County, Ala., and are still living there, the father being a prominent farmer and wagon maker. He served in the Confederate army the last year of the war. His father, Herod Seale, served in the War of 1812, was a mechanic by trade, and died in Calhoun County, Miss., in 1875. Rev. John Ford, the maternal grandfather, was a Methodist minister and died in Macon, Ga. James S. Seale is the second in a family of four sons and one daughter, and was brought up and educated in the State of Alabama, but his advantages, as far as his schooling was concerned, were very limited indeed. He learned the trade of wagon maker of his father in his youth, and in 1873 came to Monroe County, Ark., and until 1887 lived on a farm four miles north of Clarendon, since which time he has been a resident of the town, and has worked at his trade the greater part of the time and is considered an excellent carpenter and blacksmith. Besides his fertile farm of 250 acres, of which 100 acres are under cultivation, he owns an excellent house and lot in town, all of which is the result of earnest

and consistent endeavor on his part. He has always been a Democrat in his political views, and his first presidential vote was cast for Greeley, in 1872. He belongs to the Knights of Honor, and his wife, whom he married in 1875 and whose maiden name was Mattie Arnold, is a member of the Cumberland Presbyterian Church. She was born in Calhoun County, Miss., is the mother of five children, three daughters living, and is a daughter of Warren Arnold.

Miles A. Simmons, Jr., a merchant and planter of Palmer Station, is a son of Miles A. Simmons, Sr., a resident of Mississippi, who was born in Georgia in 1820, of English ancestry. He was married in 1842 to Miss Elizabeth Revel, born in the State of North Carolina in 1825. They were the parents of ten children, four of whom are still living: Charles F., Miles A., Jr. (the principal of this sketch), Virginia W. (the wife of John E. Done) and Eazer P. Mr. Simmons is the patentee and manufacturer of the famous "Simmons Liver Regulator," and has been engaged in the manufacture and sale of that medicine for thirty-nine years, now, however, being retired from business. He and his wife are living in the State of Mississippi, where they moved in 1844. He is a member of the Masonic order and of the Methodist Episcopal Church. His wife belongs to the Baptist Church. Miles A. Simmons, Jr., was born in Mississippi in 1866, and was married at the age of twenty to Miss Inez L. Smith, daughter of Capt. W. F. and Electa Smith. She was born in Springfield, Ill., in 1866. They have one son, William F. Mr. Simmons commenced clerking in his brother's drug store at the age of eighteen, and two years later bought his brother's interest, a short time after selling out to his father and removing to St. Louis, where he was engaged as book-keeper. In 1887 he came to Palmer, and was occupied in getting out railroad ties until 1889, when he started in the mercantile business, his present calling. He is also postmaster of Palmer, and is the railroad agent at that place. Besides his other interests he owns a large steam cotton-gin and cornmill, and a farm of 640 acres with some eighty acres under cultivation. Mr. Simmons is a member of the K. of H., and of the Cumberland Presbyterian Church, as is also his wife.

Stephen Simons, a progressive and successful farmer of Monroe County, is a native of Alabama, his father, William Simons, having come originally from Massachusetts. He was a bridge builder and carpenter by trade, which occupation he followed up to the late war. He then erected a steam grist-mill in Alabama, and operated it until his death in 1877. He married Susan D. Wheelock, a native of Alabama and a member of the Methodist Episcopal Church, who died in 1861. They were the parents of ten children, four still living: Stephen (our subject), Cornelia (the wife of A. S. Neeley, of Kentucky), Martin E. and John. Stephen Simons was born in 1848, and remained in his native State until 1874, when he removed to Arkansas, settling in this county. He worked at the carpenter's trade the first two years, and for three years following was engaged in the saloon business, after which he began farming on his present farm of 168 acres, with sixty acres under cultivation. He was married in 1878 to Miss Nancy A. Brown, daughter of Jesse and Mary Brown. She was born in this county in 1854. Her parents are now dead, her father having been killed in the late war, and her mother dying in 1877. Mr. Simons is an influential Democrat in political circles and a leading man in his township.

Washington Simpson, planter, Cotton Plant, Ark. Of that sturdy and independent class, the farmers of Arkansas, none are possessed of more genuine merit and a stronger character than he whose name stands at the head of this sketch. Mr. Simpson first saw the light in Morgan County, Ala., January 21, 1823, and was one of eleven children, eight sons and three daughters, born to the union of Samuel and Elizabeth (Owen) Simpson. The father was born in the Old Dominion, was a farmer by occupation, and, in connection, carried on the tanner's trade for many years. He immigrated from Alabama to La Fayette County, Miss., in 1837, and there carried on both his former occupations, until 1852, when he moved to Arkansas, locating in St. Francis County. He took up land, built a cabin, and there remained until his death, which occurred in 1860. His wife died in Monroe County, in about 1857. She was a member of the Baptist Church for many years. Of the large family born to his parents, Washington Simpson is the only one now living, although all were reared to maturity. He was married in 1847 to Miss Martha Davis, and they became the parents of seven children, of whom only three are now living: Josiah A., Allice M. and Mary E. (the widow of John C. Madox). The mother of these children died in 1860; she was a member of the Methodist Episcopal Church. Two years later Mr. Simpson took for his second wife Miss Frances Henderson, who died in 1869. In 1871 he married Miss Mary A. Anderson, who bore him nine children, six daughters and three sons, seven of whom are living: Alexander A., John W., Anna P., Mittie E., Mary O., Margaret A. and Hassie P. Mr. Simpson owns 207 acres of land, has about 120 acres under cultivation, and is a very successful farmer. In 1863 he enlisted in the infantry under Capt. Wilson, and served until the surrender at Wittsburg, in 1865. He filled the position of constable for eight years in this county, and he and Mrs. Simpson are members of the Baptist Church. Mrs. Simpson was born in La Fayette County, Miss., in 1853, and came to Arkansas with her father in 1859. He was a farmer, and died in 1862. Her mother died in 1885. Both were members of the Baptist Church.

William K. Sims is a dealer in drugs and medicines at Brinkley, Ark., and has been established in business at this point since February, 1883, his stock of goods amounting to about $2,500. He was born near Helena, Ark., in 1860, and is a son of Dr. William K. and Mary (Scaife) Sims, who were born, reared and married in the "Palmetto State," and there made their home until some years prior to the late Civil War, when they came west and settled in Phillips County, Ark. About the time of the opening of hostilities Mr. Sims died, and his family returned to South Carolina, but liking the West best, and thinking the prospects for becoming rich much better here than at their old home, they returned to Arkansas in 1868. From that time until 1883 they made their home in Phillips County, then came to Brinkley where the mother's demise occurred on November 9, 1885, she having been an earnest member of the Baptist Church for many years, as was her husband. The latter was a successful physician for many years, a graduate of his profession, and was a son of William Sims, who was a Virginian, but died in South Carolina, a well-to-do farmer. The maternal grandfather, Vida Scaipe, was of Welsh descent, and is supposed to have been born in South Carolina, but came to Phillips County, Ark., in 1868. William K. Sims is the youngest of three children born to his parents, and spent his youth in tilling the soil and acquiring a common-school education. He began for himself at the age of fourteen years as a farm hand, continuing until he was about twenty-three years old, in the meantime clerking in Helena part of the time, and previous to coming to Brinkley he clerked in a drug store in Trenton, Ark., for one year. Since establishing himself in business at Brinkley, he has become one of the leading druggists of the town, and by his thorough knowledge of drugs, his accuracy, intelligence and honesty, he has established a large and lucrative trade. From October, 1885, to October, 1889, he was postmaster of the town, being appointed to the position by President Cleveland. Mr. Sims is a Democrat, and is quite well-to-do for a young man, being the owner of an excellent business lot on Main Street.

William E. Spencer is the efficient editor of the Monroe County Sun, published at Clarendon, and owing to the admirable manner in which it is conducted it has had a most flattering increase in its circulation. It has been in existence since 1876, and has already become one of the leading newspapers in the State. Mr. Spencer was born in Minneapolis, Minn., in 1865, and is a son of Abraham and Agnes (McMurray) Spencer, who were born in Liverpool, England, and Glasgow, Scotland, respectively. They were married in the mother's native land, and in 1863 removed to Quebec, Canada, and the following year to the State of Minnesota, where their son, William E., was born. In the year 1871 they removed to Indian Bay, Ark., and in 1881 to Clarendon. Mrs. Spencer died

three years previous, having been an earnest member of the Presbyterian Church for many years. Mr. Spencer was a machinist by trade, and a member of the Baptist Church. William E. Spencer is the fourth of their five children, two sons and three daughters, and in his youth received a common-school education in Winchester, Tenn. At the early age of eight years he began learning the printer's trade in an office of his own, and after reaching a suitable age began clerking in his father's hardware store, continuing until 1886, when he began editing the Monroe County Sun, which has already become one of the well-established journals of the State, and is published in the interests of the Democrat party, of which Mr. Spencer has always been a member, his first presidential vote being cast for Cleveland. He belongs to the Arkansas Press Association and is a member of the K. of H. and K. of P. In November, 1888, he was married at Malta Bend, Mo., by the Rev. W. B. Palmore, to Miss Ella Bonner, who was born in Clarendon, is a member of the Methodist Church, a daughter of W. H. Bonner, who was a prominent farmer and resided in Monroe from 1854 until his death in 1887. He was assessor of the county from 1882 till 1886.

William Grant Sutton has been a resident of this State since 1853. He was born in Fayette County, Tenn., in 1853, but his parents came to Arkansas that year, and located in this county, where they purchased land. His parents were Thomas and Sarah (Weeks) Sutton. Thomas Sutton was born in Perquimans County, N. C., in 1804, and was a son of Thomas and Helena (Raper) Sutton, both of English descent. On coming to this county he purchased 240 acres of land, almost all in timber, which he improved and made a good farm, living upon it until his death, August 28, 1854. Mrs. Sutton was born in 1815, and was married to the father of our subject in 1831, and died in March, 1860. Thomas Sutton was the father of fourteen children, this being his second marriage; there were eleven children, three of whom are living: Susan F. (the wife of J. M. Kerr), Anna (the wife of Rev. R. B. Cavett) and William G. (our subject). The latter, the youngest of the family, was an infant at the death of his father. He now owns a fine farm of 174 acres, with sixty acres under cultivation. He is a well-known Democrat of Duncan Township, and highly spoken of by all who have become acquainted with him.

Judge James S. Thomas is an attorney at law, of Clarendon, and is a member of the legal firm of Ewan & Thomas. He born in Anson County, N. C., in 1844, and is a son of A. J. and Eliza C. (Smith) Thomas, of South Carolina and North Carolina, respectively, the former's birth occurring in 1813. They were married in North Carolina, in 1844, and moved soon after to Weakley County, Tenn., and in 1858 to Prairie County, Ark., where his wife died in October, 1867. Mr. Thomas is still living, and is a planter by trade, and a member of the Methodist Church and the A. F. & A. M. John Thomas, the grandfather, was of Welsh descent, a native of South Carolina, who died in Weakley County, Tenn. Our subject's father has been married three times, his second wife bearing him seven children, of whom James S. is the eldest. He was reared to the duties of a farm life and acquired a limited education in the country schools. In 1861 he joined Company E, First Arkansas Infantry, and was discharged at Fort Pillow on account of ill health, but soon recovered and rejoined the army, becoming a member of the Fourth Arkansas Battalion. He was captured at Island No. 10, and was confined at Camp Chase for some time, after which he was removed to Johnson's Island, and was exchanged in 1862. He was then given a position in the commissary department, and in 1863 was transferred to the Trans-Mississippi Department, and served in the quartermaster's department until the close of the war. He held all the ranks, from that of a private to captain, being made the latter in December, 1862. He surrendered at Gilmore, Tex., in June, 1865, and returned to his home and friends, and took up the study of law. After becoming thoroughly prepared to enter upon his practice, he located in Des Arc, where he was a successful practitioner until 1888, since which time he has been in Clarendon. In 1870 he was elected to repre-

sent Prairie County in the State legislature, and in 1874 was chosen tax collector, filling this position until again elected to the legislature in 1876, which position he held by re-election until 1880. In 1882 he was elected county and probate judge, and served by re-election six years, continuing during this time the practice of law. He spent five or six years in the newspaper business, being editor of the Prairie County Appeal, and afterward edited the Des Arc Citizen until his removal to Clarendon, and during his editorial career served for some time as president and vice-president of the Arkansas Press Association. He edited his papers in the interest of the Democrat party, with which he has always affiliated, and by his pen did much to sway the politics, of not only his county, but the State also. He has shown his brotherly spirit by joining the Masons and the Knights of Honor, and is a member of White River Lodge No. 37, of Des Arc in the former order and Clarendon Lodge in the latter. In 1867 he was married to Anna, a daughter of E. B. and N. N. Powell, who were born, reared and married in Tennessee. They removed to Prairie County, Ark., in 1861, and are there still living. Mrs. Thomas was born in Tennessee, and by Mr. Thomas is the mother of one son and two daughters. She has been a member of the Methodist Church for many years. Mr. Thomas is a large real-estate holder, and owns 1,500 acres of land in Prairie County. The first of the family to come to America, was shipped from Wales in a box to avoid punishment, as he had participated in a rebellion, and one of his descendants was afterward a general in the Revolutionary War.

Frank B. Toms is a planter residing near Clarendon, Ark., and was born in Perquimans County, N. C., in 1847, being the eldest of six children born to Henry C. and Susan M. (Lynch) Toms, also of that State, born February 6, 1825, and in December, 1829, respectively. They were married in their native State, in 1846, and there resided until 1851, then came to Monroe County, Ark., and settled on a woodland farm, about five miles southeast of Clarendon. Mr. Toms was a man of very limited means at that time, and came west in order to make a home for his family, and in this succeeded, for at the time of his death he was the owner of a good farm. He was a man possessing high moral principles, temperate, industrious and of exemplary habits, and his death, which occurred in 1859, while he was representing his lodge in the Masonic Grand Lodge at Little Rock, was deeply lamented, not only by his immediate family, but by all who knew him as well. His wife was a consistent member of the Methodist Church, and died in 1868. The paternal grandparents, Francis B. and Sarah Toms, were probably born and married in England, and were early emigrants to and farmers of the "Old North State." Richard and Nancy Lynch, the maternal grandparents, were also early settlers of North Carolina, from Ireland, in which country they were born, reared and married. They came to this country on account of persecution, the father having participated in a rebellion in his native land. Both died in North Carolina. Frank B. Toms and his sister Sarah, widow of A. W. Harris, are the only ones of their father's family now living. The former spent his early days on a farm, and after his father's untimely death, the principal care of the family devolved on him. This left him with but little chance of acquiring an education, but he remained faithful to his trust until his marriage, in 1877, to Fannie, a daughter of Reuben and Rebecca Harrod, natives respectively of Louisiana and Mississippi, and very early settlers of Monroe County, Ark. The father was a soldier in the Confederate States army, a farmer by occupation, and died in 1872, followed by his wife two years later. Mrs. Toms was born in Monroe County, and she and Mr. Toms are the parents of one daughter. Mr. Toms lived on the old farm, on which his father settled, until 1888, when he removed to Clarendon, where he now owns a comfortable and commodious home. His farm of 160 acres comprises some of the best land in the county, and he has eighty acres under cultivation, all being acquired by his own good management and industry. He is a Democrat, his first presidential vote being cast for Greeley, in 1872, and he is a Royal Arch Mason. He also belongs to the K. of

H., and in his religious views is a Methodist, his wife being a member of the Cumberland Presbyterian Church.

B. P. Vanderford, by reason of his association with the affairs of this county as a planter, deserves prominent mention. He is the only one living of a family of twelve children born to W. H. and Rhoda A. (Harris) Vanderford, natives of North Carolina. They removed from that State to Tennessee, and from there to Arkansas, locating in Jackson County, where he died in 1867, and his wife three years later. B. P. Vanderford was born in Buncombe County, N. C., in 1842. He was married in 1866 to Miss Mary E. Foster, a daughter of Josiah and Mary Foster, of this State. They are the parents of seven children, five still living: W. H., L. O., Jennie (the wife of J. H. Simson), B. H. and B. C. Mr. Vanderford enlisted in the Confederate army in 1861, and served until the battle of Chickamauga, in which he was wounded, being unable to again participate in active service. After the war he returned to Jackson County, and resumed farming, in 1871 removing to this county. He now owns a fine farm of 180 acres, with sixty acres under cultivation, and good buildings, etc. He is a prominent Democrat, and has served as justice of the peace since 1874, also belonging to the Knights of Honor. His wife is a member of the Methodist Episcopal Church.

Capt. Milton H. Vaughan, notary public, jeweler and photographer, of Brinkley, Ark., was born in Tipton County, Tenn., in 1839, and is a son of Edwin and Susan (Owen) Vaughan, both of whom were born near Halifax, Va. They removed to Tennessee in their youth and there became acquainted and married, the mother's death occurring about 1854, after having borne a family of eleven children, four sons and seven daughters. Mr. Vaughan afterward removed to Arkansas, where he took a second wife, and here spent the rest of his days, his death occurring in 1857 or 1858, at about the age of fifty-five years. He was a farmer by occupation and a man who possessed sterling traits of character, which won him the respect and confidence of his fellow-men. Capt.

Milton H. Vaughan was the youngest of his father's family, and in his youth received such education as usually falls to the lot of the farmer's boy. When about fifteen years of age he began learning photography in Memphis, but upon the breaking out of the Rebellion he gave up this work and assisted in organizing Company E of the Tenth Arkansas Infantry, of Springfield, Conway County, Ark., and was elected first lieutenant, being promoted to captain soon after. His brother, E. L., was lieutenant of the regiment. The first engagement in which he participated was Shiloh, but he soon after went to Louisiana and was soon after taken prisoner at the fall of Port Hudson. He was taken to Johnson's Island and kept a prisoner until June 9, 1865, when he was released and returned home. Two years were spent in active duty and two in prison. After his return to West Point, Ark., he was married in September, 1865, to Susan Oliphant, a native of Tennessee, who died in 1870, having borne four children, one son only being now alive: Thomas L. His second marriage took place in 1875, his wife, Sallie Lynch, being a daughter of William B. and Eliza J. Lynch, whose sketch will be found elsewhere in this volume. Mrs. Vaughan was born in Mississippi and by Mr. Vaughan is the mother of a daughter named Mabel. After being engaged in the jewelry business in West Point for a few years Mr. Vaughan removed to Searcy, where he made his home until after his second marriage, since which time he has been a resident of Brinkley. He has been a successful jeweler and photographer, and as far as his finances are concerned he is in independent circumstances. He has a pleasant home on New York Avenue, and his business house is commodious and substantial. He has been a notary public for the past thirteen years and has filled the position of mayor of the town several terms, has been justice of the peace one term, and has been an alderman and recorder of the city. He is an A. F. & A. M., a K. of H., and belongs to the K. & L. of H. and the K. of L. He was formerly a member of the I. O. O. F. He is a Democrat, and he and his wife are members of the Methodist Episcopal Church.

35

Capt. J. W. Walker is one of the leading planters of the county and enjoys the reputation of being, not only a substantial and progressive farmer, but an intelligent and thoroughly posted man in all public affairs. He is a native Tennesseean, born in White County, in 1837, and is a son of David and Polly (Stulls) Walker, both of whom were Virginians, and were probably married there. At an early date they removed to Hawkins County, East Tenn., thence to White County, Middle Tenn., and when the subject of this sketch was a lad, went to Van Buren County, where they resided for several years, his mother dying in February and his father in April of the same year. The father was a farmer, of Irish descent and a son of Micager Walker, who was born in Ireland and came to the United States prior to the American Revolution, and took part in that war. After living some years in Virginia he removed to Tennessee and died in Van Buren County, at the age of one hundred and seven years, his demise occurring since the close of the Civil War. Capt. J. W. Walker, the fifth of eleven children, is the only one living in Monroe County. He acquired only a moderate education in the common schools, and upon the death of his parents, began doing for himself and made his home with one man for nine years, working for wages four years and being a partner five years, becoming thoroughly familiar with stock trading. In 1860 he married Bettie Rankins, who was born in Bledsoe County, Tenn., and died in 1863, leaving one son, who died in 1885, at the untimely age of twenty-five years. Mr. Walker's second marriage took place in 1882, his wife being Mrs. Sallie Walls, a daughter of James H. and Eleanor D. Branch, natives of Wilson County, Tenn. They were married in 1840, and removed to West Tennessee, in 1851, living there eight years and going thence to Monroe County, in 1859, where Mr. Branch died, in 1867, and his wife in 1885. She was a member of the Christian Church. Mr. Branch was a well-to-do farmer. Mrs. Walker was born in Wilson County, Tenn., in 1847, and married Allen V. Walls in 1868. By her first husband she became the mother of three children, only one of whom is living. She and Mr. Walker had one child that is now deceased. Mr. Walker lacked one day of serving four years in the Confederate army, and during his term of service, while participating in different battles, was wounded four times and had five horses shot from under him. The first year he was a member of Branhan's battalion of East Tennessee Cavalry, and operated in East and Middle Tennessee and Kentucky. His battalion was afterward consolidated with Company I, Eighth Tennessee, under Gen. G. D. Dibrell, with whom he remained, operating in nearly all the Southern States east of the Mississippi River, until the close of the war. During this time he served as captain and was a gallant and faithful officer. He was in many severe engagements, among which may be mentioned Fishing Creek, Camp Goggins (Ky.), Murfreesboro, Neely's Bend, Lexington, Humboldt, Union City, Trenton, Parker's Cross Roads, Fort Donelson, Thompson's Station, Franklin, Shelbyville, Wild Cat Bridge, Chickamauga, Dalton, Resaca, Missionary Ridge, New Hope Church, Lost Mountain, Wainesboro, (S. C.), Landersville and Marietta, (Ga.). He was wounded at Camp Goggins, Wild Cat Bridge, Parker's Cross Roads and Landersville, and was captured at Wild Cat Bridge (Tenn.), August 9, 1863; being wounded severely he was at once paroled. He surrendered near Washington, Ga., May 11, 1865, and in 1866 came to Clarendon and was engaged in farming and rafting logs until in 1873, when he found employment in the sheriff's office, continuing as deputy seven years. He was elected sheriff of the county in 1884, but at the end of two years resumed farming on his land, comprising 176 acres near the town. He has in all, some 1,200 acres, about 600 under cultivation, nearly one-half of which has been acquired by his own efforts since coming to Arkansas. He raises some fine stock. He is a Democrat, though formerly a Whig, and during Cleveland's administration served one year as deputy United States marshal. He has been a member of the A. F. & A. M. for twenty years, and is now residing on the farm formerly owned by ex-Gov. Hughes. He is a member of the Methodist Episcopal Church. His wife is a member of the Cumberland Presbyterian Church.

William B. Wellborn, a merchant and an extensive land owner of Monroe County, commenced work for himself in 1871 as superintendent of a large plantation, at $50 per month. The following year he rented land and was engaged in farming one year, in 1873 embarking in the mercantile business in what is known as Duncan Station, where he has been in business ever since. He was born in Knoxville County, Miss., in 1851, the son of Jones D. and Lucy (Tate) Wellborn. The father was born in Madison County, Ala., in 1824, and was a son of Isaac S. Wellborn, of English and Irish origin. He was a planter and stockman, also owning a stage line in Monroe County, Ark., in 1855, before there were any railroads in that part of the State. He was married to Miss Lucy Tate, in Madison County, Ala., in 1848, she having been born in that county in 1827. They had a family of four children, three of whom are still living: Elizabeth I. (wife of W. W. Capps, of Memphis, Tenn.), Lucy C. (the wife of E. F. Maberry, of Prairie County, Ark.) and William B. (the principal of this article). J. D. Wellborn on leaving Alabama went to Tennessee, and from there to Mississippi in 1850, coming thence to Arkansas in 1853. He bought a farm in this county, where he made his home until his death in 1857, one year after the final summons of his wife. In addition to his business at Duncan Mr. Wellborn owns and conducts a large plantation, consisting of 1,900 acres of fine land, with 700 acres under cultivation. He was married in January, 1875, to Miss Lillian E. Kerr, daughter of W. D. and Lizzie D. Kerr; she was born in Alabama in 1856. They are the parents of five children, four of whom survive: Henry, Jennie E., Lucy A. and Barton G. He is a member of the A. F. & A. M., of the K. of P., and of the K. of G. R. Mrs. Wellborn belongs to the Methodist Episcopal Church.

Dr. Robert M. West has, by his assiduous attention to all his patients, acquired a large and steadily increasing practice, and has gained the confidence of all as a clever and scientific practitioner. He is a member of the firm of West & Thomas, of Clarendon, and was born in Henderson County, W. Tenn., July 6, 1832, being the youngest of seven sons and five daughters born to Easton and Mary E. (Simmons) West, born in North Carolina in 1775 and 1782, respectively. After their marriage, which took place in their native State, they removed to Virginia, and a few years later to West Tennessee, where they were among the early settlers. He was very active in clearing the forests, and settled on twenty-two different farms in as many years, being a resident of different counties. Both he and wife died in Humboldt, Tenn., in 1866, members of many years' standing in the Baptist Church, of which Mr. West was a deacon for seventy-two years. His father was an Irishman, and served in the Revolutionary War from North Carolina. A. L. Simmons, the maternal grandfather, was of Irish-Scotch descent, a Virginian, and also a Revolutionary soldier. Dr. Robert M. West is the only one of his father's family who is now living, to his knowledge. After remaining at home and assisting his father until he was fourteen years of age, he began working for himself as a farm hand, but at the end of two years, seeing the need of a better education, he attended a five-months' term of school, working seven months for a farmer of the region to pay for his schooling. He then concluded to try how teaching the young idea suited him, and finding that his first term was a success, and liking the work, he followed it three years in West Tennessee, in the meantime devoting his spare time to the study of medicine. In 1860 he graduated from the Medical Department of the University of Louisville, Ky., but had previously begun practicing in Tennessee, in 1858. He returned there after graduating, but in April, 1862, he joined Company H, Tenth Tennessee Cavalry, of Gen. Forrest's army, but at the end of seven months was made assistant-surgeon of the Fifteenth Tennessee Regiment, and in 1864 was transferred to the examining board of conscripts, in which capacity he served until the cessation of hostilities. He resumed his practice in Tennessee, but in 1871 came to Clarendon, where he has since practiced his profession with much success. He has been president of the Monroe County Examining Board since its organization; is Senior War-

den of Cache Lodge No. 235, A. F. & A. M.; is Past-Chancellor in the K. of P., Cowan Lodge No. 39, and is Examiner in the K. of H. and K. of P. Politically he is a Democrat, his first presidential vote being cast for James Buchanan. He is accounted one of the substantial men of Monroe County, and is the owner of 240 acres of land three miles from Clarendon, and 320 acres seven miles from the town, and also owns an elegant house in the town. He was married in October, 1860, to Mary F. Conner, who was born in Tennessee, and died in 1872, having borne two children, both now deceased. Dr. West's second marriage was consummated January 10, 1874, his wife being Miss Celena, a daughter of Lewis Wahl, a German by birth, now a resident of Milan, Tenn., aged seventy-four years. Mrs. West was born in New Albany, Ind., was reared in Kentucky, and received her education in Columbia, Tenn., being a graduate of a female college of that place. She and the Doctor have two children: Nora C. and Julius M.

Capt. J. W. Whitfield, a general merchant of Roe Roe Township, was born in Davidson County, Tenn., in 1839, and is a son of Capt. Thomas J. and Sallie L. (Dillyhunt) Whitfield, the former a Virginian, and the latter born in Davidson County, Tenn. Their marriage took place in this county, and here they made their home, with the exception of about one year spent in Texas, the father's death occurring in 1873 and the mother's in 1882, she being a member of the Baptist Church at the time of her death. Mr. Whitfield was brigadier-general of the Tennessee militia in early days, and was all through the Rebellion, being a member of the Forty-second Tennessee Infantry, Confederate States army, and was captain of Company H. He was captured at the battle of Fort Donelson and was kept a prisoner at Johnson's Island for seven months. He was then taken on a gunboat to Fortress Monroe, thence to Richmond, where he was liberated or released at the close of the war. He was a member of the A. F. & A. M. and was of English descent. The maternal grandfather, Dillyhunt, was a German and died in Davidson County, Tenn., having been a soldier in the War of 1812.

Capt. J. W. Whitfield was the fourth of nine children, five sons and four daughters, and received but little schooling in his youth. Upon the opening of the war he joined the Confederate army as captain of Company I, Forty-second Tennessee Infantry, and he and his brother, Capt. Silas D. H. Whitfield, and two younger brothers, were all in the same regiment with their father, the latter and his two eldest sons, each commanding a company. They were all captured at Fort Donelson and taken to Johnson's Island, and our subject was exchanged at Vicksburg, and soon after assisted in organizing Company G, becoming a member of Wheeler's cavalry, and operated with his regiment in Tennessee and Mississippi. In the fall of 1863 he was captured on the Tennessee River, but a few hours afterward made his escape and rejoined his command and captured the Federal who had a short time before captured him; this was in Humphreys County. From that time until the final surrender he operated in West Tennessee, and surrendered at Brownsville of that State. The most important engagements in which he participated were Fort Donelson, Fort Hudson, Johnsonville, and some spirited skirmishes. After the war he began farming in Madison County, Tenn., then returned to Middle Tennessee and was engaged in merchandising for five years, and in 1873 removed to Texas, where he followed the same occupation and also managed a cotton plantation for three years. After returning to Tennessee and residing there until 1880 he came to Lonoke County, Ark., and at the end of one year settled in Aberdeen. Since October, 1888, he has resided in Roc Roe Township, and is carrying on the mercantile business with success and also managing a farm of 100 acres. He has a good plantation in Madison County, Tenn., and a store which nets him a comfortable annual income. He is one of the prominent business men of the county, and is a man who commands the respect and esteem of all who know him. He is very fond of hunting, and much of his spare time is spent in the woods with his gun. Mr. Whitfield has always been a Democrat and voted for Jefferson Davis in 1860. He is a member in good standing of the Christian Church, and his wife,

whose maiden name was Delia Scott, and whom he married in 1862, was a member of the Methodist Church. She was born in Fayette County, Tenn., and died in June, 1887, being a daughter of George R. and Hester A. Scott, natives, respectively, of Davidson and Madison Counties, Tenn. The father was a wealthy farmer, and both he and wife died in Madison County, his death occurring in November, 1887, and hers in the winter of 1865.

Capt. Lewis N. Williams is a stock trader and farmer of Roc Roe Township, and was born in Bedford County, Tenn., in 1836, being the youngest of six sons born to William D. and Mary A. (Phillips) Williams, the former born in North Carolina, and the latter in Tennessee. They were married in the mother's native State, and here the father was engaged in farming and stock trading. His death occurred while serving in the Confederate army. His wife followed him to the grave a few years later, her death occurring in Texas while on a visit to a son. She was a member of the Presbyterian Church. Lewis N. Williams received very limited early educational advantages, and at the early age of thirteen years, left home and went to Texas, where he spent some years working on a farm and in the stock business on the frontier. In 1862 he joined Company C of a Texas Battalion, and after the fight at Elk Horn, his company was reorganized at Des Arc, and became the First Texas Legion, afterward operating east of the Mississippi River. He was made orderly-sergeant of his company, was promoted to lieutenant, and finally for meritorious conduct was raised to the rank of captain. At the evacuation of Corinth, he lost his right arm, but remained with the army about a year longer, although not on active duty. He returned to Texas after this, and ran a wagon train of about twenty ox teams in Western Texas, being engaged in hauling cotton for the Government, and at the time of the final surrender was at Brownsville, Texas. He has spent many years of his life on the frontier, and has endured many hardships and privations, and has had many hairbreadth escapes from death, having been robbed several times. His life has been an eventful and interesting one, full of excitement and romance, and in all the difficulties he has encountered in his walk through life, he has met and surmounted them all. He first came to Monroe County, Ark., in 1867, but in 1870–71 was in the stock commission business in Memphis, and while there lost all his accumulations of years, and was left $1,000 in debt. He then returned to Monroe County, engaged extensively in stock dealing, and is now one of the wealthiest men of Monroe County, being the owner of about 4,000 acres of land. He has been interested in the development of the county, morally, intellectually and socially, and has the reputation of being a man of progressive views, thoroughly posted in all public matters. He is a Democrat politically, a member of the Famous Life Association, and in 1872 was united in marriage to Miss Dora Miller, a native of Mississippi, who died in 1883. His second marriage was consummated in 1884, his wife being Miss Josie Cannon, a native of Arkansas County, and a member of the Methodist Church.

Woodfin & Henderson. Among the leading general mercantile establishments of Brinkley, Ark., none are deserving of more favorable mention and consideration than the above mentioned firm, of whom E. L. Woodfin and R. M. Henderson are the proprietors. Their house was established in 1887 and with their stock which amounts to $4,000 they do an annual business of $15,000. Mr. Woodfin was born in Marshall County, Miss., in 1851, and is a son of John and Mary (Scott) Woodfin, the former a native of Alabama and the latter of North Carolina. After spending most of their youth in Tennessee they were married there, but afterward moved to Mississippi, which State continued to be their home until 1859, at which time they came to Arkansas and settled in Cotton Plant. Mr. Woodruff was a farmer by occupation, a member of the Masonic fraternity, and died at Des Arc in 1861. His wife survives him and is a member of the Presbyterian Church. E. L. Woodfin is one of three surviving members of a family of seven children and spent his youthful days in laboring on the farm. Two years were spent in cattle dealing, which occupation proved fairly remunerative, but in 1885 he engaged in his present occupation in Brinkley. In 1875 he was married to Miss Mollie, a daughter of Benjamin and Matilda Glover, who were born, reared and married, in Limestone County, Ala., but removed to De Soto County, Miss., and in 1859 to Arkansas, locating near Wheetley, where the mother's death occurred in 1871. Mr. Glover married again and is now living at Cotton Plant occupied in farming. Mrs. Woodfin is one of five children and was born in Mississippi and for a number of years has been a member of the Old School Presbyterian Church. Mr. Woodfin is a Democrat. When starting out in life for himself in 1869 he had only $18 but now owns the old homestead of 480 acres, besides a good house and business block in Brinkley. He lost heavily during 1874, his large crop of cotton being consumed by fire, but he has retrieved his losses and is now in affluent circumstances.

CHAPTER XXI.

LEE COUNTY—RECENT ORGANIZATION—CREATIVE ACT—SEAT OF JUSTICE—OFFICERS OF TRUST—DURING
WAR TIMES—POLITICAL COMPLEXION—VALUATION—DEVELOPMENT—CHURCHES AND SCHOOLS
—PERIOD OF SETTLEMENT—LOCATION, AREA AND POPULATION—STREAMS, SOILS,
ETC.—NATURAL YIELDS—STOCK RAISING INTERESTS—SKETCH OF MARI-
ANNA AND HAYNES—NUMEROUS SELECTED SKETCHES.

Culture's hand
Has scatter'd verdure o'er the land;
And smiles and fragrance rule serene,
Where barren wild usurp'd the scene.—*Anon.*

EE, one of the more recent acquisitions to the sisterhood of counties in Arkansas, is yet comparatively new, having been created by the legislature of 1873. The territory now embraced within its limits was a portion formerly of four counties, viz.: Phillips, Monroe, St. Francis and Crittenden.

The act of organization was entitled "an act to create the county of Lee and for other purposes." The first section defining the boundaries of the new county was as follows:

"That all that portion of territory, now being in the counties of Phillips, Monroe, St. Francis and Crittenden, included within the following boundaries, viz.: Beginning at the southwest corner of Section 31 on the base line, in Township 1 north, Range 1 east, running east with base line to the Mississippi River; thence with the meanderings of said river to the east township line of Township 3 north, Range 6 east; thence north to the northeast corner of Section 1, Township 3 north, Range 6 east; thence west with the northern line of Township 3 north, Range 6 east, 3 north, Range 5 east, 3 north, Range 3 east, 3 north, Range 2 east, 3 north, Range 1 east and 3 north, Range 1 west, of the fifth principal meridian, to the northwest corner of Section 3, in Township 3 north, Range 1 west; thence south with the section lines, to the southwest corner of Section 34, Township 2 north, Range 1 west; thence east to the southeast corner of Section 36, Township 2 north, Range 1 west; thence south to the southwest corner of Section 31, Township 1, north of Range 1 east, to the place of beginning, be and the same is hereby formed into a separate and distinct county, to be known and designated as the county of Lee, to have and to exercise, as a body politic and corporate, all the rights, privileges and immunities of a separate county." It was further provided by this act that the temporary seat of justice for the new county should be located at Marianna.

It was also provided that an election should be held to elect commissioners, whose duty it should be to locate the court house, as nearly as possible in conformity with the will of the majority of the people.

A lot of ground near the center of the town was purchased and a frame building erected thereon, which was used for court purposes by the county until the erection of the present handsome and commodious public edifice.

The following are the officers who have served the county since its organization. County judges: H. N. Hutton, E. L. Black and H. N. Word. Clerks: M. H. Wing, F. H. Govan, T. C. Merwin and W. T. Derrick. Sheriffs: W. N. Furbush, C. H. Banks, E. H. B. Dupuy and V. M. Harrington. Treasurers: B. B. Nunnally, D. S. Drake, B. M. Govan and Julius Lesser. Owing to its brief existence as a separate county, the list of Lee's public servants is smaller than that of adjacent localities.

At the breaking out of the war the territory included in the present county of Lee, having as stated been embraced in Phillips, Monroe, St. Francis and Crittenden Counties, the part taken in that struggle by the people of this section appears elsewhere in the present volume. It is only necessary to say that about 300 men went from here for the Confederate army, and but a small porportion ever returned. D. C. Govan, T. C. Anderson and B. C. Brasher commanded troops from the region hereabouts, and were attached first to Hindman's legion, and afterward to the Second Arkansas Regiment of Cavalry.

The political complexion of the county may be judged from the vote for President cast in 1888, in which Cleveland received 962, Harrison 1,537 and Streeter 13 votes.

The taxable property of the county in 1880 was, in round numbers, $1,800,000, which has increased until it is now, 1889, $2,410,730, of which $1,723,-525 is real and $687,205 is personal property. This is hardly a fair criterion by which to judge its true wealth, the general rule of assessment being only 40 per cent of the actual value of the property. The county is practically out of debt, with its scrip at par. During the year just passed a magnificent court house has been erected, costing

$15,500, for which cash was paid. There is also in course of construction a substantial jail, with all the modern appliances and conveniences, which will cost about $7,000, and the money is in the treasury to meet this demand also. In 1880 the county shipped about 25,000 bales of cotton, increased in 1889 to upward of 40,000 bales. In 1880 there were 50,000 acres of improved land here, but now something over 87,000.

This county is not a whit behind its sister counties in educational facilities. It is divided into forty-three school districts, in which are erected eighty-one good substantial school-houses, thirty-eight for the white children, and forty-three for colored. The school population by the last census was 5,838, the amount expended in the conduct of the schools reaching nearly $17,000.

In the country the principal religious denominations represented are the Methodists and Baptists. Many of the neighborhoods have, in addition to their school edifices, neat and roomy churches, though in the absence of church buildings proper school-houses are used for worship. A commendable and generous rivalry is apparent among the different denominations toward the promotion of good, and the services are well attended.

The people of this section have indeed made rapid and noticeable strides in the advancement of education since the war, the adoption of the free school system having proven an important factor in the general progress and development of the community.

The early settlers of Lee County were of that class who represented true worth and unpretentious greatness. Penetrating the wilderness to carve out for themselves and their progeny homes, they brought with them the same spirit of tolerance that actuated and inspired their ancestry in founding this great Republic, many of them being the veterans of "Jackson's War."

This county was at one time the home of that lawless desperado and freebooter, John A. Murrell. Here he rendezvoused and sallied forth to prey upon the flat-boat navigators of the Mississippi. About one and a half miles northeast of Marianna stands the Lone Pine. Beneath its somber, dismally rattling boughs frequently met this outlaw chief and his clan of unworthy followers; here in council were planned numerous forays, and here they divided their illgotten spoils. Not far distant burst forth several pure and never-failing springs; and the ruins of the old blacksmith shop, where the band had their horses shod, with the corks in front, the anvil dust and iron, still remain to mark with certainty the spot.

Among the early settlers of the territory now embraced in this county, was John Patterson, who died quite recently at the advanced age of eighty-six, in a little enclosure, about one and a half miles from Marianna. He rests beside six of his wives and twenty of his children, who preceded him to the spirit land, and since his death his seventh wife has followed him. Among other pioneers were David Wills, a native of Rhode Island; James Wilson, of Missouri; Ridley Myrick, Owen Myrick, Charles Ewen, John Dillard and E. K. James, all of Tennessee; David Davis, of Kentucky, who came in 1829; A. G. McDaniel, of Kentucky, who came in 1824; Green E. Story, of Missouri; Middleton Hensley and Washington Hensley, of Indiana; also Larkin Meeks, of the same State; Thomas Adams, of Kentucky; J. Lee and Hiram Dunn, of Virginia; Andrew Dunnski, Obadiah Roberts, John Griffin and Absalom Lowrey came prior to 1829; John Lynch, Matthew Smith, William Smith and Cyrus Lyttle. In 1829 there were not to exceed forty families in the county. The most densely settled portion was on Cow Bayou. In 1835 seven families entered from the States of Illinois and Indiana, locating west of L'Anguille. In 1852 there was a large influx of immigration from the Carolinas, and a steady increase in new-comers existed until the breaking out of the war. That circumstance, here as elsewhere, for a time greatly retarded the settlement of the county. Among those who once owned large estates and numerous slaves were Col. Walter L. Otey and his brother Robert. As the more prominent of the later settlers might be mentioned: Frank Smith, Bryant Lynch, R. D. Griffith and Judge H. N. Hutton, now an influential attorney; John Hudson, one of the first blacksmiths to locate in this section; Eli T. Diamond, Berry

Parker, of Alabama; Alex. Granger, of Kentucky; Bascom Bunch, David Weatherly and R. R. Foreman, of North Carolina.

The first negroes within the present limits of the county were brought here by Samuel Bryant and Rufin Brown, the former bringing nine and the latter six. Among the most noted hunters of this section was Larkin Weeks, a recital of whose wonderful hairbreadth escapes in his numerous encounters with the denizens of the woods would furnish material for a thrilling volume.

The larger proportion of the present population of Lee are Tennesseeans. Each of the other Southern States has a fair representation, while among the thrifty and prosperous are found many from the Northern States.

Lee County is situated in the eastern portion of the State, bounded on the north by St. Francis County. On the east is the Mississippi River, on the south the counties of Phillips and Monroe, and on the west the counties of St. Francis and Monroe. It has a length of about twenty-eight miles from east to west, and a width of eighteen miles from north to south, and contains some 612 square miles of as fertile and beautiful land as any in the great Mississippi Valley—a section whose productions are only limited by its extent.

The population of the county by the census of 1880 was 13,288, which has since materially increased, at present having an estimated population of 18,000. It is divided into fifteen political divisions known as townships, named as follows: Hampton, Union, Independence, Big Creek, Bear Creek, Texas, Spring Creek, Liberty, Walnut, St. Francis, Richland, Oak Forest, Fleener, Council and Hardy. These townships contain over 700 farms, averaging 115 acres of improved land per farm, and there yet remains in the county 313,000 acres susceptible of cultivation. The principal town and county seat is Marianna, besides which are several smaller but thriving commercial centers of local import, among which may be mentioned Haynes, LaGrange, Moro, Spring Creek and Oak Forest.

The principal streams of the county are the St. Francis and the L' Anguille Rivers, the former flowing through in a southeasterly direction, and the latter entering near the center of the northern portion of the county and flowing in and emptying into St. Francis River, about two miles beyond the limits of the county.

The Mississippi River forms the entire eastern front, giving the county direct water communication with all points in the Mississippi and Ohio Valleys.

The land hereabouts lies in a level plain with the exception of Crowley's Ridge which passes through the county, entering on the northern boundary near its center and passing out in the southeast portion. The general width of this ridge is from one and one-half to three and one-half miles, with an altitude of from 250 to 325 feet above sea level.

In the southwestern and eastern portions of the county are numerous beautiful lakes of pure water abounding in the choicest fish.

Perhaps no other county in the State of equal area has a soil which in general productive properties ranks above that of this county. The whole area is susceptible of cultivation and with the exception of the land on Crowley's Ridge is alluvial, adapted to all the crops of this latitude which it produces in lavish profusion; indeed the husbandman has only to put forth but little effort when the soil laughs with its burdensome abundance.

The county is especially adapted to the great Southern staple, cotton. Here originated the celebrated world-renowned variety known as the "Taylor Cotton" which has taken the premium for length of staple and firmness of texture at every fair and exposition where it has been exhibited, notably at the World's Fair at Amsterdam, in Holland. The average yield per acre for cotton is from 350 to 700 pounds. Corn produces from thirty to seventy-five bushels per acre; small grains have never been cultivated to any great extent, but do well here, more especially oats and millet. Vegetables such as potatoes, cabbage and onions grow in the greatest abundance with but little care and cultivation. Fruits of all varieties are raised and with few exceptions do well. That berries are a sure crop is evidenced by the profusion in which they grow in

an uncultivated state. This county is the home of the grape and nowhere else does it thrive better nor produce more abundantly, the forests bordering on the rivers being festooned with the luxurious growth of vines.

Though game in the estimation of the old settler may be somewhat scarce, plenty still remains throughout the forests and cane brakes of the county, and it is no uncommon sight to see the carcass of a bear or a saddle of venison brought in for shipment to the markets of the East. Squirrels and rabbits everywhere abound; there is but one drawback to the shooting of small game in this country—its great abundance destroys the zest of the sport.

A question frequently asked, and to Northern people perhaps the hardest to satisfactorily solve, is this: If your county can produce all you claim, in such abundance and so cheaply, why has it been so backward in its development? Why have its resources lain dormant and comparatively unknown during this long lapse of years? A reply naturally is given that in the first place the system of labor here has been different from that of the North, and while the brain and inventive genius of the latter have for centuries taxed themselves in the endeavor to save human muscle, the contingency based on labor here did not demand this. The average capacity of the negroes of the South to manage and comprehend extended only to the most primitive agricultural implements, and with these they could produce a sufficient amount of cotton and corn to supply the wants and even luxuries of the planter. To minerals, fruits, stocks, timber and grass, they did not care to give attention, save in quantities for domestic purposes. The war destroying this system of labor, and impoverishing the planter, his power of recuperation has been slow; yet it would seem marvelous were one not to take into consideration the wonderful conditions of soil and climate that exist in this southland.

The average temperature of this section is about 62°, rarely reaching 100° in the summer months or falling below 42° in the winter. The average rain fall is not far from forty-five inches, the rains being generally seasonable and propitious. There has never been known an entire failure of crops in the county since its first settlement. Here the soil responds kindly and liberally to the husbandman's labors, and will yield abundant returns for his labor. A single fountain in the desert is more highly appreciated than a thousand limpid streams, bursting from every hillside in a land more favored. So in other countries a single avenue to wealth is crowded and pressed with more tenacity than are the hundred open pathways of a land which affords so much. Lee County needs further and higher development, every department of business and life demanding reinforcement. Its people are generous and hospitable, and welcome all from the North, South, East and West. The material advancement of their county is their ambition. Political affiliations are not a primary consideration, neither does denominational prejudice prove a hindrance to progress.

The invitation is to all, come and look at the fertile lands of the county, and mingle with its people.

Stock raising is rapidly coming to the front, and the general adaptation of the soil to the growth of all forage grasses will in the near future advance this industry to an important rank. That portion of the county known as "Bear Creek Bottom," in the southeast part, is a veritable paradise for stock. A large growth of clover and other fine grasses grow spontaneously and cover the entire valley. With a skirt of cane on either side, cattle, running at large in this bottom, keep fat enough for beef. The valley has the protection of the high lands of Crowley's Ridge which is covered with an immense growth of oak, hickory, beech and walnut trees, furnishing ample and never-failing mast on which hogs thrive and keep in good condition the year round.

The timber of this country is of the finest kind, and embraces the different varieties of oak, poplar, walnut, gum and ash. There are several fine sawmill plants here, the products of which add materially to the wealth of the county. The timber, however, has scarcely been touched, three-fourths of the county still being virgin forest.

Marianna, the principal town and trade center, of Lee County, and its seat of justice, is beautifully situated on the L'Anguille River, at the head of steamboat navigation. It is on a level plain with sufficient fall for good drainage. The Knobel branch of the Iron Mountain Railroad gives the town connection north and south with all the great railroad systems of the country, and makes it easily accessible to the principal markets outside. The elevation of the place is twenty-five feet above the highest water ever known in the Mississippi Valley.

Marianna was first settled about forty years ago, and perhaps a brief sketch of the origin of its location and name may not be out of place in this connection. Col. Walter H. Otey, nearly a half century ago, purchased of Mr. Harvey Harland, familiarly known as "Uncle Harvey," a tract of land situated on L'Anguille River, about three miles above the site of the present town. When the transfer was to be made it was discovered that "Uncle Harvey," from some cause, had forgotten or neglected to apprise his better half, "Aunt Mary Ann," of the proposed sale. She became quite indignant and flatly refused to sign the necessary papers to complete the transfer. After every argument and persuasion had been exhausted in the fruitless endeavor to induce the old lady to add her signature, Col. Otey struck upon the expedient of having Rev. Matt Cox, a gentleman in whom Mrs. Harland had the greatest confidence, to prevail upon her if possible to do the necessary "signing." After his persuasive eloquence had proven unsuccessful he was forced to adopt subterfuge, and suggested that Col. Otey, in consideration of her signature, should name the city, which he proposed founding, for her. This last bait was effective, and "Mary Ann" was easily changed to Marianna. Marianna No. 1 was abandoned in 1857. In 1858 the firm of Worsham & Green of the old town settled and built on the present site of the place, the legislature having declared the L'Anguille River navigable to this point. The land covering the site of the present town was owned by Dr. Green.

The growth of Marianna has kept pace with the development of the State, and it is now in a flourishing condition, doing as large, if not a larger, business in proportion to population than any other town in Arkansas. Its present population exceeds 1,500.

The new town was first incorporated August 7, 1877, and re-incorporated July 5, 1888. Being comparatively so young its rapid increase in population and wealth speaks volumes for the enterprise and pluck of the citizens and the natural productiveness of the country surrounding. In 1869 there were only five families located here, numbering twenty-two souls, and only three business houses, with an aggregate trade of $8,000. What a change in twenty years! It would seem as though the magician's wand had touched the place. The town is well and substantially built, having three large brick blocks—two-story buildings, and the trade is represented by twenty-five or thirty representative establishments, carrying stocks of from $3,000 to $40,000, with an annual patronage of $500,000. The leading firms are Lesser & Bro., Johnson & Grove, Jarratt & Co., P. E. Northern, Becker & Co., L. Shane & Co., Breckey Bros., general merchants; Fleming & Co., J. E. Stevenson, druggists; L. Benham, Hayes & Benthal, T. C. Merwin, family grocers. There are also two millinery and dress-making establishments and numerous restaurants and eating houses; a large brick livery stable furnishes as fine turn-outs as any in the State. Although the hotel accommodations would seem ample for a place of this size, the Phœnix and the Jones House, both of good size, fail to meet the requirements of the traveling public, and there is no better opening anywhere for a large first-class hotel.

Among other industries are three blacksmith and machine shops, one wagon and plow shop with steam power, two good steam gins with grist-mill attachments, one large saw and planing-mill plant with a capital of $40,000, cutting 40,000 feet of lumber per day, employing seventy-five men and adding greatly to the wealth and prosperity of the place.

The legal and medical professions number in their ranks some of the most prominent in these callings in the State.

The Index, published weekly, is a newsy, well-conducted sheet, and its editor, Mr. W. P. Weld, is a live citizen in the advocacy of all that materially helps to develop his town and county.

The secret orders are represented by the Masonic, I. O. O. F., K. of P., K. of H., K. & L. of H. and I. O. G. T., all in a flourishing condition, with good memberships.

This favored town is fully alive to the importance of religious advancement, and though its church buildings are not of the finest, they are neat and comfortable, an evidence of the existence of that spirit which stamps the moral character and excellence of the people. As a church going and church loving community it stands to-day on a plane far above a proportionate population in many older localities. The Baptists, Methodists, Presbyterians and Episcopalians each have houses of worship, and the Christian Church has an organization and contemplates building in the near future, having the funds in hand for that purpose.

The colored people have three church edifices, two Baptist and one Methodist. They also have a hall and an organized lodge of A. F. & A. M.

The Lee County Bank is owned and operated by Mr. J. Lesser, who is also county treasurer. He enjoys to a high degree the confidence and support of the citizens of the county.

There was shipped from this point in 1888, 12,-000 bales of cotton and several million feet of lumber. The new court house previously referred to and just completed at a cost of $15,500, is a magnificent pressed brick structure, and being situated on a commanding eminence, makes a creditable appearance. A new jail costing, when finished, $6,500 is nearing completion.

From an educational point of view, literary advantages are superior. There is located here a college and normal institute, conducted by Prof. Thomas A. Futrall, who ranks among the best educators of the South.

Haynes, the second town in population and importance in the county, is situated in the north central portion, on the Knobel branch of the Iron Mountain Railroad, one mile from the St. Francis County line and two miles from the L'Anguille

River, midway between Forrest City and Marianna, and about six miles from Crowley's Ridge.

The town has a population of 350, and is one of the most thrifty and progressive of places. Its commercial interests are represented by five general merchandise, two drug and several mixed stores. A hotel is creditably conducted and two blacksmith and wagon shops, one undertaker and a millinery establishment supply needed demands. There are several fine brick stores, and others in course of construction, one of which, now being put up by Hughes & Curtis, will cost $10,000.

There were shipped from this point in 1888, 5,000 bales of cotton. The aggregate business of the town for the last year is placed at $300,000. Also at this point are two steam saw-mills, and three steam cotton-gins.

A fine Baptist church finished, and a Methodist church nearing completion, are well sustained. A public hall is in connection with the school-house.

The colored people also have churches and school-houses.

P. H. Adams, a farmer and stock-dealer, was born in Lee County, Ark., in 1844, being the son of Henry and Nancy (Rolledge) Adams. Henry Adams was a native of Kentucky, but of English descent, and to his marriage fifteen children were born, only three of them now living: P. H., Thomas J. and Nancy (the wife of Thomas Kemp, a prosperous farmer of this county). Mr. Adams died in St. Francis County, in 1862, where he had resided for many years. His wife received her final summons some years previous. P. H. Adams was married to Miss Mary Upton, of Lee County, in 1866, and by her became the father of two children (both deceased). Mrs. Adams having died, for his second and present wife Mr. Adams chose Mrs. Mary J. Glidley, who bore him five children: Martha C. (the wife of J. Bowman of this county), Allie S., Mary C., Belle E. and Francis R. Mr. Adams owns 240 acres of land, with 100 improved, giving evidence of a careful and thorough cultivation. He is a Mason, and belongs to Baxton

Lodge, No. 242. In his religious faith he clings to the Baptist doctrine, being a member of that denomination. Mrs. Adams is a member of the Methodist Church, South. She is a native of Illinois, and was born in 1844, the daughter of Ames and Martha A. Smith. Her parents died in 1886 and 1887, respectively.

DeWitt Anderson has been prominently identified with the farming interests of Lee County, Ark., since 1881, and is now the owner of a fine farm comprising 400 acres. He was born in Wilson County, Tenn., in 1848, and is a son of Gen. Paulding Anderson and Martha T. (Horde) Anderson, the former of Tennessee and the latter of Virginia. She was a relative of the Morehead family, of North Carolina, and came with her parents to Tennessee when a small girl. She was a member of the Baptist Church, and at the time of her death, in 1861, was fifty-six years old. Her brother, Jesse Horde, was a leading minister of the Methodist Church, in Texas. Frank Anderson, the paternal grandfather, was a Virginian, and his father and mother were from Scotland, and settled in this country at a very early day. Paulding Anderson, the father of our subject, was one of a large family, and was reared in Tennessee, where he became well-known and arose to prominence in political matters. He held the various offices of his county, with the exception of county clerk, and was a member of both houses of the legislature several terms. He served in the Confederate army, and, after the Federals took possession of the State, he went to the South with Gov. Harris, and was an active participant in the Rebellion until 1863, at which time he was captured, and, after being kept a prisoner at Nashville for months, was released on parole. In his early life he commanded the Central State militia, and during a big rally he commanded 10,000 men, being made general at that time. He was very active in church and school matters in his youth, and for many years was one of the chief props of his church. He was finely educated, was a great reader, and up to the time of his death, which occurred in 1882, at the age of seventy-nine years, he kept thoroughly posted with the current literature of the day. He and his wife were blessed in the birth of eleven children, nine of whom lived to be grown. DeWitt Anderson is the ninth in order of birth, and is one of the three who are now living. Six of the seven sons served in the Confederate army, also two nephews and eight first cousins, and only one of the entire lot was killed, Capt. Dick Anderson, who lost his life at the battle of Murfreesboro. None of the rest were even wounded. DeWitt Anderson commanded a company the first three years of the war, being first lieutenant of Company K, Fourth Tennessee Cavalry, and participated in the battles of Shiloh, the first and second battles of Murfreesboro, Chickamauga and Perryville; was in the Georgia campaign, and was taken prisoner near Rome, Ga., being kept in captivity at Johnson's Island for nine months. After the surrender he was released and came home, again taking up his farming implements. He is now one of the prosperous farmers of Arkansas, and, as above stated, his home farm consists of 400 acres, although he owns 6,000 acres in the State, a considerable portion of which is rich bottom land. This property has all been acquired since coming to this State, as he then had no capital whatever, but his native energy and pluck. He was married in 1868 to Miss Chloe Davis, daughter of James Davis, a leading resident of Wilson County, Tenn., but he was called upon to mourn her death in 1870, her infant daughter dying soon after, at the age of six weeks. She was a consistent Christian, being a member of the Methodist Episcopal Church, and was a faithful, loving and helpful wife—so much so, that Mr. Anderson has since remained faithful to her memory, and is a widower.

Robert J. Bickerstaff is a native of Georgia, in which State he remained until thirteen years of age, going thence to Chambers County, Ala. After a twenty-three years' residence there he came to Arkansas, and settled in this county (then a part of Monroe), arriving February 26, 1859. Here he first engaged in farming, but later carried on the mercantile business in Moro, from 1871 to 1874, since which time he has resumed tilling the soil. Mr. Bickerstaff was born in Jasper County November 28, 1823, and was a son of Robert and Nancy (Roberson) Bickerstaff. Robert Bickerstaff was born in the State of Pennsylvania in 1774, but removed to Georgia about 1790, where he was married in 1797 or 1798. He was a son of a colonel in the Revolutionary War, and he himself was a soldier in the Indian War under Gen. Jackson, and was killed by the Indians at Fort Henderson in May, 1836. Mrs. Bickerstaff was born in Ireland in 1778, came to this country at the age of fourteen, and died in Georgia in 1834. They were the parents of fifteen children, six sons and nine daughters; two of the sons only are living, the subject of this sketch, and Pollard B., a farmer of Montgomery County, Ala. Robert J. Bickerstaff was married in Alabama, on January 31, 1848, to Miss Mary Dazier, of the same county as himself, she having been born June 28, 1828, as a daughter of Woody and Eliza (Compton) Dazier. They became the parents of eight children, seven sons and one daughter, four of whom are still living: Herschel, Robert, Mary L. (wife of John H. Sims) and Andrew, all farmers of this county, though the latter is also employed in Government work. Mr. Bickerstaff enlisted in 1862 in Company C, of the Twenty-third Arkansas Infantry, and after the reorganization was in the Trans-Mississippi Department, serving until the close of the war, having been thrice captured but each time made his escape. Mr. Bickerstaff owns a 240-acre farm, covered with valuable timber, with the exception of ninety acres under cultivation, and he also owns land in Van Zandt County, Tex. Although not taking an active part in politics, Mr. Bickerstaff has held the office of justice of the peace for the past two years. He has been a member of the Masonic order for forty years, and has also belonged to the Missionary Baptist Church the same length of time. Mrs. Bickerstaff is connected with the same church.

Virgil C. Bigham owes his nativity to Tennessee, though he commenced farming at the age of nineteen years in Monroe County, Ark., and has been engaged in this occupation to the present. He has also carried on the mercantile business since November, 1888. Mr. Bigham now owns 380 acres of land, with eighty acres under cultivation. He was born December 17, 1835, a son of Martin Bigham and Sallie (Breeding) Bigham, natives of the State of Tennessee. They were the parents of seven children, Virgil C. being the only one living. The father died in 1854, ten years after the death of his wife. Virgil C. Bigham was married in December, 1857, in Monroe County, to Miss Rachel Breeding, who died in 1858, leaving two children, both deceased. He married his second wife, formerly Miss Elizabeth Caplinn, of this State, in 1863. She became the mother of one daughter, also deceased. Mr. Bigham enlisted in the Confederate army, in 1862, in Company B, of the First Arkansas Battalion (Infantry), and took part in several hard fought battles, but was mostly on scout duty. He has been postmaster of Moro since October, 1889. He is well-known throughout the township as an honest and upright man.

S. A. Bishop, the subject of this sketch, was born in New Berne, N. C., April 11, 1835, his parents being Samuel and Phœbe (Hilbert) Bishop, both of New Berne, N. C., the latter dying in New Berne, N. C., at the advanced age of eighty-three years. S. A. Bishop received a high school education, and at the age of nineteen accepted a position as chief salesman in his brother's furniture store at New Berne, where he remained until December, 1857, after which he removed to Haywood County, Tenn. There on April 13, 1858, he was married to Miss Sarah W. Jones, of New Berne, N. C., she being the daughter of Dr. William M. and Rouncy Jones, nee Miss Rouncy Cooper, the two last named of Haywood County, Tenn. The result of this union was one daughter who, in 1878, married Mr. T. E. Bond, of Brownsville, Tenn., where they now reside. Mrs. Sarah W. Bishop died December 24, 1872. On October 15, 1873, Mr. Bishop was married to Miss Ida Peebles, at Brownsville, Tenn., she being the daughter of Mr. Robert and Mrs. Ann Peebles. The result of this union was four children, viz.: Samuel A. (born July 21, 1874), Lucy C. (born March 7, 1877), Robert P. (born July 14, 1879), and Ann Hilbert (born October 20, 1881). Mrs. Ida Bishop died at Marianna, Ark., October 6, 1888,

and was buried at Brownsville, Tenn. Robert P. Bishop died August 3, 1885; the other children are living, Samuel being a student of the Christian Brothers' College, St. Louis, Mo., and Lucy C. and Ann H. are with their aunt, Mrs. Lelia A. Blackwell, of Dallas, Tex. Mr. Bishop was engaged in the mercantile business first in 1865, at Dancyville, Tenn., remaining there until the spring of 1872, when he removed to Brownsville, Tenn., and continued merchandising. In the spring of 1883 he removed to Marianna, Ark., where he did a profitable and prosperous business until 1889, when he retired from business and is now engaged in collecting up his claims and winding up his business affairs. He is an example of a successful business man, of high social qualities, and is an honorable and affable gentleman.

George W. Bonner, who is one of the most successful farmers in Spring Creek Township, has been a resident of this county since 1869. He is a native of Tennessee, and the son of Williamson and Maria (Reddith) Bonner, originally from Virginia and North Carolina, respectively. Mr. Bonner was a man of considerable education, and for a number of years followed the occupation of school-teaching, during his latter days being recognized as a public man of considerable importance. For many years he was an elder in the Presbyterian Church. He was a soldier in the War of 1812. John Bonner, his father, a Virginian by birth, and a farmer and mechanic by occupation, lived to the age of eighty years. He participated in the Revolutionary War. Mrs. Bonner was the daughter of Aquilla Reddith, a native of North Carolina, who lived in that State until his death, at the age of ninety years. The subject of this sketch was born in Wilson County, Tenn., in 1828, but his early boyhood was spent in Shelby County, where his father had moved in 1832. He learned the carpenter's trade in youth, and followed that occupation for thirty years, but since that time has been engaged in farming. During the Mexican War he served seven months in Taylor's division. In 1869, moving to Arkansas, Mr. Bonner settled in what was then a part of Phillips (now Lee) County, and three years later located on the farm which he has since occupied. He was married, in 1854, to Miss Oliva A. F. Mason, who died nine years after their marriage, leaving four children, one of whom, Williamson E., only is living. Mr. Bonner was later married to Miss Mary E. Newsom, in 1865, a daughter of David Newsom, of Virginia. She was the mother of seven children at the time of her death, in 1881, six of whom are living: David T., George W., Charles Henry J., Carra A., Claudius H. and Fredonia L. He married his third and present wife, Mrs. Elizabeth J. Robertson (nee Tiller), daughter of Benjamin and Ann Tiller, natives of Alabama, in 1882. Mr. Bonner owns a farm of eighty acres, and has about fifty acres under cultivation, giving his attention to stock raising to a large extent. Himself and wife are members of the Methodist Episcopal Church, to which he has belonged for over forty years, and of which he has been a local minister for fifteen years. He has also been a member of the Masonic fraternity for thirty-nine years. A Democrat in politics, he takes an active interest in enterprises for the good of the community, to all of which he contributes largely, and is considered one of the leading farmers of Lee County.

Francis M. Bowdon is a native of Tennessee, and a son of Thomas and Parmelia (Jenkins) Bowdon, natives of South Carolina. The father was engaged in farming in Western Tennessee for a number of years, and moved from there to Lauderdale County, Ala., when our subject was a small boy, there acting as deputy sheriff. In 1841 he went to De Soto County, Miss., and remained eight years, then coming to Arkansas and locating in Lee County, where he bought timbered land and cleared up a good farm. He was a prominent politician of his community, holding the office of justice of the peace in Mississippi and also in this county. He died in Evanston, Ind., while on a trip to Lexington, Ky. He and wife were members of the Baptist Church, and were the parents of eleven children, three of whom are still living: Benjamin F. (a farmer of Randolph County, Ark.), Columbia (wife of John J. Felton, a farmer of this county) and Francis M. The latter, the principal of this sketch, and the eldest of those now living, was born

in Bedford County, Tenn., on May 23, 1827. He was married in 1855 to Miss Caroline Elders, a native of Mississippi, who died in 1862, leaving four children, one son, H. J., being the only one living, and who now has charge of his father's farm. Mariah Gilbert became his next wife, but died three years after without issue. Mr. Bowdon was married again to Miss Mollie Arnold, in 1867, who was the mother of three children: Ethel B., Francis M. and James L. He married Melvina Bertran, a native of this county, in 1869. Mr. Bowdon owns 580 acres in the county, 300 acres in the farm on which he lives, 150 acres in a good state of cultivation and well improved. All this he has made himself, by hard work and close economy.

David W. Boykin, son of Edwin and Elizabeth J. Boykin, was born in Smithfield, N. C., in August, 1839. He was educated at Trinity College, of that State, and enlisted in the Confederate army in 1862, receiving his discharge in 1865, at Appomattox Court-House, Va. In September, 1866, he removed to Arkansas and settled in Marianna, Lee County, then Phillips County, where he was for several years employed as book-keeper and salesman in a general dry-goods and grocery business. Mr. Boykin has now been living upon a fine and productive farm in Lee County, owned by his brother, Edwin A. Boykin, and himself, and is engaged in general farming and stock-raising. He has been twice married; first, to Miss Agnes Snead, of Smithfield, N. C.; next, to Mrs. Joanna M. Saunders, of Brownsville, Tenn. Mr. Boykin is of Irish descent.

William S. Bradford, M. D., prominently identified with the professional affairs of this section, owes his nativity to Tennessee, being a son of John W. and Emily (Nuckols) Bradford, also originally from that State. The Bradfords are an old family, and can trace their ancestors back to the time of their arrival in the Mayflower. William S. Bradford, the only son in a family of three children, was born in Hardeman County, Tenn., February 11, 1859. He spent his early life on the farm, and at the age of sixteen commenced clerking in a store in that county, becoming, when eighteen, proprietor of a grocery, in which business he was engaged for two years. During that time he studied medicine, and the next year attended a course of lectures at Vanderbilt College. He subsequently turned his attention to traveling, and was employed by a publishing company for eighteen months in selling their publications through Illinois, Iowa, Nebraska, Kansas, Missouri, Kentucky and Tennessee. In the spring of 1882 he went to Parker County, Tex., where he was engaged in the practice of medicine for a short time. Returning to Tennessee, he followed his profession in Hardeman County one year, and in the winter of 1883–84 attended a course of lectures at Vanderbilt College, from which he graduated in March, 1884. He then came to Arkansas and located in Lee County, where he has since been successfully occupied in the duties of his adopted calling. Dr. Bradford was married on December 2, 1885, to Miss Ida F. Halton, of Nevada County, Ark. They have one son, Wiley E. Dr. Bradford has a large and lucrative practice, and is highly thought of by the citizens of Lee County. He is a member of the Knights of Honor, and also of the Lee County Medical Association, and of the State Medical Society, having represented his county in the spring of 1888 at Fort Smith.

Dr. T. J. Brasher. An undeniable truth is that the life of any man, temperately lived, is of great benefit to the community in which he resides, when all his efforts are directed to advancing its interests, and whose career is according to the higher principles of what he conceives to be right, helping others and caring for those who are unable to do for themselves. Such a man is Dr. Brasher. Born in Christian County, Ky., on November 1, 1835, he is a son of Alexander and Margaret (Brown) Brasher, natives of Kentucky and North Carolina, respectively. The father's birth occurred in the year 1811, and during life he was engaged in that most important occupation to Kentuckians, the breeding and rearing of fine blooded horses. Being a wide-awake and prominent man, he took an active part in politics, and for many years filled the offices of probate judge and justice of the peace. He belonged to the Christian Church, and was a Mason of high degree. To him and wife were born a family of seven children, as follows: Alonzo W. (a prominent practicing physician of Hopkins County, Ky.), Rachel (the widow of Dr. T. A. Yarrell, of Kentucky), the immediate subject of this sketch, Melissa (wife of Dr. James M. Long, of Crofton, Ky.), William A., M. D. (killed at the battle of Franklin, Tenn.), Elbridge Gerry (a colonel in the Confederate army, who was killed at the battle of Shelbyville, Ky.) and Altazera (wife of David Wooldridge, a wealthy ranchman of Oregon). T. J. Brasher grew to manhood in Hopkins County, of the Blue Grass State, and after receiving a thorough practical education in the subordinate schools, took a classical course at Georgetown College, and later a medical course in the Eclectic Medical Institute of Cincinnati, Ohio, which graduated him with honors at the age of twenty-one years. After practicing his profession in the neighborhood of his nativity for about five years, he removed to Arkansas, in 1860, and located in Lee County, a portion of which at that time belonged to Monroe County. He was not long permitted to follow his peaceful pursuits, but in 1861 enrolled his services for the Confederate cause, and was made a first lieutenant in Company D, of Hindman's Legion. He participated in the engagements of Shiloh, Perryville, Franklin, Clarksville, Uniontown, and many other hotly contested battles, and in the first and two last mentioned actions received severe wounds. Because of these injuries he was rendered unfit for further active military duty, but on account of his recognized ability and worth, was appointed under Jefferson Davis, to a position in the secret service of the treasury department of the Confederate States. This important position he filled with credit to himself and honor to the cause, displaying great adaptability to the important duties devolved upon him. The year following the end of the great conflict, Dr. Brasher wedded Miss Nannie L. Edwards, a native of Tennessee, and a daughter of Charles A. Edwards. One daughter, Kate A. (the wife of James M. Maclin, of the firm of P. E. Northern & Co., of Marianna), is the result of this union. Since being a resident of Arkansas, the Doctor has practiced his profession, farmed and merchandised, and in a financial way,

Dr. T. J. Brasher,
LEE COUNTY, ARKANSAS.

as well as otherwise, has made his life a success. His portrait appropriately graces this volume. In addition to his other interests he has found time to enter quite actively into literary pursuits, contributing frequently to all local newspapers. He has also attained to considerable reputation as a writer upon romance, the woodpecker, squirrel, dog, highland terrapin, opossum, etc., these articles being widely copied throughout the Southern States.

Jesse Briley came to Arkansas in the fall of 1851, first locating in St. Francis County, and later in Lee County, being employed as a farm hand for seven or eight years. In 1859 he bought a quarter section of land, on which he lived until the breaking out of the war, when he enlisted in the Thirteenth Arkansas Infantry, but was soon after transferred to the Second Arkansas Cavalry, serving in Price's raid through Missouri. After the war he returned to his farm, which he found badly dilapidated, and was obliged to start from the bottom of the ladder, but has been very successful, now owning 700 acres of land, with 400 acres under cultivation. Besides this he owns a house and lot at Haynes, and is a stockholder in the Haynes Mercantile Company. Mr. Briley was born in North Carolina, in 1834, and was married in 1859, to Miss Emma Daniel. They are the parents of four children: Sallie, Laniar, Katie and Ida. He is a member of the Masonic order, and also of the Knights of Honor. He is a Democrat in politics, and is well known and highly respected as a citizen.

John A. Brittain is a progressive agriculturist and stockman of Union Township, Lee County, Ark., but was born in Franklin County, Tenn., in 1828, being the eldest of four children born to James and Frances (Stoveall) Brittain, who were also Tennesseeans. The family first came to St. Francis County, Ark., in 1845, and here Mr. Brittain purchased a farm on which a few improvements had been made, it being situated about one-half mile from Forrest City, which was then called Mt. Vernon. He lived in this settlement until his death April 9, 1849. He had been married twice, his first wife being the mother of our subject, but she died in 1836, and of her four children three are

36

yet living: John A., Susan (wife of Abram Noah, resides in Texas) and Frances (the widow of Rufus Williams, lives in Tennessee). Benjamin died in 1881, and his family still reside in Lee County. After the death of his first wife Mr. Brittain was married, in 1838, to Miss Annie Staples, of Tennessee, and the three children which were born to them are now deceased: Martha A. was the wife of Aaron G. McDaniels, and died in 1867, and the other two died in infancy. Mrs. Brittain died in September, 1844. John A. Brittain remained in the county of his birth, acquiring there a fair education, until 1845, when he came to this State with his father, and, after assisting him on the farm until he was twenty-one years of age, he followed clerking for a short while. Since that time he has followed the life of a farmer, and in 1851 purchased a portion of the farm on which he now resides, then consisting of forty acres. Very few improvements had at that time been made upon it, but he has since erected buildings, fences, etc., and now has his farm in a splendid condition for agricultural purposes. He has added 120 acres and has eighty acres under the plow. Cotton and corn are among his main products, but he also gives much of his attention to the propagation of stock. He was married in 1849 to Miss Mary McDaniel, a native of Arkansas, born in 1835. She has lived in three counties in this State, without having moved. She was born in Phillips County, which afterward became St. Francis County, and is now Lee County. She is a daughter of Archibald G. and Mary (Davis) McDaniel, who were born in Kentucky and moved to Arkansas in 1828, being among the first settlers of Phillips County, Mr. McDaniel being also one of the first postmasters in this portion of the State, a position he held until 1857. He and wife became the parents of thirteen children, eleven of whom lived to be over fourteen years of age, only two of whom are now living: Mary (Mrs. Brittain) and Harriett (the widow of Robert Shell). Mrs. McDaniel died in 1869. An uncle of Mrs. Brittain's, John Calvert, was one of the first settlers of this region, and was a soldier in the War of 1812. Her mother came from Kentucky to Arkansas via Memphis, Tenn., which at that time was only a camp, said to be one of the camps of the noted bandit Murrell. Mr. and Mrs. Brittain are the parents of ten children, G. B., Robert McD., Mary W., M. L., and Eliza A. being the only ones living. A. T. died at the age of twenty years, and J. B. when twenty-four years of age. In 1864 Mr. Brittain joined the Confederate army, becoming a member of Company C, Dobbins' Regiment, and was with Gen. Price through Missouri, and was in the battles of Pilot Knob, Lexington, and in numerous skirmishes. He was paroled in June, 1865, at Wittsburg, Ark. He and wife are worthy members of society and his wife is a member of the Methodist Church.

William J. Broadley is a son of Samuel W. Broadley, a native of Liverpool, England, whose father, Ferrell Broadley, also came originally from England, being proprietor of the "Fax Hall Spinning Company;" of the interests of that concern, still extensive and profitable, our subject is one of the heirs. Samuel Broadley came to America in 1849, a few years after his marriage, and was occupied in the mercantile business in the State of New York the following year. He then took the "gold fever" and went to California, leaving his family in New York, and engaged in the mining of the precious metal until 1853, when he was killed by an accident in a mine in which he was working. He was married in Liverpool to Miss Phœbe Covington, a native of that country and a daughter of Frederick Covington, a merchant, and, at the time of his death, at an advanced age, a man of considerable means. Mrs. Broadley is still living and a resident of New Orleans. She also has a brother in this country, a member of the firm of Covington & Co., of Salt Lake City. Of the children of Mr. and Mrs. Broadley, five are still living: Ida (wife of Frank S. Snell, a prominent real estate agent and broker of Denver, Colo.), Alice M. (wife of a Mr. Patton, a merchant of Memphis, Tenn.), William T. (an attorney of New Orleans), Henry J. (who is in the employ of the Government as a chemist) and William J. (the principal of this sketch). The latter was born in Steuben County, N. Y., in 1852. After his father's death his mother moved from New York, going to several places, and finally, in 1862, to Memphis, Tenn., where they lived one year; later she became located at New Orleans and still lives there. Mr. Broadley learned the trade of a machinist when a young man, at which he worked in different States, but finally settled in Lee County, where he was employed at his chosen occupation until 1887. Then he purchased his present farm, and has since turned his attention to farming. He was married, in 1879, to Miss Lorena O'Kelley, a daughter of Overton and Mary O'Kelley, natives of Alabama and Georgia, respectively. Mr. and Mrs. Broadley have four children: Frederick C., Charles O., Ida L. and William S. (now deceased). Mr. Broadley owns a fine farm of 440 acres, with nearly 300 acres under cultivation, and is engaged in raising stock. He and wife are members of the Missionary Baptist Church. He is a Democrat in politics, and is a prominent man of Spring Creek Township. He belongs to no secret societies, but before entering the agricultural list of Lee County, belonged to the Brotherhood of Locomotive Engineers.

George W. Bullard ranks among the leading agriculturists of Lee County, and although he was born in Tennessee in 1853, he has been a resident of Arkansas since he was three years old, at which time his father and mother, George T. and Elizabeth (Curts) Bullard, came here from their native State of Tennessee. They settled in St. Francis County and bought some unimproved land at $5 and $7 per acre, but rented land the first year of his stay. On this farm he resided until his death in 1875, and witnessed many changes in the growth and prosperity of the county as it was a very wild and unsettled region at the time of his locating. During the Civil War he suffered much at the hands of bushrangers who claimed to belong to the Union and Confederate armies, but did not himself serve in either army. Seven of his ten children lived to be grown and five are living at the present time: George W., Mattie J. (wife of John Lindsey), Octavia A. (wife of W. T. Inge), Margaret H. (wife of F. C. Danerhougher) and Alice L. The mother of these children still resides on the old homestead and manages her farm successfully. She is, as was her husband, a member of the Methodist Episcopal Church, South, and he was a member of Bethel Lodge No. 254, A. F. & A. M. George W. Bullard attended the common schools near his home in his youth and in 1870 entered Abernathy's School in Montgomery County, Tenn., where he acquired a sufficiently good education to fit him for the toils and cares of business life. At the age of twenty-one years he commenced the battle of life for himself but did not leave home until he was married, in 1882, to Miss Ella Davis, she being a daughter of J. P. and Mollie (Jackson) Davis, of Alabama, who came to Arkansas about 1870. She was born in 1865 and is one of two surviving members of their family of three children: Ella, Willie and James, the latter being deceased. Mr. Davis died in 1879 and Mrs. Davis in 1877, both being worthy members of the Cumberland Presbyterian Church, the former also a member of the I. O. O. F. Mr. and Mrs. Bullard have a family of three children: George W. (who was born February 11, 1884, and died August 23, 1886), Daisy Lee (born February 1, 1886) and Reuben E. (born October 21, 1889). Mr. Bullard owns a fine farm of 240 acres, of which 175 acres are nicely improved with good buildings of all descriptions. He raises annually from sixty to seventy-five bales of cotton, besides plenty of corn and hay, stock-raising also receiving a considerable portion of his attention. He is a rising young farmer and in all matters pertaining to the welfare of the county he is deeply interested. He is a member of Bethel Lodge No. 254, of the A. F. and A. M., and Lodge No. 1861, of the K. of H., at Haynes. His wife is a member of the Methodist Episcopal Church, South.

Capt. William H. Clark, of Marianna, Ark., was born in North Carolina in 1841, and in 1846 moved with his parents (James and Virginia L. (Pinnell) Clark), to Memphis, Tenn., and from there, in 1857, to Walnut Bend, Ark., where the father purchased land. The latter was born in Guilford County, N. C., in 1816, and was a painter by trade. This he followed until after he moved to Walnut Bend, where he resided up to 1867, when he died of yellow fever. He followed merchandising, and owned some land in Walnut Bend.

Clark's Landing was named in honor of him, and he owned the same. The mother was born in Virginia, in 1824, and died in Memphis, Tenn., in 1854. They were the parents of three children, Capt. William H. Clark being the eldest; and the second, James Preston, was captured in Walnut Bend during the war, and died from a fever contracted in prison. He was a member of Capt. Cowley's company, C. S. A. The youngest child died when young. Capt. William H. Clark was reared and educated in Memphis. He commenced steamboating in 1856, as clerk on the steamer Katie Frisbee, and followed this in different capacities until 1861, when he joined the Confederate army at Memphis. Previous to this, in 1859, he was appointed route agent for the United States mail, between Memphis, Tenn., and Vicksburg, Miss.,and was serving in that capacity when the war broke out. He joined the One Hundred Fifty-fourth Senior Tennessee Regiment as private, in Company B (Bluff City Greys), was a clerk in Adj.-Gen. Bragg's office, of the Army of Tennessee, under command of Gens. Bragg, J. E. Johnston and Hood, at department headquarters, and served from May, 1863, until the close of the war. He participated in the battles of Belmont, Shiloh, Corinth, Richmond (Ky.) and Perryville, with his company, the Bluff City Greys. During the fight at Richmond there were seventy-five in the company, and they captured from 125 to 150 of the enemy, and were in front all day. After the battle nearly all had their clothes torn by bullets, but no man of the company was wounded. They were sharp-shooters of Gen. Preston Smith's brigade. Capt. Clark was with the Army of Tennessee while under the commands of Gens. Braxton Bragg, J. E. Johnston, John B. Hood, G. T. Beauregard and Dick Taylor, from Murfreesboro, Tenn., to the surrender at Greensboro, N. C., serving continually in the adjutant-general's office under the different commanders. After the surrender he returned to Memphis and followed steamboating until 1876, part of the time being engaged in the cotton seed business. He was married in 1866, to Miss Maggie Harrison, who was born in Paducah, Ky. Her grandfather moved to Christian County,

Ky., in 1809 from Virginia, and was one of the owners and founders of Paducah. Her grandfather and William H. Harrison were first cousins, and the subject of this sketch was named for that president. Capt. Clark came here in 1876, and engaged in the receiving and forwarding business. By his marriage he became the father of seven children: William H., Jr., Dudley S., Emma, Maggie, Benigna, Ruth and Charles Preston. Capt. Clark is a member of the Masonic fraternity—Chapter, Council and Commandery—K. of H., and K. & L. of H. and K. of P. He and wife and all the family are members of the Episcopal Church. G. F. Clark was born in Guilford County, N. C., and was a first cousin of Abraham Clark, a signer of the Declaration of Independence, and was of Scotch descent. The grandmother on his father's side was a Lilly, and a relative of the Lillys of Halifax County, Va. The Carringtons, of Cumberland County, were relatives to the wife's father.

J. P. Curtis belongs to the firm of Hughes & Curtis, of Haynes, Ark., general merchants, the former being also engaged in farming. He was the fifth of eight children born to William and Mary (Porchman) Curtis, natives of North Carolina and Tennessee, respectively, the former of whom came to Arkansas in 1856, and settled in what was then St. Francis County, but is now Lee, where he improved an excellent farm, on which he died in 1878. Of his eight children only two are living: Elisabeth (Mrs. Bullard of Lee County) and J. P. Curtis. Two children died in infancy, and three died between the ages of thirteen and twenty-one. A sister, Mary, was the wife of Buck Dawson at the time of her death. The mother of these children died in 1875, she and her husband having been earnest members of the Methodist Episcopal Church, South, at the time of their death. J. P. Curtis was sixteen years of age upon his removal to this State, but the most of his education was received in Lee County. He was in his twenty-first year at the breaking out of the late war, and he immediately donned a suit of gray clothes, and became a member of Company D, Fortieth Tennessee, and was on active duty with the Army of Tennessee, until 1862, when he was transferred to the Fifteenth Arkansas Infantry, and served on the east side of the Mississippi River, until the fall of Port Hudson. He was captured at Island No. 10, and was sent to Camp Butler, Ill., but at the end of six months was exchanged at Vicksburg, and rejoined his command near that place. He surrendered, and was paroled at Port Hudson, July 8, 1863, and reached home on the 23d day of the same month. After remaining at home for eight months, he, in 1864, joined Col. Dobbins' command, and was with Gen. Price on his raid through Missouri, participating in a number of engagements in that State. He surrendered at Wittsburg, in January, 1865, and returned to his home, where he commenced to cultivate his father's farm, and continued so to do until the latter's death. In February, 1889, he became a member of the above named firm, doing an annual business of about $35,000, and in addition to this they also deal in cotton, and in the year 1888 ginned 1,300 bales, but only ginned about 800 bales last year, on account of poor crops. Mr. Curtis was married in 1867, to Miss M. C. Castell, of St. Francis County, a daughter of Calloway and Isabel (Simpson) Castell, who were among the early settlers of the county, and by her has reared a family of five children, three dying when small. Those living are: Mary (wife of Charles Higginbotham, of this county), Walter B. (who is attending school in Madisonville, Ky.), William, A. E. and B. E. Mr. Curtis belongs to Bethel Lodge No. 2168, of the K. of H.

D. W. Davis, one of the old settlers of this county, and son of David W. Davis, who came to this State in 1829, was born in the Old Dominion in 1816, and accompanied his father to Arkansas in the above mentioned year, settling where the younger Davis is now living. This was at that time a wilderness, and there were, in what is now Lee County, about forty families on the east side of the L'Anguille, and none on the west. In about 1835 Hardy Williams and brother, Jefferson Ezell, and two brothers, and one Mr. Burris, settled west of Haynes, in what is now Texas Township. The remaining portion of the county was an unbroken wilderness, filled with deer, bear, buffalo and many other wild animals. Where Marianna now stands there lived at that time two old Poles, Duskinuski and Coluski by name, and just south of them lived John Patterson, who was born in Helena in 1800. He lived to be eighty years of age. His sister, who was born previous to 1800, was the first white child born in Helena. Of all the early settlers of the county, Mr. Davis is the only one of the original families who is still living. He was one of eleven children born to his parents, five sons and six daughters, and is the only one surviving, although all lived to be grown and reared large families, except one sister and D. W. These children were named as follows: Mary (deceased, was the wife of A. G. McDaniel, family now resides in this and Monroe County), Solomon (deceased, family resides in Illinois), Nancy (deceased, wife of John W. Calvert, family deceased), Cornelius (deceased, family resides in this county and Arizona), Benjamin (deceased, family resides in St. Francis County), Rebecca (deceased), Rachel (deceased, wife of William West, family resides in Kansas), D. W., W. H. (deceased, family resides with D. W. Davis, except one daughter, Elizabeth, who married G. L. Rodgers), Harriet (deceased, wife of T. R. Harris) and Eliza (deceased, wife of Bryant Lynch, family resides in Lee County, Ark.). David W. Davis, Sr., died in 1837. He was born in 1761, and participated in the Revolutionary War. He was on a war ship with Capt. Peterson during the principal part of the war, and was with Gen. Wayne in the war with the Indians, being wounded in the shoulder in the last engagements. His wife was born in 1777, and died in 1861. Our subject, D. W. Davis, was educated in the subscription schools of Kentucky, and after coming to Arkansas received instruction from his father, who was an unusually good scholar for his day, and a fine mathematician. After the death of his father D. W. remained at home and took care of his mother. He was not in the war himself, but his family supplied quite a number of soldiers for the South. His father held the right of pre-emption on the land which he entered in 1836, there being about 160 acres in the original homestead, but to this our subject has

added 300 acres more, which belongs to him and the heirs of W. H. Davis. The Davis family, while being among the prominent ones of the county, never aspired to office, though one, J. C. Davis, is sheriff of St. Francis County. He is a nephew of D. W. Davis (subject). While Mr. Davis does not seek for official prominence he still manifests considerable interest in the local elections, and is a thorough Democrat. He is a liberal contributor to all matters relating to the good of the county, and is a man universally respected. Amanda Davis, widow of W. H. Davis, and daughter of Noah and Mary (Hearty) Reed, natives, respectively, of Massachusetts and Kentucky, was one of two children born to her parents. The other child, Elizabeth, married J. L. Rowland. Previous to her marriage to Mr. Reed, Mrs. Reed had married a man by the name of Ramage, and by him became the mother of two children: Lucinda (deceased, wife of Benjamin Travis), and James (who resides in Paducah, Ky.). Mr. Reed died in 1845, and Mrs. Reed in 1842. Mrs. Amanda Davis was born in 1833, and came with her father to Arkansas when quite small. She had very limited educational advantages, and at the age of twenty-two years was united in marriage to George Halbert. The result of this union was one child, W. H., who resides in Haynes. Mr. Halbert died December 17, 1856, and in July, 1858, his widow married W. H. Davis, who died November 23, 1883. Mr. and Mrs. Davis were the parents of seven children, five now living: Richard (died at the age of twenty-five years), T. Jefferson (died at the age of fifteen months), Mary E., Annie, George B., William H. and Harriet A. Mr. Davis and his brother, D. W., had always remained together, and the business interests still continue as before his death. W. H. Davis had been married previous to his union with Mrs. Halbert, to Miss Sarah J. Boon, and by her became the father of five children, only two now living: Mrs. Rodgers, of Texas, and David R., who resides in Lee County, Ark. Mrs. Davis is a member of the Methodist Episcopal Church.

Robert C. Davis has been a resident of Arkansas since a short time after the close of the Civil War, in which conflict he took part on the Confederate side, enlisting in Company A, of the Twenty-seventh Mississippi Infantry, in 1861, when only seventeen years of age. After the close of hostilities he returned to Mississippi, his native State, where he remained until 1869, then coming to this State and locating in Phillips County, and in 1880 he came to Lee County and settled upon his present farm. Mr. Davis was born in Attala County, Miss., in 1843, being a son of J. G. A. and Elizabeth J. Davis, natives of Illinois and Tennessee, respectively. His educational advantages were limited to a few months' attendance at the common schools in each year. Mr. Davis has been twice married; first, in 1866, to Miss Sarah J. Cornish, daughter of William and Elizabeth Cornish, natives of North Carolina and Georgia, respectively. Mrs. Davis died in 1871, leaving three children, two of whom are still living: Cornish R. and Rightor C. He was married to his present wife, Miss Luivia J. Alexander, in 1872. He owns 560 acres of land, 130 acres cleared and in a good state of cultivation, with good improvements upon his place. Mr. Davis is a Democrat in politics, and was appointed postmaster of Lee in 1884, having held the office since that time. He and wife are members of the Primitive Baptist Church, in which they take an active part.

W. T. Derrick, well known as the popular clerk of the circuit court of Lee County, is a native of Alabama, and a son of H. B. and Evaline (Beal) Derrick. H. B. Derrick is still living, a resident of this county, seventy-one years of age. His wife died in 1885, at the age of fifty-eight. W. T. Derrick was born in 1842, and came to Lee County with his father when a boy. He served four years in the Confederate army during the war, holding the position of lieutenant in the Army of Tennessee, and participated in seventeen different engagements. After the war he returned to this county and carried on farming until 1884, when he was elected county and circuit clerk, and was re-elected in 1886, and again in 1888, filling the offices with great credit to himself and satisfaction to his fellow-citizens. Mr. Derrick's wife was formerly Miss Mary S. Jones, also of Alabama origin. They are the parents of two children:

Maria and Robert L. He is a member of the K. of P. and of the K. of H. It is unnecessary to add that Mr. Derrick is one of the leading Democrats of the county, having held prominent offices for the past six years. He is also highly esteemed not only by those of the same political party, but by all good citizens throughout this locality.

H. B. Derrick, Jr., liveryman, Marianna, Ark. Among the active enterprises of a town like Marianna, the business of a livery stable occupies necessarily an important place, contributing as they do to the pleasure, convenience and actual necessities of the community. Among the most notable of this class in Marianna is that conducted by Mr. Derrick, which was established at this place in 1873. Mr. Derrick was born September 30, 1852, in Alabama and emigrated with his father from that State to Arkansas in 1859. Here he grew to manhood and received his education in the common schools, and at Florence and Huntsville, Ala. He first engaged in tilling the soil but later entered a store as clerk. As above stated, he opened the livery business at Marianna in December, 1873, and was very successful at this until a snow storm came and crushed in his stable. He then rebuilt and in 1876, as misfortune seemed to cling to him, he had his stable destroyed by fire, sustaining a loss of about $1,500, and in 1883 the stable was again destroyed by fire with a loss much heavier than before. Neither disheartened nor discouraged he again engaged in the business, built a brick barn and now has the best livery business in Eastern Arkansas. He also had a farm of 300 acres, after having sold some, and is one of the most practical business men of the county. He was married first in 1876 to Mrs. Ella Campbell, who is deceased. The children by this marriage are also deceased. Mr. Derrick afterward married Miss Emma Longley. Mr. Derrick is the son of H. B., Sr., and Evalyn Beal, the father a native of Alabama, born April 10, 1819. He is a farmer by occupation but is now living with his son. The latter is a member of the Methodist Episcopal Church, South.

Eli T. Diamond. Of all the old settlers in Arkansas there is no one more deserving of a place in the history of his State than Eli T. Diamond, who is also a descendant of Revolutionary heroes. His grandfather, John Diamond, was a native of Ireland and came to America in his boyhood days, being one of the first to respond to the call of his adopted country, and serving in the war for freedom until its close. He was a member of Gen. Marion's famous band in all of its brilliant achievements. After the close of the war he returned to his home in South Carolina, but, being surrounded by Tories, and unpleasantly and dangerously situated, he removed to Georgia and settled on the site of the present city of Milledgeville, once the capital, and where Robert Diamond, the father of our subject, was reared, he having been born in South Carolina during the stormy times of the Revolution. After his marriage Robert Diamond removed to Robertson County, Tenn., and then to Illinois, in 1816, under the Territorial Government, and settled in Bond County, where he died in 1852. He was one of the early settlers of that State. Nancy (Rice) Diamond, the mother of the principal of this sketch, was a daughter of James Rice, an Englishman. She was born in Virginia, on the banks of the Potomac River, and was there reared and educated, but later removed to Georgia, where she met, captured and married the father of Eli T. She died in Illinois in 1857, having borne eleven children, of whom the subject of this sketch is the only survivor. He was born in Robertson County, Tenn., April 22, 1807, and accompanied his parents to Illinois at the age of eight years, where he was brought up and educated. At the age of twenty years he went to Natchez, Miss., and lived with an uncle. Two years later he became employed as an overseer on a Mississippi plantation, being engaged in that occupation for eight years, when he bought an interest in a plantation in Washington County, Miss., but, putting too much confidence in his partner, he was bankrupted. He then moved to Chicot County, Ark., in 1840, where he was employed as overseer of a plantation until 1842, at which time he went to Desha County, again becoming interested in a large plantation. For awhile he succeeded very well, but, another financial crash overtaking him, he again lost the greater part of the earnings of

years of labor. He then (in 1844) removed to Walnut Bend, on the Mississippi River, in Phillips County. Here he lived for twenty-four years, clearing up one of the best-improved farms in that section of country, owning 700 acres of land, and while here he secured a large tract of land in the western part of Phillips (now Lee) County. A large negro debt swallowed up his Walnut Bend property, and for the third time he was sent adrift in the financial world. He then set out for his wild and untenanted home in the wilderness of Phillips County. In 1860 he bought a family of negroes, expecting to pay for them when he could sell cotton, as he had two crops unsold. When the war came on the cotton was burned by the Confederates, and the debt accumulated during the war. That struggle found him with a good home surrounded by every convenience and comfort. In 1862 Mr. Diamond brought hands to this section, which was then a wilderness, and improved some of his wild land, where he now lives, but still retained his home on the river. But the ravages of the war and the accumulation of debt compelled him to a compromise in giving up his river place, when he came west. Older in years, and with burdens and misfortunes sufficient to have paralyzed many a younger man, he began anew the work of making a home for his family, and soon the wilderness blossomed under his skill and husbandry. But the guns of Sumter were the death-knell of his high ambitions. The war gave freedom to his most valuable property, the negro, and the close of the war found him destitute of everything but the shattered remains of what had once been a magnificent property, and of which there only remains one-quarter section of land, on which he now lives with his son and his tenants, calmly awaiting the end of a well-spent life. Mr. Diamond has been twice married; first, in 1846, to Elizabeth Hall, a native of North Carolina, who died in 1857, leaving six children, three of whom survive: William H., Eli T. and Alford S. His second marriage was in February, 1868, to Miss Anna Owen, of Phillips County, who died in 1870. Mr. Diamond is a Democrat in politics, is a member of the Masonic order and of the Methodist Episcopal Church, South, to which he has belonged since twelve years of age. He is esteemed by all who know him for his goodness of heart, and for his Christian character in every day life. He has kept a diary of public events since 1844, noting down all public events. There are several large volumes of the work, and many are the facts and statements therein contained, which, in time to come, and even now, are very valuable.

James J. Dozier came originally from Georgia, being a son of Woody and Eliza (Compton) Dozier, also natives of that State. The senior Dozier was born in Warren County in 1804, and his wife four years later in Jasper County. They were married in 1828, and became the parents of ten children, seven of whom are still living: Mary C. (wife of R. J. Bickerstaff, whose biography appears in this work), Sallie F. (Mrs. Sutton, of Forrest City), Emily V. (wife of R. P. Danart, a resident of Texas), Anna C. (wife of Rev. W. H. Pasley, also a resident of Forrest City), James J., the principal of this sketch), Elizabeth (the wife of Andrew C. Wood, a farmer of St. Francis County) and Annette E. (widow of William Henderson). James J. Dozier was born in Jasper County, Ga., on July 1, 1843, but passed his boyhood days in what is now Lee County, Ala. He enlisted in the Confederate army in July, 1861, in the Thirteenth Regiment Alabama Volunteers, in which he served until the close of the war, serving as a non-commissioned officer. He participated in the battles of Seven Pines, the seven days' fight before Richmond, South Mountain, Antietam, Sharpsburg, Fredericksburg, Chancellorsville and Gettysburg, at which battle he was wounded by the explosion of a shell; he was also slightly wounded at the battle of the Wilderness. He took part in the engagements of Spottsylvania Court-House, Petersburg, Turkey Ridge, and a number of others, and was captured at High Bridge, three days before Lee's surrender, being held for three months. He came to Arkansas in January, 1867, and settled near Moro, where he now resides, on a farm of 220 acres, with about forty acres under cultivation. Mr. Dozier returned to Alabama in 1869, and was there married to Miss Olive I. Crabbe, of that State, and a daughter of Richard and Matilda (Love) Crabbe. Mr. and Mrs. Dozier are the parents of nine children, seven living: Nina, Charles E., Emma, Grover C., James R., Nora and Mattie. Mr. Dozier held the office of deputy sheriff during the years from 1880 to 1885. He is a member of the County Wheel.

J. P. Dunham was born in Effingham County, Ill., in 1845, but was reared in Shelby County, and up to the breaking out of the late war his time was occupied in attending the common schools. He dropped his books to join the Federal army and protect the grand old stars and stripes, and was a member of the First Illinois Cavalry, but at the end of one year was transferred to the Trans-Mississippi Department, and was on detached service under Steele, and was with him at the fall of Little Rock. He went from there to Pilot Knob, and shortly after the close of the war he went to Kansas and embarked in the lumber business, and also owned and operated a saw-mill on Marie des Cygnes River. In 1875 he came to Arkansas and settled in Phillips County, where he operated a saw-mill for two and a half years, which enterprise did not prove a financial success. From that time until 1888 he owned and operated a mill in Lee County, his business partner being R. D. Griffis, who was connected with him for eleven years, or until 1888, after which they sold out to a lumber company, and Mr. Dunham has since remained its manager. He owns a good house and lot, and 13,000 acres of land on Spring Creek, and is also in the lumber business. He is a Republican, a member of the Episcopal Church, and belongs to the A. F. & A. M., being a Knight Templar, and is also a member of the Royal Arcanum and the Knights of Honor and the Knights and Ladies of Honor. He was married while a resident of Kansas, to Miss Kate Rouse, by whom he has one child, Capitola. He is a son of Hy. and Mary (Ramsey) Dunham, the former of whom was born in Tennessee and is now a resident of Shelby County, Ill., a farmer by occupation.

William P. Fleming, M. D. Among the names which give standing to Marianna and conduce to the welfare of society, is that of Dr. Fleming, for he not only dispenses drugs, but also deals in hardware and furniture. He was born in Haywood County, Tenn., in 1856, but was reared in Crockett County, and received his literary education in Dyersburg Institute, of Tennessee, and the University of Louisville, Ky., graduating from the latter institution in March, 1877. He practiced medicine at Bell's Depot, Tenn., for three years, being also engaged in the drug business, but sold out in 1883 and came to Marianna, Ark., where he has since confined himself solely to the sale of drugs, his partner, Mr. Plummer, having charge of the hardware and furniture department. His store-room is 120x25 feet, and his stock of drugs is valued at about $10,000, and nets him a fair annual income. His stock of goods is quite complete, and it is safe to say that a call for any article will be promptly and accurately filled, for Dr. Fleming has few equals as a pharmacist. He was married in Memphis, Tenn., to Miss May Townsend, a daughter of D. H. Townsend, a farmer of that State, and by her has the following little family: Patrick, Guy and Walter. The Doctor is a son of Jacob and Mariah (Turpin) Fleming, the former a native of Illinois, reared in Tennessee. He is now a retired merchant and land owner near Bell's Depot, Tenn., and is sixty-five years of age. His wife was born in Tennessee, and died in 1888, aged fifty years. Anderson Turpin, the maternal grandfather, was a Tennesseean by birth.

M. H. Ford, planter and land-holder of Independence Township, is one of four children, reared by Charles F. and Betty (Hewett) Ford, his birth occurring in 1859. Charles Ford, a native of Virginia, was born in 1824, of parents who were among the F. F. V's. He passed his younger days in Virginia, where he became engaged in the mercantile business and was recognized as a man of unusual business aptitude. He was married in 1854 to Betty, daughter of John M. Hewett, of Kentucky, and to their union the following children were born: Minnie (now Mrs. Frank Govan of Marianna, and the mother of four children), Charlie (married to Miss Jessie Jackson, and resides at Marianna and they have three children), M. H.

(the subject of this sketch) and William (unmarried, the deputy clerk of Lee County). Mr. Ford immigrated to Arkansas and later on came to Lee County, where he purchased a large amount of property and became very popular, being considered as a public-spirited and progressive man, always ready to lend his substantial support to anything for the growth and eventual good of the county. He died in 1867 in Lee County, and his wife followed him about five years later. They were members of the Christian Church and highly respected by all who knew them. M. H. Ford passed his boyhood days in Arkansas, Kentucky and Quincy, Ill., his education being completed at the Gem City Business College of the latter place. Soon after he came to Arkansas and in 1881 was appointed marshal of Marianna, which position he held with creditable distinction for seven years. After retiring from office he engaged in farming and now has about 320 acres of good land on which his residence is situated, and in addition to that has over 1,000 acres, with a total of 600 acres well improved and under cultivation. Mr. Ford was married in 1885 to Miss Carrie Foreman, of Independence Township, Lee County, Ark., and to their union three children have been born: Twins (deceased) and Carrie Louise. Mr. Ford is a Democrat in his political views, and in secret societies is a member of the Knights of Pythias (charter member) and the Knights of Honor. He is a member of the Presbyterian Church, and his wife a communicant of the Episcopal Church.

Col. John I. Foreman, who was born in North Carolina, in 1829, was one of two children resulting from the union of William S. and Elizabeth E. (Williams) Foreman. The father's birth occurred in 1806, in North Carolina, where he became identified with the most prominent and wealthy planters of Pitt County, also belonging to one of the first families of that State. He was married in 1828, to Elizabeth, daughter of Dr. Williams, an eminent physician of North Carolina, who served as surgeon in the Revolutionary War. Mr. Foreman died in 1836, leaving to a young widow the management of his large fortune, which was willed without condition to her. She again married, her second husband being E. B. Freeman, clerk of the supreme court of North Carolina for many years. Mrs. Freeman having received a large fortune from her former husband, turned her attention to the education of her two sons, both of them being sent to Princeton, N. J., and graduating from the prominent college of that place. She closed her eyes to the scenes of this world in 1848. In 1851 John I. was elected to the legislature, from Pitt County, N. C., in which he served two years, and had he chose to remain, could have occupied a most enviable position in the political field. This, however, he did not care to do. Having previously paid a visit to Eastern Arkansas, he concluded that that was the place for his future home, and in 1853 he came to what is now Lee (then Phillips) County, to join his brother, who had immigrated to the State a year previous, bringing with him into the primeval forest a vast number of slaves and other property. He had purchased a large tract of land, and by the help of the slaves soon brought it from its embryo state, to that of cultivation. This property was equally enjoyed and shared by the two brothers, where they lived in great contentment until the breaking out of the war between the States. During that time they added much to their wealth, and became widely recognized as the most prosperous and popular planters in the State. They were known far and near for their generosity and support to all educational enterprises, and in fact to all movements that betokened the good and growth of the county. When the war was declared, John Foreman believing the South to be right, as a leader of the people with whom he lived, raised a company of soldiers for the Confederate army, and was attached to the Second Arkansas, Govan's regiment. Being transferred east of the Mississippi, he fought in the battle of Perryville (Ky.), and then returned to the Trans-Mississippi Department, where he was attached to Gen. Marsh Walker's staff. He was with this command at the date of Gen. Walker's death, in a duel with a well-known general. After this Mr. Foreman was not in active service, and at the closing of hostilities he returned home to find that his plantation and

all his valuable property had been destroyed by the ravages of war. Let it not for a moment be supposed that his great loss overpowered him, for he set to work with redoubled courage and a determination to succeed, and a few years witnessed the recovery of his fortunes, and an addition to his property lost. Here in this vicinity he lived for many years, occupying a warm place in the hearts of the entire community, by whom he was honored and revered, as a leading and popular citizen of this county. A mean action or an unkind word was something perfectly foreign to his loyal and generous nature. His death, which occurred in 1879, was sincerely mourned by all who knew him, and his work, which was of a lifetime in doing good to man, well deserved its reward in the commendation, ''Well done thou good and faithful servant.'' Col. Foreman was married in 1855 to Miss Arabella Armstrong, of New York City, a daughter of William and Martha Armstrong, early settlers of that city, where her father died in 1834. Her mother then immigrated to Tennessee, and then to Arkansas. Mr. and Mrs. Foreman had eight children: William H., Robert L. (M. D.), J. I., Jr., E. W., Jane, Arabella, M. K. and Bessie.

R. R. Foreman, residing in Independence Township, was born in North Carolina in 1831, being the son of William S. and Elizabeth E. (Williams) Foreman. The father was also a native of North Carolina, his birth occurring in 1806. He followed farming and merchandising with success, and was married in 1828 to Miss Elizabeth, daughter of Dr. Robert Williams, of North Carolina, a very prominent man and surgeon in the Revolutionary War, who was residing in the old North State at the date of his death. There were only two children born to the union of Mr. and Mrs. Foreman: R. R. (the subject of this sketch) and John. Mr. Foreman died in Pitt County, North Carolina, in 1836, respected and esteemed by all who knew him. Mrs. Foreman was again married, her second choice being E. B. Freeman, who was for many years previous to his death, and at that date, a clerk of the supreme court of North Carolina. Mrs. Freeman died in 1848 in her native State. R. R. Foreman received his education in the schools of North Carolina, afterward attending school at Princeton, N. J. In 1852 he came to Lee (then Phillips) County, and located on a farm about three miles from Marianna, this farm consisting of 360 acres, besides a large amount of property in another portion. He was married in 1853 to Frances C. Williams, a daughter of Dr. R. F. Williams, of North Carolina, a prominent physician who died in that State in 1852. To Mr. and Mrs. Foreman two children have been born: Elizabeth L. (born in 1861) and Mary C. (born in 1866, now the wife of M. H. Ford, of Lee County). Mr. Foreman is a member of Lodge No. 171 of the Masonic order at Marianna, and Chapter No. 54, and also a K. of H. For some years he was Worshipful Master and a charter member of the Blue Lodge, and also High Priest of the order. Mr. Foreman and family are members of the Episcopal Church. He is a man who takes a great interest in the growth of the county, and is lending his substantial support toward gaining this end, and especially is he interested in educational and religious matters, to which he contributes liberally.

G. F. Foster, M. D. Noah Foster, a native of Tennessee, was born in 1809 and passed his younger days in the schools of that State. In 1833 he moved to Panola County, Miss., where he met and married Miss Lodiska Spaulding, daughter of a prominent planter, Gideon Spaulding. Mr. Foster settled in Mississippi, where he and his wife are now residing. He has been very successful as a farmer, and is now enjoying the fruits of his industry, from which he accumulated a large property. He is a Democrat and has always taken an active interest in public enterprises. To himself and wife a family of ten children were born: Delila (now Mrs. Parker, residing in Lonoke County), Nancy (Mrs. Ruby, of Lonoke County), Elizabeth (deceased), John (dead), Thomas (living in Panola County, Mississippi, married and has a family of six children), Davis (unmarried and lives in Lee County, engaged in the mercantile business with his brother G. F., the subject of this sketch), and two children unnamed. G. F. Foster was born in Mississippi in 1847, and received a good common-school education in the schools of his native State, afterward entering the Eclectic Medical College of Mississippi, from which he graduated in 1884. He then moved to St. Francis County, Ark., where he practiced his profession with manifest success. In 1887 he embarked in the mercantile business, and by his courteous and obliging manners has won a liberal patronage from the surrounding community. His practice is among the best and wealthy class of people, by whom he is recognized as an efficient physician, and a credit to the profession. He also owns 200 acres of valuable land under a thrifty state of cultivation. Dr. Foster was married in 1884 to Miss Bradford Watson, a daughter of John and Betty Watson. Her parents were natives of Mississippi, but moved to Arkansas at an early date, about the year 1847 or 1850. To Dr. and Mrs. Foster two children have been born. The Doctor is a Democrat, and in secret societies is identified with the Masonic order, being a member of La Grange Lodge No. 108. He is a member of and an earnest worker in the Methodist Episcopal Church and lends valuable aid to all enterprises for the good of the county.

Thomas Foster was born within one mile of La Grange, the place where he now lives, on August 19, 1849, and was a son of Golden and Elizabeth Foster, natives of Mississippi. Mr. Golden Foster moved to Arkansas from Mississippi, and from there to Texas, but came back to Arkansas in 1841, where he died twenty years later. He was a large planter and acquired some property. He and his wife were members of the Methodist Episcopal Church, and were the parents of twelve children, two of whom are still living: Malissa (wife of Rev. Thomas Craig, now stationed at Desha, Independence County), and Thomas (the principal of this sketch, and the youngest in the family). There is living also a half-sister to these children, Miss Mattie Foster, the issue of their father's second marriage. Thomas Foster had three brothers in the Confederate army, one of whom was killed at Shiloh, one died from the wounds received at Gettysburg, and one while serving in the *Indian Territory. Soon after the war he commenced working to support his mother and sisters, and was employed by a Mr. Lownsbery at a small salary. In 1873 he began farming for himself, and with the push and energy, which are his principal characteristics, has been very successful as a cotton planter. In 1876 he was married to Miss Vionna Hickey, a daughter of C. W. and Elizabeth Hickey, of La Grange. They are the parents of these children: Frank U., Bettie Lou, Cleola, Thomas, Mattie May, Gustavus W., and one deceased. Mr. Foster, while not a member of any church, is the son of Methodist parents, and his leaning is toward that denomination. He is a member of the following secret orders: Masons, K. of H. and A. O. U. W. Mrs. Foster is a member of the Baptist Church.

J. T. Friar is a member of the Haynes' Mercantile Association, and was born within three miles of where he now lives, in 1844, being the fifth of six children born to J. T. and Perlyxie (Burk) Friar, natives of Tennessee, from near Knoxville. The father removed to Arkansas at an early day (about 1830), and in addition to farming also dealt in land. After his wife's death, in 1848, he married Miss Lucretia Seaborn, by her becoming the father of two children. His death occurred in 1856. His children by his first wife now only number two: Narcissus (wife of J. W. Byers) and our subject. The two half-brothers are also deceased. J. T. Friar was reared and educated in what is now Lee County, and at the early age of seventeen years entered the Confederate army, being in Capt. Dunn's company, known as the "Dead-shot" Company from St. Francis County. He served east of the Mississippi River for four years, and was in the following engagements: Shiloh, Chickamauga, Missionary Ridge, and from Dalton to Atlanta, Ga. He was also at Jonesboro, Springfield, Franklin, Nashville, and in numerous skirmishes. He surrendered at Greenville, N. C., and returned home. He was wounded by a minie ball in the thigh at the battle of Shiloh, and is still troubled by his wound. He first began working as a farm hand at $20 per month, continuing until 1867, when he was married to Mrs. Frances (McDaniel) Hughes, a daughter of Arch. McDaniel, but Mr. Friar was called upon to mourn her death about one year later, she having borne him a child, who

is also deceased. In 1868 Mr. Friar purchased eighty acres of slightly improved land, and has since added 200 acres, making him one of the best farms in the county, and in addition to this he owns some valuable town property, all of which he has made by industry and good management since the war. In 1888 he became associated with the Haynes' Mercantile Association, which is composed of farmers, and does a business of some $30,000. Mr. Friar has been careful and painstaking in the management of his farm and, indeed, is thorough in regard to everything connected with its advancement, as he is in every business to which he gives his attention. In 1869 he was married to Miss Martha Tipton, of Tennessee, a daughter of Benjamin and Mary Tipton, of that State, and by her has had eight children, four of whom are now living: Aggie, Nannie, Custer and J. T. Mr. and Mrs. Friar are members of the Baptist Church, and Mr. Friar belongs to Bethel Lodge No. 2168, K. of H.

E. F. Friend, miller and ginner, Marianna, Ark. This wide-awake and enterprising resident was originally from Alabama, where his birth occurred in 1838, and in that State he reached years of maturity, and received his education. He learned the carriage-maker's trade, but when the war broke out he cast aside his implements of peace and took up the weapons of warfare, enlisting in the Confederate service. He participated in the following prominent battles: Corinth, Shiloh, all the battles of Gens. Bragg and Johnston, and during his service never received a wound. After the war he returned to his home, and in 1871 moved to Arkansas. Previous to this he was married in Alabama to Miss Mary E. Gilbert, a native of that State, and after this union he moved to Marianna, where he worked at his trade for fifteen years, being the owner of a regular carriage and wagon shop for that length of time. He had a full plant of steam machinery for his business, and after the fire had but four left. The loss was at least $3,000. After this he embarked in the ginning and milling business, and will introduce a full line of rollers for grinding by the first of the year 1890. He still owns his farm of 320 acres, and is a prosperous and progressive citizen. To his marriage were born six children: Anna, Ola, Brent, Julia, Matie and Samuel. Mr. Friend is a member of the K. of H. and K. & L. of H., and Royal Arcanum. He is the son of David H. and Amanda (Hendricks) Friend, natives of Virginia and Alabama, respectively, the father born in 1800 and the mother in 1812. The father was one of the pioneers of Alabama, and lived to be about eighty years of age. He was a jeweler, a silversmith and a farmer by occupation. The mother died at the age of forty-five years.

Thomas A. Futrall, A. M., principal of the Marianna Male and Female Institute, located at Marianna, Ark., is one of the most prominent educators in the South. He was born in the "Old North State," in 1842, and was educated in the best schools of the East, having been at one time a pupil of the famous William J. Bingham. About the time he finished his academic course, in 1860, a war cloud appeared above the horizon, and very soon thereafter he joined the Southern army as a volunteer, and served with distinction as an officer of Gen. John R. Cooke's North Carolina Brigade of the Army of Northern Virginia during the late war between the States. He took part in all the great battles in Virginia, Maryland and Pennsylvania, and was paroled with the remnant of Gen. Lee's army at Appomattox Court House. At the close of the war he immigrated to West Tennessee, and established a classical and scientific school, which soon took rank with the best institutions of learning in the country, and gained for him a widespread reputation as a scholar and an educator, so much so, that in 1884 he was tendered his present position in the flourishing town of Marianna. Prof. Futrall has made this institution one of the most thorough and practical schools in the State, from which young men and women go out well prepared for the active duties of life. Beginning the work when comparatively young, Prof. Futrall has made teaching the business of his life, and has taught successfully for twenty-five consecutive years. In 1887, at the Chicago meeting of the National Educational Association of the United States, he was elected vice-president of the association, and was re-elected to the same position in Nashville, Tenn., in 1889, and is now, 1890, manager for the association in the State of Arkansas. He is a quiet, courteous, thoroughly posted gentleman, a ripe scholar, and is familiar with the best methods of instruction. In 1867 he was married to Miss Emma R. Headen, of Chatham County, N. C. A young family of seven interesting children, four girls and three boys, gather around the hearthstone.

Dr. J. H. Gibson, physician and surgeon. The subject of this sketch was born in Iredell County, N. C., in the year 1830. He attended the common schools of the neighborhood, and was graduated from Davidson College, a literary institution in Mecklenburg County, N. C., in the year 1853, after which he spent several years in teaching in the State of Florida. He then commenced reading medicine, and was graduated from the Medical University of Georgia, receiving the degree of M. D. in the year 1858. Subsequently entering upon the practice of his profession in his native State, he remained there until shortly before the breaking out of the late Civil War, when he came to the State of Arkansas, and located in Independence County, but the following year he enlisted in the Twenty-second Arkansas as surgeon. At the close of the war he came to Lee County, and resumed the practice of his adopted calling at La Grange, where he has since resided, and built up a large practice. In 1868 the Doctor was married to Miss Eliza Burke, a daughter of Elisha and Eliza Burke, natives of North Carolina, and who came to Arkansas in 1840. Her father represented Phillips County for a number of years in the State legislature. Dr. Gibson and wife are the parents of five children: Belo, Estelle, Burke, Minnie and Willie. Dr. Gibson is a member of the Presbyterian Church. He also belongs to the Masonic fraternity, and is Worshipful Master of the lodge at La Grange. His wife is a member of the Baptist Church. He is also justice of the peace of Richland Township, and one of the leading men of the township.

William Franklin Gill is a son of Nathaniel Y. Gill, a native of Tennessee, who made that State his home until 1849, when he removed to Mississippi, locating near Holly Springs. He was married in Tennessee to Miss Susan Bowles, also of that State. In 1854 they came to Arkansas, and engaged in farming on the plantation now owned by Mr. N. L. Graves, near Lexa. He was a hard working man, and a good manager, and in 1861 raised the largest crop of cotton per acre of any ever grown in Eastern Arkansas. Mr. Gill died in December, 1873, at the age of nearly fifty years. His wife was called to her long home in the same month, when forty-five years old. The paternal grandfather of the principal of this sketch, was a native of North Carolina, and of Irish descent, and moved to Tennessee when a young man, where he lived the remainder of his life, following the occupation of a farmer. William Franklin Gill was born near Columbia, Tenn., on January 8, 1846, being the eldest in a family of seven children, six of whom are living: William F., R. O. (also a farmer of this county), Morris (a farmer of Phillips County), John Y. (a merchant of Texas), Isaac S. (a teacher, also in Texas) and Mary P. (the wife of L. G. Howard [see sketch of William T. Howard in this work], the partner of our subject in the mercantile business in La Grange). In 1862 William F. Gill enlisted in Dobbins' regiment of Confederate Cavalry, in which he served until the close of the war, participating in all of the principal battles in Price's raid through Missouri, Kansas and the Indian Territory. After the close of the war, he went on the farm with his father, remaining with him until his marriage, on November 18, 1869. Mr. Gill labored for himself on the farm for one year, and then moved to La Grange, entering into the mercantile business with his father and brother, R. O. Gill. This was continued until his father died, when he and his brother conducted the trade until 1881, and then dissolved. Mr. Gill then went into business with Mr. L. G. Howard, his brother-in-law. They started with a very small capital, but their present large business demonstrates what can be done by true energy, combined with a large stock of common sense, good business management and honest dealings. He was married, on November 18, 1869, to Miss Bettie Underwood, a native of Tennessee, who died in March, 1874, leaving three children, two still living: Mollie and William Y. Mr. Gill married his second and present wife, Rebecca Holland, February 4, 1875. She was born in the State of South Carolina, in 1857, and is the mother of one daughter, Beulah. In addition to his store at La Grange, Mr. Gill owns 800 acres of fine land, of which 450 acres are under cultivation. All this he has made since the war. He is a member of the Royal Arcanum, of the Knights of Honor and is a prominent Democrat of Richland Township.

Robert O. Gill is one of the prominent residents of Haynes, Ark., is a money lender and a large real estate owner, having become by his own industry the owner of 960 acres of land, with about 260 acres under cultivation. His property is improved with good buildings and fences, and besides his own comfortable and pleasant home in Haynes, he owns another house and lot. He was born in Tennessee, in 1847, and is the second of seven children born to Nathaniel Y. and Susan A. (Bowles) Gill, also native-born citizens of Tennessee. They removed to Phillips County, Ark., in 1851, and settled twelve miles west of Helena, near what is known as Lexa, and there the father was manager of a plantation belonging to his uncle, Isaac Smith, and afterward worked in the same capacity for William Pillow. In 1856 he bought a farm west of Helena, known as Hude Park plantation, but sold out at the end of one year and became general manager of the plantation belonging to Mr. Pillow, remaining with him until the opening of the war, during which time he farmed on what is known as the Grant place. After the war was over he bought what is now known as the H. P. Rogers' place, and here made his home until 1867, when he became the owner of a farm three miles west of Haynes for one year, selling it then to Dr. Wood, moving in the spring of 1869 to La Grange, where he was engaged in the mercantile business until his death, December 16, 1873; his death was caused by pneumonia. His wife died December 3, 1873, and both had been members of the Baptist Church for a number of years. Six of their seven children are now living: W. F. (who is a merchant at La Grange), Robert O., Maria M., John Y. (of Texas), I. S. (of Texas), and Mary P. (wife of W. L. Howard, of La Grange). Robert O. Gill was reared and educated in Phillips and Lee Counties. He received only the advantages of a common-school education in his early youth, the turmoils of war placing it beyond the power of his parents to send him to higher institutions of learning, but by self-application and much reading he is one of the best posted and most intelligent men of the county. At the age of twenty-one years, or in 1868, he began life for himself as a farmer, but after farming on rented land for one year he began merchandising in La Grange, his capital stock amounting to $600, which he had earned the previous year. Since 1883 he has been a resident of Haynes, and until the spring of 1889 followed merchandising, but then sold out and has been following his present occupation. He is a man who favors all laudable public enterprises and in his political views is a Democrat. Socially he is a member of the K. of H., La Grange Lodge No. 2166, and has held nearly all the chairs in the local lodge. In the spring of 1875 he was married to Miss Cornelia L. Smith, a daughter of G. B. and Susan S. Smith, natives of Northern Alabama, who removed to Arkansas a few years prior to the late Civil War. Mrs. Smith died in 1888. Of the seven children born to Mr. and Mrs. Gill, two are now living: Alma L. and Robbie.

Joseph O. Gray. Payton R. Gray, a prominent and wealthy planter of Bear Creek Township, was born in Livingston County, Ky., in 1818, being a son of Presley Gray, also a Kentuckian by birth and a tiller of the soil, as was his father, originally from Virginia. Presley Gray was a member of the Cumberland Presbyterian Church, and lived until his seventy-second year. His wife, Maria (Hodge) Gray, was connected with the Baptist Church. She was the mother of seven children, all of whom are yet living, five residents of Kentucky, one of Iowa and our immediate subject, who has been a citizen of this State since 1847. He took charge of the old homestead at the age of twenty years, and two years later was married to Mrs. Eliza (Dunn) Thrailkill, who died a year after, leaving one child,

which only lived nine months. He then married Miss Maria Woods. She died shortly after his removal to Mississippi, in 1844, leaving three children, all deceased. He was next married to Mrs. Margaret S. Bohanan (nee Dickson), a native of Paris, Ky., who died in 1883. They were the parents of two children: Blanche (widow of John E. Burke, living with her father) and Joseph O. (who was born in Coahoma County, Miss., in 1848.) His father having been drafted for the Confederate service in 1863, our subject went as a substitute, and served in Dobbin's regiment of Confederate cavalry until the close of the war, operating in Eastern Arkansas and Missouri, and receiving his discharge in January, 1865. He was then employed in farming and clerking until 1872, when he entered into the mercantile business at Philips Bayou, in which he has since been engaged, with the exception of the years 1877–78. At that time farming occupied his attention. Mr. Gray married in March, 1875, Miss Mary C. Wilkins, a native of Lee County, Ark., and a daughter of Maj. Wilkins, an officer in the Confederate army, now deceased. They have had one son who is now deceased. Mr. Gray carries a stock of about $5,000, and his annual sales amount to over $40,000. He is also extensively occupied in farming, owning a half interest in 320 acres of fine land, besides some city property, and has the control of over 1,500 acres of land. Mr. Gray is also the postmaster of Philips Bayou, which position he has filled for the past eight years. In connection with his other interests he is engaged in cotton-ginning, operating two steam gins and one horse-power cotton-gin. He is a member of the A. F. & A. M. His wife is a member of the Baptist Church.

J. W. Greer's farm, comprising 160 acres, is one of the best for successful agricultural purposes to be found in this part of the county, and the manner in which it is conducted is in full keeping with the personal characteristics of its owner, a man of great energy and determination and of much perseverance. He was born in Union County, S. C., in 1836, and is a son of J. M. and Sarah A. (Sanders) Greer, the former a native of South Carolina and of English-Irish descent. The paternal grandfather, Robert Greer, and his brother, Orpha, served in the American Revolution, and the former was exiled from Ireland on account of his religious views, and after coming to the United States he settled in South Carolina, and there left a large number of descendants, several of whom served in the War of 1812. J. W. Greer spent his youth in his native State, but in 1858 came west and settled near Helena, Ark., on a farm where he remained industriously at work until the Rebellion came up. In 1861 he enlisted in the Confederate army, Company B, Twenty-third Arkansas, of which he was captain, and participated in the following battles: Corinth and the siege of Port Hudson, in which engagement he lost his left arm, it being shot off by a cannon ball. He was captured on July 9, 1863, and was retained a prisoner until the close of the war at New Orleans, Fort La Fayette, Bedloe's Island, Fort McHenry, Fort Delaware, then to Morris Island. After remaining at his old home for a number of years he came to Lee County, Ark., in 1878, and here has become well known and highly esteemed by all. He has been justice of the peace for eight years; is a member of the Cumberland Presbyterian Church, and has always tried to follow the teachings of the Golden Rule. He was married in 1885 to Mrs. Fannie R. Allen Harris, and by her has one child, Sarah F. He was first married to Elizabeth H. Patterson, who died leaving one child, Jason H.

Gen. D. C. Govan was born in Northampton County, N. C., July 4, 1829, and is a son of A. R. and M. P. (Jones) Govan, the former of whom was born in Orangeburg, N. C., and was educated in South Carolina College at Columbia, some of his schoolmates being William C. Preston, George McDuff, Langdon C. Chevies, Hugh S. Lagree and other men of the South, who afterward became noted. After graduating from the above-named college he began his career as a planter in Orangeburg District, and was elected to Congress from there about the year 1825. About 1830 he emigrated with his family westward to Tennessee, and there made his home until the removal of the Chickasaw Indians from the State of Mississippi, when he made that State his permanent abode, his

death occurring there in 1841, at the age of forty-seven years. His wife was born in North Carolina in 1801, and by Mr. Govan became the mother of a large family of children, her death occurring at the age of eighty-seven years. Gen. D. C. Govan grew to manhood in Northern Mississippi, and was prepared for college by Rev. Francis L. Hawks, and graduated from the Columbia (S. C.) College, in 1848. There was a military company kept in drill at this institution, then the best in the State, and of this company Mr. Govan was a member. Immediately upon graduating he joined his fellow-kinsman, Gen. Ben McCullough, on an expedition to California, their company consisting of twenty-one men, all of whom, with the exception of two or three, were experienced Texan and old Indian fighters. They left Mississippi on October 1 and traveled through Texas and Mexico north to Monterey, thence to the seacoast, where they took passage on board a vessel bound for the Golden Gate, and reached San Francisco late in December. They engaged in hunting and trapping until the next spring, and then found that they had accumulated sufficient money to engage in mining, which they did (with the understanding between our subject and Mr. McCullough that they were to share equally in the results of their western expedition) and fitted out a party to go to the mountains and commence operations. Just at this juncture the Territorial legislature of California passed a law imposing a tax on all foreigners mining in the Territory. California was then divided into two districts and Mr. McCullough received the appointment of collector for the Southern District, a position which he and Mr. Govan supposed would prove fabulously remunerative, and Mr. Govan took charge of the mining expedition and went up the San Joaquin River. He met with fair success in mining, and said that had they not been trying to make a competence in a few days, might have amassed a fortune. He mined on various rivers until he reached the North Fork of the American River, when he received a letter from Gen. McCullough saying that the foreign tax could not be collected, and the law was a failure, and requested him to meet him in Sacramento, where they would prepare for another mining expedition. When they reached that place the sheriff of the county had been killed and a special election was being held, whereupon Mr. McCullough became a candidate and was elected. Mr. Govan then sold out his mining outfit and became deputy sheriff, the former gentleman officiating in that capacity from October, 1850, to July, 1855, and did the first legal execution in the State of California after it had been admitted into the Union, hanging three men for highway robbery. He returned to his home in Mississippi immediately after retiring from the sheriff's office, Mr. Govan returning at the same time. The latter was married in Mississippi, in December, 1853, to Miss Mary F. Otey, a daughter of the Rt. Rev. James Otey, of Mississippi, and the following December he came to Arkansas, locating in that part of Phillips County, which subsequently became Lee County. He was a successful planter until the opening of the war, then began raising a company for the Confederate army, which afterward became a part of the Second Arkansas Regiment, under Gen. Hindman. They operated first in Southeastern Missouri, but were soon transferred to the Army of Tennessee, of which they formed the advance under Gen. Albert Sidney Johnston. Mr. Govan was appointed lieutenant-colonel in October, 1861, and at their request acted as colonel in the battles of Shiloh, Perryville and Murfreesboro, after which he was given command of a brigade, and acted as brigadier-general at Chattanooga, Missionary Ridge, Ringgold and other places, receiving his commission after these battles. He was all through the Georgia campaign, and was in some of the bloodiest fights around Atlanta, but showed through all great intrepidity and courage. In the memorable fight on July 22d, he captured the Sixteenth Iowa Regiment with its colors, and fractions of other companies. Gen. McPherson was killed in front of his command. After almost twenty years had passed away he still had the colors of the Sixteenth Iowa Regiment, and about this time entered into a correspondence with Gen. Belknap, and upon being invited to attend a Federal soldiers' reunion held at Cedar Rapids, Iowa, he did so and returned the colors to the Six-

37

teenth Iowa which he had captured, and received in return a gold-headed cane. In the battle of Chickamauga, the great-grandson of Thomas Jefferson was killed in front of Gen. Govan's command, he being Maj. Sidney Collidge, and his sword fell into the hands of Gen. Govan. It was afterward recaptured, and this led to an inquiry from Collidge's friends as to his whereabouts, and the facts of his death was related to them by Gen. Govan. The name of this intrepid general will live in the hearts of the Southern people as long as they revere the heroes who fought in their service, for he was among the bravest of the brave, and stood shoulder to shoulder with Gen. P. R. Cleburne, Cheatham and others, as far as bravery and ability as a commander is concerned. At the close of the war he returned to his plantation and here has lived a quiet and retired life ever since. Although he is very popular and much beloved by all, and could easily obtain any office he might desire and which the people of Arkansas could confer upon him, yet he has never been an aspirant for any civil office, and is of a rather retiring disposition, although he possesses the true courtesy and polished manners for which the people of the South are famous.

Francis H. Govan, intimately associated with the affairs of Lee County, as deputy clerk of the circuit court, was a member of Morgan's terrible band in his raid through Ohio. He was in the Confederate army from the beginning of the war until its close, first in the Northern Virginia division, in which he served until the seven-days' fight around Richmond, when he was transferred to the Western division, remaining in Morgan's cavalry until after his Ohio raid. He was subsequently appointed aid-de-camp on the staff of his uncle, Gen. D. C. Govan, holding that position until the cessation of hostilities, but spending the latter days of the war in the hospital on account of a wound received at the battle of Franklin. After his return from the army Mr. Govan attended the University of Mississippi, and in 1867 came to Arkansas, and located in this county, where he engaged in merchandising when not holding office. He was elected county clerk in 1874, and again in

1876, and in 1885 was appointed deputy clerk of the circuit court, which office he still occupies. He was married in this county in 1875 to Miss Minnie Ford, who was born in Kentucky in 1855. They are the parents of four children: Bettie H., Laura P., Francis H. and Eaton P. Mr. Govan's birth occurred in Mississippi in 1846, and he was reared at Holly Springs, that State, there receiving a common-school education. He is a son of E. P. Govan, a native of North Carolina, and of Scotch descent, his great-grandfather having been born in that country, though he emigrated to the United States. His grandfather, of South Carolina origin, was a member of Congress from that State. The father of our subject died in 1882, at the age of fifty-five years. His wife was a native of Connecticut, and a daughter of Rev. Francis L. Hawks, a distinguished Episcopal minister. Mr. Govan is a member of the A. F. & A. M., in which order he has risen to the rank of Knight Templar. He also belongs to the Knights of Honor and the Royal Arcanum. He is a man who enjoys the continued esteem of his acquaintances, and as a county official has discharged the duties connected with his office with entire satisfaction to all concerned, and the credit of himself. The records in his charge are a model of neatness and accuracy.

Ferdinand Louis Gustavus is one of the men who escorted Jefferson Davis and his cabinet south on their flight from Richmond. He enlisted in 1862, in a company of cavalry, which was made up and mustered in service at Memphis, Tenn., although composed mostly of men from Phillips and St. Francis County. He participated in the battles of Shiloh, Corinth, Iuka, Atlanta, and most of the battles of his division, and was in the command of Gen. J. E. Johnston, at the time of his surrender in May, 1865. Mr. Gustavus was born in Winnebago County, Wis., April 29, 1832, and was the oldest son of John G. and Charlotte A. (Koepner) Gustavus, natives of Prussia. Mr. Gustavus was born in 1806, and was reared within fifteen miles of Berlin, being married in 1830. In 1831 they emigrated to this country, and settled in Wisconsin, where they lived until their respective deaths, in 1862 and 1864. Both were members of the Lutheran Church, and were the parents of seven children, six of whom are living: Ferdinand L., Robert, Bertie, Theodore, Maria and Henry. The paternal grandfather of our subject was a soldier under Napoleon, and held the position of lieutenant in the Prussian army. Mr. Gustavus commenced farming at the age of twenty-two in the State of Wisconsin, but moved to Arkansas in 1856, where he was engaged as an overseer in Phillips County, until his enlistment in the army. After his return from the battlefield, he purchased the farm on which he still resides. The land is well adapted to the growing of cotton, corn, clover, and small grain. He was married April 14, 1867, to Lucy A. Rives, of Phillips County, where she was born January 28, 1848, being a daughter of John H. and Jane C. (Bonner) Rives, both deceased. They had a family of eight children, seven of whom survive: Mary F. (wife of C. J. McQuien, a farmer of Lee County), Jane A. (wife of Guss Roesher, also of Lee County), John H., Augusta E., Carrie L., Hattie C. and Frederick L. Mr. Gustavus is a leading Democrat, and has served his party and the people of his township as justice of the peace for the past eight years. He has been a member of the school board of this district since 1868. He and wife and four children are members of the Missionary Baptist Church. He also belongs to the Masonic fraternity, and of the Knights of Honor. Mr. Gustavus, having farmed in the Northern States as well as the Southern States, is capable of forming a correct opinion of both localities in regard to climate, soil, and general advantages and disadvantages for those who follow farming for an occupation, and in his judgment Arkansas can not be excelled.

Robert E. Hale is a direct descendant of the celebrated Chief Justice Matthew Hale of England. His parents, Richard C. and Driscilla (Mathews) Hale, were natives of Bedford County, Va. The former was born in 1798 and when a young man moved to Alabama, and afterward to Hardin County, Tenn., where he remained about ten years, then going to Pulaski County, Ill. This was the home of himself and wife until their death, Mr. Hale dying in 1848 and Mrs. Hale in 1884, at the age of ninety years. He started in life as a brick mason, but during the latter years of his career became a prominent contractor and builder, and was an influential man in Pulaski County, Ill., taking an active part in local politics. During the last four years of his life he held the office of probate judge. He was a son of Richard Hale, whose birth occurred in Virginia shortly before the Revolutionary War. Mrs. Hale was a daughter of Joseph Cromwell Mathews, formerly from South Carolina, who was a soldier in the Revolutionary War when a young man. He was married in South Carolina to Miss Penina Crisp, afterward removing to Alabama, then to the States of Tennessee, Kentucky and finally back to Texas in 1835, where they remained until their deaths, which occurred in the year 1858 at the ages of ninety-two and ninety-four years, respectively. Both were members of the Christian Church, in which they took an active part. The Mathews family trace their lineage back to Oliver Cromwell, who was one of the early ancestors of the family. The principal of this sketch was born in Lauderdale County, Ala., in 1824, being the third of three sons and three daughters. He was married in Pulaski County, Ill., in 1848, to Miss Susan J. Hawpe, a daughter of Judge George Hawpe. She was born in Hall County, Ga., in 1830. Mr. and Mrs. Hale became the parents of twelve children, four of whom are still living: James G., Lillian C., Joseph O. and William M. Mr. Hale made Illinois his home until 1855, when he came to Arkansas and located in that portion of Phillips County, which is now included in Lee County. For some years after his advent he carried on the mercantile and lumber business at Jeffersonville. The Mexican War breaking out a few years before his marriage, he enlisted in Company B of the Second Illinois Infantry, in which he served as sergeant, having command of his company at the battle of Buena Vista. Upon the commencement of the Civil War he was commissioned captain, but did not enter the service. At the time of his removal from Pulaski County, Mr. Hale held the position of county treasurer, collector and as-

sessor, and had been postmaster of Haleside for a number of years. Since locating here he has served as justice of the peace for a number of years. He is now the owner of over 1,000 acres of land, and has about 250 acres under cultivation, all made since his arrival in this county, when he had but $2.50. Mr. Hale is a member of the A. F. & A. M., but has not affiliated with the order for a number of years. He also belongs to the I. O. O. F., and he and wife are connected with the Christian Church, taking an active part in religious movements.

D. Hammond, proprietor of the Phœnix Hotel of Marianna, Ark., was born in Rochester, N. Y., November 3, 1840, and, like the majority of the natives of the "Empire State," he is enterprising in his views, is industrious and the soul of honor. After remaining in his native State and attending the common schools until he attained his twentieth year, he went to Missouri and worked as an engineer on the North Missouri Railroad for four years. When the war broke out he was running a Government train, and was captured by Price just west of Mexico, Mo., and was taken to Northeastern Arkansas, where he was paroled upon taking the oath not to aid the North during the remainder of the war. From Arkansas Mr. Hammond went to Nashville, Tenn., thence to Jackson, Mich., where he began working on the Michigan Central Railroad as an engineer between Detroit and Jackson, continuing two years. He was married to Miss Lucretia Blodgett, in Eaton Rapids, Mich., she being a native of that place, and afterward went on the road selling steam fire-engines for Clapp & Jones, of Hudson, N. Y. He followed this business some five years, and in October, 1871, during the great Chicago fire, he was on his way to St. Paul, Minn., to exhibit an engine, and was at Michigan City when the news of the fire reached him. He immediately went with his engine to the scene of the fire, and for four nights and three days never left his post, but did all in his power to assist in subduing the flames. He afterward took his engine to St. Paul, where he sold it, also two others, notwithstanding the fact that he had to encounter much competition. He finally left the road and began working with an engine in the fire department of Greenville, Mich., the city paying him $150 per month and furnishing him with a house, fuel and gas. At the end of one year he went to Fort Scott, Kan., and made his home for five years at that point. Here he put up a 100-battery steam-boiler, and ran it until it was moved to Marianna, Ark., on February 17, 1889. He put up the present engine in Marianna and managed it until a short time since, when he turned it over to his son, and became the proprietor of the Phœnix Hotel, in which he has made many needed changes and improvements. He and wife have two children: Luther and Maud. He is a Democrat, and belongs to the Brotherhood of Locomotive Engineers. His parents, S. and Clarinda (Howe) Hammond, were born in Clarendon, Vt., in 1799 and New York, in 1811, respectively. The father was a farmer, and immigrated to Missouri, locating at St. Charles, where he died in 1881, his wife dying one year later. Of their family of two sons and three daughters, all are living.

William L. Harper, physician and surgeon, Clifton, Ark. Dr. Harper is recognized throughout the county as a friend and laborer in the cause and advancement of the medical fraternity. He is a native of Georgia, his birth occurring in Gilmer County in 1864, and received his primary education in that State. At the age of nineteen years he entered the Medical College at Atlanta, graduating from that institution in his twenty-first year. He first commenced his practice in his native county, removing from there to Arkansas in 1886, and settled where he now lives. He enjoys a large and lucrative practice, which is gradually increasing, and a bright future is opening before him. He is a genial and generous gentleman, liberal in his ideas, a protector of the rights of, a strong promoter of the welfare of, and in deep sympathy with, humanity. He is a member of the Knights of Pythias at Marianna, Ark. The Doctor is the third of ten children, the result of the union of Lindsey and Margaret (Osborn) Harper, natives of Georgia. Lindsey Harper was a prominent farmer of his county and was a soldier in the late war. Returning home after his service he found himself financially ruined, but since then, by close attention to business, and by economy, he has succeeded in accumulating a comfortable competency. He and wife still reside in Georgia, and both are members of the Baptist Church. Of the ten children born to their union, eight are yet living and all reside in Georgia with the exception of Dr. William L. The maternal grandparents are both yet living, the grandfather at the age of eighty-four years and the grandmother at the age of eighty years. The former has been a minister in the Baptist Church for a number of years and has followed agricultural pursuits all his life. The paternal grandparents died during the war. The grandfather was taken from his house and shot by bushrangers, as were several other old and venerable men in the neighborhood, for the simple reason that they did not wish to part with all their property.

V. M. Harrington enjoys enviable prominence as the faithful sheriff of Lee County. A native of Delaware, he lived there until eighteen years of age, attending the common schools of the county of his birth, but having from his childhood imbibed a love of the South and Southern people, at an early age he moved to Mississippi, locating at Jackson, where he was employed as a clerk in a store until the breaking out of the war. Then he was given a position in the Confederate service at Brookhaven, Miss., and afterward was made quartermaster-sergeant in a Confederate camp. Though devoted to the South, he was at heart a Union man, and was unwilling to fight voluntarily against his country, so, after a long tramp and when nearly exhausted by hunger and fatigue, he reached the Federal lines. The Union officers tried to induce him to give them information in regard to their enemy's forces, location, etc., but having been employed by the Southern people and having lived among them, he refused to act the part of a spy. After the war he was again engaged as clerk. A Mr. Miller becoming intimately acquainted with him and interested in his welfare, furnished him with the necessary capital to enter into the mercantile business for himself. A wholesale house also offered to supply him with goods for carrying on a business of many thousand dollars, both of which offers he accepted, devoting his attention to commercial pursuits in Tennessee until 1871, at which time he sold out and removed Arkansas, locating at Palestine, St. Francis County. There he resumed the mercantile business, but soon moved to Marianna, where he went into the same occupation, carrying it on until 1886, the time of his election as sheriff of the county. He was re-elected in 1888. Mr. Harrington's wife was formerly Miss Georgia A. Wood, and she is now the mother of three children: Samuel, V. M. and James W. Mr. Harrington was born in Kent County, Del., in 1842, and was a son of Samuel and Sallie A. (Moore) Harrington. The collections of the county revenues made by Mr. Harrington as sheriff and collector of the county of the current year will aggregate 99 per cent. The lowest he has ever reached is 97$\frac{1}{2}$ per cent.

John W. Hayes, M. D., was born in Pittsboro, N. C., June 4, 1848, at which place he received his early education. He was afterward a student of the Hillsboro Military Academy, and then attended Davidson College, North Carolina, being in the Classical Department. In the third year of the Civil War he enlisted in the Confederate army, where he remained until the close, serving in the cavalry department, Company F, Thirteenth North Carolina Battalion. After peace had been declared Mr. Hayes went to Jackson, Tenn., and studied medicine under his uncle, Dr. J. G. Womack, one year, following which he attended a course of lectures at the University of Louisville, Ky., and the following year at the Washington University, graduating the next spring. Subsequently he commenced practicing medicine at Denmark, Tenn., was located there seven years, and in 1877 came to Arkansas, settling at Marianna, where he has been since engaged in attending to the calls of his adopted profession. Dr. Hayes is a son of Dr. W. A. Hayes and Jennette Womack Hayes. He was married to Miss Lou Moore, of Brownsville, Tenn., October 9, 1872. Dr. Hayes was one of the organizers of the Lee County Medical Association, which is one of the best in the State. He was elected State Medical Examiner of the K. of H., in Octo-

ber, 1884, and re-elected to fill the same consecutively for several years. He took a full course at the New York Polyclinic, in 1886; is a member of the Arkansas State Society and the American Medical Association. He has a brother also a physician, W. G. Hayes, M. D., of Bowie, Texas. Dr. Hayes and wife are the parents of two children living: Jeannette (a student at Batesville, Ark., College), and John W., Jr.

Ennes M. Henley first saw the light of day in Massac County, Ill., on January 28, 1832, and is the son of William and Malinda (Smith) Henley, natives of Tennessee and Kentucky, respectively. They were married in Illinois in 1828, and were the parents of twelve children, seven now living: Ennes M., Matilda (widow of Kennard Steward, of Lee County), John (a farmer of Illinois), Elijah (a lawyer, of Marianna and also postmaster of that city), Rebecca (the widow of Nicholas Phelps), Isaac (a farmer residing in Missouri), Mary (widow of Henry Lynn), Louisa (the wife of Simon Pierce). Mr. Henley died in Illinois, in the seventy-fifth year of his life, his wife having died one year previous. Ennes M. was reared in Illinois and received such advantages for an education as the primitive schools of the period would admit, accepting, when twenty years of age, the position of watchman on the steamer St. Francis, running on the St. Francis River. Later he worked on the Mississippi River on various boats. He settled in Monroe County, Ark., in 1859, and engaged in farming, and this has been his occupation ever since. He now owns an excellent farm in the western portion of Lee County, consisting of 240 acres, 100 of it being in a high state of cultivation. The principal products are corn and cotton, and clover and the grasses to some extent, and he is quite successful also in raising all kinds of stock. He owns a steam cotton-gin and grist-mill, valued at $1,000, a comfortable residence with modern improvements and conveniences being among his late additions. Mr. Henley was married in Monroe County December 23, 1858, to Miss Louisa F. Settles, of Giles County, Tenn. She was born in 1831, being the daughter of S. P. and Mary J. (Cunningham) Settles. Mr. Settles, a native of

Virginia, and of Irish descent, died in Arkansas in 1854. Mrs. Settles closed her eyes to the scenes of this world in 1872. To Mr. and Mrs. Henley's marriage eight children have been born: William F., James L., Andy S., Charley W. (residing in Brinkley), Mary M., Josephus B., Jason L. and Ennes W. William F. died in 1880. Mr. Henley served in the Civil War, enlisting in 1862 in Company C, Capt. John Foreman's Second Arkansas Infantry Volunteers, which was afterward Gen. Govan's command. He participated in the battles of Perryville, Missionary Ridge, Franklin, Nashville and many others of minor importance. He was mustered out of service at the surrender in 1865.

Hon. John Marshall Hewitt (deceased), of Marianna, Ark., was born in Frankfort, Ky., July 22, 1841, and was a son of John Marshall Hewitt, of that city, an eminent lawyer and for many years judge of the circuit court at Frankfort. Our subject received a classical education in the schools of his native city in his youth, but before he had attained his majority the Civil War broke out, and the following lines in regard to it are given in his own words: "The war was a bitter experience for me, for my father had two sons in the Union army and two sons in the Confederate, also one son-in-law on each side. All my old schoolmates and associates, as well as relatives in Kentucky, were about equally divided in sympathy, and one of my brothers was killed at Fort Donelson, on the Confederate side." Mr. Hewitt was a member of the Kentucky State militia when the war broke out, and in 1861 he joined the Federal army as adjutant of the Second Kentucky Cavalry, and was attached to the staff of Gen. Rousseau as assistant acting adjutant-general. He participated in the battle of Shiloh, and was captured by Gen. John Morgan, while the latter was on his first raid in Kentucky, but in the night he succeeded in effecting his escape, and returned to his command. After the war he returned to his home in Kentucky, and was admitted to the bar by the court of appeals, in 1865, and the following year he immigrated to St. Francis County, Ark., and engaged in cotton-planting. In 1873, when Lee County was formed, he moved to Marianna and resumed the practice of his profession, continuing this in connection with planting until his death. Although a Federal soldier, he was all his life an active Democrat, and although he came to Arkansas at a time when he could have had any office, or could have grown rich by affiliating with the Republican party, he would not do so, but stuck to his principles and party, unscathed by the political cyclone that swept Arkansas. He labored zealously for the advancement of the material interests of the State, and his fellow-citizens honored him for his efforts. He has been an active leader of his party, and was elected by the Democratic State Convention to the National Democratic Convention, which met at St. Louis, Mo., in 1876. In 1880 he was chosen to represent Lee County in the State legislature, and was elected speaker pro tem. In 1882 he was re-elected, and was chairman of the judiciary committee. In 1884 he was again sent to the legislature, and during the session of 1885 he was chairman of the committee of circuit and justice courts. In 1886 he was elected to his fourth term in the legislature, and was elected speaker of the house, and the Democratic State Convention, which met at the State capital in 1886, elected him president of the same. In January, 1886, he became president of the State Bar Association, but just as he had surmounted all primary obstacles, and could have grasped the highest honors of the State, his career was cut short by the hand of death February 29, 1887, his demise resulting from cancer of the tongue. Being a prominent member of the Masonic fraternity, his brother Masons kept his body in their hall for three days, that all might have an opportunity of paying due honor to his remains. His remains were taken to Memphis, Tenn., by the Commandery of Marianna, and at that city were met by the Commandery of Little Rock, and he was buried with the highest honors of his order, in Elmwood Cemetery. Determination was a marked trait of his character, and so was Christian fortitude and charity. Cut down in the meridian of manhood, at a time when it seemed possible for him to accomplish so much, his death was deeply lamented by all. Kentucky has given to Lee County many estimable citizens, but she has contributed none more highly respected or more worthy of respect, love and veneration than was Mr. Hewitt. He was married to Miss Sallie Howard, of Memphis, Tenn., and leaves her with one son to care for: John M., Jr. Mrs. Hewitt is a daughter of Wardlaw and Mary (Polk) Howard, the father a Virginian, who immigrated to Tennessee, and was an opulent commission merchant prior to the war, and was the owner of vast property in Memphis. He was an arch secessionist, and had such unbounded faith in the Confederacy that he sold the whole of Howard row in Memphis for Confederate money, which, of course, resulted in total loss. After the war he languished with broken spirits around the cotton exchange, but did not again enter active business life, and death claimed him in 1871. Mr. Hewitt's mother was born in Bolivar, Tenn., and was a daughter of William Polk, an uncle of President Polk. The Howards were an old English family, five brothers having come to America and participated in the Revolutionary War. All but one died or were killed, and he is the origin of the family in this country. One of these brothers donated the square on which Washington Monument now stands in Baltimore, Md. The grandmother of Mr. Hewitt was a sister of Uncle Ned Blackburn, of Kentucky, the father of Dr. Luke Blackburn, and Hon. J. C. Blackburn.

J. A. Holbert is one of the leading farmers and stock raisers of Lee County, Ark., and here his birth occurred in 1843, he being the second child born to James M. and Antoinette (McDaniel) Holbert, who were born in Kentucky and Arkansas, respectively, the former's birth occurring in 1809, and the latter's in 1825. The father removed to this State in 1815, and after making his home here until 1849, he went to Mississippi and died opposite to where Helena, Ark. is. Our subject and his brother, A. J., who lives in Arizona, and is the sheriff of Maricopa County, are the only children born to their parents, and the mother died on November 29, 1843. James M. Holbert was married a second time in 1845, his wife being Mary McDaniel, a daughter of Archibald McDaniel, and one child, Antoinette, blessed this union, she being now the wife of N. B. Purnell, and resides in Pike

County, Ark. After the death of Mr. Holbert his widow married a Mr. Hughes, and died during the war. J. A. Holbert received his education and rearing in St. Francis County, Ark., but at the age of seventeen years he dropped farm work and books to enter the Confederate army, enlisting in Company G, Thirteenth Arkansas Infantry, under Col. Tappin, and served east of the Mississippi River for four years, being a participant in the following engagements: Belmont, Shiloh, Corinth, Knoxville, Richmond (Ky.), Bardstown, Perryville, Atlanta and Jonesboro, where he was wounded and captured. He succeeded in effecting his escape after being retained only about twenty-four hours, and he afterward came west and joined Capt. Coats' company, under Gen. Marmaduke, and operated in Arkansas. After surrendering he was given his freedom, and returned home and began farming on his grandfather's plantation. Prior to the war he had owned quite a large area of land, and a number of slaves, and his father owned nearly 100 slaves. The former carried the mail from Wittsburg to Helena, a distance of over seventy miles (there being only four postoffices on the route), through a heavy cane-brake all the way. Although the country was very wild and unsettled at that time, Mr. Holbert says he never carried a pistol or a gun, and was never molested, either by the wild animals or Indians. He now has one of the finest farms in the county, comprising 200 acres of land, and has about 100 acres under cultivation, on which is a splendid frame residence and outbuildings. He was married in 1869 to Miss C. L. Hannah, of this county, a daughter of John and Penelpia (Lynch) Hannah, natives of Ireland and Arkansas, respectively, and by her became the father of eight children, four of whom are living: Lee, J. J., Bell and Blanche. One child died at the age of five years and three in infancy.

Joseph K. Hopkins is a native of Lee County, whither his parents had come two years before his birth. He attended the common schools of this locality until the death of his father (when he was sixteen years of age), when he commenced farming for himself. Mr. Hopkins was born in 1851, being the son of Archibald and Martha (O'Neal) Hopkins, natives of North Carolina and Alabama, respectively. Archibald Hopkins removed from the State of his birth to Greene County, Ala., when twenty years of age, and in 1849 to Arkansas, locating in this county, where he was engaged in farming until called from earth, in 1867, at the age of fifty-one. His wife died when the principal of this sketch was a child. Both were members of the Baptist Church. After her death Mr. Hopkins married Miss Lou Purcell, of Woodruff County, who is now deceased. He was a successful farmer during life, but lost heavily by the war. He was the father of three children by his first marriage, two of whom are still living: William A. (also a farmer of this county) and Joseph K. (our subject). The latter was married, in 1869, to Mrs. Emma (Burrows) Poole, a daughter of Peter Burrows and widow of William Poole. They have one son, Joseph B., who is at present helping his father in the store. Mr. Hopkins engaged in the mercantile business in 1876, and although starting with a small capital he has, by close economy and good business management, built up a satisfactory trade, and has the largest patronage of any store in this section of the township. He also owns one of the most extensive farms hereabouts, and in addition the control of a number of other fine farms. Although not an active politician, Mr. Hopkins is one of the leading Democrats in all campaign work. Mrs. Hopkins is a member of the Missionary Baptist Church.

J. P. Houston is a farmer and stock raiser of Richland Township, Lee County, Ark., and was born in what is now Lee County (then Phillips) in 1851, being the second child born to James M. and Mary J. (Simpson) Houston. The parents settled in Arkansas in 1846, and in Richland Township the same year, and here he purchased land to the extent of 160 acres, all of which was heavily timbered. He was a public-spirited citizen, a Democrat in his political views, and at the time of his death, in 1857, he was in full communion with the Methodist Episcopal Church. He was a son of Ross Houston, a Virginian, and was a second cousin of Gen. Sam Houston, of Texas. He and wife,

who was born in the "Blue Grass State," were married in Alabama in 1845, and became the parents of three children: Mary A. (now Mrs. Coffey, of St. Francis County, Ark.), J. P. and Thomas R. (who died in the State of Arkansas in 1884). Mrs. Houston is still living, and makes her home with her son, J. P. She is a member of the Methodist Church, and is a true Christian in every respect. J. P. Houston's early life was spent at farm labor and while thus engaged he learned lessons of industry and economy, which have stood him in good stead in later years. A portion of his early education was acquired in the schools of Middle Tennessee, and after attaining his twentieth year he started out in life for himself, and has since given his attention to farming, and is now residing on the old homestead, which comprises 320 acres, of which 230 are under cultivation. In 1886 he was united in marriage to Miss Tennie Hickman, a daughter of Nelson and Alabama (Moore) Hickman, who were Kentuckians, both of whom died in Alabama, the former's death occurring in 1862, and the latter's in 1867. Mr. Houston has always been a Democrat in his political views, and is interested in all matters relating to the welfare of the county in which he has so long made his home. He is a liberal patron of schools and churches, and is always found ready to assist the poor and afflicted. He and his wife have two children: Thomas Ross (born in 1886), and Anna May (born in 1888).

Hon. William L. Howard is a native of Lee County, and has always made this locality his home. Consequently he is well known and the respect accorded him is as wide as his acquaintance. His father, desiring to give his children a thorough education, William was sent to neighborhood common schools until the war, after which a private tutor was employed, who prepared him for college. He then entered Burrett College in Van Buren County, Tenn., where he took a full course. In 1874, the year of his father's death, he took charge of the old homestead, near La Grange, on which he was born on December 23, 1849, as a son of Robert W. and Malinda (Harris) Howard, natives of Virginia and Kentucky, respectively. Robert W. Howard was born in 1814, being a son of Christopher Howard, also a Virginian by birth, who died in Kentucky. He was a small boy when his father moved to the Blue Grass State, in which he was reared on a farm, remaining there until 1840, when he came to Arkansas and located in what was then Phillips County, on the St. Francis River. After giving his attention to rafting timber to New Orleans for the following two years, he purchased the plantation on which he spent the remainder of his life, dying on March 11, 1874. Mrs. Howard was born in 1824, and is still living on the old homestead. Both were members of the Baptist Church, and the parents of nine children, six of whom survive, all residents of Richland Township, this county: Virginia F. (at home with her mother), William L. (the principal of this sketch), L. G. (a merchant of La Grange, and a partner of William F. Gill, whose biography appears in this work), Addie (wife of N. D. Ramey), E. J. (now justice of the peace of this township) and Robert W. (at home). William L. Howard was married on January 16, 1875, to Miss Emma L. Crook, who was born in White County, Tenn., in 1850, and died in February, 1884, leaving four children, three now living: Ida B., Robert E. and Sallie H. He married his second and present wife, Miss Maggie Broyles, a relative of his first wife, and a native of the same county, January 14, 1886. They have a family of two children, Ethel Lee and William C. Mr. Howard has always taken a leading part in the politics of this county, and is one of its prominent Democrats. He was elected coroner in 1878, and served two years; was afterward elected justice of the peace, and filled that office the same length of time. He was then a candidate before the Democratic Nominating Convention in 1886 for sheriff, but was defeated. In 1888 he was elected to represent Lee County in the State legislature, which office he still acceptably holds. Mr. Howard, while not in public life, has followed agricultural pursuits for a livelihood, and owns a farm of 320 acres of as fine land as can be found in Lee County, besides an interest in the old homestead, consisting of 480 acres. He is a member of the Baptist Church, and Mrs. Howard belongs to the Methodist Episcopal Church, as did his first

wife. Mr. Howard is also a member of the Royal Arcanum.

Hon. H. N. Hutton, representative from Lee County, and who has been engaged in the practice of law in Arkansas for over twenty-nine years, is a graduate of the Lebanon Law School, and a very able attorney. Born in Franklin County, Tenn., in 1835, he is a son of John and Margaret (Davidson) Hutton, of Virginia and North Carolina origin, respectively. He received his literary education at Union University, Murfreesboro, Tenn., in which he took a full classical course, being a thorough scholar in Latin, Greek, and French, and from this institution was graduated on June 13, 1853. He then entered the Lebanon Law School, graduating in June, 1855, with the highest honors of his class. Mr. Hutton commenced practice at Shelbyville, Tenn., and in 1860 came to Arkansas, locating in this county, and practicing at Helena. In 1862 he enlisted in the Confederate army, serving one year as adjutant-general on Gen. D. C. Govan's staff. He then resigned his commission on account of poor health, and returned home. When the first court was organized at Helena, after the war, he was made prosecuting attorney, and at the expiration of his term of office, resumed regular law practice, in which he was engaged until 1874, when he was appointed to fill the vacancy of judge of the circuit court, caused by the death of the former incumbent, Judge Fox. The office not being in his own district, he declined to accept the position until having first communicated with the members of that circuit to see if his service would prove acceptable. Having received a favorable reply, he was installed in the office, and served until the expiration of the unexpired term. Judge Hutton removed to Arkansas before Lee County was formed, and when the question of the organization of a new county was sufficiently agitated, he was elected to draft the bill for the formation of the same to be presented to the legislature. He first drew up a bill for that purpose, calling the proposed county Coolidge, but it was defeated. He next drew up another, taking for a name Woodford, which was also defeated by the senate. He then revised the bill, substituting the name Lee, which was presented during the latter part of the session, and it passed the lower house in a few moments with great enthusiasm, and being sent to the senate also passed that body. On January 6, 1857, Mr. Hutton was married to Miss Cillie M. Mottley, a native of Tennessee, and a graduate of the Abbie Institute. They are the parents of four children: H. N., Jr., Walter S., J. T. and Herbert. Mr. Hutton, or Judge Hutton, as he is familiarly called, has devoted his time to hard study during life, and has developed a wonderful memory. In his extensive practice he never takes notes of the evidence, relying wholly on that faculty, which never fails him. He is justly considered one of Lee's substantial and worthy citizens.

A. Jastrawer, dealer in dry goods, groceries and drugs at White Hall, is a native of Prussia, being a son of Mark and Rose (Cohn) Jastrawer, also natives of that country. The former died when the principal of this sketch was a small boy, and his wife in 1875. Our subject was born in 1832 and was married in Prussia about 1863, to Miss Ester Cohn, also of that country, and who became the mother of two children, both now deceased. Mr. Jastrawer learned the shoemaker's trade while in his native country, at which he worked for a number of years. Emigrating to America about 1869 he landed at New York City, where he remained, working at his chosen calling for about one year. He then went to Memphis, Tenn., and three years later came to Forrest City, where he was engaged in the same business for several years, subsequently removing to Lee County. He first started in the mercantile business in different parts of this county, and in 1883 located at White Hall, where he has since been occupied in general merchandising, with excellent success, having acquired considerable property. He is the owner of 1,000 acres of land, of which half is under cultivation, and is enjoying a patronage of about $25,000 annually. Mr. Jastrawer is a member of the K. of H. and of two Jewish and German Lodges.

J. L. Jenkins, farmer, Haynes, Ark. On September 15, 1851, in Johnson County, Tenn., there was born to William and Sarah M. (Russel) Jenkins a son, who is taken as the subject of this sketch. William Jenkins was born in South Carolina in 1805, thence removing, in 1833, to Johnson County, Tenn. Leaving that State in 1857 he went to Dent County, Mo., where he remained the balance of his life, his death occurring July 27, 1871. He was too old to participate in the late war, but this did not prevent him from being harrassed by bushrangers. By his marriage to Miss Russel he became the father of ten children, only two now living: Sophronia J. (wife of J. D. Crabtree, resides in Golden City, Mo.,) and J. L. (who was the youngest of the family. The mother was a member of the Cumberland Presbyterian Church and died February 28, 1860. The paternal grandfather was an early settler of Tennessee, and was in one of the early wars. J. L. Jenkins passed his boyhood days in Dent County, Mo., received the benefit of a common-school education, and at the age of eighteen years commenced for himself in Dent County, where he farmed for some time on rented land. In 1872 he moved to St. Francis County, Ark., and worked for wages on a farm for two years, after which (in 1878) he purchased a portion of his present place, forty acres. To this he has since added 160 acres, and has fifty-five acres under improvement. Besides this his wife has sixty acres of an undivided farm of 120 acres, on which Mr. Jenkins now resides. He was married in 1876 to Miss Annie E. Stanfield, a native of Lee County and the daughter of Clark and Jane (Myrick) Stanfield, natives, respectively, of Alabama and Arkansas. The Myrick family were among the early settlers of Arkansas, having made their appearance here as early as 1820 or 1825, and were prominently identified with the early settlement of the country. Mr. and Mrs. Stanfield were the parents of four children, two now living: Mrs. Jenkins (the eldest) and J. M. (who resides with Mr. Jenkins). Mr. Stanfield died in 1883 and Mrs. Stanfield in 1876, the former a member of the A. F. & A. M. To the union of Mr. and Mrs. Jenkins were born five children: P. J. (deceased), Willie A., Nora L., Hattie M. (deceased) and Joseph B. Mr. and Mrs. Jenkins are members of the Methodist Episcopal Church, South, and are liberal contributors and supporters of all laudable enterprises, particularly those pertaining to religious and educational matters. Mr. Jenkins is a member of the Masonic fraternity, Cannon Lodge No. 254, and is also a member of the Knights of Honor, Lodge No. 2168.

Samuel L. Johnson has worked at farm labor since a young boy, his father having died when he was but two years of age, and the mother when the son was eighteen years old. At the age of fifteen he was employed as a farm hand in Monroe County, but shortly after started to learn the trade of blacksmithing, soon returning to farm labor, at which he was employed until he bought a farm of his own. He now owns 280 acres of fine farming land in Lee County, with half of it under cultivation. Mr. Johnson was born in Monroe County January 4, 1850, his parents, Hardin and Elizabeth (Davis) Johnson, being natives of Mississippi and South Carolina, respectively. They removed from Mississippi to Arkansas in 1842, and located in Monroe County on a farm, on which Mr. Johnson lived until his death in 1852. Two years later Mrs. Johnson married James Ganberry, and survived until 1868. Mr. and Mrs. Johnson had a family of four children, three of whom are still living: Julia (wife of William Moy, a farmer of Monroe County), Thomas B. (a resident of Illinois), and Samuel L. (the principal of this sketch). The latter was married March 20, 1880, to Miss Nannie Ruscoe, of Alabama birth, who lived only two years after her marriage, leaving two children, one of whom, Laura E., still survives. He was married to his second and present wife, Mary A. Jeffcoat, a native of this State, April 4, 1883. She was a daughter of William K. and Nancy J. (Fisher) Jeffcoat, both now deceased. By this marriage there was born one child, Bessie V. Mr. Johnson is a Democrat, and takes an active interest in the success of his party. He and wife are leading members of the Presbyterian Church, and live upright Christian lives.

John M. Johnson. The estate which Mr. Johnson now cultivates and owns, comprises 500 acres, of which 300 are under cultivation, and it is well adapted to the purposes of general farming. In his operation he displays those sterling principles so characteristic of those of Virginian nativity, of which industry and wise and judicious management are among the chief. He was born in Russell County, October 23, 1857, and is a son of Jacob Johnson, who was born in Carroll County, Va., in 1830, his wife, Malinda Foster, being also a native of that State, born in 1832. Their marriage took place in 1847, and to their union a family of seven children were born, of whom John M. is the fourth. Only three of this family are now living, and all reside in Lee County: Benjamin F. (who married Ida L. Riner), Nannie (who married H. E. Sapp) and Jacob. The father was a man of public spirit and took an interest in all worthy public enterprises wherever he lived. He served in the Confederate army during 1861–62, but in the latter year returned home and died of small-pox. He was a farmer by occupation, and at the time of his death owned a good farm of 200 acres. His widow survives him, and resides in Lee County, Ark., with her daughter. John M. Johnson received his education in the schools of Sulphur Springs, Va., but in 1877 concluded to seek his fortune in the West, and immigrated with his mother to Arkansas, locating in Lee County, where, in 1881, he began business for himself. He has a well-improved and well-stocked farm, and his management shows a thorough knowledge of the business.

S. D. Johnston is a member of that well-known general mercantile firm of Johnston & Grove, of Marianna, Ark., which has existed under the present title since 1881, having previously been Jarratt, Rodgers & Co., and Johnston, Foreman & Co. These two firms were really one and the business of both houses was kept in one set of books and as one firm. Later, the firm name was changed to Johnston, Rodgers & Co., and Johnston, Foreman & Co., and finally to Johnston & Grove. Their establishment is among the leading ones in Eastern Arkansas, and they occupy one of the main business houses in Marianna, having regularly in their employ seven men, besides assisting in the work themselves. The main room is 27x125 feet, the large stock of goods occupying parts of two other floors, and ranging from $15,000 to $20,000. Their highest annual sale, made in 1879, amounted to $140,000, but of late years have aggregated from $75,000 to $85,000. They also own two farms. Mr. Johnston is a Kentuckian by birth, born in 1849. He was reared to manhood in his native State and after acquiring a fair education in the common schools supplemented this by a course in college at Columbia, Ky., and in 1872 took a complete course in Leddin's Business College, Memphis, Tenn., graduating therefrom in October, 1872. Immediately after he came to Marianna and for some time acted as book-keeper for the mercantile firm of Jarratt & Rodgers, serving them in this capacity until 1877. Also during this time from 1884 he had a half interest in the mercantile firm of Johnston & Foreman, in Marianna, keeping the books and attending to the financial part of the business. When the two firms consolidated, the styles being then changed to Jarratt, Rodgers & Co. and Johnston, Foreman & Co., he was an equal partner in both houses. Unlike the majority of the young men of the present day he judiciously saved his money and in the investment of the same he has shown excellent judgment, and in every respect deserves the reputation he has acquired as a successful business man. He not only owns a one-half interest in the mercantile firm, but also some of the most valuable property in the city, consisting of a two-story brick store building, a valuable residence and other real estate in the business portion. He is an active worker for the upbuilding of the town and county, and has done much to assist in eliminating the whisky traffic from Marianna. He is the fire insurance agent of Marianna, representing eight of the best fire insurance companies; is an active member and official of the Methodist Church and the Royal Arcanum, a K. of H., a K. & L. of H., a commissioner of accounts for Lee County, and also belongs to the I. O. G. T. He was married in 1875 at Austin, Miss., to Miss Mollie F. Grove, and by her has two children living: Mary E. and Sarah A. He was married the second time at Brownsville, Tenn., to Miss Nita Mann, his present wife, and by her has one child: Willie Webster. J. B. Grove, the junior member of the above-named firm, was born in West Tennessee in

1849, and made his home in that State several years as salesman in a dry-goods store until about twenty years ago, when he came to Marianna, Ark., and acted as book-keeper and salesman for J. E. Wood in a general mercantile business until 1876. Wood failing in business he accepted a position as salesman for Jarratt & Rodgers, and in 1877 became a partner in the firms of Jarratt, Rodgers & Co. and Johnston, Foreman & Co., now Johnston & Grove. He is an excellent man of business, shrewd, honest and capable, and, like Mr. Johnston, has made all his money in Lee County. He is unmarried.

H. M. Jones, recognized as one of the well-to-do and enterprising farmers and stock raisers of Independence Township, was born in Limestone County, Ala. His father, Kimbrough Jones, was also a native of Alabama, and was married in 1846, to Evaline Weatherford, who bore him eight children: Sally (Mrs. J. P. Farrel, of Marianna), Betty (Mrs. Beauchamp, now dead), Margaret (the wife of J. D. Brown, of Marianna), Fannie (now the wife of Mr. Beauchamp, of Marianna), Emma (deceased), S. W., Dixie (Mrs. Harden) and H. M. (the subject of this sketch). Mr. Jones was a successful farmer, and in 1868 moved to Arkansas, settling in Lee County, where his death occurred two years later. Mrs. Jones is now living with her children in Marianna, and is a member of many years' standing of the Methodist Church. Mr. Jones settled the land owned by his father and which is now operated by him. After the father's death he assumed charge of his mother's family and the management of her estate, where his intuitive sense and excellent business qualifications were given a wide scope. His farm consists of 100 acres of valuable land, with eighty acres under cultivation, and bears evidence of careful and unceasing attention. In his political belief he is a Democrat.

Hiram C. Kellam, not unknown throughout this region, commenced life for himself at the age of thirteen, being employed as a farm hand, but on the death of his father, two years later, he served an apprenticeship with a leading blacksmith of his native county (Davis County, Ky.), and became a finished workman. After working at his trade in Illinois, he came to Arkansas and located at Moro, Lee County (then Monroe County), where he followed his adopted calling for some time. Afterward he purchased a farm, and has since followed that occupation. He was born September 4, 1851, being a son of Elisha J. and Lucinda (Kelley) Kellam, also Kentuckians by birth. E. J. Kellam was a minister of the Methodist Episcopal Church, South, and also carried on farming. During the war he was taken by the Federals and carried to Indiana, on account of his Southern principles and sympathy with the Confederate cause and died in that State in March, 1866. His wife died in 1862 at the age of fifty-two years. They were the parents of eight children, two of whom only are now living, the principal of this sketch, and Albert J., a farmer residing in the State of Texas. Mr. Kellam was married on February 27, 1876, to Miss Julia I. Boykin, of Johnson, County, N. C., and a daughter of Elmore and Jane E. (Jones) Boykin, originally from Virginia and North Carolina, respectively, both of whom are deceased, the former dying in 1867 and the latter in 1882. Mr. and Mrs. Kellam have a family of five children; Albert B., Hiram C., Lucinda, David H., and William L. and one deceased. Mr. Kellam owns a farm of 120 acres, with about sixty acres under cultivation, which he devotes principally to the raising of stock, having a large number of cattle, horses and hogs. He also owns and operates a large steam grist-mill and cotton-gin, erected at a cost of about $1,500. He is a strong Democrat and takes an active interest in politics,and has held the office of deputy sheriff of the county for the past twelve years. He is a member of the K. of P. and of the Masonic order, and belongs to the Methodist Episcopal Church, South, of which his wife is also a member.

John Lee, farmer and blacksmith, of Hardy Township, is a native of Indiana, and a son of Jonathan and Deborah (Britian) Lee. Jonathan Lee was born in Mercer County, Ky., in 1793, in which State he lived until after his marriage, learning the trade of blacksmithing. Soon after his marriage he removed to Washington County, Ind., and when the principal of this sketch was about one year old, went to Jackson County, where he died on July 16, 1862. He was a son of William Lee, of Irish descent, and a cooper and farmer by occupation. He was a native of Mercer County, Ky., and died in Washington County, Ind. Mrs. Lee came originally from West Virginia and died in Jackson County, Ind., in 1867, at the age of seventy-four. She was a member of the Baptist Church, as was also her husband, being a daughter of Samuel Britain, a native of Virginia, who died in Washington County, Ind., at the age of ninety-seven. John Lee was the youngest son in a family of eight children, four of whom are still living, the eldest son, Samuel, two daughters, and our subject. The latter was born in Washington County, Ind., in 1832. He was married in 1851, to Ludia Chilcott, who was born in Jackson County, Ind., in 1825. Her parents were John and Rachel (Robertson) Chilcott, the former a native of Virginia, removed to Jackson County, Ind., where was married and made his home the rest of his life, dying in 1848. He was a son of Eli Chilcott, of Pennsylvania, who removed to Virginia after his marriage, and died in Hardy County, that State. Mrs. Chilcott was also of Virginia birth, and died in 1835. She was a daughter of Blaze and Hannah (Hutchinson) Robertson. Mr. Robertson was born in England, the son of an English nobleman. He left home at the age of seventeen and came to America against his parents' wishes, and, having no money, though possessed of a good education, he contracted the wages which he would receive for his duties as a teacher, his chosen calling, for seven years, to pay his passage to the United States; after four years' service he was released from his contract. He then settled in Virginia, where he made his home the balance of his life. His wife, after the death of her husband, moved to Indiana, where she died. They were the parents of a large family of children, who were among the pioneer families of Jackson County, Ind. One of the daughters married a Mr. Hamilton, the first representative from that county, in the State legislature. Mr. and Mrs. Lee had five children, two sons and three daughters, all of whom survive:

Jonathan R. (a resident of Phillips County), Hannah E. (wife of S. B. Eaks), Lydia A. (wife of W. B. Jones), Sarah M. (wife of C. T. Payne) and William Samuel. Mr. Lee enlisted in January, 1865, in Company C of the One Hundred and Forty-fifth Indiana Volunteer Infantry, in which he served until the close of the war. He lived in Jackson County, Ind., until 1870, when he came to Arkansas and settled in what is now Lee County. Two years later he settled on his present farm, consisting of half a section of land, of which sixty-five acres are under a high state of cultivation, and all made since coming to this State. He is a prominent Democrat and takes an interest in the political affairs of the day. He and his wife are members of the Christian Church.

Julius Lesser, treasurer of Lee County, was born in Prussia in 1853, and emigrated to America in 1867, locating first in Memphis, Tenn., where he was employed as a clerk. In 1870 he came to Arkansas, and was employed in that occupation at Forrest City until 1875, then entering into business for himself at Marianna. In 1884 he sold out his store, and became engaged in the banking business, which he still continues. Shortly after disposing of his mercantile interest he bought it back, and associated with his brother as partner, the latter now having the management of the store. Mr. Lesser gives his attention to his banking business and official duties. He has held, with great satisfaction, the office of county treasurer for five consecutive years, having served first by appointment to fill an unexpired term, and afterward being elected. He and his brother enjoy a large patronage in their store, handling sixty per cent of all the cotton grown in the neighborhood, which they ship direct to the spinners, and not to commission men, as is the general custom. Mr. Lesser is a stockholder and director in the First National Bank of Helena, also a stockholder in another bank of that city, and one in Memphis, Tenn., and, in addition, is a stockholder in a large lumber company. He was married to Miss Lenora Raphaels, by which marriage two children were born: Harry and Blanche. Mr. Lesser is also largely interested in real estate in the city, owning several business

blocks, including the one in which his bank is situated, and pays taxes on $35,000 to $40,000 worth of real estate. He participates actively in promoting all public enterprises; is a member of the Masonic order, in which he has taken the degree of Royal Arch Mason, and is also a member of the Knights of Honor.

John Carrol Lynch was born on a farm which was then in St. Francis County, now a part of Lee County, in 1848, being a son Byant Lynch, who was born in this State in 1818, and Eliza (Davis) Lynch, of Kentucky origin, born in 1825. The principal of this sketch has spent his whole life in this county, but as his help was needed on his father's farm, his educational advantages in youth were very limited. He was married, in 1873, to Miss Lou A. Rogers, who was the mother of two daughters, one, Annie L., still living. Mr. Lynch owns 1,400 acres of land, 700 acres of which are cleared and a large part of it under cultivation. He raises very little cotton, but devotes most of his time and labor to the raising of stock, which he finds more profitable. He is a life-long Democrat and uses all means in his power to advance the interests of his party. He is a member of the Masonic order. His wife belongs to the Baptist Church. Mr. Lynch is one of the prominent and well-known men of Lee County. He has never had a sick day in ten years, nor taken a dose of medicine in that time, and during the last ten years he has increased in weight from 156 to 254 pounds.

Capt. George Marchbanks, planter, Marianna, Ark. Of that sturdy and independent class, the farmers of Arkansas, none are possessed of more genuine merit and a stronger character than he whose name stands at the head of this sketch. He has risen to a more than ordinary degree of success in his calling, and wherever known, he is conceded to be an energetic and progressive tiller of the soil, imbued with all those qualities of go-ahead-ativeness which have characterized his ancestors. He owes his nativity to Middle Tennessee, where his birth occurred on May 25, 1839, and is the son of Judge A. J. Marchbanks, of Warren County, Tenn. The father was a well-educated gentleman, had read law and was a legal practitioner all his life.

His father educated him and then disinherited him, and sent him forth to fight his own way in life. He was circuit judge of his district for more than thirty years, and was occupying that position at the breaking out of the war. He was kept a prisoner at Camp Chase, Ohio, during this eventful period, and when peace was declared he was offered the position of judge again. He died in the fall or winter of 1866. The mother was born in McMinnville, Tenn., and was a daughter of George and Elizabeth (Kenion) Savage. She died at the age of twenty-nine years, leaving five children. Capt. George Marchbanks attained his growth in Tennessee, and was sent as a cadet to West Point, to the Federal Military School. He was appointed by old Col. Savage, while the latter was in Congress, and remained at the school until the breaking out of the war. On April 1, 1861, he went South, and entered the Sixteenth Tennessee Regiment as adjutant. He was in the regular Confederate service, commanded a company, and served with the Sixteenth one year as first lieutenant. He was on Gen. Bragg's staff until late in 1862, and commanded Company K, in the Twenty-fifth Tennessee. After the campaign he was on Gen. Johnston's staff for some time, and was also on Gen. Bragg's staff for a year. He was with Maj.-Gen. B. Johnston in Virginia, was at Drury's Bluff and at the siege of Petersburg. After that campaign he was sent with his command up around Richmond, and subsequently to Wheeler's command. Later he came to Tennessee on a furlough, and was captured there, and remained in prison until the close of the war. After this he engaged in agricultural pursuits until 1870, when he came to what was then Phillips (now Lee) County, and there has tilled the soil ever since. He was a member of the legislature in 1881 and 1882. In 1883 he married Mrs. Freeman, whose maiden name was Julia Sterdivant. Mr. Marchbanks is a member of the Methodist Episcopal Church. He is the owner of 1,500 acres of land, and is also the owner of considerable town property.

George J. Mathews. Among the enterprising and prospering farmers and stock raisers of Lee County, none are more worthy of mention than George J. Mathews. He is a son of Burel and Piney (Whittaker) Mathews, and was born in Pitt County, N. C., December 24, 1820. Burel Mathews was a native of North Carolina, and followed the occupation of farming all his life. He was married in that State in 1818, to Miss Whittaker, and to their union six children were born, two now living: George J. and Roderick. Those deceased are: Richard F., William Miza A., Henry and one unnamed. Both Mr. Mathews and wife are dead. George J. Mathews first began to "paddle his own canoe" at the age of eighteen, accepting a position as overseer on a large plantation. He was married in 1841 to Miss Mary Crawford, of Martin County, N. C., who bore him four children, one living: George R. Mary A., P. A., and Elisha are deceased. Mrs. Mathews died in 1858, a member of many years standing in the Methodist Church. Mr. Mathews was married in 1862 to Mrs. Lydia Brooks, the widow of Amsley Brooks. She is a daughter of Franklin and Lydia Maye, of Tennessee, and was born in 1827. To the marriage of Mr. and Mrs. Mathews four children have been given: Marietta (the wife of Allen Wall), Kelson O., Epson J. and William F. (deceased). Mr. Mathews immigrated to Arkansas from North Carolina in 1852, settling in St. Francis County. He now owns 160 acres of good land, with 115 improved, the principal crop being corn and cotton. He has acted as marshal of St. Francis County for the past twelve years and has served as justice of the peace for six years. He is a member of the Methodist Church, having joined that denomination over twenty years ago. Politically he is a Democrat. Mrs. Mathews is a Baptist in her religious belief, and belongs to that church.

T. C. Merwin is a successful general merchant of Marianna, Ark., and is an example of the success attending hard work and honest dealing. He was born in Louisville, Ky., December 25, 1845, and is a son of A. W. and Anna L. (Chartres) Merwin, the former of whom died when our subject was small. He was a carriage dealer in Louisville, and died there in 1852, followed by his wife in 1864, her death occurring in the State of Mississippi. Of six children born to them, four lived to be grown, but T. C. Merwin is the only one now living. He and his mother moved to Mississippi in 1860, and were residing near Austin at the time of the latter's death. Mr. Merwin was educated at South Hanover College, Kentucky, and when the war broke out he joined the Confederate forces and was a member of Maj. Corley's cavalry. Shortly after he was discharged on account of physical disability, but about six weeks later he joined another command, the company being raised by Capt. Nall, of Missouri, and with this he remained until the close of the war, serving in the capacity of lieutenant, and operating in Missouri and Arkansas. On October 19, 1864, he and his men were captured by a force of Federals under McNeal, and the following morning one of his men was hanged by McNeal, at Lexington, Mo. They remained captives of war until June 18, 1865. After the war he began farming in Arkansas, and for eleven years continued to till the soil along the Mississippi River. After moving to Marianna he served as collector of taxes for two years, and was then elected circuit court clerk, and ex officio clerk of all other courts, serving by re-election until 1884. In the fall of 1885 he was appointed clerk of the State land office at Little Rock, and was installed in January, 1886, and held the position until November 1, 1889. He then resigned, and returned to Marianna, and opened his present establishment, which is proving a paying investment. He is a Democrat, a Royal Arch Mason, a K. of L., a member of the K. & L. of H., and also belongs to the R. A. He was married December 20, 1874, to Miss Laura Campbell, who was born in Woodford County, Ky., in 1852, and died June 18, 1877, leaving one child, Olie. His second wife was a Miss Emmie Govan, a niece of Gen. D. C. Govan, and a daughter of E. P. Govan, the latter a prominent planter before the war. Mr. Merwin and his present wife have had three children: Mary, Govan (who died in 1844, aged two years) and Willie. The family worship in the Episcopal Church.

Jonas Miller owns a fine farm of 240 acres in Hampton County, also a steam grist-mill and cotton-gin at Moro, Lee County. He is a native of North Carolina and a son of Moses and Rolly (Cross) Miller, also originally of that State. Mr. and Mrs. Miller made North Carolina their home until 1853, when they removed to Mississippi, and two years later came to Arkansas, locating in Monroe County. The father was a very successful farmer, always having something to sell, and not owing any man, and was well known and highly respected throughout the community until his death, in 1880, twenty-three years after the death of his wife. They were members of the Missionary Baptist Church and had a family of eight children, three still living: Carrie (wife of I. W. Burrows, of Woodruff County), Polly (wife of John Boyer, also of Woodruff County) and Jonas. The subject of this sketch was born in Cape Barrow County on July 15, 1845, and began life for himself as a farmer and miller at the age of twenty. He was married in March, 1873, to Miss Martha E. Breeding, daughter of Wesley and Mary (Brooks) Breeding. They are the parents of eight children, five still living: William, John, Elizabeth, Kate and Cricket. Mr. Miller has about 100 acres under cultivation, in cotton and corn principally, but is now turning his attention to stock raising, and consequently raising more grasses and grain. He has held the office of deputy sheriff and constable, both of which he filled with credit to himself and with perfect satisfaction to the citizens of the community.

William T. Moore, who is well known among the citizens of Richland Township, came originally from Alabama and is a son of Lewis and Willie (Riel) Moore, natives of Georgia and Alabama, respectively. Mr. Moore was of English descent, and moved to Alabama when a young man, where he was married, making that his home until 1838. Removing to Mississippi, he purchased a large plantation in Chickasaw County, and at the time of his death, in 1866, at the age of sixty-two years, was the wealthiest man, but one, in the county. His wife died in 1862, at the age of fifty-two years. She was the mother of eleven children, the following of whom now survive: Elizabeth (wife of B. F. Fitzpatrick, of Mobile, Ala.), John P. (a prominent merchant and real estate dealer, of Helena), Mary Ann (deceased, wife of Dr. J. P. Rockatt, of Mississippi), S. C. (a farmer of Chickasaw

County, Miss.), C. C. (a farmer and merchant of Houston, Miss.), James B. (a farmer of Pickens County, Ala.), Cora F. (wife of S. C. Pippen, of Helena), Dora (now Mrs. Bass, also of Helena), J. H. (who was killed at the battle of Gettysburg and was captain of Company H of the Eleventh Mississippi Infantry), and William T. (our subject). The latter, the third child of this family, was born in Greene County, Ala., on September 23, 1835; and remained home with his father until a short time before the war, when he commenced farming for himself. In 1862 he enlisted in the Confederate army, in the Forty-first Mississippi Infantry, in which he served until the close of the war, being present at the surrender at Appomattox Court House. After the war he returned to his home in Mississippi and engaged in farming, and in 1878 came to Arkansas, locating in Phillips County, where he was occupied in agricultural pursuits for a short time; subsequently he moved to La Grange. He was married in 1855 to Miss Lucy J. Buckingham, who was born near Okolona, Miss., in 1841. They were the parents of six children, four still living: John T. (who is in the mercantile business with his father), Mary (wife of J. B. Foster, agent and operator at Harper, Mo., for the Iron Mountain Railroad), Lulu B. (wife of Thomas M. Jack, surveyor and civil engineer at Helena), and George C. (at home). Mr. and Mrs. Moore are members of the Missionary Baptist Church, in which they take an active part.

James H. New traces his ancestry back to Revolutionary times, his grandfather, William New, having been a soldier in that war, in which he served as a member of Marion's famous legion. The great-grandsire, William New, came to this country in 1763, settling on the Chickasaw River, in Virginia. He had two sons, John and William. William and his two sons were also in the Revolutionary War, the former being colonel of Lee's dragoons. He was wounded on Roanoke River, while pursuing Lord Cornwallis, and died from the effects of that injury. William, pere, was in the War of 1812, and his two sons, John and William, were in the battle near Baltimore, Md.

38

James H. is also a descendant, on his mother's side, of Jesse Lee. His parents were James and Mary M. (Blankenship) New, Virginians by birth. James New, Sr., was born in Halifax County, on July 4, 1805, and was of English and Irish extraction. He was married in November, 1833, shortly after which he removed to Georgia, and remained one year, then going to Lauderdale County, Miss., where he lived until his death, on September 7, 1864. They were the parents of four children: Saleta A. (wife of John H. Anderson, of Illinois), Mary M. (widow of Irvin McRovy), John R. (a farmer of Lee County) and James H. (our subject). The latter, the next to the eldest, was born in Lauderdale County, Miss., on August 14, 1839. He commenced farming for himself at the age of twenty-two, and in 1869 came to Arkansas, and located on his present farm, which was then in Phillips County (now in Lee), composed of 160 acres of land, seventy acres being under a good state of cultivation. Mr. New was married in August, 1865, to Emily Clayton, also a native of Mississippi, who died in December, 1884, after having borne ten children, six still living: William U., Pattie L. (wife of J. A. Smith, a farmer of this county), James J., John R., Rebecca C. and Walter T. Mr. New enlisted in the secret service of the United States, in November, 1862, and was a member and non-commissioned officer of the First Mississippi Mounted Riflemen. He served until the close of the war, participating in the battles of Chickasaw Bluff, Harrisburg, and a number of others. He is a conservative Democrat, and a member of the Agricultural Wheel and Farmer's Secret Alliance. He is also ruling elder in the Cumberland Presbyterian Church, of which he has been a member eighteen years.

Rev. L. K. Obenchain, pastor of the Baptist Church of Haynes, was born in Botetourt County, Va., on January 23, 1841, being a son of Peter M. Obenchain, also of that county, and of German descent. He was reared on a farm in his native county, and received a good education in the common schools, later attending Roanoke College, and also Alleghany College, in Greenbrier County, Va. He was first located, after entering the ministry, in the mountains of Rock Bridge County, having been ordained at Mill Creek Church, where he remained three years. Coming to Arkansas in 1869, he was occupied in preaching at Phillips Bayou, and also taught school for three years, the following three years serving at Forrest Chapel. He next had charge of the Salem Church, of Phillips County, and of the churches at Marvel, Barton and Trenton for seven years. Mr. Obenchain later moved to La Grange, and had charge of that church, and also of the one at Phillips Bayou, where he had before been located. He came to Haynes, in January, 1888, and has since resided here, being the pastor of the Baptist Church at this place, and also at Oak Grove. He was married on the second Sunday of June, 1862, to Miss Sarah A. Baker, a daughter of Henry Baker, of Botetourt County, Va. They became the parents of five children, three of whom are still living: Bettie (wife of W. H. Ward, of Marvel), Edward B. and Ella D. Mr. Obenchain is a Democrat in politics, and is a member of the Masonic order, and of the Knights of Honor. His life has been devoted to the service of his Master, and no man in the county is more highly respected or honored, and by the purity of his life, and the example he sets, he is well worthy the confidence and respect which are placed in him.

R. B. Owen, a prosperous farmer of Richland Township, Lee County, is a native of Alabama, and was born in 1833, being the fifth in a family of nine children given to Richardson and Tobitha (Allin) Owen. Their names are as follows: Tobitha, Henry R., Edward T., Sarah H., R. B., Mary F., Susan E., Anna E. and Thomas Grant. Richardson Owen was born in North Carolina in 1790, and in 1820 was married to Tobitha, a daughter of Grant Allen, of Tennessee. Mr. Owen afterward settled in Alabama, where he engaged in farming, and was also a minister of the Methodist Episcopal Church and a doctor, having practiced medicine for some years previous to his death. Coming to Arkansas in 1851, he settled in Lee County, Richland Township, where he purchased 500 acres of valuable land. He was a public-spirited and progressive man, lending his support and influence to all public enterprises. In politics he was an old line Whig. R. B. Owen moved to Arkansas with his parents, and in 1862 enlisted in Capt. Anderson's company of Johnson regiment. He was soon after exchanged to Company C, Sixth Mississippi Infantry, and was a non-commissioned officer, serving as an ordnance-sergeant. He participated in the battles of Prairie Grove, Helena, Jenkins' Ferry and many others of minor importance. After the war Mr. Owen returned to Arkansas, settling in Lee County and resuming his occupation of farming, where he has since remained. He owns 310 acres of land, with 200 under cultivation. He was married in 1860 to Martha E. Sellers, a daughter of William B. and Mahala J. (Estes) Sellers, natives of Tennessee, but who immigrated to Mississippi, and then to Arkansas in 1847, settling in Lee County. Mr. Sellers died in 1858, and his wife in 1868. They were the parents of five children: William, Martha, Mary, Vianna and one deceased in infancy. To Mr. Owen's marriage five children have been born: Virginia D. (died in 1861), Helena (now Mrs. Walter Rainey, residing in Mississippi), Leila A., Mattie M. and an infant. In secret organizations Mr. Owen is identified with the Knights of Honor. He takes a great interest in all public improvements, and is especially interested in schools, in which he can see vast advancement and progress.

C. A. Otey, attorney-at-law of Marianna, is a native of Madison County, Ala., and spent his early boyhood days in the southern part of the State, but the death of his father necessitated his return to his native county, where he remained for some time, while preparing himself for entering the military school at La Grange. He attended that institution only a short time, as the Civil War broke out shortly after his entering college, when he immediately joined the Confederate army, enlisting in the Fourth Alabama Infantry, which was attached to Johnston's division of Confederate States troops and Bee's brigade. The Fourth Alabama distinguished themselves at the first general engagement, but it is to be regretted that they lost their gallant commander, Col. Jones, who sacraficed his own life as well as many of his command to save the day. Gen. Bee, after Jones had fallen, came up, and saying, "Fourth Alabama! I have seen your gallant fighting from yonder hill, and your ranks mowed thin while you held your position against fourfold odds! Follow me; Jackson has arrived, and he stands like a 'stone wall.' Let us go to his relief." So Jackson received the immortal soubriquet of Stonewall, while Bee was leading the Fourth Alabama in that charge, and he who knighted him, *the immortal Bee*, fell shot through the heart a few moments afterward. The Fourth Alabama erected a monument on the spot. The false accusation that Gen. Bee was intoxicated, which was the cause of his reckless bravery, is explained by our subject by the fact that he was seen to drink repeatedly from a flask during the engagement, but which he knows contained water, as he himself filled it for him at a spring. Mr. Otey was wounded at the battle of Gaines' Mill by a bullet, breaking his arm, which laid him up for about three months; rejoining his regiment at the battle of Antietam, he was captured at the battle of Lookout Mountain, and was a prisoner for one year, before being exchanged. At the close of the war he came to Arkansas and located at Helena, where he commenced the study of law, and was admitted to the bar in 1871, and later admitted to practice law before the Supreme Court. He then commenced the practice of law at Helena, and was shortly after elected prosecuting attorney, having filled the office of city attorney two terms. He was editor of a daily and weekly newspaper during two campaigns, from 1874 to 1879, and was in the legislature in 1887. Having become largely interested in real estate in this county, he moved to Marianna in 1883, where he has since lived. He now owns 4,000 acres of land, including a large plantation, on which is situated a general supply store, a saw-mill and steam cotton-gin, all under his general supervision. Mr. Otey was a son of Christopher and Emily (Smith) Otey, natives of Virginia and North Carolina, respectively. He was married in the State of Arkansas to Miss Kate McAnulty, a native of this county. Mr. Otey is well known and highly spoken of by all who are acquainted with him.

J. H. Parnell, of Marianna, Ark., was born in Southern Alabama, July 4, 1837, and is a son of John and Temperance Jane (Avery) Parnell, the former having been born in Putnam County, Ga., in 1806, and died in February, 1889, a farmer by occupation. He was a Whig in politics, was strongly opposed to secession, and served for some time in the capacity of magistrate. At the time of his death he weighed 225 pounds. His wife was born in South Carolina, and when young was taken to Alabama, where she grew to womanhood and met and married Mr. Parnell. She died about 1850, having borne a family of sixteen children, only the four oldest and the four youngest being now alive. Five sons were in the Confederate army, M. W. Parnell being a lieutenant under Gen. Price; Thomas J. was in the cavalry under Hood, Elijah being under Hood in the infantry, and was killed at Chickamauga; Daniel was in Jeff Davis's artillery and fired the last cannon at the battle of Bull Run, was taken prisoner to Elmira, N. Y., and after being paroled, died on his way home, his death being caused by exposure. Henry was in Forrest's army, and after procuring a furlough, came home, where he died of measles. All the brothers-in-law returned safe from the war. J. H. Parnell grew to manhood near Selma, Ala., and in his youth acquired a good English education. He farmed until the close of the war, then engaged in merchandising at Jacksonville, where he remained until 1869, when he immigrated to Osceola, Miss., and followed the same occupation there until 1882, at which time he came to Marianna, and until recently was a merchant there also. For the last six months he has been occupied in the hotel business, which is proving fairly remunerative. He owns some good property in the city and sixty acres of farming land, which is said to be quite valuable. Mr. Parnell is a Democrat, a Mason and a member of the A. O. U. W. His wife, who was Miss Mollie Rigney, was born in Marianna, Ark., in 1868, and is a daughter of Hy. and Cynthia (Webb) Rigney, who were former residents of Huntsville, Ala., the father a Confederate soldier during the Civil War. The paternal great-grandfather of Mr. Parnell was born in England, and came to America many years prior to the American Revolution, his son, the grandfather of our subject participating in that struggle.

Thomas G. Phillips, mayor of Haynes, came to Arkansas in 1855, and located in Lee County, where he was engaged in farming until the war. He enlisted in August, 1861, in the Thirteenth Arkansas Infantry, being appointed orderly sergeant of Company G, and participated in the battles of Belmont, Shiloh (where he was slightly wounded), Murfreesboro, Liberty Gap, Chickamauga, Missionary Ridge, and all of the principal battles of the Georgia campaign. He was severely wounded at Atlanta, was afterward elected second lieutenant, and rejoined his regiment just before the surrender. After the war Mr. Phillips returned to his farm, which he had purchased previous to entering the army, consisting of 327 acres of land. In 1879 he entered into the mercantile business. He carries a stock of goods invoicing about $2,500, and his annual sales will amount to $8,000 per year. He also owns the farm purchased before the war and, too, other property, in all 767 acres, with nearly 100 acres under cultivation. He has been twice married; first, to Miss Antonette Hustus, who died in 1879, leaving two children: Mollie (deceased) and Emma M. (still living). His second marriage was in 1885 to Mrs. Thompson, who died in 1887. Mr. Phillips was born in Indiana, May 21, 1832, as a son of Joseph and Sallie Phillips, natives of North Carolina and Ohio, respectively. They were the parents of eight children, all of whom survive and five of them are residents of Arkansas. Mr. Thomas Phillips is a strong Democrat. He has held the office of justice of the peace of his township, and on the incorporation of Haynes, was elected mayor, which office he still holds. He is a member of the Masonic order, and of the Knights of Honor, and belongs to the Methodist Episcopal Church, South.

George W. Pittman. Of that sturdy and independent class, the farmers of Arkansas, none are possessed of more sterling principles than he whose name heads this sketch, and as a merchant he has not his superior in the county as far as intelligent management, honesty of purpose and energy are concerned. He is a Georgian, born February 16, 1849, and is a son of James R. Pittman, also of that State, who was born, reared and married there, the last event being to Miss Bettie A. Nash. Of a family of ten children given to them, five are now living: John C., James G., Jesse W., Mary J. (wife of Thomas J. Pinkston and the mother of seven children) and Mattie B. (who is the wife of A. S. Sears and is the mother of four children). Mr. Pittman was a farmer by occupation, and in this calling became quite wealthy, being the owner of 1,700 acres of valuable and productive land at the time of his death, which occurred in 1868. He was always interested in the local politics of the community in which he resided, and also furthered the building of churches and schools with his purse as well as by his influence, and was ever considered one of the leading and public-spirited men of the county. His wife's death followed his, January 12, 1887, she having been an earnest Christian lady and a member of the Baptist Church. George W. Pittman, our immediate biographical subject, inherits English blood from his mother, and his early education was received in the schools near Georgetown, Ga. In 1874 he immigrated to Mississippi, and at the end of two years went to Louisiana, a year later returning to Mississippi. Since May, 1882, he has been a resident of Arkansas, and has successfully followed the occupations of farming and merchandising, and where he was then worth $800, he is now worth ten times as much.

Maj. E. D. Ragland is the son of Dr. Nathaniel and Elizabeth (Love) Ragland, his birth occurring in Shelby County, Tenn., in 1834. Dr. Ragland, a native of Virginia, was born in 1793, and served in the War of 1812. He attended the Philadelphia Medical College, and upon commencing the practice of his chosen profession, in 1818, selected Louisville, Ky., as the field of his labors. He was married in 1816 to Elizabeth, daughter of Mathew Love. To their union seven children were born, E. D., the subject of this sketch, being the sixth in order of birth. Their names were: James B., Louisa M. (now Mrs. Dr. B. D. Anderson of Texas), Dr. Nathaniel (who died in 1870 in De Vall's Bluff, and was a sergeant in Price's regiment), Mary E. (now Mrs. Rembert, residing in Memphis, Tenn.), Sarah V. (Mrs. Dunlap of Memphis, Tenn.), and Samuel W. (died in 1861 leaving a family.) His wife is the daughter of Avan Huntsman, a former Congressman of Tennessee. Dr. Nathaniel Ragland (father of our subject) died in 1859, and his wife in 1873. They were members of the Presbyterian Church, to which the former lent his hearty support and valuable influence. He was a man of great public spirit, and many improvements of early days in his city stand as monuments to his memory and liberality. He had the name of being the proprietor of the first drug store ever established in Memphis, and died very wealthy, his estate alone being valued at $294,000. Maj. E. D. Ragland passed his boyhood days in Shelby County and graduated from the University at Lebanon, Tenn. He was married in 1857 to Cornelia Mottley, daughter of B. F. and Martha (Doak) Mottley. Mr. Mottley was State representative of Tennessee for years, and died in 1847, his wife only surviving him three years. Mr. Ragland entered the army in 1862 as major in the Memphis Light Dragoons, attached to the Seventh Tennessee Cavalry and served three years. In 1864 he was taken prisoner of war and held eleven months, making his escape April 19, 1865. He participated in most of the principal engagements, and by his kindness and thoughtfulness to his men won from them their life-long respect and esteem. Maj. Ragland is indeed a generous man, never being behind in contributing to any worthy purpose, but his liberality does not end there, for many benevolent acts never reach the ears of the outside world, though his generous deeds are recognized by the happy recipient of his bounteous gifts. Major Ragland settled in Phillips County, Ark., in 1865 being occupied in the independent profession of farming in that locality until 1869, at which time he moved to his present home in Richland Township. He owns 160 acres of land, all cultivated and stocked with the various superior grades necessary to successfully operate a farm of that size. He is a Mason, being a member of La Grange Lodge, No. 108, and also belongs to the

Chapter at Marianna. The city council recognize in him an efficient and influential member. The Major and Mrs. Ragland are members of the Methodist Church at Marianna, Ark. He is interested in all enterprises for the development or promotion of the county, and has witnessed the growth of Marianna from a place that could only boast of one store to its present prosperous proportions.

T. J. Robinson, M. D., received a good common-school education in Tennessee, his native State, and spent two years in the study of medicine at home, after which he took a course of lectures at Nashville. He was attending Medical College at the breaking out of the war, but, with the true spirit of patriotism, enlisted in the Confederate army, serving part of the time in the hospital, though mostly engaged in active duty as a private. After the close of the war he gave his attention to farming for four years. He then entered the medical college at Louisville, Ky., and was graduated from that institution in the winter of 1868–69, after which, returning to Hardeman County, he practiced for fifteen years. Dr. Robinson later went to Texas, but within three months following he came to Arkansas and located at Marianna, Lee County, in 1883. Since that time he has built up a large practice. Dr. Robinson was born in Hardeman County, Tenn., in 1841, as a son of Jonas and Elizabeth (Chisum) Robinson, natives of the same State. Jonas Robinson was born in 1800, and died at the age of fifty-three. His wife is still living in Hardeman County, at the age of seventy-six years. The subject of this sketch was married in Tennessee to Miss Nannie Chisum, by which union were born three children: John C. (a student of the University of Louisville, Medical Department), Mary Wood and Pearl (his only daughters, aged, respectively, fifteen and four years, are his pets). The Doctor is a member of the Lee County Medical Society, of the Knights of Honor, and belongs to the Christian Church.

Capt. James W. Rodgers received a high school education in his native State of South Carolina, preparatory to entering the military academy at

West Point, to which his father wished to send him, but having chosen a mercantile life rather than that of a military nature he engaged in merchandising at Byhalia, Miss., where he opened a stock of general merchandise, and was also proprietor of a blacksmith and wagon shop. At the breaking out of the war he joined the first troops organized in his county, Company D, of the Ninth Mississippi Infantry, and the first year served at Warrington, near Pensacola, Fla. He received his discharge within the year on account of sickness, and returned home, but as soon as able organized Company E, Thirty-fourth Mississippi Infantry, which he commanded until the close of the war. He participated in the battles of Perryville, Murfreesboro, Dalton, Chickamauga, Missionary Ridge and on to Atlanta, and then went back with Hood, but was taken sick and sent to the hospital at Columbus, Miss. After his recovery he was placed in command of 600 men, and started to join Gen. Johnston's army in North Carolina, but receiving word of the surrender he paroled his men at Meridian, returned home, and again resumed his business. Upon remaining two years he came to Arkansas, and located in what is now Walnut Bend Township, Lee County, where he has since lived. Capt. Rodgers was born in Lawrence District, S. C., in 1834, being a son of Hon. James S. and Emily N. (Ware) Rodgers, also natives of that State. James S. Rodgers was a well-to-do farmer and a prominent citizen of his locality, and held the office of sheriff of Lawrence District for several years, and later for several terms was representative from that district to the State legislature. He served under Gen. Jackson in one of the early wars, and was a son of John Rodgers, a soldier in the Revolutionary War, and of Scotch-Irish descent. Mr. Rodgers was a member of the A. F. & A. M., and his death, which occurred in 1866, was much regretted by all who knew him. He was at that time a resident of Marshall County, Miss., to which he had removed in 1849. Mrs. Rodgers was a daughter of Gen. Edwin Ware, a merchant of Abbeville District, S. C., and a soldier in the Revolutionary War. She was a member of the Baptist Church, and died in 1862, leaving twelve children,

five sons and seven daughters, four of whom are still living: James W. (the principal of this sketch), Amanda (now Mrs. Du Puy), Albert S. and Flora (now Mrs. Myers). Mr. Rodgers was married in 1872 to Miss Ella Newman, daughter of Augustus and Sallie Newman, who removed from Bolivar County, Miss., to this county in 1868, and both of whom are now deceased. Mr. and Mrs. Rodgers are the parents of eight children, five surviving, all sons. Mr. Rodgers has lived on his present farm since 1886, and has it well improved. It consisted of 640 acres, with over 400 acres under cultivation. Mrs. Rodgers is a member of the Methodist Episcopal Church, to which her husband is a liberal contributor, strongly advocating Sunday-school work.

Henry Preston Rodgers. In chronicling the names of the prominent citizens of Lee County, that of Henry Preston Rodgers is accorded an enviable position. He is the son of Ebenezer and Parmelia (Jackson) Rodgers, his birth occurring in Madison County, Ill., in March, 1844. Ebenezer Rodgers was a native of Wales, born in 1790, and in 1820 came to America, locating in Howard County, Mo., where two years later he was united in marriage with Miss Jackson. During their residence in that State three children were given them, but in 1839 they moved to Illinois, where seven children were reared, making a family of ten born to their union. Mrs. Parmelia Rodgers, of English descent, first saw the light of day in Kentucky, in 1805, and after a long and consistent Christian life as a devoted wife and mother, she passed to her eternal rest, on Wednesday, March 28, 1882, at the age of seventy-seven years. Mr. Rodgers, Sr., though of Welsh parentage, was of English birth, and in 1818, being prompted by missionary zeal, came to America, locating in Kentucky, which presented a wide field for his labors. His was a grand and noble work, and his efforts for the advancement of Christianity and education have left imprints for good that will remain through time and eternity. In 1823, five years after his arrival in the United States, he organized a Baptist Church, in Capt. John Jackson's neighborhood, and subsequently became its pastor. Capt. Jackson, the father of Mrs. Rodgers, was by occupation a farmer, but entered the War of 1812, commanding a company of volunteers (Kentucky). In 1834 Rev. Mr. Rodgers moved with his family to Madison County, Ill., where he presided for a period of two years as pastor of the Baptist Church. At the expiration of that time he left the pastorate and devoted his time to missionary and association efforts throughout the State. After a long and well-spent life, he passed away, at his home in Upper Alton, Ill., at the age of sixty-four years. Henry Preston Rodgers, the subject of this sketch, received the rudiments of his education in the subscription schools of Madison County, Ill., and matriculated in the Shurtliff College in 1861, completing the junior year in 1863. In September, 1863, he entered the scientific department of the University of Michigan (Ann Arbor), and completed his education one year later. After leaving Ann Arbor Mr. Rodgers went to Memphis, but soon located in Bolivar, Tenn., where he engaged in merchandising. Finding that venture to be unsuccessful, however, he closed out his business, and accepted a position as salesman with a large and prominent firm, which he filled with credit and satisfaction. In 1870 he came to Arkansas, selecting Marianna as his place of abode, and again embarked in the mercantile business, his efforts being liberally rewarded. For ten years he was recognized as one of the most enterprising and progressive of Marianna's citizens, only retiring from business at that time to devote his attention to planting. He now owns 6,000 acres of as fine farm land as can be found in Arkansas, and 1,200 of this are in a high state of cultivation, the principal crops being corn and cotton. The soil in favorable seasons yields about one bale of cotton to the acre. The year 1877 witnessed Mr. Rodgers' marriage to Miss Mary Virginia Upshaw, a native of Arkansas, and a daughter of James R. and Bettie W. (Epps) Upshaw. To their union two children were born: Henry Preston, Jr. (born June 10, 1878), and Mary Lucile (born December 24, 1879). Mrs. Rodgers died in 1887, a lady of great culture and refinement, and a favorite among her wide circle of friends and acquaintants. In politics Mr.

Rodgers is a Democrat, and in 1883 he received the election to the State legislature, being re-elected in 1884. He holds a membership in the Episcopal Church, as did also his estimable wife. That he is popular is proven beyond a doubt, by the respect and confidence reposed in him by the entire people.

Albert S. Rodgers took part in many of the important and hard-fought battles of the Civil War, prominent among which were the engagements at Perryville, Lookout Mountain, Missionary Ridge, Murfreesboro, Atlanta, Jonesboro, Dalton, Chickamauga, Franklin and a number of others. He was wounded in the former and last three battles, and was taken prisoner at the last named, being confined in a Federal hospital for three months. Upon his recovery he was taken to Camp Chase, Ohio, where he was held until shortly after the surrender of Lee, when he was released on parole and returned home. There he engaged in farming until 1868. Coming to Arkansas he located in Lee County, and opened up a farm at Walnut Bend. Mr. Rodgers was born in Lawrence County, S. C., in 1844, and is a son of James S. and Emily R. Rodgers, both natives of that State. He was reared in Marshall County, Miss., where his father moved when he was three years of age, and which he made his home until his enlistment, when only seventeen years of age, in Company E, of the Thirty-fourth Mississippi Infantry. He was married in 1880 to Miss Scott M. Davidson, a daughter of A. W. and Susan E. (Camthes) Davidson. They are the parents of two children: Alma M. and Emma S. In connection with farming and stock raising Mr. Rodgers is engaged in the general mercantile business, and carries a stock of some $2,000, enjoying a large patronage. He is a prominent Democrat, and has held the position of deputy clerk of Lee County, and was justice of the peace for six years, but at the present time is not occupied in an official capacity. He is a member of the Masonic fraternity and of the Knights of Honor, and is a liberal patron to all public enterprises. Mrs. Rodgers is a member of the Presbyterian Church. James S. Rodgers, the father of our subject, was born in South Carolina in 1791, and lived to the ripe old age of seventy-five years. He was a soldier in the War of 1812, and was a prominent man of his county, holding the office of sheriff for several years. He owned a large plantation and at the breaking out of the war was the possessor of sixty slaves. In his family were twelve children, five sons and seven daughters. Saxon Rodgers, his father, was of South Carolina nativity, and a farmer of considerable means and influence. Mrs. Rodgers, the mother of Albert S., was a daughter of Edmund Ware, a Virginian by birth, and a general in the Revolutionary War.

John L. Rowland, who stands high in the agricultural ranks of Lee County, came originally from Tennessee, being a son of John B. and Elizabeth (Thomas) Rowland. The father was a son of Birch and Mary Rowland, natives of North Carolina, both of whom lived to be over sixty years of age. They were the parents of four sons: William (a mechanic and a master of his trade), George, David (both successful farmers and well-to do) and John B. The latter moved to St. Francis County in 1834, where he was engaged in farming, but a few years later came to Lee County. He was married before entering this State (then a Territory), to Miss Elizabeth Thomas, daughter of Lewis and Margaret Thomas, of South Carolina and Tennessee origin, respectively. Lewis Thomas was a soldier in the War of 1812, and gained distinction by his bravery, living to the age of sixty-five. John L. Rowland was born in Montgomery County, Tenn., in 1829, and was therefore five years of age when his parents moved to Arkansas. He was reared on his father's farm, and as the territory was at that time very thinly settled, and schoolhouses were few and far between, his educational advantages were very limited. He commenced farming for himself when twenty years old in this county, and in 1857 was married to Susan E. Reed, daughter of Noah and Mary (Hurley) Reed, natives of Massachusetts and Kentucky, respectively. Noah Reed was born in 1797; his wife died at the age of forty. Mr. and Mrs. Rowland have four children: Josephine (deceased), Ardella (deceased), Jessie L. and Mary. Mr. Rowland enlisted in the Confederate army in 1862, in Company B, of Holmes' regiment, in which he served throughout the war, participating in the battles of Cotton Plant, Helena and some others, but was principally engaged in skirmishing. After the war he returned home and resumed farming, and although he lost nearly all he had during that unhappy period, by hard work and close economy, together with good business management, he has accumulated considerable property, and now owns a fine farm of 540 acres, with 250 acres under cultivation. He has also a large amount of stock, to which industry he turns his attention, in preference to the more general occupation of cotton raising. Mr. Rowland is a Democrat in politics, is a member of the Masonic order, and of the Methodist Episcopal Church, South, to which his wife also belongs, they taking an active part in religious enterprises. He is a liberal contributor to all enterprises for the good of the community.

John W. Russell, who stands foremost among the farmers of Lee County, Ark., is a native of Alabama and a son of Alexander Russell, also of that State, and who was born about 1809. He was of Scotch descent, and was a farmer, tanner and shoemaker. In 1828 Miss Rebecca Ann Cartwright became his wife, a daughter of John and Polly Cartwright, both originally from Alabama, and of Irish descent. She was born in Madison County, that State, in 1815, and died in 1882, three years after the death of her husband. They were the parents of nine children, five sons and four daughters; three of these are known to be living: Joseph, Eveline (now Mrs. Holly of Alabama), and John W. The subject of this sketch was born in Limestone County, Ala., December 10, 1831, and remained in that county until his marriage, having charge of his father's farm. He has been married four times; first, in 1855, to Miss Louisa Breeding, a native of Morgan County, who died in 1877, leaving seven children, three still surviving: Samuel R., Otis P. and William W., all engaged in farming in this county. Mr. Russell was next married May 10, 1879, to Miss Susan Bickerstaff, also of Alabama, who died in 1883. His third marriage was in 1884 to Miss Dora Smith, also of the same State. She lived a year after her marriage, leaving one child, which died a short time after its mother. His fourth and present wife was Mrs. Mary A. Archy, widow of Rufus Archy, of Tennessee, to whom he was married in October, 1886. Mr. Russell enlisted in the Confederate service, in 1864, in Malone's battalion, in Johnston's army, and served until the close of the war. Coming to Arkansas in 1873, he located in this county and purchased the farm on which he still resides, now one of the finest in Lee County, consisting of 216 acres, with 150 acres under cultivation. He is also engaged in the milling business and cotton ginning. Mr. Russell is a Democrat in politics, and a member of the Methodist Episcopal Church. His wife belongs to the Cumberland Presbyterian Church.

Hartwell Scruggs, holding a prominent place among the enterprising and wealthy farmers of Richland Township, is a native of Tennessee, and was born in 1824, being the second in a family of three children, resulting from the union of Hartwell and Lucy (Howell) Scruggs. Hartwell Scruggs was born in 1800, in the Old Dominion. He moved to Tennessee, and there married about the year 1820, making it his home for many years, and giving his children such advantages for an education as could be obtained at that time. His son, Louis H., died in 1859, leaving a wife and two children; John, died in 1860, a wife and one child surviving to mourn his loss. Mr. Hartwell, Sr., moved from Tennessee to Lee County, Ark., in 1844, and settled on the St. Francis River, where he resided at the date of his death in 1845. Mrs. Scruggs died in the same year. Mr. Scruggs was a Democrat in his political views, and in religious faith, a Baptist. Hartwell, the subject of this sketch, passed his younger days in Tennessee, and came with his father to Arkansas in 1844. Two years later he embarked in rafting on the Mississippi River, following this occupation for eight years, after which he went to farming on the St. Francis River. In 1863 he enlisted in Dobbins' Regiment of Arkansas Cavalry, soon being taken prisoner of war, and was not released until 1865. In 1868 he settled in Richland Township, purchasing a farm of 200 acres, 100 acres now under cultivation. With the improvements that he made this farm is second to

none in the county, and the impression to the casual observer, or passer-by, is that thrift and prosperity predominate. Mr. Scruggs was united in marriage with Miss Amanda Morgan in the year 1847, and by her became the father of six children: Martha A., Hartwell, Cortez, Howell, Helen and Louis. Mrs. Scruggs died in 1861, and for his second wife Mr. Scruggs chose Rebecca Moore, of Virginia, who died in 1870, leaving two children: Clara and Anna. Mr. Scruggs was married in 1871 to Miss Harriet E. Haydon, a daughter of Waller and Sarah F. (Nelson) Haydon, originally from Virginia and Kentucky, respectively. By this marriage they have had eight children: Libourn R., Lucian (deceased), Horace B. (deceased), Carrie L. and Cora L. (twins—Cora is dead), Blackstone F., Edna E. and Rhuney R.. Mr. Scruggs is a man who has traveled a great deal, and who has seen life in all its different phases. He is a member of Lodge No. 108, of the Masonic order at La Grange, Lee County, and has been school director in his district for years. He takes an active interest in those movements tending to the good of the county, lending by his valuable support and influence especially to the advancement of education. He comments with pardonable pride on the development and growth of the county since he has resided here, and many of its enterprises will stand as monuments of his generous support, and interest manifested therein.

Richard D. Shackelford. One among the many prosperous and prominent farmers of Lee County is Richard D. Shackelford, who was born of honorable parentage at Murfreesboro, Tenn., on February 10, 1826. He is a son of John L. and Sarah A. (Chisenhall) Shackelford. John L. Shackelford came upon the scene of action in Virginia, on August 12, 1796; he was a mechanic by occupation, an old-time Whig in politics, and a member of the Methodist Episcopal Church, and as a pious and devout man, was much loved and respected by those who knew him. He was a Scotchman by birth, and came to this country when young, during the War of 1812, taking an active part, and doing valiant duty as a soldier. He was successful in life, and at the time of his death, which occurred on August 20, 1863, had considerable property. His wife, to whom he was married May 26, 1816, was also born in the Old Dominion, and was the mother of ten children, two sons and eight daughters, four of whom are still living: Katharine (widow of Rev. John Roberts), Tabitha (widow of William Williford), Rebecca (widow of John Walthall), and Richard D., the principal of this sketch. The latter was reared in Marengo County, Ala., where his father had removed when the son was two years of age. As that portion of the State at that time was comparatively an unsettled country, his education was of a very limited character. He began farming for himself at the age of twenty-one, and in 1847 removed to Arkansas, settling in Phillips County, about thirty miles northwest of Helena, which was at that time an uninhabited wilderness. After remaining there seven years, he removed to Woodruff County, continuing until 1862, at which time he joined the Confederate army, in Company G, of Dobbins' regiment, and served up to the close of the war. He then returned to his family in Woodruff County, but soon removed to his present location, where he has since been engaged as a farmer and mechanic. Mr. Shackelford has been twice married; first, to Miss Belvida Tully, in 1850, who died fifteen years later, having been the mother of seven children, six still living: Alice (now Mrs. Brown, of this county), Thomas E. (a farmer of Pulaski County), Mary (now Mrs. Marshall, of Ft. Smith), William R. (also a farmer of Pulaski County), Lucy (now Mrs. Ferguson, of Lee County) and Louis L. (a farmer of Pulaski County). He was then married in December of that year to Mrs. Mary E. Wilks (nee Brown), a daughter of John and Mary Brown, and a native of Mississippi. They had seven children, two of whom survive: Zula (now Mrs. McAlexander, a mechanic of Brinkley, Ark.), and Nannie, at home. Mr. Shackelford is a Democrat in politics, and a member of the Christian Church, as is also his wife, in which they take an active part, always being ready to give their time and means to worthy church and religious enterprises.

James A. Sims is a native of Mississippi, and a son of John and Isabella (Johnson) Sims, natives of Virginia and North Carolina, respectively. John Sims was a blacksmith by trade, and was also engaged in farming. He died in 1831, preceded by his wife (who was a daughter of Gilbert Johnson, a native of South Carolina) some five years. They were the parents of nine children, eight sons and one daughter: Samuel A., John P., William B., James A. (the principal of this sketch), Gilbert G., Benjamin M., Ernest W., David D. and Mary A. (wife of John W. Walker, of Warren County, Miss.). The places of residence of the brothers are not known. James A. Sims was born in Warren County, Miss., near Vicksburg, on February 5, 1817. On account of the country being then but thinly settled, his early advantages for an education were very limited. He commenced farming for himself at the age of seventeen, and in 1849 came to Arkansas, purchasing a farm in Lee County, which was at that time a part of Monroe County. Two years later he sold his farm, and removed to Clark County, where he remained thirteen years, soon returning and purchasing his present farm, then within the lines of St. Francis County. Mr. Sims was married, in 1851, to Miss Augusta C. Davis, a native of Phillips County, and a daughter of Thomas J. and Elvira (Mullen) Davis, both of whom are deceased. Mr. and Mrs. Sims are the parents of ten children, five sons and five daughters; seven of these are still living: John H., Louisa J., Florence I., William A., Robert E. Lee, Edward M. and Donnie D. Mr. Sims enlisted in the Confederate service in the summer of 1864, in the Arkansas Home Guards, in which he served until the close of the war. He and his wife are members of the Missionary Baptist Church, to which they have belonged for over thirty years. Mr. Sims is a strong, uncompromising Democrat.

Mrs. Louisa F. (Noles) Slaughter, the widow of Dr. Stanton Slaughter, was born in Maury County, Tenn., November 27, 1837. Dr. Stanton Slaughter, a native of South Carolina, was born in 1820, being a son of Arthur and Jane Slaughter, of Virginia. He received a liberal education, graduating from the New Orleans (La.) Medical College in 1846, and afterward settled in Mississippi, choosing this as the field of his labors, but subsequently immigrated to Arkansas, and located in Phillips County in 1851. He was immediately recognized as an efficient and conscientious physician, and rapidly gained an enviable position, both as a son of Æsculapius and a citizen. He was married in 1851 to Miss Mary Pollard, of Mississippi, who only lived one year. He was again married, his second wife being Miss Louisa F. Noles, a daughter of Allen J. and Eliza Noles. Mr. Noles was a native of Maury County, Tenn., and was born in 1807. He was a farmer and contractor and served as sheriff of Lewis County, Tenn., for many years. In 1829 he was married to Elizabeth Batmon, of Maury County, her birth occurring in 1809. They were the parents of eleven children, six sons and five daughters, four now living: Louisa F., Sarah E. (widow of B. M. Marbeau), James B. and Rosena (wife of Bruce Kirk, now residing in Texas). Mr. Noles died in 1887, and his wife in 1863. To Dr. and Mrs. Slaughter a family of ten children were given, seven sons and three daughters, five now living. Dr. Slaughter died in Brinkley, this State, January 26, 1885. He was a courteous and highly-cultured gentleman, well worthy the respect and esteem shown him by his wide circle of friends and acquaintances. Mrs. Slaughter owns 160 acres of excellent farm land, with over 100 acres under a successful state of cultivation. She is a bright, intelligent lady, and though by no means a masculine woman, manages her estate and business in a highly commendable manner, that might well be copied by many of the sterner sex.

G. F. Smith has been a resident of Arkansas since 1860, when he located in what was then a part of St. Francis County, but which now forms a portion of Lee County, and was one of the first men to advocate this county's formation. Born in Rutherford County, Tenn., on December 15, 1819, he was a son of William and Rebecca (Webb) Smith, natives of North Carolina and Tennessee, respectively. William Smith moved to Tennessee when a young man, where he worked at his trade, as a gunsmith, and also engaged in farming. He was a soldier in the War of 1813, and was present at the battle of New Orleans. To himself and wife

ten children were born, five sons and five daughters, two of whom only are living: G. F. and Jasper N. (a farmer of Hardeman County, Tenn.). G. F. Smith commenced farming for himself at the age of nineteen, and four years later removed to Hardeman County, where he was engaged in the same occupation until his removal to Arkansas. He first purchased 1,000 acres of land for $4,800; now he owns 3,600 acres in the western part of Lee County, and has some 700 acres under cultivation, which he devotes principally to cotton and corn. He also owns a steam grist-mill, saw-mill and cotton-gin, with a capacity of eight bales per day, which were erected at a cost of $3,000. Mr. Smith was married in Tennessee, in 1838, to Miss Elizabeth Bell, a daughter of Samuel Bell, of that county; she died in about 1840, leaving two children, both of whom are now deceased. Mr. Smith was married on January 17, 1843, to ˙Miss A. J. Smith, also of Tennessee origin, who passed away in 1878, having been the mother of one son; the latter died in 1853. His third and present wife, Miss V. M. Granger, was a daughter of A. H. and Mary Granger, and a native of Phillips County, Ark. They are the parents of four children: George F., Melvine, Philip J. and Stephen C. They are members of the Cumberland Presbyterian Church. Mr. Smith belongs to the Masonic order.

John H. Spivey first saw the light of day in Alabama, and after spending nine or ten years of his life in that State, he moved to Tennessee, remaining there about four years; the balance of his boyhood days were passed in Mississippi. He was reared on his father's farm, but received a good education in the common schools of the community in which he lived, and when grown served an apprenticeship as a mechanic, but has followed farming nearly all of his life. He was born on April 8, 1821, to the union of Temple and Charity (Hicks) Spivey. The former's birth occurred in Moore County, N. C., on September 22, 1794. He emigrated to Alabama in 1818 and was married in June, 1820, remaining in that State some ten years, when he went to Hardeman County, Tenn. Four years later he removed to the Chickasaw Nation in Mississippi, which was then occupied by

the Indians, and now forms a part of Tippah
County. In 1849 he went with his wife to Texas,
in which State they spent the balance of their lives.
Mr. Spivey was a millwright and farmer by occupation, and at the time of his death, in 1877, was
possessed of considerable property. Mrs. Spivey
was born on October 17, 1802, in North Carolina,
and died in 1873. They were members of the
Baptist Church, and had a family of sixteen children, nine sons and seven daughters, eight of
whom are still living. John H., the principal of
this sketch, removed to Monroe (now Lee) County,
Ark., in November, 1863, and was engaged in
farming until 1872, when he entered the ranks of
the merchants of this county, though he still carries on farming. In 1862 he enlisted in the Confederate army as a member of Blythe's battalion,
and participated in a number of battles and skirmishes, being wounded at the battle of Beaver
Dam Bayou, by a shot through the right arm. This
disabled him so that he was disqualified from active
duty. He was at that time a lieutenant of his company. Mr. Spivey was married in November, 1845,
in Hardeman County, Tenn., to Miss Martha A.
Howard, of Madison County, Ala., and daughter of
George and Penelope (Moore) Howard, of North
Carolina nativity. She was born on November 17,
1824, and is the mother of nine children, six sons
and three daughters, five of whom survive: Mary
E. (wife of John Ward, of Lee County), William
A. (also a farmer of Lee County), Andrew T. (a
farmer of Lincoln County, Tenn.), Luada (now
Mrs. Bickeroff) and Thaddeus F. (also of this
county. Mr. Spivey is a stanch Democrat, and
was elected justice of the peace in 1874, which
position he held six years; he has also been a notary public for eight years. He was appointed
postmaster of Moro in 1882, and discharged the
duties of that position until November of the past
year. He is an unaffiliated member of the Masonic order, in which he has taken the Royal Arch
degree, and is a member of the County Grange;
he also belongs to the Missionary Baptist Church,
as does his wife.

Jacob A. Sullivan's boyhood was spent on his
father's farm in Tennessee, and the war breaking

out during his school days his education was interrupted, and he was obliged to work at farm labor,
when he should have been receiving instructions
in the common English branches. He began
farming at the age of twenty-two, and has followed that occupation all his life. Born in Tipton
County, Tenn., in 1847, Mr. Sullivan moved to
Lee County in 1876, where he engaged in farming,
in 1881 opening up a store. He carries a stock of
general merchandise invoicing about $5,000, and
enjoys a good trade. He was married in 1869 to
Miss Mary F. Wooten, daughter of Cannon S. and
Helen Wooten. They are the parents of nine
children, six still living: James R., Isaac R.,
Charles C., Jacob S., Hugh, Mary A. and Fred.
Isaac Sullivan, the father of the principal of this
sketch, was born in Sumner County, Tenn., in
1814, and yet survives. His twin brother, Jacob
Sullivan, so closely resembles him that it is nearly
impossible to distinguish them. They are both
farmers by occupation. They have an older
brother, Nathan, who was a prominent Methodist
minister. Jacob A. Sullivan owns a farm of 160
acres of land, with 100 acres under cultivation.

Andrew J. Thompson. Foremost among the
leading farmers of Lee County, and well known
throughout Phillips and Lee Counties, is Andrew
J. Thompson, who has been a resident in this State
since 1840, and a citizen of Lee County since 1881.
Born in Garrard County, Ky., on December 12,
1828, he is a son of Davis and Gabraella (Dunn)
Thompson, natives of West Virginia and Kentucky,
respectively. Davis Thompson moved to the Blue
Grass State with his parents when a child, and remained there until 1836, when he came to Arkansas, having been appointed land agent by President Jackson, for the State of Arkansas. Locating
at Helena he moved his family four years later,
and held the position referred to until elected to
the State legislature in 1840. He was also one of
the commissioners appointed to re-establish the
line between Arkansas and Missouri. In 1846 he
enlisted for the Mexican War, starting out as a
private, but was soon promoted to the command of
his company, and was commissary of his regiment.
After the close of the war he was elected sheriff of

Phillips County, in which capacity he served four years. Mr. Thompson then retired from active life, and died in 1859. He was a son of Arthur Thompson, of Scotch and Irish descent, who died in Kentucky about 1820. Mrs. Thompson was a daughter of Benjamin Dunn, and was born in Baltimore, Md. Her father was a soldier in the Revolutionary War. Of their large family of children four are still living: Josephine (now Mrs. Hargravis, a resident of Helena), Helen (wife of Judge Hanks, of Helena), one daughter (now Mrs. C. L. Moore, also of that city) and Andrew J. (the subject of this sketch and the eldest of those living). The latter was reared and educated in Helena, remaining there until the war. After Gen. Curtis had taken Helena, Mr. Thompson passed the Federal lines and joined the Confederate army, enlisting in Dobbins' regiment, in which he was afterward promoted to second lieutenant. In December of that year (1862) he was captured by a party of the Fourteenth Illinois Cavalry and taken to Helena and then to Memphis, Tenn., where, through the influence of Senator Sebastin, he was given his freedom for a time, but was soon sent North and confined at Camp Chase, in Ohio, and then to Fort Delaware, and was held a prisoner until exchanged at Johnson's Island in December, 1864. After the war, returning to Helena, he was engaged in farming for twelve years, later ran a steam ferry, and for two years was occupied in operating a large steam cotton-gin at Helena. In 1881 he came to this county and purchased a farm on which he still lives, and has now 1,000 acres of land, with nearly 700 acres under cultivation, all made since the war by hard work and good business management. He at one time also owned a half interest in the Helena Oil Mills. Mr. Thompson was married in July, 1865, to Miss Eliza Jones, a native of Limestone County, Ala., and who died in 1868, leaving one son, Arthur Thompson, now book-keeper and general superintendent in D. H. Crebe's oil mills at Helena. His second wife, to whom he was married in 1870, was formerly Miss Sallie E. Crenshaw, also of Limestone County, Ala., and who died in 1886, leaving one daughter, Jessie F., at home. Mr. Thompson is a Democrat,

and a leader in the political movements of his township.

John J. Thompson was born in Bedford County, Tenn., January 25, 1823, and is the son of Samuel C. and Rebecca (Doty) Thompson. Samuel Thompson, a native of Virginia, was born in 1801, and married in Tennessee, about the year 1820, Miss Doty, who was born in Tennessee in 1803. They were the parents of ten children, of whom those living are: John J., Rebecca A. and Mary E.; those deceased are: William, Isaac D., Enoch G., Lucy, Henry, Nancy D. and Thomas. Mr. Thompson died in Hardeman County, Tenn., in 1862, and his wife in 1875. John J. received but limited advantages for schooling, the educational facilities at the period of his boyhood being far from satisfactory. At the age of twenty-one he began life on his own responsibility, selecting farming as his occupation, which, together with the mechanic's trade, has principally occupied him. Coming to Arkansas in 1861, he settled in Phillips County, near where he now resides in Lee County. He owns eighty acres of land with fifty in cultivation, the principal products being corn and cotton; he is also engaged to some extent in the raising of cattle and hogs. Mr. Thompson was married in Hardeman County, Tenn., on March 24, 1846, to Miss Mary R. Clift, a native of that State and county, and a daughter of Barney B. and Helsie Clift. Mrs. Thompson died in Lee County, October 23, 1886, having borne seven children: John H. (Baptist minister of Springfield, Mo.), William T. (a farmer of Lee County, Ark.) and Franklin P., Martha E., James R., Charles R. and one infant dead. Mr. Thompson served as justice of the peace for one year, and has been a member of the school board for two years. In secret organizations he is connected with the Agricultural Wheel.

Joseph S. Thompson came originally from Hardeman County, Tenn., being a son of Thomas Thompson, a native of Orange County, N. C., who died in 1830. The latter was a soldier in the War of 1812, and took part in some of the most important engagements of the war, including the battle of New Orleans. He was a farmer and blacksmith by occupation. Joseph S., the principal of this sketch, was reared in his native county until after grown to manhood. He did not have the advantages for obtaining an education which his children now enjoy, as Hardeman County was at that time but thinly settled, and there was no school-house or church in his neighborhood. He began farming for himself at the age of twenty-one, and in 1858 came to Arkansas and purchased a farm near Marianna, not moving his family here until the following year. He was first married, in 1840, to Miss Nancy Allen, of North Carolina, who died in 1861, leaving three children, Ellen (the wife of John Lovejoy, a farmer of Lee County) being the only survivor; Thomas was killed by an accidental fall from a tree, and Sarah (now deceased) was the wife of Leander Johnson. Mr. Thompson was afterward married in Woodruff County, about 1863, to Mrs. Mary McLean (*nee* Crawford), widow of William J. McLean, and a daughter of William Crawford. She died in 1874, having borne two children: Minnie (wife of Edward Gillen Waters, a farmer of this county) and William J. His third and present wife, Mrs. Susan Green, a native of Mississippi, was the daughter of William and Betsey (Coley) Dougherty. They are the parents of one son, Joseph Ritter. Mr. Thompson now owns a farm of 160 acres, with 100 acres under cultivation. He and wife are members of the Christian Church, in which they take an active part.

Phillip H. Underwood has been a resident of Lee County since four years of age. He commenced farming for himself at the death of his father, on the old homestead, which occupation he has followed since that time. He was married, in 1873, to Miss Sallie Bennett, a daughter of Thomas B. and Betty (McCloudon) Bennett, natives of North Carolina and Georgia, respectively. Mr. and Mrs. Underwood are the parents of six children: Phillip O., Delia, Ola, Robert, Jettie and Honor. Mr. Underwood was born in Maury County, Tenn., in 1848, being a son of Edward and Mary Underwood, originally from North Carolina and Tennessee, respectively. The father of our subject was born in 1809, and was one of a family of six children; he died at the age of fifty-nine, having been

a successful farmer in Tennessee, to which State he removed when a young man. There he made his home until 1852, when he came to Arkansas, and located in this county, dying here in 1868. Mr. Underwood owns a farm of 167 acres, of which he has forty-five acres under cultivation. His principal crop is cotton, but he is also engaged in stock raising on a small scale. He is a Democrat in politics, and is a prominent man of Lee County. His wife is of the Primitive Baptist faith.

Dr. William Bennett Waldrip is a native of Mississippi, his birth occurring in De Soto County (near Belmont), March 9, 1846. His father, S. G. Waldrip, of North Carolina, was born in 1818, and at an early age was apprenticed to a brick-mason, in which trade he became very proficient, in connection with farming, the latter being his principal occupation through life. He was married to Miss Martha J. Smart, of Mississippi, and by her became the father of five children, four now living: James M. (a resident farmer and brick-layer of Tate County, Miss.), William B. (our subject), Henry L. (of Tate County, Miss.), Elizabeth J. (widow of Ned Casey, now Mrs. John Gray, residing in Wheetley), Mary F. (Mrs. Henderson Freeman, died in 1885). Mr. Waldrip removed to Arkansas in 1874 and settled in St. Francis County, where he passed away in 1885. He was a member of the Masonic order, and in political views was a Whig until the death of that party, after which he became a Democrat. In his religious belief he was a Baptist, being a member of the Primitive Baptist Church. Mrs. Waldrip died in Wheetley, Ark., in 1883, having passed her sixty-seventh birthday. William B. Waldrip was reared in Mississippi, where he obtained a liberal common school education, and in 1869 began the study of his chosen profession, that of medicine—first, under the able instruction of Dr. J. M. Richro, and afterward attending the Medical Institute at Cincinnati, where he was graduated with high honors in the class of 1870. He first began to alleviate the sufferings of humanity in Marshall County, Miss., but one year later moved to Arkansas, locating in Monroe (now Lee) County in the town of Wheetley. Here he rapidly gained the confidence and respect of his fellow citizens, both as an efficient physician and friend. Some years later he moved to his present location, which is situated six miles southeast of Wheetley, and though here but a few years many improvements that owe their existence to his presence show him to be a man of enterprise and progress. In connection with his practice he is engaged in farming and stock raising, in which he has been unusually successful. He owns 1,600 acres of valuable land with 240 under cultivation, and the general appearance of his farm and its appointments is of thrift and prosperity. The Doctor was married in Monroe County, August 31, 1871, to Ada, daughter of Peter W. and Martha W. (Bladen) Hollaran, of Alabama. Mrs. Waldrip died in 1882, having become the mother of four children, one now living, Frederick E. Dr. Waldrip was again married on September 20, 1888, to Miss Katie Henley, of Illinois, and the daughter of Elijah and Emma (Crutchfield) Henley (residents of Marianna). Dr. Waldrip is a Master Mason and in politics a Democrat. He is liberal and charitable, contributing to all worthy enterprises, as far as his limited time and means will permit.

Enoch W. Wall is a native of Alabama, and a son of Enoch G. and Elizabeth J. (Chapman) Wall, originally from Georgia and Alabama, respectively. They were married in the latter State in 1853, and in 1865 removed to Arkansas, settling in Phillips County, where his wife died the following year, leaving three children, two still living: Enoch W. (the principal of this sketch) and William A. (a prominent farmer of this county). Mr. Wall was married a second time, by this union there being six children, three of whom survive: Judge J., Ada G. and Eula G. Mr. Wall was a decided Democrat, a member of the Cumberland Presbyterian Church, in which he took an active part, and also belonged to the Masonic order. He was a farmer by occupation, and was comfortably well off at the time of his death, which occurred in 1880, at the age of forty-seven years. Enoch W. Wall was born in Russell County, Ala., May 29, 1854, and was reared from the age of twelve, in Phillips County, Ark. He began life for himself at the age of twenty-two years as a farmer in Lee County, which was a part of Phillips County, where he now owns a fine farm of 340 acres, with over half under cultivation, lying in the heart of the "Arkansas Cotton Belt;" this yields him a large income from year to year. In 1880 and 1881 he was engaged in the mercantile business at Oak Forest, in connection with farming, but preferring agricultural life to that of a merchant, he sold out his store in 1881, and has since that time devoted himself exclusively to tilling the soil, in which, although having his share of losses and disappointments, he has been very successful. His pleasant home in this rich country is a full reward for the labor and care spent in its acquirement. Mr. Wall was married December 19, 1877, to Miss Lizzie D. Coleman, a native of the same State as himself, and a daughter of David and Viola F. Coleman, also of Alabama. They are the parents of three children: Enoch D., Orby G. and Laura V. Mr. Wall is a leading Democrat of the county, and holds the office of justice of the peace of his township, having served in this capacity for a number of years. His official duties he discharges with satisfaction to the citizens and with credit to himself. He is also president of the school board, and here also has won the respect and regard of his fellow men.

William A. Wall is a son of Enoch G. Wall, one of the pioneers of Lee County, who is now departed from this world, and who will be long remembered by the older citizens of the community. Enoch G. Wall was born in Georgia in 1833, and was married at the age of twenty to Miss Elizabeth J. Chapman, a native of Alabama, to which State he had removed a few years previous. There he made his home until 1865, when he removed to Arkansas, and settled in Phillips County, where his wife died the next year. She was the mother of three children, two of whom still live: Enoch W. (a well-known farmer of this county, whose biography precedes this) and William A. By a subsequent marriage six children were born, and three of these are living: Judge J., Ada G. and Eula G. Mr. Wall was actively interested in the political affairs of this county, being an outspoken Democrat. He was a member of the Cumberland Presbyterian Church, and a Master Mason; was well-known throughout the community, and was highly respected, and owned a good farm, which was well improved. He was in comfortable circumstances at the time of his death, in 1880. The subject of this article was born in Barbour County, Ala., on April 9, 1856, but has been a resident of this State since nine years of age, devoting himself to the occupation of farming since old enough to handle a plow. He commenced farming for himself at the age of twenty-one, and has been very successful, now owning 200 acres of land, with half of it under cultivation, and which is well improved and stocked, and devoted principally to the raising of cotton. Mr. Wall was married on November 26, 1882, to Miss Mary Etta Mathews, of St. Francis County, and a daughter of George J. and Lydia (May) Mathews, who now reside in Lee County. Mrs. Wall was born on July 4, 1863. They have had a family of three children, two of whom are still living: Fannie P. and Lydia J. The second child, Green, died in 1886. Mr. Wall is a leading Democrat in Texas Township, and is recognized throughout this part of the county as a hard-working, industrious man.

William A. Walton. William H. Walton, a native of North Carolina, was born in 1808. He was married in 1836 to Mary A. Wynn, also of North Carolina origin, and by her became the father of nine children: William A. (the subject of this sketch), Susan H. (widow of John H. Moore, residing in Oak Forest, Lee County), Lucy M. (wife of J. Carr), T. (a farmer and residing in Texas), John R., Annie (deceased wife of R. R. Badders), Nancy Z. (Mrs. John B. Grove, deceased), Nicholas J. and Catherine. Mr. Walton died in Lee County, Ark., in 1876, his wife passing away in Phillips County in 1863. William A. Walton was reared in North Carolina until reaching the age of fifteen, at which time he came with his parents to Arkansas. He received as good an education as could be obtained in the common schools and academies about his home, and when twenty-six years old he began life on his own responsibility, choosing farming as his occupation. He now owns one of the best and most picturesque farms in the western part of Lee County, consisting of 200 acres of land, with 115 under cultivation and well adapted to the growing of corn and cotton, which are the principal crops. He raises grasses and clover to some extent, and is quite extensively engaged in the development of stock. He has a steam gin and grist-mill valued at $1,500, and the general impression formed of the many improvements about the farm is that thrift and industry are characteristics predominating with the owner. He enlisted in May, 1861, in Company F, Capt. D. C. Govan's Second Arkansas Infantry Volunteer Cavalry, participating in the battles of Mumfordsville, Shiloh, Perryville, Stone River and Murfreesboro. He received a wound from a minie ball at the battle of Shiloh, and was also wounded at Murfreesboro by grape-shot, this entering his shoulder, which disabled him permanently. He was captured while in the hospital at Murfreesboro and taken to Louisville and then to Camp Butler, afterward being exchanged at City Point, Miss., where he remained until the close of the war. After the close of hostilities Mr. Walton resumed his agricultural pursuits, and a fair degree of success has attended his efforts, and prosperity now rules supreme. He was married in Phillips County, November 2, 1868, to Miss Nancy C. Boykin, a native of North Carolina, born February 12, 1852, and a daughter of Edwin and Jane Boykin. Nine children have blessed their union: Florence B., Charles, Mary E., John R., Edwin, and Frank D., Kismick, Carl and Paul, dead. Mr. Walton is a member of the Methodist Church, and served as justice of the peace of Texas Township for two years. He has also been a member of the school district, and is a man that takes great interest in all enterprises to which he lends his able support and influence.

John C. Ward, merchant and farmer, Haynes, Ark. This prominent business man and successful agriculturist is a native of Lee County, Ark., his birth occurring on October 2, 1866, and is the first child born to the union of Lafayette and Fannie (Adams) Ward, the father a native of Kentucky and the mother of Georgia. Lafayette Ward is one of the oldest physicians of this county now living, coming here in 1857 and settling in Phillips County (now Lee County) where his practice extended over a vast territory. He accumulated quite a nice fortune, and this he is at present enjoying. He was a soldier in the Mexican War and was also in the late war, being army surgeon of his regiment for a year or so. He entered service in the Mexican War at the age of fifteen years, was under Gen. Taylor in the First Kentucky Infantry and served during the entire time. He has been twice married; first, in 1851 to Miss Roxana Robards, of Louisville, Ky., and by her became the father of three children, all deceased. The wife died in 1862 or 1863, and in 1864 Dr. Ward married Miss Adams, who bore him three children, all deceased except John C. Ward. The mother was a member of the Cumberland Presbyterian Church and died in 1872. Dr. Ward is a member of the Catholic Church and of Irish parentage. John C. Ward was educated in the free schools of Lee County, and at the age of thirteen years entered the Catholic School on Washington Street, where he remained for one term. He then entered Miss Hattie Eunice's select school on Poplar Street, remained there but one term and then, in 1882, he attended school at Newton for some time. After this he entered the Lexington Commercial School, graduating from the same in 1886, and then returned home, where he began working for R. O. Gill. He continued with him for one year and in 1888 bought an interest in the business, and in 1889 succeeded him. Mr. Ward has been unusually successful in all his enterprises and does an annual business of $25,000. He and his father own about 4,500 acres of land with 550 acres under cultivation, on which are produced about 350 bales of cotton yearly. J. C. Ward selected for his companion in life Miss Ida Neolies, of Collierville, Tenn., and was united in marriage to her on November 4, 1889. Mr. Ward is a member of the Catholic Church, is a member of the K. of H., and is one of the leading young business men of Haynes. He contributes liberally to all worthy enterprises and is one of the promising young men of the county.

J. M. Weatherly, farmer, Marianna, Ark. The subject of this sketch needs no introduction

39

to the people of Lee County, for a long residence here and above all a career of usefulness and prominence, have given him a wide spread acquaintance. He was originally from Maury County, Tenn., where he was born in 1838, and is the son of David and Sallie J. (Taylor) Weatherly, the father a native of North Carolina and the mother of Tennessee. David Weatherly came with his parents to Tennessee when an infant, and settled with them in Maury County. After growing up he followed the occupation of farming in Tennessee until 1852, when he came to Phillips County (now Lee County) and settled close to where La Grange now is. He came here in the employ of Gen. Pillow and continued in his employ until 1857, when he purchased a farm and commenced tilling the soil, remaining thus engaged until his death, which occurred in 1889, at Haynes, where he had been living for some time. He was over seventy-nine years of age at the time of his death. Mrs. Weatherly died in 1862. Mr. Weatherly was a member of the Methodist Episcopal Church, and was a member of the Masonic fraternity. After the death of his wife Mr. Weatherly married, in 1868, Mrs. Sellers, who departed this life in 1872. Mr. Weatherly was then married to Mrs. Turner and became the father of two children, both deceased. His last wife survives him and resides in Haynes. J. M. Weatherly's school days were spent in Maury County, Tenn., and he came to this State with his father in 1852, remaining with him until his twenty-first year. In 1857 he returned to Tennessee and attended school at Columbia for two years. He afterward returned to Arkansas, taught school and commenced the study of law at Helena, Ark., under Adams & Hanks, eminent attorneys of Helena at that period. About this time the war broke out and his legal expectations were doomed for the time being. He joined the Confederate army in 1861, was one of the men who formed the company known as Hindman's legion, but was afterward attached to the Second Arkansas. He was a member of Company F, and served on the east side of the Mississippi River until after the evacuation of Corinth, when he was discharged on account of ill health. While on that side of the river he was not engaged in any battles and after returning to Helena, Ark., he could not remain there but enlisted in Company F, of Dobbins' regiment, of which he was appointed sergeant. From that he was promoted to lieutenant, and surrendered the company as first lieutenant at Wittsburg in 1865. He was in Gen. Price's raid through Missouri. After the war Mr. Weatherly returned home and engaged in school teaching, which occupation he continued for a short time. In 1869 he embarked in the mercantile business at Spring Creek, but only remained there until 1877, when he sold out and went to Palestine, St. Francis County, where he carried on farming and merchandising. He remained there until about 1880, when he moved his mill and gin machinery to Marianna, known as Ringville, where he has since been occupied in ginning, farming, and has also followed merchandising until the last year, when he sold out. He owns 160 acres of land with eighty acres under cultivation, and his average ginning yearly yields about 600 bales. Mr. Weatherly has been twice married; first, to Miss Mattie Harvey in 1873, and the fruits of this union were two children: Edgar and John H. Mrs. Weatherly died in the winter of 1877. She was a much respected and esteemed member of the Baptist Church. In 1884 Mr. Weatherly married Miss Bettie Moye, who bore him two children: Emma R. and Bettie. Mrs. Weatherly died in March, 1888, at Hot Springs, whither Mr. Weatherly had gone for the benefit of his health, her health having always been unusually good. She lived but three weeks after arriving there. Mr. Weatherly is one of the public-spirited men of this section, and favors all public improvements.

Lee Webster, one of the most extensive merchants and farmers of Lee County, is a native of Mississippi, and a son of James and Jane (Bankhead) Webster, who came primarily from Tennessee and North Carolina, respectively. Mr. Webster was a mechanic by occupation, and was reared in Mississippi, to which State his father had removed when he was a small boy. He was a man of some education, and was highly thought of by all who knew him. He died near Mount Pleasant,

Miss., at the age of sixty-five. He was a son of Walter Webster, a native of Tennessee, also a farmer by occupation, who, at the time of his death, at the age of ninety, was possessed of considerable property. Mrs. Webster was born in 1820 and died in 1871. She was the daughter of Thomas Bankhead, of Ireland originally, who came over to this country when seventeen years of age, and engaged in farming in South Carolina, where he died at the age of eighty years. The subject of this sketch was born in Marshall County, Miss., in 1849. He started in life as deputy sheriff of his native county, in 1868, which office he filled for several years. Then removing to De Soto County, he was occupied in trading on the Mississippi River until 1879, at which time he came to Lee County, and embarked in the mercantile business, and also in farming, both of which he still carries on. He is now the owner of four half sections of land, and has 800 acres under cultivation, devoted to the raising of cotton, of which he produces from 1,000 to 1,200 bales per annum. He opened up his store of general merchandise in 1879, with a capital of $1,400. The stock now averages over $6,000, and his annual sales have aggregated $35,000, though a more correct estimate would be $50,000 for the past year. He also owns and operates a steam grist-mill and cotton-gin, of fifteen bales capacity per day. Mr. Webster was married, in 1871, to Miss Alice Gruffe, who was born in Kentucky, in 1855. They had one son which died in infancy, and they have since taken several orphan children to rear, for whom he has made provisions in his will as though they were his own. The subject of this sketch being quite a young boy at the breaking out of the war never enlisted, but took part in several skirmishes near his home. He is a stanch Democrat in politics, and takes an active part in political work of his county. He has been a member of the board of supervisors for some time.

W. P. Weld, editor of the Marianna Index, was born in Cape Girardeau County, Mo., April 8, 1862. At the death of his mother, in September, 1875, the family was broken up, and after a two years' stay with relatives in Ohio, he came to this county and located. In 1882 he went to Indiana and attended the Valparaiso Normal School, from which he graduated in 1883. He then returned here and was employed as book-keeper until 1886, when he was appointed deputy sheriff, in charge of the office and collecting department, which position he held until he purchased the Index, started by John Thomas in 1874. It is a Democratic paper and the only newspaper published in this county. Mr. Weld was married in Batesville, Ark., to Miss Annie Granade, a native of this State, and only daughter of Rev. H. M. and Mrs. Anna Granade. They are the parents of one child, Jean Powell. Mr. Weld was a son of Ludovicus Weld, who was born in Vermont in January, 1802, and who came to Missouri late in the 50's, and who was a brother of Theodore D. Weld, the noted Abolitionist. He came to Arkansas, in 1879, to live with his children, and died in Woodruff County, in 1885, at the age of eighty-three years. His wife, the mother of our subject, was Miss Jane Porter, who was born in Ohio, in 1826, and was the mother of three children. Mr. Weld is a member of the Presbyterian Church, and belongs to the Royal Arcanum, Knights of Honor, Knights and Ladies of Honor and the I. O. G. T.

Jesse A. Wilkes, ex-assessor of Lee County, Ark., was born in Yalobusha County, Miss., in 1837, and in 1855 came to Arkansas, and located in Spring Creek Township, soon after entering the Arkansas Christian College, at Fayetteville, which institution he was attending at the breaking out of the late war. He immediately joined the Confederate army, and after participating in the battle of Oak Hill his company was disbanded and joined the Army of Tennessee, he being a member of Company I, Ballentine's regiment, and was at the battle of Atlanta. He was chosen as one of Capt. Harvey's scouts, and served in that capacity for about eighteen months. The close of the war found him at Atlanta, and from there he returned to Arkansas, making the journey on horseback, having gone there on horseback. He and his brother then formed a partnership, and for two years were engaged in the cotton traffic at Memphis, Tenn., and in Arkansas, but upon the death of his brother Mr. Wilkes returned to Arkansas to settle up their business here, but found things in such a bad condition that it took him some time to adjust matters satisfactorily. Since that time he has followed various callings, and acted in various business capacities, but is now giving his attention to farming, being the owner of some excellent land in Spring Creek Township, and in other places in the county. In 1885 he was elected county assessor, and held the position two years. In 1882 he married Mrs. Mary E. Pascal, who is a member of the Christian Church. Eight Wilkes brothers came from England to the United States at a very early day and settled in Virginia, and now have descendants in Tennessee, Mississippi, Arkansas, Texas and Missouri. The father of our subject was a farmer, and both he and wife died when Jesse A. was a child. The latter had one brother and one sister, both dead.

James A. Williams, M. D., who enjoys the largest practice of any physician in Haynes, was reared on a farm in St. Clair County, Ala., where he received a common-school education, later passing his time on a farm in Lee County, Miss. At the age of nineteen he was appointed deputy sheriff of Lee County, which position he held one year. He then entered the agricultural schools of Pontotoc, Miss., where he remained eighteen months, and was subsequently employed by Clifton & Hoyle, druggists, of Tupelo, one year. During this time he studied medicine, and after leaving the drug store attended a course of lectures at Vanderbilt University, at Nashville. In 1881 he came to St. Francis County and practiced with Dr. Zuber two years, then returning to the Medical College at Nashville, from which he graduated in 1883. Following this, Dr. Williams returned to St. Francis County, and in 1888 came to Haynes, where he has since been actively and successfully engaged in the practice of his profession. He was born in St. Clair County, Ala., February 12, 1857, and is a son of R. M. and Cordelia (Dill) Williams, also natives of that State. R. M. Williams enlisted in the Confederate army in 1861, in the Tenth Alabama Infantry, in which he held the position of first lieutenant, afterward being transferred to the cavalry service and serving as captain of his company. His wife died previous to his enlistment. Our subject was married in September, 1882, to Miss Julia Thompson, a daughter of James Thompson, treasurer of St. Francis County. They are the parents of three children: James Roger, Vivian and Alemeth. In politics the Doctor is a Democrat, and he is a member of the Baptist Church and of the Knights of Honor. He also belongs to the Lee and St. Francis Counties Medical Association. He is well known throughout this locality, notwithstanding the fact that he is comparatively a newcomer.

Rev. Nathaniel L. Willson is a native of North Carolina, and a son of John G. and Sophia (Norfleet) Willson, who also came from that State. J. G. Willson was born in Franklin County in 1782, and was married in September, 1818, his death occurring in Marshall County, Miss., in 1874, aged ninety-two years. His father was a native of North Carolina, and died at the age of fifty-eight, and his grandfather, of Ireland, came to this country in the early part of the eighteenth century, and took part in the Revolutionary War. The father of Mrs. Willson was of Scotland birth, a soldier in the Revolutionary War, being seventy-six years of age at the time of his decease. She was fifty-eight years old when called away from earth. Nathaniel L. Willson, the only one living of a family of eight children, was born in Person County, March 12, 182 , and remained there until fifteen years of age, at which time he removed to Marshall County, Miss., with his parents. He was engaged in managing his father's farm, and was employed in surveying a greater part of his time, after which he learned the tanner's and saddlery trade, following these occupations during the war and until his stock was destroyed by the Federal army. Since that period he has devoted his attention to agricultural pursuits, in connection with his ministerial duties. He was ordained as a minister of the Missionary Baptist Church in 1861, of which he has been a member since 1840. Removing to Arkansas in 1886, Mr. Willson purchased his present farm of 160 acres,

situated within a short distance of Moro, Lee County, of which he has sixty acres under cultivation, devoted principally to the raising of horses and cattle. He was married in De Soto County, Miss., in 1857, to Miss Nannie E. Jones, a native of South Carolina, and daughter of William and Rachel Jones. She died April 10, 1884, leaving eight children, five sons and three daughters, six of whom are still living: Priscilla M. (wife of James H. Carmichael, a farmer of De Soto County), Lafayette A. (a farmer of this county), Ethelbert W. (also engaged in farming in this county), Nannie E. (widow of A. J. Biggerstaff, of this county), John Bunyan and Berea B. Mr. Willson married his second and present wife, Mrs. Sarah E. Robbins (nee Elmore), a native of Mississippi, and a daughter of Levi and Elizabeth (Bullin) Elmore, October 11, 1887. She is also a member of the Missionary Baptist Church, which she joined when thirteen years old. Mr. Willson was initiated into the Masonic order in 1855, and has taken the Royal Arch degree. Mrs. Willson married Lee A. Robbins, in July, 1861, a native of Tennessee, who died in Lee County, Ark., in December, 1883, leaving three children, two living: Thomas L. and Shem R. Robbins. Their grandfather, Thomas Robbins, was a native of South Carolina.

John R. Wood, planter, Marianna. This prominent agriculturist of Lee County, Ark., owes his nativity to Hardeman County, Tenn., where his birth occurred November 7, 1835, and is the son of Dr. George Wood, who was born in Albemarle County, Va. Dr. Wood received his education in the University of Virginia, and graduated from the Jefferson Medical College of Philadelphia. He then went to Hardeman County, Tenn., practiced in Hickory Valley for eight or ten years, and there married the mother of our subject, Eliza Harkens, who bore him six children. On account of failing health, he gave up his practice and engaged in cultivating the soil, continuing at this for ten years, when his health had so improved that he moved to Searcy, Hardeman County, and resumed the practice of medicine. He there gave his children all good common school educations. In 1853 he and his brother bought a plantation in this county, and he abandoned his practice and moved to Arkansas in 1869. He sold the place on which Marianna now stands to his brother, and in January, 1870, when he came out he bought another farm, then in St. Francis (now Lee) County. Here he died in 1872, at the age of seventy-one years. He remained at his home in Tennessee during the war, but was a Union man. John R. Wood attended school in Bolivar and Jackson, Tenn., finishing his education in West Tennessee College, at Jackson. He wished to become a civil engineer, and after working two years at this his father had him give up the profession. In 1859 he engaged in merchandising with J. A. Jarrett, father of J. R. Jarrett, of Marianna, and continued at this business until the breaking out of the war. He then enlisted in the Confederate Army of Tennessee, was commissioned captain, but not liking the position resigned. He returned home, and there joined Gen. Forrest's regiment as a private, participating in the battles of Shiloh and Corinth, and fell back with the army to Tupelo, Miss. There his health failed him, and

he hired a substitute. He then went to Columbus, Miss., and entered the commissary department, as an agent to buy corn and beef, etc. He remained six months, when, his health still continuing bad, he went home and remained on his father's plantation, in Hardeman County, for twelve months. He then went to Memphis, and clerked in a wholesale grocery and cotton house, until the close of the war, when he returned to Hardeman County. He farmed during 1867, 1868 and 1869, and in 1870 moved to Lee County, Ark., with his father, remaining with him until after the latter's death, since which time he has carried on the farm. He was married in 1860 to Miss Paulina Guy, a native of Hardeman County, Tenn., and the fruits of this union have been five children: George, Lucy (wife of Mr. Millett), Paulina, Fannie and Mary W. After the death of his first wife Mr. Wood married, in Arkansas, Miss Mary Pugh, a native of Greene County, who bore him five children, two now living, Samuel and Thomas; those deceased were named John R., Eliza and Jane.

CHAPTER XXII.

———>+<•———

ARKANSAS COUNTY—BOUNDARY AND AREA—VALUATION—TOPOGRAPHICAL PRESENTATION—SPRINGS AND
MOUNDS—EARLY SETTLEMENT—NAMES OF PIONEERS—POPULATION—DURING WAR TIMES—BENCH
AND BAR—PROMINENT CASES—INTERESTING HISTORICAL RECORDS—TERRITORIAL OFFI-
CERS—CITIES, TOWNS, ETC.—CHURCH ORGANIZATIONS—TRANSPORTATION FACIL-
ITIES—COUNTY PAPERS—MUNICIPAL TOWNSHIPS AND POSTOFFICES—
RESOURCES—SCHOOLS—BIOGRAPHICAL MEMOIRS.

—•❖※❖•—

O, those blessed times of old, with their chivalry and state!
I love to read their chronicles, which such brave deeds relate;
I love to sing their ancient rhymes, to hear their legends told,
But, heaven be thanked—I live not in those blessed times of old.—*Brown.*

HE early boundaries of Arkansas County were defined as follows: "All that portion of the territory bounded north by the south line of the county of New Madrid, east by the main channel of the Mississippi River, south by the 33d° of north latitude, or the northern boundary line of the State of Louisiana, westwardly by the western boundary line of the Osage purchase, and by a line to commence upon the River Arkansas, where the boundary line of the Osage purchase intersects the same, thence in a direct line to the main source of the Wachita, thence south to the northern boundary line of the State of Louisiana, or 33d° of north latitude, shall compose a county, and be called and known by the name of the county of Arkansas." This bill, creating this county, was passed December 31, 1813.

The county at one time covered the whole State, but new counties being formed from time to time, it has been reduced to its present boundaries, which are as follows:

On the north by Lonoke and Prairie Counties, on the east by Monroe, Phillips and Desha Counties, White River being the dividing line, on the south by Desha and Jefferson Counties, the Arkansas River, the dividing line between Desha and Arkansas Counties, and Bayou Meto River, between Jefferson and Arkansas Counties, for about one-half the distance, and there Jefferson County is the boundary, Bayou Meto being wholly inside Arkansas County.

The county has an area of about 900 square miles, or 596,000 square acres, and of this amount 507,974 is subject to taxation, 30,440 acres being school land, and 57,587 acres being United States and State lands. The school, United States and State land is all exempt. The taxable land in the county is assessed at $1,178,850, an average rate of $2.32 an acre, and when it is taken into consideration, that $171,550 is town lots, it makes the valuation still lower. Also $131,210 to the Texas & St. Louis Railroad.

The town property is divided as follows: Stuttgart, $105,450; De Witt, $34,820; St. Charles, $15,970; Goldman, $11,880; Crockett's Bluff, $2,-410; Arkansas Post, $1,020. Total, $171,550.

The personal property is divided as follows: 4,350 horses, valued at $176,300; 24,467 cattle, valued at $183,790; 1,270 mules and asses, valued at $73,329; 2,029 sheep, valued at $3,070; 18,976 hogs, valued at $27,144; 51,092 all kinds of domestic animals valued at $463,633; all other kinds of personal property valued at $498,450, making a total of all personal property valued at $962,113. Total of all real property, $1,178,850—a grand total of $2,140,963 representing the taxable wealth of the county.

The surface is comparatively level, being one long rolling swell after another; just rolling enough to give good drainage, yet not so much so as to wash after it is put into cultivation. There is not a foot of land in the entire county that is not susceptible of cultivation. With an altitude at no place but little over 100 feet above high-water mark on the Arkansas, White and Mississippi Rivers, a gradual incline from the rivers, rises above the bottoms, so imperceptible as to be scarcely distinguishable. The line between the river bottoms and the upland is not strongly marked, as in most cases. A relief map would present a picture, wherein the timber and prairie would be the only distinctive feature. Right down the center runs Grand Prairie for forty miles, and is from ten to fifteen miles wide, crossed by numerous strips of timber, and having groves or islands of this dotted about here and there. The largest of these is Big Island, with an area of about 4,000 acres; the smallest, Young's Island, covering only about 160 acres. The one lying nearest the northern line of the county, and just east of Stuttgart, is called Lost Island; two miles south is Maple Island, and Big Island is one mile west of Maple; four miles south of Big Island is Mud Island, and five miles south of Mud Island is Angelico. Besides Grand Prairie there are several other smaller areas of grass land. In the eastern part of the county is White River Prairie, ten miles long and four miles wide. Lying just west of White River Prairie is La Grue, four miles long and one and a half wide; Halleys two miles long and one-half wide, near La Grue. These are all skirting along White River, and are but a few miles away from it. Sassafras Prairie setting in about five miles north of De Witt is two and one-half miles east and west, and two miles north and south. In the extreme southeastern corner of the county is Little Prairie, right between the Arkansas and White Rivers, being ten miles long and one and one-half miles wide; Cash Prairie, an arm of Grand Prairie, making off between Big and Little La Grue. La Grue Springs, ten miles southeast of De Witt, is quite a notable place, and its waters are said to be a sure remedy for malaria. Essies Springs has very cold water, and is favorably located, both for fishing and hunting, and is a resort of no little local celebrity, as in the summer and fall it is not unusual for fifty or seventy-five families to camp there at one time and remain for several weeks.

To the disciple of Izak Walton the streams of Arkansas County would have a wonderful fascination, as in their season fish of many varieties are easily caught.

Formerly wild game of all kinds abounded, and the earlier settlers depended as much or more on the rifle for supplies for the smoke-house as they did upon domestic animals. In fact, the numbers of wild animals, and the boldness they displayed in their depredations, made it no easy matter to raise pigs and lambs. Nor were the fur-bearing animals without numerous representatives, and this was no small source of income. Deer, bear, panther, wolves, wildcats, catamounts, beaver, otter, fox, 'coon, 'possum, mink, squirrels and rabbits were very numerous, and even now the bolder and more adventurous hunter can, by penetrating into the swamps, find game that will well repay him for his time and labor.

The feathered tribe had many representatives, turkey, prairie chicken, quail and the wood pigeon on the land, wild geese, brants, swan, crane and ducks and plover furnishing sport in the lagoons and bayous. Even now, in their season, the sportsman need not come home empty handed, who seeks the wild fowl in their haunts. Besides the game birds, there are crows, hawks, owls, black-birds, meadow-larks and, chiefest of all, the Southern mocking-bird. The game disappears as civilization encroaches on its haunts, but there are yet sequestered places where the slyest is to be found.

A group of well-known mounds is situated on the farm of Napoleon Menard, eight miles southeast of the village of Arkansas Post. The largest mound is 965 feet in circumference at the top and considerably larger at the base, and is some sixty feet in altitude, its slopes being covered with trees and bushes. This has been dug into quite extensively, and it has been thought useless to explore further. There is connected with this mound, by a ridge of earth, 300 feet long and twenty feet in diameter, a small circular mound, fifteen feet high and forty-five feet in diameter, in which are a number of houses, bearing evidence of having been occupied. Near the middle of the connecting ridge, a layer of burnt clay, 5,006 feet in diameter, was found. At one side a large quantity of fragments of earthen vessels were discovered, comprising a number of earthen bowls of various sizes, quite new looking, and of a type of ware quite distinct from that found in the fields and graves of same locality. Restorations of quite a number have been made, and the collection proves to be quite interesting. The collector argues from the position of the fragmentary vessels, that they had been placed by their owners upon the roofs of the houses, which had been destroyed by fire. Surrounding the Menard Mound is a field of twenty acres, which appears at one time to have been the site of a large number of dwellings, for at a depth of from one to two feet layers of burned clay are found. This field seems to have been one vast cemetery, the remains of skeletons being found in great numbers.

Pottery is found in abundance, and as a rule is found near the heads of the dead; but no ornaments nor instruments are to be found. The plowing of the fields has destroyed many earthen vessels, as the interments were near the surface. Noticeable is it that the pottery found with the remains is of a character quite distinct from that of the mound. It is of the class common in these regions.

In other portions of the county are mounds of various sizes and altitudes, some of them containing fragments of pottery, while in others are found bones, etc., but the Menard Mound, described above, is the most conspicuous one in regard to the race of men who erected them.

Among the early settlers was one A. B. K. Thetford, who also filled the office of sheriff of the county at one time. Thetford's ferry takes its name from him. At the time of his death he was living in Arkansas County, on the north side of Arkansas River, but this same house was, at an earlier date, on the south side of the river. The bed and current shifting left him on the north side. Some of his descendants are yet living in the adjoining counties.

The first civil government of Arkansas was located at Arkansas Post, as, in 1804, James B. Maney was appointed civil Governor, and resided there. He was followed by Stephen Warrel, and he by Robert W. Osborn, who administered the government till 1812; the Territory of Missouri being then established her authority extended over Arkansas. By an act of Congress approved in June, 1814, C. Jouette was appointed judge of Missouri Territory, his jurisdiction extending to the District of Arkansas. He resided at Arkansas Post and presided over a court held at that place.

The first settlers of Arkansas County were French, who settled near the Post of Arkansas. They were an enterprising and energetic people, mostly engaged in trade. Many of them accumulated fortunes, and their descendants now form an estimable class of society. The next in order were pioneer settlers from Kentucky and Tennessee, or their immediate descendants, a brave, self-reliant and independent people, many of them too fond of adventure and the chase to make permanent locations or valuable improvements.

They had penetrated the country beyond, and in advance of organized government, or, if within it, were too far from the officers of the law and the courts to be reached by legal process. Yet, resolutely determined to suppress crime and preserve good order, they had, by common consent, rules of government by which crime was summarily punished and contracts enforced. The payment of a debt was a matter of honor, and to their credit, be it said, the instances where contracts were violated were rare. No one felt absolved from his contract to pay, who had money or property, or could procure either.

Another phase of history and one worthy of note is, that all acts of crime and violence that were committed, and which were but too common among an uncultivated, bold and self-reliant people, were almost invariably open, defiant and under the influence of passion and resentment resulting from real or supposed wrongs. There is not a single instance of assassination, of robbery or of burglary, to be found on the Territorial records. The first settlers were miles apart, and generally along the streams, yet the prairies had a few located on their borders, and when necessity required, the cabin doors were temporarily closed by a latch or a pin, and the household goods were left for days and even weeks without molestation. In summer months, when at home, they slept with doors and windows (if they were fortunate enough to have any) wide open, in perfect security. A frank, honest and generous people, hospitable to a fault (a characteristic of their successors to-day), like the Scotch Highlanders they felt

"That guidance, and food, and rest and fire,
In vain the stranger must never require."

There were also among them gentlemen of the learned professions, merchants and traders, some of whom were educated and of refined manners, and all of them hospitable and social.

As found upon the records, dating back to 1804, these names appear: John W. Honey, Henry Cassidy, Rufus Easton, Benjamin Fooy, Joseph Stillwell, Harold Stillwell, Andrew Fagot, Perly Wallis, James B. Waterson, Daniel Mooney and Patrick Cassidy. Later, Richmond Peeler, who came to the State in 1810.

Two brothers, Benjamin S. and Rowland Haller, came from Kentucky. Benjamin was judge of the county probate courts, and up to middle life was an infidel, but when about fifty years old was

converted and began preaching. He was remarkable for his sound common sense. From the life he led he commanded the respect, esteem and confidence of the people, and at his death was mourned truly and deeply. Another character somewhat noted was Julian M. P. J. De Visart, Count De Boicarme, a Belgian, who came to Arkansas early in the 30's and settled within a few miles of where De Witt now is; here he died in 1852. His life was something of a mystery. Frederick Noteribe, who lived in and about Arkansas Post in the 40's, was the most prominent man in the county. He came to Arkansas somewhere from 1815 to 1818, and had been a soldier under Napoleon. He died in New Orleans of cholera in 1849. Prior to the advent of Noteribe came Charles Bogy, a native of Kaskaskia, Ill., who came with the Federal troops to take possession of Arkansas Post in the name of the United States in 1804. He was a man of Herculean proportions and wonderful physical endurance. The Michell brothers, from New Madrid, and Louis L. Refeld were well known in the early history of the county, and after its organization the latter was one of the representatives. John Laquer was another.

Terrence Farrelly, an Irishman, came from Pittsburg early in the 30's. He was in the sheriff's office, was probate and county judge, a member of the Territorial legislature, a member of the constitutional convention of 1836, a Whig in politics (thus rendered antagonistic to the Pope), Governor of Arkansas (appointed by Jackson), a man of commanding appearance, strongly marked Irish features, and having a rich brogue. He was for years the leader of his party in politics. A man of sterling integrity, he commanded the respect and confidence of the people to a marked degree.

The settlements here, as elsewhere in the earlier days, were made along the streams, and, as late as 1845, were miles apart. There was one at Point De Luce, another on Big La Grue, William Crockett at Crockett's Bluff, on White River; David Adams at Adams' Bluff; Severn Pepper at Preston Bluff, then called Pepper's Bluff; on Bayou Meto lived the Barkmans, Woods and Roberts; on Mill Bayou, Benjamin Wilson, Youngs,

Roby and Rodgers; in the southeastern part of the county were Walton, Ragan, Gordon, McCoy, Dunne, Barkers, Cobb and Evans, and of all these John R. Walton is the only one now living, who in 1845 had a family.

John A. Murrell's gang had more than one rendezvous in the county, but the Regulators, organized for self-protection, succeeded in ridding it of them.

From 1846 the country began to settle rapidly, especially between De Witt and White River. Perhaps this can best be shown by the census reports from 1810 to 1889: Population 1810, 1,062; 1820, 1,260; 1830, 1,426; 1840, 1,346; 1850, 3,245; 1860, 8,844; 1870, 8,268; 1880, 8,038; 1889, 11,640 (4,000 of whom are negroes).

In 1871 Arkansas County lost, perhaps, one-third of her population by two river townships being cut off to form a portion of Lincoln County.

The war put a stop to all material growth, and then came the dark days, when the people had nothing but the land and their hands to depend upon for a living. In 1867 the general destitution of the citizens, occasioned by poor crops, caused an expedient to be tried to procure food and provisions. There was issued by the county court, with the consent of the people, $5,000 in county script with which to buy food, and John C. Quertermous was selected to negotiate the issue. Failing in Louisville, Ky., he went to St. Louis, Mo., and there James H. Lucas took up the "promise to pay," and Mr. Quertermous came back with a sufficient amount to tide the folk over the hardest times Arkansas County ever experienced. But $2,000 of the $5,000 was all that was ever used. Needless is it to add that the debt was paid in full. This is the nearest approach to a bonded debt the county ever had. During the reconstruction period, from 1868 to 1874, the county financial affairs were in a very bad state. Taxes now are low. General and county tax is levied at the rate of 5 mills; State tax, 5 mills; general State purposes, 2 mills; sinking fund, 1 mill and for common schools, 2 mills. The school districts vote a special tax ranging from 2½ to 5 mills.

Subjoined is the financial statement of the county from October 1, 1888, to October 1, 1889: Amount of revenue, $13,085.65; total expenditures, $12,013.24; balance, $1,072.41. There is no county debt, and county scrip is at par.

At the breaking out of the war and before the State had seceded, many of her bravest and best citizens were not secessionists, but when the question of allegiance to the State and to the general Government was so placed that each man had to decide for one or the other, the State was paramount; and Arkansas County claims the divided honors of having raised the first company in the State. At any rate, Col. Robert H. Crockett, with 125 men, marched to Little Rock, and there made one company of the First Arkansas Regiment that went to Virginia under Gen. (then Col.) Fagan. Also Capt. David B. Quertermous organized a company that won honor and glory in the same regiment. Charles C. Goodden raised a company that was in the Trans-Mississippi Department. Capt. Samuel C. Smith raised another company that remained in Arkansas for awhile, but was afterward transferred across the river. Capt. Felix Robertson, later on, organized another company.

Loyal to their convictions, as one man they shouldered arms for the cause they advocated, and many of them died upon the field of battle, their blood eternal monuments to the bravery and valor of the men of Arkansas County. The first battle fought on the soil of the county was at St. Charles, on White River, on June 17, 1862. When that place was captured by the Federals, Col. Fitch in command of the Federals and Capt. Dunnington of the Confederates, there were but seventy-five Confederates in service and they were poorly armed; they had eight killed and wounded and ten were taken prisoners. The Federal loss was much greater. A cannon ball struck one the pipes of the steamer Mound City. The boiler exploded and out of 185 men on board, 180 were either killed or wounded.

In January, 1863, a force of 5,000 men were sent up White River as a counter-movement to attract attention from Arkansas Post, the point against which the main expedition was directed. They passed on up White River beyond St. Charles, leaving Capt. Williams there in command. On the return of the main command down the river, the officers and men of the gunboat were so infuriated at the fate of the crew of the ill-fated Mound City (claiming the Confederates killed many of them while in the water) that the town was fired and completely destroyed. It is but due to state that the land force did their best to stop the wanton destruction, but to no purpose.

The most important battle of the war in Arkansas was at Arkansas Post, which resulted in the surrender of that place, under distressing conditions to the Confederates, and after a resistance that reflected the greatest credit upon men and officers. The story is best told in the official report of Gen. Churchill, as follows:

Battle of Arkansas Post. Gen. Sherman commanding Federals; Gen. Thomas H. Churchill Confederates. Federal force estimated at 50,000, the Confederate at 7,000; 3,000 only effective men. Total killed, wounded and missing, of Federals, 1,846; Confederates, sixty killed, seventy-five or eighty wounded.

Copy of official report of Brig.-Gen. Thomas J. Churchill, Confederate States army, commanding lower Arkansas and White Rivers:

RICHMOND, Va., May 7, 1863.

GEN. S. COOPER, *Adjutant and Inspector General*, Richmond, Va.,

General: Not being in communication with Lieut.-Gen. Holmes, commanding the Trans-Mississippi Department, I herewith forward for your consideration my report of the actions of the 10th and 11th of January last, at Arkansas Post.

I have the honor to be, General, very respectfully your obedient servant, T. J. CHURCHILL.

Brig.-Gen. comd'g Lower Arkansas and White Rivers.

RICHMOND, Va., May 6, 1863.

General: On the morning of the 9th of January, I was informed by my pickets, stationed at the mouth of the cut-off that the enemy with his gunboats, followed by his fleet of seventy or eighty transports, were passing into the Arkansas River. It now became evident that their object was to attack the Arkansas Post. I immediately made every arrangement to meet him, and ordered out the whole force under my command, numbering about 3,000 effective men, to take position in some lower trenches, about one and one-quarter miles below the fort. The Second Brigade, under Col. Deshler, and the Third, under Col. Dunnington, occupied the works, while the First Brigade, under Col. Garland, was held in reserve.

Three companies of cavalry, under Capts. Denson, Nutt and Richardson, were sent in advance to watch the movements of the enemy. During the night the enemy effected a landing two miles below, on the north side of the river. The following day, about 9 o'clock, the gunboats commenced moving up the river and opened fire on our position. Having but one battery of field pieces, of six and twelve-pounders, I did not return their fire. It was here that I expected the co-operation of the guns of the fort, but owing to some defect in the powder, they were scarcely able to throw a shell below the trenches, much less the fort. About 2 o'clock, P. M., discovering that I was being flanked by a large body of cavalry and artillery, I thought it advisable to fall back under cover of the guns of the fort, to an inner line of intrenchments. The enemy advanced cautiously, and as they approached our lines were most signally repulsed. They made no further attempt that evening to charge our works, and I employed the balance of the time, till next morning, in strengthening my position and completing my intrenchments. Discovering that a body of the enemy had occupied some cabins in our old intrenchments, I ordered Col. R. I. Mills, with his regiment, to drive them from their position, which he did most successfully, capturing several prisoners. Just before dark Admiral Porter moved up with several of his ironclads to test the metal of our fort. Col. Dunnington, who commanded the fort, was ready in an instant to receive him. The fire opened, and the fight lasted nearly two hours, and finally the gunboats were compelled to fall back in a crippled condition. Our loss was slight; that of the enemy much heavier. During the night I received a telegraphic dispatch from you, ordering me "to hold out till help arrived or all dead," which order was communicated to the brigade commanders with instructions to see it carried out in spirit and letter. Next morning I made every disposition of my forces to meet the enemy in the desperate conflict which was soon to follow.

Col. Deshler with his brigade, with the regiment of Col. Dawson attached, commanded by Lieut.-Col. Hutchinson, occupied the extreme left; Col. Garland with his brigade with his right resting on the fort, while Col. Dunnington commanded the river defenses. It was near 12 o'clock before the enemy got fully into position, when he commenced moving upon my lines simultaneously by land and water. Four ironclads opened upon the fort, which responded in gallant style. After a continuous fire of three hours they succeeded in silencing every gun except one small six-pounder Parrott gun, which was on the land side. Two boats passed up and opened a cross-fire upon the fort and our lines. Still we maintained the struggle. Their attack by land was less successful. On the right they were repulsed twice in attempting to storm our works, and on the left were driven back with great slaughter in no less than eight different charges. To defend this entire line of rifle-pits, I had but one battery of small field pieces, under command of Capt. Hart, to whom great credit is due for the successful manner in which they were handled, contending as they did with some fifty pieces in his front. The fort had now been silenced about an hour, most of the field pieces had been disabled, still the fire raged furiously along the entire line, and that gallant band of Texans and Arkansans having nothing now to rely on save their muskets and bayonets, still disdained to yield to the overpowering foe of 50,000 men, who were pressing upon them from almost every direction. Just at this moment, to my great surprise, several white flags were displayed in the Twenty-fourth Regiment, Texas Dismounted Cavalry, First Brigade, and before they could be suppressed the enemy took advantage of them, crowded upon my lines, and not being prevented by the brigade commander from crossing, as was his duty, I was forced to the humiliating necessity of surrendering the balance of my command.

My great hope was to keep them in check until night, and then if reinforcements did not reach me, cut my way out. No stigma should rest upon the troops. It was no fault of theirs. They fought with a desperation and courage yet unsurpassed in this war, and I hope and trust that the traitor will yet be discovered, brought to justice, and suffer the full penalty of the law. My thanks are due to Cols. Anderson and Gillispie for the prompt measures taken to prevent the raising of the white flag in their regiments. In the Second Brigade, commanded by the gallant Deshler, it was never displayed. I had ordered Col. E. E. Portlock, commanding at St. Charles, to hasten to my relief with what troops he could spare. Capt. Alf Johnston reached the post on Saturday night, and took part in the action on the 11th. Col. Portlock made at the head of 190 men of his regiment of infantry, the unprecedented march of forty miles in twenty-four hours—and succeeded in entering our lines amidst a heavy fire from the enemy on his flanks. He was just on the eve of bringing his men into action when the surrender took place. In no battle of the war has the disparity of forces been so unequal. The enemies force was full 50,000, while ours did not exceed 3,000, and yet for two days did we signally repulse and hold in check that immense body of the enemy. My loss will not exceed sixty killed and seventy-five or eighty wounded. The loss of the enemy was from 1,500 to 2,000 killed and wounded. To the members of my staff, Maj. J. K. P. Campbell, chief commissary; Dr. C. H. Smith, chief surgeon; Capt. B. S. Johnston, adjutant-general; Capt. B. F. Blackburn, inspector-general; Capt. J. J. Gaines, chief of artillery; Capt. J. M. Rose, ordnance officer; Capt. R. H. Fitzhugh, engineer corps; Capt. A. J. Little, signal corps; Lieut. A. H. Sevier, aide-de-camp; Capts. Farr and Smith, volunteer aides, and Mr. J. E. McGuire, my thanks are due for many valuable services rendered me upon the battlefield. As for individual acts of gallantry I will make more full mention hereafter. I herewith inclose for your consideration the reports of Cols. Garland and Deshler; that of Col. Dunnington I have as yet been unable to obtain. I have the honor to be, General, very respectfully,

Your Obedient Servant,
T. J. CHURCHILL.
Brig-Gen. comd'g Lower Arkansas and White Rivers.

As there is a diversity of opinion concerning Gen. Churchill's conduct on the occasion of the surrender, it is important to state that Col. Deshler's report corroborates Gen. Churchill's. The correspondence here given shows the result of an investigation conducted by Lieut.-Gen. Holmes:

May 9, 1863.
Respectfully submitted to the President:
The strange circumstances causing the capture of Arkansas Post demand investigation. I recommend a court of inquiry, and that meanwhile, Cols. Garland and Wilkes, and, I incline to think, Gen. Churchill likewise, should be relieved from their present commands over the men surrendered.   J. A. SEDDON, *Secretary of War.*

Returned to secretary of war for consideration in connection with further information which he may have received.   J. DAVIS.

July 13, 1863.
File, to await such further information.
J. A. SEDDON, *Secretary of War.*

[Indorsement on copy forwarded through department headquarters.]

HEADQUARTERS ARKANSAS DEPARTMENT.
LITTLE ROCK, June 8, 1863.
It is impossible to imagine better conduct on the part of officers and men, and it is a matter of rejoicing with me that my hasty order was rendered nugatory before the brave Churchill was reduced to the ultima ratio, cutting his way through such immense odds. It never occurred to me when the order was issued that such an overpowering command would be devoted to an end so trivial.

Respectfully forwarded to the adjutant and inspector-general.   THOS. H. HOLMES, *Lieutenant-General.*

Col. Wilkes was the officer who first showed a white flag. The Federals land forces co-operated with about fifteen gunboats, besides about eighty transports; the gunboats were the De Kalb, Cincinnati, Louisville, Monarch, Clyde, Ratler, Lexington and Blackhawk.

The courts convene as follows: County court, first Monday in January, April, July and October of each year; probate court, third Monday in January, April, July and October; common pleas, fourth Monday in January, April, July and October; circuit court, second Monday in September and March.

The county is in the Eleventh judicial district and the Second congressional. John M. Elliott, of Pine Bluff, is the circuit judge.

In De Witt are five practicing attorneys, Hon. W. H. HalliBurton, James A. Gibson, E. L. Johnston, Robert P. Holt and John F. Park; at Stuttgart, Crockett & Wilcox, Morse & Hall and R. E. Puryear.

The first case tried in an Arkansas court of which any record was kept, is one known as The United States *vs.* Thomas Dickinson, January, 1820—indictment for rape determined before Andrew Scott, judge of the superior court held in Arkansas County. This was an indictment for rape committed on the person of Sally Hall, to which the defendant pleaded not guilty. There was a trial by jury, composed of Richmond Peeler, Charles Roberts, Manuel Roderigen, John Jordolas, Jacques Gocio, Stephen Vasseau, Nathas Vasseau, Michael Petterson, John Pertua, Manuel Pertua, Pierre Mitchell and Attica Nodall, who, after hearing the evidence and argument of counsel, retired to form their verdict, and returned the following: "We, the jury, find the defendant guilty of rape, in manner and form as charged in the indictment alleged." The counsel in defense moved an arrest of judgment for the following reasons:

1. It does not appear by the indictment that the same was found by the grand jurors of the United States. 2. No place is mentioned in the indictment where the offense was committed, nor is it mentioned in what year it was committed. 3. The assault and rape are not positively and directly charged in the indictment. 4. It is not stated to have been committed with force and arms. 5. It is not stated to have been feloniously committed. 6. It is not alleged in the indictment that Sally Hall was in the peace of God and the United States, when the offense is alleged to have been committed.

Four other reasons were given, but the court overruled the motion, and said that some of the reasons urged in arrest of judgment were not sustained by the record; that others were not

proper grounds in arrest of judgment, and that some had not been presented at the proper time, nor in the proper manner, if good at all.

The prisoner being asked if he had any reason why sentence should not be pronounced against him on the verdict of the jury, said, that he objected to any sentence because he was advised that the indictment did not properly charge any commission of felony. The court disregarded his objection, and sentenced him to suffer the penalty of the law in such cases made and provided, on February 15, 1820, between 10 o'clock A. M. and 3 o'clock P. M. of that day. A motion was made for a writ of error, *coram nobis*, but the motion was overruled. Joshua Norvell, prosecuting attorney for the United States; Jasin Chamberlain, Henry Cassidy, Alexander S. Walker and Perly Wallis for the prisoner. The sentence was not executed, the prisoner having been pardoned by James Miller, Governor of Arkansas Territory.

John Honey was commissioned judge of probate court, also judge of the several courts, and treasurer of the District of Arkansas in 1808. Benjamin Fooy was commissioned a justice of the peace, October 13, 1808; August 21, 1808, he was commissioned a judge of the courts of common pleas and quarter sessions. Joseph Stillwell on the same day was commissioned a judge of the court of common pleas and quarter sessions. August 23, 1808, Harold Stillwell was commissioned sheriff for the district of Arkansas. August 20, 1808, Francis Vaugine was commissioned presiding judge of the court of common pleas and quarter sessions. August 23, 1808, Andrew Fagot was commissioned a justice of the peace, notary public and coronor. December 17, 1808, Perly Wallis was commissioned deputy attorney general for the District of Arkansas, by John Scott, attorney general of the District of Arkansas. November 11, 1809, James B. Waterman was commissioned recorder of the District of Arkansas by Frederick Bates, acting governor of the Territory of Louisiana, also clerk of the common pleas and quarter sessions. Waterman was also commissioned judge of probate and to administer the oaths of office. September 27, 1810, Benjamin Howard commissioned Patrick Cassidy recorder, judge of probate, clerk of court of common pleas and to administer the oath of office. November 13, 1809, John St. Clair was commissioned justice of the peace, by Fred. Bates. July 23, 1811, by Benjamin Howard, Gov. Samuel Treat appointed justice of the peace. July 23, 1811, Samuel Moseby, Henry Cassidy and James Scull were appointed judges of the courts of common pleas and quarter sessions; and the same day James Scull was appointed captain of the Arkansas Battalion. July 25, Curtis Milbourn was appointed coroner, by Benjamin Howard.

January 4, 1814, William Clark, Governor of the Territory of Missouri, appointed Francois De Vaugine and Samuel Moseby judges of the courts of common pleas and quarter sessions, and January 5, 1814, Joseph Stillwell received a like appointment. January 4, 1814, Daniel Mooney was appointed sheriff by the same man. July 15, 1814, John Dodge was acting as clerk and *ex-officio* recorder.

The following are copies of several important historical records taken from the old Territorial books:

TERRITORY OF LOUISIANA, } ss.
DISTRICT OF ARKANSAS,

In the judge of probate's office, Monday, the twelfth day of December, in the year of our Lord one thousand eight hundred and eight.

It being the day appointed by my notice, set up in my office in pursuance of the provisions of a law passed by the legislature of this Territory, entitled an act directing the probate of wills and the descent of intestates, real estates and the distribution of their personal estates, and for other purposes therein mentioned,

I, John W. Honey, judge of probate for the District of Arkansas, attending in my office in the town of Arkansas, in pursuance of the above-mentioned notice for the purpose of attending to all such business which might be brought before me as judge of probate aforesaid. No business appearing to-day, I adjourn until to-morrow morning, 10 o'clock.   JOHN W. HONEY.

Tuesday, December 13, 1808.

Having adjourned to this day with an expectation of business, but no business appearing, I adjourn *sine die.*
JOHN W. HONEY, J. P., D. A.

TERRITORY OF LOUISIANA, } ss.
DISTRICT OF ARKANSAS.

The sixth day of June, in the year of our Lord one thousand eight hundred and eleven.

I, Andre Fagot, Esquire, a justice of the peace for the District of Arkansas, do hereby certify, that there personally appeared before me Elisha Welborn and Anne Fraser, who were by me lawfully joined together in the holy bonds of matrimony, agreeable to the provisions of the laws of this Territory in such cases made and provided.

In testimony whereof I have hereunto set my hand and seal on the date above written.   ANDRE FAGOT.

JOHN WEBSTER,
DAN FRASER,
SIMEON JENNINGS,   } Test.
JACOB STANLEY.

Received the above certificate on the 6th, and recorded on the 16th of June, 1811.   P. CASSIDY, *Clk.*

On the same day, by the same man, were married Louis Bogy and Frances, widow of James B. Waterman. June 19 Andre Fagot married Martin Huckington and Elizabeth Trimble. June 19, same man, David Huckington and Sarah Farril. July 1, 1811, William Findley and Polly Gray, married by Francois Vaugine. July 12, 1811, Nathaniel Bassett and Trisshena Speak married. July 14, 1811, William Dunn and E. Hampton; also John Ashey and Massey Keene. September 8, 1811, John Hendry and Lovina Armstead married.

Then dating from April 13, 1812, to March 3, 1814, twelve more couples.

Peter Lefever was the first man to take advantage of the law concerning insolvent debtors, and to place his property in the hands of the sheriff, to be sold for the benefit of his creditors, on March 1, 1810.

Commission, John Honey, recorder No. 1, Merriwether Lewis, Governor and commander-in-chief of the Territory of Louisiana, to all who shall see these presents greeting: Know ye that reposing special trust and confidence in the integrity, abilities and diligence of John Honey, Esquire, I do appoint him recorder of the District of Arkansas and empower him to discharge the duties of said office according to law; to have and to hold the said office with all the powers, privileges and emoluments to the same of right appertaining during the pleasure of the Governor of the Territory for the time being.

In testimony whereof, I have caused the seal of the Territory to be hereunto affixed. Given under my hand at St. Louis, the twenty-third (23) day of August in the year of our Lord one thousand eight hundred and eight and of the Independence of the United States, the thirty-third.

(Signed.)   MERRIWETHER LEWIS,
                   Governor of Louisiana.
[SEAL.]
(Signed.)   FREDERICK BATES,
                   Secretary of the State of Louisiana.

On the back of said commission is the following certificate:

TERRITORY OF LOUISIANA, ss.

Personally appeared before me the subscriber duly commissioned to administer oaths of office, either District or Territorial, John Honey, who took the oath to support the Constitution of the United States, also an oath to faithfully discharge all duties required of him as recorder of the District of Arkansas. Given under my hand, this 9th day of October, in the year of our Lord one thousand eight hundred and eight.

(Signed)   BERN PRATTE.

Received the above commission for record the 9th day of October, one thousand eight hundred and eight, and recorded the same November 22, A. D., one thousand eight hundred and eight. In the thirty-third year of the Independence of the United States.

JOHN W. HONEY, *Recorder.*

Other commissions are all the same style and wording.

This indenture, made this fifth day of June, in the year of our Lord one thousand eight hundred and four, between Catharine Pertuis, widow of Anthony Pinau, of the Post of Arkansaw, of the one part, and Maj. Thomas Napier, of the State of Georgia, of the other part, witnesseth, that the said Catharine Pertuis, for and in consideration of the just and full sum of $110, good and lawful money, to her in hand paid, at or before the sealing and delivery of these presents, the receipt whereof is hereby acknowledged, hath granted, bargained and sold, and by these presents doth grant, bargain and sell unto the said Maj. Thomas Napier, a certain tract or parcel of land, situate, lying and being a little above the mouth of the River St. Francis, adjoining lands of Sylvanus Phillips and Joseph Stillwell, containing 640 acres, to the only proper use, benefit and behoof of the said Maj. Thomas Napier, his heirs and assigns forever, and the said Catharine Pertuis, doth hereby warrant and forever defend the above-described tract of land against all persons claiming the same or any part thereof.

In witness whereof the said Catharine Pertuis hath hereunto set her hand and seal the day and year above written.

In presence of   CATHARINEX PERTUIS, [SEAL.]
WILLIAM CHISOLM,   VD. ANTONIE PINAU,
ANDRE FAGOT.   Marque.
A true copy.   Acknowledged before me on
JAMES B. MANY.   the 5th June, 1804.
                 JAMES B. MANY.

In the Constitutional Convention of 1836, Arkansas County was represented by Bushrod W. Lee, and Arkansas and Jefferson Counties by T. Farrelly. The one of 1861, by James L. Totten; of 1868, by John McClure and J. H. Hutchinson; of 1874, by J. A. Gibson.

The first Territorial legislature, composed of the Governor and supreme judges, was held at the Post of Arkansas from July 28 to August 3, 1819. Speaker, Charles Jonitte; clerk, George W. Scott; Robert Crittenden, acting Governor; Charles Jonitte, Robert Letcher and Andrew Scott, judges of supreme court. A special Territorial legislature was held at Arkansas Post February 7 to February 24, 1820. This session was convened by the Territorial Governor under the law which passed the Congress of the United States March 2, 1819, forming Arkansas Territory, which is properly the first real Territorial Assembly of Arkansas. A special session of the General Assembly of Arkansas was held at the Post of Arkansas October 2 to October 25, 1820. Arkansas County was represented by Sylvanus Phillips in the council, and W. B. R. Horner and W. O. Allen in the lower house. The session from October 1 to October 24, 1821, Neil McLane, council; October 6 to October 31, 1823, council, Andrew Latting; representative, Terrance Farrelly; October 3 to November 3, 1825, council, B. Harrington; representative, William Montgomery. Fifth legislature: Terrance Farrelly, in council; representative, W. Montgomery. Sixth Territorial legislature: Council, Terrance Farrelly; representative, William Montgomery. Seventh: Council, Terrance Farrelly; representative, Harold Stillwell. Eighth: Council, Terrance Farrelly; representative, Harold Stillwell. Ninth: The journals of this legislature are not to be found. First State legislature: Senate, S. C. Roane; representatives, James Maxwell and James Smith. Second: Senate, J. Smith; representatives, S. V. R. Ryan, J. Maxwell. Third: Senate, J. Smith; representative, B. L. Haller. Fourth: Senate, J. Yell; representative, Richmond Peeler. Fifth: Senate, J. Yell; representative, Harris Cross. Sixth: Senate, R. C. Byrd; representative, Harris Cross. Seventh: Senate, R. C. Byrd; representative, Lewis Redfeld. Eighth: Senate, N. B. Burrow; representative, A. H. Ferguson. Ninth: Senate, N. B. Burrow; representative, A. H. Ferguson. Tenth: A. H. Ferguson, Senate; representative, Samuel Mitchell. Eleventh: Senate, A. H. Ferguson; representative, Samuel Mitchell. Twelfth: Senate, Thomas Fletcher; representative, Samuel Mitchell. Thirteenth: Thomas Fletcher, president of Senate; representative, John T. Gibson. Fourteenth: Senate, Thomas Fletcher, who became acting Governor; representative, S. R. Richardson. Fifteenth: Senate, J. C. Mills; representative, G. C. Cressen. Special Confederate legislature: Senate, Thomas Fletcher, president of Senate; representative not given. Sixteenth: Senate, W. M. Galloway; representative, E. G. Abbott. Seventeenth: Senate, A. Hemmingway; representatives, W. S. McCoullough and T. M. Gibson. Eighteenth: Senate, A. Hemmingway; representatives, Arkansas and Prairie Counties, by E. R. Wiley, George H. Joslyn, B. C. Morgan, A. O. Epsy. Nineteenth: Senate, P. C. Dooley; representatives, Arkansas, Prairie and Lincoln, by M. M. Erwin, J. E. Preston, J. P. Eagle, D. J. Hinds. Twentieth: Senate, William Black; representative, R. C. Chaney. Twenty-first: Senate, A. H. Ferguson; representative, Robert C. Chaney. Twenty-second: Senate, A. H. Ferguson; representative, C. B. Brinkley. Twenty-third: Senate, Lecil Bobo; representative, R. C. Chaney. Twenty-fourth: Senate, Lecil Bobo; representative, A. D. Mathews. Twenty-fifth: Senate, Robert H. Crockett; representative, W. H. HalliBurton. Twenty-sixth: Senate, Thirteenth District, R. H. Crockett; representative, W. H. HalliBurton.

The following were the officers of Arkansas County from 1819 to 1890:

From 1819 to 1821, Eli I. Lewis, clerk; Henry Scull, sheriff; O. H. Thomas, coroner. From 1821 to 1823, Eli I. Lewis, clerk; Henry Scull, sheriff; T. Farrelly, coroner. From 1823 to 1825, Eli I. Lewis, clerk; James Hamilton, sheriff; Lewis Bogy, coroner. From 1825 to 1827, Eli I. Lewis, clerk; A. B. K. Thetford, sheriff; Lewis Bogy, coroner. From 1827 to 1829, Eli I. Lewis, clerk; A. B. K. Thetford, sheriff. From 1829 to 1830, A. B. K. Thetford, sheriff; Robert Fultony, coroner. From 1830 to 1832, T. Farrelly,* judge; Hewes Scull,

* There was no county judge up to this time. The office was filled by a board of three commissioners.

clerk; A. B. K. Thetford, sheriff. William Rainey, coroner; James Maxwell, surveyor. From 1832 to 1833, Hewes Scull, clerk; A. B. K. Thetford, sheriff; William Rainey, coroner; James Maxwell, surveyor. From 1833 to 1835, James H. Lucas, judge; John Maxwell, clerk; A. B. K. Thetford, sheriff; W. B. Summers, coroner; James Maxwell, surveyor. From 1835 to 1836, Benjamin L. Haller, judge; John Maxwell, clerk; William Price, sheriff; W. B. Summers, coroner; James Maxwell, surveyor. From 1836 to 1838, Benjamin L. Haller, judge; D. G. W. Leavitt, clerk; Henry McKenzie, sheriff; John Taylor, treasurer; W. B. Summers, coroner; Lewis Dixon, surveyor. From 1838 to 1840, Benjamin L. Haller, judge; George W. Stokes, clerk; John W. Pullen, sheriff; John Taylor, treasurer; Hugh C. Henton, coroner; John M. Shultz, surveyor. From 1840 to 1842, David Maxwell, judge; George W. Stokes, clerk; John L. Jones, sheriff; John Taylor, treasurer; R. D. Armstrong, coroner; John M. Shultz, surveyor. From 1842 to 1844, Benjamin L. Haller, judge; G. W. S. Cross, clerk; John L. Jones, sheriff; John Taylor, treasurer; John C. Walton, coroner; John M. Shultz, surveyor. From 1844 to 1846, John M. Shultz, judge; G. W. S. Cross, clerk; John L. Jones, sheriff; Lewis Redfield, treasurer; John M. Shultz, surveyor. From 1846 to 1848, T. HalliBurton, judge; G. W. S. Cross, clerk; John L. Jones, sheriff; Lewis Redfield, treasurer; Charles C. Young, coroner; Thomas HalliBurton, surveyor. From 1848 to 1850, John T. Hamilton, judge; G. W. S. Cross, clerk; John L. Jones, sheriff; B. L. Haller, treasurer. Lot L. Haines, coroner; Adam McCool, surveyor. From 1850 to 1852, John T. Hamilton, judge; W. H. HalliBurton, clerk; John L. Jones, sheriff; B. L. Haller, treasurer; John Larkey, coroner; Thomas HalliBurton, surveyor. From 1852 to 1854, T. T. Morrison, judge; William Redfield, clerk; J. T. Hamilton, sheriff; B. L. Haller, treasurer; Edward Syncoe, coroner; Adam McCool, surveyor. From 1854 to 1856, T. T. Morrison, judge; Zera S. Altom, clerk; P. S. Cross, sheriff; B. L. Haller, treasurer; J. E. McGraws, coroner; James Kirkpatrick, surveyor. From 1856 to 1858, T. T.

Felix D. Dale M.D.

AUGUSTA,
WOODRUFF COUNTY, ARKANSAS.

Morrison, judge; J. G. Quertermous, clerk; G. W. S. Cross, sheriff; John W. Lowe, treasurer; Jeremiah Haines, coroner; Melton D. Norton, surveyor. From 1858 to 1860, T. T. Morrison, judge; John P. Taylor, clerk; Joseph H. Maxwell, sheriff; John W. Lowe, treasurer; H. McGaughey, coroner; J. T. Clark, surveyor. From 1860 to 1862, Felix G. Allen, judge; Joseph H. Maxwell, clerk; H. K. Stephens, sheriff; John W. Lowe, treasurer; John P. Taylor, coroner; James S. Cowan, surveyor. From 1862 to 1864, A. H. Almond, judge; Joseph H. Maxwell, clerk; D. S. Morris, sheriff; H. G. Ramsour, treasurer; J. D. Strother, coroner; A. H. Stillwell, surveyor; A. J. Almond, assessor. From 1864 to 1866, R. K. Gamble, judge; Joseph H. Maxwell, clerk; R. C. Martin, sheriff; P. G. Tyler, treasurer; M. Kennedy, coroner; W. Quartermouse, surveyor; Ward Davis, assessor. From 1866 to 1868, A. H. Almond, judge; W. F. Gibson, clerk; R. C. Martin, sheriff; P. G. Tyler, treasurer; J. W. McKenen, coroner; A. G. Withers, surveyor; J. M. Price, assessor. From 1868 to 1870, B. C. Hubbard, judge; E. R. Wiley, clerk; Joseph H. Maxwell, sheriff; Michael Holt, treasurer; I. F. Chesher, coroner; William R. Lear, surveyor; J. P. Hubbard, assessor. From 1870 to 1872, Alex C. Wiley, clerk; Joseph H. Maxwell, sheriff; Michael Holt, treasurer; E. P. G. Tackett, surveyor; J. W. Johnson, assessor. From 1872 to 1874, E. P. G. Tackett, clerk; E. R. Wiley, sheriff; Samuel McCarthy, treasurer; L. S. Fields, coroner; J. Webster, surveyor; J. W. Johnson, assessor. From 1874 to 1876, Richard Gamble, judge; B. F. Quertermous, clerk; William Stillwell, sheriff; A. B. Crawford, treasurer; Dixon Adams, coroner; E. J. Connelly, surveyor; Jesse Bass, assessor. Form 1876 to 1878, R. K. Gamble, judge; B. F. Quertermous, clerk; William Stillwell, sheriff; A. B. Crawford, treasurer; John F. Brice, coroner; E. J. Connelly, surveyor; Charles L. Jansen, assessor. From 1878 to 1880, A. S. Hinson, judge; A. D. Matthews, clerk; B. N. Word, sheriff; Charles A. Johnson, treasurer; James Henderson, coroner; E. P. G. Tackett, surveyor; Charles L. Jansen, assessor. From 1880 to 1882, James H. Merritt, judge; J. J. McEvoy,

clerk; B. N. Word, sheriff; Robert Scanland, treasurer; James Wolf, coroner; C. F. Moore, surveyor; Charles L. Jansen, assessor. From 1882 to 1884, James H. Merritt, judge; J. J. McEvoy, clerk; L. C. Smith, sheriff; Robert Scanland, treasurer; J. H. Freeman, coroner; C. F. Moore, surveyor; John H. Bell, assessor. From 1884 to 1886, James H. Merritt, judge; Ben N. Word, clerk; L. C. Smith, sheriff; Robert Scanland, treasurer; L. J. Haywood, coroner; C. F. Moore, surveyor; C. L. Jansen, assessor. From 1886 to 1888, James H. Merritt, judge; Ben N. Word, clerk; L. C. Smith, sheriff; J. P. Poynter, treasurer; W. R. Hagler, surveyor; J. G. Johnson, assessor. From 1888 to 1890, James H. Merritt, judge; A. D. Matthews, clerk; Phin M. Black, sheriff; J. P. Poynter, treasurer; J. B. Rosevelt, surveyor; J. G. Johnson, assessor.

In 1881, in riding over the prairie, the observer would have little thought that, during the past year (1889) there could have arisen such a city as now graces Grand Prairie—Stuttgart. At that time neither signs nor indications of a town were in sight, the postoffice being located a mile north of the town site. But late in the fall of that year a corps of surveyors passed over this territory, driving stakes. In May of 1882, they came back and located the road; the postoffice had been removed to the house of I. N. Harper, who had planned to build a town on his farm. His scheme took practical shape, however, and early in 1882 the town was platted and named. Its growth for a few years was slow; at the end of the first year one small store building comprised the city. The pioneer merchant and owner of this store was a Mr. Bortfield. The growth up to 1866 was steady, the population at that time being about 300 people. In three years it has grown till now it will number 1,200 souls, and is the metropolis of Grand Prairie, lying at the junction of the Kansas City & New Orleans and the Grand Prairie Railroads, both now in rapid progress of construction.

The citizens of the town are from Iowa, Missouri, Illinois and Michigan; also many native Southern folk. There are not a dozen negro families to be found in the city limits, a certain tract

40

being set apart for their occupancy in the outskirts. Five churches hold regular service: the Methodist, Christian, Baptist, Mennonites and German Lutheran; two more buildings are now being erected. A good graded public school, with a principal and three assistants, trains the rising generation; and in the south part of the town is a spacious college building which was opened October 1, 1889, and under the able management of Prof. Jones is rapidly gaining an enviable reputation, and the patronage it receives speaks of great success. A bank has recently been opened under the management of T. H. Leslie. Two other large brick blocks are rapidly nearing completion, and the town is surely taking on an air of solidity. The brick and tile factory can scarcely supply the demand, although its capacity is nearly 2,000,000 brick yearly. A large saw-mill and three lumber-yards furnish all that is desirable in the way of building material to the town, and to the farmers who are rapidly settling upon the prairies adjoining. Every department of the mercantile business is represented by stocks ranging from $600 to $20,000. A Building & Loan Association has been organized. A Masonic Lodge, A. F. & A. M.; also the Odd Fellows; three hotels, livery stables, etc. The residences are new and tastefully arranged, being mostly cottages. The people are social and courteous, and intelligent. Last year over 375 carloads of hay were shipped from here, besides 2,500 bales of cotton and a few loads of fat cattle and hogs. Memphis, Cairo and Pine Bluff are the principal objective shipping points.

De Witt, the county seat, is the second town of importance in the county; is located near the center of the county. Charles W. Belnap, Leroy Montgomery and Dr. John M. Moreman were elected commissioners to locate the county seat. In 1853 W. H. HalliBurton, acting as their agent, bought the land. The following year the town was laid off, and in September, 1855, a log court house was finished and the records removed from Arkansas Post to the new town, which has been christened De Witt. A little incident in regard to the naming of this town is given: The commissioners being unable to agree on a name played a game of "seven up" to decide on whom the honor of selecting a name should fall. Leroy Montgomery won, and to him belongs the honor, as he gave the name for De Witt Clinton, of New York.

This was the first court house ever erected in the county; probate and county court were held in the new house in October of 1855.

The November term of circuit court was adjourned till the next regular term on account of insufficient accommodations and inclement weather. During the war several buildings were burned and the town was almost deserted. The present population is about 200. Its business is represented by three general merchandise stores, one grocery and one drug store. There are two church buildings belonging to the Methodists and Baptists.

The present court house was built in 1862, at a cost of $14,000; clerk's and sheriff's offices and jury rooms on the ground floor, with the court room above.

The public school building is a pleasantly located three-room building, in a modern style of architecture. Under the control of Prof. Crawford, it is one of the best schools in the State, has a high school department and many students outside of the regular district attend.

St. Charles, the main town and shipping point for the eastern part of the county, is pleasantly located on a bluff overlooking White River, and is the second town, from a commercial standpoint; it shipped 3,500 bales of cotton last year.

Arkansas Post is a little village standing on the north bank of the Arkansas River. The passing of a steamboat, now and then, breaks the monotony of the daily happenings, and the casual observer can see naught to remind him that at one time three-fourths of all the people in the Arkansas River Valley were living in and about that spot; that it has been the capital city of the Territory of Arkansas; that it was settled three years ere Philadelphia was founded; that for fifty years it was the county seat of Arkansas County; that the armies of the great Rebellion contended fiercely for its possession, and the boom of the cannon has echoed and reverberated about her. Yet such is the case; from a thriving capital to a prosperous town is not so great a step, but from a town to a tumbled down, deserted village only demonstrates the remorseless march of time. Arkansas Post is to-day but a small shipping point on the Arkansas River.

As this county has advanced with her sister counties in material welfare, so have the morals of her people been as well cared for by the different church organizations. The Methodists and Baptists are the strongest in number as well as the oldest, although the Christians and Presbyterians have many members.

Good church buildings dot the landscape all over the county, and in the towns and villages the spires mark the places of worship, as the deep-toned bells sound the hour.

There are between thirty-five and forty church buildings in the county, valued at about $20,000. Sunday-schools are held in many of them each Sabbath morning.

It is proof of the efficacy of the church teaching that here are to be found many of that truer, higher type of Christian people, with malice toward none and charity for all.

So strong is the love for law and good citizens, and for fear that the smallest possible incentive for crime might exist, the saloons were banished several years ago, and the scenes and incidents accompanying the rum traffic were also banished with the saloons.

White River on the east of the county, with a frontage of over forty miles on a direct line, affords excellent shipping opportunities for that part of the county. St. Charles, Crockett's Bluff, Mount Adams and Casco are all on this river, and from them most of the surplus is shipped, and supplies landed.

On the Arkansas River, Arkansas Post is the shipping point for the southern part of the county. Bayou Meto River is navigable in times of high water.

Of railroads, the St. Louis, Arkansas & Texas is, for about sixteen miles in the county, running northeast and southwest across the northwestern corner. The towns it touches are Stuttgart, Goldman and Payer, and at Stuttgart, the Kansas & New Orleans crosses the St. Louis, Arkansas &

Texas Railroad, and extends almost the entire length of the county. The Grand Prairie, connecting with the other two roads, now being constructed, extends from Stuttgart to Arkansas Post.

The public highways are kept up in good shape, and traverse the county in every direction.

Arkansas County boasts of the honor of publishing the first newspaper ever published in the State, for in 1819 the Arkansas Gazette made her first issue from Arkansas Post, and its publication was continued there till 1820, when it was taken to Little Rock. From that time until 1862, when the Chronicle came out, there was no paper published in the county; then the Elector in 1868, and in 1871 two papers at De Witt, the Sentinel and the De Witt Democrat.

In 1873 the Enterprise echoed the voice of the populace. Following that Col. Crockett published the Gleaner. About the same time the Arkansas County Democrat had a brief life. Then came the Arkansas Post, and in 1884 J. P. Poynter began to publish the De Witt Gazette, which enterprise he has made a success, and the paper is now recognized as the official organ of the Democratic party of the county. The Grand Prairie Journal, a newsy little paper, published by Clint. L. Price, at Stuttgart, is devoted to the interests of the town and the adjacent country.

There are twelve municipal townships in the county: LaGrue, Prairie, Keaton, Crockett, Point De Luce, Morris, Stanley, Mill Bayou, McFall, Bayou Meto, Chester and Arkansas.

The postoffices are located as follows: in LaGrue Township, De Witt (the county seat); Prairie Township, two, St. Charles and Ethel; Keaton Township, five, Bermuda, Mt. Adams, Cassco, Violet and Sassafras; Point De Luce, one, De Luce; Morris, two, Goldman and Hynum; Mill Bayou, Long Point, Prairieville and Olena; McFall, one, Stuttgart; Bayou Meto, two, Bayou Meto and Hagler; Chester, two, Tichnor and Booty; Arkansas, two, Stanley and Arkansas Post.

Of the whole surface of the county there is but very little waste land, and all is susceptible of cultivation, barring part of the two townships in the southeastern corner of the county, and they are as fine land, and would be just as valuable as any along the Arkansas River, were they not subject to overflow. About one-half the surface of the whole county is covered with a growth of fine, hard timber, consisting of white burr, black, red, pin, water, post, spanish and cow oaks; chincapin oak; white and black hickory; pecan, cypress, cottonwood, elm, sweet and black gum, soft maple, hackberry, sycamore, basswood, ash, some few beech and poplar and wild cherry. The value of these timber lands, as the railroads open up easy transportation, is hard to overestimate, and the lumber interests of the county are as yet practically undeveloped. Yet there are several large lumber plants located here, besides which several companies have been organized, and own large tracts of land.

The other half of the county is covered with prairie grass, that grows higher than the stock that feeds upon it. Now where does the raising of stock pay larger returns for the money invested than those on the prairies of Arkansas County? The winters are mild; the numerous glades and bayous furnish an abundance of water; a few weeks' work will put up hay enough to carry them over the winter months; stock is seldom fed over two or three months. Many of the best farmers are devoting their time solely to raising mules, horses, cattle and sheep. The lands along the Arkansas River, Bayou Meto and parts of White River is the cotton growing district, which produces from one to one and a-half bales per acre; corn from forty to sixty bushels; oats about the same; millet, clover and cultivated grasses make good crops. Out on the uplands and prairie not so much attention is given to cotton, yet even there it is a good crop, yielding from one-half to three-quarters of a bale per acre; corn on the prairie, from fifteen to forty bushels; oats make from forty to sixty bushels; millet, two to three tons per acre. All over the county apples, peaches, pears, plums, figs, quinces, strawberries, raspberries, gooseberries and grapes find their native home. Every, and all varieties of vegetable and garden stuffs grow to perfection, and melons are unsurpassed by any climate in the world.

Of the wild fruits and shrubs the red and black haw, hazel, elder, shumac, both black and white, wild plums of different varieties, blackberries, dewberries, strawberries, growing on the prairies; winter huckleberries, wild grapes of different kinds; the Muscadine, a large grape, growing singly, or in clusters of from three to four, having a thick skin, very palatable when cooked, and three varieties of summer grapes, somewhat smaller than the Concord, and then the winter grapes that ripen after the frost. The cutting and shipping of the prairie hay is one of the leading industries of the citizens adjacent to the railroads and the river shipping points. This is one of the few counties of the State in which the improving of the native stock has been attempted, by crossing upon thoroughbred sires. The results have been truly gratifying and are plainly seen in the improved grade of their stock.

Of the navigable streams, the Arkansas River is the largest, and flows along the southern boundary line, while along the whole eastern border is White River. Emptying into White River about eleven miles north of the southern boundary line is Big LaGrue, which has its source in Prairie County, and crosses the northern line of Arkansas County a little east of the center. Little La Grue, a tributary of the larger stream of the same name, rises about five miles northeast of Stuttgart, has a general southeast direction, flows thirty miles through the county.

Mill Bayou rises about twelve miles southeast of Stuttgart, having a general course of southeast and empties into Bayou Meto, twenty miles from its source.

The largest and most important stream that has its course within the county is Bayou Meto, which comes in from the west near the north line, where for about twenty miles it is wholly inside, and from that on is the line between this and Jefferson Counties. The streams are all bordered by a magnificent growth of hardwood timber.

The summary of the county examiner's report, 1888, for the schools of Arkansas County is as follows: White children, 2,703; colored, 1,456; total, 4,159. Enrollment, white, 717; colored, 281; total,

998. Number of districts, 45; number of districts reporting enrollment, 18; number of districts voting tax, 8; number of teachers employed, 45; number of school-houses, no report; value of school-houses, no report; number of institutes held, 1; number of teachers attending, 8.

The institute at DeWitt, only in point of numbers, however, was a failure. There were eight teachers and three directors present. The cause of such a small attendance appears to have been the usual one in such cases, indifference upon the part of the county examiner. Informâtion is that the county examiner of Arkansas County had failed to notify his directors as to the time and place of holding the institute, before my arrival there. The press of De Witt knew nothing of the matter, and, of course, did not notify the public in time.

Statement of number and salaries of teachers, year ending June 30, 1888. Number employed: males, 30; females, 15; total, 45. Average monthly salaries: Grade number 1, males, $45.00, females, $35.00; grade number 2, males, $30.00, females, $27.50; grade number 3, males, $25.00, females, $20.00.

Statement of revenue raised for the support of common schools, as shown by the report of the county treasurer, year ending June 30, 1888: Amount on hand July 1, 1887, $4,457.87; common school fund, $3,165.65; district tax, $7,198.-32; poll tax, $2,085.04; total, $16,606.88.

Revenues expended for support of common schools, and the balance on hand, year ending June 30, 1888: Teachers' salaries, $5,831.30; purchase of houses or sites, $340.60; buildings and repairing, $1,112.96; purchasing apparatus, $157.-85; total, $7,442.71; total amounts unexpended, $9,464.17.

Besides this, there is as much, if not more, money spent for subscription schools, for in many districts private schools are continued more months of the year than are the public schools. One private enterprise, a college, located in the southern part of Stuttgart, is under the direction and control of Prof. Jones, assisted by an able corps of teachers; the building is large and commodious, and was opened for the first time in October, 1889.

Jacob Alexander, book-keeper in the large dry-goods establishment of J. J. Woolfolk, of St. Charles, is a native of the Key Stone State, and a son of Jacob and Margaret (Moon) Alexander, both of whom came originally from the Emerald Isle to this country when young. They were married in Pennsylvania, and engaged in farming in Lancaster County until 1840, then removing to Ohio, which was their place of residence three years; later they went to Indiana. In 1857 Jacob Alexander came to Arkansas. In 1860, going to Independence, Missouri, he remained until the war broke out, when he joined the Federal army, being employed as scout throughout the war. He was born in 1837, and while in Indiana was apprenticed to a carpenter, and learned the trade. After the war he worked at his trade in Memphis, Tenn., until 1867, at that time coming to Arkansas and embarked in farming. In 1871 Mr. Alexander located at St. Charles, and was employed as clerk by the Farmers' Supply Company one year, afterward entering the employ of Mr. Woolfolk, where he is still engaged. He married Miss Mary Gunnell, a native of Mississippi. They are the parents of seven children, two of whom are living: Leona and Belle. Mrs. Alexander is a member of the Baptist Church. Mr. Alexander is a member of the Masonic order, and is the present Master of the lodge. He is a Republican in politics, and was nominated for sheriff in the last campaign. He has had a notary public's commission for seven or eight years, and is the owner of some property, besides which he has an interest in the store where he is employed.

Alwain M. Almond, one of the oldest settlers of Arkansas County, is a native of Tennessee, in which State he remained until twenty-eight years of age. He was married there to Martha Murphey, of Mississippi birth, and in 1857 came to Arkansas, locating in this county, where he rented land until the war. Mrs. Almond died in 1888, at the age of fifty-six years, having been the mother of eleven children, seven of whom survive: James, Sallie, William, Mollie, Mattie, Lou and Thomas. Mr. Almond's second wife was Mrs. Sallie Martin (nee Hewett), a daughter òf Caleb Hewett, who came to Arkansas in 1851. They are members of the Methodist Episcopal Church (as was also the first wife), in which he is one of the stewards. He has a fine farm, with 100 acres under cultivation. Mr. Almond was born in Franklin County, Tenn., in 1819, as a son of James and Jane (Martin) Almond, natives of North Carolina and Tennessee, respectively. James Almond moved to Tennessee when about seventeen years of age with his mother, his father having died when he was young, and engaged in farming in Franklin County. There he remained until 1845, when he removed his family to Mississippi, and six years later to Arkansas, settling on the same section of land which the principal of this sketch occupies, and where he died in January, 1857, at the age of sixty years. His wife died in 1887, when eighty-seven years old. They were members of the Methodist Episcopal Church, and were the parents of ten children, three of whom are living: John, Jonathan and Alwain M., our subject.

Jonathan N. Almond owes his nativity to Mississippi, where he passed his youth and early manhood up to the age of twenty-two years. Coming thence to Arkansas, he has since made this State his home, with the exception of two years spent in Texas, in 1863 and 1865. He bought his present place in 1853, but was not married until 1861, when he was united in the bonds of matrimony with Martha A. Burnett, a native of Arkansas, and daughter of Lemuel F. Burnett, of Pennsylvania origin. Mr. Almond was born in Franklin County, Miss., in 1831, the son of James and Jane (Martin) Almond, natives of North Carolina. They moved to Tennessee in their younger days, and in 1853 to Arkansas, locating in this county, where the father was engaged in his occupation as tanner until his death, in 1857, at the age of sixty years. His wife was born June 11, 1799, and died in December, 1887. They were members of the Methodist Episcopal Church, and were the parents of ten children. Six of the sons served in the Confederate army, and only two of them came out alive. Mr. and Mrs. Almond have a family of five children. He owns a fine farm of about 100 acres, under cultivation, on which he lives and also has

other land throughout the county, all made by hard work since coming to this county. He is a Democrat in politics and a member of the Methodist Episcopal Church, as is his wife.

P. M. Black, the well-known and faithful sheriff of Arkansas County, came originally from Peoria County, Ill., being a son of Thomas and Isabella (Brunson) Black. Thomas Black was born in Pennsylvania, and is a distant relative of John C. Black, of the United States Pension Office. He was a son of Michael Black, also of that State, and of German descent. Moving to Illinois when Thomas was a boy he located eighteen miles north of Peoria, where he owned a large farm and where he died at an old age. Thomas Black was the youngest of seven children, four still living. He remained in Illinois until 1864, when he went to Iowa and engaged in farming in Dallas County, then becoming occupied in the real estate business at Des Moines, Polk County, for five years. On May 15, 1874, he came to this county and still makes his home here. His wife died in 1881, at the age of fifty years, and had borne ten children, six of whom survive. Phineas M. Black was born January 7, 1855, was married in 1876 to Miss Carrie Stillwell, a native of this county, and a daughter of Asher and Carolina (Maxwell) Stillwell. Mr. Black started in business after his marriage with nothing but determination and a strong will-power to rely on, but has been prosperous in all of his undertakings. He was elected sheriff in 1888 and still holds the position, serving in an acceptable manner. He is also engaged in stock raising. Mr. and Mrs. Black are the parents of two children: Hattie O. and Lester A. Mr. Black is a member of the I. O. O. F. and is a stanch Democrat.

Rev. George Adam Buerkle and family, of Stuttgart, Ark., trace their ancestry back to the year 1372 to the Earl of Buerkle, whose coat-of-arms is still on exhibition. Rev. G. Adam Buerkle, was born in Plattenhardt, Germany, January 25, 1825, and her became married to Barbara Roth, who was born at the same place on May 23, 1823, and by her became the father of the following family: Carolina M. (born March 25, 1848, in Plattenhardt, married to Rev. S. Poppin), Maria

R. (born in Ann Arbor, Mich., July 14, 1853, and is the wife of Rev. F. Jelden), Eliza B. (also born in Ann Arbor, July 4, 1854, and is the wife of Rev. J. M. Johanssen), Christina (also was born in Ann Arbor, December, 20, 1856), Emanuel L. (born in Lansing, Mich., November 16, 1859), Adam F. (was born in Lansing, May 20, 1861), Carl W. and M. Luther (twins, born in Lansing February 14, 1863), Paul J. and M. Paulina (twins, born in Lansing March 17, 1865), Herman A. (born in Lansing March 31, 1867), and A. B. Clara (born in Woodville, Ohio, August 6, 1869). M. Paulina is the wife of Robert Harper. Rev. G. Adam Buerkle was educated at Esslingen, Wurtemberg, Germany, and was married during the year 1847, and in 1852 emigrated to the United States, and after spending one year in Lancaster County, Penn., he moved to Ann Arbor, Mich., and four years later to Lansing, where he made his home for ten years. He then spent twelve years at Woodville, near Toledo, Ohio, and on October 6, 1879, landed in Arkansas with his family. During 1876-77 he was president and visitor of the Evangelical Lutheran Synod of Ohio, and during 1878 he organized a colony and brought them to Grand Prairie, Ark., and caused a postoffice to be established, which was named after his former home in Germany—Stuttgart. He was postmaster at this point, with E. L. Buerkle as assistant. He has spared no pains nor expense to promote the advancement of the town and vicinity. When the St. Louis, Arkansas & Texas Railroad was being built the company seemed to have a prejudice against Stuttgart and would not stop their mail trains, but Mr. Buerkle promptly moved his postoffice to the railroad and erected a small house, which was the first house erected in the now town of Stuttgart. Owing to his age he turned the postoffice over to his assistant, who also became railroad and express agent at that place, and, notwithstanding the fact that his compensation was a mere pittance, he remained faithfully at his post and the afore-mentioned brothers now compose the well-known firm of Buerkle Bros., they being also the leading members of the Stuttgart German Brass Band; the band is more commonly known as Buerkle Brothers'

Brass Band. Rev. Buerkle, like the majority of Germans, is energetic and enterprising and in his calling has carried out these principles. He owns several thousand acres of land in Stuttgart and vicinity. He has been a minister of the Gospel for over thirty-four years and is still a worker for the Master, preaching every Sunday, and although his congregation is small, it is steadily growing.

Hon. Robert C. Chaney deserves prominent mention in the present volume as one of Arkansas County's representative citizens. His father, Rev. J. H. Chaney, was born in the State of Mississippi in 1805, in which locality he was reared and educated, there being married to Sarah B. Chambliss, on July 27, 1827. She was born on Christmas day, 1807, also in Mississippi, and was a daughter of Peter and Mary Chambliss. Shortly after his marriage Mr. Chaney moved to Louisiana, and in 1860 came to Arkansas, where he was engaged in his work of preaching the Gospel, being a local minister of the Methodist Episcopal Church. He was the principal organizer of the Hallas Chapel Church, in this county. He had been connected with the Methodist Church for forty years at the time of his death, in 1864. His wife who still survives him lives with the subject of this sketch, and is now in her eighty-second year. They were the parents of twelve children, seven of whom are living: Robert C., Sarah A., Mary F., William W., Emma K., Adaline B. and Mattie B. Robert C. Chaney was born in Louisiana on January 15, 1832. He was married in that State November 22, 1855, to Miss Caroline Dubose, of Louisiana birth, born on November 3, 1837, and who died in January, 1869, leaving nine children, four of whom survive: Holcomb D., Rosa F. (who married H. M. Dubose), Robert C., Jr., and Eugene R. On August 17, 1872, Mr. Chaney was married a second time to Miss Corene Hinman, also originally from the Creole State. She was called away from earth on October 7, 1889, leaving seven children, all living: Lee M., Ethel C., Ernest L., Beulah I., Rife P., Lucile B. and Horace P. Mr. Chaney owns 2,000 acres of land, of which 200 acres are under cultivation. He is also engaged in the mercantile business at Stanley, and though starting with about a $2,000 stock, he has by honest dealings and good management built up a large trade, enjoying a patronage of $15,000 per year. He is a prominent man in the politics of Arkansas County, and represented his county in the State legislature three terms, from 1874 to 1882. Besides this he has held the office of associate county judge, and has been postmaster of Stanley for the past six years. He is a member of the Masonic order, and belongs to the Methodist Episcopal Church, of which both of his wives were members.

Frank B. Childers is the son of John P. Childers, a native of Virginia, who was taken to Kentucky by his parents when but a young boy, where he was reared and educated, there being married to Catharine Amant, also of that State. She died in 1832, leaving twelve children, and five of them are still living: Pryor W., Thomas H., Philip G., Harmond and Frank B., the principal of this sketch. Mr. Childer's second wife, Eliza Asbury, was also a Virginian by birth. Their only child died in infancy. They were members of the Christian Church, and Mr. Childers was one of the leading men in the organization of the first church at Morgan, Ky. He did not take a very prominent part in politics, but was elected coroner, which position he held for several years. Frank B. Childers, the principal of this sketch, was born in the State of Kentucky, April 1, 1831, and came to Arkansas in December, 1865. His earthly possessions on entering consisted of the clothes which he wore and a shotgun. He now owns 360 acres of land, forty acres being under cultivation, with good buildings and stock. He was married November 9, 1871, to Miss Josephine Maxwell, of this State, who died September 25, 1879, having been the mother of one child, which died in infancy. Mr. Childers was next married to Lillie Halley, originally from Kentucky. She passed away November 10, 1885, having borne one daughter, Josephine W. On January 15, 1888, Mr. Childers was married to Mattie Rains, born in Gentry County, Mo., March 13, 1859. He did not take part in the late war, but was captured by the Federals while at home, in 1862, and carried to Ohio, where he was held until December of that year.

George W. Conine, who is actively and successfully engaged in merchandising, carries a stock of goods invoicing about $3,000 in his store at Arkansas Post. He was the second son of a family of seven children born to Richard and Jane (Bean) Conine, natives of Georgia and Louisiana, respectively. The father was born about 1808, of Irish descent. Going to Louisiana when a young man, he was there married, about 1838, and made his home the rest of his life, and at his death, in 1850, was one of the well-to-do planters of that State. Owing to unjust management of the estate, his widow and children were thrown upon their daily labor for sustenance. His wife died in 1858. She was a daughter of Rev. Christopher Bean, an Englishman by birth, who passed away in Louisiana, in 1852. George W. Conine was born in Carroll Parish, La., in 1844. He began making his own way in the world at the early age of seven years, being employed by Mr. Evin George (a wealthy farmer of that vicinity) to drive a team for his gin; afterward by James McNeal in the same community. At the age of fourteen he was employed as mail-carrier from Monroe to Lake Providence, La. In 1862 he joined the Carroll Dragoons of Louisiana Cavalry and was afterward transferred to Forrest's cavalry. He participated in the battles of Franklin, Vicksburg, the siege of Atlanta, Holly Springs and a number of hard-fought battles. He was at home on furlough at the time of the surrender. He then engaged in farming in Louisiana until 1867, when he came to Arkansas, locating at Arkansas Post. He was married in 1872 to Miss Caroline Rogers, a native of this county and a daughter of one of the early settlers. She died in 1879, leaving two children: Willie D. and Johnie W. Conine. Mr. Conine was then married to Miss Ruby Conine, a cousin of our subject, her father, Rev. Brittain Conine, being a brother of Richard Conine. She was born in the State of Alabama at Camp Hill where her mother, Jane Herren, died about 1854 and where her father, Rev. Brittain Conine, now resides and is a merchant of that place of forty or fifty years' standing, now being in his eightieth year. Ruby Conine is the mother of two children: Oscar and Hattie. Hattie died August

25, 1889, aged three years, one month and thirteen days. Sleep thou in Jesus, little Hattie, till He bids thee arise. Mr. Conine continued farming until 1881, when he engaged in the mercantile business with his sister, Mrs. Mary A. Fogee, and since her death, in 1887, has continued the business himself, the firm being known as G. W. and B. B. Conine. He also owns about 1,000 acres of land in different tracts in this county, of which about 200 acres are under cultivation. He is a strong Democrat and a highly respected citizen. His wife is a member of the Methodist Episcopal Church.

David O. Crump, an influential farmer and stock raiser of Crockett Township, is a native of Tennessee, and a son of Leaton and Martha E. (Oats) Crump, natives of Tennessee and Alabama, respectively. The father was born in Williamson County, Tenn., in 1821, and removed to Alabama when a young man. Soon after his marriage he settled in Memphis, where his wife died in 1855. (She was born near Huntsville about 1826). The following year he came to Arkansas, and located almost in the woods, near Crockett's Bluff, where he improved a good farm, and where he still resides, living with his second wife. He was one of the early settlers of this county, and has been prominent as a citizen, having held the office of justice of the peace most of the time during his location here. He served about two years in the Confederate army during the war, in Capt. William M. Mayo's company, and was in Price's raid through Missouri as quartermaster. He was captured at home, and was imprisoned at St. Charles just at the close of the war. He has been a member of the A. F. & A. M. for several years, and was connected with the County Grange. David O. Crump, the only child living of his parent's family, was born near Memphis, Tenn., in 1853, and was reared and educated in this county from the age of three years. He was married on January 6, 1880, to Miss Mary L. Gamble, daughter of Richard and Mary M. (Herring) Gamble, originally from Pennsylvania and Georgia, respectively. They were married in Mississippi in 1861, subsequently removing to Arkansas County, Ark., where the

father died in 1886, and his wife in Mississippi (while on a visit) in 1870. Mr. Gamble was a prominent merchant for many years, also serving as county and probate judge of this county some time. He was, besides justice of the peace, at the time of his death, shipping and receiving agent at Crockett's Bluff. Mrs. Crump was born in Aberdeen, Miss. Since the war period Mr. Crump has lived on a part of the old homestead, now having a farm of 420 acres, with about 225 acres under cultivation, mostly the result of his own efforts. Good improvements in the way of buildings, etc., adorn the place. He is a prominent Democrat, having voted for Tilden in 1876. He is engaged quite extensively at this time in stock raising, and at present has sixty head of cattle, sixteen horses and mules, and fifty head of hogs. He and wife are members of the Methodist Episcopal Church. Leaton Crump's father died when the son was a boy; the grandfather of David O., Samuel Oates, died in Memphis, though a resident of Alabama at that time.

G. W. Davidson is a native of Alabama, and is a son of Milus and Sophrina (Carpenter) Davidson, who were of Tennessee and Mississippi birth, respectively. Milus Davidson went to Alabama when a boy, and remained there until 1851–52, when he came to this county, here remaining until his death in 1872, at the age of fifty-two years. When the war broke out he joined the Confederate army, and served in Price's raid through Missouri, being captured by the Federals, though soon after he made his escape. Mrs. Davidson died in 1885 at the age of fifty years. Of their family of children two are still living: Melissa (now the widow of J. B. Butler, deceased), and G. W. The latter, the eldest child, was born in Lawrence County, Ala., in 1845, and was reared in this county, having come here with his parents when about six or seven years old. He commenced farming for himself at the age of twenty-one, and in 1871 bought his present farm, erecting in 1886 the mill and gin which he still owns and operates. Mr. Davidson is a Republican in politics, and a member of the County Wheel, and was nominated by the Republicans and Wheelers as sheriff of the county.

His wife was formerly Sallie E. Butler, a native of Mississippi. They are the parents of four children: William M., Anna C., George W. and Guy. Mr. and Mrs. Davidson are members of the Methodist Episcopal Church, South. Mr. Davidson was postmaster of St. Charles from 1872 to 1875. He is one of the leading farmers and millers in the community, and a highly respected citizen.

William F. Ferguson is the son of Hon. Austin H. Ferguson, a native of Virginia, who moved, when a young man, to Morgan County, Ala., there being married to Miss Catharine Walker. A few years later he went to Marshall County, Miss., where his wife died in 1840. In 1849, coming to Arkansas, he located in this county, and the following year was elected representative to the State legislature from Arkansas, Jefferson and Desha Counties, serving with such distinction that he was re-elected in 1851 and 1856. Subsequently he was chosen State senator from his district, composed of the counties of Arkansas and Monroe, which position he held for four years. His death occurred in 1884, at the age of seventy-two years. He was a member of the A. F. & A. M., and a strong Democrat in politics. William Ferguson, Sr., his father, who was of Irish descent, died in Texas, at the age of eighty-two, when the principal of this sketch was a small boy. William F. Ferguson first saw the light of day in Lawrence County, Ala., in 1836, and is the only child living of his parents' family. In 1862 he joined the Confederate army, becoming a member of what was first known as Clay's company, and after the reorganization, as Wheat's battalion, but was afterward transferred to Gen. Fagan's escort, and served as courier until the close of the war. Mr. Ferguson was married, in 1860, to Miss Hally, a daughter of Crede P. and Mary Hally, who was born in Fayette County, Tenn. After the war he engaged in farming, has since followed it, and now owns 940 acres of land, with about 200 acres under cultivation. Mr. Ferguson is an outspoken Democrat, and belongs to the Masonic fraternity.

Capt. Leroy Ferrell, retired steamboatman and stock raiser, is a native of Tennessee, and a son of David C. and Celia (Boren) Ferrell, natives of North Carolina and Tennessee, respectively. Mr. Ferrell went to Tennessee when a young man, where he was married and made his home until 1825, then removing to Gallatin County, Ill. In 1836 he came to Arkansas, and located in the wilds of Arkansas County, eight miles from Arkansas Post, then the capital of the Territory. The country at that time was full of bears, deer, panthers, wolves, etc., with a few Indians as pioneer inhabitants. The swamps were covered with cane-brakes, which grew to the height of a house, and so dense that it was almost impossible for one to pass through. Here Mr. Ferrell improved one of the finest farms in that region, but it was eventually washed away by the river. He was a blacksmith by trade, at which he worked in connection with farming and hunting, the latter occupying a large part of his time. He served in the War of 1812 under Gen. Jackson, as blacksmith, and died in 1858, when over seventy-six years of age. His wife had preceded him three years. Mr. and Mrs. Ferrell were the parents of nine children, Leroy Ferrell being the third one, and the only one living. He was born in Maury County, Tenn., in 1822, and has resided in this county since fourteen years of age. In 1842 Mr. Ferrell and an associate chartered a steamboat, which they ran about one year; since that time he has been engaged in boating on the Mississippi for about thirty-five years. Since settling in this county he has been interested in farming and stock raising, and in the mercantile business to some extent. He was married, in 1850, to Miss Eleanor Smith, a native of Indiana, who died in 1868, leaving four children; one of these (Thomas B. F.) only is living. He was born in Desha County in 1851, and was educated at the common schools, and later in the Business College at Memphis, Tenn., from which he graduated in 1870. He then commenced business for himself at New Gascony, Jefferson County, continuing until 1880, when he came to Arkansas Post. Here he has since carried on merchandising, and also owns and operates a large cotton-gin. At the present time Mr. Ferrell and his father own about 8,000 acres of land. During the war he was repeatedly urged by his friends to join the Confederate army, but although born and reared in the South, he refused to take up arms against his country. This position he firmly maintained until the close of the war, remaining at home and providing for his family and those whose supporters were in the Confederate army. Capt. Ferrell, although nearly seventy years of age, is of strong bodily health and vigor (save a slight affliction of rheumatism), is of pleasant address, and a good talker.

James A. Gibson, of the firm of Gibson & Holt, the leading attorneys of De Witt, is one of the best-known men of Arkansas County. He was reared and educated in Breckinridge County, Ky., his native State, and received a thorough common-school education, and, at the age of twenty entered the St. Mary's College, near Lebanon, Ky., but was obliged to give up his studies on account of his health. He then engaged in farming, and in 1861 came to Arkansas, locating in this county, where he engaged in farming until 1864. Returning to Kentucky, in 1867 he came back to this county and, locating in De Witt, commenced studying law. He was admitted to the bar the following year and has since been occupied in the practice of his profession, in which he has been very successful. He is one of the leading Democrats of this county and has served his party in a number of conventions and delegations. He was a member of the Constitutional Convention of 1874, has been a delegate to the State Democratic Conventions since 1872, was elected alternate delegate to the National Democratic Conventions held at Cincinnati and Chicago, and has been for the past three years, and is at present, a member of the State central committee. In 1881 he was a member of the Electoral College, and voted for Hancock and English, having been elected the year previous. Mr. Gibson was born in Breckinridge County, Ky., in 1837, and was a son of Hamilton and Letitia (Gilliland) Gibson, also natives of Kentucky. They were the parents of three children: William F. (a resident of Austin, Ark.), John T. (deceased) and James A., the principal of this sketch, who was married while in Kentucky, to Miss Hester Vertreese, a native of Missouri, but who was reared in Kentucky. They

are the parents of nine children: William H. (a graduate of the Louisville University of Medicine, of Kentucky), Sallie (now Mrs. Crockett), Albert, Blanche, John, Nannie, Benton, Claude and Tee. Mr. Gibson has been engaged in the mercantile business until a few years ago, since when he has devoted all his time to his profession. He entered into partnership with Robert P. Holt in 1882. They have an extensive real-estate business in connection with their law practice, and have now on hand over 100,000 acres of fine lands for sale. Mr. and Mrs. Gibson are members of the Baptist Church, in which they take an active part. He is a member of the Masonic order, in which he has taken the Royal Arch and Council degrees, and is also a member of the I. O. O. F. and has been Grand Master of the State and Grand Representative of the Sovereign Grand Lodge.

A. J. Gunnell was the eldest son in a family of ten children born to Benjamin and Caroline (Ayers) Gunnell, natives of Virginia and South Carolina, respectively. They were married in Jefferson County, Ala., in 1828, and in 1835–36 moved to Tippah County, Miss. The father was a blacksmith by trade and was a soldier in the War of 1812, dying in 1852, at the age of sixty-five years; his wife passed away in 1885, at the age of seventy-seven. He was a son of Nicholas Gunnell, a Virginian by birth, and a soldier in the Revolutionary War, who died in Georgia, at the age of ninety-eight. The father of Caroline Ayers, William Ayers, was born in South Carolina, and died near the place where Birmingham, Ala., now stands. He was of Irish descent. A. J. Gunnell first saw the light in Jefferson County, Ala., in 1829, being reared on a farm, and while never having had an opportunity to attend school, he has improved his spare moments and is a well-read man. In 1853 he came to Arkansas and located on the farm on which he still makes his home, consisting of 400 acres; at that time it was wild land covered with timber, but now 120 acres are under cultivation. In April, 1861, Mr. Gunnell joined the Confederate army, as a member of the First Arkansas Infantry, in which he served until the battle of Shiloh, when he was wounded and received his discharge and returned home. After his recovery he joined Company E of the Thirty-first Arkansas Infantry. He was made first lieutenant, and served until June, 1865, participating in some of the hardest fought battles of the war. After the war he returned home to find all of his property destroyed and left nearly without a home. He was married in September of the same year to Miss Amanda Luckett, daughter of John L. and Mary Luckett, originally from Kentucky and Tennessee, respectively; she was born in Mississippi. They are the parents of six children: Katie (now Mrs. Jones), Benjamin T., John Nicholas, Winfield D., Callie and Emma. When Mr. Gunnell came to this county it was impossible to raise hogs on account of the wolves and bears. The country was full of game of all kinds. He is now one of the leading men of this community and a member of the Methodist Episcopal Church, as are also his wife and two eldest children.

Jacob H. Hagler owes his nativity to Tennessee, being the son of Elcania and Martha (Sthudeed) Hagler, natives, respectively, of Tennessee and Kentucky. The father was a tailor by occupation, and a member of the Methodist Episcopal Church. After his death, which occurred in 1844, his wife immigrated to Arkansas with her children and located in this county, where she lived until her demise, in 1864. They were the parents of eleven children, only two of whom are living: Robert (a resident of Howard County), and Jacob H. (our subject). The latter was born in Henry County, Tenn., September 13, 1835. He was reared principally in this county, and was married February 24, 1859, to Miss Louisa Slaughter, of this State, a daughter of James and Elizabeth Slaughter. They have had six children: Mary J. (deceased), William J. (deceased), John L., Joseph E. (deceased), James E., and Marcas N. (deceased). The two sons living, John L. and James E., reside at home and are helping their father on the farm. Mr. Hagler entered the Confederate service in 1862, and participated in Price's raid through Missouri, taking part in a number of hard-fought battles; he was wounded at Swan Lake by a ball passing through his wrist; was also

taken sick at Pilot Knob and then received his discharge, after which he returned home and engaged in farming. This occupation he has since followed. He owns 1,000 acres of land, of which there are nearly 200 acres under cultivation, all acquired by his own industry and economy, as he started out in life with only $75. He and wife are members of the Baptist Church, and take an active part in the affairs of that denomination.

Col. William H. HalliBurton is a good example of what can be accomplished in life, when thorough determination to succeed is coupled with energy, perseverance and close application in the direction chosen. His early educational advantages were of a very meager description, and during a period of eight years he received but seven months schooling, but becoming desirous of improving himself, he began devoting all his spare moments to studying and reading, and soon became a thoroughly posted young man, and quite familiar with the "world of books." He was married while a resident of Benton County, Tenn., to Elizabeth C. Altom, a native of Greenville, S. C., and to them a family of seven children were born, two of whom are now living: Gulnare (wife of Dr. James B. Garrison, of Texas) and John. The mother of these children died August 20, 1848, at the Arkansas Post, Ark., where they had settled April 14, 1845, and for some months Mr. HalliBurton was engaged in teaching school, becoming thereby well and favorably known. In the spring of 1847 he was appointed to the office of deputy sheriff, and held the position until November of the same year, when he was appointed deputy clerk, and held the two offices from November, 1847, to December, 1850. During these years he frequently issued process in the name of the clerk, and went out and executed the same in the name of the sheriff. In the year 1850 he was elected clerk of the circuit court, and served one term of two years. He was sworn in as deputy sheriff at the April term, 1847, of the Arkansas County circuit court, and has been present, participating in the proceedings of each term of the circuit court of said county since, excepting the March terms of 1885, 1887 and 1889, when he was in attendance on the legislature of the State. He was elected to represent Arkansas County in the State legislature in 1885, and was re-elected in 1887 and 1889. In 1887 he was appointed deputy treasurer and special agent for the State to go to Washington, D. C., to settle a disputed debt between the State of Arkansas and the United States. He was elected colonel of the One Hundred and Thirteenth Regiment of Tennessee Militia, in 1838. During the Rebellion he was appointed chief collector of Confederate States war tax for the State of Arkansas by the president of the Confederacy, but did not take an active part in the war. His second wife was Hannah Jacobs, who was born in Wellsburg, Brooke County, Va., and to them were born five children, three of whom are now living: Jennie (wife of David Rasure), Kate (wife of Harry Greer) and Lucinda (at home). Mr. HalliBurton is now living with his third wife, who was a Mrs. Mary S. (Belknap) Patrick, a native of Pennsylvania. She is a member of the Cumberland Presbyterian Church, and he is a Baptist. He began the study of law when he was a young man, and in 1847 was licensed to practice, and was admitted to the bar in 1852. He has been a practicing lawyer of De Witt since 1857, and has always been considered a leading member of the legal fraternity. From 1860 to 1862, he resided in Little Rock, but has since made his home in De Witt. He was born in Stewart County, Tenn., November 4, 1816, and is a son of Thomas and Lucinda (Herndon) HalliBurton, natives, respectively, of North and South Carolina. The father inherited Scotch blood from his parents, and when about nine years of age, was taken by them to Tennessee, and from that time until 1834 he resided in Humphreys County. He was the seventh son and eleventh child of his father's family, and his marriage took place in Tennessee. He moved to Arkansas in 1845, and located in Arkansas County, where he followed merchandising until his death in 1859, at the age of sixty-three years. He was a member of the Baptist Church, and was very active in political affairs of the communities in which he resided, and while in Tennessee, was county court clerk of

Benton County, and after coming to Arkansas, held the offices of justice of the peace, county surveyor and county and probate judge. He was a Master Mason. His wife died in Humphreys County, Tenn., in the spring of 1834, having borne a family of eight children, of whom W. H. was the eldest, and is the only one now living. Mr. HalliBurton was married a second time, and of seven children born to this marriage, two are living: Mrs. Lucinda Mock, of Louisiana, and David N., of Dardanelle, Ark. The paternal grandparents were born in Virginia, but were early residents of Tennessee, and in 1834 removed to Henderson County, and made their home with a son. Here the grandmother died in her eightieth year, and the grandfather and his son soon after moved to Mississippi, in which State his demise occurred in 1841, he being ninety-one years of age. This old couple soon after their marriage had an orphan boy bound to them, and reared a family of thirteen children, and besides this they reared seven of their grandchildren to maturity, making in all twenty-one children, whom they brought up. Out of the twenty-one, twenty had families before the death of the grandparents, and the youngest of the twenty-one had attained his majority before the grandmother's death.

Nathan M. Henderson has always been interested in the welfare of the county of Arkansas, having been born here in 1848, and has ever been occupied in tilling the soil, and the manner in which he has acquired his present property denotes him to be an energetic and successful agriculturist. He is a son of James L. and Nancy C. (Henshaw) Henderson, the former a native of Georgia, born in 1825, their union taking place in the State of Mississippi in 1844. In 1846 they removed from Mississippi to Arkansas, and entered some 360 acres of land, but sold this property in 1858, and entered 360 acres more, which he also improved and of which he devoted a considerable portion to the raising of stock. He served in the Southern army during the Rebellion, and was on active duty from 1864 to the final surrender in 1865. He was a Mason, a member of the Cumberland Presbyterian Church, and died in 1867. His wife, who was born in Tennessee in 1831, is a member of the Baptist Church, and has been a widow for twenty-two years, residing on the old homestead. Their union was blessed in the birth of six sons and three daughters, only six of this family now living: Nathan M., Nelson H., James E., John O., Samuel A. and Nancy E. (the wife of W. F. Byers). Nathan M. Henderson was married to Miss Ruthie L. McAdams, of Arkansas, in 1869, but she left him a widower, in 1875, with two children to care for: James M. and Thomas J. Mr. Henderson's second marriage was consummated in 1877, his wife being Miss Seleta J. Bunyard, of Arkansas County, and their family now consists of three children: Alonzo J., Ruthie L. and Samuel M. Mr. Henderson was called upon to mourn the death of his second wife in 1888, she having been an earnest member of the Baptist Church. He married his present wife, Mrs. Mary C. Hanford, in 1888, she being also a member of the Baptist Church and the widow of Christopher Hanford. Mr. Henderson owns 325 acres of land, well furnished with excellent buildings, and a fine apple and peach orchard, and besides attending to the duties of his farm he is also engaged in operating a grist-mill and a horse-power cotton-gin. He is a deacon in the Baptist Church.

P. N. Howell, during the war, joined Company K of Col. Dick Pinson's regiment, in 1861, in the Mississippi Cavalry, serving in General Forrest's command. He took part in the battles of Shiloh, Corinth, Vicksburg and a number of others, and was captured at Vicksburg in 1863, being taken on board of a boat bound for the Northern prisons, but escaping, he rejoined his command. After the war he engaged in the grocery business at Memphis, and in 1868 was married to Miss Martha E. Wadsworth, daughter of W. P. and Julia C. Wadsworth, natives of North and South Carolina, respectively. In 1878 Mr. Howell went to Marshall County, Miss., where he remained until 1881, the time of his removal to Arkansas. Locating in this county, he embarked in farming on his present farm of 160 acres, about three miles from Crockett's Bluff, where he has about sixty-five acres under cultivation. His wife died in

1876, and in 1881 he married his second and present companion, Miss E. L. Jansen, daughter of Rev. Lewis Jansen, an Episcopal minister of Louisville, Ky. Mr. Howell is a Democrat in politics, and he and wife are members of the Methodist Episcopal Church. He was born in Anson County, N. C., in 1835, as the son of Abner and Phebe B. (Ingram) Howell. Abner Howell came originally from North Carolina. His father, Samuel Howell, who was born in Georgia, was of Scotch descent. Mr. Howell moved to Alabama in 1858, where he died in 1876, his wife surviving him two years.

Abner L. Huffman. From this brief and incomplete view of the life-record of Mr. Huffman will be seen that his life has not been uselessly nor idly spent, for from his earliest youth he has been familiar with the details of farm work. He was born in Caldwell County, N. C., September 12, 1851, and is a son of Samuel and Henrietta (Payne) Huffman, natives of South and North Carolina, born December 1, 1824, and December 23, 1829, respectively. Their marriage resulted in the birth of three sons and six daughters, all of whom are living with the exception of one. Those living are Marion L., Abner, Mary (wife of A. T. Young), Sarah (wife of W. W. Duncan), John B., Laura (wife of H. C. Synco), Annie E. and Amanda E. Samuel Huffman immigrated from North Carolina to Missouri in 1852, settling in Hickory County, where he lived until 1863, moving then to Calloway County, where his death occurred December 1, 1870, his occupation through life having been that of farming and tanning. In 1876 his widow removed to Arkansas, and died there April 7, of the following year, having for many years been an earnest and consistent member of the Methodist Episcopal Church. Abner Huffman was appointed postmaster of Hynum under Cleveland's administration, and still holds this position. He has been justice of the peace for the past five years, and is a man who has a host of warm friends. He owns eighty acres of good land, well improved with good buildings, fences and orchards.

Thomas H. Hutchinson, a druggist of De Witt, and also engaged in stock raising and farming, is a native of Canada. He started in the world for himself at the age of eighteen, having a few thousand dollars left to him by his grandfather, which he invested in vessel property on the lakes, and was engaged in the trading business for five years. Subsequently he lost all his money and property. After winding up his interests he had just money enough to take him to Arkansas, where he worked out by the day and month until 1873, then entering a homestead, keeping "bach" alone. In 1887 he married Miss Edith Fowler, of Ohio, daughter of F. F. and Mary E. Fowler, natives of Pennsylvania and Ohio, respectively. Mrs. Hutchinson died in 1878, after which Mr. Hutchinson married Bessie A. Fowler, a sister of his first wife. They are the parents of two children: Mabel and Howard F. Mr. Hutchinson was born in Ontario, Canada, in 1843, and was a graduate of Jones' Commercial College, London, Ont. His parents were Alexander B. and Sarah Ann (Titus) Hutchinson. Alexander Hutchinson was born in Canada West, in 1816, and Sarah A., his wife, in Nova Scotia, in 1824, the latter going to Canada with her parents at the age of eleven years. Alexander B. Hutchinson spent his life upon the farm he first settled, and died in 1886. They were members of the Baptist Church, and the parents of eleven children, four of whom are deceased. Thomas H. Hutchinson has two fine farms of 600 acres, stocked with over 300 head of cattle, besides horses and mules; 250 acres are in cultivation. He is a member of the I. O. O. F. and Masonic fraternities, and resides upon his farm, four miles from the county seat of Arkansas County.

Edward Lambert Johnson, attorney at law of De Witt, is a native of Mississippi, and a son of Hon. Edward and Lucinda (Dickey) Johnson, whose birthplaces were in North Carolina and Alabama, respectively. In 1861 they came to Arkansas, and located in Arkansas County, where Mr. Johnson died July 4, 1879, at the age of seventy. He was of Scotch parentage, his father having come from Scotland to this country, and settled in North Carolina. Mrs. Johnson was born in Huntsville, Ala., in 1815, and died in March, 1885. Her father, James Dickey, was of Irish descent, born in South Carolina; he died in Alabama. Mr.

and Mrs. Johnson were the parents of nine children, Edward L. being the fifth. Born in Choctaw County, Miss., in 1849, in the latter part of 1864 he enlisted in the Eighth Mississippi Cavalry, and served six months. After the close of the war he returned to Arkansas, and at the age of nineteen commenced publishing the Arkansas Elector, at De Witt, which he continued nearly two years. He then entered upon the study of law, in 1870 was admitted to the bar, and in 1877 was admitted to practice law in the supreme court. He was married in the Centennial year to Miss Kate Quertermous, a daughter of John G. and Cynthia A. Quertermous, natives of Kentucky and Arkansas, respectively. Since that time Mr. Johnson has devoted his time to the practice of his profession, having become one of the leading lawyers of this part of the State.

John W. Lemon. Samuel Lemon, the grandfather of the principal of this sketch, was one of the early settlers of Arkansas County. His son, Alexander M., was born in this county in 1820, and lived here all of his life, engaged in farming. He served through the Civil War, in the Confederate service, and was in the infantry under Capt. Jones, from Arkansas County, though during the last two years of the struggle he belonged to an independent scouting company of cavalry, in which he remained until the cessation of hostilities. He returned to this county after the war, but died the following year. His wife was Miss Clayton, a daughter of John S. Clayton, a wheelwright and carpenter, who was drowned in the Mississippi some time before the war. Mrs. Lemon is still living, and is about seventy-one years of age, having reared a family of six children. John W. Lemon was born in Arkansas Township, in 1846, and received very little education in youth, not having an opportunity of attending school. He joined the Confederate service during the last year of the civil strife, and served in Gen. Price's raid. Being at home on a sixty-days' furlough, shortly before peace was declared, he was captured by the Federals, and held at St. Charles about one month, until the close of the war. In 1866 he married Mary J. Rounsavill, a daughter of William Rounsavill. They are the parents of six children, three sons and three daughters. In 1875 he bought a farm in Bayou Meto Township, where he still owns a stock ranch, in 1886 removing to De Witt, for the purpose of giving his children better educational facilities. He started out a poor man, but now owns 700 acres of land in different farms, a good house, and ten acres in De Witt, and is an extensive stock raiser, buying and shipping from ten to twelve car-loads of cattle to market annually. He has seen the complete development of this county, having lived here for forty-three years, and has helped liberally in its development.

Maj. M. M. Massey, a native of Tennessee, is the son of Isaac H. and Elizabeth (Crockett) Massey, who were born in South Carolina and Tennessee, respectively. Isaac Massey moved to Tennessee from South Carolina with his parents when a boy of six years, and afterward made that State his home, dying on the farm upon which his father located, in 1843, at the age of forty-three years. He was an active member of and an elder in the Cumberland Presbyterian Church. His wife was related to Davy Crockett. She was born in 1801 and died in the same year as her husband. Of their family of eight children our subject is the eldest and the only one now living. He was born in Humphreys County, Tenn., August 25, 1820, and was reared and married in that county. In March, 1843, Miss Elizabeth Murphrey of the same locality became his wife. After remaining in Tennessee until 1871 they moved to Arkansas. Mr. Massey joined the Confederate army in September, 1861, and was elected lieutenant of the light artillery starting out. He was wounded at Fort Donelson, and was then assigned to fort duty and was made major of artillery, but was again in the field at the battle of Corinth, before having fully recovered from his wound, and afterward participated in a number of hard-fought battles. On his return to Humphreys County, Tenn., he was elected sheriff, which office he held with distinction for a number of years. His wife died two years after coming to Arkansas County, leaving six children, three of whom survive. Maj. Massey was married to his present wife, Mrs. Susan Smith (nee Bell),

also of Tennessee, in 1876. They have two children. The Major owns over 1,000 acres of land, partially under cultivation, and which he has well stocked. He is a member of the Masonic order, and of the I. O. O. F. Mrs. Massey is a member of the Methodist Episcopal Church, South.

George F. Mattmiller came originally from Germany to America with his parents in February, 1846, and located in Fayette County, Tenn., where he received a common-school education. In 1861 he enlisted in the Confederate army, Company A of the Thirteenth Tennessee Infantry; was taken prisoner in the first hard battle, at Belmont, Mo., and removed to Cairo, Ill., soon being exchanged, after which he rejoined his regiment and served until the close of the war. Going to Cape Girardeau County, Mo., he was first engaged in teaching school and next in working in a saw-mill, where he continued until 1870. He then sought a home in Arkansas, where he was married five years later to Miss Ophelia Stillwell, a native of this State, and a daughter of Asher and Josephine Stillwell. Mr. Mattmiller was born in Baden, Germany, on July 24, 1843, being a son of J. G. and Christina (Hammerschmidt) Mattmiller. J. G. Mattmiller was born on August 28, 1814, and emigrated to this country in 1846, settling in Tennessee. After devoting himself to farming there until 1870, he located a farm on the Arkansas River, near Arkansas Post, Ark., where he remained until his death, in December, 1883. His wife died in 1862, having been the mother of nine children, four of whom are living: George F., Christina (now Mrs. Rinklin), Joseph and Henry C. On coming to Arkansas Mr. Mattmiller, the subject of this sketch, had only $6. He now owns about 700 acres of land, with 100 acres under cultivation, and has a good cotton-gin, and is estimated to be worth about $6,000. He has no children of his own, but has adopted three orphan children. Himself and wife are members of the Methodist Episcopal Church.

John R. Maxwell is a native of Arkansas County, of which he has always been a resident, with the exception of eight years spent in the city of Cincinnati, from 1851 to 1858, where he was engaged in mechanical pursuits. In 1858 he returned home and the same year was appointed deputy sheriff, discharging the duties of that position until the breaking out of the war. Enlisting in June, 1861, in the Arkansas State troops, he served four months and immediately enlisted in the Confederate army, where he continued until the close of the war, a part of the time being on detached duty. He was elected second lieutenant in 1862, and afterward elected to captain, and participated in the battles of Wilson's Creek, Shiloh, Prairie Grove, Jenkins' Ferry and several other hard-fought engagements and a number of skirmishes. After the war Mr. Maxwell returned to this county and engaged in farming the first year, since which time he has been occupied in the mercantile business. He was born in Arkansas Post, on November 27, 1829, being the son of James and Elenor (Bringle) Maxwell, natives of North Carolina and Arkansas, respectively. Joseph Maxwell, the grandfather of the principal of this sketch, lived in Indiana, and died at the battle of Tippecanoe, in the War of 1812. He was the father of the following children: William, John, James, Nimrod, David, Mary (now Mrs. Berry), and Anna. All of the sons came to Arkansas at different periods, between 1818 and 1837. James and John were interested for a number of years in trading with the Indians along the Arkansas and White Rivers. James, the father of John R., located at Arkansas Post in 1824–25, at which time he was married, and subsequently worked at his trade of gun smithing. He was a well-educated man, and held several Government positions, being Government surveyor at the time of his death, in 1838. His wife died in 1880, at the age of seventy years. They were the parents of six children, two still living: John R. (our subject) and Cynthia Ann (widow of John G. Quertermous, of New Mexico). Joseph, one of the sons (now deceased), held the position of sheriff at the breaking out of the war, and was afterward elected county clerk, which office he filled at the time of his death, in 1872. Capt. Maxwell was married in 1869 to Miss Ann Quertermous, a native of Kentucky. They are the parents of two daughters, Vallenia and Ella. Capt. Maxwell is a strong Democrat and a leading merchant

41

of De Witt, and is recognized as one of the most influential men of this locality, being widely known and highly esteemed.

Walter F. Meacham is one of the progressive general merchants of Arkansas County, Ark., and by his superior management, good business ability and efficiency, has done not a little to advance the reputation the county enjoys as a commercial center. He was born in Anson County, N. C., September 10, 1851, and is a descendant of Jeremiah Meacham, who was also a native of North Carolina, born in 1809. The latter was one of "the horny handed sons of toil," and was of Scotch-Irish extraction. Upon reaching manhood he was married to Miss Maness, of North Carolina, and by her became the father of ten children, six of whom are now living: Walter F., Case, William R., Mary E. (wife of K. M. Hasty, of North Carolina), Elizabeth (wife of J. T. Redfern, of Thomas County, Ga.) and Jane (the wife of P. C. Davis, of Southwest Georgia). Jeremiah Meacham died in Anson County, Ga., in 1865, having been an earnest and consistent member of the Methodist Episcopal Church, as was his wife, who died in 1854. Walter F. Meacham began his own career at the age of eighteen years, and was first engaged in farming in his native State, continuing there until 1870, when he immigrated to Georgia, Bartow County, and followed the same occupation for eight years. He then concluded to push on farther westward, and came to Arkansas, locating in Lee County, where he built a large store room and engaged in the mercantile business, and also managed a livery barn with success. He now carries a stock of goods valued at about $6,000, and as he controls a large trade, his annual sales amount to some $36,000. His brother, Jesse C., was his business partner for a number of years, and was married to Miss Georgia A. Simms, of Georgia, in 1873, becoming by her the father of five children, three now living: Jerry, Arthur and Lillie. Jesse C. Meacham died in 1886, and his wife in 1884, she being a member of the Baptist Church at the time of her death.

Judge James H. Merritt came to Arkansas in 1857 and entered a small tract of land in this county, but soon after moved to De Witt, when he was appointed deputy sheriff, also engaging in the mercantile business. In 1862 he was elected collector of revenue and census taker of Arkansas County. Having been thrown from a horse and injured, he was unable to join the Confederate troops during the war, which were organized in this county, but in 1864 he became a member of Hawthorne's regiment, and was engaged in the commissary department. In 1873 he resumed merchandising, devoting his whole attention to that occupation until the fall of 1880, when he was elected county judge, a position that he still occupies. He is yet occupied in the mercantile business and carries one of the largest stocks of goods in the place. James H. Merritt was born in South Carolina in 1831, being the son of Allen and Mary (Willson) Merritt, natives of that State, as were also their parents. They removed to Alabama in 1834 and located in Fayette County, where the father was engaged in farming, and in 1844 went to Mississippi. Judge Merritt was married in 1859, to Miss Charlotte H. Stephen, of Indiana birth, daughter of Henry K. Stephen. The latter, a native of Eastern Tennessee, came to this county when Mrs. Merritt was a girl, and held a number of county offices; he was sheriff a number of years, and died in this county in 1881. Mr. and Mrs. Merritt have had eleven children, seven of whom are still living: William A., Sallie (now Mrs. Barnett), Joseph, Ella, Ange E., James H. and Maggie M. Mr. Merritt and wife belong to the Baptist Church, which they helped to organize, and are the only original members of that church now living. He is a member of the Masonic order and of the I. O. O. F., in which he takes an active part, and at the time of the organization of the County Grange was elected manager of their store. He is one of the most influential and popular men in De Witt.

John W. Miller is not unknown to the many residents of this locality. His father, John Miller, Sr., was born in Prussia in 1805, and there learned the carpenter's trade, coming to this country in 1830, and settling in Marshall County, Miss., where he was engaged in farming and in working at his trade. He was there married to Nancy Neal, who was born in Mississippi in 1815. Removing to Arkansas in 1850 Mr. Miller located in this county, where he lived until his death, in 1888. His wife still survives and makes her home with her daughter Mrs. Elizabeth Deberry. They were members of the Methodist Episcopal Church, and had a family of eight children, five of whom are living: Elizabeth (now Mrs. Deberry), Martha A. (now Mrs. Dillard), Francis Allen, George H. and John W. The latter, the next to the eldest child, was born in 1844. He commenced farming at the age of twenty-one, and is now the owner of half a section of land, 200 acres of which are under cultivation. He married Miss Mary Wallace, a native of New York State. They are the parents of the following children: Frances (wife of William Aldman), Jennie (now Mrs. Seamon), Alice (now Mrs. Allen), Josephine, Willie, Ellen, Sallie and Lucy. Mr. Miller is a Democrat in politics, and is one of the leading men of the township.

John S. Montgomery, by virtue of his long residence in Arkansas County and his popular association with its affairs, deserves prominent mention in the present volume. Leroy Montgomery, his father, came to Arkansas in 1846, and settled in the wilds of Arkansas County at a time when there were but few settlers and when the woods echoed with the cries of bears, deer, wildcats, panthers, etc. He was a hard-working man, and cleared up a large farm. In 1853, in company with Col. Charles Belknap and Dr. J. A. Moorman, he was appointed a commissioner to locate and name the county seat of Arkansas County. After deciding on the present site of De Witt for the new seat of justice they decided to play "seven up" to see who should name it, and the lot falling to Mr. Montgomery, he called it De Witt, in honor of ex-Gov. DeWitt Clinton, of New York. Mr. Montgomery died in 1865 and his wife in 1873. They were the parents of seven children, namely: Marion, L. D., A. J., J. S., R. L., L. and M. R., only two of whom are now living, R. L. and J. S. Montgomery. J. S. Montgomery married a Miss Martha A. Pryor, daughter of Isaac and Martha A. Pryor. They are the parents of three children, one son and two daughters. Mr. Montgomery has spent all his life on the farm that he still occupies, a part of which is the old place cleared up by his father, consisting of 520 acres, 160 acres of which are under cultivation. He also owns a cotton-gin and corn-mill (run by horse-power up to 1883, but since that time by steam-power). He is a Democrat in politics, and cast his first presidential vote for Horace Greeley in 1872. His eldest brother, Marion, was in the Confederate army, and in the last battle in Virginia, said, "I am going to send some of the blue home." A few moments later he was killed. John S. Montgomery is now living in the house built by his father in 1847.

Samuel A. Morgan is a native of Mississippi and is a son of Charles H. and Elenor A. (Galaher) Morgan, also originally from that State. Mr. Morgan was a farmer of Mississippi, and in 1853 or 1854 removed to Arkansas, settling near St. Charles, where he died the following year. His wife died October 16, 1878, at the age of fifty. She was married after her first husband's death to the Hon. A. H. Almond, who died in 1868. He was county and probate judge of Arkansas County for a number of years under Democratic rule. There was one child by this union, which died at the age of eight years. Her last husband was a member of the Methodist Episcopal Church, South, to which she also belonged. Samuel A. is the eldest and the only one living of three sons. James W. Morgan, his brother, died at the age of twenty-five, just in the bloom of manhood. The other two, Samuel A. and J. W., were born in Marshall County, Miss., in 1849 and 1852, respectively, but have lived in this county since four and five years of age. Samuel A. was married in 1870 to Miss A. E. Burnet, a daughter of Lemuel F. Burnet, one of the oldest settlers in this county. He was born in New Jersey in 1810, but was reared in Pennsylvania and Ohio. He was apprenticed to a gunsmith a few years before he became of age, and worked at the trade until twenty-one years old. In 1835 he came to Arkansas, remaining in Little Rock one year, thence going to Desha County, where he worked at his trade until he became blind and could not attend to his work. He married Jane E. Coose, a native of Tennessee and a daughter of John Coose. Mr. and Mrs. Burnet were the parents of fifteen children, five of whom are still living. Mr. Morgan bought his present place in 1878, and moved on it in 1881. He and his wife are members of the Methodist Episcopal Church, South, and are the parents of seven children, of whom four are living. He is a prominent Democrat and a highly respected citizen.

Richard H. Parker has been a resident of Arkansas since eighteen years of age, having settled in this county during the war, while home on a furlough. He is a son of Richard and Irena (Brown) Parker, natives of Georgia. They removed to Alabama when our subject was a small boy, and settled in Russell County, where they engaged in farming, remaining there until 1857, the time of starting for Arkansas. After coming overland, by wagon, a journey taking eight weeks, they located in Monroe County, on the west fork of Big Creek, where they entered land, and where the father lived until his death in 1863, his wife dying one year before. He was a soldier in the Indian Wars of 1835–36, and he and his wife were members of the Baptist Church. They had a family of nine children, six of whom are living. Richard H. Parker was born in Talbot County, Ga., in 1839. In 1860 he commenced farming for himself, but the war breaking out he joined the Confederate army in 1861, enlisting in a cavalry company. Three months later they were dismounted and joined Col. Matlock's regiment, serving in Price's raid through Missouri. He was captured in August, 1864, while home on a furlough, and sent to Memphis, Tenn., but having taken the oath of allegiance, was released and returned home. He was struck by a piece of shell at the battle of Helena, in the right leg, but was not seriously wounded. Returning to this county after his release, he was without property, and had four brothers and sisters to care for, and what he now possesses has been made since the war. Mr. Parker married Miss Susan Gardner, a native of Mississippi, and daughter of George W. and Stacy (Bounds) Gardner, of Tennessee. Mr. and Mrs. Parker are the parents of eight children, seven still living: Robert F., James R., Francis J., Caledolia, Theadecia E., Thadus A. and India. Mr. Parker settled on his present farm in 1868, and has it now in a good state of cultivation, and is engaged principally in stock raising. He is a Democrat in politics and a member of the school board, in which he takes an active part. He is a member of the Masonic order and of the Knights of Honor, and he and wife are members of the Missionary Baptist Church, in which they take a great interest.

M. F. Pike is prominently engaged in the mercantile business at Golden Hill, and has been postmaster of that place for the past five years. Born in Alabama, he was a son of Capt. John and Eliza (East) Pike, natives respectively of North Carolina and Tennessee. They were married in Alabama and made that their home until 1849, then coming to Arkansas and locating a claim in the woods, five miles from Mount Adams, where they spent the rest of their lives. Mr. Pike died in 1868 at the age of sixty-three, and his wife ten years later, when sixty-six years old. He was a son of Gen. Pike, a soldier and general in the War of 1812, who, a native of North Carolina, moved to Alabama when the father of our subject was a boy, and in 1855 removed to Arkansas and settled in this county, where he died in 1856. M. F. Pike was born in Madison County, Ala., in 1846, but was reared and educated in Arkansas County. He enlisted in April, 1861, in the Confederate service, and took part in a number of hard-fought battles; was captured on February 14, 1864, and taken to New Orleans, and was held captive for nearly a year. He was then exchanged at the mouth of the Red River, and joined Gen. Fagan's escort, in which he served until a short time before the close of the war, when he received his discharge and returned home. Of five brothers and two cousins who left his father's house and joined the Southern army, all returned home in safety. Mr. Pike was married on May 12, 1866, to Louisa S. Gravett, of Madison County, Ala. They are the parents of six children, one son and five daughters. Mr. Pike has a farm of 120 acres, with fifty acres under cultivation. He entered into the mercantile business in 1889 at Golden Hill, but also still continues farming. Mrs.

Pike has been a member of the Methodist Episcopal Church for a number of years.

Jesse P. Poynter, editor of the De Witt Gazette and county treasurer of Arkansas County, is a native of Kentucky, in which State he was reared and educated until fourteen years of age. Then he went to Ohio, and in 1852 came with his father and family to Arkansas, locating in Monroe County, but remained only a short time. Going thence to Memphis, Tenn., he was employed on the Memphis Bulletin until 1858, after which he returned to Monroe County. At the outbreak of the war he enlisted in the Twenty-fifth Arkansas Infantry, holding the position of first lieutenant, in which he served until 1864, when he was transferred to the Forty-seventh Arkansas Cavalry; he took part in Price's raid through Missouri, Kansas and the Indian Territory, and was appointed first lieutenant of Company K. After the war he engaged in farming, which occupation he followed until 1879, when he moved to De Witt, and was employed at his trade as printer. Mr. Poynter married Miss Amanda Coster, of Monroe County, and to them have been born three children: Walter, Ethel May and Cora. Mr. and Mrs. Poynter are members of the Methodist Episcopal Church. He is a member of the Masonic fraternity and is a Royal Arch Mason. In 1886 he was elected county treasurer, and re-elected in 1888, and fills the office with entire satisfaction to the community, and with credit to himself. In 1883, in De Witt, he started a paper called the Sentry, which he published until 1884, when he started his present paper, the De Witt Gazette, Democratic in politics, and the only paper published in this place. This ably advocates the interests of this section. Mr. Poynter was born in Kentucky, in 1835, the son of David E. and Judith B. (Moseley) Poynter, also natives of the Blue Grass State, where they lived until 1852, then coming to Monroe County, where they lived until their death. David E. Poynter was county surveyor of Monroe County for a number of years. His death occurred in 1859, at the age of fifty years, and his wife died in 1870, at the age of sixty-nine. They belonged to the Methodist Episcopal Church.

James M. Price, who is a man of substantial reputation hereabouts, spent his younger days on a farm in Tennessee, and was there married when twenty-three years of age to Elizabeth F. Woodard, a native of that State. In the fall of 1857, removing to Arkansas, he bought a farm on what is known as Big Island, on White River, three miles east of his present farm. During the war he enlisted, in 1864, in the Confederate army, in which he served as a veterinary surgeon in the artillery department, although opposed to the secession movement and favoring the emancipation of slaves. Mrs. Price, his wife, died in 1868, after having borne three children, all of whom are deceased. His present wife was formerly Miss E. J. Nicholson, a native of this county, and daughter of James A. Nicholson, originally from Alabama, and an old settler here. They are the parents of the following children: Fannie A., Sallie S., James A., Joseph H., Nancy E., Charles M., Ralph C. and one child who died in infancy. Mr. Price was born in Tennessee, July 5, 1827, being a son of John S. and Sarah B. (Hughs) Price, natives of Virginia and North Carolina, respectively. John S. Price and wife started for Tennessee soon after their marriage, going by wagon, and a part of the way having to cut a way through the woods, as there was no road; they located a claim on which they made their home for the remainder of their lives. Mr. Price died in the fall of 1842, while in South Alabama on a trading expedition. He was a member of the Masonic order, and took an active part in the politics of his country. His wife died in 1866, when over eighty years of age, having reared a family of eight children. James M. Price owns a farm of 1,000 acres, under a good state of cultivation, and also owns and operates a large cotton-gin. He was engaged in the mercantile business until August, 1889, and was the organizer of the Grange at St. Charles. He and his wife were formerly members of the Cumberland Presbyterian Church, but as there was no church of that denomination in Prairie Township, they united with the Methodist Episcopal Church. Mr. Price is a member of the I. O. O. F. and Masonic fraternities. Benjamin Price, the grand-

father of the principal of this sketch was a soldier in the Revolutionary War, and was captured by the Tories while on Long Island, and was thrown overboard from the vessel. Instead of being drowned, as they had expected, he made his escape to shore.

N. B. Price runs a general supply store at Mount Adams, and has a trade amounting to from $30,000 to $40,000 per year, carrying a stock that would invoice $8,000. He began life for himself at the age of seventeen as a clerk, continuing to be thus employed for some time, when he went into business for himself in Hardeman County, Tenn., and later in Memphis. After remaining in the latter city until 1865, he came to Mount Adams, and has since been in business at this point, attaining to a well-deserved reputation. Mr. Price was born in McNairy County, Tenn., in 1839, and was a son of Rev. William A. and Sarah A. (Duke) Price. The father was a native of Louisa County, Va., and when a young man moved to McNairy County, Tenn., where he married, and lived until coming to Arkansas in 1860. Settling near Mount Adams, he lived there until his death, which occurred in 1862, at the age of forty-seven. His wife died in February, 1889, at the age of sixty-eight. Mr. Price was a local minister of the Methodist Episcopal Church, and a member of the A. F. & A. M. N. B. Price was married in March, 1863, to Miss Emma Cooke, who died in 1865 or 1866, leaving two daughters. He was married the second time about 1868 to Miss Mollie E. Milligan, daughter of Rev. L. H. and Lovinia Milligan, and a native of Mississippi. Her father was a Baptist minister, and died in 1888. Mr. and Mrs. Price are the parents of five children, two sons and three daughters. Mr. Price owns 13,000 acres of land, largely under cultivation, and including an extensive stock ranch. He has acquired all his property by personal industry and business ability, and deserves the success to which he has risen. He has two brothers living: William M. (one of the most extensive stock and real estate men in Arkansas County) and Bryan (who is in the store with the principal of this sketch). Mr. Price has been postmaster of Mount Adams since his locating at this place. He is a member of Euclid Lodge No. 130, A. F. & A. M., and of Reynolds Chapter No. 147. Mr. Price is probably the oldest and most successful merchant in Arkansas County; he does a large retail and wholesale business, and is conceded to be a representative business man of the State. Mrs. Price is a member of the Methodist Episcopal Church, but was formerly a Baptist.

William M. Price has been a resident of Arkansas County, Ark., since 1860, having been born in McNairy County, Tenn., in 1846, the second of four children born to William A. and Sarah A. (Duke) Price, natives of Goochland County, Va., who moved to Tennessee in 1838, and in 1869 to Arkansas County, Ark., settling on a farm on the White River bottoms. Here his death occurred in 1864, his wife's death succeeding his in 1888. William M. Price was fourteen years of age when he came to Arkansas, and after assisting his father on the home farm, he engaged in agricultural pursuits for himself, continuing for two years, or until the opening of the war. In 1863 he enlisted at Monticello, Ark., for the remainder of the war, and was assigned post duty with Col. Crockett, serving in the capacity of acting-adjutant until the close of the war, when he was paroled at Little Rock and returned home, and again resumed his farming duties, making a crop the same year. In 1886 he engaged in the general mercantile business at Mount Adams, continuing with success until 1885, controlling the largest trade of any general merchant in the county. Since 1877 he has been engaged in the stock business, and not only raises stock, but buys and ships also, and has, without doubt, the largest herds of any one man in the State. He makes a specialty of raising blooded Hereford and Durham cattle, and also has a magnificent horse, a blooded Clydesdale and Cleveland Bay. His stock-farm is one of the finest on White River, and comprises about 7,000 acres of land, about 300 acres of which are under cultivation, devoted to grain and cotton, the latter averaging one bale to the acre. In addition to attending to his extensive farm, much of his time is given to the real-estate business, which has proven very profit-

able, and he has made some of the largest deals of any one man in the State, buying 12,000 acres of land at one time. He owns 20,000 acres of land in Arkansas County, which is for sale. Socially, he is a member of Euclid Lodge No. 130, A. F. & A. M. He was married in this county May 3, 1873, to Miss Sallie L. Crockett, a daughter of Col. R. H. Crockett, and by her has the following family of children: Mabel (attending Galloway College), William Mack, Cecil C., Herbert and Ernest (attending the Stuttgart Normal Institute). Mr. Price has always been interested in the advancement of schools, and is giving his children the best advantages to be had. He is president of the college board.

Benjamin F. Quertermous began life for himself at the age of sixteen as a farm hand. In 1857 he came to Arkansas and located in Arkansas County, and two years later was appointed deputy county clerk, which position he held until the opening of the war, when he enlisted in the Seventh Arkansas Battalion, being made third lieutenant of Company I. After the battle of Shiloh he was transferred to the Trans-Mississippi Department, and was promoted to first lieutenant of the Twenty-sixth Arkansas Infantry, participating in the battles of Prairie Grove, Pleasant Hill and a number of others. When peace had been declared he returned home and again served as deputy clerk until the reconstruction. In 1874 he was elected to the office of clerk of the court and was re-elected in 1876. In 1880, after a successful official career, he engaged in the mercantile business at Crockett's Bluff, where he has since lived. Mr. Quertermous was born in Meade County, Ky., in 1841, to the union of John W. and Elizabeth (Roson) Quertermous, of Kentucky and Virginia birth, respectively. John W. Quertermous was born near Louisville, Ky., in 1796. They removed to Arkansas in 1859, and located in this county, where he died in 1867, and his wife four years later. The principal of this sketch was married in 1884 to Lillie Cannon, daughter of D. S. and Josephine Cannon. She died in 1885, and in October, 1888, Mr. Quertermous married a sister of his first wife, and who is the mother of one daughter. Mrs.

Quertermous is a member of the Methodist Episcopal Church. Her husband has always voted the Democratic ticket, and cast his first presidential vote for Greeley in 1872. He has been very successful in business; starting on a small capital, he now carries a stock of over $5,000, and has a trade which will aggregate $16,000 per annum.

John W. Scott, who ably represents the prominent merchants and stock dealers of Arkansas County, is a native of Ohio, where his parents located on coming to this country from England. Launcelot and Jane (Clark) Scott, had a family of ten children. After emigrating to America, in 1831, they first stopped at Pottsville, Penn., but a year later chose a home in Ohio, where they lived until their deaths, that of the father occurring in 1852 at the age of fifty years, and the mother in 1888 at the age of sixty-seven. Mr. Scott was a coal operator by occupation, and was an educated man, holding the position of school director for a number of years in the Buckeye State. He and his wife were members of the Methodist Episcopal Church. John W. Scott was born in Athens County, Ohio, on September 26, 1838. After having received a good education at the common schools of his native county, he attended the Ohio University, and was married on May 16, 1868, to Elizabeth M. Brett, who died September, 1879. The following year he removed to Arkansas and settled in Arkansas County, where he shortly after became acquainted with and married a Miss Kingsberry. She died in August, 1885, leaving two children, Martha J. and John D., both living. He married his third and present wife, Ormitta Couch, on December 3, 1885. To them three children have been born, but only one survives, Hallie M. Mr. Scott is one of the leading merchants of Bayou Meto, and also owns a fine farm of eighty acres, mostly under cultivation. He is highly respected as a prominent and influential citizen of his township, enjoying the utmost confidence of the citizens, as is shown by the fact of his having held the position of justice of the peace for five years, and elected school director of his district, and is the present postmaster of the village, serving in this capacity for nearly two years. He is a member of the Ma-

sonic order, and he and wife are connected with the Baptist Church.

John W. Stephen is a native of this county, and a son of Henry K. Stephen, who was born in Cocke County, Tenn., on November 6, 1809. Removing to Clark County, Ill., he was married there to Sallie Sanders, of Indiana, and later came to Arkansas County, Ark., in January, 1844, where she died leaving one daughter, Charlotte E., wife of J. H. Merritt. He was married the second time to Amanda Maxwell, also a native of Indiana, in 1848. Upon locating in this county Mr. Stephen was engaged in the practice of medicine for sixteen years. He also held the office of county sheriff several years, and was a prominent man of the community. He died in April, 1881. His wife still survives him, and is the mother of six children, four of whom are living: Sarah Angeline (now Mrs. McGahhey), Joseph E., John W. and Katie J. (now the wife of E. H. Childers). John W. Stephen was born on June 11, 1858, and was married to Annie McGahhey, in July, 1881. They are the parents of five children: Normly, Arcola, Lenoire, Melissia, John L. and Lecil B. Mr. Stephen owns 364 acres of fine farming land, of which 125 acres are under cultivation; he also has a good cotton-gin. He is a member of the County Wheel and of the County Grange, in which he has held the office of Secretary. He is the present postmaster of De Luce, and has discharged the duties of this position for two years. He is a prominent Democrat in his county, and a highly respected citizen. Mr. Stephen's father, Henry K. Stephen, was a member of the Christian Church at the time of his death. Politically a Whig during the life of that party, he was afterward a Democrat.

Brian M. Stephens, intimately associated with the affairs of this county as farmer, ginner and stock raiser of Crockett Township, was a son of Dr. Brian M. Stephens and Julia Ann (Earnest) Stephens, natives of Virginia and Tennessee, respectively. They lived in the Old Dominion until our subject was about nine years of age, then moving to Tennessee. Dr. Stephens was also a son of Brian M. Stephens, a wealthy Virginia planter,

who was a son of one of the early colonists of that
State. Brian M. Stephens, Jr., was born in Frederick County, Va., in 1839, as the second son of a
family of ten children, three of whom are still living. He received a good common-school education, and had just entered Washington College,
Tennessee, at the breaking out of the war, when,
leaving his studies, he enlisted in the Confederate
army, in Company A of the Third Tennessee Infantry, known after the fall of Vicksburg as the
Third Tennessee Mounted Infantry. He participated in the battles of Bull Run, Perryville, siege
of Vicksburg, and a number of others. In 1866
he came to Arkansas, and in 1869 was married to
Miss Martha J. Ferguson, daughter of Hon. Austin H. Ferguson, and a sister of William F. Ferguson, whose biography appears in this work.
Mr. Stephens soon engaged in farming near Crockett's Bluff, and now has a farm of 160 acres, with
about 100 acres under cultivation, also owning a
good steam gin. He and wife are members of the
Methodist Episcopal Church. He belongs to the
I. O. O. F.

J. Harold Stillwell, of the substantial firm of
H. & W. J. Stillwell, the largest mercantile house
at Arkansas Post, was born in 1853, being the
son of Asher H. and Caroline (Maxwell) Stillwell. Asher Stillwell was born in 1819, the son
of Harold Stillwell; he was a prominent farmer
and stock raiser of Arkansas County all his life,
and held public office at different times, including
that of county surveyor. His death occurred in
1873, his wife having preceded him in 1857.
Harold Stillwell was probably born in the State of
New Jersey, but accompanied his father, Joseph
Stillwell, to Arkansas, in 1796, when the country
was under Spanish rule. Harold held the office of
sheriff of the Arkansas District, after the ceding
of the Louisiana Territory to the United States,
being the first sheriff ever appointed in the territory of this present State. The principal of this
biography was the first son in the family, consisting of two boys and two girls, all living. He began to earn his own livelihood at the age of twenty,
by clerking in a store, and in 1879 he and Mr.
Champion opened up a business house at Arkansas

Post, which they continued until 1881. Mr. Stillwell then retired from the business. J. Harold
Stillwell and his brother W. J. Stillwell, opened a
store at Arkansas Post, in 1883, under the firm
name of H. & W. J. Stillwell. They also own and
operate a store at Stanley, which W. J. Stillwell
has under his charge. Mr. Stillwell was married
in 1880 to Miss Ada Quertermous, of Kentucky
origin. They are the parents of six children, three
of whom are still living. He has been postmaster
of Arkansas Post since 1885, and is a stanch Democrat in politics. Mrs. Stillwell is a member of
the Christian Church.

Col. John A. Thompson is worthy of mention
as an influential citizen of Arkansas County. His
father, Alexander Thompson, was born in Virginia
in 1800, and was reared and educated in that State,
but in 1826 removed to Missouri, settling in Monroe County. He was married in 1822 to Miss
Margaret W. McKee, whose birth occurred in Mercer County, Tenn., in 1803–04. They were the
parents of three children, John A. (the youngest)
making his appearance in Monroe County, Mo.,
on January 23, 1831. His paternal grandfather
came from Ireland to America in 1778, with two
brothers, having been exiled and their property
confiscated by the Crown for participation in the
Irish Rebellion of that year. In 1849 Mr. Thompson went to California to look for gold and three
years later returned with his pockets well filled.
Going to Harrodsburg, Ky., he engaged in the mercantile business and remained until 1855, when
he exchanged his business and trade for real estate
in Monroe County, Mo. He was married shortly
before leaving Kentucky to Miss Jennie R. Lawrence, daughter of Samuel and Eliza Lawrence.
She died in July, 1856, leaving one child, which
survived but two months. Mr. Thompson was
married three years later to Henrietta Harrison
Greenwade, also a Kentuckian. In 1856 he moved
to Audrain County, Mo., where he resumed farming
until 1861, when the war broke out and he joined
the Confederate service, enlisting in the Missouri
State Militia. He soon received a commission as
lieutenant-colonel, and was assigned to the northern part of the State on recruiting duty, serving

throughout the war and taking part in a number of battles and skirmishes. In 1863 he was sent to Kentucky on recruiting duty, where he enlisted several hundred men. After the war he returned to his farm, which he found in a very bad state, all of his improvements, consisting of a good dwelling house, several tenement houses, and other buildings, having been destroyed, and his two negroes set free and gone. In 1875 he sold out and went to Colorado and embarked in sheep raising until 1883, when he returned to Missouri and carried on the same business. Two years later he came to Arkansas and located in this county, opening up a hardware store at Stuttgart; this he successfully conducted until quite recently, when he retired from active business life. Col. Thompson is a liberal donator to all enterprises for the advancement of the county or State, and is one of Stuttgart's best-known citizens.

John H. Walton, M. D., who ranks among the representative physicians of Arkansas County, was born and reared here, and at the age of twenty-one commenced the study of medicine under Dr. Morgan, a graduate of the Louisville Medical University, and a very successful physician. In 1875 he entered the Louisville Medical College, from which he graduated in 1882, subsequently returning to this county, where he has since practiced with encouraging success. Dr. Walton married Miss Ada Butler, a native of Mississippi, who died in 1884, leaving one daughter, Mary J. In politics the Doctor is Democratic. He is a member of the A. F. & A. M. Dr. Walton was born on March 24, 1853, within five miles of the place where he now lives, being the son of J. R. Walton, a resident of Austin, Lonoke County. The latter was born in Burke County, Ga., in 1813, and moved to Arkansas County, Ark., in 1835. He has lived in this State ever since and is a citizen of acknowledged worth and influence. He is a Royal Arch Mason.

Joe Webster is the son of Henry Webster, a native of England, who was born in 1813 and was married in that country, where he lived until about 1840. Then he emigrated to America and settled in Philadelphia, at which place he married his second wife, formerly Miss R. E. Lamborn, a native of Pennsylvania, and a daughter of Jonathan and Rachel Lamborn. They were the parents of three sons and one daughter, three of whom are still living, two in Pennsylvania, and one, the principal of this sketch, in Arkansas. Mr. Webster was engaged in the manufacturing business in Pennsylvania, until his death, in 1871. His wife still survives him and is now in her seventy-seventh year. Joe Webster was born in Chester County, Pennsylvania, on October 28, 1843. In 1866 he came to Arkansas and located at Pine Bluff, where he lived about one year and went to Arkansas County, where he was married one year later to Mary A. Montgomery, of Tennessee nativity, and a daughter of James G. and Rebecca J. Montgomery. They have a family of nine children: Effie, Frank, Della, Birtie and Edna (twins), Jennie, Harry, Louie and Ernest. Mr. Webster owns a fine farm of half a section of land, with forty acres under cultivation and well stocked, and is also engaged in the mercantile business. Though starting with but $500 he now carries a stock of goods invoicing $3,000, all of which he has made since coming to this State. He filled the office of county surveyor for four years, and has been the postmaster of Bayou Meto for twelve years. Mr. and Mrs. Webster are members of the Methodist Episcopal Church, South, in which they take an active part.

Morris D. Williams is the efficient postmaster of Goldman Station and was born in Wales in 1825, being a son of Daniel and Eleanor (Williams) Williams, the former a native of that country and a stone mason by trade, also a farmer, stock raiser and dairyman. To himself and wife, who was also born in Wales, a family of ten children were born, six sons and four daughters, of whom eight are now living: Thomas, Robert, Morris, Abiah, John A. (ex-circuit judge of Pine Bluff, Ark.), Elizabeth (wife of William Wright, of New York), Margaret (wife of Rollin Pridard, of Dakota) and Catherine (wife of William Roberts, of Missouri). Mary is deceased. Daniel Williams removed with his family from Wales to the United States in 1829, and landed in New York, locating in Oneida County of that State, where he engaged in farming and stock raising. He was a member of the Methodist Episcopal Church and died in full communion with this church in 1876, his demise occurring in the State of New York. His wife also belonged to that church, and died in 1880. Morris D. Williams was married in the State of New York, in 1865, to Miss Martha E. Thompson, a daughter of Abicutt and Axie Thompson, and their union resulted in the birth of one child: Maurice S. After the mother's death, which occurred in 1883, Mr. Williams resolved to emigrate westward, and in 1888 came to Arkansas and settled in Arkansas County, and was first engaged in hay pressing, being one of the leading dealers in hay in this section of the country, and this season (1889) put up about 150 tons of pressed hay. Since the election of Gen. Harrison to the presidency he has been postmaster of Goldman. He was a participant in the late war, having enlisted in the Heavy Artillery, Fifth New York, in 1862, but owing to poor health was compelled to give up service at about the end of six months. He was first lieutenant of Company I, Newport Artillery, and had circumstances permitted would have made a gallant soldier.

J. J. Woolfolk, who has been engaged in the mercantile business at St. Charles for a number of years, is a native of Georgia, and a son of Robert H. and Nancy (Beal) Woolfolk. Robert H. Woolfolk was a merchant of Augusta, Ga., and died when our subject was but one year old. His mother then removed to Alabama, and settled on a farm, but a few years later she married James N. Smith, of Mississippi. J. J. Woolfolk was born in Augusta, January 19, 1837, and was reared principally in Mississippi. Coming to Arkansas in 1857, he was employed as clerk in a store until the breaking out of the war, when he enlisted in the First Arkansas Infantry, and was wounded in the battle of Shiloh and captured. He was taken to Camp Butler, Illinois, where he was confined three months, and then exchanged. After the war, returning to St. Charles, Mr. Woolfolk was again employed as clerk for some time. He married Mrs. Wakefield (nee Leonia Willis), a native of this county, and

has had a family of seven children, six of whom are living: Maggie, John J., Robert H., Sallie, Jessie and Cassa. Mr. Woolfolk is in partnership with J. Alexander in merchandising. They carry a large stock of goods, and have a trade of about $60,000 per year. He is a Democrat in politics, and a popular citizen, meriting richly the success to which he has attained. He is an extensive land owner, having several farms, most of them under cultivation, and is said to be worth $100,000. Mr. Woolfolk and wife and children are members of the Methodist Episcopal Church.

James Word is a native of Alabama, and a son of William and Elizabeth (Bransford) Word, whose birthplace was in South Carolina. After William Word had moved to Alabama, his wife died, in 1849, and seven years later he came to Arkansas, settling near Crockett's Bluff, where he was killed in 1868, during the reconstruction. He was of English and Scotch descent, and had been a member of the I. O. O. F. for a number of years. James Word was born in Limestone County, Ala., in 1838. During the war he served over four years in the Confederate army, and participated in the battles of Bull Run, Shiloh, Murfreesboro, Chickamauga, Missionary Ridge, and a number of others. He served in the Army of Tennessee, then in Price's raid through Missouri, and after the battle of Murfreesboro was transferred to the Trans-Mississippi Division. He was wounded at the battle of Shiloh, and was captured in December, 1864, and imprisoned at Pine Bluff three months, following which he was taken to Little Rock, where he was held until the close of the war. Mr. Word was married in 1867, to Miss Kate Inman, who died in 1868. Two years later he married Miss Elizabeth Jelks, of Tennessee birth, who came to Arkansas with her parents in 1855. Mr. Word owns a fine farm of 700 acres, with 165 under cultivation, which he has made by his own efforts. He is one of the leading Democrats of his township, and a highly respected citizen.

Benjamin N. Word, a leading and prominent merchant of De Witt, came to Arkansas with his parents at the age of thirteen, and was reared to agricultural pursuits. Enlisting in the Confederate service at the opening of the war, he served until the close, and was in a number of hard-fought battles. On his return from the army he was appointed deputy sheriff, which position he filled until 1872. In 1878 he was elected to the same office for a term of four years, and in 1884 was elected clerk of the circuit court. While not filling public positions, Mr. Word has been engaged in the mercantile business, or in farming and stock raising. He is now occupied in the grocery trade, and is having a large and growing patronage. He was married on February 12, 1870, to Miss Ida Hutchinson, a native of Madison County, Tenn. They are the parents of five children: William N., James, Benjamin N., Mabel and Herbert. Mr. and Mrs. Word are members of the Methodist Episcopal Church, in which they take an active part. He was born in Limestone County, Ala., on September 18, 1840, his father being William Word, and his mother Elizabeth Bransford. Mr. Word has a brother, James Word, who lives in this county, and whose biography precedes this.

William Joseph Wright, originally from Ireland, emigrated to this country in 1846, locating in Vermont. His father, Frank Wright, was reared and educated in England, and joined the English army, in which he was soon promoted to the rank of colonel for his bravery. He was in the English army during the Revolutionary War, and led the "Twentieth Foot Regiment" at the battle of Waterloo. His wife, Mary (Hopkins) Wright, also of Ireland, was the mother of five children. William J. moved from Vermont to Kentucky in 1847, and was engaged in steamboating on the Mississippi, between Louisville, St. Louis and New Orleans, until 1852, when he was employed on railroads in different parts of the country for several years. In 1879 he bought land in Texas and engaged in farming for two years, after which, coming to Arkansas, he located at Pine Bluff, where he took a position as foreman in the shops of the Cotton Belt Railroad. He has been in the employ of that road for about seven years in various capacities, part of the time as contractor and for a time as conductor, his long experience quali-

fying him for almost any position. Mr. Wright married Miss Bridget Martin, also a native of Ireland, and they are the parents of twelve children, five living: Mary (wife of Joe Woodland, foreman of the car department of the Cotton Belt Railroad, residing at Pine Bluff), Charlotte (wife of Alexander Frenitell, also of Pine Bluff, and who holds the position of master car builder for the above railroad), Frank (an engineer on the Trans-Continental), William and Henry (both engineers on the same road). Mrs. Wright died in 1876, in the State of Mississippi, where they had resided for a short time. In 1888 Mr. Wright gave up the railroad life, in which he had been engaged nearly all his life, and bought a tract of land consisting of 760 acres, partially prairie land and the balance finely timbered. The average purchase price of this was $7.50 per acre. Since then he has sold all of the land, but forty acres of timber, at an average of $20 per acre. Subsequently purchasing the New Hampshire House, at Stuttgart, he has since improved it, making it the leading house in the county. Mr. Wright's second wife was Miss Annie M. Rowley, a native of Connecticut and of Irish descent. They have five children living: Aradeneck, Albert, Jessie, Charles and Vennefred. He is a member of the A. F. & A. M. and of the I. O. O. F. Mr. Wright, wife and children are members of the Catholic Church.

John Young, a well-known farmer of LaGrue Township, is a native of this county and a son of James and Sarena (Barkman) Young, natives of Kentucky and Arkansas, respectively. Mr. Young came to Arkansas when he was a young man, entering a tract of wild land in the Arkansas forests of this county. He was a man of slight education, his opportunities having been very limited, but he was enterprising, and an earnest worker in the Methodist Episcopal Church, to which he and his wife belonged, being a leading member in organizing the early churches of this community, not only those of his denomination, but of other religious bodies. He died in 1850, and his wife followed him in a short time. They were the parents of four children: Jacob (deceased), Sciney (deceased), Angelina B. (now Mrs. Brown) and John.

The subject of this sketch was born on January 3, 1838, and was married on November 27, 1859, to Miss Sarah E. Brown, also of this State, and a daughter of Pleasant and Elizabeth Brown. Mrs. Young died in January 22, 1889, leaving the following children: John P., Elizabeth (now Mrs. Duemore), Minnie (who married John Mitchell), Robert L., Bashia A., Effie M. and Henry L. Mr. Young enlisted in the Confederate army in 1862, and served until November, 1864, participating in a number of hard-fought battles, though he was never wounded nor captured. He owns a farm of 900 acres of fine land, and has about forty acres in cultivation. He is a member of the County Grange, and also of the County Wheel, in which he takes an active part. His wife was a member of the Methodist Episcopal Church, and well known in religious circles.

CHAPTER XXIII.

PRAIRIE COUNTY—HISTORY OF SETTLEMENT—ACT OF ORGANIZATION—PUBLIC STRUCTURES—CENTERS OF
JUDICIARY AFFAIRS—JUDICIAL DISTRICTS—COURTS—NAMES OF OFFICIAL INCUMBENTS—
POLITICAL HISTORY—LOCATION, TOPOGRAPHY, ETC.—PHYSICAL FEATURES—
SOIL AND PRODUCTIONS—RAILROADS—AGRICULTURAL WHEEL—
CIVIL WAR ITEMS—VALUATION AND TAXATIONS
TOWNS AND VILLAGES—PUBLIC SCHOOL SYS-
TEM—CHURCH ORGANIZATIONS—
PERSONAL SKETCHES.

Oft did the harvest to their sickle yield;
Their furrow oft the stubborn glebe has broke;
How jocund did they drive their team afield!
How bow'd the woods beneath their sturdy stroke!—*Gray*.

RAIRIE COUNTY'S earliest settlement, or the first in the territory now embraced within its limits, was probably made at and in the vicinity of the present Des Arc. About the year 1810 two men named Watts and East (Creoles) settled there, and five years later the Runkles, Coburns and Goforths, from Vincennes, Ind., also located. The latter parties came up the White River in dugouts. These were followed by the McAnultys and others. Formerly nearly all of the present county of Lonoke belonged to Prairie County, consequently it is proper to mention a few of the first settlers of that portion of the original county. In 1822 James Erwin, father of M. M. and Ambrose Erwin (now of Des Arc) came from North Carolina with the Furgesons and Dunaways and settled at Old Aus-

tin. Subsequently Daniel Farr, Jacob Gray, Sr., Robert Anderson and E. E. Dismukes settled in the vicinity of Brownsville, the first county seat of Prairie County. John Percifiell, Sr., or Percifull, settled a few miles east thereof. John Percifull, Jr., is the oldest man born in Prairie County, and M. M. Erwin is the next. Percifull remains in that portion of the country set off to form Lonoke, and Erwin lives at Des Arc.

Charles G. Harris was the first settler at Hickory Plains, and the next early pioneers there and in that vicinity were Dudley Glass, from Alabama, David Royster, from Virginia, and A. B. Taylor and his son-in-law, Ben. T. Embree, from Kentucky. This settlement began about the year 1846. C. S. De Vall, from Georgia and Capt. Patrick H. Wheat, the latter now of Lonoke County, were early settlers at De Vall's Bluff. Among the first settlers in the southern part of the county were Albert Evans, Sheffield Mayberry, Dr. Gibbon and Richard Pyburn. Mayberry is living at this writing. William C. Hazen was the pioneer settler in what is now the town of Hazen, and William Dedman settled on the military road, three miles south of Hazen. William McCuin was a pioneer settler in the central part of the county. The first settlers in the southwest part, near Fairmont, were Joseph Stillwell, Thomas Belcher, the Harrises and Maj. Tisdell. In the northwest part of the county, as now formed, Patton Harris, the Farrs, William Johnson, Robert Travis and some of the Bogards were among the original settlers. The pioneers of the county came mostly from the Carolinas, Tennessee, Georgia, Alabama and Mississippi.

Prairie County was organized in accordance with an act of the legislature, approved by Gov. Thomas S. Drew, November 25, 1846. The first section of the act reads as follows: " That all that part of the county of Pulaski lying east of the following described lines, viz.: Beginning at the corner of Townships 2 and 3 south, Ranges 9 and 10 west; thence east to the middle of Range 9; thence north to the line between Townships 1 and 2 south; thence west to the line between Ranges 9 and 10; thence north to the line between Townships 4 and 5 north; thence west to the line between Ranges 10 and 11 west; thence north to the Cypress Bayou, to the line dividing White and Pulaski, be and the same hereby is erected into and declared to be a separate and distinct county, to be called and known by the name of Prairie County."

Section 4 provided that on the first Monday of February, 1847, an election should be held in each township in the new county for the election of county officers; the elections to be held where the last general elections had been held, and by the same judges and clerks. A subsequent act provided that at these elections one commissioner in each township, and two at large in the county, should be elected to locate the seat of justice.

It will be seen by the first section of the act creating the county that nearly all of the territory now embraced in Lonoke County was included in Prairie County. Subsequent acts, one creating Lonoke County, in 1873, and others changing boundary lines, have reduced Prairie County to its present dimensions.

The commissioners elected for the purpose, at the first election held in the county, located the seat of justice at Brownsville, a point in what is now Lonoke County, two and a half miles northeast of the present city of Lonoke. This place was on the old military road, leading from Memphis to Little Rock. Ordinary county buildings were erected at Brownsville, and the clerk's office there was burned in September, 1852, together with a portion of the early county records. The seat of justice remained at its original site until 1868, when it was moved to De Vall's Bluff, where it continued until 1875, then being moved to Des Arc, where it now remains. The last term of the county court held at Brownsville was in April, 1868, and the first term held at DeVall's Bluff was in July, of that year. The last term of this court held at DeVall's Bluff was in July, 1875, and the first term held at Des Arc was in October, of the same year. While the county seat was at DeVall's Bluff the old wooden building standing on the bank of White River, which was erected by the Government in the winter of 1864–65 for officers' quarters, was utilized for a court house. The public buildings at Des Arc consist of a court house and jail. The former is a large two-story brick building, with a hall and offices on the first floor, and the court-room on the second. It was erected in 1883, by Messrs. Horne and White, and cost the county about $8,000. The jail is a small wooden structure, standing also on the public square with the court house.

In 1885 Prairie County was divided into two judicial districts, the Northern and Southern; the first being composed of the townships of Upper Surrounded Hill, Calhoun, Des Arc, Hickory Plains, Union, Bullard and White River; the second, or Southern, of the townships of Wattensas, Belcher, Tyler, Lower Surrounded Hill, Rockrow, Center and Hazen. De Vall's Bluff is the seat of justice for the Southern district, and there the county occupies a rented building for a court room, and a branch of the county clerk's office.

At Des Arc the courts convene as follows: County, on the first Mondays of January, April, July and October of each year; the probate, on the third, and the common pleas on the fourth Mondays of the same months; the circuit, on the first Mondays of March and September. At De Vall's Bluff the probate court convenes on the first Mondays of February, May, August and November; the common pleas on the second Mondays of the same months; and the circuit on the sixth Monday after the third Monday of February and August.

The Prairie County legal bar is composed of the following named attorneys: J. J. Ball, R. A. Moore, De Arcy Vaughan, J. G. Thweatt and J. M. McClintock.

The following is a list of the names of the officers of Prairie County, from its organization to the present writing, with dates of terms of service annexed:

Judges: W. S. Scroggs, 1846–48; H. Reynolds, 1848–52; J. Evans, 1852–54; J. S. Hunt, 1854–56; W. J. Rogers, 1856–58; J. S. Hunt, 1858–64; W. Sanders, 1864–66; E. L. Beard, 1866–68; C. K. Morton, 1868–72; board of supervisors, 1872–74; A. O. Edwards, 1874–76; W. M. Warren, 1876–78; W. L. Kirk, 1878–80; H. P. Vaughan, 1880–82; J. S. Thomas, 1882–88; J. M. Dorris, present judge, elected in 1888.

Clerks: E. M. Williams, 1846–54; W. H. England, 1854, to his death; then William Goodrum, balance of England's term, and till 1864; Robert Dodson, 1864–66; William Goodrum, 1866–68; L. Bilheimer, 1868–72; J. E. England, 1872–74; C. B. Mills, 1874–82; W. L. Willeford, present incumbent, elected in 1882, serving continuously since.

Sheriffs: A. Barksdale, 1846–48; J. A. Barksdale, 1848–52; E. E. Dismukes, 1852–58; J. M. King, 1858–60; W. A. Plunket, 1860–62; J. M. King, 1862–64; J. R. Gray, 1864–68; J. M. McClintock, 1868–72; J. J. Booth, 1872–74; H. O. Williams, 1874–78; A. S. Reinhardt, 1878–88; J. W. Brians, present officer, elected in 1888.

Treasurers: J. Percifull, 1846–48; W. Sanders, 1848–52; W. H. England, 1852–54; A. Tipkin, 1854–56; J. Robinson, 1856–58; L. Byram, 1858, to his death; W. Langford, balance of Byram's term and till 1862; George Hallum, 1862–64;

William Griffin, 1864–66; F. M. Griffin, 1866–68; R. Dingsdale, 1868–72; H. Brown, 1872–76; J. R. Reid, 1876–78; H. Brown, 1878–80; W. J. Frith, 1880–82; E. A. Winslow, 1882–84; H. R. Ward, 1884–88; S. R. Mason, present incumbent, elected in 1888.

Coroners: H. Avery, 1846–48; T. Furlow, 1848–50; C. Harvey, 1850–52; N. Kennedy, 1852–56: Benjamin Faucett, 1856–58; J. N. Henderson, 1858–60; L. Harrison, 1860–62; J. H. Quisenberry, 1862–64; Whit Kinidy, 1866–68; C. P. Landon, 1868–72; J. A. Woolen, 1872–74; J. G. Becton, 1874–78; J. B. Jamison, 1878–84; J. R. Mallory, 1884–88; William Dixon, present incumbent, elected in 1888.

Surveyors: P. Horton, 1846–48; S. J. Ragan, 1848–50; J. W. Utley, 1850–54; K. H. Williford, 1854–58; E. R. McPherson, 1858–60; E. A. Howell, 1860–62; J. R. Alexander, 1862–64; W. D. Anthony, 1866–68; C. W. Richardson, 1868–72; W. Fishburn, 1872–74; E. K. McPherson, 1874–76, R. A. Richmond, 1876–88; N. C. Dodson, present incumbent, elected in 1888.

Assessors: W. S. McCullough, 1868–74; G. J. Rubell, 1874–78; J. G. Worsham, 1878–80; T. A. Canon, 1880–82; William Homer, 1882–84; W. R. Brown, 1884–88; R. Dindsdall, present incumbent, elected in 1888.

Delegates in State conventions: 1861, B. C. Totton; 1868, Robert S. Gantt and William F. Hicks; 1874, David F. Reinhardt.

Representatives in General Assembly—James Erwin, 1848–50; B. T. Embry, 1850–52; B. C. Totton, 1852–54; E. M. Williams, 1854–56; William I. Moore, 1856–58; Hamilton Reynolds, 1858–60; John C. Davis, 1860–62; B. M. Barnes, 1862 * * * ; W. T. Jones, 1866–68. Prairie and Arkansas Counties—G. M. French, Isaac Ayers, W. S. McCullough and T. M. Gibson, 1868–70; same counties, F. R. Wiley, George H. Joslin, B. C. Morgan and A. O. Espy, 1870–72; P. C. Dooley, 1872–74. Prairie, Arkansas and Lonoke—J. P. Eagle, L. B. Mitchell and M. M. Erwin, 1872–74; J. D. Booe, 1874–76; J. S. Thomas, 1876–80; J. G. Thweatt, 1880–82; R. B. Carl Lee, 1882–86; J. D. Booe, 1886–88.

B. M. Barnes represented Prairie County in the Confederate legislature, held at Washington, in Hempstead County, from September 22 to October 2, 1864.

The votes cast in Prairie County for the candidates for Governor at the September election, in 1888, and for the candidates for President, at the November election, in the same year, were as follows: For Governor—James P. Eagle (Dem), 761; C. M. Norwood (Com. Opp.), 1,125. For President—Cleveland (Dem.), 761; Harrison (Rep.), 603; Streeter (United Labor), 165; Fiske (Prohibition), 15.

The population of Prairie County, in 1880, was 5,691 white and 2,734 colored, making a total of 8,425. It is now probably over 10,000.

Prairie County, Ark., lies in the east central portion of the State, and is bounded north by White and Woodruff Counties, east by Woodruff and Monroe Counties, south by Arkansas and west by Lonoke. The thirty-fifth parallel of north latitude passes through the northern part, and the county lies in the 92d° of longitude west from Greenwich.

It has an area of 650 square miles or 416,000 acres, one-fourth of the entire area being under fence and in cultivation. The whole county is level, undulating and rolling enough to admit of free and easy drainage, and not to wash, no hills and hollows, no gullies and ravines, no rock-cursed farms, not even a stone to become the instrument between the bad boy and the family cat. (Hon. J. G. Thweatt's description.) A large percentage of the lands of the county belongs to the State, and is subject to donation to actual settlers; a similar amount belongs to railroad companies, a very small amount to the United States, and the balance to individuals. Lands can be purchased at reasonable prices, but large tracts of the best lands are owned by non-resident speculators who hold the prices high enough to measureably retard immigration. However, there are plenty of tracts that may be secured from resident owners at prices that cannot fail to suit purchasers.

White River flows southerly and southeasterly through the northeast part of the county to a point about two-thirds of the distance from its northern boundary, and for the other third it forms the eastern boundary thereof. Cypress Bayou forms the west half of the northern boundary, and flowing thence easterly, it empties into White River near the southeast corner of Township 5 north, Range 5 west. Wattensas River enters the county from the west, and running easterly, bearing a little south, it empties into White River about twelve miles below the mouth of the Cypress Bayou. Cache River swings into the county and out again a little north of the center of its eastern boundary, and Bayou DeView, a tributary of the Cache, flows southeasterly across the northeast corner of the county. LaGrue River enters the county on the west, near the center north and south, and flows thence in a southeasterly direction to its confluence with White River. Bayou Two Prairie forms the southwestern boundary line of the county; and this and the other streams mentioned, together with their tributaries, furnish abundant drainage.

Between White and Cache Rivers there is a long tract of land slightly elevated above the river bottoms, and divided by a depression into two parts, the northern being called "Upper Surrounded Hill," and the southern "Lower Surrounded Hill." The extracts immediately following are from a description of the county prepared by Hon. J. G. Thweatt, attorney and abstractor of titles at De Vall's Bluff.

The prairie lands lie mostly south of a dividing line east and west through the county, and constitute a good portion of the Grand Prairie of Arkansas, which reaches out into other adjacent counties. There are three or four small, but rich, productive prairies lying in the northern portion of the county, with an area of 800 to 5,000 acres each. These lands are very rich and productive, and seem specially adapted to small grains of all kinds and tame grasses. They grow fine corn and splendid cotton. As fine fruit as the country produces can be found in the orchards on prairie farms. They grow fine vegetables of all kinds. The most of the untilled portion of the prairie is covered with a fine growth of wild grass, which is mowed, baled and shipped to market. The haying business here on the prairie is carried on very extensively. Thousands of tons are shipped yearly, and a great deal of money made at it. No lands are better adapted to stock raising. They furnish a natural range from the first or middle of March till fall. A few years ago these lands knew no occupant save the wild deer and semi-wild herds of cattle, and were regarded by the Southerner as worthless for agricultural purposes, but when the tidal wave of immigration began to flow from north to south, and the progressive husbandman of the Northwestern Prairies commenced to settle and develop the prairie lands of Prairie County, then that once considered trackless, treeless waste of grass lands, wherever touched by the agricultural magician, began to astonish the natives with her golden harvest fields, fruit-laden orchards and mammoth vegetable products, and to-day they are more in demand than any lands of the State, and are worth from twice to three times as much as the forest lands of Prairie County.

The county has a diversity of soil, the productiveness of which is exceedingly good. White River bottoms and the Surrounded Hills have both a dark brown and alluvial soil, very rich and fertile. The creek and branch bottoms are a dark loam, next in productiveness to the river bottoms. The ridges or uplands not covered by creek or branch bottoms are of a light brown, often dark in color and very productive. The soil of the prairie is of a dark brownish color, possessed of chemical combinations peculiar to itself. It does not produce as fine cotton as the timbered lands, but grows much finer wheat and oats, rye, tame grasses, peas, etc. The uplands, prairie and even branch and creek bottoms can, by rotation of crops and proper use of home fertilizers, be made better and more prolific every year. They are susceptible of a high state of fertilization, and will, when once fertilized, show effects of same for years.

The woodland part of the county is well and heavily timbered. In the river and creek bottoms is found an superabundance of red gum or satin wood, which will yield in some localities 30,000 feet of timber per acre; though millions of feet of white oak in the shape of staves and square timber

have been shipped from the bottoms of Prairie County, yet the supply is still unexhausted. There is some walnut, a great deal of hickory, ash, maple, pecan, sycamore, cottonwood, red elm, hackberry, etc., with an undergrowth of cane, pawpaw, tar blanket, grape and muscatine vines, rattan, etc. In the branch bottoms and on the uplands may be had white oak, hickory, red and black oak, sweet gum, black gum and in some upland localities immense brakes of post oak, some maple, red bud, persimmon, with an undergrowth of sumac, whortleberry, hazelnut, dogwood, etc.

According to the United States census of 1880, there were in Prairie County 1,127 farms, with 37,032 acres of improved lands, and the value of the farm products of the county for 1879 was $462,902, the following being the amount of the several products raised: Indian corn, 135,462 bushels; oats, 31,944 bushels; wheat, 2,214 bushels; orchard products, $9,465; hay, 263 tons; cotton, 6,977 bales; Irish potatoes, 2,100 bushels; sweet potatoes, 9,359 bushels; tobacco, 4,860 pounds. Great improvements have been made since 1880, which will appear when the census of 1890 shall be taken. Cotton is the staple product and next to it is Indian corn. The yield per acre depends very much upon the skill of the farmer. With scientific cultivation of the soil it can be made to produce from 50 to 100 per cent more than it does under the present modes of farming. Clover and the tame grasses succeed well, but these have been cultivated only to a limited extent.

The number of live stock in the county as shown by the census of 1880 was as follows: Horses, 1,525; mules and asses, 997; neat cattle, 11,008; sheep, 1,208; hogs, 15,673. The number of these animals in the county as shown by the tax books, for 1888, was: Horses, 2,640; mules and asses, 1,164; cattle, 14,111; sheep, 1,437; hogs, 7,546. These figures show a large increase in all except hogs. The comparison for the latter, however, is not fair, for the reason that in 1888 none were enumerated except those on hand when the property was listed for taxation, while those given in the census report included all raised during the year. The climate being very mild and water easily obtain-

able in abundant supply, Prairie County is especially well adapted to the raising of live stock, and recently a few individuals have begun the business
and have large herds of cattle grazing on the
prairies. This is becoming a leading industry.
Hogs fatten on the mast and live through the year
without being fed, but they are not extensively
raised. Fruits grow almost to perfection, especially
peaches, plums, pears, quinces, grapes and berries
of every variety. Apples also do well, but not so
well as in higher altitudes. Wild fruits, such as
grapes, plums, mulberries, blackberries, etc., grow
abundantly in the timbered portions of the county.

The Little Rock & Memphis Railroad crosses
Prairie County from east to west, and divides it
into nearly two equal parts. Its length within the
county is about twenty-three miles. The Cotton
Belt Railroad crosses the southeast part of the
county, running in a southwesterly direction. The
railroads constitute a considerable portion of the
taxable wealth of the county, and give excellent
shipping facilities.

On February 15, 1882, seven farmers, named,
respectively, W. W. Tedford, W. T. McBee, W.
A. Suit, John and George McBee, Bluford Loakey,
and L. F. Thasher, all of Prairie County, met at
the McBee school house, near Wattensas Creek
and at a point eleven miles north of Hazen, and
there organized the "Wattensas Farmers' Club,"
with W. W. Tedford, president, and W. T. McBee,
secretary. At the third meeting of this club its
name was changed to "Wheel," hence the origin
and name of that extensive organization. Soon
thereafter other wheels were organized, up to the
number of seven in all, four in Prairie and three in
Cleburne County. Then on August 22, the same
year, articles of incorporation were filed in the circuit court clerk's office in Prairie County. Afterward, April 9, 1883, delegates from the wheels
then existing met at the same school house where
the original club was formed, and organized the
State Wheel, with E. R. McPherson, president,
and J. T. Kirk, secretary. Articles of association
were filed in the office of the Secretary of State,
September 28, 1885. The officers of the State
Wheel, at this writing are, John P. H. Russ, of
White County, president, and R. H. Morehead, of
Hazen, Prairie County, secretary. The latter is
serving his fifth term. There are 2,109 subordinate wheels in Arkansas, and besides State and
subordinate Wheels exist in Mississippi, Tennessee, Kentucky, Indiana, Wisconsin and Missouri.

Upon the approach of the Civil War, in 1861,
the people of Prairie County were generally in
sympathy with the Southern cause, in consequence
of which a public meeting was held at Brownsville,
the then county seat, on April 22, 1861, and resolutions passed favoring an appropriation by the
county for putting it "upon a war footing." Subsequently, in the same month, the county appropriated $10,000 to arm and equip its volunteer
soldiers. Then and thereafter companies were
organized for the State and Confederate service.
The first company in what is now Prairie County
was organized at Des Arc, in the spring of 1861,
and commanded by Capt. George W. Glenn.
Other companies were organized in the territory of
Prairie County, as now formed, and commanded
respectively by Capts. John S. Pearson, John H.
Bulls, Michael Peal, Gus. Reinhardt, John Kirk and
Pat. H. Wheat. Gen. Steele, of the United States
army, took possession of the county about September 1, 1863, and from that time until the close of
the war it was in possession of Federal troops.
No battle was fought in the county, but a few
slight skirmishes took place between scouting parties of the contending armies. The county was
completely overrun and laid waste. M. M. Erwin,
of Des Arc, says that when he returned from the
war in June, 1865, there were not, as he believes,
fifteen horses left in the county. The people deserve great praise for their recovery from such
devastation.

In 1880 the real estate of Prairie County was
assessed for taxation at $865,881, and the personal
property at $461,100, making a total of $1,226,-
981, and the taxes charged thereon, for all purposes, were $23,803. In 1888 the real property
of the county was assessed at $1,147,073, and the
personal at $874,137, making a total of $2,021,210,
and the total taxes charged thereon were $28,-
677.28. By comparison, it will be seen that from

1880 to 1888, the taxable wealth of the county nearly doubled, while the taxes increased only about 20 per cent.

Prairie County has no bonded indebtedness, but owes a trifling amount on outstanding warrants. In 1886 the county was robbed of from $10,000 to $12,000. On this occasion the treasurer was found tied on the street, and alleged that he had been knocked down and tied by robbers, who took from him the keys to the safe containing the money. Upon suspicion he was indicted and tried for the crime, but was found "not guilty." No other arrests or prosecutions were made.

Des Arc—the county seat—is situated on the west bank of White River, in the northern part of the county, and contains about 800 inhabitants. The streets are wide, and run east and west and north and south, and the site is as level and beautiful as could possibly be found for a town. Judge Watkins, of Little Rock, bought a portion of the land on which the town is located, and James Erwin entered the other portion. In 1846 or 1847 Watkins surveyed and platted his portion into town lots and streets, and two years later Erwin laid his portion out into town lots. The latter opened the first store and erected the first cotton-gin and grist-mill (combined) in the place, and also the first saw-mill. The gins and mills were all run by horse power, and M. M. Erwin (son of James Erwin), now living at Des Arc, ginned the first bale of cotton. Mr. Erwin brought the machinery for his saw-mill, and a man to put it into operation, from Pittsburg, Penn. These improvements were made about the year 1847. The second store in the town was opened by Stephen Red, and the next by Frith & Jackson. In 1850 the town had a population of about 100, and during the 50's it grew so rapidly that by 1860 its population was over 2,000. M. M. Erwin opened and kept the first hotel or "inn" in the place. A daily stage line—the Butterfield—met the boats here on White River. This line extended by way of Little Rock, Fort Smith, etc., to San Francisco, Cal., and the price charged passengers from Des Arc to San Francisco was $200 in gold. Only fifty pounds of baggage was allowed each passenger.

During the Civil War Des Arc was partially destroyed. Some of the buildings were burned, and others taken down and moved by the Federal army to De Vall's Bluff. The place was then almost depopulated. The town is improving now in the way of removal of the wooden business buildings and erecting brick blocks on their sites. It is an important cotton market, and from 5,000 to 6,000 bales are annually shipped therefrom on White River. It contains eight general stores, four groceries, three drug stores, one hardware and grocery store, one undertaking store, a livery stable, two meat markets, two hotels and a boarding house; four churches for the white people, Methodist, Baptist, Presbyterian, and Cumberland Presbyterian; two churches for the colored people, Methodist and Baptist; two school-houses, one for the whites and one for the blacks; a postoffice, saw-mill, cotton-gin and grist-mill, a ferry across the river, a town hall, five warehouses for storage of cotton, a lodge each of Masons and Knights of Honor, five physicians, and a weekly newspaper, the Des Arc Citizen, which was established in September, 1854, by J. C. Morrel, and is now published by J. J. Baugh. It is an eight-column folio, neatly printed and ably edited. The town also contains several mechanics' shops, and other enterprises not here named. Its name, Des Arc (the arc), is from the French Bayou Des Arc, a sluggish stream that empties into the White River about two miles above the town, which had previously been named thus by the French settlers. The town is incorporated, and has a full set of corporate officers.

De Vall's Bluff, situated on the west side of White River and also on the Little Rock & Memphis Railroad, was named after C. S. DeVall, who entered the land upon which it is located. At the beginning of the Civil War, in 1861, it contained a store and dwelling house and a "boat landing." In the fall of 1863 it was taken possession of by a portion of the United States army, and from thence forward to the close of the war, and for some time thereafter it was held by Federal troops. Soon after the Federals took possession they made it their base of supplies for Little Rock and other points west. The White River being navigable at all seasons of the year, the supplies were shipped thereon to DeVall's Bluff and transported thence by rail to Little Rock; however when the Arkansas River was high enough supplies were shipped directly to that city on that stream. As soon as the Union army took possession of De Vall's Bluff and made it a permanent base of supplies, hundreds of refugees flocked in and claimed protection. Houses were erected for them to occupy, and by the close of the war the place contained many buildings and had a large population, mostly of refugees, who then returned to their former homes. It now contains a postoffice, two general, two drug, three grocery and one millinery store, a livery stable, two hotels, a boat oar factory, a large saw-mill, a Methodist Church, white, and a Baptist Church, colored, a school-house each for the whites and blacks, two title abstract offices, a lodge each of Masons, Knights of Pythias, Knights of Honor, Good Templars and Iron Hall.

The boat-oar factory is said to be the only one of the kind west of the Mississippi. It is controlled and managed by F. P. Wells, formerly of Michigan, and turns out about 3,000 feet, lineal measure, of finished oars per day. These are shipped to Liverpool, England, San Francisco and other distant cities. A large number of men are employed at this establishment. The saw-mill, which has capacity for cutting 20,000 feet of lumber per day, is managed by Wells & Maxwell.

De Vall's Bluff represents a wonderful amount of life insurance for so small a place. The Knights of Honor, fifty members, carry $2,000 each, aggregating $100,000; the Iron Hall, twenty-five members, carry $1,000 each, aggregating $25,000; the Knights of Pythias carry in the aggregate $35,000, and it is estimated that at least $50,000 is carried in the "old line companies," making a grand total of $210,000. In addition to the societies named the town has a branch of the Southern Building and Loan Association, of Knoxville, Tenn., the members of which carry 175 shares of $100 each. De Vall's Bluff is incorporated, and has a population of about 500. Its principal exports are cotton, boat oars and lumber.

Hazen, situated on the Little Rock & Memphis Railroad, forty-three miles east from Little Rock and seven miles west from DeVall's Bluff, has a population of about 650, and is the leading commercial point in the county. It was surveyed and laid out in 1873, and named in honor of William C. Hazen, its original proprietor. It is well laid out, with wide streets running east and west and north and south, and has around it a colony of thrifty and prosperous farmers from the North. It contains six general, two drug and two grocery stores, an undertaker's shop, two livery stables, two blacksmith shops, two real estate offices, postoffice, one meat market, two lumber yards, two hotels, a steam cotton-gin, saw and grist-mill, two school-houses (one for each race), two churches for the white people and two for the colored people. In and around the town are six hay presses and nine hay barns. The principal shipments are hay, cotton and fruit. More hay, fruit, produce and game are annually shipped from Hazen than from any other town in the county.

The Hazen Free Press, a five-column quarto weekly newspaper, is published by J. H. Taylor. It was established in May, 1889.

Hickory Plains is a village of about 100 inhabitants in the northwest part of the county, and contains a postoffice, general store, drug store, two steam cotton-gins and grist-mills, a blacksmith shop, three churches and a large public school building.

Barrettsville, located between Hickory Plains and Hazen, contains a postoffice, general store, drug store, and a steam cotton-gin, grist and saw-mill.

Surrounded Hill, or Fredonia, is on the Little Rock & Memphis Railroad, four miles east of De-Vall's Bluff, and contains two general and two grocery stores, two saloons, postoffice, two colored churches, a hotel, blacksmith shop and a steam cotton-gin and grist-mill. It is situated in one of the best cotton growing districts in the State, and ships a large amount of that commodity. It has a population of about 200, largely-colored.

Fairmount is a small post village on the prairie in the southern part of the county.

Ulm, a new village, is growing up in the south-eastern part of the county.

There are, besides the above, some other post hamlets in the county.

The workings of the free school system in Prairie County may be learned by reference to the following statistics taken from the last published report of the State superintendent of public instruction, it being for the year ending June 30, 1888:

Scholastic population: White, males, 1,247, females, 1,165, total, 2,412; colored, males, 771, females, 773, total, 1,544. Number of pupils taught in the public schools: White, males, 871, females, 784, total, 1,655; colored, males, 413, females, 460, total, 873. Number of school districts, 49. Teachers employed: Males, 42, females, 22; total, 64. Average monthly salaries paid teachers: First grade, males, $50.00, females, $37.50; second grade, males, $35.00, females, $25.00; third grade, males, $30.00, females, $25.00. Amount expended for the support of the schools: Teachers' salaries, $11,316.00; for houses and sites, $1,150.43; treasurer's commissions, $259.12; total, $12,725.55. The reader can compare the number of children enumerated with the number enrolled in the schools, make other comparisons and draw his own conclusions. The statistics show much room for improvement. The school terms in each district averaged four months for the year. After the public money is exhausted the teachers of the town schools usually teach a subscription school for several months longer.

The Methodist Episcopal Church, South, has the following organizations in Prairie County: Des Arc and Hickory Plains Circuit, with a church at each of these places, and three preaching points in the country, Rev. D. T. Holmes, pastor, and a membership of 283; Hazen Circuit, embracing Hazen, De Vall's Bluff, and one or two appointments in the country, with a membership in all of over 100, Rev. J. W. F. Scott, pastor; Wattensas Circuit, embracing seven organizations, with a combined membership of about 311, Rev. James Huddleston, pastor; the White River Circuit has appointments in both Prairie and Arkansas Counties, and a membership of 425, Rev. J. W. Berry being

pastor. A portion of the Carlisle Circuit lies in the western part of Prairie County, and a portion of the Brinkley Circuit in its eastern part.

There is a Baptist Church, with about forty-five members, at Des Arc, but at this writing they are not supplied with a pastor. Other Baptist Churches in the county, pastors and memberships, as shown by the session minutes of 1888, of the Grand Prairie Baptist Association, are as follows: Center Point, Elder B. F. House, 70; Hazen, Elder P. A. Haman, 52; Pleasant Ridge, Elder R. G. Thomas, 23; Liberty, ... about 15. Since these minutes were published the memberships have increased, and changes in pastors may have been made.

There are three organizations of the Presbyterians within the county: One at Des Arc, one at Hickory Plains, and the other at Hazen. Rev. S. I. Reid, of Lonoke, preaches at Des Arc and Hazen. The membership is small.

Of the Cumberland Presbyterian denomination there is only one organization in the county, and that is at Des Arc, where they have a very small membership, a neat little church edifice, but no pastor at this time.

A Christian Church was organized at Hazen about the year 1881. They have no edifice, but contemplate building one within a year. Elder J. A. Carter, of Lauderdale County, Tenn., preaches for them in the school-house. The membership is now 120. A Christian Church, with a small membership, was organized in August, 1889, at Barrettsville. Elder C. E. Gillespie, of Hazen, is pastor. Here, too, they worship in the school-house.

———•◦•———

A. L. Aydelott, merchant, Surrounded Hill, Ark. The mercantile trade has long constituted one of the leading features in the commercial pursuits of our country, and in this line we have in Surrounded Hill a thoroughly representative house, controlled by Mr. A. L. Aydelott, who is regarded as an upright and energetic man of business, and respected in commercial and social circles. He is the son of S. D. and Elizabeth (Herring) Aydelott, and his birth occurred in Shelby County, Tenn., on the 16th of March, 1855. S. D. Aydelott owes his nativity to Hardeman County, Tenn.; where his birth occurred November 18, 1819, and he moved with his parents to Kentucky when quite young. There he received his education, and after reaching his majority returned to his native State, and was united in marriage to Mrs. Elizabeth (Herring) Whitley. To this union were born three children: William L., Alfred L. and Johnny L. The father was a blacksmith by trade, also a merchant, and in connection carried on agricultural pursuits. He is the owner of about ninety-two acres of land near Arlington, Tenn. He and wife are now living in Shelby County, Tenn. They are members of the Old School Baptist Church, and have the esteem and respect of all who know them. During the late war the father enlisted in the Confederate army, One Hundred and Fifty-fourth Regiment Tennessee Volunteers, and was in the battles of Corinth and Shiloh. At the end of fourteen months he was discharged on account of age, returned home, and began merchandising at Memphis. A. L. Aydelott received a good practical education in the schools of Memphis, Tenn., and there remained until December, 1877, when he immigrated to Ark., and located on his present fine property. Upon his first advent into Arkansas he was without means, and began business for himself by working as sub-manager on a plantation. By 1878 he had accumulated some money, and he then returned to Tennessee, where he was united in marriage to Miss Sarah D. Gillespie, daughter of Jefferson and Mary Gillespie, on the 13th of February of that year. To this marriage have been born six children: Kate E. (deceased), Josie L., Grace A. (deceased), Ellise and Clarence (twins), and an infant, Herbert. Mr. Aydelott began merchandising in October, 1884, on a capital of $1,000, which has since been increased to $55,000; is the owner of about 600 acres of good land, and has under cultivation about 140 acres. He runs a public gin that is situated in Surrounded Hill, and which has all the latest improvements, and he also owns an interest in a saloon. Mr. Aydelott is progressive in his ideas, and his farm, which is well stocked, shows care and attention. He was a member of the K. of H., and was Dictator as long as he held membership; was also postmaster at Surrounded Hill for one term, and he is deeply interested in church and educational matters.

Philip B. Baugh, retired, was born in Lincoln County, Tenn., October 10, 1827, and is a son of James and Marina A. (Bruce) Baugh, the former a native of Virginia and the latter of North Carolina, she being a daughter of Arnold Bruce, a Frenchman. After their marriage the parents moved to Lincoln County, Tenn., and in 1837 to Mississippi, where the father's death occurred, his wife's death occurring in White County, Ark., in 1868. Philip B. Baugh resided with his father until the latter's death, and up to 1859 was engaged in following the plow in Mississippi. After moving to Arkansas he located in Des Arc and for two years, up to 1859, was engaged in the sawmill business. In January, 1862, he moved to White County, Ark., and followed farming and lumber manufacturing, also dealing in dry goods and real estate for some six years, then sold out, and in 1887 returned to Des Arc, where he is now spending his declining years in retirement from the active duties of life. He was married in Mississippi, on January 3, 1850, to Eleanor C. Lawson, a native of North Carolina, who was reared in Mississippi, a daughter of John Lawson, a native of Ireland. Mrs. Baugh died January 9, 1888, having borne and reared a family of ten children: John C. (a farmer of White County, Ark.), J. J. Baugh (whose sketch appears in this work), W. L. (a druggist of Des Arc), Alice (wife of B. S. Horton, of Searcy), Olivia (wife of A. A. Gilliam, also of Searcy), Cora (wife of Rev. A. C. Graham, a minister of the Methodist Episcopal Church), Ola and Nettie (young ladies at home), Ida Bruce (another daughter, died in September, 1887, at the age of twenty-one years, being the affianced wife of Rev. C. B. Mosley, now a missionary of the Methodist Episcopal Church, South, to Japan), and Katie Florence (who died at the age of eighteen years). Mr. and Mrs. Baugh belonged to the Methodist Episcopal Church, and Mr. Baugh is a Royal Arch Mason. He served as magistrate of White County for a number of years, also as notary public, and is holding the last-named position at the present time. During the Civil War he entered the Confederate army (in 1864), being a member of Col. Crabtree's regiment, and was with Price on his raid through Missouri, after which he was on detached service until the close of the war.

James J. Baugh, attorney and editor, Des Arc, Ark. The enviable position which the town of Des Arc occupies to-day as an industrial and mercantile center is due to the energy, enterprise and ability of the inhabitants and to the wise and judicious government of the civic authorities. Prominent among those who have made an impress on the history of the town, in more respects than one, is Mr. James J. Baugh, who is editor and publisher of the Citizen, and an able attorney of the town. Mr. Baugh is a native of Palona, Miss., where his birth occurred December 7, 1857, and he is the son of Judge P. B. and Eleanor (Lawson) Baugh, the former a native of Tennessee and the latter of North Carolina. The parents were married in the last-named State, and in 1859 moved to Arkansas, where the father first engaged in the saw-mill and lumber business at Des Arc. After residing at that place for a few years he moved to White County, but in September, 1887, returned to Des Arc, where he resides at the present time. He is sixty-two years of age, and is one of the prominent men of the county. He served as county judge of White County, and has held other positions of trust and responsibility. His wife died January 9, 1888. Their family consisted of seven daughters and three sons, all of whom grew to mature years. James J. Baugh passed his boyhood days in White County, and remained with his father until about seventeen years of age. He then entered a newspaper office at Searcy, learned the printer's trade, and then took up the study of law, being admitted at Searcy in 1880. He moved to Des Arc in 1880, bought out a newspaper business, and now owns the only paper published at Des Arc. He has been actively engaged in the newspaper business since that time, and his paper, with its crisp and trenchant editorials, commands an ever-widening area of circulation, while it carries with it that weight and authority, which a clear, calm and intelligent judgment must always secure. Mr. Baugh was appointed postmaster at Des Arc in 1885, and was acting postmaster for four years. His marriage took place at Hickory Plains, June 15, 1882, to Miss E. M. Reinhardt, a native of Des Arc, and the daughter of Daniel F. Reinhardt, who was a member of the Constitutional Convention of 1874. To Mr. and Mrs. Baugh were born two children: Lerline and Minnie Kate. Mr. Baugh is a member of the Knights of Honor and he and wife are members of the Methodist Episcopal Church.

Christian Bechler is accounted a prosperous farmer, stockman and miller, of Belcher Township, Prairie County, Ark., and like the majority of the natives of France, he is of an energetic temperament and progressive in his views. He is a man whom nature seems to have especially designed to be a farmer, for he has met with more than the average degree of success in pursuing this calling, and is now the owner of 448 acres of land, all of which is under fence. He was born in 1827, and when only fourteen years of age, became weary of life in his native land, and began to turn his thoughts to the new world across the water, where adventurous spirits could find wider scope of opportunities, and more congenial surroundings. He first landed in New Orleans, and in 1840 went to Ohio, and in 1846 to Iowa, thence to California in 1849, like so many others in search of gold. After working in the mining regions of that State, until 1852, he returned to Iowa, and the following year was married to Barbara Conrad, a daughter of Daniel and Mary (Klopfenstein) Conrad, who were natives of Switzerland, and came to America in 1820. Mrs. Bechler was born in Ohio, and after their marriage, she and Mr. Bechler set energetically to work to accumulate some means, and they still own the farm on which they first settled in Henry County, Iowa, which comprises 160 acres. In 1883 they came to Prairie County, Ark., and as above stated, own an excellent farm. They expect to make this State their home, and are interested in everything pertaining to its welfare. He is a Republican, and he and his wife are members of the Mennonite Church, and are the parents of the following family: Daniel (deceased), Benjamin J. and John (deceased), Peter, Mary (Mrs. L. J. Anderson, of Arkansas County, Ark.), Anna (Mrs. C. B. Zimmerman, of Prairie County), Jacob, Katie, Frances and Cordelia, the last two being twins. Mr. Bechler is one of a family of three sons born to Christian and Elizabeth (Bechler) Bechler, both of whom were born in Switzerland, and emigrated to France, where the father died in 1830, the mother's death occurring in New Orleans, La., in 1843. Their children are: Joseph (now deceased), Peter (a resident of Iowa) and Christian.

Capt. Jacob G. Becton is one of the experienced farmers and cotton-ginners of the county, and the property which he now owns has been accumulated by attending strictly to his chosen calling. He was born in New Berne, N. C., October 23, 1833, being a son of F. I. and Eliza (Rhodes) Becton, who were born, reared and married in North Carolina, the father being a farmer of that State. They reared their family in Jones County, and there the father died in 1843, his wife surviving him until 1845, she being married a second time, and with her last husband moved to Wayne County. Here Capt. Jacob G. Becton grew to manhood and was married here, moving some time afterward to Cumberland County, where he engaged in farming and merchandising until 1861, and in March of that year moved to Arkansas and made his home in Prairie County. In February, 1862, he enlisted in Capt. Bull's company, Lanon's regiment, but afterward became a member of Col. Craven's regiment, and was promoted from a private to the rank of captain, and participated in the battles of Baker's Creek, Corinth and a great many skirmishes. He was captured five times, and three times managed to make his escape, but the first time while held a prisoner he was kept on Johnson's Island for nine months, and the second time at Point Lookout, Md., for three weeks. The year following his return from the war he engaged in farming near Des Arc, and that he has been successful is clearly shown when we state the fact that he owns 960 acres of land, nearly all of which is in one body, 800 acres being in the home place, of which 500 acres are under cultivation. He has a good frame residence, and his outbuildings are all commodious and in excellent repair. He has been the owner of a cotton-gin at Des Arc since 1886, and has been extensively engaged in cotton-ginning since that time. In 1855 he was married to Lizzie E., a daughter of John E. Becton, of Wayne County, N. C. Captain and Mrs. Becton have lost one daughter, Emma, who was the wife of W. L. Willeford, also three infants while they were residing in North Carolina. The Captain is a Master Mason, and his wife is an earnest member of the Methodist Episcopal Church.

G. W. Belcher is a farmer, stockman and miller of Belcher Township and was born in Perry County, Ala., in 1840, the eldest of eleven children born to the marriage of Thomas M. Belcher and Rachel Mayberry. The former was a Virginian, born in 1810, and was one of six children of Bevley Belcher. He was reared in Alabama and was married there in 1837 and for fourteen years was engaged in overseeing. He then engaged in farming and has made that his chief calling up to the present time. In 1851 he came to Prairie County, Ark., and entered 240 acres of land which he has since increased to 400 acres. He has been justice of the peace for about twenty years, and has held the position of postmaster four or five years. He is a Democrat and during the turbulent times preceding the Rebellion and during the war he was a strong Union man, and was greatly opposed to secession. His wife is a native of Alabama and both are members of the Missionary Baptist Church. Their children are: G. W., Martha (who died in Texas), Jane (deceased), Louisa (wife of William M. Shuford of Austin, Texas), James (deceased), Permalie J. (wife of M. C. Mayberry of Prairie County) and several children who died in infancy. G. W. Belcher attended school in Cotton Gin, Miss., until eleven years of age, but after his removal with his parents to Arkansas his school days were cut short and July 7, 1861, he enlisted in Company C, Second Arkansas, McIntosh regiment, and for gallant and faithful service was raised to the rank of captain, in 1864, in the commissary department.

Some of the engagements in which he participated are Oak Hill, Wilson's Creek, Elkhorn, Farmington, Cumberland Gap, Richmond and others. In 1862 he was wounded in the left hand by a pistol shot and was in the hospital at Knoxville, Tenn., for some time. After the war he returned to Arkansas and was married in Claiborne Parish, La., 1866, to Miss Susan S. Hood, a daughter of Bryant and Polly Hood, of Georgia, and by her has four children: Ida, William M., John G. and Martha. Mrs. Belcher was born July 5, 1840, and died in September, 1889. She was a member of the Missionary Baptist Church, as is Mr. Belcher, and was an earnest and consistent Christian lady. Mr. Belcher is a Democrat and has served in the capacity of school director for about fifteen years and he also belongs to the Masons, being a demitted member of Aberdeen Lodge. He is a descendant of some of the oldest settlers of the State of Arkansas and his grandfather Belcher was in the American Revolution. He is a wealthy farmer and of his 800 acres of land, 300 are under cultivation.

Andrew Jackson Bowman, DeVall's Bluff, Ark. Mr. Bowman, one of the pioneers of Roc Roe Township, purchased his farm in that township, in 1874, and settled where he now resides the following year. He was born in Fairfield County, Ohio, in 1828, was the second in a family of ten children born to Peter and Susan (La Motte) Bowman, and received his education in the subscription school of Putnam County, Ohio. He assisted on his father's farm until twenty years of age, when he was married in the last-named county, in 1848, to Miss Rue Ann Burrel, a native of Putnam County, Ohio. After that he was engaged in farming, and thus continued in that county until 1856, when he settled in McLean County, near Lexington, and was quite extensively engaged in his former pursuit. In 1858 he moved to Piatt County, Ill., remained there until 1866, and then moved to Champaign County, of the same State, where he remained until March, 1875. He then came to Prairie County, Ark., bought 1,500 acres of raw land, which he cultivated and added to until at one time he owned 2,000 acres. He now has 680 acres with 320 acres under fence, and sixty under culti-

vation. He has paid considerable attention to fruit culture, has about forty acres in orchard, 2,000 apple trees and 1,000 peach trees, and all varieties of small fruit. He is a successful horticulturist, and has one of the finest orchards in Eastern Arkansas. He has over 100 varieties of apple trees, and a number of transcendent crab trees. On his farm he raises cotton, corn, rye, wheat and oats, and his farm is well adapted to the raising of stock. Mr. Bowman lost his excellent wife in Piatt County, Ill., in April, 1859. To their union were born three living children: Elias (residing in Ohio), Wesley (married and resides near his father) and Elmer (resides in Cloud County, Kas., married and engaged in farming). Mr. Bowman was married the second time in Piatt County, Ill., in 1859, to Mrs. Mary Ann Plotner (nee Foust), a native of Pickaway County, Ohio, and the fruits of this union were two living children: Letitia Ranceline and Arthur (at home). Mr. Bowman was married in Putnam County, Ohio, in 1874, to Mrs. Harriet J. (Zeller) Long (widow of Mr. Long), a native of Putnam County, Ohio, and the daughter of Andrew and Catherine (Henderson) Zeller. Mr. Zeller was born in Wurtemberg, Germany, and his wife in Pittsburgh, Penn. The father came to this country when single, and was married in Tuscarawas County, Ohio. He was a wagon and carriage manufacturer. His death occurred in Ohio, in 1852, and the mother died in Putnam County, in 1872, surviving him about twenty years. Mr. Bowman is active in politics, and his vote is cast with the Democratic party. He was magistrate while living in Champaign County, Ill., takes an active interest in educational affairs, and is a member of the school board. He and wife are members of the Methodist Episcopal Church, South. His grandparents were natives of Germany, and his father was a miller by trade. The latter went to Ohio when a young man, was married there, and there made his home for many years. Later in life he engaged in farming in Putnam County, Ohio, and there passed the closing scenes of his life, his death occurring in 1872. His wife survived him two years. Of their family the following are now living: Andrew Jackson (the subject of this sketch), Pauline (now Mrs. Cartwright, of Putnam County, Ohio), Martin (married, and is a a farmer in Putnam County), Mary (now Mrs. Todd, of Putnam County), Peter (married, and resides also in Putnam County) and John (who is married and resides in the above-mentioned county.

C. L. Bowman is a successful real-estate dealer of Hazen, Ark., and since 1879 has been a resident of and interested in the welfare of Prairie County. He was born in Knox County, Ind., in 1859, and was the eldest of four children reared by John and Martha A. (Roach) Bowman, the former of whom is a native of the Buckeye State, born in 1832. He was one of a large family of children, and in his youth he was taken by his parents, Daniel and Elizabeth Bowman, to the State of Illinois, and there his early manhood was spent. In 1852 he settled in Knox County, Ind., on a farm, but also engaged in carriage making, and in 1856 he espoused Miss Roach, whose people were Virginians and early residents of Indiana. To Mr. Bowman were born the following family of children: Calvin L., Samuel E. (who is married and living in Stuttgart, Ark.), Lydia M. and Mary G. Mr. Bowman removed with his family to Arkansas, in 1879, and after farming until 1883 he settled in Hazen and is there now living. He is a Democrat politically, and he and Mrs. Bowman are members of the Cumberland Presbyterian Church. Calvin L. Bowman, our subject, spent his early days on his father's farm in Arkansas and there received his early schooling, being an attendant at the common schools. He came to Arkansas with his parents, and was married here, in 1881, to Miss Sallie E. Back, a daughter of Jackson and Mary Back, the former of whom was killed in the Civil War, being a member of the Union army. His wife afterward married Mr. Denton, and is at present living in Hazen. Mr. Bowman and his wife have two boys: Walter P. and Clyde E. Up to 1886 Mr. Bowman farmed in White River Township, but since that time has been engaged in the real-estate business in Hazen. Besides having in his control large tracts of land belonging to others, he owns 160 acres of land and town property. He has always been interested in the upbuilding of schools and churches, and it is his earnest desire to see the country advance in every way, and he is doing all in his power to aid in its improvement. He and Mrs. Bowman are members of the Methodist Episcopal Church, South.

James W. Brians, county sheriff. Among the men who cast their fortunes in Prairie County, Ark., in January, 1867, and whose memory is treasured by the people of this region, is William J. Brians, the father of our subject. He was born in North Carolina, and was married there to Elizabeth Smith, a native of the same State, and moved with her to Mississippi in October, 1858, settling on a farm, where he remained eight years, after which he moved to Prairie County, Ark. He made his home on a farm near Butlerville, and here his death occurred in 1876, he having served for a short time in the Confederate army during the late war. His wife survives him at this writing. James W. Brians was born in Cabarrus County, N. C., September 5, 1852, and remained with his parents until he was twenty-three years of age. He was married in Prairie County, October 17, 1877, to Miss Emma Moore, a daughter of Dr. W. L. Moore, she being a native of Arkansas, born and reared in Prairie County. After their marriage they settled on a farm in the western part of the county, their home place consisting of eighty acres, sixty-one acres being in an excellent state of cultivation, on which is a good residence and other necessary farm buildings. Besides this land he also owns 160 acres in another tract, a considerable portion of which is also improved, and good residence property in the town of Des Arc. He has always supported the principles and men of the Democrat party, and in the fall of 1888 was nominated and elected by a handsome majority on that ticket to the office of county sheriff. He has held other local positions, and he and his wife are members of the Methodist Episcopal Church, South. They have one child three years of age named Bertha Emma, and have lost three children, William Moore (a son, dying on September 12, 1889, at the age of eleven years), Mary Buelah (died at the age of ten months) and Augustus Edwin (at the age of two years). Mr. Brians displays great system and neatness in the management of his farm, and everything about his place shows the progressive and intelligent citizen that he is.

Luther Brink, real-estate and tax-paying agent, Hazen, Ark. In a young and rapidly developing town like Hazen, situated as it is in the best grain and stock raising section of Arkansas, the business of dealing in real estate is necessarily a very important one, and especially so because, in addition to city property, there is a large amount of farm property constantly changing hands. A greater part of this is handled by the Shock & Brink, real-estate and tax-paying agents at Hazen, Prairie County, Ark. Mr. Brink was born in Boone County, Mo., in 1856, and was the third in a family of five children, the result of the union of C. W. and Mariam (Kelley) Brink. The father was born in Kentucky about 1828, and was one of a large family reared by H. L. Brink, a native of Kentucky, who moved to Missouri at an early day, and there followed the trade of millwright. The grandfather is still living, was in the War of 1812, is ninety-eight years of age and enjoys comparatively good health. C. W. Brink passed his boyhood days in Boone County, Mo., and was there married to Miss Kelley, daughter of James Kelley, after which he followed the trade of blacksmith. He now resides in Hinton, Boone County, Mo. His children are named as follows: W. H. (resides in Hallsville, Mo., is married and has two children), Joella D. (now Mrs. J. D. Barrett, resides in Hazen, Ark., and has four children), Luther, Lucy D. (was married and died in Boone County), and J. S. (died at the age of eighteen months. Mr. and Mrs. Brink are members of the Chirstian Church. The mother is deceased, her death occurring in 1865. The school days of Luther Brink were passed in Missouri, and later he engaged in mercantile pursuits and contracting in that State. He emigrated to Hazen in 1888, engaged in contracting and building, and perhaps the best compliment that could be paid him would be to point out those monuments of his handiwork which now grace so many of the homesteads in this county. Later he embarked in the real-estate

business with Mr. Shock, and this firm has control of a large amount of farming land, besides a number of thousand acres of timber and prairie land. Mr. Brink is a member of the Odd Fellow Lodge No. 158, Grand Pass, Saline County, where he first located, and where his membership remains. He is a notary public.

William H. Brock, farmer, was born in Hardeman County, Tenn., January 11, 1826, and is a son of Caleb Brock, a native of Virginia, but who was reared in North Carolina, being also married there to Mary Frances Jones, a Virginian, also reared in North Carolina. From the "Old North State" they moved to Tennessee, and still later went to Tippah County, Miss., and after making their home in this State for twenty-one years, being engaged in farming, they came to Arkansas (in 1855) and settled in what is now Prairie County, making a farm on the Cache River. After a short time they sold this and moved to Des Arc, where the father resided until his death, October 10, 1874, his wife surviving him until February 11, 1883, when she, too, passed away. Mr. Brock was a soldier in the War of 1812, and for his services received a pension from the Government in the latter part of his life. He was an earnest member of the Methodist Episcopal Church for many years, and gave liberally of his means in support of the same. His wife was a member of the same church, and possessed bright assurances of going to a happy home in the skies. William H. Brock (our subject) grew to manhood in Mississippi, and made his home with his father until the death of the latter, after which he took charge of his mother, caring for her until her demise. In 1862 Mr. Brock enlisted in the Confederate service as a private, but was on detached service the most of the time, conscripting and collecting Confederate money. After the war was over he returned to Des Arc, and has since followed various occupations, the most of his attention, however, being given to farming. He has 400 acres of land in four different tracts, all good land, and more or less improved, lying near Des Arc. He also owns some fine town property, a hotel, some residence property, and a livery stable, the latter being under his management in connection with his farm for fifteen years. He has served as a member of the school board, as alderman, deputy sheriff, and has had charge of the county poor and insane ever since the war. When Mr. Brock first located in Des Arc the town was in the timber.

David Brockway, senior member of the firm of Brockway & Eaton, general merchants of Hazen, Ark., was born in the Nutmeg State in 1837 and was the second child born to Pierce and Pearl (Webb) Eaton, who were also born in that State, the former's birth occurring about 1810. Upon securing a good education in the common schools of his native State, he began learning the carpenter's trade, and followed this occupation throughout life. He was married about 1834 and made his home in Hartford, Conn., his children being born there. Their names are as follows: William (who died when young), David and Mary (who became the wife of Mr. Hurlburt, of Quincy, Ill., and died one year after her marriage). The father of these children emigrated to California in 1848 and was never heard from afterward, but was supposed to have died in that State about 1848 or 1849. His wife survived him until 1853 when she, too, passed to her long home, her death occurring in the State of Virginia whither she had gone for her health. She was a daughter of Harvey Webb, a native of Connecticut. David Brockway acquired his early education in New Haven, Conn., and at the age of twenty years he started for the West to seek a fortune, and landed in McDonough County, Ill., where he made his home until 1883, at which date he came to Arkansas and settled at Hazen. He was formerly a successful farmer, but since his arrival in this State he has devoted his attention to merchandising and the lumber business, and since 1887 has been associated in business with William E. Eaton. They are also large shippers of hay and cotton and do an annual business of about $75,000. Mr. Brockway is a Republican politically, and socially, belongs to Hazen Lodge No. 361, A. F. & A. M., and the United Workmen, Good Hope (Ill.) Lodge No. 129. He was married in Illinois to Miss Rebecca Ballance, a daughter of Joseph Ballance, a native of England. Mrs. Brockway was born in Illinois and has borne

her husband five children: Mollie (Mrs. Webb, residing in Illinois), Ella (Mrs. Eaton), Pearl, Bessie and Bruce. She is a member of the Presbyterian Church.

William E. Eaton is the junior member of the firm of Brockway & Eaton, general merchants of Hazen, Ark., and was born near Viola, Mercer County, Ill., being a son of Rev. Cyrus H. and Margaret (Frazier) Eaton, the former of whom was born in the State of Virginia in 1821. He settled near Viola, Ill., about 1845, and was there married, his wife being a daughter of John and Elizabeth Frazier, who removed to Illinois from their native State, Ohio, at an early day. The family born to Mr. and Mrs. Eaton are: Martin (who is married and is a practicing physician of Fairbury, Neb.), Hugh (who is married and resides in Chicago, Ill., being engaged in the manufacturing business), John and William E. Rev. Cyrus Eaton removed to Iowa, becoming a well-known minister of that State, but is now in Oklahoma, Ind. Ty., in the interests of the church. His wife died in Hazen, Ark., in 1884. William E. Eaton was united in the bonds of matrimony to Miss Ella Brockway, and is residing in Hazen, Ark., the father of two children: Hallie and Harry. Margaret died in infancy. Mr. Eaton received his education in the Iowa College at Grinnell, and his youth was spent in that State and in Illinois. He has resided in Arkansas since 1883, and is associated with his father-in-law in the general mercantile business, and is meeting with financial success. Politically he is a Republican, and his wife is a member of the Presbyterian Church.

James T. Brown (deceased) was a man well known in Prairie County, and was respected for his straightforward course through life and for his many Christian virtues. He was born in Talladega County, Ala., April 13, 1842, and until he attained his eighteenth year he was a resident of his native State. At the opening of the Civil War he joined the Confederate forces and served until the close of the war, after which he went North to Indiana, and located in Hamilton County, where he met and afterward married Miss Elizabeth J. Fall, their union taking place September 9, 1866.

Mrs. Brown was born in Hamilton County, a daughter of D. H. and Susan (Wells) Brown, and after her marriage she and Mr. Brown were engaged in farming for about three years, after which they moved to Illinois, and a year later came to Prairie County, Ark. A year later they went to Woodruff County, but a short time after returned to Prairie County and located at Des Arc, where Mr. Brown purchased a mill and engaged in the manufacture of lumber. This business he conducted very successfully for a number of years, but in 1887 he sold his mill and turned his attention to farming once more, continuing this occupation until his death March 27, 1889. He was a man possessing fine business qualifications and was very successful in all his ventures, but gave liberally of his means to all worthy movements, and the needy were never turned empty from his door. He left a wife and two sons to mourn his death, the latter's names being: Daniel L. (who is married and resides on a farm in this county) and Edgar W. (a young man at home). Mrs. Brown has been engaged in the hotel business since the death of her husband, and her success in this undertaking does much to show what a woman can do when dependent upon her own resources. She keeps a first-class house called the Des Arc House.

Fred E. Brown is a prosperous general merchant of Des Arc, Ark., and by his superior business qualities has done much to advance the reputation which the county now enjoys as a commercial center. He was born in Choctaw County, Miss., August 27, 1858, and is a son of A. J. and Elizabeth (House) Brown, who were born, reared and married in Alabama, and removed to Arkansas in 1869, settling on a farm near Hickory Plains, where they are now residing. Fred E. Brown grew to manhood in Prairie County, and was educated in the schools of Des Arc and in a commercial college at Little Rock. He began the battle of life for himself as a clerk in Des Arc in 1879, but at the end of a few years he became a traveling salesman for a St. Louis and Memphis wholesale house and continued this occupation until 1888, when he purchased a stock of goods and engaged in business for himself. His store is now well established

and his stock of goods is large and well selected, and as he possesses good judgment, business ability and efficiency, his efforts are meeting with well-deserved success, and his outlook for the future is bright and promising. He was married in December, 1882, to Miss Ada Morrell, a daughter of J. C. Morrell, who was one of the early settlers of the State, and who established and edited the Des Arc Citizen for a number of years. Mrs. Brown was born, reared and educated in Prairie County, and is the mother of one child, Charles Frederick. She is a member of the Methodist Episcopal Church, South.

David J. Burks, farmer and ginner, Hickory Plains, Ark. Generally age and experience are essential to success and promotion, but in the example before us we have a young man who has risen without any especial fortuitous circumstances to the position of one of the successful agriculturists of the county. He was born in Logan County, Ky., June 11, 1859, and his father, W. I. Burks, is a native of the same State. The latter was married in his native State to Miss Harriet Irwin, a native of the same county and State, and followed farming in Kentucky for a number of years. He now resides at Springfield, Mo., where he is engaged in merchandising. He served through the late war as first lieutenant in the Confederate service. In 1874 he moved to Arkansas, and remained here until 1883, when he moved to Springfield, Mo. D. J. Burks came with his parents to Arkansas in 1874, and here grew to manhood. On November 22, 1878, his nuptials with Miss Emma Deener, a native of Arkansas and a daughter of Thomas and Huldah Deener, were solemnized, and to this happy union have been born two children: Willie and Irwin. After marriage Mr. Burks located on a farm, and has cultivated the soil industriously since that time. He bought a gin in the fall of 1888, and has good machinery, etc. His farm consists of about eighty acres with seventy-five acres under cultivation. He has a good residence and outbuildings, etc., and is making his way to the front.

Dr. James W. Burney, physician, surgeon and druggist, Des Arc, Ark. In a comprehensive work of this kind, dealing with industrial pursuits, sciences, arts and professions, it is only fit and right that that profession on which, in some period or other of our lives—the medical profession—all are more or less dependent, should be prominently noticed. It is the prerogative of the physician to relieve or alleviate the ailments to which suffering humanity is prone, and as such he deserves the most grateful consideration of all. A prominent physician and surgeon, who, by his own great abilities, has attained distinction in his profession, is Dr. James W. Burney. This gentleman owes his nativity to Williamson County, Tenn., where his birth occurred on November 1, 1830, but he was reared principally in Maury County, of that State. He came West, to Mississippi, in 1850, located at Mount Pleasant, and in 1855 commenced the study of medicine, under the instruction of Dr. J. D. Sale, one of the most prominent physicians of Northern Mississippi. In the winter of 1856–57 he took his first course of lectures at the Memphis Medical College, and in March, of the last-named year, located at Des Arc, where he associated himself with Dr. J. C. Goodwin, with whom he commenced the practice of medicine. The following year, in July, he volunteered his services in the terrible epidemic of yellow fever, then scourging Vicksburg, Miss., rendering valuable assistance in fighting the same. In 1859 the Doctor returned to Des Arc, resumed his practice, and on September 13, of the same year, was united in marriage to Miss Lucy C. Adams, a native of Tennessee, who was reared and educated in Memphis, and the daughter of H. S. Adams, a planter in Mississippi, a soldier in the War of 1812, and a participant in the battle of New Orleans. In 1861 the Doctor enlisted in the Confederate army as lieutenant in Col. Patterson's regiment, and the following year was promoted to the captaincy of Company K, Col. Matlock's regiment, by Gen. Hindman. He remained in active service up to 1864, when he resigned his commission and returned to Des Arc. He participated in the battle of Prairie Grove, and was in many severe skirmishes. After returning to Des Arc he engaged actively in the practice of his profession, in which he continued up to the present time. He went to Philadelphia and com-

pleted his course, graduating from the Medical Department of that renowned university in the class of February, 1870. Before and since his graduation he has enjoyed an extensive practice, proving conclusively that he is one of the most successful and skillful physicians in the State. He engaged in the drug business in 1881, and still continues that industry. Dr. Burney lost his first wife on August 6, 1878, and on December 7, 1880, he selected for his second wife Mrs. Hattie (Johnson) Richardson, a native of Alabama, but who was reared in Arkansas, and the daughter of Hanp Johnson. The fruits of this union have been two children: Alfred and Robert, aged, respectively, eight and six years. The Doctor was first vice-president of the first medical society formed in Prairie County, and is president of the board of examiners of this county, discharging the duties of this, as in all other important positions to which he has been called, with honor, fidelity, ability, and to the satisfaction of all concerned. He is a Master Mason, and he and wife are members of the Methodist Episcopal Church, South. For the past ten years the Doctor's name has been prominently mentioned by his friends in connection with a seat in our State legislature, but owing to private business and his extreme modesty, he has never given his consent to become a candidate for the position, although a prominent leader in the Democratic party. Chairman of the County Democratic Executive Committee during the dark days of reconstruction, he was ever at the helm, and landed the old scar-worn party safely and successfully to victory over all opposition. The Doctor's father, John Burney, was a native of North Carolina, and was reared in Guilford County, where he married Miss Matilda Young, a native also of North Carolina, and who was reared in the same county. The father moved to Tennessee about 1820, and was there engaged in agricultural pursuits. He was also a mechanic, and died in Henry County. His wife survived him a few years. Their family consisted of nine children, six sons and three daughters, three sons and three daughters now living, the three elder sons being deceased: J. T., R. W. and J. M. Burney. Those living are Mrs. E.

P. Warren (of Mississippi), Mary B. Burney (on the old home place in Maury County), Mrs. Sallie Glenn (of Tennessee), Thomas P. Burney (of Maury County, Tenn.), Prof. A. M. Burney (president of the Howard Female College, at Gallatin, Tenn.) and Dr. James W. Burney (the oldest of the three brothers, living at Des Arc, Ark., actively engaged in the practice of medicine and the drug business). He has practiced medicine a greater number of years than any other man ever did in Prairie County. He never smoked a cigar, never took a chew of tobacco, never shaved his face nor never drank whisky. At this date (January 1, 1890) his weight is even 200 pounds, and he is six feet in height, stout and active, as all may be who will lead a temperate life.

Joseph W. Caskey, farmer and stock raiser, Hickory Plains, Ark. Agricultural pursuits has been Mr. Caskey's principal occupation in life, and the energetic and wide-awake manner in which he has taken advantage of all methods and ideas tending to the enhanced value of his property, has had a great deal to do with obtaining the competence which he now enjoys. He first saw the light in Maury County, Tenn., on August 6, 1847, and when ten years of age came with his parents, J. J. and Nancy J. (Foster) Caskey, to Arkansas, and there grew to manhood. He is the eldest of three children, two sisters: Sarah (deceased, wife of C. C. Broyles) and Martha E. (wife of C. C. Burton). The parents were natives of Tennessee, and in 1856 moved to Arkansas, locating in Prairie County, on the farm where Joseph W. is now residing. There were but slight improvements on the place at that time, but they began working on the same, and soon many changes were to be seen. The father died in Ringgold, Ga., in 1863, and the mother followed him to the grave in 1885. Joseph W. Caskey then took charge of the home place, has 160 acres of land, with eighty acres improved, and all his buildings are good and substantial. He was married on January 18, 1872, to Miss M. J. Burton, a native of Henderson County, Tenn., and the daughter of C. A. Burton. Five children have been born to this union: L. C., James A., N. E., W. J. and Harriet R. Mr. and Mrs. Caskey are members of the Baptist Church, and he is clerk of the same.

M. M. Clark, De Vall's Bluff, Ark. Mr. Clark, another of the honored and much respected pioneers of Prairie County, was originally from Kentucky, where his birth occurred in Warren County, in April, 1829, and was the eighth in a family of thirteen children born to the union of Joseph and Sarah (Moore) Clark, natives of South Carolina. The parents were married in Warren County, Ky., in 1818, and the father followed the occupation of a farmer until his death, which occurred in 1852. His wife died in St. Louis two years later. The grandparents on both sides were pioneers of Kentucky, and the paternal grandfather, Micajah Clark, was in the Revolutionary War, as was also the maternal grandfather, Hugh Moore, who died in Kentucky, at the age of ninety-six years. M. M. Clark was early taught the duties of the farm, and received his education in the schools of Warren County, Ky. He came to Arkansas in 1854, settled in Mississippi County, near Osceola, where he purchased 161 acres of land, with ten acres cleared. He also entered 160 acres, making 320 acres in all, cleared the same, erected buildings, but in the freshet of 1858, lost everything he had. He was married in Mississippi County, Ark., in October, 1857, to Miss Temperance A. Herrell, a native of North Carolina, and in 1859 he sold out and came to Prairie County, Ark. In March, 1862, he enlisted at Des Arc, in Capt. Ball's company, McCarver's regiment, for three years, and was in the battle of Fort Pillow. After remaining there some time, he returned to Arkansas, and entered Gen. Hindman's division, Col. Glenn's regiment, participating in the battle of Oak Hill, Ark. He was with Gen. Price in his raid through Missouri. He was in the battle of Helena, where he received a bomb shell wound in the foot, and was paroled at the hospital at Helena, in July, 1864. He then returned to Prairie County, Ark., entered the cavalry service, and was in active duty during the war. After this he returned to Prairie County, Ark., and in 1870 moved into Wattensas Township, where he purchased 160 acres of land, and now has seventy acres cleared and under cultivation. His principal crops are cotton and corn. He is active in politics, and votes with the Democratic party. He has been magistrate in his township. Mrs. Clark is a member of the Methodist Episcopal Church, South. To their union were born two children: John and Mary (now Mrs. George Ray). Mr. Clark has witnessed many changes in the country since his residence here, being one of the oldest settlers in the township, and has always taken an active interest in all matters relating to the good of the county. He is deeply interested in educational matters, and has been a member of the school board for sixteen years.

B. J. Collins, merchant, Hazen, Ark. Jared Collins, the father of the subject of this sketch, was born in North Carolina in 1807, was married in about 1832 to Miss Matilda E. Witty and reared a family of five children: Sally J. (deceased, married Dr. Jerome Cockran), J. W. (was killed in a battle at Jonesboro, Ga.), O. B. (is residing at Birmingham, Ala.), Emma C. (married Mr. Steadham and now resides at Pine Bluff, Ark.) and Mattie E. (now Mrs. Lawrence, resides at Memphis, Tenn.). Mr. Collins moved to Mississippi about 1835, and settled in Hernando County, where he was engaged in the tailor's business, but later became a tiller of the soil in the same county. His wife died and he married Miss R. J. Irwin, the mother of the subject of this sketch, in 1842, and the daughter of Bashford and Sophia Irwin, natives of that grand old mother of States, Virginia. B. J. Collins is the eldest of the following children: J. W. (who is married and resides in Birmingham, Ala.), Laura A. (deceased, was the wife of Mr. G. W. Guthrie), J. D. (resides in Shubuta, Miss.), M. J. (resides in Cotton Plant, Ark.), Minnie (is the wife of Mr. Dobbins, of Hazen, Ark.), and M. J. (married and resides at Cotton Plant, Ark.). B. J. Collins was reared and educated in Mississippi, and in 1862 enlisted in Company C, Forty-second Mississippi Infantry, commanded by Col. Miller. He was discharged in 1863, and after the war was engaged in farming until 1869, when he went to Grenada, Miss., and until 1877 carried on the mercantile business. Returning to De Soto

County he remained two years, and in 1879 removed to Brinkley, Ark. In 1881 he located at Batesville, Independence County, coming thence to Prairie County, in 1887, where he engaged in merchandising with Mr. Dobbins. Mr. Collins is a member of the Methodist Episcopal Church, South, is a Democrat in his political views and is one of the successful men of the county.

William Cook, deputy county clerk, De Vall's Bluff, Ark. This representative gentleman is a native of Shenandoah Valley, Va., where his birth occurred in 1838, and is the eldest of five children, the fruits of the union of William and Sarah (Kelley) Cook, natives of the Old Dominion. The father was a merchant by occupation and followed this in Warren County, Va., for many years. William Cook, Jr., was reared in the Shenandoah Valley, received his education in his native State, and when fifteen years of age left home and went to Missouri. He then started to go overland to California, went as far as Salt Lake City, and then returned to Missouri, settling in Rockport, and was here engaged as clerk for different firms. In 1861 he joined the Confederate army, and soon after the battle of Wilson's Creek, he was assigned to Gen. McBride's regiment, Seventh Division, Missouri State Guards. He participated in the battles of Lexington, Mo., Springfield, Mo., Pea Ridge, Ark., and Corinth. He was with Gen. Price in his raid through Missouri, and was taken prisoner at Lexington, in that State. He was taken to Johnson's Island, was paroled in 1865, and then came direct to Des Arc, Prairie County, Ark., where he engaged in general merchandising under the firm of Wilson & Cook, and carried on business until 1868. He then engaged in agricultural pursuits on a farm he had purchased in the edge of Des Arc, for some years, and later was made deputy clerk of Prairie County. He is a Democrat in his political principles. Socially he is a member of the White River Lodge No. 37, A. F. & A. M., and has served in every office in the lodge, having been Worshipful Master for ten years. He is a member of Iron Hall Lodge No. 109, De Vall's Bluff, Ark. He was married in Missouri in 1861, to Miss Mattie Lewis, a native of Virginia, who died at Des Arc in 1874, leaving three children, the eldest, Lula, now Mrs. Vayden, of Des Arc. Mr. Cook was married the second time in Des Arc, in 1875, to Miss Can T. Allen, a native of Tennessee, and the result of this union was one child, who died at the age of one year. Mr. Cook was a member of the school board at Des Arc for some years, and is now one of the progressive men of De Vall's Bluff. Mrs. Cook is a member of the Presbyterian Church.

Joshua Davis. From his earliest youth, Mr. Davis has been familiar with the details of farm work, and since his fifth year has been a resident of Arkansas. He was born in Maury County, Tenn., in the year 1835, being the fourth child born to Joseph and Hannah (Lamb) Davis, the former a native of South Carolina, born in 1812. He was the youngest of his father's family, and when quite a young man he was left an orphan, and from that time onward was compelled to fight his own way in the world. He started westward, and finally settled in Tennessee, where he was married to Miss Lamb, by whom he became the father of nine children: Emma (deceased), Elizabeth, Thomas, John Abraham, Leonidas, William, all of whom are dead. Those living are: Joshua and Nancy (Mrs. Davis). Joseph Davis was a farmer and a practicing physician, and followed both these occupations throughout his residence in Arkansas, having first come here in 1840, settling in Monroe County. In 1849 he moved to Prairie County, where he purchased 160 acres of land, and later bought eighty acres more, and here made his home until 1882, when he moved to Pulaski County, and here died the following year. He was very fond of the chase, and his desires in this direction were fully satisfied, for on first coming to the State, it was a splendid hunting region. Politically he was a Democrat, and for many years he had been an earnest member of the Missionary Baptist Church. His wife, who was an earnest member of the Methodist Episcopal Church, South, died in Prairie County, Ark., in 1852. Joshua Davis was married in 1860 to Miss Emma Knowls, her people having been residents of Ohio. His wife died five days after her son Scott was

43

born, and in 1866 Mr. Davis wedded Mrs. Sarah M. (Hendrix) Sparks, widow of S. M. Sparks, and by her has had the following children: William H. (deceased), Priscilla (Mrs. Davis), Lucretia (Mrs. Sales), Leonidas and Elmira. In 1861 Mr. Davis enlisted in Capt. Garrett's company, Fifth Arkansas Regiment, and after serving until 1862, was discharged on account of ill health. Upon recovering, he enlisted in the Second Arkansas Cavalry, and in 1863 received a severe wound in the head at Big Shanty, Ga. He was also at Chickamauga, Missionary Ridge, Atlanta, Franklin and Nashville. Since his return home, he has given his time to agricultural pursuits, and now has a fine farm of 320 acres, with 120 under cultivation. Like his father he is fond of hunting, and in his political views is a Democrat. He and his wife are members of the Primitive Baptist Church.

Richard Dinsdale, county assessor, De Vall's Bluff, Ark. The locality in which De Vall's Bluff is situated is indeed fortunate in having among its citizens such a man as Richard Dinsdale is conceded to be, for his connection with the interests of the county in a quiet, but none the less effective way, has proven to be of much benefit and influence, and of no little importance. He was born in Yorkshire, England, May 10, 1835, and was the youngest of eight children, the fruits of the union of John and Isabella (Thwaite) Dinsdale, both natives of Yorkshire, England. The ancestors were farmers for generations back, and on both sides were of English descent. The father died in his native country in 1837, and the mother received her final summons in 1863. Their children were named as follows: Alexander (married at Brownmore, Yorkshire, England, was an extensive stock and dairy farmer and died, leaving one daughter, Isabella, now Mrs. Thomas Willain, of Brownmore, England), Simon (married and settled in Yorkshire, England, was a farmer, and died in 1887 or 1888, leaving one daughter, Rose, who is now Mrs. Hebden and resides in England), George (married and settled at Gale, England, was an innkeeper, and died in 1883), Ann (married Robert Pratt, and died in England in 1880), Fawcett (married, and settled near Melbourne, Australia, in 1851, where he is engaged in farming), Jane (died at the age of six years) and Richard. The latter was reared on a dairy farm in Yorkshire, England, received his education in the schools of that country, and, at the age of twenty-one years, left Liverpool, on a sailing vessel, and, after an ocean voyage of five weeks, landed at Castle Garden, New York City. From there he went direct to La Crosse, Wis., remained there one year, and, in the spring of 1857, in company with nine others, crossed overland to Blue Earth County, Minn., where he entered 120 acres, near Mankato. This he improved, and also speculated in buying and selling land. In October, 1861, he enlisted in an independent battalion of Minnesota Volunteers and was mustered into service at Fort Snelling, Minn., November 1. From there he was sent to Benton Barracks, Mo., and participated in the battle of Fort Donelson, after which he was engaged in guard duty as escort to the telegraph corps through Kentucky and Tennessee. He was discharged at St. Paul, November 30, 1864, remained there a short time, and, in January, 1865, started for De Vall's Bluff, Ark., where he was engaged in the general grocery business. This he continued until 1873. During this time he was appointed county treasurer by Powell Clayton, and served four years. He subsequently engaged in agricultural pursuits, and is the owner of 400 acres of land, while his wife has 200 acres, making 600 acres in all, with about fifty acres under cultivation. He was married at De Vall's Bluff, Ark., in 1873, to Mrs. S. A. Brooks, a native of West Tennessee, and the result of this union has been two children: Isabella (died at the age of four years) and Maggie (who died at the age of eight years). Mr. and Mrs. Dinsdale are members of the Methodist Episcopal Church, South. Socially, Mr. Dinsdale is a member of the Masonic fraternity, Hamilton Lodge No. 110, he being Worshipful Master of the lodge. He is also a member of the Chapter, a member of Occidental Council No. 1, Little Rock, and belongs to De Vall's Bluff Lodge No. 2172, K. of H., which he has represented in the Grand Lodge. He takes an active part in politics, and his vote is cast with the Republican party. He also takes a deep interest in educational matters and has been a member of the school board for years. He has been a member of the town council a number of terms. He was elected county assessor in 1888, which position he fills to the satisfaction of all.

Dobbins & Collins, general merchants, Hazen, Ark. W. G. Dobbins, senior member of the firm, was born in Warren County, N. C., in 1844, and was the fourth in a family of five children born to the union of N. J. and Rebecca (Baker) Dobbins, natives of Virginia and North Carolina. The parents were married in North Carolina in 1830, and later moved to Mississippi, where the father carried on agricultural pursuits. Their children were named as follows: Elizabeth (deceased, was the wife of John E. Brown), John J. (married and resides in Mississippi), Edward B. (was killed at the battle of Shiloh), W. G. (our subject), and Joseph S. (who is married and resides in Mississippi). N. J. Dobbins is a member of the Baptist Church, is a public-spirited citizen and an earnest Democrat. His wife died in 1888. W. G. Dobbins moved to Mississippi with his parents in 1856, received his education in the common schools and began life as a sturdy son of the soil. He was married in 1877 to Miss Minnie C. Collins, daughter of Jared and R. J. (Erwin) Collins, natives, respectively, of North Carolina and Virginia. To this union were born five children, two now living: Viola D. and Edward B. Those deceased were named: William I., Clyde and Ada I. Mr. Dobbins moved to Arkansas in 1888, and engaged in merchandising at Hazen, where he still continues. He is an active man in the building up of the country and is universally respected. He is a Democrat in politics, and he and wife are members of the Baptist Church. In 1862 Mr. Dobbins enlisted in Blythe's battalion for twelve months, State service, and in 1863 he enlisted in Chalmer's battalion Eighteenth Mississippi Cavalry. He participated in the battles of Fort Pillow, Guntown, Harrisburg and several skirmishes. At the close of the war he returned to Mississippi and there remained until coming to Arkansas.

James M. Dorris has been a resident of Prairie County for twenty-two years, but has been a resident of the State since 1859. He is a Kentuckian, born in Fulton County August 7, 1838, and is a son of Samuel H. and Anna (Howton) Dorris, who were also natives of the "Blue Grass State." The father, who was born in 1795, was a farmer throughout life, and a soldier in the War of 1812, being with Jackson at the battle of New Orleans, and died in his native State in 1847, his wife's death occurring in 1846, she being born in 1799. James M. Dorris made his home with a sister in Kentucky until about sixteen years of age, then resided with different parties until he attained his majority. His early advantages for acquiring an education were not of the best, but he read with avidity such books as came in his way, and by the time he was ready to commence his medical studies he was a well-informed and intelligent young man. He became a disciple of Æsculapius under the direction of Dr. J. B. Blanton, of Hickman, Ky., and was a conscientious and faithful student for over two years. In 1859 he came to Arkansas and located at Searcy, and until the opening of the war was occupied as a hardware merchant. In April, 1861, he enlisted in the Confederate army, as a member of Company A, of Col. Matlock's regiment, one of the best drilled, as well as one of the best fighting companies west of the Mississippi River. Capt. James A. Poe commanded the company, in which he served until the close of the war, being engaged in various detached duty the most of the time. He was a participant in a number of skirmishes, and while home in Arkansas on a furlough, the army was disbanded in Louisiana. He then returned to Searcy and again engaged in the hardware business, but sold out after one year's experience, and settled about six miles northwest of Des Arc, where he began the practice of medicine, and was one of the leading members of that "healing art" for about seventeen years. He also conducted a farm, and was engaged in raising stock, and in all these enterprises was extremely successful. During the war he lost all his property, but since that time he has accumulated a handsome competency, and is now the owner of about 1,500 acres of land, about 250 acres being in

White County. His land embraces five farms, and he has about 300 acres under cultivation and well improved. He has always been a stanch Democrat in politics, and while a resident of White County served in the capacity of associate justice in the county courts, and in September, 1888, was elected to the last-named office in Prairie County, and in this capacity has shown sterling integrity, sound judgment, broad intelligence and liberal views. His decisions are made after careful and painstaking study of the evidence and all feel that his judgment can be relied upon. While in White County the Judge was married on October 17, 1860, to Miss Fannie E. Old, a daughter of Thomas Old. She was born near Somerville, Tenn., and was there reared to womanhood. She and the Judge are members of the Methodist Episcopal Church, and are the parents of the following family: James T. (deputy sheriff of Prairie County), Samuel H., Lucien A. and Rosie (who is attending college at Gallatin, Tenn.).

Adolph Driehaus, at present a planter of Ulm, Ark., is one of the many excellent citizens of foreign birth now living in Prairie County, who, by their thrift and energy have become prosperous and substantial residents in the community in which they make their home. He was born in the city of Leer on the river Ems, on the north seacoast (German Empire), on June 25, 1831, receiving his education at several of the schools in the city, and when hardly fifteen years of age went to sea, visiting most every navigable port in the world. He served nearly three years on the old frigate, Constitution, under Commodore Mayo, stationed on the west coast of Africa to suppress the slave trade, and was honorably discharged at Portsmouth, N. H., in 1854, under F. Pierce's administration. He studied navigation and went, after a year's hard studying, to sea again for several years as second and first officer or mate, when, in 1859, he became master of the barque Five Star. After one voyage he was given command of the Goldfinder, in which vessel he went up the Pike River to Fienstien in September of 1862. When France and England were at war with China, on August 13, 1862, at 3 o'clock P. M., they were attacked by Chinese pirates in the Gulf of Pichili and Mr. Driehaus was shot through the head and severely cut up with swords and left for dead. In 1863 he commanded the clipper barque, Flying Fish, under the Siamese colors, sailing mostly between Bankok and Shanghai, when, in 1865, she was sold at Hong Kong for $35,000. While in command of this craft he met with the Confederate cruiser, Alabama, on the east coast of Borneo, commanded by Capt. Lemmon. He then paid his passage from Hong Kong to London, England, and later made a visit to his old home in Leer to see his father. In March, 1866, he left home again, being of a restless disposition, and crossed the ocean to New York, trying hard to get command of a vessel again, but times being so very dull he remained quite a while in New York without success. He then went to Illinois and Iowa to grow up with the country and made several successful land speculations. On October 6 he was united in marriage to Miss Charlotte Rennan, who bore him eight children: Emma, Mary, Robert E., Adolph H., Bertha H., John T. and two other children who died in infancy. Mr. Driehaus' children are all at home with the exception of his oldest daughter, Mrs. Alf. Shriner, who resides in Nebraska, and is the mother of one child, a daughter named Mary. Mr. Driehaus has a good farm of 240 acres, eighty acres of which are improved and well stocked. He has an excellent orchard of 800 bearing trees, and is one of the wide-awake farmers of the county. After his marriage he resided in Iowa for a short time and then moved to Nebraska where he lived for twenty years, being one of the first settlers. The Pawnee Indians were numerous there at that time. Mr. Driehaus and family are members of the Methodist Episcopal Church and he takes a deep interest in educational matters. He came to this State in December, 1888, taking possession of the property he had bought the year previous, preferring the Sunny South of this locality to the North with its blizzards.

W. T. Edmonds, farmer and ginner, De Vall's Bluff, Ark. What is usually termed genius has little to do with the success of men in general. Keen perception, sound judgment and a determined will,

supported by persevering and continuous effort, are essential elements to success in any calling. Mr. Edmonds was originally from Shelby County, Tenn., where his birth occurred on October 14, 1845, and is the son of William T. Edmonds, a native of Tennessee, and one of the early pioneers of that State. He was married in Obion County, Tenn., to Miss Mary Ann Brown, also a native of Tennessee, and the fruits of this union were nine children. The father followed farming there until his death, which occurred in 1851, the mother surviving him until 1852. He was a minister in the Methodist Episcopal Church, South, and was revered and respected by all acquainted with him. W. T. Edmonds, the fifth of the nine children born to his parents, was reared to farm life, educated in the schools of Obion and Shelby Counties, Tenn., and in August, 1861, at Dresden, Weakley County, Tenn., he enlisted in Company A, Thirty-first Tennessee Infantry, commanded by Capt. Tansey, as a private. He participated in the battles of Shiloh, Corinth, Perryville and Murfreesboro, and after that battle, under the conscript act, he was discharged and returned to West Tennessee. He there joined Gen. Forrest's cavalry, and was in the battle of Harrisburg (Miss.), Price's Cross Roads, Memphis, Franklin, Nashville, Fort Pillow, etc. He was paroled at Gainesville, Ala., in 1865, after which he returned to Memphis and engaged as salesman in a wholesale tobacco house. In 1868 he was messenger on the Mobile & Ohio Railroad for the Southern Express Company, running from Cairo to Mobile, and in 1869 he came to Prairie County, settled in Lower Hill Township, where he remained engaged in tilling the soil until 1888. He then purchased 460 acres of land, with 150 acres under cultivation, and his principal crops have been cotton and corn. He has a good cotton-gin located one and a half miles from De Vall's Bluff, and is considered one of the practical and progressive farmers of the county. He is a Democrat, politically, but is not active in politics. He is a member of the Knights of Pythias, White River Lodge No. 41, and is also a member of the Knights of Honor, De Vall's Bluff Lodge. He was married at De Vall's Bluff, Ark., on December

23, 1886, to Miss Sally Senter, a native of Hamblen County, Tenn., who was a teacher in the De Vall's Bluff schools when Mr. Edmonds met her. He and wife are members of the Missionary Baptist Church.

Martin M. Erwin is one of the progressive tillers of the soil of Prairie County, Ark., and was born in Austin in what is now Lonoke County, December 9, 1828, being a son of Oliver Erwin, a brother of A. S. Erwin. He was reared on the home farm near Austin, and his knowledge of the world was only such as could be obtained while assisting his father in tilling the soil. He was married in Pulaski County in July, 1852, to Miss Elizabeth McCraw, a daughter of Pleasant McCraw, a prominent man and a pioneer of that county. After his marriage Mr. Erwin farmed for a short time near the old home place, but in 1853 he moved to Des Arc where he has since made his home, and in addition to conducting his farm he also dealt in real estate, both occupations proving quite successful, and he is now the owner of several thousand acres of land, besides some valuable town property. In 1861 he enlisted in the Confederate army and served until he received his discharge for disability the following year. After remaining idle until 1863 he re-enlisted and was on active duty until the close of the war, participating in the battles of Mansfield, Pleasant Hill, and was with Price on his raid through Missouri. He was called upon to mourn the loss of his wife by death in 1855, and two years later he took for his second wife Miss Sania Bethell, a daughter of Dr. William Bethell, who is now deceased. Mrs. Erwin was born in Rockingham County, N. C., but was reared and educated in Dallas County, Ark. She and Mr. Erwin have one son, William Erwin, a merchant of Des Arc; and they are members of the Methodist Episcopal Church.

Ambrose S. Erwin, retired merchant, Des Arc, Ark. In these days of money-making, when life is a constant struggle between right and wrong, it is a pleasure to lay before an intelligent reader the unsullied record of an honorable man. To the youthful it will be a useful lesson, an incentive to honest industry. Ambrose S. Erwin, the subject of this sketch, is a native of Arkansas, his birth occurring at old Austin, in what is now Lonoke County, on February 26, 1834, and is the son of Hon. James and Olivia (McCaleb) Erwin, both natives of North Carolina. The father was of Irish descent and grew to manhood in his native State, where he remained until 1822. He then moved to Arkansas, settled in what is now old Austin, and erected the first house in Lonoke or Prairie Counties, being one of the first actual settlers of these counties. He resided in that vicinity and carried on agricultural pursuits until about 1850, when he, in partnership with G. C. Watkins, of Little Rock, entered the land and laid off the town of Des Arc. He then settled there, erected a residence, mill and gin, and there died on January 1, 1853. He held several prominent official positions, and was the first man to represent Prairie County in the legislature. He contracted with the United States to assist in removing the Indians west of the Mississippi and was engaged in that business for a number of years. Mrs. Erwin survived her husband a few years, dying in 1859; she was of Scotch descent. Their family consisted of three sons and one daughter, all of whom grew to mature years, but Ambrose S. and an elder brother are the only ones now living. The former attained his growth in Des Arc, and remained with his parents until they received their final summons. In 1855 he began clerking in Des Arc, and continued at this until 1859, when he formed a partnership with a Mr. P. H. Haley, in the general mercantile business and which he has continued the principal part of the time since. He began as clerk, but by his good business management has made a comfortable competence which he now enjoys, and is one of the substantial men of Prairie County. He left his business during the war, and in 1861 enlisted in Col. Churchill's regiment, serving about three months, when he was discharged. In 1862 he re-enlisted in Col. Crawford's regiment and served until the close of the war. He entered the army as a private, was promoted to the rank of lieutenant, and at the close of the war had charge of a company. He participated in the following battles: Oak Hills, Poison Springs, Mark's Mill, and was in all the battles of Gen. Price's raid through Missouri. He was captured with Gen. Marmaduke at Big Blue, but succeeded in making his escape within two hours afterward. He was at Camden and had command of couriers when peace was declared and he was disbanded at that place. Returning home after the war he formed a partnership with S. N. Jackson, which continued for three years, and then he and Mr. Plunkett formed a partnership in the mercantile business, which continued for about twenty years. Mr. Erwin was married in Des Arc, in February, 1859, to Miss Lucy Bethell, a native of Memphis, but who was reared in Arkansas, and the daughter of Dr. William Bethell. They have five children: Anna (wife of Reuben Lee), Albert L., Carrie (wife of F. P. Cates, of Little Rock), Mabel and Minnie (two young ladies at home). Mr. Erwin is a Master Mason, and he and wife and family are members of the Old School Presbyterian Church.

Albert L. Erwin, although a young man, is already recognized as a progressive and substantial merchant of Des Arc and has achieved a place among the business men of the county by no means an inferior one and one in which many older in years and experience might well feel proud to occupy. He has spent his life and received his education in Des Arc, his birth occurring here January 1, 1864, and he is a son of A. S. and Lucy Erwin, a sketch of whom appears in this work. Besides attending the schools of his native town he was also an attendant of Batesville College and after clerking in his father's store some time he formed a partnership with B. B. Bethel & Co., and was associated with this firm for two years. He then began business for himself and now has one of the best and most complete establishments in the county. His store is a long two-story brick 110x30 feet and is well fitted to supply the wants of the public. He has been married since September 20, 1885, to Iuta Ward, a native of Winona, Miss., where she was also reared and educated, being an attendent of the Ward Seminary, of Nashville, Tenn. She died September 22, 1889, leaving one son: Benj. A., a child of three years. Mr. Erwin is a member of the Presbyterian Church.

B. W. Flinn, M. D., is a physician and surgeon of prominence in Prairie County, Ark., and although he is still a young practitioner he has been very successful in alleviating the sufferings of the sick and afflicted. He was born in Darlington District, S. C., February 19, 1861, and is a son of Dr. C. J. Flinn, a native of the "Emerald Isle," but who was reared and educated in Mississippi. He was a man of superior mental endowments, and for a number of years was professor in Charleston Medical College, becoming well known as an eminent physician. In 1869 he moved to Arkansas, and located in Lonoke County, and for two years practiced his profession at Austin, moving in 1871 to Des Arc, Prairie County, where he made his home until his death, November 24, 1884. His wife, whose maiden name was Susan A. Hearron, was born and reared in South Carolina, and their marriage also took place in that State. She now resides in Des Arc. Dr. B. W. Flinn spent the greater part of his youth in Des Arc, and received the best educational advantages the town afforded, commencing, after reaching a proper age, the study of medicine with his father, and took his first course of lectures in 1879 in the College of Physicians and Surgeons at Baltimore. During 1880 and 1881 he took a course of medical lectures in a College of Memphis, Tenn., graduating in the spring of 1881, but the following year returned to this institution and took the hospital course. He then located eight miles south of Des Arc, and has since been in active practice in the county, but since March, 1884, has been a resident of the town of Des Arc. He is a member of the County Medical Society, and in 1884 was appointed county medical examiner, and still holds this position. He was married in Prairie County, March 10, 1886, to Miss Lizzie Whyte, a daughter of J. F. Whyte, she being a native of this county, and by her he has one son: Heber, who is eighteen months old. The Dr. and his wife are members of the Old School Presbyterian Church, and he is a member of the K. of H., and is medical examiner of his lodge.

F. H. Fransioli is a farmer of Belcher Township, Prairie County, Ark., and was born in Wilson County, Tenn., in 1851, and was reared to manhood in that county, being the third child born to J. A. and Mary J. (Thomason) Fransioli, the former a native of Switzerland. About the year 1820 he emigrated to America, settling in Memphis, Tenn., where he engaged in the queensware business and made his home for nearly forty years. In 1844 he married the daughter of John Thomason, a native of Mississippi, and by her became the father of the following family: Josephine (who is the wife of George Shutt and resides in Wilson County, Tenn.), Charles (who died in Arkansas County, Ark., in 1877) and our subject, F. H. Mr. Fransioli died in Cuba in 1858, whither he had gone for his health. His widow survives him and is a resident of Middle Tennessee. F. H. Fransioli spent his life, up to 1875, in the State of Tennessee, and after the year 1870 worked for himself, being engaged in farming in Wilson County. This occupation has received the greater part of his attention since coming to the State, and of his fine farm of 600 acres he has 150 acres under cultivation. He possesses those advanced ideas and progressive principles regarding agricultural life which has placed so many men at the top round of the ladder, and in looking over his well tilled farm we find that his days have not been uselessly or idly spent. He has done all in his power to promote an interest in the building of schools and churches, and has also been interested in local politics, being a member of the Democratic party. He is a Mason, and his wife, whom he married in 1879, and whose maiden name was Lucy Tittle, is a member of the Methodist Episcopal Church. She is a daughter of James and Margaret E. (Hurst) Tittle.

David Gates, De Vall's Bluff, Ark. A number of years passed in sincere and honest endeavor to thoroughly discharge every duty in the different lines of business to which his attention has been directed has contributed very materially to the success that has fallen to Mr. Gates' career in life. He was born in Bavaria, Germany, in 1845, and was the fourth in a family of five children, the fruits of the union of Mayer and Henrietta Gates, natives also of Bavaria, Germany. The father was a stock breeder, a butcher and an extensive land owner. He died in 1881, and the mother in 1883, in their native country. Ferdinand, their eldest son, came to America in 1855, settled at Hickory Plains, Prairie County, Ark., and in 1865 engaged in business at Des Arc. Later he had four stores, one at De Vall's Bluff, another at Lonoke, another at Cotton Plant and still another at Des Arc. He is closing out the one at Des Arc. He is now residing at Memphis. He was in the service for three years. Isaac, another son, came to Prairie County, Ark., in 1856, engaged in peddling until 1865, and then engaged as partner with his brother Ferdinand. In 1861 he enlisted in the Confederate army, was quartermaster and commissary in Bragg's division, and was wounded at Chattanooga and Murfreesboro. He suffered from paralysis and died in 1884. David Gates came direct to Prairie County, Ark., in 1857, and although but little over twelve years of age he commenced working for his brother on a salary. He was educated at Hickory Plains, Ark., and in 1862 he donned his suit of gray, shouldered his musket, and enlisted in Company A, Col. Glenn's regiment of infantry. He participated in the battle of Little Rock, and afterward was placed in Woodruff's battalion of artillery. He was in the battles of Mansfield and Pleasant Hill, and was with Gen. Price in his raid through Missouri. He surrendered at Marshall, Tex., in 1865, after which he returned to Prairie County, but in 1866 went to the Lone Star State, where he was engaged in the stock business and in running a wagon train. In 1868 he returned to Prairie County, and was engaged on a salary for his brother as collector and outside manager. They own a stock ranch of 480 acres, and make a speciality of raising blooded stock, especially Hereford and short-horned cattle. They also raise cotton, corn, millet and peas. The subject of this sketch owns individually about 1,200 acres, with 450 acres under cultivation. He is also engaged in raising horses. Mr. Gates was married in Des Arc in 1881 to Miss Carrie Greer, a native of Des Arc. They have two children: Stella and Fannie Pearl. Mr. Gates is a member of the K. of H. in Brinkley, and is also a member of De Vall's Bluff Lodge, No. 41, K. of P.

Dr. W. R. J. Gibbon, planter and stock raiser, Roe, Ark. Every life has a history of its own, and although in appearance it may seem to possess very little to distinguish it from others, yet Dr. Gibbon's career as a planter and physician, as well as his experience in the political affairs of the community, have contributed to give him a wide and popular acquaintance with nearly every citizen of Prairie County, if not personally, then by name, and serves to make his career a more than ordinary one. Dr. Gibbon was born in Brunswick County, Va., on March 19, 1832, and is the son of Thomas Gibbon, who was also a native of the Old Dominion, born in 1772. The father was educated in his native State, and in 1811 was there married to Miss Mary Mabry, who was born in Virginia in 1782, and was the daughter of Nathaniel and Dorotha Mabry, early settlers of Virginia. To Mr. and Mrs. Gibbon were born eleven children, five of whom lived to be grown: James L., Thomas, Lucy J., W. R. J. and Charles. The remainder died in infancy. The senior Mr. Gibbon was quite a prominent man in Brunswick County, held the office of sheriff of the same for two years, and filled many other prominent positions. He was in the War of 1812, held the position of captain, but on account of poor health was released from duty. He was member of the Masonic fraternity for about fifty years, and held most of the offices in that order. He and wife were both members of the Methodist Episcopal Church. He was a planter by occupation, and owned about 1,300 acres of land at the time of his death, which occurred in July, 1859. His wife died in 1867. Dr. W. R. J. Gibbon received his education in Stony Mount Male Academy, Brunswick County, Va., and the Virginia Military Institute, and later attended the Medical College of Virginia, graduating during the session of 1854–55. In June of the same year he immigrated to Fayette County, Tenn., practiced his profession there until December, 1856, when he immigrated to Arkansas and located in Monroe County, at Indian Bay. He was married April 24, 1856, to Miss Mary J. Wilie, a native of Pontotoc County, Miss., born March 1, 1839, and the daughter of Oliver and Susan Wilie. On May 28, 1860,

a son, Thomas E., was born to this union, and he is now residing at Los Angeles, Cal. He was educated at Austin and Lonoke, and has been practicing law for the past eight years. He is a brilliant young man and was elected to the legislature from Pulaski County, in 1885 and 1886. Dr. W. R. J. Gibbon is an extensive planter and stock dealer by occupation, and has about 320 acres of good land, with 125 acres under cultivation. He is one of the prominent men of Prairie County, has represented the same in the legislature, and is at present filling that honorary position. He is a member of the Blue Lodge, in the Masonic order, and has held the office of Master for four years of Lodge No. 185. He is also a member of the Good Templars' lodge, and is a man who takes an interest in all laudable enterprises. He and Mrs. Gibbon are members of the Methodist Episcopal Church, South, and both are liberal contributors to the same.

J. W. Grady is one of the well-known farmers and stockmen of Prairie County, and is highly respected and very popular, for his career has been of much value to this community, both in material affairs, as a public spirited citizen and otherwise. Since 1867 he has resided on his present farm of 160 acres, seventy acres of which are under cultivation, and has continuously given his attention to the calling to which he was reared, that of farming and stock raising. After coming into this new country, he had many discouragements to overcome, and many obstacles to meet in securing for himself and family a comfortable home, but this did not deter him from putting forth every energy toward the ambition of his hopes. In his efforts he was warmly aided by his good wife, whom he married in August, 1865, and whose maiden name was Sarah J. Collier, a daughter of V. H. and Hannah Collier. To Mr. and Mrs. Grady have been born eight children: William L., Caroline (now Mrs. Petty of Prairie County), James, Anna, Francis, Joseph, Mary and Jackson. The mother of these children died at her home in Prairie County, in 1887, and the following year Mr. Grady espoused Lou E. Petty, a daughter of George I. Petty, of Prairie County. Mr. Grady is a Democrat, a Master Mason, and he and wife are members of the Baptist Church. He was born in Alabama in 1841, and was the second child born to William J. and Caroline E. (Brown) Grady, the former of whom was born in the State of North Carolina about 1815. He was married there in 1835, to a daughter of Leroy Brown, a South Carolinian, and he and his wife became the parents of twelve children: Sophia E. (of Texas), J. W. (our biographical subject), Samuel H. (who lives in Mississippi), Nathaniel (also of Mississippi), Zachariah T. (of Alabama), Leroy (of Alabama), Caroline E. (Mrs. McKinney, of Alabama), Florence (Mrs. Tramell, of Alabama), Frances (who died at the age of seventeen years) and three infants (deceased). Mr. Grady moved to Alabama, shortly after he was married and reared his boys to a farm life in that State. He was a prominent Mason, and besides holding a number of official positions, he was Master of his lodge for a number of years. He was magistrate in the town where he lived, and was possessed of a keen insight into business, and very prosperous in farming. He died in Chambers County, Ala., in 1880, his wife following him to the grave five years later. The Grady's are of Irish descent, the grandfather, John Grady, having been born in the "Emerald Isle." In 1861 J. W. Grady took up arms in defense of the South, and enlisted in Company D, Eighth Confederate Cavalry, and was under Wheeler, taking part in all the engagements in which the Army of Tennessee participated.

Thomas F. Greer, farmer, stock raiser and ginner, Des Arc, Ark. Tennessee has given to Prairie County, Ark., many estimable citizens, but she has contributed none more highly respected or for conscientious discharge of duty in every relation of life, more worthy of respect and esteem than the subject of this sketch. He was born January 14, 1829, in Rhea County, and is the son of William and Tempie (Presley) Greer, both natives of Tennessee. The father followed agricultural pursuits in Tennessee a number of years and then removed to Alabama, thence to Arkansas in 1851, and settled in Prairie County, where he resided for some time. Later he removed to White County. He

died at the residence of his son, Thomas F., in 1885, and his wife died two years previous to this. Thomas F. Greer's time was divided in early life between assisting on the farm and in attending school in Alabama. He remained with his parents until twenty-one years of age, when he moved with them to Arkansas in 1851, engaging in the livery business at Des Arc, and continuing it until about 1873. He then bought land where he now resides, cleared it, and has since added to the same until he now is the owner of 640 acres of good land, with about 250 acres under cultivation. He has a good gin, ten or twelve tenement houses, and his land lies about two miles from Des Arc. Mr. Greer served about two years in the ordnance department of the Confederate army during the war. He has been twice married, first about 1853 to Miss Sarah Goodwin, a native of Middle Tennessee, who bore him four children: Isabella (wife of G. W. Blakemore), Floyd (married, and resides at Des Arc, Ark.), Annie (wife of John Thomas) and one died in infancy. Mr. Greer's second marriage occurred about 1875, to Mrs. Ellen (Brown) Bethell, a native of Memphis, Tenn., and the daughter of Col. Samuel Brown. To this union have been born two children: Daisy and Birdie. Mr. Greer is a member of the Baptist Church and his wife of the Old School Presbyterian Church. He is now also engaged in the saw-mill business.

J. A. Harr is a real-estate dealer of Fairmount, Ark., and was born in Maryland in 1854, being the fifth child born to Everhard and Martha (Coffman) Harr, the former of whom was born in Philadelphia, Penn., being one of nine children born to Isaiah Harr, an Englishman. Everhard Harr was a manufacturer of edge tools, and after working in his native city for many years he moved to Maryland. He was born in 1790, and about 1835 was married, his wife being a native of Philadelphia, and a member of the Coffman family of that city. Their children were: Isaiah (who is married and lives in Phillipsburg, Penn.), J. A., Sanford L. (a resident of Fairmount, Ark.) and James, Mary, Martha and Margaret (deceased). The early days of our subject were spent in Maryland, and his schooling was obtained in the Millersville State

Normal School of Pennsylvania. After teaching school for a number of years he determined to take Horace Greeley's advice and "Go West," thinking the advantages for a young man of push and enterprise much better here than there, and in 1877 settled in the State of Nebraska, in Colfax County. In 1882, however, he came to Fairmount, Ark., and has since been actively and successfully engaged in the real-estate business. He has under his control 240,000 acres of land, and in his deals commands the public confidence in a marked degree. He is a director of the Little Rock & Mississippi Railroad, and being public spirited and enterprising, is deeply interested in the upbuilding of the county, and is a special advocate of schools and churches. He is a Republican in his political views.

John R. Harshaw, merchant, farmer and postmaster, Hickory Plains, Ark. A number of years passed in sincere and earnest endeavor to thoroughly discharge every duty in the different branches of business to which his attention has been directed has contributed very materially to the success that has fallen to Mr. Harshaw's career in life. He came originally from Mississippi, where his birth occurred in Marshall County, on September 4, 1852, and is the son of Daniel Harshaw, a native of South Carolina. When a young man the father married Miss Mary N. Dowdle, also a native of South Carolina, and they afterward moved to Mississippi, where they resided for fifteen years. In December, 1852, they moved to Arkansas, located at Hickory Plains, Prairie County, and there the father cultivated the soil for a several years. In 1866 he engaged in mercantile pursuits with his son at this place and continued business here up to 1883. He was postmaster from 1865 up to the time of his death and was a man who had the confidence and esteem of all. His wife survives him at this writing and is now seventy years of age. Their family consisted of two sons and five daughters, all of whom grew to mature age. One son, Leroy D., was the second merchant at Hickory Plains. He went to California for his health in 1873 and died there soon after. Three of the sisters are living: Mrs. E. S. Davis (a widow),

Mrs. A. C. Harrison (also a widow) and Mrs. A. S. Reinhardt (of Des Arc). J. B. Harshaw attained his growth and received a good practical education at Hickory Plains Academy. He clerked for his father until twenty-one years of age, when he took an active interest in the store and has had charge of the business since that time. He has a large and complete stock of general merchandise, and is doing an immense business of about $30,000 annually, and handles cotton, etc. He is a clear-headed man of business and an excellent manager of all affairs of which he has the control; he has enjoyed an unsullied reputation and has materially helped the general interests and standing of Hickory Plains. He is the owner of several farms in this State and county, in all about 5,000 acres of land, and is a man whose characteristics of energy, promptness and sobriety will always secure success. He was appointed postmaster here in 1883 and holds this position at the present time. He was married at Hickory Plains on May 18, 1876, to Miss Eva Burks, a native of Kentucky, who was reared and educated near Russellville, Logan County, Ky., and who is the daughter of W. I. Burks, now of Springfield, Mo. To Mr. and Mrs. Harshaw were born five children, who are named as follows: Leroy, Mary V., Marion B., John R. and Lizzie. Mrs. Harshaw is a member of the Methodist Episcopal Church, South. Mr. Harshaw is a man of fine physique, standing six feet one inch, weighs 275 pounds, and is as pleasant and sociable a gentleman as one would care to meet.

A. J. Hendricks, a farmer and stock raiser, Hazen, Ark. Mr. Hendricks on starting out in life for himself, chose as his calling the pursuit of farming, and not without substantial results. He takes a native pride in all that he does, for this county has ever been his home, his birth occurring in 1849. His father was a native of South Carolina, was born in 1812, and was married in 1834 to Miss Rebecca L. Minton, the daughter of S. B. Minton, a native of South Carolina. Mr. Hendricks, Sr., settled in Arkansas, in 1844, entered land, and here reared his family of twelve children, all now deceased, with the exception of Matilda, A. J., B. F., Rebecca and Naomi. William, the father, was a member of the Primitive Baptist Church, was magistrate for years, and took an active interest in everything pertaining to the good of the county. He died in 1884. The mother is still living, and is an honored member of the Primitive Baptist Church. A. J. Hendricks commenced life for himself in 1869 as an agriculturist, and chose for his companion in life, Miss Amanda Sparks, daughter of David Sparks. This union resulted in the birth of nine children: Leroy F., Ernest J. and Purna. Those deceased were named: Thomas E., Albert A., Luther F., Arizona, Irene and Ursula. Mr. Hendricks now owns a good farm of 150 acres, has sixty-five under cultivation, and is one of the progressive agriculturists of the county. He is a member of the school board, and takes a deep interest in all educational matters. He is a Democrat in politics.

James W. Highfill, farmer and stock raiser, Hickory Plains, Ark. Mr. Highfill, like many of the prominent settlers of Prairie County, is a native of North Carolina, his birth occurring in Guilford County, November 27, 1848, and is the son of D. H. Highfill, a native of North Carolina, and Sarah H. (McMichael) Highfill, also a native of the same State. The family moved to Tennessee in 1851, settled in Henry County, and there resided until 1856, when in the fall of that year, they moved to Missouri. One year later they returned to Tennessee, and the parents now reside in Weakley County, where they own a good farm. J. W. Highfill's youthful days were divided between assisting on the home place and in attending school. He remained with his father until twenty-one years of age and was married December 24, 1870, to Miss Tennessee L. Ashby, a native of Wilson County, Tenn., and the daughter of James W. Ashby. The fruits of this union have been eight sons: William H., Jesse B., Charles L., Henry H., Edwin James, Walter T., John A. and Robert D. They lost one daughter in October, 1888, at the age of eighteen months. After his marriage he followed farming in Henry County, for two years, and in January, 1872, moved to Arkansas, locating on land adjoining his present property. He has a farm of 160 acres, with ninety acres under cul-

tivation, and has six acres in orchard. Mr. Highfill is serving his second term as president of Agricultural Wheel No. 2, and he is given a recognized position among the leading agriculturists of the township. He and Mrs. Highfill are members of the Missionary Baptist Church, and he is a deacon in the same. As a citizen, Mr. Highfill is respected and esteemed by all acquainted with him.

W. W. Hipolite, M. D., De Vall's Bluff. Among the people of Prairie County, as well as surrounding counties, and of the State at large, the name that heads this sketch is by no means an unfamiliar one. For many years he has been actively engaged in the practice of his chosen profession, and during this time his career as a practitioner and thorough student of medicine has won for him no less a reputation than has his personal characteristics as a citizen and a neighbor. He was born in Hornellsville, Steuben County, N. Y., August 3, 1834, and was the son of Casimir Vincent Hipolite, a native also of New York. The father was the son of Vincent Hipolite, a native of France, and at one time a surgeon in the French army. After leaving the army Vincent Hipolite resided on the Island of Hayti, where he was a large property holder, till the insurrection of 1791, when his possessions were confiscated. Owing to the fact that he was a physician his life was spared, in order that his services might be utilized in the hospital. He succeeded in escaping to New York, in one of his own vessels, accompanied by seven of his slaves, who still adhered to him. It was during the residence of Vincent Hipolite in New York that Casimir Vincent Hipolite, the father of the subject of our sketch, was born, September 12, 1796. C. V. Hipolite lost by death two wives and all his children by them, excepting a son who died some years later. He was married for the third time on June 16, 1833, to Nancy Drake, widow of Francis Drake, and whose maiden name was Nancy Parsons a native also of the same State. To them were born three children, Dr. W. W. Hipolite being the eldest; the next, Maria Antoinette, who became the wife of Dr. F. M. Weller, and died at Evanston, Ill.; the youngest, Leverett Anson Hipolite, is now a resident of Kansas. The occupation of C. V. Hipolite was that of a farmer, which he followed in the State of New York till 1851, when he removed to Northville, Mich., and thence, in 1857, to Cook County, Ill., where he continued his occupation till 1861. Owing to their advanced age, and the fact that they were alone, the father and mother of Dr. W. W. Hipolite were then induced to make their future home with him, first in Racine County, Wis., and then in De Vall's Bluff, Ark., where they died, the mother on June 24, 1870, and the father in November, 1874. The early life of Dr. W. W. Hipolite was spent on his father's farm, where he regularly attended the public school till the age of fifteen, when he entered the Academy of Fredonia, N. Y., where he remained till the fall of 1851, when he accompanied his father's family to Northville, Mich. While attending Fredonia Academy, he was, on the recommendation of the faculty, appointed to take charge of the meteorological observations at that point, by authority of the Smithsonian Institute of Washington, D. C. After his removal to Northville, Mich., he engaged in teaching school, and while thus employed commenced the study of medicine under his brother-in-law, Dr. F. M. Weller. In due time he entered the Medical Department of the University of Michigan, from which he graduated with honor, March 27, 1857. After graduation he spent some months in the office and drug store of Dr. Weller, who had in the meantime removed to Evanston, Ill. He located in Cook County, Ill., in the spring of 1858, where he built up a good practice, and remained there three years, when he removed to Racine County, Wis., and continued to practice his profession. In December, 1862, he entered the army as assistant surgeon of the Eighteenth Regiment Illinois Volunteer Infantry, having been commissioned as such by Gov. Yates, of Illinois. Soon after joining his regiment he was placed in charge of the same, the regimental surgeon having been sent on duty elsewhere. He was constantly with his regiment in its various engagements in Tennessee, and later in the Vicksburg campaign. Soon after the surrender of that stronghold he resigned and returned to his home, owing to the fact that he

had become disabled for duty from a severe attack of typho-malarial fever, followed by camp diarrhœa, and his recovery was despaired of. During several succeeding months his recovery was slow and tedious, and he was unable to engage in business. After about one year from the time he left the service, his health being sufficiently restored to enable him to again take the field, he re-entered the service by accepting a commission as assistant surgeon of the Twenty-ninth Wisconsin Volunteer Infantry. From this time till April 9, 1866, when he was finally discharged with his regiment, he saw much active service, and held many responsible positions. At one time he had charge of all the reserve artillery, Department of the Gulf, with headquarters at Kenner, La. In February, 1865, he was ordered to take charge of the hospital property of his brigade, and convey the same to Fort Gaines, Mobile Bay. In the execution of this order he embarked on board the gulf steamer George Peabody, which had on board in all about 1,000 men and nearly 200 horses and mules. After crossing the bar, at the mouth of the Mississippi River, the vessel encountered the most violent storm known there for many years, and all the horses and mules, excepting four, were put overboard, and eight men were lost. It was deemed a marvel that the vessel escaped destruction with all on board. Upon his arrival at Fort Gaines, Dr. Hipolite found waiting him a commission from President Lincoln, promoting him to the rank of major of cavalry and surgeon of the Eleventh United States Cavalry Troops. Prior to this he had successfully passed the medical examining board, United States army, at St. Louis, before which he was ordered by the surgeon-general of the army. He joined his new command at Little Rock, Ark., and served with it till April 1, 1865, when the Eleventh, the One Hundred and Twelfth and the One Hundred and Thirteenth Regiments, United States Cavalry Troops, were consolidated into a single organization, to be known as the One Hundred and Thirteenth United States Cavalry Troops, and he was retained as the surgeon of the new regiment, and was commissioned as such by President Lincoln. In the fall of 1865 he was made post-surgeon at De Vall's

Bluff, Ark., and took charge of the large hospitals at that post, and continued in charge until his final muster out. He was also surgeon-in-chief of White River District, which embraced a wide extent of territory. Upon leaving the army the Doctor resumed his practice in Wisconsin, where he remained till the spring of 1870, when he removed from Racine, Wis., to De Vall's Bluff, Ark., where he has continued to practice to the present time. He is regarded as one of the leading physicians of his State, and has held many responsible positions. He is the regularly commissioned surgeon of most of the various life insurance companies doing business there, and also of the Memphis & Little Rock Railway. He is the president of Prairie County Medical Society, a member of the Arkansas State Medical Society, and, by appointment from that organization, has for several years been a member of the board of visitors to the Medical Department of the Arkansas Industrial University; and was a delegate to the Ninth International Medical Congress, which met in Washington, D. C., in 1887. He is a Republican in politics; has been a member of the town council for a number of terms, and is at present president of the school board. While a resident of Cook County, Ill., he was married, in Chicago, to Maria Jane Parker, seven years his junior, a native of Canada, and the daughter of Lott and Roxana Parker, both natives of Massachusetts. The parents settled in Canada East, where the father engaged in farming. In the spring of 1880, being left alone, they left their life-long home in Canada, and removed to De Vall's Bluff, to be with their two daughters, Mrs. A. W. Socy being a sister of Mrs. Dr. Hipolite. The mother died in 1882, and the father still lives at the advanced age of eighty-five years. To Doctor and Mrs. Hipolite have been born five children. The first, Carrie Lorena, died at the age of five years and seven months, at De Vall's Bluff, while he was in charge of the post hospital there, the mother and children having gone there to spend the winter with him. The next, Fred A., is attending the Medical College at Little Rock, and expects to graduate in the spring of 1890. The third, Walter H., is a civil engineer and a fine draughtsman. Both sons attended school at Little Rock and at the Arkansas Industrial University, located at Fayetteville. Carrie Lorena, the only daughter now living, was named after the first-born, which died as stated. She is now the wife of T. J. Owen, a druggist at De Vall's Bluff. Charles Edward, the youngest, will be nine years of age on the last day of January, 1890. The Doctor owns a fine residence, and has one of the best equipped offices in his State. He still owns the mare "Dixie," now twenty-eight years old, on which he rode during the last year of his service in the army.

H. W. Holmes, druggist, Hazen, Ark. Mr. Holmes established the drug business in Hazen in April, 1889, and his accuracy and skill in this particular branch of industry, have won the confidence of the public, and he already commands a good trade. He came to Prairie County, Ark., in the fall of 1870, from Alabama, and here he has since resided. He owes his nativity to Madison County, Ala., where his birth occurred in 1851, and is the eldest in a family of three children, the fruits of the union of D. K. and Virginia A. (Rutherford) Holmes, natives of Virginia and Alabama, respectively. The father was reared in Lexington, Ky., read medicine in Nashville, Tenn., and took a medical course at that place, after which he practiced his profession for over twenty-five years. He has now retired, and resides at Hazen. His excellent wife departed this life in Jackson County, Ala., in 1861. H. W. Holmes remained in Alabama until twenty years of age, and received his education in the schools of Jackson County. He came with his father to Arkansas in 1870, and here he commenced clerking in a dry-goods store, at Des Arc, Prairie County, remaining in that city for about seven years. In 1884 he came to Hazen, and was engaged as book-keeper for Curtis & Co., general merchants, following this business for different firms, until he engaged in the drug business, in 1889. He was married in Des Arc, in 1882, to Miss Mamie Thompson, a native of South Carolina, and the daughter of William and Elizabeth A. (West) Thompson, natives, respectively, of North Ireland and South Carolina. Mr. Thompson came to this county in about 1872, and here his death occurred in 1887. Mrs. Thompson is now residing in Des Arc. To the union of Mr. and Mrs. Holmes have been born three living children: William T., Daniel K. and Annie Pearl. Henry W. died in February, 1888, at the age of two years and six months. Mr. Holmes is Democratic in his political views, and takes considerable interest in politics. He was recorder of Hazen for a number of years, and is also a member of the school board. He is a member of the K. of H., Hazen Lodge No. 3135, and was charter member and Reporter of the same. Mrs. Holmes is a member of the Presbyterian Church. Mr. Holmes was the founder of Hazen Free Press, and had charge of it for some time, but recently sold out. He purchased the outfit and moved it to Hazen.

Simeon Horne, retired. The life record of this gentleman will prove of more than usual interest, for his career has been of much benefit and influence among the people with whom he has resided, not only of Prairie County, but throughout the State. He was born in Jones County, Ga., August 8, 1818, and is a son of Simeon and Elizabeth (Bloodworth) Horne, natives of North Carolina, who moved from Bibb County to Georgia at an early day. Here Simeon Horne, Sr., made a farm, near where Gordon Station is now situated, and on this farm reared his family and made his home until his death, in 1819, his wife surviving him a number of years. She moved with her family to Middle Tennessee, about the year 1826, and here died two years later, in Rutherford County. Simeon Horne, our subject, was the youngest of a family of eight children and was reared to the age of fourteen years in Tennessee going, in 1832, to Tipton County, with an older brother, where he attained his majority. He learned the carpenter's and builder's trade in this county and after moving to Memphis, in 1844, worked at his trade there until his removal, in 1856, to Arkansas. He settled on a farm near Des Arc, in White River Township, and up to 1881 was actively engaged in farming and also contracting and building, but at this date gave up farm work and moved to Des Arc, where he has since made his home. His ability and skill

as a mechanic is shown by the buildings which he has erected, among which may be mentioned the county court house, the Presbyterian Church, numerous stores, county bridges, etc. His labors have been attended with excellent results, and in addition to owning 400 acres of fine farming land, with about 140 acres under cultivation, he owns a good drug store in Hazen and some valuable town property in Des Arc. He was married in Tipton County, Tenn., about 1841, to Maria, a daughter of Arthur F. Wooten, who died in that county, and he was next married in Memphis, to Sarah C., a daughter of Tillman Bettis, their union taking place October 10, 1848. Her death occurred in Prairie County, Ark., in August, 1880, leaving, besides her husband, two sons and two daughters to mourn her loss, their names being: E. P. (the widow of A. M. Morrow), Rev. T. J. (a minister of the Presbyterian Church), W. A. (a farmer of this county), and Elizabeth (wife of Dr. W. F. Williams, of Hazen). One son, Samuel B., died in 1883, after reaching mature years. Mr. Horne married his present wife in Des Arc, in 1881, she being Mrs. Mahala (Jackson) McLaren, a native of Tennessee, who came to Arkansas after reaching womanhood. Mr. Horne and his wife are members of the Presbyterian Church, in which he is an elder, and he has been a member of the Masonic fraternity since 1839, and is now a Royal Arch Mason. In 1862 he joined Col. Lemoyne's regiment of infantry and served on detached duty as regimental quartermaster, until his regiment was disbanded. He re-enlisted in 1864, becoming a member of Col. Davie's battalion, and was with Price on his memorable raid through Missouri. His company was disbanded at Clarksville, Tex., in 1865.

William A. Horne is a prosperous farmer and stockman of Prairie County, and was born in Memphis, Tenn., December 12, 1851, being a son of Simeon Horne, a sketch of whom appears in this work. William A. Horne came to Arkansas with his parents when a child of five years, and his knowledge of the world was only such as could be learned on the home farm until he attained his majority. On December 22, 1874, he was married to

Miss Sarah L. Flinn, sister of Dr. Flinn, a druggist of Des Arc, her birth having occurred in the "Palmetto State." She was brought by her parents to Arkansas when a miss of eleven years, and was here reared to womanhood and received her education. After their marriage she and Mr. Horne located on a farm near Des Arc, and this occupation has received Mr. Horne's attention up to the present time, but since 1886 they have been residing in Des Arc, in order to give their children the advantages of the town schools. Their farm comprises 300 acres of land, of which 150 are under cultivation, furnished with good buildings, fences, orchards, etc., and, in addition to attending to his land, Mr. Horne gives considerable attention to raising horses and mules, in which he has been very successful. He has served in the capacity of magistrate, is a member of the K. of H., and belongs to the Famous Life Association of Little Rock, and the Mutual Life Association of New York. He and wife have a family of seven children: Irene, Oscar C., William Flinn, Nina H., Simeon, Wigfall and Faber.

F. P. Hurt was the first man to settle on the present site of Hazen, Ark. (November, 1873), and is now express agent at that place. He was born in Tipton County, Tenn., and is the youngest of four sons born to S. T. and M. C. (Hofler) Hurt, both of whom were born in the "Old North State," the former's birth occurring in 1809 and the latter's in 1811. Their union was consummated on June 2, 1844, in the State of Tennessee, and there they reared a family of five children, whose names are as follows: Texana (who was born in 1845 and died in 1846), James N. (who was born in 1846 and died the same year), Spencer T. (born June 1, 1850, and died in 1882), Rufus K. (born in 1852 and died the following year) and F. P. (whose birth occurred in October, 1854). Mr. Hurt died in 1855, and his widow still survives him and is a resident of Hazen, Ark. F. P. Hurt has been a resident of Hazen since 1871, at which time there was only one dwelling house and a log house in the place, and for six years after locating was engaged in merchandising, but for some time past has been agent for the Southern Express Com-

pany, which position keeps him fully employed as the place has grown and improved very rapidly. Since 1881 Mr. Hurt has been married to Miss Solonia E. Price, a daughter of F. F. Price. She was born in Prairie County, and is the mother of three children: Birdie A., Sophia S. and Carrie F.

B. R. Jenkins is the popular druggist and postmaster of Barrettsville, and although a native born resident of the State of Mississippi, he has been a resident of Prairie County, Ark., since 1868. His father, J. J. Jenkins, was born in South Carolina in 1819, and was a son of Benjamin and Frances Jenkins. His youth was spent in his native State, but when a young man he removed to Northeast Mississippi, and there remained engaged in farming for about sixteen years. He was married in this State about 1842 to Miss Mary Guess, a daughter of Richard and Jane Guess, who were native Alabamians. Mr. and Mrs. Jenkins reared a family of eight children: Frances J. (died when a young lady), B. R., James (who is also deceased), Jack A. (a resident of Lonoke County, Ark.), Mary (deceased), Catherine (Mrs. Morgan, resides in Prairie County), Anna (Mrs. Chaffin, also resides in this county) and Amanda (deceased). In 1857 Mr. Jenkins removed his family to White County, Ark., and after his wife's death, in 1860, he married Mrs. Nancy Jackson, and by her reared a family of eight children: George W., John H., Samuel H., David S., Charley, Josephine, Thomas and Bettie. After residing in White County for about ten years, he came to Prairie County, and is here residing on a farm. He is a Mason, and in his political opinion is a Democrat. B. R. Jenkins has been educated in Arkansas, and in 1867 was united in marriage to Miss Louisa Hagle, but they parted by mutual consent after living together for one year. Mr. Jenkins has been a resident of Prairie County for twenty-one years, and for sixteen years was a farmer, but since 1886 has been engaged in the drug business at Barrettsville, and has been postmaster of that place since 1887. He owns 160 acres of land, and has forty acres under cultivation. He is a member of the Baptist Church.

Henry C. Jewell is a prosperous agriculturist of this region, and owing to having been a follower of the Golden Rule, he has received the esteem of his fellow-citizens. Owing to his having spent his early life on a farm, and to his advanced and progressive ideas he has done not a little to advance the farming interests hereabouts, and his farm, comprising 160 acres, is one of the best tilled in this section. He has about eighty acres under cultivation, and his residence is comfortable and his outbuildings substantial. He was born in Nelson County, Ky., September 27, 1832, and is a son of James and Nancy (Higdon) Jewell, who were born, reared and married in the "Blue Grass State." In 1839 they moved to Indiana, and opened up a farm in Vigo County, here spending the rest of their days, the mother's death occurring in March, 1845, and the father's in January, 1862. Henry C. Jewell's youth was spent in the Hoosier State, and until he was twenty years of age, he made his home with his father, going then to Illinois, and worked on a farm in Coles County. Here he was married on April 10, 1857, to Nancy Tilley, a native of Indiana, and a daughter of Moses Tilley, and began farming for himself, continuing to make Coles County his home until 1870, when he sold out and moved to Arkansas, and has since been a resident of his present farm. He and his wife are the parents of the following children: Leonard (who is married and lives in Arizona Territory), Emma (wife of Thomas Chandler), Stephen E. (also in Arizona), James, Rachel and Herschel.

Dr. B. F. Johnson has been engaged in the drug business in Des Arc since 1866, and the stock of goods which he carries is only to be found in a well-kept, reliable drug store. He was born in Prince George's County, Md., July 19, 1836, and is a son of Lloyd Johnson and Elizabeth (Walker) Johnson, who were also born in Maryland, the father being a farmer of Prince George's County until his death, in December, 1860, his wife's death occurring several years earlier. Dr. Johnson grew to manhood in Maryland, and when a young man began learning the drug business in a store in Washington, D. C., but after his father's death he came West and located at Des Arc, where he en-

gaged in the printing and newspaper business, having charge of a paper for two years, at which time the Federal soldiers took the office from him. In 1866 he engaged in the drug business, buying out an established store, and since that time he has devoted his attention to this work, with the exception of two years, when his property was destroyed by fire. The following two years were spent in general merchandising, after which he resumed the drug business, and his stock now includes drugs of all kinds, paints, oils, etc. The Doctor was married at West Point, White County, Ark., December 21, 1865, to Miss Alice Bradshaw, a daughter of W. H. Bradshaw, of White County. She was born in Dresden, Tenn., but was reared and educated in White County, Ark. Her union with the Doctor has resulted in the birth of six children: Jessie (who died when she was six years old), Boyd B., May, Eva, Herbert and Zuma. Dr. Johnson and his wife are members of the Methodist Episcopal Church, and he belongs to the Masonic fraternity and the Knights of Honor.

John R. Johnson, farmer and ginner, Hickory Plains, Ark. There are a number of men prominently identified with the agricultural affairs of this county, but none among them are more deserving of mention than Mr. John R. Johnson, who was born in Randolph County, N. C., March 30, 1839. His parents, Joseph and Katie (Brower) Johnson, were both natives of North Carolina and were married in that State. The parents moved to Tennessee about 1842, locating in Decatur County, and there tilled the soil until 1876, when he moved to Arkansas. He located in Sebastian County and resides there at the present time. His first wife died in 1878. John R. Johnson remained in Tennessee until sixteen years of age and in 1857 moved to Arkansas, locating at Fort Smith, where he resided for about fourteen months. He came to Hickory Plains in 1859 and was one of the early settlers. In 1861 he enlisted in the Confederate army, Fourth Independent Arkansas Battery as a private and was promoted to the rank of second lieutenant after the battle of Murfreesboro. Afterward he was on detached duty for twelve months on the Alabama Railroad and served

Your Respectfully
B. B. Conner

WOODRUFF COUNTY, ARKANSAS.

all through the war. He participated in the battles of Wilson's Creek, Richmond, and Murfreesboro. After the war he returned to Hickory Plains. He followed the carpenter's trade, working at the same during 1866–67, at Little Rock and in 1867 began merchandising in Pulaski County. In 1868, 1869 and 1870 he worked at his trade in Prairie County, and many monuments of his handiwork are still standing in the county, especially in Hickory Plains and vicinity. In 1870 he began selling goods here, and two years later engaged in tilling the soil, which occupation he has since carried on. He has 240 acres of land with about 145 cleared, has good buildings and is in a very prosperous condition. He built a gin in 1880, has good new machinery and is doing a good business. He is the owner of six acres of land where his gin is located and also has several lots in Des Arc. Mr. Johnson was married in Prairie County, Ark., in 1868, to Miss Fannie Holloway, a native of Fayette County, Tenn., but who was reared and educated in Hickory Plains. She is the daughter of John Holloway. Mr. Johnson is a member of the Masonic fraternity, Hickory Plains Lodge No. 95, and is Junior Deacon and Past Master in the same. He was one of the original founders of the Wheel organization and was twice unanimously elected president of the State Wheel. He was appointed and is one of the county commissioners. In 1888 he was doorkeeper of the house of representatives and in 1889 was appointed by the Governor for the Second Congressional district to the Farmers' Agricultural Congress. Mr. and Mrs. Johnson are members of the Old School Presbyterian Church and he is an elder in the same.

Charles F. King is one of the sturdy and independent tillers of the soil of Arkansas, and his property has been acquired by his own good management and industry. Like so many native Virginians he displays in his business operations those sterling principles, which mark him as one of the leading men of the county, and he is noted for his progressive views. His birth occurred near Petersburg, March 31, 1809, and he is a son of Elisha King, who was also a Virginian and served in the American Revolution, entering the army

4 4

when quite young and serving throughout the entire war. At the age of eighteen years he was married in his native State to Miss Priscilla Butler, also of that State, and there they resided until their respective deaths. Charles F. King grew to manhood in the Old Dominion, but removed to Tennessee in 1830 and located at Memphis, near which place he farmed for a number of years, then became conductor on the Charleston Road, continuing as such three years. He came to Arkansas in 1856 and settled in Prairie County, in the neighborhood of where he now lives, there being very few settlers in this section at that time. The farm which he first purchased was slightly improved, but this he afterward sold, and bought his present property which consists of 170 acres, sixty of which he is engaged in tilling. He was married in Tennessee to Miss Lucy Bettis, a native of that State, and by her has the following children: Charles Tillman (who is married) and Agnes (wife of J. B. Stallings). Mr. and Mrs. King are members of the Methodist Episcopal Church and he belongs to the I. O. O. F. Charles King, his son, was born near Memphis, Tenn., June 1, 1856, and when an infant was brought by his parents to Arkansas, and in Prairie County he grew to manhood and was educated. He was married in White County May 3, 1877, to Miss Bettie Benge, a native of Mississippi, but who received the principal part of her rearing in Arkansas. After their marriage they lived in Beebe for about one year, and since that time have resided on the farm with their father, Charles F. King, and our subject is engaged in operating his cotton-gin. He and Mrs. King are members of the Methodist Episcopal Church and are the parents of three children: Thomas O., Jennie L. and Esther I.

John W. Knauff, farmer, Des Arc, Ark. Nowhere in Prairie County is to be found a man of more energy or determined will or force of character, than Mr. Knauff possesses, and no agriculturist is deserving of greater success in the conduct and management of a farm than he. Farmville, Prince Edwards County, Va., was the scene of his birth, the same occurring on March 19, 1836, and he is the son of G. Philip Knauff, a native of Germany, and Ann E. (Bondurant) Knauff, who was of French Huguenot descent. The parents were married in Virginia, and the father was a merchant and importer of musical instruments, doing business at Farmville for a number of years. His death occurred in 1855. His wife had died previous to this, shortly after the birth of the subject of this sketch. John W. Knauff passed his youthful days in Prince Edward County, and received a good education at Hampden Sidney College. He left college after completing his junior year, on account of the death of his father, and engaged in teaching in Virginia for about two years, when he returned to college and graduated with honor. In the fall of 1858 he came West, to Arkansas and was the first engaged as principal of the male academy at Searcy, where he remained five months. He then returned to Virginia, and there remained until March, 1859, when he came to Des Arc, where he continued his former occupation of teaching near that town until 1861. In August, of that year, he enlisted in the Confederate army, First Arkansas Mounted Rifles, Col. Churchill's old regiment, and served until peace was declared. He was disbanded and paroled at Greensboro, N. C., on May 1, 1865. He enlisted as a private and musician, but no regimental bands being allowed in the Confederate army and the band to which he belonged being unwilling to serve as brigade band, each member of his band was required to serve as litter bearer or go in the ranks in time of an engagement. He always took a musket and was wounded three times in Johnston's retreat from Dalton to Atlanta, Ga., but refused to be sent to a hospital, his wounds not preventing his marching. He took part in the following battles: Oak Hill, Pea Ridge and many skirmishes; was then transferred to the east side of the river, and participated in the battles of Chickamauga, Murfreesboro, Richmond (Ky.), and all the fights in and around Atlanta. He was wounded slightly at Atlanta (Resaca), but was not disabled from service. After the war he returned to Prairie County, Ark., engaged in agricultural pursuits, and also taught school, continuing the last-named occupation up to the present time. He was married here on May 17, 1868, to Miss Emma P. Williams,

a native of Alabama, although reared principally in Prairie County, and the daughter of Elijah Williams. The fruits of this union have been seven children: Guy W., O. O., Emma Irene, Baxter T., Philip W., Hubert A. and John De W. Mr. Knauff served one term as magistrate, and is a man universally respected.

Dr. William Lee is a physician of acknowledged merit in Prairie County, and the restoration of hundreds to health and happiness is due to his skill and talent. He was born in Graves County, Ky., February 20, 1832, and is the son of Gen. Joshua and Nancy (Markham) Lee, both of whom are Virginians by birth. The father moved to the Blue Grass State in his early manhood, and was a successful tiller of the soil in Graves County for a number of years, or until 1845, when he moved to Arkansas, and for some time followed the plow in Independence County, near Batesville, on the old Independence road. Later he engaged in steamboating on the White River, but after following this occupation for a few years he decided that farming was more congenial to his tastes, as well as more remunerative, and he resumed agriculture. About this time reverses overtook him, and he disposed of his property here and moved to Louisiana, where he set energetically to work to retrieve his fortunes, and succeeded in doing so to some extent, and at the time of his death was the possessor of a comfortable competency. He died in 1855, his wife's death occurring in 1853. Dr. William Lee removed with his parents to Louisiana, and after reaching mature years determined to see a little of the world, and traveled over the greater portion of Louisiana, Texas and Georgia. Having always been possessed with a desire to study medicine, he began a systematic course of reading at Des Arc, under Dr. E. P. Nicholson and Dr. Burney, and in 1866 located six miles west of Des Arc, and has been an able practitioner of the county ever since. In connection with his practice he has been engaged in managing his small farm, situated about five miles west of the town, but recently rented his property and moved to this place. He joined the Confederate service in 1861, becoming a member of Gen. P. R. Cleburne's regiment, and from a sergeant was promoted to the rank of captain in the Trans-Mississippi Departments, Company F, of Ganse's regiment. He was a member of Cleburne's regiment until after the battle of Missionary Ridge, and during his term of service was in the fights at Scottsville (Ky.), Shiloh and Prairie Grove; in this engagement he received a wound in the lower part of the left leg, and after recovering somewhat, was transferred to the cavalry, and was with Price on his raid through Missouri. At the close of the war he returned to Des Arc, and here has since made his home. A year after his removal to Prairie County, Ark., or in June, 1859, he was married to Miss Mary Lee, a daughter of John Lee. She was born and reared in Prairie County, and here died on February 20, 1876, having become the mother of four children by the Doctor: Martha Ann (wife of Henry Boggs, of Utah), John M. (married and residing on the farm), Elizabeth and Thomas B. In December, 1885, the Doctor was married to Mrs. M. E. (Jones) Whitlock, a native of Arkansas, being here reared and educated, and a daughter of Abner P. Jones. The Doctor belongs to the Prairie County Medical Society.

William B. Lumpkin. The amount of land which this gentleman has in his possession comprises 520 acres in four different farms, and of the entire amount he has 300 acres under cultivation, and all his property well improved with good buildings. Since 1886 he has been residing in Des Arc, where he owns some valuable property, but he continues to manage his farm, and has been more successful than the average. He was born in Lawrence County, Tenn., April 14, 1840, and is a son of J. B. Lumpkin, a native of North Carolina, who came west with his parents to Tennessee when a small lad, and was here reared to manhood, educated and married, his wife's maiden name being Betsey Bryant, a native of North Carolina. After his marriage Mr. Lumpkin moved to Shelby County, but afterward settled permanently in Tipton County, where he is now residing at the age of seventy-six years, his wife's death having occurred here in 1876. William B. Lumpkin grew to maturity in Tennessee, and until he attained his majority made his home with his father. In the

latter part of 1861 he enlisted in the Confederate army, Fifty-first Tennessee Infantry, Company B, and of his company, which consisted of 104 men, he and one other man were the only ones not killed or wounded. He enlisted as a private, but became a non-commissioned officer, and took part in the battles of Chickamauga, Franklin, and was in the retreat from Chattanooga to Atlanta. At the fall of Fort Henry he was captured, and for nine months was kept in captivity at Alton, Ill., and after being exchanged rejoined his regiment, and at the final surrender was at home on furlough. He then settled down in Shelby County, and was engaged in farming up to 1879, when he sold out, and moved to Arkansas, locating in Prairie County, near Des Arc, his first purchase of land being 160 acres. He was married in Shelby County, Tenn., July 24, 1870, to Miss Nannie J. Yancey, a native of Iuka, Miss., a daughter of James Yancey, but her demise occurred on October 15, 1884, leaving besides her husband, to mourn her loss, a family of four children: Tellie, Thomas B. and Calvin P. Saddie died in September, 1887, at the age of thirteen years. Mr. W. B. Lumpkin is a member of White River Lodge of the Masonic fraternity.

Prof. Hugh McQ. Lynn, the well-known postmaster of Des Arc, Ark., was born in Chester County, S. C., April 10, 1837, and is a son of John and Elizabeth (McQuiston) Lynn, also natives of the Palmetto State, where they were reared, educated and married. In December, 1837, they moved to Tennessee, and settled in Tipton County, where the father followed agricultural pursuits until his death in January, 1886, his wife following him to the grave in April, 1889. Prof. Lynn's early youth was spent in Tipton County, and he acquired an education far beyond the average farmer's boy, owing to the fact that he was studious and persevering, and received superior advantages. He entered Erskine College, S. C., and graduated from this institution when twenty-two years of age, after which he engaged in teaching in Tipton County, holding the position of principal of an academy. After coming to Arkansas, in 1872, he engaged in teaching school in Lonoke County, continuing one year, then followed the same occupation in Des Arc for nine years, and also taught for some time at Hazen. He is an educator of more than local celebrity, and up to the spring of 1889 his entire time and attention was given to his profession, but since then he has held the position of postmaster of Des Arc, but only entered actively upon his duties on September 1, 1889. He was married in Tennessee, April 10, 1862, to Miss Martha S. Simpson, a native of that State, and by her became the father of two sons and one daughter: Dr. J. R. (of Hazen), W. C. (a book-keeper by profession) and Nannie E. (a young lady, and Mr. Lynn's principal assistant in the postoffice). At the opening of the Civil War, Mr. Lynn espoused the Confederate cause, and in May, 1861, joined the Ninth Tennessee Infantry, as a private, and served until the close of the war, being paroled at Memphis, Tenn., in July, 1865. He was in the fights at Chickamauga and Franklin, but the most of the time served on detached duty in the ordnance department. Prof. Lynn has shown his brotherly spirit by becoming a member of the Masonic fraternity, and the K. of H., and in the former organization has attained the Royal Arch degree, and has been Worshipful Master and High Priest, and in the latter order is Past Dictator. He and family are members of the Old School Presbyterian Church, and he is an elder in the same.

Robert C. McCarley. From this brief review of the life of Mr. McCarley it will be seen that his time has not been uselessly or idly spent, but that he has continued to "pursue the even tenor of his way," and is now ranked among the prosperous and enterprising farmers and merchants of the county. He was born in Lauderdale County, Ala., May 12, 1833, and he is the second in a family of five children, four sons and one daughter, born to the marriage of Thomas McCarley and Margaret Sturgeon, the former a native of Alabama, and the latter of Tennessee. They were married in Alabama, where the mother was reared, and here the father's death occurred in 1839, he having been a follower of the plow throughout life. His wife lived to be seventy-two years old, reared her family, and died in 1886. Robert C. McCarley left

home after reaching his twentieth year, and began clerking in a store in Lauderdale County, continuing until 1859, when he came to Arkansas, and settled at Des Arc, following the same occupation here for several years. After embarking in the mercantile business on his own responsibility he continued this work until the opening of the war, and in 1863 joined the Confederate service, Col. Dobbins' cavalry, and served as a private until the close of the war. Soon after enlisting he was detailed to the adjutant-general's office, but was soon after transferred to the quartermaster's department, and served in this capacity during the remainder of the war. In January, 1865, he was captured while at home on a visit, and was held a prisoner at Little Rock until the close of the war, being paroled on May 12, 1865. After the war he returned home and clerked for a while, then again engaged in business for himself, and since 1879 has carried an excellent line of general merchandise. He is the owner of 1,350 acres of land in seven different farms, and has about 400 acres under cultivation; 800 acres lie near Des Arc, and are very valuable. He has been married four times, once in Alabama, and three times in Arkansas. He has one son by his second wife (Albert by name), who is clerking in Des Arc. He married his present wife, Mrs. M. C. (Koonce) Howard, in 1876, she being a native of Tennessee, and by her has a daughter named Anna, a miss of ten years. Mr. McCarley has held a number of local offices, such as magistrate and alderman, and has been treasurer and mayor of Des Arc. He is an elder in the Cumberland Presbyterian Church, of which his wife is also a member, and he is a Master Mason, and has been a member of that order since 1860. He also belongs to the I. O. O. F.

James R. Mallory, merchant, De Vall's Bluff, Ark. Among the many industries largely developed in De Vall's Bluff within the past years, that of merchandising has taken a prominent position, as may be seen by the establishment and growth of the various houses engaged in this line of enterprise. One of the best-known and most liberally patronized establishments in the city of De Vall's Bluff is that conducted by Mr. Mallory. This gentleman was born in Granville County, N. C., on May 25, 1834, and is the son of John Mallory, a native of North Carolina, and Mollie (Coleman) Mallory, whom he had met in Tennessee. The fruits of this union were eight children, five daughters and three sons: William, Sallie, Eliza, Mary, Lucy, Caroline, James R. and John. Mr. Mallory was a local minister and was instrumental in organizing several churches in North Carolina. He died in 1861, and his wife several years previous. He was very much interested in educational as well as church matters, and contributed liberally to all laudable enterprises. James R. Mallory was educated in Oxford, N. C., and was there married to Miss Lucy Horner, in November, 1866. This union resulted in the birth of two children: Sarah and John T., both of whom reside at home. Mr. Mallory immigrated from North Carolina to Arkansas in November, 1868, located at De Vall's Bluff, and there he has since resided, engaged in mercantile pursuits with a stock valued at $10,000. He has held the position of coroner for four years and was also postmaster for nineteen months. He is a member of the K. of H., and has held the office of Reporter of that lodge. He is also a member of what is called Iron Hall, located at De Vall's Bluff, and is a Freemason, but has not affiliated with any lodge in this State. He enlisted in the Confederate army, under Gen. Lee, in 1861, and his first hard battle was at Richmond, Va. He was commissary of the Fifth North Carolina Regiment during service, and was discharged at Appomattox Court House, Va., in 1865. He then returned to his home and embarked in mercantile pursuits, which he has since continued.

Dr. Stephen R. Mason, county treasurer, De Vall's Bluff, Ark. There are few men of the present day, whom the world acknowledges as successful, more worthy of honorable mention, or whose life history affords a better example of what may be accomplished by a determined will and perseverance, than Dr. Mason. He was born in the town of Chichester, near Pittsfield, Merrimack County, N. H., in 1827, and was the fourth in a family of five children born to the union of John and Abigail Amanda (Roby) Mason, natives, also, of New Hampshire. The parents were married in that State and there the father was an operative in a cotton-factory until 1835, when he moved to the Far West and located in what is now Woodford County, Ill., near where Metamora is now located, and there bought land of the United States and improved a farm. In 1840 he moved to Bureau County, Ill., and there his death occurred in 1861. His excellent wife survived him until 1867. Dr. Stephen R. Mason remained on the home farm, where the town of Buda is now located, until sixteen years of age, and received his education in the academy at Princeton, Ill. After this he engaged in teaching school, and in the meantime read medicine with Dr. J. S. Whitmire, at Metamora, in 1847. He then alternately attended school and taught until the fall of 1849, when he entered Rush Medical College, Chicago, Ill., and graduated therefrom in the class of 1851. He then began practicing in Bureau County, near Buda, and remained there until 1853, when he located at Sheffield, Ill. Dr. Mason was married in 1852 to Miss Mary A. Brainard, a native of La Fayette, Ohio, and the daughter of Deodatus E. and Sally J. (Fry) Brainard, natives of New York. Mr. and Mrs. Brainard emigrated to Ohio and settled in Medina County at an early date. From there they moved to Bureau County, Ill., in 1841, and here the father was occupied in cultivating the soil. Both parents are now living, and reside in Buda, Ill. To the Doctor and Mrs. Mason were born five children, four now living: Ella Jane (now Mrs. W. B. Allen, of Chicago, Ill.), Ida May (now Mrs. J. W. Waterman, of Creston, Iowa), Roby E. (was an engineer on the Little Rock & Memphis Railroad a number of years, and recently on the Batesville & Brinkley Railroad, where he was killed by the engine being derailed, near Gray Station, on July 28, 1888; his widow now resides in Brinkley, Ark.), Wilbur J. (is married, resides at De Vall's Bluff, and is assistant postmaster at that place) and Harry W. (who is married and resides at Cotton Plant, Ark., being railroad agent and operator on the Batesville & Brinkley Railroad). The mother of these children died in March, 1889, and the remains of both mother and son were carried to Buda, Ill. After his marriage Dr. Mason resided in Sheffield until coming to De Vall's Bluff, in 1873, since which time he has practiced his profession. He was first appointed postmaster at De Vall's Bluff in 1881 (February 4), and served in that capacity until the spring of 1886. He was reappointed in August, 1889. He was elected county treasurer of Prairie County in 1886, was reelected in 1888, and is the present incumbent. He has been magistrate a number of times, and has held various town and school offices; he is also a member of the American Institute of Homœopathy, joining the same in 1867, and a member of the Southern Homœopathic Association. He is a member of Ames Lodge No. 142, A. F. & A. M., at Sheffield, Ill., was made a Mason in 1852 or 1853, and has also been a member of the I. O. O. F. He was a charter member of De Vall's Bluff Lodge No. 2172, Knights of Honor. In 1882 he joined the Iron Hall Association, and has drawn one final benefit of $1,000, and considers it a good thing. The Doctor is independent in his religious views, and is willing others should enjoy the same privilege.

W. E. Maxwell, merchant and manufacturer, De Vall's Bluff, Ark. This gentleman is one of the prominent business men of De Vall's Bluff, Ark., and his reputation in that capacity is well and favorably known throughout the county. He was originally from Kentucky, where his birth occurred in 1852, and is the eldest of a family of six children born to the union of J. H. and Mary M. (Cole) Maxwell, the father a native of Kentucky, and the mother of Pennsylvania. J. H. Maxwell was born in Caldwell County in 1822, and was a merchant and planter. He was married in 1849 or 1850 to Miss Cole, who was a descendant of the family of that name in Pennsylvania. Mr. Maxwell died in 1884 at De Vall's Bluff, Ark. W. E. Maxwell began business for himself by manufacturing handles at Lansing, Mich., in 1875, remaining there until 1883, when he came to De Vall's Bluff, and there, in partnership with Mr. Wells, engaged in the mill business under the firm title of Wells, Maxwell & Co. This firm is engaged in sawing all kinds of lumber, and ships a great deal of oak to foreign parts. He is also engaged in merchandising under the firm title of Maxwell & Co., and is one of the ablest business men to be found. He is the owner of considerable town property, and owns a 900-acre tract of land in the county. He is a member of the Masonic fraternity, Hamilton Lodge No. 110, De Vall's Bluff, and is a member of the Knights of Pythias, White River Lodge No. 41, of De Vall's Bluff.

S. A. Minton is a worthy agriculturist of Prairie County, Ark., and enjoys to an unlimited extent, the confidence and respect of all who know him. He has been a resident of the county since 1867, and at that date settled on forty acres of land in Center Township, and at the present time has 220 acres, 100 under cultivation. Born in the State of Alabama, in 1844, he is the third child born to J. M. and Nancy (Rainwater) Minton, both of whom were born in the "Palmetto State," the former's birth occurring in 1818, and the latter's in 1816. J. M. Minton settled in Alabama, where he followed farming and tanning, and his marriage occurred about 1836. After residing in Alabama until 1860, he came to Arkansas and settled at Austin, where he worked at the tanner's trade for about ten years, then moving to Center Township, Prairie County, where he spent his declining years, his death occurring in 1884. Politically he was a Democrat and his wife was a member of the Primitive Baptist Church. They became the parents of the following children: Emily E. (who is the wife of R. N. Sparks and resides in Centre Township), S. B. (who lives in Hazen Township is married and has eight children), S. A. (our subject), Martha G. (wife of R. N. Sparks, Sr.), Adaline (who died young), Matilda S. (died in 1868 in her nineteenth year), John P. (who also died in childhood), and M. M. T. (an infant, deceased). The mother of these children died in the year 1882. The paternal grandparents, Sylvanus and Jennie Minton, became the parents of twenty-three or twenty-four children. S. A. Minton spent his youth in Alabama and came with his father to Arkansas in 1860. The following year he enlisted in Company B, Fourth Arkansas Regiment of Infantry, and the battles in which he participated were: Richmond, Murfreesboro, Atlanta, Missionary Ridge, Chickamauga and Franklin. Upon returning to Arkansas he was married in December, 1866, to Miss Nancy A. Douglas, a daughter of Logan and Patience Douglas, and the year following moved to Prairie County, and as shown above, has become a well-to-do farmer. The children born to his union are: George J. (who died in 1887), Joseph M. (who also died in 1887), Emma C. (who is the wife of R. N. Sparks, Jr.), William F., Thomas W., Burrell S. and Ada B. Mr. Minton is a member of the Primitive Baptist Church and is an enterprising and progressive citizen.

Hon. William L. Moore, retired physician and surgeon, Hickory Plains, Ark. A plain untarnished statement of the facts embraced in the life of William L. Moore, a man well known to the people of Prairie County, Ark., is all that we profess to be able to give in this history of the county; and yet, upon examination of those facts, there will be found the career of one whose entire course through the world has been marked with singular honesty and fidelity of purpose, as well as sincere and efficient service to those whom he has been called upon to represent in different capacities. He was born in Wilson County, Tenn., near Lebanon, on August 29, 1814, and is the son of Robert and Ann L. (Duty) Moore, natives of Virginia and North Carolina, respectively. The parents were married in North Carolina, near the line, and the father cultivated the soil in Virginia until 1806, when he moved to Wilson County, Tenn. He was in the Creek War, was made major, and fell while leading his men at the battle of Talladega. The mother reared the family, and in 1819, was married the second time, to James L. McDonald. She then moved to Cotton Grove, Tenn., thence to Bolivar to educate her children, and there died in 1827. Dr. William L. Moore was reared in Tennessee, and at the age of fourteen years, entered a store to learn something of merchandising, spending the time alternately in the store earning funds and in attending school until twenty-one years of age. He received a fair education in the common and higher English branches, also studied Latin, and subsequently began the study of medi-

cine under Dr. John McCall, at Rome, Smith County, which he continued a short time. He then began studying under Dr. Alexander Goode, of Fayette County, a very prominent physician, and took his first course of lectures in 1833, 1834 and 1835. He then practiced with his preceptor for twelve months, and his home being in the corner of Fayette County, he practiced in that, and Marshall, DeSoto and Shelby Counties for twelve years, meeting with excellent success. In February, 1853, he moved to Arkansas, locating in Hickory Plains, Prairie County, where he has remained ever since. While living in Fayette County, Tenn., he was married on December 9, 1846, to Miss Mary C. Abington, a native of the Blue Grass State, and the daughter of William Abington. Five living children are the results of this union: Edwin, Dora (wife of Dr. Lindsay), Emma (wife of J. N. Brians), Ripley A. (an attorney at Des Arc) and Samuel A. They lost two daughters, one an infant, and the other nine years of age, and a son who died at the age of three years. After locating in Prairie County, Dr. Moore carried on farming in connection with his practice, and for ten years lived in Hickory Plains to educate his children. In 1856 he was elected to represent Prairie County in the legislature and served one term. During the late war, he was in the Confederate service about six months, and was first lieutenant of Totten Guards, Twenty-fifth Arkansas Battalion of Infantry, and was in the battle of Farmington. In reorganizing the Dr. was discharged and returned home. He has been a member of the Masonic Fraternity for over forty years, and all matters of benefit receive his sanction and support.

Edwin Moore, stock raiser, farmer and ginner, Hickory Plains, Ark. Mr. Moore owes his nativity to Fayette County, Tenn., where his birth occurred on May 9, 1848, and is the son of Hon. W. L. Moore, whose sketch immediately precedes this. He came with his father to Arkansas in 1853, and grew to manhood in Prairie County, where he received a fair education and this he has improved materially by self-culture. He remained with his parents until twenty-one years of age, and on March 8, 1870, was united in marriage in Prairie

County, Ark., to Miss Mattie Brians, daughter of W. J. and E. J. Brians and sister to J. W. Brians, sheriff of Prairie County, whose sketch appears elsewhere in this work. Mrs. Moore was born in North Carolina, but was reared and partly educated in Prairie County. After marriage Mr. and Mrs. Moore had nothing of this world's goods on which to commence, but they went to work with a determination to succeed, and although they had considerable to contend with they were not discouraged. They first located on a farm which they began clearing of the timber that covered it, and this they have since added to until they now own about 1,000 acres of good land with some 500 acres under cultivation. They have a good frame residence, a good gin boiler and engine and first-class outbuildings, etc. They also have a good orchard and vineyard. Mr. Moore was elected magistrate, holding the position for eight consecutive years, and was also made a member of the school board. He takes a great interest in politics and served as a delegate to the State Democratic Convention. To Mr. and Mrs. Moore were born seven children: Charles A., William E., Robert A., Emma A., James L., Henry I. and Gordon E. and the two eldest children with their parents are members of the Methodist Episcopal Church. Mr. Moore has also reared his wife's youngest brother and her mother has made her home with him since the death of Mr. Brians. Mr. Moore is a member of the Masonic fraternity.

Dr. W. P. Owens, physician and surgeon, De-Vall's Bluff, Ark. This prominent and successful practitioner owes his nativity to De Soto County, Miss., where his birth occurred August 10, 1855, and he located in Prairie County, in March, 1884, where he has since practiced his profession. He was the fourth of nine children born to the union of Joshua D. and Fannie (La Favre) Owens, natives of Alabama. The parents were married in their native State, and there the father carried on agricultural pursuits until 1835, when he moved to Mississippi, and settled in De Soto County, where they are now living. Dr. W. P. Owens was reared to farm labor, and remained under the parental roof until seventeen years of age. He

received his literary education at Lexington, Ky., and at the State University of Mississippi, at Oxford, where, after reaching the junior year, he commenced reading medicine, and then entered the College of Physicians and Surgeons, at Baltimore, Md., in September, 1878, graduating with the class of 1880. He then returned to De Soto County, commenced the practice of medicine, which he continued until 1884, and, as above stated, he then came to De Vall's Bluff, Ark., where he has since built up a good practice. He was married near Baltimore, Md., in 1879, to Miss Florence Dawson, a native of Maryland, and the daughter of Edward Thomas and Susan (Smith) Dawson, natives also of Maryland. Mr. Dawson was a merchant, and followed this pursuit the principal part of his life. His death occurred in 1878. His wife had died many years previous. To Dr. and Mrs. Owens were born four children, one living, Edward. The Doctor is not very active in politics, but votes with the Democratic party. Socially he is a member of the K. of P. Mrs. Owens is a member of the Methodist Episcopal Church, South.

Dr. A. C. Parrish, physician and surgeon, Hazen, Ark. Dr. Parrish has all the attributes essential to a successful practitioner, is the possessor of much personal popularity and is highly esteemed by all who know him. He was born in Dixon County, Tenn., in 1836, was reared to the arduous duties of the farm and received his education in the schools of his native county. He commenced reading medicine in 1849, and after continuing this for a few years he begam practicing in 1852. Since then he has been actively engaged in the practice of his profession, a period of thirty-seven years, and has met with fair success. He was married in Hickman County, Tenn., in 1848, to Miss Jane Wilson, a native of Tennessee, and to them were born eight children, three now living: Albert (married and residing in Texas), Rebecca (now Mrs. Pollard of Tennessee) and Nellie A. (now Mrs. Turner of White County, Ark.). The mother of these children died on June 3, 1862. In 1864 Dr. Parrish married Mrs. Elizabeth (Spencer) James, widow of L. James, and her death occurred in October, 1885. Three children were the result of this union: Melvin, Nola and Sudie. He married the third time in 1888 Mrs. Alice (Gwyn) HalliBurton, widow of H. HalliBurton. The Doctor came to Arkansas in 1870 and engaged in tilling the soil in connection with his practice. He has opened up several farms, built three cotton-gins and now owns a good farm of thirty acres, besides giving his children land. He votes with the Democratic party but is not active in politics. Socially he is a member of the K. of P., Hazen Lodge No. 3134, and he and lady are members of the Missionary Baptist Church.

L. M. Peak has passed the uneventful life of the farmer, and has continued to "pursue the even tenor of his way" until he is now ranked among the prosperous agriculturists of this region. He is a Kentuckian by birth, born in Scott County in 1851, and is the third child born to Dudley and Ann (Martin) Peak, the former a Kentuckian also, born in 1820. His brothers and sisters are as follows: James (deceased), John J., Leland, Madison (who died young), Dudley, Laurinda (Mrs. W. Cragg, now deceased), Pilena (Mrs. S. Cragg) and Eveline (wife of Sandy Faulkner, the supposed "Arkansaw Traveler"). Dudley Peaks pent his youth in his native State, and in 1841 was married, his wife being a daughter of William H. and Susan (Hayle) Martin, all Kentuckians. Mrs. Peak's brothers and sisters are as follows: Jane, Solon, Louis, Nettie and James. Mr. Peak and his wife were members of the Baptist Church, and became well-to-do farmers. They reared five children: Susan M. (Mrs. J. Long, the mother of four children), Emma (Mrs. J. Morris, now deceased), L. M., George and Solon, all of whom are married and live in Scott County, Ky., except L. M. Peak. The father was a public-spirited citizen, a Democrat in politics, and passed from this life in 1883, his wife dying in 1859. L. M. Peak resided in Kentucky until thirty-four years of age, and was married, in 1875, to Sallie K. Sconce, a daughter of James F. and Lou A. (Morris) Sconce, but in 1873 had begun farming for himself, and moved to Missouri. That State continued to be his home until 1885, when he came to Arkansas, and a year

later settled in Prairie County. Here he purchased land to the amount of 350 acres, and now has it all under fence, and a considerable portion of it in a good farming condition. He is a Democrat, and while a resident of Scott County, Ky., served in the capacity of constable two years. He and wife are members of the Christian Church, and are highly esteemed and valued citizens of the county.

J. M. Perry is a farmer and stock shipper of Hazen, Ark. This leading farmer of Prairie County, Ark., was born in Camden County, N. C., on August 31, 1846, and is the son of S. B. Perry, who was also born in North Carolina, in the year 1812. The father was educated in his native State, and was there married to Miss Nancy J. Rieves, also a native of North Carolina. To this union have been born thirteen children, seven of whom are still living in Arkansas, and four in North Carolina, viz.: John W., William J., Samuel, James M., Joseph E., Ann J. and Sarah H. The father, a successful agriculturist, is still living, and resides in Chatham County, N. C. He assisted materially in building up the country in the early settlement of North Carolina, and is one of the prominent citizens. His father was one of the very first settlers of that State. Mr. and Mrs. Perry are members of the Methodist Church. J. M. Perry was educated in North Carolina, and in 1863 he enlisted in the Confederate army, under Gen. Holmes, in Company A, Sixty-ninth Regiment, and his first battle was at Plymouth. He received his discharge in 1865, and returned home, where he was engaged in tilling the soil the first year. On August 10, 1865, he was united in marriage, to Miss Temperance E. Lindly, a native of North Carolina, and the daughter of Owen and Temperance Lindly. Two children have been the fruits of this union: Quincy (deceased) and Walter O. (who resides at home with his parents). Mr. Perry is a farmer by occupation, and owns about 160 acres of good land, with sixty acres under cultivation. He is a member of the Masonic fraternity, Blue Lodge, and has held the office of Junior Warden. He is a member of the Wheel, and held the office of president of the same for one year. He is a self-made man, and one who has the energy and perseverance to succeed in whatever he undertakes. When he first came to Arkansas, he was the owner of a horse and $40 in money. Now he has an excellent farm, well stocked, and is one of the substantial farmers of the county. He and Mrs. Perry are members of the Methodist Church.

J. E. Perry. There are few farms of the size, if any, in this portion of Arkansas that presents a better picture of advanced agriculture than the one referred to in the present sketch. It contains 320 acres, with 150 under cultivation, and as far as natural advantages, and the manner in which it is improved is concerned, it is probably without a superior hereabouts. The owner of this farm, Mr. Perry, was born in North Carolina in 1849, and was the eighth of a large family of children born to D. B. and Nancy J. (Rieves) Perry, and was a grandson of William and Anna Perry, the latter couple being the parents of twelve children and natives of Virginia. D. B. Perry was born in North Carolina in 1812, and from his earliest youth has been familiar with farm life, and has made that calling quite a success. He and wife are members of the Methodist Episcopal Church, South, and are still residing in North Carolina, and he is a Democrat in his political views, and is an enterprising and public-spirited man. He and Miss Rieves were married about 1832, his wife being a daughter of Reuben and Hannah Rieves, natives of North Carolina, and by her he became the father of twelve children: John, William J., Mary M. (the wife of a Mr. Campbell, is deceased), Henry H., Abner B., Samuel, James M., J. E., Isaac (deceased), Aaron D., Anna J. (Mrs. Perry) and Sarah H. (Mrs. Headen). J. E. Perry assisted in tilling the old farm in North Carolina, and during odd moments attended the common schools, acquiring thereby a fair education. In 1872 he determined to come west to court dame fortune, and settled in Prairie County, Ark., where he purchased 160 acres of land, but this land he has since increased to its above-mentioned proportions. He was married in 1876 to Miss Sallie McNeill, a daughter of Philip and Sallie (Tabb) McNeill, born in North Carolina and Tennessee, who died in 1876 and 1868, respectively. Mr.

and Mrs. Perry have a family of four children: Bessie, Henry A., Fitz Hugh and Clio C., and are expecting soon to give up farming and move to town, in order to give their children the advantages of the town schools. Mr. Perry is a Mason, E. H. English Lodge No. 237, at Walter Chapel, and belongs also to the K. of H. No. 168840 of Carlisle. He and wife have for some time been members of the Methodist Episcopal Church, South. The latter was born in 1860, in the house in which she now lives.

John W. Pettey is a manufacturer of lumber and shingles at Des Arc, and since one year old has been a resident of the State of Arkansas. He was born in De Soto County, Miss., May 11, 1854, and is a son of George I. Pettey, of Alabama, who was reared in Mississippi and was married in Shelby County, Tenn., to Barbara Ann Callis, a native of Shelby County. After their marriage they resided in Mississippi for about two years, and in the spring of 1855 moved to Arkansas and settled near Hazen, where they cleared a farm and reared their family. The father served in the Confederate army for over two years and died at his old home in September, 1880. His wife, two sons and four daughters survive him, all residents of Prairie County, the children being married. John W. Pettey grew to manhood in Prairie County, and remained with his father on the farm until twenty-six years of age, then began blacksmithing, having learned the trade at home, and from 1878 up to 1881, conducted a blacksmith, wagon and repair shop, but in the last-named year purchased his mill, and has since given his attention to the manufacture of lumber, averaging about 400,000 feet annually, the business rapidly increasing from year to year. He has overhauled his building and put in considerable new machinery this year, and is preparing to cut all the lumber and shingles for which he has demand. His brother has been associated with him in business since January, and they are honest and enterprising business men, and are bound to succeed. He was married in October, 1885, to Lelia W. Plant, a daughter of C. H. Plant, of Prairie County. Mrs. Pettey was born near Moscow, Tenn., but was reared and educated in

Prairie County, Ark., and by Mr. Pettey is the mother of two children: Earl Cecil and Homer Allen. Mr. Pettey and his wife are members of the Methodist and Christian Churches, respectively, and he is a Mason and a member of White River Lodge No. 37, of which he has been Master for two years.

Dr. George E. Pettey, physician and surgeon, Des Arc, Ark. Dr. Pettey, one of the successful practitioners of Des Arc, was born in Washington County, Tex., on January 16, 1857, and is the son of Dr. F. M. Pettey, a native of Limestone County, Ala. The father was educated at Memphis, Tenn., and afterward located in that State, where he practiced his profession for four years. He then moved to the Lone Star State, located in Washington County, but a few years later moved to Navarro County, Tex., where he practiced his profession until the breaking out of the war. He was surgeon in the army, and had charge of Galveston Hospital, where he remained until the cessation of hostilities. After the war he located in Arkansas, and is now engaged in the practice of his profession in Monroe County of that State. He married Miss Sarah A. G. Elliott, in Henderson County, Tenn., in 1848, and the result of this union was the birth of two sons and six daughters. Dr. George E. Pettey came to Arkansas with his father in 1870, attained his growth in Mississippi County, and later began the study of medicine with his father. At the age of fourteen years he entered a drug store, where he remained while studying medicine. He took his first course of lectures at the Medical Department of Vanderbilt University, Nashville, Tenn., in the winter of 1880–81, and took another course in the spring and summer of the last-mentioned year. He then passed an examination before the medical board, and began the practice of his profession at Hickman, Mississippi County, Ark., where he remained three years. From there he removed to Golddust, Tenn., where he continued in practice until October, 1887, when he went to Memphis, and took an additional course at Memphis Hospital Medical College, graduating from the same in the spring of 1888. After completing this course he came to Des Arc, Ark.,

where he is doing an extensive practice. Dr. Pettey is a surgeon of superior skill, bold, but extremely careful, giving personal attention to the most minute details of an operation. His complete success in every operation he has undertaken is sufficient warrant for the general expression that he is fast taking position as one of the leading surgeons of the State. The Doctor makes a specialty of the diseases of women and rectal diseases. He has always been studious, there being few well-known books on medicine he is not acquainted with, and by taking a number of the leading medical journals, both of this country and Europe, keeps constantly up with the times. He was married in Mississippi County, Ark., on December 24, 1879, to Miss Susan C. Lynch, a native of Arkansas, who was reared in Mississippi County, and the daughter of Esq. A. J. Lynch. To this marriage were born four children: Adah L., Mary A., Francis Allen and George E., Jr. They lost their eldest son, Francis Allen, in June, 1888. Dr. Pettey is a member of the Masonic fraternity and is now Worshipful Master of White River Lodge No. 37. He and wife are members of the Methodist Episcopal Church, South.

Capt. Augustus M. Reinhardt, farmer, stock raiser and horticulturist, Hickory Plains, Ark. This enterprising and progressive citizen was born in Lincoln County, N. C., October 20, 1825, and is the son of Hon. Michael and Mary (Moore) Reinhardt, both natives of North Carolina. Michael Reinhardt was a farmer up to 1846, when he moved to Marshall County, Miss., and there resided until his death, which occurred in 1852. He served one term as a member of the State senate, and held other positions of honor and trust, acquitting himself as an efficient, popular official, always laboring zealously for the best interests of his constituents. He also served in one of the old Indian wars. His wife died in 1828. Capt. Reinhardt went to Mississippi in the spring of 1845, and his father's family moved out in the fall of the same year. They made a crop the following year, and remained there until 1852, farming in Marshall County, when they moved to Prairie, Ark., and bought land in Hickory Plains Township. They

farmed here until the breaking out of the war, and
were also engaged in the real-estate business for
four years previous to that event. Capt. Reinhardt enlisted with the "Boys in Gray," in March,
1862, first in Col. Turnbull's infantry, and served
in that capacity up to May, when he returned
home. In 1863 he joined the cavalry, Col. Monroe's regiment, and was commissioned captain in
the First Regiment, serving until peace was declared. He participated in the fights at Mark's
Mill and Poison Springs, and also in a number of
skirmishes. Returning home after the war, he
engaged in farming and the real-estate business,
being now the owner of 1,000 acres of land, with
all but 160 acres in Prairie County. The home
place consists of 600 acres, with 300 acres under
cultivation, and the buildings on the same are substantial and pleasing to the eye. He has a beautiful yard, ornamented with trees, evergreens,
shrubs and flowers, and his orchard, of about
eighty acres, furnishes some of the finest peaches,
apples, pears and plums to be found. He has a
fine vineyard of about four acres, and shipped
about 800 baskets from the same, but retaining for
himself about as many more. He was first married in Prairie County in January, 1856, to Miss
Mary Harshaw, sister of John Harshaw, whose
sketch may be seen in this work. Mrs. Reinhardt
was born and reared in Marshall County, Miss.,
and died August 28, 1881, leaving nine children:
Henry, Anna (wife of Brainard Perkins), Mattie
(widow of Mr. Jones), Mamie, Emmett, Clara,
Sallie, John and William. Mr. Reinhardt took for
his second wife Mrs. Sallie E. (Rayburn) Harrison,
a native of Conway County, Md., where she was
educated and married. She is a member of the
Methodist Episcopal Church. Mr. Reinhardt is a
member of the Presbyterian Church, and is an
elder in the same.

Abel S. Reinhardt, like the majority of native
Mississippians, is progressive in his views and of
an energetic and enterprising temperament. He
was born in Marshall County January 4, 1847, and
is a son of D. F. and Harriet E. (Shuford) Reinhardt, both of whom were born and reared in Lincoln County, N. C. About 1844 they immigrated

to Marshall County, Miss., but a short time afterward moved to Tennessee and in 1857 settled in
Prairie County, being engaged in farming in these
three States. In October, 1888, he moved to Little Rock and there died in November of that year,
his wife having passed away many years earlier, in
1861, on October 8. He was twice married, his
second wife being a sister of his first, and she still
survives him. Mr. Reinhardt was a representative
to the last Constitutional Convention and was a man
who possessed superior natural abilities and was
universally beloved and respected. He reared nine
children to mature years, but one son, Adolphus, lost
his life at Pilot Knob in 1864, while serving in the
Confederate army. Mary (wife of Rev. R. H. Croz-
ier, of Palestine, Tex.), Emma (wife of Dr. P. E.
Thomas, of Clarendon, Ark.) and Abel S. Reinhardt
are the only ones of the family now living. The
latter received a common-school education in
Prairie County and in 1864 enlisted in the Confederate army, Col. Witt's regiment, and was with
Price on his raid through Missouri. He was badly
wounded in November of that year and was disabled for several months. After the surrender he
returned home and successfully conducted the home
farm for a number of years, but in 1876 moved to
Hickory Plains. Two years later he was elected
sheriff and collector of Prairie County, and was re-
elected in 1880, 1882, 1884 and 1886, serving in
all ten consecutive years, his majority at each time
of his re-election being large. He has been carrying on a farm all these years and he also owns a
good home in Des Arc. He was married in Prairie
County on October 30, 1871, to Miss Laura J., a
daughter of Daniel and Mary Harshaw, of Hickory
Plains, and by her has had the following children:
Alice, Katie Gray, Lillie, Gracie, Arthur Shnford
and two sons who died in infancy. Mr. and Mrs.
Reinhardt are members of the Old School Presbyterian Church and the former belongs to the
Knights of Honor.

George J. Reubell, druggist, Hazen, Ark.
This worthy and much-respected citizen of Prairie
County, Ark., was originally from New York State,
his birth occurring in the city of New York, in
1837, and was the only son born to the union of

Jacob and Mary A. (Cornelius) Reubell, natives of New York. George J. Reubell was left fatherless when but six months old, and his mother, who was a native of France, died at Staten Island, N. Y., in 1845. Grandfather Cornelius was under Napoleon in the battle of Austerlitz, and others, in the retreat from Moscow, and after Napoleon was banished to the Island of Elba he came to America, settling on Staten Island, N. Y., where he followed the occupation of a gardener. His death occurred early in 1856. George J. Reubell was reared and educated in the schools of New York City, and at the age of seventeen years he went to Madison County, Tenn., where he worked at the boot and shoe business. He also engaged in clerking, and in November, 1860, he came to Prairie County, Ark., where he resumed his trade, at Brownsville and Des Arc, until the close of the war. He also read medicine for some time. In 1866 he was engaged in selling drugs for different firms, and also filled the position as clerk in a general store. In 1874 he was appointed assessor of Prairie County, was elected the same year, and served in that capacity until 1878, when he was appointed deputy circuit clerk, filling this position until 1884. He is active in politics, and votes with the Democratic party. He is a member of the K. of H., Hazen Lodge No. 3135, and is Reporter of the same. He was also a member of the I. O. O. F. He was married in Des Arc, in 1863, to Julia A. Kilgrove, a native of Tennessee, and the daughter of James D. Kilgrove, who was also a native of North Carolina, and who came to Prairie County, Ark., in 1860. To the union of Mr. and Mrs. Reubell were born seven children: James C., Gilson B., Henry D., Mary Anna, Medora, Charles E. and Addie. In 1876 Mr. Reubell purchased eighty acres of land, and has added to the same until he is now the owner of 205 acres, with thirty-five acres under cultivation. He and Mrs. Reubell are members of the Presbyterian Church.

W. H. Richards (deceased). Of that sturdy and independent class, the farmers of Arkansas, none were possessed of more genuine merit and a stronger character than he whose name stands at the head of this sketch. His birth occurred in

Person County, N. C., February 16, 1841, and in 1871 he was married to Mrs. Harriet (Hunter) Tipton, the widow of J. A. Tipton. Moving with her shortly after to Prairie County, Ark., he purchased in Center Township 100 acres of land which he commenced immediately to improve, and soon had seventy acres under cultivation. He took an active interest in all affairs pertaining to the welfare of the county and in his political views was a Democrat. He was also a patron of education and his death, which occurred in Prairie County, January 25, 1888, was deeply lamented by all. Mrs. Richards was born in the State of Mississippi in 1835, and was there married in 1852 to William B. Higginbottom, born September 15, 1829, in Tuscaloosa County, Ala., by whom she became the mother of four children: John B. (a farmer), E. E., S. L. and Mary A. (deceased). Mr. Higginbottom removed to Clark County, Ark., in 1860, and there died in 1863, his widow afterward being united in marriage to J. A. Tipton, by whom she became the mother of one son: John. She was again left a widow in 1871 and the following year married Mr. Richards, as above stated. She was born in Mississippi in 1835, and was one of a family of twelve children born to George W. and Harriet (Bonds) Hunter, natives of North Carolina, who were married in Mississippi and spent their days in the last-named State. Mr. and Mrs. Richards became the parents of three children: Jennie E., Robert L. and Florence Idella.

Robert E. Richardson, of the well-known firm of R. E. Richardson & Co., composed individually of J. M. and R. E. Richardson, owes his nativity to Memphis, Tenn., where his birth occurred on January 28, 1848, and where he attended school until fourteen years of age. His father, Gen. Robert V. Richardson, was born in the Old Dominion, on November 4, 1820, and immigrated with his parents to Wilson County, Tenn., in 1834. He received his education in Clinton College, afterward taught school for about four years, and then commenced the study of law, opening an office at Brownsville, Tenn. Here he found the field too small for his capabilities, and later moved to Memphis, Tenn., where he became one of the prominent legal lights in the profession. He continued his chosen calling up to the time of his death, which occurred in 1869. In 1845 he was united in marriage to Miss Mary E. Avent, a daughter of James M. Avent, of Limestone County, Ala., and the fruits of this union were three children: James M., Robert E. and Philip R., the two eldest of whom reside in Prairie County, Ark. Previous to the war Gen. Richardson was one of the largest land holders in the State of Arkansas, owning at one time 100,000 acres of land. He was the inspector-general of the Tennessee Volunteers during the Mexican War, and was in service during the whole time. In 1861 he organized the Twelfth Tennessee Regiment of Tennessee Cavalry, and was assigned duty under Gen. N. B. Forrest, afterward receiving the commission of brigadier-general. Later he organized the Fourteenth, Fifteenth and Sixteenth Regiments of Tennessee Cavalry, which formed one of the principal brigades of the Army of Tennessee, and served with distinction in all the principal battles of the late war. He was paroled at Grenadier, Miss., on April 15, 1865, after which he moved immediately to New York City, where he became vice-president of the United States Cotton Company, and in his official capacity, while with the company, he was obliged to visit Europe twice on business. In 1868 he returned to Memphis, Tenn., practiced his profession there, and while on a tour of inspection of his large landed interest in Southeast Missouri, he was assassinated in Clarkton, Dunklin County, in December, 1869. Robert E. Richardson moved with his parents to Fayette County, Tenn., in January, 1862, and in the spring of the following year he joined the Confederate army as a private, Twelfth Tennessee Regiment, commanded by his father, and his first engagement was one of the most desperate cavalry charges that occurred during the war. The Twelfth Tennessee Regiment, 325 strong, fought over 3,000 Federal soldiers who were trying to capture Capt. Richardson's wagon train, consisting of sixty or seventy wagons, but the captain succeeded in drawing the enemy away from the train and went out of the fight with 100 prisoners. He was in numerous engagements over Tennessee and Mississippi during 1863, 1864 and 1865, was in secret service also during those two years, and gained much valuable information for the Confederate army. He was promoted to the rank of captain, and served in that capacity until the close of the war. He surrendered April 15, 1865, after which he returned with his father to their home, and was here engaged in tilling the soil. In 1865 he attended the Male Academy at New Castle, Tenn., and there remained until May, 1866. The same year he moved with his father's family to New York City, where the remainder of that year and the whole of 1867 he attended school at the University of New York. At the close of the last-mentioned year he moved back to Memphis, and here read law under Judge McHenry and Col. Hubbard. He remained with them for about a year, and then went to Hardeman County, Tenn., where he was engaged in cultivating the soil until 1868. In June of the same year he married Miss Annie Avent, daughter of W. T. and Nannie Avent, and afterward remained in Hardeman County for four years. In January, 1872, he moved with his family back to Memphis, and was there engaged in the wholesale grocery business, under the firm title of Scales, Richardson & Co. He became dissatisfied with his partner and sold his interest to a man named Murphy, and in 1863 he engaged as a drummer for Menken Bros., remaining with them two years when he was offered a larger salary and began working for Lowenstine Bros. He remained with this firm until after their failure, when he went to Louisville and worked in the capacity of a drummer for W. H. Walker & Co. In 1879 he and a brother crossed the Mississippi River to Arkansas and engaged in farming and merchandising in that State. In 1881 they moved to Fort Smith, and after remaining there six months became dissatisfied and moved to Prairie County, Ark., where the same year they bought out the firm of R. P. Watt & Co. Here they have remained ever since, and have gained a large trade by their honest, upright conduct. Mr. Richardson has been a member of the K. of H. for seven years; is one of the prominent citizens of the county and is a liberal contributor to all worthy enterprises. He is a member of the Methodist and his wife a member of the Baptist Church. Their family consists of the following children: Annie C., Robert V., Mattie A. and James E.

J. M. Richardson, a member of the firm of E. R. Richardson & Co., is a brother of R. E. Richardson, the subject of the preceding sketch, and is a man whose excellent business ability is acknowledged by all. He owes his nativity to Memphis, Tenn. (where his birth occurred October 16, 1850), and is the son of Gen. Robert V. Richardson (see preceding sketch). J. M. Richardson received a thorough education in Memphis, Tenn., and New York City and there he began business for himself as book-keeper, remaining thus engaged until January, 1881. He then came to De Vall's Bluff, engaged in the mercantile business on a capital of $1,200 and has been very successful, increasing the original capital to $40,-000. He is also engaged in a large ranch business, has an excellent stock farm and has some of the finest blooded animals in the State of Arkansas. He owns about 10,000 acres of good land in the State and is the man who by his wide-awake and thoroughgoing manner will succeed in whatever he undertakes. He selected as his companion in life Miss Ella Rose, daughter of Judge E. W. Rose of Giles County, Tenn., and was united in marriage to her March 18, 1874, at Pulaski, Tenn. The fruits of this union have been the following children: Ella, Gussie, Erma, Annie, Sarah, Lillian (deceased) and James M., Jr. Mr. Richardson is a member of the K. of H., has held all the offices in the gift of his lodge and has represented his lodge twice in the Grand Lodge of the State. He has been a delegate to every Democratic State convention from this county since his removal here and is a man in whom implicit confidence is placed. He and Mrs. Richardson are members of the Presbyterian Church, take a deep interest in church and school work and are liberal contributors to all worthy enterprises.

F. M. Robinson, justice of the peace, Hazen, Ark. Mr. Robinson owes his nativity to Madison County, Tenn., where his birth occurred October 10, 1835, and is now one of the much-esteemed and respected citizens of Prairie County. He is the eldest of a family of twelve children born to Henry and Jane (Golden) Robinson, the father a native of the Old Dominion, and the mother of South Carolina. They were married in Tennessee, where the father conducted a farm, and was a successful farmer. He is still living in Madison County, Tenn., but his wife died in February, 1889. He first settled in Tennessee when it was called Kentucky. F. M. Robinson passed his boyhood days in assisting on his father's farm and in attending the schools of Madison County. He selected Miss Susan Lester as his companion in life, and was married to her December 29, 1853, in Tennessee. She was the daughter of Richard and Mary (Newsom) Lester, natives, respectively, of Virginia and Tennessee. At an early date Mr. Lester settled in Tennessee, and there he and wife passed their last days. Mr. Robinson came to Prairie County in 1858, settled near Hickory Plains, and there engaged in agricultural pursuits, which occupation he has continued for twenty-five years. He enlisted at Austin, May 10, 1861, in Company C, Col. Glenn's regiment of infantry, but later was transferred to Company I, as second lieutenant of the same regiment. He was in a number of the prominent battles, Prairie Grove, Helena, Little Rock, Saline and others, and was taken prisoner at Camden, Ark., confined at Austin, and paroled in 1865, after which he returned to Prairie County, Ark. Here he engaged in tilling the soil, and this continued until 1883, when he moved to Hazen, where he followed the carpenter's business for some time, and later the undertaker's business. He owns a good business building and some lots. He takes considerable interest in politics, and votes with the Democratic party. He is recorder of the town of Hazen, and one of the commissioners of accounts of Prairie County. Mr. Robinson has also been magistrate for fourteen successive years, and has discharged all duties incumbent upon these various public offices to the satisfaction of all. To his marriage were born ten living children: Walter (married, and resides near Boston, Tex.), T. A. (engaged in merchandising in Cotton Plant, Ark.), Sam E. (married, and residing at Hope, Ark.), Ella (now Mrs. Rev. W. J. Hudspoth, State evangelist of Christian Church, of Texas, resides at Prescott, Ark.), F. C. (physician and surgeon at Kerr Station, Ark.), Emmett (married, and resides at Hazen), F. B. (resides at Cotton Plant), Minnie (resides at Prescott), Eva and Nellie (both residing at Prescott, Ark.). The mother of these children was called to her long home in March, 1886. She was a kind mother and a true helpmate to her husband.

James M. Rooker, farmer and stock raiser, Hickory Plains, Ark. Mr. Rooker is now following a calling that has for ages received undivided efforts from many worthy individuals, and one that always furnishes sustenance to the ready worker. He was originally from York County, S. C., where his birth occurred on December 11, 1833, and is the son of John B. Rooker, a native of South Carolina, and Nancy A. (McCallum) Rooker, who was born in Scotland. John B. Rooker was a mechanic, a bridge carpenter, and moved from his native State to Georgia, where he was engaged in building bridges on the first railroad from Atlanta to Chattanooga. He subsequently located on a farm in Gordon County, and there received his final summons about 1857. He served as magistrate for a number of years, and was a much respected citizen. His wife survives him, and is seventy-five years of age. James M. Rooker passed his boyhood days in Georgia, and remained with his father until of age, after which he went to Noxubee County, Miss., and was overseer on a plantation for three years. He was married on January 28, 1858, in Smith County, to Miss Mary A. Hill, a native of Noxubee County, and the daughter of Sherod Hill. To this union have been born fourteen children: Emma E. (wife of R. S. Guess), Joseph A. (lives on a farm near his father's), J. Thomas (now taking medical lectures at Little Rock), Ella E. (wife of William Webb), John W., Augustus, Cora E. (wife of J. E. Wilson), Bunyon, Leroy C., Mary O. and Martha (twins), Samuel, Ava and Elmer. They lost one child, Minnie, on November 2, 1871, at the age of four years. After his marriage Mr. Rooker bought a farm in Smith County, and tilled the soil up to the breaking out

of the late war. He enlisted in the Confederate army, Seventh Battalion Infantry, in May, 1861, and served twelve months, after which he was in the Forty-sixth Regiment Infantry, and served until the close of the war, being promoted from private to sergeant. He participated in the following engagements: Chickasaw Bayou, Port Gibson, siege of Vicksburg, where he was captured, held a prisoner until the fall and then exchanged. After this he was in the fights at Atlanta, Kenesaw Mountain, and in the fights from Dalton to Nashville. He was again captured in front of Nashville, and held at Camp Douglas until the close of the war. He received one slight wound at Vicksburg, but numerous bullets passed through his clothing. Returning to Mississippi after the war, he followed farming there for two years, and in 1868 moved to Arkansas, where he rented land in Prairie County for one year. He then purchased 160 acres, cleared it, and added to the same until he now owns 500 acres of land, with 150 acres under cultivation. He has good buildings, a fine orchard of five acres, and is one of the progressive men of the county. He has been a member of the school board for a number of years, and is deeply interested in educational matters. He and wife are members of the Baptist Church, and he is deacon in the same.

J. B. Sanders, county examiner of Prairie County, Hazen, Ark. There are many men in this county at the present day in whose lives there are but few thrilling incidents, or remarkable events, yet whose success has been a steady and constant growth, and who, possessed of excellent judgment, strong common sense and indomitable energy, have evinced in their lives and character, great symmetry, completeness and moral standing of a high order. To this class belongs Mr. Sanders, whose birth occurred in Johnson County, N. C., in 1834, and who was the second in a family of eleven children born to the union of R. T. and Eliza C. (Boone) Sanders, natives of North Carolina. The father was a man of education, having graduated from the University of North Carolina, in the class of 1828, and was a large land owner in his native State. In 1870 he moved to Prairie

County, Ark., and later in life settled at Hazen, where his death occurred in 1887. The mother had died in 1885. The father was not active in politics, but took a great interest in church work, and was moderator of the Grand Prairie Baptist Association at the time of his death. J. B. Sanders was initiated into the duties of farm life when young, and received his education in the Baptist College at Clinton, Miss., graduating with the class of 1856. He then commenced cultivating the soil, continuing at this until January, 1863, when he enlisted at De Soto County, Miss., in the Eighteenth Mississippi Cavalry, in Chalmer's division of Forrest's cavalry. Mr. Sanders participated in many of the battles and raids of Forrest's cavalry in West Tennessee and North Mississippi, and was taken prisoner at Spring Hill, Tenn., in January, 1865. He was confined at Camp Chase, Ohio, paroled there on June 13, 1865, and afterward returned to De Soto County, Miss., when he found all of his property, stock, etc., gone and he reduced from affluence to poverty. He was married in Madison County, Miss., in 1856, to Miss Ezza Denson, a native of Mississippi, and the daughter of Harvey and Jennie (King) Denson, early pioneers of Madison County, Miss. One child, Harvey, was born to this union, and he is at present and has been for nine years, a clerk in the Gates mercantile store at De Vall's Bluff, Ark. Mr. Sanders was married in De Soto County, Miss., on December 23, 1865, to Miss Lucy C. Gwyn, a native of the Old Dominion, and the daughter of James H. and Caroline S. (Ransom) Gwyn, natives also of Virginia, and both now deceased. After his second marriage Mr. Sanders settled on a farm, and in 1870, came to Prairie County, where he has been engaged in teaching most of the time for sixteen years. He takes a very great interest in educational matters and had charge of the school at Judsonia, Ark., in the winters of 1881 and 1882. He has been county examiner most of the time since 1881, and has filled that position in a highly creditable manner. He took an active part in the organization of Hazen Township, where he has resided since 1881, having bought seventy acres in the woods, and now has forty acres fairly improved. He takes considerable interest in politics and votes with the Democratic party. He was chairman of the Democratic executive committee of Prairie County for years. He is a member of the Masonic fraternity, White River Lodge, at Des Arc, Ark., and is a member of Quitmana Chapter, Hernando, De Soto County, Miss. He and Mrs. Sanders are members of the Missionary Baptist Church; Mr. Sanders being moderator of the Grand Prairie Baptist Association, comprising this and Arkansas Counties. To the marriage of Mr. and Mrs. Sanders were born seven children: Walter Troy (clerking at De Vall's Bluff), Joseph (who has been contracting for the Little Rock & Memphis Railroad, building wire fence for them since eighteen years of age), James (working for the Little Rock & Memphis Railroad), Bappy (John Thomas), Alice, Hall, and Lucy. Mr. Sanders has seen a vast change in Prairie County, from a moral as well as an educational standpoint, since his residence here. When he first came to Arkansas guns and dogs were often heard on the Christian Sabbath, but now the church and Sunday bell sounds forth instead of the hunter's call. He can say what very few can say, that he has not lost one of his own intermediate family since he came to the State, twenty years ago. This speaks well for the health of Prairie County, Ark.

William D. Shock has been a resident of Hazen, Prairie County, Ark., for only one year, yet he is well known throughout the community as a successful business man, being engaged in the real estate and lumber business. He owns about 100 lots in the town, and has about 1,200 acres of land. He was born in Missouri in 1843, being the eighth child in a family of sixteen born to Henry Shock, who was born in Kentucky in 1802. The latter was one of twelve children born to John and Mary Shock, who were of German descent and natives of Pennsylvania. The latter couple removed to Missouri at an early day and settled in Boone County, where the father followed farming and blacksmithing. He died in 1855, and his wife about 1862. Henry Shock spent his early life and school days in Missouri, and, like his father, was a successful tiller of the soil, being also a prosperous stockman. He

45

was married, first, in 1827, to Miss Mary Jackson, a daughter of Thomas Jackson, a Virginian. Five children blessed this union: John J., Thomas P., Permelia A., Joseph S. and Mary J. (the wife of S. Alverson). The mother of these children died about 1835, and three years later Mr. Shock wedded Miss Hannah L. Cox, a member of the Cox family of Kentucky, she being one of a family of seven children. To them were born eleven children: James H., Lucinda F. (widow of D. Smart, of Missouri), William D., Daniel P., Sarah and Lydia (twins, the former the wife of J. Turner, of Missouri, and the latter, Mrs. Green Gautt, also of that State), Alonzo, Theodore R., Robert A. and Milton P. Mr. Shock died in the State of his adoption in 1885, but his widow still survives him and resides on the old homestead, she being a member of the Christian Church, as was her husband. William D. Shock, the immediate subject of this biography, spent his youth in Missouri, and in 1862 left home to take part in the struggle between the North and South. After being in the service a short time he was crippled by a horse falling on him, and was compelled to go home, but upon recovering he again entered the service and in 1864 joined Company H, Marmaduke's brigade, but was afterward exchanged to the advance guard of the same brigade. After his return home he turned his attention to farming and stock raising, in Audrain County, being very successful in both occupations, but since coming to Arkansas has devoted his time to the real estate and lumber business, and now has under his control about 40,000 acres of land together with a number of town lots. He was married, in 1867, to Miss Nancy I. Gay, a daughter of John D. and Rebecca E. Gay, of Missouri, but natives of Kentucky. Mrs. Shock was born in Missouri, and her union with Mr. Shock has resulted in the birth of three children: Charles E., Olivia (who died in Missouri in 1886) and William R. The family attends the Christian Church.

J. D. Sparks is a stockman and farmer of Center Township, Prairie County, Ark., and was born in Tennessee in 1854, being the youngest of ten children born to David and Comfort (Marphat)

Sparks, the former a native of the "Old North State," born in 1808, one of a large family of children born to John Sparks. His youth was spent in his native State, but while still young he was taken to Middle Tennessee, and in this State received the most of his education. He was reared to a farm life, and in 1834 was married to Miss Marphat, she being a daughter of John Marphat, of North Carolina, who removed to Tennessee during the early history of that State. Mr. Sparks' family are as follows: Julia, Minas, Findly, Sarah, Comfort, John, William, Elmira, Amanda and Jonas D. (the immediate subject of this biography). The father was a Democrat, and a member of the Primitive Baptist Church. The early life and school days of Jonas D. Sparks were spent in Center Township, and there he was married, in 1876, to Miss Margie Anna Mills, a daughter of Thomas and Catherine Mills, natives of Tennessee. Mrs. Sparks was born in Arkansas, and has borne her husband four children: Pearl, Ross, May and Berney. In 1876 Mr. Sparks engaged in farming for himself, and by judicious management and industry has become the owner of 120 acres of land, and has about seventy under cultivation. He is a stanch Democrat in his political views, and has always been one of the public-spirited citizens of the county.

Hugh S. Stephenson is filling the office of justice of the peace at Des Arc, and by occupation is an undertaker. He was born in Maury County, Tenn., March 24, 1819, and is a son of Rev. John C. Stephenson, who was born in Tennessee, where he was reared, educated and married, the last event being to Miss Agnes Simpson, who was born in that State. Rev. Stephenson moved to Alabama at an early day, settling in the northern part of the State, where he was engaged in farming and preaching the doctrines of the Cumberland Presbyterian Church for many years; he fell in the pulpit while preaching his last sermon, and died soon after, his death being caused by the bursting of a blood-vessel, in August, 1840. His wife survived him until 1887, when she too passed from life at the age of eighty-nine years. Hugh S. Stephenson grew to manhood in Lawrence County,

Ala., and until he attained his majority, made his home with his father, learning in the meantime the carpenter's trade, at which he worked as contractor until his marriage in 1840. After moving to Sumter County in 1841, he farmed for about eight years, then put up a tannery in Pickens County, and spent eight more years in conducting this business. Northern Mississippi became his home in 1858, and until the opening of the war he was engaged in farming in De Soto County. He joined the Confederate service, Blye's battalion, but a year later he was discharged on account of disability, after which he was on detached duty the most of the time until the close of the war. He continued to make his home in Mississippi until January, 1870, when he came to Des Arc, Ark., and engaged in contracting and building, also the livery business. After following the latter business for about four years he gave it up, and in 1883 began dealing in undertaker's goods, at which he has been quite successful. In all his enterprises he has been reasonably successful, and has acquired a good home and a comfortable competency. He first filled the office of magistrate in Alabama, serving there about eight years, and discharged the duties of the same office in Mississippi for ten years, and has been justice of the peace at Des Arc for at least twelve years, and has also filled the office of alderman at this place. He joined the Masonic fraternity in Alabama, was Master of his lodge there for about eight years, and represented his lodge in the Grand Lodge of the State. He was also Master of Des Arc Lodge. He is an elder in the Cumberland Presbyterian Church, and is a consistent Christian. He was married in Alabama, in 1840, to Ann A. Whitley, a native of Alabama and a daughter of N. G. Whitley. She was born in North Carolina, but was reared in Alabama. Their children are: Lou H. (wife of A. C. Weatherall), Alice (wife of W. G. Hazen), Lula (wife of Henderson Reid), Willie H. (wife of D. J. Martinger, of Little Rock), Amos J. (at home) and Dr. Charles C. (a prominent young physician of Swan Lake). Robert H. was wounded at Shiloh, and afterward died from the effects of this wound. Mariah, who died several years ago,

was the wife of J. B. Jamison. George W., who died in 1884, at the age of twenty-eight years, and two children who died in infancy.

Jefferson J. and Frank Stratton are prosperous farmers and cotton ginners, residing at Barrettsville, and are natives of the county in which they are now residing, and sons of James E. and Comfort (Sparks) Stratton. The father was a Tennesseean, born in 1829, and his juvenile days were spent at farm work in his native State, and in attending the old time subscription schools. About 1858 he wedded the daughter of David and Comfort Sparks, Tennesseeans, and in 1856, came to Prairie County, Ark., and settled in Totten Township, and here reared his family, which consists of the following children: Thomas B. (who died in 1864), Jefferson, Frank, Lou, Dora (who died in 1880) and Eddie. The father of these children was a well-to-do and prosperous farmer, and died in Lonoke County, Ark., in 1873. He and wife were members of the Missionary Baptist Church, and his widow still survives him, and has been a resident of Center Township since 1886. He was a soldier all through the war, enlisting in 1861. Their sons, Jefferson J. and Frank, were born in 1861 and 1864, respectively, and are now young men of enterprise and push, their outlook for the future being bright and promising. In 1887 they began operating a cotton-gin, which has a capacity of twelve bales per day. Jefferson owns 160 acres of land, and has eighty acres under cultivation, while Frank lives with his mother and manages her farm of 160 acres, of which sixty acres are under the plow. Their sister Lou is now Mrs. M. L. McCune, and has three children: Quinton, Birney and Frank.

John Henry Taylor, editor of the Hazen Free Press, was born April 25, 1862, in Panola County, Tex., his parents, Thomas H. and Annie A. Taylor, being married there in 1855. The father was a Georgian, who went from the State of his birth to Texas in 1849, the mother having moved there from her native State (Alabama) with her parents in 1850. Thomas H. Taylor was one of the gallant "boys in gray," and spent four years faithfully fighting for the cause of the South. After the proclamation of peace he began the study of medicine, graduating in his profession in 1866, and two years later moved to Hopkins County, Tex., where he was successfully engaged in the practice of his profession until his death, in June, 1888, being recognized as one of the leaders of the medical fraternity. J. H. Taylor spent his early life, up to the age of sixteen years, on a farm, and became thoroughly familiar with the details and intricacies of farm labor, acquiring also that sturdy independence and honesty of purpose which is characteristic of the average farmer's boy, and which has remained among his chief characteristics up to the present day. Upon reaching the above-mentioned age he entered the office of the Sulphur Springs (Texas) Gazette as an apprentice, remaining there until he attained his twentieth year; then went to Jefferson, Marion County, Texas, and worked for two years as foreman of a book and job office for Wortham & Mullins, but thinking he could do better for himself elsewhere, he, in 1885, went North and traveled over the whole of the Eastern and Northern States, working in nearly every town containing over 10,000 inhabitants. This tour extended over a period of two years, and he acquired a keen insight into the political views of the different sections, from which he is deriving a great benefit. In the spring of 1886 he went to Waco, Tex., where he took charge of the newspaper and book and job office of Rev. J. B. Cranfill, called the Advance office. He was also foreman of the daily, and it was published in favor of the prohibition campaign, which was agitating Texas in 1887. In June, 1888, he landed in Little Rock, Ark., and in July of the same year he settled in Prairie County, and in August established the Vox Populi, a paper which he edited in a very able manner, winning considerable notoriety as a journalist. February 12, 1889, he was united in marriage to Miss Rosa Cuneo, at Hazen, Ark., and they took a trip to Texas and spent some three months sight-seeing in the Lone Star State. In May, 1889, he established and is now running the Hazen Free Press, an eight-page quarto, at a subscription price of $1 per year. This journal, under the efficient editorship of Mr.

Taylor, is already wielding a widespread influence for good, and some interesting and valuable information can always be gleaned from its columns. That a brilliant future in the field of journalism lies before Mr. Taylor is conceded by all, and he gives every promise of becoming one of the leading men of Arkansas. He is of a social and genial nature, "With malice toward none and charity for all."

Col. Nicholas B. Thweatt, farmer and horticulturist, Hickory Plains, Ark. Prominent among the enterprising and successful tillers of the soil of Prairie County, whose career has been both honorable and successful, is the subject of this sketch. His father, Howard D. Thweatt, was a native of Virginia, who went to Tennessee when a young man and was there united in marriage to Miss Elizabeth Echols, a native also of the Old Dominion. The parents moved to a farm in Williamson County, Tenn., and there reared their family. The father was a regent in the War of 1812, but was not in active service himself. He died at his son's residence in Mississippi. Col. Nicholas B. Thweatt owes his nativity to Williamson County, Tenn., where his birth occurred on May 10, 1827, and remained in his native State until seventeen years of age when he went to Mississippi, settling in Yalobusha County, where he cultivated the soil up to the breaking out of the war. In 1862 he enlisted in the Confederate army, served on detached duty most of the time (in secret service) and thus continued until cessation of hostilities. He was taken prisoner, held at Helena and there suffered much from exposure. He was in numerous tight places, but always succeeded in getting through all right. Returning to Mississippi after the war he remained there until 1867, after which he moved to Arkansas and located on his present fine property. He purchased an improved farm and now has 200 acres with 100 acres cultivated. Like the majority of farmers in that locality he has a good residence and substantial outbuildings. He has a fine orchard of six acres and has one and a half acres in vineyard. He made the first wine manufactured in Prairie County, and makes on an average from 150 to 200 gallons per year. This is a very fine quality of wine. Mr. Thweatt was married in Mississippi on December 18, 1850, to Miss Mary Hardin, a native of North Carolina, but who was reared in Mississippi, and the daughter of Redic Hardin. Mrs. Thweatt died on March 25, 1870, leaving four sons: J. G. (an attorney at De Vall's Bluff), A. (a farmer and stock raiser), Prof. H. D. (a teacher of Prairie County) and N. E. (who is on the home farm). Mr. Thweatt is a Royal Arch Mason, also belongs to the Council, and is Past Master of the same.

J. G. Thweatt, attorney, De Valls Bluff, Ark. Every life has a history of its own and although in appearance it may seem to possess little to distinguish it from others, yet the popularity attained by Mr. Thweatt in his profession as well as his political career has contributed to give him a wide and popular acquaintance with nearly every citizen of Prairie County, if not personally, then by name. He came to Prairie County, Ark., from Tallahatchee County, Miss., in January, 1867, settled near Hickory Plains, where he has since made his home. His birth occurred in Tallahatchee County, Miss., in 1852, and he was the eldest of seven children born to the union N. B. and Mary (Hardin) Thweatt, natives respectively of Tennessee and North Carolina. The father left his native State and journeyed to Mississippi when a young man, married there and in 1867 moved to Prairie County, Ark., where he engaged in agricultural pursuits. He is still living, but the mother died in Prairie County in 1869. J. G. Thweatt was early taught the duties of farm life and received his education at Hickory Plains, Prairie County. He commenced reading law at De Vall's Bluff in 1873, and two years later was admitted to the bar. He commenced the practice of law at De Vall's Bluff in 1875 and the following year moved to Des Arc, where he continued his practice. He also engaged in the real-estate business and has charge of the land of the Little Rock & Memphis Railroad in Prairie and Arkansas Counties. He has considerable land for sale in South Prairie County, both prairie and timber land, all well watered by living streams. He has sold a vast amount of land and it is advancing each year in value. Mr. Thweatt

is active in politics and in 1881 represented Prairie County in the legislature. He votes with the Democratic party and socially is a member of the K. of H. He was married in Des Arc, Prairie County, in 1882, to Miss Maggie McLaughlin, a native of Kentucky and the daughter of John and Christina (Cooper) McLaughlin, natives of Scotland and Kentucky, respectively. The father left his native country in 1839, settled in Michigan and some time later moved to New York, thence to Kentucky in 1857 and in 1870 to DeWitt, Arkansas County. He was for many years a minister in the Methodist Episcopal Church, but prior to that was an attorney. He is now located at Arkadelphia. The mother is also living. J. G. Thweatt opened his present office in January, 1888, and is one of the practical business men of the place. He has always taken an active interest in all things relating to the good of the county, especially educational and religious matters, and he and Mrs. Thweatt are members of the Methodist Episcopal Church, South. One child, Charley, is the result of this marriage.

Gen. William A. E. Tisdale. The history of the Tisdale family in this country, or rather that branch to which the subject of this sketch belongs, dates back to the great-great-grandfather, John Tisdale, who settled in Massachusetts in 1646, making his home at Taunton. His son, John, the great-grandfather, was a colonel in the Revolutionary War, and raised and equipped his regiment. His son, who also bore the name of John, was born in the "Bay State," was a gentleman of the old school, and possessed very courtly and polished manners, and in his youth was very fond of the chase. His son, Timothy, the father of our immediate subject, was born in Massachusetts, and there spent most of his life, his death occurring in 1856, at the age of fifty-eight years. He was very finely educated, being a graduate of Harvard College, and was a Congregational minister. His wife, whose maiden name was Charlotte Quintin, was also born in Massachusetts, and on her father's side is a descendant of an old Scotch family, that resided in the Lowlands. She was born in 1800, and died in 1869. Her mother was Thankful Nye, a sister of the late Senator Nye, of Nebraska. Maj. Will. A. E. Tisdale, was born near Winchester, Va., in 1838, his parents being residents of that State at the time, but in his early youth he was taken by them to Hampshire County, Mass., and at the age of fifteen years he entered West Point Military Academy, and was graduated therefrom in 1857. He was sent to the frontier as brevet-second lieutenant, and under Maj. (later Lieut.-Gen.) E. Kirby Smith, Confederate States army, went to Salt Lake, thence to San Francisco, Fort Vancouver, Walla Walla and back to the frontier, where, in 1859, he resigned on account of rheumatism and located in Clinton County, Iowa. Here he was admitted to the bar by the Hon. John F. Dillon, in April, 1861, but did not enter on his practice as the war then came up. He joined the Missouri State Militia as first lieutenant of an independent company, being mustered in by the then Capt. (afterward Gen.) Lyons, on April 23, 1861, for three months, and before the expiration of said service was made captain. He subsequently enlisted in the Fifth Iowa Infantry (in August, 1861), and remained in the army until August, 1867, serving part of the time after being crippled as Adjutant 60, United States Colored Troops, and mustered out with the volunteer rank of major-brevet-colonel, and the rank of captain in the Regulars. He received a severe wound in the thigh at the battle of Wilson's Creek, in August, 1861, and in March, 1862, at the battle of New Madrid, received a wound in the forehead over the right eye, causing the entire loss of the same. This happened while serving under Gen. John Pope, and he received a high compliment from his brigade commander, Brig.-Gen. Schuyler Hamilton. On September 19, 1862, while acting aid-de-camp at Iuka, Miss., he was wounded seven times, twice through the lungs, both balls passing in under the right arm, once through the right foot, one in the right hand, one in the right leg above the knee, breaking the bone, one in the left leg below the knee, and one in the buttock. All these wounds he received in forty minutes, and was complimented on his bravery in a special order by Gen. C. L. Mathias, his old colonel. Subsequently he served the most of the time on staff duty, holding such positions as provost-marshal, inspector-general and aid-de-camp. He commanded the military prison at Helena for some five months, and was also engineer in charge of Helena's fortifications. He arrived at Little Rock the night of the surrender of Richmond, and was assigned to duty as district provost-marshal, which position he held until August, 1865, at which time he was assigned to duty as superintendent and provost-marshal Bureau of Refugees, Freedmen and Abandoned Lands for the White River District embracing De Vall's Bluff, Augusta, Jacksonport, Batesville and Evening Shades. In October he was ordered to Little Rock to relieve Col. Sargeant, in charge of the largest district of the State. During the reconstruction he was appointed by Gen. E. O. C. Ord, as president of the board of military registration for Johnson County, which office he held until after the election for the constitution, and its adoption in March, 1868. In July of the same year he was appointed by Gen. Clayton, assistant adjutant-general for the State, and assistant mustering officer, and was sent to the district embracing the counties of Van Buren, Searcy, Newton, Carroll and Madison to muster the militia, which he accomplished in due time, and returned to Little Rock the night of November 4, in time to vote in the Congressional election held on November 5. He was one of Clayton's brigadier-generals in the military troubles, was with Gen. Upham in his skirmishes, and subsequently commanded the district composed of the counties of Greene and Craighead, where he had a skirmish with the Ku-klux gang, and on being relieved, turned over to Gov. Clayton 980 affidavits of parties who confessed to having belonged to the Ku-klux. All this time he was interested in planting on the Arkansas River, an investment that did not pan out to his advantage, and in July, 1869, he was appointed assistant assessor and deputy collector of one division of the First Congressional district, with headquarters at Jacksonport, and during this time collected some $20,000, much of which he obtained from old delinquents. In March, 1871, he was made chief assistant assessor for the district, with headquarters at De Vall's Bluff, which office he held until the fall of 1872, when he was appointed clerk of the United States Court at Helena, and held this office until March, 1875. In March, 1881, he was tendered the position of mail agent on the Memphis & Little Rock Mail Route, the duties of which position he faithfully filled until November, 1881. Since that time he has been twice elected a school director of his district, and although he has never been an aspirant for political honors, he was once nominated by the Republican party for State senator, but declined to be a candidate. He is now one of the commissioners of accounts and notary public of Prairie County. Although disabled and incapacitated for manual labor, he prides himself as being one of the "honest sons of toil," and the owner of about 1,000 acres of land. He was married November 19, 1863, to Miss Serena M. Graham, a daughter of Hon. James B. Graham and Sarah A. (Fish) Graham, the latter a relative of Hamilton Fish. Mrs. Tisdale was born in Pittsburgh, Penn., in 1844, and when about nine years old she was taken by her people to Warren, Ohio, thence to Keokuk, Iowa, at the age of eleven years. She is an accomplished singer, and at the time of her marriage was the leading soprano singer in the Congregational Church at Keokuk. She is one of nine children, all of whom are living and married, with the exception of two who died in infancy. Gen. Tisdale is the seventh son in succession in a family of nine children, the one younger than him a girl, and he and five brothers were in the Union army, three operating in the East and three in the West. Gen. and Mrs. Tisdale have had born to them a family of seven children: Launa Maria (born May 3, 1865, in Keokuk), Frank Story (born in Keokuk November 8, 1868), Maud Alice (born January 13, 1870, and died August 12, 1872, at De Vall's Bluff). The following children were also born there: Charles Henry (born August 8, 1873), Clara Mabel (born October 8, 1874, and died in September, 1875, at Fairmount), Thomas Albert (born March 8, 1877, and died August 12, 1878), and John Timothy (born May 8, 1881, and died August 12, 1881). These little ones were carefully laid away on the home place, and the especial care of their

graves and the wealth of flowers which bloom over them shows that though absent they are not forgotten. When the General first came with his family to their present home, which they called Pleasant Prairie, the people in the community obtained their mail at De Vall's Bluff, twenty-five miles away, but through the instrumentality of Hon. W. W. Whitshire, then a member of Congress, and a personal friend of the family, he had established a mail route from Lonoke to De Witt, which gave them mail once each week, and later was increased to twice a week. This office was from some cause unknown abandoned, and Gen. Tisdale had the office established at his home and it was called Des Moines, Mrs. Tisdale being postmistress until the establishment of a store at Fairmount, when she resigned in favor of Benjamin Thalheimer. The General is now Post Commander of the G. A. R. Post at Stuttgart, and is a member of the Republican Central Committee of Prairie County. In politics he is a strong Republican, and always has been from boyhood. He has in his possession a silver spoon that came from England with the first John Tisdale in 1646.

J. M. Van Zandt, M. D. One of the very foremost among the professional and active business men of Barrettsville, is acknowledged to be Dr. Van Zandt, whose personal popularity is unlimited. He was born in Wayne County, Tenn., in 1841, being the eldest of five children born to Thomas T. and Elizabeth (Wells) Van Zandt, the former of whom was born in the State of Tennessee, in 1828, and there spent his youthful days and received his education. He was a minister of the Methodist Episcopal Church, and was a member of the Southwest Missouri Conference. In 1839 he married, his wife being a daughter of George Walls, and in 1844 he moved to Ozark County, Mo., and there became pastor of a church. Of five children born to him, our subject is the eldest. The next in order of birth is John W. (who lives in Marion County, Ark., is married, and has a family of six children), James A. B. (who resides near St. Charles), Elizabeth H. (Mrs. J. L. McSwayne, residing near De Vall's Bluff) and Margaret P. (Mrs. C. E. Hayley, also residing near St. Charles). Rev. Thomas T. Van Zandt was a Democrat in his views, a member of the Masonic fraternity, and was a man whom all respected and esteemed. He met a violent death during the turbulent times of the Civil War, being killed by Jayhawkers, in 1863. His wife died in Missouri, in 1858. The paternal grandfather, Elijah Van Zandt, was born in North Carolina, and was a participant in the War of 1812. Dr. J. M. Van Zandt received his early education in the common schools of Missouri, and after reaching a proper age, began studying medicine, at McDowell's College, in St. Louis, Mo., and in 1861 began his first practice. He did not continue long, however, but the same year enlisted as third sergeant in the Missouri Cavalry State Troops, and was a participant in the fights at Oak Hill, Lexington, Pea Ridge, Prairie Grove, Hartsville, Cape Girardeau, Helena, Jenkins' Ferry and others. After the death of his father he left this command, and took charge of a company, and joined Price on his raid through Missouri, his last fight being at Newtonia, that State. He practiced his profession in Dallas County, Mo., in 1865, and the following year went to Texas, and settled in Somerville County. Not liking this location, he came to Arkansas, and after a residence in Arkansas County until 1884, he settled in Barrittsville, Prairie County, where he has since made his home. In connection with his practice he is engaged in merchandising, having commenced this enterprise in October, 1889, and is doing a prosperous business. While in Texas he was married, in 1877, to Miss Ida E. Yager, a daughter of R. L. and Elizabeth (Sanders) Yager, the former an Alabamian. Dr. and Mrs. Van Zandt are members of the Christian Church, and are the parents of two children: Nannie M. and Helen E. The Doctor has been an extensive traveler, but is thoroughly satisfied with his present location. He is a Mason, and has a demit from Little River City Lodge No. 402, Bell County, Texas.

Judge Horace P. Vaughan. On this page of the history of Prairie County, Ark., is found the life record of a man, whose career through life has been as honest in the honesty of manhood, as worthy so far as duty, well and faithfully performed goes, and as untarnished by reproach as that of any man mentioned in the history of the community. He was born in Mecklenburg County, Va., August 25, 1825, and is a son of Pleasant and Mourning E. (Dance) Vaughan, who were also Virginians. The father for a number of years was a teacher by profession, being also engaged in farming. He reared his family, consisting of a son and two daughters, in Mecklenburg County, and there died in 1883, his wife's death having occurred in 1844. Although not favored with very good educational advantages in his youth Judge Horace P. Vaughan possesses a brilliant and cultured mind and his knowledge of books and the world has been mostly acquired since reaching years of maturity. At the early age of thirteen years he began clerking and followed this occupation off and on until he came west in 1852, arriving at Somerville, Tenn., in August of that year. He followed his old occupation of clerking in that place for three years and in 1855 came to Arkansas, settling at Des Arc, where he formed a partnership with another gentleman and was engaged in the mercantile business up to the opening of the war. He was then appointed by the military board as secretary of that organization, and this position retained until the close of the war, being also paymaster-general of the State troops and private secretary to the Governor. After the close of the war he settled in Des Arc again, took up the study of law, and in 1867 was admitted to the bar and practiced his profession successfully until 1878. Before commencing the practice of law and since giving up the work he has been engaged in farming and at one time he owned a considerable quantity of valuable lands and town property, but reverses have swept much of his property away. Mr. Vaughan was elected and held the office of magistrate for a number of years, and has been mayor of the town and county judge one term, and to the excellent natural abilities possessed by Judge Vaughan are added the wisdom and experience of a useful and well-spent life and there was no reason to view his official career with disapproval when he retired from the bench. He was married in

Prairie County, Nov. 4, 1856, to Mattie E. Brock, a native of Mississippi, and a daughter of Caleb and Mary F. (Jones) Brock, who were among the first families to come to this region. Mrs. Vaughan died February 5, 1873, leaving five children: D'Arcy, Emmet, Victor, Percy and Rezzie. Victor died January 24, 1883, aged seventeen years. Judge Vaughan's second union took place in May, 1873, his wife being Mrs. Mary J. (Cox) Mizill, was born in Phillips County, Ark., and by her he is the father of five children: Blanche, Mabel, Bertha, Alzie and Horace Cox. Judge Vaughan belongs to the Methodist Episcopal Church, South, and his wife to the Missionary Baptist Church. He is also a member of the Masonic fraternity.

F. P. Wells. A sketch of Mr. Wells' life, as far as Prairie County is concerned, covers a period of but little over six years, yet he has become so thoroughly identified with the business interests of the same, and his career has been so successful that a brief sketch of his career will be of much interest to all. His birth occurred in Erie County, Penn., in 1836, he being the eldest of a family of nine children born to the marriage of J. E. Wells and Louisa Cole. The former was born in the "Green Mountain State" in 1812, and about the year 1820 removed with his father to Pennsylvania, and in that State he was reared to manhood and married, the last-named event taking place in 1835, and resulted in the birth of these children: Mittie, Charles, Jerome (deceased), Julius, Louisa, Judson, Addie, Jerome (named for his elder brother who died) and subject of sketch. Mr. Wells was a tanner by trade, and in this business became quite successful. He died in 1886, still survived by his wife, who is residing in Buffalo, N. Y. F. P. Wells' youthful days were spent in the "Keystone State," but his education was acquired in Hillsdale College, Mich. Mr. Wells is a married man, his wife having formerly been Miss Sarah M. Page, a daughter of E. Page, their union being consummated in 1861, and resulted in the birth of six children: Charles, Marie, Julius, Frank, Louise and Clara. They, with their mother, reside in Buffalo, N. Y. Mr. Wells first began manufacturing boat-oars in 1865, in Albion, Erie County,

Penn., but at a later period he removed to Lansing, Mich., where he had control of four mills for this purpose, his business there being on a very extended scale, indeed. In 1883 he established a factory at De Vall's Bluff, Ark., which establishment is the only one of the kind in the State, and it is fitted up with all the latest improved and best machinery, and has a capacity of 3,500 feet of oars per day. He ships his product to all points of the globe, and in addition to having an extensive trade with the seaport and river towns of the United States, he supplies the markets of London and Liverpool (England), Glasgow (Scotland) and Sidney and Melbourne (Australia). He manufactures pike-poles, handles of all kinds and descriptions, but makes a specialty of oars. Joseph Gordner & Sons, of London, Liverpool (England) and Glasgow (Scotland), are interested in this establishment. Mr. Wells owns a portion of 14,000 acres of woodland, and in addition to this, owns valuable property in Lansing, Mich., and Buffalo, N. Y. Mr. Wells is one of the progressive and enterprising business men of the county, whose strict attention to work, perseverance and integrity have produced such substantial results, and it is a pleasure to lay before the reader the unsullied record of such a man. He is a member of the Masonic order, and he and wife are members of the Congregational Church at Lansing, Mich.

Dr. David N. White, Hickory Plains, Ark. This much-esteemed and prominent citizen was originally from North Carolina, his birth occurring in Burk County, July 18, 1832, the son of John and Sarah P. (Duncan) White, natives of North Carolina. The father was a blacksmith by trade, and also carried on agricultural pursuits all his life. He moved to Tennessee about 1834, located into Carroll County, and there tilled the soil until his death, which occurred about 1857. His wife survived him many years, and died in Tennessee in 1879. Dr. David N. White passed his boyhood days in Carroll County, Tenn., and remained with his father until twenty-one years old. He embarked in the tanning business when a young man, continuing seven years, when he commenced the study of medicine at Shady Grove, under Dr. J. G. Boyd about 1857.

He took his first course of lectures at Nashville, Tenn., in the winter of 1860, but had previously practiced for some time with Dr. Boyd. In the last-mentioned year he located in Henderson County, and practiced in connection with Dr. H. Brown for six years. In the spring of 1866, he removed to Arkansas, located at Hickory Plains, and has been in constant practice here since that time, and had most of the practice in the neighborhood. The Doctor located on a farm when he came here and in connection with his professional duties has carried on agricultural pursuits. He was married in Henderson County, Tenn., on May 6, 1863, to Miss Martha J. Whyte, a native of Henderson County, and the daughter of Joseph Whyte. Ten children have been the fruits of this union, eight sons and two daughters: Homer L. (a physician now practicing with his father), Joseph M. W. (clerk at Des Arc), William L., David E., Lily, John T., Luther, Newton B., Fred and Mattie. The Dr. and wife are members of the Baptist Church, and have the respect and esteem of all acquainted with them. The Dr. is a member of the Masonic fraternity, White River Lodge No. 39, and is a Master Mason. He was elected a commissioner to locate the court house.

William L. Willeford is the present efficient circuit and county court clerk of Prairie County, Ark., and as his prominent characteristics are strict, honest and exceptionally fine business qualifications, his fellow-citizens have been quick to recognize his merits. His birth occurred in Giles County, Tenn., July 20, 1847, and he is a son of A. H. and Sarah W. (Cotrell) Willeford, the former a Tennesseean, and the latter a native of Alabama. A. H. Willeford removed to Alabama after reaching manhood, and there became a prominent attorney at law, and served the Government as surveyor of that State. After the celebration of his nuptials, he returned to Tennessee, but in 1851 settled in Hernando, De Soto County, Miss., where he successfully practiced law until his death, which occurred in July, 1860. His widow removed to Des Arc, Ark., in 1871, and is now residing with her son, William L. The early days of the latter were spent in Mississippi, and there he

acquired his early education, and from this State he joined the Confederate army, in 1862, being at that time only fourteen years of age. He enlisted as a private in Company K, Ninth Mississippi Infantry, and was in the battles of Shiloh, Murfreesboro, Franklin and a great many skirmishes. During the latter part of the war, he was transferred to Forrest's cavalry, and was disbanded near Selma, Ala., in 1865. He then returned to Mississippi, and began clerking in a drug store, and during the period up to 1871, he became thoroughly familiar with the details of this business. He then followed this occupation in Des Arc, in the drug store of Col. Burney, until 1875, at which time he turned his attention to farming, continuing one year, and in the fall of that year he purchased a drug store, and successfully managed it until 1882. At this date he was elected on the Democratic ticket, of which he has always been a supporter, to the office of clerk of the circuit and county court, and has been re-elected successively in 1884, 1886 and 1888, and is acknowledged by all to be the best clerk Prairie County has ever had. He has also filled other positions of trust with ability, and in every walk in life, has been straightforward, upright and conscientious. September 26, 1872, his marriage with Miss Emma Becton was celebrated. She was a daughter of J. G. and Lizzie Becton, and was born in North Carolina, her death occurring in Prairie County, Ark., October 2, 1888, leaving a family of five children to mourn her loss: Anna, Gracie, Jacob, William and Frederick. Mr. Willeford took for his second wife Miss Maggie Bacon, a Kentuckian, a daughter of Ben. and Gabriella Bacon, their union taking place April 17, 1889. Mrs. Willeford is a member of the Baptist Church, and her husband belongs to the K. of H. and the K. of P.

B. S. Willeford, merchant, Des Arc, Ark. Among the prominent business houses of Des Arc, one deserving of special mention is that conducted by Mr. Willeford, who established himself in business at this place in 1887. He owes his nativity to Pulaski County, Tenn., where his birth occurred on February 13, 1850, and is the brother of W. L. Willeford, whose sketch immediately precedes this. B. S. Willeford moved with his parents from Tennessee to Mississippi, thence to Arkansas, in 1870. Previous to this, while in Mississippi, he had been engaged in a number of business enterprises, and, after coming to Des Arc, he engaged in merchandising on his own responsibility. Although he commenced in a very small way, he soon built up an extensive trade, and now does as flourishing a business as any of the substantial men of the town. He selected for his companion in life Miss Amanda Allen, a native of Prairie County, and the daughter of Col. Allen, whom he married in December, 1878. The fruits of this union have been two children, viz.: Cannie and Ruth. Mr. Willeford has served as alderman of his ward, also filled the position of marshal, and was deputy clerk at De-Vall's Bluff for a time. He has steadily kept up that reputation for excellence, which first gave him success.

Dr. W. F. Williams, physician and surgeon, Hazen, Ark. Dr. Williams is a man who is steadily and surely making his way to the front in the medical profession and as a prominent and useful citizen. He was born in Memphis, Tenn., in December, 1850, and his parents, John S. and Frances S. (Lawrence) Williams, were natives of Virginia and Memphis, Tenn., respectively. The father came to Tennessee, a single man, engaging in the drug business under the firm name of Watson & Williams, and was married in Memphis. In 1856 he came to Prairie County, Ark., settling on a farm, where he also engaged in the practice of medicine, having graduated from the Philadelphia Medical Institute some time previous. In 1862 he enlisted as surgeon in Col. Lemoin's regiment of this State, and later consolidated into the Seventeenth Arkansas Infantry. He was transferred to the west side of the Mississippi River, was enrolling officer for several counties and was made bonding agent for Confederate script. At the close of the war he returned to Woodruff County, engaged in teaching and earned money enough to take him and his family back to Prairie County. He returned to the homestead in the winter of 1865, and resumed the practice of medicine. He was elected Secretary of the State Grange, and was Secretary

pro tem. at its organization in 1872. In the year 1875, he moved to DeVall's Bluff, Ark,, and made that his home. In 1879 he was elected Master of the State Grange. His death occurred in November, 1881. The mother died in September, 1870. The father was a member of Des Arc Lodge, No. 45, A. F. & A. M. Dr. W. F. Williams was educated at St. Johns' military school in Little Rock, Ark., attending four years, and then attended the Memphis Medical Institute, from which he graduated in March, 1886. After this he commenced the practice of medicine near Hickory Plains, and later went from there to Hazen, buying out Dr. G. W. Hudspeth. He takes a prominent part in politics and his vote is cast with the Democratic party. He was married in Prairie County, in 1873, to Miss Elizabeth Horne, a native of Tennessee, who bore him seven children, four living: Frank, Lawrence (deceased), Joseph (attending school in Water Valley, Miss.), Sim, Anna Lou (deceased), Bessie Emma and W. F., Jr. The Doctor is a member of the Masonic order, Hazen Lodge, No. 561, and he and Mrs. Williams are now connected with the Presbyterian Church at Hazen, having been members of that denomination since 1867. He was elected representative to the State Medical Association and is the present Treasurer of the County Medical Society. He takes a deep interest in the temperance cause and is one of the progressive men of the county.

Rudolph Wintker, planter, Ulm, Ark. This gentleman is another of the many esteemed citizens of foreign birth who have made their home in Prairie County. He was born in Germany on December 27, 1833, and was the son of Matthew Wintker and Wilhelmina Wortman, both natives of Germany and both members of the Lutheran Church. The father was a farmer by occupation and this pursuit carried on the principal part of his life. Rudolph Wintker left his native country with his mother and emigrated to the United States. They located first in St. Louis, but subsequently moved to Illinois, where they remained two years and then returned to St. Louis, where he learned the carpenter's trade. About 1851 he returned to Illinois, locating in Washington County, and there, on January 3, 1856, was united in marriage to Miss Mena Platt, a native of Germany. This union resulted in the birth of nine children, six of whom are living at the present time: Caroline, Franklin, Henry, Emma, Emele and Rudolph, and all reside in Prairie County. The mother of these children died on February 8, 1885, and Mr. Wintker chose for his second wife Miss Helena Eilers, and was married to her on April 16, 1889. He emigrated from Illinois to Arkansas on December 1, 1882, located where he now resides, and is the owner of 200 acres of good land, with seventy acres under cultivation. He has held the office of school director and has been justice of the peace for five years. He has also been a member of the Odd Fellows Lodge. Mr. Wintker also handles considerable real-estate and is one of the thorough-going business men of the county. He and wife are members of the Lutheran Church, and reside a short distance from the same. He makes it now a special business to sell real-estate and attend to collections.

E. F. Wylie, farmer and stock raiser, Fairmount, Ark. Of that sturdy and independent class, the farmers and stock men of Arkansas, there are none who possess more genuine merit or stronger character than he whose name stands at the head of this sketch. Mr. Wylie owes his nativity to Indiana, where his birth occurred July 8, 1830. His father (A. M. Wylie) was a native of Kentucky, born in 1819, and in that State he received his education. Subsequently he emigrated to Indiana, and there married Miss Rebecca Farmer, a native of Indiana, and the daughter of Jesse and Rhoda Farmer. The fruits of this union were ten children: Augusta C., E. F. and Julia O. The remainder died while young. The father was a farmer by occupation, and this pursuit continued the principal part of his life. His wife died in 1849, and he chose for his second wife Miss Elizabeth Young, who bore him three children: Ellen, George and Lillie. Mr. Wylie held the office of sheriff of Tipton County, Ind., for three terms, and was a man who took quite an interest in church and educational matters. He died in 1881, but his wife is still living, and resides in Illinois. He was a member of the Baptist Church, to which his wife also now belongs. E. F. Wylie received his education in Illinois and emigrated to Missouri in 1853, where he married Miss Sarah J. Richardson, on May 24, of the same year. She was born in Indiana, and by her marriage became the mother of six children: Rebecca J. (deceased), Emma C. (wife of Fulton Harris), Martha O. (wife of John Vaughn), Augustus M., Norton W., Cora A. (who resides at home) and Charles E. The mother of these children died in 1886. Mr. Wylie emigrated from Missouri to Arkansas in 1874, and located in Prairie County, where he now resides. In 1887 he married Miss Emma E. Hollaway, and to this union has been born one child, Henry W. Mr. Wylie has followed farming and stock raising nearly all his life; is the owner of 400 acres of land, with sixty acres under cultivation, and is one of the progressive and enterprising farmers of the county. He was Master of the Grange for two years, and has held the office of justice of peace for four years. He and wife are members of the Methodist Episcopal Church.

CHAPTER XXIV.

Ye pioneers, it is to you
The debt of gratitude is due;
Ye builded wiser than ye knew
The broad foundation
On which our superstructure stands.—*Pearre.*

PHILLIPS COUNTY was organized in accordance with an act of the legislature of Arkansas Territory, approved May 1, 1820. It then included a large amount of territory lying north of its present limits, which has since been organized into several counties. The county was named in honor of Sylvanus Phillips, a pioneer settler, and one of the original proprietors of the site of the present city of Helena. Soon after the county was organized, the seat of justice thereof was located at this place, and about the year 1821, Nicholas Rightor, an early settler and Government surveyor, surveyed and laid out a town on lands belonging to Sylvanus Phillips and William Russell, and it was named Helena, in honor of Miss Helena Phillips, a daughter of Sylvanus Phillips. Russell was not a settler of the county. He lived at St. Louis, Mo., was a great land speculator, and owned a part of the lands on which the city of Little Rock was located, and was one of the company that laid out the capital city. He obtained his lands by locating soldier claims on the best lands he could find, and then buying them of such claimants as did not desire to occupy them at very low prices. In this way he accumulated a vast amount of the best lands in Arkansas.

The first county building, which was a two-story log building, with a court room above and the jail below, stood on the ridge a short distance south of the present court house. The next county buildings, consisting of a small two-story frame court house and a one-story log jail, stood on the east of Main or Ohio Street, south of Porter Street. Early in the Civil War period this court house took fire and burned down (supposed to have taken fire accidentally). The county then rented a building for court purposes and county offices until the present court house was ready for occupancy. The present jail, a large two-story brick structure, was erected in 1860. It stands on a lot east of and adjoining the court house square. The court house is a large and plain two-story brick building, with halls, stairs and office rooms on the first floor and the court room on the second. It was completed in 1871, in "reconstruction" times, and is said to have cost the county much more than it should have cost. It stands in the northwestern part of the city, on a hill so elevated that a commanding view of the city can be obtained therefrom. A beautiful grass lawn surrounding the house is kept in good order.

The following is a list of names of county officers of Phillips County, from its organization to the present, with dates of terms of service annexed: Judges: J. H. McKenzie, 1829–32; J. J. McKeal, 1832–33; I. C. P. Tolleson, 1835–36; W. E. Butts, 1836–38; T. B. Hanley, 1838–40; W. E. Butts, 1840–42; A. G. Underwood, 1842–44; J. S. Hornor, 1844–46; A. G. Underwood, 1846–56; A. P. Ewarts, 1856–58; A. G. Underwood, 1858–60; J. B. Shell, 1860–62; A. P. Ewarts, 1864–65; E. G. Cook, 1865–66; George West, 1866–68; Q. K. Underwood, 1868–72; board of supervisors, 1872–74; S. J. Clark, 1874–78; M. T. Sanders, 1878–82; R. W. Nicholls, present incumbent, first elected in 1882, re-elected, and has served continuously since.

Clerks: W. B. R. Hornor, 1820–21; S. Phillips, 1821–23; S. M. Rutherford, 1823–25; H. L. Bisco, 1825–27; G. W. Fereby, 1827–29; Austin Hendricks, 1829–30; S. C. Mooney, 1830–32; J. R. Sanford, 1832–38; J. S. Hornor, 1838–42; William Kelley, 1842–44; L. D. Maddox, 1844–48; R. H. Yates, 1848–52; E. H. Cowley, 1852–62; J. H. Maxey, 1864–66; E. H. Cowley, 1866–68; S. J. Clark, 1868–74; D. W. Elison, 1874–78; —— Thompson, 1878–82; Whit Jarmin, 1882–88; James C. Rembert, present incumbent, elected in 1880.

Sheriffs: Daniel Mooney, 1820–23; George Seaborn, 1823–25; Daniel Mooney, 1825–27; H.

L. Brisco, 1827–30; F. Hanks, 1830–32; H. L. Brisco, 1832–35; M. Irvin, 1835–44; W. M. Bostick, 1844–48; D. Thompson, 1848–52; A. Thompson, 1852–58; B. W. Green, 1858–62; B. W. Green, 1864–65; J. Graves, 1865–66; B. Y. Turner 1866–68; D. C. Gordon, 1868–72; A. Barrow, 1872–74; H. B. Robinson, 1874–78; B. Y. Turner, 1878–84; E. D. Pillow, present incumbent, first elected in 1884.

Treasurers: J. B. Ford, 1836–52; E. P. Scantland, 1852–54; J. Locke, 1854–56; W. D. Hornor, 1856–58; William Lonford, 1858–60; E. K. Harris, 1860–62; R. A. Yerby, 1864–66; W. H. Crawford, 1866–68; S. H. Brooks, 1868–72; N. Straub, 1872–78; S. H. King, 1878–80; E. M. Ford, 1880–86; N. Straub, present incumbent, first elected in 1886.

Coroners: Peter Edwards, 1823–25; W. H. Calvert, 1829–32; Enor Askew, 1832–33; S. S. Smith, 1833–35; P. Pinkston, 1835–36; W. Battis, 1836–38; J. Skinner, 1838–40; A. Sanders, 1840–42; W. H. Calvert, 1842–50; M. Platt, 1850–54; J. M. Odle, 1854–56; R. Goodwin, 1856–58; W. A. Dickson, 1858–60; W. A. Thorn, 1860–62; T. Wallace, 1864–65; A. Neal, 1865–66; J. J. Mulky, 1866–68; C. Williams, 1872–74; Samuel Hill, 1874–78; T. H. Quarles, 1878–80; John Grenshaw, 1880–82; T. N. Upshaw, 1882–84; R. W. McKenny, 1884–86; C. H. Hicks, 1886–88; Abe Crawford, present incumbent, elected in 1888.

Surveyors: N. Rightor, 1823–25; N. Rightor, 1829–30; B. Burress, 1830–32; C. P. Smith, 1832–35; Charles Pearcy, 1835–36; C. P. Smith, 1836–38; H. Turner, 1838–40; J. H. Bonner, 1840–42; S. Weaver, 1842–44; S. Goodman, 1844–46; J. Thomas, 1846–48; S. K. Goodman, 1848–50; E. H. Gilbert, 1850–60; M. D. Norton, 1860–63; E. H. Gilbert, 1864–68; F. Trunkey, 1868–72; M. M. Robinson, 1872–76; W. W. Bailey, 1876–78; B. F. Thompson, 1878–82; R. A. Blount, 1882–86; Thomas M. Jacks, present incumbent, first elected in 1886.

Assessors: J. C. Watson, 1864–65; H. Campbell, 1865–66; J. A. Bush, 1866–68; H. B. Robinson, 1868–72; T. Grissom, 1872–74; A. Barrow, 1874–76; M. G. Turner, 1876–78; B. W. Green,

1878–88; M. G. Turner, present incumbent, elected in 1888.

Circuit court clerks: J. P. Clopper, 1878–80; J. F. Humphries, 1880.

Delegates in constitutional conventions: 1836, Henry L. Brisco and George W. Ferebey; 1861, T. B. Hanley and C. W. Adams; 1864, J. A. Butler, T. M. Jacks and Thomas Pearce; 1868, Joseph Brooks, Thomas Smith, William H. Gray and James T. White; 1874, J. J. Hornor, J. T. White and R. Polk.

Representatives in Territorial legislature: Daniel Mooney in council and W. B. R. Hornor in house, 1823; J. W. Calvert in council and H. L. Brisco in house, 1825; E. T. Clark in council and John Johnson in house, 1827; F. Hanks in council and E. T. Clark in house, 1829; Charles Caldwell in council and T. Hanks in house, 1831; W. T. Moore in council and M. Hanks in house, 1833.

Representatives in State legislature: J. C. P. Tolleson and J. J. Shell, 1836–38; J. J. Shell and F. Hanks, 1840–42; Elisha Burke and T. B. Hanley, 1842–44; E. Burke and F. B. Culver, 1844–46; E. Burke and Bailey Kendall, 1846–48; John Martin and W. E. Preston, 1848–50; W. E. Preston and J. C. Tappan, 1850–52; G. Geffries and A. Wilkins, 1852–54; R. B. Macon and W. D. Rice, 1854–56; Francis H. Moody, 1856–58; Thomas C. Anderson, 1858–60; J. C. O. Smith and Thomas J. Key, 1860–62; H. P. Slaughter and W. N. Mixon, 1866–67; J. A. Butler, M. Reed, J. C. Tobiast, W. H. Gray, J. J. T. White and J. K. Whitson, Phillips and Monroe, 1868–69; same counties, G. W. Hollibough, A. Mays, J. M. Peck, Austin Barrow, C. C. Waters and J. M. Alexander, Jr., 1871; same counties, J. W. Williams, Tony Grissom, John W. Fox, W. H. Furbush, G. H. W. Stewart and H. H. Robinson, 1873; same counties, T. M. Jacks, P. McGowan and W. Foreman, 1874; Phillips only, Tony Grissom, A. H. Miller and Perry Coleman, 1875; Perry Coleman, J. M. Donohoe and T. M. Jacks, 1877; Greenfield Quarles, T. B. Hanley and W. R. Burke, 1879; G. Quarles, A. G. Jarman and J. P. Roberts, 1881; S. H. Brooks, R. B. Macon

and John J. Moore, 1883; J. P. Roberts, W. R. Burke and S. H. King, 1885; R. B. Macon, James P. Clarke and J. M. Donohoe, 1887.

In 1888 the number of votes cast in Phillips County for State and National candidates for office was as follows: For Governor, at the September election, James P. Eagle (Dem.), 1,123; C. M. Norwood (Com. Opp.), 3,278. For President, at the November election, Cleveland (Dem.), 789; Harrison (Rep.), 2,123. This shows the Republicans to have a very large majority in the county, but before the September election, 1888, a compromise county ticket, composed of candidates from both parties, was put into the field, and at the election it was successful, hence the county officers are representatives of both parties, and it is said that this gives general satisfaction.

The population of the county since its inception has been, at the end of each decade, as follows: 1820, 1,197; 1830, 1,152; 1840, 3,547; 1850, 6,935; 1860, 5,931 white and 8,945 colored, making a total of 14,876; 1870, 4,871 white and 10,501 colored, total, 15,372; 1880, white 5,444, colored 15,809, total 21,253.

The county court, proper, was organized in 1829, and prior to this time the county business was transacted in the circuit court. Since 1829 there has always been a county court, but from 1872 to 1874 it consisted of a board of supervisors. The several courts of Phillips County convene in regular session at Helena at the following dates: County, on the first Monday of January, April, July and October of each year; common pleas, on the third Monday of the same months; probate, on the third Monday of February, March, August and November; circuit, on the third Monday of May and November.

As far back as 1836, the year that Arkansas became a State, the Helena bar consisted of the following resident attorneys: William K. Sebastian and John C. P. Tolleson from Tennessee; William E. Butts from New York; Thomas B. Hanley and William M. McPherson from Kentucky, and John Preston from Virginia. These were mostly young men then, and some of them lived to become distinguished throughout the State. The bar of this county has always been noted for its ability, having among its members some of the ablest lawyers and most distinguished generals the State, has produced. The resident attorneys of Phillips County, now composing its legal bar, are Gen. J. C. Tappan, Judges John J. Hornor & Son, E. C. Hornor, Jacob Trieber and M. L. Stephenson, John C. Palmer and R. W. Nicholls, Greenfield Quarles and John I. Moore, James P. Clarke, P. O. Thweatt, Jacob Fink, Samuel I. Clarke, James P. Roberts and M. G. B. Scaife. Gens. Pat. R. Cleburne and Thomas C. Hindman were once members of this bar.

Phillips County, located in East Central Arkansas, is bounded north by the base line of the public land surveys which separates it from Lee County, east by the Mississippi River which separates it from the State of Mississippi, south by Desha County, and west by Arkansas and Monroe Counties. The northwest corner of the county is at the initial point where the fifth principal meridian crosses the base line, and this meridian forms a portion of the western boundary of the county. The area is about 659 square miles, two-fifths of which is alluvial level land, and only about one-sixth of the county is improved.

Crowley's Ridge which runs through Greene, Craighead, Poinsett, Cross, St. Francis and Lee Counties, forming the divide between St. Francis and Cache Rivers, terminates in Phillips County just below the city of Helena. In the upper counties this ridge has an elevation of only a few feet above the river bottoms, but in Phillips it is very hilly and broken, the hills extending from 100 to 200 feet in height. The top of this ridge, throughout its entire length in Arkansas, is composed, for the most part of silicious clay and marl of quarternary date, usually resting on a bed of water-worn gravel. Numerous springs of good cool water flow from beneath this gravel bed along the eastern foot of the ridge near Helena. The most noted of these is the "Big Spring," two and a half miles above Helena, which forms a considerable stream where it flows from under the gravel bed at the base of the ridge.

The following section, showing the position of the material composing Crowley's Ridge, was taken in 1859 or 1860 close to Mr. Rightor's dwelling in the edge of the city of Helena, by the then State geologist, Prof. David Dale Owen: Quartenary: Yellow, silicious clay, six feet; marl, with fossil shells. At this place, the marl was traversed by two vertical cracks one inch in width, and filled with sand from the stratum beneath. Tertiary: Yellow and orange sand and gravel, twenty feet; gravel, six inches; space concealed, reddish clay, nine feet; plastic clay (potter's) local, six inches; yellowish and white sand, with some gravel, five feet; sand and gravel, fifteen feet; space concealed, twelve feet; bed of slough.

The geologist further said in his report: "In Phillips County there are many remains of old fortifications or aboriginal towns to be seen, monuments of a bygone race, of whose history no tradition known to the white man has been preserved by the occupants of the country. One of these ancient works of art, four miles west of Helena, at the terminus of Crowley's Ridge, was visited. The embankments now nearly destroyed by the washing of the rains, and the cultivation of a part of the land, were built of sun-dried clay, mixed with stems and leaves of the cane. The vegetable structure of the cane is still well preserved in the clay matrix, and I could in no instance, find any evidence of the cane's having been charred by fire, hence the conclusion that it received no greater heat than that given it by the sun. Nor is there any appearance of fashioned brick, of which it is said this wall was built. The clay and stems of cane appear to have been mixed together and molded into a wall, somewhat after the manner of a pise. The northern boundary of this enclosure is formed by the hills, and within the interior there are a number of small mounds."

Agriculturally speaking, Phillips County ranks equal to any in the State. The broad Mississippi in the southern part, interspersed with small, old lakes and bayous, is remarkably fertile. In the western part, watered by Big Creek, there is a large body of level land formed by the gradual flattening out of the Crowley's Ridge; hence, it has received the name of table lands.

A considerable district of land a few miles below Helena, is known as "Sugar-tree Ridge," so called, because of the large amount of trees of that name grown thereon. This ridge is elevated a few feet above the overflow of the Mississippi. Aside from the sugar trees, the timber growth consisted of black walnut, red oak, persimmon, white and red elm, sweet gum, mulberry and large sassafras. Here traces of old fortifications and mounds have been found, and in plowing over the latter, human bones, implements of pottery, arrow-heads and stone axes have been found. The low bottom lands of the lakes and sloughs are from ten to fifteen feet lower than the ridge land, and have a bluish-black, stiff, plastic soil when wet, but when dry it becomes mellow, and easily pulverizes under cultivation. The alluvial land adjoining the Mississippi is a sandy loam, easily cultivated, and is very productive. The hill land soil is derived from the silicious, marly, quartenary clay above the gravel. It is also very fertile. The timber growth on Crowley's Ridge originally was large poplar, beech, red and white oak, spanish oak, hickory, sweet gum, black walnut, butternut, sugar tree, honey locust and cane. The only poplar trees in Arkansas grow on Crowley's Ridge. The table lands have for the most part, a deep yellow, or mulatto soil, which is also very fertile. The principal growth is sweet gum, but on the most elevated portions are the same timbers as are found on Crowley's Ridge.

The St. Francis River empties into the Mississippi a short distance south of the northeast corner of Phillips County. Big Creek enters the county from the north about nine miles east of its northwest corner, and flows southeasterly, southerly and southwesterly, and leaves the county a little north of the center of its western boundary. Beaver Bayou heads a little east of the center of the county and flowing thence southwesterly it empties into White River. Another stream rises near the center of the county and flowing in the same direction as the latter also empties into White River. These streams, with the Mississippi on the east, and their tributaries, furnish the drainage of the county. Water is abundant for all purposes, but for domestic use spring water and cistern water are mostly used.

Improved lands can be bought at from $10 to $20, and unimproved at from $1 to $5 per acre. The yield of crops per acre is said to be as follows: Cotton, on hill lands, 600 pounds; on bottom lands, 1,000 pounds; Indian corn, on uplands, average crop, seventeen bushels; oats, twenty bushels; Irish potatoes and sweet potatoes, 100 bushels each; turnips, 200 bushels; field peas, fifty bushels per acre. Of the tame grasses, timothy, red top and orchard grass are said to yield two tons each, and clover and millet, three tons each. The yields of grain and vegetables are given according to the present system of farming, and are far below what they could be under a scientific process of farming. But very little tame grass of any kind has been cultivated in the county. The attention of the farmers is mostly devoted to the raising of cotton, and the live stock get their living by grazing the native wild grasses on the commons or ranges. In 1880, according to the United States census, there were in Phillips County, 1,311 farms and 85,379 acres of improved lands. The aggregate yield of products for 1879 were given as follows: Cotton, 29,070 bales; Indian corn, 332,585 bushels; oats, 13,410 bushels; wheat, 367 bushels; orchard products, $3,512; hay, 1,401 tons; Irish potatoes, 6,261 bushels; sweet potatoes, 21,956 bushels; tobacco, 11,172 pounds. The entire value of all the farm products raised in the county in 1879 were calculated at $1,548,538. Assuming that there has not been much change since 1880, except the increase of quantities, the above figures show conclusively what kinds of products are mostly cultivated. Cotton stands pre-eminently at the head, Indian corn next, all the other products, except sweet potatoes, being very limited.

The number of domestic animals in the county, according to the census of 1880, were as follows: Horses, 1,783; mules and asses, 2,850; neat cattle, 8,998; sheep, 2,230; hogs, 14,217. The number of these animals as shown by the assessor's returns for 1889, are as follows: Horses, 2,402; mules and asses, 3,403; neat cattle, 8,060; sheep, 1,953; hogs, 7,362. These figures show an increase in the

46

number of horses and mules, but a decrease in the number of all the others.

Fruits of all kinds, common to this latitude, can be grown as well here as in any of the other valley counties of the State. Small fruits, especially for the Northern market, could be grown here with profit. But this industry has not been developed to any considerable extent. Cotton-growing seems to be the all-absorbing industry.

The Helena branch of the Iron Mountain Railroad connects Helena with the main line at Knobel, in Clay County. This gives Phillips County a direct outlet to the North and at the several roads crossing it, to all points east or west. It enters the county from the north and traverses it about fifteen miles to its southern terminus at Helena. The Arkansas Midland Railway connects Helena with the St. Louis, Arkansas & Texas Railway at Clarendon. It traverses across the entire county, a distance of about twenty-seven miles. A transfer across the Mississippi River, connects Helena with the Louisville, New Orleans & Texas Railroad on the east side of the river, and thus gives an outlet directly by rail to the Crescent City, and to all points east of the river. These railroads and the Mississippi River, which traverses the entire eastern border of the county, constitute its shipping facilities.

The United States census of 1880 shows that the real estate of the county was then assessed at $776,-080, and the personal property at $440,640, making a total of the taxable wealth of $1,216,720. The assessor's returns for 1889, indicates the real estate to have been assessed at $2,408,495, and the personal property at $977,990, a total of $3,386,485. This shows a wonderful increase in the value of the property of the county since 1880. To get a fair estimate of the real value, the whole amount returned by the assessor should be thribbled. Property is generally assessed for taxation at only about one-third of its real value.

The county has recently issued $100,000 thirty-year funding bonds, with interest at six per cent, payable July 1, each year. A few years ago the county owed $200,000 in railroad bonds, and $60,000 in refunded script. This has been reduced so that according to the last financial report, dated July 7, 1889, the total indebtedness was $104,400.

The French and Spaniards may have made temporary settlements in the territory now composing Phillips County, long before the beginning of the nineteenth century, but if any such were made no detailed account thereof has been preserved. But that there were permanent settlers here when the century began is evident from the fact that in the year 1800, one John Patterson was born at a place about five miles above, or rather north of the site of the present city of Helena. In 1836 Judge John S. Hornor, who is now living in Helena, and who was eighty-three years of age in August, 1889, came to Helena from Virginia in 1836. His uncle, William B. R. Hornor, had settled here many years prior to that date. Other early settlers of Helena and vicinity, all of whom were here in 1836, were James H. McKenzie, from North Carolina, John J. Bowie, from Louisiana, Fleetwood Hanks, from Kentucky, who lived where his son, Judge Hanks, now resides, B. A. Porter, from Massachusetts, Dr. B. F. Odle, from New York, Henry L. Briscoe, from Virginia, who was register of the United States land office here in 1836, Boyd Bailey, from Kentucky, F. H. Cosset, George W. Fereby, from Virginia, Nicholas Rightor, Sylvanus Phillips, after whom the county was named, Judge Thomas J. Lacy, from Kentucky, and others. Lacy was then one of associate justices of the first supreme court of Arkansas. The other lawyers in Helena, in 1836, are mentioned under the head of legal bar. In 1835 John T. Jones, now known as Judge Jones, a farmer living in the county, came from Virginia, and settled first in Helena. In the summer of 1889 he and his loving wife returned on a visit to "Old Virginia," and there on August 13, at the house of their son-in-law, Maj. Morton, in Charlotte County, they celebrated their golden wedding, having lived together as husband and wife half a century.

The first settler in the Martin settlement, at the present northern boundary of the county, was James Martin, from Kentucky. There was a large family of the Martins, and some of them were early settlers of the territory farther north. The first settlers of the "Lick Creek Settlement," were William F. Moore, from Alabama, and Jesse J. Shell, from Louisiana. The latter died while a member of the legislature. James Nelson settled on the military road leading to Little Rock, on the place where his son John W. now resides. Near the Martin settlement were the pioneers, Josiah S. McKiel and Col. Elisha Burke, both from North Carolina. Burke's widow and younger children are living on the same place at this writing. Burke at one time represented this county in the lower house, and at another time this and Monroe County in the upper house of the State legislature. Bailey Kendall, from Kentucky, was the first settler west of Big Creek at the village of Trenton, and John C. Swan, from Kentucky, near the present village of Marvell. Thomas Locke and the father of James M. and Ellis Ward, and Benjamin F. Bonner, all from Tennessee, were the pioneer settlers of the northwest part of the county. The extreme southern part of the county, the lowlands, were not settled until much later than the uplands. The Indians all moved away from this part of Arkansas prior to 1836. A part of those moved to the Indian Territory from Georgia and other States, and crossed the Mississippi at Helena in 1837.

Upon the approach of the Civil War of 1861-65, many of the best and most conservative men of Phillips County deplored a disruption of the Union of the States, but after the war had actually begun, all the citizens became unanimously in favor of disunion and the establishment of a Southern Confederacy. The first companies raised in the county for the Confederate service were the Yell Rifles, commanded by Pat R. Cleburne; the Phillips Guards, commanded by Capt. W. S. Otey; the Tappan Guards, by Capt. J. C. Tappan; the Pat. Cleburne Guards, by Capt. Thomas Quinlin; the La Grange Guards, by Capt. D. C. Govan, and the Trenton Guards by Capt. J. W. Scaife. These were all raised early in 1861. Afterward other companies were organized in the county, sufficient in number, together with those named, to compose three regiments—the Second, Thirteenth and Fifteenth, Confederate States army. It must be remembered that at that time Phillips County contained the greater part of what is now Lee County, and it turned out for the Confederate service the three regiments above mentioned, two major-generals—Pat R. Cleburne and Thomas C. Hindman—and six brigadier-generals: D. C. Govan, J. C. Tappan, C. W. Adams, L. E. Polk, Dandridge McRea and Arch Dobbins.

The county remained within the Confederate lines until July, 1862, when the Federal army under Maj.-Gen. Samuel R. Curtis, first occupied Helena, and from that time forward to the end of the war the town was strongly garrisoned by Federal troops. On December 15, 1862, Brig.-Gen. W. A. Gorman, then in command at Helena, reported that an outpost of his, consisting of twenty-three men and a commissioned officer belonging to the Sixth Missouri Cavalry, were captured at a point four miles out on the St. Francis road, near the residence of ———— Turner. On January 3, following, he again reported that on the first day of the month twenty-five or thirty Texas rangers had captured another of his outposts, consisting of twenty-six men and a commissioned officer of the Twenty-eighth Iowa Regiment. In this report he censured the men captured, and recommended the officer to be disgracefully dismissed. On January 12, 1863, Lieut. James B. Bradford, with twenty-five men of the Second Wisconsin Cavalry, was sent out to a point on Lick Creek, about twelve miles west of Helena, where he was confronted by superior numbers, and being overpowered he and four of his men escaped and returned to Helena, and afterward some more of his men also, having made their escape, returned to Helena. On May 25, 1863, a skirmish between small forces at Polk's plantation, a few miles from Helena, took place. A few other small engagements were had in the county between the contending forces, aside from the battle of Helena. Helena was strongly fortified by the garrison occupying it, and was a very advantageous military post for the Union army, especially for keeping the communication of the Mississippi open to points below. In the western part of the town, on the ridge south of the present court house, was Fort Curtis, armed with siege guns, and there were redoubts armed with field-pieces, and protected by rifle-pits on the suburban hills north and west of the town, so as to effectually guard every avenue of approach. One of the redoubts was on the summit of Graveyard Hill. The Confederate General, T. H. Holmes, commanding the District of Arkansas, seeing the importance of Helena to the Union army, and the advantages it might be to the Confederate army, conceived the idea of capturing it. To this end he concentrated his army, consisting of the commands of Gens. Price, Marmaduke and others, at Clarendon, on White River, from which place he advanced upon Helena, and reached Allen Polk's plantation, five miles therefrom, on the morning of July 3, 1863. The plan of attack was for Gen Price, with his two brigades, McRea's and Parson's, to assault and take Graveyard Hill at daylight, Marmaduke, assisted by Walker's cavalry brigade, to take Rightor's Hill by daylight, and Gen. Fagan to take the battery on Hindman's Hill by daylight. Gen. B. M. Prentiss was in command of the garrison, and was well informed of the approach of the Confederates, and consequently in readiness to receive them. Arrangements had been made to hold an old-fashioned celebration in Helena on Saturday, July 4, but Gen. Prentiss issued an order to dispense with it, and for every man to be at his post of duty.

Accordingly, at 3 o'clock, A. M., of July 4, the Confederate army advanced upon the town, attacked and drove in the outposts, and by daylight the battle raged furiously. The battery on Hindman's Hill and the redoubt and battery on Graveyard Hill were captured by storm, after which a large force of Confederates passed through the ravine between these hills into the suburbs of the town, where, being exhausted and confused, they were surrounded and captured by the Federalists. The battle continued to rage until 10:30 A. M., when the Confederate commander, finding his army losing ground, retired from the field and left all in possession of the garrison. It is said that the hardest fighting took place on Graveyard Hill. In the summarized reports of the battle by the respective commanders of the armies, Gen. Holmes said that his whole force consisted of 7,646 effect-

ive men and officers, that his loss was 173 killed, 687 wounded and 776 missing, making a total of 1,636. Gen. Prentiss said that his whole garrisoned force consisted of 4,129 effective men and officers, assisted by the gunboat Tyler, commanded by Lieut.-Com. Pritchett, which rendered him valuable assistance, and that his loss consisted of fifty-seven killed, 146 wounded and thirty-six captured, making a total of 239. He reported the Confederate loss at 400 killed, 354 wounded and 774 captured in addition to the wounded, making a total of 1,528. It will be seen that, in the aggregate, Prentiss reported the Confederate loss at 108 less than Holmes did, but that they differed widely as to the number of killed and wounded. Of course, Prentiss had the best opportunity to know how many were killed, as they were all buried by his men, but it appears to be an extraordinary number in comparison with the number he reported as wounded. No other attack was ever made upon Helena.

Helena, the county seat of Phillips County, is situated on the west bank of the Mississippi River, at the foot of a range of hills, which bounds the city on the north and west, the distance from the river bank to the hills on the west being about half a mile. The site of the greater part of the city, especially the business part, is comparatively low and level. Many of the streets and business houses, and some dwelling houses, have been elevated on made land several feet above the original level. The origin of the town has been given in connection with the organization of the county. Among the early merchants of the place, who were doing business here in 1836, were John J. Bowie, F. H. Cosset and George W. Fereby. There were about half a dozen business houses in the town at that time. William B. R. Hornor, mentioned among the early pioneer settlers, was a lawyer and kept a hotel in Helena at a very early day. B. A. Porter, another of the pioneers, engaged in the lumber business about the year 1836 and erected a saw-mill in Helena. Later he moved into the country, but still continued his lumber business in the town. Waldo P. Craig erected another saw-mill about the year 1837.

The growth of Helena from its inception to the year 1838 was very slow and gradual; then, in consequence of the financial panic of 1837, the place began to decline, and for a few years more people, it is said, moved away from the town and the country round about than came into it. The population of Helena in 1840 was 250 souls. In 1844 the town and country began again to progress, but the growth was so slow that in 1860 the population of Helena had only reached about 800. It did not suffer much during the war period of 1861–65, for the reason that it was constantly held by Federal troops from its first occupancy by them in July, 1862, to the close of the war. Had it been occupied alternately by the contending armies it would have suffered much more than it did.

Since the close of the war, its growth has been gradual, but much more rapid than before. In 1880 its population, according to the United States census, was 3,652 and it is now estimated at 5,000. It contains at this writing, Baptist, Catholic, Presbyterian and Methodist churches, four schools, cotton-seed oil mills, lumber mills, cotton gins and compress, planing mills, a foundry and machine shop, an opera house capable of seating 800, three banks, gas-works, an efficient and well-equipped fire department, street railways, a telephone exchange, gas-works, two express offices, two railroad depots, ferry-boats for crossing the river, many stores of all kinds, several wholesale houses, four weekly and one daily newspaper, and all the other attributes of a city of its size.

The Helena Weekly World, a nine-column folio, was established in 1870, and is now ably published by William S. Burnett, its editor and proprietor. The Helena Daily World, a seven-column folio was established in 1871, and is published from the same office and by the same party as the Weekly World. It is claimed by its proprietor to be the oldest daily paper in the State excepting the Arkansas Daily Gazette. These papers are Democratic in politics and both are well edited. The Helena State was established October 19, 1889, by B. M. Barrington. It is a seven-column quarto, is published every Friday, and is also Democratic in principle, neat in appearance, and edited with

ability. The Southern Review, an eight-column folio, now in its fifth volume, is published weekly at Helena by the "Benevolent Church Aid and Relief Society," an association of the colored people. Rev. J. T. White is editor and manager, and J. E. Harris, business manager. The People's Friend, a six-column folio, is published weekly at Helena, by M. Kline, a colored man. It is now in its second volume. These "colored" papers bear but little upon the subject of politics.

Helena was incorporated as a city of the second class, but efforts are now being made to secure its incorporation as a city of the first class.

Directly west of Helena is the old graveyard on one of the hills partially surrounding the city. The land was owned by individuals, but by consent the people buried their dead there from the settlement of Helena until the close of the Civil War. The summit of the hill is not less than 100 feet above the level of the city. After Gen. Curtis occupied the place in 1862, he built a redoubt on this hill, as well as upon other commanding positions, and cut the timber off of them to strengthen the defenses of the city. It is said that the hardest part of the battle of Helena was fought in this graveyard, it being a very large tract of hill land. Monuments and headstones were knocked to pieces by the cannonading. After the close of the war, the timber having been removed, the ground began to wash into gullies, and soon began to disturb the sleeping dead. Then the remains of some persons who had friends and relatives living sufficiently near, were disinterred and buried elsewhere, but the remains of all others were left to their fate. Some of the gullies now reach a depth of from thirty to forty feet, graves have been completely washed away and human skulls and bones can be seen in great numbers bleaching in the gullies. Now and then a grave can be found undisturbed. It is only a question of time, however, when all will be washed away, unless otherwise removed. An improvement company, which has been organized in the city, has purchased the lands which contain the old graveyard, and contemplate leveling down the hills and using the earth to fill up the hollows and depressions of the site of the city, and laying out the lands thus made level into an addition to the city. This can be done largely with the aid of the washing of the rains. These hills contain no solid rock formation, consequently the earth can easily be loosened up and removed. This will be a great improvement to the city, both in filling up the low places and in removing the unsightly gullies.

Evergreen Cemetery, owned by a company of that name, lies at a proper distance north of the city, but it is only partially fenced and is not kept in a neat and proper condition, the stock at large being allowed to overrun it. Next to this is the Catholic Cemetery, and still farther is the Hebrew Cemetery. A small tract of land on Confederate Hill contains the remains of about 300 Confederate soldiers. This hill is one of the highest points on Crowley's Ridge, just north of the city. This cemetery is kept in order by the Phillips County Memorial Association, managed mostly by the ladies. Among the most noted men buried here are Gen. Pat. R. Cleburne, Gen. T. C. Hindman, Col. Paul F. Anderson and Maj. R. H. Cawley (a Presbyterian minister when he entered the military service).

Poplar Grove, the second town in size in the county, is situated on the Arkansas Midland Railway, seventeen miles west of Helena. It was laid out in 1872 on lands belonging to N. S. and B. Y. Turner. The first business, a general store, was established in 1873, also the postoffice, with James R. Turner, postmaster. The same year several business and dwelling houses were erected. It now contains six general stores, a drug store, a millinery store, four churches (two for the whites and two for the blacks), one cotton-gin and grist-mill combined, one saw-mill, two blacksmith shops, one livery stable, two hotels, one undertaker's shop, a white school taught ten months in the year (four months free and six months on subscription), a colored school taught four months each year (free), and a lodge each of Knights of Honor and Knights and Ladies of Honor. The school at Poplar Grove is very popular, and the people are proud of it. There are two teachers, a music teacher and ninety pupils in attendance. A number of

the pupils are from the country, and board in the village. Large quantities of cotton and cotton-seed are shipped from this point. The population of the village is about 400.

Marvell is situated on the Arkansas Midland Railway, twenty-one miles west of Helena. The first store was opened there in 1870, by Messrs. Dade & Emby. It now has five general stores, four groceries, a furniture store, an undertaking establishment, a foundry and machine shop, two blacksmith shops, a church used by the Presbyterians, Baptists and Christians, a colored Baptist and a colored Quaker church, a school-house, livery stable, hotel, and a cotton-gin, huller and grist-mill combined. The postoffice was established in 1872, with G. H. Cowan, postmaster. About 3,000 bales of cotton are shipped annually from this place. It has a lodge each of Masons and Knights of Honor. The population is about 300, one-third of which is colored.

Trenton is a small village three miles south of Poplar Grove, and contains a steam saw and grist mill and cotton-gins. Cotton and cotton-seed are shipped from here; it also has a hotel, two or three general stores and a population of about 150.

Barton is a station on the Arkansas Midland Railway, thirteen miles west of Helena, having a population of about fifty. It has a saw-mill and two or three small stores.

For the year ending June 30, 1889, the scholastic population of Phillips County was as follows: White, males, 904, females, 842, total, 1,746; colored, males, 3,360, females, 3,137, total, 6,497. Pupils taught in the public schools: White, males, 545, females, 413, total, 958; colored, males, 2,262, females, 2,151, total, 4,413. This shows only a small percentage of the scholastic population taught in the public schools, but it is partially accounted for by the fact that several private schools, especially in Helena, are maintained and patronized. There are 36 school districts in the county, and the number of teachers employed during 1888 were: White, males, 15, females, 13, total, 28; colored, males, 33, females, 18, total, 51; aggregate, 79. The average monthly salary of teachers for the last year was: White, males, of the first grade, $60, females, of the same grade, $44.25; second grade, white, males, $41.80, females, $36.75. The average term in the several schools for the last year was four months, and the amount of money spent for the support of the public schools was $14,881. The value of the school property in the county is at least $40,000. The public school-house in Helena is probably the largest one of its kind in the State. It is a two-story brick, handsome and substantial, contains ample rooms, and on the top thereof is a grand tower, in which is a fine town clock, which strikes every hour of the day. It was constructed in 1886, at a cost of $24,000. There is also in Helena a very large and commodious public school-house for the colored people. In addition to the public schools in this place is the private school taught by Prof. W. S. White, which is a mixed graded school, in which pupils are prepared for college. This school has been established for twelve years, and has now about fifty pupils. There is also the Catholic Convent school, the "Academy of the Sacred Heart," and a Kindergarten school, taught by Miss Wendland. In addition to the above, the colored people have two or three private schools, all well sustained. The scholastic population of Helena school district is 2,000. Five teachers are employed in the white public school, and the same number in the colored public school. There is also the Southland Institute, about nine miles northwest of Helena, a school for the colored people, conducted by Prof. Beard.

The Presbyterian Church in Helena was organized long before the Civil War, and the present frame church edifice was also erected before that period. During the war it was used by the Federal troops as a hospital. For some time the church has been without a regular pastor, but during 1888 Rev. A. E. Grover, of Mason, Tenn., has preached for it every alternate Sabbath. He has recently been called to and has accepted the pastorate of the church. The membership at this writing is about fifty, and the Sunday-school of forty pupils is progressing finely under the superintendence of J. R. Graham. This is the only church of this denomination in Phillips County.

The Methodists and Baptists were probably, as they have been everywhere, the pioneer Christian workers in the county, both of the societies organized in a very early day. Of the Methodist Episcopal Church, South, there is Helena Station, with a membership of from 150 to 175, with Rev. E. M. Pipkin, pastor. This station has a large brick edifice, erected in 1884, which ranks among the finest in the State. The Sunday-school connected with it has about seventy-five scholars, and is doing good work as the nursery of the church. The La Grange Circuit, containing several appointments, with an aggregate membership of about 150, with Rev. W. E. Bishop, pastor, is also in Phillips County. These constitute all the churches of this denomination within the county. The names of the Baptist Churches in the county are: Helena, Marvell, Barton, Salem, New Hope, Cypress and Level Valley. These have an aggregate membership of about 300, and those reported having Sunday-schools are Helena, Salem and New Hope. Rev. W. H. Barnes is pastor of the church at Helena.

The Catholics have a small church organization in Helena, with Rev. Father J. M. Boetzkes, priest. They have just completed a nice and comfortable brick church edifice, worth about $10,000.

The colored people have three Baptist and one Methodist Church in Helena, and several other organizations throughout the county. There may be a few other church societies in this county which have not been mentioned.

Capt. J. C. Barlow, dealer in hardware, stoves, etc., of Helena, Ark., was born in Scott County, Ky., January 3, 1836, and is a son of Thomas J. and Mildred (Cantrell) Barlow, natives of Scott and Bourbon Counties, Ky., respectively. The paternal grandfather was born in Old Virginia and the grandmother in North Carolina, but at an early period they moved to the wilds of Kentucky, making their way thither on horseback, the grandmother carrying a large cane which she pretended was a gun, and used in frightening away the Indians. She was reared on the farm once owned by Daniel Boone in the "Old North State." The grandparents on both sides died in Kentucky, and were farmers by occupation. Thomas J. Barlow was also a farmer, and after living a useful and well-spent life, quietly breathed his last in Ballard County, Ky., in 1873, his wife's death occurring in Scott County, Ky., she having borne him six children, three of whom are now living: Frances A. (wife of John W. Allison, of Bourbon County, Ky.), Joseph C. and James M. Edward was in the Confederate army and died at Montgomery, Ala. Thomas died in Kentucky and William also died there when quite young. Mr. Barlow was married twice and by his last wife had a family of three children, Clifton J. being the only one alive. J. C. Barlow was reared and favored with the advantages of the common schools in Scott County, Ky., but in 1859 came to Helena, Ark., and became a salesman in a dry-goods establishment, this work receiving his attention until the opening of the war, when he enlisted in the Phillips County Guards, and subsequently got a transfer to the Yell Rifles, with which he served until the fall of 1861, when he joined the Second Arkansas Battery, remaining with them until the close of the war. After serving for some time as first lieutenant of artillery he was appointed to the rank of captain by the secretary of war, and was a participant in all the engagements of his regiment. After the war he clerked in Memphis, Tenn., for about one year, then returned to Helena and has since been conducting a hardware establishment, this enterprise meeting with good success under his able management. He has the largest stock of goods in the town, and receives a most liberal share of public favor. He filled an unexpired term as mayor of Helena, is president of the Phillips County Fair Association, and since August 22, 1882, has held the position of colonel of the Arkansas State Guards, receiving his appointment from Gov. F. J. Churchill during the political troubles of that year. He was married in 1869 to Miss Mary J. Porter, a native of Helena, and in 1876 took for his second wife Mrs. Mary Grant, by whom he has three children: Fannie A., Harrell E. and Jo-

seph C., Jr. Capt. and Mrs. Barlow are members of the Episcopal Church.

Rev. J. M. Boetzkes, rector of St. Mary's Church, at Helena, Ark., was born in Prussia, Germany, and received his education at Muenster University, Westphalia, from which institution he was graduated in 1855, and was ordained subdeacon September 8 of the same year. The following year he embarked to America, taking passage at Havre, France, and landed at New York City after a two weeks' ocean voyage, and came directly to St. Louis, where he was ordained deacon a few months after his arrival. On September 8, 1856, he was ordained a priest of the Catholic Church, and during the late Civil War was in the service for some time in Scott County, Mo., acting as chaplain. Here he built a stone church, which was demolished during the latter part of the war. He was in the hospital service in St. Louis for about a year, and in 1865 returned to Europe, but a few months later came back to the United States and settled in the city of Philadelphia, where he occupied a position in the diocese until 1875, at which time he came to Helena, Ark. Here he was the means of erecting a fine brick church at a cost of $12,000, and on July 21, 1889, it was dedicated, the corner-stone being laid July 22, 1888. The convent at Helena has been built several years, but since Father Boetzkes' arrival he has improved it wonderfully. It is a day and boarding-school and is controlled and managed by nine Sisters of Charity who have made it one of the best institutions of the kind in the West. The training includes a comprehensive collegiate course and thoroughly fits a young lady for any position or vocation in life, the branches taught being music, the languages, all branches of mathematics, chemistry, botany, calisthenics, etc. The building is beautifully situated and commands a view of the Mississippi River, as well as the surrounding country and the grounds are tastefully laid out with magnolia and other shade trees.

R. S. Bonner, carpenter, Poplar Grove, Ark. Were it necessary for us to include in the sketch of Mr. Bonner's life any items pertaining to his ability and skill as a builder, perhaps the greatest compliment that could be paid him would be to point out those monuments of his handiwork, which now grace so many of the homesteads in this portion of the State. He was born in Alabama, in 1844, and is the fifth of ten children, the result of the union of Thomas T. and Elizabeth (Schackelford) Bonner, the father a native of North Carolina, and the mother of Alabama. Thomas T. Bonner was a carpenter and ginwright by trade, and came to Alabama when a young man. He was there married to Miss Schackelford in 1834, and of the ten children born to this union, five are now living: R. S., J. C., W. H., E. C. and R. K. Mr. Bonner was a member of the I. O. O. F., and was a much-respected citizen. He died on December 31, 1849, and the mother died in 1871. The maternal grandfather, John L. Schackelford, was a native of the Old Dominion, and moved to Alabama at an early day. His death occurred in Phillips County (now Lee County) in 1863, at the age of seventy-nine years. He was a soldier in the War of 1812. His wife died in 1874, at the age of eighty-five years. R. S. Bonner came to Arkansas in 1856, received his education in this State and Alabama, and at the age of sixteen years, or in 1861, enlisted in Company A, Thirteenth Arkansas Infantry, under Capt. Tappan (afterward Gen. Tappan), in what was known as Tappan's guards. He served in Gen. Bragg's command and was engaged in quite a number of battles, prominent among which were: Belmont, Corinth, Shiloh, Richmond, Perryville, Chickamauga, Missionary Ridge, Murfreesboro and Bell Buckle Station. He was captured close to Atlanta, in 1864, was confined at Rock Island, Ill., for four months, after which he was exchanged and returned to Arkansas. Later he served in Capt. Weatherly's company. He surrendered in 1865, and afterward engaged in farming on rented land in Phillips County, until 1876. He then bought his present place, at that time consisting of forty acres, principally wood land, and to this he has added eighty acres, with 100 acres under cultivation. However he devotes the greater part of his time to carpenter work and is the only contractor at this place, doing a large amount of building. His marriage occurred in

October, 1869, to Miss Jennie Allison, who bore him seven children, two only now living: Hettie R. and Mamie L. Five died while small. Mrs. Bonner died in 1881. She was a worthy member of the Methodist Episcopal Church. In October, 1883, Mr. Bonner married Miss Mamie Allison, a sister of his first wife, and they have two children: Olivett and Eveline H.

Charles L. Bonner, son of Charles S. Bonner, one of the pioneer settlers of this county, was born on his present place of residence in Phillips County, in 1862. His father was a native of Tennessee, as was also his mother, whose maiden name was Miss Margaret J. Gamble, and the former came to Phillips County, Ark., in 1835, when there were very few settlers. His father bought land on Big Creek, but in 1844 Charles S. purchased the place on which his son Charles L. is now residing, and which at that time consisted of 160 acres of land. He and wife were the parents of eight children, five of whom are now living: Nettie (widow of T. N. Conley), B. F., Chellie J. (wife of John W. Terry), C. L. and Loutie L. (a teacher in the Galloway Female College of Searcy, Ark.). The eldest child, Sallie E. (deceased, was the wife of W. S. Ferrill). She left one child, Charles. The father of these children died in 1876, but the mother is still living, and makes her home with her son Charles L. The latter received a good common-school education in Phillips County, and at the age of nineteen years began work for himself as a farmer, having followed this occupation the principal part of the time since. He was also engaged in the saw-mill business for some time. In 1888 he was married to Miss Sallie Allison, of Phillips County, and of the city of Helena. The maternal grandfather of Charles L. Bonner was among the early settlers of Eastern Tennessee, and was in the wars with the Indians in that section of the country. He came to Phillips County in 1840, where he resided until his death in 1874. Mr. and Mrs. Bonner and Mr. Bonner's mother are members of the Methodist Episcopal Church, South.

James T. Brame. About four generations ago, three sons named Brame, who lived in England, their native country, separated, one remaining at

home, another going to Canada, and the third
coming to America, choosing for his residence the
State of Virginia. From this son, James T.
Brame, the subject of this sketch, is a direct de-
scendant. James T. Brame was born in Virginia
November 26, 1848 and is the son of James H.
Brame, a celebrated professor, for many years con-
nected with the prominent colleges of Virginia,
but is now retired. He is the son of Thomas
Brame, and was born in Mecklenburgh County,
Va., in 1816. James H. Brame was married in
1847 to Miss Martha Baptist, born in Virginia in
1826, and a daughter of Richard H. Baptist. Mr.
Baptist was a prominent politician, having served as
State senator for sixteen years, and was filling that
position at the date of his death. He was an uncle
of Gen. A. P. Hill. Mrs. Baptist's maiden name was
Sally Goode, she being a daughter of Dr. Thomas
Goode, of Virginia. James T., our subject, was
one of eight children, five sons and three daughters, born to his parents. He was reared in Virginia, and at the age of fifteen years enlisted in the
Confederate army, Company A, First Virginia Regiment, and served until the surrender of Gen. Lee.
At the battle of Stanton River Bridge he received
a slight wound, that being the only time he was
injured, notwithstanding that he was always in the
thick of some of the most important engagements.
At the age of twenty-one he left his native home
and came to Arkansas, locating in Phillips (now
Lee) County, at Council Bend. He chose the independent occupation of farming, which has been
his work ever since, and has resided on his present
farm since 1881, under his careful management it
being second to none in the county. It consists
of 400 acres, nearly all cultivated. Mr. Brame
also oversees and cultivates 1,000 acres. In January, 1875, he was married in Memphis, Tenn., to
Miss Anna J. Peters, who was born in Camden,
Ark., in 1855, and the daughter of John B.
Peters. He was of Tennessee birth, but came to
Arkansas at an early date, and died during the
war. Mrs. Peters was Miss Paralee Jackson, of
Florence County, Ala. To Mr. and Mrs. Brame
three children have been born: Ellen G., Mary P.
and Anna. Mr. Brame is a member of the K. of

P. and A. L. of H., and in his political views is a
Democrat, though not an enthusiast, his first
presidential vote having been cast for Samuel J.
Tilden. Mr. Brame and wife are members of the
Presbyterian Church.

Nicholas Brickell, undertaker, Poplar Grove,
Ark. There are few branches of business, if any,
that require more consideration and sympathetic
feeling than that of the undertaker. Their services are only called under the most trying circumstances that can befall a family or friends, and
the utmost tact, coupled with decision and perfect,
unostentatious knowledge of the business, is required. In these points Mr. Nicholas Brickell is
well-grounded by nature and experience. He was
born in Surry County, N. C., in 1824, and is the
eldest of five children born to the union of J. B.
and Frances (Harrison) Brickell, the father a
native of South Carolina, and the mother of North
Carolina. J. B. Brickell was a cabinet workman,
and always followed that trade after his marriage.
Previous to that, however, he had followed merchandising. He was a soldier in the War of 1812,
having joined while quite young. He was married in 1822, and of the five children born to his
union, five are now living: Nicholas, D. C. (is a
manufacturer of carriages in Atlanta, Ga.), Mathias
(died in White County, Ark., and his family reside in that county), Andrew J. (resides in Tennessee), and Emma (wife of E. A. Peal, of North
Carolina. Mr. Brickell died in 1850. He was a
member of the Masonic fraternity. Mrs. Brickell
died in 1870, and was a member of the Methodist
Episcopal Church. Nicholas Brickell passed his
youthful days and received his education in his
native county, where, in later years, he learned the
cabinet-maker's trade. He began working at his
trade at the age of twenty-one years, and continued
the same in North Carolina until 1846, when, in
December of that year, he moved to Georgia, settling where Palmetto now stands, and followed the
furniture business. This he continued until 1856,
when he moved to Franklin, Heard County, Ga.,
and there followed the same business. In 1870
he moved to Trenton, Big Creek Township, Phillips County, Ark., remained there until 1871, when

he moved into the country, and farmed on rented land for three years. In 1875 he moved to his present place of residence, and here built his shop and house, besides two store houses, and has forty acres of land well improved. He was married December 2, 1847, to Miss Martha A. Sanders, daughter of Joel and Fannie (Harris) Sanders, natives, respectively, of North Carolina. Mr. and Mrs. Sanders became the parents of eight children, five now living: G. H., John, Martha A. (wife of Mr. Brickell), Margaret (widow of John Edwards, who was killed at the second battle of Manassas), and Mary. All, with one exception, residing in Georgia, whither the father had moved when his children were quite small. Mr. Sanders died in 1849, and his widow in 1856. Mrs. Brickell was born February 4, 1830, and by her marriage to Mr. Brickell became the mother of ten children, seven now living: T. J. (resides at Brinkley, Monroe County, Ark.), John C. (deceased), Georgia R. (wife of J. H. Miller, of Holly Grove, Ark.), C. W. (resides in Clarendon, Monroe County), W. P. (resides in Phillips County), J. B. (resides at Helena), Martha A. (wife of J. J. Raleigh, of Poplar Grove), Robert L., C. W. (of Clarendon, who was State senator from that senatorial district, and T. J. (who is a local minister in the Methodist Episcopal Church at Brinkley). In 1861 Mr. Brickell joined the State service in Company G, Col. Wilcoxson's regiment of State cavalry, and was in the State service for six months. He only served a short time in the regular service, being detailed to stay at home and work at his trade, making spinning wheels and looms for making cloth. Mr. Brickell is a demitted member of the Masonic fraternity, Chattahoochee Lodge No. 61, and he and wife are both members of the Methodist Episcopal Church, South, of this place. He favors all improvements for the good of the county, and extends a hearty welcome to all white immigration. He and his wife are the grandparents of thirteen children.

Hon. Samuel H. Brooks. Since locating in this county in 1866 Mr. Brooks has enjoyed the reputation of being not only a substantial and progressive farmer, but an intelligent and thoroughly posted man in all public affairs as well. He was born in Philadelphia, Penn., October 17, 1839, and is a son of John and Amelia (Fletcher) Brooks, the former a native of Bristol, Penn., and the latter of London, England. John Brooks was a merchant by occupation, and died in Cincinnati, Ohio, in 1840, at the untimely age of thirty-one years. His widow afterward married Jacob B. Furrow, of Piqua, Ohio, who followed merchandising until his death in 1884. His widow survives him, and is an earnest and devout member of the Methodist Episcopal Church. She was a child of six years when brought by her parents to the United States, and their location was made at Philadelphia, Penn., where their death occurred many years later. Mr. and Mrs. Brooks became the parents of two children: Samuel H., and Thomas P., who died in Cincinnati in 1885, being county recorder of Hamilton County at the time of his decease. Samuel H. Brooks was educated in the schools of Saint Paris, Ohio, and at the age of fourteen years left home to become a salesman in a hardware store at Piqua, Ohio, but two years later he turned his attention to the railroad business, and was ticket agent at that point for one year. He next went to Indianapolis, Ind., and became conductor on the old Belfontaine line, which is now known as the Bee line, and after serving in this capacity for about ten years he worked on the Ohio & Mississippi Railroad for a short time. He then (in 1863) joined the Second Tennessee Federal troops, organized at Memphis, Tenn., under Col. Curry, but at the end of one year he went to Mississippi and located in Coahoma County, and a year later came to Phillips County, Ark., where he has since been engaged in planting; and his well established characteristics of energy, perseverance and unbounded industry have brought him safe returns. His neat farm embraces 420 acres, and to this he is enabled to give intelligent management, but he is at present giving the most of his attention to the management of Dr. A. A. Hornor's plantation of 1,350 acres. He has always been a Democrat in politics, and in 1868 was elected county treasurer, in which capacity he served four years. In 1882 he was chosen to represent Phillips County in the State legislature. In

1862 he was united in marriage to Miss Caroline S. Shock, a daughter of Abel Shock, who made the first steam fire-engine in the United States, and discovered the fine copper fields in the region of Lake Superior. He was a native of Pennsylvania, and died in Missouri in 1874. Mrs. Brooks was born in Cincinnati, Ohio, April 28, 1840, and she and Mr. Brooks have one daughter, Amelia A., who made a roll of butter that took the premium at the Centennial Exhibition at Philadelphia in 1876. Mrs. Brooks is a member of the Presbyterian Church, and Mr. Brooks is a Mason, and belongs to the I. O. O. F.

John L. Brown is a native of this county, and has always resided here. He was educated at the common schools, acquiring a good practical learning and resided with his parents until their death, in 1869, being married to Miss Mary E. Yates, who was born in Mississippi in 1845, and died in 1884. He married his second wife in 1885, formerly Miss Lenora Phillips, of South Carolina origin. Mr. Brown was born on April 24, 1847, a son of Richard Brown, who first saw the light in White County, S. C., in 1800. In 1839 he immigrated from South Carolina to this county, where he purchased a tract of wild land, and at the time of his death, which occurred in 1864, he owned a well-improved farm. His wife was Polly Ann Stumb, who was born in Illinois in 1817, and died in 1851, leaving nine children, five of whom are still living. John L. Brown and wife are the parents of one child, Idalgo S. He owns a farm of 200 acres of land, of which 130 acres are under cultivation. His principal crop is cotton and he raises about forty bales per annum. He is a Democrat in politics, and is a highly respected citizen.

Moses Burke has been long and worthily identified with the interests of Phillips County, and no worthy history of this immediate vicinity would be complete which failed to make proper mention of his life. He was born in the house in which he now resides March 1, 1848, and is a son of Elisha and Eliza (Cail) Burke, both natives of North Carolina, the former's birth occurring July 13, 1798, and his death in Phillips County, Ark.,

June 21, 1860. His marriage took place March 24, 1825, and until 1835 or 1836 they resided in their native State, moving then to Arkansas, and soon after located on the farm on which our subject is now living. The father was a farmer all his life, and was very successful, and in connection with this work was engaged in milling, ginning, blacksmithing and wagon making, being successful in all these undertakings. While in North Carolina he represented his county several times in the State legislature, and after coming to Arkansas he represented his district in the senate three or four terms, and later was a member of the legislature from Phillips County. He was also colonel of militia in North Carolina and Arkansas for many years, and while the Whig party was in existence affiliated with that party. He was born of Irish parents, and his wife was of Scotch descent, her birth occurring on July 9, 1807. She bore her husband the following children: Eliza (wife of Dr. James H. Gibson, of La Grange, Ark.) and Moses being the only ones living. Those deceased are: Richard C. (who died in 1870 when about forty years of age), Sallie F. (wife of Joseph Neville, died in 1857 at the age of twenty years), Elisha (was accidentally killed at Helena in 1856 at the age of fourteen years), and the rest of the children, numbering three, died in infancy. Moses Burke received his early education in his home, and when only nineteen years of age he assumed the management of his mother's property, and has continued to successfully conduct it up to the present time. They now jointly own 740 acres of land, of which 400 acres are under cultivation, nearly all of it having been obtained since the war, as during that time the most of their property was demolished. Mr. Burke was married in 1878 to Miss Jenny E. Goodwin, a daughter of Sanford E. Goodwin, her birth occurring in Phillips County, in 1852, and by her he has a family of five children: Aubrey, Elisha B., Ethel, Moses Oscar and Jennie E. Mrs. Burke is a member of the Methodist Episcopal Church, and in his political views Mr. Burke is a Democrat. He is a live and enterprising agriculturist, and his long residence in this county, his industrious habits and perseverance, as well as his strict integrity and honesty of purpose, have contributed to place around him a host of friends and acquaintances.

William S. Burnett is the able editor and proprietor of the Helena Daily and Weekly World, which paper is firmly established as a representative journal of this portion of the State. Mr. Burnett's birth occurred in this county, and he has become well known for his perseverance, enterprise and progress, as well as for many other admirable traits of character, and to a very great extent he enjoys the esteem and confidence of his fellow-man. After acquiring a common-school education, he entered the office of the Democratic Star of Helena as an apprentice at the printer's trade, but completed his knowledge of the business in the Southern Shield office. He then began an independent career as publisher of the Helena Clonen, in 1864, but after conducting this paper for a short time, he sold out, and established the Des Arc Crescent, of which paper he had the management from 1866 to 1869. At the latter date, he sold this paper also and returned to Helena, where, in conjunction with Mulkey & Burke, he established the Weekly World in 1871, and afterward also began the publication of the Daily World. At a later period he sold his interest in these journals, and in 1874 he began editing the Daily Mail, but in 1876, again disposed of his paper. From that time until 1885 he gave his attention to other branches of business, then purchased the Daily World, which he is now successfully conducting, it being the second oldest daily in the State. Under his judicious management it has become recognized as an influential paper, and has done good work in advancing the interests of Eastern Arkansas. Its editorial policy has been directed by a man of good judgment, and its columns always contain something instructive and interesting. He has always supported the men and measures of the Democrat party, and has himself held responsible positions as a township and county officer.

James A. Bush, planter, Latour, Ark. Of that sturdy and independent class, the farmers of Arkansas, none are possessed of more genuine merit and a stronger character than he whose name stands at the head of this sketch; he has risen to more than an ordinary degree of success in his calling of an agriculturist and stock man, and wherever known, he is conceded to be an energetic and progressive tiller of the soil, imbued with all those qualities of go-a-head-ativeness which have characterized his ancestors. His birth occurred in Knoxville, Tenn., January 2, 1832, and he is of German descent. He remained with his parents until eighteen years of age, when he commenced to learn the blacksmith trade, working at his trade until 1860, and accumulating considerable money. He then commenced to speculate, and has continued this ever since. During the late war he served some time in Dobbin's regiment, and was in a number of sharp skirmishes. He was on picket duty when the first gunboat passed Helena, and was a brave and gallant soldier. He was discharged three times for sickness before leaving the army. His property was burned and otherwise destroyed during the late war, and he was a heavy loser. He was the owner of twenty-seven picked slaves, worth on an average of $1,500 apiece. After the war he commenced to farm, which occupation he has since continued. He is now the owner of 1,800 acres, with 1,200 under cultivation, and uses convict labor of Phillips, Monroe, Lee and St. Francis Counties. He has used this kind of labor for six years, and during that time has used 2,000 negroes, only losing one by death, and he meeting his death by burning, while trying to escape. In 1860 Mr. Bush married Miss Jennie McKinsick, a native of Marshall County, Miss., born in 1834, and the daughter of Robert McKinsick. The fruits of this union have been five living children: Lucy C. (wife of John D. Binley, of Covington, Ky., merchant, formerly traveling for a firm in St. Louis), James R. (with the East Arkansas Hedge Company, in the capacity of bookkeeper), Jesse and Walter (twins, both at home) and Maude (at school, in Memphis). Mr. Bush was formerly a Whig in politics, and is one of the enterprising citizens of the county. Although he commenced without means, by his energy and good business ability he has become one of the most successful and substantial men of the county. He is a liberal contributor to all laudable enterprises, and has recently donated a house to be used as a Union Church. He is the son of Andrew and Nancy (Agnew) Bush, and the grandson of George Bush, who was one of the most substantial men of Tennessee, and died in Knox County of that State. Andrew Bush and wife were natives of Knox County, Tenn., and North Carolina, respectively, and were married in Knoxville, Tenn., where they remained until their son, James A., was eleven years of age. Then they moved to Northern Alabama, Madison County, and later came to Arkansas, where they passed the remainder of their lives, the father dying in 1860, when sixty years of age, and the mother dying in 1878, at the age of seventy-eight years. Both were members of the Methodist Episcopal Church, South, and he was a Whig in politics. He had followed agricultural pursuits all his life, was a soldier in the War of 1812, and was in the battle of the Horse Shoe. To his marriage were born seven children, all now deceased but the subject of this sketch.

S. B. Carpenter, druggist, Helena, Ark. There is no branch of business more important in the whole list of occupations than that of the druggist. A prominent and representative establishment devoted to this branch of industry is that of Mr. S. B. Carpenter, who for a number of years has been before the public in this line. He carries a large stock of drugs, etc., and does a good business. He is a native of this county, his birth occurring in 1854, and is the son of S. B. and Margaret (Owen) Carpenter, both natives of Alabama, where their families were very prominent. The parents moved to Arkansas at a very early day, entered land, and were pioneers of the county. The father was a very successful planter, and was the owner of a great many negroes. His death occurred in 1874. Of the ten children born to this marriage our subject was the eldest, and five are now living. S. B. Carpenter, Jr., was reared in Phillips County, received his preparatory education there and then studied pharmacy in the School of Pharmacy at Cincinnati, Ohio, in 1878. Since that time he has been engaged in business for himself, and although he started on a small capital he is now in

very comfortable circumstances. He is a bright young business man, and prescriptions are compounded with care and dispatch. He is a member of the Masonic fraternity.

Calvin Clark, Helena, Ark. Indiana has given to Phillips County, Ark., many estimable citizens, but she has contributed none more highly respected, or, for conscientious discharge of duty in every relation of life, more worthy of respect and esteem than the subject of this sketch. He was born in Wayne County on July 21, 1820, and is the son of John and Anna (Price) Clark, natives of North Carolina. The father moved to Indiana from North Carolina when eighteen years of age (or in 1836) and located in Wayne County, being among the very first settlers. He first followed farming, but in later years engaged in the milling and carding business, which he carried on until his death. His wife died in 1832, and both were members of the Friends Church. Their family consisted of five children, three of whom are now living: Calvin (the eldest child), Alfred (a farmer in Indiana was formerly a merchant) and Mary Ann Hadley (wife of Jesse Hadley, of Morgan County, Ind.). Those deceased were named: Sarah (wife of William Thornburg, of Rush County, died when about thirty years of age) and Lydia (who died when twenty years old). Calvin Clark received his education in the schools of Wayne and Morgan Counties, Ind., and was but fifteen years of age when his father died. His father had married again after the death of the mother, and Calvin made his home with his step-mother until after the father's death, when he went to live with an uncle. Soon after he went to Monrovia, attended school for a time, and when eighteen years of age began teaching school in Henry County. This he continued for a number of years in the winter season, and followed farming in the summer. Later he engaged in farming near Richmond, Ind., which he continued until 1864, when he came to Arkansas and took charge of what was then known as the Orphans' Asylum, taking charge of the same until 1886. This was a school for the colored orphans, and is now known as the Southland College, under the auspices of the Friends of the United

States. Mr. Clark was married in 1844 to Miss Elida Clawson, of Indiana, who was born in 1822, and is the daughter of William and Keziah (Ward) Clawson, of North Carolina. To this union was born one living child, Eliza C. (wife of Theodore F. Wright, banker and miller of Granville, Ohio, and a partner with our subject in a plantation in this county. The children deceased were named as follows: Myra (born in 1845, and died in 1864, when a young lady) and Annie (who died in Indiana when in her sixth year). The above mentioned school was first organized by a Mrs. Clark, and her husband co-operated with her. This has been their life's work, and they can justly be proud of the same. Their school was located at Helena for two years, and in 1867 they changed it to its present location, nine miles northwest of Helena. Mrs. Clark received her education in the best schools of Indiana (at that time) and is a recorded minister in the Friends' Church. Mr. Clark is also a member of that church, being an elder in the same, and is a Republican in politics. Clark & Wright are the owners of about 1,700 acres of land, with 1,000 acres cleared.

Hon. James P. Clarke is an able lawyer of Helena, Ark., and ever since starting in this profession his career has been one of distinction and success. He is active, intelligent and energetic by nature, public-spirited, liberal-minded and generous in disposition; it is not to be wondered at that his career has been successful and honorable. He was born in Yazoo County, Miss., August 18, 1854, and is a son of Walter and Ellen (White) Clarke, who were early residents of the State of Mississippi, and there the father's death occurred in 1861, his wife also passing away in that State. Mr. Clarke was a civil engineer and contractor, and he and his wife became the parents of three children, only two of whom are living, of whom Hon. James P. is one. He received the principal part of his education and rearing in Mississippi, but also attended school in Alabama and Virginia, thus becoming quite familiar with the "world of books." He graduated from the Law Department of the University of Virginia, and since coming to Helena in 1879 has given his profession his un-divided attention, and owing to his sound views, his intelligence, and his ability as a lawyer, business has come to him unsolicited. The people of the county have not been slow to recognize his worth, and in 1886 he was elected to the State legislature, and to the State senate in 1888.

Gen. Patrick Ronayne Cleburne. The career of this gentleman and his ability as a commander, which is so noted in the annals of Confederate history, has been justly admired by friend and foe, and although erroneous impressions regarding his early life have existed, the following sketch of his career is founded on fact. He was born in Ireland, ten miles west from the the city of Cork, on St. Patrick's Day, March 17, 1828, and was a son of a popular and successful physician, who made a good living by his profession, but who spent his money too freely for the acquisition of wealth, in his favorite pursuit of amateur farming. He was married to Mary Anne Ronayne, and the subject of this sketch was named after her father, Patrick Ronayne, Esq., of Cork. Dr. Cleburne was descended from an old Tipperary family of English and Quaker stock, which settled in Ireland during Cromwell's reign. He was finely educated and was a graduate of some of the best colleges of medicine and surgery. After the death of his wife, which occurred when Patrick was about a year old, he married a Miss Stuart, a daughter of a Scotch clergyman of that name, their union being a very happy one, and his children never lacked the kind ministrations and gentle love of a mother, Patrick being an especial favorite of hers, and she was always remembered by him with veneration. The Doctor's first union resulted in the birth of three children, and the second in the birth of four. Of these, Joseph (the issue of the first marriage) died of yellow fever contracted on the west coast of Africa during a voyage, and Christopher (issue of the second marriage) was a gallant captain in the Second Kentucky Cavalry of Morgan's command, and fell at the battle of Cloyd's Farm, May 10, 1864, aged twenty-one years. The rest, with the exception of Patrick, still survive and live in this country. William, the oldest brother, is engineer of the Oregon Short Line at Omaha, Neb., and

Anne is now Mrs. Sherlock, formerly of Cincinnati, Ohio. Patrick Cleburne received his early instructions from a private tutor, and at the age of twelve years was sent to a private school kept by a Rev. Mr. Spedden, but as he was a man of very harsh measures, Patrick's efforts at acquiring a classical education were a failure. At the age of sixteen, his father died, and he then determined to turn his attention to pharmacy and apprenticed himself to a Mr. Justin, of Mallow, but upon his failure to pass the examination at Apothecary's Hall, Trinity College, Dublin, after what he considered a thorough preparation, he was so disheartened and mortified that he enlisted in the Forty-first Regiment of Infantry, then stationed at Dublin, hoping that it would soon be ordered to foreign service. His anticipations were not realized, however, and owing to the monotony and dull routine of barrack life, he turned his thoughts to America, where adventurous and ambitious spirits could find a wider scope for their talents, and although his withdrawal was decidedly opposed by Capt. (afterward Gen.) Pratt, who distinguished himself in India and the Crimea, he was immovable and purchased his discharge through the intervention of his family. In company with his brothers William and Christopher, and his sister Anne, he embarked on the vessel Bridgetown, and on the following Christmas day entered the mouth of the Mississippi River. Leaving his friends in New Orleans, he went at once to Cincinnati and engaged in business on Broadway with a druggist named Salter, but soon after left this place and located in Helena, Ark., commencing his career here as a prescription clerk in the store of Grant & Nash, purchasing, two years afterward, Mr. Grant's interest. During this time he devoted himself to the study of his profession, and also general literature, and being particularly fond of oratory became a conspicuous member of literary and debating societies. As orator of the day at a Masonic celebration, he achieved considerable local distinction, and upon the advice of friends, and also being personally inclined, he abandoned his old business and turned his attention to the study of law in the office of Hon. T. B. Hanley, and was soon after admitted to

the bar, forming in 1856 a law partnership with Mark W. Alexander, the firm being known as Alexander & Cleburne. About this time, while the violent contest between the Democratic and Know-Nothing parties was in its full vigor, Mr. Cleburne accidentally witnessed a shooting affray between T. C. Hindman, a noted speaker and leader of the Democrats, and Dorsey Rice, a bitter partisan on the Know-Nothing side, and was shot by Jamison Rice, who supposed Mr. Cleburne was a participant in the struggle. The ball passed entirely through his body, but, although almost mortally wounded, he turned and seeing James Marriott standing with pistol in his hand and supposing him to be his assailant, he coolly raised his pistol and shot him dead. He then fell himself, and was carried by friends to his home, where he struggled between life and death for many days, but finally recovered. This affair was always a source of much regret and sorrow to Mr. Cleburne, but which he was powerless to avert. In 1859 he became associated in the practice of law with L. H. Mangum and —— Scaife, the firm being Cleburne, Scaife & Mangum, they constituting one of the best and strongest legal firms of the State. Mr. Cleburne was a very successful lawyer, and very popular with the masses, this being the natural result of his own deep sympathy with humanity, making every sufferer his brother. In 1855, when Helena was visited by that terrible scourge, yellow fever, Mr. Cleburne was one of the few to remain to nurse the sick, bury the dead and help the poor, this being only one instance of his remarkable nerve and courage. He knew not what fear was. Incapable of bravado he was grand in the energy of his anger when aroused, quick as lightning in execution, and indifferent to all consequences. Personally he was the soul of honor, but was proud and sensitive in disposition, and although at heart the friend of all the world, he had few intimate friends; among these may be mentioned his brigadier-generals, Polk, Lowrey, Govan, Granberry, Hardee and Cheatham, also Gen. John C. Brown. When the Civil War became imminent Mr. Cleburne at once stepped to the front, and he was chosen captain of the Yell Rifles, and was afterward made colonel of the First Arkansas Regiment of State troops. A record of his triumphs up to the battle of Franklin is well known to every reader of current history, and will not be given here. Suffice it to say, he never suffered defeat, but achieved splendid success. In more battles than one his figure stands out prominently as the hero of the day, and his distinction was won by universal acclamation. Although he was rigid in the enforcement of discipline, the soldiers whom he commanded loved him to a man, and trusted him implicity, and were ready to follow where he led, with alacrity and confidence. The morning of November 29, 1864, saw the armies of the Tennessee ready for battle. Schofield was at Columbia, and it was Hood's purpose to outflank and outmarch him, so as to cut him off from Nashville and capture his army. With this object in view he crossed the Duck River three miles above Columbia and marched to Spring Hill, a small town on the Nashville pike midway between Columbia and Franklin. Cleburne's division was leading, with Bate immediately following him, and Brown in the rear, the first-named division being composed of four brigades. Late in the afternoon Cleburne reached the vicinity of Spring Hill, near which was a Federal fortification. A mile from this fortification ran McCuthen's Creek, and the road on which Cleburne was coming crossed this creek, and approached the turnpike at a right angle. Under the direction of Gen. Cheatham, the corps commander, and following the plan of Gen. Hood, Bate moved out to form on Cleburne's left, and Brown's brigade was moved to the right on the double quick, and made their formation. Gen. Hood then, in person, ordered Gen. Cleburne to form at the left of the road, in the cornfield at the foot of a hill, move forward and take the enemy's works, adding that Brown had formed on his right and Bate was advancing to form on his left. This order was executed rapidly, and the enemy had only time to fire one volley before Granberry and Govan were at their works, and in less than fifteen minutes, with a loss of four killed and forty-five wounded, the earthworks with some prisoners were taken. Cleburne's command was now in full view of Spring Hill, and

47

less than 300 yards from it. A Federal battery on the turnpike then commenced to shell the command, which had become somewhat scattered in pursuing the enemy, and Gen. Cleburne dispatched L. H. Mangum, the original writer of this sketch, to Granberry on the left, with directions to form his brigade so as to be prepared to move on the pike. As he gave the order he said, "I will see Govan." At that moment a shell burst over his head and wounded his horse, causing the animal to rear furiously, and Mr. Mangum paused to make the inquiry, "Are you hurt, General?" but the answer fired at him was, "No, go on, Mangum, and tell Granberry what I told you, and we will take the pike." Shortly after the brigades had formed and the battery had retreated. It was then discovered that Bate had not formed on the left, owing to the creek, through which Cleburne had waded, proving an obstruction, and as night was approaching, they were ordered to bivouac. During the night the Federal army passed along this very pike, within 200 yards of Cleburne's command, and escaped to Franklin. In the morning Hood's army began pursuing the enemy, and in the afternoon reached Winston's Ridge, where they could get a good view of Schofield's fortifications at Franklin, and their admirable nature caused Hood to look serious and consult with his officers what was best to be done. Some of his ablest generals opposed the attack, among whom was Gen. Cleburne, but, notwithstanding this, Hood ordered an immediate attack, and while on the eve of the onset, he addressed Cleburne thus: "General, I wish you to move on the enemy. Form your division on the right of the pike, with your left resting on the same. Gen. Brown will form on your left, with his right resting on the same. Give orders to your men not to fire a gun till you drive the Federal skirmishers from the first line of works in your front. Then press them and shoot them in the backs while running to the main line. Then charge the main works." To which Cleburne answered with a smile, "General, I will take the works or fall in the attempt." The first line of works was easily taken, and when his men made the final charge, Cleburne was at the front.

A message had been sent from him to L. H. Mangum to join him at once, the latter having been sent to locate a battery, and upon his return the General said, "It is too late, go on with Granberry." He then turned his horse and galloped up to Govan's brigade, this being the last time Mr. Mangum ever saw the General alive. Shortly after Cleburne's horse was shot from under him, and while in the act of mounting another which had been offered him, this, too, was shot and instantly killed. Cleburne then rushed forward on foot, and when within less than a hundred yards from the works, he fell, pierced by a minie-ball, which passed through his body and probably caused instant death. Hidden by smoke and enveloped by thunders, he sank on the couch of his glory, unattended and alone. As soon as his absence became known, the deepest anxiety was shown, and it was at first reported that he was captured, but these hopes were dissipated by the finding of Cleburne's body by a correspondent of the press, and he was taken to the home of Mr. McGavock, near by, and shortly afterward to Columbia for interment, the funeral rites being performed by Rt.-Rev. Bishop Quintard. Later his body was removed to the family burying-ground of the Polk family, at Ashwood, six miles from Columbia. Here, shadowed by the solemn forest trees, and near the river, on whose placid bosom he loved to row, he sleeps the sleep of a hero, and on the simple slab above his grave is the following inscription:

MAJ.-GEN. P. R. CLEBURNE,

Of the Confederate Army, born in County Cork, Ireland.
Killed at the battle of Franklin,
NOVEMBER 30, 1864.

William C. Cooke, who has been a resident of this county since 1873, removed here from Mississippi, settling in Cypress Township, where he purchased 160 acres of land. To this he has added other tracts, and now owns a farm of 220 acres, with 140 acres under cultivation. Mr. Cooke was a son of Thomas Cooke, who was born in March, 1800, and died in 1846, when our subject was a boy. He was married in Tennessee to Miss Alice Cathey, whose birth occurred in Tennessee, in about 1800, he dying in May, 1874, and leaving eleven children, only two of whom are living: Elizabeth O. (residing in Monroe County) and William C. (the principal of this sketch). The latter was born in Maury County, Tenn., March 17, 1830. He has been married five times; first, in 1852, to Miss Mary Graham, a native of North Carolina, who died in 1855, leaving one daughter, Alice (now Mrs. Jackson, a widow). His second marriage was in 1856 to Nancy Lock, of Mississippi; she departed this life in 1862, leaving three children, two of whom survive: Thomas and Samuel L. His third marriage, in 1865, was to the widow McCloud, who died in 1871, having borne three children, two living: Jenette and Virgil. In 1873 Cynthia Wright, of this county, became his wife, and at her death, in 1876, she was the mother of two children: Margaret A. and Jennie. Mr. Cooke's present wife was formerly Mrs. Robinson, to whom he was married in 1881. They are the parents of three children, two girls and one son: Cecil, Roy and Lucy. During the war Mr. Cooke enlisted in the Confederate army, in the Mississippi Cavalry, in 1862, in which he served until the close of hostilities. He is a stanch Democrat, and served one term as justice of the peace. He and wife are members of the Christian Church.

J. W. Clopton, wholesale grocer and cotton factor, Helena, Ark. This most enterprising and successful business man is the son of John H. and Matilda (Drake) Clopton, both of whom were born near Nashville, Tenn. They were married in that State, and in 1841 moved to Marshall County, Miss., where they resided until 1851, and then moved to Phillips County, Ark., where the father died in 1856. The mother died in 1865. Of the ten children born to their union, four are now living: Hoggatt, Jesse P., James W. (in Phillips County) and William C. (in New York City). James W. Clopton, was born in Marshall County, Miss., on March 16, 1841, and was ten years of age when he came to this county with his parents. He was educated principally in Helena, was reared partly on the farm, and at an early age began clerking, which enterprise he continued until the late Civil War. He

Yours Truly
Hoggatt Clopton

PHILLIPS COUNTY, ARKANSAS.

then enlisted in the Yell Rifles, of which the late Maj.-Gen. Cleburne was captain, and served until the close of the war. He received a gunshot in the right hand and left wrist at the battle of Shiloh, came home on a furlough, and while here he was captured and taken to Alton, Ill. After being retained for about four months, he was exchanged, and fortunately fell in with the first lot of prisoners that got through. He joined his regiment at Murfreesboro, and was second sergeant. He was in all the principal engagements, and served his cause faithfully and well. Returning home he farmed for two years, and then embarked in mercantile pursuits which he has since carried on. He has an extensive wholesale business, and is a successful business man. He was married, in 1869, to Miss Bettie Rainey, a native of Macon, Miss., by whom he has five children: Mary, Edna, Alice, James W. and Bess. Mr. Clopton is a member of the K. of P. and American Legion of Honor, is a stockholder in the People's Saving Bank and Helena Compress Company, also the Fair Association, and is president of the Chamber of Commerce.

Col. Hoggatt Clopton, Helena, Ark. A glance at the lives of many representative men, whose names appear in this volume, will reveal sketches of some honored, influential citizens, but none more worthy or deserving of mention than Col. Hoggatt Clopton. This gentleman resides three miles west of Helena, and is the owner of Clopton Hall plantations, among the largest in the county, consisting of 4,500 acres of land, with 1,700 acres under cultivation. He is also a capitalist. Col. Clopton was born near Nashville, Tenn., February 6, 1831, and is the son of John Hoggatt and Matilda C. (Drake) Clopton, the grandson of Anthony Clopton, and the great-grandson of Hugh Clopton, of Virginia. The latter, with two brothers, Will and Anthony, left England and came to America, locating in Virginia about 1700. Afterward Will returned to the land of his birth, and being the eldest of the three brothers, fell heir to Clopton Hall Manor, at Stratford-on-Avon. Anthony Clopton, grandfather of the subject of this sketch, was a native Virginian, and died in De Soto County, Miss., in 1848, when eighty-seven years of age. He

was a very successful farmer, and was among the first settlers of Davidson County, Tenn., locating at Nashville when that city was but a small trading point. He moved to Tipton County, Tenn., in 1836, and resided there until 1846, when he broke up housekeeping on account of the death of his wife, whose maiden name was Rhoda Hoggatt, and moved to Marshall County, Miss. Later he moved to De Soto County of the same State, where he passed the closing scenes of his life. He was a Whig, but took very little interest in politics. He was at one time a partner in a race course at Clover Bottom, near Nashville, Tenn., with Gen. Andrew Jackson. John Hoggatt Clopton, the father of the subject of this sketch, was born in Davidson County, Tenn., on Aug. 31, 1805, and died on July 26, 1855, in Phillips County, Ark. He was married in March, 1830, to Miss Matilda C. Drake, a native of Wilson County, Tenn., born September 15, 1813, and died June 6, 1865. They lived near Nashville, Tenn., until 1839, when they moved near Holly Springs, Marshall County, Miss., where they resided until December, 1851. After this the family moved to Phillips County, Ark. While living at Nashville Mr. Clopton was engaged in raising fine stock, especially racing stock, but also raised blooded stock of all kinds. He was the owner of a great many slaves, but sold his property at Nashville, moved to Mississippi with his slaves, and from that time until his death was occupied as a cotton planter. He was unusually successful, and although starting life with rather limited means, by his superior business ability and great energy was the possessor of a great deal of property at his death. He and wife were worthy members of the Methodist Episcopal Church, South, and on coming to Phillips County were instrumental in the building up of the Methodist Episcopal Church at Helena. He was a Whig in politics. Matilda C. (Drake) Clopton was the daughter of Brittain Drake, a native of North Carolina, whose ancestors were also English, and an old settler of Wilson County, Tenn. He was a farmer, and in his political views was a Whig. There were born to the union of John Hoggatt Clopton and wife, eight sons and two daughters, four of whom are now living: Col.

Hoggatt, Jesse P. (a prominent planter and merchant of Phillips County, Ark.), James W. (a successful merchant and planter of Phillips County, now residing in Helena), and William C. (an eminent attorney of New York City, a graduate of the University of Virginia, and also a graduate of the University of Berlin, Germany). The children deceased were named as follows: John Anthony (was born January 23, 1833, and died on July 19, 1854; he was a merchant at Helena, Ark.), Brittain D. Clopton (was born March 9, 1835, and died February 4, 1881, at Columbia, Tenn.), Charles C. (was born March 16, 1837, and died near Memphis, Tenn., December 24, 1854, while on a visit), Jack Hoggatt (was born in October, 1843, and died on May 28, 1855), Matilda L., Helena (died in April, 1858), and Fannie (who was the first of the children to die, her death occurring when but two years of age). Col. Hoggatt Clopton graduated at the University of Mississippi, in 1851, and was elected speaker to represent the Hermean Society at commencement, in which he bore the highest honor as speaker, and soon after turned his attention to planting and merchandising. He started the latter business in 1853, continued one year, and being the eldest son it became his duty to assist his father and family in planting operations. His three brothers, Jesse P., James W. and William C. were in the Confederate army, Jesse P. holding the rank of major, and James W. being in the commissary department on account of a wound received at the battle of Shiloh. William C. was but fourteen years of age when he enlisted. Col. Hoggatt entered the service in 1862, in Albert W. Johnson's regiment as lieutenant. After the war he again turned his attention to planting, and although he has experienced many heavy losses, he is now in a prosperous condition, and is one of the representative and substantial citizens of the county. His marriage to Miss Ellen S. Booker took place December 19, 1867. She was born in Columbia, Tenn., and was the daughter of James G. Booker, a Virginian by descent. She was a member of the Episcopal Church, and died in full communion with the same on May 20, 1869. Mr. Clopton has remained single since. He is a member of the

Masonic fraternity, and in politics he affiliates with the Democratic party. He is of purely English origin, and may well be proud of his ancestors, as many of them have been distinguished men. One of them, Sir Hugh Clopton by name, was Lord Mayor of London in the reign of King Henry the Eighth, and lies entombed by the side of Shakespeare, in Stratford Church on Avon. And another ancestor, Capt. John Hoggatt, his great-grandfather, commanded a company in the War for Independence, and now lies buried near Nashville, Tenn., with a record of his career written on his monument. He was of English descent, and a native of Virginia, and was a farmer by occupation. Mr. Clopton took an extensive trip all over England, Ireland, Wales and Scotland, and Continental Europe the past spring, summer and fall, and was at the tomb of Shakespeare and Sir Hugh Clopton. They were contemporaries, and are buried side by side in Stratford Church on (the river) Avon, in Warwick County, England, about 100 miles west of London.

Jesse P. Clopton, planter, Marvell, Ark. The principal part of his life Mr. Clopton has followed, with substantial success, the occupation to which he was reared and in which he is now engaged, farming. He is one of the largest land owners in Phillips County, is also one of its recognized leading agriculturists and merchants, and as a man, no less than a citizen, is highly esteemed. His birth occurred near the old Jackson Hermitage, Davidson County, Tenn., March 4, 1839, and is the son of John Haggatt and Matilda C. (Drake) Clopton, both natives of Tennessee. The parents were married in their native State but immigrated to North Mississippi in 1844 and there the father died July 26, 1855. The mother was a descendant of Sir Francis Drake, and died in this county June 6, 1865. Their marriage resulted in the birth of ten children: Haggatt (born February 6, 1831), John A. (deceased, born January 23, 1833), Brittain D. (deceased, born March 9, 1835), Charles C. (deceased, born March 28, 1837), Jesse P., James M. (born March 16, 1841), Jack M. (born October 8, 1843), Matilda L. (deceased, born November 29, 1845), William C. (born March 16, 1848) and Fannie (deceased, born January 29, 1851). Jesse P. was but twelve years of age when he moved with his parents from Mississippi to this county and here he finished his growth. He received such educational advantages as were attainable in the common schools, but afterward completed his schooling by attending Lebanon College, Tenn. After this he began the study of medicine, but the war broke out and he enlisted in the Confederate service in 1861, under Gen. Cleburne's demand, Fifteenth Arkansas Regiment. He served until he was disabled, was then discharged and was out of service for four months. He then again joined the army, was soon after captured and almost directly exchanged, being on parole for about two months. He was at the battle of Helena and was the first man shot at while performing the duties of adjutant-general. At the close of the war he returned home and engaged in tilling the soil. He was married January 7, 1864, to Miss Virginia C. Swan, a native of Phillips County, Ark. (born February 5, 1846, and the daughter of Major John C. Swan, who was born in Frankfort, Ky., on April 1, 1800. Major Swan came to this county in 1836, located eighteen miles west of Helena on what is known as the military road, and here he was extensively engaged in cultivating the soil, owning at one time over 1,000 acres in this county and as much in the State of Mississippi. He helped survey the military road at an early day and was one of the prominent and useful citizens. He was married in Helena, Ark., to Miss Permelia B. Raleigh, a native of Virginia (born November 7, 1817), and the daughter of Charles V. Raleigh. Mr. Raleigh was a native of North Carolina, and the capital of that State was named in his honor. He was a descendant of Sir Walter Raleigh. Maj. Swan died in this county December 25, 1849, and his wife died September 9, 1867. They were the parents of three daughters and one son: John R. (was a captain in the Confederate army and died at his home, a number of years after the war). Mary J. (deceased), Fannie A. (deceased) and Virginia C. (who is the youngest child). To Mr. and Mrs. Clopton were born five children, two now living: Jesse P. (deceased), Virginia (deceased), John H.

(deceased), Agnes C. and Eugenia (both at home). Mr. Clopton is the owner of 1,776 acres of land, 1,100 acres under cultivation, and raises annually from 250 to 400 bales of cotton. In March, 1872, he opened a store of general merchandise in Marvell and carries a stock of goods valued at $5,000. He buys and ships cotton and is the leading business man of Marvell. In politics, he is Democratic, casting his first presidential vote for H. Seymour, and he held the office of circuit clerk for two years. He is a member of the K. of H. and the K. & L. of H. He and his family are members of the Episcopal Church. Mr. Clopton has a large cotton-gin and saw-mill on his plantation.

Roland J. Cook, planter, Barton, Ark. Phillips County is acknowledged by all to be one of the best agricultural portions of the State, and as such its citizens are men of advanced ideas and considerable prominence. A worthy man of this class is found in the person of Roland J. Cook. He was originally from Yalobusha County, Miss., where his birth occurred October 27, 1839, and is the son of James and Frances (Brooks) Cook, natives of North Carolina and Tennessee, respectively. The father was born in 1810 and the mother in 1814. They were married in Mississippi, moved from there to Phillips County, Ark., in 1856, and located on the farm where Roland J. now resides. The principal part of this land was then covered with wood, but it was cleared by Mr. Cook and his son. James Cook was a carpenter by trade, and built the house in which our subject is now living. After coming to Arkansas he turned his attention exclusively to farming, and this continued up to the time of his death, which occurred in 1873. The mother died in 1866. The father was a Whig in politics, sympathized with the South, but never approved of secession. There were born to their marriage eight children, six now living, Roland J. being the eldest. The latter spent his school days in Mississippi and Arkansas, and in June, 1861, enlisted in the Second Arkansas (Confederate) Infantry, serving in the same until after the battle of Chickamauga, when he was severely wounded by a gunshot in the right hand and the left breast. He was orderly sergeant, and was in

many prominent engagements: Shiloh, Murfreesboro and Perryville, Ky. After being wounded
he was taken prisoner, but only retained for a
short time. Returning home after the war, he
turned his attention to farming, following the
same for one year in Mississippi, and subsequently
resumed agricultural pursuits on the old homestead, where he now lives. He is the owner of
300 acres of good land, and has 150 acres under
cultivation. In 1866 he married Miss Lucy Winbourn, daughter of Rev. A. K. Winbourn, of De
Soto County, Miss. The result of this union has
been five children. Mr. and Mrs. Cook are members of the Methodist Episcopal Church, South,
and Mr. Cook is steward in the same. He is a
member of the Masonic fraternity, the K. of H.,
and in politics is a Democrat, but is conservative
in his views.

H. P. Coolidge (deceased) was born in the State
of Maine, February 7, 1812, and while still in his
early youth was taken by his parents to the Buckeye State, settling near Cincinnati, where he was
left an orphan at an early age. When about seventeen years of age he went to Louisiana and during a residence of several years in New Orleans
was a boss mechanic, being considered the complete master of his trade. While in that city he
was married to Elizabeth J. Legier, a French lady,
and in 1842 came with her and his infant son, C.
R. Coolidge, to Helena, Ark., making the trip on a
flat-boat, intending to journey on to New Orleans
for permanent residence there. The sheriff of the
county determined to make him pay annual license
for selling his goods, but he thought it a wanton
injustice, and, although intending to remain at
Helena for one month, he paid his license and determined to settle here. He rented a store building, put in a stock of goods and soon built up a
very extensive trade, so large in fact that he determined to stay here, although his original intention had been to go back to New Orleans. Helena
continued to be his home until his death, which
occurred April 23, 1872, his wife dying November
17, 1880. Of nine children born to them, two only
lived to be grown. A daughter, who married Dr. F.
N. Barke, now a resident of Helena, died January,

1887, leaving an infant daughter, Mary E. Burke,
who lives mainly with her uncle, C. R. Coolidge, in
Helena. Only one, C. R. Coolidge, is now living.
Mr. Coolidge became known all over this section of
the country, not only in his business capacity, but
in local political matters as well, and for some time
served as county and probate judge, although he
was no office seeker. He was a man who attended
strictly to his own affairs and for his many sterling
business and social qualities was beloved by all
who knew him. At one time he was offered 400
acres of land, which is now in the heart of Memphis,
Tenn., for a small sum of money, and if he had
closed the bargain he would have been worth millions of dollars. He was very liberal with his wealth
and always gave liberally to the poor and distressed,
also to schools and churches, and all worthy public
enterprises. He was very progressive in his ideas
and always endeavored to keep out of the beaten
path, and was ever ready to adopt new ideas. He
was a stanch Union man during the war and expressed his thoughts and opinions freely and
without fear. He was a prominent Mason and Odd
Fellow and a member of the Methodist Episcopal
Church. Such a man, liberal and progressive in his
views, enterprising, industrious and public-spirited,
is a blessing to any community and deserves the
highest praise which can be given him. His son,
Charles R., has erected a monument to his memory
which was made in Italy at a cost of $6,000. It is
twenty-nine feet six inches in height and is surmounted by a life-size statue of Mr. Coolidge,
which is very finely executed. Charles R. Coolidge
was born in New Orleans in November, 1836, and
came to Helena with his parents. He was brought
up in the mercantile business, which he has always
followed. He has been very successful in all his
business undertakings and has one of the handsomest residences in the city of Helena. Like his
father he is enterprising and public-spirited and is
one of the foremost citizens of Phillips County.
He was married in 1866 to Miss Elizabeth T. Ellis,
a native of Middle Tennessee, by whom he has ten
children, nine living: Henry, Charles R., Jr., Willie, Eva, Lizzie, Andrew, Ellis, Walter and Mary.
Eva, his second child, is deceased, and a younger

daughter was named for her. Mr. Coolidge was an Odd Fellow for many years and served some time in the late war and was at one time taken prisoner.

D. H. Crebs. The Planters' Compress & Storage Company of Helena, Ark., is one of the largest establishments of the kind in Southern Arkansas, and the amount of ground used by them for the successful conduct of their establishment comprises four and three-quarters acres, it being purchased by our subject in August, 1886. He immediately erected one of the finest cotton-gins in the South, and in 1887 built a compress, which was the first erected in Helena, and the first year pressed 18,000 bales of cotton. This is a large brick structure, and was owned and operated individually by Mr. Crebs until the spring of 1889, when a stock company was organized, and took the name of the Planters' Compress Company, in which Mr. Crebs has a controlling interest, and is president of the company; J. H. Lawrens is secretary, and L. Lucy, treasurer. The cotton-gin has a capacity of twenty-five to thirty bales of cotton per day. Mr. Crebs was born in Winchester, Frederick County, Va., October 30, 1836, and is a son of Henry Crebs, who was also a Virginian, and a soldier in the War of 1812, he being then only about seventeen years of age. His father was a Revolutionary soldier, and was of Scotch birth, an early settler of Virginia. Henry was a farmer by occupation, and eventually died in the town in which he was born and reared. Of his six children, four are now living. His son, D. H., was eleven years old when his father died, then began learning the machinist's trade, and in 1862 he enlisted in Company A, Second Virginia Regiment, and was wounded at Seven Pines by a gunshot, which necessitated his remaining in a hospital for some time. He was in Mat. Marra's command, but afterward joined Col. Tanner's battalion and was in all the general engagements in which his regiment participated. After the war he was left, like all soldiers, destitute, but he worked at what he could find to do, and in 1867 came to Helena and began doing business for a Mr. Barbarbroux, of Louisville. At the end of two years the company dissolved, and Mr. Crebs then began an in-

dependent career, and is still dealing in machinery. He built the first oil mills in Helena, also the first opera house, but the latter burned down in 1885. Mr. Crebs has been one of the live business men of the place, and his interest and support in all public affairs, his honesty and industry, as well as his progressive views on all matters of importance, have won him the respect of all who know him. He is a stockholder in the First National Bank and the Peoples' Bank, and by his shrewdness and tact is one of the wealthy men of the county. He has one of the handsomest residences in the city, it being situated on a natural building site, in full view of the Mississippi River, as well as the city and surrounding country. In 1876 he was united in marriage to Miss Mary Carruth, and in 1880 took for his second wife, Miss Jennie Cook, by whom he has two children: Maggie and Harry.

Job Dean, farmer and saloon man, Trenton, Ark. Mr. Dean owes his nativity to Shelby County, Tenn., where his birth occurred in 1847, and is the first and only child born to the union of Henry and Fannie (Abington) Dean, natives, respectively, of South Carolina and North Carolina. The elder Dean was a farmer and speculator in real estate. He moved to Tennessee when a young man, and was there married in 1845 to Miss Abington. He owned a great deal of land in this county at the time of his death, which occurred in 1860. The mother died in 1850, and two years later the father married Miss Laura Hudson, of Madison County, Tenn., who bore him four children, only three of whom lived to be grown: Richard (deceased, died at the age of twenty-four years of consumption), Mary H. (deceased, wife of Tobe Hamner. She was the mother of one child, Albert, who resides in Tennessee with his father, who is a minister in the Methodist Episcopal Church), Emma (wife of T. J. Leak, of Collierville, Tenn., and the mother of four children, Dean, Tigue, Emma G. and Fletcher). Our subject was educated in the common schools of his native county, and spent two years at Black Hawk, Carroll County, Miss., where he finished his education. At the age of twenty years he left school, and when twenty-nine years of age was married to Miss Maggie Davis, of Marshall County, Miss., who bore him five children, only two now living: Henry and Mamie. After marriage Mr. Dean commenced farming in Shelby County and there remained until 1874, when he moved to Marshall County, Miss., where he was engaged in tilling the soil for two years. In 1876 he came to Phillips County, Ark., cultivated the soil, but was not very successful for the first few years. In 1880 he opened the saloon business at Trenton and still runs this in connection with a family grocery. He now owns 160 acres of land with forty acres cleared, which he rents for $200 per year. Mr. Dean is a member of the Masonic fraternity, Lebanon Lodge No. 97, K. of H., and is Vice-Dictator of that organization. Politically he is a Democrat. He favors improvements for the benefit of his county and all laudable designs for the interest of the people.

Amos W. Dougherty, the fifth son in a family of fourteen children born to Isaac and Rachel (Slimp) Dougherty, made his appearance upon the stage of life in Lauderdale County, Ala., on November, 1, 1830. At the age of five he removed with his parents to Mississippi, where he was reared, educated, and learned the carpenter's trade under an older brother. In about 1860 he came to Arkansas and located in this county, and was engaged at his trade until 1887. In 1851 he was married to Miss Lucy B. Wilkes, a native of Alabama, who died in 1865, leaving five children; one of these, Indiana V., is the wife of W. J. Day, of this county. Mr. Dougherty was married the second time, in 1866, to Miss Caroline N. Dean, of this State, she surviving until in November, 1872. His third wife, Nancy J. Slayton, to whom he was married in February, 1874, came originally from Georgia, and died in July, 1876. Mr. Dougherty was married to his last wife, Mrs. Virginia D. Andrews, in November, 1877. In 1847 he enlisted in the Mexican War and served about six months, taking part in a number of skirmishes. In 1861 his patriotism still asserted itself, and he enlisted in the Confederate army, in the Seventh Arkansas Infantry, serving until his capture in April, 1865, when he was taken to Memphis and kept until the following June. He owns a small farm of forty-nine acres, and also owns a steam cotton-gin, meeting with good success in his efforts. Mr. Dougherty is a member of the Masonic order and of the K. of H. In politics is a Democrat, and a highly respected citizen.

Isaac Ehrman, wholesale and retail liquor dealer, Helena, Ark. The trade carried on in staple articles of consumption always constitutes a most important factor in the commercial resources of a city or town, and it is therefore not surprising if it finds its natural recognition in Helena. Prominent among those engaged in it is the firm of Ehrman Brothers, who have followed this business a number of years. Isaac Ehrman is a native of Rhine, Bavaria, born on November 4, 1836, and is a son of M. and Sophia (Rubel) Ehrman, who were natives of Germany. The father came to America in 1878, and is now a resident of Memphis, Tenn., and is in the eighty-second year of his age. To his marriage were born eight children, six now living, and all in America: Isaac, Emelia (wife of Jacob Wertheimer, of Pine Bluff), Hannah (wife of J. Nathan, who is a member of the firm of Nathan & Oppenheimer, of Memphis), Mrs. Wertheimer (of Birmingham, Ala.), Mrs. Alice Wolf (of Columbus, Miss.) and Emanuel. Isaac Ehrman was reared and educated in Germany, where he remained until 1853, and when fifteen years of age, took passage at Havre, and landed at New Orleans after an ocean voyage of sixty days. He went to Fayette, Miss., and kept books for his uncle until 1860, when he returned to Europe. In 1861 he returned to Mississippi, but went from there to Memphis, Tenn., where he was engaged in the dry-goods business until 1873; was also part of the time interested in the liquor business, and at the above-mentioned date he came to Helena. He was married in 1863 to Miss Cecil Wertheimer, who bore him four children: Fannie, Ophelia, Eddie and Blanche. Mr. Ehrman is a member of the Masonic fraternity, K. of H., K. of P., Royal Arcanum, etc. He was alderman for four years, and was a stockholder in the People's Saving Bank. He is also a stockholder in the Opera House and Fair Association, and is a prominent man of Helena.

L. A. Fitzpatrick, of the firm of Jacks, Fitzpatrick & Co., wholesale druggists at Helena, was born in Chickasaw County, Miss., in November, 1848, and is the son of B. F. and E. J. (Moore) Fitzpatrick, natives of Georgia and Alabama, respectively. The parents moved to Mississippi at quite an early date, but from there went to Mobile, Ala., where they are now living, the father being a cotton factor. L. A. Fitzpatrick's time in youth was divided between assisting on the farm and in attending the common schools. In 1864 he enlisted in the Confederate army, and served one year. In 1868 he came to Helena, Ark., and began clerking in a drug store, but in 1872 he purchased an interest in the business of Jacks & Moore. In 1879 the firm title was changed to Jacks & Co., and in 1884 the present company was formed. They carry a stock of goods valued at $25,000, and do an annual business of $200,000. They are the largest dealers in drugs in Helena, and are enjoying a liberal patronage, being careful and reliable men. Mr. Fitzpatrick was married in 1872 to Miss Alzena F. Jacks, a daughter of Dr. T. M. Jacks, and to this union were born seven children living: Katie, Lotta M., Ben. F., L. A., Jr., Hopkins R., Curtis H. and Ione. Mr. Fitzpatrick is a member of the I. O. O. F., and Knights of Pythias, American Legion of Honor, Royal Arcanum and Ladies and Knights of Honor. He held the office of city treasurer for several years, and was also alderman for some time. He is a large stockholder in the Jacks Real Estate Company, the Arkansas Building Association and the Electric Light Company.

Robert FitzHugh. In reviewing the contents of this volume, no adequate idea of the agricultural affairs of Phillips County or of its substantial citizens, could be formed which failed to make mention of Mr. FitzHugh and the excellent estate which he owns. His residence tract contains 1,570 acres, and is admirably adapted to raising all kinds of grain indigenous to this climate, and besides this he owns 700 acres in another tract, and in all has 600 acres under cultivation. Everything about his property pronounces him to be an agriculturist of enterprise and progress, and such he

is acknowledged by all to be. He was born in Livingston County, N. Y., December 18, 1826, and this alone speaks volumes for him as a progressive and enterprising citizen. He is a son of Richard P. and Mary A. FitzHugh, the former a native of Maryland and the latter of York State. Robert, our subject, first moved from his native State to Ohio in 1863, thence to Michigan in 1866, and still later settled in Phillips County, Ark. In 1865 he married Miss Sarah T. Hubbard, a daughter of Dr. Hubbard, of Phillips County, and six children are the result of their union: Mary A., Richard H., Annie S., Flora B., Mabel and Foster C. Mrs. FitzHugh is a member of the Episcopal Church, and her husband is a Democrat in his political views. His father removed to York State when seventeen years of age and followed farming there, until his death in 1863, at the age of sixty-three years. His wife died in 1882, also in New York, having reached the age of sixty-seven years. Of seven children born to them, three are now living.

N. J. Fritzon, mayor of Helena and dealer in queensware, has a life record of more than usual interest and seems by nature to be a man fitted to rule. He was born across the ocean, his birth occurring in Sweden near the Baltic Sea, in October, 1838. At an early day he displayed the energy and enterprise which has since characterized his career, and his youth was spent in learning the shoemaker's trade and in studying music, in which he became very proficient, being able to play almost any instrument which was put into his hands. Life in his native land was not suited to one of his energetic and enterprising disposition, and he accordingly determined to cross the ocean and see what life in a new land had in store for him, and in 1857 first set foot on American soil at Boston, the voyage from Gothenberg to this point occupying a period of five weeks. He immediately went to Moline, Ill., thence to Rock Island, working at his trade, and the year 1859 found him in St. Louis, from which point he went to New Orleans a short time after. This city continued to be his home until the bombardment of Fort Sumter, when he returned to St. Louis, thence back to

Rock Island, Ill., where he enlisted in Company A, Ninth Illinois Cavalry, and was made chief musician and bugler of his regiment. In 1862 he was mustered out of service, by order of the war department, and was then musician for eight months on Gen. Steele's staff. In February, 1863, he came to Helena and engaged in the grocery business and this was his exclusive means of a livelihood for twenty-one years, but was a very lucrative one. His stock of queensware is very large and of an exceptionally fine quality, and as he is an honest and upright man of business, his sales are large. He has been connected with the fire department of the city since the war and for several years has been its chief. In 1888 he was elected mayor of Helena and his record as an official, as well as a business man, will bear the investigation of one and all, for not a shadow can be advanced derogatory to his reputation. He is a Royal Arch Mason, and for a number of years he has been a member of the town council and the board of health. He was married in 1867 to Miss Mary B. Nixon, by whom he has five children: Sidney H., John E., Mary B., Nelson J. and Eudora C.

Bogan N. Gist is the son of Thomas Gist, and was born in South Carolina in 1852. Thomas Gist, also a native of South Carolina, dates his existence from 1816, immigrating to what is now Lee County, S. C., in 1857, where he died in 1887. He was married in South Carolina to Miss Mary Bogan, who passed away in 1865, having borne eight children, two sons and two daughters now living. Bogan N., the eldest in order of birth, received an excellent education in the schools of his native State, afterward completing his studies at a prominent military school in Kentucky. He resided with his parents until reaching his majority, and on May 3, 1878, was married to Miss Mary Blanche Heineman, born in Mississippi, and a daughter of Charles and Mildreth Heineman. Mrs. Heineman is now living in Phillips County, Ark., and her husband died in Murfreesboro, Ala. Mr. Gist and wife are the parents of one child, Bogan N., Jr. They have resided on their present place since 1872, on which Mr. Gist erected a handsome and commodious home at a cost of $200,000. He owns about 640 acres of land, and with 500 acres under cultivation, located sixteen miles west of Helena. The farm is admirably adapted to the growing of hay, grain and vegetables, and presents a fine appearance in its carefully cultivated state. Mr. Gist is quite extensively engaged in stock raising, from which he receives a comfortable income. Politically he is a Democrat, and is a citizen of whom Phillips County may well be proud; honest, enterprising and a leader in any movement that suggests the present or future growth of the community.

Thomas Clark Glasscock, a planter and stock raiser of Cypress Township, was reared and educated in Alabama, his native State, also being married there in 1856 to Miss Isabella Couch, whose birth occurred in Morgan County, Ala., November 22, 1836. She was a daughter of Uriah and Elizabeth (Turney) Couch, both of Tennessee origin. In 1861 Mr. Glasscock enlisted in the Twenty-ninth Alabama Infantry, and served over three years. In 1867 he immigrated from Alabama to Tennessee, and two years later moved to Phillips County, Ark., and located on the farm on which he now lives, as superintendent, remaining until 1874, when he returned to Alabama, and in 1881 came back to this county and again took charge of the same plantation, consisting of 1,400 acres, with over 400 acres under cultivation. Mr. Glasscock was born in Blount County, Ala., August 11, 1837, and was a son of John R. and Martha (Rutherford) Glasscock, natives of Tennessee and Alabama, respectively. John R. Glasscock was born about 1822, a son of Gregory Glasscock, who was also born in Tennessee, of English descent, and moved to Alabama when John R. was a boy of eight years. He took part in numerous early Indian wars, and is still living in Cullman County, Ala. His wife was born in 1824, and died in 1887, having been the mother of twelve children, eight of whom are still living. Thomas C. Glasscock is a member of the Masonic order, holding the office of Worshipful Master of his lodge, and is a strong Democrat in politics. Himself and wife have no children of their own, but reared one child, Minnie M. (Mrs. Couch), who still resides with them.

James P. H. Graham is a native of North Carolina, but was reared in Mississippi, and received his education in the common schools of that State. At the age of twenty-two he commenced farming for himself, and in December, 1860, was married to Miss Sarah Cathey, whose birth occurred in Mississippi, on October 10, 1842. She died in January, 1872, being the mother of four children, one of whom, Elizabeth A. D., is still living. In November, 1872, Mr. Graham married Sarah E. Jarrett, born in Alabama, in August,1851,a daughter of Freeman and Mary (McMillen) Jarrett, and a sister of Joseph F. Jarrett, whose biography appears in this work. They are parents of seven children, five living: Mary M., Josie E., Joseph W., Mittie P. and Edner L. Our subject was born in Cleveland County, N. C., on January 27, 1838. Arthur H. Graham, his father, was born in North Carolina, on September 17, 1809, and removed to Mississippi in 1839, coming from that State to this county in 1869. He was married on January 23, 1834, to Miss Elizabeth D. S. Wray, also of North Carolina, born in 1815, and a daughter of James Wray, of English descent. She died in 1844, leaving five children, two of whom survive: James P. H. and William Walter. The senior Mr. Graham was engaged in agricultural pursuits until his death, which occurred in November, 1887. He was the son of John Graham, of Irish descent, though a native of Cleveland County, N. C. James Graham came to this county with his father in 1869, and has since resided here. He was a resident of Mississippi at the time of the breaking out of the war, and enlisted in March, 1862, in Company A of the Ninth Mississippi Infantry, serving until December, 1863, when he was taken prisoner at the battle of Missionary Ridge, and carried to Rock Island, where he was confined until May 3, 1865. He was then exchanged and received his discharge at Natchez, Miss. Although captured early in the war, he participated in four great battles of the war, Shiloh, Murfreesboro, Chickamauga and Missionary Ridge. Mr. Graham now owns a fine farm of 160 acres, with 112 acres under cultivation, upon which are improvements, buildings, orchards, &c. He is a

stanch Democrat, and although not an office seeker, was elected justice of the peace in 1884, which position he held for a year. He then resigned on account of other business matters requiring his attention. He is a member of the K. of H. and of the Christian Church, his wife belonging to the Baptist Church.

H. M. Grant, M. D., and ex-State senator, was born in Christian County, Ky., in May, 1829, and is one of two surviving members of a family of twelve children born to Joshua D. and Henrietta (McNeal) Grant, the former a native of North Carolina, and the latter of Virginia. Both parents were taken to Kentucky when young, and there they were married and spent the greater portion of their lives, the mother's death occurring in that State, and the father's in Northwest Arkansas, he being a farmer and merchant by occupation. Both grandfathers served in the War of 1812. Dr. Grant received the earlier part of his education in Kentucky, and completed his studies at McKendrie College, Lebanon, Ill. At the age of seventeen years he began his medical studies, and favored with excellent preparatory training he was enabled to at once enter upon a successful career. In 1849, when in his twentieth year, he graduated from the Louisville Medical College, and his first practice was at La Fayette, Ky., but here he only remained a short time. In 1850 he came to Helena, Ark., which only had about 200 inhabitants at that time, rented an office, and hung out his "shingle," and is now the oldest medical practitioner in the town. His success has been very gratifying, and to say that he is a superior physician and surgeon is not detrimental to other physicians of the town and county. At the opening of the war he began drilling a corps of soldiers preparatory to entering the service, but a few days before ready to begin active duty his horse fell with him, injuring him so badly that he was insensible for several days. His right arm was severely injured, and rendered him unfit for active military duty, which has always been a source of much regret to him, as he had the requisites necessary for an excellent soldier. He rendered good service, however, in dressing the wounded at different battles, and in this capacity his labors were invaluable. While on board a boat going down the river he fell asleep and came very near being drowned, as the boat was commencing to sink rapidly, and he was only saved from a watery grave by his companions pulling him out at the skylight by his injured arm. This so aggravated the difficulty that the joint became stiff, and he has never since had good use of it. He has filled the position of mayor of Helena for several terms, also councilman, and in 1866 was elected to the State senate, serving by re-election four years, and was again chosen to the position in 1880, serving another four years by re-election. He was the first mayor of Helena after the war, the last man elected to the senate before the reconstruction period, and the first white man elected after. He has always been a man of strict integrity, sterling worth, and his progressive and sound views on all public matters has made him well and favorably known to the residents of Phillips County. He was first married in the State of Illinois to Miss Sarah E. Roach, and by her had one child, who is now deceased. His second marriage was consummated in the State of Kentucky, in 1848, to Miss Sarah Griffin, by whom he also had one child: Sarah C., wife of H. P. Grant. His present wife (who was Araminta J. Blaine) is a relative of James G. Blaine. They also have one child: Lillian H. The Doctor is a Royal Arch Mason, a member of the I. O. O. F., and he and wife belong to the Episcopal Church. His sister, Mrs. Emeline S. Daniel, resides in Mount Vernon, Ill., and a brother, Judge A. M. Grant, died at that place.

Nathaniel Lee Graves, a Tennesseean by birth, has been a resident of this county since four years of age. He was born in Giles County, Tenn., in 1836, being a son of Alexander and Ann (Graves) Graves, natives of Granville County, N. C., and Henry County, Va., respectively, representatives of two distinct families. Alexander Graves came to Arkansas in 1840, and located in Phillips County, where he was engaged in farming until his death in 1863, his wife following one year later. They were the parents of seven children, three of whom are still living. The principal of this sketch was first married in March, 1869, to Miss Mary E. Boone, a daughter of O. C. Boone, a lineal descendant of the noted Daniel Boone. She died in 1876, leaving two sons: Alexander W. and Nathaniel J. Mr. Graves was married to his second wife, Florence Carson, a native of Natchez, Miss., April 1, 1878. Mr. Graves owns a fine farm of 2,560 acres of land, situated thirteen miles west of Helena, of which 1,300 acres are under cultivation. His principal crop is cotton, and he grows of this product from five to seven hundred bales per annum. He also raises considerable stock, having on hand at the present time about seventy head of horses, 125 head of cattle and 300 sheep. On his plantation there are fifty colored families and eight white families of laborers engaged in the operation of this immense plantation. Mr. Graves also owns and operates his own steam cotton-gin. He is a member of the Knights of Pythias, Knights of Honor and of the United Workman. He and wife are members of the Old School Presbyterian Church. Mr. Graves is one of the most influential men in the county, and takes an active interest in all public enterprises.

F. M. Hawkins, farmer, Vineyard, Ark. In the year 1836, in Tennessee, there was born to the union of Jehu and Sarah (Owens) Hawkins, a son, F. M. Hawkins, who was the youngest of three children, only one, our subject, now living. The parents were natives of North Carolina and Tennessee, respectively, and the father came to Arkansas in 1847, locating ten miles east of Jacksonport in Jackson County. After remaining there for four or five years he moved to Missouri and settled near Prairie City, where his death occurred sometime during the war. Mrs. Hawkins died in 1837. After the death of Mrs. Hawkins, the father married Miss Armstrong who bore him three children: Henry, Winfield and Mary. Mrs. Hawkins died in 1849 and Mr. Hawkins' third marriage was to a sister of his second wife. F. M. Hawkins was principally reared in Jackson County and received the major part of his education at home. He commenced for himself at the age of eighteen years by tilling the soil and this has been the principal pursuit through life. In 1861 he joined the army as a private and was promoted first to fifth sergeant, then to lieutenant and later to captain of the Nineteenth Arkansas Regiment and served in the Trans-Mississippi Department, Tappan's brigade and Churchill's division for nearly four years. He was in the battles of Mansfield (La.), Pleasant Hill (La.) and Jenkins' Ferry. He was captured at Arkansas Post and was sent to Camp Douglas, Chicago, where he remained until March, 1863. He then succeeded in making his escape. He returned to his company at Little Rock, and his command surrendered at Shreveport (La.) at the close of the war. Mr. Hawkins then went to Kentucky, remained there eight years and was engaged in cultivating the soil. In 1872 he came to this county and bought 117 acres of land the following year and on that he now resides. To the original tract he has added enough to make 353 acres, and now has 100 acres of deadwood, preparatory to clearing. He produces on his farm about forty bales of cotton, but devotes a great deal of his time to the raising of stock. He has some graded cattle and hogs and is also raising some horses. He was married in 1874 to Mrs. Bettie Brady (*nee* Payne) of Shelby County, Ky., and the daughter of John Payne and wife (*nee* Nugen) of the same State. Mr. Hawkins is a member of the Old School Presbyterian Church, and Mrs. Hawkins is a member of the Missionary Baptist Church.

William Harvey Henderson is a son of Hampton and Mary (Graham) Henderson, the former of whom died when William H. was about fifteen years of age. He lived with his mother until twenty-two years old, when he began farming for himself, and in 1854 was married to Miss Susan Steward, a native of Georgia, who died in the following year. Mr. Henderson married his present wife, Miss Margaret King, in January, 1860; she was born in Mississippi in 1839. They are the parents of nine children, four of whom are still living: Thomas J., James H., Sarah V. (the wife of William H. Allison, of this county) and Mary B. (wife of Allen Terry). In 1859 Mr. Henderson purchased his present farm, consisting of 160 acres, which was at that time wild land, with no improvements, and now he has over seventy acres

under cultivation. His principal crop is cotton, and he also raises considerable corn as well as cattle and hogs. He is a prominent Democrat, and himself and wife are members of the Missionary Baptist Church. Mr. Henderson was born in Gibson County, Tenn., November 14, 1831. Hampton Henderson was of English descent, his father being born in England. He moved to Tennessee when a young man, and died in 1844. His wife was a native of North Carolina, and died in 1862. They were the parents of eight children, two of whom are still living: Thomas and William H. (the principal of this sketch).

Richard B. Higgins, a planter of Phillips County of considerable prominence, is a native of Phillips County, Ark., his birth occurring October 27, 1852. His father, Richard Higgins, was born in Lexington, Ky., in 1827, and in 1846 immigrated to Crittenden County, Ark. Two years later he moved to Phillips County, where he became an extensive planter, owning at the date of his death, in 1862, over 1,300 acres of valuable land. He was the son of Joel Higgins, a Kentuckian by birth, and of Scotch-Irish descent. Richard Higgins, Sr., was married in Kentucky to Miss Elizabeth B. Brand, born in Lexington, Ky., in 1829, and is now residing in that city. By her marriage with Mr. Higgins, she became the mother of five children, the subject of this sketch being the fourth in order of birth. Richard B. received his education in the schools of Kentucky, and in 1879 was married to Miss Mary C. Rankin, of Kentucky, who was born in 1859. To their union these children have been born: Richard B. and Robert P. Mr. Higgins is farming the land which he inherited from his father, consisting of 770 acres, with 500 under a careful and successful state of cultivation. He raises over 200 bales of cotton annually, and the many improvements incident to his ownership, demonstrate his spirit of energy and progression. Mr. and Mrs. Higgins are members in high standing of the Christian Church. The former is a Democrat, having cast his first political vote for Samuel J. Tilden. He served as deputy sheriff for his county for two years, discharging the duties of that office in a highly commendable manner. In societies he is identified with the K. of P., Legion of Honor, and the United Workman.

William Hildreth, one of the most promising of Phillips County's young and prospering farmers, was born in Paris, Ky., April 23, 1855. His father, Joseph A. Hildreth, was also a native of Kentucky, where he is now residing, and recognized as among the leading planters. He is the son of John Hildreth, of Virginia nativity. Joseph A. was married to Miss Sallie Smith, of Bourbon, Ky., who died in 1878, having borne six children, three sons and three daughters, all living. William is the oldest in order of birth. In 1877 he left his home and came to Phillips County, several years later purchasing his farm on which he now resides. This farm consists of 103 acres, with over ninety acres carefully cultivated. In 1880 Mr. Hildreth was united in marriage with Miss Josie Keller, who was born in Paris, Ky., in 1856, and a daughter of Patrick and Margaret Keller. Two children have been born to their union: Mary and Belle. Mr. Hildreth is a Democrat, and a gentleman who takes an active interest in all matters pertaining to the benefit or growth of the county.

S. H. Holtzclaw, farmer and stockman, Vineyard, Ark. Phillips County is rapidly coming into a position as one of the foremost stock counties in the State, and it is but uttering a plain fact to say, that to a few men in this community is due the credit for advancing stock interests here and establishing a reputation in this department which is bound to stand for years. Mr. Holtzclaw has had not a little to do toward developing this industry, and, if for no other account, he is accorded a worthy place in this volume. He was born in Mississippi in 1849, and his parents, E. and E. (Green) Holtzclaw, were natives of North Carolina and South Carolina, and of German and English origin, respectively. E. Holtzclaw came to Mississippi in 1849, and followed farming on rented land until about 1855, when he came to Phillips County, Ark. He bought 160 acres on Big Creek, and afterward added to this amount, until he was the owner of 320 acres, with 160 acres improved. Canebrake was standing all over the table-lands at that time and game abounded in this section, even up to 1860.

From 1855 to 1865 fire was applied plentifully to the cane to drive out the panthers, bears and wildcats, for it was almost impossible to raise calves or pigs while these animals were so numerous. Mr. Holtzclaw owned about twenty-three negroes, old and young, and was one of the leading farmers of this section. He died in 1874, and his wife four years previous. Both were members of the Baptist Church. They were the parents of ten children, seven of whom lived to be grown, and four are now living: Mary J. (wife of William H. McGrew, of Phillips County), S. H. (our subject), Warren (resides in this county), Matheney (wife of William Wooten, resides in this county). S. H. Holtzclaw attained his growth and received a meager education in Phillips County, his school days being cut short by the breaking out of the war. This deficiency he has made up to a great extent since reaching manhood and by his own exertions. At the age of twenty-one years he commenced farming for himself on rented land, and this continued for three years. In 1874, or at the time of the death of his father, he assumed control of the latter's property, wound up the business, and in 1875 purchased eighty acres of fine land. Since then he has added 120 acres of land, and has 170 acres under cultivation, on which he produces about sixty-five bales of cotton, or about three-fourths of a bale per acre. He also raises plenty of corn and hay to keep the stock on his farm, and very rarely fails to have corn to sell. He was married in 1878 to Miss Maggie Chappell, of Phillips County, and the daughter of Christopher and Ann (Green) Chappell, natives of North Carolina. Her parents came to Arkansas about 1834, and settled on what is now known as the Chappell place. The father was a noted hunter in this section, and he and Uncle Bill McGraw and Andy Adams were the hunters in this county in early days, killing as many as five or six bears in one hunt. To the union of Mr. and Mrs. Holtzclaw were born five children, three now living: C. J. (deceased), H. G., Charner (deceased), Ervie Ophelia and Sylvestus. Mr. and Mrs. Holtzclaw are both members of the Christian Church.

E. C. Hornor, merchant, Helena, Ark. The

trade in general dry goods has long constituted one of the leading commercial pursuits of the country, and in this line in Helena is found a thoroughly representative house controlled by E. C. Hornor, who carries the most complete and extensive stock of goods to be had in the city. He was born in Helena April 24, 1859, and is a son of William and Anna (Reynolds) Hornor, natives of Kentucky. The father was a merchant, and was one of the early settlers of Phillips County, Ark. During the late war he was an officer in the quartermaster's department, and died while on duty. The mother is now the wife of James W. Wickersham, of Fort Smith, Ark. E. C. Hornor, the youngest of three children, received his education in Helena. He began clerking in a store when sixteen years of age, with McKenzie, Hornor & Co., and by industrious habits and economy he saved sufficient means to enable him to start in business for himself. In 1884 he invested in a small stock of goods, valued at perhaps $500, and by strict attention to business he soon built up a good trade, and now has one of the neatest and best equipped stores in the city, with a stock of goods valued at $40,000. During the year 1889 he did a business of $85,000. He employs nine men, and although he is the youngest business man in the city, he is a bright factor in the mercantile affairs of the city. He was married in December, 1887, to Miss M. Blanche Morten, of Sumnerville, Tenn., and the fruits of the union have been two sons, Morten and William Edward.

Thomas H. Hubbard. Like many, and perhaps the most of the representative citizens of Phillips County, Ark., Mr. Hubbard is a Virginian, his birth occurring in Halifax County in June, 1843, being a son of Dr. H. C. and Ann M. (Osborne) Hubbard, who were also Virginians, the former's birth occurring in 1804, and the latter's in 1809. Their respective deaths were in Cumberland and Buckingham Counties, in 1873 and 1852. Dr. Hubbard was a graduate of the Ohio Medical College at Cincinnati, Ohio, and practiced his profession in Cumberland County, Va., until his death, being also engaged in farming. After the death of our subject's mother, he married Miss Sallie P.

Swann. He and his first wife were members of the Missionary Baptist Church, and in his political views he was a Whig. Thomas H. Hubbard is the second of their five children, two now living, the other member being William O. His early schooling was received in Cumberland County, and upon the opening of the war he joined the Confederate service, and became a member of the Twenty-first Virginia Infantry, and two years later joined the Third Virginia Cavalry. He was in many battles, and was wounded at Cedar Mountain, by a gun-shot, in the breast and left arm, and surrendered at Appomattox Court House. After returning home he resumed his farming operations, but in 1870 moved to Coahoma County, Miss., and at the end of eight years removed to Phillips County, Ark. He was married, in 1880, to Miss Julia Nixon, a native of Brownsville, Miss., and by her is the father of two children: Henry C. and Louise. Mr. Hubbard is a thrifty farmer, careful, prudent and economical, and those who know him best recognize in him a good friend and neighbor. He and wife are members of the Presbyterian Church, and in his political views he is a Democrat.

Edward L. Hubbard, well and favorably known to a host of acquaintances in this community, was born in Phillips County, September 26, 1849, and during his long residence here has become well known for his many sterling qualities. He is progressive in his views, and the advanced state of the agricultural facilities of the county is due to him as well as to his neighbors. His plantation comprises 667 acres of land, and of this 300 acres are under cultivation. His opportunities for acquiring an education were above the average, for he supplemented his primary education, which he received in the State of Ohio, by attending an excellent school in St. Louis. He and his sister Sarah are the only surviving members of a family of five children, born to Dr. John M. and Adaline P. (King) Hubbard, the former a native of the "Nutmeg State," and the latter of Louisiana. The Doctor was a man of exceptionally fine mind, and was exceedingly well educated, being a graduate of Yale College and also of a medical college.

Possessing the spirit of adventure, and thinking to better his fortunes he pushed westward, and after practicing his profession for some time in Natchez, Miss., he went to Louisiana, where he married and made his home until his removal in 1837 to Phillips County, Ark. His labors to alleviate the sufferings of the sick and afflicted prospered, and the excellent health which many of the residents of the county now enjoy, is due to his skill and talent. He also gave considerable attention to planting, and became well-to-do. Owing to his fidelity to these callings his own health became wrecked, and while in St. Louis, in 1871, trying to revive his failing energies his death occurred, he being sixty years of age at the time. His wife died in Phillips County when a comparatively young woman, her demise occurring in 1852. Our immediate subject has had charge of his present property since 1872, and in his political views is a Democrat.

Obadiah B. Hudson is the son of Henry Hudson, who was born in Scotland about 1774, and after his marriage emigrated to the United States, locating in Kentucky, where he died in 1850. His second wife, Nancy Williams, was born in Tennessee in 1796, and became the mother of fourteen children, of whom O. B. Hudson, the principal of this sketch, is the only survivor. Mr. Hudson was the father of four children by his first marriage. Obadiah B. was born in McCracken County, Ky., February 8, 1836, and remained in that State until thirteen years of age. He never attended school but one day in his life, and all of the education which he received was by studying at home and by practical experience with the world. At the age of thirteen he went to Louisiana and was employed on a boat on the Mississippi River for three years. In 1858, returning to Kentucky, he commenced farming in Ballard County, and in the fall of that year was married to Susan A. Williams, a native of that county, who was born in 1844. She was a daughter of James and Cinda R. Williams. They are the parents of eleven children, seven living: Rosella (wife of John T. Moore), Mittann (wife of William F. Carliss), Imogene, Joseph S., Fred G., William T. and Maggie B. Mr. Hudson remained in Kentucky only one year after his marriage,

when he removed to Arkansas and located in Phillips County, buying a house and lot at La Grange, and was employed as a brick mason for about twelve years. At the beginning of the war he enlisted in the Confederate army and served about three months, when he was taken sick and received his discharge. In 1867 he purchased a farm of 820 acres in Phillips County, at which time he was elected collector of the county, a position the duties of which he has ably discharged for twenty-two years. In 1872 he sold his farm and removed to Helena, where he resided until 1882, then buying 160 acres of land, with 125 acres under cultivation. He has had a number of narrow escapes while performing his duties as collector, having been shot at a number of times and hit six times, once in the face, causing the loss of the right eye, twice in the body and once in the right leg, just below the knee. He is a member of the Knights of Honor and of the Methodist Episcopal Church, South, to which his wife also belongs.

W. D. Hutchinson is a worthy successor of W. D. Hutchinson, who is remembered by the old pioneers of Phillips County, as one of their respected number, now long since gone to his last resting place. Mr. Hutchinson was born in the State of Mississippi, in 1833, being a son of James A. and Catharine Hutchinson, also natives of that State. He came to Arkansas with his father in 1851, and settled in this county, where he was engaged in farming until his death, with the exception of the years which he devoted to the cause of the Confederacy. Enlisting in 1862 in Capt. Anderson's company of Dobbin's regiment, he was taken sick shortly after the battle of Helena, on July 4, 1863, and being unable to perform further active duty, received his discharge and returned home, and again engaged in farming, but died in 1867. Previous to his enlistment he was a captain of a company of militia. He was a member of the A. F. & A. M., and was in good circumstances at the time of his death, and left a farm of 320 acres to his wife and eight children, in a good state of cultivation. His wife, Mary E. (Hicks) Hutchinson, was a daughter of E. A. and Lucretia (Dickens) Hicks, originally from North Carolina. Mr. Hicks came to Phillips County in

1844, and at the time of his death was one of the largest, if not the most extensive, land owner in the county; he was also a prominent member of the I. O. O. F. Previous to his demise in 1850, he divided his property among his eight children, three of whom are still living: Mary E. (is the oldest), E. A. (of Barton, Arkansas) and Emma (wife of John Hicks, of Little Rock). Mrs. Hicks was a member of the Methodist Episcopal Church, South, and died in 1859. Of the family of eight children of Mr. and Mrs. Hutchinson, four only survive; the three daughters (residents of Memphis, Tenn.): Frances (wife of John King, is the mother of one daughter, Ada May), Mary (is the wife of James K. Wooten, and has three children: James W., Linceain and Mary C.), Emma B. (wife of Pat Rhodes) and Albert E. (a farmer of Phillips County, and who married a Mrs. Tullea (nee Meserole), and is the father of one son: Albert E. Hutchinson). Mrs. Hutchinson still resides on the old homestead, and is a highly respected lady, and a prominent member of the Methodist Episcopal Church, South, in which she takes an active part, giving her time, money and influence to all enterprises for the good of the community in which she lives.

Thomas M. Jacks, Jr., the efficient surveyor of Phillips County and one of its truly respected citizens, is a native of this county, being a son of Dr. Thomas M. and Freelove (French) Jacks. The former was born in Rutherford County, N. C., and received the rudiments of his literary education at the public schools of Huntsville, Ala., after which he attended medical college at Louisville, Ky., and Jefferson Medical College, at Philadelphia, Penn. Dr. Jack's father, Rev. David Jacks, was also a native of Rutherford County, N. C. He (Thomas M., Sr.) came to Arkansas in 1849 and settled at Sterling, at the mouth of the St. Francis River, where he engaged in the practice of his profession, and also at Phillips' Bayou. Subsequently, or in 1852, he came to Helena and was associated with Dr. Silverberg in practice, and also in the drug business. In 1866 he entered into partnership with John P. Moore in the real estate and banking business and in carrying on a drug store. He was

a very influential man in the county, and represented his district in Congress in 1863. He was in the sixty-third year of his age at the time of his death in 1883, and was the owner of immense landed estates situated in the counties of Phillips, Lee and Arkansas, and Coahoma County, Miss. The Doctor was married twice. By his first marriage, which occurred at Sterling, Ark., in 1846, he was the father of five children, two sons and three daughters, all of whom are living. Mrs. Jacks dying in 1869, Dr. Jacks was again married in 1872 to Miss Elizabeth Wills, of Helena, by whom he had one daughter and three sons, all living. Thomas M. Jacks, the fourth son of the first marriage, was born in 1855. He received a thorough education at Helena in Prof. Russell's school, then preparing himself at Phillips Academy, Andover, Mass., to enter Yale College, which he did in 1875. From this institution he graduated as a civil engineer in 1878. Returning to his home at Helena, Mr. Jacks accepted a position as civil engineer for the Iron Mountain Railroad Company, from Helena to Forrest City, and continued with them from 1879 to 1881. In 1886 he was employed by the Mobile & Birmingham Railroad Company as resident engineer, and is now consulting engineer on the levee board at Helena, also being civil engineer of Helena. He was elected surveyor of Phillips County in 1886 and re-elected in 1888. December 23, 1884, Mr. Jacks was married to Miss Lulu B. Moore, a daughter of William and Lucy Moore, of La Grange, Ark. They are the parents of one child, Claudine, three years of age. Mr. Jacks is a member of the Baptist Church, and politically is a Democrat. At this time he is connected with the Jacks-Fitzpatrick Drug & Real Estate Company of Helena.

Thomas L. Jackson, M. D., is a graduate of the Jefferson Medical College of Philadelphia. He received the foundation of his education in the common schools of Virginia, his native State, and later in the Randolph Macon College of that State, from which he graduated in the fourth year of that institution, subsequently entering the Jefferson Medical College. This he attended one year, and was graduated in 1859. Dr. Jackson was

48

born near Petersburg, Va., November 21, 1840, and is a son of Thomas and Mary H. (Morgan) Jackson, also originally of the Old Dominion. Thomas Jackson was born June 20, 1808, of English ancestry, and is a descendant of one of three brothers who came to the American colonies from England and received large grants of land. He was a son of John E. and Jane (Bailey) Jackson, also natives of the same State as our subject. John E. Jackson served seven years in the Revolutionary War, for which services his wife drew a pension from the Government after his death. The mother of Thomas L. was born in 1807, and died in 1864, fourteen years before her husband's demise. They were the parents of five sons and two daughters. Four sons are now deceased (two having died in the Confederate army), and one of the daughters. He whose name heads this sketch commenced practice near his old home in 1860, and the following spring enlisted in the Confederate army, in the First Virginia Cavalry, serving on the medical staff the greater part of the time, though he also participated in the battles of Manassas, the seven days' fight before Richmond, Fredericksburg, Spottsylvania Court House, battle of the Wilderness, Gettysburg, and was present at Lee's surrender at Appomattox Court House. After the war he returned home, and in 1874 moved to Mississippi, where he was married three years later to Miss Kate E. Pardee. She was born in the State of Michigan, March 17, 1859,. and is a daughter of George and Elizabeth Pardee. Dr. and Mrs. Jackson have five children: Bessie, Lucy, Kate H., Thomas S. and William L. Dr. Jackson practiced in Mississippi for fifteen years, until February, 1889, when he removed to Marvell, Ark., where he has since been engaged in following his chosen profession, now enjoying a patronage which amounts to about $2,500 per year. He was appointed chief health officer of Benton County, Miss., by the Governer, which position he held for six years. The Doctor is a member of the Knights of Honor, and his wife belongs to the Episcopal Church.

Dr. G. D. Jaquess, physician and druggist, Helena, Ark.. This prominent business man was born in Posey County, Ind., January 5, 1834, and is a son of Garrison and Mary (Smith) Jaquess, natives of Kentucky. The parents immigrated to Indiana about 1811, located in Posey County, and there passed their last days. The father was a farmer by occupation, and was forty-eight years of age at the time of his death. Their family consisted of seven children, six sons and one daughter, four now living: James F., T. C., W. B. and Dr. G. D. The latter assisted the father on the farm until twenty years of age, attending school during the winter seasons, and at the age of eighteen years he began the study of medicine, graduating from the Transylvania University at Lexington, Ky., in 1848. He then began practicing at Petersburg, Ind., where he remained until the war broke out, when he was made surgeon of the Eightieth Indiana Volunteers, and served in that capacity until the cessation of hostilities. He was married in 1848 to Miss Aurelia Hammond, a native of Indiana, who bore her husband two living children: Mary J. (wife of L. J. Wilkes) and Aurelia. Two sons were drowned in the Mississippi River. In 1866 Dr. Jaquess and family moved to Tunica County, Miss., where the Doctor was engaged in cotton growing for two years. Not being fitted for this he gave it up, and in 1869 came to Helena, where he was appointed postmaster by President Arthur, serving in that capacity for four years. Since that time he has been engaged in the practice of his profession, and has also carried on the drug business in connection. He is a member of the Royal Arcanum, Knights of Honor, and Knights and Ladies of Honor, and Golden Rule. He owns considerable real estate in both the country and city, and is a successful business man. He has been mayor of the city three times, and is one of the prominent Republicans of Phillips County.

Col. Amos Green Jarman. Phillips County has long had the reputation of being one of the best farming counties in the State, and not only do the farmers here give much attention to this industry, but they are generally men of enterprise and information, and take pride in the general upbuilding of the county. Prominent among those who have done their full share in advancing every interest of this section is Mr. Jarman, who came here in 1859, his first purchase of land amounting to 320 acres. Since then he has added to this tract, and now owns 1,000 acres, of which 600 are under cultivation. His homestead is beautifully located and finely improved, and as he started in life with but little means, he deserves much credit for the admirable way in which he has surmounted the many difficulties which have strewn his pathway. He lost heavily during the war, but has since recovered his losses and added much more. He is a native of Alabama.

Joseph F. Jarrett, well known in this community, was reared in Alabama until thirteen years of age, when his parents moved to this county. He was married in 1871 to Miss Mary L. Thompson, who was born in Tennessee in 1855, being a daughter of William Thompson, whose sketch appears in this work. They are the parents of nine children, seven of whom are still living: Lulu (wife of S. V. Haggard), Albert, Joseph L., Ollie, Willie, Frank and Ora. Mr. Jarrett was born in Lawrence County, Ala., in June, 1847, the son of James F. Jarrett, whose birth occurred in Alabama in 1823. He came to this county in 1860, and died here in 1879. He was a son of Freeman N. Jarrett, of Irish descent. The mother of our subject, Mary (McMillen) Jarrett, was born in Alabama in 1824 and still resides on the old homestead in this county. She bore a family of eight children, four of whom survive: Joseph F., Sarah (wife of J. P. H. Graham), Virginia (wife of W. T. Cooke) and W. B. Mr. Jarrett has a fine farm of 200 acres of land, with seventy-five acres under cultivation. He is one of Cypress Township's best farmers; is a Democrat, and he and his wife are members of the Baptist Church.

Nathan Johnson, whose interests in Phillips County are such as to give him wide acquaintance, is a native of Tennessee, and a son of Jesse C. and Elizabeth (White) Johnson, also originally from that State. Jesse C. Johnson was born in 1800, of Irish and English descent, and is still living in Wilson County, Tenn. He was a son of Samuel Johnson, of Virginia nativity. The mother of our subject died when he was only three weeks old, and

his father married the second time, Miss Polly Pryer, who is still living, and who bore twelve children, eleven surviving. Nathan Johnson was born in Wilson County, on November 9, 1847, remaining in his native State until 1875, when he removed to Arkansas, locating in Phillips County. Here he purchased a quarter section of wild land, all in the woods, and now has over half of it under cultivation. He was married in 1869 to Miss Martha Melissa Marshall, who was born in Lee County, Ga., in August, 1855, the daughter of T. J. and Mary E. (King) Marshall. They are the parents of eleven children, seven living: Mary E., Lilla P., Nora, Valley B., Jemimah, Leslie and Ollie. In addition to his farm, Mr. Johnson owns a saw-mill, grist-mill and cotton-gin all combined, which he erected about 1882, at a cost of over $4,000, and which is being liberally patronized. He also owns another farm of eighty acres, with about fourteen acres cleared, on which is situated a good dwelling-house. He is a member of the Masonic order, the Knights of Honor, and of the Legion of Honor. A leading Democrat in the township, he is one of its influential men, and with his wife belongs to the Missionary Baptist Church, in which he takes an active part.

Joseph D. Kendall, of Kentucky nativity, was born March 28, 1825, being the son of Bailey and Martha G. (Dickerson) Kendall. His father, Bailey Kendall, was born in Kentucky April 11, 1795, and his wife, originally of the same State, was born in 1806 and died in 1878. Bailey Kendall emigrated to Arkansas in 1836 and died in 1868. He was a man of no little prominence, having served as representative of Arkansas and justice of the peace for many years. He was an influential citizen, his demise robbing the county of one of its best and most popular men. Joseph D. received a liberal education in the schools of Phillips County, and in 1861 was united in marriage with Miss C. A. Yelton, of Kentucky, daughter of Jesse and Lucy (Kendall) Yelton. Mrs. Kendall was born in 1835 and died in 1867, leaving four children, one now living: Jesse L. (born February 4, 1863, residing in Helena). Mr. Kendall was again married, in 1875, to Mrs. Virginia O'Neill. She was born in 1833, and by her marriage with Mr. Kendall has borne one child: Mary (born March 22, 1878). Her maiden name was Faidley. When Mr. Kendall's father came to Arkansas he purchased the farm where our subject lives at this time. It was entirely unimproved, but is now one of the best and most carefully cultivated plantations in the county. Mr. Kendall made many improvements, transferring the property in an excellent condition to his son at the time of his death. This farm consists of 300 acres, and is admirably adapted to the growing of all grains, fruits, cotton and vegetables. He has a fine steam cotton-gin which was erected soon after the war by Mr. O'Neill, being at that time one of the first in that section of the county. Mr. Kendall's farm or rather his residence is in the corporation limits of Trenton, so he virtually lives in the city and country at the same time. He is a member of the K. of H., Trenton Lodge, and a Democrat politically. He is giving his children excellent advantages for obtaining an education, and is a liberal contributor to all enterprises. A good citizen, he is respected by the entire community.

James C. Kersey, a prominent farmer of Big Creek Township, was born in Union County, S. C., October 17, 1858, but has been a resident of Phillips County, Ark., since twelve years of age, attending the common schools of this county in youth, and later entering the Arkansas Industrial University, at Fayetteville. In April, 1886, he was married to Mary E. Copeland, who was born in Texas, in May, 1860, a daughter of Elijah and Margaret (Hennison) Copeland, both natives of Alabama. They are the parents of one son, William R. Mr. Kersey owns a fine farm of 452 acres of land, of which about half is under cultivation. His principal crop is cotton, he raising some sixty-five bales annually. In 1889 he erected a steam cotton-gin, at a cost of $1,200, for his own use and that of his neighbors. He has always voted the Democratic ticket, and cast his first presidential ticket for W. S. Hancock. Mr. Kersey's father, William Kersey, was born in Upton County, Ga., about 1832, and died in Phillips County in 1882. He was reared in Georgia, and when a young man went to South Carolina, marrying there, in 1857,

Miss Sarah H. Turner. He was a son of Robert Kersey, a native of South Carolina. Sarah H. (Turner) Kersey was born in that State in 1848, and is a sister of Nathaniel B. Turner, whose biography appears in this work. She is the mother of ten children, these still living: Anna J. (the wife of Richard Davis), Monroe, Mary A. (the wife of Thomas Hennison), Carley (wife of Wiley Clatworthy), Lee, James C. (the principal of this sketch), Ellen and Zeller (twins). In 1867 Mr. William Kersey moved to Arkansas, and purchased the farm on which the subject of this sketch now lives. He was a member of the Masonic order, and of the Baptist Church.

Hon. S. H. King, farmer and stock raiser, Poplar Grove, Ark. The King family is a very old and prominent one, and is of Scotch origin. The first to come to this country were Richard King and wife, who made their appearance here as early as 1700. They located in Philadelphia, then a small village, and here the wife died. In 1735 Samuel married Miss Margaret Barclay, of Dutch parentage, and from this honored couple the King family of the present day are descendants. He and wife were the parents of twelve children. He died in May, 1782, at the age of eighty-two years. His son, James King (the great-grandfather of our subject), was born in 1737, in New Jersey, whither his father had moved. He married Miss Sarah Hall, in 1765, in North Carolina, and they became the parents of nine children, Andrew King being their youngest son, and the grandfather of our subject. He died in 1852, at the age of seventy-four years. His son, Thomas S. N. King (the father of our subject), was born in North Carolina, in 1804, and was married in 1832, to Miss J. F. Smith, a native of Georgia, who bore him seven children, all of whom lived to be grown: Porter B. (deceased, family resides in Benton County, Ark.), Ella S. (widow of W. H. Trader, and now resides in Washington, D. C.), W. B. (resides in Madison Parish, La., engaged in farming), S. H., Elizabeth N. (deceased), Fannie S. (deceased) and Laura J. (deceased, wife of Henry W. Scull, of Pine Bluff, Ark.). Mrs. King died in 1886, at the age of seventy-two years, after a long and eventful life. Thomas S. N. King had previously been married to Miss Margaret Battle, who only lived a short time afterward. He was a minister in the Baptist Church, and was also a successful agriculturist. He moved to Mississippi in 1833, and was among the very first settlers of that State. In 1846 he moved to Arkansas, settled at Helena, this county, and was engaged in tilling the soil. He was the third Baptist minister in the county, and assisted in establishing the first three churches of that denomination there, these being New Hope, Beach Grove and Helena, which is now called the First Baptist Church of Helena. Mr. King moved to the country in 1849, and settled three miles south of Helena, where he engaged in farming, but still continued his ministerial duties. He was commissioner of schools in this county, and took a deep interest in educational matters. He died in 1869, at the age of sixty-four years. S. H. King first attended the subscription schools of Phillips County, and at the age of eighteen years entered the Union University of Murfreesboro, Tenn., where he remained three years, or until his twenty-first year. He then engaged as book-keeper for W. F. & J. T. Moore, of Helena, with whom he remained one year, and then, the war breaking out, he enlisted in the Confederate army, Gen. Cleburne's old company (called the Yell Rifles) as a private, and was promoted to the rank of sergeant while with this company. At the end of one year he was appointed commissary, with the rank of major of Preston Smith's brigade of Tennessee troops, being the first commissary that was appointed to that office with the rank of major. He had previously held the rank of captain while in the Tennessee army. Major King participated in many battles, prominent among them being Shiloh, Chickamauga, Richmond, Murfreesboro, Missionary Ridge, Atlanta, where he was wounded in both arms, and was slightly wounded in the lower part of the breast. After this he was in the battles of Franklin, Nashville, and was in the last battle fought by Gen. Joseph E. Johnston. He surrendered April 27, 1865, at Greensboro, N. C. May 16, 1865, he married Miss Sue Scaife, and in the fall of

1865 he came back to Phillips County, where he tilled the soil on rented land in a small way. In 1872 he purchased 160 acres of land, which he improved, and traded for the place on which he is now residing, then consisting of 160 acres. This he has since improved and added to, until he now owns 312 acres, with 160 acres under cultivation, and on which is a good steam cotton-gin. He gins yearly an average of 400 bales, and produces on his farm thirty-five bales yearly, together with hay, corn, etc. He is also quite a stockman, raising cattle and horses principally. Mr. and Mrs. King became the parents of two children: Lannie (wife of J. E. Davidson, resides in Marion Township) and W. F. (who resides in Cypress Township, and is a teacher by profession). Mrs. King died in May, 1868, and in 1871 he chose for his second wife Miss Sallie Cook, daughter of James and Frances (Brooks) Cook. James Cook came to Phillips County in 1875. The paternal grandmother of Mrs. King was a Bragg, an aunt of Gen. Bragg, while the maternal grandfather Brooks was one of the family of Brooks, of South Carolina, and came from England. The mother was a Paine, and a relative of Bishop Paine. James Cook and wife were the parents of eight children, six now living: Roland (on the old homestead, near Barton), Sallie (wife of Mr. King), Susan E. (wife of E. A. Hicks, of Barton), Nannie, Jennie (wife of D. H. Crebs, of Helena) and Robert (of Poplar Grove). Mr. Cook died in 1872, and his wife in 1876. To the marriage of Mr. and Mrs. King were born five children: James P., W. C., Jennie, J. W. and A. F. In 1878 Mr. King was elected county treasurer, and served one term. In 1885 he was elected to the legislature from Phillips County, and served in that capacity in a highly creditable manner. He is a member of the K. of H., Marvell Lodge No. 1628, and he and Mrs. King are members of the Baptist Church. He is one of the most prominent citizens of the county, and has the confidence and respect of all.

James H. Lanier, farmer, Helena, Ark. This prominent and much respected citizen of Phillips County, Ark., was born in Person County, N. C., on March 10, 1826, and is one of thirteen children born to the union of Lewis G. and Sarah E. (Henning) Lanier, natives of North Carolina. The father was born in 1800, and was married in his native State to Miss Henning. About 1830 they moved to Maury County, Tenn., and there the mother died in 1850, when about forty-nine years of age. The father was afterward married three times, and received his final summons in Maury County in 1880. His last wife survives him and is now living in Maury County, Tenn. The mother of our subject was a member of the Methodist Episcopal Church, and the father a member of the Masonic fraternity, and a Whig in politics. He was a well to-do farmer and stock raiser. Of their large family of children, three are now living, and James H. is fourth in order of birth. They are named as follows: James H., Joseph (a saddler, and is now living in Wynne, Ark.) and William (a farmer in Maury County, Tenn.). Those deceased were: Lewis (a farmer of Maury County), Mary (died in that county), Albert (died during the war while in the Confederate service, and it is thought his last days were spent in a Federal prison), Hugh H. (died in Maury County, Tenn.; was a farmer), Martha (died in Tennessee), Sallie (died in that State) and Rebecca (who is the eldest daughter and the wife of James H. Colburn, died in Tennessee). James H. Lanier passed his school-boy days in Maury County, Tenn., and when twenty-two years of age engaged in agricultural pursuits, which he continued only a short time until he turned his attention to mercantile pursuits, serving in the capacity of salesman at Mount Pleasant for three years. He again returned to tilling the soil, and in 1855 moved to Phillips County, Ark., serving in the capacity of overseer on the plantation of Thomas Barrows, continuing thus for three years. In 1862 he enlisted in Capt. Weatherby's company of Col. Dobbins' regiment of cavalry, and served until the close of the war, being in the commissary department during the latter part of the war. He participated in the battle of Helena ; was with Gen. Price on his raid through Missouri, and was at Pilot Knob. After the war he commenced to farm for himself, bought forty acres of land, and has added to this until he has an extensive farm. In

1858 he was united in marriage to Miss Sarah E. Lanford, a native of Alabama, born near Huntsville on November 14, 1835, and the daughter of William Lanford. The fruits of this union were two children: James R. (in the employ of Lohman & Co., at Helena) and Mittie N. (attending school at Helena). These children are deceased: William L. (died when ten years of age), Sallie R. (died at the age of eight years), Martha F. (when six years of age) and Mary L. (at the age of ten years). Mrs. Lanier has been a member of the Methodist Episcopal Church, South, since early girlhood. Mr. Lanier is a Mason, a member of the Wheel, and is a Democrat in politics. He is an enterprising and much respected citizen of the county.

Henry Lawrens is a proper representative of the energetic business men of Helena, which element has done and is doing so much for the advancement of the material interests of the city. He was born in Shelby County, Tenn., June 13, 1856, and is a son of Joseph and Margaret Lawrens, who were born in the old country and removed to America during the early part of their lives, settling in the State of Indiana. From this point they moved to Nashville, Tenn., where the father worked as engineer in a brewery; and in this city the mother's death occurred. Henry Lawrens resided in Nashville until he was fourteen years of age, when he went to Memphis and worked for some time in a cooper shop, learning the trade, and two years later came to Helena, Ark., and spent some time in working in different restaurants. In 1880 he established his present business, but began on a small scale, and now carries a large and well selected stock of dry goods, and in fact everything to be found in a general establishment. He is in every respect a self-made man as he came to this county without a dollar, and is now deservedly classed among the leading business men of the county, which reputation he has acquired by the active, intelligent management of his affairs, and by his honesty and fair dealing. He is worth at least $10,000, and instead of carrying a stock of goods valued at $156, as he did at first, his present stock is valued at $6,000 at least, and his establishment is known as the Magnolia Store. He has served as city alderman six years or three terms, and is a director in the Mutual Building and Loan Association. Socially he is a member of the K. of P. He was united in marriage November 9, 1886, to Miss Clara Dissman. Their one child is Minnie.

Silas Lingg is a member of the firm of Lingg, Lambert & Co., undertakers, of Helena, Ark., and was born in the State of Delaware, on May 21, 1849, being a son of Joseph and Judith (Ffirth) Lingg, the father a native of Switzerland, and the mother of America. Their marriage took place in the State of Delaware, and shortly after they moved to Chicago, Ill., later to Grand Detour, that State, and here Joseph Lingg was engineer of a plow factory until his death, his wife also dying there. Of eight children born to them, only two are now living. He and three brothers were in the Union army during the Rebellion, and his brother Joseph A. was killed in battle at Spottsylvania, Va. The maternal grandfather Ffirth was judge of a court in Philadelphia in 1796, and was a very intellectual and prominent man. The ancestors of the wife of Mr. Lingg's maternal grandfather settled on the site of Philadelphia, Penn., in 1623, which place is still occupied and owned by one of Silas Lingg's cousins. Nine generations of children have been born on the homestead, which is still in the family. Silas Lingg was reared and educated in Illinois, but being of a rather enterprising disposition, he went to Nebraska, and followed river life until 1875, and at present has in his possession his commission as pilot and captain of a steamboat. In 1875 he took an interest in a soda water and cider manufactory belonging to Jacks & Co., and was thus associated until 1880, when he bought out his partners, and has since managed the business alone, meeting with the best success. Since 1880 he has been in the undertaking business also, and has become thoroughly experienced in the details of this difficult branch. He is very prompt day and night, and guarantees strict and careful attention to all orders. He is a director of the People's Building and Loan Association, and socially belongs to the K. of P., the A. O. U. W. and the A. L. of H. In 1880 he was elected city treasurer, and in 1885 was chosen city marshal,

and was re-elected in 1886. He was married in 1873 to Mattie E. Gordon, by whom he has three children: Vera, Blanche E. and Silas L.

Dr. D. A. Linthicum is one of the very foremost of the professional men of the county and is acknowledged by the medical fraternity to be one of their leading members. He was born in Bardstown, Ky., June 15, 1827, and is a son of Rufus and Eliza (Anthony) Linthicum, the former a native of Maryland and the latter of the "Blue Grass State." The paternal grandfather, John Linthicum, was born in Wales, and on coming to the United States, settled in Maryland and later in Bardstown, Ky., where he followed the occupation of farming and lived until his death. The maternal grandparents were native Germans and were early settlers of Kentucky, in which State they both breathed their last. Rufus Linthicum, like our subject, was a physician and was a graduate of the Transylvania University of Lexington, Ky. He was twice married, and his first union resulted in the birth of seven children, only two of whom are now living: Dr. D. A. and Susan A., the wife of Dr. J. A. Hodge, of Henderson, Ky. To his second marriage six children were born. He practiced his profession in Henderson County, Ky., until his death in the winter of 1864, his wife having died in an adjoining county many years earlier. The subject of our sketch received the principal part of his rearing in what is now McLean County, Ky., and received an excellent knowledge of books in the Hartford Academy of that State. Having always been desirous of following in his father's footsteps, he began his medical studies under the able instructions of the latter and after receiving sufficient preparation, he entered the St. Louis Medical University, graduating in 1849. He first entered upon the practice of his profession in McLean County, Ky., where he remained until the breaking out of the war, then enlisted as a private in the Eighth Kentucky Regiment (C. A. S.), and was subsequently made surgeon of his regiment which position he held until 1862. He was then made chief surgeon of Gen. Patrick Cleburne's division of Hardee's corps of the Army of Tennessee, and served in this capacity until the final surrender. He then returned to Kentucky, where he was an active medical practitioner until 1867, when he became a resident of Helena, Ark. In 1870 he graduated from the Washington University of Baltimore, Md., and in 1872 had an honorary degree conferred upon him by his Alma Mater. He has been president of the State Medical Society of Arkansas and is a member of the American Medical Association, also of the County Medical Society. He was married in 1848 to Miss Phœbe C. Johnson, of Daviess County, Ky., and by her has had three children, of whom Dr. Theodric C. is the only one living. He is a graduate of the Kentucky School of Medicine and of the Philadelphia School of Pharmacy.

Thomas J. Lucado, planter, Marvell, Ark. One of the foremost men among the agriculturists of Phillips County is he whose name appears above, and who has borne an influential part in promoting the various interests of the county. He owes his nativity to Fayette County, Tenn., where his birth occurred November 29, 1843, and is the son of Joel Lucado. The father was a native of the Old Dominion, born in 1797, was reared in that State, and was there married to Miss Mary Johnson, a native also of Virginia, born in the same year. They moved from their native State to Tennessee about 1836, were among the early settlers of that State, and resided there until 1859, when they moved to Phillips County, Ark. He died in 1862, and his wife the year following. His father, Isaac Lucado, was born in Virginia, and there passed his entire life. He was of Spanish-English descent, and was a soldier in the Revolutionary War. Thomas J. Lucado was the youngest of twelve children born to his parents, three of whom are now living. He attained his growth in Fayette County, Tenn., received his education in the common schools of that county, and there remained with his parents until reaching his majority. He then came with them to Phillips County, Ark., and here the father purchased about 1,200 acres of land, which he owned up to the time of his death. In 1862 Thomas J. enlisted in the Confederate army, Company G, Fifth Arkansas Regiment Infantry, served three years, and received a slight wound at the battle of Prairie Grove. He was taken prisoner at the battle of Helena, removed to Alton, Ill., and from there to Fort Delaware, where he remained until April, 1865. He then returned to this county. In 1871 he was united in marriage to Miss Sarah Peterson, of Phillips County, born in 1854, and who died in 1873. Two children were born to this union, both now deceased. His second marriage took place in 1884, to Miss Molly Impey, who was born in this county in 1868, and died in 1886. In 1888 Mr. Lucado married Miss Mary Kitchens, who was born in Phillips County. Mr. Lucado has 540 acres of land, with about 250 acres in cultivation, and raises 100 bales of cotton annually. He erected a cotton-gin in 1867, but this was burned in 1876, and the one he now has, and which is run by steam, cost about $1,500. He is a Democrat in politics, and his first presidential vote was cast for Horatio Seymour. He is an honest, upright man, a substantial farmer and a highly respected citizen. He and Mrs. Lucado are members of the Baptist Church.

William M. Lowry, planter, Helena, Ark. One of the foremost men among the agriculturists of Phillips County, is he whose name appears above, and who has borne an influential part in promoting the various interests of the county. He was originally from Louisiana, his birth occurring at Milliken's Bend, September 20, 1832, and is the son of Alfred J. and Cleora C. (Hynes) Lowry, natives, respectively, of Frankfort and Bardstown, Ky. The father died at Milliken's Bend, La., in 1872, when fifty-five years of age, and the mother died in 1864 at the age of forty-two years. They were married in Bardstown, Ky., and later moved to Natchez, Miss., where they remained two years, going thence to Milliken's Bend, La. The mother died while on a visit to Louisville. The father was a graduate of St. Joseph College, Bardstown, and was a planter by occupation, raising annually from 600 to 1,000 bales of cotton. He was a member of the lower house of the legislature while residing in Louisiana, and served in that capacity for four years. He was a Mason and held an office in the Grand Lodge of the State, was a Whig at one time, but during the latter part of his life was a Democrat. Mrs. Lowry was a member of the Cumberland Presbyterian Church. Their family consisted of eight children, six of whom lived to maturity, and five of whom are living at the present time, viz.: Mrs. S. D. Tompkins (now residing in Helena), William M., Mrs. Caroline Polk (wife of Col. Cadwallader Polk, of Phillips County), F. M. (wholesale merchant at St. Louis, Mo.), Mrs. C. C. (now residing at Helena). One son, A. J. Lowry, contracted consumption during the war, and died one year after peace was declared. He was aide-de-camp to Col. Cadwallader Polk. William M. Lowry received his education at Bardstown, Ky., and remained there until three months before graduating, when he was compelled to leave St. Joseph's College, at that place on account of ill health. He went from there to New Orleans, La., where he was engaged in planting for three years, after which he returned to his father's old plantation in that State. In 1869 he came to Phillips County, and is now the owner of 520 acres of land, with 480 acres under cultivation. He was in the Confederate service a short time during the war, but was discharged on account of disability. He lost $100,000 in two years after the war, and consequently was obliged to begin over again. He has been quite successful since that time, and is one of the first cotton growers in the county. He has reared an interesting family of children, three sons attending college at Bardstown, Ky., and two daughters attending at Fayetteville, Ark. His marriage occurred in 1860, to Miss Artana Majoun, of Bayou Sarah, La., and the fruits of this union have been eight children, five now living: Bruce (carrying on the home plantation), Alfred J. (in the employ of D. H. Crebs, of Helena), Sam T. (is in the employ of J. W. Clopton, cotton broker of Helena), Jennie (at home) and Annie T. (at home). Mr. Lowry is a member of the Catholic and his wife a member of the Episcopal Church. He is a Democrat in his political opinion, and is one of the most enterprising citizens of the county, always manifesting public spirit in worthy movements.

Gen. L. H. Mangum, attorney at law, Helena, Ark. What is usually termed genius has little to do with the success of man in general. Keen perception, sound judgment, and a determined will, supported by persevering and continuous effort, are essential elements to success in any calling, and their possession is sure to accomplish the ends hoped for in the days of his youth. The jurisprudence of a commonwealth is the most necessary factor toward its growth and permanence, for, without a thorough knowledge and administration of the law no form of popular government could long exist. Gen. L. H. Mangum, by virtue of his ability as a jurist and his victories at the bar, is eminently worthy of a place in the record of successful men, and the history of his life is an important and honorable part of that of his State and country. He was born in Hillsborough, N. C., on May 26, 1837, and is the son of Priestly H. and Rebecca H. (Southerland) Mangum, natives of North Carolina. The maternal grandfather, Ranson Southerland, was a soldier in the Revolutionary War, and that family was one of the most prominent in the State of North Carolina. The Mangum family were originally from Wales, were early settlers of North Carolina, and W. P. Mangum was State senator from North Carolina for thirty years, being president of the senate during President Tyler's administration. Priestly H. Mangum was a very prominent and noted lawyer, was solicitor for a number of years, and was also a member of the North Carolina legislature for a number of years. His whole heart was in his profession, for he loved the law and had the most exalted respect for its conscientious and honorable followers, and he found very little time to mingle with politics. His reputation was that of a safe counsellor, a fearless, eloquent, earnest, and most convincing advocate. His death occurred in 1850, and the mother's in 1838. They were the parents of six children, three sons and three daughters, four of whom are now living. Wiley P. was consul-general, sent by President Lincoln to China and Japan, and held this position for twenty-one years. He died at Tientsin, China, in February, 1881. Catherine (deceased), Priestly H., Mary L. (wife of

J. J. James, of N. C.), Rebecca T. (widow of John R. Williams), and Leonard H., who is the youngest of the family. The latter remained in his native State until eighteen years of age, having previously read law, and then entered the school at Princeton, N. J., graduating from the same in 1857. The same year he came to Helena, and in 1858 was admitted to the Helena bar, afterward forming a partnership with Gen. Cleburne & Scaife, under the firm title of Cleburne, Scaife & Mangum, the same continuing thus until the breaking out of the war, when all entered the army. Mr. Mangum enlisted in the celebrated Yell Rifles, and went out as second sergeant. He was badly wounded at the battle of Shiloh, where he had several horses shot from under him, and was shot seven times, through the hip, thigh, arm and hand. He was given up to die, but rallied and returned to the army. He was then offered a captaincy, but declined to serve, and went to Gen. Cleburne's staff, where he remained until the surrender. After returning to Helena he found his library stolen, and although he had but $30 in money, he began practicing his profession and met with excellent success. This continued until he was appointed by President Cleveland chief of warrants, land and territorial accounts, and steamboat inspector accounts, holding the position for four years, and then resigned on his own account, thinking that he ought to do so to give way to the opposing party. He held the office of probate judge for a number of years, and from time to time held the circuit judge's place. He has been prominently identified with Phillips County for over thirty years, and was a member of the Democratic National Convention of 1868, held at New York, nominating Seymour and Blair, also of the convention of 1876. He served on the Committee of Resolutions and Platforms. He has been twice married, first to Miss Anna W. Nunn, by whom he had two children, one living: Wiley P., who is now in Washington City, and his second marriage was to Mrs. Fannie Metzger (nee Clements) of Helena. Personally, Gen. Mangum is upright, honorable and just in all matters concerning his political action, as well as in matters of private life. His entire career has been one to

which he may refer with pardonable pride, and just satisfaction.

Isam Manning, farmer, Poplar Grove, Ark. This much-respected and esteemed citizen was originally from Indiana, where his birth occurred in 1822, and was principally reared in Phillips County, Ark., whither he had removed with his parents in 1834. His education was received in the private schools, and when twenty-three years of age he commenced farming for himself on his own land. In 1846 he went to Mexico as a soldier in Capt Preston's Company, Col. Yell's First Arkansas Regiment, and was at the battle of Buena Vista. He was in the service one year and came home in 1847. In February of the following year he was married to Miss Lucinda Bailey, daughter of Thomas and Milly Bailey, of Kentucky, and became the father of three children, only one now living: John, who is a farmer and resides in Johnson County, Ark. Mrs. Manning died in 1857, and in May of the following year Mr. Manning was married to Miss Samantha Thomas, daughter of W. A. Thomas, a native of Georgia. To the second marriage were born eleven children, six now living: Biddie (wife of Robert McGinnis), Walter, Etta, Jessie, Edmond and Robert. In 1859 Mr. Manning bought his present property, consisting of 400 acres, and now has 200 acres improved, with a splendid frame residence, outbuildings, etc. He has a gin on his place, with which he did his own and some custom ginning until this year. He raises on his home place about thirty bales of cotton yearly, and up to this year ginned, on an average, about seventy-five bales per year. Besides his home farm, Mr. Manning is the owner of 620 acres of land, with 100 acres improved. He did not serve in the late war, but lost a great deal of property. He is a liberal donator to all laudable enterprises, and he and wife are members of the Cumberland Presbyterian Church. He is a member of the Wheel, and in his political views affiliates with Democratic party. His parents, William and Jane (Elliott) Manning, moved to Arkansas in 1834, and rented land on Big Creek, close to what is now Middle Bridge, where there was a ferry kept by a man by the name of James Hanks. The country at that time was wild and unsettled, bear, panther, wolves, deer, etc., were plenty all over the county, and Helena was a small place with only two dry-goods stores there, kept by Judge McKinzie and F. & M. Hanks. There was several saloons and grocery stores, and population numbered about 250. Mr. Manning remained here about two years, and then went to Mississippi, where he remained but one year. He never bought or entered land in this county. He died in 1843, at the age of forty-seven years. His widow afterward married in (1847) a Mr. Mosby, of Phillips County. She died in 1853, at the age of fifty-five years.

Peter Mengoz. In all ages of the world, industry, perseverance and energy, where intelligently applied, have achieved excellent results, and Mr. Mengoz is an excellent example of what can be accomplished when the spirit of determination is exercised in connection with the every-day affairs of life. His farming and stock raising operations have resulted most satisfactorily, and he now owns 1,600 acres of land and has 600 acres in a fine state of cultivation. He is also the owner of the Grand Opera House at Helena, and is a director and the main stockholder in the Fair Association. He has some fine thoroughbred horses on his plantation, and makes a specialty of Alford cattle and Berkshire hogs. Although a native of France he has become thoroughly Americanized, and takes a deep interest in the affairs of his adopted country. His birth occurred on April 27, 1837, and he is a son of Franco A. and Lucile (Vouron) Mengoz, who were born, reared, educated and married in France. After residing there until 1853 they concluded to cross the "big pond" and seek their fortune in America, and, upon reaching the United States, settled first in Stark County, Ohio, but not liking the situation, moved the following year to Iowa, and purchased land in Black Hawk County, Iowa, being among the first to locate at Gilbertville. Here the mother's death occurred in 1866, at the age of fifty-five years, and, after this event, Mr. Mengoz returned to France, and after a few years' stay there, came back to Iowa to settle up his affairs, realizing on the sale of his property quite a handsome sum of money. While in New York City, on the eve of returning to his native land, he was unfortunately robbed of all his money, and was compelled to join his son, the subject of this sketch, and with him made his home until his death, August 25, 1878, at the age of seventy-seven years. He was a stone cutter and contractor by trade, and was compelled to leave France on account of his political views, and after reaching "the land of the free and the home of the brave" gave his attention to farming exclusively. He served in the French War seven years, and he and his wife were members of the Catholic Church. Of five children born to them, their son Peter is the eldest, and only three of the family are now living: France (who has been working in the gold mines of Oregon since 1867), Mary (wife of Nicholas Deisch) and Peter. Eugene was born in 1842, was a farmer by occupation, and died in Phillips County in 1876. Charles died in France at the age of five years. Peter Mengoz received the most of his education in the schools of his native land and came with his parents to this country, remaining with them until 1858, when he came to Arkansas and became an employe of a New Orleans firm, and was foreman of different forces of men in the State of Arkansas until the opening of the war, when he joined the Confederate army and was in the commissary department, or rather wsa a contractor furnishing beef for the army. He drove his cattle from Texas, and was in this business until the close of the war, when he came to Helena and engaged in farming, but at the end of one year became a salesman in the grocery and provision house of John Meadow, remaining with him two years. He then became associated with William Baggett in the grocery business, but at the end of one year began business alone, and opened a wholesale and retail grocery, provision and liquor establishment, which he continued to conduct until 1880, when, as stated above, he retired to his plantation. His property has been acquired through his own business ability and energy since the war, as at that time what property he had accumulated was swept away. He is a devout member of the Catholic Church, socially belongs to the K. of H., and in his political views is a Democrat. In 1873 he returned to his old home in France, and visited Switzerland the same year, and in 1889 again went to Europe and traveled through England, France, Switzerland, Bavaria, Baden, also other provinces of Prussia, and then returned to the United States fully contented to make his home here for the remainder of his days. He has been quite an extensive traveler in the United States also, and in 1855 made a trip to the Rocky Mountains for a St. Louis Fur Company.

Aaron Meyers, wholesale and retail grocer, Helena, Ark. Among the most important industries of any community are those that deal in the necessaries of life, and next to bread and meat, nothing is more necessary than groceries. Helena has a number of first-class establishments doing business in this line, and prominent among the number is that conducted by Mr. Meyers. This gentleman was born in Prussia, Germany, on August 25, 1841, and is the son of Isaac and Yetta Meyers, natives of the same province. There the parents grew up, married, and received their final summons. Aaron Meyers was reared and educated at Schwarza, graduated in 1856 and the same year sailed for America. He first located at St. Louis, was engaged in the grocery business at that place until 1868, and then came to Helena, Ark., where he filled the position of salesman for some time. He was city marshal and city tax collector, and for five years filled the position of mayor of the city to the satisfaction of all. In fact he has been connected with almost every public enterprise that has taken place since he came here and has taken a deep interest in improving the city. He has been president of the Chamber of Commerce for two years, secretary of the school board for six years, president of the Helena Building & Loan Association, treasurer of the Helena Opera House, Grand Chancellor of the K. of P. of the State of Arkansas, and holds several offices in different orders. He is a director in the Fair Association and a stockholder in the opera house. He was married in 1879 to Miss Johanna Potsdamer and to them were born four children: Ellen R., Bettie M., Isaac M. and Gertrude R. Mr. Meyers was married the second time to Miss

Bianca Potsdamer, by whom he has one child, Joseph C. He and wife are church members.

P. T. R. Miller, farmer and stockman, Poplar Grove, Ark. Mr. Miller, another of the many substantial citizens of foreign birth, now residing in Phillips County, owes his nativity to Scotland, where he was born in 1848. His father, George Miller, followed agricultural pursuits the principal part of his life, but in his younger days was engaged in merchandising in his native country, Scotland, where he now resides with his wife, who was formerly Miss Elizabeth Robertson. They both enjoy good health in spite of their advanced years, he being eighty-four or eighty-five and she seventy-five years of age, and both are members of the Old School Presbyterian Church. Their family consisted of eight children, six of whom are now living and P. T. R. being the eldest. The next in order of birth, Elizabeth (is now the widow of David Walker, and lives in Scotland. Mr. Walker died in Helena, Phillips County), William A. (resides in New York City, and is entry clerk for Hilton, Hughes & Denning), James R. (came to America, but in 1881 returned to his native country and is engaged in tilling the soil), Esther (resides in Scotland), Maggie (deceased), Georgiana (in Scotland), and Daniel (deceased, who was the youngest, and who was killed by a fall from his horse in Australia). P. T. R. Miller was reared and educated in Scotland, and when nineteen years of age crossed the ocean to America, where he followed agricultural pursuits in New York State. He was afterward with the Adams Express Company as messenger until 1870, when he returned to Scotland. In 1871 he came back to America and located at Cleveland, Ohio, where he remained four years, part of the time being engaged in the cornice maker's trade, and afterward had charge of some horses. He left there in 1875 and came to Phillips County, Ark., where he has since tilled the soil. He is at present a member of the firm of Bailey & Miller, which was established in the spring of 1888. This firm has 250 acres under cultivation, the principal part of which is seeded down to grass for the summer herding of cattle. They have commodious barns with sufficient room to care for about 100 head of stock, and take it all in all, this is one of the leading stock farms in Eastern Arkansas. They have on hand a fine Holstein animal, preparatory to the breeding of fine cattle, and their intention is also to breed for market a fine grade of sheep. Mr. Miller has been twice married, first in 1877, to Miss Martha Gallatin, who died in 1878, leaving one child, Martha E. Mr. Miller's second marriage was to Mrs. Mattie Banks (*nee* Hipps), a native of Alabama, and the fruits of this union have been four children: George R., Lizzie and Henry B. and Ed W. (twins). Mrs. Miller was the mother of three children by her former marriage: Georgia A. (wife of W. P. Vernor, of Phillips County), W. H. H. and James (both at home). Mr. Miller is a member of the A. O. U. W., Junior Lodge, Helena, Ark., and Mrs. Miller is a member of the Methodist Episcopal Church, South.

John P. Moore is vice-president of the First National Bank, also of the Peoples Savings Bank, and is also a real estate and plantation supply dealer of Helena, Ark. His career is but another evidence of the possibilities young men have for advancement in the world when supported by strong resolution to rise. He was raised on a farm, though he acquired an education in the Western Military Institute of Kentucky, and in the University of Mississippi, at Oxford. His opportunities he improved and became well posted on the current literature of the day, and laid the foundation for a successful career in later days. He first began business for himself as a merchant in Aberdeen, Miss., but in 1856 sold out his business there, and came to Helena, where he opened a mercantile establishment, which he has since conducted, with the exception of the time during the Civil War, when he was obliged to suspend business. His mercantile business is now conducted under the firm name of John P. & F. Moore, Dr. Frierson Moore, his son, being the partner. He owns a vast amount of land in Arkansas and Mississippi, of which a large portion is under cultivation, and his real estate in the city of Helena is very valuable. He is a strong advocate of investments in real estate, and has been active in advancing the inter-

ests of the city and county. He was married near Aberdeen, Miss., in 1854, and is the father of four children, two sons and two daughters. His parents were Alabamians, and moved to Chickasaw County, Miss., at an early day, in which State they both died. Our subject was born in Alabama, and reared in the great State of Mississippi.

John T. Moore, the obliging and courteous postmaster of Red Store, was born in Chicot County, Ark., January 20, 1845, the son of Stephen P. and Margaret (Cassidy) Moore. Stephen P. Moore immigrated from South Carolina (where he was born in 1814) to Mississippi when only sixteen years of age, and was there married in 1840, by his union with Miss Cassidy becoming the father of seven children, two daughters and a son (John T.) now living. Mrs. Moore died in Phillips County, Ark., in 1885, at the age of seventy-one years. John T. Moore was reared in Mississippi from the age of four years, and received his education in the schools of that State. In 1875 he was married to Miss Eugenia Goodman, who was born in Mobile, Ala., in 1849, and died in Arkansas County, Ark., in 1882, leaving two children: Robert and Eugenia. Mr. Moore immigrated to Arkansas from Mississippi in 1882, which has been his home ever since. He owns 1,260 acres of land, a greater portion of it being under a successful state of cultivation. The principal crop that he grows is cotton, averaging about 140 bales annually. Mr. Moore belongs to the Baptist Church, in which he is regarded as a faithful and prominent member. He can remember and loves to recite his early adventures of hunting, many times having killed over 100 bears in a season.

William M. Neal is a real-estate and insurance agent at Helena, and a record of his life will be of more than passing interest, for he is a man of recognized worth and of a substantial and progressive spirit. He was born in Wilson County, Tenn., September 6, 1853, and is a son of William Z. and Josephine (Puckett) Neal, who were also natives of that State, the father being a man of superior education, and the founder of the Lebanon (Tenn.) Herald in 1852. This journal he continued to publish until 1872, at which time he sold out, purchasing a farm and moving thereon, and there now lives. He was internal revenue collector under Gen. Grant, and was a Whig in his political views for many years. He and wife, who is now dead, became the parents of five children, three now living, of whom our subject is the eldest. His early scholastic advantages were received in the Cumberland University at Lebanon, Tenn., and he there also learned the printer's trade, serving a four-years apprenticeship in his father's office, after which he wrote for and read proof on the Nashville Daily American for some time. He next went to Washington, Miss., and after working as a bookkeeper for a number of years he, in March, 1876, came to Helena and worked in the same capacity for the bank here, continuing to be thus occupied four years, at which time he began giving his attention to merchandising. Four years later he embarked in his present calling, and in this branch of business has become one of the leading men of the county. He handles an immense amount of real estate and owns some very valuable property himself. He represents the Manhattan Life Insurance Company; being, too, a stockholder in and secretary of the Helena & Brick Manufacturing Company, and is also a stockholder and secretary of the Mutual Building & Loan Association, which he assisted in organizing, in June, 1887, with a capital stock of $600,000. He is also secretary of the Helena Gas, Water & Power Company, which has a capital stock of $10,000. December 5, 1888, he was married to Miss Margaret Redford, who is a member of the Methodist Episcopal Church.

M. Newman, wholesale and retail dealer in liquors, etc., Helena, Ark. A very reliable as well as popular store is that of Mr. Newman, who opened the saloon business in Helena in 1874, and has every requisite and convenience in his line of business. He was born in Hesse Castle, Germany, on October 31, 1837, and is the son of William and Esther (Freudenberg) Newman, natives of Germany, where they passed their entire lives. Mr. Newman was reared in Germany, received his education at Hesse Castle, and in 1856 he sailed for America, taking passage at Bremen, and landing at New York City after a fifty-six days' ocean voyage. He remained in New Year for one year, and then traveled over nearly the entire continent, especially the Western and Southern States. In the fall of 1858 he located at Little Rock, and made his headquarters there until 1861. The following year he located at Helena, Ark., and was occupied as clerk for two years. He then engaged in the mercantile business, carried this on until 1869, and then entered into the stock business for one season. In 1871 he embarked in the cigar business, and two years later in the dairy business, which he continued for one year. After this he opened a saloon, and has since conducted the sale of liquors, cigars, etc. Mr. Newman was only seventeen years of age when he came to America, and had nothing but the clothes he was wearing. He has been quite successful, and is one of the enterprising business men of Helena, doing an extensive business in his line. He was married in 1864 to Miss Bertha Platt, and the result of this union was five children: Eli (who is now twenty-three years of age), Theresa (twenty years of age), Albert (eighteen), Willie (fifteen) and Estella (ten years of age). Mr. Newman is a Royal Arch Mason, a Knight of Pythias, belongs to the A. O. U. W., and is a member of the Knights and Ladies of Honor, Beni Brith, and Kersher Shel Barzel. He is the agent for Anheuser-Busch Brewing Company, the largest company in the South.

Judge R. W. Nicholls is an attorney at law of Helena, Ark., and his name is identified with his professional standing, the welfare and material and social happiness of Phillips County. He was born in the Parish of Assumption, La., December 9, 1849, and on his father's side is descended from an old English family of note, and inherits French blood from his mother. The paternal grandfather, Thomas C. Nicholls, was judge of a district court in Louisiana, and upon his death was succeeded by his son, R. W. (the father of our subject), who held the office until his death, at the untimely age of thirty-five years, having discharged his duties in a manner highly satisfactory to all. He was a lieutenant in the Mexican War and was aid-de-camp for Gen. Taylor. An old trunk which he carried through this engagement is in possession of his son, Judge R. W. Nicholls, and has his name engraved upon it. He was a brother of the present Gov. Nicholls, of Louisiana, who is the only one of the seven sons living, and, in fact, is the only member of his father's family who survives. R. W. was married to Miss J. M. Phillips, and by her reared one son, Judge R. W. Nicholls. The youthful days of the latter were spent in his native State, a part of his time being spent on his father's plantation and the rest of the time in the city of New Orleans, where he acquired a good common-school education, which he subsequently improved by attendance at the State University at Alexandria, where he graduated in 1869. In 1870 he came to Helena, Ark., and began the study of law, and in December of the following year was admitted to the bar. He at once entered upon a career of distinction and success, business coming to him unsolicited, and his strong, good sense, his knowledge of human nature, his calm conservatism and his genuine legal ability were soon perceived, and he gained the general confidence of the people, so much so that, in 1876, he was elected city attorney, and in 1879 was chosen mayor of Helena, and this position held by re-election until 1882. Since that time he has been county and probate judge, and selfish and personal considerations have been laid aside when the question of duty has been presented. Every enterprise of a public nature finds in him a warm advocate, and his opinion is sought and his counsel heeded, in nearly every question of a public nature, as well as on private matters. He was married, in 1873, to Miss Janie McAlpine, a native of Mississippi, and by her he has a family of three children: Winifred, George and Robert W., Jr. The Judge belongs to the I. O. O. F., the Knights of Pythias, the Knights of Honor and the Royal Arcanum. He is a grand-nephew of the famous poet, Rodman Drake, the author of "Culprit Fay."

William B. O'Shields has long had the reputation of being one of the best farmers in the county, and as a merchant his name and fame is co-extensive with Phillips and the surrounding counties. Every step of his career has been marked by acts of liberality, and he has ever displayed a vital interest in the higher development of his county, which is no doubt owing, in a measure, to his having been born here. His birth occurred on the farm where he now lives, October 5, 1851, and he is the youngest of ten children born to Isaac and Jarvey G. (Nixon) O'Shields, both of whom were born in South Carolina, the former's birth occurring about 1813, and the latter's in Phillips County, Ark., October 16, 1873. His wife died in 1863 at the age of fifty-one years. Their marriage took place in South Carolina, and in 1844 they came to Arkansas, locating in Phillips County, where he followed farming until his death, being quite successful in this calling. He inherited Irish blood from his parents, who were born in the Emerald Isle, and in his political views was first a Whig, but later became a Democrat. His wife was a member of the Methodist Episcopal Church, South, and bore him the following family of children, the names of those who are living being here given: Jennie (widow of Thomas Carter, who died while serving in the Confederate army), Thomas N. (who is a farmer and blacksmith of this county), Richard L. (also a farmer of the county), Isaac (following the same occupation here) and William B. The following are the names of those who are deceased: Nancy (wife of William Jackson), Fanny (who died after reaching womanhood), Mollie (wife of William Jackson), John, and Elizabeth (the wife of Thomas Kibby). William B. O'Shields received the most of his education in Phillips County, and supplemented a common school course by an attendance at Phillips Academy, where he acquired an excellent education. On attaining his majority he began farming for himself, and in 1881 began merchandising also, and has since followed both these occupations, his labors being attended with the best results. In his political views Mr. O'Shields is a Democrat, and on that ticket was elected, in 1878, to the position of constable, and, in 1882, to the office of justice of the peace. In 1885 he was married to Miss Mary Davidson, a daughter of John and Margaret Davidson. She was born in Helena, Ark., is a member of the M. E. Church, South. They have two children: Lottie B. and Maggie May.

E. D. Pillow, sheriff, Helena, Ark. Mr. Pillow, the popular sheriff of Phillips County, though born in Columbia, Tenn., on May 17, 1846, has been a resident of Phillips County, Ark., since 1866, and the confidence which the people have in him, is therefore intelligently placed, for in that time they have had every opportunity to judge of his character and qualifications. His parents, Jerome B. and Elvira (Dale) Pillow, were both natives of Middle Tennessee, and the grandparents were among the early settlers of that State. The paternal grandfather was in the War of 1812. The father of E. D. Pillow, Jerome Pillow, was a brother of Gen. Gideon J. Pillow, who made a lasting reputation in the Mexican War. Jerome B. was a farmer, and some time in the 40's he came to Phillips County and invested largely in real estate, although he never resided in the county. He is still living in Tennessee, and is in his eightieth year. The mother died in 1889. They were the parents of seven children: Mrs. J. W. Q. Ridley, Mrs. Lena Long, Mrs. W. D. Bethel, Mrs. John M. Gray, Mrs. Minter Parker, Edward D. and Jerome B. Edward D. Pillow, the subject of this sketch, was reared in Tennessee, and received a limited education in that State. When in his sixteenth year, or in 1862, he enlisted in Company E, First Tennessee, and served until the surrender, being but nineteen years of age when the war closed. He was in many hard-fought battles, and was a brave and daring soldier. In 1866 he came to Helena and engaged in farming, which pursuit he has since continued. He is the owner of about 3,000 acres of land, has about 1,600 acres under cultivation, and is deeply interested in the raising of cotton. In 1884 he was elected sheriff, re-elected in 1886 and 1888, and is now serving his third term. He was married to Miss Emma Rice, a daughter of Dr. F. H. Rice, and to this union were born three children: William B., Edward Rice and Camille Polk.

Allen J. Polk owes his nativity to Mecklenburg County, N. C., where his birth occurred on March 5, 1824. He is the son of Dr. William J. and Mary (Long) Polk, and the grandson of Col. William J. Polk, of Revolutionary fame. Col. Polk started out from Queens College when sixteen years of age, entered the army as lieutenant, and served in different capacities until the close of the war, when he held the rank of lieutenant-colonel. He is said to have been the first man wounded south of Lexington. He died at Raleigh, N. C. This Polk family is the same as that of James K. Polk, and our subject is a grandson of Gen. Thomas Polk, whose name is so intimately connected with the Mecklenburg Declaration of Independence, or Resolvency, of June 20, 1775. Dr. William J. Polk and wife were natives of North Carolina, born in Mecklenburg and Halifax Counties, respectively, the father on March 21, 1793, and the mother on March 10, 1797. Both died in Columbia, Tenn., the former in 1860, and the latter on September 20, 1885, at the age of eighty-nine years. They were married in North Carolina on June 1, 1818, and in 1836 moved from that State to Columbia, Tenn., where they passed the closing scenes of their lives. In 1848 Dr. Polk sent his son, Allen J. Polk, to Phillips County, Ark., to purchase land, and the latter is now living on land purchased in 1849. Dr. Polk was a graduate of Jefferson School of Medicine, but during his later years he was engaged exclusively in planting. In his political views he was a Whig, and took a deep interest in politics. He was president of the Bank of Tennessee, at Columbia, for many years, and was a man universally respected. He and wife were members of the Episcopal Church. Allen J. Polk received his education at the University of North Carolina, and in 1845 began the study of law at Columbia, Tenn., being admitted to the bar at that place in 1846. He practiced law for one year, and in 1849 commenced planting, which occupation he has since followed, although he has met with many reverses. In 1859 Mr. Polk married Miss Fitzhugh, daughter of Clark Fitzhugh, and the fruits of this union were four living children: Mrs. Susan Keesee (of Helena), Mrs. Anna Pepper (of Memphis), Zelda and Robbin. Mrs. Polk is a member of the Catholic Church. She is a grand-niece of Gen. George Rodgers Clark, who captured the Northwest Territory. Mr. Polk is a member of the Masonic order and a Democrat.

Col. Cadwallader Polk, planter, Helena, Ark. The subject of this sketch needs no introduction to the people of Phillips County, for a long residence, and, above all, a career of usefulness and prominence, have given him an acquaintance which shall last for many years. He was born in Columbia, Tenn., October 16, 1838, and is the son of Dr. William J. and Mary Rebecca (Long) Polk. [For further particulars of parents see sketch of Allen J. Polk.] Of the fourteen children born to his parents six are now living, and Col. Cadwallader Polk is sixth in order of birth, viz.: Allen, Lucius E. (was a planter at Columbia, Tenn.), Rufus (who resides at Little Rock), Mrs. Houston (wife of Russell Houston, of Louisville, Ky.), and Mary P. Branch (resides at Nashville, Tenn.). Russell Houston is attorney for the Louisville & Nashville Railroad. Col. Cadwallader Polk received his education at the University of North Carolina, graduating with honor from the same in 1858, and soon after he turned his attention to planting, which occupation he has carried on since. During the late war he enlisted as second lieutenant of the First Tennessee Confederate Infantry, and served in different capacities until promoted to the rank of colonel of an Arkansas regiment after the battle of Shiloh. He was appointed aid-de-camp to Gen. Hindman, and was in service from that time until the close of the war. While major of Hawthorn's regiment, and at the battle of Prairie Grove, he was wounded in the right cheek by a musket-ball, which came out at the left side of the neck, and soon after he was made colonel, serving in that capacity until cessation of hostilities. He was in West Virginia with Gen. Stonewall Jackson, was in the second day's fight of Shiloh, Prairie Grove, Helena and Little Rock. His regiment surrendered at Camden and Pine Bluff. He soon after turned his attention to planting, and is now the owner of 1,400 acres in the home place, with 600 acres in cotton, corn and grass. He was married March 29, 1864, to Miss Carrie Lowry, of Milliken's Bend, La., and the result of this union was six children, viz.: William J., Anna T., Walter R. (at Little Rock in the employ of the Memphis & Little Rock Railroad in

the capacity of book-keeper), Cadwallader (at home), Nena (at home), and Edward M. Mr. and Mrs. Polk are members of the Episcopal Church. Mr. Polk is a Mason, a K. T., and in his political opinions affiliates with the Democratic party. He takes a great interest in politics, but has never desired to hold office. He is now very much occupied in the rearing of stock, and has a flock of Southdowns, probably the finest in the State. He has some Almont's stock of horses, also other fine stock, and is one of the progressive and enterprising farmers of the county.

E. A. Porter, agent for the Pacific Express Company, at Helena, Ark., is a native of Helena, Ark., his birth occurring here June 5, 1865, he being a son of William and Ann A. (Hanks) Porter, the latter being a sister of Judge James M. Hanks, ex-Congressman. William Porter was born March 9, 1818, at Cincinnati, Ohio, and in his youth, or youthful days, came to Arkansas and located in Helena, owning and operating a tannery, saw and grist-mill at the mouth of the St. Francis River. He conducted this business on a very extensive scale until the opening of the war, during which time he lost nearly all his accumulations of years. After the war he set to work to retrieve his fortunes, and for some time operated a saw-mill and cotton-gin, but later on made farming his chief avocation, possessing a good farm about four miles south of Helena. He is still living (retired from the active duties of life) in Helena, and possesses the full consciousness of having fought the battle of life successfully, and can now rest from the labor and heat of the day. He has never aspired to political positions, and although his views are in accord with the Democratic party, he has never been a partisan. His son, E. A. Porter, was reared and educated in Helena, and at an early age became a messenger boy in the express service, receiving various promotions until he attained his present position of agent for the Pacific Express Company. He is a young man of push, energy and enterprise, and owing to his many other admirable business qualifications, his future success is assured. He has shown his approval of secret organizations by becoming a member of the K. of

P., being a charter member of this organization at Wynne, and he also belongs to the A. O. U. W. March 19, 1888, he espoused Miss Ida B. Dickson.

James C. Rembert is the efficient county clerk of Phillips County, Ark., and is a man whom the citizens delight to honor, for he is careful, prudent, and undeniably honest, and in every walk in life has shown himself to be eminently worthy the respect which is accorded him by all. He is a native of Shelby County, Tenn., born January 17, 1849, and is a son of Llewellyn C. and Mary (Jackson) Rembert, who were also Tennesseeans, in which State the mother died, the father's death occurring in Prairie County, Ark., he having been a worthy and fairly successful planter throughout life. James C. Rembert attended school in the State of Tennessee, until fifteen years of age, his time being also spent in assisting his father on the farm, and in 1866 he came to Helena, Ark., and was salesman in a dry goods house until 1870, when he was made chief deputy in the sheriff's office, and ably discharged the duties of that position until 1874. He then alternately acted as deputy sheriff and salesman of dry goods until 1882, when he became deputy county clerk, receiving the appointment from Gov. Hughes to fill a vacancy in April, and his labors were so satisfactory that, September 2, 1888, he was elected to the office which he still continues to hold. Every worthy enterprise of a public nature finds in him a warm advocate, and as he is a man of intelligence and thinks for himself, his views are always sound. He has been fairly prosperous in a worldly point of view, and is the owner of some excellent real estate in Helena. Socially he belongs to the A. O. U. W., the K. of P., and the Royal Arcanum. He was married, in 1871, to Miss Cortney C. Cage, and by her has three children: J. C., Jr., Bettie C. and Cortney T.

William H. Renfro (deceased) was one of the thirteen children born to the union of Talton and Elizabeth (Harrison) Renfro, his birth occurring in Maury County, Tenn., March 8, 1833. Of that large family of children only three are now living: John H. (residing in Sacramento, Cal.), D. B. (a resident of Holly Grove, Ark.) and Matilda (the widow of William Baulch). When William H. Renfro was nineteen years of age, he came to Phillips County, having accepted a position to superintend a large plantation, owned by a Mr. A. W. Smizer, which he continued to do until the breaking out of the war. He then enlisted in the Confederate army, serving two years. During the war he purchased the farm where Mrs. Renfro now resides, the place then consisting of 480 acres, with only fifty improved. Mrs. Renfro owns 200 acres of improved land, with only forty unimproved, on which are good buildings and many modern evidences of progression and prosperity. That Mr. Renfro was a popular and influential man is demonstrated beyond a doubt by the manner in which he is mentioned, and the reverence in which his memory is held. He was a quiet, law-abiding citizen, keeping pace with the world, in the even tenor of his way, and many improvements of his county stand as monuments of his liberality and support. No one ever realized, not even his own family, how largely Mr. Renfro gave in charities. On this point he was secretive, nothing abashing him more in his own eyes than when a deed of mercy was traced to its source by some grateful recipient of his generosity. He was married December 8, 1856, in this county, to Miss Amanda E. Graves, who was born in Shelby County, Tenn., December 26, 1836, and a daughter of Alexander and Annie (Graves) Graves. Mr. and Mrs. Renfro reared a family of three children: Ella R. (wife of B. Y. Turner) and Lizzie (Mrs. W. C. Brooks). One daughter is deceased. Mr. Graves (father of Mrs. Renfro), was born in Greenville, N. C., in 1800, and was married in Giles County, Tenn., having moved to that county when twenty-one years old. To his marriage eight children were born, three now living: N. L., Maggie (wife of her cousin, Joseph Graves, of this county) and Amanda (Mrs. Renfro). Mr. Graves died in Phillips County, Ark., in 1863. His wife, who was born in Louisa County, Va., in 1804, died in 1864. Mrs. Renfro manages her farm in a good business-like way. She is a supporter of all charitable movements, an earnest worker in and a highly-respected member of the Cumberland Presbyterian Church.

S. M. Reynolds, one of the prominent farmers and stock growers of Marion Township, is the sixth of a family of eight children born to the union of Thomas and Elizabeth (Winters) Reynolds, natives of Tennessee. Thomas Reynolds was a farmer by occupation and continued this pursuit in his native State until about 1848, when he moved to Franklin County, Ark. He purchased land near Ozark, Ark., continued his former pursuit, and was among the first to settle in that county. He died in 1854 and the mother the year previous. Of their eight children, four are now living: Christopher Columbus (resides in Kansas), S. M., Zach (resides in Missouri), and Robert C. (who resides at Plano, Tex.). W. D. (deceased) was in the war with Mexico, and was in the battles of Buena Vista, Marengo and at the City of Mexico at the surrender.. S. M. Reynolds was born in Greene County, Tenn., in 1846, and was reared by his brother W. D., and received his education in the common schools of Phillips and Lee Counties, Ark., as his brother moved to this State in 1859. The latter entered land and S. M. worked on the same until twenty-two years of age. In 1868 he married Miss Mary J. McGrew, of Phillips County, and the daughter of William and Sallie (Clabough) McGrew, natives of Tennessee and North Carolina, respectively. Mr. and Mrs. Reynolds are the parents of eight children: W. T., Henry L., James P., Marion F., Mary E. (deceased), Carrie A., Minnie G. and Octavus (deceased). After his marriage S. M. Reynolds moved to Sharp County, Ark., where he followed the trade of blacksmithing for about one year and then returned to Phillips County. He settled on his present property, which was owned by his wife and which consisted of 120 acres with fifty acres under cultivation. In 1862 Mr. Reynolds joined the boys in gray, Anderson's company, commanded by Dobbins, and was in the battle of Helena, July 4, 1863. He was at the surrender of Little Rock, and was also in a number of skirmishes, etc. He was captured in Phillips County, was sent to Helena and there remained for two weeks when he was paroled. This was the latter part of 1864. Mr. Reynolds is a member of the County Wheel and Farmers' Alliance, and is

Vice-President of the Subordinate Wheel. He is a member of the K. of H., Spring Creek Lodge No. 2643, and is also Vice-President of this. He and Mrs. Reynolds and three of the children are members of the Christian Church. William Reynolds, the paternal grandfather of our subject, was in the War of 1812, and the maternal grandfather, Christopher Winters, was a German, from Pennsylvania, and last resided at Charleston, Tenn.

William Rose, an old resident and substantial farmer of Searcy Township, was born in Jackson County, Ohio, on January 7, 1817, being one of eleven children born to William and Mary (Atkins) Rose. William Rose, Sr., was a native of Montgomery County, Va., and moved with his parents to Ohio when a small boy. He was reared, married and died there in 1879. He was of English-Irish descent, and his wife a direct descendant of the Germans, and died when William, Jr., was a boy. Our subject received his education in the schools of Ohio, and, when twenty-one years old, immigrated to St. Francis County, Ark., where he rented land until 1847, at that time purchasing 160 acres, on which he lived until 1870, when he came to Phillips County, settling on his present farm. This place consists of 440 acres, with 200 acres under a fine state of cultivation, and the improvements, which are numerous, show him to be of an industrious and enterprising spirit. In 1889 Mr. Williams erected a steam cotton-gin, at a cost of $1,500. His farm, situated eighteen miles southwest of Helena, is well adapted to the growing of grain, hay and cotton. He is also engaged in stock-raising, a profitable source of income. Mr. Rose was first married in St. Francis County, in 1843, to Miss Marian Castile, a native of that county, who died in 1847, having borne two children, now deceased. Mr. Rose was again married in 1850 to Miss Augustine Forbes (a cousin of the former wife). She died in 1864, and of five children born to their union only one is now living: Margaret F. (the wife of F. M. Cox, residing in Lee County). In 1865 Mr. Rose married Mrs. Emily Brown (nee Brown). His fourth wife was Martha Brown, a native of Mississippi, and who has two children by her former marriage: John L. and

Carrie. Mr. Rose is a Democrat politically, having cast his first vote for President James K. Polk. He is a member of the Cumberland Presbyterian Church, and a quiet, law-abiding citizen.

Judge M. T. Sanders, Helena, Ark. Matthew T. Sanders was born in Abbeville District, S. C., but during his childhood his parents moved to Alabama and settled in Greene County. His father, Dr. Charles P. Sanders, was a native of Charleston, and was married to Elizabeth Ann Thomson, of Anderson District, S. C. After their removal to Alabama, his father became a prominent physician and practiced his profession with great success until his death. His mother is living. The subject of this sketch was educated in part at Erskine College, S. C., but completed the collegiate course at the University of Alabama, studied law, and was admitted to the bar in 1859. The same year he located in Helena, Ark., where he began the practice of his profession. He entered the military service of the Confederate States in 1861, was afterward appointed first lieutenant of artillery, and assigned to ordnance and staff duty. At the close of the war he was a member of McNair's staff, Churchill's division, received his parole at Shreveport, La., returned to Helena in 1866, and resumed the profession of law. He soon became a successful and prominent lawyer, and enjoyed an extensive practice until he was elected to the bench. Judge Sanders has always been an active Democrat. For two years after the close of the war he was editor of the Helena Clarion, a leading Democratic journal. For several years he was chairman of the Democratic Executive Committee of his county, and in the local political revolution in Phillips County, by which the Democrats, after an exciting campaign, defeated the Republicans in 1878, he was chosen for county judge. In this administration of county affairs he relieved the tax-payers of oppressive burdens, reduced current expenses of the county 50 per centum below what they were previous to his election, and earned the lasting gratitude of the people by many wise reforms in matters affecting the welfare of the county. In 1882 Judge Sanders was a Democratic candidate for Congress in the First Congressional district, but after a partial canvass of the district withdrew from the race. In July of the same year he was nominated for circuit judge by the Democracy of the first judicial circuit, and elected the following September by a majority of more than 5,000 votes over his Republican opponent, Col. W. H. Hawes. This honor was unsought, and for that reason affords the best evidence of the confidence of the people in his ability, integrity and purity of character. He was re-elected in 1886. Judge Sanders has served nearly eight years on the bench, and by his fine legal attainments and superior administrative capacity he has proven a valuable acquisition to the judiciary of the State. He is both a Mason and an Odd Fellow, and a member of the Episcopal Church. In 1868 he was married to Miss Sallie Alexander, of Helena, Ark., and by this union has five children.

Arthur M. Scott, a well-known merchant and farmer of Spring Creek Township, came originally from Alabama, and is a son of Adam C. and Catharine (Shackelford) Scott, natives of Kentucky and Virginia, respectively. Mr. Scott was a relative of the noted Winfield Scott. He was a mechanic by trade, and died during the Mexican War, while in service. His wife is now living in Yell County, Ark., at the age of seventy-two years. They were the parents of four children, of whom our subject is the only one living. Arthur M. Scott was born in Southern Alabama, on August 12, 1837. He was reared in his native State until eleven years of age, when he came to Arkansas with his grandfather, John L. Shackelford, and has resided in this county since that time. His mother removed to this State three years later. Arthur received his education at Batesville, where he was attending school at the breaking out of the war, and then enlisted in the Confederate army, in Company C of the Fifteenth Arkansas Infantry, in which he served until the close of hostilities. He participated in the battles of Missionary Ridge, Perryville (where he was shot through the right hip and disabled for eleven months), Jonesboro, and, a number of others, and was captured at Franklin, Tenn., and taken to Camp Douglas, at Chicago, where he was held until June 16, 1865. Returning to Arkansas he engaged in farming for a year, then going to Helena, where he remained until 1869. After being engaged in clerking until 1871 he started in business for himself, opening a store of general merchandise, that he still owns, and which has proven very successful. He also leases 200 acres of land near North Creek, and on this raises annually about fifty bales of cotton, and a large amount of hay. Mr. Scott is a leading Democrat, and has served in a public capacity for a number of years. He has filled the position of justice of the peace for some four years, has been a notary public since 1879, and has held the office of postmaster of North Creek since 1872, being the present incumbent.

Jesse C. Shell, a prominent planter and an old resident of Phillips County, is a native of Louisiana, and a son of Jesse J. Shell, who was born in Orange District, S. C., May 4, 1802. His father, Jacob Shell, first saw the light of day in South Carolina in 1771, dying in Louisiana in 1833. He was under Gen. Jackson at the battle of New Orleans. His wife, Sarah Rutlidge, a descendant of Gov. Rutlidge, died in 1832. Jesse Shell, Sr., moved to this county from Louisiana, in 1833, to escape the cholera, and settling ten miles from Helena, was one of the early settlers and prominent men of the locality. He represented his county in the first legislature of the State, in 1836, and was re-elected in 1838, and again in 1840. To himself and wife were born nine children, two of whom are living: Margaret A. (the wife of Maj. Palmer, of Monroe County) and Jesse C. The latter was born in Lake Providence in 1829, but grew up in this county from his fourth year, being reared by a Mr. Mooney after his father's death, which occurred in 1841, a result of a kick from a horse. He was employed, at the age of eighteen, as a manager, and had charge of a plantation. In 1849 he went to California, was engaged in mining for two years, and then returning, he located in this county, and was appointed deputy sheriff the same year. The following year Mr. Shell was again employed as a manager, in which occupation he was employed until the war, when he enlisted in the First Arkansas Mounted Riflemen, and

served until the close of the war, being in Price's raid through Missouri. After peace was declared he commenced farming, and has since followed that calling. He was married, in 1878, to Miss Mary Ward, who was born in Preston, England, on September 8, 1852, being a daughter of Henry and Alice Ward, who lived and died in England. She came to this country with an aunt, and was reared in the city of Cincinnati and New Orleans. They were the parents of four children: Jesse R., Walter P., James H. and Margaret C. (who is deceased). Mr. Shell owns a farm of 160 acres, which is mostly under cultivation. He is a Democrat in politics, and a member of the Knights of Honor, holding the office of Protector in his lodge, and also belongs to the Knights and Ladies of Honor. He is a member of the Methodist Episcopal Church, South, and his wife of the Catholic Church.

Frank B. Sliger, president of the First National Bank of Helena, Ark., is one of the foremost business men of Phillips County, although he is young in years. His birth occurred in New Orleans, La., July 16, 1854, and he is a son of Samuel and Mary (Klock) Sliger, the former a native of Frankfort, Germany, and the latter of Strasburg. They were married in their native country, and in 1846 embarked on board a vessel bound for the United States, landing at New Orleans, where Mr. Sliger engaged in the produce business. He enlisted in the Mexican War, and is supposed to have been assassinated at the City of Mexico. Besides his wife, who afterward died in Covington, Ky., he left a family of six children, of whom Frank was fourth. His opportunities for acquiring a good education being excellent, he secured a fair general knowledge in the public schools of New Orleans. It was not long until he had to rely entirely upon his own resources for support, and although his education was very good he was young in years and unacquainted with the ways of the world, and therefore found it somewhat difficult to obtain a living for a number of years. In the spring of 1868, when only fourteen years of age, he came to Helena and immediately entered the employ of Straub & Lohmann, merchants, and is still associated with the senior partner, having been connected with him a period of twenty-two years. By economy, industry and a judicious use of his money saved, wealth soon began to come in, and he engaged in the brokerage and real-estate business, his wealth materially increasing while thus occupied. In 1884, in connection with L. Lucy, he started a private bank, but their business increased to such an extent that they were compelled to reorganize with more capital, and the National Bank was established, he becoming its president. He also deals in real estate, and owns a vast amount of land in different localities. He is public-spirited, progressive, and possesses keen perception and sound judgment, and is acknowledged by all to be one of the leading business spirits of Helena. He is a stockholder in the Planters' Compress Company, the Electric Light and Power Company, and so secure is he in the estimation of the people that he could command almost any position in their power to give, did he so wish it. He has been city treasurer for several years, was treasurer of Cotton Belt District No. 1, and as he has always been deeply interested in educational matters, he has been president of the school board for a number of years, but is now resigned. He is Grand Treasurer of the Knights of Honor of the State, is Grand Commander of the American Legion of Honor of the State, is a member of the Grand Lodge of the Knights of Pythias and the Ancient Order of United Workmen, and also belongs to the Royal Arcanum and I. O. O. F., being Noble Grand in the latter organization. He was married in March, 1886, to Miss Maggie Carpenter, by whom he has one child, Eugenia, born in March, 1887.

Edward Sonfield, merchant, Poplar Grove, Ark. Mr. Sonfield owes his nativity to Cincinnati, Ohio, where his birth occurred on May 30, 1854, and is the eldest of eleven children, the result of the union of Henry and Rosa (Kornik) Sonfield, natives of Germany. The father came to this country and settled in Cincinnati in 1850 or 1851, and was engaged in the jewelry business, following the same for ten or eleven years. He then moved to Nashville, Tenn., in 1861, embarked in the dry-goods business, which he followed until 1865, when he moved to Memphis, here continuing the same occu-

pation. He died in that city on July 27, 1873, a much-respected and honored citizen. Mrs. Sonfield still resides in Memphis, where she was married in 1879 or 1880 to S. Eichwald. To Mr. and Mrs. Sonfield were born eleven children, eight now living: Edward, Annie (wife of D. Zellner, of Memphis), Sarah (wife of M. Hirshberg, of Boston), William (salesman at Memphis), Sallie and Jennie (at home), Eugene and Leon. Those deceased were Henrietta (died when small), Julia (was accidentally burned to death at Cincinnati in 1874) and Morris (died at Memphis, in 1881, in his twenty-third year). Edward Sonfield was educated at Cincinnati and Memphis, and at the age of thirteen years was employed as cash boy for Menken Bros., of Memphis. He was then employed as salesman for several years, and from 1873 to 1876 was traveling salesman for Otto Schwill & Co. In 1870 Mr. Sonfield moved to Trenton, Phillips County, Ark., and was salesman here for several years, traveling a portion of the time. In March, 1885, he commenced merchandising for himself at Poplar Grove with a small capital, and has since done a good business, his annual sales being about $6,000. He owns a fine store-house and dwelling. He chose for his companion in life Miss Alice Myers, of Helena, Ark., the daughter of Alex. and Mary (Poe) Myers, and was united in marriage to her on March 3, 1881. Her parents were natives of Germany and Mississippi, respectively. The father came to America when a young man, settled in Holly Springs, Miss., was married there and became the father of a family of children, seven now living: Blakly (residing in Memphis), Minnie (wife of Ben. Wiley, of Helena), Alice, Samuel, Lucy, Susie and Alex (the four last at home). To Mr. and Mrs. Sonfield were born four children: The eldest, an infant, died December 21, 1881; Henrietta (died October 6, 1883), Henry (born October 29, 1884) and Julia (born December 14, 1886). Mr. and Mrs. Sonfield are both of the Jewish faith. Mr. Sonfield is a member and Reporter of the K. of H., Poplar Grove Lodge No. 2442; also Secretary of the American Legion of Honor, Hendrix Council 737, and is notary public of this county. Politically he is a Democrat.

Christopher Columbus Spain is a son of Mabry and Delilah Spain, natives of South Carolina. The former died in 1855, somewhere out West, the particulars of which were never known. C. C. Spain made his appearance in this world in Union County, S. C., on October 4, 1838. His mother dying when he was only seven weeks old, he was reared by an uncle, and in 1860 immigrated from South Carolina to Trenton, Ark., locating where he now lives in 1870. This place consists of 175 acres, with over 100 acres under cultivation. In 1875 he opened a store and engaged in the mercantile business, to which he has since given his attention. He was the prime mover in getting the postoffice of Coffee Creek established in 1878, and has been postmaster ever since. Mr. Spain has been married three times; first in 1867, to Miss Mellissa Browning, who was born in this county, on August 11, 1845, and who died on August 15, 1878, leaving four children, two still living: Ida M. and Mary E. Arthur and Christopher C. are deceased. He married his second wife, Dorathy E. Phillips, in January, 1879, who died in March, 1880. His third and present wife was formerly Sarah A. Higginbotham, to whom he was married in November, 1882, and who was born in this county on March 12, 1861. They are the parents of two children: Mellissa C. and Dortha E. Mr. Spain served as a gallant soldier in the Confederate service twelve months during the war. He is a strong Democrat, and a member of the K. of H., and he and his wife belong to the Baptist Church. He held the office of justice of the peace for over five years. In addition to his farm work Mr. Spain owns and operates a steam cotton-gin, which he erected at a cost of $1,200, and which is largely patronized.

William H. Stone is a prosperous insurance agent of Helena, Ark., and we may truthfully say that no other business calls for better judgment, keener foresight, greater caution or more honest dealing than does this. By it the penniless and dependent are protected as well as the rich, and it is one of the great interests of the age, ranking with banking, railroading, mining and mercantile pursuits. Mr. Stone is the able representative of ten different insurance companies in Helena, and is accounted one of the successful business men of the county. He was born in St. Francis County, Ark., September 30, 1841, and is a son of William H. and Caroline S. (Heslep) Stone, the former a native of Tennessee, and the latter of Kentucky. After the father's death, which occurred in Tennessee, the mother came to Helena, Ark., in 1847, and here died on March 8, 1877, just thirty years to the day after her arrival. Of their family of five children all are deceased with the exception of William H. and his brother Joseph H. The former was but six years old when brought by his mother to the county, and here he grew to honorable manhood, receiving his education in a private school. Early in the year 1861 he enlisted in the Yell Rifles and during a service of four years saw much hard service, and participated in some hardfought battles. Upon his return to Helena at the close of the war he clerked for two years, but since that time has followed his present calling, at which he has done remarkably well, being now the owner of considerable valuable real estate in the town. He has been a Mason since 1867, and also belongs to the Royal Arcanum and the Knights of Honor. In 1867 he wedded Miss Sallie L. Miles, a native of Arkansas, and by her has two children: Ellice and Clinton.

W. B. Stout, agent for the Southern Express Company, and passenger agent for the Louisville, New Orleans & Texas Railroad, owes his nativity to Paducah, Ky., where his birth occurred on November 25, 1848, and is the son of Hezekiah and Mary G. (Gholston) Stout, the father a native of Indiana, and the mother of Kentucky. The father was a prominent business and saw mill man in Indiana, Tennessee and Kentucky, and was city tax collector for a number of years in Paducah, Ky., before his death, which occurred in Paducah, in November, 1877. The boyhood days of W. B. Stout was passed in the common schools and later in college. At an early age he was employed in the Adams and Southern Express office at Paducah, and has followed this business for twenty-two years. In 1880 he was transferred to St. Louis, and remained there until coming to Helena, in 1886. He has occupied every position of trust while in the employ of this company, and now occupies both positions as express agent and passenger agent. He has much experience and thoroughly understands his business. He was married in 1880 to Miss Louisa M. Simon, of Paducah, Ky., who was born in Louisville, Ky., became a member of the Catholic Church in early life, both children being baptized in the same church. Their names are: Mamie Threasa (was born at Little Rock, Ark., January 14, 1882) and Archibald L. (was born in St. Louis, Mo., in March, 1885). Mr. Stout is a member of the K. of H., and is a stockholder in two building and loan associations, American Building & Loan Association and Tontine Savings Association; being secretary and treasurer of the same.

Maj. J. A. Tappan, hardware merchant, Helena. Ark. In Fayette County, Tenn., in January, 1847, there was born to Capt. E. S. and Sarah E. (Williamson) Tappan, a son, J. A. Tappan. The parents were both natives of Tennessee, and the father was a merchant by vocation. He was a prominent politician of Tennessee, and was a member of the legislature several terms. He was a captain in the War of 1812. J. A. Tappan was reared to maturity in his native county, receiving his education there, and when only sixteen years of age, or, in 1863, he enlisted in Company A, Sixth Tennessee Regiment, and served until the surrender. He then learned civil engineering, following the same for years, and engineered the St. Louis & St. Joe Railroad; also the Missouri, Kansas & Topeka Railroad. In 1870 he came to Helena and built the Arkansas Midland Railroad, being chief engineer of the same. He then took charge of and reconstructed the gas-works, which were $8,000 in debt, got them in good shape and turned them over with $2,500 cash. He represents W. H. Brown & Co., at Pittsburg, the largest coal dealers in the world. He engaged in the hardware business in January, 1889, and is doing a good business, carrying a large stock of goods. Their coal business is an extensive one, selling about 500,000 bushels annually. It is shipped both by river and railroad. He is a stockholder in the Fair Association. He was married in 1878 to Miss Maggie Lambert, and the fruits of this union

have been three children: Maggie, Mattie and Bessie. Mr. Tappan is a member of the I. O. O. F. Lodge, and is one of the leading and prominent men of Helena. He has done a great deal in the way of improving the city.

Reuben Terry is a native of Kentucky, and a son of John and Jane (Gray) Terry, originally from Kentucky and Virginia, respectively. John Terry was born on April 3, 1801, and died in 1833 at Evansville, Ind., while on his way from New Orleans. He was married on June 20, 1819. Reuben Terry, his father, was of Irish descent and a native of Virginia. Reuben Terry, the principal of this sketch, was born in Bourbon County, Ky., on April 1, 1821, and at the age of sixteen commenced learning the carpenter's trade, which he followed for twenty years. He was married in Indiana, in 1847, to Miss Nancy Ann Shaver, who was born in Ripley County, that State, in 1828. She died in January, 1885, having been the mother of nine children, two of whom are still living: John W. (residing in Poplar Grove) and Albert (who resides in this county) Mr. Terry's second marriage was on June 11, 1889, to Miss Fannie Jones, who was born in Tennessee, August 22, 1858. In 1872 Mr. Terry engaged in the mercantile business at Turner, this county, taking his eldest son, J. W., in partnership, the firm being known as J. W. Terry & Co. They carry a stock of $4,000, and do a business of $12,000 to $15,000 annually. He has been portmaster of this village since 1879. In 1846 he enlisted in the Mexican War, serving under Gen. Taylor, and was discharged at New Orleans in June,. 1847. He is a member of the Masonic and I. O. O. F. fraternities, and he and wife are connected with the Methodist Episcopal Church, South.

G. F. Thomin, M. D., physician and surgeon, Marvell, Ark. A prominent physician and surgeon, who by his own abilities has attained distinction in his profession, is Dr. G. F. Thomin. This gentleman was born in Cincinnati, Ohio, in 1848, and is the son of Conrad Frederick Thomin, a native of Germany, who came to America in 1824. The latter settled in Cincinnati, and embarked in the milling business, which he still continues, running a custom and merchant mill, although he is now seventy-seven years of age. He was married in Cincinnati, Ohio, to Miss Catherine Folenious, who is also living, and is now sixty-four years of age. Both are members of the Old School Presbyterian Church. Of their family of five children, four are now living: Louisa (deceased, wife of Joseph Cohn, the family now residing in Hamilton County, Ohio), Fredericka (wife of B. Buell, of the same place), Eliza (wife of Robert Wade, who is the grandnephew of Gen. B. Wade, of Ohio. He also resides in Hamilton County), G. F., and Charles F. (who resides in Ohio). G. F. Thomin was reared in Cincinnati, Ohio, and attended the free schools of that place until six years of age, when his father moved in the country, to Venice on the Great Miami River. There he attended school until sixteen years of age, when he entered Hanover College (Indiana), graduating from the same at the age of twenty years. He then entered the Ohio Medical School the same year, and at the age of twenty-one graduated from the same. In 1865 he enlisted in the United States army as one of the Ohio State National Guards, commanded by Col. Fisher, of Cincinnati, and spent most of his time while in the army on the eastern coast of Virginia. He was a drummer boy, and was discharged at Camp Denison, Ohio. The Doctor commenced practicing at Millville, Ohio, where he remained for three years, and then moved to Northeast Missouri in 1872. He practiced at Williamston, Lewis County, and remained there until December, 1884, when he located at Marvell, in Phillips County, his present home, and still has his large practice. Although he has spent a comparatively short time in this county, he enjoys a large and lucrative practice, and from all appearances the confidence in his abilities is not misplaced. The Doctor has been twice married, his first wife being Miss Nautilla Woodyard, daughter of Col. M. D. Woodyard, whom he married in 1870. Col. Woodyard commanded the United States forces from Missouri, and was under Gen. Moore. To the Doctor and wife was born but one child, who died in infancy. Mrs. Thomin died in 1872 of consumption. In

1874 Dr. Thomin married Miss Mamie K. Sprinkle, daughter of W. J. Sprinkle, of Canton, Mo., who was quartermaster under Gen. Moore. Doctor and Mrs. Thomin became the parents of three children: Ada, Frederica and Harry (deceased). The Doctor is a member of the Masonic fraternity, Marvell Lodge No. 369, of which he is Master, and he and wife are members of the Christian Church.

William Thompson, an extensive planter of Cypress Township, is a native of Tennessee, and was born in Williamson County October 22, 1821. He moved to Kentucky in 1843, and in 1855 to Greene County, Mo., coming in 1866 to this county. The first year he rented a farm, and the following year purchased a tract of wild land. Mr. Thompson was married in Kentucky about 1847 to Miss Henrietta Roper, who was born in Kentucky in 1833. She is the mother of twelve children, ten of whom are still living: Joseph E. (married to L. F. Renfraw), William A., Sarah M. (widow of Robert Henderson), Lucretia (married to J. F. Jarrett), Anna (wife of F. Dawson), Henrietta B. (wife of William McKinley), Charles F., Laura, Allie and Alice (twins). They are the grandparents of twenty-two children. Mr. Thompson owns 320 acres of land, with 140 acres under cultivation. Though upon locating in this county he had but $1 in his pocket, he is now in good circumstances, and owns a well-improved farm, stocked with cattle, mules and horses. Mr. Thompson, formerly a Whig, cast his first presidential vote for Henry Clay; he now votes the Democratic ticket. During the war he served as wagon master in the Confederate army for three years. He and wife and all but two of the children belong to the Baptist Church. Mr. Thompson is a model farmer, an old resident and a highly respected citizen.

Judge P. O. Thweatt, attorney at law. To undertake to introduce to our readers the subject of this sketch would be something entirely unnecessary, for his extensive acquaintance and long connection with the affairs of this county have rendered him well and popularly known. Born near Franklin, Williamson County, Tenn., October 10, 1834, he is a son of Harwood D. and Elizabeth

(Echols) Thweatt, who were of Welsh and English origin, and natives of the Old Dominion, their ancestors having settled in that commonwealth prior to the American Revolution. Both the paternal and maternal grandfathers participated in that war, and two of the Judge's paternal uncles died while serving in the War of 1812, and his mother's only brother died the next year of disease contracted at Pensacola. Harwood and Elizabeth Thweatt moved from Virginia to Tennessee in 1811, and located near Franklin, but in the year 1845 moved to Mississippi and settled in Yalobusha County, where both died on a farm. Two of their seven children are now living: Nichols and Judge P. O. The latter spent his youth and received his early education near what afterward became the battle-field of Franklin, he being an attendant of Harper's Academy, from which institution he graduated in 1856. From that time until 1859 he made his home in Mississippi, and at the latter date removed to Monroe County, Ark., where he spent some time in teaching school and studying law, being admitted to the bar at Clarendon, in March, 1860, and entered at once upon a successful career. His labors were interrupted, however, by the opening of the war, and in June, 1861, he went to Fort Smith and joined Churchill's regiment, but owing to his receiving a gunshot wound in the left leg, at the battle of Oak Hill, Mo., August 10, of that year, he was unfitted for active duty for the remainder of the war, but served as commissary. In 1862 he was elected county and probate judge of Monroe County, and served until the Federal troops took possession of the county, in 1863, when he went as a refugee to Texas and there remained until the war closed. In 1865 he returned to Clarendon, Ark., built him an office and resumed his law practice. In 1866 he was elected prosecuting attorney of the First Judicial District, which extended from the Missouri line to the mouth of White River, and served until the reconstruction period, when he was removed from office. Having located at Helena, he practiced alone until April, 1870, then formed a co-partnership with Judge T. B. Hanley, continuing until 1873, when he became associated with Hon. G. Quarles, which partner-

ship lasted for about ten years. His professional career was one of gratifying success, and he has built up a reputation for ability that is not merely local, but extends over a wide range. He owns two good farms, each containing several hundred acres, and his farm on Old Town Ridge comprises 800 acres, of which 400 are in cultivation; and the one on Old Town Island comprises 320 acres, of which 220 are in a high state of cultivation, and on which is erected a fine steam cotton-gin. All this has been earned through practicing his profession. He was associated for some time with his brother, W. H. Thweatt, at Clarendon, but like himself the latter enlisted in the Confederate army, was wounded at the battle of Shiloh, in 1862, and died in 1864. The Judge is a Royal Arch Mason, has passed all the chairs in the Odd Fellows lodge, and is also a member of the Knights of Pythias, the Royal Arcanum and the Legion of Honor. His marriage, which occurred on February 23, 1870, was to Mary, the only daughter of Judge J. S. Hornor, and by her he is the father of three children: Bessie, Oscar and Re, who are living, and two dead. The Judge has now in his possession a Virginia land grant, dated 1735, to a tract of land in Prince George County, Va., signed by George II., and granting a large tract of land to his ancestors on the father's side.

Joseph Woodson Thompson, farmer, Marvell, Ark. A life-long experience in the channels of agricultural pursuits has contributed not a little toward the success which has fallen to the lot of Mr. Thompson, who is acknowledged by all to be one of the enterprising and substantial citizens of the county. He is the owner of 370 acres of excellent land, and has 140 acres under cultivation, with a good orchard, fine buildings, etc. He was originally from Williamson County, Tenn., where his birth occurred on March 3, 1826, and is the son of Joseph Lee Thompson, and grandson of William and Rachel Thompson. The grandparents moved from North Carolina to Williamson County, Tenn., when Joseph was six years of age, and there he grew to manhood. William Thompson was of Scotch descent, and he was a soldier in the Revolutionary War. Joseph Thompson was married in Williamson County, Tenn., to Miss Sarah Adams, a native of Blount County, Tenn., born in 1800; she died in 1877, in Phillips County, Ark. He moved from Tennessee to Greene County, Mo., in 1856, and from there to Phillips County, Ark., in 1862. There he died July 3, 1874. They were the parents of eight children, five now living: William (in this county), Joseph W., John L. (resides in Greene County, Mo.), Mary (widow of Mr. Carter, and now resides in Fulton County, Ky.) and Samuel H. (in Monroe County, Ark.). Joseph Woodson Thompson was the third in order of birth of the children born to his parents. He attained his growth and received his education in Williamson County, Tenn., and in 1854 he went to Greene County, Mo., where he resided eight years, engaged in farming. He then enlisted in the Confederate army, in May, 1861, in Company A of the State service, and in 1862 entered the regular army in Company B, Hawthorn's regiment of infantry. About February, 1863, he was discharged on account of disability. He was in the fights of Pea Ridge and Oak Hill. After his discharge he came to this county, and here he has resided ever since. He was married here on March 27, 1882, to Mrs. Helen Pasley, a native of Phillips County, Ark., and the fruits of this union has been one child, Woodson Lee. Mrs. Thompson was born in 1852 as the daughter of William and Laura Thompson, both of whom died when their daughter was about two years old. They were married in this county, and after their death Helen was reared among strangers. She was married about 1875, to Harvey J. Pasley, who died in 1877, leaving one child, Harvey C., who now resides with Mr. and Mrs. Thompson. Mr. Thompson is Democratic in his political views, and his first presidential vote was cast for Z. Taylor. At one time he was a Whig. Mr. Thompson is a member of the Masonic order, Marvell Lodge No. 369, Royal Arch Chapter at Clarendon, Monroe County, Ark., and is also a member of the K. of H.

Mrs. Emma Ann Turner is the widow of Nathan S. Turner, who was born in Caswell County. N. C., December 28, 1825, as a son of Edmund and Mary (Slade) Turner, also natives of Caswell County. The paternal grandfather, Edmund Turner, originally from Maryland, was a soldier in the Revolutionary War, and was one of the early settlers of North Carolina. He was of English descent. Edmund Turner, Jr., removed from North Carolina in 1844, going first to Tennessee, then to Missouri, where he remained ten years, then to Mississippi, and in 1857 came to Phillips County, Ark., where he died the following year, his wife dying the same month. They were the parents of five children, two of whom only are living. Nathan S. Turner and the subject of this sketch were married in Mississippi January 7, 1852. He came to this county in 1856, and embarked in farming, and was one of the influential men of the county. He was a member of the Masonic order, in which he had taken the Royal Arch degree, and was a prominent Democrat. He died on February 28, 1874. Mrs. Emma Turner was born in Currituck County, N. C., on September 30, 1838, her parents being Daniel B. and Nancy (Gray) Lindsey, also of that county. They were married in their native State, and resided in Currituck County until 1840, when they moved to Hardeman County, Tenn., remaining five years. After removing to Mississippi, in 1856, they came to Arkansas, and located in this county. Mr. Lindsey afterward went to St. Francis County, where he died in 1868, at the age of sixty years. His wife was born in 1816, and died in December, 1858, in Monroe County, Ark. They were the parents of nine children, four of whom are still living—one son in Texas, one son in Mississippi, a daughter in Faulkner County, Ark., and the principal of this sketch. Mrs. Turner owns 285 acres of land, near the village of Poplar Grove, of which 200 acres are under cultivation. She also owns twenty-two town lots. She is now engaged in keeping a boarding house, which is largely patronized. She is the mother of two children, William T. and John B.

Nathaniel Berry Turner, a large planter of Cypress Township, is a native of South Carolina, and is the owner of 1,320 acres of land, with over 400 acres under cultivation. Besides being the owner of a steam cotton-gin, which he erected in 1873, he is quite an extensive stock-raiser, and the largest hay producer in his township. His principal crop is corn and cotton, of the last of which he raises from 100 to 160 bales annually. He was born in South Carolina, March 7, 1834, and is a son of John and Nancy (Cooper) Turner. John Turner, a native of South Carolina, died in that State in 1855. His father, Joseph Turner, was a Virginian by birth. The mother of our subject, originally from South Carolina, died in May, 1871. She bore a family of eleven children, five boys and six girls, three of whom are living in South Carolina, one in Alabama, and three in this county. The rest are now deceased. The subject of this sketch remained in his native State until 1859, when he came to Arkansas, and located in Phillips County. Here he was married, in 1868, to Miss Ellen McDowell, who was born in Mississippi, in 1847. They are the parents of eleven children, eight of whom survive: John L., Laura A., Nathaniel G., Ellis, James C., Nellie, Blanche and Liza Josie. Mr. Turner enlisted in June, 1862, in Company C, of Johnson's regiment, in which he served until the close of the war. He is a strong Democrat, and one of the influential men of his township. He has served as school director for six years, is a member of the County Wheel, and is a self-made man. When he came to this county he was employed as overseer of a gang of negroes, and had no property. Now he is one of the largest land owners in the county.

Capt. B. Y. Turner, farmer, Poplar Grove, Ark. Mr. Turner is recognized as a careful, energetic agriculturist of this community, and by his advanced ideas and progressive habits has done no little for the farming elements hereabouts. Originally from Tennessee, he was born in 1838, and is the youngest of five children, the fruits of the union of Edmond and Mary (Slade) Turner, natives, respectively, of Maryland and North Carolina. Edmond Turner moved to Tennessee about 1837, but after a residence there of one year moved to Greene County, Mo., and settled near Springfield in 1839. Springfield was at that time a very small place, the principal merchant being Daniel P. Berry, and only two or three business houses were there at that time. The section of country

between that place and the Arkansas line was very sparsely settled, and Mr. Turner was among the pioneers of that county. He remained there sixteen years, and in 1855 came to this county, settling where his son, Capt. B. Y. Turner, now lives, and on a portion of this land the city of Poplar Grove was laid out in 1878. When Mr. Turner first purchased this farm there were but thirty acres cleared, and at the time of his death he had improved only forty or forty-five acres. He died in 1858. Of the five children born to his marriage only two are now living: W. C. (who resides in California and is extensively engaged in farming and stock raising) and B. Y. Turner. The mother of these children died in 1858, within a few days of her husband. Both were members of the Methodist Episcopal Church, South. He was a member of the Masonic fraternity. B. Y. Turner was reared and educated principally in Marshall County, Miss., whither his father had moved in 1851. He attended graded school at Oxford, Miss., for two years, and afterward came with his father to this State, where he studied medicine under Dr. R. G. Dunn, and attended his first lectures at Louisville Medical College in 1855. He never practiced to any great extent, but spent the time between 1856 and 1861 engaged in farming. In the last mentioned year he joined a company known as the South Western Guards, as a private, and was elected lieutenant, and upon its organization was promoted to the rank of captain. After his company was joined to the Second Arkansas Infantry, Capt. Turner was engaged in the following battles: Green River, Shiloh, Corinth (1st) and Iuka. After the last named battle he was transferred to the west side of the Mississippi River and served in Dobbins' brigade, under Gen. Price. He was in the battles of Helena and Big Creek, and at the last place was wounded by a minie-ball in the left leg, which disabled him for some time. He was with Gen. Price through Missouri, and participated in most of the battles fought during that time. He surrendered and was paroled at Helena in July, 1865. Capt. Turner then returned home and found himself a poor man, his property consisting of two six-shooters and a black horse. He was not discouraged, however, and went to work at tilling the soil. He is now the owner of 400 acres of land, with 250 acres under cultivation, and is also the owner of a large cotton-gin and grist-mill combined. He gins annually 500 bales of cotton, and produces from his farm seventy bales annually. In 1867 he was elected sheriff (this was the first election held after the war), but was disqualified by the new constitution of 1868. Ten years later he was elected to the same office and filled this office in a highly creditable manner until 1884. Mr. Turner has been three times married; first, in 1859, to Miss Fannie Swan, who died the same year. In 1869 he married Miss Virginia A. Cowley, daughter of Edward A. Cowley, who was one of the early county and circuit clerks of Phillips County, and one of the old pioneers of Helena. To Mr. and Mrs. Turner were born two children: Edward B. (died at the age of nine years) and Virginia (who died at the age of six years). Mrs. Turner died in 1875. She was a member of the Old School Presbyterian Church. In 1879 Mr. Turner was united in marriage to Miss Ella R. Renfro, of Phillips County, and daughter of W. H. and A. A. Renfro, natives of Tennessee. Mr. and Mrs. Turner became the parents of two children: Renfro H. and Bartlett Y., Jr. Mr. Turner is a member of the Old School Presbyterian Church, and is a member of Poplar Grove Lodge of the K. of H. He is a Democrat in his political views, and is a prominent citizen. Mr. Turner is a member of the American Legion of Honor, Hendrix Lodge No. 737.

James R. Turner, livery merchant, Poplar Grove, Ark. This stable, from the large business it does, not only exemplifies the importance of the town, but reflects credit on its management. Mr. Turner engaged in this business near where he is now located, at the age of twenty-one years, and in 1873 he moved to his present place of business, having built the first business house in the village, and started the first general store. He was also appointed postmaster in his twenty-first year, and served in that capacity for twenty years. At the time he was appointed postmaster he was elected justice of the peace, which office he retained

for eight years. In January, 1868, he married Miss R. N. McCoy, a native of Phillips County, born on Christmas day, 1851, and the daughter of John and J. E. (Howard) McCoy, natives of Kentucky, who came to this State in 1840. Mr. McCoy was a short time in the Confederate army, and died in 1864. Mrs. McCoy afterward, in 1872, was united in marriage to M. A. Stripline, of this county. He died in 1877, and Mrs. McCoy now resides with her son-in-law, James R. Turner. To the latter's marriage were born seven children, four now living: Robert N., Daisy, Eva and Templin. Three died when small. Mr. Turner is a member of the Masonic fraternity, La Fayette Lodge No. 97, and he and wife are members of the K. & L. of H., Poplar Grove Lodge No. 518, he being Treasurer of the same. Mrs. Turner is a member of the Cumberland Presbyterian Church. Mr. Turner is an earnest worker for emigration, and is a member of the county emigration body called the Phillips County Emigration Society. He was born in Phillips County, Ark., in 1848, and is the third of nine children born to the union of W. R. and Elizabeth F. (Ewett) Turner, and the only one now living. The father came to this county from Maryland in 1836, settled near Helena, which was then only a small trading point, and when Indians were numerous. He bought land and tilled the soil the principal part of his life, and at one time, previous to the war, was the owner of a number of negroes. He was one of the pioneer settlers, and helped to open nearly every public road in the county. He served as justice of the peace previous to the late unpleasantness, and was for those days one of the best-educated men in the county. He was born in 1818 and died in 1877. He served for a short time in the Confederate service before the close of the war. He was twice married, first, in 1843, to the mother of the subject of this sketch, who died in 1862, and in 1863 to a sister of his first wife, Martha A. Ewett, who bore him three children, two of whom are now living: J. C. (in the store of James R. Turner) and Mrs. Emma F. Pearson (of Poplar Grove.) Mrs. Turner resides with her daughter, Mrs. Pearson.

Richard N. Venable, M. D., physician and surgeon, Poplar Grove, Ark. Among the people of Phillips, as well as surrounding counties, the name that heads this sketch is by no means an unfamiliar one, for, for many years he has been successfully occupied in the prosecution of his chosen profession. During this time his career as a practitioner and thorough student of medicine has won for him no less a reputation than has his personal characteristics as a citizen and neighbor. He was born in Virginia in 1828, and is the third of seven children, the result of the union of Henry and Margaret (Ried) Venable, natives of the Old Dominion, also. Henry Venable was a merchant and farmer of Virginia, and was postmaster of Prince Edward Court House (some member of this family has been postmaster at that place for over 100 years). He was a slave owner, having at one time fifty negroes, but devoted most of his time to merchandising. He died in 1856, in his fifty-eighth year, and Mrs. Venable died in 1870, at the age of seventy years. The maternal grandfather of the Doctor was sent by George III. to survey and sell a large tract of land, located close around Prince Edward Court House, Va. The maternal grandfather, Gilford Morton, was in the Revolutionary War, and was wounded at Guilford Court House, N. C. Of the seven children born to the marriage of Henry Venable, only three are now living, Dr. Venable being the eldest one, Andrew and Margaret (now Mrs. Hanna, of Prince Edward County, Va.). Andrew resides in Charlotte County. Dr. Venable was reared in Prince Edward County, Va., received his education at home until twelve years of age, when he entered the Washington University, later the University of Virginia, and in 1851 he entered the Jefferson Medical School of Philadelphia, graduating from the same. He then began practicing at Lynchburg, Va.; from there went to Minnesota, thence to Mississippi, and in 1876 came to Phillips County, Ark., where he settled near Poplar Grove. He has been twice married; first to Miss Caroline I. Craft, of Holly Springs, Miss., who died in 1876, and in 1883 he was united in marriage to Mrs. Wallace, who had been a resident of Phillips County for thirty years.

Dr. Venable was in the Confederate service from 1862 to 1865, was surgeon of Baldwin's brigade and the Second Texas (Moore's) brigade. During the siege of Vicksburg he was transferred to another brigade, and remained with the same until the close of the war. He was engaged in numerous battles as field-surgeon, was taken prisoner at Vicksburg but was immediately paroled. He returned to Phillips County at the close of the war, and at once resumed his practice. Dr. Venable is a man who favors all public improvements for the benefit of his county, and favors all newcomers with a hearty welcome. He and Mrs. Venable are members of the Cumberland Presbyterian Church. He is a member of the Masonic fraternity, is a K. & L. of H., Myrtle Lodge No. 518. He is a prominent physician, and has a large practice.

B. B. Waddell, president and manager of the Citizens' Street Railway and superintendent of the Highland Improvement Company, was originally from Carroll County, Tenn., where his birth occurred on August 24, 1832, and is the son of Amos and Nancy (Pratt) Waddell, the father a native of Georgia and the mother of Virginia. The parents emigrated to Tennessee about 1820, were among the first settlers, and here the mother died. In 1849 the father moved to Southern Arkansas, locating in Ashley County, where he remained for several years. He then returned to Tennessee, where he passed his last days. He was a captain in the War of 1812. Their family consisted of eleven children, four now living: Dr. A. P., Mrs. Smith (of Tennessee), B. B. and Lucinda (in Texas). B. B. Waddell attained his growth and received his education in Tennessee. In 1849 he came with his father to Arkansas, but only remained a few weeks when he returned to Memphis and entered the law office of Judge Henry G. Smith. In 1853 he was admitted to the bar and is the only one of the Memphis bar admitted at that time who is now living. He practiced law at that place until 1866, with the exception of the time during the war, after which he gave up his profession and engaged in keeping hotel until 1873. In 1861 he entered the staff of Gen. Polk, was transferred to Gen. Beauregard's staff, and remained with the same until 1864, when his health failed and he returned to Memphis. While keeping hotel he was also engaged in laying the Nicholson pavement, and made other city improvements. In 1873 he went to St. Louis, embarked in the real estate business and remained there until 1880. He then engaged as general superintendent for Thomas G. Allen & Co., of Memphis, large real estate dealers, owning fifty-two plantations, and he remained interested in this business until 1887, when he came to Helena, and with other parties purchased a large interest here, which he is now superintending. He procured the franchise and laid the street railway in 1888, and this is now in a prosperous condition. Since his residence here he has consolidated his interest and formed the Highland Improvement Company, and purchased the large hills around Helena. He is now engaged in leveling the hills and making beautiful building sites of the same. Mr. Waddell is a progressive citizen and has always rendered his services of influence in Helena by many marked improvements. While living in Memphis he was principally engaged in the management of a large plantation in connection with his law practice. He was married at Denmark, Tenn., in 1856, to Miss Fannie Tarber, by whom he has four children: Tarber, Lizzie, Paul and Anna. He is a member of the Episcopal Church.

Capt. D. R. Weedman, farmer, Poplar Grove, Ark. Mr. Weedman, one of the leading farmers of Marion Township, first saw the light in Breckinridge County, Ky., in 1833, and is the third of ten children, the result of the union of Stephen and Mary A. (Gilbert) Weedman, natives of Kentucky and Virginia, and of German-English parentage, respectively. The paternal grandfather came from Germany to America when a small boy. Stephen Weedman was a farmer and house carpenter by occupation, and followed this the latter part of his life. He was among the early settlers of Grayson County, Ky., and died in 1866, at the age of sixty years. Mrs. Weedman still lives in Meade County, Ky., is eighty-nine years of age, enjoys perfect health, and is a member of the Baptist Church, of which her husband was also a member.

Of the ten children born to their marriage only six are now living: Addison (resides in Kentucky), Amos (also resides in Kentucky), D. R., Mordecai, Miram (both residing in Kentucky), Jacob (deceased), William (deceased), Francis (resides in Kentucky), Martha (deceased), and Mary (wife of George Brands). D. R. Weedman was early taught the duties of farm life, and received his education in Breckinridge County, Ky. At the age of twenty-one years he commenced life for himself as a flat-boatman, and also learned the trade of ship carpenter. While engaged in the flat-boat business he carried on the building of flat-boats, following the same for ten years, or until thirty-one years of age. He then joined the Confederate army, Company F, First Kentucky Regiment, as a private, and was elected second lieutenant at the organization of the company. From that he was promoted to the rank of first lieutenant, and participated in the following battles: Stone River, Chickamauga, Dalton and all the cavalry fights in that section. From Dalton he went to Atlanta, Greensboro, N. C., and here his brigade was detailed as escort for Jefferson Davis and Gen. Breckinridge, and remained with them until the surrender on May 8th. This regiment was the last guard to Mr. Davis. Capt. Weedman has in his possession one of the silver dollars paid him by the Confederate States Government, just before his surrender, and has inscribed on it the following: "Last payment, C. S. A., Washington, Ga., May 8, 1865," and on the other side is, "D. R. Weedman, 1st Ky. Cav." At the termination of hostilities Capt. Weedman went to his home in Kentucky and remained in that State from June, 1865, to May, 1869, when he engaged at his trade, and also followed agricultural pursuits. He then came to Phillips County and worked at the carpenter's trade for four years. In 1874 he bought eighty acres of land, with sixty acres improved, but has since sold that, and is now the owner of 250 acres with 200 acres under improvement. The Captain was married in 1879 to Mrs. Martha A. Connelly, nee Thompson, of this county, and a native of this State, which union resulted in the birth of two children, only one, George, now living. Mr. Weedman is a member of the K. of H., Poplar Grove Lodge No. 2442, and Mrs. Weedman is a member of the K. & L. of H., Myrtle Lodge No. 518, both lodges of Poplar Grove. Capt. Weedman, like the majority of his neighbors, favors all public improvements for the benefit of his county, and extends a hearty welcome to all emigrations of whites, no matter of what nationality.

L. J. Wilkes, grocer, Helena, Ark. There are several houses in this city that are thoroughly typical, not alone of the comprehensive growth and increasing importance of Helena as the supplying center of the growing West, but whose career is a source of public pride, delineating as they do the general business enterprise and commercial sagacity of some of our leading citizens. Such a concern is that conducted by Wilkes & Ford which was established under the firm title of Wilkes & Ford in 1884. They carry a full line of groceries, etc., and are doing a good business. Mr. Wilkes was born in Putnam County, Ga., on October 25, 1852, and is the son of Rev. T. U. Wilkes, a Baptist minister who came to Arkansas about 1861, and located at Trenton, where he passed the closing scenes of his life. The mother died in Georgia. L. J. Wilkes was quite small when he came to Arkansas, and here he grew to manhood, receiving a limited schooling at Trenton, Ark. In 1871 he came to Helena and was employed as a clerk for several years. Being economical he saved money and in 1876 went into the business for himself, taking a partner. As above stated, he formed a partnership with Mr. Ford in 1884, and they are now doing a thriving business. Mr. Wilkes is a stockholder in the Home Mutual Building & Loan Association and is a wide-awake and thoroughgoing business man. He was married in 1876 to Miss Mary Jaquess, daughter of Dr. G. D. Jaquess, of Indiana, and the result of this union has been three children: George R., Luther J. and Louisa. Mr. Wilkes is a member of the First Baptist Church, his wife a member of the Methodist Episcopal Church, South.

Giles W. Wilkes, a well-known colored citizen of Big Creek Township, Phillips County, and extensively engaged in planting, was born in North Carolina about the year 1833. He was reared in Georgia and came to Phillips County, Ark., in 1861, ten years later purchasing the plantation on which he now resides. This consists of 580 acres, with 250 acres cultivated, and his spirit of progression has made his farm one of the most carefully cultivated in the community. He has many modern improvements, a good house, out-buildings, and the general impression given to the observer is that thrift and prosperity abound. Mr. Wilkes was first married, in 1866, to Miss Salina Scaile, of South Carolina, who died in 1885, having borne one child. One year later Mr. Wilkes was married to Mrs. Mary Joyce, who has two children by her former marriage: Mary and Anna. By her union with Mr. Wilkes she is the mother of two children living: Luther and James. Mrs. Wilkes owns in her name 250 acres of land, making a total of 830 acres under the skillful and efficient management of Mr. Wilkes. Himself and former wife were members of the Colored Missionary Baptist Church. The present Mrs. Wilkes is a member of the Methodist Episcopal Church, South. Mr. Wilkes is a Republican in his political views, having cast his first vote for U. S. Grant. He is an honest and industrious citizen, liberal in all his contributions to worthy enterprises, and is quite wealthy.

S. A. Wooten, wholesale and retail grocer, Helena, Ark. The grocery trade is one of the most important departments of commerce all the world over, representing as it does the staple article of consumption. In Helena it is somewhat extensively carried on, the establishments being of a general representative character. Prominent among those engaged in this trade are Messrs. Wooten & Co., who are classed among the most successful business men of Helena. S. A. Wooten owes his nativity to Tipton County, Tenn., where his birth occurred in 1858, and he is the son of Arthur and Eliza Wooten, both of whom died when our subject was an infant. He was given a good common-school education in Tennessee, and there remained until fourteen years of age, when he came to Helena, Ark. He was from early youth a boy of strong will power, and his greatest desire was to rise higher in position. He first sought employment as a clerk in a store, followed this for a number of years, and gave the best of satisfaction to his employers. Being industrious and economical he saved some money, and in 1882 embarked with his brother Charles in the mercantile business, but continued but a short time when each started out for himself. S. A. was in partnership with others for some time, and is now considered one of the leading grocers of Helena, doing an extensive trade in both the wholesale and retail. He was married in 1882 to Miss Cora Eddins, a native of Tipton County, Tenn., and three children were born to this union: Katie, Floy and Shadie. Mr. Wooten is a member of the A. O. U. W. and the Golden Rule. He carries $2,000 insurance in the Travelers, $1,000 in the Manhattan and $2,000 in the New York Life Insurance Company.

George W. Yancey has been a resident of Phillips County since sixteen years of age. He owns a farm of 140 acres, with ninety acres under cultivation, situated three and one-half miles southwest of Trenton, his principal crops being corn and hay, and he is also breeding horses, mules and cattle, which he finds to be one of the lucrative branches of agriculture. Mr. Yancey was born in Virginia, on July 4, 1855, and is a son of James E. and Mary E. (Waller) Yancey, also natives of that State. They removed to Kentucky in 1859, then to Illinois in 1867, and 1870 came to this county, engaging in farming. James E. Yancey was born in 1813, and was a son of Charles Yancey, a native of Virginia, and of English descent. He died in 1875, on the farm on which the principal of this sketch now resides. Mrs. Yancey is still living and resides with her son. She was the mother of nine children. George W. Yancey was married in 1876, to Miss Viola Crenshaw, who was born in this county in 1859. She is the mother of four children, two of whom are living: Winnie, William J. (deceased), Ann (deceased) and Berton C. Mr. Yancey is a member of the Knights of Honor, and is a Democrat in politics, having cast his first presidential vote for Tilden in 1876.

Simon Krow was born in Prussia in 1837, and emigrated to this country when seventeen years of age, locating in Cincinnati, where he was employed as book-keeper for several years. He then went to St. Louis and engaged in the mercantile business, going in 1860 to Memphis, Tenn., where he was engaged in the same branch of trade for five years. In 1865 he came to Arkansas and devoted his attention to buying cotton along the Arkansas River, trading in this manner from Fort Smith to the Mississippi. Four years later he came to Trenton and again entered into the mercantile business, in which he is still occupied, carrying a stock of from $25,000 to $30,000. He has a large and increasing trade and well deserves his success. Mr. Krow is a member of the Masonic order, and also of the Knights of Honor. In addition to his mercantile interests he is interested in the real estate business and owns considerable property, and is one of Trenton's influential and prominent citizens.

CHAPTER XXV.

SPEECH OF HON. T. F. SORRELLS ON THE DEEP WATER QUESTION—A MATTER OF PRIME IMPORTANCE—
EASTERN ARKANSAS INTERESTS—NECESSITY OF DEEP WATER—METHODS EMPLOYED, ETC, ETC.

THE following extract from the speech of Hon. Theodoric F. Sorrells, delegate to the Denver Deep Water Convention, as delivered before the Arkansas legislature, is deemed of sufficient importance to occupy the best attention of the readers of the present volume:

Gentlemen of the General Assembly: In obedience to the announcement made to-day I appear before you to address you upon the great commercial question of the age, and one to be carried out by this generation, and I do thank you for the courtesies thus extended to me in tendering me this hall for the purposes of this occasion, that I might have an opportunity of giving you a short account of my stewardship as your representative to the Denver convention in August last, as well as my views touching the probable results of the meeting of said convention. I was appointed by Gov. Simon P. Hughes as a delegate to the Inter-State Deep Water Harbor Convention at Denver, Colo., which was held there August 28, 29, 30, and 31, 1888. * * * This, to my mind, is the most important step that has been taken in forty years, and one in the right direction, and was held at a suitable time, when gentleman from every portion of the Trans-Mississippi States had an opportunity to attend and participate in the deliberations of the said convention, who may have desired to take a part in its permanent organization. No country occupied by civilized man has been suffering more than the Trans-Mississippi States for the want of a deep water harbor on the northwest coast of the Gulf of Mexico, so as to make a convenient outlet for the Trans-Mississippi States to the sea.

The inhabitants of the Trans-Mississippi States must be aroused from their commercial inactivity and change their mode of operation, and prepare for a different and more convenient commercial existence; and with a view to that end the convention assembled with 750 delegates from all the Trans-Mississippi States. After four days and night's labor the convention adopted the following resolutions:

WHEREAS, it is the sense of the States of Texas, Colorado, Kansas, Nebraska, Missouri, Iowa, Arkansas, California and Nevada, and of the Territories of New Mexico, Wyoming, Utah, Arizona, Dakota and Indian Territory, in convention assembled at Denver, Colo., under the call of his excellency, Alva Adams, governor of the State of Colorado, that the commercial, agricultural, mining, manufacturing and stock interests of all that part of the United States lying west of the Mississippi River, and the commercial and naval advantages of our country generally, demand a permanent deep water port on the northwest coast of the Gulf of Mexico; therefore be it

Resolved, 1. That the senators and representatives in Congress, from the States hereinbefore referred to, and the delegates from the Territories herein set forth, be and they are hereby most earnestly requested to procure at once a permanent available appropriation of the amount necessary to secure a deep water port on the northwest coast of the Gulf of Mexico, west of the 93½° west longitude, capable of admitting the largest vessels, and at which the best and most accessible harbor can be secured and maintained in the shortest possible time and the least cost.

2. That for the purpose of carrying into effect the foregoing resolutions, committees to consist of five from each State and three from each Territory representative in this convention, be appointed by their respective delegations; that it shall be the duties of said committees to see that the object of said resolutions be properly presented and vigorously urged before Congress, and to that end and with the view of co-operation and concert of action the chairmen of the respective committees shall be and they are hereby constituted and created a central committee.

3. That the States and Territories and commercial bodies represented in this convention approve the idea of securing deep water on the gulf coast of Texas by private capital, and they do hereby respectfully request and respectfully urge their senators, representatives and delegates in Congress to lend their united support to such bills as may be introduced for such purpose with proper safeguards for the protection, of the government, provided that the port or point suggested be one desirable for the location of a deep water harbor.

WHEREAS, the need of a deep water harbor on the coast of the Gulf of Mexico directly and vitally affects nearly one-fourth of the people of the United States, we deem the requests contained in the foregoing resolutions of such great and paramount importance as to justify their early reference to the official action of the president of the United States, in order that he may be duly and fully informed, and be able, as contemplated in the Constitution of the United States, to "give to Congress information of the State of the Union, and recommend to their consideration such measures as he shall judge necessary and expedient;" therefore be it

Resolved, that a copy of the foregoing resolutions be transmitted to the president of the United States, and that he be requested to make in his next annual message to the Congress of the United States such recommendations with reference to the location of a deep water harbor on the northwest coast of the Gulf of Mexico as to him shall seem proper and expedient.

WHEREAS, it is of vital importance to all that vast region of our country between the Mississippi River and the Pacific Ocean, including Minnesota, Oregon and Washington Territory on the north, and Arkansas, Texas and California on the south, that a harbor deep enough to float any vessel that sails the ocean, and ample enough to protect the fleet that will be required to handle the commerce of this whole region of country, nearer to it than any other Atlantic seaport, be constructed on the north-

west coast of the Gulf of Mexico as soon as practicable; and

WHEREAS, such a harbor is of such great national importance that it is worthy of an ample appropriation from Congress for its construction; and

WHEREAS, we have already adopted a request to the present members of Congress to favor such appropriations, but would make that request more emphatic; therefore,

Resolved, that the legislatures and people of all the States and Territories included in the region described be earnestly requested to elect no senators, representatives or delegates to Congress, except such as are known to be heartily in favor of such an appropriation, and will earnestly and faithfully work for it until such a harbor is completed.

After the adoption of the above resolutions and the appointment of the general committee and the State executive committees, the general committee adjourned to meet in the city of Dallas, Tex., on October 17, 1888, and a quorum being present the committee formulated and adopted the following act, to be presented to Congress:

A BILL TO ESTABLISH A DEEP WATER HARBOR ON THE COAST OF THE STATE OF TEXAS AND FOR OTHER PURPOSES:

Be it enacted by the Senate and House of Representatives of the United States of America in Congress assembled:

Section 1. That the President be and is hereby empowered and requested to appoint three engineers of the army and two engineers from civil life, who shall proceed to make a careful and critical examination of the coast of Texas and select the most eligible point for a deep water harbor, to be of ample depth, width and capacity to accommodate the largest ocean-going vessels and the commercial and naval necessities of the country, said selection to be made at one of the present ports or at a different place if the commission find one more eligible for the purposes above indicated.

Section 2. That the sum of $10,000,000, or as much thereof as may be necessary, be and the same is hereby appropriated and made a permanent and available fund for the purpose of selecting such deep water harbor and constructing the same as soon as the selection shall be made.

Section 3. That the commissioners herein provided for, not in the employ of the Government, shall receive as compensation —— dollars per day, and their expenses while traveling.

Section 4. The money hereby appropriated to be paid out of any money in the treasury not otherwise appropriated; said work to be conducted and the money expended under the direction of the secretary of war.

The reason I voted for the above act asking Congress to appropriate $10,000,000 is simply from the fact that I am opposed to the driblet system of appropriations for the improvement of rivers and harbors, for I do regard the system as having been a great drawback upon the improvement of our rivers and harbors now and heretofore so much needed. In consequence of the great and often ruinous delays caused too often by tacking appropriations for rivers and harbors on the general river and harbor bills, which is too often done by a system of demagogy, where each congressman wants some bayou or river opened up to give them a little brief local popularity that they may be returned to Congress. And so they frequently work for each other's local schemes to give each other local popularity, but with no advantage to navigation, but to the great injury of the country and the depletion of the Federal treasury.

Still this system is quite expensive and ruinous, because the work that is done under the driblet system frequently washes away between the appropriations. For instance, take the Mississippi River improvements. The unfinished levees wash away as fast as the appropriations are received; hence the labor bestowed, the money spent, and no permanent good results. For that reason I am in favor of making ample appropriations to commence and carry out the work to completion, without any delay, and for that reason I voted for an appropriation of $10,000,000, and would never be satisfied with anything less. What is $10,000,000 to such a great country as this? The difference in the price of freights in one year will more than pay for a first-class harbor on the Texas coast. But, before I commence the argument, I will say that I have no written speech prepared for this occasion, but my remarks will be drawn from my observation and study of this great commercial question for the last fifteen years, and I regret that I have not time to discuss this great question as its magnitude demands, but I will not weary your patience or impose upon your kindness and good nature. But I do unhesitatingly say that the question I present to-night is one of more importance than has been presented to the people of the

Trans-Mississippi States in forty years, and without any further delay I will subdivide the question into three divisions.

The first subdivision of the question is: Do the inhabitants of the Trans-Mississippi States need a deep water harbor on the northwest coast of the Gulf of Mexico?

The second division of the question is: Can a deep water harbor on the northwest coast of the Gulf of Mexico be built?

The third division to the question is: What will be the results to the Western Hemisphere and to the world if built?

I will now proceed to dispose of the question as indicated, by each subdivision, as the same presents itself to my understanding, and say with great earnestness that the 15,000,000 of people embraced in the Trans-Mississippi States do greatly need a deep water harbor, a great commercial entrepot, somewhere on the northwest coast of the Gulf of Mexico as an outlet, mart and market for the produce of that great country, to save the expense of the long railroad haul that those people in the Trans-Mississippi States have in order to reach the Atlantic seaboard with their produce raised in those States and Territories. The Trans-Mississippi States on 1,132,245,113 acres of land, with a population of nearly 13,233,696, and an assessed value of property of $3,296,320,568, produced in the aggregate, in 1886, 715,791,000 bushels of corn, and shipped out of the counties where grown 315,677,940 bushels. The wheat crop of the same year amounted to 30,240,500 bushels, and the crop shipped out of the counties where raised, 22,393,270 bushels.

Now, in order to determine whether the country west of the Mississippi River needs a deep water harbor on the northwest coast of the Gulf of Mexico, which question I think will be fully settled in the minds of all fair-minded men, whether they live in the East or West, as soon as I make a statement of the comparative distances and difference in the railroad haul from any given point in the Trans-Mississippi States to the Gulf of Mexico and the Atlantic seaboard, which I will proceed to give.

To Gulf Coast From—	Miles.	From New York To—	Miles.
Little Rock, Ark	440	Little Rock, Ark	1080
St. Louis, Mo	720	St. Louis, Mo	885
San Francisco, Cal	1820	San Francisco, Cal	2650
Topeka, Kas	680	Topeka, Kas	1135
Lincoln, Neb	820	Lincoln, Neb	1185
Bismark, Dak	1240	Bismark, Dak	1335
Santa Fe, N. M	760	Santa Fe, N. M	1735
Denver, Colo	920	Denver, Colo	1620
Salt Lake City	1200	Salt Lake	1960
Helena, Mont	1495	Montana	1920
Oregon City, Ore	1885	Oregon City	2440
Carson City, Nev	1480	Carson City	2380

Hence the expense of rail haul to and from the Atlantic seaboard to the cities west of the Mississippi River to any point in the Trans-Mississippi States. That a great saving in the expense of transportation by bringing the consumer and producer in close proximity with each other, and such would certainly be the case with a deep water harbor on the northwest coast of the Gulf of Mexico, and by that means obtain much lower freight rates, which would cause the producer to obtain much greater increase of profits on the productions of their farms than they have been able to do when depending alone on European countries.

By reference to the trade of Central America, West India Islands, South America and Mexico, and the trade of Mexico with foreign markets, as will fully appear from the statement of surplus grains produced in the Trans-Mississippi States alone, is almost as much surplus of wheat and corn as the balance of the United States. The truth is that the Trans-Mississippi States, including the Pacific States, do furnish almost the entire export trade of the United States; and from an accurate estimate that has been made, giving the number of horses, mules, milch cows, sheep, hogs and cattle in the United States in 1887, it will be seen that the greater portion of live stock in the United States is now west of the Mississippi River, and the greatest production of meat of the United States is furnished by the Trans-Mississippi States and Territories.

A large portion of the trade from Europe to Mexico is at this time being carried through the ports of Corpus Christi and Galveston, and it is believed that the completion of the Mexican National Railway, that runs down Galveston Island, when connected with any railway running to the city of Mexico, will turn away much of the trade from Vera Cruz and bring the same down to a deep water harbor on the Texas coast, and a suitable harbor on the Texas coast would save 1,500 miles of transportation. And the trade of Northern Mexico will in the future greatly increase the commercial business and trade of the United States.

This opinion seems to be entertained by railroad men, as they seem to be pushing their lines toward Mexico. And an immense saving would be made in the long lines of through shipments. If there was a deep water harbor on the northwest coast of the Gulf of Mexico, this would certainly control much of the trade of Mexico, because the same would pass through the ports on the Texas coast, there being no good harbor on the Mexican coast.

From the foregoing table of distances from the Texas gulf coast to the different points above indicated, and the difference between those points and a deep water harbor on the northwest coast of the Gulf of Mexico and the Atlantic seaboard, the necessity of a deep water harbor in the interest of trade and commerce on the northwest coast of the Gulf of Mexico seems to go without argument, for the opening of a gateway to the Gulf of Mexico is the commencement of a new commercial era. In the countries of North and South America, the West India Islands, Central America, Mexico and all the Trans-Mississippi States new commercial destiny that will attract the attention and consideration of the civilized world, and place in the hands of the American people the commerce of the world. Through this gateway to the Gulf of Mexico the future opens to the people of the Trans-Mississippi States a great harvest of wealth, and they are now beginning to learn the lessons before them and turn their trade away from Europe and Asia, and seek other markets, if necessity require, of their own creation in the southern climes of the Western Hemisphere, because there is an immense uncultivated country situated far beyond the control of our laws and constitution, an immense area of navigable waters, a gulf and a sea, destined to become the greatest commercial place in the Western Hemisphere, full of islands and the wealth of nature. All are struggling and striving to take an active part in the great commercial movement of this progressive age.

Still beyond there lies a vast continent, full of all that is valuable in nature; those continents and islands are our natural co-operators, and with us to become the world's benefactors, for with us under the present civilization our people are turned away from old Europe and Asia to distant continents in pursuit of trade and commerce. We are not familiar with the lands and waters of the Western Hemisphere that lie beyond and under the tropics. Our people ought to learn more of them. They have a longitudinal position in the Western Hemisphere. In the position they occupy with the people of the Trans-Mississippi States and in accordance with the requirements of a great natural commercial law of trade, mutual intercourse would maintain and wealth be amassed by exchange of products. Alexander the Great was compelled to enrich his empires with the wealth of the tropics. He, with the great tide of human beings, moved from the Persian gulf and built up great commercial harbors on the Mediterranean Sea, and thence onward to the Netherlands, and to-day has a controlling influence over England's commerce. Such we learn from history and the same has come down to us. Such a destiny now lies in sight of the people of the Trans-Mississippi States, and the rapid increase to 20,000,000 in the Trans-Mississippi States and from that to 40,000,000 in the next half century does certainly command the prompt action of those now living to make ready for the new trade and commerce now growing up between the two continents of the Western Hemisphere, and success of trade and commerce will depend upon the co-operative movements between the two countries, one with the other. If we look back through history to ancient times we will find the world full of examples to stimulate us in this great commercial enterprise. We are only required to look back through history to that dark commercial age when commerce and trade commence its final struggle with the military under the feudal despotism of Europe and Asia; when five great commercial highways were opened and traveled from the Persian gulf to the commercial markets on the Mediterranean Sea, which were the great highways traveled by Phœnecians, Jews and the merchants of Alexandria to Constantinople and other cities.

Now, if it be true in those ancient days that nations were made wealthy by the trade of Africa and the East Indies, the prospects must be much greater for the people of the Trans-Mississippi States to enrich themselves by the trade of the West Indies, Central and South America and Mexico. The trade that now opens to the people of the Trans-Mississippi States is certainly a much broader field for human enterprise than Europe and Asia affords at this time, which they have only to cultivate to make the same a great ally in trade and commerce and not a rival in any of the chosen industries of the great Trans-Mississippi States. It is certain that the universal tendency of the race of mankind upon this globe has been to make the circuit of the world upon parallel lines with the equator, seeming as by instinct to follow the sun in his movement around the planet. It is also certain that the great wealth of former ages in other nations have been obtained from the tropics. No people have ever been vitalized by civilization who have failed to exchange earth's products with different latitudes and zones. The exchange of similar products do not enrich either country. The difference in products when exchanged will create wealth in both. For instance, there is no advantage derived by the exchange of the cotton of Tennessee for the cotton of Arkansas, or the tobacco of Kentucky for that of Virginia, for these are the products of each State; and no exchange can be made that will be profitable to either. It must appear to all fair-minded men that the exchange of the products of the warm climate for those of the cold climate, such as corn, wheat, fruits and arts of industry of the North, for the sugar, coffee, cotton, rice and other productions of the South, that our people are to be mostly benefited in securing the rewards of their varied industries.

The circuit of the globe is now complete. Upon our land the chain of the world's empire has been finished; the conquest has been carried from the East to the West. Astonished at such a triumph, the Anglo-Saxon race now turns to new fields of labor on longitudinal lines. What else can be done in order to achieve their greatest possibilities in civilization and commerce? It seems to me that nothing else can be done in these progressive and grasping times. It does appear to me that man's travel on this globe has been to make the circuit of the same within the lines of the same temperature with his own home in the East; and the westward movement of the human race along the growth of progress and improvement corresponds with the movement of the sun in Zodiac. But the next great and important movement to be made must correspond to the second solar movement which is known in astronomy as the procession of the equinoxes. The varying of the sun in its ethereal pathway, what is known as the elliptic, creates the changes and variations in the seasons and revives the vegetable kingdom and causes everything to grow for man's happiness and comfort, and the varying and vibrating of the human race, north and south of the line of equal temperature, creates the immense wealth of the world and pushes forward civilization into every country.

For that reason the people of the Trans-Mississippi States have but to live in obedience to this great law of the universe to fulfill the ends of their earthly mission. The development of these facts will at once completely reorganize the present system of exchange in the Trans-Mississippi States, as well as this continent, and decrease the importance of east and west railways in comparison to those running north and south, and railways running from any of the great commercial cities of the valley, Chicago, St. Louis or Kansas City, or other kindred cities, to the Atlantic or Pacific Ocean will sink into utter significance in comparison to those running north and south and uniting the lakes with the gulf. The truth is, one good railway connecting with a good harbor on the Gulf of Mexico will be of more value to any one of the cities from which it may run than any Pacific railway that well can be built. For this reason it must appear to every candid mind that in less time than two years the trade with the West India Islands,

Central and South America will be more valuable to the Trans-Mississippi States than all the trade they will have with Europe and Asia. This statement to some persons may seem remarkable. Nevertheless time will prove it to be true. In this I desire to be fully understood. I don't intend to say that the trade of the West Indies, Central and South America will be greater than the trade of Europe and Asia, but I do say that the time will come in the near future when the people of the Trans-Mississippi States will carry on more trade with the West Indies, Central and South America, than they will with Europe and Asia.

Now let me stop and argue the case, and see if I am not correct. As a proof I will state that the greater portion of the trade of the Trans-Mississippi States, as well as the entire Mississippi Valley, at present with Europe and Asia, is confined to such products as are produced in the country where they live; and in the same latitude are to be found in all North America, in much greater quantities, all those natural products that Europe and Asia have in the same latitude. For that reason may we not suppose that the time is near at hand when the people will produce out of the same kind of raw material such fabrics and implements as they may need in their varied industries? And for that simple reason our people will no longer be forced to go to Europe and Asia for such things as can be raised and manufactured at home. Then our people will only be required to go down to the elements we do not possess in order to carry on this trade with the commercial marts and markets of the world. This will of course lead them down to the tropical regions of the globe, and for that simple reason another evidence of the commercial destiny of the people of the Trans-Mississippi States, and the surplus producer of these States following the flow of the waters to the gulf, whether carried by river or by rail. Our trade with the warm climates of the Western Hemisphere is rapidly increasing; and to keep it on the increase demands liberal legislation and far-seeing statesmanship on the part of our congressmen. No man can calculate the value of our future commerce with the Central and South American States, the

West Indies and Mexico, when these countries shall be more fully developed, the soils forced to produce and yield to their utmost capacity, the productions of which will mostly find its way to the Trans-Mississippi States. And whatever trade is carried on with Europe and Asia with the great Mississippi Valley must be done through the Gulf of Mexico.

The construction of a canal across the Isthmus of Panama, as well as the railroad from Panama to the City of Mexico, will most certainly bring the trade from the western slope and the Pacific Ocean through there and into the Caribbean Sea and the Gulf of Mexico, which is destined to become the great commercial place of the world, and thousands of ships comprising the fleets of all christendom will meet in this great commercial highway, which these waters will most certainly become.

But without a deep water harbor on the northwest coast of the Gulf of Mexico these things can never be; and with a deep water harbor on the northwest coast of the Gulf of Mexico the great commercial advantages can and will be accomplished in the near future as certain as any future event, the building of which is not a local matter, but of great national concern, being needful for national defenses, where she can erect her forts and fortifications to protect the sea coast, as we have much open coast along that line that is entirely unprotected, and the civilized world is alive to the fact that the United States has a poor navy.

I do hope I have convinced you of the necessity of a deep water harbor on the northwest coast of the Gulf of Mexico with ample sea room to accommodate the trade and commerce of the world. This is the great question, the all-absorbing question, the question of the hour with the people of the Trans-Mississippi States.

I am convinced that the thing can be done and that speedily, if Congress will make the required appropriation for that purpose, which I believe Congress will do if the people of the Trans-Mississippi States will unite and properly present the matter to Congress.

The next question to be considered is, can a deep water harbor be constructed on the northwest coast of the Gulf of Mexico with ample sea room to accommodate the trade and commerce of the civilized world? The solution of the question, to my mind, is quite easy, if we are allowed to judge the future by the past, and for our purpose we will look back through history for 2,000 or more years and see what has been done beyond the seas. Have not the nations of the Old World spent millions upon millions of dollars in the improvement of their rivers and harbors? The Danube, Seine, Oder and other rivers? The harbor at Antwerp and the Amsterdam Canal? And have we not a more powerful nation than any that ever existed beyond the Atlantic? Besides vast sums of money expended by the nations of the Old World for the improvement of their rivers and harbors, none of which is equal, in commercial importance, to a deep water harbor on the northwest coast of the Gulf of Mexico. Still our legislators hesitate to move forward in the development of this great country, as the situation demands, for the best interest of this generation and others to come.

I will call attention to two of the great canals of the globe, the character and magnitude of which require the deepest thought and the most profound consideration.

I will first mention the great imperial canal, of China, completed in the thirteenth century, which was 1,250 miles long, a distance from the northern lakes to the Gulf of Mexico, and the Chinese wall, which is 1,500 miles long. And during this century the Suez Canal was constructed, which carries the waters of the Red Sea through the Gulf of Suez into the Mediterranean Sea, which is the greatest commercial water highway for trade and commerce that has been made since the time of Pharaoh, when Joseph was carried down to Egypt. The said canal furnished more direct communication with the Eastern Hemisphere famous in those Trojan times. This canal is ninety-two miles long, twenty-six feet deep, its draught is twenty-five feet, it required thirteen years to construct it, was finished in 1869, at a cost of 17,026,000 pounds. It has a capacity for barges 400 feet long.

To the American legislator this great commercial enterprise looks wonderful, and the expense almost beyond computation. But what are they to this great country and its needs? Which canal has only been completed twenty years, and has done more to civilize and Christianize the inhabitants of the Eastern Hemisphere in this short time than had been done in a thousand years before, by bringing the people of the Eastern Hemisphere in close proximity with each other, and thereby the morals, customs, habits and intelligence of the people were improved. Within the memory of men now living many improvements have been made on the American harbors. The Erie Canal has been constructed: Milwaukee, Chicago, Buffalo, New York and many other great harbor improvements have been made, too tedious to mention in the brief time allowed me. The truth is there has never been a failure to improve any American harbor that has been undertaken. So I do unhesitatingly say that a deep water harbor can be constructed on the northwest coast of the Gulf of Mexico. There can not be a question as to the successful construction of such a harbor, if Congress will make the required appropriation, which I believe it will do, as I have before stated.

The next and last question to be considered is as to what will be the social, financial and commercial results to be attained by the construction of a deep water harbor on the northwest coast of the Gulf of Mexico. There is one thing of which I do feel certain, that at whatever place shall be constructed a deep water harbor on the northwest coast of the Gulf of Mexico, there will spring up from the sand beach one of the grandest cities in the great Southwest. It will become the great central city of the Western Hemisphere, and will soon become a grand commercial mart and market for the produce of the great new West, which is now on a boom from the Mississippi River to the Pacific Ocean. The city that will be built up there will soon stand out as one of the most flourishing cities that will adorn the American continent. Such is to my mind the character of the city that will be erected there, and there stand for the admiration and glory of succeeding generations as they pass down the stream of time, through the long vista of ages to come. And as the inhabitants of

the great Trans-Mississippi States will in future time stand on the wharves of this great coming city and look back along the pathway of bygone years, they will be ready to exclaim, as did the queen of Sheba when she visited Solomon, that "half had not been told by me to-night."

When we look back through the dim distance of former ages and take a view of the commercial marts of the ancients, those which by their commercial growth have left their footprints on the sands of time, which time can never wipe out or obliterate, and for whose supremacy and control empires have been gained and lost; when we look back through the ages to those ancient cities, see the resources that nourished and upheld them, we find that they were quite small compared to those that now cluster around, and will become tributary to a deep water harbor on the northwest coast of the Gulf of Mexico. See, for instance, who are to be her contributors from the land side, which extends from the Gulf of Mexico north to the Lake of the Woods, including eighteen States and Territories, embracing nearly one-third of the whole United States, every inch of which will be beneficiaries to a deep water harbor on the northwest coast of the Gulf of Mexico. The inhabitants of this vast country has doubled every two years, and the population of this great country comprises one-fifth of the national population. But as great as has been the growth of this great country, the same is at this time in the infancy of its future greatness.

The productions of this country are almost beyond computation at this time, and to undertake to estimate what the future productions will be, no human foresight can discover the amount of traffic and tonnage that will in the future roll down from this great country on the great railways to the wharves of this great coming city. This great city will, in a few short years, grow up to 200,000 inhabitants, and those who live will be proud of it, and gratified in feeling that they have been concerned in the inauguration of this great commercial movement, and helped to lay the foundation for their future great central city of the Western Hemisphere.

The interest and happiness of generations to come plead for its completion. Nature has pointed out the way the products of this grand and great country shall be carried to the markets of the world.

The great Creator has so arranged the mountains and the valleys between the Alleghenies and the Sierra Nevadas that the commerce of this great country, comprising the Trans-Mississippi States, shall pass down to a deep water harbor on the northwest coast of the Gulf of Mexico to reach the markets of the world without being required to make a long and expensive "rail haul" with the immense produce of the great valleys across the Alleghenies or the Sierra Nevadas to reach the seaboards of the Atlantic on the east and the Pacific on the west.

The truth is, there is no limit to the argument that can be made on behalf of a deep water harbor on the northwest coast of the Gulf of Mexico. It grasps like the seas and takes in all the shores (of the Western Hemisphere at least). A few more thoughts and I will hasten to the close of an unfinished argument upon the great commercial question now before this country.

I have now discussed this great question from the land side. It now becomes my duty to look out over and across the Gulf of Mexico and the Caribbean sea to the great countries that lie beyond, all of which will become tributary to a deep water harbor on the northwest coast of the Gulf of Mexico, which will be Central and South America, West India Islands, Mexico and Cuba, which will soon belong to the United States by purchases from Spain. So will the commerce of China and Japan come through the harbor on the gulf coast as soon as the canal is constructed through the Isthmus of Panama. All these great countries will bring their commerce through a deep water harbor on the northwest coast of the Gulf of Mexico. Such a brilliant future is not offered to any other harbor now on the globe, and all that is required to bring these grand results is an ample appropriation by Congress to carry out this grand commercial enterprise, which will contribute so much to the glory and happiness of generations unborn, and will contribute largely to the growth and commerce of the great State of Arkansas.

As soon as the deep water harbor is established on the northwest coast of the Gulf of Mexico and the bridge is built across the Mississippi River at Memphis there will be many great trunk lines of railways running from Memphis and St. Louis to the deep water harbor on the gulf coast, all of which will be forced to run through the State of Arkansas—no way to go around her. Then the southern portion of Arkansas and Northern Louisiana and Southeastern Texas will finally loom up and make Little Rock a great railroad center and an extensive manufacturing city. I might say at this point that a deep water harbor on the gulf coast of Texas will forever be more favorable to our export and import trade than any harbor on the Pacific coast. For this reason the produce of the great country lying between the Mississippi River and the Pacific Ocean will never be carried to the city of San Francisco to be shipped to the markets of Europe, for they will not ship their produce from San Francisco across the Northern Pacific and beyond the equator into the Southern Pacific, and around Cape Horn over a perilous sea of 10,000 miles to reach the Atlantic Ocean to go to Europe, in order to avoid which they will bring their produce directly down to a deep water harbor on the northwest coast of the Gulf of Mexico to tide water, where they can have free ocean to the markets of the world. For that reason the city of San Francisco can never compete with a deep water harbor on the northwest coast of the Gulf of Mexico in point of trade and commerce, whether imports or exports. So all this contributes to the future greatness of a deep water harbor on the gulf coast of Texas, and then we shall have established a permanent trade and commercial relations with all the South American States, Cuba, the West India Islands, Central America and Mexico.

No ship that sails from either shore
    While to and fro it plies,
But weaves the thread of friendship o'er
    The gulf that 'twixt us lies.

ERRATA.

The following corrections have been received since the publication of the various sketches to which they refer. The publishers regret the delay in return of biographies, thus necessitating this Errata:

Page 139. Sketch of Robert W. Canada.
3d line. Change "for a period of time" to *since January 29, 1836.*
5th line. *Malissa* for *Melissa.*
22d line. *Dialpha C.* for *Alpha C.*

Page 140. Same sketch.
24th line. *Four* years instead of *eight.*
Last line. "1830" for "1838."
2d line (second column). After Tennessee add: Coming to Arkansas.
7th line. *January* for *June.*
8th line. *Clerk for* instead of *a merchant in business with.*
17th line. *Trustee of* instead of *steward in.*
At end of sketch add: Mr. Canada was one of the judges of election in six townships of White County when Arkansas was reconstructed in 1868.

Page 141. In sketch of William H. Carodine, name should be spelled *Caradine* throughout.
18th line (second column). *James* for *Jones.*

Page 142. Same sketch. After Church add: *South.*

Page 176. Sketch of John T. Hicks.
7th line. *Lytle* should be *Lightle.*
8th line. *Twenty-eight* instead of *eighteen.*
9th line. Read after *Arkansas:* "Previous to which he read law."
10th line. Read: "After coming to Searcy he began practicing," etc.
19th line. "1857" should be "1859."

Page 177. Same sketch.
11th line. "1846" should be "1856."
13th line. "1858" should be "1859."
15th line. *Lytle* should read *Lightle.*
17th line. Before *Tennessee* insert: Fayette County.
19th line. After *Tennessee* add: In 1859.
21st line. After *residing* add: Having attained the age of eighty-seven years.
23d line. Read: After which he took a law course at the University of Virginia in 1881–82, etc.
2d line from bottom of sketch. *Episcopal* should read *Protestant Episcopal.*

Page 196. Sketch of Jefferson Pinkney Linder.
28th line (second column). *Baptist* for *Presbyterian.*
32d line. *That county* should read *Lincoln County.*
38th line. *August* should read *September.*

Page 234. Sketch of John A. Roberson.
12th line. *Mr. Roberson* should read *Mrs. Roberson.*
26th line. "110" should be "180."
6th line from bottom. "1864" for "1863."

Page 257. Sketch of Walker & Ford.
32d line. For sentence commencing "He served as, etc.," substitute: J. R. Ford served in the Confederate army as an officer in the Second Georgia Infantry. Being sent on a special mission which led him outside the Confederate lines, he was captured and tried by a court-martial as a spy; and though not found guilty he was sent to prison at Camp Chase, Ohio, and held until after the surrender. He was released on parole May 14, 1865.
6th line from bottom. *Alabama & Chattanooga* should read *Chattanooga, Rome & Columbus.*
5th line from bottom. *Merchant* instead of *salesman.*
2d line from bottom. *Benjamin* for *Robert.*

Page 258. Same sketch.
18th line. Married Miss Joanna Lane.
22d line. *December 14* for *December 4.*
23d line. *September 8* for *September 14.*

Page 387. Sketch of John N. White.
8th line (second column). After 1885 add: To the Hinton place.

Page 407. Sketch of Levi B. Boon.
11th line. For sentence commencing: The mother was afterward married, substitute: The latter was reared by a man named Boon, from whom L. B. took his name.
12th line (second column). *Stack* for *Stock.*

Page 429. Sketch of D. C. Louder.
9th line (second column). *Mr.* should be *Benoni.*
27th line. *Allicia* should be *Alice.*
28th line. *Four* should be *seven.*
Since the sketch of Mr. Louder was printed he has been called away from earth, having died November 30, 1889.

Page 475. Sketch of Col. V. B. Izard.
6th line. *W.* for *N.*
6th line from bottom. *Actively* for *successfully.*

3d line from bottom. *W.* for *N.*

13th line (second column). *Acting* for *assisting.*

Page 476. Same sketch.

3d line. *Cummings* for *Cunning.*

8th line. *James S. Izard* instead of *James.*

16th line from bottom (second column). *Rejected* for *repealed.*

Page 479. Same sketch.

4th line. Change marriage to: January 19, 1859, to Miss Mollie T. Foudren.

19th line. *Selecting* for *soliciting;* and *offices* for *affairs.*

Page 552. Sketch of Dr. W. D. Powell.

13th line. *Gurpana* should read *Georgia Ann.*

15th line. *Jennie* should read *Jimmie.*

4th line (second column). "1856" should read "1866."

5th line. "The same year" should read "in 1856."

6th line. *Sophner* should read *Shaffner.*

7th line. *H. Leona* for *Georgiana.*

9th line. After *time* add: In 1872 to Miss Lythia

A. Wardnell, a native of Illinois, and the fruits of this union were two children: Minnie, born April 15, 1873, and Lillie M., born May 13, 1875, died December 22, 1876.

9th line. After 1881 add: Mr. Powell was married the third time to Mrs.

10th line. For *Maria A. Hill* substitute "Mrs. Mahala Ann Maria Hill, daughter of William L. Eddins, of Shelby County, Tenn."

22d line. "1856" should read "1866."

Page 562. Sketch of William B. Wellborn.

9th line. *Knoxville* should read *Noxubee.*

Page 572. Sketch of P. H. Adams.

6th line from bottom. *Glidley* should read *Golightley.*

4th line from bottom. *Belle E.* should read *Bettie E.*, and *Francis* should read *Frank.*

5th, line (second column). "1844" should be "1840."

6th line. *Martha A. Smith* should be *Martha James.*

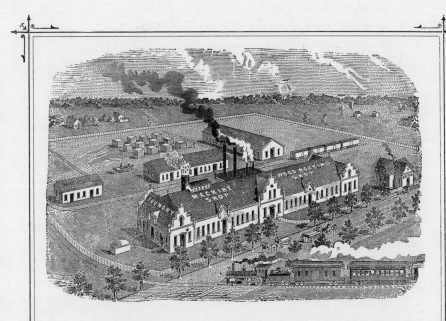

THOMAS COTTON PRESS WORKS,

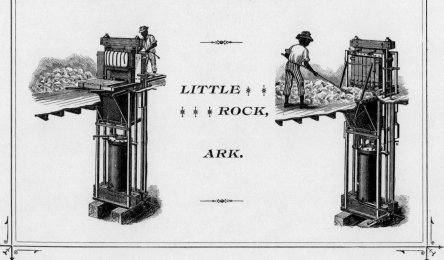

LITTLE * *

* * ROCK,

ARK.